HAVE YOU HEARD A GOOD BOOK LATELY?

Introduction to Business Instructor...

"Do your students commute to class?"

"Do your students have part- or full-time jobs?"

"Do your students come to class unprepared?"

If you answered YES! to one or more of these questions, then it's time you give your students what they have told us in focus groups they need!

Introducing...*Understanding Business* on AUDIO TAPE!

What better way to ensure that your students are prepared for each class! You now have the option of giving your students a package containing *Understanding Business*, in both print and audio format. This special package is only $14 more than the cost of the text alone.

The audio tape package contains the abridged* text of *Understanding Business*. Consider the benefits of this special package!

- Better student preparedness and more class participation!
- Increased comprehension and better performance on exams!
- Ease of use (at home, in the car, or almost anywhere)!
- Fewer excuses!

In order for your students to benefit from this opportunity you will need to order this special package. The tapes without the book are priced at over $45.00.

SPECIAL UB5E and AUDIO TAPE PACKAGE ISBN: 0-07-561888-5

AVAILABLE NOW!

*Tapes are abridged to exclude end-of-chapter material and boxed features.

Understanding Business

Understanding Business

Edition 5

William G. Nickels
University of Maryland

James M. McHugh
St. Louis Community College at Forest Park

Susan M. McHugh
Applied Learning Systems

Irwin McGraw-Hill

Boston   Burr Ridge, IL   Dubuque, IA   Madison, WI   New York   San Francisco   St. Louis
Bangkok   Bogotá   Caracas   Lisbon   London   Madrid
Mexico City   Milan   New Delhi   Seoul   Singapore   Sydney   Taipei   Toronto

Irwin/McGraw-Hill

A Division of The **McGraw·Hill** *Companies*

UNDERSTANDING BUSINESS

Copyright © 1999 by The McGraw-Hill Companies, Inc. All rights reserved. Previous editions © 1987 by Times Mirror/Mosby College Publishing; © 1990, 1993, and 1996, by Richard D. Irwin, a Times Mirror Higher Education Group, Inc. company. Printed in the United States of America. Except as permitted under the United States Copyright Act of 1976, no part of this publication may be reproduced or distributed in any form or by any means, or stored in a data base or retrieval system, without the prior written permission of the publisher.

This book is printed on acid-free paper.

international   1 2 3 4 5 6 7 8 9 0 VNH/VNH 9 3 2 1 0 9 8
domestic   1 2 3 4 5 6 7 8 9 0 VNH/VNH 9 3 2 1 0 9 8

ISBN 0-256-21980-X
ISBN 0-07-303975-6 (annotated instructor's edition)
ISBN 0-07-365714-X (Business Week edition)

Vice president and editorial director: Michael W. Junior
Publisher: Craig S. Beytien
Senior developmental editor: Laura Hurst Spell/Burrston House
Associate editor: Elizabeth M. Lindboe
Senior marketing manager: Katie Rose-Matthews
Senior project manager: Mary Conzachi
Production supervisor: Michael R. McCormick
Designer: Diane Beasley/Laurie J. Entringer
Senior photo research coordinator: Keri Johnson
Photo research: Burrston House
Supplement coordinator: Rose M. Range
Compositor: PC&F, Inc.
Typeface: 10/12 New Aster
Printer: Von Hoffman Press, Inc.

Library of Congress Cataloging-in-Publication Data

Nickels, William G.
    Understanding business / William G. Nickels, James M. McHugh,
Susan M. McHugh.—5th ed.
        p.   cm.
    Includes bibliographical references and index.
    ISBN 0-256-21980-X
    1. Industrial management.   2. Business.   3. Business—Vocational
guidance.   I. McHugh, James M.   II. McHugh, Susan M.   III. Title
HD31.N4897 1999   98-23637
650—dc21

INTERNATIONAL EDITION
Copyright © 1999. Exclusive rights by The McGraw-Hill Companies, Inc. for manufacture and
    export.
This book cannot be re-exported from the country to which it is consigned by McGraw-Hill.
The International Edition is not available in North America.

When ordering the title, use ISBN 0-07-115817-0

http://www.mhhe.com

Dedication

To all the students who will be using the concepts and principles in this text to help make this a better world for everyone. And to our friends and families who have been patient with us while we spent days and nights putting together this text and package. You make it all worthwhile.

Brief Contents

Contents

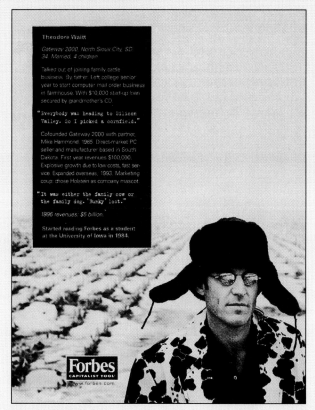

Theodore Waitt, co-founder of Gateway 2000, is an excellent example of the fuel that drives the engine of business—entrepreneurship.

Prologue:

Secrets to Your Success (Confidential for Students Using This Text) P-XXXVIII

Part 1
Business Trends: Cultivating a Business in Diverse, Global Environments

Chapter 1

Finding Opportunities in Today's Dynamic Business Environment P-24

Although still in its infancy, marketing on the Internet is a major trend in business and the number of companies using this medium increases everyday.

It's one thing to participate in recycling products, but as this ad states, there are two sides to the process. Social responsibility places demands on consumers as well as businesses.

LaVan Hawkins, founder of Urban City Foods, is one of America's most successful and socially responsible entrepreneurs. He recently presented the Baltimore City Public Schools with a check for $500,000 to establish a center for entrepreneurship.

Part 3
Business Management: Empowering Employees to Satisfy Customers

Change and competition go hand in hand in today's global business environment—even for the management and franchises of a successful giant like McDonald's. Shown here is their secret test kitchen where they developed the new Made for You food production system.

Part 4
Management of Human Resources: Motivating Employees to Produce Quality Goods and Services

Chapter 10

Motivating Employees and Building Self-Managed Teams 286

Profile: Herb Kelleher of Southwest Airlines 287

Doing the right thing! Aaron Feuerstein, owner of the fire-ravaged Malden Mills textile complex, speaks to his workers in Methuen, Massachusetts telling them that he will continue to pay their wages and health insurance while the plant is being rebuilt. Eventually, all but a few dozen employees returned to work and sales and profits in 1997 reached an all time high.

Part 5
Marketing: Developing and Implementing Customer-Oriented Marketing Plans

Chapter 13
Building Customer and Stakeholder Relationships 378

Profile: Chris Zane of Zane's Cycles 379

Chapter 14
Developing and Pricing Quality Products and Services 406

Profile: Kendrick Melrose of Toro 407

It can't be done! Obviously, the Japanese designers of this Sushi-making robot didn't subscribe to this view. Are there limits to applying technology in solving business problems?

Chapter 15

Distributing Products Efficiently and Competitively 440

Chapter 16

Promoting Products Using Integrated and Interactive Marketing Communication 470

Part 6
Decision Making: Managing Information

Chapter 17

Using Technology to Manage Information 502

Is owning or leasing office space a thing of the past?
Rather than striving for the corner office the more
impressive career achievement may be your own fully
equipped Landjet. Staying close to your customers
takes on a new meaning.

Chapter 18

Understanding Financial Information and Accounting 528

Part 7
Managing Financial Resources

Chapter 19

Financial Management 562

Chapter 20

Securities Markets: Financing and Investing 590

As this Microsoft ad implies, education is a powerful tool, and when combined with entrepreneurship the possibilities become even greater.

About the Authors

Dr. William G. Nickels is an associate professor of business at The University of Maryland, College Park. With over 30 years of teaching experience, Bill teaches introduction to business in large sections (250 students) and marketing principles (500 students) each semester. Bill has won the Outstanding Teacher on Campus Award three times, including two out of the last three years. Bill received his M.B.A. degree from Western Reserve University and his Ph.D. from The Ohio State University. He has written a principles of marketing text and a marketing communications text in addition to many articles in business publications. Bill is a marketing consultant and a lecturer on many business topics.

Jim McHugh is an associate professor of business at St. Louis Community College/Forest Park. Jim holds an M.B.A. degree and has broad experience in both education and business. In addition to teaching several sections of introduction to business each semester for 18 years, Jim maintains an adjunct professorship at Lindenwood University, teaching in the marketing and management areas at both the undergraduate and graduate levels. Jim has conducted numerous seminars in business and maintains several consulting positions with small and large business enterprises in the St. Louis area. He is also involved in a consulting capacity in the public sector.

Susan McHugh is an educational learning specialist with extensive training and experience in adult learning and curriculum development. She holds an M.Ed. degree and has completed her course work for a Ph.D. in education administration with a specialty in adult learning theory. As a professional curriculum developer she has directed numerous curriculum projects and educator training programs. She has worked in the public and private sector as a consultant in training and employee development. In addition to her role as co-author of the text, Susan designed the instructor's manual, test bank, student assessment and learning guide, and the telecourse guide.

Preface

The fourth edition of *Understanding Business* grew to be the number one textbook in the introduction to business market. In large measure, this was due to the most aggressive product development effort ever implemented, involving over 200 faculty who teach the course and hundreds of students. As a result of this massive listening and responding campaign, the number of students using *Understanding Business* doubled. Thousands of students have called it the most readable and usable text they've ever read. Furthermore, as a result of this success in the United States, the text has been translated into Spanish and Chinese and has a Canadian version called *Understanding Canadian Business*.

What does an author team or publisher do when they have such a successful text? They return to listening and responding to users (faculty and students) and nonusers. For the fifth edition, using various forums we asked over 200 faculty what changes could be made to improve the text and package. We held close-to-the-customer focus groups involving over 100 instructors in Los Angeles, San Jose, Philadelphia, Austin, Chicago, Fort Lauderdale, Orlando, Boston, and Washington, D.C. Interaction with the participants of these sessions helped us learn the wants and needs of a diverse group of intro instructors and students. Several instructors kept diaries of how the fourth edition of *Understanding Business* worked in their classrooms. This feedback was an invaluable source of insights regarding how to increase the instructional value of the text. More than 60 instructors reviewed all or part of the revised manuscript and made extensive suggestions for fine-tuning the material. Here are a few of the more significant changes made in response to this feedback.

MORE COVERAGE OF TECHNOLOGY, ESPECIALLY THE INTERNET

It is amazing how schools differ in the access their students have to the Internet. Even though some schools have limited access, the consensus of the focus groups and reviewers was that students need to know how to use the Internet to do research, apply for jobs, and prepare themselves for the jobs of the future. In response, this edition has a unique in-text guide to the Internet (an appendix to Chapter 1) called Driver's Ed for the Information Superhighway. Some students know this basic information about the Internet and how to use it, but many do not. All students should benefit from reviewing the Internet fundamentals. To help students in their research, we now provide Web addresses for the companies referenced in the text. Furthermore, we added Taking It to the Net exercises to the end of every chapter to hone research and analytical skills using the Internet. References to Internet use, intranets, and extranets are woven throughout the text. Technology and Internet issues have also been integrated throughout many of the videos accompanying the text. In addition, two of the videos deal exclusively with the Internet—Getting the Job You Want On-Line and Guide to the Internet, providing you with an exciting way to introduce students to the latest uses of the World Wide Web. An interactive Web site, developed expressly for *Understanding Business, Fifth Edition,* features on-line study aids and activities, Internet links to companies featured in the text, and more. Visit us at http://www.mhhe.com/ub5e and see for yourself.

UNIQUE FOCUS ON DEVELOPING PROFESSIONAL BEHAVIOR

The most unexpected request, and one that came from many schools, was to focus attention on the need for students to develop proper business etiquette and professional behavior. We address these important issues in the new Secrets to Your Success prologue. To highlight this important theme, which we carry throughout the text, a special video was created to show students proper professional behavior and etiquette.

KEEPING UP WITH WHAT'S NEW

Users of the fourth edition of *Understanding Business* were eager for us to maintain the currency for which the text is famous. A glance through the endnotes will show that most references are from 1997 and 1998. A few of the new current issues include:

- Economic problems in Asia
- ISO 14000
- Latest uses of the Internet, intranets and extranets
- Year 2000 problems (Y2K)
- Learning organizations
- Proposed merger of Nasdaq and Amex
- Smart cards
- Customer relationship management
- Micropreneurs and home-based businesses
- Most recent fiscal and monetary policies in the United States
- Constant change as a business dynamic
- On-line banking (including a video)

MAINTAINING CURRENCY: THE *BUSINESS WEEK* CONNECTION

One way that many instructors expect their students to stay current is to read *The Wall Street Journal, Business Week,* and other such business periodicals. Most would like to assign them in class. In many schools, however, the added cost is too much to add these resources as a requirement. In response, Irwin/McGraw-Hill has arranged with *Business Week* to provide an affordable subscription rate for students. For just a few extra dollars, students can now get *Business Week* magazine for 16 weeks and learn the latest in business strategies and practices. In order to emphasize the importance of reading current business periodicals we have added a new and unique box to each chapter called From the Pages of *Business Week*. As an added benefit, instructors will receive a free subscription for a semester as well as a weekly newsletter that provides article summaries and application questions.

INTEGRATION OF IMPORTANT CONCEPTS THROUGHOUT THE TEXT

Users and nonusers asked us to continue to incorporate and emphasize the following topics as themes throughout the text:

- Pleasing customers
- Small business and entrepreneurship
- Teams
- Ethics and social responsibility
- Quality
- Technology
- Global business
- Cultural diversity

There was a strong consensus that the importance of each of these topics requires emphasis beyond the traditional single chapter treatment. In response, we added even more small business and international examples throughout the text. For example, there are boxes called Spotlight on Small Business and Reaching Beyond Our Borders in every chapter. The fourth edition of *Understanding Business* already had more emphasis on entrepreneurship than the competition. That leadership position is maintained with examples integrated throughout, an Entrepreneurship Readiness Questionnaire, and an entire chapter on Entrepreneurship and the Challenge of Starting a Business. Many students have very little knowledge about how to generate the capital required to start and run a small business. Therefore, Chapter 22 supports the entrepreneurship theme by describing in detail how students can learn to budget, save, and invest their money to enable them, should they choose to do so, to buy or start their own business, or invest in other businesses.

EMPHASIS ON CAREERS

Our student focus groups recommended that we continue to emphasize and provide information about potential careers. In response to this request, we include unique career portfolios at the end of each part. Each portfolio includes a vignette that profiles the career development of a recent college student. The portfolios also include charts of specific careers including titles, job descriptions, requirements, potential earnings, responsibilities, and future growth possibilities.

Additionally, we continue to include the popular Getting the Job You Want appendix that describes how to search for jobs, write a resume, and respond in interviews. We've added a substantial number of examples, illustrations, and exercises that encourage students to search for jobs on the Internet.

······ ▬▬▬ ·····

NEW TO THIS EDITION: THE TEXT ON AUDIOTAPES

This new and unique feature was suggested by one of the early focus group participants and received tremendous support from subsequent groups. These audio cassettes contain the text of each chapter minus the end matter. They are designed for commuters and other students who wish to enhance their learning by listening to the text. Obviously, these tapes will be invaluable to students who are visually impaired or who have other disabilities that make reading difficult or impossible.

······ ▬▬▬ ·····

LEARNING BUSINESS SKILLS THAT WILL LAST A LIFETIME

The Secretary of Labor appointed a commission, the Secretary's Commission on Achieving Necessary Skills (SCANS), to identify the skills people need to succeed in the workplace. SCANS' fundamental purpose is to encourage a high-performance economy characterized by high-skill, high-wage employment. The commission's message to educators is: Help your students connect what they learn in class to the world outside. To help educators prepare their students for the workplace, SCANS identified five workplace competencies that should be taught: (1) Resource skills (the ability to allocate time, money, materials, space, and staff); (2) Interpersonal skills (the ability to work on teams, teach others, serve customers, lead, negotiate, and work well with people from culturally diverse backgrounds); (3) Information ability (the ability to acquire and evaluate data, organize and maintain files, interpret and communicate, and use computers to process information); (4) Systems understanding (the ability to operate within various social, organizational, and technological systems and to monitor and correct performance to design or improve systems); and (5) Technology ability (the ability to select equipment and tools, apply technology to specific tasks, and maintain and troubleshoot equipment). The pedagogical tools in the text and package are designed to facilitate these SCANS competencies.

Here are the major pedagogical devices used in the text:

- *Learning Goals.* Tied directly to the summaries at the end of the chapter and to the test questions, these learning goals help students preview what they are supposed to know after reading the chapter, and then test that knowledge by answering the questions in the summary. The study guide is also closely linked to the learning goals as part of the total integrated teaching, learning, and testing system.

- *Opening Profiles.* Each chapter begins with a profile of a person whose career illustrates an important point covered in the chapter. Not all the personalities are famous since many of them work in small businesses and nonprofit organizations. These profiles provide a transition between chapters and a good introduction to the text material.

- *Progress Checks.* Throughout the chapters there are Progress Checks that ask students to remember what they have just read. If students are not understanding and retaining the material the Progress Checks will stop them and show them that they need to review before proceeding. We have all experienced times when we were studying and our minds wandered. Progress Checks are a great tool to prevent that from happening for more than a few pages.

- *Critical Thinking Questions.* These unique inserts, found throughout each chapter, ask students to pause and think about how the material they are reading applies to their own lives. This device is an excellent tool for linking the text material to the student's past experience to enhance retention. It greatly increases student involvement in the text and course as recommended by SCANS.

- *Informative Boxes.* Each chapter includes several, fully integrated boxed inserts that apply the chapter concepts to particular themes, including small business, legal issues, making ethical decisions, and global business. Although numerous additional examples of such topics are integrated throughout the text, these boxes provide highlighted applications of key concepts in particular areas. The *Business Week* boxes, new to this edition, were developed in cooperation with *Business Week* magazine. The ethics boxes, titled Making Ethical Decisions, pose questions that require students to evaluate their own ethical behavior as recommended by SCANS.

- *Key Terms.* Key terms are developed and reinforced through a four-tiered system. They are introduced in boldface, repeated and defined in the margin, listed at the end of each chapter with page references, and defined in a comprehensive glossary at the end of the text. The glossary also contains another unique feature recommended and endorsed by the focus groups. All American slang expressions used in the text, such as *in the red,* or *the bottom line,* are now included. Students from other countries enjoy learning American slang, but often need some help in translating it since these expressions are not found in most dictionaries. And for the first time the entire end-of-text glossary is available in Spanish and can be shrinkwrapped (free of charge) with the text.

- *Cross-Reference System.* This system, unique to this text, refers students back to the **primary discussion** and examples of all key concepts. A specific page reference appears each time a key concept occurs in a chapter subsequent to its original discussion. This feature allows students to quickly review or study that concept (if necessary) in context in order to improve their comprehension of the material. It also eliminates the need to continuously revisit and restate key concepts, thus reducing overall text length.

- *Photo and Illustration Essays.* More and more students today are becoming visual learners. Consequently, we have made a conscientious effort to enhance the illustration program in this edition. Each photo and illustration in the text is accompanied by a caption in the form of a short paragraph that clearly demonstrates the relevance of the visual to the material in the text. The accompanying descriptions, most of which contain application or critical thinking questions, help the student understand what is being shown in the graphic and how it is related to the concept or topic being illustrated. In order to enhance their pedagogical value, many of these photos were commissioned specifically for use in this edition.

- *Interactive Summaries.* The end-of-chapter summaries are directly tied to the learning goals and are written in a unique question and answer format. Answering the questions and getting immediate feedback helps prepare students for quizzes and exams. The students in our focus groups were extremely positive about this format.

- *Taking It to the Net Exercises.* New to this edition, these optional exercises at the end of every chapter allow students to explore and research topics and issues on the Web. Additional exercises can be found on the UB5/e Web site.

- *Developing Workplace Skills.* The Developing Workplace Skills section provides a diverse array of activities designed to increase student involvement in the learning process. Some of these miniprojects require library or Internet searches, but many of them involve talking with people to obtain their reactions and advice on certain subjects. Students then come to class better prepared to discuss the topics at hand. These assignments can be divided among groups of students, which will enable them to learn a great deal from outside sources and about teamwork without any one student having to do too much of the work. These are the types of learning experiences that facilitate the SCANS competencies.

- *Practice Cases.* Each chapter concludes with a short, optional case to allow students to practice managerial decision making. They are intentionally brief and meant to be discussion starters rather than take up the entire class period. The answers to the cases are in the instructor's manual. Again these examples of real-world problem solving will help students achieve the SCANS competencies.

- *Video Cases.* Video cases are provided for each chapter. These are placed at the end of the chapter and are optional as assignments. They feature companies of various sizes in both the services and manufacturing sectors. Each showcases processes, practices, and managers that highlight and bring to life the key concepts, and especially the themes of the fifth edition.

- *Package Options.* Various packages are available to ensure your students that they are getting the most value for their money. In addition to the *Business Week* package, where students get *Business Week* for the lowest price anywhere, faculty can order a package that includes a CD-ROM containing other business books worth hundreds of dollars. Talk to your Irwin/McGraw-Hill representative for the package that best suits your students.

In short, thanks to you and your colleagues, the number one text is now even better. It is the text that others benchmark for quality, readability, usability, and currency.

···· ▬▬▬ ····
THE BEST INSTRUCTIONAL MATERIALS

Perhaps it is because we use these materials in our own classrooms that we were so meticulous with the preparation of the various instructional materials. Jim teaches traditional-size classes of 30–50 students in an urban community, and Bill teaches classes of 250 in large lecture halls in a four-year institution. As a result, everything in the fifth edition is designed to help instructors be more effective and make this course more practical and interesting for students. Based on our own research and the feedback from the focus groups involving users of every major competitor, we can state without hesitation that no introductory business text package is as market responsive, easy to use, and fully integrated as this one. To accomplish this integration, the authors carefully designed, contributed to and reviewed the instructor's manual and test bank. They also prepared the new acetates and the accompanying annotations and notes. Additional supplements were prepared by outstanding practitioners who used the materials in their own classes, and all have been reviewed by the text authors.

···· ▬▬ ····
KEY SUPPLEMENTS FOR INSTRUCTORS

NEW! Instructor's Orientation Video. If you are a course coordinator, part-time or first-time instructor, or experienced teacher frustrated by the breadth and complexity of the various supplements available for use with *Understanding Business,* your ship has come in! We offer you so many instructional tools, it's extremely difficult to absorb them all at once (as we heard over and over at the focus groups). So we've put together this simple orientation video (approximately 30 minutes in length) that walks you through the whats, wheres, and whys of each supplement—a perfect tool for part-time faculty or as an orientation to effective use of classroom supplements for anyone. If you are currently using or considering *Understanding Business* you owe it to yourself to review this video. Contact your Irwin/McGraw-Hill representative for copies.

Instructor's Manual. All material in the Instructor's Manual has been widely praised by new instructors, part-timers, and experienced educators alike for its quality, comprehensiveness, and ease of use. Many instructors tell us that the IM is a valuable time-saver that makes them look good in class. The Instructor's Manual is unique in its thorough integration with both the text and package. Each chapter opens with a description of the differences between the fourth and fifth editions in order to facilitate the conversion of your own teaching notes to the new edition. After a short topic outline of the chapter and listing of the chapter objectives and key terms, you will find a **resource checklist** with all of the supplements that correspond to that chapter. Consequently, there is no need to flip through half a dozen sources to find which supplementary materials are available for each chapter.

To make the system even easier to use, the detailed lecture outline (in large type) contains marginal notes recommending where to use acetates, supplementary cases, lecture enhancers (additional examples), and critical thinking exercises. Space is also available to add personal notes of your own so that they too may be integrated into the system.

Each chapter contains lecture enhancers—short article summaries that provide additional examples—allowing you to examine topics and concepts from different angles and to implement the latest business and social issues. Supplementary cases, similar to those in the text, are provided for each chapter for use as outside assignments and/or classroom discussions. The critical thinking exercises require students to analyze and apply chapter concepts, a tremendous aid in getting students more involved in the learning process. The Instructor's Manual has been revised and reformatted by Gayle Ross, of Copiah-Lincoln Community College.

Annotated Instructor's Edition (AIE). The AIE is a reproduction of the student edition of the text with the addition of marginal notes that suggest where to use various instructional tools such as the overhead transparencies, supplementary cases, and lecture enhancers. It also identifies the activities that facilitate the SCANS competencies.

Test Bank. This part of our Integrated Teaching and Testing System always receives more attention from users and reviewers than any other supplement. We're keenly aware that the success of your course depends on tests that are comprehensive, accurate, and fair, and we have provided questions that measure recall, and require students to apply the material to real-world situations. **The Nickels/McHugh/McHugh Test Bank is like no other on the market.** It is designed to test three levels of learning.

1. Knowledge of key terms.
2. Understanding of concepts and principles.
3. Application of principles.

A rationale for the correct answer and the corresponding text page add to the uniqueness of our 4,000 plus-question Test Bank. The Fifth Edition Test Bank (again, thanks to reviewers and focus group suggestions) contains questions for many of the boxed inserts in the text and all appendices. Another helpful tool is our unique Test Table. This chart helps you develop balanced tests by quickly identifying items according to objective and level of learning.

For the ultimate in ease, each chapter concludes with a Quick Quiz. These 10-item tests are ready for reproduction and distribution for testing or for outside assignments. The Test Bank was revised by the very capable team of Dennis Shannon and Jim McGowen of Belleville Area College.

Computest 4. The Test Bank also comes in a computerized version. This enhanced test-generation software allows users to add and edit questions; save and reload multiple test versions; select questions based on type, difficulty, or key word; and utilize password protection. It supports over 250 printers; links graphics, tables, and text to a series of questions; supports numerous graphics including special characters, complex equations, subscripts, superscripts, bolds, underlines, and italics; and can run on a network.

Teletest. For those who prefer not to use the computerized test-generator, Irwin/McGraw-Hill provides a Teletest Service. Using a toll-free phone number, you can order an exam prepared from the *Understanding Business* Test Bank. A master copy of the exam, with answer key, is sent first class mail the same day it is requested. Fax is also available within 30 minutes of the request.

Overhead Transparency Acetates. Over 260 original acetates, none of which reproduce textual exhibits, augment the concepts and examples presented in the text. These acetates enable you to illustrate and enhance your lectures with colorful visual aids. Detailed annotations regarding content and suggested uses for each acetate are found on both the acetate divider sheets and in the Instructor's Manual. The contents of this package are also available in an electronic (PowerPoint) format—see below.

Transparency Masters. In addition to the acetates, all important charts, graphs, and tables **in the text** are reproduced as transparency masters for your easy use in the classroom.

Microsoft PowerPoint Slides. Over 260 electronic slides keyed to the text are available. These slides can be modified with PowerPoint.

NEW VIDEOS for Most Chapters. In their report, SCANS stated that video and multimedia materials are essential to creating the realistic contexts in which the competencies are used. Video cases are available for every chapter and most segments are 8 to 15 minutes in length and are suitable for classroom, home, or lab viewing. Detailed notes regarding content, running time, suggestions for use, and answers are included in the multimedia resource guide. NEW videos for this edition include: Business Etiquette; Starbucks; Guide to the Internet; Breaking Down the Great Wall; Ethics Vignettes; Urban-City Foods; Jay Goltz, Artists Frame Service; Lou Gerstner and the IBM Turnaround; Southwest Airlines; American President's Line; Airwalk; Getting the Job You Want on the Internet; and On-line Banking.

NEW! Presentation CD-ROM. Much of the instructor's manual, the PowerPoint® slides, video clips, lecture outlines, and more are compiled in electronic format on a CD for your convenience in customizing multimedia lectures.

NEW! Media Resource Guide. If you're wondering how to go about incorporating media into your introduction to business classroom, let this guide be your answer by providing helpful instruction on how to use all media components. In addition, **this manual contains teaching notes and test questions for each of the videos.**

NEW! Telecourse Guide. Do you teach Introduction to Business in a telecourse? Now you can use the Telecourse Guide to make your job easier. This guide gives you step-by-step instructions and hints as to how to use UB5/e with telecourse material.

NEW! Distance Learning Course Management Tool. What if you could place all of your course materials on-line? You could assign quizzes, post homework assignments, even track student progress with ease. And you could do it all from your computer. Now you can! McGraw-Hill Learning Architecture (MHLA) is a course administration tool that allows instructors to place materials on the Web. MHLA provides a structure for presenting effective and efficient instructional activities. For a demo of this exciting new technology, visit our Web site at http://www.mhla.net.

NEW! Web Site: www.mhhe.com/ub5e. Instructors will find a wealth of information on the book's home page, including PowerPoint slides, lecture materials from the instructor's manual, and other teaching resources.

···· ▬ ····
KEY SUPPLEMENTS FOR STUDENTS

REDESIGNED! Student Assessment and Learning Guide. Written by Barbara Barrett of St. Louis Community College/Meramec, the Student Assessment and Learning Guide contains both objective (multiple-choice) and various forms of open-ended questions that require the student to write out his or her personal summary of the material. The guide gives students the opportunity not only to prepare for tests, but also to develop and practice their business knowledge and skills. The following materials are provided for every chapter: learning goals, chapter outline, key terms and definitions, retention questions, critical thinking questions, and a practice test.

NEW! Concept Mastery and Exam Prep Disk. This new software by Jim McGowen and Dennis Shannon provides an excellent and convenient resource for giving students experience with computers while at the same time allowing them to pre-test their comprehension of key concepts. Shrink-wrapped with every new copy of the text, this 3.5 disk contains numerous practice exam questions for every chapter, modeled on the test items in the *Understanding*

Business testing system. If your students use this software, they should be better prepared for exams, as well as more computer savvy.

NEW! Spanish/English Glossary. The entire end-of-text glossary has been translated into Spanish and is now available free of charge to be shrinkwrapped with the text.

REVISED! Stock Market Experience. This manual was developed and fine-tuned by John A. Knappenberger out of his own approach to teaching students about the buying and selling of stocks in a free enterprise system in his Introduction to Business course at Mesa State College. In addition to exposing students to the basic principles of investment, the manual provides coverage of using electronic spreadsheets and the Internet to manage a stock portfolio.

NEW! Mind-Q Internet CD-ROM. This interactive software helps students learn to use the Internet at their own pace.

Essentials of Business CD-ROM. This CD-ROM provides access to eight best-selling business textbooks, including *Understanding Business.* All texts are hyperlinked across disciplines, allowing students to retrieve information in a cross-functional format. Also included on this CD are a variety of business forms and templates. In addition, students will find a dynamic tutorial on New Venture creation.

NEW! Text on Audio Tape. A 15-cassette version of the text that allows students to prepare for class or review for tests while commuting, jogging, or wherever and whenever they like!

NEW! ZAPITALISM! From LavaMind, this new software is an exciting business simulation with great color graphics. Zapitalism! will entertain students while teaching them important business concepts such as supply and demand, advertising, risk management, stock market, pricing, capital expenditures, taxes, pleasing customers, and more.

NEW! Web Site: www.mhhe.com/ub5e. Students will make the most of their experience with *Understanding Business* by visiting the book's dedicated home page, developed by Russell Baker of Florida Metropolitan University—Tampa College. There they will find additional resources to help them succeed both in and outside of the classroom, including chapter quizzes and review materials, Internet exercises, links to companies and organizations featured in the text, tips on conducting an on-line job search, and more.

We are extremely proud of the text and the integrated teaching and testing system that you have helped us develop over the years. The many accolades from loyal text and supplements users are gratifying and rewarding. As evidenced by the unprecedented level of feedback solicited from users and non-users alike we continue to strive to provide the strongest instructional package to help you support the text in the classroom. We firmly believe that no course in college is more important than the introduction to business course. That's why we enjoy teaching it so much and why we are willing to work with you and to spend so much time helping others make this the best course on campus.

Bill Nickels
Jim McHugh
Susan McHugh

Acknowledgments

We have been blessed to work with a great team of professionals in making this fifth edition and package a reality. At Irwin/McGraw-Hill, Craig Beytien again served as our executive editor. As manager of the project, it was Craig's job to recruit the best team members, and as always he did an outstanding job. Many thanks to Liz Lindboe, Associate Editor, for her insights and contagious enthusiasm that kept us going through the harried crunch time.

Glenn Turner and Meg Turner of Burrston House were steadfast in their roles as developmental editors. Their persistence in gathering market research and their diligence in keeping us focused on priorities were indispensable in assuring that the product responds to your needs. They conducted the focus groups and managed the text reviews that proved so helpful in revising the text and the supplements. They, along with their colleague Donna Arsenoff, also conducted and managed a comprehensive photo search that included commissioning over 50 custom-made photos to illustrate key points.

The beautiful new text design was created by the talented Diane Beasley. Mary Conzachi did a splendid job of keeping the production of the text on schedule. Laura Hurst-Spell kept all of the complex pieces of the supplements package under control. We are particularly grateful to Laura for coordinating the development of the dynamic new video package. Many thanks to Rose Range and Betty Hadala for all their efforts in producing the finest supplemental materials. We also want to thank Janet Renard for her excellent copyediting. Of course, we must thank Matt McGuire, Sayre Berkshire, and Nan Drews for processing those all important expense reports.

As we've previously stressed, many dedicated educators contributed to the text and package. Dennis Shannon and Jim McGowen of Belleville Area College revised the Test Bank. Gayle Ross of Copiah-Lincoln Community College gave the Instructor's Manual a face-lift. Barbara Barrett of St. Louis Community College/Meramec revised the Study Guide. John Knappenberger of Mesa State College wrote the new Stock Market Experience. Pete Giuliani of Franklin Community College, Columbus, Ohio, contributed lists of related Web sites to the Instructor's Manual. Russell Baker of Florida Metropolitan University—Tampa College developed the Web site.

Many more people than we can ever acknowledge worked behind the scenes to translate our manuscript into the text you see; we thank them all.

Having a great text and package doesn't mean a thing if we don't find a way to get it to you. Kurt Strand, Director of Marketing, has been tireless in his support of this project. Our exceptional marketing manager, Katie Rose-Matthews, has a passion for this project that rivals our own. Her excitement and energy were infectious as she spread the word of the project's progress to the sales reps. We appreciate the renowned service and commitment of these dedicated sales reps as much as you do.

We have many instructors, **more than ever before**, to thank for contributing to the development of *Understanding Business*. An exceptional and creative group of reviewers dedicated many long hours to critiquing the previous edition and subsequent drafts of this edition. Their innovative and insightful recommendations and contributions were invaluable in making this edition a stronger instructional tool. Their contributions appear on every page of this revision. Our sincere thanks to the following reviewers.

···· ▬▬▬ ····

REVIEWERS OF THE FIFTH EDITION

Larry Aaronson, *Catonsville Community College*

Maria Aria, *Camden County College*

Glenann Arnold, *Pueblo Community College*

Barry Ashmen, *Bucks County Community College*

Hal Babson, *Columbus State Community College*

Herm Baine, *Broward Community College*

Russell Baker, *Florida Metropolitan University*

Charles Beavin, *Miami Dade—North*

Michael Bejtlich, *Cape Cod Community College*

Larry Benke, *Sacramento City College*

Marcel Berard, *Community College of Rhode Island*

Patricia Bernson, *County College of Morris*

John Berry, *Antelope Valley College*

Barbara Boyington, *Brookdale Community College*

Steven E. Bradley, *Austin Community College—Riverside*

Harvey S. Bronstein, *Oakland Community College*

Joseph Brum, *Fayetteville Technical Community College*

Barrett R. Burns, *Houston Community College*

Sam Chapman, *Diablo Valley College*

Barbara Ching, *Los Angeles City College*

Nancy Christenson, *Brevard Community College—Cocoa*

Robert Clobes, *St. Charles County Community College*

Bobbie Corbett, *Northern Virginia Community College—Annandale*

John Courtney, *University of Maryland, University College*

William W. Crandell, *College of San Mateo*

Lawrence Danks, *Camden County College*

Burton V. Dean, *San Jose State University*

Jack Dilbeck, *Ivy Tech State College*

Fran Emory, *Northern Virginia Community College—Woodbridge*

Shad Ewart, *Anne Arundel Community College*

Bob Farris, *Mt. San Antonio College*

Robert Fineran, *East-West University*

H. Steven Floyd, *Manatee Community College*

John Foster, *Montgomery College*

Barry Freeman, *Bergen County Community College*

Roger Fremier, *Monterey Peninsula College*

Lucille S. Genduso, *Nova Southeastern University*

James George, Jr., *Seminole Community College*

Tom Gilbertson, *Baker College*

Julie Giles, *DeVry Institute of Technology DuPage Campus*

Peter Giuliani, *Franklin University*

Eileen Glassman, *Montgomery College*

Don Gordon, *Illinois Central College*

Ron Gordon, *Florida Metropolitan University*

Gary Greene, *Manatee Community College—South*

Paula Gulbicki, *Middlesex Community College*

Jim Hagen, *Cornell University*

Billye Hansen, *University of Central Oklahoma*

Dennis Hansen, *Des Moines Area Community College*

Paula W. Hansen, *Des Moines Area Community College*

Lewis Jerome Healy, Jr., *Chesapeake College*

Chuck Hiatt, *Central Florida Community College*

David Hickman, *Frederick Community College*

Nathan Himelstein, *Essex County College*

Jim Isherwood, *Community College of Rhode Island*

Henry Jackson, *Delaware County Community College*

William Jedlicka, *William Rainey Harper College*

M. E. "Micki" Johnson, *Nova Southeastern University*

Mike Johnson, *Delaware County Community College*

Allen Kartchner, *Utah State University*

J. Roland Kelley, *Tarrant County Junior College*

Emogene King, *Tyler Junior College*

James H. King, *McLennan Community College*

Gregory Kishel, *Rancho Santiago Community College*

Patricia Kishel, *Cypress College*

Charles C. Kitzmiller, *Indian River Community College*

Karl Kleiner, *Ocean County College*

Anne Kostorizos, *Middlesex Community College*

Pat Laidler, *Massasoit Community College*

Fay Lamphear, *San Antonio College*

Thomas Lerra, *Quinsigamond Community College*

Murray Levy, *Glendale Community College*

Richard Lewis, *Lansing Community College*

Tom Lifvendahl, *Cardinal Stritch College*

Stephen Lindsey, *Citrus College*

Donald Linner, *Essex County College*

Corinne B. Linton, *Valencia Community College*

Paul James Londrigan, *Charles Mott Community College*

Larry Martin, *Community College of Southern Nevada*

Randolph L. Martin, *Germanna Community College*

Thomas Mason, *Brookdale Community College*

Bob Matthews, *Oakton Community College*

Paul McClure, *Mt. San Antonio College*

Jimmy McKenzie, *Tarrant County Junior College*

Noel McKeon, *Florida Community College at Jacksonville, Downtown*

Pat McMahon, *Palm Beach Community College—Glades*

Richard Morrison, *Northeastern University*

William Morrison, *San Jose State University*

Ed Mosher, *Laramie County Community College*

Carolyn Mueller, *Ball State University*

Winford C. Naylor, *Santa Barbara City College*

Sharon Nickels, *St. Petersburg Junior College*

Carolyn Nickeson, *Del Mar College*

David Oliver, *Edison Community College*

Kenneth Olson, *County College of Morris*

Robert A. Pacheco, *Massasoit Community College*

Teresa Palmer, *Illinois State University*

Janis Pasquali, *University of California—Riverside*

John P. Phillips, *Northern Virginia Community College—Manassas*

Marie Pietak, *Bucks County Community College*

Alison Adderley-Pittman, *Brevard Community College—Melbourn*

Marva H. Pryor, *Valencia Community College*

Brooke Quigg, *Pierce Junior College*

Charles C. Quinn, *Austin Community College—Northridge*

Don Radtke, *Richard J. Daley College*

Robert Redick, *Lincoln Land College*

Jim Reinemann, *College of Lake County*

Ali Roodsari, *Baltimore City College*

Linda Roy, *Evergreen Valley College*

Maurice M. Sampson, *Community College of Philadelphia*

Nick Sarantakes, *Austin Community College*

Wallace J. Satchell, *St. Phillips College*

Marilyn Schwartz, *College of Marin*

Greg Service, *Broward Community College—North*

Phyllis Shafer, *Brookdale Community College*

Dennis Shannon, *Belleville Area College*

Charles R. Shatzer, *Solano Community College*

Mark Sheehan, *Bunker Hill Community College*

Lynette Shishido, *Santa Monica College*

Leon Singleton, *Santa Monica College*

Sol A. Solomon, *Community College of Rhode Island*

Russell Southall, *Laney College*

Lynda St. Clair, *Bryant College*

Kenneth Steinkruger, *DeVry Institute of Technology—Chicago*

David Stringer, *DeAnza College*

Charles I. Stubbart, *Southern Illinois University*

Bill Syvertsen, *Fresno City College*

Daryl Taylor, *Pasadena City College*

Gary W. Thomas, *Anne Arundel Community College*

Lynda Thompson, *Massasoit Community College*

Susan Thompson, *Palm Beach Community College—Central*

J. Robert Ulbrich, *Parkland College*

Sal Veas, *Santa Monica College*

Robert Vandellen, *Baker College—Cadillac*

Mike Vijuk, *William Rainey Harper College*

Martha Villarreal, *San Joaquin Delta College*

Cortez Walker, *Baltimore City Community College*

W. J. Waters, *Central Piedmont Community College*

Martin Welc, *Saddleback College*

William A. Weller, *Modesto Junior College*

James H. Wells, *Daytona Beach Community College*

Richard Westfall, *Cabrillo College*

Aimee Wheaton, *Regis University*

Mary E. Williams, *University of Central Oklahoma*

Joyce Wood, *Northern Virginia Community College*

Ron Young, *Kalamazoo Valley Community College,*

···· ▬ ····

REVIEWERS AND OTHER PARTICIPANTS IN THE DEVELOPMENT OF PREVIOUS EDITIONS

Milton Alderfer, *Miami-Dade Community College,* Dennis G. Allen, *Grand Rapids Community College,* Dan Anderson, *Sullivan Jr. College,* Kenneth Anderson, *Charles S. Mott Community College,* John Anstey, *University of Nebraska—Omaha,* Ed Aronson, *Golden West College,* Larry Arp, *University of Southern Indiana,* Doug Ashby, *Lewis & Clark Community College,* Harold Babson, *Columbus State Community College,* Xenia Balabkins, *Middlesex Community College* Michael Baldigo, *Sonoma State University,* John Balek, *Morton College,* Barbara Barrett, *St. Louis Community College,* Richard Bartlett, *Muskigan Area Technical*

College, Lorraine Bassette, *Prince George's Community College*, Alec Beaudoin, *Triton College*, Jade Beavers, *Jeferson State Community College*, John Beem, *College of DuPage*, Dean Bittick, *East Central College*, Carol Bibly, *Triton College*, John Blackburn *The Ohio State University*, Jim Boeger, *Rock Valley College* Mary Jo Boehms, *Jackson State Community College*, John Bowdidge, *Southwest Missouri State University*, Stephen Branz, *Triton College*, Robert Brechner, *Miami-Dade Community College*, Harvey Bronstein, *Oakland Community College*, Debbie Brown, *Santa Fe Community College*, Joseph Brum, *Fayetteville Technical Community College*, Thomas Buchl, *Northern Michigan University*, Albert Bundons, *Johnson County Community College*, Dennis Butler, *Orange Coast Community College*, Ron Bytnar, *South Suburban College*, Willie Caldwell, *Houston Community College*, J. Callahan, *Florida Institute of Technology*, B.J. Campsey, *San Jose State University*, Professor Carman, *Bucks County Community College*, Mary Margaret Cavera, *Davenport College*, Sandra Cece, *Triton College*, Bruce Charnov, *Hofstra University*, Bonnie Chavez, *Santa Barbara City College*, William Chittenden, *Texas Tech University*, Larry Chonko, *Baylor University*, Jill Chown, *Mankato State University*, Michael Cicero, *Highline Community College*, J. Cicheberger, *Hillsborough Community College*, Monico Cisneros, *Austin Community College*, James Cocke, *Pima County Community College*, Professor Connell, *Montgomery County Community College*, Jeffrey Conte, *Westchester Community College*, Ron Cooley, *South Suburban College*, Allen Coon, *Robert Morris College*, Doug Copeland, *Johnson County Community College*, John Coppage, *Saginaw Valley State University*, Bobbie Corbett, *Northern Virginia Community College*, James Cox, *Jefferson Community College*, Bruce Cudney, *Middlesex Community*

College, C. Culbreth, *Brevard Community College*, Clifford Davis, *SUNY—Cobleskill*, R.K. Davis, *University of Akron*, Vincent Deni, *Oakland Community College*, Kathleen Denisco, *SUNY—Buffalo*, S. Desai, *Cedar Valley College*, Katherine Dillon, *Ocean County College*, Samuel DiRoberto, *Penn State University—Ogontz*, Ronald Eggers, *Barton College*, Pat Ellsberg, *Lower Columbia College*, Ted Erickson, *Normandale Community College*, Alton Evans, *Tarrant County Community College*, John Evans, *New Hampshire College*, C.S. Everett, *Des Moines Area Community College*, Al Fabian, *IVY Tech*, Karen Fager, *Umpqua Community College*, Frank Falcetta, *Middlesex Community College*, S. Fante, *Central Florida Community College*, Edward Fay, *Canton College of Technology*, Janice Feldbauer, *Austin Community College*, David Felt, *Northern Virginia Community College—Manassas*, Bob Ferrentino, *Lansing Community College*, Robert Fishco, *Middlesex County Community College*, Charles FitzPatrick, *Central Michigan University*, Jane Flagello, *DeVry Institute of Technology—Lombard*, Steve Floyd, *Manatee Community College*, John Foster, *Montgomery College*, Leatrice Freer, *Pitt Community College*, Michael Fritz, *Portland Community College*, Thomas Frizzel, *Massasoit Community College*, Alan Gbur, *Richard J. Daley College*, Eileen Baker Glassman, *Montgomery College*, Bernette Glover, *Olive Harvey College*, Patricia Graber, *Middlesex County College*, Mike Graves, *Portland Community College*, Joe Gray, *Nassau Community College*, Gary Green, *Manatee Community College*, Roberta Greene, *Central Piedmont Community College*, Stephen Griffin, *Tarrant County Junior College*, Donald Gordon, *Illinois Central College*, John Gubbay, *Moraine Valley Community College*, Johnathan Gueverra, *Newbury College*, James J. Hagel, *Davenport College*, Dan Hall, *East Central College*, Daniel Hallock,

St. Edward's University, Clark Hallpike, *Elgin Community College,* Ron Halsac, *Community College Allegheny North,* E. Hamm, *Tidewater Community College,* Bob Harmel, *Midwestern State University,* Gene Hastings, *Portland Community College,* Frederic Hawkins, *Westchester Business Institute,* Joseph Hecht, *Montclair State College,* Douglas Heeter, *Ferris State University,* Michael Heim, *Lakewood Community College,* Sanford B. Helman, *Middlesex County College,* Tim Helton, *Joliet Junior College,* Edward Henn, *Broward Community College,* Dave Hickman, *Frederick Community College,* George Hicks, *Muskigan Area Technical College,* Nathan Himmelstein, *Essex County College,* Eric Hoogstra, *Davenport College,* B. Hoover, *Brevard Community College,* Vince Howe, *University of North Carolina— Wilmington,* Joseph Hrebenak, *Community College Allegheny County,* Tom Humphrey, *Palomar College,* Howard Hunnius, *John Tyler Community College,* Robert Ironside, *North Lake College,* James Isherwood, *Community College of Rhode Island,* Gloria Jackson, *San Antonio College,* Paloma Jalife, *SUNY—Oswego,* Bill Jedlicka, *Harper College,* Paul Jenner, *Southwest Missouri State University,* Gene Johnson, *Clark College,* Michael Johnson, *Delaware County Community College,* Wallace Johnston, *Virginia Commonwealth University,* John Kalaras, *DeVry Institute of Technology,* Alan Kardoff, *Northern Illinois University,* Norman Karl, *Johnson County Community College,* Allen Kartchner, *Utah State University,* Bob Kegel, *Cypress College,* Warren Keller, *Grossmont College,* Jim Kennedy, *Angelina College,* Daniel Kent, *Northern Kentucky University,* Professor Kern, *Reading Area Community College,* Robert Kersten, *St. Louis Community College—Florissant Valley,* Betty Ann Kirk, *Tallahassee Community College,* John A. Knarr, *University of Maryland—European Division,*

Barbara G. Kreichbaum, *Hagerstown Business College,* Patrick C. Kumpf, *University of Cincinnati,* Kenneth Lacho, *University of New Orleans,* Jay LaGregs, *Tyler Junior College,* Professor Lander, *Montgomery County Community College,* Roger Lattanza, *University of New Mexico,* Donna Lees, *Butte College,* Jim Lentz, *Moraine Valley Community College,* George Leonard, *St. Petersburg Junior College,* Joseph Liebreich, *Reading Area Community College,* Ellen Reynolds Ligons, *Pasadena City College,* Yet Mee Lim, *Alabama State University,* Donald Linner, *Essex County College,* John Lloyd, *Monroe Community College,* Thomas Lloyd, *Westmoreland County Community College,* Paul Londrigan, *C.S. Mott Community College,* Patricia Long, *Tarrant Junior College,* Anthony Lucas, *Allegheny Community College,* Joyce Luckman, *Jackson Community College,* Judith Lyles, *Illinois State University,* Jerry Lynch, *Purdue University,* Rippy Madan, *Frostburg State University,* Richard Maringer, *University of Akron—Wayne College,* Alan Marks, *DeVry Institute of Technology,* Bob Mathews, *Oakton Communitiy College,* Christine McCallum, *University of Akron— Wayne College,* Diana McCann, *Kentucky College of Business,* Mark M. McCarthy, *Davenport College,* Carl Meskimen, *Sinclair Community College,* Duane Miller, *SUNY— Cobleskill,* Herbert Miller, *Indiana University—Kokomo,* Terrance Mitchell, *South Suburban College,* Joyce Mooneyhan, *Pasadena City College,* Willy Morris, *Northwestern Business College,* William Motz, *Lansing Community College,* Micah Mukabi, *Essex County College,* Gary R. Murray, *Rose State College,* Herschel Nelson, *Polk Community College,* Sharon J. Nickels, *Saint Petersburg Junior College,* Elaine Novak, *San Jacinto College,* Phil Nufrio, *Essex County College,* Edward O'Brien, *Scotsdale Community College,* Eugene O'Connor, *California Polytechnical University—San Luis*

Obispo, Cletus O'Drobinak, *South Suburban College,* Katherine Olson, *Northern Virginia Community College,* Susan Oleson, *Central Piedmont Community College,* J. Ashton Oravetz, *Tyler Junior College,* George Otto, *Truman College,* Nikki Paahana, *DeVry Institute of Technology,* Mike Padbury, *Arapahoe Community College,* Dennis Pappas, *Columbus State Community College,* Dennis Pappas, *Columbus Technical Institute,* Knowles Parker, *Wake Technical Community College,* Patricia Parker, *Maryville University,* Darlene Raney Perry, *Columbus State,* Stephen Peters, *Walla Walla Community College,* A. Pittman, *Brevard Community College,* Joseph Platts, *Miami-Dade Community College,* Wayne Podgorski, *University of Memphis,* Raymond Pokhon, *M A T C,* Robert Pollero, *Ann Arundel Community College,* Geraldine Powers, *Northern Essex Community College,* Roderick Powers, *Iowa State University,* Renee Prim, *Central Piedmont Community College,* Donald Radtke, *Richard J. Daley College,* Anne Ranczuch, *Monroe Community College,* Richard Randall, *Nassau Community College,* Richard J. Randolph, *Johnson County Community College,* Betsy Ray, *Indiana Business College,* Mary E. Ray, *Indiana Business College,* Robert Redick, *Lincoln Land Community College,* Scott Reedy, *Brookes College,* James Reinemann, *College of Lake County,* Carla Rich, *Pensacola Junior College,* John Rich, *Illinois State University,* Doug Richardson, *Eastfield College,* Karen Richardson, *Tarrant County Junior College,* Bob Roswell, *Jackson Community College,* Jeri Rubin, *University of Alaska,* Jill Russell, *Camden County College,* Karl Rutkowski, *Peirce Jr. College,* Tom Rutkowski, *SUNY—Cobleskill,* Cathy Sanders, *San Antonio College,* Nicholas Sarantakes, *Austin Community College,* Billie Sargent, *National College,* Wallace Satchell, *St. Phillip's College,* Gordon Saul, *National Business College,* Larry Saville, *Des Moines Area Community College,* Kurt Schindler, *Wilbur Wright College,* Dennis Schmitt, *Emporia State University,* Jim Seeck, *Harper College,* Daniel C. Segebath, *South Suburban College,* Patricia A. Serraro, *Clark College,* Guy Sessions, *Spokane Falls Community College,* Dennis Shannon, *Belleville Area Community College,* Richard Shapiro, *Cuyahoga Community College,* Nora Jo Sherman, *Houston Community College,* Donald Shifter, *Fontbonne College,* Leon Singleton, *Santa Monica College,* Jerry Sitek, *Southern Illinois University,* Michelle Slagle, *The George Washington University,* Noel Smith, *Palm Beach Community College,* Bill Snider, *Cuesta College,* Paul Solomon, *San Jose State University,* Carl Sonntag, *Pikes Peak Community College,* Rieann Spence-Gale, *Northern Virginia Community College,* Richard Stanish, *Tulsa Junior College,* Emanual Stein, *Queensborough Community College,* Scott Steinkamp, *Northwestern Business College,* Carl Stem, *Texas Tech University,* Robert Stivender, *Wake Technical Community College,* David Stringer, *DeAnza College,* Jacinto Suarez, *Bronx Community College,* Paul Sunko, *Olive Harvey College,* George Sutcliffe, *Central Piedmont Community College,* Lorraine Suzuki, *University of Maryland—Asian Division,* Carl Swartz, *Three Rivers Community College,* James Taggart, *University of Akron,* Merle E. Taylor, *Santa Barbara City College,* Verna Teasdale, *Prince George's Community College,* Ray Tewell, *American River College,* Susan Thompson, *Palm Beach Community College,* Darrell Thompson, *Mountain View College,* Vern Timmer, *SUNY—Alfred,* Amy Toth, *Northampton County Area Community College,* Robert Ulbrich, *Parkland College,* Pablo Ulloa, *El Paso Community College,* Richard Van Ness, *Schenectady County Community College,* Heidi Vernon-Wortzel, *Northeastern University,* Janna P. Vice, *Eastern Kentucky*

University, Michael Vijuk, *Harper College*, William Vincent, *Santa Barbara City College*, Philip Weatherford, *Embry-Riddle Aeronautical University*, Pete Weiksner, *Lehigh County Community College*, Henry Weiman, *Bronx Community College*, Bernard Weinrich, *St. Louis Community College—Forest Park*, Bill Weisgerber, *Saddleback College*, Sally Wells, *Columbia College*, Donald White, *Prince Georges Community College*, Walter Wilfong, *Florida Technical College*, Dick Williams, *Laramie County Community College*, Paul Williams, *Mott Community College*, Gayla Jo Wilson, *Mesa State College*, Wallace Wirth, *South Suburban Community College*, Judy Eng Woo, *Bellevue Community College*, Bennie Woods, *Burlington County College*, Greg Worosz, *Schoolcraft College*, William Wright, *Mt. Hood Community College*, Merv Yeagle, *Hagerstown Junior College*, C. Yin, *DeVry Institute of Technology*, Ned Young, *Sinclair Community College*, Ron Young, *Kalamazoo Valley Community College*, C. Zarycki, *Hillsborough Community College*, Richard Zollinger, *Central Piedmont College*.

In the fourth edition, it was our honor to receive direct input from a very special group of users—students. These introduction to business students gave up their time to visit with us in a day-long session in order to help us better meet the needs of students that will follow them. We thank the following for sharing their ideas and course experiences:

Carol Griesbach, *Rock Valley Community College*

Leslie Hanson, *Moraine Valley Community College*

Ken Kuh, *Moraine Valley Community College*

Tom Martin, *Harper College*

Kathy Sarich, *DeVry Institute of Technology*

Kevis Smith, *Olive Harvey College*

Donna Wendling, *Elgin Community College*

The fifth edition is once again superior to its predecessors due to involvement of these committed instructors and students. We thank them all.

Bill Nickels
Jim McHugh
Susan McHugh

Understanding Business

Secrets to Your Success (Confidential for Students Using This Text)

Prologue

film
Bus
Etiquette

This is an exciting and challenging time to be studying business. Never before have there been more opportunities to become a successful businessperson anywhere in the world. And never before have there been more challenges. Success in any venture comes from understanding basic principles and learning to apply those principles effectively. There are some secrets to success that can make the task easier and give you an edge over the competition. The purpose of this prologue and of the entire text is to help you learn these principles and some of the secrets of success that will help you not only in this course but in your entire career.

Experts say it is likely that today's college graduates will hold seven or eight different jobs in their lifetime. That means you will have to be flexible and adjust your strengths and talents to new opportunities as they become available. Many of the best jobs of the future don't even exist today. Learning has become a lifelong job. You will have to constantly update your skills if you want to achieve and maintain a leadership position.

This book and this course together may be one of your most important learning experiences ever. They're meant to help you understand business so that you can use business principles throughout your life. But you don't have to be in business to use business principles. You can use marketing principles to get a job and to sell your ideas to others. You can use your knowledge of investments to make money in the stock market. Similarly, you'll be able to use management skills and general business knowledge wherever you go and in whatever career you pursue. What you learn now could help you be a success the rest of your life.

◄ CONSIDER USING TM 1
Chapter Outline

•••• ▬▬▬ ••••

YOU ALREADY KNOW ONE SECRET: THE VALUE OF A COLLEGE EDUCATION

The gap between the earnings of high school graduates and college graduates is growing every year. It now ranges from 60 to 70 percent.[1] That is, college graduates may make 70 percent more than high school graduates. Thus, what you invest in a college education is likely to pay you back many times. That

◄CONSIDER USING OT TRANS-
PARENCY P-1
Business Training For the 21st Century

College students in general make from 60 to 70 percent more money in their lifetimes than high-school graduates. College not only prepares you for the jobs of the future, it also gives you the chance to network with other college graduates who may help you find jobs in the future. What can you do while in college to optimize the networking benefits it provides?

doesn't mean there aren't good careers available to non-college graduates. It just means that those with an education are more likely to have higher earnings over their lifetime.

To get the most out of your college education, you must become familiar with computers. We encourage you to take any opportunity that arises to use the computer and to learn the latest computer applications, including word processing, desktop publishing, and e-mail, as well as using the Internet. The investment you make in college and in developing computer skills will likely be quite rewarding. It will be even more valuable if you study your text carefully and make the effort to complete all the exercises in the study guide.

···· ▬▬ ····

THE SECRET TO STARTING A SUCCESSFUL CAREER

CONSIDER USING OT TRANS-
PARENCY P-2 ➤
Key Career Questions

Almost all of us want to find a rewarding career and to be successful and happy. We just find it hard to decide what that career should be. Even many of those who have relatively successful careers continue to look for something more fulfilling, more challenging, and more interesting. If you're typical of many college students, you may not have any idea what career you'd like to pursue. That isn't necessarily a big disadvantage in today's fast-changing job market. There are no perfect or certain ways to prepare for the most interesting and challenging jobs of tomorrow, many of which have yet to be created. Rather, you should continue your college education, develop strong computer skills, improve your verbal and written communication skills, and remain flexible while you explore the job market.

One purpose of this text is to introduce you to the wide variety of careers available in business and management. You'll learn about production, marketing, finance, accounting, management, economics, and more. At the end of the course, you should have a much better idea about what careers would be best for you and what careers you would *not* enjoy. Not only that, you'll be prepared to use basic business terms and concepts that are necessary to achieving success in any organization—including government agencies, charities, and social causes—or in your own small business.

CONSIDER USING LECTURE
ENHANCER P-1 ➤
Success of Women Entrepreneurs

··· GETTING STARTED ···

A great place to start in your career search is with a course like this one. Each chapter in this book will begin with a profile of someone in the business world. Each section of the book ends with a profile of a recent student who used the concepts he or she learned in this course to begin a career. Many of the people you'll meet in the profiles learned the hard way that it's easy to fail in business if you don't know what you're doing. Reading these stories is a good way to learn from the experiences of others.

··· ASSESSING YOUR SKILLS AND PERSONALITY ···

The earlier you can do a personal assessment of your interests, skills, and values, the better it will be for you in finding some career direction. In recognition of this need, many colleges offer self-assessment programs. About 300 schools use a software exercise called the System for Interactive Guidance and Information (SIGI). A different version, called DISCOVER, is used at about 400 other schools. Both SIGI and DISCOVER feature self-assessment exercises, create personalized lists of occupations based on your interests and skills, and provide information about different careers and the preparation each requires.

The Strong-Campbell Interest Inventory and the Meyers-Briggs personality indicator can be used to supplement DISCOVER and SIGI, and to reinforce the results. Visit your college's placement center, career lab, or library and learn what programs are available for you.

It would be helpful to use one or more self-assessment programs early in this course so you can determine, while you're learning about the different business fields, which ones most closely fit your interests and skills. Self-assessment will help you determine the kind of work environment you'd prefer (for example, technical, social service, or business); what values you seek to fulfill in a career (for example, security, variety, or independence); what abilities you have (for example, creative/artistic, numerical, or sales); and what important job characteristics you stress most (for example, income, travel, or amount of job pressure).

Even if you're one of the 40 percent or more of college students who are over 25 years old, an assessment of your skills will help you choose the right courses and career path to follow. Many others have taken such tests because they are not satisfied with what they're doing and are seeking a more rewarding occupation. Armed with the results of your self-assessment, you too are more likely to make a career choice that will be personally fulfilling.

Many people return to college to improve their skills in areas such as computers and writing. Others return because they realize, once they enter the marketplace, how important a college education is. Can you see the advantage of going back to school periodically over your career to keep your skills current?

••• LEARNING PROFESSIONAL BUSINESS STRATEGIES •••

Business professionals have learned the importance of networking and of keeping files on subjects that are important to them. These are two secrets to success that students should begin practicing now. One thing that links students in all colleges is the need to retain what they learn in business courses. While it's important for you to learn about various careers and businesses, you may tend to forget such data. You need a strategy to help you remember what you've learned. It's also extremely important to keep the names of contact people at various organizations. In addition, you may want to keep facts and figures of all kinds about the economy and business-related subjects. These are all reasons why you should develop resource files.

An effective way to become an expert on almost any business subject is to set up your own information system. Eventually you may want to store data on computer disks for retrieval on your personal computer and to access professional databases as businesspeople do. Meanwhile, it's effective to establish a comprehensive paper filing system.

If you start now, you'll soon have at your fingertips information that will prove invaluable for use in term papers and throughout your career. Few college students do this filing, and, as a consequence, most lose much of the information they read in college or thereafter. *Developing this habit is one of the most effective ways of educating yourself and having the information available when you need it.* The only space you'll need to start is a 12-inch by 12-inch corner of your room to hold a portable file box. In these files you might put your course notes, with the names of your professors and the books you used, and so on. You may need this information later for employment references. Also, be sure to keep all the notes you make when talking with people about careers, including salary information, courses needed, and contacts.

Each time you read a story about a firm that interests you, either cut it out of the publication or photocopy it and then place it in an appropriate file. You

◄ **CONSIDER USING OT TRANSPARENCY P-3**
How to Grow a Career

◄ **CONSIDER USING OT TRANSPARENCY P-4**
Career Expectations and Opportunities Analysis

◄ **CONSIDER USING OT TRANSPARENCY P-5**
Six Keys to Career Self-Reliance

A simple file system can provide you with some useful advantages over students who do not keep such files. You will have at your fingertips articles that will be valuable in completing class assignments, the names of people you can use to network, the names of the best professors on campus so you can schedule them, and other resource information you deem worthwhile. What additional benefits do you see from keeping interesting information from newspapers, magazines, and similar sources?

might begin with files labeled Careers, Small Business, Economics, Management, and Resource People. You might summarize the article briefly on a Post-it note and stick this summary on the front for later reference.

You definitely want to have a personal data file titled Credentials for My Résumé or something similar. In that file, you'll place all reference letters and other information about jobs you may have held. Soon you'll have a tremendous amount of information available to you. You can add to these initial files until you have your own comprehensive information system.

Businesspeople are constantly seeking ways to increase their knowledge of the business world and to increase their investment returns. One way they do so is by watching television shows such as "Wall $treet Week," Adam Smith's "Money World," and the "Nightly Business Report." Watching such programs is like getting a free graduate education in business. Try viewing some of these shows or listening to similar shows on the radio, and see which ones you like best. Take notes and put them in your files. Another way, one of the best, to increase your business knowledge is to read your local newspaper. Keep up with the business news in your local area so you know what jobs are available and where.

ANOTHER SECRET WEAPON: GOOD MANNERS

Good manners are back, and for a good reason. As the world becomes increasingly competitive, the gold goes to the team that shows off an extra bit of polish. The person who makes a good impression will be the one who gets the job, wins the promotion, or clinches the deal. Manners and professionalism must become second nature to anyone who wants to achieve and maintain a competitive edge.[2]

"Too often professionals spend their energies becoming experts in their particular field, often neglecting other concerns, including fashion and etiquette," says Susan Huston, an etiquette instructor. "They look great on paper and many even get through the interview, then they get in the workplace and may not fit in. They have reached their destination and their behavior becomes critical, but they haven't learned how to present themselves well."[3]

One source of irritability and rude behavior within a company may result from downsizing and the extra work and stress it produces.[4] Even under stressful conditions, however, it is important to maintain your composure at work and not lose your temper.

The lesson is this: You can have good credentials, but a good presentation is everything. You can't neglect etiquette, or somewhere in your career you will be at a competitive disadvantage because of your inability to use good manners or to maintain your composure in tense situations.

••• LEARNING TO ACT LIKE A PROFESSIONAL •••

You can learn a lot about good and bad manners from watching professional sports. During the 1997 basketball playoff series, for example, Michael Jordan of the Chicago Bulls showed that true professionals accept responsibility for the team and never give up. Whenever the game was on the line, the team turned to Michael for the important shot, and, more often than not, he made it.

CNBC's popular "pre-game" financial news program "Squawk Box" helps viewers keep up with business news by taking them live inside the trading rooms of major investment banks and onto the floor of the New York Stock Exchange. The show's hosts track the strategies of Wall Street investment professionals and interview prominent business-people before trading begins each morning. What have you personally learned from watching this or similar business shows on TV?

You can probably think of contrasting examples of sports stars who have earned a bad reputation by not acting professionally (e.g., spitting, swearing, criticizing teammates in front of others, and so on). People in professional sports are fined if they are late to meetings or refuse to follow the rules established by the team and coach. Business professionals also must follow set rules; many of these rules are not formally written anywhere, but every successful businessperson learns them through experience.

You can begin the habits now that will make for great success when you start your career. Those habits include the following:

1. *Making a good first impression.* "You have seven seconds to make an impression. People see your clothes before you even open your mouth. And make no mistake, everything you say following those first few moments will be weighed by how you look," says image consultant Aleysha Proctor.[5] You don't get a second chance to make a good first impression. Skip the fads and invest in high-quality, classic clothes. Remember, "high-quality" is not necessarily the same as "expensive." Take a clue as to what is appropriate at any specific company by studying the people there who are most successful. What do they wear? How do they act?

2. *Focusing on good grooming.* Be aware of your appearance and its impact on those around you. Consistency is essential. You can't project a good image by dressing up a few times a week and then show up looking like you're getting ready to mow a lawn. Wear appropriate, clean clothing and accessories. It is not appropriate, for example, for men to wear hats inside of buildings. It is also not appropriate, usually, to wear wrinkled shirts or to have shirttails hanging out of your pants.

3. *Being on time.* When you don't come to class or to work on time, you're sending a message to your teacher or boss. You're saying, "My time is more important than your time. I have more important things to do than be here." In addition to the lack of respect tardiness shows to your teacher or boss, it rudely disrupts the work of your colleagues. Promptness may not be a priority in some circles, but in the workplace

promptness is essential. But being punctual doesn't always mean just being on time. Executive recruiter Juan Menefee recalls a time he arrived at 7:40 A.M. for an 8:00 A.M. meeting only to discover he was the last one there. "You have to look around, pay attention to the corporate culture and corporate clock," says Menefee. To develop good work habits and get good grades, it is important to get to class on time and not leave early.

4. *Practicing considerate behavior.* Considerate behavior includes listening when others are talking, and not reading the newspaper or eating in class. Don't interrupt others when they are speaking. Wait for your turn to present your views in classroom discussions. Of course, eliminate all words of profanity from your vocabulary. Use appropriate body language by sitting up attentively and not slouching. Sitting up has the added bonus of helping you stay awake! Professors and managers get a favorable impression from those who look and act alert. That may help your grades in school and your advancement at work.

5. *Being prepared.* A businessperson would never show up for a meeting without reading the materials assigned for that meeting and being prepared to discuss the topics of the day. To become a professional, one must practice acting like a professional. For students, that means reading assigned materials before class, asking questions and responding to questions in class, and discussing the material with fellow students.

From the minute you enter your first job interview until the day you retire, people will notice whether you follow the proper business etiquette. Just as traffic laws enable people to drive more safely, business etiquette allows people to conduct business with the appropriate amount of dignity. How you talk, how you eat, and how you dress all create an impression on others.

Business etiquette may have a different meaning in different countries. It is important, therefore, to learn the proper business etiquette for each country you visit. Areas that require proper etiquette include greeting people (shaking hands is not always appropriate); eating (Europeans, for example, often hold their knives and forks while eating); giving gifts; handling business cards; and conducting business. Honesty, high ethical standards, and good character (e.g., reliability and trustworthiness) are important ingredients to success in any country. Ethics is so important to success that we will include ethics discussions throughout the text.

···· ▬▬▬ ····

THE SECRET OF THE RESOURCES FOR THIS COURSE

College courses are best at teaching you concepts and ways of thinking about business. However, to learn firsthand about real-world applications, you will need to explore and interact with actual businesses. Textbooks are like comprehensive tour guides in that they tell you what to look for and where to look, but they can never replace experience.

This text, then, isn't meant to be the only resource for this class. In fact, it's not even the primary resource. Your professor will be much better than the text at responding to your specific questions and needs. This book is just one of the resources he or she can use with you to satisfy your desire to understand what the business world is all about. There are six basic resources for the class in addition to the text and study guide:

1. *The professor.* One of the most valuable facets of college is the chance to study with experienced professors. Your instructor is more than a teacher of facts and concepts. As mentioned above, he or she is a resource who's there to answer questions and guide you to the answers for others. It's important for you to develop a friendly relationship with all of your professors. One reason for doing so is that many professors get job leads they can pass on to you. Professors are also excellent references for future jobs. By following the rules of dress and etiquette outlined above, you can create a good impression, which will be valuable should you ask a professor to write a good letter of recommendation for you. Finally, your professor is one more experienced person who can help you find and access resource materials, both at your college and in the business world.

2. *The text,* Understanding Business, *and the study guide that comes with it.* The study guide will help you review and interpret key material and give you practice answering test questions. Even if your professor does not assign the study guide, you may want to complete it anyhow. Doing so is one way of competing successfully with the other students.

3. *Outside readings.* We recommend that you review the following magazines and newspapers as well as other resources during the course and throughout your career: *The Wall Street Journal, Forbes, Inc., Business Week, Fortune,* the *Harvard Business Review, Nation's Business, Black Enterprise,* and *Entrepreneur.* As mentioned earlier, you may also want to read your local newspaper's business section to keep up with current issues. If you're not familiar with these sources, it's time to get to know them. You don't necessarily have to become a regular subscriber, but you should learn what information is available in these sources over time, especially information that will help you get a job. All of these sources are probably available free of charge in your school's learning resource center or the local public library. One secret to success in business is staying current, and these magazines will help you do so.

4. *Your own experience and that of your classmates.* Many college students have had experience working in business or nonprofit organizations. Talking together about those experiences exposes you to many real-life examples that are invaluable for understanding business. Don't rely totally on the professor for answers to the cases and other exercises in this book. Often there is no single "right" answer, and your classmates may open up new ways of looking at things for you. Part of being a successful businessperson is knowing how to work with others. College classrooms are excellent places to practice this skill. Some professors provide opportunities for their students to work together in small groups. Such exercises build teamwork as well as presentation and analytical skills. If you have students from other countries in your class, working with them can help you learn about different cultures and different approaches to handling business problems. There is strength in diversity, so seek out people different from yourself to work with on teams.

◄ CONSIDER USING OT TRANS-
PARENCY P-6
Planning a Return to the Workforce

◄ CONSIDER USING OT TRANS-
PARENCY P-7
Where Are the Jobs of the Future?

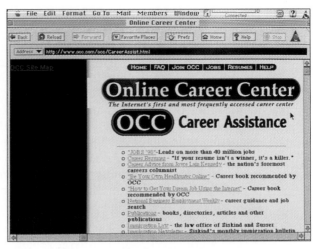

(Left) When shopping in a local mall or on the Internet, think about possible careers in the companies you visit or research. What kind of career are you now planning? What courses will you have to take to pursue that career? Have you taken a broad selection of courses that will enable you to switch careers if you so choose? Many people consider Harley-Davidson an icon among American companies, but would it be a desirable place to work?

(Right) More and more people today are turning to the Internet to find job openings and to learn about companies that interest them. If you have not learned how to "surf" the Net yet, now is the time to start. Find someone on campus who can help you learn and search for a computer you can use. Even if you're already surfing, you should continue to learn better and faster ways of finding the information you want. If you are computer wise, would you be willing to help someone in your class become more computer literate?

5. *Outside contacts.* One of the best ways to learn about different businesses is to personally visit them. Who can tell you more about what it's like to start a career in accounting than someone who's doing it now? The same is true of other jobs. The world can be your classroom if you let it. When you go shopping, for example, think about whether you would enjoy working in and managing a store. Talk with the clerks and the manager to see how they feel about the job. Think about the possibilities of owning or managing a restaurant, an auto body shop, a health club, a print shop, or any other establishment you visit. If something looks interesting, talk to the employees and learn more about their jobs and the industry. Soon you may discover fascinating careers in places such as the zoo or a health club or in industries such as travel or computer sales. In short, be constantly on the alert to find career possibilities, and don't hesitate to talk with people about their careers. Typically, they'll be pleased to give you their time because they're talking about their favorite subject—themselves.

6. *The Internet.* Never before have students had access to information as easily as they do today. What makes information gathering so easy now is the Internet. Once you've learned to surf the Internet, you will find more material than you could use in a lifetime. On the Internet you can search through library catalogs all over the world, find articles from leading business journals, view paintings from leading museums, and more—much more. Throughout this text we will present information and exercises that will help you gain experience using the Internet. But don't rely on the text for all your knowledge. Talk with your friends and acquaintances and learn as much as you can about how to use the Internet. This resource is likely to become even more important in the future. The information changes rapidly, and it is up to you to stay current. If you don't already know how to use the Internet, learn to do so now!

To find information about careers or internships try the following sites:

National Assembly of Voluntary Health and Social Welfare Organizations: http://www.nassembly.org (database of more than 2,000 internships in nonprofit organizations, for the summer and throughout the year).

Riley Guide: http://www.dbm.com/jobguide/

Online Career Center: http://www.occ.com

Career Mosaic: http://careermosaic.com

America's Job Bank: http://www.ajb.dni.us

Yahoo! Classifieds: http://classifieds.yahoo.com

The Main Quad: http://develop.mainquad.com

7. *The library or learning resource center.* The library is a great complement to the Internet as a valuable resource. Work with your librarian to learn how to best access the information you need. For example, it is a valuable exercise to research the resources you might use to begin a successful career search. While you're in college, you may want to work as an intern in various firms to get a better idea of what people do in various careers. Some schools offer a cooperative education program where you go to school for a while and then work for a while in a local firm. If your school doesn't offer such a program, you can create one on your own. The following are sources you can use for finding out about such jobs and other career choices:

◄ CONSIDER USING OT TRANSPARENCY P-8
Enrollments in Higher Education

◄ CONSIDER USING OT TRANSPARENCY P-9
Number of Students Completing 4-Year Degrees

Peterson's Hidden Job Market 1998 (Princeton, N.J.: Peterson's Guides).

Adams Job Almanac 1998 (Holbrook, Mass.: Adams Publishing).

John W. Wright, *The American Almanac of Jobs and Salaries,* 1997–98 edition (New York: Avon Books).

Timothy Butler and James Waldroop, *Discovering Your Career in Business* (Reading, Mass.: Addison-Wesley, 1997).

LaVerne L. Ludden, *Job Savvy* (New York: JIST Works, 1998), for information on how to make a good impression and on problem solving.

Dana Morgan and Robert Goldenkoff, *Federal Jobs* (New York: Macmillan General Reference, 1997).

Ollie Stevenson, *The Colorblind Career* (Princeton, N.J.: Peterson's, 1997).

Richard Nelson Bolles, *What Color Is Your Parachute?* (Berkeley, Calif.: Ten Speed Press, 1998).

Ronald L. Krannich, *Change Your Job/Change Your Life* (Manassas Park, Va.: Impact Publications, 1997).

For help in résumé writing and other career enhancements, see the following sources:

Kate Wendleton, *Job-Search Secrets* (New York: Five O'Clock Books, 1997).

Margaret Riley, Frances Roehm, and Steve Oserman, *The Guide to Internet Job Searching* (Lincolnwood, Ill.: VGM Career Horizons, 1997).

Résumés for College Students and Recent Graduates (Lincolnwood, Ill.: VGM Career Horizons, 1997).

Caryl Rae Krannich and Ronald Krannich, *Interview for Success* (Manassas Park, Va.: Impact Publications, 1997).

Camille Lavington, *You've Only Got Three Seconds* (New York: Doubleday, 1997).

John T. Molloy, *Dress for Success* (New York: Warner Books, 1998).

···· ▬ ····

THE SECRET TO GETTING THE MOST FROM THIS TEXT (AND AN A IN THE COURSE)

Many learning aids appear throughout this text to help you understand the concepts:

1. *List of Learning Goals at the beginning of each chapter.* Reading through these Learning Goals will help you set the framework and focus for the chapter material. Since every student at one time or another has found it difficult to get into studying, the Learning Goals are there to provide an introduction and to get your mind into a learning mode.

2. *Self-test questions.* Periodically within each chapter, you'll encounter set-off lists of questions headed Progress Check or Critical Thinking. These questions give you a chance to pause, think carefully about, and recall what you've just read. We've all experienced having our minds wander while we read. The Progress Checks will help you realize whether you're really absorbing the material. They're also an excellent review device. The Critical Thinking questions are designed to help you relate the material to your own experiences. They should help you think about the meaning of what you have just read in relation to your own life. Research has shown that it is much easier to retain information and concepts if you can relate to them personally.

3. *Key terms.* Developing a strong business vocabulary may be one of the most important and useful outcomes of this course. To assist you, all key terms in the book are highlighted in boldface type. Key terms are also defined in the margins, and page references to these terms are given at the end of each chapter. A full glossary is located in the back of the book. You should rely heavily on these learning aids in adding the key terms to your vocabulary.

4. *Boxes.* Each chapter contains a number of boxes that offer extended examples or discussions of concepts in the text. This material is designed to highlight key concepts and to make the book more interesting to read. One of the questions most frequently asked by our students is "Will the stuff in the boxes be on the test?" Make sure you read the boxes whether your instructor tests you on them or not—they're often the most interesting parts! The boxes cover major themes of the

Because life really is mostly essay questions, this text includes a couple of critical thinking exercises in every chapter to encourage you to generate your own thoughts about the issues raised in the chapter. Can you see the benefit of pausing to answer such questions as you read? In the first place, it will put the material into your own context. Secondly, it will keep you aware of the issues and force you to think about your own perspectives.

FRANK & ERNEST® by Bob Thaves

book: (1) ethics (Making Ethical Decisions); (2) entrepreneurship (From the Pages of *Business Week* Magazine); (3) small business (Spotlight on Small Business); (4) legal environment of business (Legal Briefcase); and (5) global business (Reaching Beyond Our Borders).

5. *End-of-chapter summaries.* The summaries are not mere reviews of what has been said in the text. Rather, they're written in question-and-answer form, much like a classroom dialogue. This format makes the material more lively and should help you remember it better. The summaries are directly tied to the Learning Goals so that you can see whether you've accomplished the chapter's objectives.

6. *Developing Workplace Skills exercises.* Regardless of how hard textbook writers and professors try to make learning easier, the truth is that students tend to forget most of what they read and hear. To really remember something, it's best to do it. That's why there are Developing Workplace Skills sections at the end of each chapter. The purpose of Developing Workplace Skills questions is to suggest small projects that reinforce what you've read and help you develop the skills you need to succeed in the workplace. These activities will help you develop skill in using resources, interpersonal skills, skills in managing information, skills in understanding systems, and computer skills.

7. *Taking It to the Net exercises.* The Internet exercises serve two purposes: to enhance your understanding of the concepts presented in the chapter and to build your Internet skills. Many of these exercises involve interactive activities that help you apply the chapter's concepts. It is important to remember that the Internet is constantly evolving and that Internet addresses (known as uniform resource locators, or URLs) are subject to constant and frequent change. If an address in a Taking It to the Net exercise is no longer available to you, you can impress your instructor by finding a Web site with similar information and completing the exercise there.

8. *Practicing Management Decisions.* The management decision cases give you another chance to think about the material and apply it in real-life situations. Don't skip the cases even if they're not reviewed in class. They're an integral part of the learning process because they enable you to think about and apply what you've studied.

If you use all of these learning aids plus the study guide, you will not simply "take a course in business." Instead, you will have actively participated in a learning experience that will help you greatly in your chosen career. The most important secret to success may be to enjoy what you are doing and to do your best in everything. You can't do your best without taking advantage of all the learning aids that are available to you.

Now you know the secrets to succeeding in this course and in your career. Begin applying these secrets now to gain an edge on the competition. Good luck. We wish you the best.

Bill Nickels
Jim McHugh
Susan McHugh

Getting the Job You Want

Appendix

▶ CONSIDER USING TM 2
Appendix Outline

One of the most important objectives of this text is to help you succeed in your career. First of all, you have to decide what job you want. We'll help you in this decision by explaining what people do in the various business functions: accounting, marketing, human resource management, finance, and so on.

As we indicated earlier, it helps to do a self-assessment to determine what kind of career would be best for you. You also should go to the library and do some background research into organizations that need people with your skills and knowledge.

If you're older and looking for a new career, your self-assessment has probably revealed that you have both handicaps and blessings that younger students do not have. First of all, you may already have a full-time job. Working while going to school is exhausting. Many older students must juggle family responsibilities in addition to the responsibilities of school and work. But take heart. You have also acquired many skills from these experiences. Even if they were acquired in unrelated fields, these skills will be invaluable as you enter your new career.

Whether you're beginning your first career or your latest career, it's time to develop a strategy for finding and obtaining a personally satisfying job.

···· ▬▬▬ ····

A JOB SEARCH STRATEGY

◄ CONSIDER USING OT ACETATE A-10
Fastest Growing Areas in Job Growth For the Next 15 Years

Several good books are available that provide guidance for finding the right job. This appendix has drawn from them to summarize the important steps:

1. *Complete a self-analysis inventory.* Some self-analysis inventories were discussed in the Prologue. See Figure A.1 for a sample personal assessment. If you want to do an assessment on your own, see Richard

┌   FIGURE **A.1**   ┐
····

A PERSONAL ASSESSMENT SCALE

Interests

1. How do I like to spend my time?
2. Do I enjoy being with people?
3. Do I like working with mechanical things?
4. Do I enjoy working with numbers?
5. Am I a member of many organizations?
6. Do I enjoy physical activities?
7. Do I like to read?

Abilities

1. Am I adept at working with numbers?
2. Am I adept at working with mechanical things?
3. Do I have good verbal and written communication skills?
4. What special talents do I have?
5. In which abilities do I wish I were more adept?

Education

1. Have I taken certain courses that have prepared me for a particular job?
2. In which subjects did I perform the best? The worst?
3. Which subjects did I enjoy the most? The least?
4. How have my extracurricular activities prepared me for a particular job?
5. Is my GPA an accurate picture of my academic ability? Why?
6. Do I want a graduate degree? Do I want to earn it before beginning my job?
7. Why did I choose my major?

Experience

1. What previous jobs have I held? What were my responsibilities in each?
2. Were any of my jobs applicable to positions I may be seeking? How?
3. What did I like the most about my previous jobs? Like the least?

4. Why did I work in the jobs I did?
5. If I had it to do over again, would I work in these jobs? Why?

Personality

1. What are my good and bad traits?
2. Am I competitive?
3. Do I work well with others?
4. Am I outspoken?
5. Am I a leader or a follower?
6. Do I work well under pressure?
7. Do I work quickly, or am I methodical?
8. Do I get along well with others?
9. Am I ambitious?
10. Do I work well independently of others?

Desired job environment

1. Am willing to relocate? Why?
2. Do I have a geographic preference? Why?
3. Would I mind traveling in my job?
4. Do I have to work for a large, nationally known firm to be satisfied?
5. Must I have a job that initially offers a high salary?
6. Must the job I assume offer rapid promotion opportunities?
7. In what kind of job environment would I feel most comfortable?
8. If I could design my own job, what characteristics would it have?

Personal Goals

1. What are my short- and long-term goals? Why?
2. Am I career-oriented, or do I have broader interests?
3. What are my career goals?
4. What jobs are likely to help me achieve my goals?
5. What do I hope to be doing in 5 years? In 10 years?
6. What do I want out of life?

Source: Eric N. Berkowitz, Roger A. Kerin, Steven Hartley, and William Rudelius, *Marketing*, 3rd ed. (Homewood, Ill.: Richard D. Irwin, 1992), p. 663.

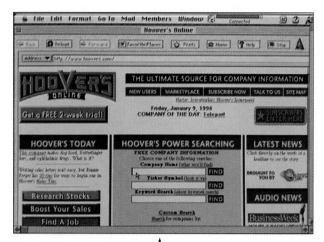

More and more job seekers are finding employment opportunities using the Internet. This Web site contains information about companies that could help you determine the industry in which you would like to work. Other sites list companies currently looking for workers, offer help in creating a résumé, and provide many additional kinds of advice on conducting a job search. Check out the sites discussed in the text to learn what is available. Are you willing to move to another city (or country) if you find an attractive job there?

Nelson Bolles, *What Color Is Your Parachute?* (Berkeley, Calif.: Ten Speed Press, 1998). Career Navigator is a software program that will walk you through five modules of job-seeking strategies from "Know Yourself" to "Land That Job."

2. *Search for jobs you would enjoy.* If your school has a placement office, begin there. Even after you've found a job, keep interviewing people in various careers. Career progress demands continuous research.

3. *Begin the networking process.* You can start with your family, relatives, neighbors, friends, professors, and local businesspeople. Be sure to keep a file of your contacts that includes each person's name, address, phone number, and place of employment; the person who recommended the contact to you; and the relationship between the source person and the contact.

4. *Begin investigating companies on the Internet.* The Riley Guide (http://www.dbm.com/jobguide/) will give you details about finding jobs on the Internet. Also check out Jobtrak (http://www.jobtrak.com), which lists jobs for college graduates. Hoovers (http://www. hoovers.com) offers short company reports. The Security and Exchange Commission's Edgar database (http:www,sec.gov/edgarhp.htm) provides financial details about companies.

5. *To find companies looking for people, get back on the Internet.* Worldwide News (http://www.worldwidenews.com) has hundreds of on-line newspapers from around the world where you can look in the classifieds. CareerPath (http://www.careerpath.com) contains ads from over 30 newspapers. The Monster Board (http://www.monster.com) has a personal job-search agent that will narrow the listings down to jobs that match your profile. Also, check out CareerMosaic at (http://www.careermosaic.com).

6. *Prepare a good cover letter and résumé.* Samples are provided in this appendix. Post your résumé on the Internet. Be sure to use industry action words in your résumé (see Figure A.2) because companies use key words to scan résumés. Having experience working in teams, for example, is important to many companies.

FIGURE **A.2**

• • • •

SAMPLE ACTION WORDS TO USE IN YOUR RÉSUMÉ AND JOB INTERVIEWS

Managed	Wrote	Budgeted	Improved
Planned	Produced	Designed	Increased
Organized	Scheduled	Directed	Investigated
Coordinated	Operated	Developed	Teamed
Supervised	Conducted	Established	Served
Trained	Administered	Implemented	Handled

7. *Develop interviewing skills.* We'll give you some clues as to how to do this later in the appendix.

8. *Keep after companies in which you have an interest.* Show your interest by calling periodically or sending e-mail and letting the company know you are interested. Send follow-up letters. Indicate your willingness to travel to various parts of the country or the world to be interviewed. Get to know people in the company and learn from them whom to contact and what qualifications to emphasize.

••• THE JOB SEARCH •••

The placement bureau at your school is a good place to begin reading about potential employers. On-campus interviewing is by far the number one source of jobs (see Figure A.3). Figures for the Internet are not yet available, but it is becoming a good place to find jobs. Another good source of jobs involves writing to companies and sending a good cover letter and résumé. You can identify companies to contact in your library or on the Internet. Check such sources as the *Million Dollar Directory* or the *Standard Directory of Advertisers.* Your library and the Internet may also have annual reports that will give you even more information about your selected companies.

A very important source of jobs is networking, that is, finding someone in a firm to recommend you. You find those people by asking friends, neighbors, family members, and others if they know anyone who knows someone, and then you track those people down, interview them, and seek their recommendation.

◄ **CONSIDER USING TM 3**
Where College Students Find Jobs
(Figure A1-3)

SOURCE OF JOB	PERCENTAGE OF NEW EMPLOYEES
On-campus interviewing	49.3%
Write-ins	9.8
Current employee referrals	7.2
Job listings with placement office	6.5
Responses from want ads	5.6
Walk-ins	5.5
Cooperative education programs	4.8
Summer employment	4.7
College faculty/staff referrals	4.5
Internship programs	4.5
High-demand major programs	4.4
Minority career programs	2.9
Part-time employment	2.4
Unsolicited referrals from placement	2.1
Women's career programs	2.1
Job listings with employment agencies	1.9
Referrals from campus organizations	1.8

┌ FIGURE **A.3** ┐
• • • •
WHERE COLLEGE STUDENTS FIND JOBS

When looking for a job, be sure to check the sources listed in the figure. Use those sources that will guarantee your success as you begin your job search. Total is over 100 percent because students use multiple sources.

Source: J. Singleton and P. Scheetz, *Recruiting Trends,* Michigan State University.

"there is a **magical moment** when . . . Cypresses and red-tile roofs appear; you hear the screech of cicadas and catch the scent of wild thyme and lavender . . . against a backdrop of harsh, brightly lit landscapes that inspired . . . Cézanne and van Gogh."

Travel services and tourism represent the largest nongovernmental industry in the United States. As the population of the United States ages and more and more people are retired, there will be greater demand for recreation, travel, and tourism services. Have you given any thought to working in such a diverse field? What types of career preparation would be desirable or necessary?

Other good sources of jobs include the want ads (be sure to check them out on the Internet), job fairs, summer and other internship programs, placement bureaus, and walking into firms that appeal to you and asking for an interview. The *Occupational Outlook Quarterly,* produced by the U.S. Department of Labor, says this about job hunting:

> *The skills that make a person employable are not so much the ones needed on the job as the ones needed to get the job, skills like the ability to find a job opening, complete an application, prepare the résumé, and survive an interview.*

Before you read on, check the Interview Rating Sheet in Figure A.4. Note what recruiters want. Interviewers will be checking your appearance (clothes, haircut, fingernails, shoes); your attitude (friendliness is desired); your verbal ability (speak loud enough to be heard clearly); and your motivation (be enthusiastic). Note also that interviewers want you to have been active in clubs and activities and to have set goals. Have someone evaluate you on these scales now to see if you have any weak points. You can then work on those points before you have any actual job interviews.

It's never too early in your career to begin designing a résumé and thinking of cover letters. Preparing such documents reveals your strengths and weaknesses more clearly than most other techniques. Your résumé lists all your education, work experience, and activities. By preparing a résumé now, you may discover that you haven't been involved in enough outside activities to impress an employer. That information may prompt you to join some student groups, to become a volunteer, or to otherwise enhance your social skills.

You may also discover that you're weak on experience, and seek an internship or part-time job to fill in that gap. In any event, it's not too soon to prepare a résumé. It will certainly help you decide what you'd like to see in the area marked Education and, if you haven't already done so, help you choose a major and other coursework. Given that background, let's discuss how to prepare these materials.

••• WRITING A RÉSUMÉ •••

A résumé is a document that lists information an employer would need to evaluate you and your background. It explains your immediate goals and career objectives. This information is followed by an explanation of your educational background, experience, interests, and other relevant data.

If you have exceptional abilities but don't communicate them to the employer on the résumé, those abilities aren't part of the person the employer will evaluate. You must be comprehensive and clear in your résumé if you are to communicate all your attributes.

Candidate: "For each characteristic listed below there is a rating scale of 1 through 7, where '1' is generally the most unfavorable rating of the characteristic and '7' the most favorable. Rate each characteristic by *circling* just *one* number to represent the impression you gave in the interview that you have just completed."

Name of Candidate _____

1. Appearance

Sloppy	1	2	3	4	5	6	7	Neat

2. Attitude

Unfriendly	1	2	3	4	5	6	7	Friendly

3. Assertiveness/Verbal Ability

a. Responded completely to questions asked

Poor	1	2	3	4	5	6	7	Excellent

b. Clarified personal background and related to job opening and description

Poor	1	2	3	4	5	6	7	Excellent

c. Able to explain and sell job abilities

Poor	1	2	3	4	5	6	7	Excellent

d. Initiated questions regarding position and firm

Poor	1	2	3	4	5	6	7	Excellent

e. Expressed thorough knowledge of personal goals and abilities

Poor	1	2	3	4	5	6	7	Excellent

4. Motivation

Poor	1	2	3	4	5	6	7	High

5. Subject/Academic Knowledge

Poor	1	2	3	4	5	6	7	Good

6. Stability

Poor	1	2	3	4	5	6	7	Good

7. Composure

Ill at ease	1	2	3	4	5	6	7	Relaxed

8. Personal Involvement/Activities, Clubs, Etc.

Low	1	2	3	4	5	6	7	Very high

9. Mental Impression

Dull	1	2	3	4	5	6	7	Alert

10. Adaptability

Poor	1	2	3	4	5	6	7	Good

11. Speech Pronunciation

Poor	1	2	3	4	5	6	7	Good

12. Overall Impression

Unsatisfactory	1	2	3	4	5	6	7	Highly satisfactory

13. Would you hire this individual if you were permitted to make a decision right now?

Yes   No

FIGURE A.4

• • • •

INTERVIEW RATING SHEET

Some employers use an interview rating sheet like the one in this figure. When you go for a job interview, put your best foot forward.

◄ **CONSIDER USING TM 4**
Interview Rating Sheet (Figure A1-4)

Your résumé is an advertisement for yourself. If your ad is better than the other person's ad, you're more likely to get the interview. In this case, *better* means that your ad highlights your attributes in an attractive way.

In discussing your education, for example, be sure to include your extra-curricular activities such as part-time jobs, sports, or clubs. If you did well in school, put down your grades. The idea is to make yourself look as good on paper as you are in reality.

◄ **CONSIDER USING LECTURE ENHANCER A-1**
More Resume Guidelines

◄ **CONSIDER USING LECTURE ENHANCER A-2**
Using the Internet for Resumes

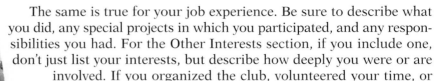

The same is true for your job experience. Be sure to describe what you did, any special projects in which you participated, and any responsibilities you had. For the Other Interests section, if you include one, don't just list your interests, but describe how deeply you were or are involved. If you organized the club, volunteered your time, or participated more often than usual in an organization, make sure to say so in the résumé. See Figure A.5 for a sample résumé.

••• WRITING A COVER LETTER •••

A cover letter is used to announce your availability and to introduce the résumé. The cover letter is probably one of the most important advertisements anyone will write in a lifetime—so it should be done right.

First, the cover letter should indicate that you've researched the organization in question and are interested in a job there. To get the attention of the reader and show your interest, tell what you know about the organization and what sources you used in the first paragraph.

You may have heard people say, "It's not what you know, but whom you know that counts." This is only partly true, but it's important nonetheless. Even if you don't know anyone, you can get to know someone. You do this by calling the organization (or better yet, visiting its offices) and talking to people who already have the kind of job you're hoping to get. Ask about training, salary, and other relevant issues. Then, in your cover letter, mention that you've talked with some of the firm's employees and that this discussion increased your interest. You thereby show the letter reader that you know someone, if only casually, and that you're interested enough to actively pursue the organization. This is all part of networking.

Second, in the description of yourself, be sure to say how your attributes will benefit the organization. For example, don't just say, "I will be graduating with a degree in marketing." Say, "You will find that my college training in marketing and marketing research has prepared me to learn your marketing system quickly and begin making a contribution right away." The sample cover letter in Figure A.6 will give you a better feel for how this looks.

Third, be sure to "ask for the order." That is, say in your final paragraph that you're available for an interview at a time and place convenient for the interviewer. Again, see the sample cover letter in Figure A.6 for guidance; notice in this letter how Yann subtly shows that she reads business publications and draws attention to her résumé.

Principles to follow in writing a cover letter and preparing your résumé include the following:

- Be self-confident. List all your good qualities and attributes.

- Don't be apologetic or negative. Write as one professional to another, not as a humble student begging for a job.

- Research every prospective employer thoroughly before writing anything. Use a rifle approach rather than a shotgun approach. That is, write effective marketing-oriented letters to a few select companies rather than to a general list.

- Have your materials prepared by an experienced keyboarder if you are not highly skilled yourself. If you have access to a word processing system with a letter-quality laser printer, you can produce individualized letters efficiently.

FIGURE **A.5**

. . . .

SAMPLE RÉSUMÉ

◄ **CONSIDER USING TM 5**
Sample Résumé (Figure A-5 on text
page P-19)

Yann Ng
345 Big Bend Boulevard
Kirkwood, Missouri, 63122
314-921-5385

Job objective: Sales representative in business to business marketing

Education:

St. Louis Community College at Meramec
A.A. in Business (3.6 grade point average)
Served on Student Representative Board

University of Missouri, St. Louis
B.S. in Business: Marketing major (3.2 grade point average, 3.5 in major)
Earned 100 percent of college expenses working 35 hours a week.
Member of Student American Marketing Association
Vice President of Student Government Association
Dean's List for two semesters

Work experience:

Schnuck's Supermarket: Worked checkout evenings and weekends for four years while in
school. Learned to respond to customer requests quickly, and communicate with them in
a friendly and helpful manner.

Mary Tuttle's Flowers: For two summers, I made flower arrangements, managed sales
transactions, and acted as Assistant to the Manager. I trained and supervised three
employees. Often handled customer inquiries and complaints.

Special skills:
I am fluent in Vietnamese, French, and English. I'm proficient at using WordPerfect and
Word. I've developed my own Web site (www.yan@stilnet.com) and use the Internet
often to do research for papers and for personal interests.

Other interests:
I'm an excellent cook and often prepare meals for my family and friends. I enjoy reading
the classics. I play the piano and do aerobics. I've traveled extensively in Asia, Europe,
and America. I also enjoy doing research on the Internet.

References furnished upon request

- Have someone edit your materials for spelling, grammar, and style.
  Don't be like the student who sent out a second résumé to correct
  "some mixtakes." Or another who said, "I am acurite with numbers."
- Don't send the names of references until asked. Put "References furnished on request" at the bottom of the last page of your résumé.

FIGURE **A.6**

• • • •

**SAMPLE
COVER LETTER**

➤ **CONSIDER USING TM 6**
Sample Cover Letter (Figure A-6)

Yann Ng
345 Big Bend Boulevard
Kirkwood, Missouri, 63122
314-921-5385

Dear Mr. Karlinski: [Note: it's best to know whom to write by name.]

Recent articles in *Inc.* and *Success* magazine have praised your company for its innovative products and strong customer orientation. I'm familiar with your creative display materials. In fact, we've used them at Mary Tuttle's Flower Shop, where I have worked for the last two summers. I talked to Christie Bouchard, your local sales representative, and she told me all about your products and your training program at Premier Designs.

Christie mentioned the kind of salespeople you are seeking. She said you want men and women with proven sales ability. I've had great success making and selling flower arrangements at Mary Tuttle's, and I've learned customer relations at Schnuck's. As you know, they have one of the best customer-oriented training programs in the industry. Christie also said that you wanted self-motivated people with leadership ability. I've paid my way through college working nights and summers. I was selected to be on the Student Representative Board at St. Louis Community College at Meramec and was active in student government at Missouri. I have also paid my own way to Asia, Europe, and the Americas. I am very independent and self-motivated.

I know that I could be a successful salesperson at Premier Designs. I'll be in the Chicago area the week of January 4–9. What time and date would be most convenient for you to discuss career opportunities at Premier? I'll phone your secretary to set up an appointment.

Sincerely,

Yann Ng

PREPARING FOR JOB INTERVIEWS

➤ **CONSIDER USING LECTURE ENHANCER A-3**
Grade Honesty Becoming More Important

Companies usually don't conduct job interviews unless they're somewhat certain that the candidate has the requirements for the job. The interview, therefore, is pretty much a make-or-break situation. If it goes well, you have a greater chance of being hired. Therefore, you must be prepared for your interviews. There are five stages of interview preparation:

- How would you describe yourself?
- What are your greatest strengths and weaknesses?
- How did you choose this company?
- What do you know about the company?
- What are your long-range career goals?
- What courses did you like best? Least?
- What are your hobbies?
- Do you prefer a specific geographic location?

- Are you willing to travel (or move)?
- Which accomplishments have given you the most satisfaction?
- What things are most important to you in a job?
- Why should I hire you?
- What experience have you had in this type of work?
- How much do you expect to earn?

FIGURE A.7
• • • •
BE PREPARED FOR
THESE FREQUENTLY
ASKED QUESTIONS

◄ CONSIDER USING TM 7
Sample Interview Questions (Figure A1-8)

1. *Research the prospective employer.* Learn about the industry the firm is in, its competitors, its products or services and their acceptance in the market, and the title of your desired position. You can find such information in the firm's annual reports, in *Standard & Poor's*, Moody's manuals, and various business publications such as *Fortune, Business Week*, and *Forbes*. Ask your librarian for help, or search the Internet. You can look in the *Reader's Guide to Business Literature* to locate the company name and to look for articles about it. This important first step shows you have initiative and interest in the firm.

2. *Practice the interview.* Figure A.7 lists some of the questions frequently asked in interviews. Practice answering these questions and more at your college's placement office and with your roommate, parents, or friends. Don't memorize your answers, but be prepared—know what you're going to say. Also, develop a series of questions to ask the interviewer. Figure A.8 shows sample questions you might ask. Be sure you know whom to contact, and write down the names of everyone you meet. Review the action words in Figure A.2 and try to fit them into your answers.

   For a fun way to practice answering interview questions, sit in the hot seat at http://www.kaplan.com/career on the Internet. This interactive site asks typical interview questions and gives you three alternative responses. Choose the wrong one and the interview is over. Continued correct responses will earn you an interview with the next supervisor.

3. *Be professional during the interview.* "You don't have a second chance to make a good first impression," the saying goes. That means you should look and sound professional throughout the interview. Do your homework and find out how managers dress at the firm. Then buy an

FIGURE A.8
• • • •
SAMPLE QUESTIONS TO
ASK THE INTERVIEWER

- Who are your major competitors, and how would you rate their products and marketing relative to yours?
- How long does the training program last, and what is included?
- How soon after school would I be expected to start?
- What are the advantages of working for this firm?
- How much travel is normally expected?
- What managerial style should I expect in my area?
- How would you describe the working environment in my area?

- How would I be evaluated?
- What is the company's promotion policy?
- What is the corporate culture?
- What is the next step in the selection procedures?
- How soon should I expect to hear from you?
- What other information would you like about my background, experience, or education?
- What is your highest priority in the next six months and how could someone like me help?

1. **Ability to communicate.** Do you have the ability to organize your thoughts and ideas effectively? Can you express them clearly when speaking or writing? Can you present your ideas to others in a persuasive way?

2. **Intelligence.** Do you have the ability to understand the job assignment? Learn the details of operation? Contribute original ideas to your work?

3. **Self-confidence.** Do you demonstrate a sense of maturity that enables you to deal positively and effectively with situations and people?

4. **Willingness to accept responsibility.** Are you someone who recognizes what needs to be done and is willing to do it?

5. **Initiative.** Do you have the ability to identify the purpose for work and to take action?

6. **Leadership.** Can you guide and direct others to obtain the recognized objectives?

7. **Energy level.** Do you demonstrate a forcefulness and capacity to make things move ahead? Can you maintain your work effort at an above-average rate?

8. **Imagination.** Can you confront and deal with problems that may not have standard solutions?

9. **Flexibility.** Are you capable of changing and being receptive to new situations and ideas?

10. **Interpersonal skills.** Can you bring out the best efforts of individuals so they become effective, enthusiastic members of a team?

11. **Self-knowledge.** Can you realistically assess your own capabilities? See yourself as others see you? Clearly recognize your strengths and weaknesses?

12. **Ability to handle conflict.** Can you successfully contend with stress situations and antagonism?

13. **Competitiveness.** Do you have the capacity to compete with others and the willingness to be measured by your performance in relation to that of others?

14. **Goal achievement.** Do you have the ability to identify and work toward specific goals? Do such goals challenge your abilities?

15. **Vocational skills.** Do you possess the positive combination of education and skills required for the position you are seeking?

16. **Direction.** Have you defined your basic personal needs? Have you determined what type of position will satisfy your knowledge, skills, and goals?

Source: "So You're Looking for a Job?" The College Placement Council.

appropriate outfit. When you meet the interviewers, greet them by name, smile, and maintain good eye contact. Sit up straight in your chair and be alert and enthusiastic. If you have practiced, you should be able to relax and be confident. Other than that, be yourself, answer questions, and be friendly and responsive.

When you leave, thank the interviewers and, if you're still interested in the job, tell them so. If they don't tell you, ask them what the next step is. Maintain a positive attitude. Figure A.9 outlines what the interviewers will be evaluating.

4. *Follow up on the interview.* First, write down what you can remember from the interview: names of the interviewers and their titles, any salary figures mentioned, dates for training, and so on. Put the information in your career file. You can send a follow-up letter thanking each interviewer for his or her time. You can also send the interviewers a letter of recommendation or some other piece of added information to keep their interest. "The squeaky wheel gets the grease" is the

operating slogan. Your enthusiasm for working for the company could be a major factor in getting hired.

5. *Be prepared to act.* Know what you want to say if you do get a job offer. You may not want the job once you know all the information. Don't expect to receive a job offer from everyone you meet, but do expect to learn something from every interview. With some practice and persistence, you should find a rewarding and challenging job.

···· ▬▬ ····
BE PREPARED TO CHANGE JOBS

If you're like most people, you'll find that you'll follow several different career paths over your lifetime. This is a good thing in that it enables you to try different jobs and stay fresh and enthusiastic. The key to moving forward in your career is a willingness to change jobs, always searching for the career that will bring the most personal satisfaction and growth. This means that you'll have to write many cover letters and résumés and go through many interviews. Each time you change jobs, go through the steps in this appendix to be sure you're fully prepared. Good luck.

Tim—
Starbucks

Finding Opportunities in Today's Dynamic Business Environment

LEARNING GOALS

After you have read and studied this chapter, you should be able to

1 Describe how businesses and nonprofit organizations add to a country's standard of living and quality of life.

2 Explain the importance of entrepreneurship to the wealth of an economy and show the relationship of profit to risk assumption.

3 Examine how the economic environment and taxes affect businesses.

4 Illustrate how the technological environment has affected businesses.

5 Identify various ways that businesses can meet and beat competition.

6 Demonstrate how the social environment has changed and what the reaction of the business community has been.

7 Analyze what businesses must do to meet the global challenge.

8 Compare the new quality standards and identify what businesses are doing to meet those standards.

9 Review how trends from the past are being repeated in the present and what such trends will mean for the service sector.

Luther and Lenora Cain left farm life to find more opportunity in the business world. Luther found a job as a porter and Lenora as a maid. In fact, to earn enough to rear a family, Luther took on three jobs, including one as a chauffeur at Coca-Cola. Soon he became the chauffeur and personal valet to the president of Coca-Cola.

Herman Cain is Luther and Lenora's son. He learned from his parents that hard work and dedication pay off in the long run. He finished high school second in his class and attended Morehouse College, working after school and summers to help pay his tuition. His father had saved enough money to buy a grocery store, and Herman worked in that store for a while. Inspired by Dr. Martin Luther King, Cain went on to get a master's degree at Purdue University and landed a job at Coca-Cola as an analyst. Four years later, he and his supervisor moved to Pillsbury, where in another five years he was vice president for corporate systems and services. His goal was to become president of a firm.

The president of Pillsbury told Cain that he would most likely reach his goal by rising up through the ranks at Burger King, a division of the company. But that meant starting from the bottom, flipping hamburgers and giving up his company car and nice office! Cain hoped it was the right thing to do and, as it turned out, it was. He completed the usual two-year training program in nine months and was named Burger King's vice president of the Philadelphia region, in charge of 450 units. It had been a slow-growing region, but Cain turned it into the company's best one for growth, sales, and profit.

Cain was so successful at Burger King that he became the president of Pillsbury's Godfather's Pizza. Having reached his goal, Cain began his work as president by streamlining operations. Unprofitable units were closed, and others were made more efficient. Eventually Cain and a partner bought Godfather's from Pillsbury for $50 million. Since then, the value of the company has doubled.

Cain says that service is the driving force behind his business. His number one rule is, "The customer is always right." He also says that if you love what you are doing, you will be successful. Following that philosophy, Cain became the first black president of the National Restaurant Association.

Now Cain is working hard to support his community. He supports an outreach program for troubled teens and gives speeches about what it takes to be a success. Many young people think the fast-food industry offers only dead-end jobs. Herman Cain doesn't see it that way. He sees such jobs as a chance to eventually run something—to own something. He sees opportunity.

The first chapter of this text explores trends in business, including today's trend toward *entrepreneurship*, which is defined as assuming the risk of starting and managing a business. As you read through this chapter, think of the many opportunities businesses provide for creating jobs, building wealth, and fostering community.[1]

 PROFILE

Herman Cain of Godfather's Pizza

WHAT IS A BUSINESS?

A **business** is any activity that seeks profit by providing goods and services to others. Businesses provide us with necessities such as food, clothing, housing, medical care, and transportation, as well as many other things that make our lives easier and better. Businesses also provide people with the opportunity to become wealthy, as Herman Cain's story in the opening profile clearly shows. Sam Walton of Wal-Mart began by opening one store in Arkansas and, over

business
Any activity that seeks profit by providing needed goods and services to others.

◄ **LG 1.**
Describe how businesses and nonprofit organizations add to the standard of living and quality of life.

Ellen Wessel is part of a savvy group of female entrepreneurs who are setting the pace in the fast growing $21 billion women's sports equipment and apparel market. Her company, Moving Comfort, Inc., now has sales in excess of $12 million. The keys to her success: listening to customers, hiring women athletes as advisers, and paying attention to female physiology.

time, became the richest person in America a few years ago. (His heirs now have billions of dollars.) Bill Gates started Microsoft and is now the richest person in the world.

••• BUSINESSES CAN PROVIDE WEALTH AND A HIGH ••• QUALITY OF LIFE FOR ALMOST EVERYONE

➤ **CONSIDER USING TA 1-2**
Objectives of Business

Entrepreneurs like Sam Walton and Bill Gates not only became wealthy themselves but also provided employment for other people. Wal-Mart is currently the nation's largest private employer.[2] Employees pay taxes that the federal government and local communities use to build hospitals, schools, roads, playgrounds, and other facilities. Taxes are also used to keep the environment clean and to support people in need. Businesses also pay taxes to the federal government and local communities. Thus, the wealth businesses generate helps everyone in the communities. The nation's businesses are part of an economic system that helps to create a higher standard of living and quality of life for everyone in the country.

standard of living
The amount of goods and services people can buy with the money they have.

The term **standard of living** refers to the amount of goods and services people can buy with the money they have. For example, the United States has one of the highest standards of living in the world, even though workers in some other countries, such as Germany and Japan, make more money per hour. How can that be? Prices for goods and services in Germany and Japan are higher, so what a person can buy in those countries is less than what people in the United States can buy with the same amount of money. The United States has such a high standard of living largely because of the wealth created by its businesses.

quality of life
The general well-being of a society.

The term **quality of life** refers to the general well-being of a society in terms of freedom, clean environment, education, health care, safety, free time, and everything else that leads to satisfaction and joy. Maintaining a high quality of life requires the combined efforts of businesses, government agencies, and nonprofit organizations. The more money businesses create, the more is available for such causes.

Presently, many people in the United States are sacrificing a higher standard of living (having more things) for a higher quality of life (having more time). They are buying smaller homes and smaller cars, and are taking more vacations and spending more time with their families. As you approach your career, how can you balance having a high standard of living with maintaining a high quality of life?

··· NONPROFIT ORGANIZATIONS USE BUSINESS PRINCIPLES ···

Not everything that makes life easier and better is provided by businesses. Nonprofit organizations such as government agencies, public schools, civic associations, charities, and social causes help make our country and the world more responsive to all the needs of citizens. A **nonprofit organization** is an organization whose goals don't include making a personal profit for its owners. Nonprofit organizations often do strive for gains, but such gains are used to meet the stated social or educational goals of the organization, not to enrich the owners.

nonprofit organization

An organization whose goals do not include making a profit for its owners.

If you want to work in a nonprofit organization, you'll need to learn business skills such as information management, leadership, marketing, and financial management.[3] Therefore, the knowledge and skills you can acquire in this and other business courses will be useful for careers in any organization, including a nonprofit one. Because such crossover is possible, many businesspeople volunteer their expertise in nonprofit organizations. Others change careers to run nonprofit organizations that require the same skills they had been using in the business world. Melissa Bradley, for example, started a consulting firm her first year out of college. When she was 23, revenues reached a million dollars. Seeing the opportunity that entrepreneurship offers, Melissa sold her consulting firm to launch The Entrepreneurial Development Institute (TEDI), an organization in Washington, D.C., that teaches entrepreneurship to at-risk young people.[4]

Following college, Melissa Bradley achieved success early in her career. She learned that the same skills that lead to success in for-profit businesses can be carried over to nonprofit organizations. She has now dedicated her career to teaching these skills to others.

Businesses, nonprofit organizations, and volunteer groups often strive to accomplish the same objectives. All such groups can help feed people, provide them with clothing and housing, clean up the environment and keep it clean, and improve the standard of living and quality of life for all. To accomplish such objectives, however, this nation's businesses must remain competitive with the best businesses in the rest of the world.

THE IMPORTANCE OF ENTREPRENEURSHIP TO WEALTH

An **entrepreneur** is a person who risks time and money to start and manage a business. Look at what entrepreneurs of the past have done to create wealth. The state of Delaware doesn't need to charge a sales tax on retail purchases because of the great wealth created by E. I. Du Pont, a chemicals entrepreneur.

entrepreneur

A person who risks time and money to start and manage a business.

◀ **LG 2.**
Explain the importance of entrepreneurship to the wealth of an economy and show the relationship of profit to risk assumption.

The Du Pont Company today has over 114,000 employees and along with Hercules, another chemical company, is one of the two largest employers in Delaware. Texas has long been a relatively rich state because of entrepreneurs who took the risk of finding oil there. Now the leading companies in the state include Exxon, Shell, Tenneco, and Coastal. Who are the largest employers in your state? What do those businesses contribute to society?

··· OPPORTUNITIES FOR ENTREPRENEURS ···

Millions of business owners in our nation's history have taken the entrepreneurial risk and succeeded, and entrepreneurs continue to come from all over the world to prosper in America. Ezzat Reda is from Lebanon. He and his younger brother, Hussein, now own one of the best-stocked magazine stores of its kind in Manhattan. In the early 1990s the number of Latino-owned businesses in the United States grew by 76 percent—a faster rate than that of any other category of business. The next-highest level of minority-business growth was for businesses owned by Asians, Pacific Islanders, American Indians, and Alaskan Natives; these businesses grew by 61 percent. Some 30 percent of Koreans who have immigrated to the United States own their own businesses.[5] Other Asians are also prospering in business. In short, tremendous opportunities exist for those men and women willing to take the risk of starting a business.[6] For more on women in small business, see the case at the end of the chapter.

downsizing
Making organizations more efficient by laying off workers.

▶ **CONSIDER USING CRITICAL THINKING EXERCISE 1-1**
How Much Profit?

One factor contributing to the increasing numbers of entrepreneurs in the United States today is corporate downsizing. **Downsizing** means laying off or letting go of some workers or managers to make a business more efficient. Some layoffs and cutbacks are due to businesses' need to reduce costs to become more competitive; others result from new strategies for assigning (outsourcing) nonessential work to other firms.[7] *Entrepreneur* magazine points out, however, that downsizing is creating new opportunities for entrepreneurs who can provide business services such as advertising, building maintenance, computer-related services, and security services.

profit
Earnings above and beyond what a business spends for salaries, expenses, and other costs.

While the Fortune 1,000 companies (the 1,000 largest firms in the United States) cut 4.2 million jobs between 1986 and 1996, small businesses added 9.2 million jobs to the economy.[8] As the Spotlight on Small Business box demonstrates, for those individuals such as Evan Kemp who understand the business system and how it works, the 21st century will provide more opportunities—and more challenges—than ever before.

··· MATCHING RISK WITH PROFIT ···

Profit is money a business earns above and beyond what it pays out for salaries and other expenses. For example, if you were to rent a vending cart

People who take the risk of opening and managing a store often create wealth for themselves and their families. In addition, they create jobs and wealth that the community can use to build schools and other projects. What kind of businesses are opening and closing in your area? What impact will such changes have on the community?

Spotlight on Small Business

http://solutions@disability.com

Business: From Disability to Opportunity

Evan J. Kemp was head of the Equal Employment Opportunity Commission and played a major role in passing the 1991 Americans With Disabilities Act. That act made it possible for many more disabled Americans to find good jobs.

The needs of disabled Americans have created a huge market for specially designed or adapted products (there are some 48 million people with various disabilities). Mr. Kemp understands this market because he has muscular dystrophy. He created Evan Kemp Associates (EKA) to serve people in similar circumstances. EKA has three subsidiaries. EKA Communications publishes a newsletter for the disabled. EKA Marketing & Distribution designs marketing and advertising strategies for companies planning to sell to the disabled. It operates the Disabilities Mall on the Internet where products for the ▲ disabled are available. The third subsidiary is made up of retail stores that sell wheelchairs, scooters, and other supplies for the disabled. It also converts vans and autos to make them accessible.

The company has revenues of about $6 million. EKA is just one of hundreds of thousands of small businesses that are providing more jobs and more wealth in the United States. While larger businesses may be eliminating some workers, small businesses are creating more jobs, so the net result is more jobs and more opportunities for everyone.

Source: Karen Riley, "Businessman with Disability Knows Firsthand His Market's Special Needs," *The Washington Times*, August 7, 1995, p. A14; and John Godfrey, "Small-Business Population Booms," *Home Office Computer*, July, 1997, p. 21.

---

and sell hot dogs this summer, you would have to pay for the cart, for the hot dogs and other materials, and for someone to run the cart while you were away. After you paid your employee and yourself, paid for the food and materials you used, paid the rent on the cart, and paid your taxes, any money left over would be profit. Keep in mind that profit is over and above the money you pay yourself in salary. You could use any profit you make to rent a second cart and hire another employee. After a few summers, you might have a dozen carts employing dozens of workers.

Not all businesses make a profit. A **loss** occurs when a business's costs and expenses are more than its revenues. **Revenue** is the money a business earns by selling goods and services. If a business loses money over time, it will likely have to close, putting its employees out of work.

Starting a business therefore involves risk. **Risk** is the chance an entrepreneur takes of losing time and money on a business that may not prove profitable. Not all companies make the same amount of profit. Those companies that take the most risk may make the most profit. It's risky to open a fast-food franchise in the inner city because insurance and land costs there are usually high. On the other hand, the chance of making substantial profits is also good because there's less competition. As a potential business owner, you want to invest your money in a company that's likely to make a lot of profit but that isn't too risky. You need to do research (e.g., talking to other businesspeople) to find the right balance between risk and profit.

loss
When a business's costs and expenses are more than its revenues.

revenue
The value of what is received for goods sold, services rendered, and other sources.

risk
The chance you take of losing time and money on a business that may not prove profitable.

• What is profit, and who gets the profits businesses make? What is the difference between revenue and profit?

Progress Check

- What is risk, and how is it related to profit?
- What is the difference between standard of living and quality of life?

••• THE ROLE OF THE FACTORS OF PRODUCTION •••
IN CREATING WEALTH

factors of production
The resources used to create wealth: land, labor, capital, entrepreneurship, and knowledge.

U.S. businesses can remain competitive with the best businesses in the rest of the world only if they manage the factors of production carefully. **Factors of production** are the resources businesses use to create wealth. Today businesses use five major factors of production: (1) land (and other natural resources); (2) labor (workers); (3) capital (e.g., machines, tools, and buildings); (4) entrepreneurship; and (5) knowledge. (See Figure 1.1.)

Traditionally, business texts have emphasized only four factors of production: land, labor, capital, and entrepreneurship, but management expert and business consultant Peter Drucker says that the most important factor of production in our economy "is and will be knowledge." Almost all of the young workers in the Silicon Valley area of California are knowledge workers.[9] That is, they are paid for what they know and can do. Many have become millionaires while still in their 20s. Such results should motivate today's college students to get as much education as possible to prepare themselves for knowledge-oriented jobs. To become as rich as Bill Gates and other billionaires, however, they will have to become entrepreneurs.

If you were to analyze rich countries versus poor countries to see what causes the differences in the levels of wealth, you'd have to look at the factors of production in each country. Such analyses have revealed that some poor countries often have plenty of land and natural resources. Russia and China, for example, both have vast areas of land with many resources, but they are not rich countries. Therefore, land isn't the critical element for wealth creation. For example, Japan is a rich country but is poor in land and other natural resources.

Most poor countries have many laborers, so it's not labor that's the primary source of wealth today. Laborers need to find work to make a contribution; that is, they need entrepreneurs to provide jobs for them. Furthermore, more capital is becoming available in world markets. Thus, money for machinery and tools is available, so capital isn't the missing ingredient. Capital is not productive without entrepreneurs to put it to use.

Clearly, then, what makes rich countries rich today is a combination of entrepreneurship and the effective use of knowledge. Lack of entrepreneurship and the absence of knowledge among workers, along with the lack of freedom, contribute to keeping poor countries poor. The box called Legal Briefcase discusses the importance of freedom to economic development.

▼ CONSIDER USING TM 9
The Five Factors of Production
Text Figure 1-1

┌ FIGURE **1.1** ┐
• • • •
THE FIVE FACTORS OF
PRODUCTION

Land:	Land and other natural resources are used to make homes, cars, and other products.
Labor:	People have always been an important resource in producing goods and services, but many people are now being replaced by technology.
Capital:	Capital includes machines, tools, buildings, and other means of manufacturing.
Entrepreneurship:	All the resources in the world have little value unless entrepreneurs are willing to take the risk of starting businesses to *use* those resources.
Knowledge:	Information technology has revolutionized business, making it possible to quickly determine wants and needs and to respond with desired goods and services.

Legal Briefcase

http://www.cipe.org/index95.html

Freedom Equals Prosperity

A recent study found that the freer a country is, the wealthier its citizens are. Freedom includes freedom from excess taxation, government regulations, and restrictions on trade. One country that had great freedom, Hong Kong, also had the highest per capita income ($27,202). (It will be interesting to see how much freedom Hong Kong is able to maintain now that it has become a part of the People's Republic of China—as of July, 1997.)

The United States is a relatively free country as well, and its per capita income is $27,178. The per capita gross domestic product for the 23 freest countries was $14,829. For the least free, it was $2,541. As a country introduces more freedom, its economy also begins to grow. The countries that have introduced freedom recently include Russia and El Salvador. They are likely to experience rapid economic growth as a result, all other things being equal.

The legal environment of a country therefore has much to do with the economic environment. More freedom equals more prosperity for all. Therefore, businesses must work closely with government to minimize taxes and maximize economic freedom. The legal environment of business is a critical part of any economic growth plan. That is why this text focuses on legal issues throughout. By reading about such issues in the context of various business functions, you will see how important the legal system is to business.

Source: Donald Lambro, "Wrong Way Turn on Economics," *Washington Times*, June 9, 1997, p. A.19; and Peter Brimelow, "Freedom Pays," *Forbes*, June 16, 1997, pp. 142–143; and Bruce R. Scott, "How Do Economies Grow?," *Harvard Business Review*, May–June 1997, pp. 156–64.

Entrepreneurship also makes some states and cities in the United States rich while others remain relatively poor. The business environment either encourages or discourages entrepreneurship. In the following section, we'll explore what makes up the business environment and how to build an environment that encourages growth and job creation throughout the world.

···· ▬ ····

THE BUSINESS ENVIRONMENT

The business environment has a tremendous effect on the success (or failure) of entrepreneurs. Figure 1.2 identifies five environmental factors that are key to business growth and job creation:

1. The economic environment, including taxes and regulation.
2. The technological environment.
3. The competitive environment.
4. The social environment.
5. The global business environment.

◀ LG 3.
Examine how the economic environment and taxes affect businesses.

Business grows and prospers in a healthy environment. The result is job growth and the wealth that makes it possible to have both a high standard of living and a high quality of life. The wrong environmental conditions, on the other hand, lead to business failure, loss of jobs, and a low standard of living

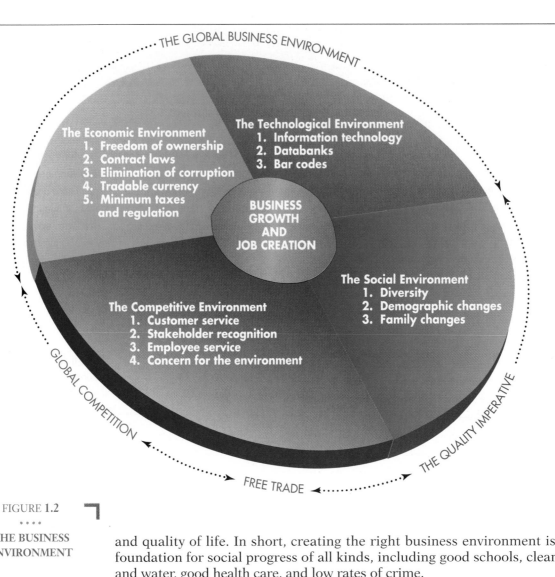

The Economic Environment
1. Freedom of ownership
2. Contract laws
3. Elimination of corruption
4. Tradable currency
5. Minimum taxes and regulation

The Technological Environment
1. Information technology
2. Databanks
3. Bar codes

BUSINESS GROWTH AND JOB CREATION

The Competitive Environment
1. Customer service
2. Stakeholder recognition
3. Employee service
4. Concern for the environment

The Social Environment
1. Diversity
2. Demographic changes
3. Family changes

THE GLOBAL BUSINESS ENVIRONMENT
GLOBAL COMPETITION
FREE TRADE
THE QUALITY IMPERATIVE

FIGURE **1.2**
· · · ·
**THE BUSINESS
ENVIRONMENT**

▲ CONSIDER USING TM 10
The Business Environment
Text Figure 1-2

➤ CONSIDER USING TA 1-3
How Government Affects Business

➤ CONSIDER USING TA 1-4
Government As An Overseer and
Regulator

and quality of life. In short, creating the right business environment is the foundation for social progress of all kinds, including good schools, clean air and water, good health care, and low rates of crime.

··· THE ECONOMIC ENVIRONMENT ···

People are willing to start new businesses if they feel that the risk isn't too great. Part of that risk involves the economic system and how government works with or against businesses. Government can do a lot to lessen the risk of starting businesses and thus increase entrepreneurship and wealth. One way for government to promote entrepreneurship is to allow private ownership of businesses. In some countries, most businesses are owned by the government and thus there's little incentive for people to work hard or create profit. All around the world today, however, various countries are selling government-owned businesses to private individuals to create more wealth. Let's explore what else the government can do to foster entrepreneurial growth.

- The government can lessen the risks of entrepreneurship by passing laws that enable businesspeople to write contracts that are enforceable in court. Many countries don't yet have such laws, making the risks of starting a business that much greater.

- The government can establish a currency that's tradable in world markets. One element preventing Russia from joining world markets and gaining economic strength is its lack of a tradable currency.

- The government can focus on eliminating corruption in business and government. It's hard to do business in many poor countries because the governments are so corrupt. It's very difficult in such countries to get permission to build a factory or open a store without a government permit, which is obtained largely through bribery of public officials.[10] Corrupt business leaders can threaten competitors and minimize competition. There are many laws in the United States to minimize corruption, and businesses can flourish as a result.

- The government can keep taxes and regulations to a minimum. Entrepreneurs are looking for a high return on investment, including the investment of their time. If the government takes away much of what a business earns through high taxes, the returns may no longer be worth the risk. This is true even within rich countries. States and cities that have high taxes and regulations may drive entrepreneurs out while states and cities with low taxes attract entrepreneurs. This is happening all across the United States and the world.[11]

The economic environment is so important to businesses that we'll devote all of Chapter 2 to that subject. There you'll learn more about the influence of government on business success and failure.

•••• ▬▬▬ ••••

THE TECHNOLOGICAL ENVIRONMENT

The most successful college graduates of tomorrow will be those who can find their way on the information superhighway. The **Internet** is a network of computer and telecommunications equipment that links people throughout the world into one unified communications system. Information on almost any topic imaginable is now available through the Internet. To access such information, you must be able to use computers and other telecommunications equipment.

If you haven't ventured onto the information superhighway yet, now is the time. Many schools offer Internet access in their computer labs. Find out where they are on your campus and when they are available to you. The appendix "Driver's Ed for the Information Superhighway" at the end of this chapter can guide you on your journey. Each chapter in this book offers Internet exercises called "Taking It to the Net" that will send you to fascinating places all over the world.

••• THE IMPORTANCE OF INFORMATION TECHNOLOGY •••

Many companies now have a chief information officer (CIO), who is the person responsible for getting workers and managers information they need to turn their company into a world-class competitor. The CIO must provide information about customers, competitors, and the changing business environment. Denis O'Leary is the CIO at Chase Manhattan, which has operations in

There is much that governments can do to promote entrepreneurship. One of the greatest obstacles to starting a small business is adequate capital. Most entrepreneurs use their own financial resources or borrow from friends and family. Some are fortunate enough to get support from the Small Business Administration. Nita and Pravin Patel, recent immigrants from India, were able to purchase a pharmacy in Philadelphia using SBA-backed funds.

◄ CONSIDER USING TA 1-5
Did You Know?

Internet
A connection of tens of thousands of interconnected computer networks that includes 1.7 million host computers.

◄ LG 4.
Illustrate how the technological environment has affected businesses.

◄ CONSIDER USING LECTURE ENHANCER 1-1
The Internet Is Here To Stay

◄ CONSIDER USING LECTURE ENHANCER 1-2
The Job Skill Gap

◄ CONSIDER USING TA 1-6
Projected Required Average Skill Level by 2000

39 states and 50 countries. When O'Leary was 40, he supervised 30,000 of the bank's 67,000 employees. Chase has over 60,000 desktop computers. The phone center handles some 130 million calls a year. Managing information flows in a company like that is one of the most important jobs in the world.[12]

Information management is becoming the most important part of most businesses. The problem today, however, is that few businesses are now managing information well. The information manager's most important role is to establish information flows between businesses and their customers. Because information technology (IT) has become such a central part of an organization's success, we'll devote Chapter 17 to that issue. Information technology (linked computers, cellular phones, modems, and the like) will be used in the future to monitor the business environment so that firms can quickly adapt to changing conditions.

▲ CONSIDER USING TA 1-7
Current Skill Level of Workers

▼ CONSIDER USING LECTURE ENHANCER 1-3
Keeping the Customer Happy

••• RESPONDING TO CUSTOMERS •••

Regardless of the occupation you choose, chances are you will be more productive using the latest in technology, including computers, modems, fax machines, pagers, and the like. Many farmers are doing just that. They can hook up to satellites to learn which fields need watering. They can also get on-line information about the latest in fertilizers and farm equipment. What careers can you think of that would be enhanced by information now available on the Internet?

Technology has also made it possible for businesses to become much more responsive to customers. For example, businesses are now marking goods with bar codes, those series of lines that you see on most grocery goods. Those bar codes tell retailers what size product you bought, what color, and at what price. A scanner at the checkout counter reads that information and puts it into a databank. A **databank** is an electronic storage file where information is kept. One use of databanks is to store vast amounts of information about consumers. For example, a retailer may ask for your name, address, telephone number or if you would like to be on their mailing list. That information is added to the databank. Soon retailers know what you buy and for whom you buy it.

Using this information, companies can send you catalogs and other direct mail advertising which offers the kind of products you might want, as indicated by your past purchases. Databases enable stores to carry only the merchandise that the local population wants. They also enable stores to carry fewer items, and less inventory, saving them money.[13]

Electronic data interchange (EDI) is a system by which sales data from bar codes on various products are sent directly to manufacturers, which then replace the purchased items quickly. Using EDI, the flow of information from retailers to manufacturers is seamless. That is, there are no barriers to communication. Likewise, the flow of goods from manufacturers to retailers is much smoother. The growing use of EDI technology is making it possible for businesses to save time and money, resulting in less expensive products. Thus, technology now makes it possible for businesses and consumers to receive the right ads about the right products at the right time for them to make a purchase. Moreover, the price is usually more attractive because the new distribution process is so efficient. We'll discuss distribution systems in detail in Chapter 15.

databank
Electronic storage file for information.

➤ LG 5.
Identify various ways that businesses can meet and beat competition.

•••• ▬▬▬ ••••

THE COMPETITIVE ENVIRONMENT

Competition among businesses has never been greater than it is today. Some companies have found a competitive edge by focusing on making high-quality products.[14] The goal for many companies is zero defects—no mistakes in making the product. Some companies, such as Motorola in the United States and Toyota in Japan, have come close to meeting that standard. However, simply making a quality product isn't enough to allow a company to stay competitive

Marketing on the Internet

Business Week magazine did a survey in 1997 to determine what people were doing on the Internet. They found that most of the Internet users surveyed had seen ads online and half of them had clicked on an ad for more information. But only 19 percent had purchased anything after viewing a cyberad.

What attracted people to Internet ads were interesting graphics, offers of information, and promises of a free product or service. About 70 percent felt that Internet ads were at least "somewhat helpful." A remain-

ing problem with Internet marketing, however, is that 65 percent of the respondents were "not willing at all" to share personal and financial information about themselves so that ads could be targeted to an individual's specific tastes. It seems that people don't completely trust the Internet yet and are not as likely to purchase something advertised there as on TV or other media.

Source: Keith H. Hammonds, "A Lot of Looking, But Not Much Buying," *Business Week*, October 6, 1997, p. 140.

in world markets. Companies now have to offer both quality products and outstanding service at competitive prices. That is why General Motors (GM) is building automobile plants in Argentina, Poland, China, and Thailand. Combining excellence with low-cost labor and minimizing distribution costs have resulted in larger markets and long-term growth for GM.[15] The differences between yesterday's traditional businesses and today's world-class businesses are shown in Figure 1.3.

••• COMPETING BY DELIGHTING THE CUSTOMER •••

Manufacturers and service organizations throughout the world have learned that today's customers are very demanding. Not only do they want good quality at low prices, but they want great service as well. In fact, products in the

TRADITIONAL BUSINESSES	WORLD-CLASS BUSINESSES
Customer satisfaction	Delighting the customer[1]
Customer orientation	Customer and stakeholder orientation[2]
Profit orientation	Profit and social orientation[3]
Reactive ethics	Proactive ethics[4]
Product orientation	Quality and service orientation
Managerial focus	Customer focus

FIGURE 1.3

••••

HOW COMPETITION HAS CHANGED BUSINESSES

1. *Delight* is a term from total quality management. *Bewitch* and *fascinate* are alternative terms.

2. Stakeholders include employees, stockholders, suppliers, dealers, and the community; the goal is to please *all* stakeholders.

3. A social orientation goes beyond profit to do what is right and good for others.

4. *Proactive* means doing the right thing before anyone tells you to do it. *Reactive* means reacting to criticism after it happens.

Making Ethical Decisions

http://www.depaul.edu/ethics/bentmba.html

Ethics Begin with You

Television, movies, and the print media all paint a dismal picture of ethics among businesspeople, government officials, and citizens in general. It is easy to criticize the ethics of these people. It is more difficult to see the moral and ethical misbehavior of your own social group. What are some of the behaviors of your friends that you find morally or ethically questionable?

One of the major trends in business today is that many companies are creating ethics codes to guide their employees' behavior. We feel this trend toward improving ethical behavior is so important that we've made it a major theme of this book. Throughout the text you'll see boxes like this one, called Making Ethical Decisions. The boxes contain short descriptions of situations that pose ethical dilemmas and ask what you would do to resolve them. The idea is for you to think

about the moral and ethical dimensions of every decision you make.

Here is your first ethical dilemma: Soon you will be taking exams in this course. Suppose you didn't prepare for one of the tests as thoroughly as you should have. As luck would have it, on exam day you are sitting in the desk right in front of the instructor, who just happened to leave the answer key sticking out of his book. The instructor is called out of the room and everyone else is concentrating intently on his or her own work. No one will know if your eyes wander toward the answer key. A good grade on this test will certainly help your grade point average. What is the problem in this situation? What are your alternatives? What are the consequences of each alternative? Which alternative will you choose? Is your choice ethical?

➤ **CONSIDER USING LECTURE ENHANCER 1-4**
How to Build a Strong Ethical Base

➤ **CONSIDER USING CRITICAL THINKING EXERCISE 1-2**
Making Ethical Decisions

21st century will be designed to "fascinate, bewitch, and delight" customers, exceeding their expectations. Every manufacturing and service organization in the world should have a sign over its door telling its workers that the customer is king. Business is becoming customer-driven, not management-driven as in the past.[16] This means that customers' wants and needs must come first. Successful organizations must now listen to customers to determine their wants and needs, then adjust the firm's products, policies, and practices to meet these demands. It is important to consider the moral and ethical practices of the firm as well. The box on Making Ethical Decisions discusses the trend toward creating ethics codes in business.

••• COMPETING BY MEETING THE NEEDS ••• OF THE COMMUNITY

It is possible for businesses today to please their customers and still not meet some needs of the community in which they operate. For example, in their efforts to please employees and customers, firms may take actions that pollute the environment. Such an outcome is highly undesirable in today's business environment. World-class organizations in the future must attempt to meet the needs of all their stakeholders. **Stakeholders** are all the people who stand to gain or lose by the policies and activities of an organization. Stakeholders include customers, employees, stockholders, suppliers, dealers, people in the local community (e.g., community interest groups), environmentalists, and elected government officials.[17] (See Figure 1.4.) All of these groups are affected by the products, policies, and practices of the firm, and their concerns need to be addressed.

stakeholders
Those people who stand to gain or lose by the policies and activities of an organization.

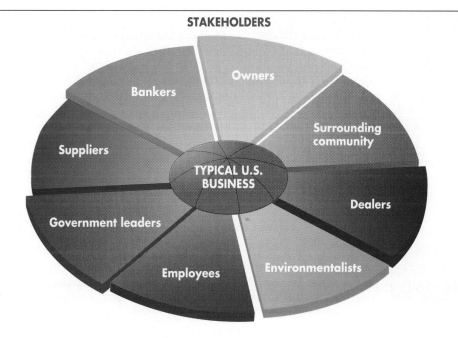

STAKEHOLDERS

Owners

Bankers

Surrounding community

Suppliers

TYPICAL U.S. BUSINESS

Dealers

Government leaders

Employees

Environmentalists

FIGURE **1.4**

• • • •

A BUSINESS AND ITS STAKEHOLDERS

Often the needs of a firm's various stakeholders will conflict. For example, paying employees more may cut into stockholders' (owners') profits. Balancing such demands is a major role of business managers.

◄ CONSIDER USING TM 11
A Business and Its Stakeholders
Text Figure 1-4

The challenge of the 21st century will be for organizations to work together to ensure that all stakeholders' needs are considered and satisfied as much as possible. Such an ambitious goal calls for both world-class employees and world-class organizational leaders.

Critical Thinking

Many current business books talk about having teams of employees work together to satisfy the needs of all stakeholders, including the community. Some recommend having environmentalists and community leaders sit in on team discussions so that businesses can respond quickly to community needs. What community needs aren't being met by businesses in your area? Can you see the benefit of having community leaders sit in on planning sessions to see that those needs are met? What, if any, drawbacks to such a policy can you see from the company's perspective?

··· COMPETING BY RESTRUCTURING AND ··· MEETING THE NEEDS OF EMPLOYEES

To meet the needs of customers, firms must give their frontline workers (office clerks, front-desk people at hotels, salespeople, etc.) freedom to respond quickly to customer requests. This is called *empowerment,* and we'll be talking about that process throughout this book. In this chapter, we simply want to acknowledge that many businesses must reorganize to make their frontline people more effective than they are now. Many firms have formed cross-functional teams to allow people from various departments to work together. These teams have learned to work without close supervision; thus, they are often called self-managed cross-functional teams.[18] One aspect of the downsizing we mentioned earlier has been the elimination of managers as lower-level workers learn to work in self-managed teams. Companies that have implemented self-managed teams will expect a lot more from their lower-level workers than they did in the past. Because they will have less management oversight, such workers will need more education. Furthermore, lower-level employees will need to receive higher pay and be treated more as partners in the firm. Increasingly,

◄ CONSIDER USING TA 1-8
Growing Number of Telecommuters

◄ CONSIDER USING LECTURE ENHANCER 1-5
Teams Lead to Responsiveness

As a consumer, you will appreciate the trend in business to empower frontline workers to delight their customers. What this means is that the person who deals with you at the counter or in sales will be authorized to act on your requests or will have the power to quickly find someone who can. In most cases they will not have to consult with their manager, thus ensuring that the company's response will be faster and more efficient. Which organizations would you like to see implement this concept first?

➤ LG 6.
Demonstrate how the social environment has changed and what the reaction of business has been.

demography
The statistical study of human population to learn its size, density, and other characteristics.

multiculturalism
Process of optimizing the contribution of people from different cultures.

➤ CONSIDER USING TA 1-9
Dealing With a Multicultural Workforce

➤ CONSIDER USING LECTURE ENHANCER 1-6
The Aging of the Baby Boomers

managers' jobs will be to train, support, coach, and motivate lower-level employees.[19] As many companies have discovered, it sometimes takes years to restructure an organization so that managers are willing to give up some of their authority and employees are willing to assume more responsibility.

Employees with increased responsibility are likely to demand increased compensation based on performance. Often, in larger firms, that will mean giving employees partial ownership of the firm. It will also mean developing entirely new organizational structures to meet the changing needs of customers and employees. We'll discuss such organizational changes and models in Chapter 8.

··· COMPETING BY CONCERN FOR THE ··· NATURAL ENVIRONMENT

In their rush to give consumers what they want and need, managers must be careful that they cause minimal damage to the natural environment. Business and government leaders throughout the coming years will be discussing issues such as the potential benefits and hazards of nuclear power, recycling, the management of forests, the ethical treatment of animals, and the protection of the air we breathe and the water we drink. Environmentalism must not be a social cause of a few; it must be a major focus of everyone, and it's becoming increasingly so.

···· ▬▬▬ ····

THE SOCIAL ENVIRONMENT

Demography is the statistical study of the human population with regard to its size, density, and characteristics. In this book, we're particularly interested in the demographic trends that most affect businesses and career choices. We're going through major changes in the United States that are dramatically affecting how we live, where we live, what we buy, and how we spend our time. Furthermore, tremendous population shifts are leading to new opportunities for some firms and to declining opportunities for others.

··· MULTICULTURALISM AND ITS ADVANTAGES FOR BUSINESS ···

The Bureau of the Census predicts that the U.S. population in 2050 will be very different from what it is today. First, our population will increase by approximately 50 percent: 383 million versus 260 million today. As the population grows, today's students will find an increased demand for a wide variety of goods and services.

Second, the population's makeup in the year 2050 will also be very different from what it is today. The Hispanic and Latino population will increase from 9 percent of the total to 21 percent, and the Asian population will rise from 3 percent to 11 percent. Think of the business opportunities and challenges such shifts will create. In a business context, **multiculturalism** is the process of optimizing (in the workplace) the contributions of people from different cultures. Having a multicultural population provides an opportunity for all U.S. citizens to learn to work with people of all nations. That should give Americans an advantage when it comes to negotiating and working with people in global markets.

Moreover, a diverse population can provide ideas, concepts, and cultural norms to enrich the business culture. A diverse population is a strong population.

Just as a healthy forest is made up of diverse trees and bushes so that a disease that affects one will not affect all, a strong business population is made up of people of all different ages, creeds, experiences, and national origins. There is strength in different views and perspectives. All in all, one of the reasons the United States is strong is because of its diversity and openness to people from all countries.

▼ CONSIDER USING TA 1-10
The Changing Workforce

••• THE INCREASE IN THE NUMBER OF ••• OLDER AMERICANS

By 2030, the entire baby-boom generation (the 76 million people born from 1946 to 1964 who make up almost one-third of the current U.S. population) will be senior citizens.

Americans aged 45 to 54 are currently the richest group in U.S. society. They spend more than others on everything except health care and thus represent a lucrative market for restaurants, transportation, entertainment, education, and so on. What do such demographics mean for you and for businesses in the future? Think of the products the middle-aged and elderly will need—medicine, nursing homes, assisted-living facilities, adult day care, home health care, recreation, and the like—and you'll see opportunities for successful businesses of the 21st century. Older citizens will demand more and better health care, more recreation and travel, and new and different products and services of all kinds. Businesses that cater to them will have the opportunity for exceptional growth in the near future.

▲ CONSIDER USING LECTURE ENHANCER 1-7
Older People Are Becoming More Influential

A diverse workforce brings many different perspectives to every issue that is faced by an organization. That diversity of views helps assure an organization that it will not ignore any constituency in its internal and external policies. Thus diversity strengthens an organization and is the source of ads like this one.

◄ CONSIDER USING CRITICAL THINKING EXERCISE 1-3
The Effects of Trends

◄ CONSIDER USING TA 1-11
U.S. Population by Generations

◄ CONSIDER USING SUPPLEMENTAL CASE 1-1
Dealing With Changing Family

telecommuting
Working at home and keeping in touch with others in the workforce using telecommunications.

••• TWO-INCOME FAMILIES •••

Several factors have led to a dramatic growth in two-income families. The high costs of housing and of maintaining a comfortable lifestyle have made it difficult if not impossible for many households to live on just one income. Furthermore, many women today simply want a career outside the home.[20]

One result of this trend is a host of programs that companies are implementing to assist two-income families. IBM and Procter & Gamble, for example, have pregnancy benefits, parental leave, flexible work schedules, and elder care programs. Some companies offer referral services that provide counseling to parents in search of child care or elder care. Such trends are creating many new opportunities for graduates in human resource management.

Many employers provide child care benefits of some type; some of these programs, such as the one at Johnson Wax, are on-site. Such centers are expensive to operate and often cause resentment from employees who don't use the benefits. The resentment has led companies to offer cafeteria benefits packages, which enable families to choose from a "menu" of benefits. A couple may choose day care instead of a dental plan, for instance.

Many companies are increasing the number of part-time workers to enable mothers and fathers to stay home with children and still earn income. Others allow workers to stay home and send their work in by telecommunications. This is called **telecommuting**.[21] The net result of these trends is increased

productivity
The total output of goods and services in a given period of time divided by work hours (output per work hour).

Progress Check

One of the current trends in business is to get employees close to the customer where they can respond quickly to customer wants and needs. Thus there is less need for workers to have office space. Instead, they work out of their homes. They maintain contact with others through the computer, phone, e-mail, and other electronic means. This is called telecommuting. As an increasing number of workers no longer need to commute to work, it may eventually lead to a population shift away from big cities to smaller ones where the living is less expensive and not as congested. In what businesses have you seen evidence of telecommuting in your locale?

opportunity for men and women to enhance their standard of living and raise a family.[22] They also create many job opportunities in day care, counseling, and other related fields. You'll learn more about what's happening in human resource management in Chapters 11 and 12.

▲ CONSIDER USING LECTURE ENHANCER 1-8
Men, Families, and "Women's Issues"

- What are the five factors of production?
- How can government encourage entrepreneurial growth?
- How does information technology help businesses to be more customer-oriented?
- What are stakeholders? Discuss how a business can compete by being more responsive to all its stakeholders.

▼ LG 7.
Analyze what businesses must do to meet the global challenge.

···· ▬▬▬ ····

THE GLOBAL ENVIRONMENT

The global environment of business is so important that we show it as surrounding all other environmental influences. (See Figure 1.2.) Perhaps the number one global environmental change in recent years is the growth of international competition and the increase of free trade among nations. Japanese manufacturers like Honda and Mitsubishi have won much of the market for automobiles, videocassette recorders, TV sets, and other products by offering global consumers better-quality products than those of U.S. manufacturers. This competition has hurt many U.S. industries, and many jobs have been lost.

Today manufacturers in countries such as China, India, South Korea, and Mexico can produce high-quality goods at low prices because their workers are paid less money than U.S. workers and they've learned quality concepts from Japanese, German, and U.S. producers. Late in 1997, however, Thailand, Malaysia, Hong Kong, Japan, South Korea, and other countries had banking problems that caused a major upheaval in global markets. These problems affected all nations, showing the interdependence of countries today.

U.S. manufacturers have been analyzing the best practices from throughout the world and many have implemented the most advanced quality method. In fact, U.S. workers in many industries are now more productive than workers in Japan and other countries. **Productivity** is the volume of goods and services that one worker can produce. Better technology, machinery, and tools enable each worker to be more productive.[23]

U.S. businesses are rapidly changing their ways of operating to become world-class competitors. The Ford Taurus, the Chrysler Minivan, and the Oldsmobile Aurora are now competitive with the best automobiles in the world. Companies such as Disney, Federal Express, Intel, and Microsoft, as well as many smaller companies, are as good or better than competing organizations anywhere in the world. But businesses have gone beyond simply competing with organizations in other countries by learning to cooperate with international firms. That cooperation has the potential to create rapidly growing world markets that can generate prosperity beyond most people's expectations. The challenge is tremendous, but so is the will to achieve.

··· GLOBAL OPPORTUNITIES AND ··· FREE-TRADE AGREEMENTS

In 1994 the United States signed the North American Free Trade Agreement (NAFTA), increasing trade between the United States, Canada, and Mexico. Previously, there were trade restrictions among the three countries that made it hard to sell goods and services across the borders. Now it's easier for U.S. auto manufacturers to sell cars in Mexico and for Mexican companies to export their goods, such as cement, to the United States. The goal is to allow consumers and businesses in all three countries to benefit from unrestricted trade. Some U.S. companies are expected to lose business to Mexican and Canadian companies, but other companies such as Wal-Mart are expected to gain markets. It will take years for the results to be clear.

Since NAFTA was passed, the United States has created some 2.5 million jobs a year and unemployment has dropped to 4.6 percent. Many of the new jobs pay high wages because export industries pay about 13 percent more than those in manufacturing generally.[24] Mexico's economy has been up and down since the passage of the agreement, but much of that fluctuation has been due to conditions not related to NAFTA. In general, one can say that NAFTA has been neither the success imagined by some nor the disaster proposed by others and that the more open borders may lead to better economies for all three countries.

Global trade means opportunities and challenges for every country. The United States is a huge market that attracts product from all over the world. In this photograph employees are assembling telephones for AT&T in Laredo, Mexico. The wages and profits made from selling goods to the United States can be used to buy more goods and services from the United States as well as its competitors. Thus it's possible for all countries to benefit from free trade and global competition. That doesn't mean that every individual and every firm will benefit. Some will lose out to foreign competitors. What are some of the essential resources for success in global competition?

Free trade among nations can work like free trade among different areas of one country. Note, for example, how prosperous people are in the United States as a result of free trade between the states. Many jobs were lost in recent decades when companies shifted production from the Northeast to states like North Carolina, but overall the country continued to prosper. Trying to protect manufacturers from international competition often leads to stagnation and the inability to compete globally.

Most European leaders recognize the benefits of free trade as well. As a consequence, free-trade agreements have been negotiated among the various European countries (the European Union, or EU). As the agreements are successfully completed, European trade is likely to grow much faster than it has grown in recent years. Figure 1.5 lists current members of the EU; more countries may join as the benefits of free trade become apparent.

Trade agreements have also been established in Asia, South America, and other parts of the world. World trade agreements and the global environment in general are so important to businesses today that Chapter 3 is devoted entirely to global business. A key issue in the United States today, for example, is whether or not to give the President freedom to sign free-trade agreements with other countries without changes being made by Congress. This is called fast-track legislation. It was defeated in 1997, but it could come up again.

 CONSIDER USING SUPPLEMENTAL CASE 1-2
The Travel and
Tourism Industry

··· HOW GLOBAL CHANGES AFFECT YOU ···

The free-trade agreement signed in 1994 will lead to many career opportunities for American college graduates. As businesses expand to serve global markets, new jobs will be created in both manufacturing and service industries.

Reaching Beyond Our Borders

http://www.webmasters.co.nz

Competing in Cyberspace—Keeping Up with Technology

Tropical Jim's Remake-Shop is a small business that designs Web sites for businesses. About 90 percent of his customers are American companies. Where is Tropical Jim's located? In Caracas, Venezuela. Jim Macintyre, the owner, says that the firm wasn't profitable until it began to sell in the U.S. market. Part of his success is due to the fact that salaries in Caracas are 10 percent of U.S. salaries.

Tropical Jim's has to compete for U.S. business with another Web designer based in New Zealand: Web-Masters Ltd. Frank ven der Velden, the owner, says that U.S. businesses aggressively search the Internet to find companies that offer the best value for the services they want. That search is conducted worldwide, and a company in Venezuela or New Zealand, although far away, has an equal chance of being selected.

Many small firms in the United States are just getting started with Internet marketing. They are often shocked to find that there are dozens of foreign companies already set up in their industry offering good quality at low prices. How to compete? The answer is to provide quality on-line customer service. That means that the Web site is so attractive that companies aren't tempted to go any further in their search for a good supplier. To make a Web site attractive, a company must offer product specifications, answers to frequently asked questions, references, easy-to-follow ordering instructions, and more.

Small businesses in America, therefore, must keep up with the latest in technology or risk losing business to foreign suppliers that have less expensive labor and ready access to the market. That means hiring people who can bring the business up-to-date on Internet marketing, including the use of databases and other technological tools. Later in the text, we will explain in detail the use of database marketing and other cutting-edge developments. At this point, it is important to note that competition, even for the smallest businesses in the service sector, is now *global*. Global competition is here. Students interested in a career in small business must become computer literate and be familiar with all the latest communication technology or risk being obsolete upon graduation.

Source: Fred Hopgood, "Foreign Exchange," *Inc. Tech* 1997, no. 2, pp. 85–88, and Michael D. Donahue, "Adapting the Internet to the Needs of Business," *Advertising Age,* February 2, 1998, p. 26.

▶ **CONSIDER USING LECTURE ENHANCER 1-9**
Global Opportunities for the Smaller Competitor

▶ **CONSIDER USING TM 12**
Members of the European Union
Text Figure 1-5

Exports are expected to continue to increase under NAFTA and other new trade agreements, which will lead to expansion of the job market both in the United States and globally.

Global trade also means global competition. The students who will prosper are those who are prepared for the markets of tomorrow. That means that you must prepare yourself now to compete in a rapidly changing environment.

FIGURE **1.5**
• • • •

MEMBERS OF THE EUROPEAN UNION

Austria	**Germany**	**Luxembourg**
Belgium	**Great Britain**	**Netherlands**
Denmark	**Greece**	**Portugal**
Finland	**Ireland**	**Spain**
France	**Italy**	**Sweden**

Rapid changes create a need for continuous learning. In other words, be prepared to continue your education throughout your career. Colleges will offer updated courses in computer technology, telecommunications, language skills, and other subjects you'll need to stay competitive. Students have every reason to be optimistic about job opportunities in the future if they prepare themselves well.

···· ━━━ ····

THE QUALITY IMPERATIVE

As mentioned earlier, one consequence of global competition is that no country dares fall behind other countries in providing high-quality products. Quality production techniques have been in place for over a decade in countries such as Japan, the United States, and Germany. A U.S. citizen, W. Edwards Deming, was instrumental in introducing quality concepts worldwide. Using his techniques top-quality manufacturers are able to make products with almost no defects and to make them quickly. Global consumers will fast become accustomed to such quality.

Quality in today's firms is defined as providing customers with goods and services that go beyond the expected. At IBM, for example, quality is defined as meeting customers' demands, both inside and outside the organization, for defect-free products, services, and business processes. Consumers are increasingly demanding the best quality at the lowest price. Much of Wal-Mart's success has come because the company provides such value. Companies that can't provide the combination of high quality and low price will be less able to compete in the 21st century. Even small businesses, such as Custom Research Inc., are able to compete with large firms because of quality.

··· **THE QUALITY STANDARD: THE BALDRIGE AWARDS** ···

In the United States, a standard was set for quality with the introduction of the Malcolm Baldrige National Quality Awards in 1987. To qualify for one of these awards, a company has to show quality as measured three ways: (1) by customer satisfaction, (2) by product and service quality, and (3) by quality of internal operations. Among other things, the Baldrige Awards require companies to increase employee involvement, measure themselves against industry leaders, and shorten the time it takes to introduce new products. A major criterion for earning the award is whether customer wants and needs are being met, and customer satisfaction ratings are better than those of competitors. As you can see, focus is shifting away from just making quality goods and services to providing top-quality customer service in all respects.

··· **QUALITY, ISO 9000, AND ISO 14000 STANDARDS** ···

The new global measures for quality are called ISO 9000 standards. **ISO 9000** is the common name given to quality management and assurance standards published by the International Organization for Standardization (ISO). Prior to the establishment of such standards in 1987, there were no international standards of quality against which to measure companies. Now ISO standards, established in Europe, provide a "common denominator" of business quality accepted around the world.

What makes ISO 9000 so important is that the European Union, the group of European countries that are establishing free-trade agreements, is demanding that companies that want to do business with the EU be certified by ISO

◄ **LG 8.**
Compare the new quality standards and identify what businesses are doing to meet those standards.

quality
Providing customers with high-quality goods and services that go beyond the expected.

ISO 9000
Quality management and assurance standards published by the International Organization for Standardization (ISO).

➤ CONSIDER USING LECTURE
ENHANCER 1-10
The Impact of the Baldrige Awards

standards. There are several accreditation agencies in Europe and in the United States that can certify that a company meets standards for all phases of its operations, from product development through production and testing to installation.

Those companies that qualify for a Baldrige Award will have little trouble passing the certification process for ISO 9000, but most U.S. companies have a long way to go to qualify. It's no longer enough to have a total quality program to compete in certain areas of the world. Now in order to do so that program must be certified by international standards.

ISO 14000
A collection of the best practices for managing an organization's environmental impacts.

ISO 14000 is a collection of the best practices for managing an organization's impact on the environment. ISO 14000 is an environmental management system (EMS). Certification in both ISO 9000 and ISO 14000 would show that a firm has a world-class management system in both quality and environmental standards. In the past, people in firms were assigned separately to meet both standards. Today, ISO 9000 and 14000 standards have been blended so that an organization can work on both at once.[25]

•••• ▬▬▬ ••••

THE EVOLUTION OF AMERICAN BUSINESS

➤ LG 9.
Review how trends from the past are being repeated in the present and what that will mean for the service sector.

Many managers and workers are losing their jobs in major manufacturing firms. Businesses in the United States have become so productive that fewer workers are needed in the industrial sector (i.e., industries that produce goods). **Goods** are tangible products such as computers, food, clothing, cars, and appliances.

goods
Tangible products such as houses, food, and clothing.

Due to the increasing impact of technology and global competition, shouldn't we be concerned about the prospect of higher unemployment and lower incomes in the future? Where will the jobs be when today's students graduate? These important questions force us to look carefully at the U.S. economy and its future.

➤ CONSIDER USING TA 1-12
Ethical Questions to Ask

••• PROGRESS IN THE AGRICULTURAL AND ••• MANUFACTURING INDUSTRIES

The United States has been a leader in economic development since the beginning of the 1900s. The agricultural industry led the way, providing food for the United States and much of the world. That industry became so efficient through the use of technology that the number of farmers has dropped from about a third of the population to less than 2 percent. The number of farms in the United States declined from some 5.7 million at the turn of the century to about 2 million today. However, average farm size is now about 455 acres versus 160 acres in the past. In other words, agriculture is still a major industry in the United States. What has changed is that millions of smaller farms have been replaced by some that are huge, some that are large, and some that are small but highly specialized. The loss of farm workers was not a negative sign. It was instead an indication that U.S. agricultural workers were the most productive in the world, and they still are even though there are fewer of them.

Many farmers who lost their jobs went to work in factories. The manufacturing industry, much like agriculture, used technology to become more productive. The consequence, as in farming, was the elimination of many jobs. Again, the loss to society is minimal if the wealth created by increased productivity and efficiency creates new jobs elsewhere, and that's exactly what has happened over the past 50 years. Many workers in the industrial sector found jobs in the service sector. In fact, as noted earlier, the unemployment rate in the United States went as low as 4.6 percent in 1998. Those who can't find jobs today are largely people who need retraining and education to match job opportunities that now exist. We'll discuss the manufacturing sector and production in more detail in Chapter 9.

··· PROGRESS IN SERVICE INDUSTRIES ···

Many workers who could no longer find employment in manufacturing were able to find jobs in the service industry. **Services** are intangible products (i.e., products that can't be held in your hand) such as education, health care, insurance, recreation, and travel and transportation. In the past, the dominant industries in the United States produced goods (steel, railroads, machine tools, etc.). Today, the leading firms are in services (legal, telecommunications, entertainment, financial, etc.). Travel and tourism is now the nation's number two employer and its leading export. Tourism accounts for about 10 percent of all jobs in the United States.[26]

Since the mid-1980s, the service industry has generated almost all of our economy's increases in employment. Although service-sector growth has slowed, it remains the largest area of growth. Chances are very high that you'll work in it at some point in your career. Figure 1.6 lists many service-sector jobs. Look it over to see where the careers of the future are likely to be. Retailers like The Gap are part of the service sector. Each new store creates many managerial jobs for college graduates.

Another bit of good news is that there are more high-paying jobs in the service sector than in the goods-producing sector. High-paying service-sector jobs can be found in health care, accounting, finance, telecommunications, architecture, law, and software engineering. Projections are that the service sector will grow slowly in the coming decades. (See Figure 1.7.) Some sectors, such as telecommunications, will grow rapidly, while others, such as advertising, may have much slower growth. The strategy for college graduates is to remain flexible, to find out where the jobs are being created, and to move when appropriate.

Most people thought that the service era in the United States would last a lot longer, but it seems to be losing out to a new era in the 21st century. The new era could be described as a global revolution that will affect all sectors of the economy: agricultural, industrial, and service. The global "information revolution" is breaking down barriers between nations. As a result, global competition will intensify, but so will the opportunity for international cooperation.

··· YOUR FUTURE IN THE GLOBAL ECONOMY ···

We're now in the midst of an information-based global revolution that will alter the way business is done in the future. It's exciting to think about the role you'll play in that revolution. You may be a leader; that is, you may be one of the people who will implement the changes and accept the challenges of world competition based on world quality standards. This book will introduce you to some of the concepts that will make such leadership possible.

"This is MY PHiLADELPHiA"
Bill Cosby

" I love WARM places, like PHILADELPHIA. The SMILES I get for free when I'm antiquing in the nearby COUNTRYSIDE, warm. The cheesesteaks on SOUTH STREET, warm. Go ahead, you can walk it off later SHOPPING in the largest mall on the East Coast. Even one of the COOLEST clubs here is called WARMDADDY'S. (It's a BLUES thing.) But there's nothing warmer than the hearts of THE PEOPLE who live here, in THE FRIENDLIEST CITY in America. My friends, come visit THE WARMEST PLACE ON EARTH. "

PHiLADELPHiA. *The place that* LOVES YOU BACK.

Touch history, take in the countryside, enjoy the nightlife, the museums, the art and most of all, the people. Come love a place that will love you back. For your free getaway planner, call 1-888-GO-PHILA.

Pennsylvania Memories last a lifetime

A major consideration when choosing a job is deciding where you would like to work. Different cities in the United States advertise not only to attract visitors, but businesses and workers as well. A case in point is Philadelphia, with its investment in a new convention center, development of Penn's Landing, and recent facelift of its South Broad Street area—all of which are being carried out in an attempt to convince businesses and employees to stay in the city or relocate there. How important do you think the location of a job will be in your employment decision?

services
Intangible products such as education, health care, and insurance.

Remember that most of the concepts and principles that make businesses more effective and efficient are applicable in government agencies and nonprofit organizations as well. This is an introductory business text, so we'll tend to focus on business. Nonetheless, we'll remind you periodically that you can apply these concepts in other areas. Business can't prosper in the future without the cooperation of government and social leaders throughout the world.

FIGURE **1.6**
••••
**WHAT IS THE
SERVICE SECTOR?**

There's much talk about the service sector, but few discussions actually list what it includes. Here's a representative list of services as classified by the government:

Lodging Services

Hotels, rooming houses, and other lodging places
Sporting and recreation camps
Trailering parks and camp sites for transients

Personal Services

Laundries	Child care
Linen supply	Shoe repair
Diaper service	Funeral homes
Carpet cleaning	Tax preparation
Photographic studios	Beauty shops
Health clubs	

Business Services

Accounting	Exterminating
Ad agencies	Employment agencies
Collection agencies	Computer programming
Commercial photography	Research and development labs
Commercial art	Management services
Stenographic services	Public relations
Window cleaning	Detective agencies
Consulting	Interior design
Equipment rental	

Automotive Repair Services and Garages

Auto rental	Tire retreading
Truck rental	Exhaust system shops
Parking lots	Car washes
Paint shops	Transmission repair

Miscellaneous Repair Services

Radio and television	Welding
Watch	Sharpening
Reupholstery	Septic tank cleaning

Motion Picture Industry

Production	Theaters
Distribution	Drive-ins

Amusement and Recreation Services

Dance halls	Racetracks
Symphony orchestras	Golf courses
Pool halls	Amusement parks
Bowling alleys	Carnivals
Fairs	Ice skating rinks
Botanical gardens	Circuses
Video rentals	

Health Services

Physicians	Nursery care
Dentists	Medical labs
Chiropractors	Dental labs

Legal Services

Educational Services

Libraries	Correspondence schools
Schools	Data processing schools

Social Services

Child care	Family services
Job training	

Noncommercial Museums, Art Galleries, and Botanical and Zoological Gardens

Selected Membership Organizations

Business associations
Civic associations

Financial Services

Banking	Investment firms (brokers)
Insurance	
Real estate agencies	

Miscellaneous Services

Architectural	Surveying
Engineering	Utilities

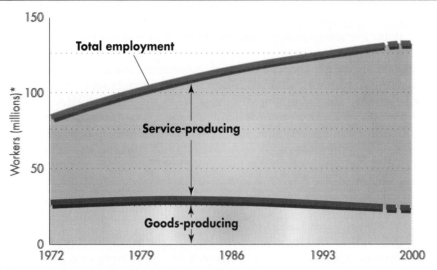

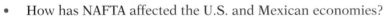

*Includes wage and salary workers, the self-employed, and unpaid family workers.

Source: *Occupational Outlook Handbook,* U.S. Department of Labor.

Progress Check

- How has NAFTA affected the U.S. and Mexican economies?
- What are the Baldrige Awards?
- What is the difference between the ISO 9000 and ISO 14000 standards?
- If the service sector is in decline, where will future job opportunities be?

SUMMARY
· · · · · ·

1. A business is any activity that seeks profit by providing goods and services to others.
   - *Where does the money come from that people use to buy goods and services?*
   Businesses and their employees create the wealth that people use to buy goods and services. Businesses also are the source of funds for government agencies and nonprofit organizations that improve the quality of life of society. The quality of life of a country refers to the general well-being of its people because of freedom, a clean environment, safety, schools, health care, free time, and other things that lead to satisfaction and joy. Thus, business adds to both quality of life and standard of living by creating the wealth needed to fund progress in these areas.

   1. Describe how businesses and nonprofit organizations add to a country's standard of living and quality of life.

2. People are willing to take the risk of starting businesses if they feel that the risk isn't too great.
   - *What is the importance of profit, loss, and risk to a business?*
   Profit is money a business earns above and beyond the money that it spends for salaries, expenses, and other costs. Businesspeople make profits by taking risks. *Risk* is the chance you take of losing time and money on a business that may not prove profitable. A *loss* occurs when a business's costs and expenses are more than its revenues. If a business loses money over an extended period of time, it will likely have to close, putting its employees out of work.
   - *What factors of production do businesses use to create wealth?*
   Businesses use five factors of production: land, labor (workers), capital, entrepreneurship, and knowledge. Of these, the most important are entrepreneurship and knowledge.

   2. Explain the importance of entrepreneurship to the wealth of an economy and show the relationship of profit to risk assumption.

3. Examine how the economic environment and taxes affect businesses.

3. Economic factors affect business by increasing or decreasing the risks of starting a business.
   - ***What are some things that government can do to lessen the risk of starting businesses?***
   Part of that risk involves the way that government treats businesses. There's much a government can do to lessen the risk of starting businesses: allow private ownership of businesses, pass laws that enable businesspeople to write contracts that are enforceable in court, establish a currency that's tradable in world markets, focus on the elimination of corruption in business and government, and keep taxes and regulations to a minimum. From a business perspective, lower taxes mean lower risks, more growth, and more money for workers and the government

4. Illustrate how the technological environment has affected businesses.

4. The most successful college graduates of tomorrow will be those who can find their way on the Internet.
   - ***How has technology benefited businesses and consumers?***
   Information technology (linked computers, cellular phones, modems, and the like) are used by business to monitor the business environment so that firms can quickly adapt to changing conditions. Technology has also made it possible for businesses to become much more responsive to consumers. Bar codes tell retailers what size product you bought, what color, and at what price. Using that information, the retailers can send you catalogs and direct mail pieces offering you exactly what you want, as indicated by your past purchases.

5. Identify various ways that businesses can meet and beat competition.

5. Competition among businesses has never been greater than it is today.
   - ***What are some ways in which businesses meet and beat competition?***
   Some companies found a competitive edge in the 1980s by focusing on making quality products. By the early 1990s, meeting the challenge of making a quality product was not enough to stay competitive in world markets. Companies had to offer quality products and outstanding service at competitive prices. World-class organizations meet the needs of all their stakeholders. Modern businesses have teams of employees who work together to satisfy the needs of all stakeholders, including employees, the community, and people concerned about the natural environment.

6. Demonstrate how the social environment has changed and what the reaction of the business community has been.

6. The United States is going through a social revolution that's having a dramatic impact on how we live, where we live, what we buy, and how we spend our time.
   - ***How have such social changes affected businesses?***
   Changes in society are resulting in new opportunities for some firms and declining opportunities for others. As the world population grows, there will be many new opportunities for businesses to sell more products and services. Moreover, a diverse population provides businesses with ideas, concepts, and cultural norms that enrich the business culture. Because many more women have entered the labor force, companies have implemented a variety of programs to assist two-income and single-parent families. Many employers provide child care benefits of some type to keep their valued employees.

7. Analyze what businesses must do to meet the global challenge.

7. The number one global environmental change is growth of international competition and the opening of free trade among nations.
   - ***How can businesses meet the global challenge?***
   Many businesses in the United States have met the challenge of quality. Now they're moving to form alliances with businesses all over the globe to take advantage of the best business practices in the world. Free-trade

agreements are expected to create even more opportunities and challenges. In 1994 the North American Free Trade Agreement (NAFTA) expanded trade between the United States, Canada, and Mexico, and other such agreements being negotiated today are opening the world to free trade and the potential for achieving greater prosperity.

8. ISO 9000 and ISO 14000 refer to quality management and assurance standards published by the International Organization for Standardization.
   • ***How important is quality to the future of businesses?***
   Quality in today's firms is defined as providing customers with goods and services that go beyond the expected. Quality and service will be the two major competitive factors in the 21st century. If you include service in quality, then quality is the competitive advantage for the future. ISO 14000 standards assure the community that a company is doing its best to protect the environment while making quality goods and services.

8. Compare the new quality standards and identify what businesses are doing to meet those standards.

9. The United States has been a leader in economic development since the beginning of the 1900s.
   • ***What is the history of our economic development and what does it tell us about the future?***
   What has sustained America as the world's economic leader is the development and use of technology to improve productivity. Productivity is the volume of goods and services one worker can produce. Due to productivity gains, the agricultural sector was able to produce more food with fewer workers. Those displaced agricultural workers eventually went to work in factories producing more industrial goods. Improved productivity resulting from technology and increased competition from foreign firms combined to reduce the need for factory workers and contributed to the development in the United States of a service economy.

9. Review how trends from the past are being repeated in the present and what that will mean for the service sector.

KEY TERMS
• • • • • •

business 1	**ISO 9000** 19	**quality of life** 2
databank 10	**ISO 14000** 20	**revenue** 5
demography 14	**loss** 5	**risk** 5
downsizing 4	**multiculturalism** 14	**services** 21
entrepreneur 4	**nonprofit**	**stakeholders** 12
factors of	**organization** 3	**standard of living** 2
production 6	**productivity** 16	**telecommuting** 15
goods 20	**profit** 4	
Internet 9	**quality** 19	

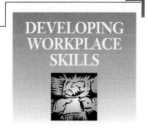

DEVELOPING WORKPLACE SKILLS

1. This text describes the growth trend in the numbers of businesses in the service sector. Look through your local phone book and list five businesses that provide services in your area. This text also describes how certain demographic and social changes affect businesses. Look at your list of local service businesses and consider how these trends affect them. Distinguish the businesses that are negatively affected from those that are positively affected. Be prepared to explain your answers.

2. Research current business publications to identify which countries have the fastest growing economies. Choose one of the countries and describe its standard of living and quality of life. If you chose to find a job there, what language would you need to speak? Compose a list of other skills you'll need to prosper in that country.

3. Plan for educational advancement throughout your business career by creating a timeline that shows the key steps you need to take in order to meet your goals.

4. Determine which nonprofit organizations in your community might offer you the best chance to learn the kind of skills you'll need in the job you hope to have when you graduate. How could you best allocate your time to allow you to volunteer at that organization? Write a letter that inquires about their program and opportunities for volunteering.

5. Use a computer word processing program to write a one-page report on how technology will change society in the next 10 years. Use a computer graphics program or hand-draw a chart that illustrates the increase of personal computers used in American homes since 1980.

**TAKING IT
TO THE NET**

(This exercise requires using the Internet. If you do not know how to use this powerful computer network, you need to read the appendix "Driver's Ed for the Information Superhighway.")

Purpose of this exercise: To gather data regarding trends in population and the social environment and to analyze how these changes affect American businesses. To answer the following questions, explore the Census Bureau's homepage on the Internet at http://www.census.gov/.

Questions:

(Be sure to include the URL of the Web site where you found the answer to these questions—you can find the URL in the address box of your browser.)

1. Select the Population Clock from the Census Bureau's Homepage. Record the time and population for the United States.

2. What is the fastest growing occupation? What could contribute to the increase in this profession? Hint: The Bureau of Labor Statistics is a great place to search for occupational growth statistics. You will find occupations with the largest job growth from now to 2006.

3. What percentage of consumer expenditures is for food? Transportation? What does the information tell you about the standard of living in the United States? Hint: There is a search feature within the Census Bureau's Web site. The Bureau of Labor Statistics also has a search feature. There are even consumer expenditure surveys found within this site.

4. What percentage of mothers receiving Aid to Families with Dependent Children (AFDC) were never married? What is the amount of AFDC benefits received in your city? How does this number compare with the national average? The AFDC site lists information on various parts of the country. What explanation can you give for this trend? Hint: Try searching for AFDC (Aid to Families with Dependent Children).

5. Return to the U.S. Census Bureau's homepage. What is the population of the nation now? Record the population and the time. If you are doing this project individually, you should collect at least 10 different population counts. Be sure to record the day and the time you collect each one. If you would like to put the data in chart form, the entire class's data can be used to make a graph. What does this chart tell you about the U.S. population? How could businesses use this information?

Practicing Management Decisions

The Wall Street Journal reported in 1996 that approximately 5.9 million women-owned businesses were operating in the United States. This constitutes about one-third of small businesses. Together these businesses employed more people than all the Fortune 500 companies combined. In the 1990s, women were forming small businesses at twice the rate of men. In other words, much of the future growth of small businesses in the United States will be managed by women, and small businesses are the ones creating most of the new jobs.

One reason so many women are starting their own businesses is that some feel that corporations have established a "glass ceiling" (an invisible barrier) that prevents women (and minorities) from reaching top levels of management. A recent study, for example, found that among 4,000 executives in a variety of U.S. companies, only 19 were women. Many firms are working to correct this problem, but progress has been slow. The U.S. Department of Labor is working to establish rules for government contractors that would eliminate any glass ceilings that they perceive.

Women entrepreneurs are frequently the business leaders in developing countries. Women tend to be the ones to take the risk of starting small businesses. To encourage their growth, the women's World Bank encourages banks to make loans to women by backing 75 percent of each loan. The focus has been on ownership of very small businesses (microenterprises) but is now shifting to larger firms. The Foundation for International Community Assistance (FINCA) makes small loans to women in less-developed countries. Some 65,000 loans are now outstanding.

CASE
• • • • • •
WOMEN ENTREPRENEURS IN SMALL BUSINESS
• • • • • •

The loan recipients use the money to start businesses or put it into community banks that lend money to other entrepreneurs.

Women in America are soon expected to own 50 percent of all small businesses. Women now make up 55 percent of the enrollment in higher education, so they may be better trained than men for tomorrow's executive positions if they major in business and related subjects.

Decision Questions

1. The number of women in developing countries who are becoming entrepreneurs is increasing. What can the governments of these developing countries do to promote and encourage such risk taking among their entrepreneurs?
2. What progress, if any, can you cite in breaking the glass ceiling for women in U.S. businesses, government agencies, and nonprofit organizations?
3. What advantages and/or disadvantages do you see from women taking over top positions in business, nonprofit organizations, and government?
4. Minority women are one of the fastest-growing categories of small-business owners. What effect will such a trend have on the economy in general?

Source: Stephanie N. Metha, "Hear Them Roar," *The Wall Street Journal,* November 11, 1996, pp. A1 and A5; Peter Behr, "Women-Owned Businesses Proliferating, Finding Credit Easier to Get, Study Says," *Washington Post,* April 9, 1997, p. C10; and Wendy Zellner, Resa W. King, Veronica N. Byrd, Gail DeGeorge, and Jane Birbaum, "Women Entrepreneurs," *Business Week,* April 18, 1994, pp. 104–110.

Many of us dream of starting a business and watching it grow. Howard Schultz, CEO of Starbucks, made his dreams come true. Schultz bought the original Starbucks coffee shop in Seattle in 1987 and rapidly propelled it to a business that made net sales of $465 million in 1995. What are the reasons for Schultz's incredible success?

First, Schultz did not make Starbucks a copycat of typical American coffee shops. Instead, Schultz sought to model Starbucks after the

VIDEO CASE
• • • • • •
STARBUCKS

neighborhood coffee bars he frequented while in Italy. The coffee introduced at Starbucks also had a stronger flavor than most Americans were used to. Though the risks were high for serving beverages that might seem strange to local tastes, Schultz saw the profit potential inherent in such a venture. In fact, Americans have come to love the flavor of Starbucks coffee so much that the company has made the flavor available in a soft drink, and even a beer!

Schultz also had the personal background to help him succeed as an entrepreneur. A self-described "poor kid from Brooklyn," he grew up in federally subsidized housing and knew he wanted something better. Schultz also possesses a high tolerance for ambiguity, by his willingness to embrace risk. Most importantly, he believed in himself and believed success was possible.

Schultz's treatment of his employees is almost certainly another factor in Starbucks' success. Starbucks' 12,000 employees are called "partners" and all of them, even part-time employees, are offered stock options and health coverage. Schultz believes such treatment breeds self-esteem in the workplace, and it also seems to keep his employees loyal and hard-working.

Schultz also showed incredible tenacity in sticking with Starbucks and seeing it grow to its current status, where it serves an estimated three million customers each week. He pursued his venture despite losing $3 to $4 million for the first three years of business. Schultz also stuck with this dream even while dealing with the stress of starting a new family while losing money on his business.

Ten years ago we wouldn't have understood an order for a "grande latte." Today, with a new Starbucks opening almost every day, and an estimated 2,000 stores by the year 2000 (including outlets in Japan), the nomenclature of Starbucks truly has become part of the culture of our country. Forty-two-year-old Howard Schultz has masterfully managed Starbucks from start-up to success. Time will tell how Schultz will handle Starbucks' future, but given his attitude and past success, Starbucks will likely be around for a long time.

Discussion Questions

1. How does Schultz attempt to meet the needs of his employees? How might his action affect Starbucks' employee performance?
2. How will the competitive environment affect the future performance of Starbucks?
3. How did Shultz balance risk and profit potential while pursuing his vision of Starbucks?

Driver's Ed for the
Information Superhighway

using internet to find a job

Appendix

Never cruised the World Wide Web? Want to learn some basic tips? The purpose of this appendix is to help ease novices toward the on-ramp to the information superhighway. If you are an experienced Internet user, you may just want to skim this material for features you haven't used yet. The material is arranged in a question-and-answer format so that you can easily jump to a topic you would like to know more about. Don't worry if you have never so much as pressed an Enter key—we won't get too technical for you. You don't have to understand the technical complexities of the Internet to travel on the information superhighway. But, as in learning to drive, it's usually a good idea to learn which end of the car to put the gas in.

Technology changes so quickly that writing about how to use the Internet is like washing the windows of the Empire State Building—as soon as you're finished it's time to start over again. For this reason we've tried to keep the discussion as general as possible and not give too many specific steps that may be out of date by the time you read this. The important thing to remember is that you can't break anything on the information superhighway, so just jump right in, explore the on-line world, and have fun!

···· ■ ····

WHAT IS THE INTERNET?

*The **Internet** is a network of networks. It involves tens of thousands of interconnected computer networks that include millions of host computers.* The Internet is certainly not new. The Pentagon began the network in 1969 when the world feared that a nuclear war would paralyze communications. The computer network was developed to reach far-flung terminals even if some

connections were broken. The system took on a life of its own, however, and grew as scientists and other academics used it to share data and electronic mail. No one owns the Internet. There is no central computer; each message you send from your computer has an address code that lets any other computer in the Internet forward it to its destination. There is no Internet manager. The closest thing to a governing body is the Internet Society in Reston, Virginia. This is a volunteer organization of individuals and corporate members who promote Internet use and oversee development of new communication software. See Figure A1.1 for a description of how the Internet works.

WHAT IS THE WORLD WIDE WEB, AND HOW IS IT DIFFERENT FROM THE INTERNET?

The World Wide Web (WWW, or the Web) is a means of accessing, organizing, and moving through the information in the Internet. Therefore, the Web is part of the Internet. Think of the Internet as a gigantic library and the Web as the Dewey Decimal System. Until the creation of the World Wide Web in 1993, it was as though that gigantic library simply threw all of its books and other materials into mountainous piles. If you wanted to find something on the Internet, you needed to type in a complex code representing the exact address of the site you wanted.

The basic difficulty of navigating the Internet without the Web is twofold: (1) the traffic signs on the Internet are written in Unix, and (2) there is no defined structure for organizing information. Unix is an operating system that was designed long before anyone thought of the term *user-friendly*. And, since the Internet does not require a prescribed structure for entering information, even experienced users have difficulty retrieving information without a tool like the Web.

When the Web evolved, the game changed. Not only did the Web add graphics and sound, which breathed life into the dreary text-only Internet,

The Internet is a network of networks that connects an estimated 20 million users in 137 countries to one of 1.7 million central computers. Historically, the primary users have been scientists, researchers, students, and academics who tap in from their personal computers, terminals, or workstations. But general use is soaring. Rock star Billy Idol, the White House staff, and late night host David Letterman are well-known Internet users.

In some cases, users pull information directly from one of the desired computers. To reach certain desired computers a user may have to travel through other computers.

If a user is not at an institution with a direct connection to a desired computer that is part of Internet, that person will dial into an intermediary computer, known as a service provider.

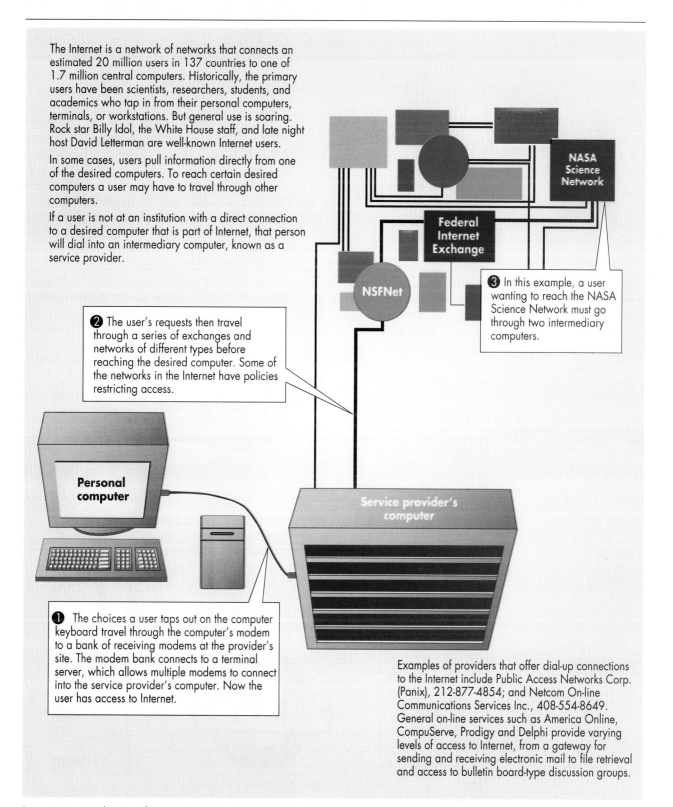

NASA Science Network

Federal Internet Exchange

NSFNet

❸ In this example, a user wanting to reach the NASA Science Network must go through two intermediary computers.

❷ The user's requests then travel through a series of exchanges and networks of different types before reaching the desired computer. Some of the networks in the Internet have policies restricting access.

Personal computer

Service provider's computer

❶ The choices a user taps out on the computer keyboard travel through the computer's modem to a bank of receiving modems at the provider's site. The modem bank connects to a terminal server, which allows multiple modems to connect into the service provider's computer. Now the user has access to Internet.

Examples of providers that offer dial-up connections to the Internet include Public Access Networks Corp. (Panix), 212-877-4854; and Netcom On-line Communications Services Inc., 408-554-8649. General on-line services such as America Online, CompuServe, Prodigy and Delphi provide varying levels of access to Internet, from a gateway for sending and receiving electronic mail to file retrieval and access to bulletin board-type discussion groups.

Source: Peter Lewis, "Taking Care of Business," *St. Louis Post-Dispatch,* December 15, 1993, p. 11D. Reprinted with permission of the *St. Louis Post-Dispatch,* copyright 1993.

but it also made navigating parts of the Internet easy even for beginners. Now Web cruisers don't need to know Unix in order to travel the Net. You can go from place to place on the Web simply by clicking on a word or a picture called hypertext. Hypertext allows any part of any document to be linked to any other document, no matter where it is, allowing you to jump around from place to place with a click of the mouse. Hypertext links are usually shown in a contrasting color on the computer screen (see Figure A1.2). *Cruising* or *surfing* means following hypertext links from page to page on the Web.

···· ▬▬▬ ····

WHAT DO I NEED TO BE ABLE TO GET ON THE WEB?

The first thing you need in order to cruise the information superhighway is a computer with a modem (a device that connects your computer with other computers via phone lines) and a Web browser. There are other ways to connect to the Internet, but until they become more widely available, more economical, and/or more user-friendly, most of us will use modems and standard phone lines to access the Net. Many schools offer students Internet service, so check out what is available at your school. You may have already paid computer-service fees that include Internet connection, so get your money's worth and get on-line now. If you can't connect through your school, you can connect to the Net by signing up with an Internet service provider (ISP). Your ISP will give you the phone number and a set of directions for connecting your computer to the Net. At this time most ISPs provide unlimited access to the Internet for a flat monthly fee.

┌─   ─┐
   FIGURE **A1.2**

   ····

**HYPERTEXT LINKS AND
A UNIFORM RESOURCE
LOCATOR (URL)**

➤ **CONSIDER USING TM 14**
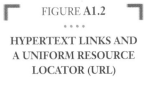
Hypertext Links and a Uniform Resource
Locator (URL)

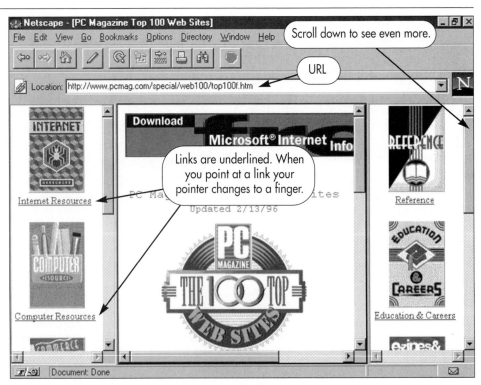

Source: Fritz J. Erickson and John A. Vonk, *Effective Internet* (Burr Ridge, Ill.: Irwin, 1996), p. 14.

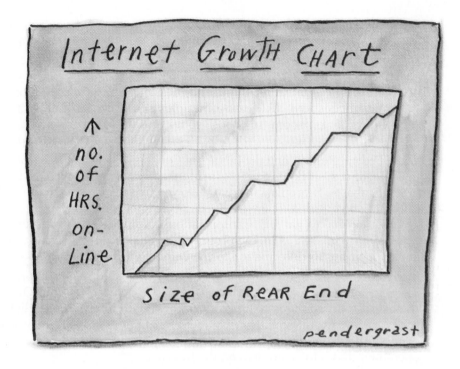

WHAT IS A WEB BROWSER?

A Web browser is a program or application that provides you with a way to access the World Wide Web. The first graphical Web browser that allowed pointing and clicking was Mosaic, developed by Eric Bina and Marc Andreessen at the National Center for Supercomputing Applications. Andreessen, an undergraduate at the time, later went on to fame and fortune as the developer of Netscape Navigator. Mosaic was based on a code written by Tim Berners-Lee of CERN, the European laboratory for particle physics.

WHICH IS THE BEST BROWSER?

Currently, the two most popular Web browsers are Netscape Navigator and Microsoft Internet Explorer. At the time of this writing, the best browser is the one you have access to—in other words, neither one has a clear advantage over the other. The case may be different by the time you read this. If we had to predict the future, we would have to say that both Netscape and Microsoft will continue to improve their browsers to compete with each other and that Web users will benefit from the competition as the browsers become more powerful and easier to use.

WHY WOULD I WANT TO CRUISE THE INTERNET?

You can use the Internet to:

- *Communicate on-line.* You can communicate with others through the following:

  News groups. These are special-interest groups in which you can get advice or just share thoughts with people.

Electronic mail (e-mail). E-mail lets you stay in touch with friends, trade files, and do business, all from the comfort of your computer desktop.

Internet relay chat (IRC). IRCs allow you to chat with other people all over the world in real time (that is, talk with someone else while you are both on the line rather than send messages that are read later). Live and uncensored, IRC can sometimes sound like a junior high school boys' locker room, so choose your chats wisely.

- *Gather information.* Internet users can tap into such diverse institutions as the Federal Reserve and the Library of Congress. Some Web sites offer news headlines, stock market information, access to encyclopedias, and other databases. Search engines can help you find the sites that have the information you need. There are special Web sites that offer push technology that makes gathering information automatic: after you tell it what you are interested in, the program searches the Web periodically and then pushes the information to you without your having to ask for it.

- *Shop.* Forgot your mom's birthday? No problem. Get on-line and order roses to be delivered to her door before she disinherits you. Or, if things get too bad, book a flight out of town with a few mouse clicks and a credit card number. Note, however, that credit card security is a concern that is getting lots of attention as more and more businesses open their doors to customers on the Internet.

- *Play games (after you finish studying, of course).* You can play games against another person or against the computer while you're on-line.

···· ▬▬▬ ····

CAN YOU TELL ME HOW TO CRUISE THE WEB WITHOUT TURNING ME INTO A COMPUTER MAJOR?

There are only four simple things you need to know about to navigate the Web: (1) Web addresses, (2) directories and search engines, (3) links, and (4) the Back Page button.

···· ▬▬▬ ····

WHAT ARE WEB ADDRESSES?

Every Web site has an address called a uniform resource locator (URL). Go back to Figure A1.2 and look at the top of the browser window. See the line that starts with http://? That's the URL for the page. To get to any Web site, you just type its address in the space for the URL entry in your Web browser. This means, or course, that you know the exact URL. It is important to know that the Web is constantly evolving and therefore URLs often change as new sites are added and old ones dropped. Sometimes a new URL is supplied when you visit an old site, but often it is not, in which case you reach a dead end.

···· ▬▬▬ ····

WHAT IF I DON'T KNOW WHICH SITE I NEED, MUCH LESS ITS URL?

To find topics that interest you, you can use one of several Web directories or search engines. Once you are at the search engine's home page, all you have to do is to enter the key words for the topic you want and you will quickly receive a list of links to sites related to your request. Some of the most popular directories and search engines are Yahoo!, Infoseek, Lycos, Alta Vista, Excite, and WebCrawler. (You can find the URLs for these sites in Taking It to the Net, Exercise 1, at the end of this appendix.)

WHAT DO I NEED TO KNOW ABOUT LINKS?

Once you're at a site, the two main ways to cruise around are by clicking on an icon button link or on a text link. One way to tell if something is a link is to place your cursor over the graphic icon or text. If it changes into a hand, then you know it is a live link. When you click on a link, you will be sent to another Web site or to another page on the current Web site.

WHAT IF I WANT TO GET BACK TO SOMEPLACE I'VE BEEN?

If you want to go back to a site you have left recently, you can just click on the Back Page button in your browser. This will lead you back through the exact same page route you traveled before. Or you can enter the desired site's URL. If you are on the same Web site, you can choose the home page link or one of the section icons to take you back to the home page or another section.

WHERE DO I GO WHEN I CLICK ON SOMETHING?

When you're navigating the Net, you can go from a Web page in Paris to one in Peru. What happens? When you click on a link, your computer sends out a request for information to another server. That server, which may be next door or across the planet, interprets your request, finds the information (text, graphics, or entire Web pages), and then breaks it up into packets. The server sends the packets to your computer, where your browser puts them back together and you see the Web page, all in the blink of an eye (or an eternity—they don't call it the World Wide Wait for nothing).

WHY DOES IT TAKE SO LONG TO MOVE FROM ONE PLACE TO ANOTHER ON THE WEB?

The speed with which you reach other Internet sites depends not only on the speed and size of your phone line and computer but also on the speed and size of phone lines and computers at the other site. You won't get to class any faster in a Ferrari than in a bus if you're locked in a traffic jam. The same is true on the information superhighway. Sometimes your computer will seem to take forever to get to a site or to open an image. If this happens, you can click the Stop button on your menu bar and try again later when the Internet may be less busy.

HOW CAN I COMMUNICATE WITH OTHERS ON-LINE?

You can reach out and touch your fellow Internet surfers via newsgroups, e-mail, or an IRC.

WHAT ARE NEWSGROUPS?

The Usenet is a global network of discussion groups known as newsgroups. Newsgroups are collections of messages from people all over the world on any subject you can imagine (and some you'd rather not imagine). Newsgroups are divided into categories indicated by the first letters of their name. There are many different category prefixes, but the main ones you will see are comp (computer), sci (science), rec (recreation), soc (society), and alt (alternative). Under these headings are thousands of subcategories from alt.alien.visitors to za.humour.

HOW DO I JOIN A NEWSGROUP?

Web browsers have built-in newsreading capabilities. You first need to go to the Mail and News options menu and enter your server information, which is usually something like "news.myserver.com" (contact your Internet service provider to find out exactly what it is). There are also options for organizing how you read your messages. Some people like their messages "threaded" (meaning all postings on a particular topic are grouped together), while others prefer to sort their messages by date.

When you find a group you like, don't jump into the conversation right away. Take time to read the frequently asked questions (FAQ) list for that group first. The FAQ list includes the questions that most newcomers ask. After you read the FAQs, you should read at least a week's worth of postings to get a feel for the group and what kinds of discussions its members have. Remember, you may be joining discussions that have been going on for a year or more, so you may feel like the new kid on the block for a while. Most newsgroups are quite friendly if you follow these few basic rules.

Web browsers, like the one for America Online shown here, offer advice to newsgroup newbies (new users). Notice that AOL suggests that you begin by reading netiquette hints so that you mind your on-line manners and don't jump into newsgroups on the wrong foot.

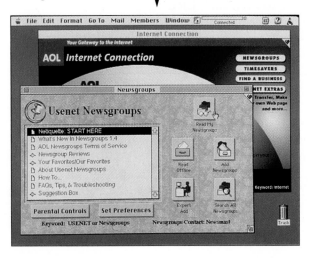

HOW DO I SEND E-MAIL?

As with "snail mail" delivered by the U.S. postal system, e-mail is delivered to its recipient by an address. An Internet e-mail address has two parts: the user name and the name of the computer on which that user has an account. For example, Professor Ulysses R. Smart's e-mail address at Ignatius Kendall University may be ursmart@iku.edu. The symbol "@" is pronounced "at." The suffix ".edu" indicates that the address is an educational institution.

There are several e-mail software packages available. Netscape and Internet Explorer include e-mail capabilities. To compose a message, click on the Mail button (see Figure A1.3). Enter the e-mail address of the person to whom you are writing in the *To:* field. Enter the subject of your message in the *Subject:* field. If you want others to receive the message, enter their e-mail addresses in the *CC:* field and separate each e-mail address with a comma. Next, enter the body of the message in the large space. When you have completed your message, click on the Send button. To check for new messages received, simply click on the Get Mail button. If you have received new mail,

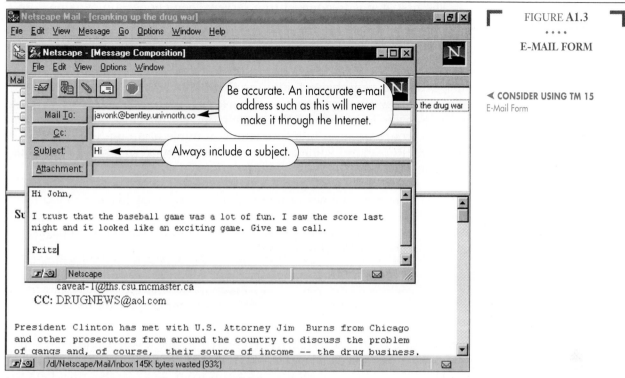

FIGURE **A1.3**

••••

E-MAIL FORM

◀ **CONSIDER USING TM 15**
E-Mail Form

Source: Fritz J. Erickson and John A. Vonk, *Effective Internet* (Burr Ridge, Ill.: Irwin, 1996), p. 56.

the subject and sender will be displayed in a window. Click on a message to display its contents.

You can also send files with your e-mail. To send files from a graphics program or word processor, simply choose *attach file* and navigate your hard drive to find the file you want to send.

One of the more interesting ways to take advantage of e-mail is to join one or more mailing lists (or listservs, to use the technical term).

•••• ▬▬ ••••

WHAT ARE LISTSERVS?

Listservs, or mailing lists, are similar to Usenet newsgroups. Unlike newsgroups, though, listserv discussions are delivered to your in-box as e-mail, and responding is as easy as punching your Reply button (which sends the message to everyone on the mailing list). To find a mailing list that piques your interest, try the mailing list directory Listz at www.listz.com. Be careful, though, mailing lists can quickly jam your in-box.

•••• ▬▬ ••••

WHAT IS IRC?

Internet relay chat (IRC) is an Internet protocol that allows you to have real-time conversations with other people around the world. As with newsgroups, it's best at first to observe, or "lurk," and see how the others on the IRC channel interact. To use an IRC channel you must have a chat "client" or program. The two most popular freeware chat clients are PIRCH for Windows and Ircle for the Mac.

The first step is to connect to a server. Then choose a nickname, join a room (or "channel"), and start lurking away. All IRC channels start with the # sign, and most servers have a channel called #newbie where you can ease into the swing of things.

There are Web sites devoted to some of the more popular IRC networks such as DalNet, AnotherNet, and the UnderNet. All of them have extensive information on IRC and how to use it. Not all IRC is idle chat. Many people have discovered ways to use IRC to help one another by developing virtual support groups on-line. Talk City is one example of an on-line community that uses IRC as a vehicle for people to draw support in a safe and friendly environment.

IRC is one of the most popular uses for the Internet, but could easily be replaced by Internet phones, or more advanced Web chat, like America Online's Virtual Places (VP). VP's attraction is that you create an on-screen avatar, or 3-D representation of yourself. Then you can go to designated Web pages and chat with other people who have VP.

···· ▬▬ ····

HOW DO YOU USE SEARCH ENGINES?

You'll always get better results from a search engine if you define what you're searching for as specifically as possible. The two easiest ways to narrow your search are by adding and subtracting terms from your search string. Let's say you want to read more about the death of Princess Diana. If you search Yahoo! for Princess Di, you may get back 78 (or more) site matches. However, you can focus the search a little more by adding another search word. Just typing in the word itself isn't good enough, though. In order to receive only sites that contain both Princess Di and the other word, you have to use the word *and* to link them. If you search for "and death" you get four matches—all memorials to the princess.

If adding search items doesn't narrow the field enough, try subtracting them—tell the search engine what *not* to look for. Say you're looking for business opportunities. You search for *business and opportunity* and get overwhelmed by more than 2,500 site matches, most of which are Amway-type, multilevel marketing operations (commonly known as MLMs). You can narrow your search by asking for these items to be excluded. For example, use the word *not* instead of *and*. This time you search for *business and opportunity not mlm* and get just seven items back.

A third way to define your search more closely is to put your search term in quotes. That tells the search engine that you're looking for exactly those words in exactly that order.

Don't worry about remembering all these surfing tips. Most search engines have an Advanced Options menu that lists ways to search using a form. Also, many search engines offer specific instructions on how to make the most of your search on their site.

If you try different search engines to look for the same topic, you'll get different results. That's because the search engines are different. Each search engine uses its own program (called a bot or crawler) to search the Web. Not only do these programs use different methods of searching and indexing, but they start from different points on the Web. You probably will also get different results if you search on a directory rather than a search engine, again because of the different approach to indexing sites. To explore more about the differences in search engines, try doing the Taking It to the Net exercises at the end of this appendix.

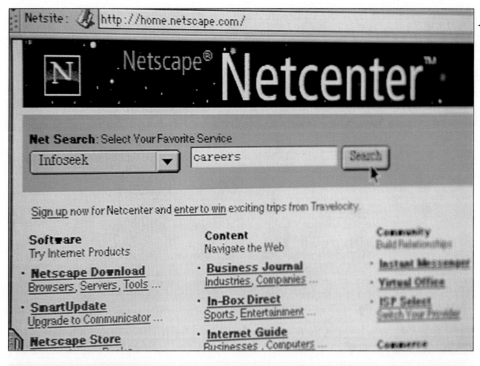

(top) When you don't know where to go to find the information you want on the Internet, a search engine such as Infoseek can point you in the right direction. Suppose you're looking for career guidance, simply key the word "careers" in the search box and click Search. (bottom) Ask and you shall receive! In this case you received more than you bargained for. Infoseek found 1,391,273 pages that include your search word, careers. You could browse through some of them by clicking the listed links. For example, clicking the Career Resource Center link shown at the bottom of the screen will send you to that web site. Or you could refine your search by clicking "Search only within these pages" and entering in a more specific topic as "resumes."

···· ▬▬ ····

DO I HAVE TO BE ON-LINE TO SURF THE WEB?

Why watch and wait for your favorite sites to download when you can browse while you sleep? You can do this using a program like Freeloader, Pointcast, Webwacker, or After Dark Online. These programs allow you to set a time and a list of Web sites, and the program goes to work, downloading page after page, graphic after graphic, and leaving them neatly on your desktop, to be surfed at your leisure.

Visit our web site at http://www.mhhe.com/ub5e and look for on-line help in understanding the concepts you'll be reading about in this text. If you like, send us an e-mail message letting us know what you like about the book and the web site. If there is something you think we should change, let us know that too!

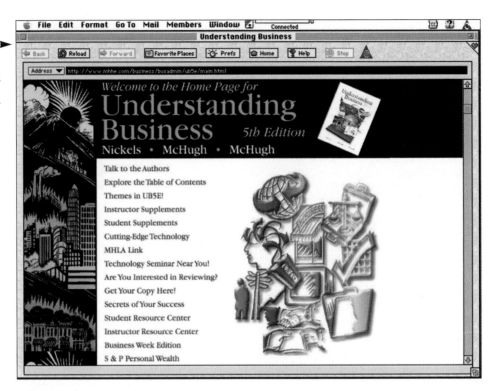

•••• ▬▬▬ ••••

WHERE CAN I GO TO LEARN MORE ABOUT THE WEB?

The best way to learn how to do something is by doing it, so the best place to learn about the Web is on the Web. It's time for you to put the pedal to the metal and get yourself onto the information superhighway. The following Web sites can help you learn more about the Web:

Newbie-U (New User University): www.newbie-u.com

How Do I Explore the Web?: www.squareonetech.com/hdiesplor.html

Cyberspace Companion: www.w3aces.uiuc.edu/AIM/scale

Learn the Net: www.learnthenet.com

Exploring the World Wide Web: www.gactr.uga.edu/exploring

TAKING IT TO THE NET

Purpose

To compare and gain experience using search engines. Finding information on the Internet can be difficult. Most novice searchers end up retrieving either way too much information or none at all. Searchers may do better if they take the time to learn some basic principles. Use one or both of the following exercises to gain the experience you need for a smoother ride on the information superhighway.

Exercise 1

Pick a topic. Use six different search engines to search for information on your chosen topic. Make sure you use the same terms for each engine. Note the characteristics of the engines you use. Present your results in a one-page summary that includes the following information: characteristics of each engine, the advantages/disadvantages of each engine, and which search engine was your favorite and why. URLs for some popular search engines are as follows:

AltaVista: http://www.altavista.digital.com

Excite: http://www.excite.com

HotBot: http://www.hotbot.com

Infoseek: http://www.infoseek.com

Lycos: http://www.lycos.com

WebCrawler: http://www.webcrawler.com

Exercise 2

Read the article "The Right Search Engine: IW Labs Test," by David Haskin, reprinted on *Internet World*'s Web site. You can find the article at the following address: http://www.iw.com/1996/05/showdown.html.

Using the information you read in the article, locate the home pages of NBC and the *New York Times*. Search for each company's home page using AltaVista, Excite, and Infoseek. Describe the results you reached with each. Which of these three search engines made it easiest for you to find the desired URL? What is the URL for each company's home page?

Economics: The Creation and Distribution of Wealth

Chapter

2

LEARNING GOALS

*After you have read and studied this chapter,
you should be able to*

1 Explain how wealth is created in an economy.

2 Discuss the major differences between capitalism, socialism, communism, and a mixed economy.

3 Describe how the free-market system works.

4 Use key terms (e.g., GDP and productivity) to explain the U.S. economic condition.

5 Describe monetary policy and its importance to the economy.

6 Discuss fiscal policy and its importance to the economy.

Rosa Alvardo is one of the founders of a village bank in Guatemala. There are now some 132 such banks in Guatemala that lend money to women to start their own businesses. Alvardo used her own bank loan to start a business selling underwear and cosmetics. She used some of her savings to take a technical course in cake baking to expand her product line.

Alvardo's village bank is one of a global chain of village banks sponsored by the Foundation for International Community Assistance (FINCA). Alvardo and the other bankers give microloans (which start at $50 and are usually less than $300) to women so that they can start their own businesses. Each loan must be paid back, with interest, by the end of a four-month cycle. Furthermore, each borrower must save at least 20 percent of her loan amount during the cycle. For a $50 loan, this comes to $10. Those borrowers who repay the loan (95 percent do) are able to borrow more money—up to $300. That $300 is enough capital to create one to three full-time jobs in the developing countries where the programs are at work.

The banks are started by FINCA but are run by the women themselves, who not only borrow money from the banks but also collect the money and give one another advice about running their businesses. Some 77 percent of the borrowers have never saved any money before. The microloans enable the borrowers to greatly improve their lives through the buildup of wealth. Alvardo says this about the community bank: "I learned how to save. I increased the money I had to spend on my business, my working capital. And now I can buy more food and clothes and books for my children."

As a result of village bank loans, Maria Julia Ducal is able to sell undergarments sewn by her daughter. Corin Galses runs a hardware store in her home, selling cement, bricks, and other construction materials. Conception Pinero Ortiz sells meat, milk, bread, and other staples from her home-based convenience store, where her older children work. Mabel Calderon sells ponchos, greeting cards, and artificial flowers. Her savings enabled her to add a room to her house.

The story of how these women have used village banking to start their own businesses shows that entrepreneurs can be found everywhere. What they lack, often, is just a few dollars to get their businesses going. Those few dollars create jobs and add wealth to the community. Given the proper economic environment, such businesses may eventually lead to prosperity for an entire country.

PROFILE

Rosa Alvardo— Village Banker

Source: Patricia B. Kelly, "The Real Profits of Village Banking," *Americas*, November/December 1996, pp. 38–43, and personal contact with FINCA, February 1998.

···· ▬ ····

THE IMPORTANCE OF THE STUDY OF ECONOMICS

Have you ever wondered why some countries are rich and others are poor? Why, for example, is South Korea relatively wealthy and North Korea not? Why are people in Taiwan relatively wealthy and people in China mostly poor? Such questions are part of the subject of economics. In this chapter, we shall explore the various economic systems of the world and how they either promote or hinder business growth, the creation of wealth, and a higher quality of life for all.

◀ **LEARNING GOAL 1.**
Explain how wealth is created in an economy.

◀ **CONSIDER USING TM 16**
Chapter Outline

◀ **CONSIDER USING LECTURE ENHANCER 2-1**
The Need for Economic Education

Reaching Beyond Our Borders

http://infomanage.com/entrepreneur/

Pablo Tesak, Entrepreneur from El Salvador

When Pablo Tesak came to El Salvador in 1951, the majority of consumer products there were imported from the United States and Europe. Tesak decided to develop a line of snack products for the poor people of El Salvador. He knew these snacks would have to be simple and cheap. Tesak began making such snacks and prospered. Later, a civil war in the country caused dissent among his workers. In order to stabilize his work force Tesak raised salaries, but even so he discovered that his employees needed more.

To keep his workers and increase their productivity, Tesak opened a "price club" for his workers. He arranged to buy local products from nearby factories and make them available to employees at cost, with interest-free monthly payments. The club now sells beds, refrigerators, and other household goods to employees and provides them with services such as medical care, English courses, and a summer camp for children. Tesak then set up a $500,000 home credit line so that his employees could borrow money to buy homes. As a result of these new benefits, employee morale and productivity increased substantially. Tesak learned that entrepreneurship can flourish even in the most trying of conditions, with hunger, war, poverty, and disease as constant threats.

> **CONSIDER USING OT ACETATE 2-1**
> The Four "Whats" of an Economic System

> **CONSIDER USING LECTURE ENHANCER 2-2**
> The Study of Economics

> **CONSIDER USING OT ACETATE 2-2**
> Key Principles of Economics

> **CONSIDER USING OT ACETATE 2-3**
> Economics: Macro and Micro

The success of the American business system is due to an economic and political climate that allows businesses to operate freely. Any change in the U.S. economic or political system has a major influence on the success of the business system. The world economic situation and world politics, such as the recent banking crisis in Asia, also have a major influence on businesses in the United States.[1] Therefore, to understand business, you must also understand basic economics and politics.

Rosa Alvardo is just one of millions of men and women (called entrepreneurs) who are willing and able to create jobs and wealth if given the chance. That chance comes when a market system is introduced and people are provided with a little money to get started. The Reaching Beyond Our Borders box about Pablo Tesak will give you an idea of how a small business can grow and help whole communities prosper.

The three basic objectives of this chapter are to teach you (1) how the free enterprise system works to create wealth and prosperity, (2) how free markets differ from government-controlled markets in the distribution of wealth, and (3) some basic terms and concepts from economics so that you'll understand what they mean when you encounter them in business periodicals.

••• WHAT IS ECONOMICS? •••

economics
The study of how society chooses to employ resources to produce goods and services and distribute them for consumption among various competing groups and individuals.

Economics is the study of how society chooses to employ resources to produce goods and services and distribute them for consumption among various competing groups and individuals. Businesses may contribute to an economic system by inventing products that greatly increase available resources. For example, businesses may discover new energy sources, new ways of growing food, and new ways of creating needed goods and services. Just recently, for example, a new kind of rice plant was developed that will greatly increase rice production.

There's no way to create peace and prosperity in the world by merely dividing the resources we have today among the existing nations. There aren't enough known resources available to do that. *Resource development* is the study of how to use technology to increase resources and to create the conditions that will make better use of those resources.

▼ CONSIDER USING LECTURE ENHANCER 2-3
The Spirit of Adam Smith

••• THE ECONOMIC THEORY OF WEALTH CREATION: ••• ADAM SMITH

The Scottish economist Adam Smith was one of the first people to imagine a system for creating wealth through the promotion of entrepreneurship. Rather than divide fixed resources among competing groups and individuals, Smith envisioned creating *more* resources so that everyone could become wealthier. The year was 1776. Adam Smith's book *An Inquiry into the Nature and Causes of the Wealth of Nations* is often called simply *The Wealth of Nations*.

Adam Smith is considered the father of capitalism. **Capitalism** is an economic system in which all or most of the means of production and distribution (e.g., land, factories, railroads, and stores) are privately owned (not owned by the government) and are operated for profit. In capitalist countries, businesspeople decide what to produce; how much to pay workers; how much to charge for goods and services; whether to produce certain goods in their own countries, import those goods, or have them made in other countries; and so on. No country is purely capitalist. Often the government gets involved in issues such as determining minimum wages and setting farm prices, as it does in the United States. But the *foundation* of the U.S. economic system is capitalism, as it is in most other leading countries.

Adam Smith believed that *freedom* was vital to the survival of any economy, especially the freedom to own land or property and the freedom to keep the profits from working the land or running a business. He believed that people will work hard if they know they will be rewarded (have incentives) for doing so. He made the desire for improving one's condition in life the basis of his theory. According to Smith, as long as farmers, laborers, and businesspeople (entrepreneurs) could see economic reward for their efforts (i.e., receive more money in the form of profits), they would work long hours. As a result of those efforts, the economy would prosper, with plenty of food and all kinds of products available to everyone.

Adam Smith developed a theory of wealth creation more than 200 years ago. His theory relied on entrepreneurs working to improve their lives. To make money, they would provide goods and services, as well as jobs, for others.

••• THE "INVISIBLE HAND" •••

Under Adam Smith's theory of capitalism, businesspeople don't necessarily deliberately set out to help others. They work primarily for their own prosperity and growth. Yet, like an **invisible hand**, as people try to improve their own situation in life, an economy grows and prospers through the production of needed goods, services, and ideas. Thus, the invisible hand turns self-directed gain into social and economic benefits for all.

How is it that people working in their own self-interest produce goods, services, and wealth for others? The only way farmers in a given area can become wealthy is to sell some of their crops to others. To become even wealthier, farmers would have to hire others to produce more food. As a consequence, people in that area would have plenty of food available and some would have jobs on the farms. So the farmers' efforts to become wealthy lead to jobs for some and food for all.

capitalism
An economic system in which all or most of the means of production and distribution are privately owned and operated for profit.

invisible hand
The term coined by Adam Smith to describe the social benefits that come from businesspeople trying to improve their own lives.

Wealth in the United States is not distributed equally. Thus one sees such contrasts as a homeless person sleeping in the snow in front of the Washington monument in Washington, D.C. Many businesspeople feel a social responsibility to share their wealth with the less fortunate through charitable giving and through company policies that support education and other programs to keep people out of poverty. What further steps would you have businesspeople take to end homelessness?

➤ **LEARNING GOAL 2.**
Discuss the major differences between capitalism, socialism, communism, and a mixed economy.

➤ **CONSIDER USING SUPPLEMEN-TAL CASE 2-1**
Foundations of the Capitalist System **(SCANS)**

The same principles apply to shoemakers, hatmakers, furniture makers and house builders. To increase wealth for their families, such manufacturers work hard and hire others. As a consequence, nearly everyone in the area would have access to homes, furniture, and so on, and everyone who was willing and able to work would have a job. That is how Adam Smith felt wealth would be created. Experience has shown that he was right.[2]

Smith assumed that as people became wealthier, they would naturally reach out to help the less fortunate in the community, as Pablo Tesak did (review the Reaching Beyond Our Borders box on page 44). That has not always happened in the past. Today, however, many U.S. businesspeople are becoming more concerned about social issues and their obligation to return to society some of what they've earned.[3]

THE HISTORY OF BUSINESS AND ECONOMICS

Following the ideas of Adam Smith, businesspeople in the United States, Europe, Japan, Canada, and other countries began to create more wealth than had ever been created before. They hired others to work on their farms and in their factories, and their nations began to prosper as a result. Businesspeople soon became the wealthiest people in society.

Great disparities in wealth began to appear. Businesspeople owned large homes and fancy carriages, while workers lived in more humble surroundings. Nonetheless, there was always the promise of better times. If you wanted to be wealthy, all you had to do was start a successful business of your own. Of course, it wasn't that easy—it never has been. Then and now, you have to accumulate some money to buy or start a business, and you have to work long hours to make it grow. But the opportunities have always been there.

••• THE SEARCH FOR EQUALITY •••

Free-market capitalism (capitalism without any government regulation) naturally leads to inequality of wealth. Business owners and managers will make more money and have more wealth than workers will. Similarly, people who are old, disabled, or sick may not be able to start and manage a business. Others may not have the talent or the drive to start and manage a business or farm. What does society do about such inequality? Not all people are as generous as Pablo Tesak. In fact, the desire to produce as much as possible and to create as much wealth as possible led some businesspeople to use such practices as slavery and child labor. Living conditions for workers throughout the world were modest at best in the 1800s.

Furthermore, free-market capitalism may lead to environmental damage as businesses pollute streams and the air and cause other environmental problems. Clearly, some government rules and regulations are necessary to make sure that the environment is protected and that people who are unable to work get the basic care they need.

••• THE BIRTH OF COMMUNISM •••

The German political philosopher Karl Marx saw the wealth created by capitalism, but he also noted the poor working and living conditions of laborers in the 1800s. He decided that workers should take over ownership of businesses and share in the wealth. In 1848 he wrote *The Communist Manifesto,* outlining the process. Marx thus became the father of communism. **Communism** is a system in which the state (the government) makes all economic decisions and owns all the major forms of production. One problem with communism is that the government has no way of knowing what to produce. As a result, shortages of many items may develop, including shortages of food and basic clothing. Another problem with communism is that it doesn't inspire businesspeople to work hard because the government takes most of the earnings. Communism, therefore, is slowly disappearing as an economic form among the world's nations.

Communist countries today include China, North Korea, and Cuba. North Korea is now suffering severe economic depression, and many people there are starving. Other countries are sending them food to survive. The people in Cuba are also suffering from the lack of goods and services readily available in most other countries. Some parts of the former Soviet Union remain communist, but the movement there is toward free markets.[4] The same is true in parts of China. China has seen the success of Hong Kong and its free markets and has experimented with such freedom in certain regions. Those regions have prospered greatly while the rest of China has grown only slowly. Meanwhile, however, Cuban leader Fidel Castro declared that Cuba would remain communist in 1997.

Socialism is an economic system that combines ideas from both capitalism and communism. We'll explore that system next.

communism
A system in which the state makes all economic decisions and owns all the major forms of production.

◄ **CONSIDER USING LECTURE ENHANCER 2-4**
Red Dawn for Hong Kong

◄ **CONSIDER USING LECTURE ENHANCER 2-5**
Post-Communist Russia: Some Statistics

◄ **CONSIDER USING CRITICAL THINKING EXERCISE 2-1**
Standard of Living Comparison
(SCANS)

···· ■ ····

THE ATTRACTION OF SOCIALISM

Socialism is an economic system based on the premise that some businesses should be owned by the government. Private businesses and individuals are taxed relatively steeply to pay for social programs. Socialists acknowledge the major benefit of capitalism—wealth creation—but believe that wealth should be more evenly distributed. They believe that the government should be the agency to create a more even distribution of wealth.

Socialism became the guiding economic platform for countries such as Holland, Sweden, France, and much of the rest of the world. In some countries, such as Canada, businesses were expected to prosper, but businesses and workers also had to pay extremely high taxes.[5] In other countries, most major businesses are run by the government. Socialist nations also rely heavily on the government to provide education, health care, retirement benefits, unemployment benefits, and other social services.

socialism
An economic system based on the premise that some businesses should be owned by the government.

··· THE NEGATIVE CONSEQUENCES OF SOCIALISM ···

Socialism creates more equality than capitalism does, but it takes away some of businesspeople's incentives to start work early and leave work late. The motto of socialism is "From each according to his ability, to each according to his needs." Thus, those who work hard and prosper must share with those who don't work so hard or those who don't have such well-paying jobs. Marginal tax rates in Sweden once reached 85 percent. (The marginal tax rate is the rate you pay on the additional money you earn after a certain income level.) Thus, professional tennis players, doctors, lawyers, business owners, and others who make a lot of money are taxed very highly. As a consequence, many of them leave socialist countries for other countries with lower taxes, such as the United States and England.

◄ **CONSIDER USING SUPPLEMENTAL CASE 2-2**
Economic Consequences of Communist Systems
(SCANS)

It has turned out that socialism hasn't created the jobs or the wealth that capitalism has. Over the past decade or so, socialist countries have simply not kept up with the United States in job creation or wealth creation. While the unemployment rate in the United States dropped below 5 percent in 1997, the unemployment rates in Spain, France, and most other European countries were over 10 percent.[6]

••• THE TREND TOWARD MIXED ECONOMIES •••

The nations of the world have largely been divided between those that followed the concepts of capitalism and those that adopted the concepts of communism or socialism. Thus, to sum up the preceding discussion, the two major economic systems vying for dominance in the world today can be defined as follows:

1. **Free-market economies** exist when the marketplace largely determines what goods and services get produced, who gets them, and how the economy grows. *Capitalism* is the popular term used to describe this economic system. It's based on principles from Adam Smith.

2. **Command economies** exist when the government largely decides what goods and services will be produced, who will get them, and how the economy will grow. *Socialism* and *communism* are the popular terms used to describe variations of this economic system. Both are based on principles from Karl Marx.

The experience of the world has been that neither free-market nor command economies have resulted in optimum economic conditions. Free-market mechanisms haven't been responsive enough to the needs of the old, the disabled, or the elderly; nor did they protect the environment. Therefore, over time, voters in free-market countries, such as the United States, elected officials who adopted many social and environmental programs such as social

free-market economies
Economic systems in which decisions about what to produce and in what quantities are decided by the market, that is, by buyers and sellers negotiating prices for goods and services.

command economies
Economic systems in which the government largely decides what goods and services will be produced, who will get them, and how the economy will grow.

Capitalism and entrepreneurship are expanding throughout the world as this small T-shirt business in Russia demonstrates. Given the right political climate, it is possible for the economies of many of the former Soviet-bloc countries to grow and prosper and eventually join the world's economic powers. What advantages and disadvantages do you see from other countries becoming economically stronger?

security, welfare, unemployment compensation, and various clean air and water acts.

Socialism and communism, on the other hand, didn't always create enough jobs or wealth to keep economies growing fast enough. As a consequence, communist governments are disappearing and socialist governments have been cutting back on social programs and lowering taxes on businesses and workers. The idea is to generate more business growth and thus more revenue.

The trend, then, has been for so-called capitalist countries to move toward more socialism and for so-called socialist countries to move toward more capitalism. We say "so-called" because there are no countries that are purely capitalist or purely socialist. All countries have some mix of the two systems. The trend toward capitalism in socialist countries slowed recently as countries, such as France and Canada, moved back toward socialism.[7] But the long-term global trend is toward a blend of capitalism and socialism.

The net effect of capitalist systems moving toward socialism and socialist systems moving toward capitalism is the emergence throughout the world of mixed economies. **Mixed economies** exist where some allocation of resources is made by the market and some by the government. Most countries don't have a name for such a system. If the dominant way of allocating resources is by free-market mechanisms, then the leaders of such countries still call their system capitalism. If the dominant way of allocating resources is by the government, then the leaders call their system socialism. Figure 2.1 on ➤P. 50◄ compares the various economic systems.

Like most other nations of the world, the United States has a mixed economy. The degree of government involvement in the economy is a matter of some debate in the United States today. The government has now become the largest employer in the United States. The number of workers in the public sector is more than the number in the entire manufacturing sector. There's much debate about the role of government in health care, schools, business regulation, and other parts of the economy. The government's goal is to grow the economy while maintaining some measure of social equality. That goal is very hard to attain. Nonetheless, the basic principles of freedom and opportunity should lead to economic growth that is sustainable.

Government has a great effect on businesses in the United States and throughout the world. Later in the chapter, we'll explore many issues having to do with the U.S. government and the economy. Keep in mind as you read this material that the foundation of the U.S. economy is capitalism. The government serves as a means to *supplement* that basic system as it tries to promote both economic growth and social equality. Changes in the U.S. tax codes may significantly affect the economy over the next few years.

This is an interesting time to monitor the relationship between business and government in the United States. This is also an interesting time to watch how the Internet affects such relationships worldwide. The Internet is expected to unite all the world economies into one electronic mall where the economic systems of the individual countries involved will be less critical to business success. We explore that notion in the Spotlight on Small Business box on ➤P. 51◄.

mixed economies
Economic systems in which some allocation of resources is made by the market and some is made by the government.

◄ **CONSIDER USING LECTURE ENHANCER 2-6**
Shenzhen: China Experiments With Economic Reform

Progress Check

- What's the most important resource for wealth creation?
- What did Adam Smith mean by the "invisible hand," and how does it create wealth for a country?
- What led to the emergence of socialism?
- What are some negative consequences of socialism?

	CAPITALISM	**MIXED ECONOMY**	**SOCIALISM**	**COMMUNISM**
Social and economic goals	Private ownership of land and business. Liberty and the pursuit of happiness. Free trade. Emphasis on freedom and the profit motive for economic growth.	Private ownership of land and business with government regulation. Government control of some institutions (e.g., mail). High taxation for defense and the common welfare. Emphasis on a balance between freedom and equality.	Public ownership of major businesses. Some private ownership of smaller businesses and shops. Government control of education, health care, utilities, mining, transportation, and media. Very high taxation. Emphasis on equality.	Public ownership of all businesses. Government-run education and health care. Emphasis on equality. Many limitations on freedom, including freedom to own businesses, change jobs, buy and sell homes, and to assemble to protest government actions.
Motivation of workers	Much incentive to work efficiently and hard because profits are retained by owners. Workers are rewarded for high productivity.	Incentives are similar to capitalism except in government-owned enterprises, which have few incentives. High marginal taxes can discourage overtime work.	Capitalist incentives exist in private businesses. Government control of wages in public institutions limits incentives.	Very little incentive to work hard or to produce quality goods or services.
Control over markets	Complete freedom of trade within and among nations. No government control of markets.	Some government control of trade within and among nations (trade protectionism). Government regulation to ensure fair trade within the country.	Some markets are controlled by the government and some are free. Trade restrictions among nations vary and include some free-trade agreements.	Total government control over markets except for illegal transactions.
Choices in the market	A wide variety of goods and services is available. Almost no scarcity or oversupply exists for long because supply and demand control the market.	Similar to capitalism, but scarcity and oversupply may be caused by government involvement in the market (e.g., subsidies for farms).	Variety in the marketplace varies considerably from country to country. Choice is directly related to government involvement in markets.	Very little choice among competing goods.
Social freedoms	Freedom of speech, press, assembly, religion, job choice, movement, and elections.	Some restrictions on freedoms of assembly and speech. Separation of church and state may limit religious practices in schools.	Similar to mixed economy. Governments may restrict job choice, movement among countries, and who may attend upper-level schools (i.e., college).	Very limited freedom.

FIGURE **2.1**

. . . .

COMPARISONS OF KEY ECONOMIC SYSTEMS

➤ **LEARNING GOAL 3.**
Describe how the free-market system works.

. . . . ▬▬ . . . .

THE FOUNDATIONS OF CAPITALISM

Some students have difficulty understanding how the free-market system works or what its benefits and drawbacks are. Without that understanding, however, citizens can't determine what the best economic system is. You should learn how the U.S. economy works and what mechanisms exist to promote economic growth. Let's begin the process by exploring how the free-market system works.

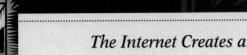

Spotlight on Small Business

The Internet Creates a One-World Market

The World Wide Web (WWW) is a relatively new phenomenon, but one that will have a profound effect on the world's economies. In the past, a small business was fairly confined in its market reach. It couldn't afford to advertise nationally, much less globally. In such a setting, it was possible for a country to become rather isolated from other countries, and the government could regulate businesses closely. Today, however, even small businesses have established Web sites where they can reach global markets quickly and easily.

Woodmere Camera in Lynbrook, New York, for example, sells rare, hard-to-find cameras. The market for such cameras is global, but Woodmere had no way to reach that market in the past. Today, however, Woodmere has established a Web site (http://www.woodcam.com) where customers can shop in an on-line catalog, request information by e-mail, and place orders by filling out an electronic order form.

Think of what such developments mean to the economies of various countries. Whether the country itself is capitalist or socialist makes little difference to World Wide Web entrepreneurs. They can establish their own businesses quickly and easily on the Internet. People in one country can also work for people in another country—over the Internet. For example, a software developer in India can work for a California company and send his or her work to the company over the Internet. Similarly, a software developer in Oklahoma can work for a high-tech company in Maryland. The link is by Internet. Where people live, therefore, no longer affects where they work. What has developed because of the Internet is a global market with global workers making global products.

To whom shall the worker in India pay income taxes: India or the United States? Or both? Who pays worker benefits? When someone is unemployed in India, should he or she be counted in the unemployment figures in the United States? That question may sound silly now, but it may not be in an era when workers can live anywhere in the world. The World Wide Web will have a profound effect on all the economies of the world and will likely force all countries to adopt a similar economic system or risk becoming a social isolate in the world economy. What will that world economic system be? What will the rights of workers be? What union and environmental rules will apply? As you can see, the next few years will present tremendous challenges and opportunities to those who understand economics and business.

Source: Tim McCollum, "Making the Internet Work for You," *Nation's Business,* March 1997, pp. 6–13.

Individuals living in a capitalist (free-market) system have four basic rights:

- *The right to private property.* This is the most fundamental of all rights under capitalism. It means that individuals can buy, sell, and use land, buildings, machinery, inventions, and other forms of property. They can also pass property on to their children.

- *The right to own a business and to keep all of that business's profits after taxes.*

- *The right to freedom of competition.* Within certain guidelines established by the government, individuals are free to compete with other individuals or businesses by offering new products and promotions. To survive and grow, businesses need laws and regulations, such as the laws of contracts, which ensure that people will do what they say they'll do.

- *The right to freedom of choice.* People are free to choose where they want to work and what career they want to follow. Other freedoms of choice include where to live and what to buy or sell.

As the price of fish and other such products rise, producers typically have a greater incentive to work longer or do what's required to increase the supply. However, when more people have ready access to fish, the price of fish begins to drop. Can you explain why the price of gasoline is so low these days, using the concept of supply and demand?

Given these rights and freedoms, how do businesspeople know what goods to produce and in what quantity? What role do we, as consumers, play in the process? How do businesses learn about changes in consumer desires? These questions and more are answered next.

••• HOW FREE MARKETS WORK •••

The free-market system is one in which decisions about what to produce and in what quantities are made by the market, that is, by buyers and sellers negotiating prices for goods and services. You and I and other consumers in the United States and in other relatively free markets send signals to tell producers what to make, how many, in what color, and so on. We do that by choosing to buy (or not to buy) certain products and services.

For example, if all of us decided we wanted more fish, we would signal the fishing industry to provide more fish. As demand for fish goes up, the price goes up as well, because people are willing to pay more than before. People in the fishing industry notice this price increase and know they can make more money by catching more fish. Thus, they have incentive to get up earlier and fish later. Furthermore, more people go fishing or start fish farms. These are people who previously couldn't make enough profit fishing or raising fish, but now can because of the higher price. The kind of fish they catch or raise depends on the kind of fish we request in the store.

The same process occurs with most other products. The price tells producers how much to produce. As a consequence, there's rarely a long-term shortage of goods in the United States. If something is wanted but isn't available, the price tends to go up until someone begins making that product, sells the ones already on hand, or makes a substitute.

••• HOW PRICES ARE DETERMINED •••

The preceding discussion about how free markets work is an important part of economics. The main point is that, in a free market, prices are not determined by sellers; they are determined by buyers and sellers negotiating in the mar-

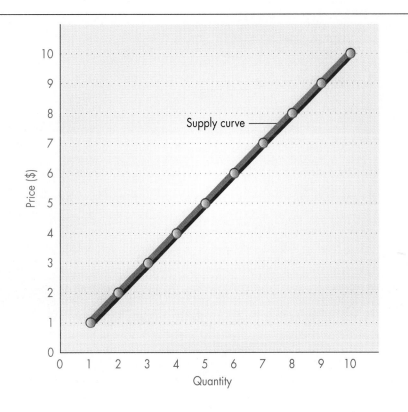

FIGURE 2.2
• • • •

THE SUPPLY CURVE AT VARIOUS PRICES

The supply curve rises from left to right. Think it through. The higher the price of fish goes (the left margin), the greater the quantity that the fish industry will be willing to supply.

◀ CONSIDER USING TM 17
The Supply Curve at Various Prices

ketplace. A seller may want to receive $10 a pound for fish, but the quantity demanded at that price may be quite low. The lower the price, the higher the quantity demanded is likely to be. How is a price determined that is acceptable to both buyers and sellers? The answer is found in the economic concepts of supply and demand.

··· SUPPLY ···

Supply refers to the quantity of products that manufacturers or owners are willing to sell at different prices at a specific time. Generally speaking, the amount supplied will increase as the price increases because sellers can make more money with a higher price.

    Economists show this relationship between quantity supplied and price on a graph. Figure 2.2 shows a simple supply curve. The price of an item in dollars is shown vertically on the left of the graph. Quantity is shown horizontally at the bottom of the graph. The various points on the graph indicate how many fish sellers would provide at different prices. For example, at a price of $2 a pound, people in the fish industry would provide only two fish, but at $8 a pound, they would supply eight fish. The line connecting the dots is called a supply curve (shown as a line to simplify understanding). The supply curve indicates the relationship between the price and the quantity supplied. All things being equal, the higher the price, the more the fishing industry will be willing to supply.

··· DEMAND ···

Demand refers to the quantity of products that people are willing to buy at different prices at a specific time. Generally speaking, the quantity demanded will decrease as the price increases. Again, the relationship between price and

supply
The quantity of products that manufacturers or owners are willing to sell at different prices at a specific time.

demand
The quantity of products that people are willing to buy at different prices at a specific time.

▸ FIGURE 2.3
. . . .

THE DEMAND CURVE
AT VARIOUS PRICES

A simple demand curve
showing the quantity of
fish demanded at dif-
ferent prices. The
demand curve falls from
left to right. It is easy to
understand why. The
higher price of fish,
the lower the quantity
demanded. As the price
falls, the quantity
demanded goes up. We
drew the line straight so
you could see the
relationships more
clearly.

▸ CONSIDER USING TM 18
The Curve at Various Prices

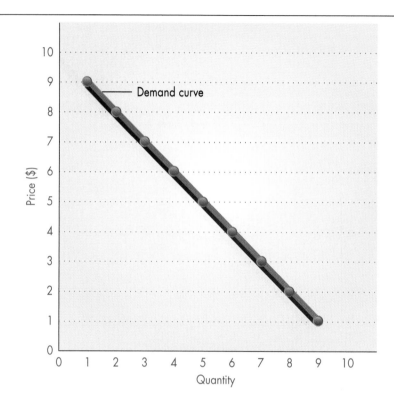

quantity demanded can be shown in a graph. Figure 2.3 shows a simple
demand curve. The various points on the graph indicate the quantity demanded at various prices. For example, at a price of $8, the quantity demanded is
just two fish. But if the price were $2, the quantity demanded would increase
to eight. The line connecting the dots is called a demand curve. It shows the
relationship between quantity demanded and price.

••• EQUILIBRIUM POINT •••

▸ CONSIDER USING LECTURE
ENHANCER 2-7
Supply and Demand: Coffee

It should be clear to you after reviewing Figures 2.2 and 2.3 that the key factor
in determining the quantity supplied and the quantity demanded is price.
Sellers prefer a high price and buyers prefer a low price. If you were to lay one
of the two graphs on top of the other, the supply curve and the demand curve
would cross. At that crossing point, the quantity demanded and the quantity
supplied would be equal. Figure 2.4 illustrates that point. At a price of $5, the
quantity demanded and the quantity supplied are equal. That crossing point is
known as the equilibrium point. In the long run, that price would become the
market price. Market price, then, is determined by supply and demand.

What would happen if the seller moved his or her price up to $6? At that
price, the buyer would be willing to buy only four fish, but the seller would be
willing to sell six fish. Similarly, if the price were cut to $4, then buyers would
be willing to buy six fish, but sellers would be willing to sell only four. In a free
market, prices will tend to move toward the equilibrium price.

Proponents of a free market would argue that, because supply and
demand interactions determine prices, there is no need for government
involvement or government planning. If surpluses develop (i.e., quantity supplied exceeds quantity demanded), a signal is sent to sellers to lower the price.
If shortages develop (i.e., quantity supplied is less than quantity demanded), a
signal is sent to sellers to increase the price. Eventually, supply will again
equal demand if nothing interferes with market forces.

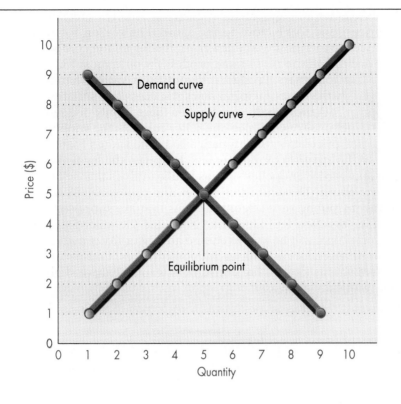

FIGURE 2.4
••••
THE EQUILIBRIUM
POINT

The interaction of quantity demanded and supplied is the equilibrium point. When we put supply and demand curves on one graph, we find that they interact at a price where the quantity supplied and the quantity demanded are equal. This is therefore called the equilibrium point. In the long run, the market price will tend toward the equilibrium point.

◀ **CONSIDER USING TM19**
The Equilibrium Point

◀ **CONSIDER USING OT ACETATE 2-4**
Competitive Market Structures

••• COMPETITION WITHIN FREE MARKETS •••

In a free market, organizations compete with one another to offer consumers the best products at the best price. Competition is thus a major component of the free enterprise system. Competition exists in different degrees, ranging from perfect to nonexistent. Economists generally agree that four different degrees of competition exist: (1) perfect competition, (2) monopolistic competition, (3) oligopoly, and (4) monopoly.

Perfect competition exists when there are many sellers in a market and no seller is large enough to dictate the price of a product. Under perfect competition, sellers produce products that appear to be identical. Agricultural products are often considered to be the closest examples of perfect competition at work. You should know, however, that there are no true examples of perfect competition. Today, government price supports and drastic reductions in the number of farms make it hard to argue that even farming is an example of perfect competition.

Monopolistic competition exists when a large number of sellers produce products that are very similar but are perceived by buyers as different. Under monopolistic competition, product differentiation (the attempt to make buyers think similar products are different in some way) is a key to success. Think about what that means for just a moment. Through tactics such as advertising, branding, and packaging, sellers try to convince buyers that their products are different from those of competitors. Actually, the competing products may be similar or even interchangeable. Under monopolistic competition, individual sellers set prices. The fast-food industry is an example of monopolistic competition.

An **oligopoly** is a form of competition in which just a few sellers dominate a market. Generally, oligopolies exist in industries that produce products such as breakfast cereal, beer, automobiles, soft drinks, aluminum, and aircraft. One reason some industries remain in the hands of a few sellers is that the initial

perfect competition
The market situation where there are many sellers of nearly identical products and no seller is large enough to dictate the price of the product.

monopolistic competition
The market situation where there are a large number of sellers that produce similar products, but the products are perceived by buyers as different.

oligopoly
A form of competition where the market is dominated by just a few sellers.

investment to enter an oligopolistic industry is usually tremendous. In an oligopoly, prices tend to be close to the same. The reason for this is simple. Intense price competition would lower profits for all the competitors, since a price cut on the part of one producer would most likely be matched by the others. Product differentiation, rather than price, is usually the major factor in market success in a situation of oligopoly.

A **monopoly** occurs when there is only one seller for a product or service. Since one seller controls the supply of a product, the price may rise dramatically. In the United States, laws prohibit the creation of monopolies. However, the legal system does permit approved monopolies such as public utilities that sell gas, water, and electric power. These utilities' prices and profits are usually monitored carefully by public service commissions that are supposed to protect the interest of buyers. New legislation may soon end the monopoly status of utilities, and consumers will be able to choose among utility providers. This is likely to result in fewer, larger utilities and lower prices. Competition works best when organizations know what consumers want. Next we shall explore how consumer wants are expressed.

Monopolistic competition means that there are many similar products competing for the same market, as in the market for hamburgers in the United States. What are some of the techniques being used by U.S. fast-food marketers like McDonald's and Burger King to differentiate their products from the competition? Is price one of those competitive tools?

monopoly
A market in which there is only one seller.

➤ CONSIDER USING LECTURE ENHANCER 2-8
Handicaps of the U.S. Economy

···· ▬▬ ····

WORLD MARKETS: SUPPLY AND DEMAND

Every day throughout the world billions of consumers are sending signals to millions of producers telling them what they (the consumers) want. The signals are sent by the prices of various goods and services. The signals are sent very quickly, so that there should be little delay in ending surpluses and shortages.

In the real world, however, there are many interferences to the free exchange of goods and services among countries. Consequently, some countries have surpluses (e.g., the United States has a surplus of many crops) and others suffer from shortages (many countries, North Korea for example, lack sufficient food). A global free-market system would seem to be a good system for improving the world's economic condition. Given the advantages of such a system, there must be offsetting disadvantages or else the nations of the world would move more quickly toward becoming one unified free market.

··· LIMITATIONS OF THE FREE-MARKET SYSTEM ···

The free-market system, with its freedom and incentives, was a major factor in creating the wealth that developed countries now enjoy. Some people even talk of the free-market system as an economic miracle. Capitalism, more than any other system, provides opportunities for the poor to work their way out of poverty. Capitalism also encourages businesses to be more efficient so that they can successfully compete on price and quality. Thus, capitalism has brought prosperity to the United States and to much of the rest of the world, but it has brought inequality as well.

As soon as Poland introduced capitalist principles in 1990, inequality increased dramatically. The new entrepreneurs (mostly manufacturers and store owners) became wealthy, while the average worker didn't. Such inequality has caused much national and world tension since the 1800s. As explained earlier in this chapter, governments intervened in free-market systems to create more social fairness and a more even distribution of wealth. That's how mixed economies got started.

Government entities at the state, local, and federal levels (or the equivalent in countries other than the United States) take a large share of total national output and reallocate it to create more equality. Some money goes to schools, some goes to help those who are unemployed, and so on. The economic question becomes, How much money should be available to the government for national defense and social welfare, and how much should be left to free-market forces to provide incentives for more output? If more is left to business, then the economic pie may grow faster and there will be more money to distribute. But if free markets allocate all money, then some people who can't participate in the capitalist system may suffer. A major question is, What's the proper blend of government involvement and free markets? We'll discuss that issue in the next section of this chapter.

Progress
Check

- What are the four basic rights a person has under capitalism?
- What is the signal businesspeople use to know what to produce and in what quantity?
- How are prices determined?
- What are the limitations to a free-market system?

Critical
Thinking

Adam Smith anticipated that businesspeople would be like Pablo Tesak (see the Reaching Beyond Our Borders box, p. 44) and would voluntarily support those in need. In the past, churches, temples, and other nonprofit organizations took a leadership position in supporting those in need. If the government were to stop supporting the needy, would private and nonprofit organizations provide the extra needed support? What are the advantages and disadvantages of the government being the major source of welfare?

···· ▬▬▬ ····

UNDERSTANDING THE ECONOMIC SYSTEM OF THE UNITED STATES

Over the past few years, while most of the world has moved toward freer markets, the United States has been moving toward having more social programs. Recently, for example, new programs were proposed to help fund the first years of college and to provide day care for the children of workers. Furthermore, there has been much conflict between business leaders and government leaders. Many business leaders believe that taxes are too high and there are too many government regulations. Government leaders have been divided as to the direction the government should take. Some believe that the government should be more involved in health care, education, and environmental issues. Others believe there should be less involvement. Those subjects have dominated political debate throughout the latter half of the 20th century and are likely to continue into the 21st century.

Because of such uncertain economic policies, the U.S. economic system is in a state of flux. The following sections will introduce the terms and concepts you'll need to understand the issues facing government and business leaders today. As an informed citizen, you can then become a leader in helping to create a world economy that is best for all.

··· KEY ECONOMIC INDICATORS ···

◄ CONSIDER USING LECTURE
ENHANCER 2-9
Economic Indicators

Three major indicators of economic conditions are (1) the gross domestic product (GDP), (2) the unemployment rate, and (3) the price indexes. When you read business literature, you'll see these terms used again and again. It will greatly increase your understanding if you learn the terms now.

A nation's gross domestic product (GDP) does not include those sales of goods and services that are not reported to the government. These activities include the sale of illegal copies of branded goods that are sold in flea markets. It also includes such things as informal baby sitting, day care, or lawn mowing services that take in cash and fail to report their earnings to the government. How much money do you suppose is involved in illegal transactions involving drugs, counterfeit copies of branded items, and other such transactions?

gross domestic product (GDP)
The total value of goods and services produced in a country in a given year.

unemployment rate
The number of civilians who are unemployed and tried to find a job within the prior four weeks.

➤ **CONSIDER USING LECTURE ENHANCER 2-10**
Creating Jobs

➤ **LEARNING GOAL 4.**
Use key terms (e.g., GDP and productivity) to explain the U.S. economic condition.

GROSS DOMESTIC PRODUCT (GDP)   **Gross domestic product (GDP)** is the total value of goods and services produced in a country in a given year. If GDP growth slows or declines, there are often many negative effects on businesses. A major influence on the growth of GDP is how productive the workforce is, that is, how much output workers create with a given amount of input.

Almost every discussion about a nation's economy is based on GDP. The total U.S. GDP in 1997 was over $6 trillion. The level of U.S. economic activity is actually larger than the GDP figures show because the figures don't take into account illegal activities (e.g., sales of illegal drugs). The high GDP in the United States is what enables Americans to enjoy such a high standard of living.

Note: Until recently, the major figure used in the United States to measure output was gross national product (GNP). The GNP is equal to the GDP plus the net result of trading with other nations, along with similar factors. The United States stopped using GNP as a measure because the rest of the world used GDP and Americans wanted to be able to compare nations using the same measure.

THE UNEMPLOYMENT RATE   The **unemployment rate** refers to the number of civilians at least 16 years old who are unemployed and tried to find a job within the prior four weeks. The U.S. unemployment rate in 1998 was the lowest in years, below 5 percent. There are four types of unemployment: frictional, structural, cyclical, and seasonal.

Frictional unemployment refers to those people who have quit work because they didn't like the job, the boss, or working conditions and who haven't yet found a new job. It also refers to those people who are entering the labor force for the first time (e.g., new graduates) or are returning to the labor force. There will always be some frictional unemployment because it takes some time to find a new job or a first job. Frictional unemployment has little negative effect on the economy.

Structural unemployment refers to unemployment caused by the restructuring of firms or by a mismatch between the skills (or location) of job seekers and the requirements (or location) of available jobs (e.g., coal miners in an area where mines have been closed). Structural unemployment calls for industry retraining programs to move workers into growth industries. One problem has been that many high-paying jobs in firms such as steel mills have been lost and some workers have found only lower-paying jobs in the service sector.

Cyclical unemployment occurs because of a recession or a similar downturn in the business cycle (the ups and downs of business growth and decline over time). This type of unemployment lasts until the economy recovers and businesses begin rehiring.

Seasonal unemployment occurs where demand for labor varies over the year, as with the harvesting of crops.

The United States tries to protect those who are unemployed because of factors such as recessions and industry shifts. Nonetheless, for a variety of factors, many of these individuals do not receive unemployment benefits.

Would the United States be better off today if we hadn't introduced modern farm machinery? There would be more people employed on the farm if we hadn't. Would the world be better off in the future if we didn't introduce new computers, robots, and machinery? They do take away jobs in the short run. What happened to the farmers who were displaced by machines? What will happen to today's workers who are being replaced by machines?

THE PRICE INDEXES   The **consumer price index (CPI)** consists of monthly statistics that measure the pace of inflation (consumer prices going up) or deflation (consumer prices going down). Costs of about 400 goods and services—including housing, food, apparel, and medical care—are computed to see if they are going up or down. The CPI is an important figure because some government benefits, wages and salaries, rents and leases, tax brackets, and interest rates are all based on it. A recent panel of economists appointed by the Senate Finance Committee reported that the CPI is overstated by 1.1 percent. The reason for the overstatement, supposedly, is the failure to take into account that some new products, such as computers, are faster or better but don't cost more and that consumers shop for lower-cost goods when the price of substitutes is raised.[8] Thus, if corn goes up, people buy peas instead. There is a call for an adjustment of the CPI because overstating inflation figures has negative effects on the economy. Watch the newspapers to see the conclusion.

The producer price index (PPI) measures prices at the wholesale level. Prices were dropping on the PPI during 1997, indicating that inflation was not going to be a problem.[9] Other indicators of the economy's condition include housing starts, retail sales, and changes in personal income. You can learn more about such indicators by reading business periodicals and listening to business broadcasts on radio and television.

The government plays a major role in trying to maintain growth in the economy without causing prices to increase too much. How the government does that and how much of the GDP the government should have to work with are two critical issues.

••• DISTRIBUTION OF GDP •••

The income earned from producing goods and services goes to the people who own businesses (such as stockholders) in the form of dividends and to the government in the form of taxes. Some countries take a much larger percentage of GDP for the government than other countries. The question in the United States each year is, How much of GDP should go to the government and how much should go to businesses and the owners of businesses?

In the United States, the percentage of GDP given to the government at all levels (federal, state, and local) was about 20 percent in the early 1950s. By 1997, that figure had risen to about 33 percent. When you count all fees, sales taxes, and more, the government share can exceed 50 percent. Is that figure too high

◄ **CONSIDER USING OT ACETATE 2-5**
What Makes Up the Consumer Price Index?

Critical Thinking

consumer price index (CPI)
Monthly statistics that measure changes in the prices of about 400 goods and services that consumers buy.

Even though the unemployment rate in the United States fell below 5 percent, there are still people in many parts of the country who are without a job or who are working in part-time positions hoping to find a better, full-time job. Would it be wise for those people to move to the parts of the country where the unemployment rate is really low? What are some of the factors that make such moves difficult?

Use of modern farm equipment has led to a substantial decrease in the number of workers needed on a farm. Similarly, the latest in manufacturing equipment has eliminated many factory jobs. Would it be wise for companies in the United States to forgo the latest advances in technology and new equipment in order to provide more jobs for people? What would be the consequences?

or not high enough? That is a subject of debate among economists and politicians in the United States. The answers will have a great effect on businesses and you. It is important, therefore, to understand the basic terms and concepts so you can vote intelligently and help the country to continue prospering. One source of prosperity is increased productivity.

••• PRODUCTIVITY IN THE UNITED STATES •••

Productivity is the total volume of goods and services one worker can produce in a given period of time. An increase in productivity means that a worker can produce more goods and services than before. The higher productivity is, the lower costs are in producing goods and services, and the lower prices can be. Therefore, businesspeople are eager to increase productivity.

At the beginning of the 20th century in the United States, one out of three workers was needed to produce enough food to feed everyone and create some surplus for world use. Today it takes fewer than 2 out of 100 workers to produce far greater quantities of food that contribute a much larger share to world production. What made the difference? The answer is that the use of tractors, chemical fertilizers, combines, silos, and other machines and resources (capital) raised farmers' productivity.

Now that we're in a service economy, productivity is an issue, because service firms are so labor intensive. Machinery helps labor increase productivity. Spurred by foreign competition, productivity in the manufacturing sector is rising rapidly. But manufacturing provides just over 20 percent of our economy's output. It's the nonmanufacturing sector (the service sector) that appears to be holding back productivity gains.

••• PRODUCTIVITY IN THE SERVICE SECTOR •••

In the service sector, computers, word processors, and other machines are making service workers more productive. The United States is ahead of much of the world in service productivity. However, one problem with the service industry is that an influx of machinery may add to the *quality* of the service provided but not to the *output per worker* (productivity).

For example, you've probably noticed how many computers are being installed on college campuses. They add to the quality of education but don't necessarily boost professors' productivity. The same is true of some new equipment in hospitals, such as CAT scanners. They improve patient care but don't necessarily increase the number of patients that can be seen. In other words, today's productivity measures fail to capture the increase in quality caused by new technology.

The United States and other countries need to develop new measures of productivity for the service economy, measures that include quality as well as quantity of output. Otherwise, it will appear that the United States isn't making much progress toward improving the quality of life when, in fact, it's likely that the quality of life is continuing to improve. New measures would prove the case, one way or the other. The rising stock market through the 1990s was largely due to increased profits from businesses, profits made possible by productivity increases.

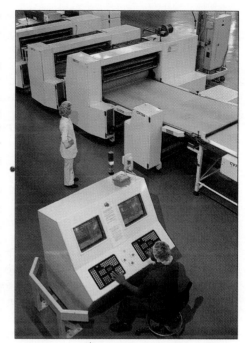

Shown here is the latest in computerized dough processing at a Nabisco plant in Richmond, Virginia. It is easy to gauge productivity increases in manufacturing that are due to the use of the newest machinery. That's because the output is increased dramatically and can be accurately measured. In the service industry, on the other hand, output is often more difficult to measure. For example, what changes in productivity have you noted in sit-down restaurants where computers are used to process food orders?

INFLATION AND THE CONSUMER PRICE INDEX

One measure of the strength of an economy is its ability to control inflation. **Inflation** basically refers to a general rise in the price level of goods and services over time. It is sometimes described as too many dollars chasing too few goods. That is, the quantity demanded is going up and so prices go up.

As explained earlier, the consumer price index (CPI) measures changes in the prices of about 400 goods and services that consumers buy. The CPI measures the price of an average market basket of goods for an average family over time. Among the items included in the basket of goods are food, automobiles, clothing, homes, furniture, drugs, and medical and legal fees. The consumer price index is closely followed because so many companies and government programs base their salary and payment increases on it.

Disinflation describes a condition where the increase in prices is slowing (the inflation rate is declining). That was the situation in the United States throughout the early 1990s. **Deflation** means that prices are actually declining. It occurs when countries produce so many goods that people cannot afford to buy them all (too few dollars chasing too many goods). That was the condition that led to the banking collapse in much of Asia late in 1997.[10] We'll discuss the implications of that collapse later in the text.

••• THE ISSUE OF RECESSION VERSUS INFLATION •••

A **recession** is two or more consecutive quarters of decline in the GDP. When a recession occurs, prices fall, people purchase fewer products, and more businesses fail. A recession has many negative consequences for an economy: high unemployment, increased business failures, and an overall drop in living standards. A **depression** is a severe recession. It is usually accompanied by deflation. For years (since the Great Depression of the 1930s) the government has put much of its effort into preventing another recession or depression. Whenever business has slowed or unemployment has increased, the Federal Reserve has pumped money into the economy to revive it. We'll explain that process next.

inflation
A general rise in the prices of goods and services over time.

disinflation
A condition where price increases are slowing (the inflation rate is declining).

deflation
A situation where prices are actually declining.

recession
Two consecutive quarters of decline in the GDP.

depression
A severe recession.

➤ **CONSIDER USING LECTURE ENHANCER 2-11**
The Great Depression: Capitalism in Crisis

There's much debate about the future of the U.S. economy as the government tries to keep employment high, inflation low, and businesses growing. To fight inflation and recession, the government and the Federal Reserve System try to manage the economy. To understand the economic situation in the United States and the world today with regard to inflation, recession, unemployment, and other economic matters, you must understand the government's and the Federal Reserve System's roles. Two terms that are crucial to your understanding are *monetary policy* and *fiscal policy*.

THE ISSUE OF MONETARY POLICY

monetary policy
The management of the money supply and interest rates.

Monetary policy is the management of the money supply and interest rates. In learning about monetary policy, the first thing one must understand is the role of the Federal Reserve System (the Fed). The Fed is one of the sources of money in the economy; it can add or subtract money from the economy as it sees fit. For example, the Fed can increase the interest rate on money it lends to banks if it thinks such action is warranted. Banks would pass this increase on to borrowers, thus slowing the economy as businesses and households borrow less. The Federal Reserve System is a private organization that operates independently of the president and Congress and has the goal of keeping the economy growing without causing inflation. It does that by trying to manage the money supply and interest rates. (Chapter 21 discusses the Fed in more detail.)

➤ **CONSIDER USING OT ACETATE 2-6**
How Inflation Affects Buying Power

••• TIGHT VERSUS LOOSE MONETARY POLICY •••

➤ **LEARNING GOAL 5.**
Describe monetary policy and its importance to the economy.

Having too much money in the economy sometimes causes inflation. When that happens, the Fed usually cuts the money supply and increases interest rates. That makes less money available for spending and discourages businesses and consumers from borrowing money (because of high interest rates). When businesses find it hard to borrow money, they often cut back on production and lay off workers or cut workers' hours. In either case, this slows the economy and lowers inflation. When unemployment gets too high, the Federal Reserve may put more money into the economy and lower interest rates. This stimulates spending and encourages business growth, which leads to the hiring of more people.

When you read that the Fed is "loosening up on the money supply" or lowering interest rates, it means that the Fed is trying to stimulate the economy (i.e., increase both consumer spending and business investment). A "tight monetary policy" is one in which the Fed is restricting the supply of money and increasing credit costs to lower inflation. During the mid-1990s, the Federal Reserve raised interest rates a little and threatened to raise them even more to slow the economy. If the economy slows too much, a recession could occur. If the economy doesn't slow, inflation could take place. Thus, the Fed plays a major role in keeping the economy growing at just the right rate.

➤ **LEARNING GOAL 6.**
Discuss fiscal policy and its importance to the economy.

THE ISSUE OF FISCAL POLICY

fiscal policy
Government efforts to keep the economy stable by increasing or decreasing taxes or government spending.

Fiscal policy refers to the federal government's efforts to keep the economy stable by increasing or decreasing taxes and/or government spending. For many years, the government has tended to raise taxes to fund more and more social and defense programs. The result is an increasing federal debt. Politi-

Proponents for maintaining a strong international military posture believe that due to political instability in various parts of the world the United States must continue to allocate a large percentage of federal tax revenues to its defense system, and especially to high-tech weapons. What do you perceive as the economic advantages and disadvantages of developing and maintaining such expensive weapons?

cians have debated whether to lower the debt through more taxes, less spending, or both. Most politicians believe that the debt needs to be lowered because the money paid for interest on the debt is so high that it drains money from the economy that could be used for better purposes.

··· HOW TAXES AND SPENDING AFFECT BUSINESSPEOPLE ···

A major issue in most political campaigns concerns fiscal policy—taxes and spending. Tax rates on those with the highest reported incomes in the United States were raised in the early 1990s. Many of those people are major investors in business. Higher taxes thus lowered the amount available for investment. Later in the 1990s, tax rates were lowered on some investment income to boost the economy. The long-term effect on businesses should be positive, but this remains to be seen.

What's important for you to understand at this point is that fiscal policy has a major influence on businesses and businesspeople. Employees and the entire economy eventually feel the effects as businesspeople decide whether to hire more people and invest more money.

Government spending is also an issue today. The government is spending more each year, even though the rate of growth in spending is slowing. All the talk about "balancing the budget" tends to obscure the fact that the government goes on spending more each year. An equivalent example is a person who says he or she is going on a diet by gaining weight for the next few years and losing it later on—several years in the future. Would you trust such a person to really lose weight later? Similarly, some people are skeptical that the government will really balance the budget sometime in the near future. It will be especially difficult if the Federal Reserve slows the economy. You can learn more about this issue and fiscal policy in general by reading the business section of your daily paper or *The Wall Street Journal*.

◄ CONSIDER USING OT ACETATE 2-7
How Does the Government Get Its Money?

◄ CONSIDER USING OT ACETATE 2-8
What $1 Billion Can Buy

··· THE FEDERAL DEFICIT ···

The **federal deficit** is the difference between federal revenue and federal spending in any given year. There was much concern about deficit spending throughout the 1980s and mid-1990s. Government spending was exceeding revenue by hundreds of billions of dollars every year. Therefore, a major topic of conversation in the 1990s was: How can we cut the budget deficit? Each year there's a federal deficit; the amount not paid is added to the national debt. The **national debt**, then, is the sum of all the federal deficits over time.

federal deficit
The difference between federal revenue and federal spending in any given year.

national debt
The sum of all the federal deficits over time.

FIGURE **2.5**

· · · ·

**1998 GOVERNMENT
REVENUE AND EXPENSES**

Most of the government's
revenue comes from you
and me and other tax-
payers in the form of
taxes and social security
payments. Corporate tax
provides a much smaller
revenue source. The bulk
of spending goes to indi-
viduals in the form of
welfare, social security,
and related programs.
Defense takes 15 percent.
The national debt
gobbles up 14 percent of
every dollar in interest
payments.

► **CONSIDER USING TM 20**
1998 Government Revenue and
Expenses

► **CONSIDER USING CRITICAL
THINKING EXERCISE 2-2**
Balancing the Federal Budget **(SCANS)**

► **CONSIDER USING OT ACETATE
2-9**
How Much Is the Federal Debt

► **CONSIDER USING OT ACETATE
2-10**
Top Expenditures of the Federal
Government

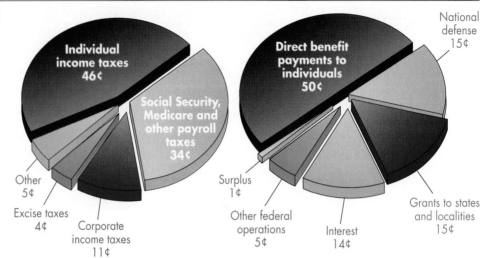

··· THE NATIONAL DEBT ···

Government spending has exceeded government income for so long that the
national debt is now about $5.5 trillion.[11] That's about $20,000 for every man,
woman, and child in the United States, or $80,000 for a family of four. What
does a trillion dollars look like? If you had a stack of $1,000 bills in your hand
only four inches high, you'd be a millionaire. A trillion dollars would be a
stack of $1,000 bills 67 miles high. If we were able to pay off the national debt
in one payment, we would need a stack of $1,000 bills over 300 miles high.

Most people believe that something must be done about the national debt,
and soon. The questions are, How did the national debt get so enormous?
What can be done about it? First, let's look at how the national debt got so
large. Figure 2.5 gives some details about the sources of government funds
and the way that money is spent. Expenditures for government programs are
growing faster than the economy's ability to support those programs. Most
government programs have automatic increases built into them, so spending
goes up automatically every year. Since World War II, every dollar of legislated
higher taxes has been matched by $1.28 to $1.58 in higher spending. The way
to have smaller deficits, therefore, isn't just to raise taxes. Spending must be
cut as well.[12] (Figure 2.6 shows how the national debt is growing.) For the latest update on the size of the national debt, log on to the Internet and go to
http://www.brillig.com/debt_clock. This site gives the new debt every second
and how much of that debt you and other U.S. citizens owe.

One question that economists, government officials, and ultimately you
and other taxpayers must answer is: What are our national priorities? That is,
do we want a strong military capability, including nuclear weapons and a
strategic defense system, and how much are we willing to pay for such a capability? Can we shift some defense money to domestic programs and international aid? These are the kinds of questions being posed in the media.

A huge chunk of federal income goes for social security payments. Social
security wasn't originally meant to be a retirement program, but a supplement
to savings. Many people now ignore that fact and rely on social security for
survival. Given this, do you think it's reasonable for the government to reduce
these benefits, or should people retire later and lessen the burden on social
security? These will be major issues throughout the coming years.

Millions of people receive medicare treatment, school lunches, medicaid, food stamps, housing subsidies, low-cost student loans, or other government-paid (taxpayer-paid) assistance. Certain industries—for example, dairy farmers and gas and oil companies—receive subsidies or tax deductions to support their production. What is the national priority regarding such payments? Should the government continue such payments and expand the programs when hard times come, or should such payments be limited somehow? Are such payments more or less important than defense or social security? What should the policy be if such payments threaten the economy by siphoning too much money from business? These are the issues you'll be seeing in the various media. How they are dealt with will have a direct effect on you (in taxes) and on business.

◄ **CONSIDER USING OT ACETATE 2-11**
The Changing Composition of the Federal Budget

••• JUST TAX THE RICH AND PAY OFF THE DEBT? •••

For years, economics was defined as the allocation of *scarce* resources among competing groups and individuals. No two groups would seem more in competition in a society than the rich and the poor. The feeling among many people is that the rich got rich by exploiting the poor (labor). In their search for more equality, some people suggest increasing taxes on the rich and giving the additional money to the poor. Such was the thinking behind most socialist governments.

◄ **CONSIDER USING SUPPLEMEN-TAL CASE 2-3**
Just Tax the Rich and Pay Off the Debt? (Revisited) **(SCANS)**

The problem with such thinking is that there simply aren't enough wealthy people making enough money so that by increasing their taxes the government would be able to pay for all its programs. A few years back, *Forbes* magazine reported that if the federal government took 100 percent of the income of the 35,875 millionaires in the United States, the increase in revenue would run the government for just 12 days. If the total wealth of the 400 richest people in the United States were confiscated, it would pay for just three months.

Wealthy people make most of their money from investing in businesses. If the government were to increase their taxes, that investment money would no longer be there, and the economy would slow. Therefore, it's clear that taxing the rich isn't a solution to the government's problems. The tax burden always falls on the middle class, those people who are struggling to pay their mortgages, send their kids to school, and so forth. Increasing their taxes makes

◄ **CONSIDER USING TM 21**
The National Debt

FIGURE 2.6
••••
THE NATIONAL DEBT

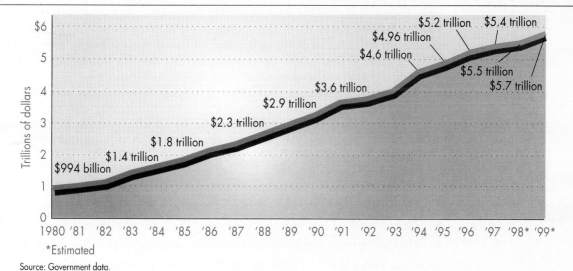

*Estimated

Source: Government data.

Making Ethical Decisions

http://www.nolo.com/chunktax/tax8.html

Exploring the Tax Laws

Imagine that you've been out of school for a while and you and your spouse are now earning $50,000 a year. To get to that point, you both paid your way through college. You look forward to buying a home, cars, and other goods and services that you've been postponing all these years to get your education.

You decide to buy a nice home. The government allows you to deduct all the mortgage interest charges on that home and the property taxes from your taxable income. That makes the payments much easier at first. In fact, almost all the money you're paying into the home the first few years goes for taxes and mortgage interest, and all of that is tax deductible. That means that you won't have to pay the government as much in taxes.

You also feel that you should give some money to your religious group and other charities. The money you give these nonprofit organizations is also deductible from your taxes if you itemize such deductions. You read in the

paper that you and other people who buy homes and give money to charity are receiving unfair tax breaks. After all, poor people can't get deductions for the rent they pay and they can't afford to give to charity. Some people feel that you shouldn't receive a "government subsidy" to buy your home. You, on the other hand, feel that you're paying enough in taxes, but you want to give your fair share.

Should the tax laws of the United States be changed to eliminate such deductions? Some people can buy tax-free bonds, get deductions for interest payments on their homes, receive deductions for money given to charity, and get tax breaks to rent out a second home. Businesses can write off some entertainment and travel expenses, and more. What percentage of a person's income should go to the government? Should everyone pay equally or should the rich pay more? What are the moral and ethical reasons for your position?

▲ SCANS

---

them poorer, and nobody feels better off. That's why recent tax bills have cut the taxes on the middle class or offered them more benefits, such as a start in college for their children.

The only long-term solution to meeting government needs is for the economy to grow, as it has been recently. That increases the size of the pie and makes it possible for everyone to have more without taking it from someone else. The problem is that growth strategies are directly in conflict with goals of more equality. Growth often comes from cutting taxes on the rich. That encourages them to invest more and to make the economy grow. The box Making Ethical Decisions explores tax deductions for homeowners and asks some questions to stimulate your thinking on such matters.

The economic goal in the future is to keep the economy growing so that more and more people can rise up the economic ladder, pay their share of taxes, and cut the federal deficit and debt. By slowing government growth, the economy can catch up. As productivity increases, the potential for growth is very high.

Progress Check

- What's the difference between a recession and a depression?
- How does the Federal Reserve manage the economy using monetary policy?
- How does the government manage the economy using fiscal policy?
- How big is the U.S. national debt? What's the difference between the federal deficit and the national debt?

SUMMARY
. . . . . .

1. Economics is the study of how society chooses to employ resources to produce various goods and services and to distribute them for consumption among various competing groups and individuals.

- *How can wealth be created in a society so that more is available for distribution?*

Adam Smith called the mechanism for creating wealth and jobs an invisible hand. Under his system of capitalism, nobody deliberately sets out to help others. In fact, they work only for their own prosperity and growth. Yet, like an invisible hand, through people trying to improve their own situation in life, an economy grows and prospers through the production of needed goods, services, and ideas.

1. Explain how wealth is created in an economy.

2. Capitalism is an economic system in which all or most of the means of production and distribution (e.g., land, factories, railroads, and stores) are privately owned and operated for profit. Socialism is an economic system based on the premise that most businesses should be owned by the government.

- *Discuss the major differences between capitalism, socialism, and communism.*

The major difference between capitalism, communism, and socialism is the involvement of the government. Under capitalism, the government isn't very involved in the distribution of wealth and much freedom is given to businesspeople. Under communism, almost all economic decisions are made by the government and the government owns most businesses. Under socialism, the government owns and controls many key businesses; private businesses and individuals are taxed relatively steeply to pay for social programs such as health care, education, unemployment insurance, and social security.

2. Discuss the major differences between capitalism, socialism, communism, and a mixed economy.

3. The free-market system is one in which decisions about what to produce and in what quantities are made by the market; that is, by buyers and sellers negotiating prices for goods and services.

- *Describe how the free-market system works.*

Buyers tell sellers what to produce and in what quantity by the buying decisions they make in the marketplace. When buyers demand more goods, the price goes up, signaling suppliers to produce more. The higher the price, the more goods and services are produced. Price, then, is the mechanism that allows free markets to work.

3. Describe how the free-market system works.

4. Three major indicators of economic conditions are (1) the gross domestic product (GDP), (2) the unemployment rate, and (3) the price indexes.

- *What are the key terms used to describe the U.S. economic system?*

Gross domestic product (GDP) is the total value of a country's output of goods and services in a given year. The unemployment rate refers to the number of civilians at least 16 years old who are unemployed and who tried to find a job within the most recent four weeks. The consumer price index measures changes in the prices of about 400 goods and services that consumers buy. It contains monthly statistics that measure the pace of inflation (consumer prices going up) or deflation (consumer prices going down). Productivity is the total volume of goods and services one worker can produce in a given period.

4. Use key terms (e.g., GDP and productivity) to explain the U.S. economic condition.

5. Describe monetary policy and its importance to the economy.

5. Monetary policy is the management of the money supply and interest rates.
   • ***What is the importance of monetary policy to the economy?***
   When unemployment gets too high, the Federal Reserve may put more money into the economy and lower interest rates. This stimulates spending and encourages business growth, which leads to the hiring of more people. On the other hand, when unemployment is low and prices are rising, the Fed may take money out of the economy and raise interest rates. This slows spending, and businesses hire fewer workers.

6. Discuss fiscal policy and its importance to the economy.

6. Fiscal policy refers to government efforts to keep the economy stable by increasing or decreasing taxes and/or government spending.
   • ***Why is fiscal policy important to the economy?***
   The government in recent years has tended to raise taxes to fund more social programs. The government is trying to cut spending to balance the budget (that is, make income equal spending). But such attempts have been rather unsuccessful; Congress merely cut the growth in spending rather than spending itself. The result is an increasing federal debt. The debate is whether to lower the debt through more taxes, less spending, or both.

KEY TERMS

capitalism 45
command economies 48
communism 47
consumer price index (CPI) 59
demand 53
deflation 61
depression 62
disinflation 61
economics 44

federal deficit 63
fiscal policy 62
free-market economies 48
gross domestic product (GDP) 58
inflation 61
invisible hand 45
mixed economies 49
monetary policy 62

monopolistic competition 55
monopoly 56
national debt 63
oligopoly 55
perfect competition 55
recession 62
socialism 47
supply 53
unemployment rate 58

DEVELOPING WORKPLACE SKILLS

1. What are some of the disadvantages of living in a free society? How could such disadvantages be minimized? What are the advantages? Write a short essay describing why a poor person in India might reject capitalism and prefer a socialist state. How could the United States overcome this situation to broaden the base of the free-market system? Two students could debate capitalist versus socialist societies to further reveal the issues.

2. Identify one widely debated economic issue and discuss the various viewpoints with your classmates and instructor. Choose a position and be ready to defend it by researching facts and figures to support it. Have you set up a filing system yet to maintain such information?

3. The text discusses three major indicators of an economy's health: gross domestic product (GDP), unemployment rate, and the price indexes. The text also describes the close relationship of productivity to GDP. Each of these indicators rises and falls during periods of recession and periods of growth. Devise a chart that illustrates whether each economic indicator goes up, goes down, or remains the same during a condition of economic recession or growth.

4. Most of the world's nations are moving toward some variation of a mixed economy. What do you see as the primary differences between the emergence of mixed economies and pure capitalism? Which would you favor and recommend? Why?

5. Now that some welfare in the United States has been moved from the federal to the state level, more input may be expected from local religious organizations and businesses. What are the advantages and disadvantages of having the government care for people versus the local citizens through charitable organizations? Write a two-page paper explaining your position.

TAKING IT TO THE NET

Purpose

To compare the value of the dollar based on variances in the consumer price index.

Exercise

Do your parents ever tire of telling you how much things cost back in their day? Sure things were cheaper then, but the value of a dollar was different too. Think about something you bought today (think of anything—shoes, soda, candy bar, haircut—whatever). How much did the good or service you bought today cost your parents when they were your age? Find out by using the handy tool on the Woodrow Federal Reserve Bank's Web site (http://woodrow.mpls.frb.fed.us/economy/calc/cpihome.html). The calculator uses the Consumer Price Index to compare the value of the dollar in different years. Enter the cost of the item you bought today, the year you would like to compare it with, and presto you'll find out how Mom and Pop could get along on such a small paycheck. (For an even bigger shock, compare the current dollar to the dollar in your grandparents' day!)

1. How much would a $50 pair of jeans bought in 1997 cost the year you were born?

2. How much would a $6 an hour job in 1997 have earned in 1970?

3. How much would a $12,000 1997 car have cost the year you got your first driver's license?

Practicing Management Decisions

No formula is more useful for understanding inflation than the rule of 72. Basically, the idea is to quickly compute how long it takes the cost of goods and services to double at various compounded rates of growth. For example, if houses were increasing in cost at 9 percent a year, how long would it take for the price of a home to double? The answer is easy to calculate. Simply divide 72 by the annual increase (9 percent) and you get the approximate number of years it takes to double the price (eight years). If houses go up in price by 12 percent, it only takes about six years to double in price (72 ÷ 12 = 6), and so on. Don't ask why this formula works; it would only confuse you. Just understand that it does. Of course, the same calculation can be used to predict how high food prices or auto prices will be 10 years from now.

CASE
• • • • • •
THE RULE OF 72
• • • • • •

Here's an example of how you can use the rule of 72. Let's say you wanted to buy a house for $100,000 but found interest rates so high that you'd end up paying almost $500,000 for the house after 30 years (assuming no money down). It sounds as if you'd be paying way too much for the house, given the information so far. But if you calculate how much the house may be worth after 30 years, you may change your mind. If housing prices increase 10 percent a year, prices will double approximately every seven years (72 ÷ 10 = 7.2). In 30 years, then, the price will double about four times (30 ÷ 7 = 4.3). Your $100,00 house would then sell for about $1.6 million in 30 years. Here's how you calculate that: $100,000 × 2 = $200,000 × 2 = $400,0000 × 2 = $800,000 × 2 = $1,600,000.

Since you would have paid less than $500,000, the home would be a good deal (assuming a 10 percent increase per year). If the price went up only 6 percent a year, what would the price be after 30 years? It would double in 12 years (72 ÷ 6 = 12), so it would double about 2.5 times in 30 years. In other words, it would be worth about $600,000, still more than you paid for it.

Discussion Questions

1. If the cost of a college education is about $15,000 per year now, what will it cost your children per year if costs go up 9 percent a year and your children go to college 24 years from now?

2. If the value of a home doubles in 12 years, what is the annual rate of return? (Hint: use the rule of 72 in reverse.)

3. If a bank is charging you 7 percent to borrow money for your mortgage, how do you know whether or not you will make money on the home when you sell it?

4. If interest on the national debt is 7 percent a year, how long would it take for the debt to double? How long would it take if interest rates went up to 8 percent?

China, with its 1.2 billion people and staggering abundance of natural resources, is expected to become the world's largest economy in the next millennium. This transition to global economic power will not be easy for the communist giant since China has not historically embraced an open-door policy to world traders. For a 50-year period, China chose a self-imposed isolation, with its goal to become economically self-sufficient. The shift from communist to free-market trade policies seems like a mountain too steep to climb, but China enjoyed an enormous boost in its climb in the summer of 1997. After 150 years of British control, Hong Kong, the capitalist Mecca of the far east, returned to China's rule. This much publicized shift in political control could be the best thing to ever happen economically to China.

Hong Kong has been a powerful engine in driving capitalism into high gear in many Asian markets. During the past 15 years, Hong Kong has grown from the 23rd to the 8th largest trade entity in the world. It has become a global center for finance, distribution, and trade and has established a complex and functioning business structure to compete in world markets. This efficient functioning infrastructure caused many of the world's leading corporations to set up shop in Hong Kong. The Hong Kong business community also developed vast knowledge in governmental trade strategies and how to implement

VIDEO CASE

• • • • • •

BREAKING DOWN THE GREAT WALL

policies for economic growth. By gaining the trade facilities of Hong Kong, China can open its previously closed doors much wider and make effective use of the important theory of comparative advantage.

Still, the economic shift to unrestricted free trade policies from a closed society is bound to cause some concern and fear in China. It's essential that the government establish specific trade strategies to confront and deal with these concerns. Trade policies involving tariffs, subsidies, import quotas, local content requirements, and administrative trade policies will need to be adapted for both political and economic reasons. By forging close ties with Hong Kong business leaders, China can take a giant step in bridging gaps and removing wedges that have separated the nation from global markets in the past.

Discussion Questions

1. Hong Kong's reentry into China should help the Chinese economy make use of the economic theory of comparative advantage. How might China make use of this important global economic theory? Cite some examples.

2. What adjustments will China need to make to conform to the cultural, economic, and social practices of other countries?

3. If the Chinese impose stiff trade policies, what might be the reaction of their global trading partners?

Competing in Global Markets

Chapter

3

LEARNING GOALS

After you have read and studied this chapter, you should be able to

1 Discuss the increasing importance of the global market and the roles of comparative advantage and absolute advantage in international trade.

2 Explain how the marketing motto "Find a need and fill it" applies to global markets, and understand key terms used in international business.

3 Describe the current status of the United States in global business.

4 Illustrate the strategies used in reaching global markets.

5 Evaluate the hurdles of trading in world markets.

6 Debate the advantages and disadvantages of trade protectionism.

7 Explain the role of multinational corporations in global markets.

The road to global trade is not always clear even to experienced and successful businesspeople. Take Dary Rees for example. Rees watched domestic sales for her Miami-based tabletop and home accessories business taper off in 1995. Her problem was one that many businesses might envy. It seemed Rees's product line, which ranged from $15 saltshakers to $2,000 chandeliers, had saturated the U.S. market. Market penetration was so extensive that retailers such as Nordstrom's and Henri Bendel complained about a lack of exclusive distribution.

Luckily, Rees spotted an advertisement in the National Women Business Owners newsletter that announced a trade mission to Amsterdam and London sponsored by the U.S. Commerce Department. Although the trip cost $6,000, she felt the investment could pay off handsomely. She decided to take some import-export courses offered by the local World Trade Center in Miami and the United Parcel Service. She investigated the Export

Hotline & TradeBank, which provides market data for 50 industries in 78 countries (http://www.exporthotline.com)—and off she went.

The rest is history. The U.S. ambassadors helped forge strategic alliances with key contacts, and by the end of the trade mission Rees had contacted a British distributor to serve retail clients in the United Kingdom and another distributor in Holland to take care of accounts in Holland, Belgium, and Luxembourg. After the success of the European trip Rees decided to crack the Asian market and proceeded on a trade mission to Hong Kong, Singapore, and Taiwan. Today her company is doing $100,000 worth of business in the region.

Rees represents a growing number of successful U.S. businesspeople who have identified the vast opportunities that exist in global markets. The future of U.S. economic growth is tied to global trade. This chapter will help you prepare for a seat on Rees's next trade mission.

PROFILE

Dary Rees, Global Entrepreneur

THE DYNAMIC GLOBAL MARKET

Do you dream of traveling to exotic cities like Paris, Hong Kong, Rio de Janeiro, or Cairo? Years ago, the closest most Americans would get to working in these cities was in their dreams. However, the situation has changed. Today it's hard to find a major U.S. company that does not cite international expansion as a link to future growth.[1] Also, a recent study noted 91 percent of the companies doing business globally believe it's important to send employees on global assignments.[2]

Have you thought about the possibilities of a career in international business? Maybe a few facts will make the possibility more interesting: There are about 260 million people in the United States, but there are about 6 billion potential customers in the 193 countries in the global market. Of the 6 billion people in the world, approximately 75 percent live in developing areas where technology, education, and per capita income still lag.[3]

Today Americans buy over $100 billion worth of goods from Japan. American Express Card usage is on the rise in Germany, Saudi Arabia, and other markets. Sales of pagers made by Motorola in the People's Republic of China increased from 100,000 in 1991 to over 8 million in 1996. The company notes this is the fastest-growing global market for its pagers in the world.[4]

◄ CONSIDER USING TM 22
Chapter Outline

◄ LEARNING GOAL 1.
Discuss the increasing importance of the global market and the roles of comparative advantage and absolute advantage in international trade.

◄ CONSIDER USING OT ACETATE 3-1
Growing World Population

importing
Buying products from another country.

exporting
Sellling products to another country.

Of the approximately six billion people that live in 193 countries on this planet, about one in five live in China. Pictured here is a crowded street in Shanghai City, China bustling with activity. It's no wonder that the United States and other industrialized countries are eager to expand trade with this emerging market. General Motors, Coca-Cola, Motorola, and Boeing are just a few of the U.S. firms that have made significant investments in China.

The United States is the largest importing nation in the world. It is the largest exporting nation as well. **Importing** is buying products from another country. **Exporting** is selling products to another country. Competition in exporting is very intense. The United States must compete against aggressive exporters such as Germany, Japan, and China.

These facts show that international trade is big business today and will be even more important in the new millennium. Therefore, it is important you prepare yourself for the global challenge. Ask yourself these questions: Are you studying a foreign language in school? Have you talked with anyone about the excitement and rewards of traveling to and trading with other countries? Do you recognize the many challenges the United States will face as we approach the year 2000? Many colleges offer students the opportunity to study abroad. If you are interested talk with your counselor, instructor, or faculty advisor.

The purpose of this chapter is to expose you to global business, including its potential and its problems. The demand for students with training in international business is almost certain to grow as the number of businesses that take the leap into the global market increases. Maybe you will decide that a career in international business is your long-term goal.

···· ▬▬▬ ····

WHY TRADE WITH OTHER NATIONS?

There are several reasons why one country would trade with other countries. First, no nation, even a technologically advanced one, can produce all of the products that its people want and need. Second, even if a country became self-sufficient, other nations would demand trade with that country to meet the needs of their people. Third, some nations have an abundance of natural resources and a lack of technological know-how. Other countries (for example, Japan and Switzerland) have sophisticated technology but few natural resources. Trade relations enable each nation to produce what it is most capable of producing and to buy what it needs in a mutually beneficial exchange relationship. This happens through the process of free trade. **Free trade** is the movement of goods and services among nations without political or economic obstruction.

••• THE THEORIES OF COMPARATIVE •••
AND ABSOLUTE ADVANTAGE

International trade is the exchange of goods and services across national borders. Exchanges between and among countries involve more than goods and services, however. Countries also exchange art, athletes, cultural events, medical advances, space exploration, and labor. The guiding principle supporting free economic exchange was suggested by 19th-century economist David Ricardo, who proposed the **comparative advantage theory**.[5] This theory states that a country should produce and sell to other countries those products that it produces most effectively and

COMPANY	EXPORTS AS A PERCENTAGE OF TOTAL SALES
Boeing	57.5%
Sun Microsystems	49.2
Intel	39.1
Caterpillar	32.8
Hewlett-Packard	22.6
Chrysler	19.1
General Electric	13.2

FIGURE **3.1**
· · · ·
SUCCESSFUL U.S. EXPORTERS

◄ **CONSIDER USING TM 23**
Successful U.S. Exporters
(Figure 3.1 on text page 75)

efficiently, and should buy from other countries those products it cannot produce as effectively or efficiently.

The United States has a comparative advantage in producing many goods and services, such as high-tech products and engineering services. Figure 3.1 lists the most successful U.S. exporters. On the other hand, the United States does not have a comparative advantage in producing some shoes, coffee, toys, and many other products that it imports. Through specialization and trade, the United States and its trading partners can realize mutually beneficial exchanges.

A country has an **absolute advantage** if it has a monopoly on the production of a specific product or is able to produce it more efficiently than all other nations. For instance, South Africa once dominated diamond production. Today there are very few instances of absolute advantage in the global economy.

· · · · ▬▬▬ · · · ·

GETTING INVOLVED IN GLOBAL TRADE

Students often wonder which U.S. firms are best for finding a job in international business. Naturally the discussion focuses on large multinational firms (e.g., Boeing, Ford, IBM, and Du Pont) that have large multinational accounts. But the real potential in global markets may be with small businesses. Today in the U.S. economy, small businesses generate about half of the private-sector commerce but account for only 20 percent of exports.[6] However, with the help of the U.S. Department of Commerce, 8,000 companies expanded their exports in 1996 alone.[7]

Getting started is often a matter of observation, determination, and risk. What does that mean? First of all, it is important to research and study global markets in which you are interested in doing business. The college library, the Internet, or your fellow classmates are often a good first stop. If you have the opportunity, travel to get some feel for the culture and lifestyles in various countries to see if global business appeals to you.

For example, several years ago a traveler in one country of Africa noticed that there was no ice available for drinks, for keeping foods fresh, and so on. Further research showed that, in fact, there was no ice factory for hundreds of miles, yet the market seemed huge. The man returned to the United States,

free trade
The movement of goods and services among nations without political or economic obstruction.

comparative advantage theory
Theory which asserts that a country should produce and sell to other countries those products that it produces most efficiently.

absolute advantage
When a country has a monopoly on producing a product or is able to produce it more efficiently than all other countries.

◄ **CONSIDER USING LECTURE ENHANCER 3-1**
Is Free Trade Still the Answer?

◄ **CONSIDER USING LECTURE ENHANCER 3-2**
Arguments for and Against Free Trade

◄ **CONSIDER USING OT ACETATE 3-2**
Largest Global Companies in the World by Industry

found some willing investors, and returned to Africa to build an ice-making plant. Much negotiation was necessary with the authorities (negotiation best done by locals who know the system), and the plant was built. Now the man is indeed wealthy and the country has available a needed resource.

··· IMPORTING GOODS AND SERVICES ···

Students often find that importing goods into the United States can be quite profitable. Foreign students attending U.S. colleges and universities often notice that some products widely available in their countries are not available in the United States, or are more costly here. By working with foreign producers and finding some working capital, these students have become major importers while still in school.

Several years ago, executives from Minnetonka, Inc., of Chaska, Minnesota, were browsing in a German supermarket when they noticed a fascinating new product—toothpaste in a pump dispenser. The company contacted Henkel, the German manufacturer, and together they introduced the product into the United States as Check-Up toothpaste. It became so popular that Colgate, Crest, and other major brands soon followed with their own versions of the pump.

··· EXPORTING GOODS AND SERVICES ···

Once you decide to get into international trade, you will be surprised at what you can sell overseas. Who would think, for example, that a U.S. firm could sell beer in Germany, where so many good beers come from? Yet right around the corner from a famous beer hall in Munich you can buy Samuel Adams Boston Lager. Thousands of cases have been sold, and a local licensing agreement will assure more sales to come. American brewing giant Anheuser-Busch took the hint. It purchased the largest brewer in central China and began selling its flagship Budweiser product in major Chinese cities.[8] But you haven't heard anything yet. Can you imagine selling sand to the Middle East? Meridan Group sells a special kind of sand used in swimming pool filters. And a Rhode Island fishery even sells sushi to Japan.

So what can you sell to other countries? Just about anything of quality you can sell in the United States. You can sell snowplows to the Saudi Arabians. Why? They use them to plow sand off their driveways. Just about any good or service that is used in the United States is needed in other countries, and the competition is often not nearly as stiff for most of them. Also, exporting is a terrific boost to the economy. The U.S. Department of Commerce estimates that every $1 billion in U.S. exports generates 25,000 jobs at home.[9]

But don't be misled: selling in global markets is not necessarily easy. We shall discuss a number of hurdles later in this chapter. Often adapting products to specific global markets is potentially profitable but difficult. A good example of this is in the box, Reaching Beyond Our Borders.

If you are interested in exporting, write for "The Basic Guide to

One of the ways to participate in global exchanges is to import products from other countries. This picture shows Marjorie Filmyer, owner of the Tullycross Fine Irish Imports of Philadelphia, meeting with a representative of the Beleek China Company at the Dublin, Ireland Showcase—the national trade show for buyers and sellers of Irish handcrafts. Would owning or managing a store like Tullycross appeal to you as a career possibility?

Reaching Beyond Our Borders

Looking for a Kick from the Global Market

Nike is the number one athletic shoe seller in the United States. Its products, made by foreign contractors, are sold in over 100 foreign countries. The objective of the Beaverton, Oregon–based enterprise is to compete with Coca-Cola and McDonald's to become the best-known brand name on the planet. To reach this goal, however, appealing to the fans of the most popular sport in the world is a must. Therefore, soccer has become the number one priority for Nike.

Nike President Thomas E. Clarke's office spotlights action photos of soccer players wearing Nike's swoosh logo. "Once we set our sights on being a global company, we had to focus on soccer," explains Clarke. And focus they did, spending hundreds of millions of dollars to gain sponsorship of world-class players and teams. The record-setting $200 million paid for sponsorship of Brazil's national team literally staggered the soccer

world. Yet Clarke confidently stated, "You never overpay for things that are good. This is our most important international deal."

Nike's goal is to become the leader in soccer footwear, apparel, and equipment by the World Cup 2002. However, its competitors Adidas, Umbro, and Puma do not intend to step aside. Adidas, the market leader, still retains sponsorship of many top teams and players, including sponsorship of World Cup 1998 in France. Nike's in-your-face advertisements and heavy-handed promotion tactics have also caused some concern in the soccer world. Still, the company plans to get a big kick out of the global market in the 21st century.

Source: Roger Thurow, "In Global Drive, Nike Finds Its Brash Ways Don't Always Pay Off," *The Wall Street Journal*, May 5, 1997, pp. A1–A10; and Linda Himmelstein, "The Swoosh Heard around the World," *Business Week*, May 12, 1997, pp. 76–80.

Exporting," which is available from the U.S. Government Printing Office, Superintendent of Documents, Washington, D.C. 20402. More advice can be found in *Business America*, a trade magazine published by Commerce's International Trade Administration. You can order it from the U.S. Government Printing Office as well. Also, call the Small Business Administration at (617) 350–5096 and ask for a copy of *Exportise*, or dial the Export Hotline for a free exporting kit: (800) USA–XPORT. A visit to your campus library, including a tour on the Internet, is also a big help.

◄ CONSIDER USING OT ACETATE 3-3
Comparing the U.S., China, and India

••• MEASURING GLOBAL TRADE •••

In measuring the effectiveness of global trade, nations carefully follow two key indicators: balance of trade and balance of payments. The **balance of trade** is the relationship of exports to imports. A *favorable balance of trade,* or trade surplus, occurs when the value of exports exceeds that of imports. An *unfavorable balance of trade,* or **trade deficit**, occurs when the value of imports exceeds that of exports. It is easy to understand why countries prefer to export more than they import. If I sell you $200 worth of goods and buy only $100 worth, I have an extra $100 available to buy other things. However, I'm in an unfavorable position if I buy $200 worth of goods and sell only $100.

The **balance of payments** is the difference between money coming into a country (from exports) and money leaving the country (for imports) plus money flows from other factors such as tourism, foreign aid, military expenditures, and foreign investment. The amount of money flowing into or out of a

balance of trade
The relationship of exports to imports.

trade deficit
Buying more goods from other nations than are sold to them.

balance of payments
The difference between money coming into a country (from exports) and money leaving the country (for imports) plus money flows from other factors such as tourism, foreign aid, military expenditures, and foreign investment.

country for tourism and other reasons may offset a trade imbalance. The goal is always to have more money flowing into the country than flowing out of the country. This is called a *favorable balance of payments.*

To make certain trade is being conducted globally on a fair basis, laws have been enforced to prohibit unfair practices, such as dumping. **Dumping** is the practice of selling products in foreign countries for less than you charge for the same products in your own country. This tactic is sometimes applied to unload surplus products in foreign markets or to gain a foothold in a new market by offering products for lower prices than domestic competitors do. South Korea and Japan, for example, have been accused of dumping.[10] U.S. laws against dumping specify that foreign firms must price their products to include 10 percent overhead costs plus 8 percent profit margin. Dumping can take time to prove, however. There's also evidence that some governments offer financial incentives to certain industries to sell goods in global markets for less. Charges of dumping have been made against manufacturers of several products, including steel, motorcycles, and computer flat-panel screens.

Now that you understand some basic terms, we can begin discussing global business in more depth. The first questions to address are how and what the United States is doing in world trade. Before doing so, however, let's check your progress.

dumping
Selling products for less in a foreign country than is charged in the producing country.

➤ **CONSIDER USING OT ACETATE 3-4**
Nations That Have Not Converted to the Metric System

Progress Check

- Can you explain why statistics (world population, size of market, etc.) support the expansion of U.S. businesses into global markets?
- Evaluate the concept of comparative advantage and state some examples of this concept in actual global markets.
- How do you determine the difference between a nation's balance of trade and its balance of payments?

···· ▬▬▬ ····

TRADING IN GLOBAL MARKETS: THE U.S. EXPERIENCE

➤ **LEARNING GOAL 3.**
Describe the current status of the United States in global business.

➤ **CONSIDER USING LECTURE ENHANCER 3-3**
International Relations Gunboat Style

Fully 95 percent of the world's population lies outside the United States. However, the United States historically has never been very active at exporting. How can this be true when the United States is the world's largest exporter? Even though the United States exports the largest volume of goods, we export a much lower percentage of our products than other countries do. (Figure 3.2 lists the major trading economies in the world.) In the early 1980s, no more than 10 percent of American businesses exported products. However, slow economic growth in the United States and other economic factors lured more businesses to global markets in the late 1980s and early 1990s. Today most large businesses are involved in global trade, and growing numbers of small businesses are going global as well.

Although the United States is the world's largest exporter, it does not export a significant percentage of its gross domestic product (GDP). In other words, compared to other industrialized economies such as Japan, Taiwan, and Switzerland, the United States does not depend on exporting as much. For many years the United States exported more goods and services than it imported. In 1985, however, the United States bought more goods from other nations than it sold to other nations. Remember that this is called a trade deficit or unfavorable balance of trade. The United States had run its highest

THE MAJOR TRADING ECONOMIES OF THE WORLD

European Union	Republic of Korea
United States	Singapore
Japan	Taiwan
Hong Kong and China	Switzerland
Canada	

Source: 1996 World Trade Organization.

FIGURE **3.2**

••••

THE MAJOR
TRADING ECONOMIES
OF THE WORLD

◄ CONSIDER USING TM 24
The Major Trading Economies of the
World
(Text Figure 3.2, page 79)

trade deficits with Japan and China. In 1997 the merchandise trade deficit with Japan stood at over $40 billion; the trade deficit with China was close to $37 billion.[11]

Another way economists measure a nation's economic activity is to compare the amount of money a country owes to foreign creditors and the value of what foreign investors own in the country with the money foreigners owe to it, and the value of what is owned in foreign markets. During the 1980s, it was widely reported that the United States had become a **debtor nation**, that is, a country that owes more money to other nations than they owe it. This caused quite a stir when the information was first reported. Some even felt the United States was on the road to economic ruin. However, contrary to those gloomy interpretations, it is not necessarily a bad sign when foreign businesses invest here. It means the United States is perceived as a strong economic leader, and foreign investors are willing to invest in our market by building new plants here. What has emerged is a trend toward more foreign direct investment in the United States.

Foreign direct investment is the buying of permanent property and businesses in foreign nations. Visible examples of foreign direct investment in the United States include the purchase of Pebble Beach Golf Club in California by the Japanese and the opening of the Mercedes plant in Vance, Alabama.[12] Those who view foreign investment in the United States as a sign of strength contend that foreign firms are investing in the United States because the American economy has been very strong throughout the 1990s. Property, buildings, and stock in U.S. firms have simply been more attractive than those in other countries. The time to worry is when investors find other countries more attractive. Figure 3.3 lists the nations with the largest direct foreign investment in the United States.

◄ CONSIDER USING SUPPLEMEN-
TAL CASE 3-1
Entering the Import/Export Business
(SCANS)

debtor nation
Country that owes more money to other nations than they owe it.

◄ CONSIDER USING OT ACETATE
3-5
Checklist for Exporters

foreign direct investment
Buying of permanent property and businesses in foreign nations.

▼ CONSIDER USING TM 25
Countries with the Highest Foreign Direct
Investment in the United States
(Text Figure 3.3 on page 79)

United Kingdom	$110 billion
Japan	$80 billion
Netherlands	$68 billion
Canada	$38 billion

Source: U.S. Commerce Department.

FIGURE **3.3**

••••

COUNTRIES WITH THE
HIGHEST FOREIGN
DIRECT INVESTMENT IN
THE UNITED STATES

Critical
Thinking

You have read that some 95 percent of the world's population lives outside the United States, but still many U.S. companies do not engage in world trade. Why is that? What do such figures indicate about the future potential for increasing U.S. exports? What do they say about future careers in international business?

STRATEGIES FOR REACHING GLOBAL MARKETS

▶ **LEARNING GOAL 4.**
Illustrate the strategies used in reaching global markets.

An organization may participate in international trade in many ways, including exporting, licensing, creating subsidiaries, contract manufacturing, franchising, joint venturing, and countertrading. Each of these strategies provides opportunities for people interested in becoming involved in global markets.

••• EXPORTING •••

Export Assistance Centers (EACs)
Created to provide hands-on exporting assistance and trade-finance support for small and medium-sized businesses.

With global competition intensifying, the U.S. government realized it needed to change its business-as-usual approach in aiding small and medium-sized businesses desiring to export. **Export Assistance Centers (EACs)** were created to provide hands-on exporting assistance and trade-finance support for small and medium-sized businesses.[13] To date, 14 EAC hub offices exist, with further expansion planned. EACs represent the future of federal export promotion efforts. Still, many U.S. firms are reluctant to go through the trouble of establishing trading relationships. Therefore, it makes sense that some specialized organization would step in to negotiate such exchanges for them. These specialists are called **export trading companies**. An export trading company serves the role of matching buyers and sellers from different countries and provides other services (such as dealing with documentation and custom's offices) to ease the export of products into foreign markets. Export trading companies often provide internships or part-time opportunities for students interested in careers in global business. Learning a foreign language in school and taking courses related to international trade are good ways to attract the attention of an export trading firm.

export trading companies
Companies that attempt to match buyers and sellers from different countries.

▶ **CONSIDER USING LECTURE ENHANCER 3-4**
Harley-Davidson Cigarettes

••• LICENSING •••

licensing
Agreement in which a producer allows a foreign company to produce its product in exchange for royalties.

▶ **CONSIDER USING LECTURE ENHANCER 3-5**
Drug Dealing, Swiss Style

▶ **CONSIDER USING LECTURE ENHANCER 3-6**
The Growth in Pet Food Exports

▶ **CONSIDER USING OT ACETATE 3-6**
Proposed Global Labor Standards

A firm may decide to compete in a growing global market by **licensing** to a foreign company the right to manufacture its product or use its trademark on a fee (royalty) basis. The company generally sends representatives to the foreign producer to help set up the production process. It may also assist in such areas as distribution and promotion.

A licensing agreement can be beneficial to a firm in several different ways. Through licensing, an organization can gain additional revenues from a product that it would not have normally generated domestically. In addition, foreign licensees often must purchase start-up supplies, component materials, and consulting services from the licensing firm. Coke and Pepsi often enter foreign markets through licensing agreements that typically extend into long-term service contracts. Even the Royal Canadian Mounted Police entered into a licensing agreement with the Walt Disney Company to market products bearing Mounties images.[14] One final advantage of licensing worth noting is that licensors spend little or no money to produce and market their products. These costs come from the licensee's pocket. Therefore, licensees generally work very hard to see that the product succeeds in their market.

However, as you may suspect, licensing agreements may provide some disadvantages to a company. One major problem is that often a firm must grant licensing rights to its product for an extended period, maybe as long as 20 years. If a product experiences remarkable growth in the foreign market, the bulk of the revenues goes to the licensee. Perhaps even more threatening is that a licensing firm is actually selling its expertise in a product area. If a foreign licensee learns the technology, it may break the agreement and begin to produce a similar product on its own. If legal remedies are not available, the licensing firm may lose its trade secrets, not to mention the agreed-upon royalties.

••• CREATING SUBSIDIARIES •••

As the size of a foreign market expands, a firm may want to establish a foreign subsidiary. A **foreign subsidiary** is a company that is owned by another company (called the parent company) in a foreign country. Such a subsidiary would operate much like a domestic firm, with production, distribution, promotion, pricing, and other business functions under the control of the foreign subsidiary's management. Of course, the legal requirements of both the home and host countries would have to be observed. The primary advantage of a subsidiary is that the company maintains complete control over any technology or expertise it may possess. Nestlé is one example of a major firm with many foreign subsidiaries. The Swiss company has spent billions to acquire foreign subsidiaries such as Carnation in the United States and Perrier in France.[15]

The major shortcoming associated with creating a subsidiary is that the company is committing a large amount of funds and technology within foreign boundaries. Should relations with the host country falter, the firm's assets could be taken over by the foreign government.

••• CONTRACT MANUFACTURING •••

Contract manufacturing involves the production of private-label goods by a foreign company to which a company then attaches its brand name or trademark. This is also referred to as outsourcing. Many well-known firms such as Levi Strauss and Nike practice contract manufacturing. The consumer electronics industry also makes extensive use of this practice.[16] In such a situation, the firm or its foreign producer can handle the product's distribution or promotion. Through contract manufacturing a company can often experiment in a new market without heavy start-up costs. If the brand name becomes a success, the company has penetrated a new market with reduced risk.

••• FRANCHISING •••

Franchising is popular both domestically and in global markets. We will discuss franchising in depth in Chapter 5. Firms such as McDonald's, 7-Eleven, and Dunkin' Donuts have many global units operated by foreign franchisees. McDonald's alone has almost 9,000 outlets globally, in 101 countries.[17]

Franchisors have to be careful to adapt in the countries they serve. For example, KFC's first 11 Hong Kong outlets failed within two years. Apparently the chicken was too greasy and messy to be eaten with fingers by the fastidious people of Hong Kong. McDonald's made a similarly disastrous mistake when entering the Amsterdam market. It originally set up operations in the suburbs, as it does in the United States, but soon learned that Europeans mostly live in the cities. Therefore, McDonald's began to open outlets downtown. Domino's Pizza originally approached the global market with a one-pie-

Millions of times a day around the world, things do go better with Coke. In fact Coca-Cola generates almost 80 percent of its total sales in global markets. Many of these sales are the result of licensing agreements Coke has with many companies in various countries. This is an example of the refreshing taste of Coke in the familiar red and white can in the Chinese market.

foreign subsidiary
A company owned by another company (parent company) in a foreign country.

contract manufacturing
Production of private-label goods by a company to which another company then attaches its brand name or trademark.

◄ CONSIDER USING LECTURE ENHANCER 3-7
Beijing Big Mac

Nike is an example of a company that makes extensive use of contract manufacturing. Here workers in China package the famous "swoosh" brand shoes for shipment back to the United States. While contract manufacturing helps companies reduce labor costs, criticism has grown concerning the use of child labor and other workplace violations. Nike has pledged to remedy any human rights violations involved in the manufacture of its products. What can consumers do to encourage companies to observe basic human rights?

fits-all approach. The company found out the hard way that Germans like small individual pizzas, not large pies, and Japanese customers enjoy squid and sweet mayonnaise pizza. The company now sells franchises to business-people with local savvy—a move that boosted sales from $16 million in 1986 to $503 million in 1996.[18]

••• INTERNATIONAL JOINT VENTURES •••

A **joint venture** is a partnership in which companies (often from two different countries) join to undertake a major project. According to Coopers & Lybrand, a New York–based international professional services firm, such strategic alliances are helping companies grow much faster than their counterpart companies that are not participating.[19] Joint ventures can even be mandated by governments as a condition of doing business in their country. It is, for example, often hard to gain entry into a country like China, whose economy is centrally planned; joint ventures often help. For example, the Campbell Soup Company formed joint ventures with Japan's Nakano Vinegar Company and Malaysia's Cheong Chan Company to expand its rather low market share in both countries.[20] Joint ventures are nothing new in international trade. Xerox Corporation and Fuji Photo Film Company have enjoyed a 34-year joint venture relationship that shows no signs of deteriorating.[21] But perhaps the most visible examples of joint ventures are found in the cooperation between major department stores and foreign producers of TV sets, VCRs, CD players, and other such goods. The foreign company produces the goods, and U.S. corporations provide the distribution and promotion expertise. In the United States, names such as Panasonic, Samsung, and Sony are as familiar as GE and Westinghouse because of joint ventures.

The benefits of international joint ventures are clear—shared technology, shared marketing expertise, entry into markets where foreign goods are not allowed unless produced locally, and shared risk. The drawbacks are not so obvious. An important one is that one partner can learn the other's technology and practices and go off on its own as a competitor. Also, over time, the technology may become obsolete or the joint venture may be too large to be as flexible as needed.

joint venture
A partnership in which companies (often from two or more different countries) join to undertake a major project.

bartering
The exchange of goods or services for goods or services.

countertrading
Bartering among several countries.

••• COUNTERTRADING •••

One of the oldest forms of trade is called **bartering**, the exchange of merchandise for merchandise or service for service with no money involved. **Countertrading** is more complex than bartering in that several countries may be involved, each trading goods for goods or services for services. It has been estimated that countertrading accounts for 25 percent of all international exchanges.

Examples of bartering agreements are many. Chrysler traded its vehicles in Jamaica for bauxite. McDonnell Douglas (before becoming part of Boeing Corporation) traded jets in Yugoslavia for canned hams. General Motors has traded vehicles with China for industrial gloves and cutting tools. Counter-trading involves more combinations than the bartered agreement. For example let's say that Jamaica wanted vehicles from Chrysler but Chrysler did not have a need for bauxite. In a countertrade agreement, Chrysler may trade vehicles to Jamaica, which then trades bauxite to China, which then exchanges industrial gloves and cutting tools with Chrysler. Through this countertrade, all parties receive a mutually beneficial exchange.

Barter is especially important to poor countries that have little cash available for trade. Such countries may barter or countertrade with all kinds of raw materials, food, or whatever other resources they have. With many emerging economies still in a state of flux, there is no question that bartering and countertrading will continue in global markets into the 21st century. Trading products for products helps businesses avoid some of the problems and hurdles that exist in global markets. Unfortunately, businesspeople must vault many hurdles in global markets. That's what we will look at next.

◄ CONSIDER USING LECTURE ENHANCER 3-8
Cultural Differences

◄ CONSIDER USING OT ACETATE 3-7
U.S. Foreign Direct Investments

HURDLES OF TRADING IN GLOBAL MARKETS

Succeeding in any business takes work and effort, due to the many hurdles that exist in all markets. Unfortunately, the hurdles get higher and more complex in global markets. This is particularly true in dealing with differences in cultural perspectives, societies and economies, laws and regulations, and fluctuations in currencies. Let's take a look at each of these formidable hurdles.

◄ LEARNING GOAL 5.
Evaluate the hurdles of trading in world markets.

◄ CONSIDER USING LECTURE ENHANCER 3-9
Ground Breaking and The Smiling Pig

••• CULTURAL DIFFERENCES •••

If you hope to get involved in international trade, you will have to be aware of the cultural differences among nations. Different nations have very different ways of conducting business, and American businesspeople are notoriously bad at adapting. In fact, American businesspeople have consistently been accused of **ethnocentricity**, which means they feel our culture is superior to all others and our job is to teach others the American way of doing things. In contrast, foreign businesspeople are very good at adapting to U.S. culture. Let us give you a couple of examples of how American businesses had difficulty in adapting to important cultural differences.

Religion is an important part of any society's culture and can have a significant impact on business operations. McDonald's and Coca-Cola unfortunately offended Muslims by putting the Saudi Arabian flag on their packaging. The flag's design contains a passage from the Koran, and Muslims feel their Holy Writ should never be wadded up and thrown away.[22] Consider the tragedies in Bosnia and the Middle East, where clashes between religious communities have hurt these economies. In Islamic countries, dawn-to-dusk fasting during the month of Ramadan causes workers' output to drop considerably. Also, the requirement to pray five times daily can affect output. For example, an American manager in Islamic Pakistan toured a new plant under his control in full operation. He went to his office to make some preliminary forecasts of production. As he was working, suddenly all the machinery in the plant stopped. He rushed out expecting a possible power failure and instead found his production workers on their prayer rugs. He returned to his office and proceeded to lower his production estimates.

ethnocentricity
The feeling that one's culture is superior to all others.

◄ CONSIDER USING OT ACETATE 3-8
Cultural Differences in Global Markets

The influence of religion can even extend to the workplace. Here we see workers in a Michigan warehouse taking time off the job to pray at the required time of day as specified by their religion.

global marketing
Selling the same product in essentially the same way everywhere in the world.

➤ **CONSIDER USING OT ACETATE 3-9**
Did You Know?

➤ **CONSIDER USING SUPPLEMENTAL CASE 3-2**
Differences in Management Methods (**SCANS**)

Cultural differences can also have an impact on such important business factors as human resource management. In Latin American countries, workers believe that managers are placed in positions of authority to make decisions and be responsible for the well-being of the workers under their control. Consider what happened to one American manager in Peru who neglected this important cultural characteristic and believed workers should participate in managerial functions. This manager was convinced he could motivate his workers to higher levels of productivity by instituting a more democratic decision-making style. Shortly after his new style was put in place, workers began quitting their jobs in droves. When asked why, the Peruvian workers said the new production manager and supervisors did not know their jobs and were asking the workers what to do. All stated they wanted to quit and find new jobs, since obviously this company was doomed because of incompetent managers.

Without question, cultural differences present a significant hurdle for global managers. The reality of growing cultural diversity in the U.S. workplace highlights differences and distinctions even in our domestic market. Therefore, learning about important cultural perspectives on time factors, change, competition, natural resources, achievement, and even work itself in global markets can be of great assistance. Today firms often provide classes and training for managers and their families on how to adapt to different cultures and avoid culture shock. Involvement in courses in cultural variations and anthropology can assist you in understanding foreign cultures.

Cultural differences affect not only management behaviors but global marketing strategies as well. **Global marketing** is the term used to describe selling the same product in essentially the same way everywhere in the world. Some companies have developed universal (global) appeals. Brand names such as Coca-Cola, Disney, IBM, Ford, and Toyota have widespread global appeal and recognition. Other companies, unfortunately, have hit the hurdles and stumbled. Some past experiences reveal the problems of a global marketing strategy. For example, translating a theme into a different language can be disastrous. To get an idea of the problems companies have faced with translations, take a look at Figure 3.4.

Thousands of similar stories could be told. The truth is that many U.S. companies often fail to think globally. For example, U.S. auto producers often don't adapt automobiles to drive on the left side of the road, as is done in many countries, and they often print instructions only in English. Also, the

┌   FIGURE **3.4**   ┐
· · · ·

OOPS, DID WE SAY THAT?

A global marketing strategy can be very difficult to implement. Look at the problems these well-known companies encountered in global markets.

- Pepsi Cola attempted a Chinese translation of "Come Alive, You're in the Pepsi Generation," that read to Chinese customers as, "Pepsi Brings Your Ancestors Back From the Dead."
- Coor's Brewing Company put its slogan "Turn It Loose," into Spanish and found it translated as "Suffer From Diarrhea."
- Perdue Chicken used the slogan "It Takes a Strong Man to Make a Chicken Tender," that was interpreted in Spanish as "It Takes an Aroused Man to Make a Chicken Affectionate."
- KFC's patented slogan "finger-lickin good," was understood in Japanese as "Bite Your Fingers Off."
- On the other side of the translation glitch, Electrolux, a Scandinavian vacuum manufacturer tried to sell its products in the U.S. market with the slogan "Nothing Sucks Like An Electrolux."

United States is one of only five nations in the world that refuses to conform to the metric system. The problems go on and on. Since global marketing works only in limited cases, it's critical that U.S. exporters thoroughly research their objectives before attempting to penetrate global markets.

••• SOCIETAL AND ECONOMIC DIFFERENCES •••

Certain social and economic realities are often overlooked by American businesses. A sound global philosophy is never to assume that what works in one country will work in another.[23] Take Kids 'R' Us, the clothing subsidiary of Toys 'R' Us, for example. The company missed the mark in Puerto Rico by banking heavily on back-to-school sales. What company planners failed to understand is that Puerto Rican kids all wear uniforms to school. The close association of Puerto Rico to the United States made the company think the market was identical to ours. Turner Broadcasting's Cartoon Network did not make the same mistake. It linked seven of its cartoon characters with the traditional wishes of the Chinese New Year: Droopy Dog for happiness, Popeye for health, Richie Rich for wealth, Captain Planet for prosperity, Penelope Pitstop for style, and Winsome Witch and Scooby Doo for wisdom and luck.[24]

Surely it's hard for us to imagine buying chewing gum by the stick instead of by the package. However, in economically depressed nations like Haiti this buying behavior is commonplace because customers have only enough money to buy small quantities. What might seem like an opportunity of a lifetime may in fact be unreachable due to economic conditions.

Technological constraints may also make it difficult or impossible to carry on effective trade. For example, some less developed countries have such primitive transportation and storage systems that international food exchange is ineffective, because the food is spoiled by the time it reaches those in need. American exporters must also be aware that certain technological differences affect the nature of exportable products. For example, how would the differences in electricity available (110 versus 220 volts) affect an American appliance manufacturer wishing to export?

••• LEGAL AND REGULATORY DIFFERENCES •••

In any economy, the conduct and direction of business is firmly tied to the legal and regulatory environment. In the United States business is heavily impacted by various federal, state, and local laws and regulations. In global markets, several groups of laws and regulations may apply. This makes the task of conducting world business even tougher. What businesspeople find in global markets is a myriad of laws and regulations that are often inconsistent. Important legal questions related to antitrust rules, labor relations, patents, copyrights, trade practices, taxes, product liability, child labor, prison labor, and other issues are written and interpreted differently country by country. To compound problems, American businesspeople are required to follow U.S. laws and regulations in conducting business affairs. For example, some legislation such as the **Foreign Corrupt Practices Act of 1978** can create hardships for American businesspeople in competing with other foreign competitors. This law specifically prohibits "questionable" or "dubious" payments to foreign officials to secure business contracts. In many countries, corporate bribery is acceptable and perhaps the only way to secure a lucrative contract.

Meters, liters, kilograms . . . the metric system is the standard system of measurement used throughout the world; throughout the world, that is, except in the United States. The United States is one of five nations in the world that has not adopted the metric standard as its system of weights and measures. What disadvantages, if any, does this present to companies who export or import goods to the United States?

◄ **CONSIDER USING OT ACETATE 3-10**
Favorite Campbell Soups

◄ **CONSIDER USING LECTURE ENHANCER 3-10**
Japan and Music Copyrights

Foreign Corrupt Practices Act of 1978
Law that prohibits "questionable" or "dubious" payments to foreign officials to secure business contracts.

From the Pages of BusinessWeek

www.europa.eu.int

Merger Mania Rocks the Continent

The offers are coming fast and furious; a proposed $39 billion merger between two consumer-products giants; the proposed merging of two large publishers intended to create one of the world's largest communications groups; multi-billion dollar offers to take over major retail and insurance firms. This was typical of the action on Wall Street in the 1980s when newspapers regularly featured such headlines of U.S. corporate mergers. Well is Wall Street at it again? No, this time it's Europe where mergermania is just beginning.

Europe has historically been a market of divided countries and borders with individual companies prospering in their domestic markets. It was like each country was its own niche where domestic producers ruled the roost. Well that was before the dream of European cooperation finally manifested itself in the establishment of the European Union (EU). Today the new European business vision is a single market, operating under one currency, with a specific set of regulations. The reality of this single market in Europe has companies scrambling to face new business challenges. European managers for example are finding that cutting costs and focusing

on a huge multi-cultural market forces them to think on a European if not a global scale. One way to make the transition to this new market is to consolidate different companies' cultures and strengths by merging them into one firm.

The fear on the continent is as companies join together and consolidate their expertise and resources, some countries will suffer a loss of jobs. Thus far, European managers have mainly involved companies driven by the industrial logic of combining companies in the same business sector with minimal plans of job loss. Still the idea of the unfriendly takeovers and megamergers between firms in different industries hovers as a possibility. Where is the merger action in Europe likely to be? Banks, auto parts manufacturers, small, regional food companies, maybe even a major Continental carmaker like Mercedes or BMW could get swept into the flurry. Mergermania is just the beginning of how the EU is going to change the way Europe does business.

Source: John Rossant, "Why Merger Mania is Rocking the Continent," *Business Week*, October 27, 1997, p. 64.

To be a successful trader in foreign countries, it's often important to contact local businesspeople in other countries and gain their cooperation and sponsorship. Since foreign bureaucracies are often stumbling blocks to successful international trade, local businesspeople can help to penetrate those barriers. In some situations you must find a local sponsor who can pay the necessary fees to gain government permission to conduct business.

••• PROBLEMS WITH CURRENCY SHIFTS •••

> **CONSIDER USING CRITICAL THINKING EXERCISE 3-1**
> Currency Shifts (**SCANS**)

The global market does not have a universal currency. Mexicans shop with pesos, Germans with deutsche marks, South Koreans with won, the British with pounds, and Americans with dollars. Globally, the U.S. dollar is considered the world's dominant and most stable form of currency. This doesn't mean, however, that the dollar always retains the same value.

exchange rate
The value of one currency relative to the currencies of other countries.

For example, today one dollar may be exchanged for 3 deutsche marks, but tomorrow you may only get 2.5 marks for your dollar. The **exchange rate** is the value of one nation's currency relative to the currencies of other countries. Changes in a nation's exchange rates can have important implications in global markets. For example, a *high value of the dollar* means that a dollar would be traded for more foreign currency than normal. The products of foreign pro-

Making Ethical Decisions

http://www.letlink.co.uk

Deciding the Fate of Nightie Nite's Nightgowns

As a top manager of Nightie Nite, a maker of children's sleepwear, you are aware of all the U.S. government regulations that affect your industry. A recently passed safety regulation prohibits the use of the fabric that you have been using for young girls' nightgowns for the past 15 years. Apparently the fabric does not have sufficient flame-retardant capabilities to meet U.S. government standards. In fact, last week Nightie Nite lost a lawsuit brought against it by the parents of a young child severely burned because the nightgown she was wearing burst into flames when she ventured too close to a gas stove. Not only did you lose the lawsuit, but you may also lose your nightshirt if you don't find another market for the warehouse full of nightgowns you have in inventory. You realize that some countries do not have such restrictive laws concerning products sold within their borders. You are considering exporting your inventory of products barred in the United States to these countries. What are your alternatives? What are the consequences of each alternative? What will you do?

▲ SCANS

ducers would become cheaper because it takes fewer dollars to buy them. The cost of U.S.-produced goods, however, would become more expensive to foreign purchasers because of the dollar's high value. Lowering the value of the dollar means that a dollar is traded for less foreign currency than normal. Therefore, foreign goods become more expensive because it takes more dollars to buy them. It also makes American goods cheaper to foreign buyers because it takes less foreign currency to buy American goods. Global markets operate under a system called **floating exchange rates**, in which currencies "float" according to the supply and demand in the market for the currency. This supply and demand for currencies is created by global currency traders that create a market for a nation's currency based on the perceived trade and investment potential of the country. At certain times, however, countries themselves will intervene and adjust the value of their currencies. Both Mexico and Japan devalued their currencies in the mid-1990s. **Devaluation** is lowering the value of a nation's currency relative to other currencies.

Changes in currency values cause many problems. Consider a company like Nestlé, which has factories in 74 countries. Labor costs can vary considerably as currency values shift. The H. B. Fuller Company has 43 plants in 27 foreign countries making paints, adhesives, and coatings. Mr. Fuller feels that the most dramatic problem he faces is in the currency area, "since you can't control currency, you must learn to control your business." Mr. Fuller now uses currency fluctuations to his advantage by buying raw materials from sources with currencies lowered in value.

Understanding currency fluctuations and financing opportunities is vital to success in the global market. Banks traditionally have led the way in financing export operations in the United States. However, American banks are not always willing to provide export financing, and U.S. exporters have to turn to foreign banks and other sources for financing. This is often especially true for small and medium-sized businesses (companies with under 500 employees with revenues less than $25 million) that lack the size and stature of large corporations. These companies must be creative and scour the globe for financing. Fortunately, a growing number of U.S. government, multilateral, and interregional agencies are available to provide financing. (A partial list of these organizations is included in Figure 3.5).

floating exchange rate
Value of currencies that fluctuate according to the supply and demand in the market for the currency.

devaluation
Lowering the value of a nation's currency relative to other currencies.

FIGURE **3.5**

• • • •

U.S. GOVERNMENT,
MULTILATERAL, AND
INTRAREGIONAL
SOURCES OF GLOBAL
FINANCING

➤ **CONSIDER USING TM 26**
U.S. Government, Multilateral, and
Interregional Sources of Global Financing
(Figure 3.5 on text page 88)

➤ **LEARNING GOAL 6.**
Debate the advantages and disadvantages of trade protectionism.

Export-Import Bank   This bank makes loans to exporters that can't secure financing through private sources and to foreign countries that use the funds to buy American goods.

International Finance Corporation (IFC)   This organization makes loans to private businesses when they can't obtain loans from more conventional sources. It's affiliated with the World Bank.

International Development Association (IDA)   This organization makes loans to private businesses and to member countries of the World Bank.

Inter-American Investment Corporation (IIC)   This organization operates as an autonomous merchant banking corporation that will give preference to small and midsized companies that wish to expand.

European Bank for Reconstruction and Development   Based in London, this bank has a mandate to devote 60 percent of its investment activity to private-sector loans.

Overseas Private Investment Corporation   This organization sells insurance to U.S. firms that operate overseas. It covers damages caused by war, revolution, or insurrection; inability to convert local currencies to U.S. dollars; and expropriation (takeover by foreign governments).

 Critical Thinking

Many countries in the world are called less-developed countries. Why are they less developed? Is it because they lack natural resources? Then how do you explain the success of Japan, which has few natural resources?

trade protectionism
The use of government regulations to limit the import of goods and services; based on the theory that domestic producers can survive and grow, producing more jobs.

•••• ▬▬▬ ••••

TRADE PROTECTIONISM

Trade protectionism is the use of government regulations to limit the import of goods and services. Countries often use trade protectionist measures to protect their industries against dumping and foreign competition that hurts domestic industry. Protectionism is based on the theory that such practices will help domestic producers survive and grow, producing more jobs. Generally, it is not a good idea. As we said in the previous section, cultural differences, societal and economic factors, legal and regulatory requirements, and currency shifts are all hurdles to those wishing to trade globally. What is often a much greater barrier to international trade is the overall political atmosphere between

Filling up with premium might get you the same grade of gasoline throughout the world, but it's not going to cost the same price market by market. Taxes and the availability of the product are major reasons gasoline prices can vary in foreign markets. Currency valuation can also make the price of a product like Mobil's gasoline fluctuate for consumers in foreign countries. For example, if the value of the U.S. dollar is high, the cost of gasoline in a station such as this will be lower than you might expect. The opposite is true if the dollar is lower in relation to another nation's currency.

nations. This barrier is best understood through a review of some economic history of world trade.

Business, economics, and politics have always been closely linked. In fact, economics was once referred to as "political economy," indicating the close ties between politics (government) and economics. For centuries, businesspeople have tried to influence economists and government officials. Back in the 16th, 17th, and 18th centuries, nations were trading goods (mostly farm products) with one another. Businesspeople at that time advocated an economic principle called mercantilism. Basically, the idea of **mercantilism** was to sell more goods to other nations than you bought from them, that is, to have a favorable balance of trade. This results in a flow of money to the country that sells the most. Governments assisted in this process by charging a tariff (basically a tax) on imports, making imported goods more expensive.

There are two different kinds of tariffs: protective and revenue. **Protective tariffs** are designed to raise the retail price of imported products so that domestic goods will be more competitive. These tariffs are meant to save jobs for domestic workers and to keep industries from closing down entirely because of foreign competition. **Revenue tariffs**, on the other hand, are designed to raise money for the government. Revenue tariffs are commonly used by developing countries. Today there is still considerable debate about the degree of protectionism a government should practice.

Import quotas limit the number of products in certain categories that can be imported into a nation. The United States has import quotas on a number of products, such as beef, sugar, and steel. Again, the goal is to protect industry in order to preserve jobs. An **embargo** is a complete ban on the import or export of a certain product. The ban on the sale of Cuban cigars and the ban on imports of Iraqi oil into the United States are examples. The United States also prohibits the export of some products. The Export Administration Act prohibits the exporting of goods that would endanger national security. Political considerations have caused many countries to establish embargoes.

Nontariff barriers are not as specific as tariffs and embargoes but can be just as detrimental to free trade. Countries will even set restrictive standards that detail exactly how a product must be sold in a country. For example, in Denmark, butter must be sold in cubes not tubs. J. W. Kisling, chairman of Multiplex Company, a maker of beverage-dispensing equipment with offices in Germany, France, Taiwan, England, and Canada, feels that a good deal of trade is stifled by nontariff barriers such as ISO (International Organization for Standardization) requirements ➤ P. 19 ◀. James Thwaits, president of international operations of the 3M Company, concurs and goes so far as to state that as much as half of all trade is limited by *nontariff barriers*. For instance, Japan has some of the lowest tariffs in the world, yet American businesses find it difficult to establish trade relationships with the Japanese. Even foreign companies offering high-quality products and services have difficulty penetrating Japanese markets because of the Japanese tradition of forging semipermanent ties with suppliers, customers, and distributors. Often this is done through a Keiretsu, which is a close knit group of Japanese companies within an industry.[25] The Japanese believe that stable alliances provide economic payoffs by nurturing long-term strategic thinking and mutually beneficial cooperation. Hence imported goods have been blocked from the market. The U.S. government has investigated such practices and once threatened a possible trade war with Japan over these restrictions.

In Japan, the price charged by rice farmers is protected by the government through import quotas that limit the amount of foreign rice that can be imported into the country. The United States has protested such trade actions in Japan and insists that exporting to the Japanese market is hindered by both tariff and nontariff barriers. Do you know of any U.S. products protected by import quotas?

mercantilism
The economic principle advocating the selling of more goods to other nations than a country purchases.

protective tariff
Import tax designed to raise the price of imported products so that domestic products are more competitive.

revenue tariff
Import tax designed to raise money for the government.

import quota
Limiting the number of products in certain categories that can be imported.

embargo
A complete ban on the import or export of certain products.

General Agreement on Tariffs and Trade (GATT)
Agreement among 124 countries which provided a forum for negotiating mutual reductions in trade restrictions.

World Trade Organization (WTO)
Replaced the GATT agreement and was assigned the duty to mediate.

common market
A regional group of countries that have no internal tariffs, a common external tariff, and a coordination of laws to facilitate exchange; an example is the European Union.

The European Union (EU) is a common market dedicated to dismantling economic borders in Europe early in the next century. In doing so the EU will become a market larger than the United States in both population and GDP. But its ambitions do not stop there. The European Monetary Union hopes to put currencies such as the French franc, Italian lira, British pound sterling, and other member currencies to pasture by 2002 and replace them with a new currency called the euro. Take a close look at this currency; some economists predict the euro may replace the dollar as the dominant medium of exchange in global markets.

Such constraints could be viewed as good reasons to avoid world trade. But these same constraints could also be viewed as a tremendous opportunity. The General Agreement on Tariffs and Trade (GATT) was established to deal with such trade questions. Let's look at the issues involved in the GATT agreement and establishment of the World Trade Organization (WTO).

••• GENERAL AGREEMENT ON TARIFFS ••• AND TRADE (GATT) AND WTO

In 1948, the **General Agreement on Tariffs and Trade (GATT)** was established. This agreement among 23 countries provided a forum for negotiating mutual reductions in trade restrictions. In short, government leaders from nations throughout the world have cooperated to create monetary and trade agreements that facilitate the exchange of goods, services, ideas, and cultural programs. In 1986, the Uruguay Round of GATT talks was convened to renegotiate trade agreements. After eight years of meetings, 124 nations agreed to a new GATT agreement. The U.S. House of Representatives and Senate approved the pact in 1994. The new GATT agreement lowers tariffs on average by 38 percent worldwide, and also extends GATT rules to new areas such as agriculture, services, and the protection of patents. On January 1, 1995, the **World Trade Organization (WTO)**, headquartered in Geneva, Switzerland, replaced GATT and assumed the primary task of mediating trade disputes. As an independent institution, the WTO has authority over key cross-border trade issues and global business practices.[26] The WTO is the first attempt at establishing a truly global mediation center where trade issues can be resolved within a period of 18 months instead of languishing for years.

Before you get too excited though, it's important to note the GATT agreement did not resolve many of the internal national laws that impede trade expansion. For example, critical areas such as intellectual property (trademarks and copyrights), and financial services were not addressed. The GATT's achievements were impressive, and the expectations of the WTO are admirable but many problems will remain.

••• COMMON MARKETS •••

One of the issues not resolved by the GATT talks is the concern that regional agreements such as NAFTA and common markets such as the European Union (EU) will create regional alliances at the expense of global expansion. A **common market** is a regional group of countries that have no internal tariffs, a common external tariff, and the coordination of laws to facilitate exchange among countries.

As mentioned in Chapter 1, the EU is a group of nations in Europe that dissolved their economic borders in the early 1990s. Europe expects to become a vast $8.4 trillion market of some 320 million people who trade freely and live and work where they please. Europeans see such integration as the only way to compete with the United States and Japan for world markets.

The path to unification has been slow and difficult, yet significant progress has been made. The European Monetary Union (EMU) even hopes to have a new currency, "the euro," in place by 2002. If this happens, francs, marks, guilders, and possibly even lire and pesetas will be supplanted by this new currency.[27] C. Fred Bergsten,

To Tariff or Not to Tariff

Some feel that tariffs are necessary to protect national markets from foreign competition. Some of the arguments they use are as follows:

- Tariffs save jobs. Tariffs should be used to keep cheap foreign labor from taking over American jobs.
- Tariffs are imposed on the United States by its competitors. To make competition fair we have to take mutual measures.
- Tariffs protect industries (automobiles, aerospace, and shipbuilding) vital to a nation's security and are needed for defense.
- Tariffs protect new domestic industries from established foreign competition (often called the infant-industry argument).

Critics of tariff policies argue:

- Tariffs reduce competition and restrain international trade.
- Tariffs increase inflationary pressure, raise consumer prices, and stimulate inflation.
- Tariffs support special-interest groups such as local manufacturers.
- Tariffs lead to foreign retaliation and subsequent trade wars.

Debates over tariffs and trade restrictions are a major part of international politics. Help yourself by staying current on this issue, because the future of global trade may very well depend on them.

director of the Washington-based Institute for International Economics, has even suggested the euro could replace the dollar as the dominant international monetary unit.[28]

However, the idea of free movement of labor, shared social programs, new and strange tax systems, a new currency, and shared professional standards is rather scary to countries that historically are more used to fighting with one another than working as an economic unit. The leaders of the EU counter that shared economic interests are the best way to keep the peace.

One advantage for Americans is that English has become Europe's common business language. Some American observers, however, fear that a European protectionist state may emerge. Early signs have not justified those fears.

◄ **CONSIDER USING CRITICAL THINKING EXERCISE 3-2**
Trade Protectionism (**SCANS**)

◄ **CONSIDER USING OT ACETATE 3-11**
Who's Got the Worst Reputation Globally?

••• THE NORTH AMERICAN FREE •••
TRADE AGREEMENT (NAFTA)

One of the most debated issues of the early 1990s was the **North American Free Trade Agreement (NAFTA)**, which was discussed briefly in Chapter 1. Opponents, led primarily by organized labor and billionaire Ross Perot, promised nothing short of economic disaster if the U.S. Congress passed this treaty. The primary questions surrounded the issues of U.S. employment, exports, and the environment. Perot and organized labor predicted a "giant sucking sound" of jobs and capital leaving the United States. In contrast, NAFTA proponents forecast a vast new market for exports that would create jobs and opportunities in the long term. After NAFTA's passage in the Congress, President Clinton signed the treaty into law and the combination of the United States, Canada, and Mexico created a market of over 370 million people with a gross domestic product of $7.2 trillion.[29]

North American Free Trade Agreement (NAFTA)
An agreement through which the United States, Canada, and Mexico formed a free trade area.

◄ **CONSIDER USING LECTURE ENHANCER 3-11**
Vintage NAFTA

free-trade area
Market in which nations can trade freely without tariffs or other trade barriers.

NAFTA creates a **free-trade area** where nations can lower trade barriers with each other while maintaining independent trade agreements with non-member countries. Since 1994, NAFTA has experienced both success and difficulties. Two-way trade between the United States and Mexico has grown 23 percent, but the devaluation of the Mexican peso in 1995 forced the United States to commit $30 billion in aid to Mexico. Also, while all sides agree that trade among the member nations will likely grow over the next five years, concerns persist involving job loss and creation, child labor law violations, environmental concerns, and the long-term strength of the peso.[30] The debate begun in the early 1990s concerning NAFTA is far from being resolved.

Still, the certainty of the emergence of economic blocs like NAFTA has changed the landscape of global trade. Some observers have even suggested expansion of NAFTA into a Free Trade Area of the Americas by the year 2005 or even a Transatlantic Free Trade Area in union with the European Union. Such suggestions have global economists concerned that as the world divides itself into certain major trading blocs, poorer countries that don't fit into one of the blocs will suffer.

Progress Check

- What are the major hurdles to successful global trade?
- What exactly is meant by ethnocentricity?
- Identify at least two cultural and societal differences that can affect global trade efforts.
- What are the advantages and disadvantages of trade protectionism? Of tariffs?

MULTINATIONAL CORPORATIONS

multinational corporation
An organization that manufactures and markets in many different countries and has multinational stock ownership and multinational management.

There has been much discussion about the power of multinational corporations such as General Motors and Royal Dutch Shell. It may be hard to imagine but the annual sales of these two multinational companies are larger than the gross domestic products of nations such as Pakistan, Venezuela, and Turkey. It is helpful to first understand what they are and what they mean for global business. A **multinational corporation (MNC)** is an organization that does manufacturing and marketing in many different countries; it has multinational stock ownership and multinational management. The more multinational a company is, the more it attempts to operate without being influenced by restrictions from various governments. Multinational corporations are typically extremely large corporations, but caution should be exercised before calling any large company multinational. Not all firms involved in global business are multinationals. A business could be exporting everything it produces, thus deriving 100 percent of its sales and profits globally, but that alone would not make it a multinational. Only firms that have manufacturing capacity or some other physical presence in various nations can be called multinational.

THE FUTURE OF GLOBAL TRADE

Global trade grows more interesting each day. New and expanding markets present new opportunities for trade and development. Nowhere is this more true than in the emerging nations in Asia, particularly the People's Republic of China.

China is the world's most populous country, with more than 1.2 billion people; it also has the world's fastest-growing economy.[31] Some economists go as far as to predict that in the next 20 years, China's economy will overtake that of the United States. John Naisbitt, author of *Megatrends Asia,* makes it clear that Asia, and especially China, is where Western nations should set their sights if they wish to prosper in the new millennium. This is obviously the reason General Motors recently invested $1.6 billion to build a new plant in Shanghai; the company expects car sales to increase by 20 percent annually through 2000 and to reach 3 million within a decade.[32] Coca-Cola has invested $550 million in China and plans to have 23 bottling plants by the end of 1997. The company plans to hit $1 billion in sales by 2000.[33] Just a few years ago, such

investment potential in China was considered to be too risky and not worth the effort. Today U.S. companies are flocking to China and are obviously eager to trade with the Chinese.

However, concerns remain about China's one-party political system, its human-rights policies, the growing trade imbalance, and the repatriation of Hong Kong, which became a part of China on July 1, 1997. Some members of the U.S. Congress have even proposed removing China's most-favored-nation (MFN) status, a distinction granted that permits a country to take advantage of relatively low import duties. To date this has not happened.

Since the fall of Communism, Russia has been a prize coveted by many global traders. Like China, Russia presents enormous opportunities. Philip Morris, RJR Nabisco, Coca-Cola, Bristol-Myers, and Gillette are firms that have established manufacturing facilities in Russia. Despite the many political and social problems still present, firms are clearly attracted by Russia's 150 million potential customers, who are craving Western goods.

Though China, Japan, and Russia attract most of the attention in Asia, U.S. businesses should not forget the rest of the continent. Taiwan is now the 13th largest trading nation in the world.[34] The U.S. decision to resume trade with Vietnam presents another opportunity for global expansion. Add India, Indonesia, Thailand, Singapore, the Philippines, Korea, and Malaysia to the growing list of emerging markets in Asia, and it's easy to see the great potential the Asian market holds for U.S. business, and for you. However, difficulties in the financial markets in Asia in late 1997 reminded businesses that this is still an area of the world with high risk.[35]

··· GLOBALIZATION AND YOU ···

Whether you aspire to be future entrepreneurs, managers, or business leaders, you must now think globally as you plan your career. As this chapter points out, global markets are huge and overflowing with opportunity. By studying foreign languages, learning about foreign cultures, and taking business courses you can develop a global perspective on your future. The potential of global markets does not belong only to the multinational corporations. Small businesses are often better prepared to take the leap into global markets than are large, cumbersome corporations saddled with bureaucracies. Also, don't forget the potential of franchising which we will examine in Chapter 5.

Can you hear it? It's the giant sucking sound predicted by H. Ross Perot if the U.S. Congress approved the North American Free Trade Agreement. Well, the debate continues about the results of NAFTA since it was approved by the government in 1994. Here, organized labor relays its position concerning the trade agreement. The issue of NAFTA is certain to be on the front burner in the future as proponents vow to expand the scope of the treaty and opponents promise a battle to the bitter end. Stay tuned!

◄ **LEARNING GOAL 7.**
Discuss the role of multinational corporations in global markets.

◄ **CONSIDER USING OT ACETATE 3-12**
Familiar Multinational Companies

◄ **CONSIDER USING OT ACETATE 3-13**
What's the Second Most Valuable Language in Global Business?

Spotlight on Small Business

http://msm.byu.edu/programs/mba/

Utah's Economy Goes Global

Can you name a state with explosive growth in global trade, lots of foreign-language-speaking citizens, and an emerging breed of global entrepreneurs? Bet you didn't answer Utah! After all, Utah has a population of only 1.9 million and is hundreds of miles away from the closest seaport. Still, Utah is booming—and a good deal of its growth is in global trade, thanks in many ways to the influence of the Mormon faith.

For over 100 years the Mormon Church has been sending young people overseas for a two-year mission. Many stay on in foreign countries and capitalize on the language skills and contacts they develop. Others return home and do the same thing. Kent Derricott left on a mission to Japan 20 years ago. During those years, in addition to his mission work, he has been a TV commentator, a cable TV infomercial pitchman, and a documentary producer in Japan. Vaun Andrus also did his mission in Japan in the 1970s. He returned home to advise Japanese banks about U.S. investments and real estate. Now ▲

back in Utah, he has developed a home shopping network that reaches into Japan. At Evans & Sutherland Computer Company near the University of Utah, a bevy of Mormon missionaries speak Mandarin with the Taiwanese air force and Hebrew with Israeli businesspeople. In fact 30 percent of the people in Utah speak a foreign language. At Brigham Young University, as many as 75 percent of its MBA students are bilingual. This advantage has created a competitive edge for many businesses in Utah.

Utah is benefiting as many of its young people learn foreign languages and build cultural and societal awareness on their missions. It should be the mission of entrepreneurs in other states to follow this lead as they approach global markets.

Source: Bernard Wysocki, "Utah's Economy Goes Global, Thanks in Part to Role of Missionaries," *The Wall Street Journal*, March 28, 1996, pp. A1–A6.

Progress Check

> **LECTURE ENHANCER 3-12**
> Web Watch: Big Emerging Markets

- What is a multinational corporation (MNC)? Can you name at least three multinational corporations?
- What are the major risks of doing business in countries like the People's Republic of China or Russia?
- What might be some important factors that will have an impact on global trading?

SUMMARY
• • • • •

1. Discuss the increasing importance of the global market and the roles of comparative advantage and absolute advantage in international trade.

1. The world market for trade is huge. Some 95 percent of the people in the world live outside the United States.
   - ***Why should nations trade with other nations?***
   (1) No country is self-sufficient, (2) other countries need products that prosperous countries produce, and (3) there is a world imbalance of natural resources and technological skills.
   - ***What is the theory of comparative advantage?***
   The theory of comparative advantage contends that a country should produce and then sell those products it produces most efficiently but buy those it cannot produce as efficiently.
   - ***What is absolute advantage?***
   Absolute advantage means that a country has a monopoly on a certain product or can produce the product more efficiently than any other country can. There are few examples of absolute advantage.

2. Students can get involved in world trade through importing and exporting. They do not have to work for big multinational corporations.
   - **What kinds of products can be imported and exported?**
   Just about any kind of product can be imported and exported. The most important thing for a potential importer or exporter to remember is to find a need and fill it.
   - **What terms are important in understanding world trade?**
   Exporting is selling products to other countries. Importing is buying products from other countries. The balance of trade is the relationship of exports to imports. The balance of payments is the balance of trade plus other money flows such as tourism and foreign aid. Dumping is selling products for less in a foreign country than in your own country. Trade protectionism is the use of government regulations to limit the importation of products. See other terms on the Key Terms list at the end of this chapter to be sure you know the important ones.

   2. Explain how the marketing motto "Find a need and fill it" applies to global markets, and understand key terms used in international business.

3. It was widely reported during the late 1980s and early 1990s that the United States was a "debtor nation." In fact, it was called the largest debtor nation in the world. However, the United States was attracting a good deal of foreign direct investment. The United States was never in the gloomy position many claimed. Its market was perceived by other nations as being more lucrative and attractive for investment.
   - **What's the best way to look at debt figures in global markets?**
   The best way to determine whether or not a nation is a net debtor is to look at income flows among nations. When income from foreign investments exceeds outgo, a nation is not likely a debtor. Also, if direct foreign investment is growing, the nation may show a debt position but the market is perceived as viable for foreign investment.

   3. Describe the current status of the United States in global business.

4. A company can participate in world trade in a number of ways.
   - **What are some ways in which a company can get involved in international business?**
   Ways of entering world trade include exporting, licensing, creating subsidiaries, contract manufacturing, franchising, international joint ventures, and countertrading.

   4. Illustrate the strategies used in reaching global markets.

5. There are many restrictions on foreign trade.
   - **What are some of the hurdles that can discourage participation in international business?**
   Potential stumbling blocks to world trade include cultural differences, societal and economic differences, legal and regulatory differences, and fluctuations in different currencies.

   5. Evaluate the hurdles of trading in world markets.

6. Political differences are often the most difficult hurdles to international trade.
   - **What is trade protectionism?**
   Trade protectionism is the use of government regulations to limit the import of goods and services, based on the theory that domestic producers can survive and grow, producing more jobs. The tools of protectionism are tariffs, import quotas, and embargoes.
   - **What are tariffs?**
   Tariffs are taxes on foreign products. There are two kinds of tariffs: protective tariffs, which are used to raise the price of foreign products, and revenue tariffs, which are used to raise money for the government.
   - **What is an embargo?**
   An embargo prohibits the importing or exporting of certain products.

   6. Debate the advantages and disadvantages of trade protectionism.

> • *Is trade protectionism good for domestic producers?*
> That is debatable. Trade protectionism hurt the United States badly during the Great Depression because other countries responded to U.S. tariffs with tariffs of their own.
> • *Why do governments continue such practices?*
> The theory of mercantilism started the practice of trade protectionism and it has persisted, in a lesser form, ever since.

7. Explain the role of multinational corporations in global markets.

7. Multinational corporations have a huge impact on world trade.
   • *How do multinational corporations differ from other companies that participate in international business?*
   Unlike other companies that are involved in exporting or importing, multinational corporations also have manufacturing facilities or other types of physical presence in various nations.

KEY TERMS
......

absolute advantage 75
balance of payments 77
balance of trade 77
bartering 82
common market 90
comparative advantage theory 74
contract manufacturing 81
countertrading 82
debtor nation 79
devaluation 87
dumping 78
embargo 89
ethnocentricity 83
exchange rate 86
Export Assistance Centers (EACs) 80

export trading companies 80
exporting 74
floating exchange rates 87
Foreign Corrupt Practices Act of 1978 85
foreign direct investment 79
foreign subsidiary 81
free trade 74
free-trade area 92
General Agreement on Tariffs and Trade (GATT) 90
global marketing 84
import quota 89
importing 74

International Organization for Standardization (ISO) 89
joint venture 82
licensing 80
mercantilism 89
multinational corporation (MNC) 92
North American Free Trade Agreement (NAFTA) 91
protective tariff 89
revenue tariff 89
trade deficit 77
trade protectionism 88
World Trade Organization 90

DEVELOPING WORKPLACE SKILLS

1. Visit an Oriental rug dealer or some other importer of foreign goods. Talk with the owner/manager about the problems and joys of being involved in international trade. Compile a list of advantages and disadvantages. Then get together with others in the class and compare notes.

2. Using a computer word-processing program, write a short essay describing the benefits and disadvantages of trade protectionism. Have your class divide into two sides and debate this issue: "Resolved: that the United States should increase trade protection to save American jobs and American companies."

3. Many U.S. firms have made embarrassing mistakes when trying to sell products overseas. Sometimes the product is not adapted to the needs of the country, sometimes the advertising makes no sense, sometimes the color or packaging is wrong, and so forth. Discuss the steps U.S. businesses

should follow to be more responsive to the needs of foreign markets. Discuss your list with others, and together form a plan for improving U.S. trade overseas.

4. I. M. Windy is a candidate for the U.S. House of Representatives from your district. He just delivered an excellent speech at your college. He spoke at great length on the topic of tariffs. His major arguments were that we need tariffs to

a. Provide revenues.

b. Protect our young industries.

c. Encourage Americans to buy U.S.-made products because it is patriotic.

d. Keep us militarily strong.

e. Protect American workers and wages.

f. Help us maintain a favorable balance of trade.

g. Create a favorable balance of payments.

Do you agree with Mr. Windy? Evaluate each of the candidate's major points by indicating whether you consider it valid or invalid. Justify your position.

5. Many U.S. firms have made embarrassing mistakes when trying to sell products in global markets. Sometimes the product is not adapted to the needs of the host nation, sometimes the advertising makes no sense, sometimes the product color is wrong, and so forth. Discuss the steps U.S. businesses should follow to be more responsive to the needs of foreign markets. Discuss your list with other class members, and together form a plan for improving U.S. trade practices.

TAKING IT TO THE NET

Purpose of this exercise: To compare the shifting exchange rates of various countries and to predict the effects of such exchange shifts on international trade.

Questions

One of the difficulties of engaging in international trade is the constant shift in exchange rates. How much do exchange rates change over a 30-day period? Research this by choosing five countries and recording the exchange rate for the currency of each (Austria's schilling, Italy's lira, Japan's yen, Mexico's peso, etc.) for 30 days. The rates are available on the Internet at www.washingtonpost.com/wp-srv/business/longterm/stocks/currency.htm. Chart the amount of foreign currency per dollar. What effect would these currency shifts have on your company's trade with each of these countries?

Practicing Management Decisions

No topic in this chapter generates more differing opinions than that of trade protectionism. In fact, in the presidential election of 1996, protectionism was a hotly debated subject and NAFTA was again in the headlines. Underdog Republican candidate Pat Buchanan won the New Hampshire primary

CASE
• • • • •
PROTECTING OR RISKING YOUR FUTURE
• • • • •

and several party caucuses by focusing on this issue. Stories in newspapers and commentators on television began referring again to "Smoot-Hawley." The question many began to ask was, "What is Smoot-Hawley and why does this term appear ever so often?" Some history may help clarify the issue.

The date: June 13, 1930 (Friday the 13th). The time: 2:13 P.M. The place: the U.S. Senate. The Great Depression had started, and the air was full of talk about trade protection. Over 1,000 economists warned the government that protectionism was dangerous and petitioned it not to pass the Smoot-Hawley Act. (Hawley was a professor of economics at Willamette University. Smoot was a banker and wool manufacturer.) But, by a vote of 44 to 42, the bill passed. It was an act conceived by Republican congressmen, passed by a Republican Congress, and signed into law by conservative Republican President Herbert Hoover.

The act imposed duties of up to 60 percent on almost everything imported into the United States. The concept was to protect the western beet sugar farmer by raising the duty for sugar; protect the northwestern wheat farmer by raising the duty on wheat; and protect the Imperial Valley cotton farmer by raising the duty on cotton from Egypt. The list continued: cattle and dairy products, hides, shoes, velvet, silk, china, pocket knives, watch parts, and so on.

The result was that world trade fell by one-third, and a global trade war started. Exports dropped from $4.8 billion to $1.7 billion from 1929 to 1932. Imports dropped from $5.4 billion to $2.4 billion. Other countries were plunged into depression also as world trade fell. In 1934, Congress passed the Reciprocal Trade Agreement Act to reduce tariffs, but the effort was too little, too late.

The issue of world trade regulation continued. Years after Smoot-Hawley, from 1987 until 1993, the GATT discussions often reached impasse points or stalemates. A collapse of the negotiations would have actually pleased protectionists. Instead, the GATT agreement was passed by 124 nations in 1994. Still, the growth of several key trading blocs such as NAFTA and the EU raised the fear that a new wave of protectionism might surface. These trading blocs allow for free trade among nations in the same trading bloc, but may lead to greater protectionist legislation and less free trade between nations in competing trading blocs. Many wonder if Smoot-Hawley is lifting its head again.

Decision Questions

1. Why do you suppose some politicians are pushing for trade protection? What are the economic conditions that would call for protectionism?
2. Is there a lesson to be learned from the early 1930s concerning restrictive legislation on world trade? What forces could cause Congress to reverse itself on this issue?
3. What should the role of the U.S. government be with regard to world trade? How much effort should be made to protect American workers from foreign competition? When should such efforts take effect?

Source: Louis S. Richman, "What's Next after GATT's Victory?" *Fortune*, January 10, 1994, pp. 66–71; Tim Lang, "The New Protectionism: Global Trade Rules Protect Corporations," *The Nation*, July 15, 1996, p. 29; and John McGinnis, "Restraining Leviathan: If Free Trade Is Federalism's Heir, Protectionism Is the Best Way to Ensure a Future for Big Government," *National Review*, March 11, 1996, p. 40.

Coca-Cola and Pepsi are major competitors throughout the world as well as in the United States. When it comes to Japan, however, Coke is the clear winner. Why? The sale of soft drinks in Japan began on military bases after WWII. However, the rapid growth stage didn't begin until 1957 when a Japanese businessperson bought a license to manufacture Coke in Japan.

What made Coke a success in Japan over time was its willingness to partner with local businesspeople. Rather than simply being a multinational firm, Coke was successful in becoming a multilocal firm. That is, it found partners in various cities and worked closely with them to develop sales in those areas.

VIDEO CASE
• • • • • •
SELLING COCA-COLA IN JAPAN

As many U.S. firms have found, it wasn't easy to break into the Japanese market. For one thing, Coke wanted to sell directly to retailers. That simply was not—and *is* not—the tradition in Japan. The tradition is to sell through a whole series of middlemen that control the distribution.

When trying to sell in a different country, it is fundamentally important to adapt as much as possible to the local culture. Coca-Cola did that by setting up in-house social clubs like those in other Japanese firms. It also helped employees buy homes with low-interest loans. Every effort was made to adjust to the tastes of the local people, including the creation of a 50 percent juice drink.

Relationship marketing is especially important in Japan, where negotiations take time, and patience is truly a virtue. Consensus building is the norm, and that requires more time than U.S. firms are used to investing. Nonetheless, the payoff can be extraordinary. For example, Coke has approximately 1,000,000 dealers and 700,000 vending machines in Japan as a result of its patience and care in establishing local relationships.

Pepsi, on the other hand, remains a minor competitor due to its failure to invest the time necessary to establish local partners and relationships. Consequently, Pepsi's market penetration in Japan continues to be hindered and shallow.

Discussion Questions

1. What evidence can you cite showing that foreign firms have been very careful to adapt to U.S. culture when marketing their products here?

2. Many U.S. firms have had difficulty establishing relationships in Japan. Do you think that they could learn from Coke's experience and try again? Would a similar approach work for U.S. automakers?

3. Talk with a local storeowner or manager who sells products from various parts of the world. Ask him or her what foreign manufacturers do to establish and maintain good relationships with that store and its suppliers.

Demonstrating Ethical Behavior and Social Responsibility

Chapter 4

LEARNING GOALS

After you have read and studied this chapter, you should be able to

1 Explain why legality is only the first step in behaving ethically.

2 Ask the three questions one should answer when faced with a potentially unethical action.

3 Describe management's role in setting ethical standards.

4 Distinguish between compliance-based and integrity-based ethics codes and list the six steps in setting up a corporate ethics code.

5 Define social responsibility and examine corporate responsibility to various stakeholders.

6 Analyze the role of American businesses in influencing ethical and social responsibility in global markets.

"I don't have to look too far to find heroes. I just look around my factories, and I see people who wanted to change and people who helped them," Nancy Bierk confides. Bierk owns Ad Impressions, a company that makes festive garters for theme parks and restaurants, and Logo Masters, a factory that makes T-shirts.

"My greatest asset is my people. They are a very special group," boasts Bierk. What makes them special? For one thing Nancy hires people few other managers would even consider hiring. Some are ex-convicts and others are former alcoholics or drug users. Some are from war-torn countries and are struggling to learn English and to fit into a new culture. Many are women. "I hired women who had been told they were worthless, women whose husbands had walked out on them after 30 years of marriage, women who had been on welfare for years," Bierk says.

Bierk says the employee who taught her the most was a former drug dealer who spent 15 of his 29 years in jail. "I learned from him about the society inside our society, a society that does not look to the rest of us for direction or control," said Bierk. "I also learned that the lives of many young African-American men were being wasted."

Bierk pairs some of those young men with immigrants from Russia and Bosnia and tells all of them they will find guidance at work. Someday they will serve as mentors to others in the workplace and in their communities.

"You can make money and help people too," declares Bierk. Bierk is not alone in her declaration. A growing number of business executives realize that a social vision can also mean big profits. In 1997, President Bill Clinton presented the Business Enterprise Award, a corporate social responsibility award, to Olmec Toys, seller of millions of dollars' worth of ethnic dolls. Awards were also presented to Donna Klein, the work life director at Marriott Hotels; McCay Nursery, for allowing migrant workers to share in profits; Motorola Inc., for paying more than $160 million to train employees; and Max De Pree, of furniture maker Herman Miller Inc., for sharing company gains with employees.

In this chapter we will explore the moral and ethical responsibilities of businesspeople. This is a new era in business, an era when social responsibility is receiving top attention.

PROFILE

Nancy Bierk, Ad Impressions and Logo Masters

Source: Patricia Corrigan, "Hiring Heroes," *St. Louis Post-Dispatch*, May 4, 1997, pp. 1E and 8E; and "Business Role Model," *Jet*, March 19, 1997, p. 5.

MANAGING BUSINESS ETHICALLY AND RESPONSIBLY

Knowing what is right and wrong and behaving accordingly is what ethical behavior is all about. Ethical behavior can influence your success in business. In fact, it was ranked the most important personal attribute of graduates in a 1994 survey of chief financial officers.[1]

Social responsibility is a business's concern for the welfare of society as a whole. In this chapter we will look at ethics from both an individual and an organizational perspective, and then we will look at how organizations show social responsibility.

◄ CONSIDER USING TM 27
Chapter Outline

◄ LEARNING GOAL 1.
Explain why legality is only the first step in behaving ethically.

social responsibility
A business's concern for the welfare of society as a whole.

► **CONSIDER USING LECTURE ENHANCER 4-1**
Experiment or Exploitation?

► **CONSIDER USING SUPPLEMEN- TAL CASE 4-1**
Ethics in Hollywood and the Entertainment Industry (**SCANS**)

► **CONSIDER USING LECTURE ENHANCER 4-2**
Is It Possible to Teach Ethics?

ethics
Standards of moral behavior, that is, behavior that is accepted by society as right versus wrong.

► **CONSIDER USING OT ACETATE 4-1**
Classifying Business Decisions According to Ethical and Legal Relationships

Water pollution is one of the major environmental concerns in the United States today. Here you see water loaded with phosphate from Florida sugar cane fields gushing into a river. What effect will the phosphate have on the environment downstream, on water consumers, other businesses, and so on? The federal government has proposed a tax for clean-up to be paid by the sugar cane growers. What do you think is the most ethical way of dealing with this problem?

LEGALITY IS ONLY THE FIRST ETHICAL STANDARD

Some people wonder if being ethical these days means not getting caught doing something illegal. The "ethical" question seems to have become, Was it legal? A society gets itself in trouble when it considers ethics and legality to be the same. Ethics and legality are two very different things. Although following the law is an important first step, ethical behavior requires more than that. Ethics reflects people's proper relations with one another: How should people treat others? What responsibility should they feel for others? Legality is more limiting. It refers to laws we have written to protect ourselves from fraud, theft, and violence. Many immoral and unethical acts fall well within our laws.

The word *ethics* can be defined several different ways. Some philosophers and theologians distinguish between ethics and morals. They have presented such a variety of distinctions, however, that to use any one of them invites confusion with the others. Therefore the words *ethical* and *moral* are used interchangeably here. You can learn more about the distinction between ethics and morals by taking a philosophy course. For our purposes, we define **ethics** as the standards of moral behavior, that is, behavior that is accepted by society as right versus wrong.

••• PERSONAL ETHICS BEGIN AT HOME •••

It is easy to criticize business for its moral and ethical shortcomings, but we must be careful in our criticism to note that Americans in general are not too socially minded, either. A recent book, *The Day America Told the Truth*, revealed that most Americans have few moral absolutes: Many decide situationally whether it's all right to steal, lie, or drink and drive. Two-thirds of the population reported never giving any time to the community. Nearly one-third said they never contributed to a charity. Both managers and workers cited low managerial ethics as a major cause of our competitive woes. Employees reported that they often violate safety standards and goof off as much as seven hours a week. Our young people learn from such behavior: two-thirds of U.S. high school seniors said they would lie to achieve a business objective.[2]

It is always healthy when discussing moral and ethical issues to remind ourselves that ethical behavior begins with you and me. We cannot expect society to become more moral and ethical unless we as individuals commit to becoming more moral and ethical ourselves.

The purpose of the Making Ethical Decisions boxes you see throughout the text is to demonstrate to you that it is important to keep ethics in mind whenever you are making a business decision. The choices are not always easy. Sometimes the obvious solution from an ethical point of view has drawbacks from a personal or professional point of view. For example, imagine that your supervisor has asked you to do something you feel is unethical. Imagine also that you just took out a mortgage on a new house to make room for your first baby, due in two months. Not carrying out your supervisor's request may get you fired. What would you do? Sometimes there is no desirable alternative. Such situations are called *ethical dilemmas* because you must choose between equally unsatisfactory alternatives. It can be very difficult to maintain a balance between ethics and other factors such as pleasing stakeholders or advancing in your career.

It is helpful to ask yourself the following questions when faced with an ethical dilemma:[3]

◄ CONSIDER USING LECTURE ENHANCER 4-3
Social Responsibility Reality Check at Levis

◄ LEARNING GOAL 2.
Ask the three questions one should answer when faced with a potentially unethical action.

1. *Is it legal?* Am I violating any law or company policy? Whether you are gathering marketing intelligence, designing a product, hiring or firing employees, planning on how to get rid of waste, or using a questionable nickname for a secretary, it is necessary to think of the legal implications of what you do. This is the most basic step in behaving ethically in business, but only the first one.

2. *Is it balanced?* Am I acting fairly? Would I want to be treated this way? Will I win everything at the expense of another party? Win-lose situations often end up as lose-lose situations. There is nothing like a major loss to generate retaliation from the loser. Within a company, imbalances can eventually lead you to use your limited resources to combat the competition in the "backroom" rather than to compete in the marketplace. Every situation cannot be completely balanced, but it is important to the health of our relationships that we avoid major imbalances over time. An ethics-based businessperson has a win-win attitude. In other words, such a person tries to make decisions that benefit all parties involved.

3. *How will it make me feel about myself?* Would I feel proud if my family learned of my decision? Would I be able to discuss the proposed situation or action with my immediate supervisor? The company's clients? How would I feel if my decision were announced on the evening news? Will I have to hide my actions or keep them secret? Has someone warned me not to disclose my actions? Am I feeling unusually nervous? Decisions that go against our sense of right and wrong make us feel bad—they corrode our self-esteem. That is why an ethics-based businessperson does what is proper as well as what is profitable.

There are no easy solutions to ethical problems. Individuals and companies that develop a strong ethics code and use the three ethics-check questions presented above have a better chance than most of behaving ethically.

Critical Thinking

Think of a situation you were involved in recently that tested your ethical behavior. For example, maybe your best friend "forgot" about a term paper due the next day and asked you if he could copy and hand in a paper you wrote for another instructor last semester. What are your alternatives, and

A picture says a thousand words—but not always the truth! NBC used photographs of a rigged GM truck bursting into flames upon impact from another car to illustrate the truck's fuel tanks' defects. The use of setup pictures undermined the story the network wanted to promote. Upon pressure from GM, NBC acknowledged the bogus footage. GM is satisfied that NBC was adequately humbled, but how does this affect your confidence level in NBC's news reporting?

what are the consequences of each one? Would it have been easier to resolve this dilemma if you had asked yourself the three questions listed above? Try answering them now and see if you would have made a different choice.

> CONSIDER USING LECTURE
ENHANCER 4-4
Ethical Decisions Involve a Moral Choice

••• ETHICS IS MORE THAN AN INDIVIDUAL CONCERN •••

Some managers think that ethics is a personal matter—that either individuals have ethical principles or they don't. These managers feel that they are not responsible for an individual's misdeeds and that ethics has nothing to do with management. But a growing number of people think that ethics has *everything* to do with management. Individuals do not usually act alone; they need the implied, if not the direct, cooperation of others to behave unethically in a corporation.

For example, in 1992, Sears, Roebuck & Company was besieged with complaints about its automotive services. Sears management had tried earlier to improve the performance of its auto centers by introducing new goals and incentives for its employees. The increased pressure on the Sears employees to meet these quotas caused them to become careless and to exaggerate the need for repairs. Did the managers say directly, "Deceive the customers"? No, but the message was clear anyway. The goals and incentives created an environment in which mistakes did occur and managers did not make efforts to correct the mistakes. Sears settled pending lawsuits by offering coupons to customers who paid for certain services between 1990 and 1992. The estimated cost to Sears was $60 million. Such misbehavior does not reflect a management philosophy that intends to deceive. It does, however, show an insensitivity or indifference to ethical considerations. In an effort to remedy this insensitivity, Sears replaced 23,000 pages of policies and procedures with a simple booklet called "Freedoms & Obligations," which discusses the company's code of business conduct from a commonsense approach.[4]

> CONSIDER USING OT ACETATE
4-2
Factors that Influence Managerial Ethics

Making Ethical Decisions

http://www.bbb.org

Psst, Kid, Look at This!

Joe Camel took a lot of heat from people who said his ads appealed to adolescents and encouraged them to smoke. Converse is on the run from people who say the name of its basketball shoe Run'N'Gun might encourage adolescent violence, especially in inner cities where handguns are as common as basketballs. Liquor producers are swallowing the criticism of folks who say their new drinks with sweet taste, brightly colored labels, and cutesy names like Tahitian Tangerine and Dixie Jazzberry could encourage adolescents to start drinking. Look on the back page of the May 1997 edition of *Spin*

magazine and you'll see a cartoon ad for Gordon's vodka. Almost 50 percent of *Spin* readers are under 21.

All of the offending companies respond that they are not encouraging adolescent misbehavior. What do you think? Do you think the companies are trying to make adolescents their new customers? If so, is such luring ethical? What are the companies' responsibilities to the well-being of the young members of society?

Sources: David Leonhardt, "How Big Liquor Takes Aim at Teens," *Business Week*, May 19, 1997, p. 92; Walter Shapiro, "Tobacco Debate Should Light Fire Under Congress, *USA Today*, March 20, 1998, p. 4A.

▲ SCANS

··· ORGANIZATIONAL ETHICS BEGINS AT THE TOP ···

Ethics is caught more than it is taught. That is, people learn their standards and values from observing what others do, not what they say. This is as true in business as it is at home. Corporate values are instilled by the leadership and example of strong top managers.[5]

IBM, Xerox, McDonald's, Marriott, and dozens of other companies are known to have strong, effective, and ethical leadership.[6] Within these firms, a high value system has become pervasive, and employees feel they are part of a corporate mission that is socially beneficial. On the other hand, corporate standards can work the other way, too, as you learned from the Sears example. Even managers with strong personal values may place their concern for the corporation's profits ahead of those values.

Any trust and cooperation between workers and managers must be based on fairness, honesty, openness, and moral integrity. The same can be said about relationships among businesses and among nations. A business should be managed ethically for many reasons: to maintain a good reputation; to keep existing customers; to attract new customers; to avoid lawsuits; to reduce employee turnover; to avoid government intervention (the passage of new laws and regulations controlling business activities); to please customers, employees, and society; and simply to do the right thing.

◄ **LEARNING GOAL 3.**
Describe management's role in setting ethical standards.

◄ **CONSIDER USING LECTURE ENHANCER 4-5**
Management Philosophy at Philly Coca-Cola

◄ **CONSIDER USING OT ACETATE 4-3**
Who Are the Most Generous Business Tycoons?

◄ **LEARNING GOAL 4.**
Distinguish between compliance-based and integrity-based ethics codes and list the six steps in setting up a corporate ethics code.

◄ **CONSIDER USING OT ACETATE 4-4**
Why People Volunteer

◄ **CONSIDER USING CRITICAL THINKING EXERCISE 4-1**
Ethical Dilemmas (**SCANS**)

SETTING CORPORATE ETHICAL STANDARDS

Formal corporate ethics codes are popular these days. Companies without them are scrambling to develop and commit their corporate values to paper. Companies that already have codes are rushing to keep them current and to make sure all employees know and understand them.[7] Figure 4.1 offers a sample from one company's code of ethics.

FIGURE 4.1

• • • •

OVERVIEW OF
LOCKHEED MARTIN'S
CODE OF ETHICS

➤ CONSIDER USING TM 28
Overview of Lockheed Martin's Code of
Ethics

➤ CONSIDER USING TM 29
Strategies for Ethics Management

TREAT IN AN ETHICAL MANNER THOSE TO WHOM LOCKHEED MARTIN HAS AN OBLIGATION

We are committed to the ethical treatment of those to whom we have an obligation.

For our employees we are committed to honesty, just management, and fairness, providing a safe and healthy environment, and respecting the dignity due everyone.

For our customers we are committed to produce reliable products and services, delivered on time, at a fair price.

For the communities in which we live and work we are committed to acting as concerned and responsible neighbors, reflecting all aspects of good citizenship.

For our shareholders we are committed to pursuing sound growth and earnings objectives and to exercising prudence in the use of our assets and resources.

For our suppliers we are committed to fair competition and the sense of responsibility required of a good customer.

This excerpt from Lockheed Martin's Web page is an overview of the stakeholders to whom Lockheed Martin has an obligation to treat in an ethical manner. To see the company's complete code of ethics go to their Web site at http://www.lmco.com/exeth/ethset.html.

**compliance-based
ethics codes**

Ethical standards that emphasize preventing unlawful behavior by increasing control and by penalizing wrongdoers.

**integrity-based
ethics codes**

Ethical standards that define the organization's guiding values, create an environment that supports ethically sound behavior, and stress a shared accountability among employees.

Although ethics codes vary greatly, they can be classified into two major categories: compliance-based and integrity-based. **Compliance-based ethics codes** emphasize preventing unlawful behavior by increasing control and by penalizing wrongdoers.[8] Whereas compliance-based ethics codes are based on avoiding legal punishment, **integrity-based ethics codes** define the organization's guiding values, create an environment that supports ethically sound behavior, and stress a shared accountability among employees. See Figure 4.2 for a comparison of compliance-based and integrity-based ethics codes.

To be effective, all ethics codes must be enforced; that is, employees must be held responsible for their behavior. A long-term improvement of America's business ethics calls for a six-step approach:

1. Top management must adopt and unconditionally support an explicit corporate code of conduct.

2. Employees must understand that expectations for ethical behavior begin at the top and that senior management expects all employees to act accordingly.

3. Managers and others must be trained to consider the ethical implications of all business decisions.

FIGURE 4.2

• • • •

STRATEGIES FOR ETHICS
MANAGEMENT

As you can see from this chart, integrity-based ethics codes are similar to compliance-based ethics codes in that both have a concern for the law and use penalties as enforcement. Integrity-based ethics codes move beyond legal compliance to create a "do-it-right" climate that emphasizes core values such as honesty, fair play, good service to customers, a commitment to diversity, and involvement in the community. These values are ethically desirable, but not necessarily legally mandatory.

Features of compliance-based ethics codes

Ideal:	Conform to outside standards (laws and regulations)
Objective:	Avoid criminal misconduct
Leaders:	Lawyers
Methods:	Education, reduced employee discretion, controls, penalties

Features of integrity-based ethics codes

Ideal:	Conform to outside standards (laws and regulations) and chosen internal standards
Objective:	Enable responsible employee conduct
Leaders:	Managers with aid of lawyers and others
Methods:	Education, leadership, accountability, decision processes, controls, and penalties

4. An ethics office must be set up. Phone lines to the office should be established so that employees who don't necessarily want to be seen with an ethics officer can inquire about ethical matters anonymously.

5. Outsiders such as suppliers, subcontractors, distributors, and customers must be told about the ethics program. Pressure to put aside ethical considerations often comes from the outside, and it helps employees resist such pressure when everyone knows what the ethical standards are.

6. The ethics code must be enforced. It is important to back any ethics program with timely action if any rules are broken. That is the best way to communicate to all employees that the code is serious and cannot be broken.

corporate philanthropy
Dimension of social responsibility that includes charitable donations.

corporate responsibility
Dimension of social responsibility that includes everything from hiring minority workers to making safe products.

corporate policy
Dimension of social responsibility that refers to the position a firm takes on social and political issues.

Progress Check

- When faced with ethical dilemmas, what questions can you ask yourself that might help you make ethical decisions?
- What are the six steps to follow in establishing an effective ethics program in a business?

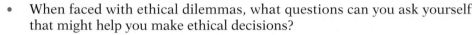

CORPORATE SOCIAL RESPONSIBILITY

As we said at the beginning of the chapter, corporate social responsibility is the concern businesses have for the welfare of society. The social performance of a company has several dimensions:

- **Corporate philanthropy** includes charitable donations to nonprofit groups of all kinds. Strategic philanthropy involves companies making long-term commitments to one cause, such as McDonald's founding and support of Ronald McDonald Houses.[9] Philanthropy isn't limited to large corporations. The box on page 109 describes how small businesses can become involved.

- **Corporate responsibility** includes everything from hiring minority workers to making safe products, minimizing pollution, using energy wisely, providing a safe work environment, and more.

- **Corporate policy** refers to the position a firm takes on social and political issues.

So much news coverage is devoted to the social problems caused by corporations that people tend to get a one-sided negative view of the impact that companies have on society. Few people know, for example, that Xerox has a program called Social Leave, which allows employees to leave for up to a year and work for a nonprofit organization. While on Social Leave, the employee gets full salary and benefits and has job security. IBM and Wells-Fargo Bank have similar programs. In fact, many companies are jumping on the "volunteerism bandwagon" by allowing employees to volunteer their help part-time to social agencies of all kinds. One of the goals of the President's Summit for America's Future, led by Colin Powell in 1997, was to increase the numbers of corporate volunteers.[10] Volunteer America designed a Web-based program to match nonprofit organizations that need volunteers with

Businesses may be "shot down" if they ignore their responsibilities to all stakeholders. Disney surrendered to historians and citizens who believed that a proposed theme park in the midst of Civil War battlefields in Virginia would adversely affect local communities and the environment. A group called Protect Historic America pointed out that the site was important to all Americans—not just Virginians—and should be protected from the impact of the theme park.

Some corporate employees extend their commitment to stakeholders outside of the company. Here we see Lori Wingerter, a GM environmental engineer and chairperson of GREEN (Global Rivers Environmental Education Network), teaching students how to help clean up rivers. People like Lori believe that social responsibility means working to improve the quality of life both in and out of the office.

Mattel introduced Share a Smile Becky as Barbie's friend with a disability so that Barbie's world would reflect the rich diversity of the real world. To celebrate the new doll, Mattel presented $10,000 checks to the National Parent Network on Disabilities and the National Lekoteck Center. After the doll's release, the company was embarrassed to discover that existing Barbie Dream Houses proved not to be disability-accessible when Becky's wheelchair failed to fit through doorways. Mattel admitted its blunder and will redesign the playhouse. But what can the children who already own a home or vehicle do with the inaccessible toys?

people looking for volunteer opportunities. The Volunteer America URL is www.volunteeramerica.com . See the Taking It to the Net exercise at the end of this chapter for directions to a similar Web site.

Two-thirds of the MBA students surveyed by a group called Students for Responsible Business said they would take a lower salary to work for a socially responsible company. But when the same students were asked to define a socially responsible company, things got complicated. It appears that even those who want to be socially responsible can't agree on what it involves.[11]

Maybe it would be easier to understand social responsibility if we looked at the concept through the eyes of the stakeholders to whom businesses are responsible: customers, investors, employees, and society in general.[12]

••• RESPONSIBILITY TO CUSTOMERS •••

One responsibility of business is to satisfy customers by offering them goods and services of real value. A recurring theme of this book is the importance of pleasing the customers. This responsibility is not as easy to meet as it seems. Keep in mind that three out of five new businesses fail—perhaps because their owners failed to please their customers. One of the surest ways of failing to please customers is not being up front with them. For example, in 1988 a consumer magazine reported that the Suzuki Samurai was likely to roll over if a driver swerved violently in an emergency. When Suzuki executives denied there was a problem, sales plummeted. In contrast, Daimler Benz suffered a similar problem in 1997 during a test simulating a swerve around a wayward elk, when its new A-class "Baby Benz" rolled over. The company quickly admitted a problem, came up with a solution, and committed the money necessary to put that solution into action. In addition, they continued to answer questions in spite

Spotlight on Small Business

http://www.giftsinkind.org

Myths about Small-Business Philanthropy

Many entrepreneurs have a hard time determining how to start a charitable-giving program in their businesses. Often this is because of misconceptions.

Myth 1: Charities need cash, so struggling small businesses can't help them without jeopardizing their own cash flow.
Reality: Sure, charities need money. But they also need equipment (such as used computers), food, clothing, and volunteers.

Myth 2: If your business is small, you can't make a significant difference.
Reality: If you target your involvement to small programs within your community, you'll be able to have a notable impact. For instance, one Chicago manufacturer invested just $1,500 in a new local early-childhood literacy program that rewarded inner-city parents with grocery money when they read to their children.

Myth 3: Charity organizers will pay attention only to large contributors with well-known names.
Reality: Nonprofits look for ways to form partnerships with both large and small companies. For example, Dine Across America, a fund-raising effort for a national antihunger organization, received funding for administrative expenses from American Express. But more important, it was small businesses—restaurants and food wholesalers—that donated the food and labor.

Business owners who don't know how to locate nonprofit organizations that need donations can call Gifts in Kind International (703-836-2121), which serves as a middleman by collecting clothing, office equipment, and other useful materials and distributing them to more than 50,000 nonprofit organizations and schools across the nation.

Sources: Jill Andresky Fraser, "How to Give Wisely," *Inc.,* February 1997, p. 104. "America's Spirit of Giving," *Portland Oregonian,* October 1, 1997, p. A12.

---

of aggressive press coverage. Since the test flip, only 2 percent of the orders for the vehicle have been canceled. The solution cost the company $59 million in 1997 and will cost $118 million each year thereafter. Analysts say those costs will probably eliminate any profit on the vehicle. However, the quick resolution of the problem protected the company's reputation, thus allowing its other models to become such hits that Daimler's net earnings remained the same.[13]

··· RESPONSIBILITY TO INVESTORS ···

American economist Milton Friedman made a classic statement when he said that corporate social responsibility means making money for stockholders.[14] "Ethical behavior is good for shareholder wealth," says Robert Agate, president of Colgate-Palmolive Co. Those cheated by financial wrongdoing are the shareholders themselves.[15]

Some people believe that before you can do good you must do well; others believe that by doing good, you can also do well.[16] For example, Bagel Works, a New England–based company with eight stores now and more planned, has a dual-bottom-line approach that focuses on the well-being of the planet as well as profits. With sales in excess of $3 million in 1995, Bagel Works received national recognition for social responsibility. Its mission involves commitments to the environment and to community service. In addition to environmentally protective practices such as promoting in-store recycling, composting, using

◄ **LEARNING GOAL 5.**
Define social responsibility and examine corporate responsibility to various stakeholders.

◄ **CONSIDER USING LECTURE ENHANCER 4-7**
Putting His Money Where His Mouth Is

◄ **CONSIDER USING LECTURE ENHANCER 4-8**
Different Views of Corporate Responsibility

◄ **CONSIDER USING CRITICAL THINKING EXERCISE 4-2**
Surveying Public Interest Organizations **(SCANS)**

organically grown ingredients, and using nontoxic cleaners, donations for community causes are included in each store's budget.

Many people believe that it makes financial as well as moral sense to invest in companies that are planning ahead to create a better environment. By choosing to put their money into companies whose goods and services benefit the community and the environment, investors can improve their own financial health while improving society's health.[17]

••• RESPONSIBILITY TO EMPLOYEES •••

Businesses have several responsibilities to employees. First, they have a responsibility to create jobs. It's been said that the best social program in the world is a job.[18] It is better to teach people to fish than to give them fish.

Once a company creates the jobs, it has an obligation to see to it that hard work and talent are fairly rewarded. Employees need realistic hope of a better future, which comes only through a chance for upward mobility. People need to see that hard work, goodwill, ingenuity, and talent pay off. As Ellen Marram, president of Seagram's Beverage Group, says, "While growing one's business is important, I think it's equally important to grow one's employees."[19]

Companies also have a responsibility to maintain job security or, if layoffs are impossible to avoid, companies should give employees warning. Some companies offer laid-off employees assistance in finding new jobs. Such loyalty to employees pays off in the long run. Consider the experience of Harman International Industries. The Harman management tries to guarantee job security for its 4,300 employees by finding other tasks for them to do during assembly-line downtime rather than lay them off. For instance, workers might be asked to make wall clocks with the circular pieces of wood that were cut out of every speaker box. When the factory was destroyed by a 1994 earthquake, the employees proved their loyalty by getting the factory up and running again in just a few days.[20]

••• RESPONSIBILITY TO SOCIETY •••

One of business's major responsibilities to society is to create new wealth. If businesses don't do it, who will? More than a third of working Americans receive their salaries from nonprofit organizations that in turn receive their funding from others, who in turn receive their money from business. Foundations, universities, and such own billions of shares in publicly held companies. As those stock prices increase, more funds are available to benefit society.

Paul Newman donates all of the profits from the sale of his Newman's Own products to charity. Newman uses his entrepreneurial talents as well as his celebrity to help the less fortunate.

Businesses are also responsible for promoting social justice. Business is perhaps the most crucial institution of civil society. For its own well-being, business depends on its employees being active in politics, law, churches, arts, charities, and so on. For example, some of the folks at the General Electric plastics division helped their community while developing their own team-building skills. Rather than heading to a resort hotel to participate in some isolated team-building activities, the group went into the neighborhood surrounding their offices and helped rebuild the community, barn-raising style. The result back on the job was a sense of team camaraderie that proved as lasting as the buildings that were rebuilt.[21]

Of course, business is responsible for helping to make its own environment a better place. Printing companies in the Great Lakes region have joined the Great Printers Project because they know their industry is a major source of pollution. Working in cooperation with their unions, suppliers, and customers, the companies have taken steps to set standards for incorporating prevention into environmental protection even if it means a short-term expense increase.[22]

Many corporations are publishing reports that document their net social contribution. To do that, a company must measure its social contributions and subtract its negative social impacts. We shall discuss that process next.

••• SOCIAL AUDITING •••

It is nice to talk about having organizations become more socially responsible. It is also hopeful to see some efforts made toward creating safer products, cleaning up the environment, designing more honest advertising, and treating women and minorities fairly. But is there any way to measure whether organizations are making social responsiveness an integral part of top management's decision making? The answer is yes, and the term that represents that measurement is *social auditing.*

A **social audit** is a systematic evaluation of an organization's progress toward implementing programs that are socially responsible and responsive. One of the major problems of conducting a social audit is establishing procedures for measuring a firm's activities and their effects on society. What should be measured? See Figure 4.3 for an outline of business activities that could be considered socially responsible.

There is some question as to whether positive actions should be added (e.g., charitable donations, pollution control efforts) and then negative effects subtracted (e.g., pollution, layoffs) to get a net social contribution. Or should just positive actions be recorded? In general, social responsibility is becoming one of the aspects of corporate success that business evaluates, measures, and develops.

In addition to the social audits conducted by the companies themselves, there are four types of groups that serve as watchdogs regarding how well companies enforce their ethical and social responsibility policies:

1. *Socially conscious investors* who insist that companies extend the company's own high standards to all their suppliers.

2. *Environmentalists* who apply pressure by naming names of companies that don't abide by the environmentalists' standards.

◄ **CONSIDER USING LECTURE ENHANCER 4-12**
How Far We've Come

◄ **CONSIDER USING CRITICAL THINKING EXERCISE 4-3**
Social Responsibility Successes and Failures
(SCANS)

◄ **CONSIDER USING OT ACETATE 4-9**
Three Concepts of Social Responsibility

◄ **CONSIDER USING OT ACETATE 4-10**
Most Admired Companies by Industry

◄ **CONSIDER USING LECTURE ENHANCER 4-13**
The CEP's Corporate Conscience Awards

◄ **CONSIDER USING TM 30**
Examples of Socially Responsible Business Activities

social audit
A systematic evaluation of an organization's progress toward implementing programs that are socially responsible and responsive.

- Community-related activities such as participating in local fund-raising campaigns, donating executive time to various nonprofit organizations (including local government), and participating in urban planning and development.
- Employee-related activities such as equal opportunity programs, flextime, improved benefits, job enrichment, job safety, and employee development programs. (You'll learn more about these activities in Chapters 11 and 12.)
- Political activities such as taking a position on issues such as nuclear safety, gun control, pollution control, and consumer protection; and working more closely with local, state, and federal government officials.
- Support for higher education, the arts, and other nonprofit social agencies.
- Consumer activities such as product safety, honest advertising, prompt complaint handling, honest pricing policies, and extensive consumer education programs.

FIGURE 4-3
••••
SOCIALLY RESPONSIBLE
BUSINESS ACTIVITIES

3. *Union officials* who hunt down violations and force companies to comply to avoid negative publicity.

4. *Customers* who take their business elsewhere if a company demonstrates unethical or socially irresponsible practices.

···· ▬▬ ····

INTERNATIONAL ETHICS AND SOCIAL RESPONSIBILITY

Ethical problems and issues of social responsibility are not unique to the United States. Top business and government leaders in Japan were caught in a major "influence peddling" (read bribery) scheme in Japan. Similar charges have been brought against top officials in South Korea and the People's Republic of China. What is new about the moral and ethical standards by which government leaders are being judged? They are much stricter than in previous years. Top leaders are now being held to a higher standard.

Government leaders are not the only ones being held to higher standards. Many American businesses are demanding socially responsible behavior from their international suppliers by making sure their suppliers do not violate U.S. human rights and environmental standards. For example, Sears will not import products made by Chinese prison labor. Phillips–Van Heusen Corp. said it would cancel orders from suppliers that violate its ethical, environmental, and human rights code. Dow Chemical expects its suppliers to conform to tough American pollution and safety laws rather than just to local laws of their respective countries. McDonald's denied rumors that one of its suppliers grazes cattle on cleared rain forest land but wrote a ban on the practice anyway.

In contrast to companies that demand that their suppliers demonstrate socially responsible behavior are those that have been criticized for exploiting workers in less developed countries. Nike, the world's largest athletic shoe company, has been accused by human rights and labor groups of treating its workers poorly while lavishing millions of dollars on star athletes to endorse its products. Cartoonist Gary Trudeau featured an anti-Nike campaign in his popular Doonesbury syndicated series. A 1997 Ernst & Young report on the company's operations in Asia indicated that thousands of young women, labored 10$\frac{1}{2}$ hours a day, six days a week, in excessive heat, noise, and foul air, for slightly more than $10 a week. The report also found that workers with skin or breathing problems caused by the factory conditions had not been transferred to departments free of chemicals. More than half the workers who dealt with dangerous chemicals did not wear protective masks or gloves. Nike officials say they are working to improve conditions, but their critics say they are not doing enough quickly enough.[23]

Children provide cheap labor in some countries. Here we see a young girl sewing in a Mexican factory. Often the factories are hot, noisy, and filled with polluted air. Such conditions are regulated in the United States. Some U.S. companies require their foreign suppliers to improve working conditions. Is it ethical for American companies to demand that their suppliers in other countries comply with our moral standards?

The justness of requiring international suppliers to adhere to American ethical standards is not as clear-cut as you might think. Is it always ethical for American companies to demand compliance with our moral standards? What about countries where child labor is an accepted part of the society, where families depend on the children's salaries for survival? What about foreign companies doing business in the United States? Should they expect American companies to comply with their ethical standards? What about multinational corporations? Since they are not a part of a given society, do they then not have to conform to any society's standards? Why is Sears applauded for not importing goods made in Chinese prisons when there are many

Reaching Beyond Our Borders

http://www.pathfinder.com

Far from Giving Them the Shirt Off Your Back

Sometimes companies that try to be socially responsible still face more criticism than praise. Even Phillips–Van Heusen Corp. (PVH), the clothing company that has developed a reputation as a champion of human rights for overseas workers, can't escape criticism. For example, PVH has taken unusual steps to improve working conditions in Guatemala. Its 650 employees get subsidized lunch, free on-site health care, and school supplies for their children. Sewing workers sit in ergonomic chairs and make higher wages than workers in other companies. The company has even contributed more than $1.5 million to improve the nutrition, facilities, and teacher education at Guatemalan schools. "We are paying the highest wages in that country," says CEO Bruce Klatsky. Unfortunately, those wages are still only about half of what it takes for a family of five to escape poverty in Guatemala. "Simply being the best plantation owner isn't exactly something to brag about," contends Stephen Coats, executive director of the U.S./Guatemala Labor Education Project.

General Motors (GM) is facing similar criticism in Mexico. In addition to paying the standard wage, GM is helping thousands of its workers buy their first homes.

GM matches employee contributions toward a 26 percent down payment and helps push employee mortgage applications to the top of long waiting lists. GM's wages are in line with the average Mexican manufacturing pay, but critics charge that $1.33 an hour leaves workers struggling to support families. Not everyone is a critic though. Noel Castro Monreal, a 24-year-old GM technician says about his new 400-square-foot home, "This is much better, a thousand times better." Such feelings will help GM boost morale and reduce turnover. GM requires workers buying houses to stay in its plants five years or repay the down payment.

These situations show how difficult it is for companies doing business in developing countries to make the right business decisions while responding to increasing demands to be socially responsible.

Sources: Rebecca Blumenstein and Dianne Solis, "GM's Mexican Houses on Shaky Ground," *The Wall Street Journal Interactive Edition,* June 20, 1997; and Wendy Bounds, "Critics Confront a CEO Dedicated to Human Rights," *The Wall Street Journal,* February 24, 1997, p. B1.

prison-based enterprises in the United States? None of these questions are easy to answer, but they give you some idea of the complexity of social responsibility issues in international markets.[24]

One important thing to remember is that it isn't enough for a company to be right when it comes to ethics and social responsibility. It also has to convince its customers that it's right.

◀ CONSIDER USING SUPPLEMENTAL CASE 4-3
France's AIDS Scandal (**SCANS**)

Progress Check

- What is corporate social responsibility, and how does it relate to each of business's major stakeholders?
- What is a social audit, and what kinds of activities does it monitor?

SUMMARY

1. Ethics goes beyond obeying laws. It also involves abiding by the moral standards accepted by society.
   - *How is legality different from ethics?*
   Ethics reflects people's proper relation with one another. Legality is more limiting. It refers to laws written to protect us from fraud, theft, and violence.

1. Explain why legality is only the first step in behaving ethically.

2. Ask the three questions one should answer when faced with a potentially unethical action.

2. It is often difficult to know when a decision is ethical.

   • *How can we tell if our business decisions are ethical?*
   Our business decisions can be put through an ethics check by asking three questions: (1) Is it legal? (2) Is it balanced? and (3) How will it make me feel?

3. Describe management's role in setting ethical standards.

3. Some managers think ethics is an individual issue that has nothing to do with management, while others believe ethics has *everything* to do with management.

   • *What is management's role in setting ethical standards?*
   Managers often set formal ethical standards, but more important are the messages they send through their actions. Management's tolerance or intolerance of ethical misconduct influences employees more than any written ethics codes do.

4. Distinguish between compliance-based and integrity-based ethics codes and list the six steps in setting up a corporate ethics code.

4. Ethics codes can be classified as compliance-based or integrity-based.

   • *What's the difference between compliance-based and integrity-based ethics codes?*
   Whereas compliance-based ethics codes are based on avoiding legal punishment, integrity-based ethics codes define the organization's guiding values, create an environment that supports ethically sound behavior, and stress a shared accountability among employees.

5. Define social responsibility and examine corporate responsibility to various stakeholders.

5. Social responsibility is the concern businesses have for society.

   • *How do businesses demonstrate corporate responsibility toward stakeholders?*
   Business is responsible to various stakeholders, including customers, investors, employees and society in general. (1) Business's responsibility to customers is to satisfy them with goods and services of real value. (2) Business is responsible for making money for its investors. (3) Business has several responsibilities to employees: to create jobs, to maintain job security, and to see that hard work and talent are fairly rewarded. (4) Business has several responsibilities to society: to create new wealth, to promote social justice, and to contribute to making its own environment a better place.

   • *How are a company's social responsibility efforts measured?*
   A corporate social audit measures the effects of positive social programs and subtracts the negative effects of business (e.g., pollution) to get a net social benefit.

6. Analyze the role of American businesses in influencing ethical and social responsibility in global markets.

6. Many customers are demanding that companies deal only with other companies that share a commitment to environmental and human rights issues.

   • *How can companies influence the ethical behavior of their international suppliers?*
   Companies like Sears, Phillips–Van Heusen, and Dow Chemical will not import products from companies that do not meet their ethical and social responsibility standards.

KEY TERMS
• • • • • •

compliance-based
  ethics codes 106
corporate
  philanthropy 107

corporate policy 107
corporate
  responsibility 107
ethics 102

integrity-based ethics
  codes 106
social audit 111
social responsibility
  101

1. What influences have helped shape your personal code of ethics and morality? What influences, if any, have pressured you to compromise those standards in recent years? Think of an experience you had at work or school that tested your ethical standards. What did you decide to do to resolve your dilemma? Now that time has passed, are you comfortable with the decision you made? If not, what would you do differently?

2. Newspapers and magazines are full of stories about individuals and businesses that are *not* socially responsible. What about those individuals and organizations that *do* take social responsibility seriously? We don't normally read or hear about them. Do a little investigative reporting of your own. Identify a public interest power group in your community and identify its officers, objectives, sources and amount of financial support, size and characteristics of its membership, and examples of its recent actions and/or accomplishments. You should be able to choose from environmental groups, animal protection groups, political action committees, and so on. Call the local chamber of commerce, the Better Business Bureau, or local government agencies for help. Try using one of the Internet search engines to help you find more information.

3. You are manager of a coffeehouse called The Morning Cup. One of your best employees desires to be promoted to a managerial position; however, the owner is grooming his slow-thinking son for the promotion your employee seeks. This nepotism may hurt a valuable employee's chances for advancement, but complaining may hurt your own chances for promotion. What do you do?

4. Contact a local corporation and ask for a copy of its written ethics code. Would you classify its code as compliance-based or integrity-based? Explain.

5. Where do you see leadership emerging to improve the moral standards of the United States? What could you do to support such leadership?

Purpose

To encourage students to help others through community service

Exercise

One of the most common reasons people give for not contributing more of their time to their community is that they don't know where to go to volunteer. You can find out about volunteer options in your zip code by visiting the Internet site http://www.servenet.org .

1. Go to the section dealing with issues and read one article about a topic that interests you. Write a brief summary of the article and add how you might become involved in community activities that address your chosen issue.

2. Use the site's search tools to see what types of volunteer options are available in your area. If your area is not yet included in the site's database, choose a nearby zip code so that you have an idea of what types of agencies you can contact to offer your services. The best way to learn about volunteering is by volunteering, so put your community service plan into action by offering your services to one of the agencies in your area.

Practicing Management Decisions

CASE

······

GOT A DEADLINE? CLICK HERE

······

Have a term paper due soon? With the advent of the World Wide Web, plagiarism is as easy as point and click. Some Web sites list thousands of term papers on hundreds of topics—and the papers are waiting to be downloaded 24 hours a day. A Boston University law student posed as a student wanting to buy a term paper to see how easily it could be done. The student reached eight companies in seven states and paid fees ranging from $45 to $175. The university charged the companies in federal court with wire fraud, mail fraud, racketeering, and violating a Massachusetts law that bans the sale of term papers.

Some Web sites are not affected by current laws because they offer the papers for free. The sites receive money from advertisers who buy space on the sites. The owner of one of the Web sites says that the papers on his site show the substandard writing skills of many college students. You get the idea from the papers on the site that students get rewarded for length. They write pages and pages of junk, yet many instructors accept them.

The owner also says the bad papers say something about the mediocre assignments that some professors give year after year. He thinks it is absurd that class assignments can be so vague that a student can go to the Internet and find a generic essay on it. He thinks he is doing education a favor by forcing professors to give more specific writing assignments and to require extensive footnotes.

If recycling term papers is so easy, why do professors bother assigning them? While the writing style used for term papers is different from that used in the workplace, writing develops critical thinking skills and the ability to express thoughts and ideas. Tom Rocklin, director of the Center for Teaching at the University of Iowa puts it this way: "I have sat down with a group of businesspeople, and they say what they are looking for in new hires are skills developed by a traditional liberal arts education. Discussion, reading, and extended writing are a crucial part of that."

Decision Questions

1. Would you consider submitting a paper from one of these Web sites as your own? Why or why not?
2. Do you agree with the Web site owner who said he is "improving" education by exposing these papers as the mediocre results of mediocre assignments? Justify your answer.
3. View this issue through the eyes of your professor. The Web sites are out there and your students have access to them. What would you do to discourage your students from plagiarism?

Sources: Patrice M. Jones, "Internet Term Papers Write New Chapter on Plagiarism," *Chicago Tribune*, December 8, 1997, Section 1, p. 1. Dale Singer, "School Cheating Would be a Crime Under Missouri Lawmaker's Bill," *St. Louis Post Dispatch*, March 9, 1998, p. B1.

VIDEO CASE

······

ETHICS IN THE WORKPLACE

In college, you learn how to do many things the right way. For example, in accounting and math classes, you learn how to prepare financial statements and solve quadratic equations. With time and study, you learn how to do these things in a technically proficient manner. You face a much tougher challenge, however, in learning *how to do the right thing* when faced with ethical dilemmas. Imagine working as an accountant for a manufacturing firm that looks like it's going to miss its budget projections for the first time in three years. Missing projections frustrates everyone, but the situation becomes even more intolerable when a major customer places a large order for delivery the next quarter. If the order had only

been four weeks prior, that order could have been filled this quarter and would put the projections over the top. A foreman suggests you record the order for the present quarter to put the company over. He advises, "If we don't get the order delivered this quarter who's going to know anyway?"

Ethical questions abound in all business departments and disciplines. For example, how far should you go to promote a product? Suppose you are urged to design a blatantly sexist campaign just because it will please the client. Should you go along with such a suggestion even if it violates what you consider to be good taste and respect? When is the proper time to follow your own beliefs as opposed to following "orders"?

Decisions involving finance are not much easier. Consider the challenge of investing funds for clients. Is it important that you invest your client's money in a high-yield company even if that company has a reputation for questionable ethical behavior? Or should you consider a socially responsible firm that offers a bit lower yield but over the long-term offers more value to the environment?

What do you do if you see someone else violating what you believe to be ethical standards? Should you report such infractions to others? What could be the consequences of your behavior?

Discussion Questions

1. What are other difficult ethical issues you may face on the job?
2. What do you think happens to people that follow their ethical standards completely, when such standards go against the wishes of their supervisors? Would you advise such people to compromise?
3. How would you personally handle all the situations presented above? Why would you behave in the manner you chose?

Working within the
Legal Environment of
Business

Appendix

It was P. T. Barnum who framed the motto "there's a sucker born every minute." Without some legal oversight and control, it would be easy for some consumers to become the prey Barnum talked about. Here we see what appears to be outrageous claims being made by a weight loss program. The legal system protects consumers' rights to safety by forcing producers of such products to prove the claims they are making are actually true.

THE NEED FOR LAWS

Imagine a society without laws. Just think, no speed limits to control how fast we drive, no age restrictions on the consumption of alcoholic beverages, no limitations on who can practice medicine—a society in which people are free to do whatever they choose, with no interference. Obviously, the more we consider this possibility, the more unrealistic we realize it is. Laws are an essential part of a civilized nation. Over time, the depth and scope of the body of laws must change to reflect the needs and changes in society. The **judiciary** is the branch of government chosen to oversee the legal system.

The world of business is also governed by laws. In fact, the government seems to be stepping in more and more to govern the behavior of business-people. Thus, you see more laws and regulations regarding sexual harassment on the job, the hiring and firing of employees, the granting of unpaid leave for family emergencies, and enforcement of environmental and safety laws. As you may suspect, businesspeople prefer to set their own standards of behavior. However, business has not been perceived as implementing acceptable practices fast enough. To hasten the process, the government has expanded its control and enforcement procedures. In this appendix we will look at some of the laws and regulations now in place. You cannot obey or understand the law unless you know what the law is.

BUSINESS LAW

Business law refers to rules, statutes, codes, and regulations that are established to provide a legal framework within which business may be conducted and that are enforceable by court action. A businessperson should be familiar with the laws regarding product liability, sales, contracts, fair competition, consumer protection, taxes, and bankruptcy. Let 's start at the beginning and discuss the foundations of the law.

··· STATUTORY AND COMMON LAW ···

There are two major kinds of law: statutory law and common law. Both are important for businesspeople.

Statutory law (written law) includes state and federal constitutions, legislative enactments, treaties of the federal government, and ordinances. You can read these laws, but many are written in such a form that their meaning must be determined in court. That is one reason there are so many lawyers.

Common law is the body of law that comes from decisions handed down by judges. Common law is often referred to as *unwritten law,* because it does not appear in any legislative enactments, treaties, and so forth. What judges have decided in previous cases is very important to today's cases. Such decisions are called precedent, and they guide judges in the handling of new cases. Common law evolves through decisions made in trial courts, appellate courts, and special courts. Lower courts must abide by the precedents set by high courts such as the U.S. Supreme Court. In law classes, therefore, students study case after case to learn about common law as well as statutory law.

··· ADMINISTRATIVE AGENCIES ···

Branches of government called administrative agencies issue many rules, regulations, and orders. **Administrative agencies** are institutions created by Congress with delegated power to pass rules and regulations within their mandated area of authority. Since Congress creates administrative agencies, it can also terminate them. Some administrative agencies hold quasi-legislative, quasi-executive, and quasi-judicial powers. This means the agency is allowed to pass rules and regulations within its area of authority, conduct investigations in cases of suspected rules violations, and hold hearings when it feels the rules and regulations have been violated. Administrative agencies issue more rulings and settle more disputes than do courts. Figure A.1 lists and describes the power and functions of several leading federal administrative agencies within the executive branch of government. How many of these agencies have you heard about?

TORT LAW

The tort system is an example of common law at work. A **tort** is a wrongful act that causes injury to another person's body, property, or reputation. Although torts often are noncriminal acts, victims can be awarded compensation. This is especially true if the conduct that caused harm is considered intentional. An intentional tort is a willful act that results in injury. *Negligence* deals with unintentional behavior that causes harm or injury. World Rio Corporation was ordered to pay $4.5 million to nearly 53,000 African-American women who sued the former maker of a widely advertised hair care product because the

---

judiciary
The branch of government chosen to oversee the legal system.

business law
Rules, statutes, codes, and regulations that are established to provide a legal framework within which business may be conducted and that are enforceable by court action.

statutory law
State and federal constitutions, legislative enactments, treaties, and ordinances (written laws).

common law
The body of law that comes from judges' decisions; also referred to as *unwritten law.*

◄ **CONSIDER USING TM 31**
Appendix Outline

administrative agencies
Institutions created by Congress with delegated power to pass rules and regulations within their mandated area of authority.

◄ **CONSIDER USING OT ACETATE B-1**
Sources of U.S. Law

◄ **CONSIDER USING OT ACETATE B-2**
The Categories of Business Law

tort
A wrongful act that causes injury to another person's body, property, or reputation.

FIGURE **A.1**

• • • •

FEDERAL REGULATORY
AGENCIES

➤ **CONSIDER USING TM 32**
Federal Regulatory Agencies

AGENCY	FUNCTION
Federal Trade Commission (FTC)	Enforces laws and guidelines regarding unfair business practices and acts to stop false and deceptive advertising and labeling.
Food and Drug Administration (FDA)	Enforces laws and regulations to prevent distribution of adulterated or misbranded foods, drugs, medical devices, cosmetics, veterinary products, and hazardous consumer products.
Consumer Products Safety Commission	Ensures compliance with the Consumer Product Safety Act and seeks to protect the public from unreasonable risk of injury from any consumer product not covered by other regulatory agencies.
Federal Communications Commission (FCC)	Regulates wire, radio, and TV communication in interstate and foreign commerce.
Environmental Protection Agency (EPA)	Develops and enforces environmental protection standards and researches the effects of pollution.
Federal Power Commission (FPC)	Regulates rates and sales of natural gas producers, wholesale rates for electricity and gas, pipeline construction, and imports and exports of natural gas and electricity to and from the United States.

product liability
Part of tort law that holds businesses liable for negligence in the production, design, sale, or use of products they market.

Under product liability laws, manufacturers can be assessed damages for a product's effects even if they were unaware of the danger. This is referred to as strict liability and means without regard to fault. Therefore, even if the producers of Fen-Phen did not know of the dangers of their product before placing it on the market, they can be legally liable for the harm caused this littlest victim.

product caused baldness, green scalps, and other health problems.[1] Such product liability is one of the most controversial areas of tort law related to business actions. Let's look briefly at this issue.

••• PRODUCT LIABILITY •••

Few issues in business law have caused as much debate as product liability. **Product liability** is covered under tort law and holds businesses liable for negligence in the production, design, sale, or use of products they market. At one time the legal standard for measuring product liability was if a producer *knowingly* placed a hazardous product on the market. Today, many states have extended product liability to the level of strict liability. Legally, this means *without regard to fault*. Therefore, a company could be liable for damages (financial compensation) caused by placing a product on the market with a defect even if the company did not know of the defect at the time of sale. The rule of strict liability has caused serious problems, particularly for the manufacturers of chemicals and drugs. A producer may place a drug or chemical on the market that everyone agrees is safe. Years later, a side effect or other health problem could emerge. Under the doctrine

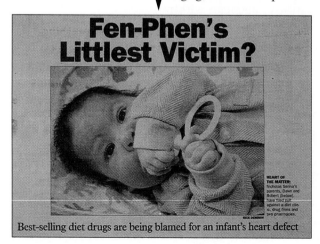

Best-selling diet drugs are being blamed for an infant's heart defect

of strict liability, the manufacturer can be held liable. Insurance companies and businesses are calling for relief from huge losses from such damage suits by lobbying Congress to set limits on the amounts of damages for which they are liable should their products harm consumers.

···· ▬▬▬ ····
LAWS PROTECTING IDEAS: PATENTS, COPYRIGHTS, AND TRADEMARKS

Many people, including students, invent products they feel are of commercial value, and then they wonder what to do next. One step may be to apply for a patent. A **patent** is a document that gives inventors exclusive rights to their inventions for 20 years. (The term of patents was increased from 17 to 20 years in 1995 as a result of the GATT Uruguay Round legislation.)[2] Patent owners may sell or license the use of the patent to others. Filing a patent with the U.S. Patent Office requires a search to make sure the patent is truly unique, followed by the filing of forms. The advice of a lawyer is usually recommended. See Figure A.2 for a review of patent laws. Penalties for violating a patent can be very severe. Several years ago Polaroid was able to force Kodak to recall all of its instant cameras because Polaroid had several patents that Kodak violated. Kodak lost millions of dollars, and Polaroid maintained market leadership in instant cameras.

How good are your chances of receiving a patent if you file for one? Some 65 percent of patent applications are approved, costing the inventor a minimum of $6,600 in fees over the life of the patent. The time it takes to process a patent is just over 20 months.[3] That figure may increase, however, since the growth in patents requested is outstripping the number of examiners in the U.S. Patent & Trademark Office. Less than 2 percent of inventors file on their own; the rest hire a lawyer. If you file successfully, you can make a lot of money if someone violates your patent. For example, Robert Kearns won millions of dollars from Ford and Chrysler for a patent on intermittent windshield wipers.

Critics argue that some inventors intentionally delay or drag out a patent application and wait for others to develop the technology. After others develop the technology, the inventors surface to claim the patent, and demand large fees.

patent
A document that gives inventors exclusive rights to their inventions for 20 years.

◄ **CONSIDER USING OT ACETATE B-4**
Leaders in Patents in the U.S.

◄ **CONSIDER USING LECTURE ENHANCER B-1**
Lloyd's of London Offering Patent Insurance

◄ **CONSIDER USING LECTURE ENHANCER B-2**
Rumble at the Patent Office

◄ **CONSIDER USING OT ACETATE B-5**
Types of Patents Issued

◄ **CONSIDER USING TM 33**
Patent Law

- A U.S. patent is enforceable for 20 years from its issue date. An issued patent excludes others from making, using, or selling a patented product or using a patented process.

- A patent defines its protected product or process in claims that set forth the required elements and features of that product or process. An unauthorized product or process that incorporates *all* of the claimed elements and features typically infringes the patent—even if the product or process utilizes additional elements or features not set forth in the claims.

- A patent must be issued before it can be infringed, which means that a patent pending has no legal effect—it serves only as an advance warning.

- A patent application general takes twenty months to be processed, and is kept secret by the Patent & Trademark Office up until the time the patent is issued.

- If the Patent & Trademark Office or a court determines that a claimed invention has been marketed for more than a year before a patent application is filed, the patent will be rejected or declared invalid.

Sources: *Inc.* magazine (July 1988). Copyright ©1988 by *Inc.* Publishing Company, 38 Commercial Wharf, Boston, MA 02110 and Rodney Ho, "Investors Battle Big Firms over Patent Secrets Bill," *The Wall Streeet Journal,* March 18, 1997, p. A1.

⌐ FIGURE **A.2** ¬
····
PATENT LAW

copyright
Exclusive rights to materials such as books, articles, photos, and cartoons.

trademark
A legally protected name, symbol, or design (or combination of these) that identifies the goods or services of one seller and distinguishes them from those of competitors.

➤ **CONSIDER USING LECTURE ENHANCER B-3**
Is Your Product Warranty Complete?

➤ **CONSIDER USING LECTURE ENHANCER B-4**
Negotiable Instrument Forgery and the UCC

From Peoria, Illinois, to Capetown, South Africa, Coca-Cola is one of the best known words in the world. It's not surprising then that this world famous brand name is a registered trademark of the Coca-Cola Company. If you look closely, the small circle at the end of the word Cola with the "R" inside signifies this company has exclusive legal protection to use this name and symbol.

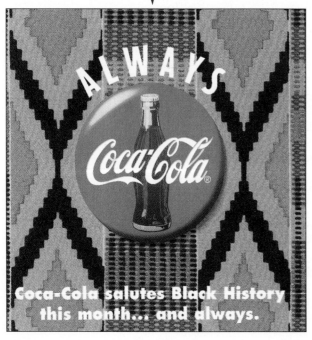

This is referred to as a *submarine patent*. One engineer has reportedly collected millions of dollars in royalties for a series of long-delayed patents, including one that was the forerunner of the bar-code scanner.[4] Congress has proposed changes to current patent law that would require patent applications be made public after 18 months regardless of whether a patent has been granted.[5]

A **copyright** protects an individual's rights to materials such as books, articles, photos, and cartoons. Copyrights are filed with the Library of Congress and involve a minimum of paperwork. They last for the lifetime of the author or artist plus 50 years. You may charge a fee to anyone who wishes to use your copyrighted material.

A **trademark** is a legally protected name, symbol, or design (or combination of them) that identifies the goods or services of one seller and distinguishes them from those of competitors. Trademarks generally belong to the owner forever, so long as they are properly registered and renewed every 20 years. Some well-known trademarks include the Golden Arches of McDonald's and the NBC peacock. We will discuss trademarks in more detail in Chapter 14.

···· ■ ····

SALES LAW: THE UNIFORM COMMERCIAL CODE

At one time, laws involving businesses varied from state to state, making interstate trade extremely complicated. Today, all states have adopted the same commercial law. The **Uniform Commercial Code (UCC)** is a comprehensive commercial law that covers sales laws and other commercial laws. Since all states have adopted the law, the UCC simplifies trading across state lines. The UCC has 11 articles, which contain laws covering sales; commercial paper such as promissory notes and checks; bank deposits and collections; letters of credit; bulk transfers; warehouse receipts, bills of lading, and other documents of title; investment securities; and secured transactions. We do not have space to discuss all of these articles, but we would like to tell you about at least two of them: (1) Article 2, which contains laws regarding warranties, and (2) Article 3, which covers negotiable instruments.

··· WARRANTIES ···

A warranty guarantees that the product sold will be acceptable for the purpose for which the buyer intends to use it. **Express warranties** are specific representations by the seller that are relied upon by the buyer regarding the goods. The warranty you receive in the box with a clock, toaster, or VCR is the express warranty. It spells out the seller's warranty agreement. **Implied warranties** are legally imposed on the seller. It is implied, for example, that the product will conform to the customary standards of the trade or industry in which it competes.

Warranties offered by sellers can be either full or limited. A full warranty requires a seller to replace or repair a product at no charge if the product is defective; limited warranties typically limit the defects or mechanical problems that are covered. Many of the rights of buyers, including the acceptance and rejection of goods, are spelled out in Article 2 of the UCC. Both buyers and sellers should become familiar with the UCC. You can read more about it in business law books in the library or on the Internet.

••• NEGOTIABLE INSTRUMENTS •••

Negotiable instruments are forms of commercial paper (such as checks) that are transferable among businesses and individuals and represent a promise to pay a specified amount. Article 3 of the Uniform Commercial Code states that negotiable instruments must (1) be written and signed by the maker or drawer, (2) be made payable on demand or at a certain time, (3) be made payable to the bearer or to order, and (4) contain an unconditional promise to pay a specified amount of money. Checks or other forms of negotiable instruments are transferred (negotiated for payment) when the payee signs the back. This is referred to as an endorsement.

CONTRACT LAW

If I offer to sell you my bike for $35 and later change my mind, can you force me to sell the bike, saying we had a contract? If I lose $120 to you in a poker game, can you sue in court to get your money? If I agree to sing at your wedding for free and back out at the last minute, can you claim we had a contract? These are the kinds of questions that contract law answers.

A **contract** is a legally enforceable agreement between two or more parties. **Contract law** specifies what a legally enforceable agreement is. Basically, a contract is legally binding if the following conditions are met:

1. *An offer is made.* An offer to do something or sell something can be oral or written. If I agree to sell you my bike for $35, I have made an offer. That offer is not legally binding, however, until other conditions are met.

2. *There must be voluntary acceptance of the offer.* The principle of mutual acceptance means that both parties to a contract must agree on the terms. If I use duress in getting you to agree to buy my bike, the contract would not be legal. Duress occurs if there is coercion through force or threat of force. You couldn't use duress to get me to sell my bike, either. Even if we both agree, though, the contract is still not legally binding without the following.

3. *Both parties must give consideration.* **Consideration** means something of value. If I agree to sell you my bike for $35, the bike and the $35 are consideration, and we have a legally binding contract. If I agree to sing at your wedding and you do not give me anything in return (consideration), we have no contract.

4. *Both parties must be competent.* A person under the influence of alcohol or drugs, or a person of unsound mind (one who has been legally declared incompetent), for example, cannot be held to a contract. In many cases, a minor may not be held to a contract, either. For example, if a 15-year-old agrees to pay $10,000 for a car, the seller will not be able to enforce the contract.

5. *The contract must be legal.* Gambling losses are not legally collectible. If I lose money to you in poker, you cannot legally collect. The sale of illegal drugs is another example of an unenforceable contract.

Uniform Commercial Code (UCC)
A comprehensive commercial law adopted by every state in the United States; it covers sales laws and other commercial laws.

express warranties
Specific representations by the seller regarding the goods.

implied warranties
Guarantees legally imposed on the seller.

negotiable instruments
Forms of commercial paper (such as checks) that are transferable among businesses and individuals and represent a promise to pay a specified amount.

contract
A legally enforceable agreement between two or more parties.

contract law
Laws that specify what constitutes a legally enforceable agreement.

◄ CONSIDER USING OT ACETATE B-3
Criteria for a Valid Contract

consideration
Something of value; consideration is one of the requirements of a legal contract.

6. *The contract must be in proper form.* An agreement for the sale of goods worth $500 or more must be in writing. Contracts that cannot be fulfilled within one year also must be put in writing. Contracts regarding real property (land and everything attached to it) must be in writing.

••• BREACH OF CONTRACT •••

breach of contract
When one party fails to follow the terms of a contract.

Breach of contract occurs when one party fails to follow the terms of a contract. Both parties may agree to end a contract, but if just one person violates the contract, the following may occur:

1. *Specific performance.* The person who violated the contract may be required to live up to the agreement if money damages would not be adequate. For example, if I legally offered to sell you a rare painting, I would have to sell you that painting.

damages
The monetary settlement awarded to a person who is injured by a breach of contract.

2. *Payment of damages.* The term **damages** refers to the monetary settlement awarded to a person who is injured by a breach of contract. If I fail to live up to a contract, you can sue me for damages, usually the amount you would lose from my nonperformance. If we had a legally binding contract for me to sing at your wedding, for example, and I failed to come, you could sue me for the cost of hiring a new singer.

3. *Discharge of obligation.* If I fail to live up to my end of a contract, you could agree to drop the matter. Generally you would not have to live up to your end of the agreement either.

Lawyers would not be paid so handsomely if the law were as simple as implied in these rules of contract. In fact, it is always best to have a contract in writing even if not required under law. The offer and consideration should be clearly specified, and the contract should be signed and dated. A contract does not have to be complicated as long as it has these elements: (1) it's in writing, (2) mutual consideration is specified, and (3) there is a clear offer and agreement.

LAWS TO PROMOTE
FAIR AND COMPETITIVE PRACTICES

One objective of legislators is to pass laws that the judiciary will enforce to ensure a competitive atmosphere among businesses and promote fair business practices. Chapter 2 explained how competition is a cornerstone of the free-market system. In the United States, the Justice Department's antitrust division and other government agencies serve as watchdogs to ensure that competition among sellers flows freely and that new competitors have open access to the market.

There was, however, a time when businesses operated under relatively free market conditions. Big businesses were able to drive smaller competitors out of business with little recourse. The following discussion shows how government responded to these troubling situations and how business must deal with them today.

••• THE INTERSTATE COMMERCE •••
ACT OF 1887

When the railroads started to grow after the Civil War, their managers thought little about what was good for the country and a great deal about what was good for the railroads. The public complained enough about such practices as the railroads agreeing among themselves to fix prices that Congress passed the Interstate Commerce Act in 1887. The act stipulated that the railroad rates must be "reasonable"; prohibited discriminatory rates, rebates, and other forms of favoritism; and outlawed price-fixing agreements between railroads. The act established the Interstate Commerce Commission (ICC) to enforce these provisions. In the fall of 1995, President Bill Clinton signed the Interstate Commerce Commission Termination Act, which abolished the 107-year-old ICC. Certain continuing responsibilities of the ICC were transferred to the Department of Transportation and the Surface Transportation Board.[6]

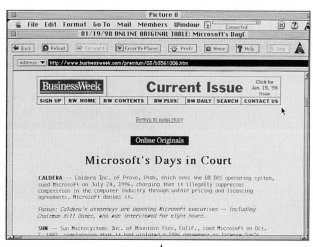

Competition is the cornerstone of the free-market system. In the United States the antitrust division of the Department of Justice is assigned the official task of ensuring markets are competitive and open. In 1997, the Department of Justice turned its sights on software giant Microsoft and investigated charges that the company illegally suppressess competition in the computer industry.

••• THE SHERMAN ANTITRUST ACT OF 1890 •••

In the late 19th century, big oil companies, big railroads, big steel companies, and other large firms dominated the U.S. economy. People were afraid that such large and powerful companies would crush any competitors and then charge high prices. It was in that atmosphere that Congress passed the Sherman Antitrust Act in 1890. The Sherman Act was designed to prevent large organizations from stifling the competition of smaller or newer firms. The Sherman Act forbids the following: (1) contracts, combinations, or conspiracies in restraint of trade, and (2) actual monopolies or attempts to monopolize any part of trade or commerce. Because of the act's vague language, there was some doubt about just what practices it prohibited. The following laws were passed later to clarify some of the legal concepts in the Sherman Act.

- *The Clayton Act of 1914.* The Clayton Act prohibits exclusive dealing, tying contracts, interlocking directorates, and buying large amounts of stock in competing corporations. *Exclusive dealing* is selling goods with the condition that the buyer will not buy goods from a competitor (when the effect lessens competition). A tying contract requires a buyer to purchase unwanted items in order to purchase the desired items. An interlocking directorate occurs when a board of directors includes members of the board of competing corporations.

- *The Federal Trade Commission Act of 1914.* The Federal Trade Commission Act prohibits unfair methods of competition in commerce. This legislation set up the five-member Federal Trade Commission (FTC) to enforce compliance with this act. The involvement of the FTC depends on the members on the board at the time. The FTC conducted three times as many investigations and brought twice as many cases in the 1990s as it did during the 1980s.

- *The Robinson-Patman Act of 1936.* The Robinson-Patman Act prohibits price discrimination. One interesting aspect of the Robinson-Patman Act is that it applies to both sellers and buyers who "knowingly" induce or receive an unlawful discrimination in price. It also stipulates that certain types of price-cutting are criminal offenses punishable by fine and imprisonment. This act applies to business-to-business transactions and does not apply to consumers in business transactions.

- *The Wheeler-Lea Amendment of 1938.* The Wheeler-Lea Amendment gave the FTC additional jurisdiction over false or misleading advertising. It also gave the FTC power to increase fines if its requirements aren't met within 60 days.

As the years have passed, the laws have grown more precise and the punishment more definite. Congress is continuing to monitor business practices and to pass laws to regulate those practices when necessary.

···· ▬▬ ····
LAWS TO PROTECT CONSUMERS

consumerism
A social movement that seeks to increase and strengthen the rights and powers of buyers in relation to sellers.

Consumerism is a social movement that seeks to increase and strengthen the rights and powers of buyers in relation to sellers. President John F. Kennedy proposed four basic rights of consumers: (1) the right to safety, (2) the right to be informed, (3) the right to choose, and (4) the right to be heard. These rights will not be maintained if consumers passively wait for organizations to recognize them; they will come partially from consumer action in the marketplace. Consumerism is the people's way of getting their fair share in marketing exchanges. Although consumerism is not a new movement, it has taken on new vigor and direction throughout the 1990s. Figure A.3 lists the major consumer protection laws.

···· ▬▬ ····
TAX LAWS

taxes
How the government (federal, state, and local) raises money.

Mention the word *taxes* and most people frown. That's because taxes affect almost every individual and business in the United States. **Taxes** are how the government (federal, state, and local) raises money. Traditionally, taxes have been used primarily as a source of funding for government operations and programs. They have also been used as a method of encouraging or discouraging taxpayers from doing something. For example, if the government wishes to reduce the use of certain classes of products (cigarettes, beer, etc.), it passes

To raise revenue for specific social objectives or programs, or to discourage increasing consumption or use of specific products such as alcoholic beverages or tobacco, the government often passes additional taxes on the manufacturer, retailer, or both on these selected items. Added tax revenues raised from such *sin taxes* go toward funding the specific objective or program. Suggestions have been made to increase the tax on cigarettes by as much as $1 per pack to discourage teenagers from smoking.

what are referred to as *sin taxes*. The additional cost of the product from increased taxes *perhaps* discourages additional consumption. In other situations, the government may encourage businesses to hire new employees or purchase new equipment by offering a tax credit. A tax credit is an amount that can be deducted from a tax bill.

Taxes are levied from a variety of sources. Income (personal and business), sales, and property are the major bases of tax revenue. The federal government receives its largest share of taxes from income. States and local communities often make extensive use of sales taxes. The tax policies of states and cities are taken into consideration when businesses seek to locate operations. Tax policies also affect personal decisions such as retirement. Figure A.4 highlights the primary types of taxes levied on individuals and businesses.

◄ CONSIDER USING TM 34
Consumer protection laws

FIGURE A.3
....
CONSUMER
PROTECTION LAWS

LEGISLATION	PURPOSE
Pure Food and Drug Act (1906)	Protects against the adulteration and misbranding of foods and drugs sold in interstate commerce.
Food, Drug, and Cosmetic Act (1938)	Protects against the adulteration and sale of foods, drugs, cosmetics, or therapeutic devices and allows the Food and Drug Administration to set minimum standards and guidelines for food products.
Wool Products Labeling Act (1940)	Protects manufacturers, distributors, and consumers from undisclosed substitutes and mixtures in manufactured wool products.
Fur Products Labeling Act (1951)	Protects consumers from misbranding, false advertising, and false invoicing of furs and fur products.
Flammable Fabrics Act (1953)	Prohibits the interstate transportation of dangerously flammable wearing apparel and fabrics.
Automobile Information Disclosure Act (1958)	Requires auto manufacturers to put suggested retail prices on all new passenger vehicles.
Textile Fiber Products Identification Act (1958)	Protects producers and consumers against misbranding and false advertising of fiber content of textile fiber products.
Cigarette Labeling Act (1965)	Requires cigarette manufacturers to label cigarettes as hazardous to health.
Fair Packaging and Labeling Act (1966)	Makes unfair or deceptive packaging or labeling of certain consumer commodities illegal.
Child Protection Act (1966)	Removes from sale potentially harmful toys and allows the FDA to pull dangerous products from the market.
Truth-in-Lending Act (1968)	Requires full disclosure of all finance charges on consumer credit agreements and in advertisements of credit plans.
Child Protection and Toy Safety Act (1969)	Protects children from toys and other products that contain thermal, electrical, or mechanical hazards.
Fair Credit Reporting Act (1970)	Requires that consumer credit reports contain only accurate, relevant, and recent information and are confidential unless a proper party requests them for an appropriate reason.
Consumer Product Safety Act (1972)	Created an independent agency to protect consumers from unreasonable risk of injury arising from consumer products and to set safety standards.
Magnuson–Moss Warranty–Federal Trade Commission Improvement Act (1975)	Provides for minimum disclosure standards for written consumer product warranties and allows the FTC to prescribe interpretive rules and policy statements regarding unfair or deceptive practices.
Alcohol Labeling Legislation (1988)	Provides for warning labels on liquor saying that women shouldn't drink when pregnant and that alcohol impairs our abilities.
Nutrition Labeling and Education Act (1990)	Requires truthful and uniform nutritional labeling on every food the FDA regulates.

FIGURE **A.4**

· · · ·

TYPES OF TAXES

➤ CONSIDER USING TM 35
Types of taxes

TYPE	PURPOSE
Income taxes	Taxes paid on the income received by businesses and individuals. Income taxes are the largest source of tax income received by the federal government.
Property taxes	Taxes paid on real and personal property. *Real property* is real estate owned by individuals and businesses. *Personal property* is a broader category that includes any movable property such as tangible items (wedding rings, equipment, etc.) or intangible items (stocks, checks, mortgages, etc.). Taxes are based on their assessed value.
Sales taxes	Taxes paid on merchandise when it's sold at the retail level.
Excise taxes	Taxes paid on selected items such as tobacco, alcoholic beverages, airline travel, gasoline, and firearms. These are often referred to as *sin taxes*. Income generated from the tax goes toward a specifically designated purpose. For example, gasoline taxes often help the federal government and state governments pay for highway construction or improvements.

· · · · ━━━ · · · ·

BANKRUPTCY LAWS

bankruptcy
The legal process by which a person, business, or government entity unable to meet financial obligations, is relieved of those obligations by having the court divide any assets among creditors, freeing the debtor to begin anew.

➤ CONSIDER USING OT ACETATE B-6
The Average Person Who Files Bankruptcy

➤ CONSIDER USING LECTURE ENHANCER B-5
Bankruptcy Reform Proposals: Only Strong Will Survive

Bankruptcy is the legal process by which a person, business, or government entity unable to meet financial obligations is relieved of those debts by a court. The court divides any assets among creditors, allowing creditors to get at least part of their money and freeing the debtor to begin anew. The U.S. Constitution gives Congress the power to establish bankruptcy laws. There has been bankruptcy legislation since the 1890s. Two major amendments to the bankruptcy code include the Bankruptcy Amendments and Federal Judgeships Act of 1984 and the Bankruptcy Reform Act of 1994. The 1984 legislation allows a person who is bankrupt to keep part of the equity (ownership) in a house, $1,200 in a car, and some other personal property. The Bankruptcy Reform Act of 1994 amends more than 45 sections of the bankruptcy code and creates reforms that speed up and simplify the process.[7]

In 1996 a record 1.2 million Americans filed for bankruptcy.[8] This was the first time bankruptcies exceeded 1 million in a year.[9] The United States averaged only 250,000 bankruptcies per year in the 1960s and 1970s. The number of bankruptcies picked up in the late 1980s and grew tremendously in the 1990s. Bankruptcy attorneys say the increase in filings is due to a lessening of the stigma of bankruptcy, the changing economy, an increase in understanding of bankruptcy law and the protection it offers, increased advertising by bankruptcy attorneys, and the ease with which some consumers can get credit. Over 90 percent of bankruptcy filings each year are by individuals.

Bankruptcy can be either voluntary or involuntary. In **voluntary bankruptcy** cases the debtor applies for bankruptcy, whereas in **involuntary bankruptcy** cases the creditors start legal procedures against the debtor. Most bankruptcies today are voluntary because creditors usually want to wait in hopes that they will be paid all of the money due them rather than settle for only part of it.

Bankruptcy procedures begin when a petition is filed with the court under one of the following sections of the Bankruptcy Code:

voluntary bankruptcy
Legal procedures initiated by a debtor.

involuntary bankruptcy
Bankruptcy procedures filed by a debtor's creditors.

Chapter 7—"straight bankruptcy" or liquidation (used by businesses and individuals).

Chapter 11—reorganization (used by businesses and some individuals).

Chapter 13—repayment (used by individuals).

Chapter 7 calls for straight bankruptcy, which requires the sale of nonexempt assets of debtors. Under federal exemption statutes, a debtor may be able to retain up to $7,500 of equity in a home ($15,000 in a joint case); up to $1,200 of equity in an automobile; up to $4,000 in household furnishings, apparel, and musical instruments; and up to $500 in jewelry. States may have different exemption statutes. When the sale of assets is over, the resulting cash is divided among creditors, including the government. Almost 70 percent of bankruptcies follow these procedures.[10] Chapter 7 stipulates the order in which the assets are to be distributed among the creditors. First, creditors with *secured* claims receive the collateral for their claims or repossess the claimed asset. Then *unsecured* claims are paid in this order:

1. Costs involved in the bankruptcy case.
2. Any business costs incurred after bankruptcy was filed.
3. Wages, salaries, or commissions (limited to $2,000 per person).
4. Employee benefit plan contributions.
5. Refunds to consumers who paid for products that weren't delivered (limited to $900 per claimant).
6. Federal and state taxes.

The remainder (if any) is divided among unsecured creditors in proportion to their claims. See Figure A.5 for the steps used in liquidating assets under Chapter 7.

Chapter 11 allows a company to reorganize and continue operations while paying only a limited proportion of its debts. The company does not have to be insolvent in order to file for relief under Chapter 11. The Bankruptcy Reform Act of 1994 extends a "fast-track" procedure for small businesses filing under Chapter 11. Under certain conditions, the company can sell assets, borrow

FIGURE **A.5**

· · · ·

HOW ASSETS ARE DIVIDED IN BANKRUPTCY

This figure shows that the creditor (the person owed money) selects the trustee (the person or organization that handles the sale of assets). Note that the process may be started by the debtor or the creditors.

◄ **CONSIDER USING TM 36**
How Assets Are Divided in Bankruptcy

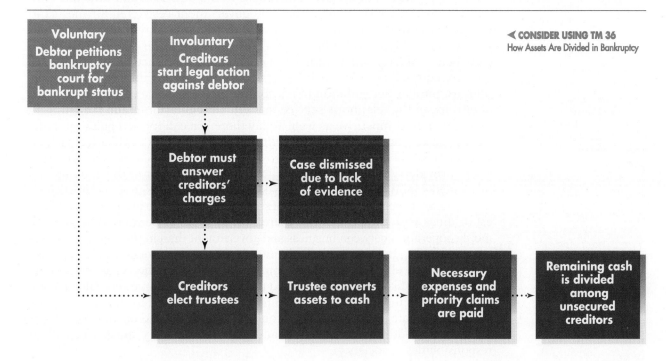

In the fourth quarter of 1997, Manhattan Bagel filed a voluntary bankruptcy petition under Chapter 11 of the bankruptcy law. Under Chapter 11, a company can continue to operate while it tries to work out a plan for paying off its debts. Unfortunately the track record for companies filing Chapter 11 and returning successfully to the market is not encouraging. Let's hope Manhattan Bagel is able to roll in the dough again.

deregulation
Government withdrawal of certain laws and regulations that seem to hinder competition.

money, and change officers to strengthen its market position. A trustee appointed by the court to protect the interests of creditors usually supervises all such matters. Chapter 11 is designed to help both debtors and creditors find the best solution.

Under Chapter 11, a company continues to operate but has court protection against creditors' lawsuits while it tries to work out a plan for paying off its debts. In theory, Chapter 11 is a way for sick companies to recover. In reality, less than 25 percent of Chapter 11 companies emerge healthy—usually only the big ones with lots of cash available to start with. In 1991, the U.S. Supreme Court gave individuals the right to file bankruptcy under Chapter 11.

Chapter 13 permits individuals, including small-business owners, to pay back creditors over a three-to-five-year period. Chapter 13 proceedings are less complicated and less expensive than Chapter 7 proceedings. The debtor files a proposed plan for paying off debts to the court. If the plan is approved, the debtor pays a court-appointed trustee in monthly installments as agreed upon in the repayment plan. The trustee then pays each creditor.

···· ▬▬▬ ····

DEREGULATION

By 1980, the United States had developed laws and regulations covering almost every aspect of business. There was concern that there were too many laws and regulations, and that these laws and regulations were costing the public money (see Figure A.6). Thus began the movement toward deregulation. **Deregulation** means that the government withdraws certain laws and regulations that seem to hinder competition. Perhaps the most publicized examples of deregulation have been those in the airlines and in the telecommunications industry. At one time, the government restricted airlines as to where they could land and fly. When such restrictions were lifted, the airlines began competing for different routes and charging lower prices. This was a clear benefit to consumers, but it put tremendous pressure on the airlines to be more competitive. New airlines were born to take advantage of the opportunities. Similar deregulation in telecommunications gave consumers a flood of options in the telephone service market. Deregulation made the trucking industry more competitive as well. Today there is a call for deregulation in the electric power industry and other utilities.[11] Such changes could affect virtually every U.S. city and citizen as the cost of power changes as well as the number of providers.[12] There is also a call for new regulations in the banking and investments industries that would make financial markets more competitive.

It seems some regulation of business seems necessary to assure fair and honest dealings with the public. But there now appears to be more dialogue and more cooperation between business and government than in the past. Businesses have adapted to the laws and regulations, and have done much toward producing safer, more effective products. Competition is getting fierce, as many small and innovative firms have been started to capture selected markets. Global competition is also increasing. Business and government need to continue to work together to create a competitive environment that is fair and open. If businesses do not want additional regulation and government, they must accept their responsibilities to society.

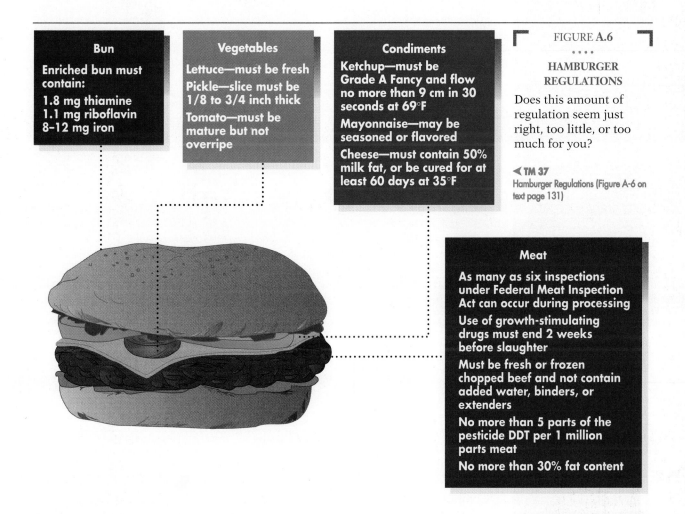

Bun

Enriched bun must contain:

1.8 mg thiamine
1.1 mg riboflavin
8–12 mg iron

Vegetables

Lettuce—must be fresh

Pickle—slice must be 1/8 to 3/4 inch thick

Tomato—must be mature but not overripe

Condiments

Ketchup—must be Grade A Fancy and flow no more than 9 cm in 30 seconds at 69°F

Mayonnaise—may be seasoned or flavored

Cheese—must contain 50% milk fat, or be cured for at least 60 days at 35°F

Meat

As many as six inspections under Federal Meat Inspection Act can occur during processing

Use of growth-stimulating drugs must end 2 weeks before slaughter

Must be fresh or frozen chopped beef and not contain added water, binders, or extenders

No more than 5 parts of the pesticide DDT per 1 million parts meat

No more than 30% fat content

FIGURE **A.6**
· · · ·
HAMBURGER REGULATIONS

Does this amount of regulation seem just right, too little, or too much for you?

◄ TM 37
Hamburger Regulations (Figure A-6 on text page 131)

KEY TERMS
· · · · · ·

administrative agencies 119
bankruptcy 128
breach of contract 124
business law 119
common law 119
consideration 123
consumerism 126
contract 123
contract law 123

copyright 122
damages 124
deregulation 130
express warranties 123
implied warranties 123
involuntary bankruptcy 128
judiciary 119
negotiable instruments 123

patent 121
product liability 120
statutory law 119
taxes 126
tort 119
trademark 122
Uniform Commercial Code (UCC) 123
voluntary bankruptcy 128

Forms of Business Ownership

Chapter 5

LEARNING GOALS

After you have read and studied this chapter,
you should be able to

1 Compare the advantages and disadvantages of sole proprietorships.

2 Describe the differences between general and limited partners, and compare the advantages and disadvantages of partnerships.

3 Compare the advantages and disadvantages of corporations, and summarize the differences between C corporations, S corporations, and limited liability companies.

4 Define and give examples of three types of corporate mergers and explain the role of leveraged buyouts and taking a firm private.

5 Outline the advantages and disadvantages of franchises and discuss the opportunities for diversity in franchising and the challenges of international franchising.

6 Explain the role of cooperatives.

I n 1964 Tony Conza borrowed $2,000 to open his first sandwich shop with two of his old schoolmates in Hoboken, New Jersey. Three years later they had 10 stores. What they didn't have was enough experience to manage the business. The growing losses pushed the partners out, but Conza's self-confidence told him to stick with it. He hired an operations expert to help him learn management skills. As the business grew stronger, he hired a lawyer to prepare franchise arrangements. By 1983, there were 150 franchises and revenues approaching $1 million a year. Conza went public that year, putting Blimpie stock on the open market.

Blimpie added only 50 new franchises in the next five years. Conza grew restless. He felt that he let the details of managing deflate his entrepreneurial passion. He vowed to change from a manager drowning in day-to-day details into a leader who could create a vision and inspire his employees and franchisees to maximize their talents. Conza chose a team of his senior managers to revise goals for the company and then delegated the new responsibilities to meet those goals to his managers. Since then, Blimpie has more than tripled in size, to more than 700 stores. Now there are Blimpie outlets in such diverse places as on campus at the University of Texas at Austin; in a bowling alley in Collinsville,

PROFILE

Tony Conza of Blimpie International Sandwich Shops

Illinois; on some Delta airline flights; and in a hospital in Atlanta, Georgia. Conza adds a personal touch to Blimpie advertising by appearing in national radio and regional television ads.

In 1997, Conza hired a consultant to help find another food brand to franchise in combination with Blimpie. One reason he did so was that the company had to pass up some choice retail sites because they were too large for Blimpie outlets by themselves. If two brands share space, more sites become feasible. Blimpie won't be the first company to offer co-branded outlets. For example, Allied Domecq Ltd. of Britain combines some of its Dunkin' Donuts and Baskin-Robbins units.

Conza's business started as a partnership, changed to a sole proprietorship, changed again to a franchise operation, and finally changed to a franchise corporation. Each form of ownership has its advantages and disadvantages. You will learn about them all in this chapter.

Sources: Louis S. Richman, "Rekindling the Entrepreneurial Fire," *Fortune*, February 21, 1994, p. 112; Jeffrey A. Tannenbaum, "Putting a Face with a Name Gives Ads Personal Touch," *The Wall Street Journal*, July 17, 1997, p. B2; "Blimpie International Hires Financial Consultant for Mergers," Dow Jones News Service, May 13, 1997; and Jeffrey A. Tannenbaum, "Blimpie Seeks to Gain Synergies from a Franchise Acquisition," *The Wall Street Journal Interactive Edition*, May 20, 1997.

BASIC FORMS OF BUSINESS OWNERSHIP

◄ **CONSIDER USING TM 38**
Chapter Outline

◄ Consider Using LECTURE ENHANCER 5-1
Why Government Ownership

Like Tony Conza, hundreds of thousands of people start new businesses in the United States every year. Chances are, you have thought of owning your own business or know someone who has. One key to success in a new business is knowing how to get the resources you need to start. You may need to take on partners or find other ways of obtaining money. To stay in business, you may need help from someone with more expertise than you have in certain areas, or you may need to raise more money to expand. How you form your business can make a tremendous difference in your long-term success. You can form a business in several ways. The three major forms of business ownership are (1) sole proprietorships, (2) partnerships, and (3) corporations.

Due in part to the services provided by firms such as BellSouth, minority and woman-owned businesses have many opportunities for success in today's markets *if* they can provide quality goods and services at competitive prices.

sole proprietorship
A business that is owned, and usually managed, by one person.

partnership
A legal form of business with two or more owners.

corporation
A legal entity with authority to act and have liability separate from its owners.

➤ **LEARNING GOAL 1.**
Compare the advantages and disadvantages of sole proprietorships.

It can be easy to get started in your own business. You can begin a word processing service out of your home, open a car repair center, start a restaurant, or go about meeting other wants and needs of your community. An organization that is owned, and usually managed, by one person is called a **sole proprietorship**. That is the most common form of business ownership.

Many people do not have the money, time, or desire to run a business on their own. They prefer to have someone else or some group of people get together to form the business. When two or more people legally agree to become co-owners of a business, the organization is called a **partnership**.

There are advantages to creating a business that is separate and distinct from the owners. A legal entity with authority to act and have liability separate from its owners is called a **corporation**.

As you will learn in this chapter, each form of business ownership has its advantages—and disadvantages. It is important to understand these advantages and disadvantages before starting a business. Keep in mind that just because a business starts in one form of ownership, it doesn't always stay in that form. Many companies start out in one form (like Blimpie International sandwich shops), then add or drop a partner or two, and eventually become corporations, limited liability companies, and/or franchisors. Let's begin our discussion by looking at the most basic form of ownership—the sole proprietorship.

···· ▬ ····

SOLE PROPRIETORSHIPS

··· ADVANTAGES OF SOLE PROPRIETORSHIPS ···

Sole proprietorships are the easiest kind of businesses for you to explore in your quest for an interesting career. Every town has some sole proprietorships you can visit. Talk with some of the people in them about the joys and frustrations of being on their own. Most will mention the benefits of being their own boss and setting their own hours. Other advantages they mention may include the following:

1. *Ease of starting and ending the business.* All you have to do to start a sole proprietorship is buy or lease the needed equipment (e.g., a saw, a word processor, a tractor, a lawn mower) and put up some announcements saying you are in business. It is just as easy to get out of business; you simply stop. There is no one to consult or to disagree with about such decisions. You may have to get a permit or license from the local government, but often that is no problem.

2. *Being your own boss.* "Working for others simply does not have the same excitement as working for yourself." That's the way sole proprietors feel. You may make mistakes, but they are your mistakes—and so are the many small victories each day.

3. *Pride of ownership.* People who own and manage their own businesses are rightfully proud of their work. They deserve all the credit for taking the risks and providing needed goods or services.

4. *Retention of profit.* Other than the joy of being your own boss, there is nothing like the pleasure of knowing that you can earn as much as possible and do not have to share that money with anyone else (except the government, in taxes).

5. *No special taxes.* All the profits of a sole proprietorship are taxed as the personal income of the owner, and the owner pays the normal income tax on that money. (However, owners do have to file an estimated tax return and make quarterly payments.)

◄ **CONSIDER USING OT ACETATE 5-1**
Advantages and Disadvantages of Sole Proprietorships

••• DISADVANTAGES OF SOLE PROPRIETORSHIPS •••

Not everyone is equipped to own and manage a business. Often it is difficult to save enough money to start a business and keep it going. The costs of inventory, supplies, insurance, advertising, rent, utilities, and so on may be too much to cover alone. There are other disadvantages of owning your own business:

1. *Unlimited liability—the risk of losses.* When you work for others, it is their problem if the business is not profitable. When you own your own business, you and the business are considered one. You have **unlimited liability**; that is, any debts or damages incurred by the business are your debts and you must pay them, even if it means selling your home, your car, and so forth. This is a serious risk, and one that requires thought and discussion with a lawyer, insurance agent, and others.

2. *Limited financial resources.* Funds available to the business are limited to the funds that the one (sole) owner can gather. Since there are serious limits to how much money one person can raise, partnerships and corporations have a greater probability of recruiting the needed financial backing to start a business and keep it going.

3. *Difficulty in management.* All businesses need some management; that is, someone must keep inventory records, accounting records, tax records, and so forth. Many people who are skilled at selling things or providing a service are not so skilled in keeping records. Sole proprietors may have no one to help them. It is often difficult to find good, qualified people to help run the business. A common complaint among sole proprietors is that good employees are hard to find.

4. *Overwhelming time commitment.* It is hard to own a business, manage it, train people, and have time for anything else in life. This is true of any business, but a sole proprietor has no one to share the burden with. The owner must spend long hours working. The owner of a store, for example, may put in 12 hours a day, at least six days a week. That is almost twice the hours worked by a salaried laborer. Imagine how this time commitment affects the sole proprietor's family life. Tim DeMello, founder of the successful company Wall Street Games Inc., echoes countless other sole proprietors when he says, "It's not a job, it's not a career, it's a way of life."[1]

5. *Few fringe benefits.* If you are your own boss, you lose the fringe benefits that come from working for others. You have no health insurance, no disability insurance, no sick leave, no vacation pay, and so on. These benefits may add up to 30 percent or more of a worker's income.

unlimited liability
The responsibility of business owners for all of the debts of the business.

◄ **CONSIDER USING LECTURE ENHANCER 5-2**
The Development of Sears and Roebuck

6. *Limited growth*. If the owner becomes incapacitated, the business often comes to a standstill. Expansion is often slow since a sole proprietorship relies on its owner for most of its creativity, business know-how, and funding.

7. *Limited life span*. If the sole proprietor dies or retires, the business no longer exists unless it is sold or taken over by the sole proprietor's heirs.

➤ **LEARNING GOAL 2.**
Describe the differences between general and limited partnerships and compare the advantages and disadvantages of partnerships.

Talk with few local entrepreneurs about the problems they have faced in being on the own. They are likely to have many interesting stories to tell, such as problems getting loans from the bank, problems with theft, and problems simply keeping up with the business. These problems are also reasons why many sole proprietors choose to find partners to share the load.

Critical Thinking

Have you ever dreamed of opening your own business? If you did, what would it be? What talents or skills do you have that you could use? Could you start a business in your own home? How much would it cost to start? Could you begin part-time while you worked elsewhere? What satisfaction and profit could you get from owning your own business? What would you lose?

PARTNERSHIPS

general partnership
A partnership in which all owners share in operating the business and in assuming liability for the business's debts.

limited partnership
A partnership with one or more general partners and one or more limited partners.

general partner
An owner (partner) who has unlimited liability and is active in managing the firm.

limited partner
An owner who invests money in the business but does not have any management responsibility or liability for losses beyond the investment.

limited liability
The responsibility of a business' owners for losses only up to the amount they invest; limited partners and shareholders have limited liability.

master limited partnership (MLP)
A partnership that looks much like a corporation in that it acts like a corporation and is traded on the stock exchanges like a corporation, but is taxed like a partnership and thus avoids the corporate income tax.

A partnership is a legal form of business with two or more owners. All states except Louisiana have adopted the Uniform Partnership Act (UPA) to replace laws relating to partnerships. The UPA defines the three key elements of any general partnership as (1) common ownership, (2) shared profits and losses, and (3) the right to participate in managing the operations of the business.

There are several types of partnerships: (1) general partnerships, (2) limited partnerships, and (3) master limited partnerships. A **general partnership** is a partnership in which all owners share in operating the business and in assuming liability for the business's debts. A **limited partnership** is a partnership with one or more general partners and one or more limited partners. A **general partner** is an owner (partner) who has unlimited liability and is active in managing the firm. A **limited partner** risks an investment in the firm, but enjoys limited liability and not legally help manage the company. **Limited liability** means that limited partners are not responsible for the debts of the business beyond the amount of the investment—their liability (debts they must pay) is limited to the amount they invest to the company; their personal assets are not at risk.

A new form of partnership, the **master limited partnership (MLP)**, looks much like a corporation in that it acts like a corporation and is traded on the stock exchanges like a corporation, but it is taxed like a partnership and thus avoids the corporate income tax. Two well-known MLPs are Burger King and Perkins Family Restaurants.

• ADVANTAGES OF PARTNERSHIPS •••

There are many advantages to having one or more partners in a business. Often, it is much easier to own and manage a business with one or more partners. Your partner can cover for you when you are sick or go on vacation. Your partner may be skilled at inventory control and accounting, while you do the selling or servicing. A partner can also provide additional money, support, and expertise. Some of the people who are enjoying the advantages of partnerships today are doctors, lawyers, dentists, and other professionals. Partnerships usually have the following advantages:

1. *More financial resources.* When two or more people pool their money and credit, it is easier to pay the rent, utilities, and other bills incurred by a business. A limited partnership is specially designed to help raise capital (money). As mentioned earlier, a limited partner invests money in the business but cannot legally have any management responsibility and has limited liability.

2. *Shared management and pooled knowledge.* It is simply much easier to manage the day-to-day activities of a business with carefully chosen partners. Partners give each other free time from the business and provide different skills and perspectives. Some people find that the best partner is a spouse. That is why you see so many husband-and-wife teams managing restaurants, service shops, and other businesses.

3. *Longer survival.* A study reported in *Forbes* magazine found that of 2,000 businesses started since 1960, partnerships were four times as likely to succeed as sole proprietorships. Having a partner watching over him or her can help a businessperson become more disciplined.

Collette Renfro owns and has developed a very successful business, The Blackberry Harvest Dollhouse Museum Shoppe in Homewood, IL. As a sole proprietor she has the freedom to make all her own business decisions that she would not necessarily have if she had a partner. But this increased freedom also includes increased risks. Just as Collette gets to keep all the profits, she must also pay for any mistakes she makes. What are some of the key decisions she has to make on a frequent basis?

••• DISADVANTAGES OF PARTNERSHIPS •••

Anytime two people must agree on anything, there is the possibility of conflict and tension. Partnerships have caused splits among families, friends, and marriages. Let's explore the disadvantages of partnerships:

1. *Unlimited liability.* Each *general* partner is liable for the debts of the firm, no matter who was responsible for causing those debts. You are liable for your partners' mistakes as well as your own. Like a sole proprietor, general partners can lose their homes, cars, and everything else they own if the business is sued by someone or if it goes bankrupt. Many states are allowing partners to form limited liability partnerships (LLPs) to end this disadvantage.

2. *Division of profits.* Sharing the risk means sharing the profit, and that can cause conflicts. For example, two people form a partnership; one puts in more money and the other puts in more hours. Each may feel justified in asking for a bigger share of the profits. Imagine the resulting conflicts.

3. *Disagreements among partners.* Disagreements over money are just one example of potential conflict in a partnership. Who has final authority over employees? Who hires and fires employees? Who works what hours? What if one partner wants to buy expensive equipment for the firm and the other partner disagrees? Potential conflicts are many. Because of such problems, all terms of partnership should be spelled out in writing to protect all parties and to minimize misunderstandings. The Spotlight on Small Business box on the next page offers a few tips about choosing a partner.

4. *Difficult to terminate.* Once you have committed yourself to a partnership, it is not easy to get out of it. Sure, you can end a partnership by just saying "I quit." However, questions about who gets what and what

◄ **CONSIDER USING LECTURE ENHANCER 5-3**
Are Partners Bad for Business?

◄ **CONSIDER USING OT ACETATE 5-2**
Advantages and Disadvantages of Partnerships

◄ **CONSIDER USING LECTURE ENHANCER 5-4**
Put Partnership Agreements in Writing

Spotlight on Small Business

http://www.inc.com/idx_t_xb.html

Choose Your Partner

Suppose you need money and want help running your business, and you decide to take on a partner. You know that partnerships are like marriages and that you won't really know the other person until after you live together. How do you choose the right partner? Before you plunge into a partnership, do three things:

1. Talk to people who have been in successful—and unsuccessful—partnerships. Find out what worked and what didn't. Ask them how conflicts were resolved and how decisions were made.

2. Interview your prospective partner very carefully. What skills does the person have? Are they the same as yours, or do they complement your skills?

What contacts, resources, or special attributes will the person bring to the business? Do you feel the same about family members working for the business? Do you share the same vision for the company's future?

3. Evaluate your prospective partner as a decision maker. Ask yourself, "Is this someone with whom I could happily share authority for all major business decisions?"

Just like most good marriages, the best way to avoid major conflicts is to begin with an honest communication of what each partner expects to give and get ▲ from the partnership.

> **CONSIDER USING CRITICAL THINKING EXERCISE 5-1**
> Picking Partners (**SCANS**)

happens next are often very difficult to solve when the business is closed. Surprisingly, law firms often have faulty partnership agreements and find that breaking up is hard to do. How do you get rid of a partner you don't like? It is best to decide that up front in the partnership agreement. The box called How to Form a Partnership gives you more ideas about what should be included in partnership agreements.

The best way to learn about the advantages and disadvantages of partnerships is to interview several people who have experience with such agreements. They will give you insights and hints on how to avoid problems.

One common fear of owning your own business or having a partner is the fear of losing everything you own if the business loses a lot of money or someone sues the business. Many businesspeople try to avoid this and the other disadvantages of sole proprietorships and partnerships by forming corporations. We shall discuss this basic form of business ownership next.

Progress Check

- Most people who start a business in the United States are sole proprietors. What are the advantages and disadvantages of sole proprietorships?

- What are some of the advantages of partnerships over sole proprietorships?

- Why would unlimited liability be considered one of the biggest drawbacks to sole proprietorships and general partnerships?

- What is the difference between a limited partner and a general partner?

HOW TO FORM A PARTNERSHIP

It's not hard to form a partnership, but it's wise for each prospective partner to get the counsel of a lawyer experienced with such agreements. Lawyers' services are usually expensive, so would-be partners should read all about partnerships and reach some basic agreements before calling a lawyer. One good book that covers the basics of forming a partnership is *The New Jacoby & Meyers Practical Guide to Everyday Law* (Fireside Press/Simon & Schuster, 1994).

For your protection, be sure to put your partnership agreement in writing. The Model Business Corporation Act recommends including the following in a written partnership agreement:

1. The name of the business. Many states require the firm's name to be registered with state and/or county officials if the firm's name is different from the name of any of the partners.

2. The names and addresses of all partners.

3. The purpose and nature of the business, the location of the principal offices, and any other locations where the business will be conducted.

4. The date the partnership will start and how long it will last. Will it exist for a specific length of time or will it stop when one of the partners dies or when the partners agree to discontinue?

5. The contributions made by each partner. Will some partners contribute money, while others provide real estate, personal property, expertise, or labor? When are the contributions due?

6. The management responsibilities. Will all partners have equal voices in management or will there be senior and junior partners?

7. The duties of each partner.

8. The salaries and drawing accounts of each partner.

9. Provision for sharing of profits or losses.

10. Provision for accounting procedures. Who'll keep the accounts? What bookkeeping and accounting methods will be used? Where will the books be kept?

11. The requirements for taking in new partners.

12. Any special restrictions, rights, or duties of any partner.

13. Provision for a retiring partner.

14. Provision for the purchase of a deceased or retiring partner's share of the business.

15. Provision for how grievances will be handled.

16. Provision for how to dissolve the partnership and distribute the assets to the partners.

•••• ▬▬▬ ••••

CORPORATIONS

◄ **CONSIDER USING LECTURE ENHANCER 5-5**
The Fortune List of Most Admired Corporations

Although the word *corporation* makes people think of big businesses like General Motors, IBM, Ford, Exxon, GE, Westinghouse, and USX (formerly U.S. Steel), it is not necessary to be big in order to incorporate (start a corporation). Obviously, many corporations are big. However, incorporating may be beneficial for small businesses also.

A **conventional (C) corporation** is a state-chartered legal entity with authority to act and have liability separate from its owners. What this means for the corporation's owners (stockholders) is that they are not liable for the debts or any other problems of the corporation beyond the money they invest. Owners no longer have to worry about losing their house, car, or other property because of some business problem—a significant benefit. A corporation not only limits the liability of owners, it enables many people to share in the ownership

conventional (C) corporation
A state-chartered legal entity with authority to act and have liability separate from its owners.

Making Ethical Decisions

Are You Your Brother's Keeper?

Imagine that you and your partner own a construction company. You receive a bid from a subcontractor that you know is 20 percent too low. Such a loss to the subcontractor could put him out of business. Accepting the bid will certainly improve your chances of winning the contract for a big shopping center project. Your partner wants to take the bid and let the subcontractor suffer the consequences of his bad estimate. What do you think you should do? What will be the consequences of your decision?

▲ SCANS

➤ **LEARNING GOAL 3.**
Compare the advantages and disadvantages of corporations and summarize the differences between C corporations, S corporations and limited liability companies.

➤ **CONSIDER USING OT ACETATE 5-3**
Advantages and Disadvantages of Corporations

(and profits) of a business without working there or having other commitments to it. See the box below for a description of various types of corporations

··· ADVANTAGES OF CORPORATIONS ···

Most people are not willing to risk everything to go into business. Yet for a business to grow and prosper and create abundance, many people would have to be willing to invest their money in it. The way to solve this problem was to create an artificial being, an entity that existed only in the eyes of the law—a corporation. Let's explore some of the advantages:

1. *More money for investment.* To raise money, a corporation sells ownership (stock) to anyone who is interested. This means that millions of people can own part of major companies like IBM, Xerox, and General Motors and smaller companies as well. If a company sold 10 million

---

CORPORATE TYPES

You may find some confusing types of corporations when reading about them. Here are a few of the more widely used terms:

An *alien corporation* does business in the United States, but is chartered (incorporated) in another country.

A *domestic corporation* does business in the state in which it's chartered (incorporated).

A *foreign corporation* does business in one state, but is chartered in another. About one-third of all corporations are chartered in Delaware because of its relatively attractive rules for incorporation. A foreign corporation must register in states where it operates.

A *closed (private) corporation* is one whose stock is held by a few people and isn't available to the general public.

An *open (public) corporation* sells stock to the general public. General Motors and Exxon are examples of public corporations.

A *quasi-public corporation* is a corporation chartered by the government as an approved monopoly to perform services to the general public. Public utilities are examples of quasi-public corporations.

A *professional corporation* is one whose owners offer professional services (doctors, lawyers, etc.). Shares in professional corporations aren't publicly traded.

A *nonprofit corporation* is one that doesn't seek personal profit for its owners.

A *multinational corporation* is a firm that operates in several countries.

shares for $50 each, it would have $500 million ava[i]lable to build plants, buy materials, hire people, manufacture prod[uct]s, and so on. Such a large amount of money would be difficult t[o rai]se any other way. Corporations may also find it easier to obtain lo[ans] since lenders find it easier to place a value on the company when [the]y can review how the stock is trading.

2. *Limited liability.* A major advantage of corporations [is th]e limited liability of owners. Corporations in England and Canad[a hav]e the letters *Ltd.* after their name, as in British Motors, Ltd. Th[is] stands for limited liability and is probably the most significant [advan]tage of corporations. Remember, limited liability means tha[t the o]wners of a business are responsible for losses only up to the am[ount t]hey invest.

3. *Size.* That one word summarizes many of the advant[ages] of some corporations. Because they have the ability to raise l[arge] amounts of money to work with, corporations can build large, m[od]ern factories with the latest equipment. They can also hire experts [or] specialists in all areas of operation. Furthermore, they can buy othe[r] corporations in other fields to diversify their risk. (What this means [i]s that a corporation can be involved in many businesses at once so th[a]t if one fails, the effect on the total corporation is lessened.) In short, a major advantage of corporations is that they have the size and resources to take advantage of opportunities anywhere in the world. Corporations do not have to be large to enjoy the benefits of incorporating. Many doctors, lawyers, and individuals, as well as partners i[n] a variety of businesses, have incorporated. There are many small c[or]porations in the United States.

◄ CONSIDER USING LECTURE ENHANCER 5-6
Going Public

4. *Perpetual life.* Because corporations are separate from those who own them, the death of one or more owners does not terminate the corporation.

5. *Ease of ownership change.* It is easy to change the owners of a corporation. All that is necessary is to sell the stock to someone else.

6. *Ease of drawing talented employees.* Corporations can attract skilled employees by offering such benefits as stock options (the right to purchase shares of the corporation for a fixed price).

7. *Separation of ownership from management.* Corporations are able to raise money from many different investors without getting them involved in management. The corporate hierarchy looks like Figure 5.1 on the next page.

The pyramid in Figure 5.1 shows that the owners/shareholders are separate from the managers and employers. The owners elect a board of directors. The directors select the officers. They, in turn, hire managers a[n]d employees. The owners thus have some say in who runs the corporation, b[ut] no control.

••• DISADVANTAGES OF CORPORATIONS •••

There are so many sole proprietorships and partnerships in the United States that it is clear that there must be some disadvantages to incorporating. Otherwise, more people would incorporate their businesses. The following are a few of the disadvantages:

1. *Initial cost.* Incorporation may cost thousands of dollars and involve expensive lawyers and accountants. There are less expensive ways of incorporating in certain states (see the subsection call[ed] Individuals

FIGURE **5.1**
. . . .
**HOW OWNERS AFFECT
MANAGEMENT**

Owners have an influence on how business is managed by electing a board of directors. The board hires the top managers (or fires them). It also sets the pay for top managers. Top managers then select other managers and employees with the help of the human resources department.

◄ CONSIDER USING TM 39
How Owners Affect Management

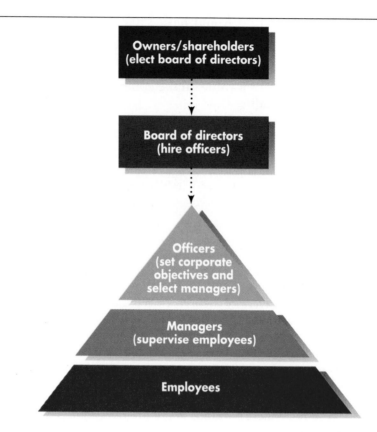

➤ CONSIDER USING OT ACETATE
5-4
Who Makes Up Corporate Boards?

Can Incorporate later in this chapter), but most people do not have the time or confidence to go through this procedure without the help of a lawyer.

2. *Paperwork.* The papers filed to start a corporation are just the beginning. Tax laws demand that a corporation prove that all its expenses and deductions are legitimate. A corporation therefore must process many forms. A sole proprietor or a partnership may keep rather broad accounting records; a corporation, on the other hand, must keep detailed records, the minutes of meetings, and more.

3. *Two tax returns.* If an individual incorporates, he or she must file both a corporate tax return and an individual tax return. The corporate return can be quite complex and usually requires the assistance of a certified public accountant (CPA).

4. *Size.* Size may be one advantage of corporations, but it can be a disadvantage as well. Large corporations sometimes become too inflexible and too tied down in red tape to respond quickly to market changes.

5. *Difficulty of termination.* Once a corporation is started, it's relatively hard to end.

6. *Double taxation.* Corporate income is taxed twice. First the corporation pays tax on income before it can distribute any to stockholders. Then the stockholders pay tax on the income (dividends) they receive from the corporation. States often tax corporations more harshly than other enterprises. Sometimes they levy special taxes that apply to corporations, but not to other forms of business.

7. *Possible conflict with board of directors.* Some conflict may brew if the stockholders elect a board of directors that disagrees with the present

HOW TO INCORPORATE

The process of forming a corporation varies somewhat from state to state. The articles of incorporation are usually filed with the secretary of state's office in the state in which the company incorporates. The articles contain

- The corporation's name.
- The names of the people who incorporated it.
- Its purposes.
- Its duration (usually perpetual).
- The number of shares that can be issued, their voting rights, and any other rights the shareholders have.
- The corporation's minimum capital.
- The address of the corporation's office.
- The name and address of the person responsible for the corporation's legal service.
- The names and addresses of the first directors.
- Any other public information the incorporators wish to include.

Before a business can so much as open a bank account or hire employees, it needs a federal tax identification number. To apply for one, get an SS-4 form from the IRS.

In addition to the articles of incorporation listed, a corporation also has bylaws. These describe how the firm is to be operated from both legal and managerial points of view. The bylaws include

- How, when, and where shareholders' and directors' meetings are held, and how long directors are to serve.
- Directors' authority.
- Duties and responsibilities of officers, and the length of their service.
- How stock is issued.
- Other matters, including employment contracts.

Source: Stephen L. Nelson, "How Not to Incorporate," *Home Office Computing*, February 1994, pp. 28–30.

management. Since the board of directors chooses the company's officers, an entrepreneur could find himself forced out of the very company he founded. This is what happened to Steve Jobs at Apple Computer.

Many people are discouraged by the costs, paperwork, and special taxes corporations must pay. Partners may feel that the hassles of incorporation outweigh the advantages.

◄ CONSIDER USING OT ACETATE 5-5
The World's Largest Public Companies

◄ CONSIDER USING OT ACETATE 5-6
America's Oldest Companies

••• INDIVIDUALS CAN INCORPORATE •••

A corporation does not need to have hundreds of employees or thousands of stockholders. Individuals (e.g., doctors, lawyers, plumbers, and movie stars) can also incorporate. By doing so, they may save on taxes and receive other benefits of incorporation. Many firms incorporate in Delaware because it is relatively easy to do so there. A book called *How to Form Your Own Corporation without a Lawyer for Under $500* by Ted S. Nicholas (Enterprise Publications) tells you the steps to take. The box above outlines how to incorporate.

••• S CORPORATIONS •••

One issue that has received much attention in recent years is the formation of S corporations. An **S corporation** is a unique government creation that looks like a corporation but is taxed like sole proprietorships and partnerships. S corporations have the benefit of limited liability. The paperwork and details of S corporations are similar to those of regular corporations. S corporations have shareholders, directors, and employees, but the profits are taxed as the personal income of the shareholders—thus avoiding the double taxation of conventional corporations.

Avoiding the double corporate tax rate was enough reason for 1.6 million small U.S. companies to operate as S corporations. The benefits of S

S corporation
A unique government creation that looks like a corporation but is taxed like sole proprietorships and partnerships.

Here we see a nonprofit corporation in action as American Red Cross director Elizabeth Dole tours the flooded downtown area of Grand Forks, ND, in April 1997. The Red Cross is there when disaster strikes. Nonprofit corporations get tax breaks because of the good work they do.

corporations change every time the tax rules change. The best way to learn all the benefits for a specific business is to go over the tax advantages and liability differences with a lawyer, an accountant, or both.

Not all businesses can become S corporations. In order to qualify, a company must

1. Have no more than 75 shareholders.
2. Have shareholders who are individuals or estates and are citizens or permanent residents of the United States.
3. Have only one class of outstanding stock.
4. Not have more than 25 percent of income derived from passive sources (rents, royalties, interest, etc.).

Changes in the Small Business Jobs Protection Act of 1996 have made the formation and operation of S corporations easier. The legislation increased the maximum number of shareholders from 35 to 75 and allowed tax-exempt organizations such as charities to own shares in S corporations after January 1, 1998.[2] Perhaps the most sweeping change made by the 1996 act was the new opportunity for S corporations to own subsidiaries. Let's say that you have a manufacturing business that is set up as an S corporation and you want to truck your own products. Trucking firms have a high potential for accidents and liability lawsuits. However, under the new rules, you can limit your liability by making your trucking operations a subsidiary of the manufacturing company. That way if the worst happens, and the trucking company loses a lawsuit for a terrible accident, your liability is limited to your investment in the trucking company. Your manufacturing investment remains safe from the trucking liability.[3]

S corporations aren't attractive to all businesses. Since the top tax rate for S corporations (39.6 percent) is almost five points higher than the highest corporate rate (35 percent), fast-growing small businesses are switching to C corporation status to avoid the higher taxes. They don't intend to pay dividends to owners because they need the money for new investment. Thus, they are not subject to double taxation. Many of the slower-growing businesses, on the other hand, have been keeping the S corporation form of ownership. However, many businesses are being attracted to the newest form of business ownership: limited liability companies (LLCs). The committee responsible for the S Corporation Reform Act proposal identified the rise of LLCs as one of the most important reasons for passing the legislation. Some commentators assert that without reform S corporations would be unable to compete for capital with LLCs. We shall discuss LLCs next.

••• LIMITED LIABILITY COMPANIES •••

Billed as the "business entity of the future," a **limited liability company (LLC)** is similar to an S corporation but without the special eligibility requirements. The concept of limited liability companies is so new that many states have just recently passed legislation regarding them. LLCs were introduced in Wyoming in 1977 and were recognized by the IRS as a partnership for federal income tax purposes in 1988. By the fall of 1996, all 50 states and the District of Columbia recognized LLCs. In 1995 the National Conference of Commissioners on Uniform State Laws approved the final version of the Uniform Limited Liability Company Act. The number of LLCs has risen dramatically since 1988, when there were less than 100 filings. Between September 2, 1988 (when the IRS passed its ruling), and December 31, 1995, over 210,000 businesses filed to become LLCs. It is notable that New York did not begin accepting LLC applications until October 24, 1994, and yet by December 31, 1994 (less than 10 weeks), it registered over 1,000 LLCs.[4]

Why the drive toward LLCs? LLCs offer the best of all corporate worlds for many new businesses: personal-asset protection (normally available only to shareholders of C corporations), choice to be taxed as partnership or as corporation (partnership-level taxation was previously a benefit normally reserved for partners or S corporation owners), and flexible ownership rules (which S corporations lack).[5] Until the new rules, LLCs were taxed as corporations. This was a positive factor for some businesses, but a negative one for others. Now LLCs can tell the IRS how they want to be taxed: as a partnership or as a corporation.[6] LLCs are so new that anyone considering starting one may want to do some research before making a final decision. Information about LLCs is available from the Association of Limited Liability Companies in Washington, D.C. (202-965-6565). The Commerce Clearing House also has a user-friendly introduction called *A Guide to Limited Liability Companies;* call 1-800-835-5224 for information. Another recommended guidebook on LLCs is *The Essential Limited Liability Company Handbook* (Oasis Press, 1-800-228-2275). You can review answers to frequently asked questions about LLCs on the Web at http://www.hia.com/llcweb/ll-faq.html.

Figure 5.2 on the next page lists the advantages and disadvantages of the major forms of business ownership.

limited liability company (LLC)
A company similar to an S corporation but without the special eligibility requirements.

◀ CONSIDER USING LECTURE ENHANCER 5-7
Lloyd's of London Goes Limited

◀ CONSIDER USING TM 40
Comparison of Forms of Business Ownership

Progress Check

- What are the major advantages and disadvantages of incorporating a business?

- What is the role of owners (stockholders) in the corporate hierarchy?

- If you buy stock in a corporation and someone gets injured by one of the corporation's products, can you be sued? Why or why not? Could you be sued if you were a general partner in a partnership?

Critical Thinking

In the past, forming a corporation was the only way to achieve limited liability. Why would most sole proprietors and partners be expected to form limited liability companies in the future rather than corporations?

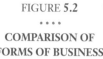

FIGURE **5.2**
....
COMPARISON OF
FORMS OF BUSINESS
OWNERSHIP

		Partnerships		Corporations		
	Sole Proprietorship	**General Partnership**	**Limited Partnership**	**Conventional Corporation**	**S Corporation**	**Limited Liability Company**
Documents needed to start business	None, may need permit or license	Partnership agreement (oral or written)	Written agreement. Must file certificate of limited partnership	Articles of incorporation, bylaws	Articles of incorporation, bylaws, must meet criteria	Articles of organization and operating agreement; no eligibility requirements
Ease of termination	Easy to terminate: just pay debts and quit	May be hard to terminate, depending on the partnership agreement	Same as general partnership	Hard and expensive to terminate	Same as conventional corporation	May be difficult, depending upon operating agreement
Length of life	Terminates on the death of owner	Terminates on the death or withdrawal of partner	Same as general partnership	Perpetual life	Same as conventional corporation	Same as partnership
Transfer of ownership	Business can be sold to qualified buyer	Must have other partner(s)' agreement	Same as general partnership	Easy to change owners; just sell stock	Can sell stock, but with restrictions	Can't sell stock
Financial resources	Limited to owner's capital and loans	Limited to partners' capital and loans	Same as general partnership	More money to start and operate; may sell stocks and bonds	Same as conventional corporation	Same as partnership
Risk of losses	Unlimited liability	Unlimited liability	Limited liability	Limited liability	Limited liability	Limited liability
Taxes	Taxed as personal income	Taxed as personal income	Same as general partnership	Corporate, double taxation	Taxed as personal income	Taxed as personal income
Management responsibilities	Owner manages *all* areas of the business	Partners share management	Can't participate in management	Separate management from ownership	Same as conventional corporation	Varies
Employee benefits	Usually fewer benefits and lower wages	Often fewer benefits and lower wages; promising employee could become a partner	Same as general partnership	Usually better benefits and wages, advancement opportunities	Same as conventional corporation	Varies

···· ▬ ····

CORPORATE EXPANSION:
MERGERS AND ACQUISITIONS

Merger mania continues to strike corporate America. In 1996 merger activity hit an all-time high of more than $660 billion. There were more than 10,000 mergers worth at least $1 million. That's nearly twice the dollar volume and number of deals of the peak year of the 1980s.[7] Put another way, 1996 mergers occurred at the rate of more than one per hour, around the clock, all year long.[8] Not only were there many mergers, there were many megamergers. We saw such megadeals as the $37 billion marriage of MCI Communications and WorldCom and the $23.6 billion union of Bell Atlantic and Nynex.[9] The trend is a result of major changes in the entertainment, drug, and telecommunications industries. Most of the new deals involve companies trying to expand within their own fields to save costs, enter new markets, position for international competition, or adapt to changing technologies or regulations.

What's the difference between mergers and acquisitions? A **merger** is the result of two firms forming one company. Sounds like a marriage, doesn't it? An **acquisition** is one company buying the property and obligations of another company. It is more like buying a house than entering a marriage.

There are three major types of corporate mergers: vertical, horizontal, and conglomerate. A **vertical merger** is the joining of two firms involved in different stages of related businesses. Think of a merger between a bicycle company and a company that produces wheels. Such a merger would ensure a constant supply of wheels needed by the bicycle company. It could also help ensure quality control of the bicycle company's product. A **horizontal merger** joins two firms in the same industry and allows them to diversify or expand their products. An example of a horizontal merger is the merger of a bicycle company and a tricycle company. The business can now supply a variety of cycling products. A **conglomerate merger** unites firms in completely unrelated industries. The primary purpose of a conglomerate merger is to diversify business operations and investments. The acquisition of a restaurant chain by a bicycle company would be an example of a conglomerate merger. Figure 5.3 on the next page illustrates the differences in the three types of mergers.

Rather than merge or sell to another company, some corporations decide to maintain control of the firm internally. For example, Steve Stavro, the majority owner and head of a group that invested in the Maple Leaf Gardens Ltd. (owners of the Toronto Maple Leafs hockey team), decided to take the firm private. Taking a firm private involves the efforts of a group of stockholders or management to obtain all the firm's stock for themselves. In the Maple Leaf Gardens situation, Stavro's investors group successfully gained total control of the company by buying all of the company's stock. For the first time in 65 years, investors in the open market can no longer purchase stock in the Maple Leafs.[10]

Suppose the employees in an organization feel there is a good possibility they may lose their jobs. Or what if the managers believe that corporate performance could be enhanced if they owned the company? Do either of these groups have an opportunity of taking ownership of the company? Yes— they might attempt a leveraged buyout. A **leveraged buyout (LBO)** is an attempt by employees, management, or a group of investors to purchase an organization primarily through borrowing. The

merger
The result of two firms forming one company.

acquisition
A company's purchase of the property and obligations of another company.

vertical merger
The joining of two companies involved in different stages of related businesses.

horizontal merger
The joining of two firms in the same industry.

conglomerate merger
The joining of firms in completely unrelated industries.

leveraged buyout (LBO)
An attempt by employees, management, or a group of investors to purchase an organization primarily through borrowing.

They shook on it and agreed on a merger that resembles a mouse catching a cat. The mouse is WorldCom and the cat is MCI. WorldCom was considered an obscure second-tier provider of long-distance telephone service until it managed to outmaneuver gigantic British Telecommunications in its efforts to buy MCI, the second largest long-distance company. The mouse that roared, fast-rising WorldCom, is now the result of merging over 80 different companies.

➤ CONSIDER USING TM 41
Types of Mergers

➤ LEARNING GOAL 4.
Define and give examples of three types of corporate mergers and explain the role of leveraged buyouts and taking a firm private.

➤ CONSIDER USING OT ACETATE 5-7
The Top Mergers in the U.S.

➤ CONSIDER USING SUPPLEMENTAL CASE 5-1
Mergers (SCANS)

➤ CONSIDER USING LECTURE ENHANCER 5-8
Pepsi Pulls Back from Diversification

➤ CONSIDER USING LECTURE ENHANCER 5-9
The Price of Freedom

➤ CONSIDER USING LECTURE ENHANCER 5-10
Employee Owners at Garden State Brickface

FIGURE 5.3

• • • •

TYPES OF MERGERS

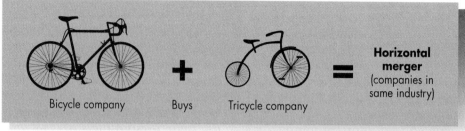

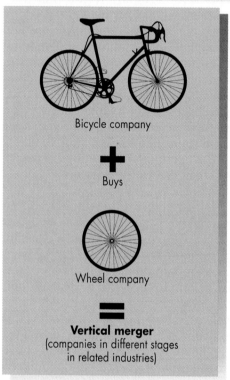

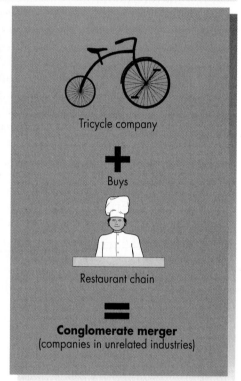

funds borrowed are used to buy out the stockholders in the company. The employees, managers, or group of investors now become the owners of the firm.

Merger mania isn't restricted to American companies. For example, foreign companies are gobbling up U.S. food companies. British candy and soft drink producer Cadbury Schweppes bought the largest American root beer producer, A&W, for $334 million. Unilever, a Dutch company, bought Kraft General Foods' ice cream division (makers of Breyer's and Sealtest). Why the buying binge? Some analysts suggest the spree was brought on by a slumping dollar, depressed stock prices, sluggish U.S. spending, and increasing globalization. Foreign companies have found that the quickest way to grow is to buy an established operation and bring the brands and technology back to Europe.

• • • • ▬▬▬▬ • • • •

SPECIAL FORMS OF BUSINESS OWNERSHIP

In addition to the three basic forms of business ownership, we shall discuss two special forms of ownership: franchises and cooperatives. Let's look at franchises first.

FRANCHISES

Basically, a **franchise agreement** is an arrangement whereby someone with a good idea for a business (the **franchisor**) sells the rights to use the business name and to sell a product or service (the **franchise**) to others (the **franchisee**) in a given territory.

Some people are more comfortable not starting their own business from scratch. They would rather join a business with a proven track record through a franchise agreement. A franchise can be formed as a sole proprietorship, partnership, or corporation. Some of the best-known franchises are McDonald's, Wendy's, 7-Eleven, and Holiday Inn.

Eight million people in the United States work in a franchise. Franchising accounts for 40 percent of all national retail sales (about $750 billion).[11] In fact, 1 out of 12 American businesses is a franchise, and a new franchise opens every eight minutes of each business day. The most popular businesses for franchising are restaurants (more than 80 percent of all franchises), retail stores, hotels and motels, and automotive parts and service centers.[12]

When you think of franchising, however, don't confine your thoughts to the United States. Some enterprising entrepreneurs have had great success taking American franchises overseas. For example, McDonald's has nearly 21,000 restaurants in 101 countries. Ranked as the world's greatest brand by the Interbrand Group, an independent branding consultant, McDonald's plans to accelerate its global business by adding as many restaurants outside the United States in the next 4 years as it did in the last 30 years.[13]

franchise agreement
An arrangement whereby someone with a good idea for a business sells the rights to use the business name and sell its products or services to others in a given territory.

franchisor
A company that develops a product concept and sells others the rights to make and sell the products.

franchise
The right to use a specific business's name and sell its products or services in a given territory.

franchisee
A person who buys a franchise.

◄ CONSIDER USING SUPPLEMENTAL CASE 5-2
Opportunities in Franchising
(SCANS)

··· ADVANTAGES OF FRANCHISES ···

Franchising has penetrated every aspect of American and global business life by offering products and services that are reliable, convenient, and cost-effective. The growth experienced in franchising throughout the world could not have been accomplished by accident. Franchising clearly has some advantages:

This may look like the set of Camelot, but it is actually the Holiday Inn in downtown Edinburgh, Scotland. Holiday Inn franchises try to complement the environment of the areas they serve. What are the payoffs for such efforts? What do you think the local reaction would have been if the franchise tried to build the typical American-style hotel in this area?

➤ **CONSIDER USING OT ACETATE 5-8**
Franchise Success Versus Independent Business Success

➤ **LEARNING GOAL 5.**
Outline the advantages and disadvantages of franchises and discuss the opportunities for diversity in franchising and the challenges of international franchising.

➤ **CONSIDER USING TM 42**
Additional Benefits and Drawbacks of Franchising

1. *Management and marketing assistance.* A franchisee (the person who buys a franchise) has a much greater chance of succeeding in business because he or she has an established product (e.g., McDonald's hamburgers); help with choosing a location and promotion; and assistance in all phases of operation. It is like having your own store with full-time consultants available when you need them. Furthermore, you have a whole network of peers who are facing similar problems and can share their experiences with you. Some franchisors are helping their franchisees succeed by helping their local marketing efforts rather than having them depend solely on national advertising. For example, Mail Boxes Etc. provides its 2,500 franchisees with a software program that will help them build data banks of customer names and addresses. The customers then will be targets for direct-mail blitzes.[14]

2. *Personal ownership.* A franchise operation is still your store, and you enjoy much of the incentives and profit of any sole proprietor. You are still your own boss, although you must follow more rules, regulations, and procedures than you would with your own privately owned store.

3. *Nationally recognized name.* It is one thing to open a new hamburger outlet or ice cream store. It is quite another to open a new McDonald's or Baskin-Robbins. With an established franchise, you get instant recognition and support from a product group with established customers from around the world.

4. *Financial advice and assistance.* A major problem with small businesses is arranging financing and learning to keep good records. Franchisees get valuable assistance and periodic advice from people with expertise in these areas. In fact, some franchisors will even provide financing to potential franchisees they feel will be valuable parts of the franchise system. For example, SRA International Inc., an executive-recruiting franchise, eases entry for selected new franchisees by allowing $20,000 of the $35,000 initiation fee to be paid from revenue over a period of two years or more.[15]

5. *Lower failure rate.* Historically, the failure rate for franchises has been lower than that of other business ventures. More recently, however, franchising has grown so rapidly that many weak franchises have entered the field. A 1993 study done for the Entrepreneurial Growth and Investment Institute in Washington found that three-fourths of all franchises fail within 10 years.[16] Conflicting research by Arthur Andersen & Co. shows that only 14 percent of new franchises fail in the first five years, compared to 62.2 percent of all new businesses in the same period.[17] You will have to decide whose numbers you choose to accept.

••• DISADVANTAGES OF FRANCHISES •••

It almost sounds like the potential of franchising is too good to be true. However, you should carefully research any franchise before buying. You must be sure to check out any such arrangement with present franchisees and possibly discuss the idea with an attorney. Some disadvantages of franchises include the following:

1. *Large start-up costs.* Most franchises will demand a fee just for the rights to the franchise. Fees for franchises can vary considerably. Start-

One of the disadvantages of owning a franchise is that you are at the mercy of your franchisor's decisions. The nerves of many McDonald's franchisees were fried when the franchise's 1997 55-cent sandwich promotion produced disappointing results. The company's drive to have a store convenient to everywhere also shook up existing franchisees when new stores ate away at their businesses.

up costs for a Jazzercise outlet range from $2,000 to $3,000. Compare that to the $600,000 or more needed to start a McDonald's restaurant.

2. *Shared profit.* The franchisor often demands a large share of the profits, or a percentage commission based on sales, not profit. This share demanded by the franchisor is generally referred to as a *royalty.*

3. *Management regulation.* Management assistance has a way of becoming managerial orders, directives, and limitations. Franchisees may feel burdened by the company's rules and regulations, and lose the spirit and incentive of being their own boss with their own business. One of the biggest changes in franchising in recent years is the banding together of many franchisees to resolve their grievances with franchisors rather than each fighting their battles alone. For example, Meineke franchisees joined forces to sue franchisor Meineke Muffler Discount Shops Inc. for fraudulently pocketing money they gave the company for advertising. The judge awarded the group of franchise owners $601 million, the largest judgment ever in a franchise case.[18] Even the venerable McDonald's is not immune to organized disgruntled franchisees. A number of franchisees who say meals are no longer happy at McDonald's have formed an organization called Consortium Members Inc. that is working on gaining approval of legislation that would mandate standards for franchisee-corporate relationships. One of the things the group is unhappy about is McDonald's forcing franchisees to go along with badly formed marketing plans (such as the confusing and disappointing 55-cent sandwich promotion).[19]

4. *Coattail effects.* What happens to your franchise if fellow franchisees fail? Quite possibly you could be forced out of business even if your particular franchise was profitable. This is often referred to as a *coattail effect.* The actions of other franchisees clearly have an impact on your future growth and level of profitability. Franchisees must also

◄ **CONSIDER USING OT ACETATE 5-9**
The Franchise Agreement

◄ **CONSIDER USING OT ACETATE 5-10**
Where Franchisees Get Financing

◄ **CONSIDER USING OT ACETATE 5-11**
How to Avoid a Franchise Lemon

FIGURE **5.4**

. . . .

**ADDITIONAL BENEFITS
AND DRAWBACKS OF
FRANCHISING**

The start-up fees and
monthly fees can be
killers. Ask around.
Don't be shy. This is the
time to learn about
opportunities.

BENEFITS	DRAWBACKS
• Nationally recognized name and established reputation	• High initial franchise fee
• Help with finding a good location	• Additional fees may be charged for marketing
• A proven management system	• A monthly percentage of gross sales may go to the franchisor
• Tested methods for inventory and operations management	• Possible competition from other nearby franchisees
• Financial advice and assistance	• No freedom to select decor or other design features
• Training in all phases of operation	• Little freedom to determine management procedures
• Promotional assistance	• Many rules and regulations to follow
• Periodic management counseling	
• Proven record of success	
• It's your business!	

look out for competition from fellow franchisees. For example, TCBY
franchisees' love for frozen yogurt thawed as the market became
flooded with new TCBY stores. McDonald's franchisees complain that
due to the McDonald's Corps relentless growth formula, some of the
new stores have cannibalized business at existing locations, squeezing
franchisees' profits per outlet.[20]

5. *Restrictions on selling.* Unlike owners of private businesses who can
   sell their companies to whomever they choose on their own terms,
   many franchisees face restrictions in the reselling of their franchises.
   In order to control the quality of their franchisees, franchisors often
   insist on approving the new owner, who must meet their standards.

6. *Fraudulent franchisors.* Contrary to common belief, most franchisors
   are not large systems like McDonald's. Many are small, rather obscure
   franchises that prospective franchisees may know little about. Most
   franchisors are honest, but there has been an increase in complaints to
   the Federal Trade Commission about franchisors that delivered little
   or nothing of what they promised.

Figure 5.4 summarizes the benefits and drawbacks in franchising, and the
box on the next page gives you some tips on buying a franchise.

••• DIVERSITY IN FRANCHISING •••

There's a strong likelihood that women and minorities will assume a much
larger role in franchising than they have in the past. A survey by Women in
Franchising indicates that women own 30 percent of the country's franchised
businesses. Women aren't just franchisees anymore either; they are becoming
franchisors as well. The top-rated franchise companies Decorating Den and
Jazzercise, for example, are owned by women.

When women have difficulty obtaining financing for expanding their businesses, they often turn to finding franchisees to sidestep expansion costs. For
example, Marilyn Ounijan, founder and CEO of Careers USA, claims that having franchisees pay for inventory and other costs of growing a business
allowed the company to grow from her office in her home to 22 locations

BUYING A FRANCHISE

Since buying a franchise is a major investment, be sure to check out a company's financial strength before you get involved. Watch out for scams, too. Scams called *bust-outs* usually involve people coming to town, renting nice offices, taking out ads, and persuading people to invest. Then they disappear with the investors' money. For example, in San Francisco a company called T.B.S. Inc. sold distributorships for in-home AIDS tests. It promised an enormous market and potential profits of $3,000 for an investment of less than $200. The test turned out to be nothing more than a mail-order questionnaire about lifestyle.

A good source of information about franchise possibilities is available from Franchise Watchdog in Burlington, Vermont. It compares what franchisors have to offer, including fees and support services, and also rates franchisors by sampling franchisees. Another good resource for evaluating a franchise deal is the handbook *Investigate before Investing,* available from International Franchise Association Publications.

Checklist for Evaluating a Franchise

The franchise

Did your lawyer approve the franchise contract you're considering after he or she studied it paragraph by paragraph?

Does the franchise give you an exclusive territory for the length of the franchise?

Under what circumstances can you terminate the franchise contract and at what cost to you?

If you sell your franchise, will you be compensated for your goodwill (the value of your business's reputation and other intangibles)?

If the franchisor sells the company, will your investment be protected?

The franchisor

How many years has the firm offering you a franchise been in operation?

Does it have a reputation for honesty and fair dealing among the local firms holding its franchise?

Has the franchisor shown you any certified figures indicating exact net profits of one or more going firms that you

personally checked yourself with the franchisee? Ask for the company's disclosure statement.

Will the firm assist you with

A management training program?
An employee training program?
A public relations program?
Capital?
Credit?
Merchandising ideas?

Will the firm help you find a good location for your new business?

Has the franchisor investigated you carefully enough to assure itself that you can successfully operate one of its franchises at a profit both to itself and to you?

You, the franchisee

How much equity capital will you need to purchase the franchise and operate it until your income equals your expenses?

Does the franchisor offer financing for a portion of the franchising fees? On what terms?

Are you prepared to give up some independence of action to secure the advantages offered by the franchise? Do you have your family's support?

Does the industry appeal to you? Are you ready to spend much or all of the remainder of your business life with this franchisor, offering its product or service to the public?

Your market

Have you made any study to determine whether the product or service that you propose to sell under the franchise has a market in your territory at the prices you'll have to charge?

Will the population in the territory given to you increase, remain static, or decrease over the next five years?

Will demand for the product or service you're considering be greater, about the same, or less five years from now than it is today?

What competition already exists in your territory for the product or service you contemplate selling?

Sources: *Franchise Opportunities Handbook* (U.S. Department of Commerce); Derek Dingle, "Franchising's Fast Track to Freedom," *Money Extra,* 1990, pp. 35–44; and Jeffrey Kolton, "Know the Score: Ten Questions You Should Ask Before Buying A Franchise," *Success,* November 1997, pp. 98–101.

throughout the country. Franchising provided Careers USA a cost-effective way to enter new markets.

Black Enterprise magazine publisher Earl Graves encourages African Americans to look for opportunities in franchising in his book *How to Succeed in Business without Being White.* Franchising opportunities seem perfectly attuned to the needs of aspiring minority businesspersons.[21] The Commerce Department's Federal Minority Business Development Agency provides minorities with training in how to run franchises.

Henry and Paula Feldman operate their franchise, Money Mailer, Inc., from their home. What advantages does a home-based franchisee enjoy that a home-based entrepreneur may not?

▶ **CONSIDER USING LECTURE ENHANCER 5-11**
Home Is Where the Money Is

▶ **CONSIDER USING OT ACETATE 5-12**
Benefits of Home-Based Businesses

••• HOME-BASED FRANCHISES •••

Home-based businesses offer many obvious advantages, including relief from the stress of commuting, extra time for family activities, and low overhead expenses. But one of the disadvantages of owning a business based at home is the feeling of isolation. Unlike home-based entrepreneurs, home-based franchisees feel less isolated. Experienced franchisors share their knowledge of building a profitable enterprise with franchisees. For example, when Henry and Paula Feldman decided to quit sales jobs that kept them on the road for weeks, they wanted to find a business to run at home together. The Feldmans started their home-based franchise, Money Mailer, Inc., with nothing more than a table and a telephone. Five years later, they owned 15 territories, run from an office full of state-of-the-art equipment. They grossed more than $600,000 during their fifth year. Henry says that the real value of being in a franchise is that the systems are in place. "You don't have to develop them yourself. Just be willing to work hard, listen, and learn. There's no greater magic than that."

••• FRANCHISING IN INTERNATIONAL MARKETS •••

The attraction of global markets has carried over into franchising. Today, American franchisors are counting their profits in pesos, lira, francs, won, deutsche marks, krona, baht, yen, and many other global currencies. More than 450 of the 3,000 franchisors have outlets overseas. Canada is by far the most popular target because of proximity and language. Many franchisors are finding it surprisingly easy to move into South Africa and the Philippines. Even though franchisors find the costs of franchising high in these markets, the costs are counterbalanced by less competition and a rapidly expanding consumer base.

Newer, smaller franchises are going international as well. Smaller franchises such as SpeeDee Oil Change & Tune-Up, Rug Doctor Pro, and Merry Maids have all ventured into the international market. What makes franchising successful in international markets is what makes it successful in the United States: convenience and a predictable level of service and quality.

Franchisors must be careful to adapt to the region. In France, the people thought a furniture-stripping place called Dip 'N' Strip was a bar that featured strippers. In general, however, U.S. franchises are doing well all over the world and are adapting to the local customs and desires of consumers. See the Reaching Beyond Our Borders box for a look at how McDonald's adapts in foreign countries.

••• USING TECHNOLOGY IN FRANCHISING •••

Franchisors are speeding onto the information superhighway in an effort to meet the needs of both their customers and their franchisees. For example, U.S. Web Corp. set up its Web site to streamline processes of effective communication for its employees, customers, and vendors. It built an intranet to allow communication among its 50 franchisees, almost eliminating paperwork. Using the Web site, every franchisee has immediate access to every subject that involves the franchise operation, even the forms to fill out. There is a chat room for franchisees to leave messages and comments for each other. All

Reaching Beyond
Our Borders

Would You Like Fries with That?

You've been studying all night and your stomach is growling so loud that it's scaring your dog. How does a nice hot McDonald's mutton burger sound? Well if you were in India right now, you could zip on down to the Golden Arches for a Maharaja Mac. That's two all-mutton patties, special sauce, lettuce, cheese, pickle and onions, all on a sesame-seed bun. Don't bother asking "Where's the beef?" in India. The large Hindu population in India believes cows are sacred.

You won't find any pork, either, since the Muslim population believes pork is unclean. But you will find other new taste sensations on the menu such as rice-based vegetable burgers—flavored with peas, carrots, red peppers, beans, and coriander and other spices. Vegetable McNuggets are bite-sized, unspiced versions of the vegetable patties served with McMasala and other sauces.

The taste of the West will take a bite out of most Indians' budget. A Maharaja Mac costs 41 rupees ($1.15) and a mutton burger costs 12 rupees ($.39), but the per capita income in India is only about $480 (18,626 rupees) a year.

McDonald's has adapted its menu to local tastes elsewhere in the world. Thai customers can get

Samurai Pork Burgers topped with a sweet barbecue sauce, and burgers in Japan come garnished with a fried egg. But the effort to appeal to Indians goes further, perhaps because the market is so volatile. McDonald's learned a lesson from the experiences of KFC, whose opening in Bangalore set feathers flying—protesting farmers tore up the restaurant, saying the company would plunder the agriculture of the country. To avoid similar problems, the mutton for Maharaja Macs comes from Indian sheep, the potatoes for the fries from Indian farms, and the Coke from an Indian bottler. However, not everyone is concerned about where the food comes from. "As long as the food's good, I don't care," said 19-year-old Pankresh Mathur as he demonstrated to the other diners just how fast a Maharaja Mac could be gulped down.

Sources: Dan Biers and Miriam Jordan, "McDonald's Finally Arrives in India, but without Big Mac," *The Wall Street Journal Interactive Edition*, October 14, 1996; Evelan Tan Powers, "New Delhi McDonald's Skips the Beef," *USA Today*, October 14, 1996, p. 2B; and Associated Press, "Despite Billions Served, India Offers McDonald's New Market," *The Wall Street Journal Interactive Edition*, October 13, 1996.

---

franchisees are kept up-to-date on company news via e-mail. The company has found that the Internet is a great way of disseminating information and is revolutionizing franchisor support and franchisee communications.[22]

◀ **CONSIDER USING LECTURE ENHANCER 5-12**
Joining Hands Across the Waters: Strategic Alliances

◀ **LEARNING GOAL 6.**
Explain the role of cooperatives.

◀ **CONSIDER USING LECTURE ENHANCER 5-13**
Coops Allow Small Businesses to Compete Against Big Ones

COOPERATIVES

Some people dislike the notion of having owners, managers, workers, and buyers as separate individuals with separate goals. These people have formed a different kind of organization to meet their needs for things such as electricity, child care, housing, health care, food, and financial services. Such an organization, called a **cooperative**, is owned and controlled by the people who use it—producers, consumers, or workers with similar needs who pool their resources for mutual gain. There are 47,000 cooperatives in the United States today. Some co-ops ask members/customers to work in the organization so many hours a month as part of their duties. Members democratically control these

cooperative
A business owned and controlled by the people who use it—producers, consumers, or workers with similar needs who pool their resources for mutual gain.

The Gentle Strength Cooperative specializes in healthful natural foods. What advantages does a farmer gain by belonging to such a cooperative? What benefits can cooperatives offer their customers?

businesses by electing a board of directors that hires professional management. You may have one of the country's 4,000 food cooperatives near you. If so, stop by and chat with the people and learn more about this growing aspect of the U.S. economy. If you are interested in knowing more about cooperatives, contact the National Cooperative Business Association (1-800-636-6222).

There is another kind of cooperative in the United States, set up for different reasons. These cooperatives are formed to give members more economic power as a group than they would have as individuals. The best example of such cooperatives is a farm cooperative. The idea at first was for farmers to join together to get better prices for their food products. Eventually, however, the organization expanded so that farm cooperatives now buy and sell fertilizer, farm equipment, seed, and other products needed on the farm. This has become a multibillion-dollar industry. The cooperatives now own many manufacturing facilities. Farm cooperatives do not pay the same kind of taxes that corporations do, and thus have an advantage in the marketplace.

To give you some idea of the size of farm cooperatives, let's look at Farmland Industries, Inc. As the country's largest farm cooperative, the company reports an annual revenue of $4.5 billion. Its 1,800 member cooperatives include 250,000 farmers in 19 states. Farmland Industries owns manufacturing facilities, oil wells and refineries, fertilizer plants, feed mills, and plants that produce everything from grease and paint to steel buildings. It also offers insurance, financial, and technical services and owns a network of warehouses.

In spite of debt and mergers, cooperatives are still a major force in agriculture today. Some top farm co-ops have familiar names such as Land O Lakes, Sunkist, Ocean Spray, Blue Diamond, Associated Press, Ace Hardware, True Value Hardware, Riceland Foods, and Welch's.

> **CONSIDER USING CRITICAL THINKING EXERCISE 5-2**
Choosing a Form of Business Ownership **(SCANS)**

•••• ━━━━ ••••

WHICH FORM OF OWNERSHIP IS FOR YOU?

As you can see, you may participate in the business world in a variety of ways. You can start your own sole proprietorship, partnership, corporation, or cooperative—or you can buy a franchise. There are advantages and disadvantages to each. However, there are risks no matter which form you choose. Before you decide which form is for you, you need to evaluate all the alternatives carefully.

The miracle of free enterprise is that the freedom and incentives of capitalism make risks acceptable to many people, who go on to create the great corporations of America. You know many of their names: J. C. Penney, Malcolm Forbes, Richard Warren Sears and Alvah C. Roebuck, Levi Strauss, Henry Ford, Thomas Edison, and so on. They started small, accumulated capital, grew, and became industrial leaders. Could you do the same?

Progress Check

- What are some of the factors to consider before buying a franchise?
- What opportunities are available for starting a global franchise?
- What is a cooperative?

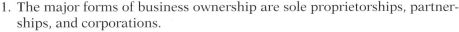

SUMMARY
• • • • • •

1. The major forms of business ownership are sole proprietorships, partnerships, and corporations.

   - ***What are the advantages and disadvantages of sole proprietorships?***
   The advantages of sole proprietorship include ease of starting and ending, being your own boss, pride of ownership, retention of profit, and no special taxes. The disadvantages include unlimited liability, limited financial resources, difficulty in management, overwhelming time commitment, few fringe benefits, limited growth, and limited life span.

1. Compare the advantages and disadvantages of sole proprietorships.

2. The three key elements of a general partnership are common ownership, shared profits and losses, and the right to participate in managing the operations of the business.

   - ***What are the main differences between general and limited partners?***
   General partners are owners (partners) who have unlimited liability and are active in managing the company. Limited partners are owners (partners) who have limited liability and are not active in the company.
   - ***What does unlimited liability mean?***
   Unlimited liability means that sole proprietors and general partners must pay all debts and damages caused by their business. They may have to sell their houses, cars, or other personal possessions to pay business debts.
   - ***What does limited liability mean?***
   Limited liability means that corporate owners (stockholders) and limited partners are responsible for losses only up to the amount they invest. Their other personal property is not at risk.
   - ***What is a master limited partnership?***
   A master limited partnership is a partnership that acts like a corporation but is taxed like a partnership. Burger King is a well-known master limited partnership.
   - ***What are the advantages and disadvantages of partnerships?***
   The advantages include more financial resources, shared management and pooled knowledge, and longer survival. The disadvantages include unlimited liability, division of profits, disagreements among partners, and difficulty of termination.

2. Describe the differences between general and limited partners, and compare the advantages and disadvantages of partnerships.

3. A corporation is a state-chartered legal entity with authority to act and have liability separate from its owners.

   - ***What are the advantages and disadvantages of corporations?***
   The advantages include more money for investment, limited liability, size, perpetual life, ease of ownership change, ease of drawing talented employees, and separation of ownership from management. The disadvantages

3. Compare the advantages and disadvantages of corporations, and summarize the differences between C corporations, S corporations, and limited liability companies.

include initial cost, paperwork, size, difficulty of termination, double taxation, and possible conflict with a board of directors.

* *Why do people incorporate?*

Two important reasons for incorporating are special tax advantages and limited liability.

* *What are the advantages of S corporations?*

S corporations have the advantages of limited liability (like a corporation) and simpler taxes (like a partnership). In order to qualify for S corporation status, a company must have fewer than 75 stockholders; its stockholders must be individuals or estates and U.S. citizens or permanent residents; and the company cannot have more than 25 percent of its income derived from passive sources.

* *What are the advantages of limited liability companies?*

Limited liability companies have the advantage of limited liability without the hassles of forming a corporation or the limitations imposed by S corporations. LLCs may choose whether to be taxed as partnerships or corporations.

---

4. Define and give examples of three types of corporate mergers and explain the role of leveraged buyouts and taking a firm private.

4. The number of mergers increased during the mid-1990s.

* *What is a merger?*

A merger is the result of two firms forming one company. The three major types of mergers are vertical mergers, horizontal mergers, and conglomerate mergers.

* *What are leveraged buyouts, and what does it mean to "take a company private"?*

Leveraged buyouts are attempts by managers and employees to borrow money and purchase the company. Individuals who, together or alone, buy all of the stock for themselves are said to take the company private.

---

5. Outline the advantages and disadvantages of franchises and discuss the opportunities for diversity in franchising and the challenges of international franchising.

5. A person can participate in the entrepreneurial age by buying the rights to market a new product innovation in his or her area.

* *What is this arrangement called?*

An arrangement to buy the rights to use the business name and sell its products or services in a given territory is called a franchise.

* *What is a franchisee?*

A franchisee is a person who buys a franchise.

* *What are the benefits and drawbacks of being a franchisee?*

The benefits include a nationally recognized name and reputation, a proven management system, promotional assistance, and the pride of ownership. Drawbacks include high franchise fees, managerial regulation, shared profits, and transfer of adverse effects if other franchisees fail.

* *What are the opportunities for women and minorities in franchising?*

Women are buying franchises at a faster rate than men are. In fact, women now own 30 percent of the nation's franchises. Minority franchise ownership is not growing as quickly, largely due to trouble getting the large start-up capital needed to purchase a franchise.

* *What is the major challenge to international franchises?*

It is often difficult to transfer an idea or product that worked well in the United States to another culture. It is essential to adapt to the region.

---

6. Explain the role of cooperatives.

6. People who dislike organizations in which owners, managers, workers, and buyers have separate goals often form cooperatives.

* *What is the role of a cooperative?*

Cooperatives are organizations that are owned by members/customers. Some people form cooperatives (Farmland, for example) to give members more economic power than they would have as individuals. Small businesses often form cooperatives to give them more purchasing, marketing, or product development strength.

acquisition 147	**franchisor** 149	**limited partnership** 136
conglomerate merger 147	**general partner** 136	**master limited partnership** 136
conventional (C) corporation 139	**general partnership** 136	**merger** 147
cooperative 155	**horizontal merger** 147	**partnership** 134
corporation 134	**leveraged buyout** 147	**S corporation** 143
franchise 149	**limited liability** 136	**sole proprietorship** 134
franchise agreement 149	**limited liability company (LLC)** 145	**unlimited liability** 135
franchisee 149	**limited partner** 136	**vertical merger** 147

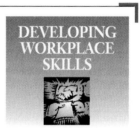

DEVELOPING WORKPLACE SKILLS

1. Research businesses in your area and identify companies that use each of the following forms of ownership: sole proprietorships, partnerships, corporations, and franchises. Arrange interviews with managers from each form of ownership and get their impressions, hints, and warnings. How much does it cost to start? How many hours do they work? What are the specific benefits? Share the results with your class.

2. Have you thought about starting your own business? What opportunities seem attractive? Think of a friend or friends whom you might want for a partner or partners in the business. List all the financial resources and personal skills you will need to launch the business. Then make separate lists of the capital and personal skills that you and your friend(s) might bring to your new venture. What capital and personal skills do you need, but neither of you have? Develop an action plan to obtain them.

3. Let's assume you want to open one of the following new businesses. What form of business ownership would you choose for each business? Why?

   a. Video game rental store.

   b. Wedding planning service.

   c. Software development firm.

   d. Computer hardware manufacturing company.

4. Review the Yellow Pages for your area and find a business cooperative in your community. Arrange a visit to find out how it was formed, who may belong to it, and how it operates.

5. Obtain an annual report of a large corporation from your library or by writing the company. What are the firm's annual sales? Net income (profit)? Number of common shareholders? Profit shareholders receive in dividends?

TAKING IT TO THE NET

Purpose

To explore current franchising opportunities and to evaluate the strengths and weaknesses of a selected franchise.

Exercise

Go to the Web site Be the Boss: The Ultimate Franchising Web Site (http://www.betheboss.com).

1. Take the interactive self-test in the Web site's Getting Started section to see if franchising is a good personal choice for you.

2. Use the search tool on this Web site to find a franchise that has the potential of fulfilling your entrepreneurial dreams. Navigate to the profile of the franchise you selected. Explore the franchise's Web site if such a link is available. Refer to the questions listed in the box Buying a Franchise on p. 153 in this text and assess the strengths and weaknesses of your selected franchise. (Hint: The Web site also contains tips for evaluating a franchise listing.)

3. Do the franchise profile and Web site give you enough information to answer most of the questions in the Buying a Franchise box? If not, what other information do you need, and where can you obtain it?

Practicing Management Decisions

The idea of starting a cooperative to meet a social need is not a new one in the United States. The first formal American co-op, the Philadelphia Contributionship for the Insurance of Homes from Loss by Fire, was organized by Benjamin Franklin in 1752 and is still operating. Today, cooperatives usually evolve because some need has not been met by the other three forms of business: proprietorships, partnerships, or corporations. For example, many homes in rural areas are serviced by telephone and electric co-ops because no one else would provide those services back in the 1930s when they were needed for farmers to enjoy the benefits of new technology.

Today the need is for child care and care of the aged. Because such needs are not being met by traditional organizations or are being offered at too great a cost, new cooperatives are emerging. A group of agricultural leaders in Texas, for example, has started a co-op to meet the special needs of retired people who want small houses with less upkeep; greater security; easy access to health care, shops, and recreational facilities; and so forth.

Similarly, child care cooperatives are emerging in various places to assist parents in finding a good, reliable place to leave their children as they work. In a child care cooperative, the parents select a board of directors, help determine what kind of services will be provided, and volunteer in various ways to keep costs down.

Smaller, independent druggists and other small businesses rely on cooperatives to allow

CASE
 • • • • • •
SHOULD COOPERATIVES GO CORPORATE?
 • • • • • •

them to compete with mass merchandisers. They usually form some kind of co-op wholesale facility where they can get goods for less.

Some of the larger cooperatives, though, are in farming. Names you may be familiar with include Land O Lakes, Sunkist, Ocean Spray, Blue Diamond, and Welch's. Ocean Spray is a farmer-owned cooperative that is now the number three juice marketer in the United States. Because of the growth in sales of co-ops such as Ocean Spray, many of the top cooperatives are thinking of selling shares to the public. They would thus become corporations much like the big companies they compete with, such as Coca-Cola.

Decision Questions

1. What are some of the advantages and disadvantages of a cooperative's changing to a corporation? What would be the major reason for a co-op to do so?

2. What is the future of cooperatives that provide housing and other services to the elderly? What are some of the differences you would expect to see at a cooperative housing development versus a corporate one?

3. What advantages do you see in the fact that members of a cooperative often volunteer their time to help in the running of the organization?

4. Might farmers lose some control over the production and marketing of their goods if farm cooperatives were to begin going corporate?

La-Van Hawkins has come a long way from the tough Chicago projects of his childhood to a luxury waterfront condo in Baltimore, but the trip wasn't an easy one. By observing what was going on around him, Hawkins saw opportunity where others saw only despair. Hawkins started his career sweeping floors for minimum wage in a fast-food restaurant. Many young people shun such jobs because they believe there is no future in a minimum wage job. La-Van Hawkins' story shows us that such beliefs are not only untrue, but they are keeping young people from experiencing the real opportunities that are available in today's economy.

A minimum wage job enables young people to prove they are reliable workers. On the job they can learn skills and work habits that can transfer to almost any company. Hawkins may have started by sweeping floors, but that was only a start. He worked his way up the employment ladder to assistant manager at a KFC franchise. He continued to succeed and ultimately became the director of operations and regional manager, supervising 80 KFC stores in the Philadelphia/Baltimore markets. Hawkins was constantly learning and observing. He was so successful that the Checkers operations lured him away to supervise their stores.

What was most apparent to Hawkins was the need to open fast-food stores in the inner city. Four years later he owned or operated 43

VIDEO CASE

· · · · · ·

LA-VAN HAWKINS OF URBAN CITY FOODS

Checkers restaurants in four inner cities.

Burger King was the next franchisor to court Hawkins. The unique feature of Hawkins' arrangement with Burger King is that, unlike other franchisees, Hawkins has a great deal of control over the image and products in his franchises. His franchises have flashier colors based on African art, new menu choices, and hip hop music.

Soon Hawkins will operate 125 restaurants in urban areas. If Hawkins' company, Urban City Foods, reaches its goal, it will be the number one Burger King franchisee by 2001. By 1996, the Urban City Burger Kings boasted $200 million in sales—nearly double the national Burger King average.

Discussion Questions

1. Why do you think Burger King allowed Hawkins and Urban City Foods to control the image and products in their stores? How is the Urban City/Burger King agreement different than most other franchise agreements?

2. What opportunities do you see in your community to become an entrepreneur and employ people from your area?

3. What are some of the conditions in the inner city that make running a franchise more difficult there? What can business and city officials do to improve such conditions?

Entrepreneurship and Starting a Small Business

Chapter

6

LEARNING GOALS

After you have read and studied this chapter, you should be able to:

1 Explain why people are willing to take the risks of entrepreneurship, list the attributes of successful entrepreneurs, and describe the benefits of entrepreneurial teams and intrapreneurs.

2 Discuss the importance of small business to the American economy and summarize the major causes of small-business failure.

3 Summarize ways to learn about how small businesses operate.

4 Analyze what it takes to start and run a small business.

5 Outline the advantages and disadvantages small businesses have in entering global markets.

David Marcheschi wanted something to give him the boost he needed for late-night college studying, but he didn't like the taste of either coffee or soda. "Why couldn't someone caffeinate plain water?" he wondered. He mentioned his idea to a friend. It so happened that his friend's father owned a beverage company with a staff chemist. The chemist agreed to see what he could do. In a few weeks, the chemist perfected the formula for Water Joe, spring water with the caffeine kick of an eight-ounce cup of coffee.

Marcheschi created a label and prepared to launch his product, but he couldn't find anyone to bottle it because it required special equipment. After two years of meeting with bottlers all over the country, in 1995 Marcheschi finally found a water company that had an existing water distribution system. The company agreed to form a partnership with Marcheschi, so Water Concepts LLC was born without the high start-up costs Marcheschi expected.

"Our product fulfills the niche of coffee and then some," Marcheschi says. It is a hit among the frenetic, caffeine-addicted futures traders at the Chicago Stock Exchange, where water is the only beverage allowed on the trading floor. Other customers include athletes looking for an energy boost, bands performing late at night, and dental patients

PROFILE

David Marcheschi of Water Concepts LLC

tired of having teeth stained brown by coffee. "People are making lemonade or orange juice with it," he explains. Some really strung-out fans use it to brew coffee or to freeze as ice cubes for colas.

In 1996, a year after full-scale production, Water Joe was shipping 400,000 bottles each week across the country and had annual sales of $12 million. Water Joe is now available in all 50 states and also in Germany and Guam. If it isn't in a store near you, Water Joe's web site http://www.waterjoe.com will help you appeal to your local stores by providing an adaptable form letter for you to send to store managers.

In early 1998, Marcheschi sold half of his stake in the company so that he could pursue other interests, but he still earns royalties on Water Joe. Marcheschi took a risk and it paid off. Stories about people taking risks by starting their own businesses are commonplace in this age of the entrepreneur. As you read about such risk takers in this chapter, maybe you'll be inspired to become an entrepreneur yourself.

Sources: Gianna Jacobson, "A Jolt of Inspiration," *Success,* February 1997, p. 21. Bob Hansen, "Water to Go," *Metro Santa Cruz,* July 2–9, 1997, and Burney Simpson, "Chicago Businessman Making a Mark With Caffeinated Water," *The Nando Times: Business Archive,* January 17, 1998.

···· ▬ ····

THE AGE OF THE ENTREPRENEUR

A 1996 poll of college seniors showed that 51 percent of the men and 31 percent of the women were more attracted to starting their own businesses than to joining the corporate ranks.[1] Generation X people (now in their 20s and early 30s) seems to share the pragmatic view that in this time of post-downsized America it doesn't make sense to work in a company where your reward can just as soon be a pink slip as a promotion or bonus. Why not get a piece of the action by working in your own company? One study of 200 entrepreneurs ages 18 to 35 revealed that the average respondent had already started 2.3 businesses. Two-thirds of them said they used their own savings to start their companies.[2] Colleges around the country are responding to this trend by offering more courses on the subject of entrepreneurship. **Entrepreneurship** is accepting the risk of starting and running a business. Explore this chapter and think about the possibility of entrepreneurship in your future.

◀ **CONSIDER USING TM 43**
Chapter Outline

◀ **CONSIDER USING LECTURE ENHANCER 6-1**
Jennie Bettles of SameSky Inc.

entrepreneurship
Accepting the risk of starting and running a business.

➤ **CONSIDER USING LECTURE ENHANCER 6-2**
Who Is the Most Admired Entrepreneur?

➤ **CONSIDER USING OT ACETATE 6-1**
How Did They Begin?

➤ **CONSIDER USING LECTURE ENHANCER 6-3**
For These Entrepreneurs, Business Is Kids' Stuff

THE JOB-CREATING POWER OF ENTREPRENEURS IN THE UNITED STATES

One of the major issues in the United States today is the need to create more jobs. You can get some idea about the job-creating power of entrepreneurs when you look at some of the great American entrepreneurs from the past and the present. The history of the United States is the history of its entrepreneurs. Consider just a few of the many entrepreneurs who have helped shape the American economy:

- Du Pont was started in 1802 by Éleuthère Irénée du Pont de Nemours. Some 18 shareholders provided $36,000 in start-up money.
- Avon started in 1886 on $500 David McConnell borrowed from a friend.
- George Eastman launched Kodak in 1880 with a $3,000 investment.
- Procter & Gamble was formed in 1837 by William Procter and James Gamble with a total of $7,000 in capital.
- Ford Motor Company began with an investment of $28,000 by Henry Ford and 11 associates.

The stories are all about the same. One entrepreneur or a couple of entrepreneurs had a good idea, borrowed a few dollars from friends and family, and started a business. That business now employs thousands of people and helps the country prosper.

The United States still has plenty of entrepreneurial talent. Names such as Steve Jobs (Apple Computer), Ross Perot (Electronic Data Systems), Michael Dell (Dell Computer), Bill Gates (Microsoft), Howard Schultz (Starbucks), Craig McCaw (McCaw Cellular Communications), Scott Cook (Intuit), and Ted Turner (Cable News Network) have become as familiar as those of the great entrepreneurs of the past.[3]

➤ **LEARNING GOAL 1.** Explain why people are willing to take the risks of entrepreneurship; list the attributes of successful entrepreneurs; and describe the benefits of entrepreneurial teams and intrapreneurs.

➤ **CONSIDER USING OT ACETATE 6-2**
Why People Start Their Own Businesses

➤ **CONSIDER USING LECTURE ENHANCER 6-4**
Tomima Edmark: Inventor and Entrepreneur

WHY PEOPLE TAKE THE ENTREPRENEURIAL CHALLENGE

Taking the risks of starting a business can be scary and thrilling at the same time. John Simon, founder of a medical-device company, describes it as "almost like bungee-jumping. You might be scared, but if you watch six other people do it and they survive, you're then able to do it yourself."[4] Some of the many reasons people are willing to take the risks of starting a business are the following:

- *Opportunity.* The opportunity to share in the American dream is a tremendous lure. Many people new to this country may not have the necessary skills for working in today's complex organizations. However, they may have the initiative and drive to work the long hours demanded by entrepreneurship. The same is true of many corporate managers who left the security of the corporate life (either by choice or as a result of corporate downsizing) to run businesses of their own.
- *Profit.* Profit is another important reason to become an entrepreneur. At one time the richest person in America was Sam Walton, the entrepreneur who started Wal-Mart. Now the richest person in America is

William Henry Gates III, the entrepreneur who founded Microsoft Corporation.

- *Independence.* Many entrepreneurs simply do not enjoy working for someone else. Many lawyers, for example, do not like the stress and demands of big law firms. Some have found more enjoyment and self-satisfaction in starting their own businesses.[5]

- *Challenge.* Some people believe that entrepreneurs are excitement junkies who flourish on taking risks. Nancy Flexman and Thomas Scanlan, however, in their book *Running Your Own Business,* contend that entrepreneurs take moderate, calculated risks; they are not just gambling. In general, though, entrepreneurs seek achievement more than power.

Growing up in a ghetto, Karl Kani dreamed of becoming the Ralph Lauren of the streets, so he designed his own clothes and had them custom-made. Kani started selling his creations from his car in front of New York City nightclubs and local basketball tournaments. Now Kani's fashions are sold by such upscale stores as Nordstrom and Macys and his company had 1995 sales of $69 million. Entrepreneurs like Kani look for opportunities overlooked by others.

••• WHAT DOES IT TAKE TO BE AN ENTREPRENEUR? •••

Would you succeed as an entrepreneur? You can learn the managerial and leadership skills needed to run a firm. However, you may not have the personality to assume the risks, take the initiative, create the vision, and rally others to follow your lead. Those traits are harder to learn or acquire. A list of entrepreneurial attributes you would look for in yourself includes the following:

1. *Self-directed.* You should be thoroughly comfortable and thoroughly self-disciplined even though you are your own boss. You will be responsible for your success or possible failure.

2. *Self-nurturing.* You must believe in your idea even when no one else does, and be able to replenish your own enthusiasm. When Walt Disney suggested the possibility of a full-length animated feature film, *Snow White,* the industry laughed. His personal commitment and enthusiasm caused the Bank of America to back his venture. The rest is history.

3. *Action-oriented.* Great business ideas are not enough. The most important thing is a burning desire to realize, actualize, and build your dream into reality.

4. *Highly energetic.* It's your business, and you must be emotionally, mentally, and physically able to work long and hard.

5. *Tolerant of uncertainty.* Successful entrepreneurs take only calculated risks (if they can help it). Still, they must be able to take some risks. Remember, entrepreneurship is not for the squeamish or the person bent on security.

It is important to know that most entrepreneurs don't get the ideas for their products and services from some flash of inspiration. Rather than a flash, the source of innovation is more like a flashlight. Imagine a search party, walking around in the dark, shining the light, looking around, asking questions, and looking some more. The late Sam Walton used such a flashlight approach. He visited his stores and those of competitors and took notes. He'd see a good idea on Monday, and by Tuesday every Wal-Mart manager in the country knew about it. He expected his managers to use flashlighting too. Every time they traveled on business, they were expected to come back with at least one idea

◄ CONSIDER USING OT ACETATE
6-3
Who Starts Businesses?

◄ CONSIDER USING CRITICAL THINKING EXERCISE 6-1
What Does It Take to Be an Entrepreneur? (**SCANS**)

◄ CONSIDER USING LECTURE ENHANCER 6-5
Charles Babbage: 19th Century Entrepreneur

► CONSIDER USING TM 44
Advice for Potential Entrepreneurs

FIGURE 6.1
· · · ·
ADVICE FOR POTENTIAL ENTREPRENEURS

- Research your market, but don't take too long to act.
- Work for other people first and learn on their money
- Start out slowly. Start your business when you have a customer. Maybe try your venture as a sideline at first.
- Set specific objectives, but don't set your goals too high. Remember, there's no easy money.
- Plan your objectives within specific time frames.
- Surround yourself with people who are smarter than you—including an accountant and an outside board of directors who are interested in your well-being and who'll give you straight answers.
- Don't be afraid to fail. Former football coach Vince Lombardi summarized the entrepreneurial philosophy when he said, "We didn't lose any games this season, we just ran out of time twice." New entrepreneurs must be ready to run out of time a few times before they succeed.

Source: Joseph Mancuso, "The Right Stuff: Do You Have What It Takes to Start Your Own Business?" *The Wall Street Journal's Managing Your Career,* Spring 1991 pp. 15–19.

worth more than the cost of their trip. "That's how most creativity happens," says business author Dale Dauten. "Calling around, asking questions, saying 'What if?' till you get blisters on your tongue."[6] If you are interested in seeing whether you have the entrepreneurial spirit in your blood, take the entrepreneurial test on page 191. There is also some advice for would-be entrepreneurs in Figure 6.1.

Critical Thinking

Do you know anyone who seems to have the entrepreneurial spirit? What about him or her makes you say that? Are there any similarities between the characteristics demanded of an entrepreneur and those of a professional athlete? Would an athlete be a good prospect for entrepreneurship? Why or why not? Could teamwork be important in an entrepreneurial effort?

··· ENTREPRENEURIAL TEAMS ···

entrepreneurial team
A group of experienced people from different areas of business who join together to form a managerial team with the skills needed to develop, make, and market a new product.

► CONSIDER USING SUPPLEMEN-
TAL CASE 6-1
3M Company, Intrapreneurial Leader
(**SCANS**)

► CONSIDER USING OT ACETATE
6-4
The Most Common Type of Home-Based Businesses

► CONSIDER USING LECTURE
ENHANCER 6-6
Listen To Your Entrepreneur

An **entrepreneurial team** is a group of experienced people from different areas of business who join together to form a managerial team with the skills needed to develop, make, and market a new product. A team may be better than an individual entrepreneur because it can combine creative skills with production and marketing skills right from the start. Having a team also can assure more cooperation and coordination among functions.

One of the exciting new companies developed in the 1980s was Compaq Computer. It was started by three senior managers at Texas Instruments: Bill Murto, Jim Harris, and Rod Canion. All three were bitten by the entrepreneurial bug and decided to go out on their own. They debated what industry to enter but finally decided to build a portable personal computer that was compatible with the IBM PC.

The key to Compaq's early success was that the company was built around this "smart team" of experienced managers. The team wanted to combine the discipline of a big company with an environment where people could feel they were participating in a successful venture. The trio of corporate entrepreneurs recruited seasoned managers with similar desires. All the managers worked as a team. For example, the company's treasurer and top engineer contributed to production and marketing decisions. Everyone worked together to conceive, develop, and market products.

Today, Compaq is the most successful of all PC makers in building powerful systems while keeping costs down to ensure healthy profit margins.[7] The person who took Compaq worldwide, Eckhard Pfeiffer, was recruited from Texas Instruments. That has become a pattern in the last few decades. Entrepreneurs such as the three from Compaq often turn their companies over to professional managers once the companies reach a certain size. Often such a change is good for the firm because new ideas are introduced and new entrepreneurial spirit is instilled.

◄ CONSIDER USING LECTURE
ENHANCER 6-7
Breeding Entrepreneurship on the Net.

••• MICROPRENEURS AND HOME-BASED BUSINESSES •••

Not every person who starts a business has the goal of making a lot of money and growing a world-class business. Some are interested in simply enjoying a balanced lifestyle while doing the kind of work they want to do. Business writer Michael LeBoeuf calls such business owners **micropreneurs**. While entrepreneurs are committed to the quest for growth, micropreneurs know they can be happy even if their companies never appear on the lists of top-ranked businesses.

Many micropreneurs are home-based business owners. In 1996, there were an estimated 27 million American home-based business owners.[8] They are writers, consultants, video producers, architects, bookkeepers, and such. In fact, the development of this textbook involved many home-based business owners. The authors, the developmental editors, the copy editor, and even the text designer operate home-based businesses. Many home-based businesses are owned by people who are trying to combine career and family.

Simply because micropreneurs don't have the ambition to create world-class businesses doesn't mean they don't make attractive profits. LeBoeuf estimates that the average income of home-based business owners is almost twice that of the average employee and that 20 percent of home-business households earn more than $75,000 a year.[9] LeBoeuf advises those who wish to get out of an office building and into a home office to focus on finding opportunity instead of accepting security, getting results instead of following routines, earning a profit instead of earning a paycheck, trying new ideas instead of

micropreneurs
Those who are willing to accept the risk of starting and managing the type of business that remains small, lets them do the kind of work they want to do, and offers them a balanced lifestyle.

Ernestina Galindo owns her own tortilla factory in Austin, Texas. Why do you think Ernestina chose to operate her factory in the United States rather than in her native country?

avoiding mistakes, and creating a long-term vision instead of seeking a short-term payoff.[10]

··· ENCOURAGING ENTREPRENEURSHIP ···
—WHAT GOVERNMENT CAN DO

To encourage more entrepreneurs to come to the United States, the government passed the Immigration Act of 1990. It created a category of "investor visas" that allows 10,000 people to come to the United States each year if they invest $1 million in an enterprise that creates or preserves 10 jobs. Some people are promoting the idea of increasing the number of such immigrants. They believe the more entrepreneurs that can be lured to the United States, the more jobs will be created and the more the economy will grow.

The Yee sisters make quite an entrepreneurial team. The six sisters knew first-hand that there was a scarcity of cosmetics that blend with the yellow skin tones of many of the 3.8 million Asian women in the United States. The sisters developed a line of 20 cosmetic items, Jane became Zhen's model, and Susan used her home as Zhen's warehouse. Their $100,000 mail-order business has just expanded to Nordstrom's prestigious cosmetic department.

Leighlonn and Jane Yee

真

z h ē n

Formulated Just For You.

A unique collection of quality cosmetics for Asians founded by Asians, the Yee sisters.

The Zhen collection offers a wide selection of foundation formulas in shades for your unique skin tone. All mineral oil free and hypo allergenic.

We also offer a complete selection of cosmetics in a color palette to enhance your eyes and lips at a remarkable price.

Our philosophy is to provide 100% satisfaction.

Call 1-800-457-8455
for a free catalog. Give us a try and receive a free lipstick with your first order. Join the growing number of satisfied customers.

The YEE sisters and mom

For distribution information contact us at
612-753-9538

Z H Ē N

Making Ethical Decisions

http://www.ethicscentre.com/home.htm

Going Down with the Ship

Suppose you have worked for two years in a company and you see signs that the business is beginning to falter. You and a co-worker have ideas about how to make a company like your boss's succeed. You are considering quitting your job and starting your own company with your friend. Should you approach other co-workers about working for your new venture? Will you try to lure your old boss's customers to your own business? What are your alternatives? What are the consequences of each alternative? What is the most ethical choice?

▲ SCANS

One way to encourage entrepreneurship is through enterprise zones that feature low taxes and government support. The government could have a significant effect on entrepreneurship by offering investment tax credits that would give tax breaks to businesses that make the kind of investments that would create jobs. The government could also institute a plan of public investment to rebuild the nation's infrastructure (bridges, roads, etc.). Such money would go to businesses that would then hire people whose spending would stimulate economic growth.

Progress Check

- Can you name some of the famous entrepreneurs from the past and some from the present?
- Why are people willing to take the risks of entrepreneurship?
- What are the advantages of entrepreneurial teams?
- How do micropreneurs differ from entrepreneurs?

••• ENTREPRENEURSHIP WITHIN FIRMS •••

Entrepreneurship in a large organization is often reflected in the efforts and achievements of intrapreneurs. **Intrapreneurs** are creative people who work as entrepreneurs within corporations. The idea is to use a company's existing resources—human, financial, and physical—to launch new products and generate new profits.[11] At 3M Company, for example, managers are expected to devote 15 percent of their time to thinking up new products or services.[12]

Have you seen those bright-colored Post-it Notes people use to stick messages up on a wall? That product was developed by Art Fry, a 3M employee. He needed to mark the pages of a hymnal in a way that wouldn't damage the book or fall out. He came up with the idea of the sticky paper. The 3M labs soon produced a sample, but distributors thought the product was silly, and market surveys were negative. Nonetheless, 3M kept sending samples to secretaries of top executives. Eventually, after 12 years, the orders began pouring in, and Post-its became a $12 million winner. The company continues to update the product and now offers Post-it Notes made from recycled paper. Post-it Notes have gone international as well. The notepads sent to Japan are long and narrow to accommodate vertical writing. Now you can even use Post-it Notes electronically—the software program Post-it Software Notes allows you to type notes and store them on memo boards, embed them in documents, or send them through e-mail.[13]

intrapreneurs
Creative people who work as entrepreneurs within corporations.

◄ CONSIDER USING OT ACETATE 6-5 AND OT ACETATE 6-6
Take the Intrapreneur Quiz

◄ CONSIDER USING LECTURE ENHANCER 6-8
Intrapreneur Versus Entrepreneur

1 We've been on a roll for 67 years.

2 Now we've popped up with another big idea. It's an ingenious dispensing system that pops up strips of tape – pre-cut, one at a time, right into your hand. New Scotch™ Pop-up Tape Strips make gift wrapping easier, especially when you've got your hands full. We're making tape even more handy, because we make the leap *from need to...*

3M *Innovation*

©3M 1997   For more information, call 1-800-3M-HELPS, or Internet: http://www.mmm.com

Not one to stick with the same old tape, 3M has a reputation for encouraging intrapreneurship by requiring employees to devote at least 15 percent of their time to thinking up new products. The company introduced its precut Pop-up Tape Strips just in time for the 1997 Christmas gift-wrapping season.

> **LEARNING GOAL 2.** Discuss the importance of small business to the American economy and summarize the major causes of small-business failure.

small business
A business that is independently owned and operated, is not dominant in its field of operation, and meets certain standards of size in terms of employees or annual receipts.

> **CONSIDER USING LECTURE ENHANCER 6-9** The Small Advantage

> **CONSIDER USING LECTURE ENHANCER 6-10** The Emotional Challenges of Starting a Business

> **CONSIDER USING OT ACETATE 6-7** How Much Capital Do Entrepreneurs Have to Start Their Businesses?

Hewlett-Packard calls its intrapreneurial approach the Triad Development Process. The idea is to link the design engineer, the manufacturer, and the marketer (the Triad) in a cross-functional team from the design phase on. Everything, even the assembly line, shuts down if the Triad team wants to test an innovation.

The classic intrapreneurial venture is the Skunkworks of Lockheed Martin Corp. The Skunkworks is a top-secret research and development center that turned out such monumental products as America's first fighter jet in 1943 and the Stealth fighter in 1991.

···· ━━ ····

GETTING STARTED IN SMALL BUSINESS

Let's suppose you have a great idea for a new business, you have the attributes of an entrepreneur, and you are ready to take the leap into business for yourself. How do you start a business? How much paperwork is involved? That is what the rest of this chapter is about. We will explore small businesses, their role in the economy, and small-business management. It is easier to identify with a small neighborhood business than with a giant global firm, yet the principles of management are similar. The management of charities, government agencies, churches, schools, and unions is much the same as the management of small and large businesses. So, as you learn about small-business management, you will make a giant step toward understanding management in general. All organizations demand capital, good ideas, planning, information management, budgets (and financial management in general), accounting, marketing, good employee relations, and good overall managerial know-how. We shall explore these areas as they relate to small businesses and then, later in the book, apply the concepts to large firms, even global organizations.

> **▼ CONSIDER USING OT ACETATE 6-8**
> What Sources Did You Use to Get Start-up Capital?

··· SMALL VERSUS BIG BUSINESS ···

The Small Business Administration (SBA) defines a **small business** as one that is independently owned and operated, is not dominant in its field of operation, and meets certain standards of size in terms of employees or annual receipts (e.g., less than $2 million a year for service businesses). A small business is considered "small" only in relation to other businesses in its industry. A wholesaler may sell up to $22 million and still be considered a small business by the SBA. In manufacturing, a plant can have 1,500 employees and still be considered small. For example, before its merger with Chrysler, American Motors was considered small because it was tiny compared to Ford, General Motors, and Chrysler. Let's look at some interesting statistics about small businesses:

- There are about 24.5 million full- and part-time home-based businesses in the United States.
- Nearly 750,000 tax-paying, employee-hiring businesses are started every year.[14]

- Of all nonfarm businesses in the United States, almost 97 percent are considered small by SBA standards.
- Small businesses account for over 40 percent of the gross domestic product (GDP).
- The total number of U.S. employees who work in small business is greater than the populations of Australia and Canada combined.
- About 80 percent of Americans find their first jobs in small businesses.
- The number of women owning small businesses has increased rapidly. Women now own nearly 6 million small businesses. That's more than one-third of all small businesses and a 43 percent increase from 4.1 million in 1987.[15]
- The number of small businesses owned by minority women surged to 1.1 million in 1996. That represents a 153 percent growth in nine years, more than three times the increase in businesses in general.[16]

As you can see, small business is really a big part of the U.S. economy. How big a part? We'll explore that question next.

••• IMPORTANCE OF SMALL BUSINESSES •••

In the 1980s large companies lost 4.1 million jobs; in 1996 alone, small businesses created almost a million new jobs.[17] Ninety percent of the nation's new jobs in the private sector are in small businesses. That means there is a very good chance that you will either work in a small business someday or start one. A quarter of the small businesses polled for a 1996 study listed "lack of qualified workers" as one of their biggest obstacles to growth.[18]

Dun & Bradstreet reports that the biggest employment increases in 1994 were in services (979,000), manufacturing (776,000), retail (468,000), and construction (349,000). The smallest job increases were in transportation, public utilities, mining, and government.[19] Did you notice that manufacturing firms are producing almost as many jobs as service firms? Why is this? Many analysts believe that the declining value of the dollar has spurred a revival in American exports as they become less expensive in global markets. As a result, small manufacturers that supply exporting industries are the winners in the 1990s.

In addition to providing employment opportunities, small firms believe they offer other advantages that larger companies do not. Owners of small companies report that their greatest advantages over big companies are their more personal customer service and their ability to respond quickly to opportunities.[20] As big businesses cut employees, they often find they do not have the staff they need and are increasingly contracting with small companies to temporarily fill their needs; this is outsourcing.

As you can see, bigger is not always better. Picture a hole in the ground. If you fill it with big boulders there are many empty spaces between them. However, if you fill it with sand, there is no space between the grains. That's how it is in business. Big businesses don't serve all the needs of the market. There is plenty of room for small companies to make a profit filling those niches.

••• SMALL-BUSINESS •••
SUCCESS AND FAILURE

You can't be naive about business practices, or you'll go broke. There is some debate about how many new small businesses fail each year. Conventional wisdom says that four out of five businesses (80 percent) fail in their first five years, yet the SBA reports a 62 percent death rate within six years. However, a

Spotlight on Small Business

http://www.sbaonline.sba.gov/

Causes of Small-Business Failure

- Plunging in without first testing the waters on a small scale.
- Underpricing or overpricing goods or services.
- Underestimating how much time it will take to build a market.
- Starting with too little capital.
- Starting with too much capital and being careless in its use.
- Going into business with little or no experience and without first learning something about it.
- Borrowing money without planning just how and when to pay it back.
- Attempting to do too much business with too little capital.
- Not allowing for setbacks and unexpected expenses.
- Buying too much on credit.

- Extending credit too freely.
- Expanding credit too rapidly.
- Failing to keep complete, accurate records, so that the owners drift into trouble without realizing it.
- Carrying habits of personal extravagance into the business.
- Not understanding business cycles.
- Forgetting about taxes, insurance, and other costs of doing business.
- Mistaking the freedom of being in business for one-self for the liberty to work or not, according to whim.

Sources: Service Corps of Retired Executives (part of the Small Business Administration); Judith Gross, "Autopsy of a Business," *Home Office Computing,* October 1993, pp. 52–60; and John Case, "The Dark Side: Births and Deaths," *Inc.,* May 15, 1996, pp. 80–81.

study by economist Bruce Kirchhoff shows that the failure rate is only 18 percent over the first eight years. Kirchhoff contends that the other failure rates resulted from misinterpretations of Dun & Bradstreet statistics. When small-business owners went out of business to start new and different businesses, they were included in the "business failure" category when obviously that is not the case. Similarly, when a business changed its form of ownership from partnership to corporation, it was considered a failure. Retirements of sole owners were also included in the "business death" category.[21] All in all, the good news for entrepreneurs is that business failures are much lower than has traditionally been reported.

Although the chances of business survival may be greater than some used to think, keep in mind that even the most optimistic interpretation of the statistics shows that nearly one out of five businesses that fails is left owing money to creditors. As you can see in the box listing causes of small-business failure above, many small businesses fail because of managerial incompetence and inadequate financial planning.

Choosing the right type of business is critical to success. Many of the businesses with the lowest failure rates require advanced training to start—veterinary services, dentists' offices, physicians' offices, and so on. While training and degrees may buy security, they do not tend to produce much growth. If you want to be both independent and rich, you need to go after growth. The businesses with the highest odds of significant growth are in manufacturing. But these are not easy businesses to start and are even more difficult to keep going.

In general it seems that the easiest businesses to start are the ones that tend to have the least growth and the greatest failure rate. The easiest businesses to keep alive are difficult ones to get started. And the ones that can

Spotlight on Small Business

Situations for Small-Business Success

Small businesses are more likely to succeed when

- The customer requires a lot of personal attention, as in a beauty parlor.
- The product is not easily made by mass-production techniques (e.g., custom-tailored clothes or custom auto-body work).
- Sales are not large enough to appeal to a large firm (e.g., a novelty shop).

- The neighborhood is not attractive because of crime or poverty. This provides a unique opportunity for small grocery stores, liquor stores, and laundries.
- A large business sells a franchise operation to local buyers. Don't forget franchising as an excellent way to enter the world of small business.

make you rich are the ones that are both hard to start and hard to keep going. See the box above to get an idea of the business situations that are most likely to lead to success.

When you decide to start your own business, you must think carefully about what kind of business you want. You are not likely to find everything you want in one business—easy entry, security, and reward. Choose those characteristics that matter the most to you; accept the absence of the others; plan, plan, plan; and then go for it!

Critical Thinking

Imagine yourself starting a small business. What kind of business would it be? How much competition is there? What could you do to make your business more attractive than those of competitors? Would you be willing to work 60 to 70 hours per week?

···· ▬ ····

LEARNING ABOUT SMALL-BUSINESS OPERATIONS

◄ **LEARNING GOAL 3.** Summarize ways to learn about how small businesses operate.

Hundreds of would-be entrepreneurs of all ages have asked the same question: "How can I learn to run my own business?" Many of these people had no idea what kind of business they wanted to start; they simply wanted to be in business for themselves. That seems to be a major trend among students today. Therefore, here are some hints for learning about small business.

··· LEARN FROM OTHERS ···

Your search for small-business knowledge might begin by investigating your local community college for such classes. One of the best things about such courses is that they bring together entrepreneurs. One of the best ways to learn how to run a small business is to talk to others who have already done it. They will tell you that location is critical. They will caution you not to be undercapitalized (not have enough money to start). They will warn you about the problems of finding and retaining good workers. And, most of all, they will tell you to keep good records and hire a good accountant and lawyer before you start. This free advice is invaluable.

••• GET SOME EXPERIENCE •••

➤ CONSIDER USING OT ACETATE 6-9
Hours Worked Per Week the First Year in Business

There is no better way to learn small-business management than by becoming an apprentice or working for a successful entrepreneur. In fact, 42 percent of small-business owners got the idea for their businesses from their prior jobs. The rule of thumb is: Have three years' experience in a comparable business.

Many new entrepreneurs come from corporate management. They are tired of the big-business life and/or are being laid off because of downsizing. Such managers bring their managerial expertise and enthusiasm with them.

Getting experience before you start your own business isn't a new concept. In fact, way back in 1818, Cornelius Vanderbilt sold his own sailing vessels and went to work for a steamboat company so he could learn the rules of the new game of steam. After learning what he needed to know, he quit, started his own steam shipping company, and became the first American to accumulate $100 million.

By starting a business part-time, during your off hours or on weekends, you can experience the rewards of working for yourself while still enjoying a regular paycheck.

Warren McLean has come a long way from his boyhood home in Harlem. McLean founded the Metropolitan Economic Development Association in 1971. Honored as a top supporter of entrepreneurship in 1997 by *Inc.* magazine, McLean has helped more than 3,000 minority-owned businesses in Minneapolis-St. Paul.

••• TAKE OVER A SUCCESSFUL FIRM •••

Small-business management takes time, dedication, and determination. Owners work long hours and rarely take vacations. After many years, they may feel stuck in their business. They may think they can't get out because they have too much time and effort invested. Consequently, there are millions of small-business owners out there eager to get away, at least for a long vacation.

This is where you come in. Find a successful businessperson who owns a small business. Tell him or her that you are eager to learn the business and would like to serve an apprenticeship, a training period. At the end of that period (one year or so), you would like to help the owner/manager by becoming assistant manager. As assistant manager, you would free the owner to take off weekends and holidays, and to take a long vacation—a good deal for him or her. For another year or so, work very hard to learn all about the business—suppliers, inventory, bookkeeping, customers, promotion, and so on. At the end of two years, make the owner this offer: He or she can retire or work only part-time, and you will take over the business. You can establish a profit-sharing plan for yourself plus a salary. Be generous with yourself; you will earn it if you manage the business. You can even ask for 40 percent or more of the profits.

The owner benefits by keeping ownership in the business and making 60 percent of what he or she earned before—without having to work. You benefit by making 40 percent of the profits of a successful firm. This is an excellent deal for an owner about to retire who is able to keep his or her firm and a healthy profit flow. It is also a clever and successful way to share in the profits of a successful small business without any personal money investment.[22]

If profit sharing doesn't appeal to the owner, you may want to buy the business outright. How do you determine a fair price for a business? Value is based on (1) what the business owns, (2) what it earns, and (3) what makes it unique. Naturally, your accountant will need to help you determine the business's value.

If your efforts to take over the business through either profit sharing or buying fail, you can quit and start your own business fully trained.

···· ▬▬ ····

MANAGING A SMALL BUSINESS

◄ **LEARNING GOAL 4.** Analyze what it takes to start and run a small business.

The Small Business Administration has reported that 90 percent of all small-business failures are a result of poor management. The problem is that the term *poor management* covers a number of faults. It could mean poor planning, poor record keeping, poor inventory control, poor promotion, or poor employee relations. Most likely it would include poor capitalization. This chapter gives us a chance to explore the functions of business in a small-business setting so you can become one of the successful owners. The functions we shall explore are the following:

◄ **CONSIDER USING LECTURE ENHANCER 6-11**
On-Line@ BUREAUCRACY.CA

- Planning your business.
- Financing your business.
- Knowing your customers (marketing).
- Managing your employees (human resource development).
- Keeping records (accounting).

Although all of the functions are important in both the start-up phase and the management phase of the business, the first two functions—planning and financing—are the primary concerns when you start your business. The remaining functions are the heart of the actual running of the business, once it is started.

◄ **CONSIDER USING LECTURE ENHANCER 6-12**
There's No Substitute for a Business Plan (I)

◄ **CONSIDER USING LECTURE ENHANCER 6-13**
There's No Substitute for a Business Plan (II)

··· BEGIN WITH PLANNING ···

It is amazing how many people are eager to start a small business but have only a vague notion of what they want to do. Eventually they come up with an idea for a business and begin discussing the idea with professors, friends, and other businesspeople. It is at this stage that the entrepreneur needs a business plan. A **business plan** is a detailed written statement that describes the nature of the business, the target market, the advantages the business will have in relation to competition, and the resources and qualifications of the owner(s). A business plan forces potential owners of small businesses to be quite specific about the products or services they intend to offer. They must analyze the competition, calculate the money needed to start, and cover other details of operation. A business plan is also mandatory for talking with bankers or other investors.

business plan
A detailed written statement that describes the nature of the business, the target market, the advantages the business will have in relation to competition, and the resources and qualifications of the owner(s).

Michael Celello, president of the People's Commercial Bank, says that fewer than 10 percent of prospective borrowers come to a bank adequately prepared. He offers several tips to small-business owners, including picking a bank that serves businesses the size of yours, having a good accountant prepare a complete set of financial statements and a personal balance sheet, making an appointment before going to the bank, going to the bank with an accountant and all the necessary financial information, and demonstrating to the banker that you're a person of good character: civic minded and respected

◄ **CONSIDER USING CRITICAL THINKING EXERCISE 6-2**
Writing a Business Plan (**SCANS**)

in business and community circles. Finally, he says to ask for all the money you need, be specific, and be prepared to personally guarantee the loan.

••• WRITING A BUSINESS PLAN •••

A good business plan takes six months to write, but you've got to convince your readers in five minutes not to throw the plan away.[23] While there is no such thing as a perfect business plan, prospective entrepreneurs do think out the smallest details. Jerrold Carrington of Inroads Capital Partners advises that one of the most important parts of the business plan is the executive summary. The summary has to catch the reader's interest. Bankers receive many business plans every day. "You better grab me up front," says Carrington.[24] The box on p. 177 gives you an outline of a comprehensive business plan.

Sometimes one of the most difficult tasks in undertaking complex projects such as writing a business plan is knowing where to start. There are many computer software programs on the market now to help you get organized. One highly rated business-plan program is Plan Write by Business Resource Software.[25]

Getting the completed business plan in the right hands is almost as important as getting the right information in the plan. Finding the right hands requires research. Next we will discuss some of the many sources of money available to new business ventures. All of them call for a comprehensive business plan. The time and effort you invest before starting a business will pay off many times later. With small businesses, the big payoff is survival.

••• GETTING MONEY TO FUND A SMALL BUSINESS •••

Entrepreneurs, like most people, often are not highly skilled at obtaining, managing, and using money. Inadequate capitalization or poor financial management can destroy a business, even when the basic idea behind the business is good and the products are accepted in the marketplace. One of the secrets of finding the money to start your business is knowing where to look for it.

An entrepreneur has several potential sources of capital: personal savings, relatives, former employers, banks, finance companies, venture capitalists, government agencies such as the Small Business Administration (SBA), the Farmers Home Administration, the Economic Development Authority, and more. You may even want to consider borrowing from a potential supplier to your future business. Helping you get started may be in the supplier's interest if there is a chance you will be a big customer later.

States are becoming stronger supporters of entrepreneurs as they create programs that invest directly in new businesses. Often, state commerce departments serve as clearinghouses for such investment programs. States are also creating incubators and technology centers to reduce start-up capital needs. **Incubators** are centers that offer new businesses low-cost offices with basic business services such as accounting, legal advice, and secretarial help. The number of incubators in the United States now exceeds 800.[26]

Technology-minded entrepreneurs often have the best shot at attracting start-up capital. Not only are such potential businesses more attractive to venture capitalists and state governments, but also the federal government has several grant programs that provide funds for computer-related ventures.

Other than personal savings, individual investors are the primary source of capital for most entrepreneurs. Such investors provide 6 of every 10 dollars

Married couple Shafalika Saxena and Robert Holdheim used their marketing expertise and knowledge of the herbal-medicine practice called ayurveda to turn their business, Better Botanicals, into a successful all-natural, herbal personal-care products business. The retail store, wholesale and mail order business had projected sales of $1.3 million for 1997. Their goal is to reach the $20 million mark in five years.

➤ CONSIDER USING OT ACETATE 6-10
How to Get a Yes From a Banker

➤ CONSIDER USING LECTURE ENHANCER 6-14
Angels On-Line

incubators
Centers that offer new businesses low-cost offices with basic business services.

OUTLINE OF A COMPREHENSIVE BUSINESS PLAN

A good business plan is between 25 and 50 pages long and takes at least six months to write.

Cover letter

Only one thing is certain when you go hunting for money to start a business: You won't be the only hunter out there. You need to make potential funders want to read *your* business plan instead of the hundreds of others on their desks. Your cover letter should summarize the most attractive points of your project in as few words as possible. Be sure to address the letter to the potential investor by name. "To whom it may concern" or "Dear Sir" is not the best way to win an investor's support.

Section 1—Executive Summary

Begin with a two-page or three-page management summary of the proposed venture. Include a short description of the business, and discuss major goals and objectives.

Section 2—Company Background

Describe company operations to date (if any), potential legal considerations, and areas of risk and opportunity. Summarize the firm's financial condition, and include past and current balance sheets, income and cash-flow statements, and other relevant financial records (you will read about these financial statements in Chapter 18). It is also wise to include a description of insurance coverage. Investors want to be assured that death or other mishaps do not pose major threats to the company.

Section 3—Management Team

Include an organization chart, job descriptions of listed positions, and detailed résumés of the current and proposed executives. A mediocre idea with a proven management team is funded more often than a great idea with an inexperienced team. Managers should have expertise in all disciplines necessary to start and run a business. If not, mention outside consultants who will serve in these roles and describe their qualifications.

Section 4—Financial Plan

Provide five-year projections for income, expenses, and funding sources. Don't assume the business will grow in a straight line. Adjust your planning to allow for funding at various stages of the company's growth. Explain the rationale and assumptions used to determine the estimates. Assumptions should be reasonable and based on industry/historical trends. Make sure all totals add up and are consistent throughout the plan. If necessary, hire a professional accountant or financial analyst to prepare these statements.

Stay clear of excessively ambitious sales projections; rather, offer best-case, expected, and worst-case scenarios. These not only reveal how sensitive the bottom line is to sales fluctuations but also serve as good management guides.

Section 5—Capital Required

Indicate the amount of capital needed to commence or continue operations and describe how these funds are to be used. Make sure the totals are the same as the ones on the cash-flow statement. This area will receive a great deal of review from potential investors, so it must be clear and concise.

Section 6—Marketing Plan

Don't underestimate the competition. Review industry size, trends, and the target market segment. Sources like *American Demographics* magazine and the *Rand McNally Commercial Atlas and Marketing Guide* can help you put a plan together. Discuss strengths and weaknesses of the product or service. The most important things investors want to know are what makes the product more desirable than what's already available and whether the product can be patented. Compare pricing to the competition's. Forecast sales in dollars and units. Outline sales, advertising, promotion, and PR programs. Make sure the costs agree with those projected in the financial statements.

Section 7—Location Analysis

In retailing and certain other industries, the location of the business is one of the most important factors. Provide a comprehensive demographic analysis of consumers in the area of the proposed store as well as a traffic-pattern analysis and vehicular and pedestrian counts.

Section 8—Manufacturing Plan

Describe minimum plant size, machinery required, production capacity, inventory and inventory-control methods, quality control, plant personnel requirements, and so on. Estimates of product costs should be based on primary research.

Section 9—Appendix

Include all marketing research on the product or service (off-the-shelf reports, article reprints, etc.) and other information about the product concept or market size. Provide a bibliography of all the reference materials you consulted. This section should demonstrate that the proposed company won't be entering a declining industry or market segment.

Sources: Eric Adams, "Growing Your Business Plan," *Home-Office Computing*, May 1991, pp. 44–48; and Carolyn Brown, "Becoming Your Own Boss: Developing a Solid Business Plan," *Essence*, March 1997, pp. 83–86.

for firms with fewer than four employees and sales of under $150,000 a year. About $56 billion in risk capital comes from these "business angels" each year. Computer networks are now available that link entrepreneurs with such potential investors.

venture capitalists
Individuals or companies that invest in new businesses in exchange for partial ownership of those businesses.

Investors known as **venture capitalists** may finance your project—for a price. Venture capitalists may ask for a hefty stake (as much as 60 percent) in your company in exchange for the cash to start your business. If the venture capitalist demands too large a stake, you could lose control of the business. Small companies raised a record $10.1 billion in venture capital in 1996.[27] Experts recommend that you talk with at least five investment firms and their clients in order to find the right venture capitalist. You can get a list of venture capitalists from the Small Business Administration. Ask for the "Directory of Operating Small Business Investment Companies." You can also follow the ups and downs of venture capital availability in *Inc.* magazine.

Two good books about finding venture capital are Robert J. Gaston's *Finding Private Venture Capital for Your Firm* (New York: John Wiley & Sons, 1989) and G. Steven Barrill and Craig T. Norback's *The Arthur Young Guide to Raising Venture Capital* (Blue Ridge Summit, Pa.: Liberty House, 17294).

••• THE SMALL BUSINESS ADMINISTRATION (SBA) •••

The Small Business Administration (SBA) is a valuable source of expertise on starting a new business. The SBA may provide the following types of financial assistance:

- *Direct loans*—loans made directly to selected small-business owners who have difficulty securing conventional loans (e.g., disabled owners, veterans, and other special cases).

- *Guaranteed loans*—loans made by a financial institution that the government will repay if the borrower stops making payments. The maximum individual loan guarantee is capped at $750,000.[28]

- *Participation loans*—combination direct and guaranteed loans. The SBA will guarantee part of the loan and will lend the balance directly.

In 1992 the Small Business Administration (SBA) started the microloan program to help aspiring entrepreneurs like Karla Brown. With her $19,000 SBA microloan in hand, Karla rented a small store in Boston that earned sales of $100,000 in 1996. Any ideas how you can take advantage of this entrepreneur-friendly program?

- *Loans from Minority Enterprise Small Business Investment Companies (MESBICs)*—finance companies that make loans to minority-owned businesses.

- *Loans from the Women's Financing Section*—guaranteed loans to qualified women for less than $50,000, created by the Women's Business Ownership Act of 1988.

- *Loans from the Women's Prequalification Pilot Loan Program*—loans to businesses that are at least 51 percent owned and operated by women; loan size is limited to $250,000.

- *Microloans*—amounts ranging from $100 to $25,000 (average $10,000) to people such as single mothers and public housing tenants.

The SBA started the microloan demonstration program in 1992. The program is administered by 101 nonprofit organizations chosen by the SBA in all states except Wyoming. Rather than base the awarding of loans on collateral, credit history, or previous business success, these programs decide worthiness on the basis of belief in the borrowers' integrity and the soundness of their business ideas. The SBA microloan program helps people like Karla Brown start their own businesses. Newly divorced and facing a mountain of debt, Brown needed to find a way to support her daughter. She bought two buckets of flowers and headed to the subway to sell them. She made enough money to keep a steady inventory, but she needed help from her friends to pay her bills. She thought she could make a living if she could take her flowers out of the subway and into a store. She obtained a $19,000 SBA microloan and rented a store in the heart of Boston. In 1996, Brown's flower shop brought in $100,000 in sales.[29]

You may also want to consider requesting funds from **Small Business Investment Companies (SBICs)**. SBICs are private investment companies licensed by the Small Business Administration to lend money to small businesses. An SBIC must have a minimum of $1 million in capital and can borrow up to four dollars from the SBA for each dollar of capital it has. It lends to or invests in small businesses that meet its criteria. Often SBICs are able to keep defaults to a minimum by identifying a business's trouble spots early; giving entrepreneurs advice; and, in some cases, rescheduling payments.

Perhaps the best place for young entrepreneurs to start shopping for an SBA loan is a Small Business Development Center (SBDC). SBDCs are funded jointly by the federal government and individual states and are usually associated with state universities. SBDCs can help you evaluate the feasibility of your idea, develop your business plan, and complete your funding application—all for free.[30]

If you want to know what loan officers look for when reviewing SBA guaranteed loan applications, invest $69 for the book *SBA Lending Made Easy*, put out by the American Bankers Association (800-338-0626) to help out loan officers. The SBA recently reduced the size of its application from 150 pages to 1 page for loans under $50,000.[31]

You may want to write or call the SBA in Washington, D.C., for the latest information about SBA programs. The SBA's address is 1441 L Street NW, Washington, D.C. 20005. The telephone number of the Small Business Answer Desk is 800-U-ASK-SBA. The SBA Home Page (http://www.sbaonline.sba.gov) gives detailed information on the agency and other business services.[32]

Obtaining money from banks, venture capitalists, and government sources is very difficult for most small businesses. (You will learn more about financing in Chapter 19.) Those who do survive the planning and financing of their new ventures are eager to get their businesses up and running. Your success in

◄ CONSIDER USING OT ACETATE 6-11
Top Priorities of Small Business

Small Business Investment Companies (SBICs)
Private investment companies licensed by the Small Business Administration to lend money to small businesses.

◄ CONSIDER USING SUPPLEMENTAL CASE 6-2
Can Small Farms Be Profitable? (SCANS)

◄ CONSIDER USING LECTURE ENHANCER 6-15
FedEx Targets Its Customers

running a business depends on many factors. Three important factors for success are knowing your customers, managing your employees, and keeping efficient records.

Progress Check

There are nine sections in the business plan on p. 177. This is probably the most important document a small-business owner will ever make. Can you describe at least five of those sections now? The Small Business Administration gives reasons why small businesses fail financially. Can you name three?

market
People with unsatisfied wants and needs who have both the resources and the willingness to buy.

Care for some rigo janci? Helen Fletcher's customers didn't until she changed the name of her Hungarian dessert to Raspberry Rhapsody. Now she can't keep the chocolate confection in stock. Fletcher says changing the name shows how important it is to listen to customers. "My main job is to think like my clients think and get ahead of their needs."

··· KNOWING YOUR CUSTOMERS ···

One of the most important elements of small-business success is knowing the market. In business, a **market** consists of people with unsatisfied wants and needs who have both the resources and the willingness to buy. For example, we can confidently state that most of our students have the willingness to take a Caribbean cruise during their spring break. However, few of them have the resources necessary to satisfy this want. Would they be considered a good market for the local travel agency to pursue?

Once you have identified your market and its needs, you must set out to fill those needs. The way to meet your customers' needs is to offer top quality at a fair price with great service. Remember it isn't enough to get customers—you have to keep them. As Victoria Jackson, founder of the $50 million Victoria Jackson Cosmetics Company, says of the stars who push her products on television infomercials, "All the glamorous faces in the world wouldn't mean a thing if my customers weren't happy with the product and didn't come back for more." Everything must be geared to bring the customers the satisfaction they deserve.

You will gain more insights about markets in Chapters 13 and 14. Now let's consider the importance of effectively managing the employees who help you serve your market.

··· MANAGING EMPLOYEES ···

As a business grows, it becomes impossible for an entrepreneur to oversee every detail, even if he or she is putting in 60 hours per week. This means that hiring, training, and motivating employees is critical.

It is not easy to find good, qualified help when you offer less money, skimpier benefits, and less room for advancement than larger firms do. That is one reason employee relations is such an important part of small-business management. Employees of small companies are often more satisfied with their jobs than are their counterparts in big business. Why? Quite often they find their jobs more challenging, their ideas more accepted, and their bosses more respectful. Over 90 percent of the top growth companies listed by *Inc.* magazine share ownership and profits with their employees.

Often entrepreneurs reluctantly face the reality that to keep growing, they must delegate authority to others. Nagging questions such as "Who should be delegated authority?" and "How much control should they have?" create perplexing problems.

This can be a particularly touchy issue in small businesses with long-term employees, and in family businesses. As you might expect, entrepreneurs who have built their companies from scratch often feel compelled to promote employees who have been with them from the start—even when those employees aren't qualified to serve as managers. Common sense probably tells you this could be detrimental to the business.

The same can be true of family-run businesses that are expanding. Attitudes such as "You can't fire family" or you must promote someone because "they're family" can hinder growth. Entrepreneurs can best serve themselves and the business if they gradually recruit and groom employees for management positions. By doing this, entrepreneurs can enhance trust and support of the manager among other employees and themselves.

When Heida Thurlow of Chantal Cookware suffered an extended illness, she let her employees handle the work she once had insisted upon doing herself. The experience transformed her company from an entrepreneurial company into a managerial one. She says, "Over the long run that makes us stronger than we were."[33] You'll learn more about managing employees in Chapters 7 through 12.

··· KEEPING RECORDS ···

Small-business owners often say that the most important assistance they received in starting and managing the business involved accounting. A businessperson who sets up an effective accounting system early will save much grief later. Computers make record keeping 100 percent easier and enable a small-business owner to follow the progress of the business (sales, expenses, profits) on a daily basis. An inexpensive computer system can also help owners with other record-keeping chores, such as inventory control, customer records, and payroll.

◄ CONSIDER USING CRITICAL THINKING EXERCISE 6-3
What If? (**SCANS**)

A good accountant is invaluable in setting up such systems and showing you how to keep the system operating smoothly. Many business failures are caused by poor accounting practices. A good accountant can help make decisions such as whether to buy or lease equipment and whether to own or rent the building. Help may also be provided for tax planning, financial forecasting, choosing sources of financing, and writing up requests for funds.

Other small-business owners may tell you where to find an accountant experienced in small business. It pays to shop around for advice. You'll learn more about accounting in Chapter 18.

··· LOOKING FOR HELP ···

Small-business owners have learned, sometimes the hard way, that they need outside consulting advice early in the process. This is especially true of legal, tax, and accounting advice but may also be true of marketing, finance, and other areas. Most small and medium-size firms cannot afford to hire such experts as employees, so they must turn to outside assistance (see the box on p. 182).

A necessary and invaluable aide is a competent, experienced lawyer—one who knows and understands small businesses. Partners have a way of forgetting agreements unless the contract is written by a lawyer and signed. Lawyers can help with a variety of matters, including leases, contracts, and protection

If I'd Only Known Then . . .

If friends and family are offering business advice, cover your ears. Comprehensive Business Services Inc., a national accounting franchise, asked 250 small-business

owners whom they consulted for advice when they launched their companies—and whom they'd recommend now. The consensus: Go with the pros.

	Actually Consulted	Recommend Consulting
Accountant/bookkeeper	55%	87%
Financial planner/ attorney	64	77
Banker	47	58

	Actually Consulted	Recommend Consulting
Investment adviser	9	29
Family and friends	48	11

Source: Edith Hill Updike, ed., "Some Friendly Advice," *Business Week's Enterprise Online*, December 22, 1997.

> **CONSIDER USING LECTURE ENHANCER 6-16**
> Relinquishing the Reins

> **CONSIDER USING OT ACETATE 6-12**
> Major Concerns of Small Business

Service Corps of Retired Executives (SCORE)
An SBA office with 13,000 volunteers who provide consulting services for small businesses free (except for expenses).

Active Corps of Executives (ACE)
SBA volunteers from industry, trade associations, and education who counsel small businesses.

against liabilities. Lawyers don't have to be expensive. In fact, there are several prepaid legal plans that offer services (such as drafting legal documents) for an annual rate of $150 to $350. Lenders that offer legal plans for small businesses include Lawphone (800-255-3352), Prodigy (800-284-5933), AT&T Home Office Network (800-446-6311), and Caldwell Legal (800-222-3035).

Marketing decisions should be made long before a product is produced or a store opened. An inexpensive marketing research study may help you determine where to locate, whom to select as your target market, and what would be an effective strategy for reaching those people. Thus, a marketing consultant with small-business experience can be of great help to you.

Two other invaluable experts are a commercial loan officer and an insurance agent. The commercial loan officer can help you design an acceptable business plan and give you valuable financial advice as well as lend you money when you need it. An insurance agent will explain all the risks associated with a small business and how to cover them most efficiently with insurance and other means (e.g., safety devices and sprinkler systems).

An important source of information for small businesses is the **Service Corps of Retired Executives (SCORE)**. This SBA office has 13,000 volunteers who provide consulting services for small businesses free (except for expenses).[34] You can find a SCORE counselor by calling your local SBA office or SCORE's Washington, D.C., number, (202) 205-6762. The SBA also sponsors volunteers from industry, trade associations, and education who counsel small businesses. They are called the **Active Corps of Executives (ACE)**.

Often a local college has business professors who will advise small-business owners for free or a small fee. Some universities have clubs or programs that provide consulting services by MBA candidates for a nominal fee. For example, Columbia University's Small Business Consulting Group charges only $15 an hour for the consulting services of a team of three MBA students with complementary skills in marketing, finance, and management.

It also is wise to seek the counsel of other small-business owners. Other sources of counsel include chambers of commerce, the Better Business Bureau, national and local trade associations, the business reference section of your

There are many opportunities to start small businesses outside the United States. Often, the competition is not nearly as stiff. This KFC in Bangkok, Thailand, for example, will not have many similar stores nearby. With over 6 billion people in the world market, there are many, many opportunities to take a successful concept from the United States to another country.

library, and many small-business-related sites on the Internet. Many entrepreneurs are using computer bulletin boards for advice and support as well as for a way to find clients.

GOING INTERNATIONAL: SMALL-BUSINESS PROSPECTS

There are only about 265 million people in the United States, but nearly 6 billion people in the world. Obviously, the world market is potentially a much larger, much more lucrative market for small businesses than the United States alone. In spite of that potential, most small businesses still do not think internationally. Only 20 percent of small-business executives say they export.[35] By Commerce Department estimates, there are 18,000 manufacturers (most of them small) that could export their products but don't. Only 2,000 U.S. firms are responsible for 80 percent of our exports. Figure 6.2 lists the industries with the highest potential in global markets.

Why are these companies missing the boat to the huge global markets? Primarily because the voyage involves a few major hurdles: (1) Financing is often difficult to find, (2) many would-be exporters don't know how to get started, (3) potential global businesspeople do not understand the cultural differences of prospective markets, and (4) the bureaucratic paperwork can bury a small business.

◄ LEARNING GOAL 5.
Outline the advantages and disadvantages of small businesses entering global markets.

◄ CONSIDER USING OT ACETATE 6-13
Eight Ways to Improve Your Company Profit

◄ CONSIDER USING TM 45
U.S. Industries with the Highest Potential in International Markets

FIGURE 6.2
U.S. INDUSTRIES WITH THE HIGHEST POTENTIAL IN INTERNATIONAL MARKETS

1. Computers and peripherals (hardware)
2. Telecommunications equipment and systems
3. Computer software and services
4. Medical instruments, equipment, and supplies
5. Electronic parts
6. Analytical and scientific laboratory instruments
7. Industrial process control instruments
8. Aircraft and parts and avionics and ground support equipment
9. Automotive parts and service equipment and accessories
10. Electronic production and test equipment
11. Electronic power generation and distribution systems and transmission equipment
12. Food processing and packaging equipment and machinery
13. Safety and security equipment
14. Printing and graphic arts equipment
15. Water resources equipment

Reaching Beyond Our Borders

Yes, You Can Make Money Exporting, But It's a Workout

When Krescenthia David finally got her exercise video onto Wal-Mart and Kmart shelves she thought she had it made. But the shoppers were already saturated with thousands of different workout tapes ranging from Cindy Crawford to Richard Simmons. When David found out that there were only about 10 exercise videos in the Japanese market, she recast her video and began exporting. In 1996 about 90 percent of her sales were in Japan.

David's three-employee firm is only one of thousands of small companies that have gone global in recent years. The companies are attracted by the fast-growing foreign markets, lower trade barriers, and stepped-up export-promotion help from state and federal government sources.

Companies that export are 9 percent less likely to go bankrupt than those that don't, and employees of ▲

exporting companies earn 13 to 16 percent more than the national average. But the risks from exporting are considerable as well: fluctuating currencies, impenetrable cultures, faraway customers, delayed payments, and antiquated business practices.

How can a small business succeed in global markets? Experts cite several critical factors: Do lots of homework at the beginning. Invest heavily in your overseas expansion. Tap into a network of professionals who understand the quirks of international trade. And understand that going global is a long-term commitment. It may take as long as three years to see any return on investment.

Sources: Laura M. Litvan, "Small Firms Go International," *Investor's Business Daily,* February 26, 1997, p. A1; and Christopher Farrell, "So You Think the World Is Your Oyster," *Business Week,* June 9, 1997, pp. 4–ENT.

Besides the fact that most of the world's market lies outside the United States, there are other good reasons for going international. For instance, exporting products can absorb excess inventory, soften downturns in the domestic market, and extend product lives. It can also spice up dull routines. See the Reaching Beyond Our Borders box to learn how one entrepreneur smothering in a crowded U.S. market found breathing room in a foreign market.

Small businesses have several advantages over large businesses in international trade:

- Overseas buyers enjoy dealing with individuals rather than with large corporate bureaucracies.
- Small companies can usually begin shipping much faster.
- Small companies provide a wide variety of suppliers.
- Small companies can give more personal service and more undivided attention, because each overseas account is a major source of business to them.

The growth potential of small businesses overseas is phenomenal. The pioneers in overseas expansion were franchised organizations such as McDonald's, Avis, Hertz, KFC, and Hanna car washes. Other entrepreneurs who saw the opportunity to start small businesses in foreign countries soon followed them. For example, John Stollenwerk found customers for his Wisconsin-made shoes in Italy, and Ohio's Andrew Bohnengel opened an entire world for his tape company by adopting the metric standard.

There is an abundance of inexpensive information about exporting. A good place to start is with the Commerce Department. Other sources of information include the SBA, banks, local freight forwarders, export management companies, and export trading companies. "Exportise," a step-by-step guide to exporting, is available from the Small Business Foundation. You can contact the SBA Office of International Trade at (202) 634-1500.

Progress Check

- Why do many small businesses avoid doing business overseas?
- What are some of the advantages small businesses have over large businesses in selling in global markets?

SUMMARY
• • • • • •

1. There are many reasons people are willing to take the risks of entrepreneurship.
   - ***What are a few of the reasons people start their own businesses?***
   Reasons include profit, independence, opportunity, and challenge.
   - ***What have modern entrepreneurs done to assure longer terms of management?***
   They have formed entrepreneurial teams that have expertise in the many different skills needed to start and manage a business.
   - ***What is a micropreneur?***
   Micropreneurs are people willing to accept the risk of starting and managing the type of business that remains small, lets them do the kind of work they want to do, and offers them a balanced lifestyle.
   - ***What is intrapreneuring?***
   Intrapreneuring is the establishment of entrepreneurial centers within a larger firm where people can innovate and develop new product ideas internally.

1. Explain why people are willing to take the risks of entrepreneurship, list the attributes of successful entrepreneurs, and describe the benefits of entrepreneurial teams and intrapreneurs.

2. Of all the nonfarm businesses in the United States, almost 97 percent are considered small by the Small Business Administration.
   - ***Why are small businesses important to the U.S. economy?***
   Small business accounts for over 40 percent of GDP. Perhaps more important to tomorrow's graduates, 80 percent of American workers' first jobs are in small businesses.
   - ***What does the "small" in small business mean?***
   The Small Business Administration defines a small business as one that is independently owned and operated, not dominant in its field of operation, and meets certain standards of size in terms of employees or sales (depends on the size of others in the industry).
   - ***Why do many small businesses fail?***
   Many small businesses fail because of managerial incompetence and inadequate financial planning. See the box on p. 172 for a list of causes of business failure.

2. Discuss the importance of small business to the American economy and summarize the major causes of small-business failure.

3. Most people have no idea how to go about starting a small business.
   - ***What hints would you give someone who wants to learn about starting a small business?***
   First, learn from others. Take courses and talk with some small-business owners. Second, get some experience working for others. Third, take over a successful firm. Finally, study the latest in small-business management techniques, including the use of computers for things like payroll, inventory control, and mailing lists.

3. Summarize ways to learn about how small businesses operate.

4. Analyze what it takes to start and run a small business.

4. Writing a business plan is the first step in organizing a business.
   - ***What goes into a business plan?***
   See the box on p. 177.
   - ***What sources of funds should someone wanting to start a new business consider investigating?***
   A new entrepreneur has several sources of capital: personal savings, relatives, former employers, banks, finance companies, venture capital organizations, government agencies, and more.
   - ***What are some of the special problems that small-business owners have in dealing with employees?***
   Small-business owners often have difficulty finding competent employees and grooming employees for management responsibilities.
   - ***Where can budding entrepreneurs find help in starting their businesses?***
   Help can be found from many sources: accountants, lawyers, marketing researchers, loan officers, insurance agents, the SBA, SBDCs, SBICs, and even college professors.

5. Outline the advantages and disadvantages small businesses have in entering global markets.

5. The future growth of some small businesses is in foreign markets.
   - ***What are some advantages small businesses have over large businesses in global markets?***
   Foreign buyers enjoy dealing with individuals rather than large corporations because (1) small companies provide a wider variety of suppliers and can ship more quickly and (2) small companies give more personal service.
   - ***Why don't more small businesses start trading internationally?***
   There are several reasons: (1) Financing is often difficult to find, (2) many people don't know how to get started, (3) many do not understand the cultural differences of foreign markets, and (4) the bureaucratic red tape is often overwhelming.

KEY TERMS
......

Active Corps of Executives (ACE) 182
business plan 175
entrepreneurial team 166
entrepreneurship 163

incubators 176
intrapreneurs 169
market 180
micropreneurs 167
Service Corps of Retired Executives (SCORE) 182

small business 170
Small Business Investment Companies (SBICs) 179
venture capitalists 178

DEVELOPING WORKPLACE SKILLS

1. Find past issues of *Entrepreneur, Success,* and *Inc.* magazines. Read about the entrepreneurs who are heading today's dynamic new businesses. Have several students in the class write profiles about various entrepreneurs and report to the class.

2. Get the 80-page 1993 federal government publication "Small Business Handbook" (item number 574A) by sending $1 to S. James, Consumer Information Center-4A, P.O. Box 100, Pueblo, Colorado 81002. The booklet will come in handy as you read later chapters of this text, since it covers such management issues as minimum and overtime pay, child labor laws, employment of alien workers, veterans, and family leave. Discuss this handbook in class.

3. Select a small business that looks attractive as a career possibility for you. Talk to at least three people who manage such businesses. Ask them how they started their businesses. Ask about financing; personnel problems

(hiring, firing, training, scheduling); accounting problems; and other managerial matters. Pick their brains. Let them be your instructors. Share your findings with the class, including whether the job was rewarding, interesting, and challenging—and why or why not.

4. Contact your local Small Business Administration office and visit it if you can. Learn as much as possible about the programs and brochures offered there.

5. Choose a partner from among your classmates and put together a list of factors that might mean the difference between success and failure of a new company entering the business software industry. Can small start-ups realistically hope to compete with companies such as Microsoft and Intel? Discuss the list and your conclusions in class.

TAKING IT TO THE NET

Purpose

To identify SBA services available locally and to examine the importance of small businesses to your local economy.

Exercise

Go to the Small Business Administration Web site (http://www.sbaonline.sba.gov). Find the following information about SBA services available near you:

1. What is the address and phone number of the SBA office nearest you?

2. Are there any SBA-sponsored special events scheduled in your area? If so, what are they?

3. Is there a Small Business Development Center in your area? Where?

4. Identify the lenders licensed to participate in the Small Business Investment Company (SBIC) program. If you needed to borrow $100,000 to start your business, which lender would you approach? Which would you approach to borrow $500,000?

5. Is there a One Stop Capital Shop available in your state? What services does it offer?

6. What does your state's small-business profile tell you about the importance of small business to your state's economy? Justify your answer by including figures regarding the percentage of businesses that are considered small businesses, the increase or decrease of business start-ups, the increase or decrease of business failures, the increase or decrease of new jobs, and the percentage of new jobs in your state that are in small business.

Practicing Management Decisions

CASE
• • • • • •
BMOC: STARTING A SMALL BUSINESS AT SCHOOL
• • • • • •

Many students do not wait until they complete school before they try to get their feet wet in small-business management. Many students go beyond the planning stage and actually run their businesses while still in school. For example, high school senior Jason Bernard runs his drawing firm, called Architectural Rendering, from his bedroom. Other young people look around, see thousands of students, and try to develop small businesses that would appeal to students. For example, some students assemble and sell Home Emergency Kits for students returning in the fall. The kits contain items like pens, chocolate chip cookies, aspirin, and other college "necessities." The kits are sold to the parents and distributed to students the first week of class as a start-the-year-right gift from home.

Some students produce and sell calendars with pictures of beautiful women or male "hunks" on campus. Others sell desk mats with advertising messages on the sides. Some students become salespeople for beer companies, cosmetic companies, and other traditional firms. They, too, feel as if they are in their own business on campus, because they have exclusive sales rights but don't have to assume as many risks.

One student earns more than his professors by selling ice cream from a truck. Others try to learn the retail business by delivering pizza or other fast foods. Some students have started moving services, moving students' goods from home to school and back.

Dick Gilbertson considered such options when he was a student at Indiana University. He felt students might enjoy having food other than pizza and subs delivered to the dorms. His research showed that students preferred McDonald's hamburgers and Taco Bell burritos. Students said they were willing to pay $1.00 more for a Big Mac, fries, and a Coke rather than ride the mile or so to McDonald's. Mr. Gilbertson's company, Fast Breaks, now serves the 13,000 students at his school. Guess who his partner is? A professor of entrepreneurship at Indiana University.

Jimmy Enriquez was busy getting a degree in accounting at the University of Texas when he started two companies. One is a construction-site cleaning business run by his sister. It has 15 employees, grosses about $4,000 a week, and has expanded to Dallas and Houston. The other business is a vending company that leases Foosball games. Foosball was dead when Jimmy and his brother Rocky started. But they started Foosball leagues, let beginners play for free, and built a prosperous business. Jimmy's advice to potential entrepreneurs:

If you wait until you're out of school and working for somebody else, you're going to get used to that big car—and you're not going to want to gamble with that stuff. It's better to start a company when you're a student, while you're still used to driving a junker and living like a dog.

Jimmy started an entrepreneur club at the University of Texas that has 260 members. There are now more than 350 entrepreneurship clubs on college campuses. The Association of Collegiate Entrepreneurs published a list of the top 100 businesses started by people under 30. All are worth over $1 million.

College campuses aren't the only places to find guidance in entrepreneurship. The National Foundation for Teaching Entrepreneurship to Handicapped and Disadvantaged Youth in Newark, New Jersey, trains former drug dealers, street toughs, and special-education students to sell goods and services. Their businesses range from sneakers and lingerie to manicures and car repair. Maybe you should consider getting started now, too.

Decision Questions

1. What are the advantages and potential problems of starting a business while in school?
2. What kinds of entrepreneurs are operating around your school? Talk to them and learn from their experiences.
3. What opportunities exist for satisfying student needs at your school? Pick one idea, write a business plan, and discuss it in class (unless it is so good you don't want to share it; in that case, good luck).

Starting with $5,000 he saved from summer jobs and a determination to succeed, Jay Goltz built his business the hard way—from the ground up. Goltz was fresh out of college with an accounting degree when he started Artists' Frame Service in 1978. Artists' Frame Service is now a $9 million business employing 120 people at its main location, a 35,000 square-foot showroom and production facility in Chicago. The custom picture-framing facility is 30 times the size of the industry average, making it the world's largest.

┌ **VIDEO CASE** ┐

JAY GOLTZ, ARTISTS' FRAME SERVICE

People are willing to take the risks of starting a business for many reasons, including profit, independence, challenge, and opportunity. Goltz recognized the opportunities in picture framing since most frame shops at that time did not focus on modern management principles. Goltz maintains that most successful businesses aren't based on new concepts, but rather are great executions of old businesses. He uses Nike as an example. People have been making gym shoes for 75 years; Nike just executed it better. Picture framing was not a new concept, but Goltz started

Artists' Frame Service with the theory that pleasing customers was the key to business success. He believed that better service and higher quality framing were the keys to pleasing customers. He offered his customers lower prices through aggressive purchasing and increased volume of framing materials. He decided to give his customers a one-week turnaround compared to other shops that took six to eight weeks.

Goltz actively shares his business acumen with other entrepreneurs through his Boss School seminars. Since he was "out on his own" from the beginning of his career, Goltz can explain the emotional and intellectual transition from a seat-of-the-pants start-up to the building of a well-run organization.

Goltz believes that customer service and execution require a fundamental understanding of business principles, such as leveraging your assets and having the appropriate skills in marketing, management, and finance. These skills can be acquired through classes and experience. It is much more difficult to develop the personality traits needed to be a successful entrepreneur, tolerant of uncertainty, self-directed, self-nurturing, highly energetic, and action oriented.

Success has not gone unnoticed for Jay Goltz. He has received numerous awards: the Minority Advocate of The Year Award in 1989; named one of the top 100 young entrepreneurs in the United States by ACE (Association of Collegiate Entrepreneurs) in 1988; finalist in the Arthur Anderson Entrepreneur Awards in 1989; and Arthur Anderson's Entrepreneur Hall of Fame in 1992. Goltz attributes his success to taking care of customers. "Service is the cheapest commodity you can provide, yet it's the surest way to success. Take care of customers and the rest will take care of itself."

Discussion Questions

1. Why do you think entrepreneurs like Jay Goltz succeed when so many others fail?
2. Can a person develop the personality traits necessary to be a successful entrepreneur? How?
3. How important is a business plan in getting started in a business such as Artist's Frame Service? Explain.

Entrepreneur Readiness Questionnaire

Appendix

Not everyone is cut out to be an entrepreneur. The fact is, though, that all kinds of people with all kinds of personalities have succeeded in starting small and large businesses. There are certain traits, however, that seem to separate those who'll be successful as entrepreneurs from those who may not be. The following questionnaire will help you determine in which category you fit. Take a couple of minutes to answer the questions and then score yourself at the end. Making a low score doesn't mean you won't succeed as an entrepreneur. It does indicate, however, that you may be happier working for someone else.

Each of the following items describes something that you may or may not feel represents your personality or other characteristics about you. Read each item and then circle the response (1, 2, 3, 4, or 5) that most nearly reflects the extent to which you agree or disagree that the item seems to fit you.

➤ **CONSIDER USING TM 46**
Entrepreneur Readiness Questionnaire

Scoring: Give yourself one point for each 1 or 2 response you circled for questions 1, 2, 6, 8, 10, 11, 16, 17, 21, 22, 23.

Give yourself one point for each 4 or 5 response you circled for questions 3, 4, 5, 7, 9, 12, 13, 14, 15, 18, 19, 20, 24, 25.

Looking at my overall philosophy of life and typical behavior, I would say that . . .	Response				
	Agree Completely (1)	Mostly Agree (2)	Partially Agree (3)	Mostly Disagree (4)	Disagree Completely (5)
1. I am generally optimistic.	1	2	3	4	5
2. I enjoy competing and doing things better than someone else.	1	2	3	4	5
3. When solving a problem, I try to arrive at the best solution first without worrying about other possibilities.	1	2	3	4	5
4. I enjoy associating with co-workers after working hours.	1	2	3	4	5
5. If betting on a horse race I would prefer to take a chance on a high-payoff "long shot."	1	2	3	4	5
6. I like setting my own goals and working hard to achieve them.	1	2	3	4	5
7. I am generally casual and easy-going with others.	1	2	3	4	5
8. I like to know what is going on and take action to find out.	1	2	3	4	5
9. I work best when someone else is guiding me along the way.	1	2	3	4	5
10. When I am right I can convince others.	1	2	3	4	5
11. I find that other people frequently waste my valuable time.	1	2	3	4	5
12. I enjoy watching football, baseball, and similar sports events.	1	2	3	4	5
13. I tend to communicate about myself very openly with other people.	1	2	3	4	5
14. I don't mind following orders from superiors who have legitimate authority.	1	2	3	4	5
15. I enjoy planning things more than actually carrying out the plans.	1	2	3	4	5
16. I don't think it's much fun to bet on a "sure thing."	1	2	3	4	5
17. If faced with failure, I would shift quickly to something else rather than sticking to my guns.	1	2	3	4	5
18. Part of being successful in business is reserving adequate time for family.	1	2	3	4	5
19. Once I have earned something, I feel that keeping it secure is important.	1	2	3	4	5
20. Making a lot of money is largely a matter of getting the right breaks.	1	2	3	4	5
21. Problem solving is usually more effective when a number of alternatives are considered.	1	2	3	4	5
22. I enjoy impressing others with the things I can do.	1	2	3	4	5
23. I enjoy playing games like tennis and handball with someone who is slightly better than I am.	1	2	3	4	5
24. Sometimes moral ethics must be bent a little in business dealings.	1	2	3	4	5
25. I think that good friends would make the best subordinates in an organization.	1	2	3	4	5

Source: Kenneth R. Van Voorhis, *Entrepreneurship and Small Business Management* (New York: Allyn & Bacon, 1980).

Add your points and see how you rate in the following categories:

21–25   Your entrepreneurial potential looks great if you have a suitable opportunity to use it. What are you waiting for?

16–20   This is close to the high entrepreneurial range. You could be quite successful if your other talents and resources are right.

11–15   Your score is in the transitional range. With some serious work you can probably develop the outlook you need for running your own business.

6–10   Things look pretty doubtful for you as an entrepreneur. It would take considerable rearranging of your life philosophy and behavior to make it.

0–5   Let's face it. Entrepreneurship isn't really for you. Still, learning what it's all about won't hurt anything.

Part 2

Business Formation

When you drive through any town or city, you see dozens, often hundreds and thousands, of small businesses. The kinds of businesses are as varied as the people who own and operate them. If you were to interview the owners, you would also find a great variety of reasons for choosing a specific business, for settling in a certain location, and for choosing business ownership as a way of life.

Many people become entrepreneurs today because they see the risks as similar to working for someone else—but the rewards much greater. The workplace as a whole is becoming increasingly risk-intensive. Many jobs are riskier propositions than they would have been 10 years ago. Downsizing and restructuring are just two reasons that job security assumptions are changing. The incentive for some risk-taking with a payoff of independence, high job satisfaction, and possible high profits just might be more enticing to you in the future than it already is now.

One of the first objections people often have when encouraged to start their own business is that "Everything has already been tried." That simply isn't true. You have probably seen ideas of your own that were put into practice by someone else—someone else who made all the profits. Although the number of possibilities seem smaller than, say, 50 years ago, the opportunities for new, creative business ideas are still lurking in a veiled reality somewhere, awaiting discovery by an innovative entrepreneur—maybe you.

••• SKILLS •••

You will need certain qualities to succeed, no matter what type of business you choose to start.

1. You must be willing to take risks. This doesn't mean being reckless; it means being comfortable with trying things that could possibly fail. It means feeling that you control your own fate—that you affect circumstances at least as much as they affect you.

2. You must be able to see the possibilities in new ways of doing things. You need to be able to "see the big picture" with both creativity and practicality. An entrepreneur cannot be too set in the old ways of doing things—or of perceiving reality.

3. You need to be a self-starter—someone who doesn't need to have others tell you what to do and when. An entrepreneur should be motivated. Getting up in the morning should be exciting and challenging rather than threatening or depressing.

4. You need to be ambitious and competitive. Entrepreneurs often have to work hard and long hours, especially in the first few years in business. A successful entrepreneur sees himself or herself as a winner and *expects* to win. You also need the health and physical stamina to work long hours day after day.

5. You need to be someone who is not easily discouraged. Many successful businesspeople have experienced setback after setback, but they refuse to see setbacks as "failures." An entrepreneur should see setbacks as lessons that won't have to be learned again.

••• CAREER PATHS •••

Entrepreneurs get started in many ways. One way is to purchase an existing business. Another is to get involved with a franchise operation. Still another is to create an original idea and develop it on your own. Whatever starting point you choose, remember that entrepreneurship usually offers rewards that are commensurate with the energy you are willing to put into the enterprise. Beyond that, the career path is up to you, the entrepreneur.

SOME POSSIBLE POSITIONS FOR WOULD-BE ENTREPRENEURS

Opportunity	Earnings	Investment	Tasks and responsibilities/ Career path	Growth possibilities
Home-based, owner-run businesses	Low at first, but great potential.	Will vary; usually very low compared with other entrepreneurial ventures.	Bookkeeping, marketing, customer relations, organization of business. Must be self-motivated and able to see opportunities.	Home-based businesses promise to be a fast-growing trend through the year 2006.
Franchising	Considerably higher than nonfranchise operations from the first month of operation.	Varies roughly from $10,000–several million, depending on size and scope of franchise.	Most franchisees provide considerable training and support for the beginning of operations. Owner must accept less freedom, but trades that for a greater chance of success. Opportunities in fast foods, office backup, auto repair, and many others.	Franchising will continue to be popular well into the next century. One of 12 businesses is a franchise.
Small business consultant	Earnings vary greatly, based on number of contacts and ability to market the service.	Can work for large consulting firms and thus not actually be in business. Operating on one's own, very little investment necessary.	Act as adviser to businesses in various stages of success or failure. A degree in business will help your credibility greatly. Should have a background of both experience and education. Eventually should have master's degree in business (MBA).	The demands for consultants will continue to grow, especially in the areas of international business and high technology.
Franchise director	Usually depends on the number of franchises in the territory and the size and scope of the overall operation.	Once on its feet, your business can grow using mostly the investment of others (franchisees).	Provide direction for the franchisee, provide training, and help the franchisee become successful. Many franchisors start by working first for another franchise to learn the strategies necessary for success.	Franchising will continue to be popular well past the year 2006.

Babette Haggerty's School for Dogs

Name: Babette Haggerty-Brennan

Age: 29

Position/title: Owner

Salary range: $35,000–$100,000+

Time in this position: Since 1989

Major factors in the decision to take this position: I started training dogs in my family business in 1989. I left home and started college. In order to support myself, I started training on my own. My success snow-balled into the business it is today.

Company name: Babette Haggerty's School for Dogs

Company's web address: I don't have a web site yet.

Company description: I have a "day school for dogs," where owners can drop their dogs off during work hours. I play, feed, and train the dogs. In addition, I provide classes for dog obedience, problem solving, and even theatrical training. I also have a German Shepherd Dog Import service in order to help German Shepherds find good homes.

Job description: I evaluate and train the dogs to help make them more manageable. I also am responsible for running the daily and long-term operations of the business.

Career paths: I started as an assistant trainer with my family's business in New York City. I was them promoted to trainer, and finally kennel manager. I gained valuable experience in dog training and managing people.

When I moved away from home and went back to school, I decided to start my own business. Although I still do many of the things I did before, I am now responsible for the entire business.

Ideal next job: I would like to expand my business by providing larger, more-comprehensive dog school housing. In addition, I would like to add more products and services including full-scale pet supplies, pet grooming, and an adoption agency for pets. My goal is to become the premier pet stop in Palm Beach County.

Best part of your job: I love dogs, and I love the flexibility of working for myself.

Worst part of your job: The worst part of my job is the long hours. The larger the business becomes, the more responsibility I have, and the more hours I have to work.

Educational background: College—Marketing Major

Favorite course: Marketing

Best course for your career: Take *lots* of business courses. In addition, my hands-on experience as a dog trainer was really valuable.

Compliments of Professor Susan Thompson, Palm Beach Community College-Central

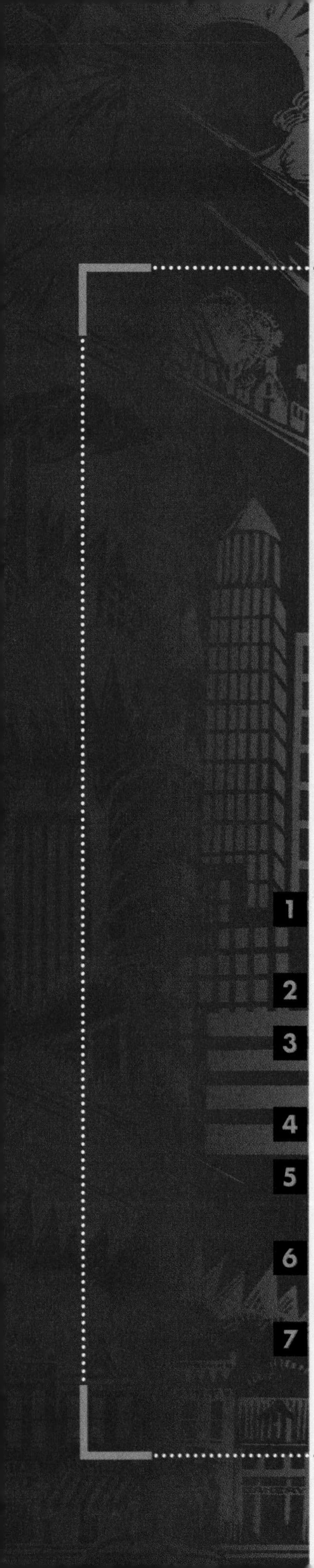

Management, Leadership, and Employee Empowerment

Chapter

7

LEARNING GOALS

After you have read and studied this chapter, you should be able to

1 Explain the four functions of management and why the role of managers is changing.

2 Relate the planning process to the accomplishment of company goals.

3 Describe the organizing function of management and illustrate how the function differs at various management levels.

4 Summarize the five steps of the control function of management.

5 Explain the differences between managers and leaders, and compare the characteristics and uses of the various leadership styles.

6 Describe the three general categories of skills needed by top, middle, and first-line managers.

7 Illustrate the skills aspiring managers need to develop to be successful in the future.

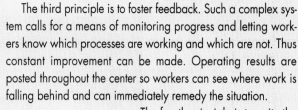

Lynn Mercer manages a product realization center (PRC) that designs, develops, and manufactures wireless products at Lucent Technologies. She directs her center through the use of broad goals and specific measurements of performance, managing through the changes that are the only constant in the market for digital cellular base stations. In such a fast-paced environment, the center finds it best to rely on self-direction in the work force. The PRC must be doing something right: they haven't missed a single delivery deadline, and total labor costs are just 3 percent of product cost. Ms. Mercer and other managers at Lucent apply some rather basic principles that businesses in the future are likely to follow.

The first principle is to hire people who have proven themselves to be self-starters and team players. Candidates are interviewed to see that they meet those requirements. Ms. Mercer knows that the company can teach new employees needed skills, but what can't be taught are initiative, curiosity, and collegiality—the basic necessities of a self-directed work force. Teams select their own leaders to maintain quality and to oversee training, scheduling, and communications with other teams.

The second principle is to create a mission from above and methods from below. That is, management sets the mission for the center, but employees are free to find the means to accomplish that mission within a framework of guidelines. (Giving employees the freedom to make decisions and implement changes on their own is known as empowerment.) Thus the process of bringing the product to market and the product itself are continuously being changed and bettered. The process is so flexible that none of the manufacturing equipment is bolted to the floor. Thus equipment can be moved quickly and easily. Employees are committed to speed, innovation, candor, and deep respect for other colleagues.

 PROFILE

Lynn Mercer of Lucent Technologies

The third principle is to foster feedback. Such a complex system calls for a means of monitoring progress and letting workers know which processes are working and which are not. Thus constant improvement can be made. Operating results are posted throughout the center so workers can see where work is falling behind and can immediately remedy the situation.

The fourth principle is to unite the inside and outside. That is, employees must have access to customers. Assemblers know the destination of every product they produce. By participating in customer visits to the center and going to customer forums, trade shows, and customer work sites, employees get to know customers personally. Such relationship-building is critical in maintaining customer loyalty.

The fifth and final principle is to reward teamwork. A yearly corporate bonus of up to 15 percent is one incentive to accomplish team objectives. Ms. Mercer works to promote the feeling of teamwork so that everyone works together to accomplish the goals of the firm.

Lucent Technologies is just one of many companies that are operating in an environment that we have called "constant whitewater." That is, the competitive environment changes so rapidly that one must constantly adjust as a kayaker must adjust to the constant challenges a wild river presents. No manager can tell a worker what to do in such situations because the environment changes too rapidly. Similarly, no one can tell the kayaker ahead of time how to adjust to each situation, because the river currents change by the second. In each situation, the idea is to find people who are talented, flexible, and creative and to give those people freedom to innovate and find their own way to the end.

Sources: Thomas Petzinger, Jr., "How Lynn Mercer Manages a Factory That Manages Itself," *The Wall Street Journal,* March 7, 1997, p. B1, and private correspondence with the firm, 1998.

THE NEW APPROACH TO CORPORATE MANAGEMENT

Lynn Mercer is just one of many managers who are radically changing the whole approach to business management.[1] Changes are necessary because of global competition, technological innovation, and customer demands.[2] Many

◄ CONSIDER USING TM 47
Chapter Outline

◄ CONSIDER USING LECTURE ENHANCER 7-1
The Mother of Management

Managers and workers today often dress much the same. They may work in teams where everyone has an important say in what and how things are done. The workforce is also diverse, with people of all ages, ethnic backgrounds, and so on. Can you see the advantages of having everyone work together as a team rather than in boss/employee relationships?

> **CONSIDER USING OT ACETATE 7-1**
> The Process of Management

> **CONSIDER USING LECTURE ENHANCER 7-2**
> The Function of A Manager

top managers have delegated some of their authority to lower-level managers and employees who can respond quickly to consumer requests. Foreign competitors once had the reputation for being more responsive to the market and bringing out innovations earlier than American firms. U.S. companies have responded by restructuring and changing their management styles in order to regain their leadership positions in the global marketplace.

The acceleration of technological change has increased the need for a new breed of worker, one who is more educated and more skilled than workers in the past. New workers demand more freedom of operation and different managerial styles. The increasing diversity of the workforce is creating additional challenges.[3]

In short, the next century will begin with corporate housecleaning—a time to get rid of the old managerial styles that have been accumulating in the attic and to introduce a new way of operating. Such changes, not easy to make, will cause major disruptions in business. Because the workforce is becoming much more self-directed than ever before, many managerial jobs are being eliminated through downsizing. The corporate term for this is *rightsizing,* but for the managers and others, a better term would be *shocking loss of job and income.*

Lucent Technologies, once part of AT&T, is only one of hundreds of firms that have gone through sweeping organizational and managerial changes. As a result of these changes, U.S. firms are becoming leaner and meaner, and are ready to take on world competition. After the downsizing of the 1980s, firms began rehiring managers and workers in the 1990s, but the new hires needed different skills, especially skills in communication, teamwork, leadership, decision making, problem solving, and information technology. In the following sections, we'll describe what you will need to know about management to stay competitive in the new global marketplace.

> **CONSIDER USING OT ACETATE 7-2**
> Sources of Management Information

••• MANAGERS ARE NO LONGER JUST BOSSES •••

Management could be called the art of getting things done through organizational resources (e.g., workers, financial resources, and equipment). At one time, managers were called bosses, and their job was to tell people what to do and watch over them to be sure they did it. Bosses tended to reprimand those who didn't do things correctly and generally acted stern and "bossy." Many managers still behave that way. Perhaps you've witnessed such behavior. Today, progressive management is changing. Managers are being educated to guide, train, support, motivate, and coach employees rather than to boss them around.[4] Most modern managers emphasize teamwork and cooperation rather than discipline and order giving.[5] Managers in some high-tech firms and in progressive firms of all kinds dress more casually than before, are more friendly than before, and generally treat employees as partners rather than unruly workers.

In general, management is experiencing a revolution. Managers in the future are likely to be working in teams, to be evaluated by those below them as well as those above, and to be assuming completely new roles in the firm. We'll discuss these roles and the differences between managers and leaders in detail later in the chapter.

What this means for you and other graduates of tomorrow is that management will demand a new kind of person; a skilled communicator and team player as well as a planner, coordinator, organizer, and supervisor. These trends will be addressed in the next few chapters to help you decide whether management is the kind of career you would like.

◄ **LEARNING GOAL 1.**
Explain the four functions of management and why the role of managers is changing.

◄ **CONSIDER USING CRITICAL THINKING EXERCISE 7-1**
Management Functions (**SCANS**)

··· THE DEFINITION AND FUNCTIONS OF ··· CUSTOMER-ORIENTED MANAGEMENT

Well-known management consultant Peter Drucker says managers give direction to their organizations, provide leadership, and decide how to use organizational resources to accomplish goals. Such descriptions give you some idea of what managers do. Our definition of *management* provides the outline of this chapter: **Management** is the process used to accomplish organizational goals through planning, organizing, leading, and controlling people and other organizational resources. This definition spells out the four key functions of management: (1) planning, (2) organizing (which includes staffing), (3) leading (traditionally called directing), and (4) controlling (see Figure 7.1).

Planning includes anticipating trends and determining the best strategies and tactics to achieve organizational goals and objectives. One of those objectives is to please customers. The trend today is to have planning teams to help

management
The process used to accomplish organizational goals through planning, organizing, directing, and controlling people and other organizational resources.

planning
A management function that involves anticipating trends and determining the best strategies and tactics to achieve organizational objectives.

Planning
- Setting organizational goals.
- Developing strategies to reach those goals.
- Determining resources needed.
- Setting standards.

Organizing (staffing)
- Allocating resources, assigning tasks, and establishing procedures for accomplishing goals.
- Preparing a structure (organization chart) showing lines of authority and responsibility.
- Recruiting, selecting, training, and developing employees.
- Placing employees where they'll be most effective.

Leading (directing)
- Guiding and motivating employees to work effectively to accomplish organizational goals and objectives.
- Giving assignments.
- Explaining routines.
- Clarifying policies.
- Providing feedback on performance.

Controlling
- Measuring results against corporate objectives.
- Monitoring performance relative to standards.
- Taking corrective action.

┌   FIGURE **7.1**   ┐
· · · ·

WHAT MANAGERS DO

Some modern managers perform all of these tasks with the full cooperation and participation of workers. Empowering employees means allowing them to participate more fully in decision making.

◄ **CONSIDER USING TM 48**
What Managers Do

organizing
A management function that involves designing the organizational structure, attracting people to the organization (staffing), and creating conditions and systems that ensure that everyone and everything work together to achieve the objectives of the organization.

leading
A management function that involves creating a vision for the organization and guiding, training, coaching, and motivating others to work effectively to achieve the organization's goals and objectives.

controlling
A management function that involves determining whether or not an organization is progressing toward its goals and objectives, and taking corrective action if it is not.

Progress Check

> **CONSIDER USING LECTURE ENHANCER 7-3**
Apple Computer Defines Itself

> **LEARNING GOAL 2.**
Relate the planning process to the accomplishment of corporate goals.

vision
An explanation of why the organization exists and where it's trying to head.

mission statement
An outline of the fundamental purposes of an organization.

monitor the environment, find business opportunities, and watch for challenges. Planning is a key management function because the other functions often depend on having a good plan.

Organizing includes designing the structure of the organization, attracting people to the organization (staffing), and creating conditions and systems in which everyone and everything work together to achieve the organization's goals and objectives. Today's organizations are being designed around the customer. For example, a top executive of AT&T recently said, "I think it's important that we communicate how customer-driven and customer-focused we're going to be."[6] The idea is to design the firm so that everyone is working to please the customer at a profit.

Leading means creating a vision for the organization and guiding, training, coaching, and motivating others to work effectively to achieve the organization's goals and objectives. The trend is to empower employees, giving them as much freedom as possible to become self-directed and self-motivated. Often that means working in teams. Teamwork aids communication, improves cooperation, reduces internal competition, and maximizes the talents of all employees on a project.[7] The traditional concept of managers as directors is giving way to that of managers as team leaders.

Controlling is determining whether an organization is progressing toward its goals and objectives, and taking corrective action if it's not. Basically, it means measuring whether what actually occurs meets the organization's goals. In the past, the greatest attention was given to corporate profits. The trend today is to also measure customer satisfaction.[8]

The four functions just addressed—planning, organizing, leading, and controlling—are the heart of management, so let's explore them in more detail. The process begins with planning; we'll look at that right after the Progress Check.

• What were some of the factors that have forced managers to change their organizations and managerial styles?

• What's the definition of *management* used in this chapter, and what are the four functions in that definition?

···· ▬ ····

PLANNING: CREATING A VISION

Planning, the first managerial function, involves setting the organizational vision, goals, and objectives. Leaders are expected to create a vision for the firm. A **vision** is more than a goal; it's the larger explanation of why the organization exists and where it's trying to head. A vision gives the organization a sense of purpose and a set of values that, together, unite workers in a common destiny.[9] Managing an organization without a vision can be counterproductive. It's like motivating everyone in a rowboat to get really excited about going out on the water, but not giving them any direction. As a result, the boat will just keep heading off in different directions rather than speeding toward an agreed-on goal. Usually employees work with managers to design a mission statement that reflects the organization's vision. A **mission statement** outlines the fundamental purposes of the organization. For example, the mission statement of Country Kitchen restaurants reads as follows:

Leaders create a vision for the firm. A clear vision motivates everyone because it explains why the organization exists and where it is going. Planning meetings enable leaders to share their vision with others. Working together, members of the firm often prepare a mission statement to communicate the organization's fundamental purposes.

We make a very simple promise to our guests: that our Country Kitchen is a warm, friendly place where you'll always feel welcome, just like in your mom's kitchen. Come in any time of the day for meals cooked the way you like them, made from only the finest ingredients and always served with a smile. Good food, satisfying helpings, and fair prices.

The mission statement becomes the foundation for setting goals and training employees. **Goals** are the broad, long-term accomplishments an organization wishes to attain. Goals need to be mutually agreed on by workers and management. Thus, goal setting is often a team process. At General Electric, the goal is to be number one in every business the company undertakes.[10]

Objectives are specific, short-term statements detailing how to achieve the goals. One of your goals for reading this chapter, for example, may be to learn basic concepts of management. An objective you could use to achieve this goal is to plan to answer correctly the chapter's Progress Check questions.

Planning is a continuous process. It's unlikely that a plan that worked yesterday would be successful in today's market. Most planning follows a pattern. The procedure you would follow in planning your life and career is basically the same as that used by businesses for their plans. Planning answers several fundamental questions for businesses:

1. What is the situation now? What is the state of the economy and other environments? What opportunities exist for meeting people's needs? What products and customers are most profitable? Why do people buy (or not buy) our products? Who are our major competitors? What threats are they to our business? (These questions are part of what is called **SWOT analysis.** SWOT stands for strengths, weaknesses, opportunities, and threats.)

2. Where do we want to go? How much growth do we want? What is our profit goal? What are our social objectives? What are our personal development objectives?

3. How can we get there from here? This is the most important part of planning. It takes three forms (see Figure 7.2):

goals
The broad, long-term accomplishments an organization wishes to attain.

objectives
Specific, short-term statements detailing how to achieve the goals.

◄ **CONSIDER USING LECTURE ENHANCER 7-4**
Planning Failure

SWOT analysis
An analysis of an organization's strengths, weaknesses, opportunities, and threats.

FIGURE 7.2
....

PLANNING FUNCTIONS
Very few firms bother to make contingency plans. If something changes the market, such companies are slow to respond. Strategic planning and tactical planning are practiced in most firms. The examples on the right are for a hypothetical breakfast cereal called Fiberrific.

➤ **CONSIDER USING TM 49**
Planning Functions

FORMS OF PLANNING

STRATEGIC PLANNING
Broad
long-range
goal-setting
by top managers

TACTICAL PLANNING
Specific
short-range
objectives/identification
by lower managers

CONTINGENCY PLANNING
Backup plans in case
primary plans fail

EXAMPLES OF PLANNING FOR FIBERRIFIC

STRATEGIC PLAN
Goal set by president: to make Fiberrific the preferred breakfast of health-conscious consumers

TACTICAL PLAN
Objective set by director of research and development: To develop a dry cereal that provides 100% of the adult RDA of vitamins, minerals, and fiber by the end of the year

CONTINGENCY PLAN
Objective set by director of research and development: If dry cereal doesn't meet the market needs, develop a comparable breakfast bar by the end of the year

strategic (long-range) planning
The process of determining the major goals of the organization and the policies and strategies for obtaining and using resources to achieve those goals.

tactical (short-range) planning
The process of developing detailed, short-term decisions about what is to be done, who is to do it, and how it is to be done.

a. **Strategic (long-range) planning** determines the major goals of the organization as well as the policies, procedures, and strategies for obtaining and using resources to achieve those goals. In this definition, policies are broad guides to action, and strategies determine the best way to use resources. At the strategic planning stage, the company decides which customers to serve, what products or services to sell, and the geographic areas in which the firm will compete.

In today's "constant whitewater" environment, long-range planning is becoming more difficult and ineffectual because changes are occurring so fast that plans set for years into the future may soon be obsolete. Therefore, such plans are often being replaced by ones that allow for quick responses to customer needs and requests. The long-range goal is to be flexible and responsive to the market.

b. **Tactical (short-range) planning** is the process of developing detailed, short-term strategies about what is to be done, who is to do it, and how it is to be done. Tactical planning is normally done by managers or teams of managers at lower levels of the organization, whereas strategic planning is done by the top managers of the firm (e.g., the president and vice presidents of the organization). Tactical planning, for example, involves setting annual budgets and deciding on other details and activities necessary to meet the strategic objectives. If the strategic plan, for example, is to sell more trucks in the South, the tactical plan might be to fund more research of southern truck drivers' wants and needs, and planning advertising to reach those people.

Operational planning is the process of setting work standards and schedules necessary to implement the tactical objectives. For example, an operational plan may include setting specific dates for certain truck parts to be completed and the quality demanded.

c. **Contingency planning** is the process of preparing alternative courses of action that may be used if the primary plans don't achieve the organization's objectives. The economic and competitive environments change so rapidly that it's wise to have alternative plans of action ready in anticipation of such changes. For example, if an organization doesn't meet its sales goals by a certain date, the contingency plan may call for more advertising or a cut in prices at that time.

The leaders of market-based companies (companies that respond quickly to changes in competition or to other environmental changes) set direction, not detailed strategy. The idea is to stay flexible, listen to customers, and seize opportunities when they come, whether they were planned or not. The opportunities, however, must fit into the company's overall goals and objectives or the company could lose its focus.

Progress Check

* What's the difference between strategic, tactical, and contingency planning?
* Why would organizations today be less concerned about strategic planning than they once were? What has become of even greater concern? Could strategic planning get in the way if an organization wants to be flexible enough to respond to market changes?

···· ▬▬▬ ····

ORGANIZING: CREATING A UNIFIED SYSTEM

◄ **LEARNING GOAL 3.**
Describe the organizing function of management and illustrate how the function differs at various management levels.

After managers have planned a course of action, they must organize the firm to accomplish their goals. Basically, organizing means allocating resources (such as funds for various departments), assigning tasks, and establishing procedures for accomplishing the organizational objectives. When organizing, a manager develops a structure or framework that relates all workers, tasks, and resources to one another. That framework is called the *organization structure*. Most organizations draw a chart showing the company's internal relationships. This is called an *organization chart*. Figure 7.3 shows a simple one. The organization chart outlines who reports to whom and who's responsible for each task. The problem of developing an organization structure will be discussed in more detail in Chapter 8. For now, it's important to know that the corporate hierarchy may include top, middle, and first-line managers.

Top management (the highest level of management) consists of the president and other key company executives who develop strategic plans. Terms you're likely to see often are chief executive officer (CEO), chief operating officer (COO), and chief financial officer (CFO). The CEO is often the president of the firm and is responsible for all top-level decisions in the firm. CEOs are responsible for introducing changes into an organization. The COO is responsible for putting those changes into effect. His or her tasks include structuring, controlling, and rewarding to ensure that people carry out the leader's vision. The CFO is responsible for obtaining funds, budgeting, collecting funds, and other financial matters.

Middle management includes general managers, division managers, and branch and plant managers (in colleges, deans and department heads) who

operational planning
The process of setting work standards and schedules necessary to implement the tactical objectives.

contingency planning
The process of preparing alternative courses of action that may be used if the primary plans do not achieve the objectives of the organization.

top management
Highest level of management, consisting of the president and other key company executives who develop strategic plans.

middle management
The level of management that includes general managers, division managers, and branch and plant managers who are responsible for tactical planning and controlling.

supervisory (first-line) management
Managers who are directly responsible for supervising workers and evaluating their daily performance.

are responsible for tactical planning and controlling. As mentioned earlier, many firms have eliminated some middle managers through downsizing. **Supervisory (first-line) management** includes those who are directly responsible for supervising workers and evaluating their daily performance; they're often known as *first-line managers* because they're the first level above workers (see Figure 7.4).

An important part of organizing is staffing, getting the right people on the organizational team. You may be more familiar with the term *personnel management* to describe that function. Today it's called *human resource management* because it's as important to develop employees' potential as it is to recruit good people in the first place. We'll discuss human resource management in Chapter 11.

••• THE CUSTOMER-ORIENTED ORGANIZATION •••

▼ CONSIDER USING TM 50
Typical Organization Chart

FIGURE 7.3
• • • •
TYPICAL ORGANIZATION CHART
This is a rather standard chart with managers for major functions and supervisors reporting to the managers. Each supervisor manages three employees.

A dominating question of the past 20 years or so has been how to best organize a firm to respond to the needs of customers and other stakeholders. Stakeholders include anyone who's affected by the organization and its policies and products. That includes employees, customers, suppliers, dealers, environmental groups, and the surrounding communities. The consensus seems to be that smaller organizations are more responsive than large organizations. Therefore, many large firms are being restructured into smaller, more customer-focused units.

Domino's Pizza, for example, is a chain of 4,500 highly independent outlets that encourage managers to regard themselves as individual entrepreneurs. Meanwhile, Domino's headquarters takes responsibility for all paperwork.

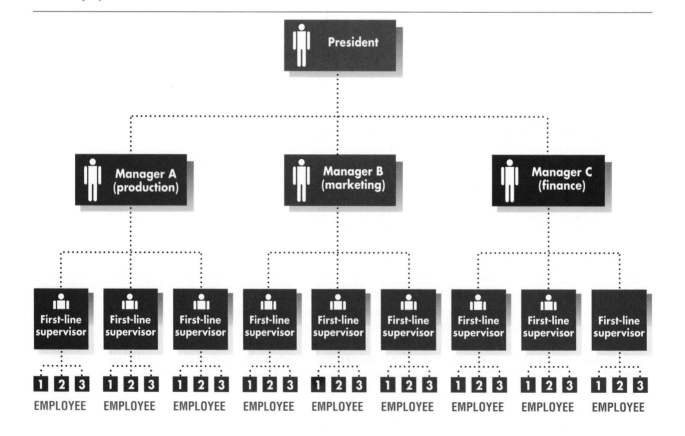

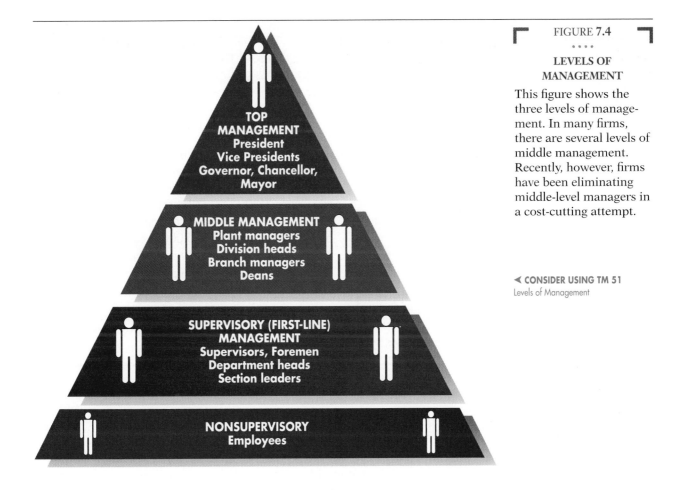

FIGURE **7.4**

● ● ● ●

**LEVELS OF
MANAGEMENT**

This figure shows the
three levels of manage-
ment. In many firms,
there are several levels of
middle management.
Recently, however, firms
have been eliminating
middle-level managers in
a cost-cutting attempt.

◄ **CONSIDER USING TM 51**
Levels of Management

Thus, managers can focus on one of their most important roles: meeting the needs of customers.

Like large firms, small businesses such as the independent tire dealer Direct Tire Sales also realize the importance of pleasing customers. Among other services, Direct Tire lends cars to customers whose own cars are in the shop, fixes flats for free on all tires purchased, and guarantees linings and brake pads for the life of the car. They'll even pick up the tab for the cab ride home for customers who have their brakes changed. But what really brings people in to Direct Tire is the customer lounge. The spotless, tastefully decorated room sports an aquarium, hot coffee, fresh doughnuts, and current magazines. Customers ignore the 10 to 15 percent premium they pay for Direct Tire's exceptional service. The dealership was awarded the *Modern Tire Dealer*'s Dealer-of-the-Year award.

Other firms, both large and small, are equally customer-oriented. The industries they represent include investment banking, health care, construction, engineering, and more. The point is that companies are no longer organizing to make it easy for *managers* to have control. Instead, they're organizing so that *customers* have more influence. The change to customer orientation is

◄ **CONSIDER USING LECTURE
ENHANCER 7-5**
Attributes of Excellent Companies

◄ **CONSIDER USING OT ACETATE
7-3**
Why the Cuts in Middle Management?

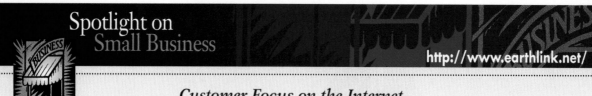

Spotlight on Small Business

http://www.earthlink.net/

Customer Focus on the Internet

Sky Dayton and a friend wrote their first business plan, for a candy store, when Dayton was 10 years old. At 19, he opened his first store, Café Mocha. Today, he is head of EarthLink, the nation's third largest Internet service provider with over 350,000 members. How does the company succeed in the face of tremendous competition from other Internet providers? "We keep our eye on the customer. That's where our focus is, and it's the key to our success," Dayton says.

Companies now do about $1.4 billion worth of business on the Internet, and that is expected to reach $3.3 billion by the year 2000. Small businesses have ▲

just as much potential for succeeding as large businesses. The key is to focus on what consumers want and then give it to them, as Sky Dayton did with his companies. Some 10,000 new sites are opening every day. Judy Cannon started her search engine registration company in 1997 and had $70,000 in sales the first year. The message these entrepreneurs have for traditional firms is this: Get on the Internet if you want to be a leader in the future.

Sources: Robert McGarvey, "Sky's the Limit," *Entrepreneur,* January 1998, pp. 117–131, and Frances Huffman, "Spreading the Word," *Entrepreneur,* March 1998, pp. 152–155.

> **CONSIDER USING SUPPLEMEN-TAL CASE 7-1**
> Team Concepts in a Small Service Firm **(SCANS)**

> **CONSIDER USING OT ACETATE 7-4**
> Management Planning Levels and Time Spans

> **CONSIDER USING SUPPLEMEN-TAL CASE 7-2**
> Changing the Paradigm **(SCANS)**

being aided by technology. For example, establishing a dialogue with customers on the Internet enables some firms to work closely with customers and respond quickly to their wants and needs. The box called Spotlight on Small Business explores the value of the Internet to small businesses, and the need for a customer focus.

••• ORGANIZATION INVOLVES MULTIPLE FIRMS •••

In the past, the goal of the organization function in the firm was to clearly specify who does what *within the firm.* Today, the organizational task is much more complex because firms are forming partnerships, joint ventures, and other arrangements that make it necessary to organize the *whole system,* that is, several firms working together.[11]

There 's no way an organization can provide high-quality goods and services to customers unless suppliers provide world-class parts and materials with which to work. Thus, managers have to establish close relationships with suppliers. To make the entire system work, similar relationships have to be established with those organizations that sell directly to consumers—retailers.

Firms are striving to have all of their processes (e.g., order processing and delivery) as good as those in the best companies in the world. Often that means finding other firms to perform various functions. Top management must contact those firms and work closely with them to coordinate processes. None of this was possible 20 years ago, because the information technology simply wasn't available. Today, however, firms throughout the world are linked by computers and communications technology so that they operate as one.

It makes no sense to introduce the latest management concepts and try to make them work in an organization that's not designed well. And one organization working alone is often not as effective as many organizations working together.

Many small businesses are pooling their efforts in such fields as marketing and distribution.[12] Many are forming purchasing cooperatives so they can buy in bulk and get better prices from suppliers. Creating a unified system out of multiple organizations will be one of the greatest management challenges of the 21st century. We'll discuss this issue in more depth in Chapter 8.

••• EMPOWERING WORKERS •••

After the plans are made and the connections between firms are negotiated, traditional managers direct the workers in activities to meet the goals and objectives of the organization. In traditional organizations, directing involves giving assignments, explaining routines, clarifying policies, and providing feedback on performance.

In traditional organizations, all managers, from top managers to first-line supervisors, direct employees. The process of directing is quite different, however, at the various levels of the organization. The top managers are concerned with the broad overview of where the company is headed. Their immediate subordinates are middle managers, who are responsible, in turn, for directing employees to meet company objectives. Top managers' directions to subordinates, therefore, are characteristically broad and open-ended. The further down the corporate ladder, the more specific the manager's directions become. First-line managers traditionally allocate much of their time to giving specific, detailed instructions to employees.

Progressive managers are less likely than traditional managers to give specific instructions to employees. Rather, they're more likely to empower employees to make decisions on their own. **Empowerment** means giving employees the authority and responsibility to respond quickly to customer requests.[13] In cooperation with employees, managers will set up teams that will work together to accomplish objectives and goals. The manager's role will be less that of a boss and more that of a coach, assistant, counselor, or team member.[14] **Enabling** is the term used to describe giving workers the education and tools they need to assume their new decision-making powers.

Honeywell Inc.'s defense-avionics plant says on-time product delivery improved to 90 percent in the late 1990s (from below 40 percent in the 1980s) because of empowered teams. Part of Dell Computer Corporation is set up so that one team builds an entire computer system, and that leads to maximum quality.[15]

You'll learn more about such teams in Chapter 8. For now it's important to know that self-managed teams function as independent elements of the firm

empowerment
Giving employees the authority and responsibility to respond quickly to customer requests.

enabling
Giving workers the education and tools they need to assume their new decision-making powers.

Dell Computer Corporation is one of today's market leaders in the design and marketing of personal computers. It reached that position by emphasizing quality, speed, and customer responsiveness. Part of Dell's success is due to its ability to build custom computers. What advantages do you see to using teams to quickly assemble and ship a computer system that exactly matches what the customer wants?

with an inherent group intelligence of their own. Because they think and act on their own and seek out any information they need, such teams are sometimes known as *smart teams*. One purpose of smart teams is to respond quickly to customer needs and market changes. Another purpose is to empower those who know the most about products and what makes them good (the employees themselves) to do what needs to be done to provide customers with world-class products.

···· ▬▬ ····

CONTROLLING

➤ **LEARNING GOAL 4.**
Summarize the five steps of the control function of management.

▼ **CONSIDER USING TM 52**
The Control Process

⌐   FIGURE 7.5   ⌐
···· ¬

THE CONTROL PROCESS

The whole control process is based on clear standards. Without such standards, the other steps are difficult, if not impossible. With clear standards, performance measurement is relatively easy and the proper action can be taken.

The control function involves measuring performance relative to objectives and standards and then taking corrective action when necessary. Thus, the control process (see Figure 7.5) is the heart of the management system because it provides the feedback that enables managers and workers to adjust to any deviations from plans and to changes in the environment that have affected performance. Controlling consists of five steps:

1. Setting clear performance standards.
2. Monitoring and recording actual performance (results).
3. Comparing results against plans and standards.
4. Communicating results and deviations to the employees involved.
5. Taking corrective action when needed.

The control system's weakest link tends to be the setting of standards. To measure results against standards, the standards must be specific, attainable, and measurable. Vague goals and standards such as "better quality," "more

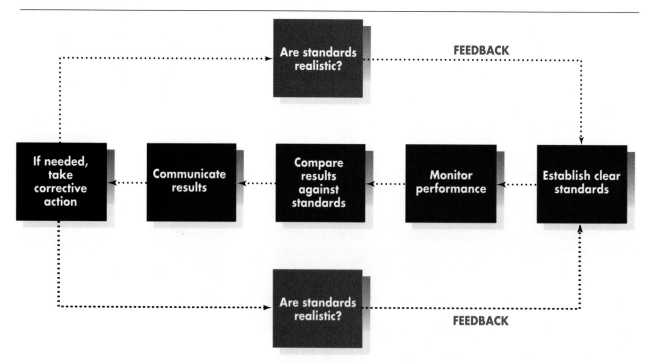

efficiency," and "improved performance" aren't sufficient because they don't describe in enough detail what you're trying to achieve. For example, let's say you're a runner and you have made the following statement: "My goal is to improve my distance." When you started your improvement plan last year, you ran two miles a day. Now you run 2.1 miles a day. Did you meet your goal? Well, you did increase your distance, but certainly not by very much. A more appropriate statement would be "My goal is to increase my running distance from two miles a day to four miles a day by January 1." It's important to have a time period established when goals are to be met. The following examples of goals and standards meet these criteria:

- Cutting the number of finished product rejects from 10 per 1,000 to 5 per 1,000 by March 31.
- Increasing the number of times managers praise employees from 3 per week to 12 per week.
- Increasing sales of product X from 10,000 per month to 12,000 per month by July.

One way to make control systems work is to establish clear procedures for monitoring performance. Naturally, management shouldn't be burdened with such control procedures unless the goals are important enough to justify such reporting. Most managers have seen, for example, elaborate accident reports that took hours of management time merely to say "All is well." To minimize paperwork, accident reports could be limited to certain kinds of serious cases.

••• NEW CRITERIA FOR MEASUREMENT: •••
CUSTOMER SATISFACTION

The criteria for measuring success in a customer-oriented firm is the satisfaction of both internal and external customers. **Internal customers** are individuals and units within the firm that receive services from other individuals or units.[16] For example, the field salespeople are the internal customers of the marketing research people who prepare research reports for them. **External customers** include dealers, who buy products to sell to others, and ultimate customers such as you and me, who buy products for their own personal use. One goal today is to go beyond satisfying customers to "delighting" customers with unexpectedly good products and services.

Other criteria of organizational effectiveness may include the firm's contribution to society or improvements in the quality of air and water surrounding the business.[17] The traditional measures of success are usually financial, defined in terms of profits or return on investment. Certainly these measures are still important, but they're not the whole purpose of the firm. The purpose of the firm today is to please employees, customers, and other stakeholders. Thus, measurements of success must take all these groups into account. Firms have to ask questions such as these: Do we have good relations with our employees, our suppliers, our dealers, our community leaders, the local media, our stockholders, and our bankers? What more could we do to please these groups? Are the corporate needs (such as making a profit) being met as well?

internal customers
Individuals and units within the firm that receive services from other individuals or units.

external customers
Dealers, who buy products to sell to others, and ultimate customers (or end users), who buy products for their own personal use.

Feedback from external customers is invaluable in helping a firm respond to their needs, especially those that go beyond the basic good or service. Was the service prompt, friendly, and helpful? What new services or products need to be offered? What would you like to see changed? Do you fill out such forms to let businesses know how you feel? If we all did, businesses would be able to serve us much better.

••• A CORPORATE SCORECARD •••

A broad measurement tool that has grown in popularity in the last few years is called a *corporate scorecard*. In addition to measuring customer satisfaction, the corporate scorecard measures financial progress, return on investment, and all else that needs to be managed for the firm to reach its final destination—profits.[18] One scorecard, for example, might follow customer service (Is it getting better or worse?) and, at the same time, product defects. Corporate scorecards often use software that enables everyone in the firm to see the results and work together to improve them. As a consequence, about 65 percent of U.S. companies are experimenting with such a measurement system. Some companies, like Shell Oil, use strictly financial measures of success. Others, like Motorola, use a more balanced approach. That is, they measure both financial progress and other, softer issues, such as employee and customer satisfaction. No company can prosper in the long run without a balanced approach that measures both financial growth and employee and customer satisfaction. That doesn't mean, however, that better financial controls don't help make the company stronger and better able to serve both customers and employees.

LEADERSHIP: VISION AND VALUES

In the literature of business there's a trend toward separating the notion of management from that of leadership. A person could be a good manager and not a good leader. Another could be a good leader without being a good manager. One difference between managers and leaders is that managers strive to produce order and stability while leaders embrace and manage change. **Leadership** is creating a vision for others to follow, establishing corporate values and ethics, and transforming the way the organization does business in order to improve its effectiveness and efficiency.[19] *Management* is the carrying out of the leadership's vision.

In the future, all organizations will need leaders who can supply the vision as well as the moral and ethical foundation for growth. They will also need managers who share in the vision and know how to get things done with the cooperation of all employees. The workplace is changing from a place where a few dictate what to do to others to a place where all employees work together to accomplish common goals. Furthermore, managers must lead by doing, not just by saying. The Making Ethical Decisions box shows how some corporate leaders are "walking the walk" when it comes to charitable giving as opposed to just "talking the talk."

In summary, leaders must

1. *Have a vision and rally others around that vision.* In doing so, the leader should be openly sensitive to the concerns of followers, give them responsibility, and win their trust.

leadership
Creating a vision for others to follow, establishing corporate values and ethics, and transforming the way the organization does business in order to improve its effectiveness and efficiency.

➤ **LEARNING GOAL 5.** Explain the differences between managers and leaders, and compare the characteristics and uses of the various leadership styles.

When a company puts its motto of total customer service in its ad, everyone in the organization must be ready to meet the goal. Ads of this type express a company's philosophy and commitment, but also create high customer expectations. If the goal is met, however, the rewards are high too. Can you see how a commitment of this type can unite employees in a common cause and generate enthusiasm and motivation?

Making Ethical Decisions

http://www.loctite.com/

Leading by Example

The popular press does not report it much, but many business leaders are quite generous when it comes to giving away the money they earn. Robert Krieble, for example, made millions of dollars. He was the founder of Loctite, a company that makes metal-locking adhesives. When people asked Krieble why he drove a Ford Festiva instead of a more expensive car, he replied, "The less money I spend on myself, the more I have to give away."

He endowed a chair in chemistry at John Hopkins University. But Krieble was most interested in freedom and the opportunity it provided for people to make their own money. So he supported the Heritage Foundation and the Free Congress Foundation. He also flooded Russia with computers and fax machines, believing that information about the rest of the world would bring down communism there, which it did.

Bill Gates of Microsoft has said that he will give about $10 million to each of his children, but will give most of the rest of his $37 billion to charity. Home Depot chairman Bernard Marcus intends to leave $850 million in stock to the Marcus Foundation, which supports education and the handicapped. These modern-day managers follow in the footsteps of other business leaders who have given generously to charity. That includes Andrew Carnegie, who gave away the equivalent (in today's figures) of $3.5 billion to libraries and other causes. In other words, some business leaders make a lot of money, but much of that money is given away to charity and the community. By being so generous with their money, such business leaders set an example for their employees and for all of us. From whom much is given, much is expected.

Are you willing to make a commitment now to donate 5 to 10 percent of your aftertax income to charitable causes? What would be the consequences of such a decision?

Sources: Dana Wechsler Linden and Dyan Machan, "The Disinheritors," *Forbes*, May 19, 1997, pp. 152–160, and Paul Craig Roberts, "Financing Freedom with What He Earned," *The Washington Times*, May 14, 1997, p. A13.

2. *Establish corporate values.* These values include a concern for employees, for customers, and for the quality of the company's products. When companies set their business goals today, they're defining the values of the company as well.

3. *Emphasize corporate ethics.* Ethics include an unfailing demand for honesty and an insistence that everyone in the company gets treated

▲ SCANS

◄ CONSIDER USING LECTURE ENHANCER 7-6
Servant Leaders

◄ CONSIDER USING TM 53
Managers Vs. Leaders

MANAGERS	LEADERS
Do things right	Do the right thing
Command and control	Inspire and empower
Seek stability and predictability	Seek flexibility and change
Are internally focused	Are externally oriented
Work within the firm	Coordinate the whole system
Are locally oriented	Are globally oriented
Think mostly of workers	Think mostly of customers and other stakeholders

Reaching Beyond Our Borders

Global Management

Managers work within organizational boundaries. Leaders set those boundaries and constantly change the organization to meet new challenges. Today's excellent corporations, more often than not, are reflections of their leaders. The leaders of successful corporations have had a vision of excellence and have led others to share that vision. Business schools are seeing a mood change these days. As students read about countries that make up the former Soviet Union going to a market economy and Eastern Europeans opening their doors to Western businesses, they're demanding to know more about global business management. Many young people know they'll be involved in international business even if they never leave the United States. They also know that American companies are looking to business schools for managers who know how to work in the new global context.

How are business schools responding to this student demand? Many are revamping their existing curriculum by integrating international examples into basic courses. This reduces the need for specific international courses. The idea is to bring international dimensions into the mainstream.

Still, some students demand more. They feel that global enterprise is too important to be mixed in with other courses, and they want courses that are entirely international. Many business schools now offer exchange programs with business schools in other countries. Professors are encouraged to participate in international research and to gain teaching experience overseas. Students are encouraged—and in some cases required—to study foreign languages. Students have caught the international fever and have passed the sense of urgency on to colleges.

> **CONSIDER USING LECTURE ENHANCER 7-7**
> Coping With an Intolerable Boss

fairly. That's why we've stressed ethical decision making throughout this text. Many businesspeople are now making the news by giving away huge amounts to charity, thus setting a model of social concern for their employees and others.

4. *Not fear change, but embrace it.* The leader's most important job may be to transform the way the company does business so that it's more effective and efficient.

As you think about leadership, keep in mind, too, that it is now a global issue. The box called Reaching Beyond Our Borders will give you some idea about how international leadership is being approached today.

••• CREATING A LEARNING ORGANIZATION •••

learning organization
An organization skilled at creating, acquiring, interpreting, retaining, and transferring knowledge; it also purposefully modifies its behavior based on new knowledge, including that which it gains from making mistakes.

A **learning organization** is one skilled at creating, acquiring, interpreting, retaining, and transferring knowledge; it also purposefully modifies its behavior based on new knowledge, including that which it gains from making mistakes. Most companies today are good at acquiring information; they are not as good at interpreting, retaining, and transferring knowledge or at changing their behavior based on that knowledge. That is where leadership comes in. When trying to transfer knowledge from one department to another, for example, there is often resistance to the new ideas. Workers tend to dismiss ideas that were not generated in their own department. Leaders who stress continuous improvement, set up cross-functional teams (see Chapter 8), and reward people for innovation and risk taking tend to create winning organizations.[20] Some firms have added a chief information officer (CIO) to their staffs to make sure that information exchange is implemented widely and freely.

··· LEADERSHIP STYLES ···

Nothing has challenged researchers in the area of management more than the search for the "best" leadership traits, behaviors, or styles. Thousands of studies have been made just to find leadership traits, that is, characteristics that make leaders different from others. Intuitively, you would conclude about the same thing that researchers have found: results of most studies on leadership have been neither statistically valid nor reliable. You and I know that some leaders are well-groomed and tactful while others are unkempt and abrasive—yet the latter may be just as effective as the former.

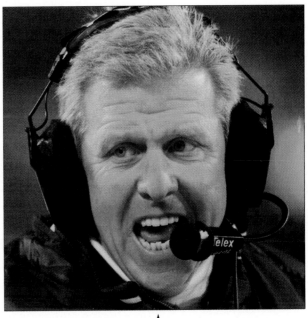

There is no single best leadership style to be used with all people in all situations. New York Jets coach Bill Parcells may appear to be an autocratic leader during games, but he, like all good leaders, seeks the advice of others when needed and allows some players more freedom than others. What kind of leadership style works best for motivating you?

Just as there's no one set of traits that can describe a leader, there's also no one style of leadership that works best in all situations. Let's look briefly at a few of the most commonly recognized leadership styles and see how they may be effective:

1. **Autocratic leadership** involves making managerial decisions without consulting others. Such a style is effective in emergencies and when absolute followership is needed, for example, when fighting fires. Autocratic leadership is also effective with some new, relatively unskilled workers who often need clear direction and guidance.

2. **Participative (democratic) leadership** consists of managers and employees working together to make decisions. Research has found that employee participation in decisions may not always increase effectiveness, but it usually increases job satisfaction. Many new, progressive organizations are highly successful at using a democratic style of leadership where traits such as flexibility, good listening skills, and empathy are dominant. Organizations that have successfully used this style include Wal-Mart, Federal Express, IBM, Xerox, and AT&T. Many smaller organizations also use participative leadership.

3. **Laissez-faire (free-rein) leadership** involves managers setting objectives and employees being relatively free to do whatever it takes to accomplish those objectives. In certain organizations, where managers deal with doctors, engineers, and other professionals, the most successful leadership style is often laissez-faire. The traits needed by managers in such organizations include warmth, friendliness, and understanding. More and more firms are adopting this style of leadership.

Individual leaders rarely fit neatly into just one of these categories. Researchers Tannenbaum and Schmidt illustrate leadership as a continuum with varying amounts of employee participation, ranging from purely boss-centered leadership to subordinate-centered leadership (see Figure 7.6).

Which leadership style is best? Research tells us that successful leadership depends largely on who's being led and in what situations.

autocratic leadership
Leadership style that involves making managerial decisions without consulting others.

participative (democratic) leadership
Leadership style that consists of managers and employees working together to make decisions.

laissez-faire (free-rein) leadership
Leadership style that involves managers setting objectives and employees being relatively free to do whatever it takes to accomplish those objectives.

➤ **CONSIDER USING CRITICAL THINKING EXERCISE 7-2**
Leadership Styles (**SCANS**)

➤ **CONSIDER USING OT ACETATE 7-5**
Manager's Empowerment Checklist

➤ **CONSIDER USING OT ACETATE 7-6 AND OT ACETATE 7-7**
Take the Empowerment Quiz

➤ **CONSIDER USING LECTURE ENHANCER 7-8**
A Manager's Expectations: The Self-Fulfilling Prophecy

➤ **CONSIDER USING TM 54**
Various Leadership Styles

It also supports the notion that any leadership style, ranging from autocratic to laissez-faire, may be successful depending on the people and the situation.

In fact, a manager may use a variety of leadership styles depending on whom he or she is dealing with in a given situation. A manager may be autocratic but friendly with a new trainee; democratic with an experienced employee who has many good ideas that can only be fostered by a flexible manager who's a good listener; and laissez-faire with a trusted, long-term supervisor who probably knows more about operations than the manager does.

There's no such thing as a leadership trait that is effective in all situations, or a leadership style that always works best. A truly successful leader has the ability to use the leadership style most appropriate to the situation and the employee involved (see Figure 7.7).

··· THE TREND TOWARD SELF-MANAGED TEAMS ···

The trend in the United States is toward placing more workers on teams, many of them self-managed.[21] That means that more planning, organizing, and controlling are being delegated to lower-level managers. This leaves more time for top managers to focus on leadership, with its emphasis on vision and empowerment. What will these trends mean for managers and leaders in the 21st century? It means, for one thing, that the trend will continue away from autocratic leadership toward laissez-faire leadership, although both will still be used effectively. This is a real challenge for traditional managers, because often it means giving up their traditional "bossy" style of management. It also means developing and training employees to assume greater responsibility in planning, teamwork, and problem solving.

More managers in the future will be empowering *teams* rather than individual employees. This is an entirely different role for many managers, one that will take some time to develop. In the end, however, the concept of self-managed teams will enable U.S. manufacturers and service organizations to compete with any other in the world. The box called From the Pages of *Business Week* talks about some of the physical changes being made in offices to accommodate the new team approach.

⌐ **FIGURE 7.6** ¬
· · · ·
VARIOUS LEADERSHIP STYLES

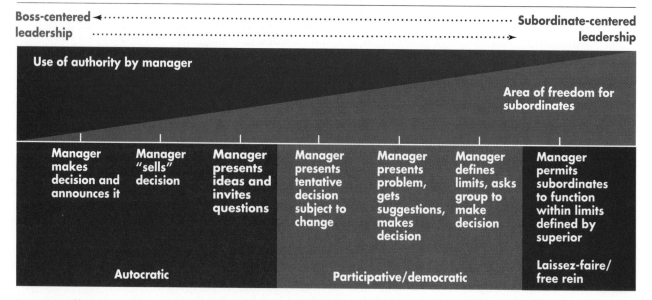

Boss-centered ◄·· **Subordinate-centered**
leadership ···► **leadership**

Use of authority by manager						
						Area of freedom for subordinates
Manager makes decision and announces it	**Manager "sells" decision**	**Manager presents ideas and invites questions**	**Manager presents tentative decision subject to change**	**Manager presents problem, gets suggestions, makes decision**	**Manager defines limits, asks group to make decision**	**Manager permits subordinates to function within limits defined by superior**
Autocratic			**Participative/democratic**			**Laissez-faire/ free rein**

··· LEADERSHIP TEAMS ···

Employees are not the only ones who will be working in teams in the future. Intensified competition and globalization are making the present style of leadership obsolete. Korn/Ferry International, a worldwide executive research firm, did a recent study of managers. They looked at 160 international companies and did intensive interviews with 75 senior executives. The executives said that within 10 years only 14 percent of the companies would be run by one leader. In the majority of cases, the companies would be run by a *team of leaders.*[22]

FIGURE 7.7

····

RULES OF LEADERSHIP

THE 12 GOLDEN RULES OF LEADERSHIP

1. *Set a good example.* Your subordinates will take their cue from you. If your work habits are good, theirs are likely to be too.

2. *Give your people a set of objectives and a sense of direction.* Good people seldom like to work aimlessly from day to day. They want to know not only what they're doing but why.

3. *Keep your people informed* of new developments at the company and how they'll affect them. Let people know where they stand with you. Let your close assistants in on your plans at an early stage. Let people know as early as possible of any changes that will affect them. Let them know of changes that won't affect them but about which they may be worrying.

4. *Ask your people for advice.* Let them know that they have a say in your decisions whenever possible. Make them feel a problem is their problem too. Encourage individual thinking.

5. *Let your people know that you support them.* There's no greater morale killer than a boss who resents a subordinate's ambition.

6. *Don't give orders.* Suggest, direct, and request.

7. *Emphasize skills, not rules.* Judge results, not methods. Give a person a job to do and let him or her do it. Let an employee improve his or her own job methods.

8. *Give credit where credit is due.* Appreciation for a job well done is the most appreciated of "fringe benefits."

9. *Praise in public.* This is where it will do the most good.

10. *Criticize in private.*

11. *Criticize constructively.* Concentrate on correction, not blame. Allow a person to retain his or her dignity. Suggest specific steps to prevent recurrence of the mistake. Forgive and encourage desired results.

12. *Make it known that you welcome new ideas.* No idea is too small for a hearing or too wild for consideration. Make it easy for them to communicate their ideas to you. Follow through on their ideas.

THE SEVEN SINS OF LEADERSHIP

On the other hand, these items can cancel any constructive image you might try to establish.

1. *Trying to be liked rather than respected.* Don't accept favors from your subordinates. Don't do special favors in trying to be liked. Don't try for popular decisions. Don't be soft about discipline. Have a sense of humor. Don't give up.

2. *Failing to ask subordinates for their advice and help.*

3. *Failing to develop a sense of responsibility in subordinates.* Allow freedom of expression. Give each person a chance to learn his or her superior's job. When you give responsibility, give authority too. Hold subordinates accountable for results.

4. *Emphasizing rules rather than skill.*

5. *Failing to keep criticism constructive.* When something goes wrong, do you tend to assume who's at fault? Do you do your best to get all the facts first? Do you control your temper? Do you praise before you criticize? Do you listen to the other side of the story?

6. *Not paying attention to employee gripes and complaints.* Make it easy for them to come to you. Get rid of red tape. Explain the grievance machinery. Help a person voice his or her complaint. Always grant a hearing. Practice patience. Ask a complainant what he or she wants to do. Don't render a hasty or biased judgment. Get all the facts. Let the complainant know what your decision is. Double-check your results. Be concerned.

7. *Failing to keep people informed.*

Source: "To Become an 'Effective Executive,' Develop Leadership and Other Skills," *Marketing News*, April 1984, p. 1.

From the Pages of **BusinessWeek**

http://www.shareholder.com/alcoa/

Teaming from Anywhere

The trend toward teams has led companies to completely alter their office arrangements so that individuals can have separate offices and still meet in teams when needed. At the aluminum company Alcoa, senior executives work in open cubicles and gather around a communications center with televisions, fax machines, newspapers, and tables to encourage impromptu meetings. Alcoa had downsized, reengineered, customer-focused, and changed its old hierarchical structure, but still wasn't getting the results it wanted. The physical environment simply wasn't designed for teamwork. So the company moved to a new facility.

Small start-up companies in Silicon Valley and huge companies like IBM and Mobil are all creating new office designs for the 21st century. *Business Week* says, ▲

"Privacy is being replaced with productivity, hierarchy with teamwork, and status with mobility." People can now work anywhere, anytime, in their offices, automobiles, or homes. Teams are linked by computers so that team members can be anywhere and still operate as part of the team. Computer networks have made it possible for managers and employees to stay at home and still be constantly in touch with other team members, all over the world. Can you picture a time when huge office buildings are a thing of the past and employees will live and work where they please, while linked by computer? That is rapidly becoming a reality for many firms.

Source: Joan O'C. Hamilton, Stephen Baker, and Bill Vlasic, "The New Workplace," *Business Week,* April 29, 1996, pp. 106–117.

Progress Check

- What are some characteristics of leadership today that make leaders different from traditional managers?
- Explain the differences between autocratic and democratic leadership styles.
- What is a self-managed team and how does it operate?

Critical Thinking

Do you see any problems with a democratic managerial style? Can you see a manager getting frustrated when he or she can't be bossy? Can someone who's trained to give orders (e.g., a military sergeant) be retrained to be a democratic manager? What problems may emerge? What kind of boss would you be? Do you have evidence to show that?

•••• ▬▬▬ ••••

TASKS AND SKILLS AT DIFFERENT LEVELS OF MANAGEMENT

> ➤ **LEARNING GOAL 6.**
> Describe the three general categories of skills needed by top, middle, and first-line managers.

Few people are trained to be good managers. A person learns how to be a skilled accountant or sales representative or production-line worker, and then—because of his or her skill—is selected to be a manager. The tendency is for such managers to become deeply involved in showing others how to do things, helping them, supervising them, and generally being very active in the operating task.

Top managers	Technical skills	**Human relations skills**	**Conceptual skills**
Middle managers	**Technical skills**	**Human relations skills**	**Conceptual skills**
First-line managers	**Technical skills**	**Human relations skills**	Conceptual skills

FIGURE **7.8**
• • • •

SKILLS NEEDED AT VARIOUS LEVELS OF MANAGEMENT

All managers need human relations skills. At the top, managers need strong conceptual skills. First-line managers need strong technical skills. Middle managers need to have a balance between technical and conceptual skills.

The further up the managerial ladder a person moves, the less his or her original job skills are required. At the top of the ladder, the need is for people who are visionaries, good planners, organizers, coordinators, communicators, morale builders, and motivators. Figure 7.8 shows that a manager must have three categories of skills:

1. Technical skills.
2. Human relations skills.
3. Conceptual skills.

Let's pause here to clarify the terms:

- **Technical skills** involve the ability to perform tasks in a specific discipline or department such as selling (marketing) or software development (information systems).
- **Human relations skills** involve communication and motivation; they enable managers to work through and with people. Such skills also include those associated with leadership, coaching, morale building, delegating, training and development, and help and supportiveness.
- **Conceptual skills** involve the ability to picture the organization as a whole and the relationships among its various parts. Conceptual skills are needed in planning, organizing, controlling, systems development, problem analysis, decision making, coordinating, and delegating.

Looking at Figure 7.8, you'll notice that first-line managers need to be skilled in all three areas. Most of their time is spent on technical and human relations tasks (assisting operating personnel, giving directions, and so forth). First-line managers spend little time on conceptual tasks. Top managers, on the other hand, need to use few technical skills. Instead, almost all of their time is devoted to human relations and conceptual tasks. One who is competent at one level of management may not be competent at higher levels and vice versa. The skills needed are different at different levels.

Spend some time reviewing the definitions of *conceptual skills* and *human relations skills*. Note that the word *delegating* is in our description of human relations skills. Another one of the key managerial tasks is decision making. Because delegating and decision making are so important, we'll explore them in more detail.

◄ **CONSIDER USING TM 55**
Skills Needed at Various Levels of Management

technical skills
Skills that involve the ability to perform the tasks in a specific discipline or department.

human relations skills
Skills that involve communication and motivation; they enable managers to work through and with people.

conceptual skills
Skills that involve the ability to picture the organization as a whole and the relationships among its various parts.

Many management experts believe that the organizations that will succeed in the future will use teams and empower them to make decisions. Such teams can respond to market changes faster and design better products. Schwinn is a company whose future will depend on how effectively its teams perform and use the freedom management has given them.

delegating
Assigning authority and accountability to others while retaining responsibility for results.

decision making
Choosing among two or more alternatives.

••• DELEGATING: BECOMING A ••• TEAM LEADER

The most difficult task for most managers to learn is **delegating** (assigning authority and accountability to others while retaining responsibility for results). Remember, managers are usually selected from those who are most skilled at doing what the people they manage are doing. In many tasks, the inclination is for managers to pitch in and help or do the job themselves. Of course, this keeps workers from learning and having the satisfaction that comes with accomplishment. A great leader is one whose workers say, "We did it ourselves." To delegate effectively, therefore, a manager must:

1. Select the appropriate person or people to do the job.

2. Assign the task.

3. Give the authority to complete the job.

4. Make those people who assume the task responsible for getting it completed on time.

As we noted earlier, most progressive managers of the 21st century will be team leaders. They will set specific goals in cooperation with a team of workers, set up feedback and communication procedures (control procedures), and minimize the tendency to continually look over the team's shoulder to make sure team members are doing things the manager's way. Employees will be empowered, that is, given the freedom to decide the hows and wheres of completing specific tasks as long as the goals are accomplished on time.

Tom Stendahl of Schwinn Cycling & Fitness says that when he and his co-workers brought Schwinn out of bankruptcy they didn't have time to set up sophisticated administrative and reporting structures. Instead, they split up the business into pieces, such as bikes, parts and accessories, and fitness. Then they hired the best people they could find and said: "Here it is guys, go out and shape the world. You have total freedom." By building a company that way, Stendahl says, you build a company that can move extremely fast.[23]

••• DECISION MAKING: FINDING THE BEST ••• ETHICAL ALTERNATIVE

Decision making is choosing among two or more alternatives. It sounds easier than it is in practice. In fact, decision making is the heart of all the management functions: planning, organizing, leading, and controlling. As Figure 7.9 shows, the rational decision-making model is a series of steps managers should follow to make logical, intelligent, and well-founded decisions. These seven Ds of decision making are

1. Define the situation.

2. Describe and collect needed information.

3. Develop alternatives.

4. Decide which alternative is best.

5. Develop agreement among those involved.

6. Do what is indicated.

7. Determine whether the decision was a good one and follow up.

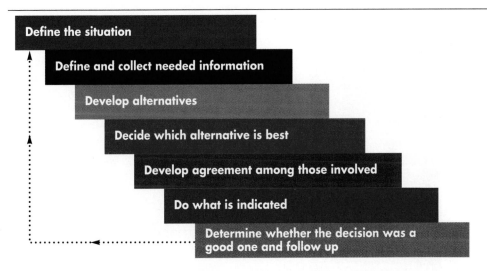

Define the situation

Define and collect needed information

Develop alternatives

Decide which alternative is best

Develop agreement among those involved

Do what is indicated

Determine whether the decision was a good one and follow up

FIGURE 7.9

THE DECISION-MAKING PROCESS

An important step in the decision-making process is to choose the best *ethical* alternative. Other alternatives may generate more money but be immoral or improper in some way. After an evaluation is made of the decision, the whole process begins again.

The best decisions are based on sound information. That's why ours is known as the Information Age. Managers often have computer terminals at their desks so they can easily get internal records and external data of all kinds. But all the data in the world can't replace a manager who's creative and makes brilliant decisions. Decision making is more an art than a science. It's the one skill most needed by managers and leaders in that all the other functions depend on it.

LEARNING MANAGEMENT SKILLS

Now that we have discussed some of the broad categories of skills needed by various levels of management, we can look at the more specific skills an aspiring manager needs to learn. Remember that customer satisfaction is the key to success in almost all businesses.

In general, it's a good idea for anyone interested in business to take as many courses as possible in oral communication, writing, computers, and human relations. In all managerial jobs, communication and human relation skills are the ones in greatest demand. Naturally, it's also important to develop technical skills in some selected area. Figure 7.10 lists the six types of skills students need to develop in order to improve their managerial potential: verbal skills, writing skills, computer skills, human relations skills, time management skills and other technical skills.

••• VERBAL SKILLS •••

Most managerial duties involve communicating with others. Managers have to give talks, conduct meetings, make presentations, and generally communicate their ideas to others. To prepare for such tasks, you should take oral communication courses and become active in various student groups. It helps to become an officer and assume responsibility for conducting meetings and giving speeches. It also helps to join a choir or other group to become comfortable performing in front of others.

At least half of communication is skilled listening. A good manager mixes with other managers, workers, clients, stockholders, and others outside the firm. He or she listens to recommendations and complaints and acts on them. Active

◄ **CONSIDER USING TM 56**
The Decision-Making Process

◄ **CONSIDER USING LECTURE ENHANCER 7-9**
World Class Bad Decisions

◄ **CONSIDER USING LECTURE ENHANCER 7-10**
Problem Solving for Decision Makers

◄ **LEARNING GOAL 7.**
Illustrate the skills aspiring managers need to develop to be successful in the future.

◄ **CONSIDER USING OT ACETATE 7-8**
Required Skills of a Quality Manager

FIGURE **7.10**

• • • •

EVALUATING YOUR MANAGEMENT POTENTIAL

If you find yourself needing improvement in any of these areas, it's a good idea to take courses or read books to improve yourself. The best time to do this is *before* you seek work so that you're fully prepared when you go job hunting.

➤ **CONSIDER USING TM 57**
Evaluating Your Management Potential

Evaluating your management potential

Skill needed	Personal evaluation			
	Excellent	Good	Fair	Need work
Verbal skills				
Writing skills				
Computer skills				
Human relations skills				
Time management skills				
Other technical skills				

listening requires asking questions, listening to the answers, and feeding back what you've heard to let others know you're truly interested in what they say.

••• WRITING SKILLS •••

Managers must be able to write clearly and precisely. Much of what they want others to do must be written in memos, reports, policies, and letters. Much of what was communicated in the past by phone or letter is now communicated by e-mail or fax. While secretaries often wrote and corrected letters in the past, managers themselves must now send their own e-mail and fax messages. Consequently, organizations everywhere are complaining about the inability of many college graduates to write clearly. If you develop good writing skills, you will be miles ahead of the competition. That means taking courses in grammar, composition, and keyboarding. To learn to write, you must practice writing! It helps to write anything: a diary, letters, notes, and so on. With practice, you develop the ability to write easily—just as you speak. With this skill, you will be more prepared for a career in management.

••• COMPUTER SKILLS •••

➤ **CONSIDER USING LECTURE ENHANCER 7-11**
Why Good Employees Can Be Bad Managers

The office of the future will be an office full of computers and related technology. As implied above, memos, charts, letters, e-mail and fax messages, and most other communication efforts will involve the computer. The truly efficient manager of the future will be able to take advantage of the continuing developments in technology. That includes being able to surf the Internet to find needed facts and figures quickly.

••• HUMAN RELATIONS SKILLS •••

A manager works with people, and that means that good managers know how not only to get along with people but also to motivate and inspire them. People skills are learned by working with people. That means aspiring managers should join student groups; volunteer to help at their church, temple, or local charities; and get involved in political organizations. They should try to assume leadership positions where they are responsible for contacting others, assigning them work, and motivating them. Good leaders begin early by assuming leadership positions in sports, community groups, and so on.

··· MANAGING DIVERSITY ···

Managing diversity means building systems and a climate that unite different people in a common pursuit without undermining their diversity. Diversity includes but also goes beyond differences in race, gender, ethnicity, sexual orientation, and disabilities. If people are to work on teams, they have to learn to deal with people who have different personalities, different priorities, and different lifestyles.[24] In the past, firms tended to look for people much like the people already working at the firm. Today such recruiting would probably be illegal, and it certainly would be less than optimal.

Research has shown that heterogeneous (mixed) groups are more productive than homogeneous (similar) groups in the workplace. Men and women, young and old, and all other mixes of people can learn not only to work together but also to do so successfully.[25] Furthermore, it is often quite profitable to have employees who match the diversity of customers so that cultural differences are understood and matched effectively. In the future, managers must learn how to deal effectively with people from many different cultures. Managers will also be asked to work in foreign countries. The more you can do now to learn other languages and work with diverse cultural groups, the better off you'll be when you become a manager.

managing diversity
Building systems and a climate that unite different people in a common pursuit without undermining their diversity.

··· TIME MANAGEMENT SKILLS ···

One of the most important skills new managers must learn is how to budget their time effectively.[26] Managers need to control many demands on their time: telephone interruptions, visits from colleagues, questions from team members, meetings scheduled by top management, and so on. Time management courses or workshops will help you develop such skills as setting priorities, delegating work, choosing activities that produce the most results, doing your work when you're at your best, and dealing with interruptions.

◄ **CONSIDER USING LECTURE ENHANCER 7-12**
Time Management Tips

◄ **CONSIDER USING LECTURE ENHANCER 7-13**
Leadership Advantage: A Boss With Daughters

This photo shows a meeting of Nike's Diversity Council. When you make and sell shoes in countries throughout the world, it is important to have the input of people from all cultures and with all viewpoints. Nike is under careful scrutiny from the media and must respond with the same responsiveness and quality that they put into their products. Can you see how a diverse workforce would help in such responsiveness?

➤ **CONSIDER USING OT ACETATE 7-9**
Tips for the New Manager

➤ **CONSIDER USING OT ACETATE 7-10**
Key Management Challenges in the Future

➤ **CONSIDER USING LECTURE ENHANCER 7-14**
Management Lessons from Revolutionary Companies

··· TECHNICAL SKILLS ···

To rise through the ranks of accounting, marketing, finance, production, or any other functional area, it is important to be proficient in that area. Therefore, students should choose some area of specialization. To rise to top management, it's a good idea to supplement undergraduate studies with a master of business administration (MBA) or a degree in government, economics, or hospital administration. More and more students are going on to take advanced degrees; you, too, may need such a degree to keep up with your colleagues.

···· ▬▬▬ ····

MANAGERS AND LEADERS ARE NEEDED EVERYWHERE

One exciting thing about studying management and leadership is that it prepares people for a career in any organization.[27] Managers and leaders are needed in schools, churches, charities, government organizations, unions, associations, clubs, and all other organizations. Naturally, an important need for managers and leaders is in business.

When selecting a career in management, a student has several decisions to make:

- What kind of organization is most desirable? That is, would it be best to work for a government, business, or nonprofit organization?

- What type of managerial position seems most interesting? A person may become a production manager, a sales manager, a human resource manager, an accounting manager, a traffic (distribution) manager, a credit manager, and so on. There are dozens of managerial positions from which to choose. In the future, graduates are likely to move among several different functions, so it pays to have a broad education in business.

- What type of industry is most appealing: sporting goods, computers, auto, tourism, aircraft, or what? Would it be more interesting to work for a relatively new firm or an established one? What courses and training are needed to prepare for various managerial careers? Only careful research will help you answer these questions.

Management will be discussed in more detail in the next few chapters. Let's pause now, review, and do some exercises. Management is doing, not just reading.

Critical Thinking

What kind of management are you best suited for: human resource, marketing, finance, accounting, production, credit, or what? Why do you feel this area is most appropriate? Would you like to work for a large firm or a small business? Private or government? In an office or out in the field? Would you like being a manager? If you aren't sure, read on and see what's involved.

Progress Check

- Which managerial skills are used more by supervisors than by top managers, and vice versa?

- What are the seven Ds of decision making?

1. Many managers are changing their approach to corporate management.
   - **_What reasons can you give to account for these changes in management?_**
   The three major reasons given in this text for management changes are (1) global competition, (2) technological change, and (3) customer demands. Managers are now being trained to guide and coach employees rather than boss them. The trend is toward working with employees as a team to meet organizational goals.
   - **_What are the four functions of management?_**
   Management is the process used to pursue organizational goals through (1) planning, (2) organizing (which includes staffing), (3) leading (formerly called directing), and (4) controlling.

1. Explain the four functions of management and why the role of managers is changing.

2. The planning function involves the process of setting objectives to meet the organizational goals.
   - **_What's the difference between goals and objectives?_**
   Goals are broad, long-term achievements that organizations aim to accomplish, whereas objectives are specific, short-term plans made to help reach the goals.
   - **_What are the three types of planning, and how are they related to the organization's goals and objectives?_**
   Strategic planning is broad, long-range planning that outlines the goals of the organization. Tactical planning, on the other hand, is specific, short-term planning that lists organizational objectives. Operational planning is part of tactical planning and involves setting specific timetables and standards. Contingency planning involves developing an alternative set of plans in case the first set doesn't work out.
   - **_How are organizations changing to become more customer-oriented?_**
   Organizations are becoming smaller so that they can respond more quickly to customers. Furthermore, each firm is striving to have every process as good as the best companies in the world. Often that means finding other firms to do various processes. Top management must make contact with those firms and work closely with them to coordinate processes so that customers get the highest-quality goods and services possible.

2. Relate the planning process to the accomplishment of company goals.

3. The traditional directing function of management involves giving assignments, explaining routines, clarifying policies, and providing feedback on performance.
   - **_What changes are occurring in this area?_**
   In general, the functions of planning, organizing, and controlling are being assigned to lower and lower levels of the firm. Top managers are spending more time on setting and selling a vision for the firm, creating a mission statement, and responding to changes in the environment.

3. Describe the organizing function of management and illustrate how the function differs at various management levels.

4. The control function of management involves measuring employee performance against objectives and standards and taking corrective action if necessary.
   - **_What are the five steps of the control function?_**
   Controlling incorporates (1) setting clear standards, (2) monitoring and recording performance, (3) comparing performance with plans and standards, (4) communicating results and deviations to employees, and (5) taking corrective action if necessary.

4. Summarize the five steps of the control function of management.

• *What qualities must standards possess to be used to measure performance results?*
Standards must be specific, attainable, and measurable.

5. Explain the differences between managers and leaders, and compare the characteristics and uses of the various leadership styles.

5. Executives today must be more than just managers; they must be leaders as well.
• *What's the difference between a manager and a leader?*
A manager plans, organizes, and controls functions within an organization. A leader has vision and inspires others to grasp that vision, establishes corporate values, emphasizes corporate ethics, and doesn't fear change.
• *Describe the various leadership styles.*
Figure 7.6 shows a continuum of leadership styles ranging from boss-centered to subordinate-centered leadership.
• *Which leadership style is best?*
The best (most effective) leadership style depends on the people being led and the situation. The challenge of the future will be to empower self-managed teams to manage themselves. This is a move away from autocratic leadership.

6. Describe the three general categories of skills needed by top, middle, and first-line managers.

6. Managers must be good planners, organizers, coordinators, communicators, morale builders, and motivators.
• *What skills must a manager have to be all these things?*
Managers must have three categories of skills: (1) technical skills (ability to perform tasks such as bookkeeping or selling), (2) human relations skills (ability to communicate and motivate), and (3) conceptual skills (ability to see organizations as a whole and how all the parts fit together).
• *Are these skills equally important at all management levels?*
The skills needed are different at different levels. Top managers rely heavily on human relations and conceptual skills and rarely use technical skills, while first-line supervisors need strong technical and human relations skills but use conceptual skills less often (see Figure 7.8).

7. Illustrate the skills aspiring managers need to develop to be successful in the future.

7. Now that you've examined what managers do, you may be considering a career in management.
• *What skills should aspiring managers be developing now to help them become better managers in the future?*
They will need to develop six skills to sharpen their managerial potential: (1) verbal skills, (2) writing skills, (3) computer skills, (4) human relations skills, (5) time management skills, and (6) technical skills.

KEY TERMS
......

autocratic leadership 213
conceptual skills 217
contingency planning 203
controlling 200
decision making 218
delegating 218
empowerment 207
enabling 207
external customers 209

goals 201
human relations skills 217
internal customers 209
laissez-faire (free-rein) leadership 213
leadership 210
leading 200
learning organization 212
management 199

managing diversity 221
middle management 203
mission statement 200
objectives 201
operational planning 203
organizing 200
participative (democratic) leadership 213

DEVELOPING WORKPLACE SKILLS

1. Compare and contrast working as a manager in the following types of organizations: government, business, and nonprofit. To learn the advantages and disadvantages of each, talk to managers from each area and share what you learn with the class.

2. Interview two or more managers of local businesses (preferably of different sizes) and find out what they spend the majority of their time doing. Is it planning, organizing, controlling, or leading? Use a computer graphics program to construct a pie chart (or hand-draw one) illustrating the average amount of time managers spend on each type of activity. If you have a chance to talk with different levels of managers, it would be interesting to create a chart comparing their allocation of time. Discuss the results with the class.

3. Discuss the disadvantages of becoming a manager. Does the size of the business make a difference? Prepare a two-page report of your findings.

4. Review *Business Week, Forbes, Inc.,* and other business journals and read about key executives and managers. How much do they make? (See *Business Week*'s annual survey.) How many hours do they work? Do you believe they earn their pay? Be prepared to give a two-minute presentation to the class about your findings and beliefs.

5. Review Figure 7.7 and discuss managers you have known, worked for, or read about who have practiced each style. Which did you like best? Why? Which were most effective? Why?

TAKING IT TO THE NET

Purpose

To test your ability to make appropriate supervisory decisions.

Exercise

Go to the Leadership Challenge part of the Positive Employee Relations Council Web site (http://www.perc.net/Background.html). This simulation involves you in fictional but realistic situations. It is broken down into moves or steps. The objective is to finish with the least number of steps and a high score. You will discover that this simulation is a maze of related decisions and interacting problems. You will find that effective supervisory decisions bring you closer to the end of the challenge, and weaker decisions inhibit your efforts, require additional steps, and get you further involved. Print the scorecard to record your results.

1. How did you score?

2. Improve your score by taking the challenge again using what you learned on the first round to make wiser decisions.

Practicing Management Decisions

How do you apply free-market principles to an organization? To find out, you might explore Koch Industries, a company involved in oil, chemicals, and agriculture. It has grown to be bigger than both Motorola and Intel, so the company must be doing something right. Charles Koch (pronounced *coke*) is the leader of the organization. He believes in market-based management and has applied it at his company.

Autocratic techniques don't work in the world of economics, Mr. Koch figures, so why would they work in a major corporation? Mr. Koch wants each employee to feel like the owner of his or her job. Thus, employees have freedom to operate the property under their individual control, sell it or improve it, and earn a return on it. This means that refinery operators schedule flows as they see fit, as long as the process remains efficient. A new engineer has the right to move people and spend money as he or she chooses.

Since different people have different skills, no two people doing the same job are expected to have the same output. All employees are encouraged to use their strengths in their own unique ways. Operating divisions are under no obligation to use internal services such as training. The training department, therefore, must do a better job than any outside training company or risk losing its role in the firm. Similarly, the training department is free to set its own prices when providing internal services. Thus, departments within the firm can work out a deal, and two different departments may be charged different prices for basically the same service. In short, a free-market atmosphere is created within the firm.

How well do free-market principles work in management? Well, Koch Industries has become the number two private firm in the United States using those principles. It may be an interesting

CASE
· · · · · ·
MARKET-BASED MANAGEMENT AT KOCH INDUSTRIES
· · · · · ·

exercise, therefore, to try to imagine what it would be like to work in and manage a firm where freedom is the dominant philosophy and each employee is free to create his or her own job description and to partner with others as needed.

Decision Questions

1. Giving employees the freedom to own their own jobs creates all kinds of incentives for the employee to work hard as long as the rewards match the effort. What is your reaction to paying employees based on their output rather than their job assignment? That is, an employee could assume many jobs or work with many people to make as large a contribution as possible to the firm.

2. Under communist economies, there is a saying, "We pretend to work and they pretend to pay us." This means that workers in such societies do not put forth their best effort and are not paid well either. Do you believe that most workers would work harder and better if given more freedom and if paid according to what they produce rather than to their job description?

3. The University of Virginia has a program for selected students that has no majors and no requirements. Each student in the program is free to choose his or her own curriculum. What would prevent the university from giving the same freedom to all students? What would be the advantages and disadvantages for both the students and the university?

4. A "learning organization" is one where each employee is encouraged to seek more education and then share that learning with others so that changes can be made continuously. Do most managers seem to encourage or discourage such a procedure? Discuss.

To compete in today's dynamic market, an organization has to have leadership and management that are in tune with the needs of customers and other stakeholders. Lou Gerstner of IBM is one of those managers. IBM was a lumbering giant whose markets were being taken by smaller, more flexible, customer-oriented firms, but

VIDEO CASE
· · · · · ·
LOU GERSTNER OF IBM

Gerstner brought a new vision to the firm and used the four functions of management to implement that vision and make the firm more responsive.

The four functions of management are: (1) planning; (2) organizing, including staffing; (3) leading; and (4) controlling. At the planning stage, Gerstner had a vision of a company that made computers more user friendly. Emphasis was placed on problem solving, not just building bigger and faster computers. More emphasis was placed on software and what it could do to make life easier. For example, IBM is developing programs that will link all your home appliances; your refrigerator will have an Internet address and will e-mail the service department if it needs repair. A large part of his vision was the development of the Internet and the company's own intranet. Now, all employees are linked electronically and have access to company data.

Gerstner knew that long-term success would rely on bringing in the right people. Technically, that is called staffing, and it is part of the organizing function. Gerstner reached outside the firm to find managers who were not steeped in the IBM tradition, but were more attuned to customers and their wants and needs. Richard Thoman, for example, had worked with Gerstner at American Express and other companies. He became the senior vice president for the IBM PC company. Thoman's strong sense of values and ethics led them through a difficult time when a flawed chip showed up in their PCs. He halted sale of the PCs and worked with other firms to develop a better one. In the long run, this decision proved to be the right one.

The real test of an executive's worth, however, is in his or her success at leadership. Gerstner is a man with strong moral values. Leadership means that everyone in the organization buys into your vision and works together to make it happen. To develop the communication necessary to build internal relationships, Gerstner focused on building the company's intranet so that communication flows were free and easy. All employees have access to him via e-mail, and Gerstner reads and responds to those messages.

Finally, a leader must have control over the organization. But how do you measure success in an organization that is trying new things? The answer is to focus on the customer and customer satisfaction. However, IBM also needed to raise its profits to keep its stockholders happy. Also, employee morale was low because so many had been dismissed from the company because of declining profits and slow growth. By 1996, IBM was reporting a profit for the first time in three years. Morale at IBM is now higher, stockholders are happy with the rapid increase of the stock price, and customers are pleased with the new goods and services IBM is providing.

Lou Gerstner is just one of the many new corporate leaders who have led U.S. businesses successfully into a new era of global competition. They still apply the same functions, but they have a different vision, a vision that includes empowering employees, building internal and external communications, and leading the organization to closer and better relationships with customers.

Discussion Questions

1. What specific management skills did Gerstner use to make IBM a more responsive organization? Explain.

2. Is the job of a manager of a small business different from a manager of a large corporation like IBM? What are the similarities and differences?

3. What are some of the ways Gerstner is making use of technology in his job as a top manager? How will managers of the future use technology to make their companies world-class competitors?

Organizing a Customer-Driven Business

Chapter

8

LEARNING GOALS

After you have read and studied this chapter, you should be able to

1 Describe the traditional hierarchical, bureaucratic organization and how it is being restructured.

2 Explain the organizational theories of Fayol and Weber.

3 Discuss the various issues connected with organizational design.

4 Describe the differences between line, line-and-staff, matrix, and cross-functional organizations.

5 Explain the benefits of turning organizations upside down and inside out.

6 Give examples to show how organizational culture and the informal organization can hinder or assist organizational change.

Mei-Lin Cheng and Julie Anderson are both managers at Hewlett-Packard, one of America's most admired companies. They work at HP's North American distribution organization, which manages the flow of billions of dollars' worth of products, from personal computers to toner cartridges, from order to delivery. But Cheng and Anderson had a problem: HP was taking 26 days for products to reach customers, while competitors were shipping out PCs within a couple of days.

Since customer responsiveness is one of the most important competitive advantages today, HP had to do something to improve its response time.

Cheng and Anderson assumed responsibility for reengineering the process of orders. Once they had permission to make certain necessary changes, the two women assembled a team of 35 people from HP and two other companies and gave them total freedom to do what was needed to improve the process.

A pilot program was able to cut delivery time from 26 to 8 days for one of HP's bigger customers. The customer was then able to cut inventories by 20 percent and increase its service level to its customers.

The two women were able to accomplish this objective by changing all the rules. There was no longer any hierarchy, no titles, no job descriptions, no plans, no step-by-step measures of progress. Instead, team members were encouraged to do whatever it took to make the system work better and faster. Diversity of views and systems thinking were encouraged. The first month was one long meeting, during which employees decided what to do and how to do it. The result, at first, was chaos. Team members included people from Andersen Consulting and

PROFILE

Mei-Lin Cheng and Julie Anderson of Hewlett-Packard

Menlo Logistics. Menlo is the company's transportation and distribution partner. The system they were trying to implement, from SAP (a German company), was designed to create a unified database covering everything from the customer's order through the credit check, manufacturing, shipping, warehousing, and billing. Then orders were traced through the firm to find where the stoppages were. Then each road block was eliminated until the whole process went smoothly and quickly.

As a consequence of this reengineering process, everyone in the organization has learned to learn. The firm is now capable of responding quickly to other challenges. Employees have learned to work and think in teams. In short, the HP's distribution organization is now a learning system where everything gets better over time and people are happier and more productive.

The HP experience is just one example of the major changes taking place in organizations today. The old system where bosses tell others what to do is being replaced by a system where everyone participates, and specialization by function (e.g., production, marketing, finance) is being replaced by cross-functional teams (people from various departments working together). The implications are tremendous for today's business students. They must be prepared to work in teams and to be self-motivated and self-directed. This chapter will look at past systems and how and why they are changing so that you will get some feel for what the future will bring.

Sources: Stratford Sherman, "Secrets of HP's 'Muddled' Team," *Fortune*, March 18, 1996, pp. 116–20. Debra Phillips, "Rush Hour," *Entrepreneur*, February 1998, pp. 114–18.

THE CHANGING ORGANIZATIONAL HIERARCHY

Moving from a boss-driven to an employee-driven or team-driven company isn't easy. Managers often resist giving up their authority over workers, while workers often resist the responsibility that comes with self-management. Nonetheless, many of the world's leading organizations are moving in that

◄ **CONSIDER USING TM 58**
Chapter Outline

◄ **LEARNING GOAL 1.** Describe the traditional hierarchical, bureaucratic organization structure and how it is being restructured.

FIGURE **8.1**
• • • •

**A TYPICAL
HIERARCHICAL
ORGANIZATION
STRUCTURE**

➤ **CONSIDER USING TM 59**
A Typical Organizational Structure
(Figure 8.1 on text page 230)

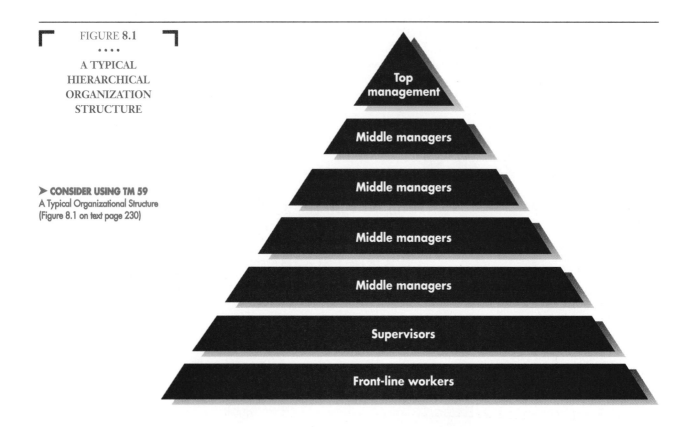

organizational design
The structuring of workers so that
they can best accomplish the firm's
goals.

hierarchy
A system in which one person is at
the top of the organization and
many levels of managers are
responsible to that person.

➤ **CONSIDER USING LECTURE
ENHANCER 8-1**
Get Organized

bureaucracy
An organization with many layers
of managers who set rules and
regulations and oversee all
decisions.

➤ **CONSIDER USING OT ACETATE
8-1**
Purpose of an Organization Chart

➤ **CONSIDER USING LECTURE
ENHANCER 8-2**
A Dilbert View of Downsizing

direction.[1] They're trying to develop an organizational design that best serves the needs of customers, stockholders, employees, and the community.

Organizational design is the structuring of workers so that they can best accomplish the firm's goals. In the past, many organizations were designed so that managers could control workers, and most organizations are still organized that way, with everything set up in a hierarchy. A **hierarchy** is a system in which one person is at the top of the organization and many levels of managers are responsible to that person. Since one person can't keep track of thousands of workers, the top manager needs many lower-level managers to help. Figure 8.1 shows a typical hierarchical organization structure.

Some organizations have had as many as 10 to 14 layers of management between the chief executive officer (CEO) and the lowest-level employees. If employees wanted to introduce work changes, they would ask their supervisors, who would ask their managers, who would ask the manager above them and so on. Eventually a decision would be made and passed down from manager to manager until it reached the employee. Such decisions could take days, weeks, or months. **Bureaucracy** is the term used for an organization with many layers of managers who set rules and regulations and oversee all decisions. But bureaucracy is on its way out.

Recently, a study found that 28 percent of companies surveyed have no more than four layers of management. Five years ago, only 8 percent had such few layers. It should be noted, however, that 8 percent of the companies still had over eight layers of management.[2] So, as you can see, organizations are eliminating managers and giving more power to lower-level employees. This process is called downsizing because it allows the organization to operate with fewer workers. According to a recent study, many companies that have downsized have not experienced the full impact they anticipated on earnings or a long-run rise in the price of their stock.[3] To understand why downsizing is occurring in spite of its frequent failure to increase long-term profits, it helps to review the history of how bureaucracy got started in the first place. (See Figure 8.2 on page 234.)

••• THE FUNDAMENTALS OF •••
BUREAUCRACY

In a bureaucratic organization, a chain of command goes from the top down. There are many rules and regulations that everyone is expected to follow. Such an organizational setup is a good idea when workers are relatively uneducated and managers are trained to make all decisions. To make the process easier, organizations are set up by function. That is, there are separate departments for design, engineering, production, marketing, finance, human resource management, accounting, legal issues, and so on.

Bureaucracies encourage people to specialize in one function on the job, which they prepare for by specializing in school. Communication among departments is minimal. Career advancement for the typical employee means moving up within a function. For example, one might move up from salesperson to sales trainer to sales manager to regional manager to marketing manager to marketing vice president. Such a career progression doesn't regularly expose people to other functions in the firm and therefore doesn't create much interfunctional cooperation.

In the past, such an organization structure worked well because employees could specialize in one area and learn it well. The problem today is that such organizations aren't very responsive to customers. Employees tend to follow the rules and aren't very flexible in responding to customer wants and needs. Leading firms such as IBM, GM, and Kodak have found that slow response to consumer demands cuts dramatically into sales, so they have responded by restructuring their firms. **Restructuring** means redesigning an organization so that it can more effectively and efficiently serve its customers. Often that means breaking down barriers between functions. It may also mean giving more authority to lower-level employees and ending top-down management. Those organizations that have made such changes have regained market leadership.[4] Many others are quickly following their lead.

There are still many remnants of bureaucracy among today's organizations. Most universities, for example, are still slow to adapt to customer (student) wants and needs. So are most government agencies. Often you can see the consequences of bureaucracy in agencies such as the Department of Motor Vehicles or the U.S. Postal Service. Such agencies are starting to explore new ways of organizing. Otherwise, they may lose their function to more efficient organizations. For example, the U.S. Postal Service knows that the postal service in England has been taken over by private firms.

COMPANIES KEEP DOWNSIZING

Total Layoffs by U.S. Companies

Companies keep downsizing despite the fact that such actions have not favorably affected long-term profits for most firms. In Fact, many firms are now eagerly hiring more middle management.

restructuring
Redesigning an organization so that it can more effectively and efficiently serve its customers.

Critical Thinking

Start noticing how many clerks and other customer-contact people say things like "That's not our policy" or "We don't do things that way" when you request some unusual service. Such answers are the result of bureaucratic rules and regulations that employees are forced to follow. Imagine a day when employees are free to adjust to the wants and needs of customers. What organizational changes would have to be made? Would the results be worth the effort?

··· ▬ ····

HOW ORGANIZATIONS HAVE EVOLVED

► CONSIDER USING SUPPLEMEN-
TAL CASE 8-1
Restructuring Hits Management Positions
(SCANS)

► CONSIDER USING LECTURE
ENHANCER 8-3
Bureaucracy Strangles Intrapreneurship

► CONSIDER USING LECTURE
ENHANCER 8-4
Bob Felton Hates Bureaucracy

To understand traditional managers and their approach to business, you have to understand traditional organization theories. In the next few sections, we'll review those theories. Then we'll outline the new approaches that will guide organizations in the 21st century.

··· THE BACKGROUND OF ORGANIZATIONAL THEORY ···

Until this century, most organizations were rather small, the processes for producing goods were rather simple, and organizing workers was fairly easy. Not until the 20th century and the introduction of mass production did business organizations become complex and difficult to manage. The bigger the plant, the more efficient production became, or so it seemed. The concept was called economy of scale. It meant that companies could produce goods more inexpensively if they could purchase raw materials in bulk, and the average cost of goods went down as production levels increased.

Along with mass production, organization theorists emerged. In France, Henri Fayol published his book *Administration industrielle et générale* in 1919. It was popularized in the United States in 1949 under the title *General and Industrial Management.* Max Weber (pronounced *Vay-ber*) was writing about organization theory in Germany about the same time Fayol was writing his books in France. Note that it was only about 50 years ago that organization theory became popular in the United States.

► LEARNING GOAL 2. Explain the
organizational theories of Fayol and
Weber.

··· FAYOL'S PRINCIPLES OF ORGANIZATION ···

Fayol introduced such principles as the following:

Unity of command. Each worker is to report to one, and only one, boss. The benefits of this principle are obvious. What happens if two different bosses give you two different assignments? Which one should you follow? To prevent such confusion, each person is to report to only one manager.

Hierarchy of authority. Each person should know to whom they should report. Managers should have the right to give orders and expect others to follow.

Division of labor. Functions are to be divided into areas of specialization such as production, marketing, and finance.

Subordination of individual interests to the general interest. Workers are to think of themselves as a coordinated team. Goals of the team are more important than the goals of individual workers.

Authority. Managers have the right to give orders and the power to exact obedience. Authority and responsibility are related: Whenever authority is exercised, responsibility arises.

Degree of centralization. The amount of decision-making power vested in top management should vary by circumstances. In a small organization, it's possible to centralize all decision-making power in the top manager. In a larger organization, however, some decision-making power should be delegated to lower-level managers and employees on both major and minor issues.

Clear communication channels. Everyone should know to whom they should report.

Order. Materials and people should be placed and maintained in the proper location.

Equity. A manager should treat employees and peers with respect and justice.

Esprit de corps. A spirit of pride and loyalty should be created among people in the firm.

Management courses in colleges throughout the world taught these principles for years, and they became synonymous with the concept of management. Organizations were designed so that no person had more than one boss, lines of authority were clear, and everyone knew to whom they were to report. Naturally, these principles tended to become rules and policies as organizations grew larger. That led to rather rigid organizations and a feeling among workers that they belonged to an inflexible system rather than to a group of friendly, cooperative workers joined together in a common effort.

••• MAX WEBER AND ORGANIZATIONAL THEORY •••

Max Weber used the word *bureaucrats* to describe middle managers whose function was to implement top management's orders. His book *The Theory of Social and Economic Organizations* appeared in the United States in the late 1940s. Weber's concept of a bureaucratic organization basically consisted of three layers of authority: (1) top managers, who were the decision makers; (2) middle managers (the bureaucracy), who developed rules and procedures for implementing the decisions; and (3) workers and supervisors, who did the work. (See Figure 8.2 for an illustration of a bureaucratic organization.)

It was Weber who promoted the pyramid-shaped organization structure that became so popular in large firms. Weber put great trust in managers and felt that the firm would do well if employees simply did what they were told. The less decision making employees had to do, the better. Clearly, this is a reasonable way to operate if you're dealing with relatively uneducated and untrained workers. Often, such workers were the only ones available at that time; most employees did not have the kind of educational background and technical skills that most of today's workers have.

Weber's principles of organization were similar to Fayol's. In addition, Weber emphasized

Job descriptions.

Written rules, decision guidelines, and detailed records.

Consistent procedures, regulations, and policies.

Staffing and promotion based on qualifications.

Weber believed that large organizations demanded clearly established rules and guidelines that were to be followed precisely. Although the word *bureaucrat,* as used by Weber, didn't have any negative connotations, the practice of establishing rules and procedures has sometimes become so rigid that *bureaucracy* has become almost a nasty name for an organization with many managers who seem to do nothing but make and enforce rules.

In summary, together Fayol and Weber introduced organizational concepts such as (1) unity of command (one employee, one boss); (2) division of labor (specialized jobs); (3) job descriptions; (4) rules, guidelines, procedures, and policies; (5) clear lines of authority and communication; (6) placement of

When you go to a store and the clerk says, "I'm sorry I can't do that, it's against company policy," you can blame Max Weber and his theories. At one time less-educated workers were best managed, it was believed, by having them follow many strict rules and regulations monitored by managers or supervisors. Are there industries or businesses today where you think it would be desirable or necessary to continue to use such controls?

◄ CONSIDER USING CRITICAL THINKING EXERCISE 8-1
Organization Chart (**SCANS**)

◄ CONSIDER USING OT ACETATE 8-2 AND OT ACETATE 8-3
Is a Bureaucratic Organization for You?

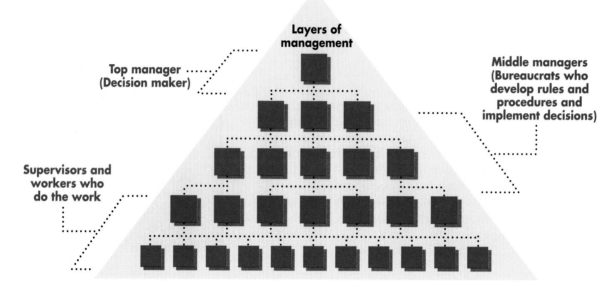

materials and people in some established order; (7) the establishment of departments; (8) detailed record keeping; (9) the establishment of an esprit de corps (a feeling of enthusiasm and devotion to the firm); and (10) the assignment of a limited number of people to each manager. You can see the benefits of such concepts. What's needed today is a way to implement those concepts while still maintaining employees' freedom and incentive to work productively on their own.

•••• ▬▬▬ ••••

DESIGNING MORE RESPONSIVE ORGANIZATIONS

It wasn't until the late 1970s that management began the process of reorganizing firms, making them smaller, less complex, and more efficient. That process continues today. As we explained in Chapter 7, new technologies, international competition, and consumer demand forced companies to change. In designing more responsive organizations, firms have had to deal with the following organizational issues: (1) tall versus flat organization structures, (2) span of control, (3) departmentalization, and (4) centralization versus decentralization.

••• TALL VERSUS FLAT ORGANIZATION STRUCTURES •••

In the early 20th century organizations grew bigger and bigger, adding layer after layer of management until they came to have what are called tall organization structures. This means, simply, that the organization chart would be quite tall because of the various levels of management. The organization structure of the U.S. Army is an example of how tall an organization can get. There are many layers of management between a private and a general (e.g., sergeant, lieutenant, captain, major, colonel). You can imagine how a message may be distorted as it moves up from officer to officer.

Business organizations, such as General Motors, took on the same style of organization as the military. They were divided into regions, divisions, centers, and plants. Each plant might have several layers of management. The net effect was a huge complex of managers, management assistants, secretaries,

General Motors.

"If the people who make the car don't fit together, the car won't either."

Welcome to the Excel training course. Before it's over, Saturn's Dennis Bowman will take these General Motors employees on a real adventure. They'll scale walls. Walk across high wires. Plunge backwards into the waiting arms of their coworkers. And take away some valuable lessons about trust, cooperation and seeing things from the other person's point of view. Developed by Saturn, Excel is now used throughout General Motors. It's turning out graduates who know the power of teamwork. Who go a little further to build quality automobiles. And who believe that the right way to treat a customer is the way you'd want to be treated yourself.

One of the most important goals of organizations today is teamwork. This concept was a key part of Fayol's principles. Teamwork builds trust, cooperation, and joint commitments to achieve the firm's objectives. Are you working in teams while in school in order to develop the team-building skills that companies will need in the future?

assistant secretaries, supervisors, trainers, and so on. The cost of keeping all these managers and support people was quite high. The paperwork they generated was enormous, and the inefficiencies in communication and decision making became intolerable.

The development of computers helped to bring more efficiency to large operations. But more important was the trend to eliminate several layers of management. Throughout the 1990s, companies have fired managers and tried to become more efficient. This trend toward trimming management positions is likely to continue into the next century.

Those organizations that do cut management are tending to create teams. Business majors therefore need to practice working and thinking in teams. You may get a job because of functional expertise (e.g., as a finance major), but your career is likely to take you into many different areas of the firm and demand more general skills. You may thus have to be a jack-of-all-trades and a master of at least one.

◀ CONSIDER USING LECTURE ENHANCER 8-6
The Return of the Middle Manager

◀ CONSIDER USING LECTURE ENHANCER 8-7
Decentralization, Span of Control

••• CHOOSING THE APPROPRIATE SPAN OF CONTROL •••

Span of control refers to the optimum number of subordinates a manager supervises or should supervise. There are many factors to consider when determining span of control. At lower levels, where work is standardized, it's

span of control
The optimum number of subordinates a manager supervises or should supervise.

possible to implement a wide span of control (15 to 40 workers). However, the number gradually narrows at higher levels of the organization because work is less standardized and there's more need for face-to-face communication. Variables in span of control include the following:

1. *Capabilities of the manager.* The more experienced and capable a manager is, the broader the span of control can be. (More workers can report to that manager.) But too wide a span can result in loss of control.

2. *Capabilities of the subordinates.* The more the subordinates need supervision, the narrower the span of control should be. (Fewer workers report to one manager.)

3. *Complexity of the job.*

    a. *Geographical closeness.* The more concentrated the work area is, the broader the span of control can be.

    b. *Functional similarity.* The more similar the functions are, the broader the span of control can be.

    c. *Need for coordination.* The greater the need for coordination, the narrower the span of control might be.

    d. *Planning demands.* The more involved the plan, the narrower the span of control might be.

    e. *Functional complexity.* The more complex the functions are, the narrower the span of control might be.

> **CONSIDER USING CRITICAL THINKING EXERCISE 8-2**
You, The Manager (**SCANS**)

Other factors to consider include the professionalism of superiors and subordinates and the number of new problems that occur in a day. In business, the span of control varies widely. The number of people reporting to the president may range from 1 to 80 or more. The trend is to expand the span of control as organizations get rid of middle managers. It's possible to increase the span of control as employees become more professional, as information technology makes it possible for managers to handle more information, and as employees take on more responsibility for self-management.

••• ADVANTAGES AND DISADVANTAGES OF •••
DEPARTMENTALIZATION

departmentalization
The dividing of organizational functions into separate units.

Departmentalization is the dividing of organizational functions into separate units. The traditional way to departmentalize organizations is by function. Functional structure is the grouping of workers into departments based on similar skills, expertise, or resource use. There might be, for example, a production department, a transportation department, a finance department, an accounting department, a marketing department, a data processing department, and so on. Such units enable employees to specialize and work together more efficiently. Advantages of such a structure include the following:

1. Skills can be developed in depth, and employees can progress within a department as their skills develop.

2. Economies of scale can be achieved in that all the resources needed can be centralized and various experts can be located in that area.

3. There's good coordination within the function, and top management can easily direct and control various departments' activities.

As for disadvantages,

1. There's a lack of communication among the different departments. For example, production may be isolated from marketing so that the

people making the product do not get the proper feedback from customers.

2. Individual employees begin to identify with their department and its goals rather than with the goals of the organization as a whole.

3. The company's response to external changes is slow.

4. People aren't trained to take different managerial responsibilities; rather, they tend to become narrow specialists.

Given the limitations of departmentalization, businesses are now trying to redesign their structures to optimize skill development while increasing communication among employees in different departments. The goal, remember, is to better serve customers and to win their loyalty.

••• DIFFERENT WAYS TO DEPARTMENTALIZE •••

In the past, companies have tried various ways to departmentalize to better serve customers. Figure 8.3 shows five ways a firm can departmentalize. Companies may use a variety of methods of departmentalization in structuring the same company. One form of departmentalization is by product. A book publisher might have a trade book department (books sold to people in a specific business or trade), a textbook department, and a technical book department. Customers for each type of book are different, so separate development and marketing processes are created for each type.

The most basic way to departmentalize, as we discussed above, is by function. This text is divided by business functions because such groupings are most common. Production, marketing, finance, human resource management, and accounting are all distinct functions calling for separate skills. Companies are now discovering, however, that functional separation isn't always the most responsive form of organization.

It makes more sense in some organizations to departmentalize by customer group. A pharmaceutical company, for example, might have one department that focuses on the consumer market, another that calls on hospitals (institutional market), and another that targets doctors.

Some firms group their units by geographic location because customers vary so greatly by region. The United States is usually considered one market area. Japan, Europe, and Korea may involve separate departments.

The decision about which way to departmentalize depends greatly on the nature of the product and the customers served. A few firms find that it's more efficient to separate activities by process. For example, a firm that makes leather coats may have one department cut the leather, another dye it, and a third sew the coat together.

••• CENTRALIZATION VERSUS ••• DECENTRALIZATION OF AUTHORITY

Imagine for a minute that you're a top manager for a retail company such as J. C. Penney. Your temptation may be to preserve control over all your stores in order to maintain a uniform image and merchandise. You've noticed such control works well for McDonald's; why not J. C. Penney? The degree to which an organization allows managers at the lower levels of the managerial hierarchy to make decisions determines the degree of decentralization that an organization practices.

Most larger companies in the past were divided into separate and distinct departments. While some of those departments, such as engineering and design, have merged, others, such as the legal department, often remain separate. What advantages, if any, can you see for having the legal department work closely with other departments such as product design and human resource management?

◄ CONSIDER USING OT ACETATE 8-5
How to Improve Organizational Structure

◄ CONSIDER USING LECTURE ENHANCER 8-8
Delegation and Mistakes

◄ CONSIDER USING LECTURE ENHANCER 8-9
A Japanese Manager Interprets Responsibility

FIGURE 8.3
• • • •
WAYS TO DEPARTMENTALIZE

A computer company may want to departmentalize by geographic location (countries), a manufacturer by function, a pharmaceutical company by customer group, a leather manufacturer by process, and a publisher by product. In each case the structure must fit the firm's goals.

➤ **CONSIDER USING TM 61**
Ways to Departmentalize (Figure 8.3 on text page 238)

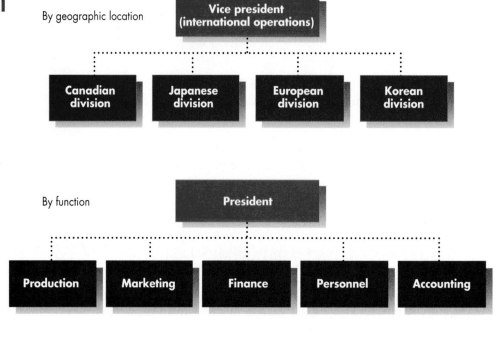

By geographic location

Vice president (international operations)

Canadian division — Japanese division — European division — Korean division

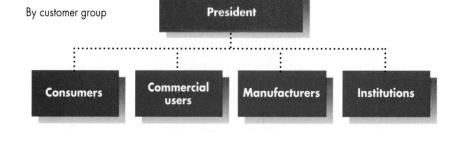

By function

President

Production — Marketing — Finance — Personnel — Accounting

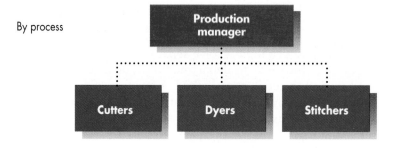

By customer group

President

Consumers — Commercial users — Manufacturers — Institutions

By process

Production manager

Cutters — Dyers — Stitchers

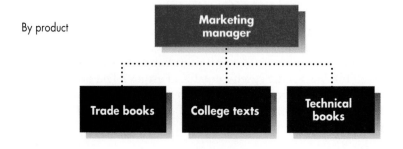

By product

Marketing manager

Trade books — College texts — Technical books

Centralized authority occurs when decision-making authority is maintained at the top level of management at the company's headquarters. **Decentralized authority** occurs when decision-making authority is delegated to lower-level managers and employees who are more familiar with local conditions than headquarters' management could be.

At J. C. Penney, for example, customers in California are likely to demand clothing styles different from those demanded in Minnesota or Maine. It makes sense, therefore, to give store managers in various cities the authority to buy, price, and promote merchandise appropriate for each area. Such a delegation of authority is an example of decentralized management.

On the other hand, McDonald's feels that purchasing, promotion, and other such decisions are best handled centrally. There's little need for each McDonald's restaurant to carry different food products. McDonald's therefore would lean toward centralized authority. Today's rapidly changing markets, added to global differences in consumer tastes, tend to favor more decentralization and thus more delegation of authority. McDonald's, for example, has learned that its restaurants in England should provide tea, those in Germany should provide beer, those in Japan should provide rice, and so on. Rosenbluth International is a service organization in the travel industry. It too has decentralized so that its separate units can offer the kinds of services demanded in each region while still getting needed resources from corporate headquarters.[5]

centralized authority
When decision-making authority is maintained at the top level of management at the company's headquarters.

decentralized authority
When decision-making authority is delegated to lower-level managers more familiar with local conditions than headquarters' management could be.

Progress Check

- What is bureaucracy and why has it led to the need for restructuring organizations?
- How many of Fayol's principles can you name?
- What principles did Weber add?
- What are the trends in tall versus flat organizations, narrow versus wide spans of control, departmentalization, and centralization versus decentralization of authority?

···· ▬▬ ····

ORGANIZATION MODELS

Now that we've explored the basic principles of organizational design, we can explore in depth the various ways to structure an organization. We'll look at four forms of organization: (1) line organizations, (2) line-and-staff organizations, (3) matrix-style organizations, and (4) cross-functional, self-managed teams. Figure 8.4 compares their advantages and disadvantages.

◄ **LEARNING GOAL 4.**
Describe the differences between line, line and staff, matrix, and cross-functional organizations.

◄ **CONSIDER USING LECTURE ENHANCER 8-10**
The First American Organization Chart

··· LINE ORGANIZATIONS ···

A line organization has direct two-way lines of responsibility, authority, and communication running from the top to the bottom of the organization, with all people reporting to only one supervisor. The most obvious example is the U.S. Army, which has a clear line of authority going from general to colonel to major to lieutenant to sergeant to corporal to private. A private reports to a corporal, the corporal to a sergeant, and so on back up to the generals. A line organization has the advantages of having clearly defined responsibility and authority, being easy to understand, and providing one supervisor for each person. The principles of good organizational design are met. In addition to the U.S. Army, most small companies are organized this way.

However, a line organization may have the disadvantages of being too inflexible, of having few specialists or experts to advise people along the line,

> CONSIDER USING LECTURE
ENHANCER 8-11
Managing the Boss

of having lines of communication that are too long, and of being unable to handle the complex decisions involved in an organization with thousands of sometimes unrelated products and literally tons of paperwork.

··· LINE-AND-STAFF ORGANIZATIONS ···

To minimize the disadvantages of simple line organizations, many organizations today have both line and staff personnel. A couple of definitions will help:

line personnel
Employees who perform functions that contribute directly to the primary goals of the organization.

staff personnel
Employees who perform functions that assist line personnel in achieving their goals.

Line personnel perform functions that contribute directly to the primary goals of the organization (e.g., making the product, distributing it, and selling it). **Staff personnel** perform functions that advise and assist line personnel in performing their goals (e.g., marketing research, legal advising, and personnel).

Many organizations have benefited from the expert advice of staff assistants in areas such as safety, quality control, computer technology, human resource management, and investing. Staff positions strengthen the line positions and are by no means inferior or lower-paid. Having people in staff positions is like having well-paid consultants on the organization's payroll.

▾ CONSIDER USING TM 62
Organization Types (Figure 8.4 on text page 240)

FIGURE 8.4

····

ORGANIZATION TYPES

Each form of organization has its own advantages and disadvantages.

··· MATRIX ORGANIZATIONS ···

Both line and line-and-staff organization structures suffer from a certain inflexibility. Both allow for established lines of authority and communication, and both work well in organizations with a relatively unchanging environment and slow product development, such as firms selling consumer products like

	Advantages	**Disadvantages**
Line	Clearly defined responsibility and authority	Too inflexible
	Easy to understand	Few specialists to advise
	One supervisor for each group of employees	Long lines of communication
		Unable to handle complex questions quickly
		Tons of paperwork
Line-and-staff	Expert advice from staff to line personnel	Potential overstaffing
	Establishes lines of authority	Potential overanalyzing
	Encourages cooperation and better communication at all levels	Lines of communication can be blurred
		Staff frustrations because of lack of authority
Matrix	Flexible	Costly and complex
	Encourages cooperation among departments	Can confuse employees
	Can produce creative solutions to problems	Requires good interpersonal skills and cooperative managers and employees
	Allows organization to take on new projects without adding to the organization structure	Difficult to evaluate employees and to set up reward systems
Cross-functional, self-managed teams	Greatly increases interdepartmental coordination and cooperation	Some confusion over responsibility and authority
	Quicker response to customers and market conditions	Perceived loss of control by management
	Increased employee motivation and morale	Difficult to evaluate employees and set up reward systems
		Requires self-motivated, highly trained workers

In high-tech industries, technology and competition changes so rapidly that often traditional forms of organization simply won't work. They are being replaced with project management teams and other arrangements that bring together employees from many different areas of the firm. What do you see as the benefits and drawbacks of constant change for employees in high-tech industries?

toasters and refrigerators. In such firms, clear lines of authority and relatively fixed organization structures are assets that ensure efficient operations.

Today's economic scene, however, is dominated by high-growth industries (e.g., robotics, biotechnology, and aerospace) unlike anything seen in the past. In such industries, competition is stiff and the life cycle of new ideas is short. Emphasis is on new-product development, creativity, special projects, rapid communication, and interdepartmental teamwork. The economic, technological, and competitive environments are rapidly changing.

From those changes grew the popularity of the matrix organization. In a **matrix organization**, specialists from different parts of the organization are brought together to work on specific projects, while still remaining part of a line-and-staff structure. (See Figure 8.5 for a diagram of a matrix organization.) In other words, a project manager can borrow people from different departments to help design and market new product ideas.

Matrix organization structures were first developed in the aerospace industry at firms such as Boeing and Lockheed. The structure is now used in banking, management consulting firms, accounting firms, ad agencies, and school systems. Although it works well in some organizations, the matrix style doesn't work in others. Advantages of a matrix organization structure include the following:

- It gives flexibility to managers in assigning people to projects.
- It encourages interorganizational cooperation and teamwork.
- It can result in creative solutions to problems such as those associated with new-product development.
- It provides for more efficient use of organizational resources.

As for disadvantages,

- It's costly and complex.
- It can cause confusion among employees as to where their loyalty belongs—to the project manager or to their functional unit.
- It requires good interpersonal skills and cooperative employees and managers.

matrix organization
Organization in which specialists from different parts of the organization are brought together to work on specific projects but still remain part of a traditional line-and-staff structure.

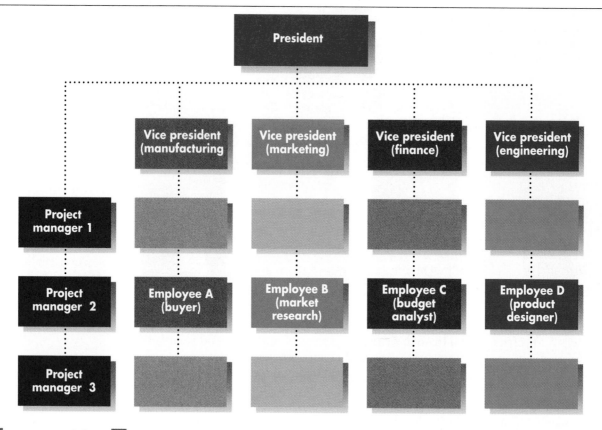

FIGURE 8.5

· · · ·

**A MATRIX
ORGANIZATION**

In a matrix organization, project managers are in charge of teams made up of members of several departments. In this case, project manager 2 supervises employees A, B, C, and D. These employees are accountable not only to project manager 2, but also to the head of their individual departments. For example, employee B, a market researcher, reports to project manager 2 *and* to the vice president of marketing.

Λ **CONSIDER USING TM 63**
A Matrix Organization (Figure 8.5 on text page 242)

cross-functional teams
Groups of employees from different departments who work together on a semipermanent basis.

If it seems to you that matrix organizations violate some traditional managerial principles, you're right. Normally a person can't work effectively for two bosses. (Who has the real authority? Which directive has the first priority: the one from the project manager or the one from the employee's immediate supervisor?) In reality, however, the system functions more effectively than you might imagine. To develop a new product, a project manager may be given temporary authority to "borrow" line personnel from engineering, production, marketing, and other line functions. Together, they work to complete the project and then return to their regular positions. Thus, no one really reports to more than one manager at a time.

The effectiveness of matrix organizations in high-tech firms has led to the adoption of similar concepts in many firms, including such low-tech firms as Rubbermaid. Rubbermaid now turns out an average of one new product every day using the team concept from matrix management.

· · · · ▬▬▬ · · · ·

CROSS-FUNCTIONAL, SELF-MANAGED TEAMS

The matrix style of organization inspired the use of cross-functional teams. **Cross-functional teams** are groups of employees from different departments who work together on a semipermanent basis (as opposed to the temporary teams established in matrix-style organizations). Often the teams are empowered to make decisions on their own without having to seek the approval of management. That's why the teams are called self-managed.[6] The barriers between design, engineering, marketing, distribution, and other functions fall as interdepartmental teams are created.

Mercantile Stores has gone to cross-functional teams at its headquarters. People at Mercantile headquarters no longer work independently but instead work concurrently with others. The whole office design was changed so that everyone would have easy access to everyone else.

Technology is increasing the trend toward cross-functional teams. As their computers are linked to show the same material at the same time, employees from different functions in different buildings (sometimes in different countries) can now work simultaneously on the same project.

◄ CONSIDER USING SUPPLEMEN-
TAL CASE 8-2
Creating Cross-Functional Teams
(SCANS)

◄ CONSIDER USING OT ACETATE
8-6
Tips for Team Leaders

••• LIMITATIONS OF CROSS-FUNCTIONAL TEAMS •••

Setting up cross-functional teams isn't easy. Managers of functional areas will often resist the move toward teams. Furthermore, team members are often unsure of what their duties are, how they'll be compensated, and who's responsible if mistakes are made. Working on a team takes different skills from working alone. Therefore, additional training is needed to prepare employees for teamwork.[7] The change to such teams is often so disruptive that a company may falter for years while the changes are being made. That has been the case at IBM, for example.

The most common problem with teams is that companies rush out and form the wrong kind of team for the wrong kind of job. Figure 8.6 illustrates five different types of teams. Another problem is that teams can be overused. Cross-functional teams aren't the answer to every management difficulty. Some problems can be solved faster by a single person. For example, making creative people sit in a team meeting and wait to reach a consensus can stifle creativity.

◄ CONSIDER USING OT ACETATE
8-7 AND OT ACETATE 8-8
Ways to Destroy Team Efforts

••• CROSS-FUNCTIONAL TEAMS LEAD TO NETWORKING •••

Cross-functional teams work best when the voice of the customer is brought into organizations. That's why it's a good idea to include customers on cross-functional product development teams. To ensure that suppliers and distributors are part of the process, they should be included on the team as well. Now you have cross-functional teams that go beyond organizational boundaries.

Some firms' suppliers and distributors are in other countries. Thus, cross-functional teams may share market information across national boundaries. The government may encourage the networking of teams, and government coordinators may assist such projects. In that case, cross-functional teams break the barriers between government and business.

Whether it involves customers, suppliers and distributors, or the government, **networking** is using communications technology and other means to link organizations and allow them to work together on common objectives.

◄ CONSIDER USING LECTURE
ENHANCER 8-12
Cross-Functional Teams for Small
Companies

◄ CONSIDER USING LECTURE
ENHANCER 8-13
Self-Organizing: Another Approach to
Structure

networking
Using communications technology and other means to link organizations and allow them to work together on common objectives.

••• EXTRANETS LINK COMPANY INTRANETS •••

The latest trend is to link firms on the extranet. An **extranet** is an extension of the Internet that connects suppliers, customers, and other organizations via secure Web sites. It is made up of linked intranets. An **intranet** is a set of communication links within companies that travel over the Internet.[8] Service organizations like Wells Fargo Bank and manufacturing firms like Silicon Graphics both use intranets. Although intranets are used mostly at larger firms, smaller firms are using them as well.[9] The idea is to link everyone in the firm electronically so they can communicate freely and work together on projects. For example, workers at Hallmark Cards once pasted creative ideas on a bulletin board

extranet
An extended Internet that connects suppliers, customers, and other organizations via secure Web sites.

intranet
A set of communication links within companies; the links travel over the Internet.

FIGURE **8.6**

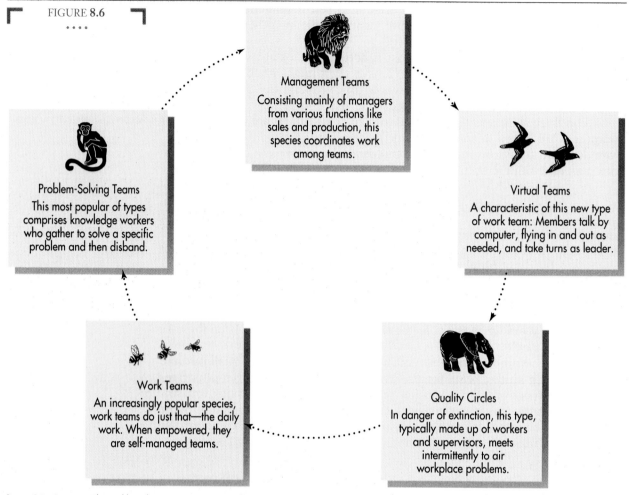

Source: Brian Dumaine, "The Trouble With Teams," *Fortune.* September 5, 1994, pp. 86–92.

▲ **CONSIDER USING TM 64**
Different Types of Teams (Figure 8.6 on text page 244)

for others to comment on. Because of limited space on the board, old cards were simply not available for easy comparison. Today, old and new cards are available on the intranet, where comments can be made and cards can be adapted by anyone. Any information a Hallmark employee wants others in the firm to see can be placed on the intranet.[10] Such information can also be made available to employees at suppliers and dealers if they are part of a linked intranet system (an extranet).

Progress Check

- Can you cite the advantages and disadvantages of line, line-and-staff, matrix, and cross-functional organizational forms?
- Why do cross-functional teams often lead to networking?
- What are extranets and intranets?

➤ **LEARNING GOAL 5.** Explain the benefits of turning organizations upside down and inside out.

➤ **CONSIDER USING SUPPLEMENTAL CASE 8-3**
Empowering Employees at Frito-Lay (**SCANS**)

···· ▬▬▬ ····

THE RESTRUCTURING PROCESS AND TOTAL QUALITY

It's not easy to move from an organization dominated by managers to one that relies heavily on self-managed teams. How you restructure an organization depends on the status of the present system. If the system already has a customer focus but isn't working well, a total quality management approach may work.

Total quality management (TQM) is the practice of striving for customer satisfaction by ensuring quality from all departments in an organization.[11] Total quality management calls for continuous improvement of present processes. Processes are sets of activities strung together for a reason, such as the process for handling a customer's order. **Continuous improvement** means constantly improving the way the organization does things so that customer needs can be better satisfied.[12]

It's possible, in an organization with few layers of management and a customer focus, that new computer software and employee training could lead to a team-oriented approach with few problems. In bureaucratic organizations with many layers of management, however, TQM is not suitable. Continuous improvement doesn't work when the whole process is being done incorrectly. When an organization needs dramatic changes, only reengineering will do. **Reengineering** is the fundamental rethinking and radical redesign of organizational processes to achieve dramatic improvements in critical measures of performance. Note the words *radical redesign* and *dramatic improvements*.[13]

At IBM credit corporation, for example, the process for handling a customer's request for credit once went through a five-step process that took an average of six days. By completely reengineering the customer-request process, IBM credit cut its processing time from six days to four hours! In reengineering, narrow, task-oriented jobs become multidimensional. Employees who once did as they were told now make decisions on their own. Functional departments lose their reason for being. Managers stop acting like supervisors and instead behave like coaches. Workers focus more on the customers' needs and less on their bosses' needs. Attitudes and values change in response to new incentives. Practically every aspect of the organization is transformed, often beyond recognition. Because of the complexity of the process, many reengineering efforts fail.

total quality management (TQM)
The practice of striving for customer satisfaction by ensuring quality from all departments in an organization.

continuous improvement
Constantly improving the way the organization does things so that customer needs can be better satisfied.

reengineering
The fundamental rethinking and radical redesign of organizational processes to achieve dramatic improvements in critical measures of performance.

Critical Thinking

Given the dramatic changes that occur when companies adopt cross-functional, self-managed teams, what would prevent the majority of companies from adopting such an organization structure? Given the flexibility and high education requirements of empowered employees, what changes must occur in U.S. schools to prepare students for such jobs?

··· TURNING THE ORGANIZATION UPSIDE DOWN ··· TO EMPOWER EMPLOYEES

Many firms are discovering that the key to long-term success in a competitive market is to empower ⇒ P. 207 ⇐ front-line people (often in teams) to respond quickly to customer wants and needs. That means major restructuring of the firm to make front-line workers the most important people in the firm. For example, doctors have long been treated as the most important people in hospitals, pilots are the focus of airlines, and professors are the central focus of universities, whereas front-desk people in hotels, clerks in department stores, and tellers in banks haven't been considered key personnel. Instead, managers were considered the key people, and they were responsible for "managing" the front-line people. The organization chart in a typical firm looked something like the pyramid in Figure 8.7.

The most advanced service organizations have turned the traditional organization structure upside down. An **inverted organization** has contact people at the top and the chief executive officer at the bottom. There are few layers of management, and the manager's job is to assist and support front-line people, not boss them around. Figure 8.8 shows the inverted organization structure.

inverted organization
An organization that has contact people at the top and the chief executive officer at the bottom of the organization chart.

FIGURE 8.7

••••

TRADITIONAL
ORGANIZATION CHART

▲ CONSIDER USING TM 65
Traditional Organizational Chart (Figure
8.7 on text page 246)

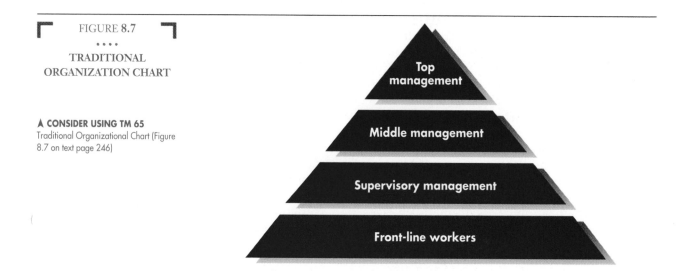

➤ CONSIDER USING OT ACETATE
8-9
The Four "R's" of Organizational
Transformation

➤ CONSIDER USING OT ACETATE
8-10
The Trend Toward Outsourcing

A good example of an inverted organization is NovaCare, a provider of rehabilitation care. At its top are some 5,000 physical, occupational, and speech therapists. The rest of the organization is structured to serve those therapists. Managers consider the therapists to be their bosses, and the manager's job is to support the therapists by arranging contacts with nursing homes, handling accounting and credit activities, and providing training.[14]

Companies based on this organization structure support front-line personnel with internal and external databanks, advanced communication systems, and professional assistance. Naturally, this means that front-line people have to be better educated, better trained, and better paid than in the past. It takes a lot of trust for top managers to implement such a system—but when they do, the payoff in customer satisfaction and in profits is often well worth the effort. In the past, managers controlled information, and that gave them power. In more progressive organizations, everyone shares information and that gives everyone power.

••• TURNING THE ORGANIZATION •••
INSIDE OUT (OUTSOURCING)

**competitive
benchmarking**
Rating an organization's practices,
processes, and products against the
world's best.

In the past, organizations have tried to do everything themselves. That is, each organization had a separate department for accounting, finance, marketing, production, and so on. Today's organizations are turning inside out. Total quality management demands that organizations benchmark each function against

FIGURE 8.8

••••

AN INVERTED
ORGANIZATION
STRUCTURE

➤ CONSIDER USING TM 66
An Inverted Organization Structure
(Figure 8.8 on text page 246)

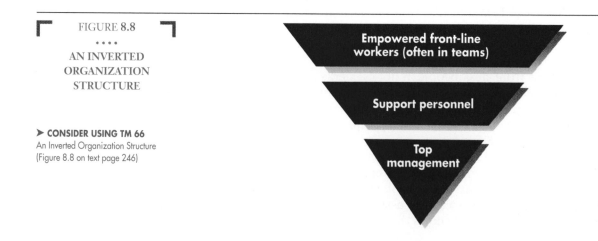

Making Ethical Decisions

http://www.benchnet.com

When Does Benchmarking Become Unethical?

There is nothing illegal or unethical about researching your competitors and other companies to learn their best practices and then using those best practices in your own firm. In fact, that is one of the key strategies for staying competitive in today's rapidly changing marketplace. But when does such research become unethical? For example, is it ethical to hire away a company's best researchers to get the secrets they have learned on the job? Most companies would say no. Is it ethical to place an em-

ployee in another firm so he or she can learn as much as possible about that firm's operations? Again, most firms would say no.

So how far can you go in spying on and learning about another organization? Your firm asks you to take a leave of absence and go to work for a competitor to find out as many secrets as you can. If you take the assignment, you will get a good promotion when you return. What will you do? What might the consequences be?

▲ SCANS

the best in the world. **Competitive benchmarking** is rating an organization's practices, processes, and products against the world's best.[15] If the organization can't do as well as the best, it will try to outsource the function to an organization that is the best. **Outsourcing** is assigning various functions, such as accounting and legal work, to outside organizations.[16] Some functions, such as information management and marketing, may be too important to assign to outside firms. In that case, the organization should benchmark on the best firms and reengineer their departments to try to be equally good. It is important to monitor benchmarking efforts so that they don't overreach the bounds of ethical behavior. The box called Making Ethical Decisions explores that issue.

When a firm has completed its outsourcing process, the remaining functions are the firm's core competencies. **Core competencies** are those functions that the organization can do as well as or better than any other organization in the world.[17] Gallo Winery, for example, doesn't grow most of its own grapes. Instead, it sticks to what it does best: producing and marketing (which includes distributing) wine products. Gallo spends more money on market research than its primary competitors do and thus knows more about the market for wines. It also has the most up-to-date information and distribution system. Gallo isn't as skilled in retailing and promotion, so it outsources those functions. The box called From the Pages of *Business Week* on page 249 discusses how small and large businesses combine globally through outsourcing to become world-class competitors.

••• CREATING INTERNAL CUSTOMERS •••

Some departments in organizations are reluctant to join the total quality revolution. They would rather function the old way, in which each department had its own agenda and method of operating. Executives who believe in total quality management have a way of transforming such departments. They create customers within the firm (internal customers), although such programs are not always popular.[18] To improve such internal services, management sets up buy-sell relationships among teams and business units in the organization.

outsourcing
Assigning various functions, such as accounting and legal work, to outside organizations.

core competencies
Those functions that the organization can do as well or better than any other organization in the world.

Working in an inverted organization such as Avis is much different from working in a firm with a more traditional structure. As a frontline person, you are given more responsibility and are expected to make more decisions.

DuPont has a program to outsource business to minority firms called TEMPO, which stands for To Encourage Minority Purchasing Opportunities. Over the last four years, DuPont has purchased $1.6 billion in goods and services from such firms. Can you see how outsourcing helps build communities?

If the team isn't happy with the products and services provided by an internal unit (such as a marketing research report), the team can purchase those services from outside vendors. This creates a competitive situation between, for example, the internal accounting department and outside public accounting firms. This competition forces internal units to become more internally customer-oriented or lose their business to outsiders.[19] For service businesses, such as health care firms, serving internal customers is critical because the actual caregivers need effective support to successfully treat their patients. For example, nurses require precise information from physicians regarding the types, timing, and proper doses of medicines they deliver.

From the Pages of BusinessWeek

http://www.nations bank.com/

Strategic Outsourcing

Recently, a story in *Business Week* magazine said, "Strategic outsourcing is emerging as one of the fastest-growing management tools of the decade." Larger companies are outsourcing some functions to smaller, more specialized companies that can perform those functions faster and more efficiently. That enables companies to compete globally and stay current with the latest changes in markets and technology. Manufacturing and service organizations are getting involved, as are for-profit and nonprofit organizations.

For example, NationsBank outsourced its entire mail operations to Pitney Bowles Management Services. Ralcorp, a major food manufacturer, outsourced the development of its information technology to a partnership consortium led by Cap Gemini. Price Waterhouse has established Centres of Excellence in the United States, Europe, Latin America, and Asia to meet the growing demand for business process outsourcing services. The U.S. Marine Corps turned to Learning International to learn the best practices for recruiting. In short, businesses and government agencies small and large are combining their expertise to provide the best products and services possible to markets around the world.

Source: Emily Leinfuss for the Outsourcing Institute in *Business Week*, December 15, 1997, pp. 67ff.

ESTABLISHING A SERVICE-ORIENTED CULTURE

Figure 8.9 summarizes the changes that occur as an organization moves from being bureaucratic to being customer-oriented. Any organizational change is bound to cause some stress and resistance among members of the firm. Therefore, any change should be accompanied by the establishment of an organizational culture that facilitates such change. **Organizational culture** may be defined as widely shared values within an organization that provide

◄ **LEARNING GOAL 6.**
Give examples to show how organizational culture and the informal organization can hinder or assist organizational change.

organizational culture
Widely shared values within an organization that provide coherence and cooperation to achieve common goals.

BUREAUCRATIC	CUSTOMER-FOCUSED
Coordination from the top	Self-management
Top-down chain of command	Bottom-up power relationships
Many rules and regulations	Employees free to make decisions
Departmentalization by function	Cross-functional teams
Specialization	Integration and cooperation
One firm does it all	Outsourcing
Management controls information	Information goes to all
Largely domestic orientation	Global orientation
Focus on external customers	Focus on both internal and external customers

FIGURE 8.9
. . . .
BUREAUCRATIC VERSUS CUSTOMER-FOCUSED ORGANIZATIONAL STRUCTURES

◄ **CONSIDER USING TM 67**
Bureaucratic Versus Customer-Focused Organization Structure (Figure 8.9 on text page 249)

Spotlight on Small Business

http://www.careerlink.org/emp/mut/corp.htm

Fun Night at the Ice Cream Parlor

Amy's ice cream parlors in Austin and Houston, Texas, attract a lot of customers because of their offbeat corporate culture. On any given night, you might see the servers juggling with their serving spades, tossing scoops of ice cream to each other, or break-dancing on the freezer top. If there is a long line, they pass out samples or give a free cone to any customer who will sing, dance, recite a poem, or otherwise entertain those in line. Employees might be wearing pajamas (Sleep-over Night) or masks (Star Wars Night). Lighting may be provided by candles (Romance Night) or strobe lights (Disco Night). You get the idea. It's fun at Amy's—for the employees and for the customers. Corporate culture can go a long way toward making a small company a success or a failure. Ask Amy Miller.

Sources: John Case, "Corporate Culture," *Inc.*, November 1996, pp. 42–53. Kenneth Hein, "Funny Business," *Incentive*, April 1998, pp. 14–20.

> **CONSIDER USING LECTURE ENHANCER 8-14**
> Effects of Corporate Culture on Performance

coherence and cooperation to achieve common goals. Usually the culture of an organization is reflected in stories, traditions, and myths.

It's obvious from visiting any McDonald's restaurant that every effort has been made to maintain a culture that emphasizes "quality, service, cleanliness, and value." Each restaurant has the same feel, the same look, the same atmosphere. In short, each has a similar organizational culture.

An organizational culture can also be negative. Have you ever been in an organization where you feel that no one cares about service or quality? The clerks may seem uniformly glum, indifferent, and testy. The mood often seems to pervade the atmosphere so that patrons become moody and upset. It may be hard to believe that an organization can be run so badly and survive, especially a profit-making organization. Are there examples in your area?

The very best organizations have cultures that emphasize service to others, especially customers. The atmosphere is one of friendly, concerned, caring people who enjoy working together to provide a good product at a reasonable price. Those companies that have such cultures have less need for close supervision of employees, not to mention policy manuals; organization charts; and formal rules, procedures, and controls. Within that atmosphere, self-managed teams can develop and flourish. The key to productive culture is mutual trust. You get such trust by giving it. The very best companies stress high moral and ethical values such as honesty, reliability, fairness, environmental protection, and social involvement. The box called Spotlight on Small Business looks at how one small organization successfully implemented a customer-oriented culture.

Thus far, we've been talking as if organizational matters were mostly controllable by management. The fact is that the formal organization structure is just one element of the total organizational system. In the creation of organizational culture, the informal organization is of equal or greater importance. Let's explore this notion next.

> **CONSIDER USING LECTURE ENHANCER 8-15**
> The Informal Organization Is Very Important

formal organization
The structure that details lines of responsibility, authority, and position; the structure shown on organization charts.

informal organization
The system of relationships and lines of authority that develops spontaneously as employees meet and form power centers; the human side of the organization that does not appear on any organization chart.

••• THE INFORMAL ORGANIZATION •••
HELPS CREATE TEAMWORK

All organizations have two organizational systems. One is the **formal organization**, which is the structure that details lines of responsibility, authority, and position. It's the structure shown on organization charts. The other is the **informal**

organization, which is the system of relationships that develop spontaneously as employees meet and form power centers. It consists of the various cliques, relationships, and lines of authority that develop outside the formal organization. It's the human side of the organization that doesn't show on any organization chart.

No organization can operate effectively without both types of organization. The formal system is often too slow and bureaucratic to enable the organization to adapt quickly. However, the formal organization does provide helpful guidelines and lines of authority to follow in routine situations.

The informal organization is often too unstructured and emotional to allow careful, reasoned decision making on critical matters. It's extremely effective, however, in generating creative solutions to short-term problems and providing a feeling of camaraderie and teamwork among employees.

In any organization, it's wise to learn quickly who the important people are in the informal organization. Typically, there are formal rules and procedures to follow for getting certain supplies or equipment, but those procedures may take days. Who in the organization knows how to obtain supplies immediately without following the normal procedures? Which secretaries should you see if you want your work given first priority? These are the questions you need to answer in order to work effectively in many organizations.

The informal organization's nerve center is the grapevine (the system through which unofficial information flows between and among managers and employees). The key people in the grapevine usually have considerable influence in the organization.

In the old "us-versus-them" system of organizations, where managers and employees were often at odds, the informal system often hindered effective management. In the new, more open organizations, where managers and employees work together to set objectives and design procedures, the informal organization can be an invaluable managerial asset that often promotes harmony among workers and establishes the corporate culture. That's a major advantage, for example, of self-managed teams.

As effective as the informal organization may be in creating group cooperation, it can still be equally powerful in resisting management directives. Employees may form unions, go on strike together, and generally disrupt operations. Learning to create the right corporate culture and to work within the informal organization is a key to managerial success.[20]

◄ **CONSIDER USING OT ACETATE 8-11**
What Are the Effects of Downsizing?

◄ **CONSIDER USING OT ACETATE 8-12**
What Are the Effects of Downsizing?

◄ **CONSIDER USING OT ACETATE 8-13**
Examples of Informal Group Norms

The right corporate culture can make a company a fun place to work and shop. A good example is Amy's ice cream parlors. The employees may seem to be simply acting silly, but the corporate culture of "fun" leads to good publicity, friendly relations with the community, willing workers, and more (read profit). Have you ever experienced or are you aware of an organization where the corporate culture made everyone feel good about the company and the work experience?

Progress Check

- What's the difference between continuous improvement and reengineering?
- What does it mean to turn an organization chart upside down? Inside out?
- What's an internal customer?
- How important is the informal organization to the success of organizational change?

SUMMARY

· · · · ·

1. Describe the traditional hierarchical, bureaucratic organization and how it is being restructured.

1. Organizational design is the coordinating of workers so that they can best accomplish the firm's goals.
   - *What is the traditional organization like, and how is it being restructured?*
   The typical organization is hierarchical and bureaucratic. Restructuring means redesigning an organization so that it can more effectively and efficiently serve its customers. Often that means breaking down the barriers between functions. It may also mean giving more authority to lower-level employees and ending top-down management.

2. Explain the organizational theories of Fayol and Weber.

2. The 20th century saw the introduction of the concept of economy of scale. *Economy of scale* means that companies can produce goods more inexpensively if they can purchase raw materials in bulk; the average cost of each item goes down as production levels increase.
   - *What concepts did Fayol and Weber contribute?*
   Fayol introduced principles such as unity of command, hierarchy of authority, division of labor, subordination of individual interests to the general interest, authority, clear communication channels, order, and equity. Weber added principles of bureaucracy such as job descriptions, written rules and decision guidelines, consistent procedures, and staffing and promotions based on qualifications.

3. Discuss the various issues connected with organizational design.

3. Organizational issues that have led to design changes include (1) tall versus flat organization structures, (2) span of control, (3) departmentalization, and (4) centralization versus decentralization.
   - *What are the basics of each?*
   The problem with tall organizations is that they slow communications. The trend is to eliminate managers and flatten organizations. The span of control becomes larger as employees become self-directed. Departments are often being replaced or supplemented by matrix organizations and cross-functional teams. In matrix organizations, people can be borrowed from departments to be put on project teams. Cross-functional teams have been very effective in making organizations faster and more responsive to the market. They've also led to decentralization of authority.

4. Describe the differences between line, line-and-staff, matrix, and cross-functional organizations.

4. The four forms of organization explored in the text are (1) line organizations, (2) line-and-staff organizations, (3) matrix organizations, and (4) cross-functional, self-managed teams.
   - *What are the advantages of each?*
   A line organization has the advantages of having clearly defined responsibility and authority, being easy to understand, and providing one supervisor for each person. Most organizations have benefited from the expert advice of staff assistants in areas such as safety, quality control, computer technology, human resource management, and investing. Matrix organizations give flexibility to managers in assigning people to projects and

encourage interorganizational cooperation and teamwork. Cross-functional, self-managed teams are more permanent and have all the benefits of the matrix style.

5. Reengineering is the fundamental rethinking and radical redesign of organizational processes to improve critical measures of performance.

   - ***What are the benefits of turning organizations upside down and inside out?***

   By turning organizations upside down, more authority and responsibility are given front-line workers so they can better serve customers. Managers serve workers instead of the other way around. Outsourcing is assigning various functions, such as accounting and legal work, to outside organizations. By setting up competition between internal and external functions, a corporation can identify its core competencies.

   5. Explain the benefits of turning organizations upside down and inside out.

6. Organizational culture may be defined as widely shared values within an organization that provide coherence and cooperation to achieve common goals.

   - ***How can organizational culture and the informal organization hinder or assist organizational change?***

   The very best organizations have cultures that emphasize service to others, especially customers. The atmosphere is one of friendly, concerned, caring people who enjoy working together to provide a good product at a reasonable price. Companies with such cultures have less need for close supervision of employees; policy manuals; organization charts; and formal rules, procedures, and controls. This opens the way for self-managed teams.

   6. Give examples to show how organizational culture and the informal organization can hinder or assist organizational change.

KEY TERMS
· · · · · ·

bureaucracy 230
centralized
 authority 239
competitive
 benchmarking 246
continuous
 improvement 245
core competencies 247
cross-functional
 teams 242
decentralized
 authority 239

departmentalization
 236
extranet 243
formal organization 250
hierarchy 230
informal
 organization 250
intranet 243
inverted
 organization 245
line personnel 240
matrix
 organization 241

networking 243
organizational
 culture 249
organizational
 design 230
outsourcing 247
reengineering 245
restructuring 231
span of control 235
staff personnel 240
total quality
 management (TQM)
 245

DEVELOPING WORKPLACE SKILLS

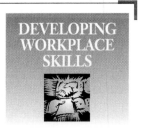

1. There is no way to better understand the effects of having many layers of management on communication accuracy than to play the game of Message Relay. Choose seven or more members of the class and have them leave the classroom. Then choose one person to read the following paragraph and another student to listen. Then call in one of the students from outside and have the "listener" tell him or her the paragraph aloud. Then bring in another student and have the new listener repeat the paragraph to him or her. And so on. Do not allow anyone in the class to offer corrections as each listener becomes the storyteller in turn. In this way, all the students can hear how the facts become distorted over time. The distortions and mistakes are often quite humorous, but they are not so funny in organizations such as Ford, which once had 22 layers of management.

Here's the paragraph:

Dealers in the Midwest region have received over 130 complaints about steering on the new Commander and Roadhandler models of our minivans. Apparently, the front suspension system is weak and the ball joints are wearing too fast. This causes slippage in the linkage and results in oversteering. Mr. Berenstein has been notified, but so far only 213 out of 4,300 dealers have received repair kits.

2. Write a two-page paper describing some informal organization with which you are familiar (at school, at work, etc.). What have you noticed about how those groups help or hinder progress in the organization?

3. Imagine you are working for Kitchen Magic, an appliance manufacturer that produces, among other things, dishwashers for the home. Imagine further that a competitor introduces a new dishwasher that uses sound waves to clean dishes. The result is a dishwasher that cleans even the worst burnt-on food and sterilizes the dishes and silverware as well. You need to develop a similar offering fast or lose the market. Write a memo to management outlining the problem and explaining your rationale for recommending use of a cross-functional team to respond quickly.

4. If you were free to start over, how would you organize your college or university? Would you have the same departments? Whom would you hire? Compose two lists, one explaining why the school should reorganize and the other why it might oppose restructuring. Discuss this issue with the class.

5. As discussed in this chapter, many of the work groups of the future, including management, will be cross-functional and self-managed. To practice working in such a group, break your class up into groups of five or so students. (Try to find students with different backgrounds and interests.) Each group must work together to prepare a report on the advantages and disadvantages of working in teams. Many of the problems and advantages should emerge in your group as you try to complete this assignment.

TAKING IT TO THE NET

Purpose

To evaluate George Ritzer's theories presented in his text *The McDonaldization of Society*.

Exercise

The McDonaldization of Society updates Max Weber's theories. Dr. George Ritzer extends Weber's ideas to the fast-food industry and today's society. The book discusses how our society has become rationalized to such a point that there are very few escapes. This home page outlines the theory of *McDonaldization* and lists sources that complement Ritzer's work (http://www.sociology.net/mcdonald/index.html).

1. What are the five dominant themes outlined in McDonaldization? (Hint: You'll need to dig deeper in the Web site to find reference to the fifth theme.)

2. Ritzer and other links offer examples that support his theories. Can you think of other such examples from your own experience?

3. Do you agree with Ritzer that McDonaldization will continue to dominate, or do you see other trends that may come to the fore? Explain.

Practicing Management Decisions

CASE

• • • • • •

IBM OUTSOURCES THE MANUFACTURING OF PCs

• • • • • •

Few companies are better known for their manufacturing expertise than IBM. Nonetheless, even IBM has to adapt to the dynamic marketplace of today. In the area of personal computers, for example, IBM was unable to match the prices or speed of delivery of mail-order firms such as Dell Computer. Dell built machines after receiving orders for them and then rushed the computers to customers. IBM, on the other hand, made machines ahead of time and hoped that the orders would match its inventory. If there was no match, IBM ended up with old computers that lost their value very quickly.

To compete against firms like Dell, IBM had to custom-make computers for its business customers, but IBM was not particularly suited to do such work. However, IBM did work with several distributors that were also having their problems. The distributors were trying to custom-make IBM machines but were forced to carry a heavy inventory of parts and materials to do so. Furthermore, distributors were tearing IBM computers apart and putting them back together with other computer companies' parts to produce custom-made computers for large customers like Georgia-Pacific and Dow Chemical.

IBM decided to allow its distributors to store parts and materials and then custom-make computers to customer demand, as Dell does. In other words, IBM outsourced about 60 percent of its commercial PC business. As a result, distributors such as Inacom Corporation are more profitable and IBM is able to offer custom-made PCs competitive in price with those of Dell and other direct-mail companies.

To make delivery faster, some direct-mail companies have outsourced their delivery systems to experts in the field. Thus, companies known for their production expertise are outsourcing some production and companies known for their fast delivery don't do their own delivery. What next? Companies are outsourcing their information system function, their accounting function, their human resource function, and more. Furthermore, they are outsourcing these functions to companies all over the world. The world has become a network of linked organizations that are specialists in relatively narrow fields. A product may be designed by one company in Italy, produced by another company in China, distributed by a company from the United States, and marketed by a company from England. The products may be available in stores in almost every country.

Discussion Questions

1. What technological changes in the world have forced companies to outsource various functions, and what technological innovations allow them to do so with little inconvenience?
2. What effects will outsourcing have on trade relationships among countries?
3. Would it be true to describe the business environment today as a global environment? What words would you use to describe the links among companies in many different countries?
4. How much influence will the Internet have on world trade and outsourcing among countries? What does the Internet provide that wasn't available before?

Sources: John B. Hayes, "Watch Out, Dell," *Forbes*, March 24, 1997, p. 84; and "Leveraging the Outsourcing Advantage," advertisement in *Forbes*, October 21, 1996, pp. 215–49.

VIDEO CASE

• • • • •

BIG APPLE BAGELS AND THE SAINT LOUIS BREAD COMPANY

In the past many businesses were organized according to concepts and structures learned from the military and the church. There were clear lines of authority and responsibility, and people at the top made virtually all decisions. To maintain control over employees, certain bureaucratic rules and regulations were passed that didn't allow employees much flexibility in decision making or in responding to customer wants and needs.

Today's organizations, in order to remain competitive, are being restructured to be more responsive to customers. This means that many layers of management, especially those in the middle, are being eliminated (middle managers are now equated with bureaucracy). It also means that front-line workers are being empowered and challenged to respond to customer wants and needs quickly. The literature is full of stories about GM, Motorola, and other big companies and their reengineering processes. However, stories about smaller firms are less common.

Big Apple Bagels and the Saint Louis Bread Company are two examples of smaller organizations that have been restructured to meet the needs of today's marketplace. As Big Apple Bagels grew, it tried to maintain its open-door policy so that everyone could have access to top management. But the larger a firm becomes, the more difficult this is. As the firm grew larger, it decentralized authority, allowing its stores to innovate by creating their own variety of bagels.

The Saint Louis Bread Company has had a similar experience. The process of radically changing organizational structure is called reengineering. At the Saint Louis Bread Company, that process called for the introduction of high technology for production processes and for gathering information on the latest advances and product features in cash registers.

The Saint Louis Bread Company is now striving to become boundaryless. This means that the divisions or boundaries between jobs and functions are being eliminated through the implementation of cross-functional self-managed teams. The focus is on the customer, and front-line workers are now empowered to be responsive to customers and give them what they want without resorting to the slow process of involving management.

Discussion Questions

1. Which of Fayol's principles of organization still appear to be used at Big Apple Bagels and the Saint Louis Bread Company, and which do not? Why do you suppose this has happened?
2. Weber was the founder of concepts such as written rules, job descriptions, and consistent procedures. Why are these principles no longer as effective as they once were in meeting the needs of customers?
3. To what extent has information technology changed the way organizations can be and are structured?

Using the Latest Technology to Produce World-Class Products and Services

Chapter

9

LEARNING GOALS

After you have read and studied this chapter, you should be able to

1. Describe the production process and explain the importance of productivity.

2. Explain the importance of site selection in keeping down costs and identify the criteria used to evaluate different sites.

3. Classify the various production processes and tell how materials requirement planning links organizations in performing those processes.

4. Describe manufacturing techniques such as just-in-time inventory control, flexible manufacturing, lean manufacturing, and competing in time.

5. Show how CAD/CAM improves the production process.

6. Illustrate the use of PERT, Gantt charts, and TQM in production planning.

7. Explain the importance of productivity in the service sector.

Tom Smith is the owner of Tom Smith Industries (TSI), a company that molds thermoplastic material in Englewood, Ohio. As one of the small manufacturers that is creating most of the new jobs in the manufacturing sector, TSI is one of those companies that will make or break the United States in the 21st century.

What makes such companies competitive is their use of the latest in manufacturing technology. Smith's first use of technology was to upgrade the company's internal management system. At the time, facility-wide tasks like job scheduling were handled manually, by moving cards around on a master board. The first computer program didn't work very well, and Smith went to an IBM AS/400 computer to run manufacturing resource planning (MRP) software. Using this computer and some new software, company personnel from billing, production scheduling, shipping, and other departments can now refer to the same order information in the same database. Thus, administrative chores are much more efficient.

Because Smith is interested in customer service, TSI is connected to business customers by electronic data interchange (EDI). This allows for an on-line exchange of information with the company's customers about orders, shipping, billing, and other issues. Once orders are received, the IBM computer generates work orders for the manufacturing department based on the promised shipping date. The computer program puts many processes in motion at once: raw-materials purchasing, press scheduling (making

the products), and billing. The computer eliminates much human error and sends out warnings if the company falls behind in its production processes.

TSI now uses a computer-numeric-controlled (CNC) machine tool to cut each mold component according to a computer program. The computer programs are based on computer-aided manufacturing (CAM) software.

What makes TSI competitive today, however, is the use of computer-aided design (CAD) to create plastic parts that compete with more traditional metal parts. Engineers share two CAD stations that are linked so that engineers can job-share.

Using the latest in technology, TSI has been able to grow and prosper. The facility it built two years ago now runs three shifts five days a week, and Smith is looking to double his capacity.

The message of this Profile is that even small firms are using the latest in computer equipment to stay competitive in a global marketplace. That means that tomorrow's college graduates must be familiar with computers and be highly adaptable to a rapidly changing technological environment. One purpose of this chapter is to familiarize you with the language of manufacturing and the latest techniques for staying ahead of competition.

 PROFILE

Tom Smith of Tom Smith Industries

Sources: Jeffrey Zygmont, "When Slow and Steady Wins the Race," *Inc. Technology*, 1996, no. 4, pp. 72–76; and Walter Pettigrew, "Rebuild, Retrofit, Remanufacture," *Quality Digest*, January 1998, pp. 44–47.

AMERICA'S MANUFACTURING BASE

The heart of the free enterprise system in the United States has always been its manufacturers. Names such as General Motors, USX (formerly U.S. Steel), Westinghouse, and Navistar (formerly International Harvester) have represented the finest in production technology since the turn of the century. But, as we enter into a new century, we're in a new era in the industrial revolution. Today manufacturing generates less than one-fourth of the U.S. gross domestic

◄ CONSIDER USING TM 68
Chapter Outline

◄ LEARNING GOAL 1. Describe the production process and explain the importance of productivity.

What will happen when the majority of production jobs are performed by machines and robots such as this one at Airbus Industries in Toulouse, France? Are there enough service sector jobs to absorb the men and women whose jobs will be replaced? Would it be best if all of us worked fewer hours so that everyone could have a job? These are some of the questions that the increased use of technology requires us to address.

➤ **CONSIDER USING LECTURE ENHANCER 9-1**
America's New Manufacturing Base

➤ **CONSIDER USING LECTURE ENHANCER 9-2**
The First Copying Machine

➤ **CONSIDER USING OT ACETATE 9-1**
The Production and Operations Process

product (the total output of goods and services). Goods-producing activities (e.g., manufacturing and construction) employed only 19.1 percent of the labor force in the 1990s, down from 26.1 percent in 1972.[1]

Bethlehem Steel and other traditional manufacturing leaders declined through much of the past 20 years. Foreign manufacturers captured huge chunks of the market for basic products such as steel, cement, machinery, and farm equipment using the latest in production techniques. That competition forced U.S. companies to greatly alter their production techniques and managerial styles. You read about the managerial changes in Chapter 8. In this chapter, we'll explore the changes that have occurred in production. Many U.S. firms are now as good or better than competitors anywhere in the world. What have American manufacturers done to regain a competitive edge? They've implemented all of the following:

1. A customer focus.
2. Cost savings through site selection.
3. A faster response to the market through flexible manufacturing.
4. More savings on the plant floor through lean manufacturing.
5. Computer-aided manufacturing and other modern practices.
6. Total quality management.
7. Better control procedures.

We'll discuss these developments in detail in this chapter. You'll see that production and operations management have become challenging and vital elements of American business. The rebuilding of America's manufacturing base will likely remain a major business issue in the near future. There will be debates about the merits of moving production facilities to foreign countries. Serious questions will be raised about replacing workers with robots and other machinery. Major political decisions will be made regarding protection of American manufacturers through quotas and other restrictions on free trade. Regardless of how these issues are decided, however, tomorrow's college graduates will face tremendous challenges (and career opportunities) in redesigning and rebuilding America's manufacturing base.

FIGURE **9.1**
• • • •
THE PRODUCTION
PROCESS
The production process
consists of taking the
factors of production
(land, etc.) and using
those inputs to produce
goods, services, and
ideas. Planning, routing,
scheduling, and the
other activities are the
means to accomplish the
objective—output.

••• THE BASICS OF PRODUCTION MANAGEMENT •••

One purpose of this chapter is to introduce the basic concepts and issues in production management. **Production and operations management** includes all the activities managers do to create goods and services. In today's firms, most of what gets done actually falls into the service category. For example, a very small percentage of the people working for manufacturers are actually on the assembly line. The rest do service work in areas such as accounting, finance, law, and so on. Therefore, the concepts that apply to service organizations, such as a consumer orientation, apply generally to manufacturing organizations as well.

New production techniques make it possible to custom-make products for individual industrial buyers.[2] The job then becomes one of getting closer to customers to find out what their product needs are. In other words, we will need effective marketing combined with effective production and management to keep U.S. producers number one in the world.

The United States remains a major industrial country and is likely to become even stronger. This means tremendous opportunities for careers in production and operations management. Today there are relatively few college students majoring in production and operations management, inventory management, and other careers involving manufacturing and mining. That means more opportunities for those student entrepreneurs ➡ P. 4 ⬅ who can see the future trends and have the skills to own or work in tomorrow's highly automated, efficient factories and mines. To prepare for a career in production and operations management, you must learn the basics of production. That's the subject of an entire course or courses, but in this chapter we'll simply present some of the fundamentals you should know.

••• PRODUCTION AND PRODUCTIVITY •••

Common sense and some experience have already taught you much of what you need to know about production and operations management. You know what it takes to write a term paper or prepare a dinner. You need a place to work, you need money to buy the materials, and you need to be organized to get the task done. The same is true of production. It uses basic inputs to produce outputs (see Figure 9.1). **Production** is the creation of finished goods and services using the factors of production (inputs): land, labor, capital, entrepreneurship, and knowledge ➡ P. 6 ⬅. Production creates what is known as form utility (*utility* means value added). **Form utility** is the value added by the creation of finished goods and services using raw materials, components, and other inputs.

Production is a broad term that describes the creative process in all industries that produce goods and services. These industries include mining, lumbering, manufacturing, education, and health care. Manufacturing is one part

production and operations management
The set of activities managers do to create goods and services.

⬆ CONSIDER USING TM 69
The Production Process

◀ CONSIDER USING LECTURE ENHANCER 9-3
Harley-Davidson Goes with its Strengths

production
The creation of finished goods and services using the factors of production: land, labor, capital, entrepreneurship, and knowledge.

form utility
The value added by the creation of finished goods and services using raw materials, components, and other inputs.

➤ CONSIDER USING LECTURE
ENHANCER 9-4
Gold from Old Computers

of production. It means making goods by hand or with machinery as opposed to extracting things from the earth (mining and fishing) or producing services.

To be competitive, manufacturers must keep the costs of inputs down. That is, the costs of workers, machinery, and so on must be kept as low as possible. Similarly, the amount of output must be relatively high. *Productivity* is the term used to describe output per unit of input ➤ P. 16 ◀. *Output* could mean goods like cars and furniture, or services such as education and health care. In either case, the question is the same: How does a producer keep costs low and still produce more (that is, increase productivity)? This question will dominate thinking in the manufacturing and service sectors for years to come.

···· ▬▬ ····

KEEPING COSTS LOW: SITE SELECTION

➤ LEARNING GOAL 2. Explain the
importance of site selection in keeping
down costs and identify the criteria used
to evaluate different sites.

➤ CONSIDER USING OT ACETATE
9-3
Leading U.S. Manufacturing States

A major issue of the recent past has been the shift of manufacturing and service organizations from one city or state to another in the United States or to foreign sites.[3] Such shifts sometimes result in pockets of unemployment in some parts of the country and the world and lead to tremendous economic growth in others.

Why would entrepreneurs spend millions of dollars to move their facilities from one location to another? One major reason some businesses move is the availability of cheap labor or the right kind of skilled labor. Even though labor cost is becoming a smaller percentage of total cost in some highly automated industries, cheap labor remains a key reason many less technologically advanced producers move their plants. For example, cheap labor is one reason why some firms are moving to Malaysia, Mexico, and other countries with low wage rates. Some of these firms have been charged with exploiting children and using unsafe labor practices in the countries where they have set up factories. To maintain high ethical and moral standards, it is important for firms to maintain the same quality standards and fair labor practices wherever they produce goods or services. The issue of using foreign labor to produce goods is likely to last well into the next century. The box called Legal Briefcase discusses in detail a company that has become involved in such issues.

Within the United States, too, moving firms to find inexpensive labor has been an issue for years. The southern part of the United States has attracted many manufacturers because the region has mostly nonunion labor. In general, such workers demand lower wages and fewer fringe benefits. By moving south, U.S. businesses can compete more effectively with those foreign producers that have much lower labor costs.

Businesses are often called greedy and uncaring when they move production facilities. But the very survival of U.S. manufacturing depends on its ability to remain competitive, and that means either cheaper inputs or increased outputs from present inputs (increased productivity).

Cheaper natural resources are another major reason for moving production facilities. Companies usually need water, electricity, wood, coal, and other basic resources. By moving to areas where such resources are cheap and plentiful, firms can significantly lower costs—not only the cost of buying such resources but the cost of shipping as well. Water shortages in the West, for example, often discourage manufacturing plants from locating there.

Reducing time-to-market is another decision-making factor.[4] As manufacturers attempt to compete globally, they need sites that allow products to move through the system quickly, at the lowest costs, so that they can be delivered rapidly to customers. Information technology (IT) is so important to quick response that many firms are seeking countries with the most advanced information systems.

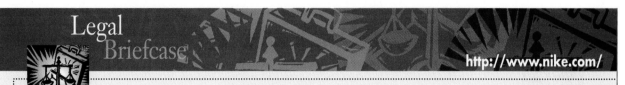

Legal Briefcase

http://www.nike.com/

Nike's Indonesian Factory

In their search for cheap labor, many companies have taken their production facilities to other countries or have outsourced production to foreign firms. One well-known company that does this is Nike. Some 1.2 million pairs of Nike shoes are made at the Nikomas Gemilang factory in Serang, outside of Jakarta, Indonesia. Working conditions inside the plant have been much discussed in the U.S. media, including in the satirical comic strip Doonesbury. It is true that overtime is mandatory there and that conditions are hard. Some workers faint from exhaustion. Independent unions are outlawed.

Nike makes sure that the workers receive minimum wage (according to Indonesian standards), and many workers get medical care and free meals. Others get transportation fees. Since Nike now operates in a world economy, should there be global laws protecting workers? U.S. workers are protected by the Occupational Safety and Health Act of 1970. Note that this is a relatively recent law. How quickly should less-developed countries be expected to pass similar laws? What obligation does Nike have to see that all of its workers, anyplace in the world, are treated fairly and decently?

··· LOCATING CLOSE TO MARKETS TO ···
SERVE CUSTOMERS BETTER

One reason businesses choose to remain in an area such as Chicago, New York, New Jersey, or California is to be where their customers are. Much of the buying power of the United States is still centered in the Midwest, Northeast, and Far West (California). By locating close to their customers, businesses lower transportation costs and can be more responsive to customer needs for service. It's especially important for service organizations to be located in urban areas where they can serve their customers best.

Many businesses are building factories in foreign countries to get closer to their international customers. That's a major reason why Honda builds cars in Ohio and Mercedes builds them in Alabama. When U.S. firms select foreign sites, they consider whether they are near airports, waterways, and highways so that raw materials and finished goods can be moved quickly and easily. Businesses also study the quality of life for workers and managers. Quality-of-life questions include these: Are there good schools nearby? Is the weather nice? Is the crime rate low? In short, site location has become a critical issue in production and operations management. The box called Making Ethical Decisions explores one of the major ethical issues involved.

◄ **CONSIDER USING LECTURE ENHANCER 9-5**
American Eagle Brick: Competing Across Borders

··· SITE SELECTION IN THE FUTURE ···

New developments in information technology (computers, modems, e-mail, voice mail, teleconferencing, etc.) are giving firms and employees more flexibility than ever before in choosing locations while staying in the competitive mainstream. **Telecommuting**, working from home via computer and modem, is a major trend in business. It is estimated that about 20 million workers are now telecommuting or soon will be. Companies that no longer need to locate near sources of labor will be able to move to areas such as the countryside, where land is less expensive and the quality of life may be nicer.[5]

◄ **CONSIDER USING CRITICAL THINKING EXERCISE 9-1**
Site Selection (**SCANS**)

telecommuting
Working from home via computer and modem.

Making Ethical Decisions

http://www.rcorp.com

Stay or Leave?

ChildrenWear Industries has long been the economic foundation for its hometown. Most of the area's small businesses and schools support ChildrenWear, either by supplying the materials needed for production or by training its employees. ChildrenWear learned that it can increase profits by half if it were to move its production facilities to Asia. Closing ChildrenWear operations in its hometown would cause many of the town's businesses to fail and schools to close, leaving a great percentage of the town unemployed, with no options for reemployment there. As a top manager at ChildrenWear, you must help decide whether the plant should be moved, and, if so, when to tell the employees about the move. The law says that you must tell them at least 60 days before closing. What alternatives do you have? What are the consequences of each? Which will you choose?

One big incentive to locate or relocate in a particular city or state is the tax situation and degree of government support.[6] Some states and local governments have higher taxes than others, yet many engage in fierce competition by giving tax reductions and other support, such as zoning changes and financial aid, so that businesses will locate there. Allen-Edmonds Shoe Corporation, for example, had trouble getting employees to work at its Port Washington plant, 25 miles north of Milwaukee. To get closer to workers, it located a plant in Milwaukee. That made workers happy because they made $12.50 an hour, and it made Allen-Edmonds happy because it received $150,000 in state development zone tax credits.[7]

Once a location is selected, production can begin. As we go through the production process, we'll discuss how it can be improved to become more competitive.

Mercedes now makes one of its newest models in Alabama so they can be close to the U.S. market. Similar plants of other international automobile manufacturers are located in several other states. Are you buying an American car when it is made in America, even if it has a name like Honda or Mercedes? Such questions show that the global marketplace has arrived and companies feel free to produce goods and services when and where it is least expensive or best for marketing to do so.

Companies now talk less about "work at home" programs and more about "work anywhere, anytime" programs. Computers in various formats, fax machines, cellular phones, networks, e-mail, and voice mail are making telecommuting a way of doing business that satisfies strategic goals of spending more time with customers and decreasing commute time. What are some of the disadvantages of telecommuting?

◄ **LEARNING GOAL 3.** Classify the various production processes and how materials requirement planning links organizations in performing those processes.

◄ **CONSIDER USING LECTURE ENHANCER 9-6**
The Green Eavesdropper

◄ **CONSIDER USING CRITICAL THINKING EXERCISE 9-2**
Production Processes (**SCANS**)

◄ **CONSIDER USING OT ACETATE 9-2**
Synthetic and Analytic Production Systems

PRODUCTION PROCESSES

There are several different processes manufacturers use to produce goods. Andrew S. Grove, chief executive officer of Intel, uses a great analogy to explain production:

> *To understand the principles of production, imagine that you're a chef . . . and that your task is to serve a breakfast consisting of a three-minute soft-boiled egg, buttered toast, and coffee. Your job is to prepare and deliver the three items simultaneously, each of them fresh and hot.*

Grove goes on to say that the task here encompasses the three basic requirements of production: (1) to build and deliver products in response to the demands of the customer at a scheduled delivery time, (2) to provide an acceptable quality level, and (3) to provide everything at the lowest possible cost.

Using the breakfast example, it's easy to understand two manufacturing terms: process and assembly. **Process manufacturing** physically or chemically changes materials. For example, boiling physically changes the egg. The **assembly process** puts together components (eggs, toast, and coffee) to make a product (breakfast). These two processes are called synthetic systems. **Synthetic systems** either change raw materials into other products (process manufacturing) or combine raw materials or parts into a finished product (assembly process).

The reverse of a synthetic system is an analytic system. An **analytic system** breaks down raw materials into components to extract other products. For example, crude oil can be reduced to gasoline, wax, and jet fuel. So, the system used in production will be either synthetic or analytic.

In addition, production processes are either continuous or intermittent. A *continuous process* is one in which long production runs turn out finished goods over time. As the chef in our diner, for example, you could have a conveyor belt that lowers eggs into boiling water for three minutes and then lifts them out on a continuous basis. A three-minute egg would be available whenever you wanted one. A chemical plant, for example, is run on a continuous process.

process manufacturing
Production process that physically or chemically changes materials.

assembly process
Production process that puts together components.

synthetic systems
Systems that either change raw materials into other products (process manufacturing) or combine raw materials or parts into a finished product (assembly process).

analytic system
Manufacturing system that breaks down raw materials into components to extract other products.

Manufacturing is a complex process involving many steps. The Decorators Supply Corporation, for example, makes detailed replicas of hand carvings. The raw material is called compo (figure on left). It is made of hide glue and molasses. Kneading makes it soft and pliable. Artisans then shape the compo in molds and do the finishing work by hand (figure on right). This is called process manufacturing.

> **CONSIDER USING OT ACETATE 9-4**
How Productivity Varies in Automobile Production

enterprise resource planning (ERP)
Computer-based production and operations system that links multiple firms into one integrated production unit.

It usually makes more sense when responding to specific customer orders (job-order production) to use an *intermittent process*. This is an operation where the production run is short (one or two eggs) and the machines are changed frequently to make different products (like the oven in a bakery or the toaster in the diner). Manufacturers of custom-designed furniture would use an intermittent process.

Today most new manufacturers use intermittent processes. Computers, robots, and flexible manufacturing processes allow firms to turn out custom-made goods almost as fast as mass-produced goods were once turned out.[8] We'll discuss how they do that in detail later in the chapter.

••• MATERIALS REQUIREMENT PLANNING: •••
THE RIGHT PLACE AT THE RIGHT TIME

One thing for certain about the technological changes now taking place in manufacturing is that they've resulted in an entirely new terminology for production and operations management. One important term from the past is *materials requirement planning (MRP)*, a computer-based production and operations management system that uses sales forecasts to make sure that needed parts and materials are available at the right place and the right time. In our diner, for example, we could feed the sales forecast into the computer, which would specify how many eggs or how much coffee to order and then print out the proper scheduling and routing sequence.

MRP was most popular with companies that made products with a lot of different parts. MRP quickly led to MRP II, an advanced version of MRP that allowed plants to include all the resources involved in the efficient making of a product, including projected sales, personnel, plant capacity, and distribution limitations. MRP II was called, in contrast, *manufacturing resource planning* because the planning involved more than just material requirements.

The newest version of MRP is now called **enterprise resource planning (ERP)**. ERP is a computer-based production and operations system that links multiple firms into one integrated production unit. The software enables the monitoring of quality and customer satisfaction as it's happening. ERP is much more sophisticated than MRP II because it monitors processes in *multiple* firms at the same time. For example, it monitors inventory at the supplier as well as at the manufacturing plant.[9]

Eventually, such programs will link suppliers, manufacturers, and retailers in a completely integrated manufacturing and distribution system that will be constantly monitored for the smooth flow of goods from the time they're ordered to the time they reach the ultimate consumer. Companies now using such systems include Coors Ceramics (structural products); Phoenix Designs (office systems and furniture); and Red Devil (sealants, caulks, and hand tools).

Progress Check

- What is production?
- What are the major factors that determine where a plant locates?
- Can you explain the differences among the following production processes: process, assembly, analytic, continuous, and intermittent?
- What is enterprise resource planning?

···· ▬▬ ····

MODERN PRODUCTION TECHNIQUES

◄ **LEARNING GOAL 4.** Describe manufacturing techniques such as just-in-time inventory control, flexible manufacturing, lean manufacturing, and competing in time.

The ultimate goal of manufacturing and process management is to provide high-quality goods and services instantaneously in response to customer demand. Traditional organizations were simply not designed to be so responsive to the customer. Rather, they were designed to make goods efficiently. The whole idea of mass production was to make a large number of a limited variety of products at very low cost. As a result of such techniques, the Ford Motor Company, for example, increased its output in 1909 from 17,771 autos to 202,667. By 1924, Ford was producing 1.8 million autos a year. Prices for autos dropped from $950 in 1909 to $550 in 1913 to $355 (with an automatic starter added) in 1923.[10]

Over the years, low cost often came at the expense of quality and flexibility. Furthermore, suppliers didn't always deliver when they said they would, so manufacturers had to carry large inventories of raw materials and components. Such inefficiencies made U.S. companies subject to foreign competitors who were using more advanced production techniques. The box called Reaching Beyond Our Borders discusses how companies compare themselves with the world's leading companies to find the best practices possible.

As a result of global competition, largely from Japan and Germany, companies today must make a wide variety of high-quality custom-designed products at very low cost. Clearly, something had to change on the production floor to make that possible. Also, something had to change in supplier–producer relationships. Six major developments have radically changed the production process in the United States: (1) just-in-time inventory control, (2) new purchasing agreements, (3) flexible manufacturing, (4) lean manufacturing, (5) mass customization, and (6) competing in time.

The American Productivity & Quality Center provides a Web site where companies can go to find other companies to benchmark. This service enables companies to compare their practices and procedures with the best in the world. Do you think you could improve your grades if you were to compare your study practices and procedures with the best students in the world? How could you begin such a process?

··· JUST-IN-TIME INVENTORY CONTROL ···

One major cost of production is holding parts, motors, and other items in warehouses. To cut such costs, the Japanese implemented a concept called

Reaching Beyond
Our Borders

http://www.apqc.org

Benchmarking the Best

Today's trend toward globalization means that the world's best manufacturers can enter almost any market at almost any time. In other words, if you aren't one of the world's best manufacturers, you're likely to go out of business. In fact, you can be one of the world's best producers and still lose the bulk of your business if you aren't also one of the most innovative and cost-efficient producers. Mercedes and BMW, for example, have long been known as two of the best car manufacturers in the world. Along came Lexus and Infiniti not only to challenge their technological lead but to offer similar quality at a much lower price. Consequently, Mercedes was forced to produce less expensive car models. If Mercedes hadn't responded, it would have continued to lose its market share.

Even being an industry leader doesn't ensure world dominance for long. Japan, for example, introduced high-definition television (HDTV) in 1988 at the Olympics in Seoul, Korea. U.S. manufacturers considered this a challenge much like the old challenge to get to the moon. Working together, U.S. manufacturers developed a better technology that leapfrogged Japanese products. European companies are doing the same. Similarly, IBM once led the world in computer technology, but it's now ▲

just one of many competitors, no longer the dominant industry leader.

Staying on top means meeting the world's standard (that is, benchmarking on the best companies in the world). A company must compare each one of its processes to that same process as practiced by the best. It must then bring its processes up to the world-class standard or outsource the process to someone who can. But it can't rest there; it must empower its workers to become the best in the world and to continuously improve processes and products to maintain a leadership position. Often that means the company must develop products that will make its own products obsolete. So be it. If it doesn't do so, someone else will. The American Productivity and Quality Center has an International Benchmarking Clearinghouse where companies can learn the best practices of companies throughout the world. The center's phone number is (713) 681-4020.

Sources: "Two New Benchmarking Studies Released," *Quality Digest*, January 1997, p. 10, and Vicki J. Powers, "Selecting a Benchmarking Partner: Five Tips for Success," *Quality Digest*, October 1997, pp. 37–41.

> **CONSIDER USING LECTURE ENHANCER 9-7**
> The New Reality: Reevaluating Just-In-Time Inventory Techniques

> **CONSIDER USING OT ACETATE 9-5**
> What's had the Biggest Effect on Productivity?

just-in-time (JIT) inventory control, which they learned from U.S. quality consultants. The idea is to have suppliers deliver their products "just in time" to go on the assembly line. A minimum of inventory is kept on the premises. Some U.S. manufacturers have adopted the practice and are quite happy with the results.

Here's how it works: A manufacturer sets a production schedule using enterprise requirement planning (ERP), or one of the other systems just described, and determines what parts and supplies will be needed. It then informs its suppliers of what will be needed. The supplier must deliver the goods just in time to go on the assembly line. Naturally, this calls for more effort on the supplier's part (and more costs). Efficiency is maintained by having the supplier linked by computer to the producer so that the supplier becomes more like another department in the firm than a separate business. The supplier delivers its materials just in time to be used in the production process, so a bare minimum must be kept in storage just in case the delivery is held up for some reason.

The latest version of JIT is called JIT II. This system is designed to create more harmony and trust than has been the case at times with JIT. In JIT II there is much more sharing of information. In fact, an employee from the supplier may work full-time at the buyer's plant handling the smooth flow of materials.

You can imagine how the system would work in Andrew Grove's breakfast example. Rather than ordering enough eggs, butter, bread, and coffee for the week and storing it, the chef would have his suppliers deliver a certain amount every morning. That way the food would be fresh and deliveries could be varied depending on customer demand. An employee from the supplier would be on hand at all times to ensure freshness.

ERP and JIT systems make sure the right materials are at the right place at the right time at the cheapest cost to meet both customer and production needs. That's the first step in modern production innovation. The second step in innovation is to change the production process itself. We'll discuss those changes next.

◄ CONSIDER USING OT ACETATE 9-6
Production and Operations Management: Functions and Tools

··· NEW PURCHASE AGREEMENTS ···

Purchasing is the function in the firm that searches for quality material resources, finds the best suppliers, and negotiates the best price for quality goods and services. In the past, manufacturers tended to deal with many different suppliers with the idea that materials would be available from someone if one supplier or another couldn't deliver. Today, however, manufacturers are relying more heavily on one or two suppliers. The relationship between suppliers and manufacturers is much closer, with suppliers often locating their facilities near the manufacturer. The purchasing department is responsible for finding such suppliers, negotiating long-term contracts with them, and getting the best price possible. The next step in innovation is to change the production process itself. We'll discuss those changes next.

purchasing
The function in the firm that searches for quality material resources, finds the best suppliers, and negotiates the best price for goods and services.

··· FLEXIBLE MANUFACTURING ···

Flexible manufacturing is the design of machines to do multiple tasks so that they can produce a variety of products. Ford Motor Company, for example, uses flexible manufacturing at its Romeo, Michigan, plant. As many as six variations of V-8 and V-6 engines can be built from the same machinery.

Allen-Bradley Company, Inc., a maker of industrial automation controls, uses flexible manufacturing to build motor starters. Orders come in daily and within 24 hours, 26 machines are used to manufacture, test, and package the starters—which are thus untouched by human hands. The machines are so flexible that a special order, even a single item, can be included in the assembly without slowing down the process.

flexible manufacturing
The design of machines to do multiple tasks so that they can produce a variety of products.

Critical Thinking

Earlier we talked about continuous processes versus intermittent processes. Can you see how flexible manufacturing makes it possible for intermittent processes to become as fast as continuous processes? What are the implications for saving time on the assembly line, saving money, and cutting back on labor?

··· LEAN MANUFACTURING ···

Lean manufacturing is the production of goods using less of everything compared to mass production: less human effort, less manufacturing space, less investment in tools, and less engineering time to develop a new product. A company becomes lean by continuously increasing its capacity to produce high-quality goods while decreasing its need for resources.

General Motors, for example, abandoned its assembly-line production process to make the Saturn automobile. The fundamental purpose of restructuring was to dramatically cut the number of worker-hours needed to build a car. The changes GM made were many, but the most dramatic was to switch to modular construction. This means that most parts are preassembled into a

lean manufacturing
The production of goods using less of everything compared to mass production.

The Sunrise Medical Mobility Products Division in Fresno, California is one of those organizations that practices mass customization. That is, they can design products that exactly meet your requirements and get them to you quickly. This photo shows their power wheel-chair assembly line. What advantages do you see to having customized products rather than mass-produced goods?

> **CONSIDER USING OT ACETATE 9-7**
How to Increase Team Productivity

robot
A computer-controlled machine capable of performing many tasks requiring the use of materials and tools.

few large components called modules. Workers are no longer positioned along miles of assembly line. Instead, they're grouped at various workstations, where they put the modules together. Rather than do a few set tasks, workers perform a whole cluster of tasks. Trolleys carry the partly completed car from station to station. Such a process takes up less space and calls for fewer workers—both money-saving steps. Suppliers were asked to provide a wider variety of parts and to subassemble certain parts before shipping them.

Finally, GM greatly expanded its use of robots in the manufacturing process. A **robot** is a computer-controlled machine capable of performing many tasks requiring the use of materials and tools. Robots, for example, spray-paint cars and do welding. Robots usually are fast, efficient, and accurate. However, robots and machinery can never completely replace creative workers.

⋯ MASS CUSTOMIZATION ⋯

mass customization
Tailoring products to meet the needs of individual customers.

Mass customization means tailoring products to meet the needs of individual customers. The National Bicycle Industrial Company in Japan, for example, makes 18 bicycle models in more than 2 million combinations, with each combination designed to fit the needs of a specific customer. The customer chooses the model, size, color, and design. The retailer takes various measurements from the buyer and faxes the data to the factory, where robots handle the bulk of the assembly.[11]

More and more manufacturers are learning to customize their products. For example, General Nutrition Centers (GNC) has put machines in some of its stores that enable customers to custom-design their own vitamins, shampoo, and lotions. Porsche 911 sports cars are offered with custom colors, custom leathers (including leather from a customer's own herd), custom wood inlays, and custom accessories like refrigerators and compartments for revolvers. You can buy custom-made books with your children's names inserted in key places or create custom-made greeting cards. The Custom Foot stores use infrared scanners to precisely measure each foot so shoes can be crafted to fit perfectly. InterActive Custom Clothes (http://www.ic3d.com) offers a wide variety of options in custom-made jeans, including four different color rivets.[12]

Spotlight on Small Business

http://www.cresearch.com

Speeding Up Research

Since 1988, only 30 firms have won the Malcolm Baldrige National Quality Award. Eight of those honorees were small businesses. But only one small business in the area of professional services has ever won. That firm is Custom Research Inc. (CRI), which won the award in 1996. The company's strategic plan called for cross-functional work teams to deliver customer-focused, quality service.

To compete for the Baldrige award, the company took a good look at its internal processes. The target was to reduce by 50 percent the time it took to complete a project. The company managed to reach that goal by using teams of six to eight people to do all the work for a particular client. CRI worked to establish a close relationship with its clients; the top 39 customers now bring in 90 percent of the company's business. The company earned the loyalty of those customers by having a goal of 92 percent "memorable experience." That is, CRI met or exceeded customer expectations 92 percent of the time. This company's experience shows that competing in time and improving internal processes are both as important to service organizations as they are to major manufacturers.

Sources: Kevin T. Higgins, "Never-Ending Journey," *Marketing Management*, Spring 1997, pp. 4–7, and Elizabeth R. Larson, "Profiles in Quality: the 1997 Baldrige Award Winners," *Quality Digest*, January 1998, pp. 26–29.

Mass customization is coming to services as well. Capital Protective Insurance (CPI), for example, sells customized risk-management plans to companies. Only the latest in computer software and hardware makes it possible for CPI to develop such custom-made policies.[13] Health clubs now offer custom-made fitness programs for individuals, travel agencies provide custom-designed vacations, and some colleges offer custom-designed curricula for students. Actually, it is much easier to custom-design service programs than it is to custom-make products, because there is no fixed tangible good that has to be adapted. Each customer can specify what he or she wants and, within the limits of the service organization, those needs can be met as specified.

••• COMPETING IN TIME •••

Competing in time is essential to competing at all in a global marketplace. Ford estimates that, to match the best, it must be 25 percent faster than it is now in creating new products. Using the latest in technology, Ford should have no problem meeting that goal. The following section explores dramatic changes that are making the production process much faster and are restoring American competitive strength in manufacturing. These changes include computer-aided design and computer-aided manufacturing (CAD/CAM). They enable firms to compete in time and in efficiency. The box called Spotlight on Small Business shows how one small firm applied these concepts to become more competitive.

◀ **CONSIDER USING SUPPLEMENTAL CASE 9-1**
Competing in Time at Digital Equipment Corporation
(**SCANS**)

◀ **LEARNING GOAL 5.** Show how CAD/CAM improves the production process.

••• COMPUTER-AIDED DESIGN AND MANUFACTURING •••

If one development in the recent past changed production techniques and strategies more than any other, it was the integration of computers into the design and manufacturing of products. The first thing computers did was help in the design of products; this is called **computer-aided design (CAD)**. The latest CAD systems allow designers to work in 3D (three dimensions).[14] The next

computer-aided design (CAD)
The use of computers in the design of products.

Through computer-assisted design (CAD), engineers can create automobile designs without paper. Design modifications can be made quickly. When CAD is tied to the manufacturing and management accounting systems, managers have a powerful tool for planning. What are some of the ways in which this technology has changed industry?

computer-aided manufacturing (CAM)
The use of computers in the manufacturing of products.

➤ **CONSIDER USING SUPPLEMENTAL CASE 9-2**
The Automation of General Motors (**SCANS**)

➤ **CONSIDER USING LECTURE ENHANCER 9-8**
Computer-Integrated Manufacturing for Small Business

➤ **CONSIDER USING LECTURE ENHANCER 9-9**
People Problems on the Plant Floor

step was to involve computers directly in the production process; this is called **computer-aided manufacturing (CAM)**.

CAD/CAM, the use of both computer-aided design and computer-aided manufacturing, made it possible to custom-design products to meet the needs of small markets with very little increase in cost. A producer programs the computer to make a simple design change, and that change can be incorporated directly into the production line.

Computer-aided design and manufacturing are invading the clothing industry. A computer program establishes a pattern and cuts the cloth automatically. Soon, a person's dimensions will be programmed into the machines to create custom-cut clothing at little additional cost. Computer-aided manufacturing is used to make cookies in those new fresh-baked cookie shops. On-site, small-scale, semiautomated, sensor-controlled baking makes consistent quality easy.

Computer-aided design has doubled productivity in many firms. The problem in the past was that computer-aided design machines couldn't talk to computer-aided manufacturing machines directly. It's one thing to design a product; it's quite another to set the specifications to make a machine do the work. Recently, however, new software programs have been designed to unite CAD with CAM: the result is computer-integrated manufacturing (CIM). The new software is expensive, but it cuts as much as 80 percent of the time needed to program machines to make parts, and it eliminates many errors.

Critical Thinking

Computer-aided design and computer-aided manufacturing (CAD/CAM) have revolutionized the production process. Now, everything from cookies to cars can be designed and manufactured much more cheaply than before. Furthermore, customized changes can be made with very little increase in cost. What will such changes mean for the clothing industry, the shoe industry, and other fashion-related industries? What will they mean for other consumer and industrial goods industries? How will you benefit as a consumer?

Progress Check

- What is just-in-time inventory control?
- How does flexible manufacturing differ from lean manufacturing?
- What is meant by competing in time?

THE COMPUTERIZED FACTORY

Because of new ideas such as CAD/CAM, the United States is now on the brink of a new era in production and operations management. The force behind the change is new technology, especially computers and robots. Terms you'll be seeing over the next decade include the following:

1. *Computer-aided engineering (CAE).* CAE includes the designing and analysis of products, the programming of robots and machine tools, the designing of molds and tools, and the planning of the production process and quality control. In the past, engineering involved a lot of paperwork—blueprints, drawings, and so forth. Many inefficiencies resulted from the shuffling of such papers from desk to desk to shop floor and so on. Today, the whole engineering process from conception to production can be and is being done by computer in some firms.

2. *Flexible manufacturing systems (FMS).* These are totally automated production centers that include robots, automatic materials handling equipment, and computer-controlled machine tools that can perform a variety of functions to produce different products. GM's new plants use flexible manufacturing systems.

3. *Design for manufacturability and assembly (DFMA).* This innovation is based on the premise that the best-engineered part may be no part at all. Reducing the number of parts needed to build a product reduces the product's cost. Savings come from less time to assemble, ease in installation and maintenance, and less field service. NCR's newest electronic cash register has only 15 parts (85 percent fewer parts from 65 percent fewer vendors than its previous model). The terminal takes only one-fourth of the time previously required to assemble it.

4. *Computer-aided acquisition and logistics support (CALS).* This communications system allows manufacturers to send design specifications to suppliers over a phone line directly to the machine that will do the work. This system makes it possible to reduce inventories even further because new parts can be ordered and processed at once, and sent almost immediately.

What you should learn from all this is that factories are being fully automated. That is, most of the jobs that traditionally have been involved in the manufacturing process are being eliminated. Everything from customer order processing, to inventory control planning, to forecasting through production, quality control, and shipping is being made more productive through the use of computers and robots. The remaining workers are and will be highly skilled technical workers who have the training needed to use and develop such equipment.

···· ▬ ····

CONTROL PROCEDURES: PERT AND GANTT CHARTS

◄ **LEARNING GOAL 6.** Describe the use of PERT and Gantt charts in production planning.

◄ **CONSIDER USING TM 70** PERT Chart for a Video

An important function of a production manager is to be sure that products are manufactured and delivered on time. The question is, How can one be sure that all of the assembly processes will go smoothly and end up completed by the required time? A popular technique for maintaining some feel for the progress of production is one that was developed in the 1950s for constructing nuclear submarines: the **program evaluation and review technique (PERT)**. PERT is a method for analyzing the tasks involved in completing a given project, estimating the time needed to complete each task, and identifying the minimum time needed to complete the total project.

The steps involved in using PERT are (1) analyzing and sequencing tasks that need to be done, (2) estimating the time needed to complete each task, (3) drawing a PERT network illustrating the information from steps 1 and 2, and (4) identifying the critical path. The **critical path** is the sequence of tasks that takes the longest time to complete. This word *critical* is used in this term

program evaluation and review technique (PERT)
A method for analyzing the tasks involved in completing a given project, estimating the time needed to complete each task, and identifying the minimum time needed to complete the total project.

critical path
The sequence of tasks that takes the longest time to complete.

Gantt chart
Bar graph showing production managers what projects are being worked on and what stage they are in on a daily basis.

quality control
The measurement of products and services against set standards.

┌   FIGURE 9.2   ┐
        • • • •

    PERT CHART FOR
      A VIDEO

The minimum amount of time it will take to produce this video is 15 weeks. To get that number, you add the week it takes to pick a star and a song to the four weeks to design a set, the two weeks to purchase set materials, the six weeks to construct the set, the week before rehearsals, and the final week when the video is made. That's the critical path. Any delay in that process will delay the final video. Delays in other processes (e.g., selecting and choreographing dancers and costume design) wouldn't necessarily delay the video because there are more weeks in the critical path than are needed for those processes.

because a delay in the time needed to complete this path would cause the project or production run to be late.

Figure 9.2 illustrates a PERT chart for producing a music video. Note that the squares on the chart indicate completed tasks and the arrows leading to the squares indicate the time needed to complete each task. The path from one completed task to the other illustrates the relationships among tasks. For example, the arrow from "set designed" to "set materials purchased" shows that designing the set must be completed before the materials can be purchased. The critical path (indicated by the bold black arrows) reflects that producing the set takes more time than auditioning dancers and choreographing dances as well as designing and making costumes. The project manager now knows that it's critical that set construction remain on schedule if the project is to be completed on time, but short delays in the dance and costume preparation shouldn't affect the total project.

A PERT network can be made up of thousands of events over many months. Today, this complex procedure is done by computer. Another, more basic, strategy used by manufacturers for measuring production progress is a Gantt chart. A **Gantt chart** is a bar graph that clearly shows what projects are being worked on and how much has been completed (on a daily basis). Figure 9.3 shows a Gantt chart for a doll manufacturer. The chart shows that the dolls' heads and bodies should be completed before the clothing is sewn. It also shows that at the end of week 3, the dolls' bodies are ready, but the heads are about half a week behind. All of this calculation was once done by hand. Now the computer has taken over. Using a Gantt-like computer program, a manager can trace the production process minute by minute to determine which tasks are on time and which are behind so that adjustments can be made to allow the company to stay on schedule.

••• TOTAL QUALITY IN PRODUCTION MANAGEMENT •••

Quality control is the measurement of products and services against set standards. Earlier in America, quality control was often done at the end of the production line. It was done by a quality control department. Today things have changed. Quality now means satisfying customers by building in and ensuring quality from product planning to production, purchasing, sales, and service. Emphasis is placed on customer satisfaction, so quality is everyone's concern, not just the concern of the quality control people at the end of the assembly

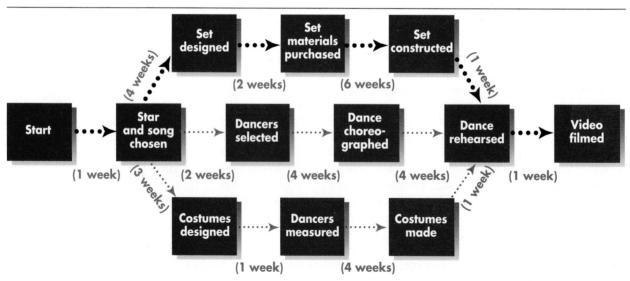

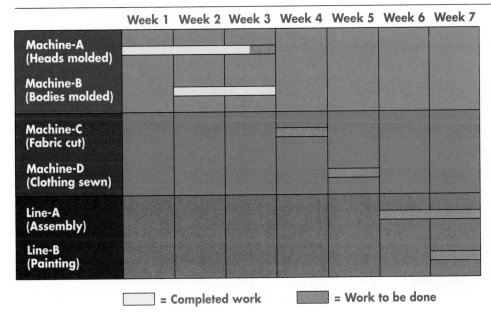

	Week 1	Week 2	Week 3	Week 4	Week 5	Week 6	Week 7
Machine-A (Heads molded)							
Machine-B (Bodies molded)							
Machine-C (Fabric cut)							
Machine-D (Clothing sewn)							
Line-A (Assembly)							
Line-B (Painting)							

☐ = Completed work   ▨ = Work to be done

FIGURE 9.3

· · · ·

A GANTT CHART FOR A DOLL MANUFACTURER

A Gantt chart enables a production manager to see at a glance when projects are scheduled to be completed and what the status now is. For example, the dolls' heads and bodies should be completed before the clothing is sewn, but they could be a little late as long as everything is ready for assembly in week 6. This chart shows that at the end of week 3, the dolls' bodies are ready, but the heads are about half a week behind.

▲ CONSIDER USING TM 71
A GANTT Chart for a Doll Manufacturer

line. In total quality management (TQM), everybody is permitted and expected to contribute to change ⇒ P. 245 ⇐.

The purpose of quality control is to make the consumer happy. Therefore, a TQM program begins by analyzing the market to see what quality standards need to be established. Quality is then designed into products, and every product must meet those standards every step of the way in the production process. The following are examples of how quality is being introduced into the production process:

- Motorola set a goal of attaining "six sigma" quality—just 3.4 defects per million products.

- In the past, Xerox found 97 defects for every 100 copiers coming off the assembly line. Now it finds only 12. As a consequence, it raised its market share for small-business copiers from 1 percent to 20 percent.

- Holiday Inn authorized its hotel staff to do almost anything to satisfy an unhappy customer, from handing out gift certificates to eliminating the charge for a service. Managers were given the authority (empowered) to waive charges for the night's stay if the customer was still unhappy.

Dozens of other manufacturers and service organizations could be discussed here, but you get the idea: the customer is ultimately the one who determines what the standard for quality should be. American businesses are getting serious about providing top customer service, and many are already doing it.

W. Edwards Deming taught quality principles to managers throughout the world. His principles included continuous improvement, ceasing the dependence on inspection to improve quality, and breaking down barriers between staff areas. He taught statistical quality control to American managers during WW II and to the Japanese in the post-war period. Do you use any quality principles in your work?

··· MEASURING PRODUCTIVITY ···
IN THE SERVICE SECTOR

The greatest productivity problems in the United States are reported to be in service organizations. While productivity growth was relatively good for manufacturers during the 1980s and 1990s, it was reported to be next to nothing for service organizations. You've already learned that over 7 of 10 U.S. jobs are now in the service sector, with more to

Productivity in the service sector has substantially improved in the last few years, but government statistics have not been able to capture the quality differences that have occurred. For example, this waitress is using a touch screen video display that shows her menus and enables her to place orders quickly and efficiently. Such machines make her job easier and result in better service to customers. Although faster, friendlier, better service is being provided at hospitals, schools, and other organizations, there are few measurements that capture those quality differences.

➤ **CONSIDER USING LECTURE ENHANCER 9-10**
How to Improve Total Quality a Little at a Time

➤ **CONSIDER USING SUPPLEMENTAL CASE 9-3**
Quality America Is Back (**SCANS**)

➤ **CONSIDER USING LECTURE ENHANCER 9-11**
Incentives for Quality at GE

➤ **LEARNING GOAL 7.** Explain the importance of productivity in both the manufacturing and service sectors.

come. A truly strong America must therefore be progressive in introducing the latest technology to services as well as to manufacturing.

There's strong evidence that productivity in the service sector is rising, but the government simply doesn't have the means to measure it. The quality of service may be greatly improving, but quality is difficult to measure. The traditional way to measure productivity involves tracking inputs (worker-hours) compared to outputs (dollars). New information systems must be developed to measure the quality of goods and services, the speed of their delivery, and customer satisfaction.

Using computers is only the beginning of improving service sector productivity. Think about labor-intensive businesses like McDonald's and Burger King, where automation plays a big role in controlling costs and improving service. Today at Burger King, customers fill their own drink cups from soda machines, which allows workers to concentrate on preparing the food. And, because the people working at the drive-up window now wear headsets instead of using stationary mikes, they aren't glued to one spot anymore and can do four or five tasks while taking an order.

Most of us have been exposed to similar productivity gains in banking. For example, people in many towns no longer have to wait in long lines for tellers to help them deposit and withdraw money. Instead, they use automated teller machines (ATMs), which usually involve little or no waiting and are available 24 hours a day.

Another service that was once annoyingly slow was the checkout counter at the grocery store. The new system of marking goods with universal product codes enables computerized checkout and allows cashiers to be much more productive when providing this service.

Airlines are another service industry experiencing tremendous productivity increases through the use of computers for everything from processing reservations, to serving prepackaged meals on board, to standardizing the movements of luggage, passengers, and so on. You may have used an automated ticketing machine or ticketless boarding to avoid the congestion at airline ticket counters.

In short, operations management has led to tremendous productivity increases in the service sector. Those gains haven't been reflected in national productivity figures because the government doesn't yet know how to accurately measure them. Nonetheless, service workers are losing jobs to machines just as manufacturing workers are. Again, the secret to obtaining and holding a good job is to acquire appropriate education and training. That message can't be repeated too frequently.

••• SERVICES GO INTERACTIVE •••

The service industry has always taken advantage of new technology to increase customer satisfaction. Jet travel enabled Federal Express to deliver goods overnight. Computer databases enabled AT&T to have individualized customer service. Cable TV led to pay-per-view services. And now interactive computer networks, such as the Internet and the World Wide Web, are revolutionizing services. Interactive services are already available from banks, stock brokers, travel agents, and information providers of all kinds. Consumers may soon be involved in all kinds of interactive systems, including participating in community and national decision making.[15]

You can now buy a greater variety of books and CDs on the Internet than you can in retail stores. You can also search for and buy new and used automobiles and new and used computers. As computers and modems get faster, the Internet may take over much of traditional retailing.[16] In short, the service sector is experiencing the same kind of revolution as the manufacturing sector. The success of service organizations in the future will depend greatly on establishing a dialogue with consumers so that service organizations can adapt to consumer demands faster and more efficiently. Such information systems (to make a dialogue easier) have been developed and should prove highly useful.

••• PREPARING FOR THE FUTURE •••

What does technological innovation mean to you? It means that, as a college student, you will have marvelous new learning opportunities. It means new career choices and a higher standard of living and quality of life. But it also means preparing for such changes. Clearly, the workplace will be dominated by computers, robots, and other advanced machinery. Even the service sector will require the widespread use of handheld computers.

If all this sounds terribly cold and impersonal, then you recognize one of the needs of the future. People will need much more contact than before with others outside the work environment. There will be new demands for recreation, social clubs, travel, and other diversions. The America of the next century will be radically different from the America of the 1990s. It will take both technically trained people and people skilled in human relationships to guide us through the transition.

Carnegie-Mellon University now requires a course in manufacturing management for its master of business administration degree. Other courses are offered in robotics and manufacturing strategy. Some students act as consultants to manufacturers in the Pittsburgh area. Stanford University has its Institute for Manufacturing and Automation. Georgia Tech has a program in computer-integrated manufacturing. Such programs will become commonplace as other schools follow these in introducing such courses at both the undergraduate and graduate levels.

Other schools are training students to manage the new high-tech workforce. Emphasis is on participative management and the design of attractive work environments. All this will come together in the next decade to bring a new era in both the manufacturing and the service sectors. You have every reason to be optimistic about the future for both U.S. and world economic growth because of these changes. You can also expect to find many exciting new careers in America's new industrial boom.

Progress Check

- Draw a PERT chart for making a breakfast of three-minute eggs, buttered toast, and coffee. Which process would be the critical path, the longest process? How could you use a Gantt chart to keep track of production?

- Why has service productivity lagged behind industrial productivity, and what can be done about it?

SUMMARY

• • • • •

1. Production and operations management consists of those activities managers do to create goods and services.

  * ***Describe the production process and explain the importance of productivity.***

  Production is the creation of finished goods and services using inputs—land, labor, capital, entrepreneurship, and knowledge. *Productivity* is the term used to describe output per unit of input. Output could mean goods like cars and furniture, or services such as education and health care.

1. Describe the production process and explain the importance of productivity.

◄ CONSIDER USING LECTURE ENHANCER 9-12
Productivity Bottleneck in the Office: The Keyboard

◄ CONSIDER USING LECTURE ENHANCER 9-13
Who's Best at Service?

◄ CONSIDER USING OT ACETATE 9-8 AND OT ACETATE 9-9
Changing Employer Productivity Expectations

◄ CONSIDER USING LECTURE ENHANCER 9-14
Productivity and Quality in Nonprofit Organizations

◄ CONSIDER USING LECTURE ENHANCER 9-15
The Virtual Factory

2. Explain the importance of site selection in keeping down costs, and identify the criteria used to evaluate different sites.

2. A major issue of the 1990s has been the shift of manufacturing and service organizations from one city or state to another in the United States or to foreign countries.

• *Why is site selection so important, and what criteria are used to evaluate different sites?*

The very survival of U.S. manufacturing depends on its ability to remain competitive, and that means either cheaper inputs, such as cheaper costs of labor and land, or increased outputs from present inputs (increased productivity). Cheaper labor and land are two major criteria for selecting the right sites. Other criteria include whether (1) resources are plentiful and inexpensive, (2) skilled workers are available or are trainable, (3) taxes are low and the local government offers support, (4) energy and water are available, (5) transportation costs are low, and (6) the quality of life and quality of education are high.

3. Classify the various production processes and tell how materials requirement planning links organizations in performing those processes.

3. Process manufacturing physically or chemically changes materials. Assembly processes put together components. These two processes are called synthetic systems.

• *Are there other production processes?*

Yes, the reverse of a synthetic system is called an analytic system. Analytic systems break down raw materials into components to extract other products. In addition, production processes are either continuous or intermittent. A continuous process is one in which long production runs turn out finished goods over time. An intermittent process is an operation where the production run is short (e.g., one or two eggs) and the machines are changed frequently to produce different products.

• *What relationship does materials requirement planning (MRP) have with the production process?*

A manufacturer sets a production schedule. It then informs its suppliers of what will be needed. The supplier must deliver the goods just in time to go on the assembly line, making the supplier part of the process.

• *How have purchasing agreements changed?*

Purchasing agreements are now longer term and involve fewer suppliers who supply quality goods and services at better prices in return for getting the business.

4. Describe manufacturing techniques such as just-in-time inventory control, flexible manufacturing, lean manufacturing, and competing in time.

4. Flexible manufacturing is the design of machines to do multiple tasks so that they can produce a variety of products.

• *What's the relationship between flexible manufacturing and lean manufacturing?*

Lean manufacturing is the production of goods using less of everything compared to mass production: half the human effort, half the manufacturing space, half the investment in tools, half the engineering time to develop a new product. Flexible manufacturing enables the firm to use less equipment to make more goods; thus, it could be considered part of lean manufacturing.

• *What is mass customization?*

Mass customization means making custom-designed goods for all customers. Flexible manufacturing makes mass customization possible. Given the exact needs of a customer, flexible manufacturing machines can produce a customized good as fast as mass-produced goods were once made. Mass customization is also important in service industries.

• *How do competing in time and just-in-time (JIT) fit into the process?*

Getting your product to market before your competitors is essential today, particularly in the electronics sector. Thus, competing in time is critical.

JIT inventory control allows for less inventory and fewer machines to move goods. This allows for more flexibility and faster response times.

5. Computer-aided design combined with computer-aided manufacturing (CAD/CAM) has made it possible to custom-design products to meet the tastes of small markets with very little increase in cost.
   - ***How do CAD/CAM systems work?***
   Design changes made in CAD are instantly incorporated into products (CAM). The linking of the two systems—CAD and CAM—is called computer-integrated manufacturing (CIM).

5. Show how CAD/CAM improves the production process.

6. The program evaluation and review technique (PERT) is a method for analyzing the tasks involved in completing a given project, estimating the time needed to complete each task, and identifying the minimum time needed to complete the total project.
   - ***How can I learn to draw a PERT chart? Is there any relationship between a PERT chart and a Gantt chart?***
   Figure 9.2 (p. 274) shows a PERT chart. A Gantt chart (Fig. 9.3, p. 275) is a bar graph that clearly shows what projects are being worked on and how much has been completed on a daily basis. Whereas PERT is a tool used for planning, Gantt is a tool used to measure progress.

6. Illustrate the use of PERT, Gantt charts, and TQM in production planning.

7. Because the United States is a service society now, automation of the service sector is extremely important.
   - ***Why is service productivity not increasing as rapidly as manufacturing productivity?***
   One important reason service productivity hasn't increased as rapidly as manufacturing productivity is that the service sector is labor-intensive. Keep in mind, however, that productivity and quality are improving in the service sector but are harder to measure than the outputs of the industrial sector.

7. Explain the importance of productivity in the service sector.

KEY TERMS

analytic system 265
assembly process 265
computer-aided design (CAD) 271
computer-aided manufacturing (CAM) 272
critical path 273
enterprise resource planning (ERP) 266
flexible manufacturing 269
form utility 261
Gantt chart 274
lean manufacturing 269
mass customization 270
process manufacturing 265
production 261
production and operations management 261
program evaluation and review technique (PERT) 273
purchasing 269
quality control 274
robot 270
synthetic systems 265
telecommuting 263

DEVELOPING WORKPLACE SKILLS

1. Mass customization means that you will be able to purchase custom-designed goods and services for about the same price as mass-produced items. Discuss how these changes will affect your own purchases of goods and services such as shoes, vacations, and video games.

2. Compose a list of the applications of advanced technology in the service sector that have already occurred; include as many as you can. Using this information, brainstorm further uses of technology in areas such as recreation, travel, retailing, wholesaling, insurance, banking, finance, and government. Prepare a two-minute summary report to give to your class.

3. Prepare a two-page paper on the advantages and disadvantages of producing goods overseas using inexpensive labor. Be sure to mention the moral and ethical issues discussed in this chapter.

4. Debate the following proposition: Should or can U.S. manufacturers limit in some fashion the growth and spread of computers and robots used in manufacturing in order to save jobs for U.S. workers? Take the side of this issue that would be opposite your normal position.

5. Think about some of the experiences you have had with service organizations recently, including your school, and select one incident where you had to wait for an unreasonable length of time to get what you wanted. Prepare a letter to a manager of that organization explaining how he or she could make the operation more efficient and customer-oriented.

TAKING IT TO THE NET

Purpose

To illustrate production processes, using the production of M&Ms as an example.

Exercise

Take a tour of the M&Ms factory and visit the company store at http://www.m-ms.com/factory/index.html .

1. Is the production of M&Ms an example of an intermittent or continuous production process? Justify your answer.

2. Should the M&M production process be classified as a synthetic or an analytic system? Explain.

3. Is mass customization used in M&M production? If so, how?

Practicing Management Decisions

CASE
· · · · · ·
VISUALIZING THE VIRTUAL FACTORY
· · · · · ·

To prepare for the future, you need to be able to visualize various scenarios and then prepare yourself to work in one of them. The future of manufacturing can be found at Boeing. The AeroTech Service Group built a highly effective virtual factory for McDonnell Douglas, which is now part of Boeing. A virtual factory is a community of many actual factories linked by an electronic network that enables them to operate as one—flexibly and inexpensively—from anywhere in the world. Imagine, if you can, what this factory of the future looks like.

Begin by imagining McDonnell Douglas's internal network of computers linking some 50 employees within the company. Imagine further that some suppliers wanted access to this network to better supply McDonnell Douglas what it needed when it needed it. Now imagine that the suppliers were so impressed with the network that they wanted their suppliers to join as well. The result? Several thousand people all joined in one complex network.

It sounds simpler than it is. For one thing, some of the companies in the McDonnell Douglas virtual factory are very small and thus have limited computer capacity. Somehow, those small companies must be able to communicate with huge companies that have the very latest in computer systems. Furthermore, imagine the problem of maintaining some sense of security with regard to information. Once a company has two-way access to another company's computers, it can obtain just about any information it wants. A network must be secure so that only desired information can be accessed. Finally, workers in different places in the world must be able to work together in real time (that means at the same time).

Now let your imagination go wild. Imagine a design firm designing a product and sending that image in three-dimensional form to a manufacturing firm that makes some design changes of its own. A physical model of the product can be constructed quickly from the computer program. If the model is approved by everyone concerned, the product can be produced using computer-integrated manufacturing. The buyer can be involved in the whole process, adding input to the design. Parts for the product will arrive just in time to go on the assembly line. A delivery firm will pick up the product and deliver it on the same day it is produced.

All of the data exchanged go over the same extranet → P. 243 ←. That is, the data are exchanged over linked Internet systems. There are very few such systems now operative in the world, but many are being developed. In other words, the world is becoming linked by an electronic web that will tie some companies together in long-lasting relationships while allowing other companies to come and go as needed.

In the virtual factory there are no permanent companies, no permanent linkages. Suppliers come and go as needed. Production facilities come on line as needed, as do delivery firms. Even individual employees will become virtual. That is, consultants and experts will join the network, make their contribution, and leave.

Discussion Questions

1. What skills will be needed by employees in a virtual environment?
2. Since many companies will be virtual, there will be fewer long-term contracts and more subcontracting. Long-term employment may become a thing of the past. How can you learn to prosper in an environment that is looking for part-time experts?
3. What effects will the linking of companies have on global politics? Where are companies most likely to locate? What does that mean for manufacturing in the United States? In less-developed countries?
4. What problems do you anticipate as companies become more and more reliant on computer networks?

Sources: David M. Upton and Andrew McAfee, "The Real Virtual Factory," *Harvard Business Review*, July–August 1996, pp. 123–33; and Heath Row, "This 'Virtual' Company Is for Real," *Fast Company*, January 1998, pp. 48–50.

When you think of manufacturing firms, names like GM and IBM come to mind. But there are thousands of smaller manufacturers in the marketplace that provide us with many of the products that make life more enjoyable. Certainly guitars are one of those products. Washburn Guitars in Chicago, Illinois, is a manufacturing company that uses the intermittent process of production. That is, Washburn makes a few of one model of guitar and then shifts production to a different model. The process is called small-batch manufacturing.

Even though Washburn makes only a few products each day (about 15 guitars), the company still needs to use the latest in production techniques to stay competitive. For example, it uses flexible manufacturing. The Washburn production facility has a machine that is capable of doing many different tasks: building guitar necks, drilling holes for the fretboard, and so on.

Washburn also follows the total quality concepts that other, larger firms follow. When planning the production process, the company keeps in mind the need for profits. Therefore, the popular, more expensive guitars take precedence over less expensive items. Today, all of Washburn's acoustic guitars are made overseas, but the company has plans to make them in a new facility in

VIDEO CASE

● ● ● ● ● ●

THE PRODUCTION PROCESS AT WASHBURN GUITARS

Nashville, Tennessee. Total quality management and modern production techniques now make it possible to manufacture acoustic guitars in the United States and still stay competitive on price.

When making career plans, it is important to include smaller firms like Washburn Guitars in your thoughts. It is often exciting to work in a small, relatively intimate environment, especially if the firm practices participative management and other modern techniques.

Discussion Questions

1. What small manufacturing facilities are located in or near your city or town? Visit them and see for yourself what it's like to work for a small manufacturer.
2. Do you think that a guitar is the kind of item that lends itself well to continuous process manufacturing? Why?
3. One of the more important aspects of small-batch manufacturing is scheduling. What kinds of scheduling techniques have you learned in this chapter that you could use in a business similar to Washburn?
4. Does a career in production management seem attractive to you? Why or why not?

Part3

Management

Management is the people part of business. Although managers are also responsible for managing finance, information, and various processes, their main responsibility is to the people who work for them. The managers are the people who run the organization. Without managers, there would be no business.

As everything else in the human realm is constantly changing, so is management and our attitudes toward it. Management careers have always been among the most challenging and fulfilling in the field of business. They still are. And the role of managers is changing rapidly as we approach the end of the century.

••• SKILLS •••

Managers today need different skills from those they needed a generation ago. Today's managers must know how to be both team players and team leaders. They cannot get away with the "jump when I say jump" mentality of the past. More than ever, managers need to be effective communicators. They especially need to know how to listen, to hear, and to understand the needs of both their subordinates and their own managers. They also need the ability to organize and to keep others organized and to possess the know-how to motivate workers.

••• CAREER PATHS •••

Today's management opportunities often start out as management training positions that later develop into full-blown management opportunities. Both government and larger companies have management training programs. Some of these organizations will hire workers through campus recruiters. Others look for skills that can be acquired outside the classroom. Another common way to become a manager is to start as an employee and work your way up the management ladder. College courses and other forms of management training are often available tuition-free to the ambitious employee.

Once a manager is hired, the progress into middle and top management is far from automatic. As one gets closer to the top, there are fewer and fewer opportunities. Getting to the top, then, means learning to be competitive and good at what you do. Understanding office politics is also certainly a plus, though some companies are more political than others.

As a manager moves up in an organization, his or her responsibilities and authority increase. Becoming an integral part of planning and running an organization brings excitement as well as rewards.

SOME POSSIBLE POSITIONS IN MANAGEMENT

Job title	Salary	Job duties	Career path	Prospects
General manager; CEO; executive vice president	Amount varies widely. Top companies: $5.7 million average; median $714,000.	Establish the organization's general goals and policies. Act as liaison with other companies; direct the individual department or division; direct supervisor in motivation and control of workers.	Most general managers and top CEOs have college degrees, but some do not. Qualifications vary widely. Most vacancies are filled by promoting lower-level managers up through the ranks.	Average growth in opportunities through year 2006, but competition is keen.
Management trainee	Mid $20,000 (to start).	Learn basic responsibilities of a manager, training for the specific industry. Work in closely supervised situations in departments such as production, sales, research and development, finance. Training period usually specified and is treated as probationary.	Usually, a two-year associate degree is the minimum. Four-year degrees are preferred. Previous management experience can be helpful, though some companies want applicants to have none, so they can be trained the company way.	Outlook through 2006 is good.
Supervisor, blue collar	Median is $33,280	Manage and train employees; keep track of time and scheduling, oversee use of equipment and materials. Work with union when union is present.	Knowledge of the technical part of the workers' task is the most important knowledge area. A two- or four-year degree is usually an aid in obtaining promotion.	Outlook through 2006 is fair to average. No growth is expected because of downsizing.
Management consultant	Varies greatly, based on reputation of consulting firm.	Act as an adviser and analyst of management concerns in host organizations.	Degree and work experience help market credibility of the consultant. However, knowledge of the industry and self-confidence are most important qualities.	Demand will increase through 2006, especially in firms doing business internationally.

Source: *Occupational Outlook Handbook*, 1998–1999 Edition: Bureau of Labor Statistics.

Automotive Services Network, Inc., Holler Automotive Group

Name: Cynthia Manner

Age: 44

Position/title: Customer Relations Manager

Salary Range: $30,000

Time in this position: 1 year

Major factors in the decision to take this position: I wanted to develop my management skills and demonstrate those to others.

Company name: Automotive Services Network, Inc. Holler Automotive Group

Company's web address: www.automotiveservice.com

Company description: Automotive Service Network (ASN) is an administrative support group for nine dealerships. In addition, we handle three NAPA part stores and two independent body shops.

Job description: As head of Customer Relations Department, I am responsible for planning, supervising, and implementing office procedures. I am also responsible for staff training, employee motivation to improve efficiency, and performance evaluations.

Career paths: Three years of teaching at a Montessori school taught me the value of breaking projects into specific tasks. I then worked in a personnel department at a telecommunications company for 16 years. I developed day to day clerical office skills. Transferring into Customer Service allowed the opportunity to expand my telephone communication skills and how to deal effectively with dissatisfied customers in both sales and service. After working six-months as a Customer Relations Representative in one of the dealerships, I saw the benefits and opportunity to develop an in-house Customer Relations Department. I independently developed and proposed the formation of the department. They promoted me to manage the new department. I have been hiring and training my new staff.

Ideal next job: I would like to be an independent consultant.

Best part of your job: The best part of my job is the freedom given to me by my employer to develop the strategic plan in initiating the in-house customer relations department.

Worst part of your job: The worst part of my job are the frustrations associated with the difficulty of extracting the day-to-day details of how the company is operated so I can integrate that knowledge into the Customer Relations Department.

Educational background: As a single mother of two boys, it took me six years to obtain a double degree in Business Administration and Management and Organizational Communication.

Favorite course: My favorite course was Humanities, which addressed all aspects of the Baroque and Renaissance Era along with Greek and Roman Cultures. It introduced me to a special aspect of history.

Best course for your career: Computer and Report Writing along with all of my general business courses were valuable.

Compliments of Professor Marva Pryor, Valencia Community College

Motivating Employees and Building Self-Managed Teams

Chapter

10

LEARNING GOALS

After you have read and studied this chapter,
you should be able to

1 Explain Taylor's scientific management.

2 Describe the Hawthorne studies and relate their significance to human-based management.

3 Identify the levels of Maslow's hierarchy of needs and relate their importance to employee motivation.

4 Differentiate among Theory X, Theory Y, and Theory Z.

5 Distinguish between the motivators and hygiene factors identified by Herzberg.

6 Explain how job enrichment affects employee motivation and performance.

7 Identify the steps involved in implementing a management by objectives (MBO) program.

8 Explain the key factors involved in expectancy theory.

9 Examine the key principles of equity theory.

The sky is not always friendly, but it does seem to shine for one airline. Southwest Airlines has continued flying high while other airlines have struggled to stay aloft. It's the only airline that has remained profitable every year since 1973. The company now ranks as the fifth largest airline among all global carriers. Analysts credit much of this achievement to the engaging management style of the company's unconventional chairman, CEO Herb Kelleher. Known to show up dressed as Elvis or the Easter Bunny, Kelleher is the jokemeister of the airline industry. He is usually at the center of Southwest's employee activities. Asked once to speak to a group about the accomplishments he's most proud of, Kelleher took the podium and said, "Well, I'm here to tell you that I *am* proud of a couple of things. First, I'm very good at projectile vomiting." Such unorthodox statements rarely fail to capture his audience's attention.

But it's his employees' attention that Kelleher has most of the time. Under his coaching the company has been a consistent winner of the Service Triple Crown —highest customer satisfaction, most on-time flights, and best baggage handling. Kelleher's employees are far more productive than employees of competing airlines. Per worker, Southwest flies more planes and serves more passengers than other airlines do. Southwest employees also pitch in wherever needed. Pilots might work the boarding gate if things back up; ticket agents might haul luggage to get the plane out on time. Employees even began a voluntary payroll deduction program to defray fuel costs when prices accelerated during the Gulf war. Southwest workers (approximately 90 percent of whom are union members) are paid competitively.

PROFILE

Herb Kelleher of Southwest Airlines

How does Kelleher do it? For starters, he actively avoids hierarchy. He has managers spend time in the trenches once a month, he de-emphasizes the importance of rules relative to good judgment, and he promotes the company as a "family." The result is the promotion of creativity and employee judgment, which ultimately leads to greater employee productivity and job satisfaction.

Fun plays a major role in motivating Southwest employees. Fun can be more than just having a good time—it can develop employees who are happy, productive, and intensely loyal. Fun can be promoted either through events such as the good old weekly barbecue or by simply making it known that a sense of humor is a highly valued trait. Kelleher believes that a sense of humor is more than just fun—it reduces stress.

His employees say Kelleher motivates them because he doesn't just say that people are his most important resource, he acts on it. Kelleher says, "You have to work harder than anybody else to show them you are devoted to the business. It's also important to be with your employees through all their difficulties, and show that you are interested in them personally. They may be disappointed in their country. Even their family might not be working out the way they wish it would. But I want them to know that Southwest will always be there for them."

Source: Anne Bruce, "Southwest: Back to the FUNdamentals," *HR Focus*, March 1997, p. 11, Donna Rosato, "Today's Topic: Putting Humor to Work in the Workplace Guest CEO Herb Kelleher of Southwest Airlines," *USA Today*, February 23, 1998, p. 5B, and Janet Kidd Stewart, "Laughing Matter Does It Pay to Orchestrate Fun at Work," *Chicago Tribune*, February 1, 1998, p. 7.

◄ **CONSIDER USING TM 72**
Chapter Outline

THE IMPORTANCE OF MOTIVATION

No matter where you end up being a leader—in school, in business, in sports, in the military, wherever—the key to your success will be motivating others to do their best. That's no easy task today when so many people feel bored and uninterested in their work. Yet people are willing to work, and work hard, if they feel that their work makes a difference and is appreciated. People are

intrinsic reward
The good feeling you have when you have done a job well.

extrinsic reward
Something given to you by someone else as recognition for good work; extrinsic rewards include pay increases, praise, and promotions.

➤ **CONSIDER USING LECTURE ENHANCER 10-1**
The Secret of Men and Motivation

motivated by a variety of things, such as recognition, accomplishment, and status. **Intrinsic reward** is the good feeling you have when you have done a job well. An **extrinsic reward** is something given to you by someone else as recognition for good work. Such things as pay increases, praise, and promotions are examples of extrinsic rewards. Although ultimately motivation—the drive to satisfy a need—comes from within an individual, there are ways to stimulate people that bring out the natural drive to do a good job.

The purpose of this chapter is to teach you the concepts, theories, and practice of motivation. The most important person to motivate, of course, is yourself. One way to do that is to find the right job in the right organization, one that enables you to reach your goals in life. The whole purpose of this book is to help you in that search and to teach you how to succeed once you get there. One secret of success is to recognize that everyone else is on a similar search. Naturally, some are more committed than others. The job of a manager is to find that commitment, encourage it, and focus it on some common goal.

This chapter will begin with a look at some of the traditional theories of motivation. You will learn about the Hawthorne studies because they created a whole new interest in worker satisfaction and motivation. Then you'll look at some assumptions about employees: Are they basically lazy, or are they willing to work if given the proper incentives? You will read about the traditional theorists. You will see their names over and over in the business literature and courses: Taylor, Mayo, Maslow, McGregor, and Herzberg. Finally, you will look

Herb Kelleher of Southwest Airlines has a way of getting his employees' attention. How do you think the way Kelleher interacts with his employees affects their motivation to perform? Does his style appeal to you?

at the modern applications of motivation theories and the managerial procedures for implementing them.

··· EARLY MANAGEMENT STUDIES (TAYLOR) ···

Several books in the 19th century presented management principles, but not until the early 20th century did there appear any significant works with lasting implications. One of the most well-known, *The Principles of Scientific Management*, was written by Frederick Taylor and published in 1911. This book earned Taylor the title Father of Scientific Management. Taylor's goal was to increase worker productivity so that both the firm and the worker could benefit from higher earnings. The way to improve productivity, Taylor thought, was to scientifically study the most efficient way to do things and then teach people those methods; this became known as **scientific management**. Three elements were basic to Taylor's approach: time, methods, and rules of work. His most important tools were observation and the stopwatch. It's Taylor's ideas that today determine how many burgers McDonald's expects its flippers to flip and how many callers the phone companies expect operators to assist.[1]

A classic Taylor story involves his study of men shoveling rice, coal, and iron ore with the same type of shovel. Taylor felt that different materials called for different shovels. He proceeded to invent a wide variety of sizes and shapes of shovels and, with stopwatch in hand, measured output over time in what were called **time-motion studies**—studies of the tasks performed to complete a job and the time needed to do each task. Sure enough, an average person could shovel more (from 25 tons to 35 tons per day) with the proper shovel using the most efficient motions. This finding led to time-motion studies of virtually every factory job. As the most efficient ways of doing things were determined, efficiency became the standard for setting goals.

Taylor's scientific management became the dominant strategy for improving productivity in the early 1900s. Hundreds of time-motion specialists developed standards in plants throughout the country. One follower of Taylor was H. L. Gantt. He developed charts by which managers plotted the work of employees a day in advance down to the smallest detail. (See Chapter 9 for a discussion of Gantt charts.) Frank and Lillian Gilbreth used Taylor's ideas in a three-year study of bricklaying. They developed the **principle of motion economy**, which showed that every job could be broken down into a series of elementary motions called a therblig (Gilbreth spelled backward with the *t* and *h* transposed). They then analyzed each motion to make it more efficient.

Scientific management viewed people largely as machines that needed to be properly programmed. There was little concern for the psychological or human aspects of work. Taylor felt simply that workers would perform at a high level of effectiveness (that is, be motivated) if they received high enough pay.

As mentioned earlier, some of Taylor's ideas are still being implemented. Management guru Peter Drucker even calls Taylor's ideas "the most lasting contribution America has made to Western thought since *The Federalist Papers*."[2] Some companies still place more emphasis on conformity to work rules than on creativity, flexibility, and responsiveness. For example, United Parcel Service (UPS) tells drivers how fast to walk (three feet per second), how many packages to pick up and deliver a day (average of 400), and how to hold their keys (teeth up, third finger). Drivers even wear "ring scanners," electronic devices on their index fingers wired to a small computer on their wrists that shoot a pattern of photons at a bar code on a package to let a customer trolling the Internet know exactly where his or her package is at any given moment.[3] See the Legal Briefcase box on page 290 for more about scientific management at UPS.

◄ **LEARNING GOAL 1.** Explain Taylor's scientific management.

◄ **CONSIDER USING SUPPLEMENTAL CASE 10-1**
Using Compensation to Motivate (**SCANS**)

scientific management
Studying workers to find the most efficient way of doing things and then teaching people those techniques.

time-motion studies
Studies of the tasks performed to complete a job and the time needed to do each task.

◄ **CONSIDER USING OT ACETATE 10-1**
Intrinsic Versus Extrinsic Rewards

principle of motion economy
Theory that every job can be broken down into a series of elementary motions.

◄ **CONSIDER USING LECTURE ENHANCER 10-2**
Gilbreth's Motion Study

Legal Briefcase

http://www.ups.com/

Scientific Management Is Alive and Well at UPS

United Parcel Service (UPS) is truly a powerhouse of a company. With over $20 billion in revenues and 335,000 employees, UPS is the world's largest package distribution company. The company grew from a small bicycle-messenger service in 1907 to today's mammoth delivery service by dictating every task for its employees. Drivers are required to step out of their trucks with their right foot, fold their money faceup, and carry packages under their left arm. If they are considered slow, their supervisor rides with them, prodding them with stopwatches and clipboards. Drivers long accepted such direction, taking comfort in $20-per-hour wages, generous benefits, and an attractive profit-sharing plan.

The need to improve productivity to meet increased competition from other delivery services prompted UPS to add 20 new services that require more skill. Drivers must learn an assortment of new codes and billing systems and deliver an increasing number of packages that have special-handling and time-sensitive requirements. All of this pressure, however, has taken its toll. Many UPS drivers suffer from anxiety, phobias, or back strain, and UPS has twice the injury rate of other delivery companies. In 1994, UPS settled a $3 million OSHA complaint that it did not provide adequate safety for workers who handle hazardous wastes.

UPS's CEO Kent (Oz) Nelson says UPS is using new technologies and better planning to achieve greater productivity without overloading employees. Competition ▲

from services such as Federal Express (where workers earn 30 to 50 percent less than UPS workers) also requires greater efficiency. Nelson says that the variety of new services require drivers to remember more things. Because the jobs require more thinking, the company has begun hiring a new breed of skilled, college-educated workers.

In August 1997, the Teamsters Union, which represents 200,000 of UPS's employees, called a nationwide strike against the company because workers and managers couldn't reach agreement on a new contract. The Teamsters said they wanted better wages and pensions, and a safer workplace. They also wanted the company to limit its use of part-time workers, who receive fewer benefits, and provide more full-time jobs. The 15-day strike ended when the union and UPS managers agreed on a five-year deal that created 10,000 new full-time jobs from existing part-time positions, increased full-time pay by $3.10 an hour, and retained the pension plan. Do you think the new breed of UPS workers will be more or less tolerant of the company's rules and demands?

Source: "U.S. Teamsters OK Strike as UPS Talks Continue," *The Wall Street Journal Interactive Edition*, July 15, 1997; Aaron Bernstein, "At UPS, Part-Time Work Is a Full-Time Issue," *Business Week*, June 16, 1997, p. 88; "Teamsters to Pressure UPS Through Rallies in U.S. and Europe," *The Wall Street Journal*, May 22, 1997, and "Alexis Herman Praise for UPS Strike Settlement," *Jet*, September 8, 1997, pp. 4–5.

> **CONSIDER USING OT ACETATE 10-2**
> Does Company Morale Affect Motivation?

> **LEARNING GOAL 2.** Describe the Hawthorne studies and relate their significance to human-based management.

The benefits of relying on workers to come up with creative solutions to productivity problems have long been recognized, as we shall discover next.

••• THE HAWTHORNE STUDIES (MAYO) •••

One of the studies that grew out of Taylor's research was conducted at the Western Electric Company's Hawthorne plant in Cicero, Illinois. The study began in 1927 and ended six years later. Let's see why it was one of the major studies in management literature.

Elton Mayo and his colleagues from Harvard University came to the Hawthorne plant to test the degree of lighting associated with optimum productivity. In this respect, theirs was a traditional scientific management study; the idea was to keep records of the workers' productivity under different levels of illumination. But the initial experiments revealed a problem: The productivity of the experimental group compared to that of other workers doing the same job went up regardless of whether the lighting was bright or dim. This was true even when the lighting was reduced to about the level of moonlight. These results confused and frustrated the researchers, who had expected productivity to fall as the lighting was dimmed.

A second series of experiments was conducted. In these, a separate test room was set up where temperature, humidity, and other environmental factors could be manipulated. In the series of 13 experimental periods, productivity went up each time; in fact, it increased by 50 percent overall. When the experimenters repeated the original condition (expecting productivity to fall to original levels), productivity increased yet again. The experiments were considered a total failure at this point. No matter what the experimenters did, productivity went up. What was causing the increase?

In the end, Mayo guessed that some human or psychological factor was involved. He and his colleagues then interviewed the workers, asking them about their feelings and attitudes toward the experiment. The researchers' findings began a profound change in management thinking that continues today. Here is what they concluded:

- The workers in the test room thought of themselves as a social group. The atmosphere was informal, they could talk freely, and they interacted regularly with their supervisors and the experimenters. They felt special and worked hard to stay in the group. This motivated them.

- The workers were involved in the planning of the experiments. For example, they rejected one kind of pay schedule and recommended another, which was used. The workers felt that their ideas were respected

◄ **CONSIDER USING OT ACETATE 10-3**
Five Personal Qualities Related to Job Motivation

◄ **CONSIDER USING LECTURE ENHANCER 10-3**
Recognition: Making Heroes

MAGNET WIRE INSULATING DEPARTMENT

This picture from inside the Hawthorne plant is a classic in the study of motivation. It was at the Hawthorne plant that Elton Mayo and his research team from Harvard University gave birth to human-based motivational theory. Before the studies at Hawthorne, workers were often programmed to behave like human robots.

and that they were involved in managerial decision making. This, too, motivated them.

- The workers enjoyed the atmosphere of their special room and the additional pay they got for more productivity. Job satisfaction increased dramatically.

Hawthorne effect
The tendency for people to behave differently when they know they are being studied.

Researchers now use the term **Hawthorne effect** to refer to the tendency for people to behave differently when they know they're being studied. The Hawthorne study's results encouraged researchers to begin to study human motivation and the managerial styles that lead to more productivity. The emphasis of research shifted away from Taylor's scientific management to Mayo's new human-based management.

Mayo's findings led to completely new assumptions about employees. One of those assumptions, of course, was that pay was not the only motivator. In fact, money was found to be a relatively low motivator. That change in assumptions led to many theories about the human side of motivation. One of the best-known motivation theorists was Abraham Maslow, whose work we discuss next.

···· ▬▬▬ ····

MOTIVATION AND MASLOW'S HIERARCHY OF NEEDS

➤ **LEARNING GOAL 3.**
Identify the levels of Maslow's hierarchy of needs and relate their importance to employee motivation.

▼ **CONSIDER USING TM 73**
Maslow's Hierarchy of Needs

Maslow's hierarchy of needs
Theory of motivation that places different types of human needs in order of importance, from basic physiological needs to safety, social, and esteem needs to self-actualization needs.

Abraham Maslow believed that to understand motivation at work, one must understand human motivation in general. It seemed to him that motivation arises from need. That is, people are motivated to satisfy *unmet* needs; needs that have been satisfied no longer provide motivation. He thought that needs could be placed on a hierarchy of importance.

Figure 10.1 shows **Maslow's hierarchy of needs**, whose levels are as follows:

Physiological needs: basic survival needs, such as the need for food, water, and shelter.

┌   FIGURE **10.1**   ┐
· · · ·
MASLOW'S HIERARCHY OF NEEDS

Maslow's hierarchy of needs is based on the idea that motivation comes from need. If a need is met, it's no longer a motivator so a higher-level need becomes the motivator. This chart shows the various levels of need

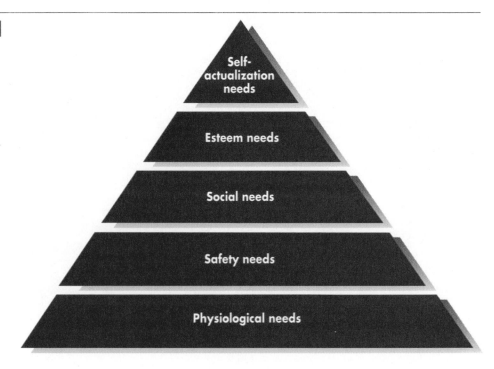

Safety needs: the need to feel secure at work and at home.

Social needs: the need to feel loved, accepted, and part of the group.

Esteem needs: the need for recognition and acknowledgment from others, as well as self-respect and a sense of status or importance.

Self-actualization needs: the need to develop to your fullest potential.

When one need is satisfied, another, higher-level need emerges and motivates the person to do something to satisfy it. The satisfied need is no longer a motivator.[4] For example, if you just ate a full-course dinner, hunger would no longer be a motivator. Also, lower-level needs (e.g., thirst) may emerge at any time they are not met, and take our attention away from higher-level needs such as the need for recognition or status.

Most of the world's workers struggle all day simply to meet the basic physiological and safety needs. In developed countries, such needs no longer dominate, and workers seek to satisfy growth needs (social, esteem, and self-actualization needs).

To compete successfully, U.S. firms must create a work environment that motivates the best and the brightest workers. That means establishing a work environment that includes goals such as social contribution, honesty, reliability, service, quality, dependability, and unity.

◄ **CONSIDER USING LECTURE ENHANCER 10-4**
Maslow's Further Study of Motivation

◄ **CONSIDER USING CRITICAL THINKING EXERCISE 10-1**
Maslow's Hierarchy of Needs

◄ **CONSIDER USING LECTURE ENHANCER 10-5**
The Big Thrill Motivation

Your job right now is to finish reading this chapter. How strongly would you be motivated to do that if you were sweating in a 105-degree room? Imagine now that your roommate turns on the air-conditioning. Now that you are more comfortable, are you more likely to read? Look at Maslow's hierarchy of needs to see what need would be motivating you at both times. Can you see how helpful Maslow's theory is in understanding motivation by applying it to your own life?

Critical Thinking

Andrew Grove of Intel is one of the 10 best executives in the United States. He has a Ph.D. and is a best-selling author. Grove believes in the concepts of Maslow and contends that managers can use his theory to improve workers' performance.

••• APPLYING MASLOW'S THEORY •••

Andrew Grove, CEO and chairman of Intel, has observed Maslow's concepts in action in his firm. One woman, for example, took a low-paying job, which did little for her family's standard of living. Why? Because she needed the companionship her work offered (social/affiliation need). One of Grove's friends had a midlife crisis when he was made a vice president. This position had been a lifelong goal, and when the man reached it he had to find another way to motivate himself (self-actualization need). People at a research and development lab were motivated by the desire to know more about their field of interest, but they had little desire to produce results, and thus little was achieved. Grove had to find new people who wanted to learn in order to achieve results.

Once one understands the need level of employees, it is easier to design programs that will trigger self-motivation. Grove believes that all motivation comes from within. He believes that self-actualized persons are achievers. Personally, Grove was motivated to earn a doctorate from the University of California at Berkeley and to write a best-selling book, *Only the Paranoid Survive*.[5] He also proceeded at Intel to design a managerial program that emphasized achievement. Now Intel's managers are highly motivated to achieve their objectives because they feel rewarded for doing so.[6]

Progress
Check

- What are the similarities and differences between Taylor's scientific management and Mayo's Hawthorne studies?
- How did Mayo's findings influence scientific management?
- Can you draw Maslow's hierarchy of needs? Label and describe the parts.
- According to Andrew Grove, what is the ultimate source of all motivation?

> **LEARNING GOAL 4.**
Differentiate among Theory X, Theory Y, and Theory Z.

···· ▬▬▬ ····

McGREGOR'S THEORY X AND THEORY Y

The way managers go about motivating people at work depends greatly on their attitudes toward workers. Douglas McGregor observed that managers' attitudes generally fall into one of two entirely different managerial styles, which he called Theory X and Theory Y.

> **CONSIDER USING LECTURE ENHANCER 10-6**
Personality Traits of CEOs and Army Generals

> **CONSIDER USING SUPPLEMENTAL CASE 10-2**
Theories Z and Y: That's How the Cookie Crumbles (**SCANS**)

••• THEORY X •••

The assumptions of Theory X management are as follows:

- The average person dislikes work and will avoid it if possible.
- Because of this dislike, workers must be forced, controlled, directed, or threatened with punishment to make them put forth the effort to achieve the organization's goals.
- The average worker prefers to be directed, wishes to avoid responsibility, has relatively little ambition, and wants security.
- Primary motivators are fear and money.

The natural consequence of such attitudes, beliefs, and assumptions is a manager who is very "busy" and who hangs over people telling them what to do and how to do it. Motivation is more likely to take the form of punishment for bad work rather than rewards for good work. Workers are given little responsibility, authority, or flexibility. Those were the assumptions behind Taylor's scientific management and other theorists who preceded Taylor. That is why management literature focused on time-motion studies that calculated the "one best" way to perform a task and the "optimum" time to be devoted to a task. It was assumed that workers needed to be trained and carefully watched to see that they conformed to the standards.

> **CONSIDER USING LECTURE ENHANCER 10-7**
Type A Managers

Theory X management still dominates some organizations. Many managers and entrepreneurs still suspect that employees cannot be fully trusted and need to be closely supervised.[7] No doubt you have seen such managers in action. How did this make you feel? Were these managers' assumptions accurate regarding the workers' attitudes?

> **CONSIDER USING LECTURE ENHANCER 10-8**
Motivation and Creativity

••• THEORY Y •••

Theory Y makes entirely different assumptions about people:

- Most people like work; it is as natural as play or rest.
- Most people naturally work toward goals to which they are committed.
- The depth of a person's commitment to goals depends on the perceived rewards for achieving them.

- Under certain conditions, most people not only accept but also seek responsibility.

- People are capable of using a relatively high degree of imagination, creativity, and cleverness to solve problems.

- In industry, the average person's intellectual potential is only partially realized.

- People are motivated by a variety of rewards. Each worker is stimulated by a reward unique to that worker (time off, money, recognition, etc.).

Rather than emphasize authority, direction, and close supervision, Theory Y emphasizes a relaxed managerial atmosphere in which workers are free to set objectives, be creative, be flexible, and go beyond the goals set by management.[8] A key technique in meeting these objectives is empowerment ⇒ P. 207 ⇐. Empowerment gives employees the ability to make decisions and the tools to implement the decisions they make. For empowerment to be a real motivator, management should follow these three steps: (1) find out what people think the problems in the organization are, (2) let them design the solutions, and (3) get out of the way and let them put those solutions into action.

Often employees complain that they're asked to become involved in company decision making, but their managers fail to actually empower them to make decisions. Have you ever worked in such an atmosphere? How did that make you feel?

The trend in many U.S. businesses is toward Theory Y management. One reason for this trend is that many service industries are finding Theory Y helpful in dealing with on-the-spot problems. Dan Kaplan of Hertz Rental Corporation would attest to this. He empowers his employees in the field to think and work as entrepreneurs. Leona Ackerly of Mini Maid Inc. agrees: "If our employees look at our managers as partners, a real team effort is built."[9]

···· ▬ ····

OUCHI'S THEORY Z

In addition to the stated reasons for the trend toward Theory Y management, another reason for a more flexible managerial style is to meet competition from foreign firms such as those in Japan, China, and the European Union. In the 1980s, William Ouchi, a professor of business at UCLA, wrote a best-selling book on management called *Theory Z: How American Business Can Meet the Japanese Challenge.* The book highlighted how organizations in Japan are run quite differently from those in the United States. Out of the Japanese system evolved a concept called Theory Z.[10] Major elements of Theory Z include virtually lifelong employment, collective decision-making, slow evaluation and promotion, and few levels of management.

Following Ouchi, several U.S. firms attempted to adopt aspects of this managerial style. Harold Geneen, however, reviewed Theory Z when he was CEO of ITT and concluded that Theory Z would not work as well in the United States as in Japan because of cultural differences. He questioned

The flexible style of Theory Z managers encourages employee creativity. John Allegretti (center) convinced Hyatt vice president Don DePorter (left) to let him start a recycling project. It was so successful that Hyatt let Allegretti develop and run a new waste-consulting company for Hyatt, called ReCycleCo Inc. Hyatt president Thomas J. Pritzker (right) endorses such intrapreneurship.

THEORY X	THEORY Y	THEORY Z
1. Employees dislike work and will try to avoid it.	1. Employees view work as a natural part of life.	1. Employee involvement is the key to increased productivity.
2. Employees prefer to be controlled and directed.	2. Employees prefer limited control and direction.	2. Employee control is implied and informal.
3. Employees seek security, not responsibility.	3. Employees will seek responsibility under proper work conditions.	3. Employees prefer to share responsibility and decision making.
4. Employees must be intimidated by managers to perform.	4. Employees perform better in work environments that are nonintimidating.	4. Employees perform better in environments that foster trust and cooperation.
5. Employees are motivated by financial rewards.	5. Employees are motivated by many different needs.	5. Employees need guaranteed employment and will accept slow evaluations and promotions.

┌   FIGURE **10.2**   ┐

• • • •

A COMPARISON OF THEORIES X, Y, AND Z

▲ **CONSIDER USING TM 74**
A Comparison of Theories X, Y, and Z

➤ **LEARNING GOAL 5.**
Distinguish between motivators and hygiene factors indentified by Herzberg.

➤ **CONSIDER USING OT ACETATE 10-4**
Most Common Motivators Used by Businesses in the U.S.

➤ **CONSIDER USING CRITICAL THINKING EXERCISE 10-2**
The Payoff (SCANS)

➤ **CONSIDER USING OT ACETATE 10-5**
How Do Workers Feel About Reward and Incentive Programs?

whether Americans would trade their heritage of personal freedom and individual opportunity for the ingrown paternalism, humility, and selflessness of the Japanese system. Geneen's estimation proved accurate—Theory Z principles were never widely adopted in U.S. business.

Judge for yourself, a job for life in a firm may sound good until you think of the implications: no chance to change jobs and no opportunity to move up quickly through the ranks. Since there are fewer layers of management in Japan, there are fewer management positions. These facts emphasize that the appropriate managerial style is one that matches the culture, the situation, and the specific needs of individual employees. (See Figure 10.2 for a summary of Theories X, Y, and Z.)

What *are* the factors that motivate workers in the United States? That is the question we address next.

•••• ▬▬▬ ••••

HERZBERG'S MOTIVATING FACTORS

Theories X, Y, and Z are concerned with styles of management. Another direction in managerial theory is to explore what managers can do with the job itself to motivate employees (a modern-day look at Taylor's research). In other words, some theorists are more concerned with the content of work than with style of management. They ask: Of all the factors controllable by managers, which are most effective in generating an enthusiastic work effort?

The most discussed study in this area was conducted in the mid-1960s by Frederick Herzberg.[11] He asked workers to rank various job-related factors in the order of importance relative to motivation. The question was, What creates enthusiasm for workers and makes them work to full potential? The results showed the most important factors that motivate workers to be (1) sense of achievement, (2) earned recognition, (3) interest in the work itself, (4) opportunity for growth, (5) opportunity for advancement, (6) importance of responsibility, (7) peer and group relationships, (8) pay, (9) supervisor's fairness, (10) company policies and rules, (11) status, (12) job security, (13) supervisor's friendliness, and (14) working conditions.

Herzberg noted that the factors receiving the most votes were all clustered around job content. Workers like to feel that they contribute (sense of achievement was number one). They want to earn recognition (number two) and feel

MOTIVATORS	HYGIENE (MAINTENANCE) FACTORS
(These factors can be used to motivate workers.)	(These factors can cause dissatisfaction, but changing them will have little motivational effect.)
Work itself	Company policy and administration
Achievement	Supervision
Recognition	Working conditions
Responsibility	Interpersonal relations (co-workers)
Growth and advancement	Salary, status, and job security

FIGURE 10.3
• • • •
HERZBERG'S MOTIVATORS AND HYGIENE FACTORS
There's some controversy over Herzberg's results. For example, sales managers often use money as a motivator. Recent studies have shown that money can be a motivator if used as part of a recognition program.

◄ CONSIDER USING TM 75
Herzberg's Motivators and Hygiene Factors

their jobs are important (number six). They want responsibility (which is why learning is so important) and want recognition for that responsibility by having a chance for growth and advancement. Of course, workers also want the job to be interesting.

Herzberg noted further that factors having to do with the job environment were not considered motivators by workers. It was interesting to find that one of those factors was pay. Workers felt that the absence of good pay, job security, friendly supervisors, and the like could cause dissatisfaction, but the presence of those factors did not motivate them; they just provided satisfaction and contentment in the work situation.

The conclusions of Herzberg's study were that certain factors, called **motivators**, did cause employees to be productive and gave them a great deal of satisfaction. These factors mostly had to do with job content. Herzberg called some other elements of the job **hygiene factors** (or maintenance factors). These had to do mostly with the job environment and could cause dissatisfaction if missing, but would not necessarily motivate employees if increased. See Figure 10.3 for a list of both motivators and hygiene factors.

Combining McGregor's Theory Y with Herzberg's motivating factors, we come up with these conclusions:

- Employees work best when management assumes that employees are competent and self-motivated (Theory Y). Theory Y calls for a participative style of management.

- The best way to motivate employees is to make the job interesting, help them to achieve their objectives, and recognize that achievement through advancement and added responsibility.

motivators
Factors that cause employees to be productive and that give them satisfaction.

hygiene factors
Factors that can cause dissatisfaction if missing but do not necessarily motivate employees if increased.

••• APPLYING HERZBERG'S THEORIES •••

Pat Blake, a Sunnen Products Co. employee, says that what makes her happy to work extra hours or learn new skills is less tangible than money or bonuses—it's a kind word from her boss. "When something good happens, like we have a shipping day with so many thousands of dollars going out the door, they let us know about that," Blake says. "It kind of makes you want to go for the gold."[12] Improved working conditions (such as better wages or increased security) are taken for granted after workers get used to them. This is what Herzberg meant by hygiene (or maintenance) factors: their absence causes dissatisfaction, but

◄ CONSIDER USING LECTURE ENHANCER 10-9
Motivation and Rewards

◄ CONSIDER USING TM 76
Comparison of Maslow's Hierarchy of Needs and Herzberg's Theory of Factors

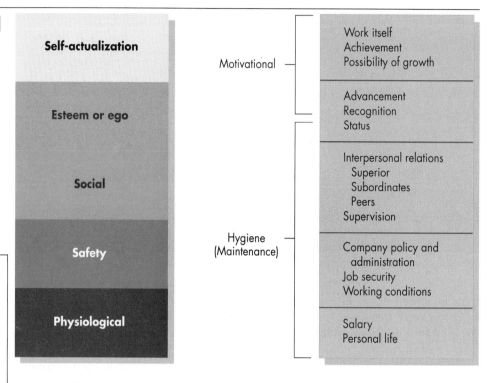

FIGURE 10.4
· · · ·
COMPARISON OF
MASLOW'S HIERARCHY
OF NEEDS AND
HERZBERG'S THEORY OF
FACTORS

Sometimes it's hard to believe that money doesn't motivate. NBA players like Kevin Garnett make lots of money (his long-term contract pays him $120 million), but when he's on the court, is it the money or the challenge of competition that makes him play harder? What else do you think drives him to the net?

their presence (maintenance) does not motivate. The best motivator for some employees is a simple and sincere "I really appreciate what you're doing."

Many surveys conducted to test Herzberg's theories have supported Herzberg's finding that the number one motivator is not money but a sense of achievement and recognition for a job well done. If you're skeptical about this, think about the limitations money has as a motivating force. Most organizations review an employee's performance only once a year and allocate raises at that time. To inspire and motivate employees to perform at their highest level of capability, achievements and progress toward goals must be recognized more than once a year.[13] In the National Survey of the Changing Workforce conducted by the Families and Work Institute in New York, salary ranked 16th in a list of items considered very important in rating jobs. A study prepared by Robert Half International, a staffing and recruitment firm in Menlo Park, California, identified limited praise and recognition as the primary reason employees leave their job.[14] The Spotlight on Small Business box on p. 299 profiles how one manager motivates employees in low-paying jobs. A review of Figure 10.4 shows that there is a good deal of similarity in Maslow's hierarchy of needs and Herzberg's theory of factors.

· · · · ▬ · · · ·
JOB ENRICHMENT

Both Maslow's and Herzberg's theories were extended by job enrichment theory. **Job enrich-**

Spotlight on Small Business

http://www.subway.com/

Motivating Low-Wage Workers

Both large and small companies would agree that attracting and keeping skilled employees is essential for growing a successful business. Most employers, however, realize this is easier said than done. The situation can even hit crisis proportions in certain service industries such as fast food, where businesses depend on entry-level, low-wage workers and employee turnover can reach 200 percent in a year. Motivational theorists such as Frederick Herzberg have concluded that money is generally not a good long-term motivator in the workplace, but can you possibly motivate a worker who is earning only minimum wage?

Steve Lauer, owner of eight Subway Sandwich shops asked that very question. At Lauer's Subway shops the majority of employees are under age 20 and earn slightly above the minimum wage. He found that workers missing shifts was a particular problem, as was a general feeling of indifference toward the job. To make matters worse, turnover numbers soared in June when college students left their Subway jobs to return home for the summer. When Lauer's employee turnover numbers surpassed 200 percent, he decided it was time to do something.

Realizing that half of his workers quit within their first 30 days, Lauer set out to lower the stress level of new employees. To help put new workers at ease, he assigned managers or designated trainers to spend at least 20 hours with them during their first two weeks on the job. He also decided that managers would evaluate employees at ▲

the end of the first 30 days rather than at the end of the quarter. In addition to these changes, Lauer placed special emphasis on an employee's one-year anniversary. After one year on the job, workers are invited to the company's holiday party and summer picnic; they receive one week of paid vacation, a service pin, a Subway sweatshirt, and a different-colored uniform. Length of service is denoted by three different uniform colors and has become a source of pride among employees. He also insists that managers give potential employees a realistic job preview so that applicants know what to expect if they choose to work for the company.

Lauer's actions reduced employee turnover to less than 100 percent at several of his stores. While such

actions are not guaranteed to work in every situation, Lauer's story does prove that a concerted effort to expand employee motivation can be successful even in the most difficult of situations. What's required of small-business owners is sensitivity, common sense, and a good measure of psychology to motivate low-wage workers successfully.

Sources: Roberta Maynard, "How to Motivate Low-Wage Workers," *Nation's Business,* May 1997, pp. 35–39 and Phyllis Berman, "Sweaty Equity," *Forbes,* December 1, 1997, p. 164.

---

ment is a motivational strategy that emphasizes motivating the worker through the job itself. Work is assigned to individuals so that they have the opportunity to complete an identifiable task from beginning to end. They are held responsible for successful completion of the task. The motivational effect of job enrichment can come from the opportunities for personal achievement, challenge, and recognition. Go back and review Maslow's and Herzberg's work to see how job enrichment grew out of those theories.

Five characteristics of work are believed to be important in affecting individual motivation and performance:

1. *Skill variety.* The extent to which a job demands different skills.

2. *Task identity.* The degree to which the job requires doing a task with a visible outcome from beginning to end.

3. *Task significance.* The degree to which the job has a substantial impact on the lives or work of others in the company.

job enrichment
A motivational strategy that emphasizes motivating the worker through the job itself.

◄ **LEARNING GOAL 6.** Explain how job enrichment affects employee motivation and performance.

► **LEARNING GOAL 7.** Identify the steps involved in implementing a management by objectives (MBO) program.

job simplification
Process of producing task efficiency by breaking down the job into simple steps and assigning people to each of those steps.

job enlargement
Job enrichment strategy involving combining a series of tasks into one assignment that is more challenging and interesting.

Enriching jobs motivates workers by appealing to personal values such as achievement, challenge and recognition. Sherwin Williams is a company committed to the principles of job enrichment. At the Sherwin Williams Richmond, Kentucky, plant self-managed work teams are trained to perform different tasks and have clear autonomy over how their jobs are organized. The program begun in 1975 has been so successful in reducing absenteeism, turnover, and increasing productivity it has been expanded to many of the company's other plants and distribution centers.

job rotation
Job enrichment strategy involving moving employees from one job to another.

goal-setting theory
Theory that setting specific, attainable goals can motivate workers and improve performance if the goals are accepted, are accompanied by feedback, and are facilitated by organizational conditions.

4. *Autonomy*. The degree of freedom, independence, and discretion in scheduling work and determining procedures.

5. *Feedback*. The amount of direct and clear information that is received about job performance.

Variety, identity, and significance contribute to the meaningfulness of the job. Autonomy gives people a feeling of responsibility, and feedback contributes to a feeling of achievement and recognition.

Sherwin-Williams, North America's largest manufacturer of paints and varnishes, began a job enrichment program in its Richmond, Kentucky, plant in 1975. Employees are grouped into self-managed teams, and the members are trained to do all of the jobs assigned to their team. The teams have autonomy to

decide where members work, what they do, and how they train other team members; the teams are also responsible for results. Compensation is based on a pay-for-knowledge system, and team members' performance is evaluated by their team leaders and peers. Employees are made to feel responsible for the entire production process.

Sherwin-Williams's program has been extremely successful. Overall, absenteeism runs less than 2 percent. Turnover is very low, and productivity is 30 percent higher than at similar plants. Cost per gallon of paint is 45 percent lower than at traditionally managed paint plants. The firm has expanded the Richmond program to other plants and distribution centers.

As mentioned above, job enrichment is based on Herzberg's higher motivators such as responsibility, achievement, and recognition. It stands in contrast to **job simplification**, which produces task efficiency by breaking down the job into simple steps and assigning people to each of those steps. There isn't much motivation in doing boring, repetitive work, but some managers who still operate on the Taylor level of motivation use job simplification. In fact, job simplification is sometimes necessary, particularly with people learning new skills.

Another type of job enrichment used for motivation is **job enlargement**, which combines a series of tasks into one assignment that is more challenging and interesting. For example, Maytag, the home appliance manufacturer, redesigned its work so that employees could assemble an entire water pump instead of just one part. **Job rotation** also makes work more interesting and motivating by moving employees from one job to another. One problem with job rotation, of course, is having to train employees to do several different operations. However, the resulting increase in employee morale and motivation offsets the additional costs.

Job enrichment is one way to ensure that workers enjoy responsibility and a sense of accomplishment. Another way is to get everyone to agree on specific company objectives.

···· ▬▬▬ ····

GOAL-SETTING THEORY AND MANAGEMENT BY OBJECTIVES

Goal-setting theory is based on the notion that the setting of specific, ambitious, but attainable goals will lead to high levels of motivation and performance if the goals are accepted, accompanied by feedback, and facilitated by organizational conditions. All members of an organization should have some basic agreement about the overall goals of the organization and the specific objectives to be met by each department and individual. It follows, then, that there should be a system to involve everyone in the organization in goal setting and implementation.

Peter Drucker developed such a system in the 1960s. Drucker asserted, "Managers cannot motivate people; they can only thwart people's motivation because people motivate themselves."[15] Thus, he designed his system to help employees motivate themselves. Called **management by objectives (MBO)**, it is a system of goal setting and implementation that involves a cycle of discussion, review, and evaluation of objectives among top and middle-level managers, supervisors, and employees. Large corporations such as the Ford Motor Company used MBO and taught the method to the U.S. Defense Department. MBO then spread to other companies and government agencies. When implemented properly, MBO meets the criteria of goal-setting theory and can be quite effective. MBO calls on managers to formulate goals in cooperation with everyone in the organization, to commit employees to those goals, and then to monitor results and reward accomplishment. There are six steps in the MBO process (see Figure 10.5). Can you tell how the model is intended to help workers motivate themselves?

MBO was widely used in the 1960s, and the management literature of the 1970s was packed with articles about MBO, but very little was written about it in the 1980s and 1990s. Some critics of MBO now see it as being out of date and inconsistent with contemporary management thought and practice. Does that mean that MBO isn't used any longer? Not according to one 1995 study, which found that 47 percent of the organizations surveyed use some form of MBO.[16]

MBO is most effective in relatively stable situations where long-range plans can be made and implemented with little need for major changes. It is also important to MBO that managers understand the difference between helping and coaching subordinates. *Helping* means working with the subordinate and doing part of the work if necessary. *Coaching* means acting as a resource—teaching, guiding, and recommending—but not helping (that is, not participating actively or doing the task). The central idea of MBO is that employees need to motivate themselves.

Problems can arise when management uses MBO as a strategy for *forcing* managers and workers to commit to goals that are not really mutually agreed on but are set by top management. Employee involvement and expectations are important.

Victor Vroom identified the importance of employee expectations and developed a process called expectancy theory. Let's examine this concept next.

···· ▬▬▬ ····

MEETING EMPLOYEE EXPECTATIONS: EXPECTANCY THEORY

According to Victor Vroom's **expectancy theory**, employee expectations can affect an individual's motivation.[17] Therefore, the amount of effort employees

management by objectives (MBO)
A system of goal setting and implementation that involves a cycle of discussion, review, and evaluation of objectives among top and middle-level managers, supervisors, and employees.

expectancy theory
Victor Vroom's theory that the amount of effort employees exert on a specific task depends on their expectations of the outcome.

▼ CONSIDER USING TM 77
Management by Objectives

⌐ FIGURE 10.5 ¬
····
MANAGEMENT BY OBJECTIVES

The critical step in the MBO process is the one where managers sit down with workers, discuss the objectives, and get the workers to commit to those objectives in writing. Commitment is the key!

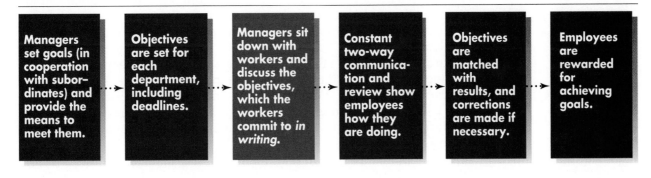

| Managers set goals (in cooperation with subordinates) and provide the means to meet them. | Objectives are set for each department, including deadlines. | Managers sit down with workers and discuss the objectives, which the workers commit to *in writing*. | Constant two-way communication and review show employees how they are doing. | Objectives are matched with results, and corrections are made if necessary. | Employees are rewarded for achieving goals. |

Yoplait yogurt managers grew a thriving business by setting goals for themselves that were even higher that those set by their parent company, General Mills. They surpassed their goals and were rewarded with bonuses that amounted to about half their annual salaries. Explain how this example relates to Vroom's expectancy theory.

exert on a specific task depends on their expectations of the outcome. Vroom contends that employees ask three questions before committing maximum effort to a task: (1) Can I accomplish the task? (2) If I do accomplish it, what's my reward? (3) Is the reward worth the effort?

Think of the effort you might exert in your class under the following conditions: Your instructor says that to earn an A in the course you must achieve an average of 90 percent on coursework plus jump 8 feet high. Would you exert maximum effort toward earning an A if you knew you could not possibly jump 8 feet high? Or what if your instructor said students could earn an A in the course but you know that this instructor has not awarded an A in 25 years of teaching? If the reward of an A seems unattainable, would you exert significant effort to try to attain one? Better yet, let's say that you read in the newspaper that businesses actually prefer C-minus students to A-minus students. Does the reward of an A seem worth it? Now think of the same type of situations that may occur on the job.

Expectancy theory does note that expectation varies from individual to individual. Employees therefore establish their own view in terms of task difficulty and the value of the reward. Researchers David Nadler and Edward Lawler modified Vroom's theory and suggested that managers follow five steps to improve employee performance:

1. Determine what rewards are valued by employees.
2. Determine each employee's desired performance standard.
3. Ensure that performance standards are attainable.
4. Guarantee rewards tied to performance.
5. Be certain that rewards are considered adequate.[18]

➤ **LEARNING GOAL 8.** Explain the key factors involved in expectancy theory.

equity theory
Theory that employees try to maintain equity between inputs and outputs compared to others in similar positions.

➤ **CONSIDER USING OT ACETATE 10-6**
How to Use Expectancy Theory

➤ **CONSIDER USING OT ACETATE 10-7**
Employee Questions About Expectancy to Motivation

➤ **CONSIDER USING OT ACETATE 10-8**
Six Keys to Motivation

➤ **LEARNING GOAL 9.** Examine the key principles of equity theory.

···· ▬▬▬ ····
TREATING EMPLOYEES FAIRLY: EQUITY THEORY

Equity theory deals with the question "If I do a good job, will it be worth it?" It has to do with perceptions of fairness and how those perceptions affect employees' willingness to perform. The basic principle is that employees try to maintain equity between inputs and outputs compared to others in similar positions. Equity comparisons are made from the information that is available through personal relationships, professional organizations, and so on.

When workers do perceive inequity, they will try to reestablish equitable exchanges in a number of ways. For example, suppose you compare the grade you earned on a term paper with your classmates' grades. If you think you received a lower grade compared to the students who put out the same effort as you, you will probably react in one of two ways: (1) by reducing your effort on future class projects or (2) by rationalizing (e.g., by saying "Grades are overvalued anyway!"). If you think your paper received a higher grade than comparable papers, you will probably (1) increase your effort to justify the higher reward in the future or (2) rationalize by saying "I'm worth it!" In the workplace, inequity leads to lower productivity, reduced quality, increased absenteeism, and voluntary resignation.

Remember that equity judgments are based on perceptions and are therefore subject to errors in perception. When workers overestimate their own contributions—as happens often—they are going to feel that any rewards given out for performance are inequitable. Sometimes organizations try to deal with this by keeping salaries secret, but secrecy may make things worse; employees are likely to overestimate the salaries of others in addition to overestimating their own contribution. In general the best remedy is clear and frequent communication. Managers must communicate as clearly as possible the results that are expected and what will follow when those results are achieved or not.

Progress Check

- Briefly describe the managerial attitudes behind Theories X, Y, and Z.
- Employees at small firms seem relatively happy with their jobs, yet about half plan to leave in a few years. Why might this be so?
- Relate job enrichment to Herzberg's motivating factors.
- What are the six steps in management by objectives?
- Evaluate expectancy theory? Can you think of situations where expectancy theory could apply to your efforts or lack of effort?

···· ▬▬ ····

IMPLEMENTING THE NEW CONCEPTS: MOTIVATION THROUGH COMMUNICATION

Management by objectives teaches us that, in any organization, one key to successful management and motivation is the establishment and maintenance of open communication so that both managers and workers understand the objectives and work together to achieve them. Communication in the organization must flow two ways. The problem is that communication often flows only one way: from top management down. One-way communication takes the form of directives, policies, announcements, memos, rules, procedures, and the like.

The flow upward, from workers to managers, is usually severely restricted. Rarely do organizations have any formal means of upward communication

◄ **CONSIDER USING LECTURE ENHANCER 10-10**
Learning Corporate Language

◄ **CONSIDER USING LECTURE ENHANCER 10-11**
Doublespeak

◄ **CONSIDER USING LECTURE ENHANCER 10-12**
Body Language

Job enrichment motivates workers by appealing to personal values such as achievement, challenge, and recognition. Harley-Davidson is a company committed to the principles of job enrichment. At Harley-Davidson, self-managed teams of workers are trained to perform different tasks and have clear autonomy over how their job is organized. The team is also responsible for its own results.

➤ CONSIDER USING SUPPLEMENTAL CASE 10-3
How Corporate Culture Motivates
(SCANS)

➤ CONSIDER USING LECTURE ENHANCER 10-13
The Myth of Top Management Teams

➤ CONSIDER USING LECTURE ENHANCER 10-14
Rethinking the Corporation

equivalent to directives and announcements. Instead, the burden falls on workers to initiate contact with supervisors and present their ideas and suggestions. As you might imagine, few people in any organization are willing to tell the boss when things are not going well. Children don't tell parents when they've broken something, students don't tell teachers when someone has goofed, and employees don't tell bosses. Such a system creates an atmosphere of "us against them," in which workers feel united in their distrust and avoidance of managers. To create an atmosphere of "us working together," managers have to become active listeners and valued assistants to workers. Such a change often demands radical retraining of managers and careful creation of new attitudes and beliefs among workers.

Teamwork does not happen by itself. The whole organization must be structured to make it easy for managers and employees to talk to one another. Procedures for encouraging open communication include the following:

- Top managers must first create an organizational culture that rewards listening. They must create places to talk (e.g., conference rooms), and they must show employees that talking with superiors counts—by providing feedback, adopting employee suggestions, and rewarding upward communication—even if the discussion is negative. Employees must feel free to say anything they deem appropriate.

- Supervisors and managers must be trained to listen. Most people receive no such training in school or anywhere else, so organizations must do the training themselves or hire someone to do it.

- Barriers to open communication must be removed. Having separate offices, parking spaces, bathrooms, dining rooms, and so on only places barriers between managers and workers. Other barriers are different dress codes and different ways of addressing one another (e.g., calling workers by their first names and managers by their last). Removing such barriers may require imagination and a willingness on the part of managers to give up their special privileges.

- Efforts to facilitate communication must be actively undertaken. Large lunch tables where all organization members eat, conference rooms, organizational picnics, organizational athletic teams, and other such outings all allow managers to mix with each other and with workers.

Leaders who don't commit themselves to fostering openness and who continue to create barriers to communication often pay a heavy price. William Agee, CEO of Morrison Knudson, moved his headquarters to Pebble Beach, California, and left his managers and employees in distant Idaho. This created a spirit of distrust and open resentment that eventually cost Agee his position.[19]

Let's see how some organizations are addressing the challenge of open communications.

••• OPEN COMMUNICATION AND SELF-MANAGED TEAMS •••

Companies with highly motivated workforces usually have several things in common. Among the most important are open communication systems and self-managed teams. These are both features at the Ford Motor Company. Kenneth Kohrs, vice president of car product development at Ford, says that an inside group known as "Team Mustang" sets the guidelines for how production teams should be formed. Given the challenge to create a car that would make people dust off their old "Mustang Sally" records and dance into the showrooms, the 400-member team was also given the freedom to make decisions

Making Ethical Decisions

Motivating Temporary Employees

You work as a manager for a Highbrow's, a rather prestigious department store. Each year, in order to handle the large number of shoppers at Christmastime, you must hire temporary employees. Because of store policy and budget constraints, all temporaries must be discharged on January 10. As you interview prospective employees, you give the impression that the store will hire at least two new full-time retail salespeople for the

coming year. You hope that this will serve to motivate the temporary workers and even foster some competition among them. You also instruct your permanent salespeople to reinforce the falsehood that good work during the Christmas season is the path to full-time employment. Is this an ethical way to try to motivate your employees? What are the dangers of using a tactic such as this?

▲ SCANS

without waiting for approval from headquarters or other departments. The team moved everyone from various departments into cramped offices under one roof of an old warehouse. Draftsmen sat next to accountants, engineers next to stylists. Budgetary walls that divided departments were knocked down as department managers were persuaded to surrender some control over their subordinates.

When the resulting Mustang convertible displayed shaking problems, suppliers were called in, and the team worked around the clock to solve the problem. The engineers were so motivated to complete the program on schedule and under budget that they slept on the floors of the warehouse. The senior Ford executives were tempted to overrule the program, but they stuck with their promise not to meddle. The team solved the shaking problem and still came in under budget and a couple of months early.[20]

To implement such groups or teams, managers at most companies must reinvent work. This means respecting workers, providing interesting work, rewarding good work, developing workers' skills, allowing autonomy, and decentralizing authority. Such principles are particularly important to the many workers who are members of what has been called Generation X.[21] In the process of reinventing work, it is essential that managers behave ethically toward all employees. The Making Ethical Decisions box illustrates the problem managers may face when filling temporary positions.

••• CHANGING ORGANIZATIONS IS ••• NOT EASY

We have come a long way from the time-motion studies of Frederick Taylor. The work of Maslow, Mayo, Herzberg, Vroom, and others has taught some managers to treat employees as associates and to get them more involved in decision making. This increases motivation and leads to greater productivity.

Highly motivated work teams depend on open communications and self-management. Ford Motor Company provided such an atmosphere for its 400 member "Team Mustang" work group. The work team, the company, and consumers all came out on top with this market-winning automobile.

215-HP 4.6L OHC V-8, 4-WHEEL POWER DISC BRAKES, PASSIVE ANTI-THEFT SYSTEM, AND SPORT-TUNED SUSPENSION ARE ALL STANDARD.   www.ford.com

THIS HORSE IS ROCKING.

MUSTANG GT   HAVE YOU DRIVEN A FORD LATELY?

Other managers, however, have been brought up under a different system. Those from the military are used to telling people what to do rather than consulting with them, and those from the football-coach school of management tend to yell and direct rather than consult and discuss.

Furthermore, employees often are not used to participative management ➤ P. 213 ◀. The transition from Theory X to Theory Y management, from Taylor to Herzberg, is still going on. It is important, then, to have examples to follow when trying to implement the new approaches.

Miller Brewing Company and Mary Kay Cosmetics are glowing examples of companies that succeeded at taking a lead in employee motivation, customer service, and establishment of a general partnership with employees. Let's review the experience of these two companies to see what lessons we can learn.

••• A MODEL FOR THE FUTURE: EMPLOYEE EMPOWERMENT •••

Miller Brewing Company is the second largest brewer in the United States. It opened its brewery of the future in Trenton, Ohio, with a mandate to develop a totally new workplace design that abandoned the rigidity of traditional brewery operations. The company decided to experiment by employing self-directed, cross-functional teams of 6 to 19 employees. The teams were assigned to handle brewing, packaging, and distribution.

To keep communications open, the company established an electronic mailbox for each employee and gave each team its own local area network terminal. In the daily operations at the brewery, employees rotated jobs, routinely backed up each other, and learned exactly how their actions affected the other employees. Workers enjoyed the freedom and flexibility offered at the plant, and the Trenton brewery enjoyed a 30 percent increase in productivity in comparison to Miller's other breweries. The top union official at the plant says, "We're partners in the business. We don't just make beer, we manage day-to-day operations. At this facility we have so many different tasks we don't check our brains at the door." According to company officials, "that's what teamwork is all about. Employees can't just say this is my job and my job only."[22]

Mary Kay Ash started her $613 million cosmetics company in 1963 when the promotion she had been working toward was given to her male assistant, whom she had just spent nine months training. She vowed to run a company that would treat women right, not "ruin their self-esteem" or limit how much money they could make. Developing women's leadership potential was a priority at Mary Kay Cosmetics from the start. Many Mary Kay consultants are refugees from corporate America. There are lawyers, a Harvard MBA, and even a pediatrician in the Mary Kay ranks.

But everyone starts off on the same foot. If you were a rocket scientist in your last job, great—but you still need to buy a beauty case and start calling your friends. Your earnings will increase as your sales do and as you recruit more Mary Kay employees, who are known as consultants. More important, though, is the emotional compensation the job provides.

Every summer, for example, more than 36,000 Mary Kay beauty consultants invade Dallas, Texas, to participate in a three-day sales rally called Seminar—at which there is plenty of emotion. Seminar is part convention, part *Hello Dolly*. Caught up in the Mary Kay enthusiasm, the women laugh, cry, and sing as the company doles out diamonds and pink Cadillacs under enough spotlights and sequins to rival any Broadway musical. Color-coded suits, badges, sashes, crowns, and other emblems show how far each person has come—like military insignia, they immediately indicate who's done what.

Despite the glitter of the diamonds and cars given out at Seminar, the most treasured rewards are the vacations, which often offer consultants

➤ CONSIDER USING OT ACETATE 10-9
How Often Do Employees Feel Stressed on the Job?

➤ CONSIDER USING LECTURE ENHANCER 10-15
Employee Control on the Assembly Line

➤ CONSIDER USING OT ACETATE 10-10
Warning Signs of Employee Stress

➤ CONSIDER USING LECTURE ENHANCER 10-16
The Consequences of Stress

special treatment. On one trip to London, Mary Kay got Harrods to close for an hour so that only Mary Kay consultants could shop there. Mary Kay Ash herself goes on many of these trips. Her consultants consider her to be uniquely approachable. "Mary Kay calls you her daughter and looks you dead in the eye. She is so sincerely concerned about your welfare that you feel you can do anything," reports one consultant. Mary Kay consultants are trained to treat their customers with the same kind of interest. They remember their customers' birthdays, send them notes, and find other ways to show concern. Mary Kay is not just a job, it's a way of life.[23]

LEARNING FROM MILLER BREWING'S AND MARY KAY'S EXPERIENCES

Understanding what motivates employees is the key to success in companies such as Miller Brewing Company and Mary Kay. Miller Brewing Company learned at its Trenton plant that teamwork promotes a self-starting philosophy among employees that encourages them to be superior. In fact, someone at the plant said the letters in *TEAM* stand for "Together, Everyone Achieves More."[24]

Mary Kay Ash developed not just a business but a true American success story. She believes that success in business depends on believing in yourself and showing interest in your employees and your customers. The best way to lead is by example, and Mary Kay is a model for employees and for managers in all types of firms.

The lessons we can learn from the Miller Brewing Company and Mary Kay examples include the following:

- The growth of industry and business in general depends on a motivated, productive workforce.

- Motivation is largely internal, generated by workers themselves; giving employees the freedom to be creative and rewarding achievement when it occurs will release their energy.

- The first step in any motivational program is to establish open communication among workers and managers so that the feeling generated is one of cooperation and teamwork. A family-type atmosphere should prevail.

> **CONSIDER USING OT ACETATE 10-11**
> Where Are Workers Most Satisfied With Their Jobs?

••• MOTIVATION IN THE FUTURE •••

Today's customers expect high-quality, customized goods and services. That means employees must provide extensive personal service and pay close attention to details. Employees will have to work smart as well as hard. No amount of supervision can force an employee to smile or to go the extra mile to help a customer. Managers need to know how to motivate their employees to meet customer needs.

Tomorrow's managers will not be able to use any one formula for all employees. Rather, they will have to get to know each worker personally and tailor the motivational effort to the individual. As you learned in this chapter, different employees respond to different managerial and motivational styles. This is further complicated by the increase in global business and the fact that managers now work with employees from a variety of cultural backgrounds. Different cultures experience motivational approaches differently, and therefore the manager of the future will have to study and understand these cultural factors in designing a reward system. The Reaching Beyond Our Borders box on page 308 describes how Digital Equipment dealt with these cultural issues within global teams.

In general, motivation will come from the job itself rather than from external punishments or rewards. Motivation is certainly difficult if employees do not

Reaching Beyond Our Borders

http://www.digital.com/

The Challenge of Global Work Teams

The new global economy has altered the world landscape by bringing products and services to every corner of the earth and helping many people in less-developed countries improve their quality of life. Business globalization has also resulted in the creation of global work teams, a rather formidable task.

Even though the concept of teamwork is nothing new, building a harmonious global work team is new and can be complicated. Global companies must recognize differing attitudes and competencies in the team's cultural mix and the technological capabilities among team members. For example, a global work team needs to determine whether the culture of its members is high-context or low-context. In a high-context team culture, members build personal relationships and develop group trust before focusing on tasks. In the low-context culture, members often view relationship building as a waste of time that diverts attention from the task. Koreans, Thais, and Saudis (high-context cultures), for example, often view American team members as insincere due to their need for data and quick decision making.

When Digital Equipment Corporation decided to consolidate its operations at six manufacturing sites, the company recognized the need to form multicultural work teams. Realizing the challenge it faced, Digital hired an internal organization-development specialist to train the team in relationship building, foreign languages, and valuing differences. All team members from outside the United States were assigned American partners and invited to spend time with their families. Digital also flew the flags of each employee's native country at all its manufacturing sites. As communication within the teams increased, the company reduced the time of new-product handoffs from up to three years to just six months.

Understanding the motivational forces in global organizations and building effective global teams is still new territory for most companies. Experiments such the one at Digital Equipment will be closely evaluated by other companies. Developing group leaders who are culturally astute, flexible, and able to deal with ambiguity is a challenge businesses must face in the 21st century.

Source: Sylvia Odenwald, "Global Work Teams," *Training and Development*, February 1996, pp. 54–60 and Vijay Govindarajan and Anil Gupta, "Success is All in the Mindset," *Financial Times*, February 27, 1998, p. 2.

value their jobs.[25] Managers need to give workers what they need to do a good job: the right tools, the right information, and the right amount of cooperation.

Will happy workers improve corporate performance? The Gallup Organization recently surveyed 55,000 workers in order to match employee attitudes with company results. The survey found four attitudes that, taken together, correlate strongly with higher profits. Specifically, the most successful companies are those in which workers feel that (1) they are given the opportunity to do what they do best every day, (2) their opinions count, (3) their fellow workers are committed to quality, and (4) there is a direct connection between their work and the company's mission.[26]

Motivation doesn't have to be difficult. It begins with acknowledging a job well done. You can simply tell those who do such a job that you appreciate them, especially in front of others. It's unfortunate that there are too few "high fives" in business.[27] After all, the best motivator is frequently a sincere "Thanks, I appreciate what you have done."

Progress
Check

- What are several steps firms can take to increase internal communications and thus motivation?
- What problems may emerge when trying to implement participative management?
- Why is it important today to adjust motivational styles to individual employees? Are there any general principles of motivation that today's managers should follow?

SUMMARY

● ● ● ● ● ●

1. Frederick Taylor was one of the first people to study management.
   - ● *What is Frederick Taylor known for?*

   Frederick Taylor is the father of scientific management. He did time-motion studies to learn the most efficient way of doing a job and then trained workers in those procedures. He published his book, *The Principles of Scientific Management,* in 1911. The Gilbreths and H. L. Gantt were followers of Taylor.

1. Explain Taylor's scientific management.

2. Management theory moved away from Taylor's scientific management and toward theories that stress human factors of motivation.
   - ● *What led to the more human managerial styles?*

   The greatest impact on motivation theory was generated by the Hawthorne studies in the late 1920s and early 1930s. In these studies, Elton Mayo found that human factors such as feelings of involvement and participation led to greater productivity gains than did physical changes in the workplace.

2. Describe the Hawthorne studies and relate their significance to human-based management.

3. Abraham Maslow studied basic human motivation and found that motivation was based on needs; he said that a person with an unfilled need would be motivated to satisfy it and that a satisfied need no longer served as motivation.
   - ● *What were the various levels of need identified by Maslow?*

   Starting at the bottom of Maslow's hierarchy of needs and going to the top, the levels of need are physiological, safety, social, esteem, and self-actualization.
   - ● *Can managers use Maslow's theory?*

   Yes; they can recognize what unmet needs a person has and design work so that it satisfies those needs.

3. Identify the levels of Maslow's hierarchy of needs and relate their importance to employee motivation.

4. Douglas McGregor held that managers will have one of two opposing attitudes toward employees. They are called Theory X and Theory Y. William Ouchi introduced Theory Z in response to McGregor.
   - ● *What are Theory X and Theory Y, and when were they developed?*

   Theory X assumes that the average person dislikes work and will avoid it if possible. Therefore, people must be forced, controlled, and threatened with punishment to accomplish organizational goals. Theory Y assumes that people like working and will accept responsibility for achieving goals if rewarded for doing so. McGregor published these theories in 1970.
   - ● *What is Theory Z?*

   Theory Z comes out of Japanese management and stresses long-term employment, among other factors.

4. Differentiate among Theory X, Theory Y, and Theory Z.

5. Distinguish between the motivators and hygiene factors identified by Herzberg.

5. Frederick Herzberg found that some factors are motivators and others are hygiene (or maintenance) factors; hygiene factors cause job dissatisfaction if missing but are not motivators if present.
  * ***What are the factors called motivators?***
  The work itself, achievement, recognition, responsibility, growth, and advancement.
  * ***What are hygiene (maintenance) factors?***
  Factors that do not motivate but must be present for employee satisfaction, such as company policies, supervision, working conditions, interpersonal relations, and salary.

6. Explain how job enrichment affects employee motivation and performance.

6. Job enrichment describes efforts to make jobs more interesting.
  * ***What characteristics of work affect motivation and performance?***
  The job characteristics that influence motivation are (1) skill variety, (2) task identity, (3) task significance, (4) autonomy, and (5) feedback.
  * ***Name two forms of job enrichment that increase motivation.***
  Job enrichment strategies include job enlargement and job rotation.

7. Identify the steps involved in implementing a management by objectives (MBO) program.

7. One procedure for establishing objectives and gaining employee commitment to those objectives is called management by objectives (MBO).
  * ***What are the steps in an MBO program?***
  (1) Managers set goals in cooperation with subordinates, (2) objectives are established for each department, (3) managers and workers together discuss the objectives and commit themselves in writing to meeting them, (4) two-way communication and review show workers how they're doing, (5) feedback is provided and corrections are made if necessary, and (6) employees are rewarded for achieving goals.

8. Explain the key factors involved in expectancy theory.

8. According to Victor Vroom, employee expectations can affect an individual's motivation.
  * ***What are the key elements involved in expectancy theory?***
  Expectancy theory centers on three questions employees often ask about performance on the job: (1) Can I accomplish the task? (2) If I do accomplish it, what's my reward? (3) Is the reward worth the effort?

9. Examine the key principles of equity theory.

9. According to equity theory, employees try to maintain equity between inputs and outputs compared to other employees in similar positions.
  * ***What happens when employees perceive that their rewards are not equitable?***
  If employees perceive that they are underrewarded they will either (1) reduce their effort or (2) rationalize that it isn't important. If they perceive that they are overrewarded, they will either (1) increase their effort to justify the higher reward in the future or (2) rationalize by saying "I'm worth it!" Inequity leads to lower productivity, reduced quality, increased absenteeism, and voluntary resignation.

KEY TERMS
• • • • • •

equity theory 302	job enlargement 300	**motivators** 297
extrinsic reward 288	**job enrichment** 299	**principle of motion economy** 289
expectancy theory 301	**job rotation** 300	
goal-setting theory 300	**job simplification** 300	**scientific management** 289
Hawthorne effect 292	**management by objectives (MBO)** 301	
hygiene factors 297		**time-motion studies** 289
intrinsic reward 288	**Maslow's hierarchy of needs** 292	

DEVELOPING WORKPLACE SKILLS

1. Talk with several of your friends about the subject of motivation. What motivates them to work hard or not work hard in school and on the job? How important is self-motivation to them?

2. Look over Maslow's hierarchy of needs and try to determine where you are on the hierarchy. What needs of yours are not being met? How could a company go about meeting those needs and thus motivate you to work better and harder?

3. One of the newest managerial ideas is to let employees work in self-managed teams. There is no reason why such teams could not be formed in colleges as well as businesses. Discuss the benefits and drawbacks of dividing your class into self-managed teams for the purpose of studying, doing cases, and so forth.

4. Think of all the groups with which you have been associated over the years—sports groups, friendship groups, and so on—and try to recall how the leaders of those groups motivated the group to action. Did the leaders assume a Theory X or a Theory Y attitude? How often was money used as a motivator? What other motivational tools were used and to what effect?

5. Herzberg concluded that pay was not a motivator. If you were paid to get better grades, would you be motivated to study harder? In your employment experiences, have you ever worked harder to obtain a raise or as a result of receiving a large raise? Do you agree with Herzberg? Assume you are a sales manager in a large department store. Use a word processor to write a memo to your sales representative explaining and advocating the company's recent decision to reduce salaries and increase bonus potential for sales personnel.

TAKING IT TO THE NET

Purpose

To assess your personality type using the Keirsey Character Sorter and to evaluate how well the description of your personality type fits you.

Exercise

Sometimes understanding differences in employees' personalities helps managers understand how to motivate them. Find out about your personality by going to the Keirsey Character Sorter Web site (http://keirsey.com/) and answer the 36-item questionnaire. The test identifies four temperament types: Guardian, Artisan, Idealist, and Rational. (Disclaimer: The Keirsey Temperament Sorter, like *all* personality tests, is only a preliminary and rough indicator of personality.)

1. After you identify your personality, read the corresponding personality portrait. How well or how poorly does the identified personality type fit?

2. Sometimes the test does not accurately identify your personality, but it may give you a place to start looking for a portrait that fits. After you have read many of the portraits, ask a good friend or relative which of the portraits best describes you.

Practicing Management Decisions

Winning the Malcolm Baldrige National Quality Award is no small feat. To be awarded the Baldrige award a company must excel in three major measurements of quality: (1) customer satisfaction, (2) product and service quality, and (3) quality of internal operations. Previous winners have included such companies as Solectron and the General Motors Saturn Division.

Taking home the Baldrige award was the last thing on the minds of Judith Corson and her partner, Jeffrey Pope, when they evaluated the situation at their Minneapolis-based market research firm Custom Research in the early 1990s. The two partners faced a market full of client companies that had downsized and were asking more of Custom Research. The problem for Corson and Pope was that Custom Research was experiencing a flattening of growth and the firm had neither the resources it needed to expand its employee base nor the technological capacity it needed to meet the growing demands. The business partners were facing the hard reality that to survive in the market they would have to provide better management of clients' work with their current staff and resources. Corson and Pope realized they had to do something quickly.

The two partners decided to abandon the traditional departmentalized structure of the organization and group their 100 or so employees into account teams. Each account team would have an account and research team leader assigned to facilitate the direction of the team. In just a short time communication and the tracking of work improved. Workers were more interested and involved, and clients were expressing satisfaction at a job well done. The business began to thrive.

But after the system had been in place for a couple of years, the partners saw a problem developing. Team members were becoming limited, learning only about the clients or the business categories handled by their group. Corson and Pope swung into action again. They decided that once or twice a year, employees would be reorganized into new teams with their size determined by the volume of work at hand.

Using the team approach at Custom Research has changed things quite a bit. The firm watched its billings go from $10 million in 1985 to $22 million in 1996. Revenue per full-time employee has risen by 70 percent. The firm meets or exceeds its client expectations on 97 percent of its projects and is rated by 92 percent of its clients as better than the competition. Such outstanding performance enabled Custom Research to become the smallest and first professional-services firm to receive the prestigious Malcolm Baldrige Award.

Decision Questions

1. Why do you think worker performance increased so significantly at Custom Research?
2. What principles of motivation seemed to work well for Corson and Pope in increasing employee productivity?
3. Would you like to work in a team-centered organization or in a more traditional organizational setting? Why?

Source: Roberta Maynard, "A Client-Centered Firm's Lesson in Team Work," *Nation's Business*, March 1997, p. 32 and Dale Dauten, "For Success, Put Yourself in Your Customer's Shoes," *Chicago Tribune*, January 11, 1998, p. 10.

If a company is to succeed in today's service-oriented economy, it must have workers motivated to satisfy customers and solve problems. One of the companies best known for its motivated employees is Southwest Airlines. Southwest Airlines has a remarkably low turnover rate (a mere 7.5 percent) and a highly productive workforce. Here's why.

• *Strong company culture.* The Southwest company culture is one of hard work and productivity. The airline's positive work environment encourages employees to give their full attention to serving customers and getting the job done—and to have a little fun doing so. This is the company's philosophy and the brainchild of Southwest's co-founder and chief executive officer, Herb Kelleher. Whether Herb is leading a company rap song or clothed in full regal splendor leading a line dance at one of the company's many parties, Herb is the company leader and inspiration.

- *Job stability*. In its 25-year history, Southwest has never laid off anyone. Employees have been known to pass up higher pay at other airlines in exchange for more security and a better work environment at Southwest.

- *Empowerment*. Some Southwest workers cite empowerment as the most important job benefit. Southwest encourages employees to hold their own meetings and solve their own problems without the interference of company managers. The employees (as well as customers) are generally included in the company's hiring process as well.

- *Opportunities for growth*. Because employment at Southwest is stable, employees are reasonably sure that they will have the time and the opportunity to grow at the airline. Pilots, for instance, expect a steady stream of promotions over the years, provided they acquire the appropriate skills and flying experience. Other employees can advance their careers by attending classes at the "university for people," run by Southwest's "people department."

- *Incentives*. Southwest can offer employees one particularly attractive incentive: discounted or free travel. Those employees with no absences or late arrivals over a three-month period, for instance, receive two free, space-available airline tickets. They can use these tickets any way they wish, even give them away to a friend.

- *Compensation*. Southwest is 83 percent union, so most of its salary and wage structure is stated in the union contract. In that respect the pay structure is similar to other airlines. What is unique about Southwest is its profit-sharing plan, which is Kelleher's means of sharing the wealth. When the company is profitable, as it has been in each of the past 25 years, a certain percentage of that profit is put into the company's profit-sharing fund. As a result of the investments and Southwest's excellent financial performance over the years, a number of 18- to 20-year veteran employees have become millionaires.

So how long can Southwest Airlines keep flying high? As long as its motivated, highly productive workers keep the throttle at full speed ahead. With markets to conquer and customers raving, the future of Southwest is on cloud nine.

Discussion Questions

1. Do Southwest Airlines employees seem more motivated by intrinsic or extrinsic rewards? Explain.
2. Herzberg distinguishes between hygiene factors and motivators. Which factors identified by Herzberg as motivators are used at Southwest Airlines?
3. How do the principles of Vroom's expectancy theory relate to Southwest Airlines?

Human Resource Management: Finding and Keeping the Best Employees

Chapter 11

LEARNING GOALS

*After you have read and studied this chapter,
you should be able to*

1 Explain the importance of human resource management and describe current issues in managing human resources.

2 Summarize the six steps in planning human resources.

3 Describe methods that companies use to recruit new employees and explain some of the issues that make recruitment challenging.

4 Outline the six steps in selecting employees.

5 Illustrate the use of various types of employee training and development methods.

6 Trace the six steps in appraising employee performance.

7 Summarize the objectives of employee compensation programs and describe various pay systems and fringe benefits.

8 Explain scheduling plans managers use to adjust to workers' needs.

9 Describe the ways employees can move through a company: promotion, reassignment, termination, and retirement.

10 Illustrate the effects of legislation on human resource management.

Immigration, race relations, changing family structures, new lifestyles, and longer life span have given managers and workers a need to examine the opportunities and challenges of workforce diversity. Madye Whitehead and Charles Henson created a business called Design Alternatives that offers managers help in understanding and managing, diversity. Design Alternatives training sessions highlight what diversity really is and why it is an asset in a company.

Whitehead says, "The training is designed to make people more understanding of differences—not just between white and black co-workers, but differences among men and women, ethnic groups, younger and older workers and those with different sexual orientations. This also involves understanding the differences within the workplace of those with and without children, married and not married, and religious differences."

Diversity training is not easy in the beginning of the sessions. "A good 80 percent of the people don't want to be there. And that's because they believe they don't have a problem and that it's someone else who has a problem," says Whitehead. But after a session, most people will see the value of the training and will use it on the job.

Since its beginning, Design Alternatives has grown about 20 percent a year, with 1996 sales of more than $1 million, 12 full-time workers, and more than 100 contingent (temporary) workers.

PROFILE

Madye H. Whitehead and Charles Henson of Design Alternatives

In 1997, Whitehead and Henson decided to divide Design Alternatives into two separate companies to better meet the needs of their customers. Design Alternatives now focuses on recruitment and placement, and Strategic Vision focuses on training.

The new goal of Design Alternatives is to focus on building careers rather than finding jobs for their recruits. The company specializes in recruiting qualified workers in the technical and professional market segments for both permanent and temporary positions. One out of 10 American workers is what economists call a contingent worker—a person hired to meet an unexpected or temporary challenge. Some analysts contend that contingent workers increase companies' flexibility and therefore their competitiveness. However, detractors contend that the drive for cost cutting and flexibility crashes head-on into another important aspect: the belief that competitive success is based on retaining a motivated, creative, empowered workforce. They believe this goal will never be met by a largely disposable workforce.

Companies such as Design Alternatives and Strategic Vision help employers find and keep the best employees through recruiting and training. That's what this chapter is all about. It discusses present and future challenges of human resource development.

Sources: William Flannery, "Diversity by Design," *St. Louis Post-Dispatch,* September 23, 1996, p. 3BP; and telephone conversations with Charles Henson, February 3, 1998 and March 3, 1998.

WORKING WITH PEOPLE IS JUST THE BEGINNING

Students have been known to say they want to go into human resource management because they want to "work with people." It is true that human resource managers work with people, but they are also deeply involved in planning, record keeping, and other administrative duties. To begin a career in human resource management, you need to develop a better reason than "I

◄ **LEARNING GOAL 1.** Explain the importance of human resource management and describe current issues in managing human resources.

◄ **CONSIDER USING TM 78** Chapter Outline

FIGURE **11.1**

• • • •

HUMAN RESOURCE
MANAGEMENT

Note that human
resource management
includes motivation as
discussed in Chapter 10
and union relations as
discussed in Chapter 12.
As this shows, human
resource management is
more than hiring and
firing personnel.

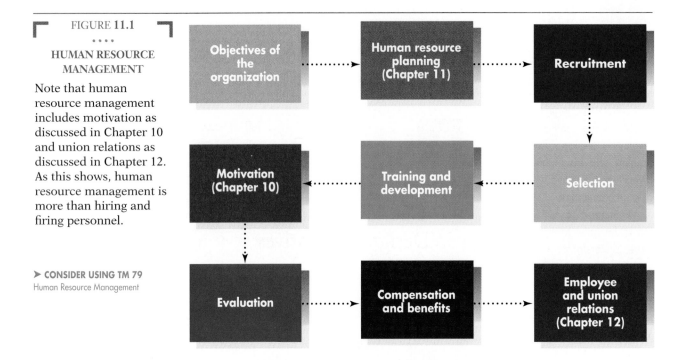

➤ **CONSIDER USING TM 79**
Human Resource Management

**human resource
management**
The process of evaluating human
resource needs, finding people to
fill those needs, and getting the best
work from each employee by
providing the right incentives and
job environment, all with the goal
of meeting the objectives of the
organization.

➤ **CONSIDER USING OT ACETATE
11-1**
The Job of Human Resource
Management

➤ **CONSIDER USING OT ACETATE
11-2**
What Attracts Workers to Specific
Employers?

➤ **CONSIDER USING LECTURE
ENHANCER 11-1**
Wanted: A Global Boss

want to work with people." This chapter will discuss various aspects of human
resource management, which involves recruiting, hiring, training, evaluating,
and compensating people. **Human resource management** is the process of
evaluating human resource needs, finding people to fill those needs, and getting
the best work from each employee by providing the right incentives and job
environment, all with the goal of meeting the objectives of the organization (see
Figure 11.1). Let's explore some of the trends in the area of human resource
management.

••• DEVELOPING THE ULTIMATE RESOURCE •••

One reason human resource management is receiving increased attention now
is that the U.S. economy has experienced a major shift from traditional manufacturing industries to service and high-tech manufacturing industries that
require more technical job skills. This shift means that many workers must be
retrained for new, more challenging jobs. For example, when Crown Zeller-
bach modernized a Louisiana pulp mill, it set up a training facility nearby and
paid workers full wages while they learned new skills. The following are other
examples:

- Hewlett-Packard spent $1 million to move 350 workers to new jobs,
  and Boeing enrolled laid-off electronics technicians in college to learn
  new microprocessor skills. The idea in each company was to retrain
  existing workers before going outside for skilled employees.

- At Motorola, continuous learning is built into the culture. The company's training programs are run from Motorola University in Schaum-
  burg, Illinois, with regional campuses in Phoenix, Arizona, and Austin,
  Texas. That the employees have learned to learn is evidenced by so
  many employees volunteering to participate in the company's "Total
  Customer Satisfaction" competition that the plant had to close during
  presentation week.

- Stelco, Inc., has been contracted to conduct management retraining for Bohumin Steel & Wire Co. in the Czech Republic. The company is converting its management and sales methods from those suitable for a communist-controlled economy to techniques designed for a free-market system.

Some people have called employees the ultimate resource, and when you think about it, nothing could be more true. People develop the ideas that eventually become the products that satisfy our wants and needs. Take away their creative minds, and leading firms such as IBM, GE, Hewlett-Packard, and GM would be nothing. The problem is that human resources have always been relatively plentiful, so there was little need to nurture and develop them. If you needed qualified people, you simply went out and hired them. If they didn't work out, you fired them and found others. But *qualified* labor is more scarce today, and that makes recruiting more difficult.

Historically, most firms assigned the job of recruiting, selecting, training, evaluating, compensating, motivating, and, yes, firing people to the various functional departments. For years, the personnel department was viewed more or less as a clerical function responsible for screening applications, keeping records, processing the payroll, and finding people when necessary.

Today the job of human resource management has taken on an entirely new role in the firm. In the future it may become the most critical function in that it will be responsible for dealing with all aspects of the most critical resource—people. In fact, the human resource function has become so important that it is no longer the function of just one department; it is a function of all managers. Most human resource functions are shared between the professional human resource manager and the other managers.[1] What are some of the challenges in the human resource area that managers face?

Every Difference Makes a Difference

AT GAP INC., WE BELIEVE IN CREATING AN ENVIRONMENT WHERE EVERYONE'S UNIQUE TALENTS ARE VALUED AND RESPECTED.

Gap Inc.

www.gap.com

As the workforce expands to include workers from a widening variety of backgrounds, the goal of the human resource manager is to create an environment in which the diverse talents of all employees are valued and developed.

••• THE HUMAN RESOURCE CHALLENGE •••

The changes in the American business system that have had the most dramatic impact on the workings of the free enterprise system are the changes in the labor force. The ability of the U.S. business system to compete in international markets depends on new ideas, new products, and new levels of productivity—in other words, on people with good ideas. The following are some of the challenges and opportunities being encountered in the human resource area:

◄ CONSIDER USING LECTURE ENHANCER 11-2
The Clerical Evolution

- Shortages in people trained to work in the growth areas of the future, such as computers, biotechnology, robotics, and the sciences.
- A huge population of skilled and unskilled workers from declining industries, such as steel and automobiles, who are unemployed or underemployed, and who need retraining. Underemployed workers are those who have higher-level skills than their current jobs require.

Human resource managers must forecast human resource needs and conduct formal and informal inventories to evaluate how prepared they are to meet these anticipated changes. At Rockwell International, advanced technology has compounded this challenge and caused human resource managers to devote increased efforts to training and developing its workforce in high-tech jobs.

- A growing percentage of new workers who are undereducated, poor, and unprepared for jobs in the contemporary business environment.
- A shift in the age composition of the workforce, including aging baby boomers, many of whom are deferring retirement.
- A complex set of laws and regulations involving hiring, safety, unionization, and equal pay that require organizations to go beyond profit orientation and be more fair and socially conscious.
- An increasing number of single-parent and two-income families, resulting in a demand for day care, job sharing, maternity leave, and special career advancement programs for women.
- A shift in employee attitudes toward work. Leisure time has become a much higher priority, as have concepts such as flextime and a shorter workweek.
- Continued downsizing that is taking a toll on employee morale as well as increasing the demand for temporary workers.
- A challenge from overseas labor pools whose members are available for lower wages and subject to many fewer laws and regulations. This results in many jobs being shifted overseas. The Reaching Beyond Our Borders box discusses the new human resource challenges faced by global businesses.
- An increased demand for benefits tailored to the individual.
- A growing concern over such issues as health care, elder care, day care (discussed in Chapter 12), equal opportunities for people with disabilities, and special attention given to affirmative-action programs.

Given all of these issues, and others that are sure to develop, you can see why human resource management has taken a more central position in management thinking than ever before. Let's see what is involved.

Critical Thinking

Based on the complex situations you'd be addressing, does human resource management seem like a challenging career area? Do you see any other issues,

Reaching Beyond Our Borders

http://www.shrm.org/

Working with Employees in Different Countries

We talked about the fact that, in many U.S. companies, employees are increasingly coming from diverse backgrounds. But how do human resource managers deal with employees in, say, an office in Spain, a service center in Brazil, or a new plant in Korea? How do they cope with hiring employees from other countries for a company's headquarters in the United States? Human resource people managing a global workforce begin by understanding the customs, laws, and local business needs of every country in which the organization operates.

Varying cultural and legal standards can affect a variety of human resource functions:

- *Compensation.* Salaries must be converted to and from foreign currencies. Often employees with international assignments receive special allowances for relocation, children's education, housing, travel, or other business-related expenses.

- *Health and pension standards.* Human resource managers must consider the different social contexts for benefits in other countries. For example, in the Netherlands the government provides retirement income and health care.

- *Paid time off.* Cultural differences can be quite apparent when it comes to paid time off. For example, four weeks of paid vacation is the standard of many European employers. But other countries do not have the short-term and long-term absence policies we

have in the United States. They do not have sick leave, personal leave, or family and medical leave. Global companies need a standard definition of what time off is.

- *Taxation.* Different countries have varying taxation rules, and the payroll department is an important player in managing immigration information.

- *Communication.* When employees leave to work in another country they often feel a disconnection from their home country. Wise companies use their intranet and the Internet to help these faraway employees keep in direct contact. Several companies use these tools for posting both job vacancies and notices to help returning employees find positions back in the United States.

Michael Losey, president and CEO of the Society for Human Resource Management, says, "Human resource policies will be influenced more and more by conditions and practices in other countries and cultures. Human resource managers will need to sensitize themselves and their organizations to the cultural and business practices of other nations and to move away from the assumed dominance and/or superiority of American business practices."

Sources: Sandra E. O'Connell, "Systems Issues for International Business," *HR Magazine*, March 1997; and Maureen Minehan, "What the Future Holds for HR," *HR Magazine*, March 1997.

such as the compensation of cross-functional teams, that are likely to affect this function? What have been your experiences in dealing with people who work in human resource management? Would you enjoy working in such an environment?

•••• ▬▬▬ ••••

DETERMINING YOUR HUMAN RESOURCE NEEDS

◄ **LEARNING GOAL 2.** Summarize the six steps in planning human resources.

All management, including human resource management, begins with planning. Six steps are involved in the human resource planning process:

1. *Preparing forecasts of future human resource needs.*

FIGURE **11.2**

• • • •

JOB ANALYSIS

A job analysis yields two important statements: job descriptions and job specifications. Here you have a job description and job specifications for a Fiberrific cereal sales representative.

➤ CONSIDER USING TM 80
Job Analysis

Job Analysis

Observe current sales representatives doing the job.

Discuss job with sales managers.

Have current sales reps keep a diary of their activities.

Job Description	**Job Specifications**
Primary objective is to sell Fiberrific to food stores in Territory Z. Duties include servicing accounts and maintaining positive relationships with clients. Responsibilities include	Characteristics of the person qualifying for this job include

Job Description

- Introducing the new cereal to store managers in the area.
- Helping the store managers estimate the volume to order.
- Negotiating prime shelf space.
- Explaining sales promotion activities to store managers.
- Stocking and maintaining shelves in stores that wish such service.

Job Specifications

- Two years' sales experience.
- Positive attitude.
- Well-groomed appearance.
- Good communication skills.
- High school diploma and two years of college credit.

➤ CONSIDER USING SUPPLEMEN-
TAL CASE 11-1
Human Resource Planning and Women
Workers (**SCANS**)

job analysis
A study of what is done by employees who hold various job titles.

job description
A summary of the objectives of a job, the type of work to be done, the responsibilities and duties, the working conditions, and the relationship of the job to other functions.

job specifications
A written summary of the minimum qualifications required of workers to do a particular job.

➤ CONSIDER USING OT ACETATE
11-7
Information Sought on Job Descriptions
versus Job Specifications

2. *Preparing a human resource inventory of the organization's employees.* This inventory should include ages, names, education, capabilities, training, specialized skills, and other information pertinent to the specific organization (e.g., languages spoken). Such information reveals whether or not the labor force is technically up-to-date, thoroughly trained, and so forth.

3. *Preparing a job analysis.* A **job analysis** is a study of what is done by employees who hold various job titles. Such analyses are necessary in order to recruit and train employees with the necessary skills to do the job. The results of job analysis are two written statements: job descriptions and job specifications. A **job description** specifies the objectives of the job, the type of work to be done, the responsibilities and duties, the working conditions, and the relationship of the job to other functions. **Job specifications** are a written summary of the *minimum* qualifications (education, skills, etc.) required of a worker to fill specific jobs. In short, job descriptions are statements about the job, whereas job specifications are statements about the person who does the job. See Figure 11.2 for hypothetical examples of a job description and job specifications.

4. *Assessing future demand.* Because technology changes rapidly, training programs must be started long before the need is apparent. Human resource managers who are proactive, that is, who anticipate the future needs of their organization, make sure that trained people are available when needed.

5. *Assessing future supply.* The labor force is constantly shifting: getting older, becoming more technically oriented, attracting more women, and so forth. There are likely to be increased shortages of some workers in

the future (e.g., computer and robotic repair workers) and oversupply of others (e.g., assembly-line workers).

6. *Establishing a strategic plan.* The plan must address recruiting, selecting, training and developing, appraising, compensating, and scheduling the labor force. Because the previous five steps lead up to this one, this chapter will focus on these elements of the strategic human resource plan.

···· ▬▬▬▬ ····

RECRUITING EMPLOYEES FROM A DIVERSE POPULATION

Recruitment is the set of activities used to obtain a sufficient number of the right people at the right time; its purpose is to select those who best meet the needs of the organization. One would think that, with a continuous flow of new people into the workforce, recruiting would be easy. On the contrary, recruiting has become very difficult, for several reasons:

- Sometimes, people with the necessary skills are not available; in this case, workers must be hired and then trained internally.[2]

- The emphasis on corporate culture, teamwork, and participative management makes it important to hire people who not only are skilled but also fit in with the culture and leadership style of the organization.

- Some organizations have unattractive workplaces, have policies that demand promotions from within, operate under union regulations, or offer low wages, which makes recruiting and keeping employees difficult or subject to outside influence and restrictions.

Because recruiting is a difficult chore that involves finding, hiring, and training people who are an appropriate technical and social fit, human resource managers turn to many sources for assistance (see Figure 11.3). These sources are classified as either internal or external. Internal sources include employees who are already within the firm (and may be transferred, promoted, etc.) and employees who can recommend others to hire. Using internal sources is less expensive than recruiting outside the company. The greatest advantage of hiring from within is that it helps maintain employee morale. However, it isn't always possible to find qualified workers within the company, so human resource managers must use external recruitment sources such as advertisements, public and private employment agencies, college placement bureaus, management consultants, professional organizations, referrals, and walk-in applications. While most external sources are straightforward, some may involve difficult decisions; the Making Ethical Decisions box presents questions about recruiting employees from competitors.

Recruiting qualified workers may be particularly difficult for small businesses that don't have enough staff members to serve as internal sources and may not be able to offer the sort of competitive compensation that attracts external sources. The Spotlight on Small Business box on page 323 outlines some of the ways small businesses can address their recruiting needs. The newest tools for recruiting employees are Internet services such as CareerMosaic, The Monster Board, and Jobtrak (see the Taking It to the Net exercise at the end of this chapter).[3]

◀ **LEARNING GOAL 3.** Describe methods companies use to recruit new employees and explain some of the issues that make recruitment challenging.

recruitment
The set of activities used to obtain a sufficient number of the right people at the right time; its purpose is to select those who best meet the needs of the organization.

◀ **CONSIDER USING OT ACETATE 11-4**
Skills Employers Are Seeking

◀ **CONSIDER USING TRANS-PARENCY MASTER 81**
Employee Sources (Figure 11.3 on text page 322)

◀ **LEARNING GOAL 4.** Outline the six steps in selecting employees.

Making Ethical Decisions

http://www.jit-recruiting.com/

Recruiting Employees from Competitors

As human resource manager for Technocrat, Inc., it is your job to recruit the best employees. Your most recent human resource inventory indicated that Technocrat currently has an abundance of qualified designers and that several lower-level workers will soon be eligible for promotions to designer positions as well. In spite of the surplus of qualified designers, you are considering offering a similar posi- ▲ tion to a designer who is now with a major competitor. Your thinking is that the new employee will be a source of information about the competition's new products. What are your ethical considerations in this case? Will you lure the employee away from the competition even though you have no need for a designer? What will be the consequences of your decision?

▢ FIGURE **11.3** ▢   ▲ SCANS

• • • •

EMPLOYEE SOURCES

Internal sources are often given first consideration. So it's useful to get a recommendation from a current employee of the firm for which you want to work. College placement offices are also an important source. Be sure to learn about such facilities early so you can plan a strategy throughout your college career.

• • • • ▬▬▬ • • • •

SELECTING EMPLOYEES WHO WILL BE PRODUCTIVE

Selection is the process of gathering information and deciding who should be hired, under legal guidelines, for the best interests of the individual and the organization. The cost of selecting and training employees has become prohibitively high in some firms. Think of what's involved: interview time, medical exams, training costs, unproductive time spent learning the job, moving expenses, and so on. It's easy to see how selection expenses can amount to over $50,000 for a

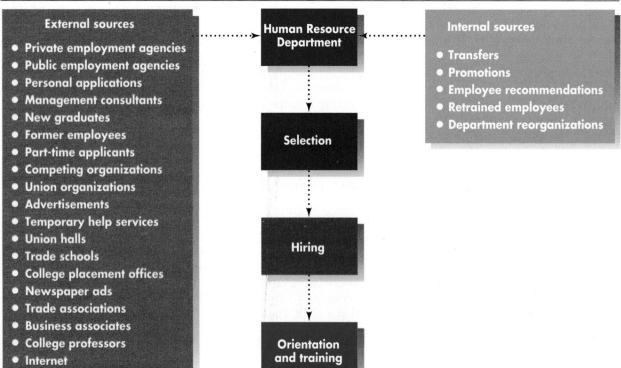

External sources
- Private employment agencies
- Public employment agencies
- Personal applications
- Management consultants
- New graduates
- Former employees
- Part-time applicants
- Competing organizations
- Union organizations
- Advertisements
- Temporary help services
- Union halls
- Trade schools
- College placement offices
- Newspaper ads
- Trade associations
- Business associates
- College professors
- Internet

Human Resource Department

Selection

Hiring

Orientation and training

Internal sources
- Transfers
- Promotions
- Employee recommendations
- Retrained employees
- Department reorganizations

Spotlight on Small Business

Small Businesses Must Compete to Attract Qualified Workers

It's harder now than ever before for businesses to find qualified employees, and it is becoming more expensive. Small-business owners across the country agree that competition for qualified employees is intensifying. Small businesses want top talent but often can't afford corporate-level benefits or expensive recruiters to hunt them down. Despite the hurdles, small-business management consultants say there are many ways to lure desirable workers:

- *Transform ads into promotional tools.* For example, Ecoprint, a small print shop in Maryland, brags about the benefits of working for this collegial company in its advertisements.

- *Post job openings on the Internet.* Running a 20-line ad on an on-line service like CareerMosaic or The Monster Board costs $100 to $150 for 30 days. A comparable ad in the *New York Times* can cost $1,728 for only a week.

- *Let your staff help select hires.* The more people involved in the interview process, the better chance you have to find out if the person has the personality and skills to fit in.

- *Create a dynamic workplace to attract local, energetic applicants.* Sometimes word of mouth is the most effective recruiting tool.

- *Test-drive an employee.* Hiring temporary workers can allow you to test candidates for a few months before deciding whether to make an offer or not.

- *Hire your customer.* Loyal customers sometimes make the smartest employees.

- *Check community groups and local government agencies.* Don't forget to check out state-run employment agencies. The new welfare-to-work programs may turn up excellent candidates you can train.

- *Lure candidates with a policy of promotions and raises.* Most employees want to know that they can move up in the company. Give employees an incentive for learning the business.

Sources: "Break the Rules to Hire Smart," *Your Company,* February 3–17, 1997; and "Netting a Job," *PC Magazine,* February 4, 1997, p. 10.

---

manager. It can even cost one and a half times the employee's annual salary to recruit, process, and train an entry-level worker.[4] In the United States, the amount businesses spent on training alone skyrocketed from $30 billion in 1991 to $55 billion in 1996.[5] Thus, the selection process is an important element in any human resource program. A typical selection process would involve six steps:

1. *Obtaining complete application forms.* Once this was a simple procedure with few complications. Today legal guidelines limit the kinds of questions that may appear on an application form. Nonetheless, such forms help the employer discover the applicant's educational background, past work experience, career objectives, and other qualifications directly related to the requirements of the job.

2. *Conducting initial and follow-up interviews.* A staff member from the human resource department often screens applicants in a first interview. If the interviewer considers the applicant a potential employee, the manager who will supervise the new employee interviews the applicant as well. It's important that managers prepare adequately for the interview to avoid selection decisions they may regret. Certain mistakes, such as asking an interviewee about his or her family, no matter how innocent the intention, could be used as evidence if that applicant later files discrimination charges.

selection
The process of gathering information and deciding who should be hired, under legal guidelines, for the best interests of the individual and the organization.

◄ CONSIDER USING OT ACETATE 11-3
What Not to Ask in Job Interviews

◄ CONSIDER USING LECTURE ENHANCER 11-3
Hiring Methods Employers Use Most

◄ CONSIDER USING LECTURE ENHANCER 11-4
Memorable Job Interview

As advances in technology change the skills needed to succeed in the workplace, fewer workers possess the required skills. Demand for technology-proficient workers has human resource managers scrambling. UPP Business Systems is a Chicago-based company that specializes in recruiting software programmers and systems analysts for special project assignments in large companies.

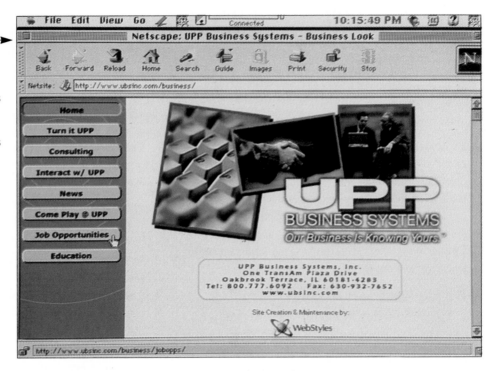

▶ CONSIDER USING LECTURE
ENHANCER 11-5
Testing and Diversity

3. *Giving employment tests.* Employment tests have been severely criticized as potential sources of illegal discrimination. Nonetheless, organizations continue to use them to measure basic competencies in specific job skills (e.g., welding, word processing) and to help evaluate applicants' personalities and interests. In using employment tests, it's important that they be directly related to the job. This will make the selection process more efficient and generally satisfy legal requirements.[6]

4. *Conducting background investigations.* Most organizations now investigate candidates' work record, school record, credit history, and refer-

Internet job search services such as The Monster Board are the newest tools used to recruit employees and/or search for jobs. Can't find a job that interests you? You can enter the type of job and the region of the country you are interested in, and The Monster Board will notify you by e-mail when a position becomes available. Check it out at http://www.monster.com.

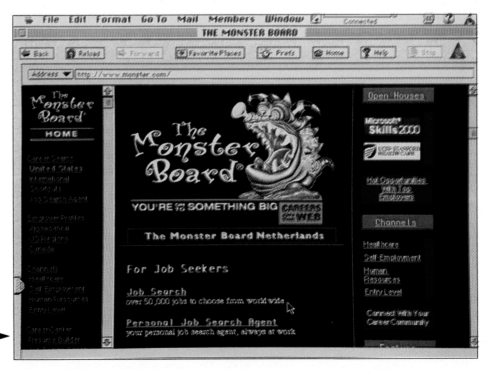

ences more carefully than they have in the past. It is simply too costly to hire, train, and motivate people only to lose them and have to start the process over. Background checks help weed out those candidates least likely to succeed and identify those most likely to succeed in a given position.

5. *Obtaining results from physical exams.* There are obvious benefits in hiring physically and mentally healthy people. However, medical tests cannot be given just to screen out individuals. In some states, physical exams can be given only after an offer of employment has been accepted. In states that allow preemployment physical exams, the exams must be given to everyone applying for the same position. There has been some controversy about preemployment testing to detect drug or alcohol abuse, as well as screening to detect carriers of the AIDS virus. Eighty percent of U.S. companies now test both current and potential employees for drug use.[7]

6. *Establishing trial periods.* Often an organization will hire an employee conditionally. This enables the person to prove his or her worth on the job. After a specified period (perhaps six months or a year), the firm may either permanently hire or discharge that employee based on evaluations from supervisors. Although such systems make it easier to fire inefficient or problem employees, they do not eliminate the high cost of turnover.

The selection process is often long and difficult, but it is worth the effort to select new employees carefully because of the high costs of replacing workers. The process helps ensure that the people an organization hires meet the requirements in all relevant areas, including communication skills, education, technical skills, experience, personality, and health.[8]

··· HIRING CONTINGENT WORKERS ···

When more workers are needed in a company, human resource managers may want to consider creative staffing alternatives rather than simply hiring new permanent employees. A company with a varying need for employees, from hour to hour, day to day, week to week, and season to season may find it cost-effective to hire contingent workers.[9] **Contingent workers** are defined as workers who do not have the expectation of regular, full-time employment. Such workers include part-time workers, seasonal workers, temporary workers, independent contractors, interns, and co-op students.[10]

A varying need for employees is the most common reason for hiring contingent workers. Companies may also look to hire contingent workers when full-time employees experience downtimes, there is a peak demand for labor, and quick service to customers is a priority. Companies in which the jobs require minimum training or that are located in areas where qualified contingent workers are available are most likely to consider alternative staffing options.[11]

Temporary staffing has evolved into a $40 billion industry. According to the Bureau of Labor Statistics about 1 of every 10 U.S. workers is employed in an alternative working arrangement.[12] Contingent workers receive few benefits; they are rarely offered health insurance, vacation time, or private pensions. They also earn $178 per week less than permanent workers.[13] On the positive side, about 40 percent of those on temporary assignments are eventually offered full-time positions. Managers see using temporary workers as a way of weeding out poor workers and finding good hires.[14] Furthermore, in an era of downsizing and rapid change, some contingent workers have even found that "temping" can be less insecure than full-time employment.

◄ CONSIDER USING OT ACETATE 11-5
Why Companies Use Temporary Workers

contingent workers
Workers who do not have the expectation of regular, full-time employment.

◄ CONSIDER USING LECTURE ENHANCER 11-6
Jillian Perlberger, Temporary Employee

◄ CONSIDER USING OT ACETATE 11-6
Do Employers Feel Workers Are "Ready" for Work?

◄ LEARNING GOAL 5. Illustrate the use of various types of employee training and development methods.

Progress Check

training and development
All attempts to improve productivity by increasing an employee's ability to perform.

employee orientation
The activity that introduces new employees to the organization; to fellow employees; to their immediate supervisors; and to the policies, practices, and objectives of the firm.

on-the-job training
Training program in which the employee immediately begins his or her tasks and learns by doing, or watches others for a while and then imitates them, all right at the workplace.

apprentice programs
Training programs involving a period during which a learner works alongside an experienced employee to master the skills and procedures of a craft.

• What is human resource management?
• What are the six steps in human resource planning?
• What factors make it difficult to recruit qualified employees?
• What are the six steps in the selection process?

···· ▬▬▬ ····

TRAINING AND DEVELOPING EMPLOYEES FOR OPTIMUM PERFORMANCE

Because employees need to learn how to work with new equipment such as word processors, computers, and robots, companies are finding that they must offer training programs that often are quite sophisticated. **Training and development** include all attempts to improve productivity by increasing an employee's ability to perform. Training is short-term skills oriented; whereas development is long-term career oriented. But both training and development programs include three steps: (1) assessing the needs of the organization and the skills of the employees to determine training needs; (2) designing training activities to meet the identified needs; and (3) evaluating the effectiveness of the training. Some common training and development activities are employee orientation, on-the-job training, apprenticeship, off-the-job training, vestibule training, job simulation, and management training.

• **Employee orientation** is the activity that initiates new employees to the organization; to fellow employees; to their immediate supervisors; and to the policies, practices, and objectives of the firm. Orientation programs include everything from informal talks to formal activities that last a day or more and include scheduled visits to various departments and required reading of lengthy handouts.

In the vestibule training session shown here, students learn how to repair automobiles by getting down and dirty. Do you think this is a more effective way of learning than reading a manual illustrated with detailed diagrams? Why?

• **On-the-job training** is the most fundamental type of training. The employee being trained on the job immediately begins his or her tasks and learns by doing, or watches others for a while and then imitates them, right at the workplace. Salespeople, for example, are often trained by watching experienced salespeople perform. Naturally, this can be either quite effective or disastrous, depending on the skills and habits of the person being watched. On-the-job training is obviously the easiest kind of training to implement and can be effective where the job is relatively simple, such as clerking in a store, or repetitive, such as collecting refuse, cleaning carpets, or mowing lawns. More demanding or intricate jobs require a more intense training effort.

• **Apprentice programs** involve a period during which a learner works alongside an experienced employee to master the skills and procedures of a craft. Some apprenticeship programs also involve classroom training. Many skilled crafts, such as bricklaying and plumbing, require a new worker to serve as an apprentice for several years. Trade unions often require new workers to serve apprenticeships to ensure excellence among their members as well as to limit entry to the union. Workers who successfully complete an apprenticeship earn the classification of *journeyman*. In the future, there are likely to be more but shorter apprenticeship programs to prepare people for skilled jobs in changing industries. For example, auto repair

John Cleese, the Monty Python comic, co-founded Video Arts Inc., a company that develops multi-media business training. The innovative CD-ROMs provide witty but highly effective training that's available 24 hours a day, all year long. The program also monitors what workers input and is ready to give them instructions if they become confused about what to do next. What advantages does such technological guidance have over the guidance of a human supervisor? What disadvantages?

will require more intense training as new automobile models include more advanced computers and other electronic devices.

- **Off-the-job training** occurs away from the workplace and consists of internal or external programs to develop any of a variety of skills or to foster personal development. Training is becoming more sophisticated as jobs become more sophisticated. Furthermore, training is expanding to include education (through the Ph.D.) and personal development—subjects may include time management, stress management, health and wellness, physical education, nutrition, and even art and languages.

- **Vestibule training** is done in schools where employees are taught on equipment similar to that used on the job. Such schools enable employees to learn proper methods and safety procedures before assuming a specific job assignment in an organization. Computer and robotics training is often completed in a vestibule school.

- **Job simulation** is the use of equipment that duplicates job conditions and tasks so that trainees can learn skills before attempting them on the job. Job simulation differs from vestibule training in that the simulation attempts to duplicate the *exact* combination of conditions that occur on the job. This is the kind of training given to astronauts, airline pilots, army tank operators, ship captains, and others who must learn highly skilled jobs off the job.

off-the-job training
Training that occurs away from the workplace and consists of internal or external programs to develop any of a variety of skills or to foster personal development.

vestibule training
Training done in schools where employees are taught on equipment similar to that used on the job.

job simulation
The use of equipment that duplicates job conditions and tasks so that trainees can learn skills before attempting them on the job.

••• MANAGEMENT DEVELOPMENT •••

Managers need special training. To be good communicators, they especially need to learn listening skills and empathy. They also need time management, planning, and human relations skills.

Management development, then, is the process of training and educating employees to become good managers and then monitoring the progress of their managerial skills over time. Management development programs have sprung up everywhere, especially at colleges, universities, and private management development firms. Managers participate in role-playing exercises; solve various

management development
The process of training and educating employees to become good managers and then monitoring the progress of their managerial skills over time.

management cases; and are exposed to films, lectures, and all kinds of management development processes.[15] In some organizations, managers are paid to take college-level courses through the doctoral level.

Management development is increasingly being used as a tool to accomplish business objectives. For example, Ford Motor Company is using education to teach executives how to be more responsive to customers. Most management training programs also include several of the following:

➤ CONSIDER USING LECTURE ENHANCER 11-7
Mimic Your Way Upward

- *On-the-job coaching.* This means that a senior manager will assist a lower-level manager by teaching him or her needed skills and generally providing direction, advice, and helpful criticism.
- *Understudy positions.* Job titles such as *undersecretary* and *assistant* are part of a relatively successful way of developing managers. Selected employees work as assistants to higher level managers and participate in planning and other managerial functions until they are ready to assume such positions themselves.
- *Job rotation.* So that they can learn about different functions of the organization, managers are often given assignments in a variety of departments. Through job rotation top managers gain a broad picture of the organization, which is necessary to their success.
- *Off-the-job courses and training.* Managers periodically go to schools or seminars for a week or more to hone their technical and human relations skills. Such courses expose them to the latest concepts and create a sense of camaraderie as the managers live, eat, and work together in a college-type atmosphere. Case studies and simulation exercises of all kinds are often part of such training.

••• NETWORKING •••

networking
The process of establishing and maintaining contacts with key managers in one's own organization and other organizations and using those contacts to weave strong relationships that serve as informal development systems.

mentor
An experienced employee who supervises, coaches, and guides lower-level employees by introducing them to the right people and generally being their organizational sponsor.

Networking is the process of establishing and maintaining contacts with key managers in one's own organization and in other organizations and using those contacts to weave strong relationships that serve as informal development systems. Of equal or greater importance to potential managers is a **mentor,** a corporate manager who supervises, coaches, and guides selected lower-level employees by introducing them to the right people and generally being their organizational sponsor. In reality, an informal type of mentoring goes on in most organizations on a regular basis as older employees assist younger workers.[16] However, many organizations, such as Merrill Lynch and Federal Express, use a formal system of assigning mentors to employees considered to have strong potential.[17]

It's also important to remember that networking and mentoring can go beyond the business environment. For example, college is a perfect place to begin networking. Associations you nurture with professors, with local businesspeople, and especially with your classmates might provide you with a valuable network you can turn to for the rest of your career.

••• DIVERSITY IN MANAGEMENT DEVELOPMENT •••

As women moved into management, they also learned the importance of networking and of having mentors. But since (even now) most older managers are male, women often have more difficulty than men do in finding mentors and entering the network. Women managers won a major victory when the U.S. Supreme Court ruled that it was illegal to bar women from certain clubs (long open to "men only") where business activity and contact-making flows. More and more, women are now entering established networking systems or, in some instances, creating their own.[18]

Similarly, African-American managers are learning the value of networking. Working together, African-Americans are forming pools of capital and new opportunities that are helping many individuals overcome traditional barriers to success. *Black Enterprise* magazine sponsors several networking forums each year for African-American professionals; call (800) 54-FORUM for information.

Companies that take the initiative to develop female and minority managers understand three crucial principles: (1) grooming women and minorities for management positions isn't about legality, morality, or even morale; it is about bringing more talent in the door—the key to long-term profitability; (2) the best women and minorities will become harder to attract and retain, so the companies that start now will have an edge later; and (3) having more women and minorities at all levels means that businesses can serve their increasingly female and minority customers better. If you don't have a diversity of people working in the back room, how are you going to satisfy the diversity of people coming in the front door?

···· ▬▬▬ ····

APPRAISING EMPLOYEE PERFORMANCE TO GET OPTIMUM RESULTS

◄ **LEARNING GOAL 6.** Trace the six steps in appraising employee performance.

Managers must be able to determine whether or not their workers are doing an effective and efficient job, with a minimum of errors and disruptions. They do so by using performance appraisals. A **performance appraisal** is an evaluation in which the performance level of employees is measured against established standards to make decisions about promotions, compensation, additional training, or firing. Performance appraisals consist of these six steps:

performance appraisal
An evaluation in which the performance level of employees is measured against established standards to make decisions about promotions, compensation, additional training, or firing.

◄ **CONSIDER USING OT ACETATE 11-8**
Major Uses of Performance Appraisals

1. *Establishing performance standards.* This is a crucial step. Standards must be understandable, subject to measurement, and reasonable.

2. *Communicating those standards.* Often managers assume that employees know what is expected of them, but such assumptions are dangerous at best. Employees must be told clearly and precisely what the standards and expectations are and how they are to be met.

◄ **CONSIDER USING CRITICAL THINKING EXERCISE 11-1**
Appraise Your Own Performance (**SCANS**)

3. *Evaluating performance.* If the first two steps are done correctly, performance evaluation is relatively easy. It is a matter of evaluating the employee's behavior to see if it matches standards.

◄ **CONSIDER USING LECTURE ENHANCER 11-8**
Appraisal Anxiety: The Agony and the Ecstasy of Annual Reviews

4. *Discussing results with employees.* Most people will make mistakes and fail to meet expectations at first. It takes time to learn a new job and do it well. Discussing an employee's successes and areas that need improvement can provide managers with an opportunity to be understanding and helpful and to guide the employee to better performance. Additionally, the performance appraisal can be a good source of employee suggestions on how a particular task could be better performed.

5. *Taking corrective action.* As an appropriate part of the performance appraisal, a manager can take corrective action or provide corrective feedback to help the employee perform his or her job better. Remember, the key word is *performance.* The primary purpose of conducting this type of appraisal is to improve employee performance if possible.

6. *Using the results to make decisions.* Decisions about promotions, compensation, additional training, or firing are all based on performance evaluations. An effective performance appraisal system is a way of satisfying certain legal conditions concerning such decisions.

Effective management means getting results through top performance by employees. That is what performance appraisals are for—at all levels of the

FIGURE 11.4

••••

MAKING APPRAISALS AND REVIEWS MORE EFFECTIVE

1. **DON'T** attack the employee personally. Critically evaluate his or her work.
2. **DO** allow sufficient time, without distractions, for appraisal. (Take the phone off the hook or close the office door.)
3. **DON'T** make the employee feel uncomfortable or uneasy. *Never* conduct an appraisal where other employees are present (such as on the shop floor).
4. **DO** include the employee in the process as much as possible. (Let the employee prepare a self-improvement program.)
5. **DON'T** wait until the appraisal to address problems with the employee's work that have been developing for some time.
6. **DO** end the appraisal with positive suggestions for employee improvement.

➤ **CONSIDER USING TM 82**
Making Appraisals and Reviews More Effective

organization.[19] Even top-level managers benefit from performance reviews made by their subordinates. The latest form of performance appraisal is called the 360-degree review because it calls for feedback from all directions in the organization: up, down, and all around.[20] Figure 11.4 illustrates how managers can make performance appraisals more meaningful.

 Progress Check

• Can you name and describe four training techniques?
• What is the primary purpose of a performance appraisal?
• What are the six steps in a performance appraisal?

➤ **LEARNING GOAL 7.** Summarize the objectives of employee compensation programs and describe various pay systems and fringe benefits.

•••• ▬▬▬ ••••

COMPENSATING EMPLOYEES: ATTRACTING AND KEEPING THE BEST

Companies don't just compete for customers; they also compete for employees. Compensation is one of the main marketing tools companies use to attract qualified employees, yet it is one of the largest operating costs for many organizations. The long-term success of a firm—perhaps even its survival—may depend on

One of the least popular tasks that managers perform is performance appraisal. However, such appraisals are effective if clear standards are established and communicated. With such standards, appraisals are easier and more effective in improving productivity.

how well it can control employee costs and optimize employee efficiency. For example, service organizations such as hospitals, airlines, and banks have recently struggled with managing high employee costs. This is not unusual since these firms are considered labor intensive. That is, their primary cost of operations is the cost of labor. Manufacturing firms in the auto and steel industries have asked employees to take reductions in wages to make the firm more competitive. Many employees have agreed, even union employees who have traditionally resisted such cuts. They know that not to do so is to risk going out of business and losing their jobs forever. In other words, the competitive environment is such that compensation and benefit packages are being given special attention. In fact, some experts believe that determining how best to pay people has replaced downsizing ⇒ P. 4 ⇐ as the human resources challenge of the late 1990s.

A carefully managed compensation and benefit program can accomplish several objectives:

- Attracting the kinds of people needed by the organization, and in sufficient numbers.

- Providing employees with the incentive to work efficiently and productively.

- Keeping valued employees from leaving and going to competitors, or starting competing firms.

- Maintaining a competitive position in the marketplace by keeping costs low through high productivity from a satisfied workforce.

- Providing employees with some sense of financial security through insurance and retirement benefits.

··· PAY SYSTEMS ···

How an organization chooses to pay its employees can have a dramatic effect on efficiency and productivity. Some of the different pay systems are as follows:

- Salary systems are systems of fixed compensation computed on weekly, biweekly, or monthly pay periods (e.g., $1,500 per month or $400 per week). It's probable that many of you who graduate from college will be paid a salary.

- Hourly wage or daywork is the system used for most blue-collar and clerical workers. Often employees must punch a time clock when they arrive at work and when they leave. Hourly wages vary greatly. The federal minimum wage is $5.15, and top wages go as high as $20 to $30 per hour for skilled craftsmen. This does not include benefits such as retirement systems, which may add up to 30 percent or more to the total package.

- In a piecework system, employees are paid according to the number of items they produce rather than by the hour or day. This type of system creates powerful incentives to work efficiently and productively.

- Commission plans, which are often used to compensate salespeople, actually resemble piecework systems; the commission is based on some percentage of sales.

- Bonus plans are used for executives, salespeople, and other employees. They earn bonuses for accomplishing or surpassing certain objectives. There are two types of bonuses: monetary and cashless. Money is always a welcome bonus. Cashless rewards include written thank-you notes, appreciation notes sent to the employee's family, movie tickets, flowers, time off, gift certificates, shopping sprees, and other types of recognition.[21]

◄ CONSIDER USING LECTURE ENHANCER 11-9
Teamwork Calls for Team Compensation

◄ CONSIDER USING CRITICAL THINKING EXERCISE 11-2
Expanding the Workforce (SCANS)

- Profit-sharing plans give employees some share of the company's profits over and above their normal pay. Ninety-nine percent of the Fortune 500 companies use some sort of performance-based incentives. These companies set goals with the input from employees ahead of time. Bonuses are based on progress in meeting the goals.[22]

Managers want to find a system that compensates employees fairly. Many companies still use the pay system devised by Edward Hay for General Foods. Known as the Hay system, this compensation plan is based on job tiers, each of which has a strict pay range. In some firms, you're guaranteed a raise after 13 weeks if you're still breathing. Conflict can arise when an employee who is performing well earns less than an employee who is not performing well simply because the latter has worked for the company longer.

John Whitney, author of *The Trust Factor*, believes that companies should begin with some base pay and give all employees the same percentage merit raise. Doing so, he says, sends out the message that everyone in the company is important.[23] Fairness remains the issue. What do you think is the fairest pay system?

••• COMPENSATING TEAMS •••

Thus far we've talked about compensating individuals. What about teams? Since you want your teams to be more than simply a group of individuals, would you compensate them as you would individuals? If you can't answer that question immediately, you are not alone. A 1996 team-based pay survey found that managers continue to be more positive about the use of teams (87 percent) than about how to pay them (41 percent). This suggests that team-based pay programs are not as effective or as fully developed as managers would hope.[24] Measuring and rewarding individual performance on teams while at the same time rewarding team performance can be tricky. Nonetheless, it can be done. Football players are rewarded as a team when they go to the play-offs and to the Super Bowl, but they are paid individually as well. Companies are now experimenting with and developing similar incentive systems.

Jay Schuster, co-author of an ongoing study of team pay, found that when pay is based strictly on individual performance, it erodes team cohesiveness and makes it less likely that the team will meet its goals as a collaborative effort. Schuster recommends basing pay on team performance.[25] Skill-based pay and profit-sharing are the two most common compensation methods for teams.

Skill-based pay is related to the growth of both the individual and the team. Base pay is raised when team members learn and apply new skills. For example, Baldrige Award winner Eastman Chemical Co. rewards its teams' proficiency in technical, social, and business knowledge skills. A cross-functional compensation policy team defines the skills. The drawbacks of the skill-based pay system are twofold: the system is complex, and it is difficult to correlate skill acquisition and bottom-line gains.[26]

In most gain-sharing systems, bonuses are based on improvements over a previous performance baseline. For example, Behlen Manufacturing calculates its bonuses by dividing quality pounds of product by man-hours. Quality means no defects; any defects are subtracted from the total. Workers can receive a monthly gain-sharing bonus of up to $1 an hour when their teams meet productivity goals.[27]

It is important to reward individual team players also. Outstanding team players—those who go beyond what is required and make an outstanding individual contribution to the firm—should be separately recognized for their additional contribution. Recognition can include cashless as well as cash rewards.

A good way to avoid alienating recipients who feel team participation was uneven is to let the team decide which members get what type of individual award. After all, if you really support the team process, you need to give teams freedom to reward themselves.

••• FRINGE BENEFITS •••

Fringe benefits include sick-leave pay, vacation pay, pension plans, and health plans that provide additional compensation to employees beyond base wages. Fringe benefits in recent years grew faster than wages. In fact, employee benefits can't really be considered "fringe" anymore. While such benefits only accounted for 1.7 percent of payrolls in 1929, in 1995 they were 32.5 percent of payrolls. U.S. companies now spend an average of approximately $13,000 a year per employee for benefits. Many employees request more fringe benefits instead of more salary, to avoid higher taxes. This has resulted in much debate and much government investigation.

Fringe benefits can include everything from paid vacations to health care programs, recreation facilities, company cars, country club memberships, day care services, and executive dining rooms. Managing the benefit package will be a major human resource issue in the future. Employees want packages to include dental care, mental health care, elder care, legal counseling, eye care, and shorter workweeks.

To counter these growing demands, many firms are offering **cafeteria-style fringe benefits** plans, in which employees can choose the benefits they want, up to a certain dollar amount. Choice is the key to flexible, cafeteria-style benefits plans. At one time, most employees' needs were similar. Today, employees are more varied and more demanding. Some employees may need child care benefits, whereas others may need relatively large pension benefits. Rather than giving all employees identical benefits, managers can equitably and cost-effectively meet employees' individual needs by allowing employees some choice.

The cost of administering benefits programs has become so great that a number of companies are hiring outside companies to run their employee benefits plans (outsourcing). IBM, for example, decided to spin off its human resources and benefits operation into a separate company called Workforce Solutions. Workforce Solutions provides customized services to each of IBM's independent units. The new company saves IBM $45 million each year.[28] Workforce Solutions now handles benefits for other organizations such as the National Geographic Society. In addition to saving money, many companies now outsource their benefits plan administration to avoid the growing complexity and technical requirements involved in administering benefits plans.

To put it simply, benefits are as important to wage negotiations now as salary. In the future, benefits may become even more important than salary.

fringe benefits
Benefits such as sick-leave pay, vacation pay, pension plans, and health plans that represent additional compensation to employees.

◄ **CONSIDER USING OT ACETATE 11-10**
Unusual Benefits Offered to Workers

◄ **CONSIDER USING OT ACETATE 11-9**
Employers Offering Family-Friendly Benefits

cafeteria-style fringe benefits
Fringe benefits plan that allows employees to choose the benefits they want up to a certain dollar amount.

◄ **CONSIDER USING LECTURE ENHANCER 11-10**
Changing Family Issues: Caring for a Dependent Adult

SCHEDULING EMPLOYEES TO MEET ORGANIZATIONAL AND EMPLOYEE NEEDS

By now, you are quite familiar with the trends occurring in the workforce that result in managers and workers demanding more from jobs in the way of flexibility and responsiveness. From these trends have emerged several new or renewed ideas such as flextime, in-home employment, and job sharing. Let's see how these innovations affect the management of human resources.

◄ **LEARNING GOAL 8.** Explain scheduling plans managers use to adjust to workers' needs.

◄ **CONSIDER USING OT ACETATE 11-11**
Percentage of Employers That Grant Family Leave

••• FLEXTIME PLANS •••

flextime plan
Work schedule that gives employees some freedom to choose when to work, as long as they work the required number of hours.

core time
In a flextime plan, the period when all employees are expected to be at their job stations.

➤ **CONSIDER USING LECTURE ENHANCER 11-11**
Irregular Hours and Worker Health

➤ **CONSIDER USING LECTURE ENHANCER 11-12**
Flextime in the Real World

➤ **CONSIDER USING TM 83**
A Flextime Chart

compressed workweek
Work schedule that allows an employee to work a full number of hours per week but in fewer days.

```
┌      FIGURE 11.5      ┐
          • • • •
   A FLEXTIME CHART
```

At this company, employees can start any time between 6:30 and 9:30 A.M. They later take a half hour for lunch and can leave between 3:00 and 6:30 P.M. Everyone works an eight-hour day. The blue arrows show a typical flextime day.

A **flextime plan** gives employees some freedom to choose when to work, as long as they work the required number of hours. Nearly 90 percent of large U.S. companies offer some version of flextime.[29] The most popular plans allow employees to come to work at 7:00, 8:00, or 9:00 A.M. and leave between 4:00 and 6:00 P.M. Usually flextime plans will incorporate what is called core time. **Core time** refers to the period when all employees are expected to be at their job stations. For example, an organization may designate core time as between 9:30 A.M. and 11:00 A.M. and between 2:00 and 3:00 P.M. During these hours all employees are required to be at work (see Figure 11.5). Flextime plans, like job-sharing plans, are designed to allow employees to adjust to the demands of the times; two-income families find them especially helpful. The federal government has experimented extensively with flextime and found it to be a boost to employee productivity and morale.

There are some real disadvantages to flextime as well. Flextime is certainly not for all organizations. For example, it cannot be offered in assembly-line processes where everyone must be at work at the same time. It also is not effective for shift work.

Another disadvantage to flextime is that managers often have to work longer days in order to assist and supervise employees. Some organizations operate from 6:00 A.M. to 6:00 P.M. under flextime, a long day for supervisors. Flextime also makes communication more difficult; certain employees may not be there when others need to talk to them. Furthermore, if not carefully supervised, some employees could abuse the system, and that could cause resentment among others. You can imagine how you'd feel if half the workforce left at 3:00 P.M. on Friday and you had to work until 6:00 P.M.

Another popular option used in 24 percent of the companies surveyed is a **compressed workweek.** That means that an employee works a full number of hours in fewer days. For example, an employee may work four 10-hour days and then enjoy a long weekend instead of working five 8-hour days with a traditional weekend. There are the obvious advantages of working only four days and having three days off, but some employees get tired working such long hours, and productivity could decline. Many employees find such a system of great benefit, however, and are quite enthusiastic about it.

Although flexible schedules are offered by so many companies, few employees take advantage of them. Most workers report that they resist using the programs because they fear it will hurt their careers. Managers send a signal that if employees change their hours they are not serious about their careers.[30]

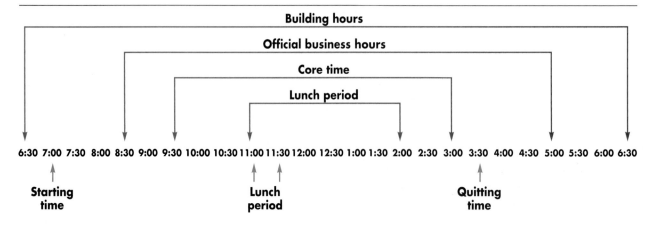

··· HOME-BASED AND OTHER ··· MOBILE WORK

Nearly 27 million U.S. workers work at home. Home-based workers can choose their own hours, interrupt work for child care and other tasks, and take time out for various personal reasons. Working at home can even be good for your career. A 1993 study for the Small Business Administration found that home-based workers get promoted at greater rates than office-bound workers.[31] Working at home isn't for everyone, however. To be successful, a home-based worker must have the discipline to stay focused on the work and not be easily distracted.

Telecommuting can be a cost saver for employers. For example, IBM used to have a surplus of office space, maintaining more offices than there were employees. Now the company has more mobile workers, with employees telecommuting, "hoteling" (being assigned to a desk through a reservations system), and "hot-desking" (sharing a desk with other employees at different times). About 10,000 IBM employees now share offices, typically with four people to an office.

Mobile workers create virtual offices that run computer and communications technology from their homes, cars, and other new work sites. Mobile workers can use pagers, portable computers, fax machines, cell phones, and network services to conduct business wherever it is convenient instead of being limited to a desk in a central office. What types of businesses in your area will benefit most from virtual offices?

··· JOB-SHARING PLANS ···

Job sharing is an arrangement whereby two part-time employees share one full-time job. The concept has received great attention as more and more women with small children have entered the labor force. Job sharing enables parents to work part-time while their children are in school and then return to the home when the children come home. Job sharing has also proved beneficial to students, older people who want to work part-time before fully retiring, and others who can only work part-time. The benefits include:

- Employment opportunities to those who cannot or prefer not to work full-time.
- A high level of enthusiasm and productivity.
- Reduced absenteeism and tardiness.
- Ability to schedule people into peak demand periods (e.g., banks on payday) when part-time people are available.

However, as you might suspect, disadvantages include having to hire, train, motivate, and supervise twice as many people and to prorate some fringe benefits. Nonetheless, most firms that were at first reluctant to try job sharing are finding that the benefits outweigh the disadvantages. Forty-four percent of the companies responding to a 1996 survey said that they offer some types of job sharing.[32]

job sharing
An arrangement whereby two part-time employees share one full-time job.

◄ **CONSIDER USING OT ACETATE 11-12**
Job-Oriented Motivational Techniques

◄ **CONSIDER USING OT ACETATE 11-13**
Company's Reasons for Establishing Flexible Work Plans

What effects have dual-career families had on the human resource function? What problems can arise when family members work together in the same firm? What is your reaction to employees who date one another?

Critical Thinking

Progress Check

- Can you name and describe five alternative compensation techniques?
- What advantages do compensation plans such as profit sharing offer an organization?

➤ **LEARNING GOAL 9.** Describe the ways employees can move through a company: promotion, reassignment, termination, and retirement.

➤ **CONSIDER USING LECTURE ENHANCER 11-13**
Caught in the Crossfire: Managing Family Firms

···· ▬ ····
MOVING EMPLOYEES UP, OVER, AND OUT

Employees don't always stay in the position they were initially hired to fill. They may excel and move up the corporate ladder or fail and move out the front door. In addition to promotion and termination, employees can be moved by reassignment and retirement.

··· PROMOTING AND REASSIGNING EMPLOYEES ···

Many companies find that promotion from within the company improves employee morale. Promotions are also cost-effective in that the promoted employees already familiar with the corporate culture and procedures do not need to spend valuable time on basic orientation.

Due to the prevalence of flatter corporate structures, there are fewer levels for employees to reach now as compared to the past. Therefore, it is more common today for workers to move *over* to a new position than to move *up* to one. Such transfers allow employees to develop and display new skills and to learn more about the company overall. This is one way of motivating experienced employees to remain in a company with few advancement opportunities.

➤ **CONSIDER USING SUPPLEMENTAL CASE 11-2**
The Dangers of Firing Employees (**SCANS**)

··· TERMINATING EMPLOYEES ···

As we discussed in previous chapters, downsizing and restructuring, increasing customer demands for greater value, and the relentless pressure of global competition and shifts in technology have human resource managers struggling to manage layoffs and firings. Even as companies regain financial strength, however, they are hesitant to rehire permanent employees. Why? One reason is that the cost of terminating employees is prohibitively high. The cost of firing comes from lost training costs as well as damages and legal fees paid in wrongful discharge suits. To save money, many companies are either using temporary employees or outsourcing certain functions.

At one time the prevailing employment doctrine was "employment at will." This meant that managers had as much freedom to fire workers as workers had to leave voluntarily. Most states now have written employment laws that limit the at-will doctrine to protect employees from wrongful firing; for example, employers can no longer fire an employee simply because that person exposed the employer's illegal actions, refused to violate a law, or was a member of a minority or other protected group. This well-meaning legislation restricted management's ability to terminate employees as it increased workers' rights to their jobs. In some cases, workers fired for using illegal drugs have sued on the ground that they have an illness (addiction) therefore they are protected by laws barring discrimination against the handicapped.[33] See Figure 11.6 for advice about how to minimize the chance of wrongful-discharge lawsuits.

➤ **CONSIDER USING LECTURE ENHANCER 11-14**
Using the Exit Interview as Control

··· RETIRING EMPLOYEES ···

In addition to laying off employees, another tool used to downsize companies is to offer early retirement benefits to entice older (and more expensive) workers to resign. Such benefits usually involve such financial incentives as one-time cash payments (golden handshakes). The advantage of offering early retirement benefits over laying off employees is that early retirement offers increase the morale of the surviving employees. Retiring senior workers also increases promotion opportunities for younger employees. (Although you may

Consultants offer this advice to minimize the chance of a lawsuit for wrongful discharge:

- Prepare before hiring by requiring recruits to sign a statement that retains management's freedom to terminate at will.

- Don't make unintentional promises by using such terms as *permanent employment.*

- Document reasons before firing and make sure you have an unquestionable business reason for the firing.

- Fire the worst first and be consistent in discipline.

- Buy out bad risks by offering severance pay in exchange for a signed release from any claims.

- Be sure to give employees the true reasons they are being fired. If you do not, you cannot reveal it to a recruiter asking for a reference without risking a defamation lawsuit.

- Disclose the reasons for an employee's dismissal to that person's potential new employers. For example, if you fired an employee for dangerous behavior and you withhold that information from your references, you can be sued if the employee commits a violent act at his or her next job.

Sources: "When Firing Can Backfire," *The Washington Post,* March 2, 1997, p. H4; and Edward Felsenthal, "Justices Let Former Employees Sue over Bad References," *The Wall Street Journal Interactive Edition,* February 18, 1997.

FIGURE 11.6

• • • •

HOW TO AVOID WRONGFUL DISCHARGE LAWSUITS

have yet to begin your career, keep in mind for later that studies have shown that if you're offered early retirement, you should accept the first offer, when employers are more likely to feel guilty and, therefore, generous.)

◄ **CONSIDER USING TM 84**
How to Avoid Wrongful Discharge Lawsuits

LAWS AFFECTING HUMAN RESOURCE MANAGEMENT

◄ **LEARNING GOAL 10.** Illustrate the effects of legislation on human resource management.

Legislation has made hiring, promoting, firing, and managing employee relations in general very complex and subject to many legal complications and challenges. Let's see how changes in the law have expanded the role and the challenge of human resource management.

The U.S. government had little to do with human resource decisions until the 1930s. Since then, though, legislation and legal decisions have greatly affected all areas of human resource management, from hiring to training and working conditions (see the Legal Briefcase box on p. 338). These laws were passed because many businesses would not exercise fair labor practices voluntarily.

One of the most important pieces of social legislation ever passed by Congress was the Civil Rights Act of 1964. This act was passed with much debate and was actually amended 97 times before final passage. Title VII of that act brought the government directly into the operations of human resource management. Title VII prohibits discrimination in hiring, firing, compensation, apprenticeships, training, terms, conditions, or privileges of employment based on race, religion, creed, sex, or national origin. Age was later added to the conditions of the act. The Civil Rights Act of 1964 was expected to stamp out discrimination in the workplace. However, specific language in the act often made its enforcement quite difficult. With this in mind, Congress took on the task of amending the law.

In 1972, the Equal Employment Opportunity Act (EEOA) was added as an amendment to Title VII. It strengthened the Equal Employment Opportunity

◄ **CONSIDER USING OT ACETATE 11-14 AND OT ACETATE 11-15**
What Do You Know About Equal Employment Opportunity Law?

◄ **CONSIDER USING LECTURE ENHANCER 11-15**
Personal Appearance Discrimination

Legal Briefcase

http://www.eeoc.gov/welcome.html

Government Legislation

National Labor Relations Act of 1935. Established collective bargaining in labor–management relations and limited management interference in the right of employees to have a collective bargaining agent.

Fair Labor Standards Act of 1938. Established a minimum wage and overtime pay for employees working more than 40 hours a week.

Manpower Development and Training Act of 1962. Provided for the training and retraining of unemployed workers.

Equal Pay Act of 1963. Specified that men and women doing equal jobs must be paid the same wage.

The Civil Rights Act of 1964. Outlawed discrimination in employment based on sex, race, color, religion, or national origin.

Age Discrimination in Employment Act of 1967. Outlawed personnel practices that discriminate against people aged 40 to 69. An amendment outlaws company policies that require employees to retire before age 70.

Occupational Safety and Health Act of 1970 (OSHA). Regulated the degree to which employees can be exposed to hazardous substances and specified the safety equipment to be provided by the employer.

Equal Employment Opportunity Act of 1972. Strengthened the Equal Employment Opportunity Commission (EEOC) and authorized the EEOC to set guidelines for human resource management.

The Comprehensive Employment and Training Act of 1973. Provided funds for training unemployed workers (was known as the *CETA program*).

Employee Retirement Income Security Act of 1974. Regulated company retirement programs and provided a federal insurance program for bankrupt retirement plans.

Immigration Reform and Control Act of 1986. Required employers to verify the eligibility for employment of *all* their new hires (including U.S. citizens).

Supreme Court ruling against set-aside programs (affirmative action), 1989. Declared that setting aside 30 percent of contracting jobs for minority businesses was reverse discrimination and unconstitutional.

Older Workers Benefit Protection Act, 1990. Protects older people from signing away their rights to things like pensions or to fight against illegal age discrimination.

Civil Rights Act of 1991. Applies to firms with over 15 employees. It extends the right to a jury trial and punitive damages to victims of intentional job discrimination.

Americans with Disabilities Act (1992 implementation). Employers must not discriminate against qualified disabled individuals in hiring, advancement, or compensation and must adapt the workplace if necessary.

Family and Medical Leave Act of 1993. Businesses with 50 or more employees must provide up to 12 weeks of unpaid leave per year upon birth or adoption of employee's child or upon serious illness of parent, ▲ spouse, or child.

> **CONSIDER USING LECTURE ENHANCER 11-16**
Dismantling the Glass Ceiling

affirmative action
Employment activities designed to "right past wrongs" by increasing opportunities for minorities and women.

Commission (EEOC), which was created by the Civil Rights Act of 1964. Congress gave rather broad powers to the EEOC. For example, the commission was permitted to issue guidelines for acceptable employer conduct in administering equal employment opportunity. Also, specific record-keeping procedures, as set forth by the EEOC, became mandatory. In addition, the commission was vested with the power of enforcement to ensure that these mandates were carried out. The EEOC became a formidable regulatory force in the administration of human resource management.

Probably the most controversial program enforced by the EEOC concerns **affirmative action;** that is, activities designed to "right past wrongs" by increasing opportunities for minorities and women. Interpretation of the affirmative-action law eventually led employers to actively recruit and give preference to women and minority group members. As you might expect, interpretation of the law was often controversial, and enforcement difficult. Questions persisted about the legality of affirmative action and the effect the program could have in creating a sort of reverse discrimination in the workplace.[34] **Reverse discrimination** has been defined as discrimination against whites or males. Charges of reverse discrimination have occurred when companies have been perceived as unfairly giving preference to women or minority group members in hiring and promoting. The term has generated much heated debate.

The Civil Rights Act of 1991 expanded the remedies available to victims of discrimination by amending Title VII of the Civil Rights Act of 1964. Now victims of discrimination have the right to a jury trial and punitive damages. One still-open question is whether or not companies would have to establish "quotas" in hiring.[35] Human resource managers continue to follow court cases closely to see how the law is enforced. This issue is likely to persist for years to come.

··· LAWS PROTECTING THE DISABLED ··· AND OLDER EMPLOYEES

The courts have continued their activity in issues involving human resource management. As you read above, the courts look carefully into any improprieties concerning possible discrimination in hiring, firing, training, and so forth specifically related to race or sex. The Vocational Rehabilitation Act (1973) extended the same protection to people with disabilities. Today, businesses cannot discriminate against people on the basis of any physical or mental handicap.

The Americans with Disabilities Act (ADA) of 1990 requires that disabled applicants be given the same consideration for employment as people without disabilities. It also requires that businesses make "reasonable accommodations" for people with disabilities. This means doing such things as modifying equipment or widening doorways. Reasonable accommodations are not always expensive. For about $6 a month, a company can rent a headset phone that allows someone with cerebral palsy to talk on the phone and write at the same time. The ADA also protects disabled individuals from discrimination in public accommodations, transportation, and telecommunications.

Equal opportunity for people with disabilities promises to be a continuing issue into the next decade. Most companies are not having trouble making structural changes to be accommodating; what they are finding difficult are the cultural changes. Employers used to think being fair meant treating everyone the same. Now they believe *accommodation* means that they must treat different people differently. In 1997, the EEOC issued new guidelines for the ADA that tell employers how they are supposed to treat workers and applicants with mental disabilities. The accommodations include putting up barriers to isolate people readily distracted by noise, reassigning workers to new tasks, and making changes in supervisors' management styles.[36]

Older employees are also guaranteed protection against discrimination in the workplace. Courts have ruled against firms in unlawful-discharge suits where age appeared to be the major factor in the dismissal. Additionally, protection

Some analysts submit that affirmative action sometimes results in reverse discrimination. To combat such discrimination, there have been proposals to repeal affirmative action. Leaders such as Jesse Jackson defend affirmative action and protest the policies of companies that do not actively support the advancement of minority groups.

reverse discrimination
Discrimination against whites or males in hiring or promoting.

In America, everyone should have equal opportunity. The Americans with Disabilities Act of 1990 (ADA) requires businesses, including public transportation systems, to make "reasonable accommodations" to people with disabilities. Why might some businesses oppose these laws?

through the Age Discrimination in Employment Act outlawed mandatory retirement in most organizations before age 70. Many companies are voluntarily phasing out mandatory retirement after age 70 as well.

••• EFFECTS OF LEGISLATION •••

Clearly, legislation affects all areas of human resource management. Such legislation ranges from the Social Security Act of 1935, to the Occupational Safety and Health Act (OSHA) of 1970, to the Employment Retirement Income Security Act (ERISA) of 1974. Human resource managers must read *The Wall Street Journal, Business Week,* and other current publications to keep up with all human resource legislation and rulings.

We have devoted so much space to civil rights and related legislation because such decisions have greatly affected human resource programs and will continue to do so. It's apparent that a career in human resource management offers a challenge to anyone willing to put forth the effort. In summary:

- Employers must know and act in accordance with the legal rights of their employees or risk costly court cases.
- Legislation affects all areas of human resource management, from hiring and training to compensating employees.
- Court cases have made it clear that it is sometimes legal to go beyond providing equal rights for minorities and women to provide special employment (affirmative action) and training to correct discrimination in the past.
- New court cases and legislation change human resource management almost daily; the only way to keep current is to read the business literature and become familiar with the issues.

Progress Check

Can you explain what was covered by the following laws?
- The Civil Rights Act of 1964.
- The Equal Employment Opportunity Act of 1972.
- The Americans with Disabilities Act of 1990.

SUMMARY
• • • • • •

1. Explain the importance of human resource management, and describe current issues in managing human resources.

1. Human resource management is the process of evaluating human resource needs, finding people to fill those needs, and getting the best work from each employee by providing the right incentives and job environment, all with the goal of meeting organizational objectives.
   * ***What are some of the current challenges and opportunities in the human resource area?***
   Many of the current challenges and opportunities revolve around the changing demographics of workers: more women, minorities, immigrants, and older workers. Other challenges concern a shortage of trained workers and an abundance of unskilled workers; skilled workers in declining industries requiring retraining; changing employee work attitudes; and complex laws and regulations.

2. Like all other types of management, human resource management begins with planning.
   • **What are the steps in human resource planning?**
   The six steps are (1) preparing forecasts of future human resource needs; (2) preparing a human resource inventory of the organization's employees; (3) preparing a job analysis; (4) assessing future demand; (5) assessing future supply; and (6) establishing a plan for recruiting, hiring, educating, and appraising, compensating, and scheduling employees.

2. Summarize the six steps in planning human resources.

3. Recruitment is the set of activities used to obtain a sufficient number of the right people at the right time to select those who best meet the needs of the organization.
   • **What methods do human resource managers use to recruit new employees?**
   Recruiting sources are classified as either internal or external. Internal sources include hiring from within the firm (transfers, promotions, etc.) and employees who recommend others to hire. External recruitment sources include advertisements, public and private employment agencies, college placement bureaus, management consultants, professional organizations, referrals, and walk-in applications.
   • **Why has recruitment become more difficult?**
   Legal restrictions complicate hiring and firing practices. Finding suitable employees can also be made more difficult if companies are considered unattractive workplaces.

3. Describe methods that companies use to recruit new employees, and explain some of the issues that make recruitment challenging.

4. Selection is the process of gathering and interpreting information to decide which applicants should be hired.
   • **What are the six steps in the selection process?**
   The steps are (1) obtaining complete application forms; (2) conducting initial and follow-up interviews; (3) giving employment tests; (4) conducting background investigations; (5) obtaining results from physical exams; and (6) establishing a trial period of employment.

4. Outline the six steps in selecting employees.

5. Employee training and development include all attempts to improve employee performance by increasing an employee's ability to perform through learning.
   • **What are some of the procedures used for training?**
   They include employee orientation, on- and off-the-job training, apprentice programs, vestibule training, and job simulation.
   • **What methods are used to develop managerial skills?**
   Management development methods include on-the-job coaching, understudy positions, job rotation, and off-the-job courses and training.
   • **How does networking fit in this process?**
   Networking is the process of establishing contacts with key managers within and outside the organization to get additional development assistance.

5. Illustrate the use of various types of employee training and development methods.

6. A performance appraisal is an evaluation of the performance level of employees against established standards to make decisions about promotions, compensation, additional training, or firing.
   • **How is performance evaluated?**
   The steps are (1) establish performance standards; (2) communicate those standards; (3) evaluate performance; (4) discuss results; (5) take corrective action when needed; and (6) use the results for decisions about promotions, compensation, additional training, or firing.

6. Trace the six steps in appraising employee performance.

7. Summarize the objectives of employee compensation programs and describe various pay systems and fringe benefits.

7. Employee compensation is one of the largest operating costs for many organizations.
   • ***What kind of compensation systems are used?***
   They include salary systems, hourly wages, piecework, commission plans, bonus plans, and profit-sharing plans.
   • ***What types of compensation systems are appropriate for teams?***
   The most common are gains-sharing and skill-based compensation programs. It is also important to reward outstanding individual performance within teams.
   • ***What are fringe benefits?***
   Fringe benefits include such items as sick leave, vacation pay, pension plans, and health plans that provide additional compensation to employees.

8. Explain scheduling plans managers use to adjust to workers' needs.

8. Workers' increasing need for flexibility has generated new innovations in scheduling.
   • ***What scheduling plans can be used to adjust to employees' need for flexibility?***
   Such plans include job sharing, flextime, compressed workweeks, and working at home.

9. Describe the ways employees can move through a company: promotion, reassignment, termination, and retirement.

9. Employees often move from their original positions in a company.
   • ***How can employees move within a company?***
   Employees can move up (promotion), over (reassignment) or out (termination or retirement) of a company.

10. Illustrate the effects of legislation on human resource management.

10. There are many laws that affect human resource planning.
   • ***What are those laws?***
   See the Legal Briefcase box on p. 338 and review the section on laws. This is an important subject for future managers to study.

KEY TERMS
......

affirmative action 338	**fringe benefits** 333	**off-the-job training** 327
apprentice programs 326	**human resource management** 316	**on-the-job training** 327
cafeteria-style fringe benefits 333	**job analysis** 320	**performance appraisal** 329
compressed workweek 334	**job description** 320	
	job sharing 335	**recruitment** 321
contingent workers 325	**job simulation** 327	**reverse discrimination** 339
core time 334	**job specifications** 320	
	management development 327	**selection** 323
employee orientation 326	**mentor** 328	**training and development** 326
flextime plan 334	**networking** 328	**vestibule training** 327

DEVELOPING WORKPLACE SKILLS

1. If you experience a typical career you are likely to have about eight different jobs in your lifetime. Therefore, you will have to prepare several résumés and cover letters. Write a cover letter and a résumé you would use to gain an entry-level position in your local area. Ask your instructor to critique them.

2. Read several current business periodicals to find information on the latest court rulings involving fringe benefits, affirmative action, and other human resource issues. Compose a summary of your findings. What seems to be the trend? What will this mean for tomorrow's college graduates?

3. Recall the various training programs you have experienced. Think of both on-the-job and off-the-job training sessions. What is your evaluation of such programs? Write a brief critique of each. How would you improve them? Share your ideas with the class.

4. Look up the current unemployment figures for individual states. Are there pockets of very high unemployment? What do you think causes such uneven figures? What can be done to retrain workers whose skills are obsolete because of a restructured economy? Is that the role of government or of business? Discuss. Could government and business cooperate in this function?

5. Find several people who work under flextime or part-time systems and interview them regarding their experiences and preferences. Using this information, draft a proposal to your company's management advocating an option for a four-day workweek. Debate this proposal with the class.

TAKING IT TO THE NET

Purpose

To use job-search Web sites to identify employment options and to compare the services offered by several recruiting-related sites.

Exercise

There are many recruiting-related sites on the Internet. You can find links to such sites at http://www.teleport.com/~erwilson/jobserch.html. Select three job-search Web sites. Use the search feature in each site to try to identify a position for which you might qualify after graduation.

1. Did the sites generate any employment possibilities for you?

2. Do some sites offer services that the others don't? Compare the strengths and weaknesses of each site. Include such criteria as variety of occupations in the database, volume of jobs, number of employers, geographical locations, ease of use, supplemental job hunting advice, and unique features.

Practicing Management Decisions

CASE

• • • • • •

DUAL-CAREER PLANNING

• • • • • •

Carey Moler is a 32-year-old account executive for a communications company. She is married to Mitchell Moler, a lawyer. Carey and Mitchell had not made any definite plans about how to juggle their careers and family life until Carey reached age 30. Then they decided to have a baby, and career planning took on whole new dimensions. A company named Catalyst talked to 815 dual-career couples and found that most of them, like the Molers, had not made any long-range career decisions regarding family lifestyle.

From the business perspective, such dual-career families create real concerns. There are problems with relocation, with child care, and so on that affect recruiting, productivity, morale, and promotion policies.

For a couple such as the Molers, having both career and family responsibilities is exhausting. But that is just one problem. If Carey is moving up in the firm, what happens if Mitchell gets a terrific job offer a thousand miles away? What if Carey gets such an offer? Who is going to care for the baby? What happens if the baby becomes ill? How do they plan their vacations when there are three schedules to balance? Who will do the housework?

Dual careers require careful planning and discussion, and those plans need to be reviewed over time. A couple who decide at age 22 to do certain things may change their minds at 30. Whether or not to have children, where to locate, how to manage the household—all such issues and more can become major problems if not carefully planned.

The same is true for corporations. They, too, must plan for dual-career families. They must give attention to job sharing, flextime, paternity leave policies, transfer policies, nepotism rules, and more.

Decision Questions

1. What are some of the issues you can see developing because of dual-career families? How is this affecting children in such families?

2. What kind of corporate policies need changing to adapt to these new realities?

3. What can newlywed couples do to minimize the problems of dual careers? What are the advantages of dual careers? Disadvantages? How can a couple achieve the advantages with a minimum number of problems?

Workers today face a host of challenges and obstacles in the workplace. Longer hours, less job security, and balancing career and family are just a few factors that can raise workers' stress levels to a boiling point. But workers are not alone. Managers also feel the pressure. Managers know that contented, happier workers tend to be more productive workers. The challenge is to provide employees with the resources that will result in a motivated, empowered workforce. Examples of companies that use a number of creative perks to motivate workers include:

- S.C. Johnson Company in Racine, Wisconsin, encourages its workers and supervisors in the customer service department to fight pressure and stress on the job by going to war with each other. It's not unusual for a supervisor and worker to arm themselves with full battle gear (water soakers) and fight it out to the drenching end.

- CIGNA Insurance Company employees who don't have the energy at the end of a 10-hour workday to face the challenge of preparing a meal for the family at home, can place take-home meal orders with the company chef. The company also offers an exercise physiologist to help employees suffering from stress.

- Salomon Smith Barney employees can visit a physician in their office building and have a prescription delivered to them right at the office.

- Wilton-Connor Packaging Company employees can bring their laundry to work with them and have it done for $1 per load (ironing is 25 cents extra). The company also provides the services of a handyman to perform

VIDEO CASE
• • • • • •
WORKPLACE TRENDS

jobs such as painting at employees' homes. The only cost to the employee is the cost of the paint.

- Andersen Consulting provides its employees a rather sophisticated perk. The company employs a concierge to run errands (such as shopping) for employees loaded down with other responsibilities.

- Coca-Cola and Home Depot offer wellness and exercise programs to reduce stress and enhance employee health at the same time. Management at Coca-Cola found that employees that participated in such activities used fewer sick days and tended to be more productive on their jobs. Home Depot found the same results and now provides exercise facilities and classes on-site for employees to help them stop smoking, learn to eat and exercise right, manage work and home, and so on. Such applications are highly recommended by officials at the Center for Disease Control in Atlanta.

The development of happier, more productive workers seems to support the investment and time in all of these innovative efforts.

Discussion Questions

1. What are the advantages and disadvantages of companies offering creative perks and special programs to workers in the workplace?

2. Do you think the number and variety of perks will continue to grow or do you think this is just a management fad that will fade in the future?

3. What other perks might companies consider to lower stress levels and increase employee productivity?

Dealing with Employee–Management Issues and Relationships

Chapter 12

LEARNING GOALS

After you have read and studied this chapter,
you should be able to

1 Trace the history of organized labor in the United States and discuss the major legislation affecting labor unions.

2 Outline the objectives of labor unions.

3 Describe the tactics used by labor and management during conflicts and discuss the role of unions in the future.

4 Explain some of the controversial employee–management issues such as executive compensation; comparable worth; child care and elder care; AIDS, drug testing, and violence in the workplace; and employee stock ownership plans (ESOPs).

When you hear names like Chainsaw Al, Rambo in Pinstripes, and the Terminator, your thoughts may well turn to the lineup of villains performing in the World Wrestling Federation. Well, think again. Al Dunlap, current CEO of Sunbeam Corporation and former CEO of Scott Paper Company, has been tabbed with all these titles. Mr. Dunlap stands out as a symbol of controversy in the 1990s, feared by communities and workers, yet admired by shareholders and Wall Street analysts.

Dunlap is a graduate of the U.S. Military Academy at West Point. He climbed his way up the corporate ladder as a hard-nosed paper-company executive in the 1970s. From there he advanced to the role of hatchet man for corporate takeover specialists Kohlberg-Kravis and Sir James Goldsmith in the 1980s. It was Goldsmith who dubbed him Rambo in Pinstripes. It wasn't until the 1990s, however, that Dunlap achieved Wall Street superstar status. As CEO of Scott Paper Company, he took a money-losing operation and transformed it in just two short years into a $9 billion operation before he sold to Kimberly-Clark. For his efforts Dunlap personally earned more than $100 million. However, after firing 11,200 workers at Scott Paper, he also gained the nickname Chainsaw Al.

The Scott Paper deal made Dunlap a hero to some and a heartless villain to others. Stockholders watched the value of the company grow $6.5 billion in just 20 months. Many employees, however, saw years of loyal service washed away as Dunlap slashed costs. At Sunbeam Dunlap has enacted a similar plan, laying off 6,000 employees and closing or selling 18 factories and 37 warehouses. Wall Street expects Dunlap to either sell Sunbeam, merge it with another firm, or acquire a complementary company. Sunbeam employees expect more cuts and layoffs.

Al Dunlap is truly a controversial figure who arouses varied emotions among different groups in the workplace. While critics suggest that Chainsaw Al needs to show compassion for the "little guy," Dunlap defends his actions as part of his job and shareholders find the returns he produces attractive.

Such controversies are the subject of this chapter. Workplace issues such as labor–management relations, executive pay, and comparable worth will dominate the headlines and the thoughts of business managers and workers throughout the coming years.

 PROFILE

Al Dunlap of Sunbeam Corporation

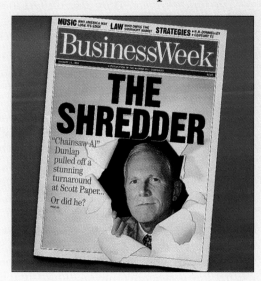

Sources: Patricia Sellers, "Can Chainsaw Al Really Be a Builder?" *Fortune*, January 12, 1998, pp. 118–20; Jonathan R. Laing, "Does Chainsaw Al Have a Truly Revived Operation—Or Something Else in His Sights?" *Barron's*, June 16, 1997, p. 29; Matthew Schifrin, "The Dunlap Effect," *Forbes*, March 24, 1997, p. 42; Barbara Ettorre, "Flash! Mississippi Town Twice Escaped Being Dunlapped!" *Management Review*, February 1997, p. 9.

EMPLOYEE–MANAGEMENT ISSUES

The relationship between managers and employees has never been smooth. Management has the responsibility to produce a profit through maximum productivity. Managers have to make hard decisions that often do not let them win popularity contests. Labor is interested in fair and competent management, human dignity, and a reasonable share in the wealth their work generates. Many issues affect the relationship between managers and employees: executive compensation, comparable worth, child care and elder care, AIDS, drug testing, violence in the workplace, and employee stock ownership plans (ESOPs).

◄ CONSIDER USING TM 85
Chapter Outline

◄ CONSIDER USING LECTURE ENHANCER 12-1
David Stern: NBA Commissioner

◄ CONSIDER USING CRITICAL THINKING EXERCISE 12-1
Are Unions Good or Bad for Business? (SCANS)

The 1990s were not the best of times for labor unions. Membership continued to dip and unions continued to fall behind in certification elections. The teamsters strike at United Parcel Service in 1997, however, seemed to rejuvenate the lagging labor movement. Do you think the teamsters' victory against UPS is a sign that organized labor is back on the upswing? Why?

▶ **LEARNING GOAL 1.**
Trace the history of organized labor in the United States and discuss the major legislation affecting labor unions.

unions
Employee organizations that have the main goal of representing members in employee–management bargaining over job-related issues.

▶ **CONSIDER USING OT ACETATE 12-1**
Why Employees Join or Don't Join Unions

This chapter discusses such issues. Like all other managerial challenges, these issues must be worked out through open discussion, goodwill, and compromise. It is important to know both sides of the issues, however, in order to make reasoned decisions.

Any discussion of employee–management relations in the United States probably should begin with a discussion of unions. **Unions** are employee organizations that have the main goal of representing members in employee–management bargaining over job-related issues. Workers formed unions to protect themselves from intolerable work conditions and unfair treatment from owners and managers. They also united to secure some say in the operations of their jobs. As the number of union members grew, workers gained more negotiating power with managers and more political power as well.

Historically, employees turned to unions to assist them in gaining specific rights and benefits. Labor unions were responsible for the establishment of minimum wage laws, overtime rules, child-labor laws, and more. After this, however, union strength waned. In the 1990s, unions have failed to regain the power they once had and membership has continued to decline. While many labor analysts forecast that unions may again regain strength among workers, others suggest unions have seen their brightest days. Still, there's no question that the future role and position of unions will arouse emotions and opinions that contrast considerably. Let's briefly look at some contrasting viewpoints concerning labor unions and then look at other key issues affecting employee–management relations.

···· ▬▬▬ ····

LABOR UNIONS FROM DIFFERENT PERSPECTIVES

Are labor unions essential in the American economy today? This question is certain to evoke emotional responses from various participants in the workplace. An electrician carrying a picket sign in New York might elaborate on the dangers to our free society if employers continue to try to "bust" authorized unions. Small manufacturers would likely embrace a different perspective and complain about having to operate under union wage and benefit obligations in a growing global economy.

Most historians generally agree that the union movement of today is an outgrowth of the economic transition caused by the Industrial Revolution of the 19th and early 20th centuries. The workers who once toiled in the fields, dependent on the mercies of nature for survival, suddenly became dependent on the continuous roll of the factory presses and assembly lines for their living. Breaking away from an agricultural economy to form an industrial economy was quite difficult. Over time workers learned that strength through unity (unions) could lead to improved job conditions, better wages, and job security.

Today, critics of organized labor maintain that few of the inhuman conditions that once dominated U.S. industry can be found in the workplace. They charge that organized labor has in fact become a large industrial entity in itself and that the real issue of protecting workers has become secondary. The legal system and current management attitudes, they say, minimize the chances that the sweatshops of the late 19th and early 20th centuries will reappear. A short discussion of the history of labor unions will cast a better light on these differing positions.

◄ CONSIDER USING LECTURE ENHANCER 12-2
Doctors to Unionize?

••• THE EARLY HISTORY OF ORGANIZED LABOR •••

The presence of formal labor organizations in the United States dates back to the time of the American Revolution. As early as 1792, cordwainers (shoemakers) in Philadelphia met to discuss the fundamental work issues of pay, hours, conditions, and job security (many of the same issues that dominate labor negotiations today). The shoemakers were a **craft union**, which is an organization of skilled specialists in a particular craft or trade. They were typical of the early labor organizations formed before the Civil War in that they were local or regional in membership. Also, most were established to achieve some short-range goal such as curtailing the use of convict labor as an alternative to available local labor. Often after a specific objective was attained, the labor group disbanded. This situation changed dramatically in the late 19th century with the expansion of the Industrial Revolution.

◄ CONSIDER USING LECTURE ENHANCER 12-3
The Complicated Legacy of Henry Ford

craft union
An organization of skilled specialists in a particular craft or trade.

The Industrial Revolution changed the economic structure of the United States. Enormous productivity increases gained through mass production and job specialization made the United States a true world economic power. This growth, however, brought problems for workers in terms of productivity, hours of work, wages, and unemployment.

◄ CONSIDER USING LECTURE ENHANCER 12-4
No More Homework. Please!

Workers were faced with the reality that production was vital. If you failed to produce, you lost your job. People had to go to work even if they were ill or had family problems. Over time, the increased emphasis on production led firms to expand the hours of work. The length of the average workweek in 1900 was 60 hours, but 80 hours was not uncommon for some industries. Wages were low and the use of child labor was common. Furthermore, periods of unemployment were hard on families who lived on subsistence wages. As you can sense, these were not short-term issues that would easily go away. The workplace was ripe for the emergence of national labor organizations.

The first truly national labor organization was the **Knights of Labor**, formed by Uriah Smith Stephens in 1869. By 1886, the Noble Order of the Knights of Labor claimed a membership of 700,000 members. The Knights of Labor offered membership to all working people, including employers, and promoted social causes as well as labor and economic issues. The intention of the Knights of Labor was to gain significant *political* power and eventually restructure the entire U.S. economy. The organization fell from prominence after being blamed for a bomb that exploded during a labor rally at Haymarket Square in Chicago in 1886, which killed eight policemen.

Knights of Labor
The first national labor union; formed in 1869.

A rival group, the **American Federation of Labor (AFL)**, was formed in 1886. By 1890, the AFL, under the dynamic leadership of Samuel Gompers, had moved to the forefront of the labor movement. The AFL was an organization of craft unions that championed fundamental labor issues. The AFL intentionally limited membership to skilled workers (craftspeople), assuming they would have better bargaining power in attaining concessions from employers. It's important to note that the AFL was never one big union. Rather, it functioned as a federation of many individual unions that could become members, yet keep their separate union status. Over time, an unauthorized committee in the AFL, called the Committee of Industrial Organization, began to organize workers in **industrial unions**, which consisted of unskilled and semiskilled

American Federation of Labor (AFL)
An organization of craft unions that championed fundamental labor issues.

industrial unions
Labor organizations of unskilled and semiskilled workers in mass-production-related industries such as automobiles and mining.

Many believe a turning point for organized labor occurred in the 1980s when members of PATCO (Professional Air Traffic Controllers' Organization) were fired by President Ronald Reagan for going on strike. The President further ordered the hiring of replacement workers to replace the striking controllers. How do you feel about the use of replacement workers?

Congress of Industrial Organizations (CIO)
Union organization of unskilled workers; broke away from the AFL in 1935 and rejoined it in 1955.

workers in mass-production industries such as automobiles and mining. John L. Lewis, president of the United Mineworkers Union, led this committee.

Lewis's objective was to organize both craftspeople (craft unions) and unskilled workers (industrial unions). In 1935 when the AFL rejected his proposal, Lewis broke away to form a new, rival organization called the **Congress of Industrial Organizations (CIO)**. The CIO soon rivaled the AFL in membership, partly because of the passage of the National Labor Relations Act (Wagner Act) that same year (see Figure 12.1). For 20 years, the two organizations struggled for leadership in the labor movement. It wasn't until passage of the Taft-Hartley Act in 1947 (see Figure 12.1) that the two organizations saw the benefits of a merger. In 1955, under the leadership of George Meany, 16 million labor members united to form the AFL–CIO. Today, the AFL–CIO includes affiliations with 78 labor unions.[1]

> **learning goal 2.**
> Outline the objectives of labor unions.

•••• ━━━━ ••••

LABOR LEGISLATION AND COLLECTIVE BARGAINING

The growth and influence of organized labor in the United States has depended on two major factors: the law and public opinion. Figure 12.1 outlines five major federal laws that have had a significant impact on the rights and operations of labor unions. (Take a few moments and read the basics involved in each of these laws before going on.)

collective bargaining
The process whereby union and management representatives put together a contract for workers.

The National Labor Relations Act (Wagner Act) provided labor with legal justification to pursue key issues such as collective bargaining that were strongly supported by Samuel Gompers and the AFL. **Collective bargaining** is the process whereby union and management representatives put together a contract for workers. The Wagner Act expanded labor's right to collectively bargain and legally obligated employers to meet at reasonable times and bargain in good faith with respect to wages, hours, and other terms and conditions of employment. Gompers believed collective bargaining was the key to attaining a fairer share of the economic pie for workers. He further believed that collective bargaining would enhance the well-being of workers by improving work conditions on the job.

> ➤ **CONSIDER USING OT ACETATE 12-3**
> Union Membership by Industries

FIGURE **12.1**
· · · ·
MAJOR LEGISLATION
AFFECTING
LABOR–MANAGEMENT
RELATIONS

Norris–La Guardia Act, 1932	Prohibited courts from issuing injunctions against nonviolent union activities; outlawed contracts forbidding union activities; outlawed the use of yellow-dog contracts by employers. (Yellow-dog contracts were contractual agreements forced on workers by employers whereby the employee agreed not to join a union as a condition of employment.)
National Labor Relations Act (Wagner Act), 1935	Gave employees the right to form or join labor organizations (or to refuse to form or join); the right to collectively bargain with employers through elected union representatives; and the right to engage in labor activities such as strikes, picketing, and boycotts. Prohibited certain unfair labor practices by the employer and the union, and established the National Labor Relations Board to oversee union election campaigns and investigate labor practices. This act gave great impetus to the union movement.
Fair Labor Standards Act, 1938	Set a minimum wage and maximum basic hours for workers in interstate commerce industries. The first minimum wage set was 25 cents an hour, except for farm and retail workers.
Labor–Management Relations Act (Taft-Hartley Act), 1947	Amended the Wagner Act; permitted states to pass laws prohibiting compulsory union membership (right-to-work laws); set up methods to deal with strikes that affect national health and safety; prohibited secondary boycotts, closed-shop agreements, and featherbedding (the requiring of wage payments for work not performed) by unions. This act gave more power to management.
Labor–Management Reporting and Disclosure Act (Landrum-Griffin Act), 1959	Amended the Taft-Hartley Act and the Wagner Act; guaranteed individual rights of union members in dealing with their union, such as the right to nominate candidates for union office, vote in union elections, attend and participate in union meetings, vote on union business, and examine union records and accounts; required annual financial reports to be filed with the U.S. Department of Labor. One goal of this act was to clean up union corruption.

◄ **Consider Using Tm 86**
Major Legislation Affecting Labor-Management Relations (Figure 12.1 on text page 351)

The Wagner Act also established an administrative agency, the National Labor Relations Board (NLRB), to oversee labor–management relations. The NLRB provides guidelines and offers legal protection to workers who seek to vote on "organizing" a union to represent them in the workplace. The formal process in which a union is recognized by the NLRB as the authorized bargaining agent for a group of employees is called **certification**. Figure 12.2 describes the steps involved in a union-organizing campaign. The Wagner Act also provided workers with a clear process to remove a union as the workers' representative. **Decertification** (also described in Figure 12.2) is the process by which workers take away a union's right to represent them.

certification
Process of a union's becoming recognized by the NLRB as the bargaining agent for a group of employees.

decertification
The process by which workers take away a union's right to represent them.

··· OBJECTIVES OF ORGANIZED LABOR ···

As you might suspect, the objectives of organized labor frequently change according to shifts in social and economic trends. For example, in the 1970s the primary objective of labor unions was to obtain additional pay and benefits for their members. Throughout the 1980s, objectives shifted toward issues related

FIGURE **12.2**
· · · ·

STEPS IN UNION-ORGANIZING AND DECERTIFICATION CAMPAIGNS

Note that the final vote in each case requires that the union receive over 50 percent of the *votes cast.* Note, too, that the election is secret.

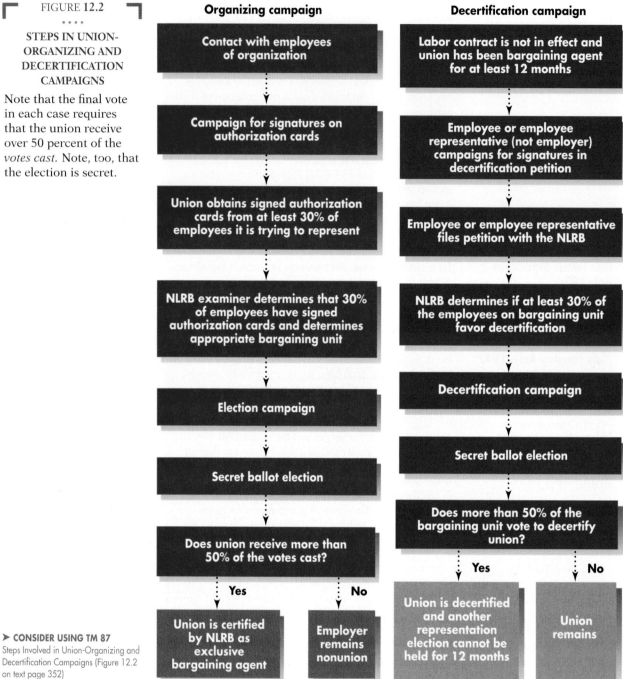

Organizing campaign

Contact with employees of organization

Campaign for signatures on authorization cards

Union obtains signed authorization cards from at least 30% of employees it is trying to represent

NLRB examiner determines that 30% of employees have signed authorization cards and determines appropriate bargaining unit

Election campaign

Secret ballot election

Does union receive more than 50% of the votes cast?

Yes   No

Union is certified by NLRB as exclusive bargaining agent

Employer remains nonunion

Decertification campaign

Labor contract is not in effect and union has been bargaining agent for at least 12 months

Employee or employee representative (not employer) campaigns for signatures in decertification petition

Employee or employee representative files petition with the NLRB

NLRB determines if at least 30% of the employees on bargaining unit favor decertification

Decertification campaign

Secret ballot election

Does more than 50% of the bargaining unit vote to decertify union?

Yes   No

Union is decertified and another representation election cannot be held for 12 months

Union remains

> **CONSIDER USING TM 87**
Steps Involved in Union-Organizing and Decertification Campaigns (Figure 12.2 on text page 352)

negotiated labor–management agreement
Settlement that sets the tone and clarifies the terms under which management and labor agree to function over a period of time.

to job security and union recognition. In the 1990s, unions also focused on job security, but the issue of global competition and its effects often took center stage. The AFL–CIO, for example, was a major opponent of the North American Free Trade Agreement (NAFTA) passed by Congress in 1994. It also was instrumental in encouraging Congress in 1997 to deny President Bill Clinton's request to speed up trade agreements through what is called fast-track legislation.

The **negotiated labor–management agreement** sets the tone and clarifies the terms and conditions under which management and labor agree to

FIGURE **12.3**

· · · ·

**ISSUES IN A
LABOR–MANAGEMENT
AGREEMENT**

Labor and management
often meet to discuss and
clarify the terms that
specify employees'
functions within the
company. The topics
listed in this figure are
typically discussed
during these meetings.
Notice that the union is
concerned about the
employees' benefits and
rights.

◄ **CONSIDER USING TM 88**
Issues in a Labor-Management
Agreement (Figure 12.3 on text
page 353)

1. Management rights
2. Union recognition
3. Union security clause
4. Strikes and lockouts
5. Union activities and responsibilities
   a. Dues checkoff
   b. Union bulletin boards
   c. Work slowdowns
6. Wages
   a. Wage structure
   b. Shift differentials
   c. Wage incentives
   d. Bonuses
   e. Piecework conditions
   f. Tiered wage structures
7. Hours of work and time-off policies
   a. Regular hours of work
   b. Holidays
   c. Vacation policies
   d. Overtime regulations
   e. Leaves of absence
   f. Break periods
   g. Flextime
   h. Meal time allotments
8. Job rights and seniority principles
   a. Seniority regulations
   b. Transfer policies and bumping
   c. Promotions
   d. Layoffs and recall procedures
   e. Job bidding and posting
9. Discharge and discipline
   a. Suspension
   b. Conditions for discharge
10. Grievance procedures
    a. Arbitration agreement
    b. Mediation procedures
11. Employee benefits, health, and welfare

function over a specific period of time. Negotiations cover a wide range of topics and can often be quite lengthy. Figure 12.3 provides a list of topics commonly negotiated by labor and management before reaching an agreement.

A **union security clause** stipulates that employees who reap benefits from a union must either join or pay dues to the union. After passage of the Wagner Act, organized labor sought strict security in the form of the closed-shop agreement. A **closed-shop agreement** specified that workers had to be members of a union before being hired for a job. To labor's dismay the Labor–Management Relations Act (Taft-Hartley Act) outlawed this practice in 1947 (see Figure 12.4). Today labor clearly favors the union shop agreement as the most effective means of ensuring workers' security. Under the **union shop agreement**, workers do not have to be members of a union to be hired for a job, but must agree to join the union within a prescribed period (usually 30, 60, or 90 days) of time. Under a contingency called the **agency shop agreement**, employers may hire nonunion workers who are not required to join the union, but these workers must pay a special union fee or pay regular union dues. Unions justify payment of a fee or dues under an agency shop agreement because all workers are represented at the bargaining table, not just the union members.

The Taft-Hartley Act recognized the legality of the union shop but granted individual states the power to outlaw such agreements through passage of **right-to-work laws**. To date, 21 states have passed such legislation (see Figure 12.5). In a right-to-work state, an **open shop agreement** gives workers the option to join or not join a union, if one is present in the workplace. Furthermore, if they choose not to join the union that is certified in their workplace, they cannot be forced to pay a fee or dues to the union.

In the future, the focus of union negotiations will no doubt continue to shift as issues such as child and elder care, worker retraining, two-tiered wage plans, employee empowerment, and even integrity and honesty testing further challenge union members' rights in the workplace. Unions also intend to carefully monitor global agreements such as NAFTA to see that U.S. jobs are not lost.

◄ **CONSIDER USING LECTURE ENHANCER 12-5**
Unions in Small Business

union security clause
Provision in a negotiated labor–management agreement that stipulates that employees who benefit from a union must either join or pay dues to the union.

closed-shop agreement
Clause in a labor–management agreement that specified that workers had to be members of a union before being hired (outlawed in 1947).

union shop agreement
Clause in a labor–management agreement that says workers do not have to be members of a union to be hired, but must agree to join the union within a prescribed period.

agency shop agreement
Clause in a labor–management agreement that says employers may hire nonunion workers who are not required to join the union but must pay a union fee.

right-to-work laws
Legislation that gives workers the right, under an open shop, to join or not join a union if it is present.

open shop agreement
Agreement in right-to-work states that gives workers the option to join or not join a union, if one exists in their workplace.

FIGURE **12.4**

· · · ·

DIFFERENT FORMS OF UNION CONTRACTS

Passed in 1947, the Taft-Hartley Act stated that employees don't have to be members of a union before being hired. Prior to this act, union membership could be a condition for employment. Now most union contracts are union shop agreements.

▶ **CONSIDER USING TM 89**
Different Forms of Union Contracts
(Figure 12.4 on text page 354)

TYPE OF CONTRACT	DESCRIPTION
Union shop	The majority of union contracts are of this type. The employer can hire anyone, but employees must join the union to keep their jobs.
Agency shop	Employers may hire anyone. Employees need not join the union, but are required to pay a union fee. Less than 10 percent of union contracts are of this nature.
Closed shop (no longer used)	The Taft–Hartley Act made this form illegal. Only union members could be hired under this system.
Open shop	Union membership is voluntary for new and existing employees. Those who don't join the union don't have to pay union dues. Few union contracts are of this type.

Labor unions play a role in countries other than the United States as well. The status of labor unions in Germany represents that of unions in much of Western Europe. The box called Reaching Beyond Our Borders on page 355 discusses such unions in more detail.

▼ **CONSIDER USING TM 90**
States with Right-to-Work Laws (Figure 12.5 on text page 354)

FIGURE **12.5**

· · · ·

STATES WITH RIGHT-TO-WORK LAWS

··· RESOLVING LABOR–MANAGEMENT DISAGREEMENTS ···

The rights of labor and management are outlined in the negotiated labor–management agreement. Upon acceptance by both sides, the agreement becomes a guide to work relations between the firm's employees and managers. However, signing the agreement doesn't necessarily end the employee–management

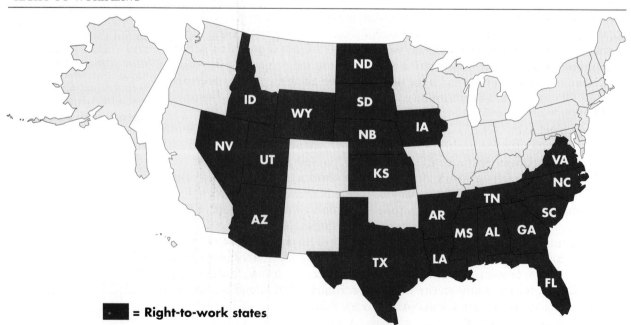

■ = **Right-to-work states**

Reaching Beyond Our Borders

http://www.access.digex.net/miner/index.html

German Labor Unions Face a Global Economy

German union members have long been the envy of unionized workers around the world. Union workers in Germany lead the world in vacation time and paid holidays. They also enjoy the shortest workweek in the industrialized world. Still, the average German worker calls in sick twice as often as the average American worker and enjoys "healthy" sick-pay benefits. Additionally, the passage of the Codetermination Act of 1976 stated that corporations and limited partnerships with more than 2,000 employees be run by supervisory boards composed of representatives of management and labor. With union representation on corporate boards, German workers enjoyed lucrative labor pacts and became the highest paid industrial workers in the world. However, the mood seems to be shifting, and German labor unions are beginning to experience many of the same difficulties faced by their fellow members in the United States.

Take, for example, I. G. Metall, Germany's largest labor union; its membership has declined by 20 percent over the past five years. The once-feared union conceded that the high unemployment rate in Germany had something to do with the rising price of labor. It then did the unthinkable and allowed firms to offer jobs to the long-term unemployed at a wage rate temporarily below the negotiated minimum. Some argue these downturns are only temporary, but Klaus Zwickel, leader of I. G. Metall, sounds a more somber note. He claims the union will not recapture its lost members and that shifts are occurring in the job market that will clearly affect the union's future.

Germany's job future, like that of the United States, is in businesses such as software, telecommunications, environmental technology, and the like. Workers in many of these industries unfortunately see labor unions as relics from the past. Business leaders also see Germany at a crossroads. They feel the country must make significant changes in its labor agreements—as England did in the 1980s—or suffer the results in a tough global market. Wolfgang Schroeder, a strategic advisor to I. G. Metall, warns that Germany cannot be the exception in global markets where competition has intensified. Time will tell if the German unions go the way of their counterparts in the United States and England, where the power and ranks of unions have dwindled over the past 10 years.

Sources: "Leading from Behind," *The Economist*, January 27, 1996, pp. 60–62; and Greg Steinmetz, "Head of German Trade Group Lambastes High Wages with Wit and One-Liners," *The Wall Street Journal Europe*, March 21, 1997, p. 1.

---

negotiations. As you might suspect, there are sometimes differences concerning interpretations of the labor–management agreement. For example, managers may interpret a certain clause in the agreement to mean that they are free to select who works overtime. Union members may interpret the same clause to mean that managers must select employees for overtime based on employee seniority. If controversies such as this cannot be resolved between the two parties, a grievance may be filed.

A **grievance** is a charge by employees that management is not abiding by or fulfilling the terms of the negotiated labor agreement according to how they perceive it. Overtime rules, promotions, layoffs, transfers, job assignments, and so forth, are generally sources of employee grievances. Handling such grievances demands a good deal of contact between union officials and managers. Grievances do not imply that a company has broken the law. In fact, the vast majority of grievances are negotiated and resolved by **shop stewards** (union officials who work permanently in an organization and represent employee interests on a daily basis) and supervisory-level managers. However, if a grievance is not settled at this level, formal grievance procedures will begin. Figure 12.6 illustrates the different steps the formal grievance procedure could follow.

◀ **CONSIDER USING CRITICAL THINKING EXERCISE 12-2**
Union Negotiations (SCANS)

◀ **CONSIDER USING OT ACETATE 12-5**
Percentage of Union Certification Elections Won

grievance
A charge by employees that management is not abiding by the terms of the negotiated labor agreement.

shop steward
A union official who works permanently in an organization and represents employee interests on a daily basis.

FIGURE 12.6

• • • •

THE GRIEVANCE RESOLUTION PROCESS

The grievance process may move through several steps before the issue is resolved. At each step, the issue is negotiated between union officials and managers. If no resolution comes internally, an outside arbitrator may be mutually agreed on. If so, the decision by the arbitrator is binding (legally enforceable).

➤ **CONSIDER USING TM 91**
The Grievance Resolution Process (Figure 12.6 on text page 356)

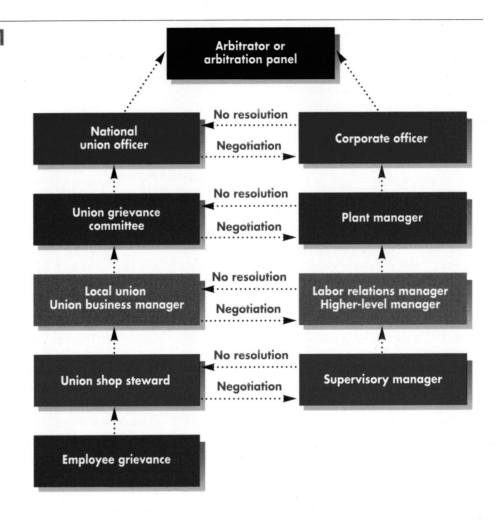

••• MEDIATION AND ARBITRATION •••

bargaining zone
Range of options between the initial and final offer that each party will consider before negotiations dissolve or reach an impasse.

mediation
The use of a third party, called a mediator, who encourages both sides to continue negotiating and often makes suggestions for resolving the dispute.

arbitration
The agreement to bring in an impartial third party (an arbitrator) to render a binding decision in a labor dispute.

➤ **CONSIDER USING OT ACETATE 12-4**
Factors that Affect the Collective Bargaining Process

During the negotiation process, there is generally what's called a **bargaining zone**, which is a range of options between the initial and final offer that each party will consider before negotiations dissolve or reach an impasse. If labor–management negotiators aren't able to agree on alternatives within this bargaining zone, mediation may be necessary. **Mediation** is the use of a third party, called a mediator, who encourages both sides to continue negotiating and often makes suggestions for resolving a work dispute. However, it's important to remember that mediators make suggestions, not decisions. Elected officials, attorneys, and college professors are often called on to serve as mediators in a labor dispute.

Another option used to resolve labor–management conflicts is arbitration. **Arbitration** is the agreement to bring in an impartial third party (an arbitrator) to render a binding decision in a labor dispute. Many of the negotiated labor–management agreements in the United States call for the use of an arbitrator to end labor disputes. The arbitrator must be acceptable to both labor and management. The nonprofit American Arbitration Association is the dominant force in dispute resolution.[2] You may have heard of baseball players filing for arbitration to resolve a contract dispute with their teams.

···· ▬▬▬ ····

TACTICS USED IN LABOR–MANAGEMENT CONFLICTS

If labor and management reach an impasse in collective bargaining and negotiations break down, either side or both sides may use specific tactics to enhance their objectives and perhaps sway public opinion. The primary tactics used by organized labor are the strike and the boycott. Unions might also use pickets and work slowdowns to get desired changes. Management, on the other hand, may implement lockouts, injunctions, and even strikebreakers. In the following sections, we will look briefly at each of these strategies.

··· UNION TACTICS ···

The strike has historically been the most potent tactic unions use to achieve their objectives. A **strike** is when workers collectively refuse to go to work. Strikes attract public attention to a labor dispute and at times cause operations in a company to slow down or totally shut down. You may remember the delivery slowdowns caused by the United Parcel Service strike in 1997. (See the box From the Pages of *Business Week.*) Strikers may also picket, which means they will walk around outside the organization carrying signs and talking with the public and the media about the issues. Strikes have often led to resolution of a labor dispute; however, they also have generated violence and extended bitterness since emotions on both sides frequently reach a boiling point. The United Auto Workers' strike against Caterpillar, for example, caused a great deal of bitterness on both sides throughout the 1990s.

The public often realizes how important a worker is when he or she goes on strike. If you waited for a package to arrive that didn't get there on time because of the UPS strike, you know what we mean. Try to imagine what an economic and social disaster it would be if doctors and nurses at a large hospital went on strike, or all police officers in a town left work at once. Many states prohibit such job actions, but police officers, firefighters, teachers, and others often engage in "sick-outs" or the "blue flu," where the members of the union don't strike but refuse to come to work on the pretext of illness. Employees of the federal government, such as postal workers, can organize unions but are denied the right to strike. In fact, under the provisions of the Taft-Hartley Act, the president can ask for a cooling-off period to prevent a strike in what's considered a critical industry. During a **cooling-off period**, workers return to their jobs while the union and management continue negotiations. The cooling-off period can last up to 80 days. Fortunately U.S. presidents have not had to invoke this power since early 1978.

◄ **LEARNING GOAL 3.**
Describe the tactics used by labor and management during conflicts and discuss the role of unions in the future.

◄ **CONSIDER USING LECTURE ENHANCER 12-6**
Additional Tools Used by Labor to Fight Management

◄ **CONSIDER USING OT ACETATE 12-6**
Use of the Strike is Diminishing

strike
A union strategy in which workers refuse to go to work; the purpose is to further workers' objectives after an impasse in collective bargaining.

cooling-off period
When workers in a critical industry return to their jobs while the union and management continue negotiations.

◄ **CONSIDER USING LECTURE ENHANCER 12-7**
Does the Right to Strike Mean Anything Anymore?

◄ **CONSIDER USING LECTURE ENHANCER 12-8**
The Declining Power of the Picket Line

◄ **CONSIDER USING LECTURE ENHANCER 12-9**
Additional Tools Used by Management to Fight Labor

In some European nations, labor unions have the power to virtually shut down the economy. This happened in France in late 1997 when 300,000 striking truckers tied up the hub of Europe's highway system with 150 roadblocks. Some consider the French truck-drivers' union to be the most powerful in the world. Could a situation similar to this happen in the United States?

From the
Pages of **BusinessWeek**   http://www.aflcio.org/
home.htm

Labor Flexes Its Muscles

The United Parcel Service's strike in August 1997 proved that unions could not be taken for granted. After nearly 20 years of siding with companies, the public supported the striking UPS Teamsters by about a 2-to-1 margin against the company, even though the strike caused major inconveniences for many people. The victory helped revitalize organized labor and encouraged the AFL–CIO's leadership to consider expanding its use of "capital power" to win workplace concessions from management.

In total, labor union retirement funds hold approximately $1.4 trillion (that's right—*trillion*) in corporate stock. This accounts for about 14 percent of all outstanding shares of stock in the United States. If the AFL–CIO can persuade various pension trustees to act in concert, labor unions would become the largest bloc of organized shareholders in the nation. To support such efforts, the AFL–CIO has established an Office of Investment to find out just how much stock labor can influence.

By law, a union must share control of its members' pension funds with management-appointed pension fund trustees. The union trustees, however, tend to be more active. Pension managers are concerned about the influence labor could exert by using its retirement funds; they know they may be caught between management and labor interests. William Patterson, head of the Office of Investment for the AFL–CIO, has already put top management on notice to prepare for battles over CEO pay, workplace health and safety, labor supplier standards, the use of part-time workers, and other issues important to union members. It appears an energized labor movement is ready to move from the picket lines to the boardrooms. Stay tuned.

Sources: Aaron Bernstein, "'Working Capital': Labor's New Weapon," *Business Week*, September 29, 1997, pp. 110–12; and Paul Magnusson, Nicole Harris, Linda Himmelstein, Bill Vlasic, and Wendy Zellner, "A Wake-Up Call for Business," *Business Week*, September 1, 1997, pp. 28–29.

The strike is losing its popularity as a labor tactic. While there were 470 strikes in 1952, there were only approximately 30 strikes in 1996, the fewest in 50 years.[3] Both labor and management seek to avoid strikes if at all possible. Nonetheless, as strikes in air and ground transportation, publishing, aerospace and auto manufacturing, overnight delivery, and professional sports have illustrated, the strike is not yet dead as a labor tactic.

Unions also use boycotts in an attempt to obtain their objectives. Boycotts can be classified as primary or secondary. A **primary boycott** is when organized labor encourages both its members and the general public not to buy the product(s) of a firm involved in a labor dispute. A **secondary boycott** is an attempt by labor to convince others to stop doing business with a firm that is the subject of a primary boycott. For example, if a union initiates a boycott against a supermarket chain because that chain carries the products produced by the target of a primary boycott, this would be considered a secondary boycott. Labor unions can legally authorize primary boycotts but the Taft-Hartley Act prohibits the use of secondary boycotts.

••• MANAGEMENT TACTICS •••

Like labor, management also uses specific tactics to achieve its contract goals. Historically management used tactics such as **yellow-dog contracts** (which required employees to agree as a condition of employment not to join a union) and **lockouts** (which put pressure on unions by temporarily closing the

primary boycott
When a union encourages both its members and the general public not to buy the products of a firm involved in a labor dispute.

secondary boycott
An attempt by labor to convince others to stop doing business with a firm that is the subject of a primary boycott.

yellow-dog contracts
A contract that required employees to agree as a condition of employment not to join a union.

lockouts
When management temporarily closes the business to put pressure on unions.

business and denying employment to the workers) to counter what it considered unreasonable labor demands. However, the Norris–La Guardia Act of 1932 outlawed yellow-dog contracts, and lockouts are rarely used today (though you may remember the sight of major league baseball players locked out of spring training in 1990 and the National Hockey League players locked off the ice in 1994). Management most often uses injunctions and strikebreakers to defeat labor demands it sees as excessive.

An **injunction** is a court order directing someone to do something or to refrain from doing something. Management has sought injunctions to order striking workers back to work, limit the number of pickets that can be used during a strike, or otherwise deal with actions that could be detrimental to the public welfare. For a court to issue an injunction, management must show a "just cause," such as the fear of violence erupting or the possible destruction of property.

The use of strikebreakers has been a particular source of hostility and violence in labor relations. **Strikebreakers** (called scabs by unions) are workers who are hired to do the jobs of striking employees until the labor dispute is resolved. Employers have had the right to replace strikers since a 1938 Supreme Court ruling, but it wasn't until the 1980s that this tactic was frequently used.

injunction
A court order directing someone to do something or to refrain from doing something.

strikebreakers
Workers hired to do the jobs of striking workers until the labor dispute is resolved.

••• THE FUTURE OF UNIONS AND ••• LABOR–MANAGEMENT RELATIONS

Many new labor–management issues have emerged that affect labor unions. Increased global competition, advanced technology and the changing nature of work have changed and threatened the jobs of many workers.[4] To save jobs, many unions have even granted concessions or **givebacks** to management. In such acts, union members give back previous gains from labor negotiations. It's obvious that for unions to grow they will have to adapt to a workforce that is increasingly culturally diverse, white collar, female, foreign born, and professional. The AFL–CIO, for example, plans to specifically target membership campaigns to women in traditionally low-paying fields, such as health care and garment sewing.[5] It's also interesting to note that the largest labor organization in the United States is the National Education Association (NEA), which represents over 2 million members. The Spotlight on Small Business box on page 360 discusses the movement of doctors toward union membership.

givebacks
Concessions made by union members to management; gains from labor negotiations are given back to management to help employers remain competitive and thereby save jobs.

◄ CONSIDER USING LECTURE ENHANCER 12-10
Ways for Unions to Reverse Its Slide

Organized labor is evidently at a crossroads. The unionized share of the nonfarm workforce has declined from a peak of 35.5 percent in 1945 to just 14.5 percent today (see Figure 12.7).[6] The role of unions in the 21st century is likely to be quite different from the role they assumed in the past. Union members know as well as anyone the necessity for U.S. firms to remain competitive with foreign firms and will likely do their part in maintaining

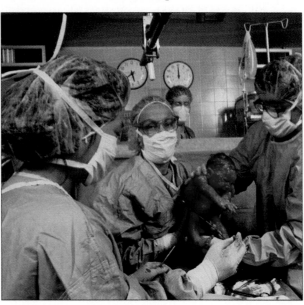

As health care costs increase, doctors continue to feel pressure from cost cutting measures that limit what they can charge and from outside interference that infringes on their ability to make medical decisions. This pressure has caused doctors to evaluate the benefits of unionizing. The Florida-based Federation of Physicians & Dentists continues to sign up more private practice physicians each year. Should workers like doctors have the right to strike?

Spotlight on Small Business

http://www.opeiu.org/index.htm jay

Look for the Union Stethoscope

Ever imagine entering a doctor's office and not saying "Ahhhhh" but instead asking to see the doctor's union card? This might not be as absurd as it may sound. Many private-practice physicians are leaning toward the idea of unionizing so they can collectively bargain with health care payers. It seems that many physicians see themselves as belonging to a profession that is under extreme duress, according to Jay Porcaro, leader of the Podiatrists' Union. His union is affiliated with the AFL–CIO, as is the Federation of Physicians and Dentists, a group based in Tallahassee, Florida, that has signed up more than 2,000 private-practice doctors primarily in Florida and Connecticut. According to Porcaro, when you look for representation it's hard to beat the collective bargaining skills of the AFL–CIO.

Pro-union doctors, however, may run into an obstacle tougher to cure than the common cold—antitrust law. It seems that antitrust law bars competitors from joining together to set prices and working conditions. Mark Whitener, deputy director of the Federal Trade Commission's bureau of competition warns, "If doctors are just trying to keep prices up and control the market, that's ▲

illegal." The FTC has in fact accepted a judicial consent order that barred doctors in Billings, Montana, from negotiating with the Billings Physician Hospital Alliance concerning fee schedules. Legal experts even hint that groups of independent doctors could face criminal prosecution if they try to bargain collectively without forming a fully managed care joint venture. Still, many healers in white coats, intent on gaining collective bargaining muscle, plan to lobby Congress. The American Medical Association has explored the collective bargaining option but warns private-practice physicians that unionized bargaining activity is presently illegal.

The future of organized labor promises to be interesting. Who knows, someday the president of the AFL–CIO may be called away from the annual Labor Day parade to perform an emergency appendectomy.

Sources: Harris Meyer, "Look for the Union Label," *Hospitals & Health Networks*, December 5, 1996, pp. 69–72 and "Union Files Appeal with Labor Board on Doctors Campaign to Organize; UFCW Local 56 Wants Hearing on Doctors Right to Join Union," *PR Newswire*, February 5, 1998.

U.S. competitiveness. Unions in the future will probably assist management in training workers, redesigning jobs, and assimilating the new workforce; that is, they will recruit and train foreign workers, unskilled workers, former welfare recipients, and others who may need special help in adapting to the job requirements of the 21st century. Concepts such as continuous improvement, constant creative innovation, and employee involvement programs cannot be implemented without the cooperation of employees. Unions have taken a leadership role in making that happen. In exchange for cooperating with management, unions can achieve improved job security, profit sharing, and sometimes higher wages. How organized labor handles these major challenges may well define the future for unions.

> **CONSIDER USING LECTURE ENHANCER 12-11**
Strike Pays Off in Las Vegas

Progress Check

- What kinds of workers are joining unions today, and why are they joining?
- What are the major laws that affected union growth, and what is covered in each?
- Why do the objectives of unions change over time?
- What are the major tactics used by unions and by management to assert their power in contract negotiations?

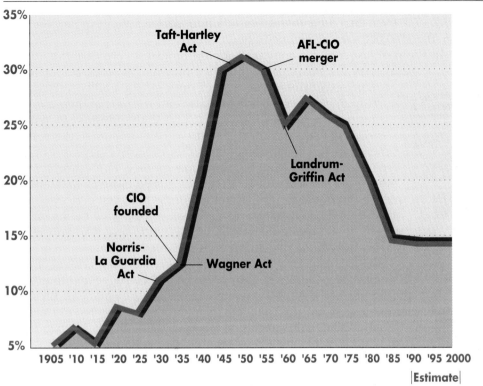

┌─   FIGURE **12.7**   ─┐

• • • •

**UNION MEMBERSHIP AS
A PERCENTAGE OF THE
NONAGRICULTURAL
WORKFORCE, 1905–2000**

Union membership as a
percentage of the work-
force grew rather
steadily until the 1950s.
Since then it has
declined rather steadily.
There may be a reversal
of the trend if unions can
recruit service workers
such as teachers, nurses,
and doctors.

•••• ▬▬▬ ••••

CONTROVERSIAL
EMPLOYEE–MANAGEMENT ISSUES

This is an interesting time in the history of employee–management relations.
Organizations are involved in downsizing and outsourcing, and the government
is taking a much more active role in mandating what benefits and assurances
businesses must provide to workers. Due to budget cuts, the government has
eliminated some social benefits to workers. Businesses, on the other hand, are
being urged to provide additional benefits. In other instances, general issues of
fairness are questioned. Let's look at a few of the controversies, starting with the
issue of executive compensation.

••• THE ISSUE OF EXECUTIVE COMPENSATION •••

How much should a top executive earn? Tiger Woods putts his way to over $16
million a year, Arnold Schwartzenegger flexes his way to over $30 million a year,
and Oprah Winfrey talks her way to over $100 million a year. Countless other
top performers in sports, movies, and entertainment have long walked away
with hefty paychecks, with few complaints from the public that supports them.

Is it out of line, then, that Lawrence Coss, the chief executive of Green Tree
Financial Corporation, should make $102 million a year or that Andrew Grove of
Intel should make almost $97 million a year?[7] In Chapter 2 we explained that the
U.S. free enterprise system is built on incentives that allow executives to make
that much. Throughout the 1990s, however, government, boards of directors,
and stockholders have challenged this fundamental principle and argued that
executive compensation is getting out of line. In 1996, the total compensation

◄ **CONSIDER USING TM 92**
Union Membership as a Percentage of
the Nonagricultural Workforce, 1905-
2000

◄ **CONSIDER USING OT ACETATE
12-2**
Declining Participation in Unions

◄ **LEARNING GOAL 4.**
Explain some of the controversial
employee–management issues such as
executive compensation, comparable
worth, child-care and elder care, AIDS,
drug testing, and violence in the workplace, and employee stock ownership
plans (ESOPs).

◄ **CONSIDER USING SUPPLEMEN-
TAL CASE 12-1**
Unions Turn to the Service Industry for
Growth (SCANS)

◄ **CONSIDER USING SUPPLEMEN-
TAL CASE 12-2**
Closing Union Stores and Factories
(SCANS)

◄ **CONSIDER USING OT ACETATE
12-7**
What Chief Executives Earn in Other
Countries

▶ CONSIDER USING OT ACETATE
12-8
The Hourly Wages of Selected CEO's

Is over $2 million per week plus all the rides you can handle at Disneyland a fair wage? That's what Disney CEO Michael Eisner earned from his total compensation package. Eisner however is not unique. Many other executives also receive over $100 million in compensation for a single year as more companies tie top managers' compensation to company performance and stock options. Is this a fair or unfair wage system?

▶ CONSIDER USING OT ACETATE
12-9
The Pay Gap is Narrowing

(salary, bonuses, and stock options) of an average CEO of a major company was $5,781,300. Even after adjustments for inflation, this represents a huge increase from the $160,000 average compensation in 1960.[8]

In the past, executive compensation and bonuses were generally determined by the firm's profitability or increase in stock price. Today, many executives receive stock options (the ability to buy company stock at a set price at a later date) as part of their compensation. The assumption in using such options as part of executive compensation is that the CEO will raise the price of the firm's stock. The problem is that executive pay continues to soar, even when the company does poorly. For example, CEO Anthony J. O'Reilly, of H. J. Heinz, earned close to $109 million over a three-year period, even though the financial performance of his firm had been spotty and the stock price lagged behind that of other firms in the industry.[9] Many observers question how corporate boards can justify such a questionable increase.

Management consultant Peter Drucker has been critical of executive pay levels since the mid-1980s, when he suggested that CEOs should not earn much more than 20 times the salary of the company's lowest-paid employee. Some companies have followed Drucker's advice. For example, at Herman Miller Inc., a Michigan producer of office furniture, the chief executive is limited to 20 times the average worker's pay. Unfortunately, many companies have turned a deaf ear to this suggestion. In fact, if you were a hot dog vendor making minimum wage at any of the Walt Disney theme parks, it would take you 17,852 years to make as much as CEO Michael Eisner earned in 1996.[10] Today the average chief executive of a major corporation makes 209 times the pay of a typical American factory worker.[11]

Since firms compete globally, looking at what executives in other countries make may prove revealing. American CEOs typically earn two to three times as much as executives in Europe and Canada.[12] Some European companies often have workers on the board of directors. Since boards set executive pay, this could be a reason why the imbalance between starting pay and top pay is less for European executives. In Japan, the CEO of a large corporation makes approximately 40 times what the average factory worker makes (compared to 209 times in the United States). Also, in Japan chief executives do not generally receive stock options.

It's important to recognize that most U.S. executives are responsible for billion-dollar corporations and work 70-plus hours a week. Many can show their stockholders that their decisions turned potential problems into success (Disney's stock has increased 2,400 percent since Michael Eisner became CEO, and Coke's market value rose from $4 billion to $150 billion during the late Robert Goizueta's tenure.)[13] Clearly, there is no easy answer to the question of what is fair compensation for executives. What's your opinion? You may be one of those executives someday.

 Critical Thinking

The high pay for top executives creates tremendous incentives for lower-level executives to work hard to get those jobs. The high pay also creates resentment among some workers, stockholders, and consumers. What's your position on top-executive compensation? Should it be more equitable? Does it matter that many athletes and TV stars continue to sign exorbitant deals in the millions of dollars?

··· THE ISSUE OF COMPARABLE WORTH ···

An issue equally as challenging as executive pay is that of pay equity for women. This question has taken on steadily increasing importance as more women have entered the labor force. In 1890, women made up only 15 percent of the labor force. In 1997, the rate was about 50 percent.[14] Among the many issues that have accompanied women's move into the labor force is that of pay equity, or comparable worth. **Comparable worth** is the concept that people in jobs that require similar levels of education, training, or skills should receive equal pay.

Comparable worth goes beyond the concept of equal pay for equal work. The Equal Pay Act of 1963 already requires companies to give equal pay to men and women who do the same job. It's against the law, for example, to pay a female nurse less than a male nurse. Rather, the issue of comparable worth centers on comparing the value of jobs such as nurse or librarian (traditionally women's jobs) with jobs such as truck driver or plumber (traditionally men's jobs). Such a comparison shows that "women's" jobs tend to pay less—sometimes much less.

Today, women earn approximately 71 percent of what men earn, though the disparity varies considerably by profession and level of education.[15] In the past, the primary explanation for this disparity was that women only worked 50 to 60 percent of their available years once they left school, whereas men, on the whole, worked all of those years. This changed in the 1990s as fewer women left the workforce for an extended period of time. Another explanation is that many women try to work as well as care for their families and therefore fall off the career track. This is especially true in professions such as medicine and law. Other women opt for more flexible jobs that pay less, such as bookkeeping, nursing, or secretarial work. One of the main explanations, however, is that women make less because the labor market is not perfectly competitive and some degree of gender bias still exists.[16]

The idea of comparable worth is to correct past discrimination by raising the pay in so-called women's jobs. To help them determine appropriate pay levels, some firms have started comparable-worth analyses. AT&T, for example, evaluated 20 categories of employment using 14 measurements and altered the base pay in several jobs traditionally held by women. Other firms also implemented changes. Evidence shows that it's difficult to determine if comparable worth would lead to better market equilibrium. Many women even appear poised to do better than men as specific sectors, such as health care, drive the new economy. Nonetheless, comparable worth promises to be an ongoing issue as women continue as a large percentage of the labor force in the 21st century.

··· THE ISSUE OF SEXUAL HARASSMENT ···

Sexual harassment refers to unwelcome sexual advances, requests for sexual favors, and other conduct of a sexual nature (verbal or physical). It became a major issue in the workplace in the 1980s. The furor intensified in 1991, with the nationally televised confirmation hearings of Supreme Court Justice Clarence Thomas, who was accused of sexual impropriety by a former employee, an attorney and college professor named Anita Hill. The debate was further accelerated by the resignation of U.S. Senator Bob Packwood, accused of sexual

◄ CONSIDER USING SUPPLEMEN-
TAL CASE 12-3
Marked for the Mommy Track (SCANS)

comparable worth
The concept that people in jobs that require similar levels of education, training, or skills should receive equal pay.

sexual harassment
Unwelcome sexual advances, requests for sexual favors, and other conduct of a sexual nature (verbal or physical).

Executive compensation and comparable worth have attracted the attention of analysts in the workplace. Well, what about minimum wage workers that toil at the bottom rung of the market structure? As this graph highlights, these workers have perhaps fared worse than any other workers. Do you feel the minimum wage should be increased?

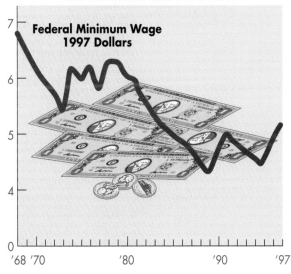

ADJUSTED FOR INFLATION, THE MINIMUIM WAGE IS DOWN

Federal Minimum Wage
1997 Dollars

Female workers at the Mitsubishi plant in Normal, Illinois, protest against the company's lack of enforcement of sexual harassment policies. Sexual harassment refers to unwelcome sexual advances, requests for sexual favors, and other conduct (either verbal or physical) of a sexual nature. In 1998, the U.S. Supreme Court expanded the scope of sexual harassment by ruling that sexual harassment can even extend to situations involving same-sex harassment.

▶ **CONSIDER USING LECTURE ENHANCER 12-12**
Sexual Harassment: The Rules Have Changed

▶ **CONSIDER USING OT ACETATE 12-10**
Types of Sexual Harassment

misconduct, and by the bombardment of charges against the U.S. military, including a case involving the U.S. Army's highest-ranking enlisted person.[17] And by now it's likely that no one in the country is unaware that the president of the United States was accused of sexual harassment by a former state employee in Arkansas named Paula Jones. The case is now under appeal.

Both men and women are covered under the Civil Rights Act of 1991, which governs sexual harassment. Women, however, file the majority of sexual harassment cases. The number of sexual harassment complaints filed annually with the Equal Employment Opportunity Commission grew from 6,000 in 1990 to over 15,000 in 1996.[18] In 1997, the U.S. Supreme Court expanded the debate by agreeing to hear a case involving same-sex harassment.

A person's conduct on the job can be considered sexually harassing if (1) an employee's submission to such conduct is made either explicitly or implicitly a term or condition of employment; (2) an employee's submission to or rejection of such conduct is used as the basis for employment decisions affecting the worker's status; or (3) the conduct unreasonably interferes with a worker's job performance or creates an intimidating, hostile, or offensive working environment. In evaluating charges of sexual harassment the key word seems to be *unwelcome,* a term the courts have hotly debated.[19] There's no question that managers and workers are now much more sensitive to comments and behavior of a sexual nature. EEOC statistics report that sexual harassment is the fastest growing area of employee complaint.[20]

The Thomas hearings and subsequent disclosures involving companies such as the Mitsubishi Motor Manufacturing Company of America introduced managers to the concept of a *hostile workplace,* which is any workplace where behavior occurs that would offend a reasonable male or female.[21] The U.S. Supreme Court in 1996 broadened the scope of what can be considered a hostile work environment.[22] A major problem is that workers and managers often know that a policy concerning sexual harassment exists but have no idea what it says. Former U.S. Labor Secretary Lynn Martin suggests that companies offer management training, require sexual harassment workshops for all employees, and revamp the human resource department if necessary to ensure compliance. Employing such efforts may save businesses millions of dollars in lawsuits and make the workplace more productive and harmonious. Nonetheless, it's safe to bet sexual harassment is likely to remain an important issue into the 21st century.

Progress Check

- How does top-executive pay in the United States compare with that in other countries?
- What's the difference between comparable worth and equal pay for equal work?
- How is sexual harassment defined, and when does sexual behavior become illegal?

Critical Thinking

Should college football coaches be paid the same as college volleyball coaches? That is, are their jobs of comparable worth? How would that affect the supply and demand for football coaches? What role should the market play in determining wages?

••• THE ISSUE OF CHILD CARE •••

Child care was an important issue in the 1990s and promises to remain a concern into the 21st century. Responsibilities for child care subsidies, child care programs, and even child care leave are being debated in both the private and public sectors of the economy. Federal child care assistance has risen significantly and is expected to increase with the changes in the recently passed welfare reform act. Workplace changes have already occurred such as the Family and Medical Leave Act, which permits up to 12 weeks of unpaid leave per year to qualified workers following the birth of a child. Some taxpayers question whether single workers or single-income families should subsidize dual-income families who must pay for child care. Still, the need for child care today is obvious. According to the U.S. Census Bureau a sizable percentage of today's 50 million working women is likely to become pregnant during their working years. Child care–related employee absences could cost American businesses billions of dollars annually. It's obvious that child care issues are critical in the workplace and will not go away. The question is, Who should provide child care services and who should pay for them?

◄ **CONSIDER USING LECTURE ENHANCER 12-13**
Group Child Care

The number of companies that offer child care as an employee benefit is growing. Some of the more extensive child care programs are offered at large firms such as Fleet Financial Services, Johnson & Johnson, Stride Rite, and Campbell Soup. Some companies even provide emergency child care services for employees whose children are ill or whose regular child care arrangements are disrupted.[23] Time Warner, for example, offers both in-home and office-based emergency care year-round.

Small companies are competing for available talent with creative programs that meet specific employee needs and yet cost considerably less. For example, Haemonetics Corporation in Braintree, Massachusetts, set up Camp Haemonetics, a summer camp for its employees' children, who often had been bored during the summer. The kids come to work with their parents and then get bused off for swimming, hiking, and so forth at a nearby state park. At noon, they come back for lunch with Mom or Dad, and then return for more camp activities until about 5:00 P.M. Working parents have made it clear that safe, affordable child care is an issue on which they will not compromise. Companies have responded by providing:

- Discount arrangements with national child care chains.

- Vouchers that offer payments toward whatever type child care the employee selects.

- Referral services that help identify high-quality child care facilities to employees.

- On-site child care centers where parents can visit children at lunch or lag times during the workday.

- Sick-child centers to care for moderately ill children.

As single-parent and two-income households continue to grow, it will be interesting to follow this very important workplace issue. However, a new workplace storm is brewing over the issue of elder care. Let's look at this next.

••• THE ISSUE OF ELDER CARE •••

➤ **CONSIDER USING OT ACETATE 12-11**
Percentage of Workers Responsible for an Aging Relative

➤ **CONSIDER USING OT ACETATE 12-12**
What Companies Are Providing in Elder Care

The workforce in the United States is aging. By 2005, 40 percent of U.S. workers will be aged 40 to 58.[24] Many of these workers will not have to concern themselves with finding care for children. However, they will confront another problem: how to care for older parents and other relatives. Statistically, the number of households with at least one adult providing elder care has tripled in the past 10 years. Expectations persist that over the next five years 18 percent of the U.S. workforce will be involved in the time-consuming and stressful task of caring for an aging relative.[25] Sally Coberly, a specialist on aging at the Washington Business Group, predicts that in coming years elder care will have a greater impact on the workplace than child care. Some firms are beginning to experience this effect already. At U.S. West, a work/family referral service, employee requests for elder care have begun to outnumber those for child care. Unfortunately, the situation is not expected to get any better but rather to grow considerably worse with reductions in medicare and medicaid placing more burdens on family caregivers.[26]

Andrew Scharlach, a professor of aging at the University of California at Berkeley, estimates that elder care costs employers billions of dollars in lost output and replacement costs. These costs are expected to rise even higher as more experienced and high-ranking employees become involved in caring for older parents. Businesses realize these older workers are often more critical to the company than the younger workers affected by child care problems. Some companies note that transfer and promotion decisions are especially difficult for employees whose elderly parents need ongoing care. With an aging workforce, this issue is not expected to go away.

••• THE ISSUES OF AIDS, DRUG TESTING, AND ••• VIOLENCE IN THE WORKPLACE

➤ **CONSIDER USING LECTURE ENHANCER 12-14**
Handling AIDS Discrimination

➤ **CONSIDER USING OT ACETATE 12-13**
Should Drug Testing Be Done in the Workplace?

The spread of acquired immune deficiency syndrome (AIDS), though declining, is still a top national concern. AIDS is a leading cause of death for Americans between the ages of 25 and 44—a group that represents almost half of the nation's workforce.[27] Such statistics have caused businesses to direct their attention to the issue of AIDS, since no one predicts a quick victory over this disease. The U.S. Center for Disease Control launched a program called Business Responds to AIDS, which explains how companies can teach employees about the basics of AIDS and how to deal with it on the job.[28] Certainly the development of such clear-cut policies is needed to confront this critical issue.

One of the more controversial employee–management policies concerns the mandatory testing for the human immunodeficiency virus (HIV), which is the virus that causes AIDS. Preemployment medical testing cannot be used

Making Ethical Decisions

http://www.bbb.org//library/
ethical.html

Should You Keep the Tap Flowing?

You are the owner of a small regional brewery that serves a specialized market in three Midwest states. In the past you have considered automating one of the brewery's operations, the racking room, because it could easily be robotized. However, the employees in the racking room have been loyal and hardworking. In the past they even voted down union representation, feeling it could cause difficulties for your plant. Also, you are aware that the possibility of finding alternative employment for these workers is slim.

The other day, however, you heard that one of the employees in the racking room was diagnosed as having the HIV antibody. You realize that this person's medical bills could escalate to over $250,000 over the course of the illness, not to mention missed workdays, production slowdowns, co-worker concerns, and so forth. Without question, insurance premiums for your firm will increase. You are also aware that, legally, this employee cannot be dismissed because of this medical misfortune. But you do have the option of closing the racking room, pleading the necessity to automate. Of course, all of the employees in this department would lose their jobs. What would you do? Is your decision good for the business? Is your decision ethical?

▲ SCANS

selectively to screen out anyone who may be HIV-positive. If administered, the tests must be given to all potential employees across the board. More and more firms are insisting on mandatory HIV testing because an AIDS-afflicted employee can cost an employer an enormous amount in terms of insurance, losses in productivity, increased absenteeism, and turnover. Many firms have gone beyond preemployment testing and suggested that all existing employees should be tested for the HIV antibody. Managers argue that the information they would gain would allow for the development of a uniform and humanitarian AIDS policy at the workplace. Nevertheless, this issue, like others, has no easy answer. The Making Ethical Decisions box asks how you would deal with a worker who has AIDS.

Some companies feel that alcohol and drug abuse are even more serious workplace issues because substance abuse involves far more workers than AIDS does. The U.S. Department of Health and Human Services supports these concerns and estimates that businesses lose up to $312 billion a year due to substance abuse in the workplace.[29] Such losses have caused drug testing at work to grow at a rapid pace. Over 80 percent of major companies now test workers and job applicants for substance abuse.

Many responded to the cry for help in the fight against HIV in the 1990s. Such support enabled researchers to make some remarkable gains in the battle against this dreaded disease. "Business Responds to AIDS" is an educational program for businesses developed by the Center for Disease Control in Atlanta—an agency of the federal government. Do you feel government or private industry should be the leader in the war against HIV?

◄ CONSIDER USING OT ACETATE
12-14
Major Types of Workplace Violence

Employers are also struggling with a growing trend toward violence in the workplace. The U.S. Department of Labor cites homicide as the number two

➤ CONSIDER USING LECTURE
ENHANCER 12-15
ESOPs Are Supposed to Build Employee
Loyalty, But . .

**employee stock
ownership plans
(ESOPs)**
Programs that enable employees to
buy part or total ownership of the
firm.

Over 50 years ago, Louis Kelso believed making his employees owners of the company would increase their performance. He established the concept of ESOPs (employee stock ownership plans), which has expanded today to over 10,000 companies offering such opportunities to workers. Fifty-four percent of United Airlines is owned by its employees, who can truly boast, "Fly our friendly skies." Why are so many companies still reluctant to provide ESOPs?

cause of job-related fatalities.[30] In 1986, a postal service employee in Oklahoma killed 14 fellow workers before taking his own life. Since then, 24 other postal employees have perished on the job at the hands of fellow employees. Still, many executives and managers don't take workplace violence seriously and believe that reports of it are primarily media hype. According to an American Management Association study, 69 percent of its member companies do not provide any formal training for dealing with prevention of violence in the workplace.[31] However, other organizations, such as the U.S. Postal Service, have recognized the threat and have begun to hold focus groups for employee input and hire managers with strong interpersonal skills to deal with growing employee violence.

While issues such as AIDS, drug testing, and violence present a somewhat grim picture of the workplace, many employees are assuming new roles within their companies. In fact, some are becoming owners. Let's see how this is happening.

••• THE ISSUE OF EMPLOYEE •••
STOCK OWNERSHIP PLANS (ESOPs)

No matter how hard workers fight for better pay, they will never become as wealthy as the people who actually own the company. At least that is the theory behind **employee stock ownership plans (ESOPs)**. An ESOP is a program that enables employees to buy part or total ownership of the firm. Louis O. Kelso conceived the idea of ESOPs about 50 years ago. His plan was to turn workers into owners by selling them stock. Using this concept, he helped the employees of a newspaper buy their company. Since then, the idea of employees

Come meet the 54,000 new owners of United. Come fly our friendly skies.
UNITED AIRLINES

taking over all or some of the ownership of their companies has gained much favor. Many people consider ESOPs examples of capitalism at its best. The facts are, however, that ESOPs have had mixed results.

BENEFITS OF ESOPs ESOPs enjoyed considerable growth in the 1980s, stalled in the first half of the 1990s, and have recently been revived. According to the National Center for Employee Ownership, there are just under 10,000 businesses with ESOPs, covering over 10 million workers.[32] Approximately 90 percent of ESOPs are in privately held companies, and 10 percent are in publicly traded companies.[33] Employee participation in ownership has emerged as an important issue in many different industries and every type of company.

Some familiar organizations with ESOPs include United Airlines, Avis, and Publix Super Markets. Publix, in fact, has the nation's largest ESOP, with 97,000 employees owning 44 percent of the company.[34] Small businesses are joining their larger counterparts and enjoying the growth ESOPs can provide in encouraging and increasing worker productivity. Giving employees a share in the profits of the firm motivates them to enhance their involvement in the firm and increases morale.

The bold ESOP leap that encouraged the 76,000 employees of United Airlines to work together in finalizing the sale of 54 percent of the airline to its employees seems to be paying off. Productivity at United is rising and grievances from employees have plunged. Machinists Union leader Ken Thiede admits many of his fellow union members watch the United stock very closely.[35] It would be misleading, however, to say that ESOPs are easy to implement or that they are an unqualified success. Let's look at the other side of ESOPs.

PROBLEMS WITH ESOPs Not all ESOPs work as planned. They can be used to refinance a firm with employees' money without giving employees added participation or more job security. Weirton Steel's ESOP was once praised as an ideal model. Unfortunately, over time the mood of Weirton employees has changed from cooperation to confrontation. Though workers agreed to several wage reductions and job cuts and sold 33 percent of their stock to finance a $550 million modernization, the company still lost money. Union leaders now say that company executives no longer even talk with them.[36] At Avis, employee-owners (as participants in ESOPs are called) complain of having no representation on the company's board and no voting rights. In fact, at 85 percent of the companies with ESOPs, employees do not have voting rights and rarely have a strong voice on the company's board of directors.

In summary, the goals of ESOPs are good—employee ownership, employee pride, better customer relations, and so on—but the implementation of such programs is often less than satisfactory. ESOPs are not for every company and certainly entail a degree of risk. When used correctly, however, ESOPs can be a powerful strategy for improving corporate profitability and increasing employee satisfaction, participation, and income.

Firms that have healthy employee–management relations have a better chance to prosper. As managers, taking a *proactive approach* is the best way to ensure workable employee–management environments. The proactive manager anticipates potential problems and works toward resolving those problems before they get out of hand.

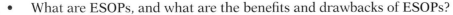

Progress Check

- What are some of the issues related to child care and elder care, and how are companies addressing those issues?
- What are ESOPs, and what are the benefits and drawbacks of ESOPs?

SUMMARY
......

1. Trace the history of organized labor in the United States and discuss the major legislation affecting labor unions.

1. There were organized labor unions in the United States before the American Revolution.
   * ***What was the first union?***
   The cordwainers (shoemakers) organized a craft union of skilled specialists in 1792. The Knights of Labor, which was formed in 1869, was the first national labor organization.
   * ***How did the AFL–CIO evolve?***
   The American Federation of Labor (AFL), formed in 1886, was an organization of craft unions. The Congress of Industrial Organization (CIO), a group of unskilled and semiskilled workers, broke off from the AFL in 1935. Over time, the two organizations saw the benefits of joining together and thus became the AFL–CIO in 1955.

2. Outline the objectives of labor unions.

2. Much legislation has been passed to balance the power of labor and management.
   * ***What are the provisions of the major legislation affecting labor unions?***
   See Figure 12.1 on p. 351.

3. Describe the tactics used by labor and management during conflicts and discuss the role of unions in the future.

3. The objectives of labor unions shift in response to changes in social and economic trends.
   * ***What topics typically appear in labor–management agreements?***
   See Figure 12.3 on p. 353.
   * ***What are the tactics used by unions and management in conflicts?***
   Unions can use strikes and boycotts. Management can use injunctions and lockouts.
   * ***What will unions have to do to cope with declining membership?***
   In order to grow, unions will have to adapt to a workforce that is becoming more white-collar, female, and culturally diverse. To help keep American businesses competitive in international markets, unions must soften their historic "us-versus-them" attitude and build a new "we" attitude with management.

4. Explain some of the controversial employee–management issues such as executive compensation; comparable worth; child care and elder care; AIDS, drug testing, and violence in the workplace; and employee stock ownership plans (ESOPs).

4. The median salary of top executives of major industrial companies is around $5.7 million a year.
   * ***What is a fair wage for managers?***
   The market and the businesses in it set managers' salaries. What is fair is open to debate.
   * ***What is comparable worth?***
   Comparable worth is the demand for equal pay for jobs requiring similar levels of education, training, and skills.
   * ***Isn't pay inequity caused by sexism?***
   There is evidence on both sides of that question, but government or corporate actions indicate that some remedial action will be taken regardless of causes.
   * ***How are some companies addressing the child care issue?***
   Responsive companies are providing day care on the premises, emergency care when scheduled care is interrupted, discounts with child care chains, vouchers to be used with employee's chosen care center, and referral services.
   * ***What is elder care, and what problems do companies face with this growing problem?***
   Workers with older parents or other relatives often need to find some way to care for them. It's becoming a problem that will perhaps outpace the need

for child care. Workers who need to care for dependent parents are generally more experienced and vital to the mission of the organization. The cost to business is very large and growing.

* **What are some concerns surrounding AIDS and mandatory HIV testing?**

An employee with AIDS can cost an employer an enormous amount in terms of insurance increases, losses in productivity, increased absenteeism, and employee turnover. Employees may question the accuracy of HIV tests and may see the tests as an infringement on their personal right to privacy.

* **How well are employee stock ownership plans (ESOPs) working?**

ESOPs have had mixed results, but the overall trend is favorable. Some 10,000 businesses now have ESOPs. Properly implemented, such plans can increase morale, motivation, commitment, and job satisfaction. The problem is that many firms have used ESOPs as a capital-raising scheme and have not given employees more participation in management. The issue of the administration of ESOPs will be a major one in the next decade.

KEY TERMS

· · · · · ·

agency shop agreement 353
American Federation of Labor (AFL) 349
arbitration 356
bargaining zone 356
certification 351
closed-shop agreement 353
collective bargaining 350
comparable worth 363
Congress of Industrial Organizations (CIO) 350
cooling-off period 357

craft union 349
decertification 351
employee stock ownership plans (ESOPs) 368
givebacks 359
grievance 355
industrial unions 349
injunction 359
Knights of Labor 349
lockouts 358
mediation 356
negotiated labor–management agreement 352
open shop agreement 353

primary boycott 358
right-to-work laws 353
secondary boycott 358
sexual harassment 363
shop steward 355
strike 357
strikebreakers 359
unions 348
union security clause 353
union shop agreement 353
yellow-dog contracts 358

DEVELOPING WORKPLACE SKILLS

1. Many college faculty members do not belong to a union. Faculty pay in many disciplines has fallen way behind pay in industry. Talk with several professors about their feelings toward unions. Assuming faculty salaries aren't increased to match industry, do you think unions will eventually be able to recruit more faculty members?

2. Debate the following in class: "Business executives receive a total compensation package that is far beyond their value." Take the opposite side of the issue from your normal stance to get a better feel for the other point of view.

3. Find the latest information on legislation related to child care, parental leave, and elder care benefits for employees. What are the trends? What will the cost to businesses be of these new programs? On balance, do you support or reject such legislation? Why?

4. Develop a list of three employee-management issues not covered in this chapter. Compare your list with others. Pick one or two popular ones and debate them in class.

5. Should businesses and government agencies be required to provide child care for employees? What about health care? What if some employees would prefer not to have the company provide child care because they have no children? Devise a fringe benefits system that you consider fair for both employers and for employees with a variety of needs.

TAKING IT TO THE NET

Purpose

To compare the salaries of CEOs of major corporations in the United States with those of U.S. workers, to assess the justification of such salaries, and to compose a letter in support or opposition to the Income Equity Act of 1997.

Exercise

Visit the AFL–CIO Web site at http://www.aflcio.org/home.htm. Navigate through the site and find information regarding salaries of CEOs of major corporations in the United States.

1. How much have the salaries of CEOs fluctuated in recent years compared to the salaries of workers? Include the URL of where you found the information that supports your answer.

2. The AFL–CIO site offers a number of reasons for CEO pay increases. List these reasons. Find evidence that supports the union's perspective. Can you offer arguments opposing its position? Include the source of the information that supports your answer.

3. U.S. Representative Martin Olav Sabo introduced the Income Equity Act of 1997, which limits the tax deductibility of executive compensation to 25 times that of the lowest-paid full-time employee in the same firm. The bill doesn't limit pay, but it prevents the government from subsidizing excessive pay through the business tax deduction and gives companies an incentive to examine their pay practices. Has Congress passed other legislation that limits executive compensation? If so, what was it? Do you support or oppose the passage of the Income Equity Act? Write a letter to your congressional representative stating your position.

4. Explore beyond the AFL–CIO site and see if you can find out whether the Income Equity Act of 1997 passed.

Practicing Management Decisions

As you learned in this chapter, the strike is a major weapon used by unions to obtain their objectives in a contract dispute. During a strike, workers will generally set up picket lines to inform the general public about the contract impasse. In fact, organized labor's fundamental purpose often is to win public support for its position.

In years past, companies would rarely try to replace striking workers with strikebreakers (called scabs by the union). Many unionists felt this trend

CASE
• • • • • •
ATTENTION PLEASE: SUBSTITUTING FOR STRIKING WORKERS, REPLACEMENT WORKERS!
• • • • • •

shifted when President Ronald Reagan replaced striking air traffic controllers with nonunion controllers in the 1980s. Businesses felt that Reagan legitimatized the process of replacing striking workers. Furthermore, a loophole in the National Labor Relations Act made the process legal. Today it's not uncommon for firms to advertise for replacement workers if they believe a strike may be forthcoming. Caterpillar, for example, advertised for replacement workers when the United Auto Workers threatened a strike against the company.

Needless to say, unions are very much opposed to firms hiring replacement workers during a strike. At some companies, the replacement workers became full-time replacements, taking the jobs of former union workers. President Bill Clinton promised to sign a law prohibiting the use of permanent replacement workers if it reached his desk. Labor unions spent over $35 million in the election of 1996 trying to regain control of the Congress from the Republicans. The unions felt a Democratic Congress would be more sympathetic to their cause. But the Republicans maintained a majority in both houses of Congress, dooming any possibility of such legislation reaching the president's desk.

Still, the issue did not die. President Clinton used his constitutional power and signed an executive order barring federal contractors from using replacement workers, a decision (applauded by organized labor) that affected some 26 million workers employed by federal contractors. The order was overturned, however, by the U.S. Court of Appeals, which rejected the ban imposed through the executive order of the president. The right of federal contractors to replace striking workers was reaffirmed. The question now remains in the court of popular opinion.

Decision Questions

1. Should companies have the legal right to replace striking workers? If so, should replacement workers be permitted to keep their jobs after the labor dispute has ended?
2. What are some potentially negative effects of replacing striking workers?
3. Does either the company or the union really ever win during a strike? What are some of the negative effects of strikes for both the company and the union?
4. Would you cross a picket line and fill the job of a striking worker? Why or why not?

Sources: David Warner, "A Bill to Outlaw Replacing Strikers," *Nation's Business*, June 1993, p. 56; and William H. Miller, "Big Victory," *Industry Week*, February 19, 1996, p. 69; and "A Business Win," *Industry Week*, June 3, 1996, p. 62.

Labor and management working harmoniously together—sounds like an impossible dream. Well, the impossible dream is a reality at the Saturn plant in Spring Hill, Tennessee. At this facility workers and managers have joined together in a unique union-management partnership that's governed by a slender 18-page labor agreement that gives workers a voice in planning and operating decisions at the company. This new work culture at Saturn has both management and workers beaming.

What makes this accomplishment even more unique is that all the workers at the Saturn plant come from other General Motors plants around the country, including some locations that were a hotbed of hostility between the union and management. At the Saturn facility, workers feel they have a clearer voice in how their jobs are structured and more control over the final product that leaves the plant. Union workers also believe empowerment and the effective use of teams are key factors in managing quality and enhancing productivity.

Michael Bennett, president of the United Autoworkers Local 1853 at the plant, credits both management and the union for the change in the Saturn work environment. He concedes that his

VIDEO CASE

. . . . . .

SATURN: CAN OIL AND WATER REALLY MIX?

role and that of fellow union members has changed and admits that he represents not only the union members but also GM customers and stockholders. His management counterpart, Robert Boroff, vice president of production, admits to some problems adjusting his style from traditional management practices, but agrees the team approach is working at Saturn. Both men feel that the key to the plant's long-term growth is maintaining an aura of compromise where solutions are acceptable to all. Since its entry into the market in the 1980s, Saturn has maintained a set of key concepts as its base of operations. These concepts include:

* Everyone in the company has ownership and is responsible for its successes and failures.
* Equality is practiced not just preached.
* People are the company's most important asset.
* Barriers to doing a good job have been eliminated.
* Union and management are partners, sharing responsibility for ensuring the success of the company.
* People have authority to do their job.

How have operations at Saturn fared? Saturn turned a profit for General Motors just three years after the company began. In 1997, Saturn was the only small car on the GM roster that was making money. Ask any member of a work team at Saturn about their jobs and they agree resoundingly about two things: they will go out of their way to help a fellow team member and product quality is the goal. When asked about the competition in this intensely competitive industry, Saturn workers smile and ring out in a loud chorus. Bring 'em on.

Discussion Questions

1. What key elements are needed in a company such as Saturn to make such unique labor/management relations work?

2. Do you think the Saturn experiment is an example of a workplace fad or an indicator of how future labor/management agreements will function?

3. Which side has the toughest job adjusting to such a revolutionary type work arrangement such as Saturn?

Part4

Management of Human Resources

Human resources are the people in an organization. How those people are hired, managed, and treated is the responsibility of human resource managers. These key people used to be called personnel managers or directors—and still are in some companies. They are personnel specialists who help to make management more effective in hiring and in overall job satisfaction. Many organizations are too large to allow close contact between top management and most subordinates. In such firms, human resource people provide this link.

Human resource specialists select, interview, and recommend prospective employees for job openings. They are involved in training for both employees and managers. Human resource personnel will often be directly involved in writing training guides, and they keep everyone in the organization informed about training opportunities. A director of human resources may manage several departments in larger companies, including equal employment opportunity specialists and recruitment specialists.

••• SKILLS •••

A human resource manager must have a thorough knowledge of current laws. Since the early 1960s, many new laws affecting employment have been passed, especially in the area of equal employment opportunity. Not knowing the law can damage a company and even cause it to lose credibility with the public.

Like other managers, human resource mangers need the ability to organize themselves and to keep others organized. They also need good communications skills, both oral and written. Since human resource planning is an integral part of the job, they must also be good planners, able to project both long- and short-term needs. Good human resource managers should also like to persuade and influence the actions of others. Often they have to sell their ideas on such issues as creative training programs, changing company traditions, and staffing changes.

Other skills are more specific to the careers in the area. For example, training specialists need skills in teaching and developing training programs. Directors of labor relations need to have extensive training in labor union operations and law. Human resource planning specialists must be adept at forecasting future trends and planning for them.

••• CAREER PATHS •••

In today's workplace, most companies want to hire college graduates, even for entry-level human resource positions. An increasing number of colleges offer programs that lead to a human resources management degree. Graduate programs leading to master's and doctoral degrees are also numerous. Human resource management is also one field that hires many women and minorities.

Entry-level jobs include administrative assistant, human resource assistant, or office assistant. Even with the academic training that is required, experience in a human resource department is important for success as a human resource manager. Just as in other management positions, promotion to the top in a large organization is likely to be competitive—and even political.

SOME POSSIBLE POSITIONS IN HUMAN RESOURCE MANAGEMENT

Job Title	Salary	Job Duties	Career Path	Prospects
Training specialist	Median: $37,200	Assess needs for training, plan and implement training programs. Conduct orientation and on-the-job training programs.	A background in teaching or psychology is helpful. Degree in human resource management can also help. Often will be promoted into management within human resource department.	Average growth through 2006.
Employment interviewer/ counselor	Median $20,000 (to start)	Act as broker, bringing job and applicant together.	College degree desirable. Jobs are available in state employment agencies and in private career placement companies.	Average growth through 2006.
Employee benefits specialist	Median: $38,300	Administer programs in health insurance, retirement plans, profit sharing, etc. Apply ever-changing federal laws to the process.	Begin by following orders of human resource manager; given more responsibility with experience.	Above average growth through 2006.
Labor relations specialist	$25,300 (to start)	Assist management in conducting negotiations with the union and help in labor–management disputes.	Entry-level specialists deal with minor grievances and other minor labor–management issues. After experience, they become involved in higher-level negotiations.	Below average growth due to declining union membership.

Source: *Occupational Outlook Handbook,* 1998–1999 Edition, Bureau of Labor Statistics.

Trans Union Corporation

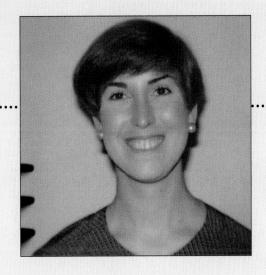

Name: Kathleen A. McGrath

Age: 38

Position/title: Human Resource Consultant

Salary range: $40,000–$50,000

Time in this position: $1\frac{1}{2}$ years

Company name: Trans Union Corporation

Company's web address: www.tuc.com

Company description: A division of the Chicago-based Marmon Group, Trans Union is the nation's leading provider of consumer credit information. Its annual sales exceed $500 million.

Job description: As a consultant, I counsel corporate associates, managers, and field representatives on using existing policies and procedures in a variety of areas (benefits, training, compensation, international, etc.) in order to address important company concerns and objectives. I must recommend improvements in procedures, training, and tools when necessary.

I am also expected to develop and interpret policies in more complex areas, such as relocation and salary increases, as well as ensure that services are delivered to associates in a timely way, and that our policies are administered in accordance with the law.

Planning is also my responsibility. I develop and manage our strategic plans for year-long projects, which include open enrollment, hiring costs, and salary administration guidelines.

Career path: I studied physical therapy for three years at Illinois State University. I participated in management training at Hart, Schaffner & Marx until they went out of business in 1989. I joined Kohl's department store as an assistant store manager and was promoted to store manager. I worked at Kohl's for two years. I then returned to college and worked in HR through a work-study program. I became HR assistant for DFT Lighting, a leading manufacturer of light fixtures.

Ideal next job: My ideal next job would be a senior HR consultant or a team leader.

Best part of your job: Several things I like about my job include using consulting skills to assist customers, bringing new concepts and ideas to support the common goal of the customer, and supporting an information technology staff of approximately 350 people.

Worst part of your job: I have been truly happy with every aspect of my job.

Educational background: I received an associate's degree in business from William Rainey Harper College in 1991. I then completed the SHRM Human Resources General Certification in 1995.

Favorite course: My management and human resource courses were my favorite.

Best course for your career: Human resource management courses and information systems courses benefited me the most in the experience I needed for my current position.

Recommended by Prof. Mike Vijuk, William Rainey Harper College

Marketing: Building Customer and Stakeholder Relationships

Chapter 13

LEARNING GOALS

After you have read and studied this chapter, you should be able to

1 Define marketing and summarize the steps involved in the marketing process.

2 Describe marketing's changing role in society and the merging of the marketing concept with total quality management.

3 Describe how relationship marketing differs from traditional marketing.

4 List the four Ps of marketing.

5 Apply the four parts of the marketing research process to a business problem.

6 Differentiate between consumer and industrial markets.

New marketing techniques have enabled small retailers to compete with the giants such as Wal-Mart and Sears. Zane's Cycles in Branford, Connecticut. is a good example. Chris Zane, the owner, began the shop when he was still a teenager. Early on, he learned that to keep customers a store has to offer outstanding service and more. The principle behind such service is a concept called relationship marketing.

Most stores focus on making a sale, and follow-up service is given little thought. The goal is to make the transaction, and that is the end of it; thus, such an approach is called transactional marketing.

With relationship marketing, on the other hand, the goal is to keep a customer for life. Zane attracts customers by setting competitive prices. He keeps them by giving them free lifetime service on their bicycles. He also provides free coffee and sells helmets to young people at cost to encourage safety.

Zane keeps a database on customers so he knows what they need and when they will need it.

For example, if he sells a bicycle with a child's seat, he knows that soon that customer may be buying a regular bicycle for the child and he can send out an appropriate brochure at just the right time. Zane encourages people to give him their names, addresses, and other such information by offering to make exchanges without receipts for those people whose transaction information is in the database.

Zane also establishes close community relationships by providing scholarships for local students. Because of his competitive prices, great service, and community involvement, Zane's customers recommend his shop to others. No large store can compete with Zane's in the areas of friendly service and personal attention to each customer. That is what the new style of marketing is all about.

PROFILE

Chris Zane of Zane's Cycles

Sources: Michael Barrier, "Ties That Bind," *Nation's Business*, August 1997, pp. 12–18; and Charlotte Mulhern, "Word on the Street," *Entrepreneur*, February 1998, p. 12.

WHAT IS MARKETING?

From an organizational perspective, such as Zane's Cycles, **marketing** is the process of determining customer wants and needs and then providing customers with goods and services that meet or exceed their expectations. More simply, the goal of the marketing process is to

FIND A NEED AND FILL IT

In the past, businesses made products first and only then thought about selling and distributing those products. In other words, production came first. In an era when the customer is king, that approach is obsolete. In such an environment, marketing comes first. Businesses now try to determine exactly what consumers need or want and then provide the goods and services that fill those needs and wants.[1] Knowing what customers want is much easier today because past purchases can be recorded in a database (an electronic file). For example, a grocery store that uses such a database knows what each customer has purchased over the last few months. Such purchases may include dog food, baby food, and diapers. From that information, the store knows that the customer likely has small children and a dog. Using that information, the store

marketing
The process of determining customer wants and needs and then providing customers with goods and services that meet or exceed their expectations.

◄ **LEARNING GOAL 1**
Define marketing and summarize the steps involved in the marketing process.

◄ **CONSIDER USING TM 93**
Chapter Outline

◄ **CONSIDER USING LECTURE ENHANCER 13-1**
What Is Marketing?

GTE Sprint has the right idea when it comes to marketing: "Find a Need and Fill It." They know that listening to customers is as important as talking. "We hear you loud and clear" is an effective slogan if implemented properly.

Our sentiments exactly.

At GTE Sprint, we make it our business to understand yours. So we consult with the only real experts: business-people just like you. What helps you manage your long distance system? What gets in the way? Can we simplify it? Can we save you even more money? Then we use the answers to create valuable new services.

Sprint' Advanced WATS is a good example. With Advanced WATS you don't have to predict

for more than you really use, even during telephone "rush hours." And our new lower rates make Advanced WATS a better bargain than ever.

Call GTE Sprint. Tell us about your needs. And we'll give you some concrete examples of how we can fill them.

GTE SPRINT
We hear you loud and clear.

can send out coupons and advertisements specifically designed to appeal to families with small children and a pet. Supermarkets and other stores use a variety of means to get customer data, but the most common is to offer some kind of discount program to those willing to provide it.

••• NONPROFIT ••• ORGANIZATIONS USE MARKETING ALSO

Marketing is a critical part of almost all organizations, whether profit or nonprofit. Charities use marketing to raise funds or to obtain other resources. For example, the Red Cross might have a promotion to collect blankets after a major storm. Churches use marketing to attract new members and to raise funds. Politicians use marketing to get votes. States use marketing to attract new businesses and tourists. Many states, for example, have competed to get automobile plants from other countries to locate in their area. Schools use marketing to attract new students. Other organizations, such as unions and social groups, also use marketing.

➤ CONSIDER USING OT ACETATE 13-1
The ABCs of Marketing

Critical Thinking

Using the concept of "Find a need and fill it," what could your college do to attract more students? What needs might a religious organization try to meet to attract new members? Can you see the importance of listening to people to determine their wants and needs before you do any marketing?

➤ CONSIDER USING LECTURE ENHANCER 13-2
Small Business Planning Stays Flexible

➤ LEARNING GOAL 2
Describe marketing's changing role in society and the merging of the marketing concept with total quality management.

➤ CONSIDER USING LECTURE ENHANCER 13-3
Holy Marketing!

•••• ▬▬▬ ••••

UNDERSTANDING THE MARKETING PROCESS

One of the best ways for you to understand marketing is to take one product and follow the marketing process that led to the development and sale of that product (see Figure 13.1). You may start the process by remembering that the basis of marketing is finding a need and filling it. So your first step is to find a need. Imagine that you and your friends don't eat big breakfasts. You want something for breakfast that's fast, nutritious, and good tasting. Some of your friends eat Quaker's 100% Natural cereal but you and others are not happy with its sugar content.

You ask around among your acquaintances and find a huge demand for a good-tasting breakfast cereal that's nutritious, high in fiber, and low in sugar. That leads you to conduct a more extensive marketing research study to determine whether there's a large market for such a cereal. Your research supports your hypothesis: there's a large market for a high-fiber cereal. "Aha," you say to yourself, "I've found a need." You've now completed one of the first steps in marketing. You've researched consumer wants and needs and found a need for a product that's not yet available.

··· DESIGNING A PRODUCT ··· TO MEET NEEDS

The next step is to develop a product to fill that need. A **product** is any physical good, service, or idea that satisfies a want or need. In this case, your proposed product is a multigrain cereal made with an artificial sweetener. It's a good idea at this point to do *concept testing*. That is, you develop an accurate description of your product and ask people whether the concept (the idea of the cereal) appeals to them. If it does, you might go to a manufacturer that has the equipment and skills to design such a cereal, and begin making prototypes. *Prototypes* are samples of the product that you take to consumers to test their reactions. The process of testing products among potential users is called **test marketing**.

If consumers like the product, you may turn the production process over to an existing manufacturer or you may produce the cereal yourself. *Outsourcing*, remember, is the term used to describe the allocation of production and other functions to outside firms ➤ P. 247 ◄. The idea is to retain only those functions that you can do best and outsource the rest.[2]

Once the product is made, you have to design a package, think up a brand name for the product, and set a price. A **brand name** is a word, letter, or group of words or letters that differentiates one seller's goods and services from those of competitors. Cereal brand names, for example, include Cheerios, Team Flakes, and Raisin Bran. You name your cereal Fiberrific to emphasize the high fiber content and terrific taste. We'll discuss the product development process, including packaging, branding, and pricing, in Chapter 14. Now we're simply sketching the whole process to get an overall picture of what marketing is all about.

··· GETTING THE PRODUCT ··· TO CONSUMERS

Once the product is manufactured, you have to choose how to get it to the consumer. You may want to sell it directly to supermarkets or health food stores, or you may want to sell it through organizations that specialize in distributing food products. Such organizations are traditionally called marketing middlemen or intermediaries because they're in the middle of a series of organizations that distribute goods from producers to consumers. We'll discuss such marketing intermediaries and distribution in detail in Chapter 15. The box called From the Pages of *Business Week* will give you some insight into the role of marketing intermediaries.

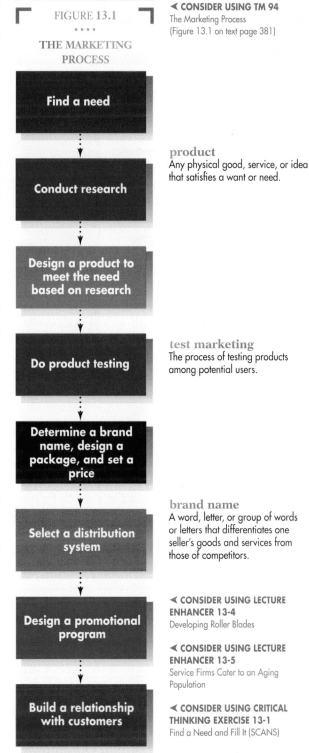

FIGURE 13.1
····
THE MARKETING PROCESS

- Find a need
- Conduct research
- Design a product to meet the need based on research
- Do product testing
- Determine a brand name, design a package, and set a price
- Select a distribution system
- Design a promotional program
- Build a relationship with customers

◄ **CONSIDER USING TM 94**
The Marketing Process
(Figure 13.1 on text page 381)

product
Any physical good, service, or idea that satisfies a want or need.

test marketing
The process of testing products among potential users.

brand name
A word, letter, or group of words or letters that differentiates one seller's goods and services from those of competitors.

◄ **CONSIDER USING LECTURE ENHANCER 13-4**
Developing Roller Blades

◄ **CONSIDER USING LECTURE ENHANCER 13-5**
Service Firms Cater to an Aging Population

◄ **CONSIDER USING CRITICAL THINKING EXERCISE 13-1**
Find a Need and Fill It (SCANS)

From the Pages of **BusinessWeek**

http://www.amazon.com

The Role of Intermediaries in Virtual Bookstores

Amazon.com is known as the "earth's biggest bookstore" because it offers some 2.5 million books. But the truth of the matter is that this Internet-based "store" stocks only a couple of thousand books in its warehouse and fills only about 5 percent of its orders itself. The rest of the orders are filled by a dozen wholesalers that store books for Amazon.com. Wholesalers are marketing intermediaries that sell to retailers, such as bookstores. The largest of these wholesalers is Ingram Book Group. It provides about 60 percent of the books sold by Amazon.com.

Ingram provides books to other Internet providers as well. Ingram stores nearly 500,000 titles, the largest inventory carried by anyone. The company ships almost all the orders it receives on the same day it receives them. About 85 percent of all orders are received by the retailers within 24 hours. Retail stores and on-line retailers pay the wholesale markup to Ingram, which amounts to a couple of percentage points above what they pay publishers. Amazon.com is considering increasing its own warehous-

ing facilities to take advantage of these profits. Other on-line sellers may do the same. Ingram, then, like all intermediaries, will face more competition and will have to come up with a deal that is so attractive that on-line stores will use them rather than build their own facilities. Virtual selling gets real when it comes to distribution.

Sources: Anthony Bianco, "Virtual Bookstores Start to Get Real," *Business Week*, October 27, 1997, pp. 146–48; Heather Green, Gail De George and Amy Barrett, "The Virtual Mall Gets Real," *Business Week*, January 26, 1998, pp. 90–91.

••• ESTABLISHING A RELATIONSHIP •••
WITH CUSTOMERS

promotion
All the techniques sellers use to motivate people to buy products or services.

➤ **CONSIDER USING OT ACETATE 13-2**
Who wins the Prize for Customer Service?

One of the last steps in the marketing process is to promote the product to consumers. **Promotion** consists of all the techniques sellers use to motivate people to buy products or services. They include advertising, personal selling, publicity, and various sales promotion efforts, such as coupons, rebates, samples, and cents-off deals. Promotion is discussed in Chapter 16.

The last step in the marketing process consists of relationship building with customers. That includes responding to any suggestions they may make to improve the product or its marketing. Postpurchase service may include exchanging goods that weren't satisfactory and making other adjustments to ensure consumer satisfaction, including recycling. Marketing is an ongoing process. A company must continually adapt to changes in the market and to changes in consumer wants and needs.

TOTAL QUALITY AND
THE MARKETING CONCEPT

Marketing has changed over time as the wants and needs of consumers have changed. A brief review of marketing's history will show its adaptability and give you a glimpse of what's likely to come next.

••• THE MARKETING CONCEPT •••

After World War II ended in 1945, there was tremendous demand in the United States for goods and services among the returning veterans who were starting a new life with new families. These postwar years launched the baby boom (a sudden jump in the birthrate) and a boom in consumer spending. Competition for consumers' dollars was fierce. Business owners recognized the need to be more responsive to consumers, and a philosophy emerged called the **marketing concept**. The marketing concept had three parts:

1. *A customer orientation:* Find out what consumers want and provide it for them.

2. *A service orientation:* Make sure everyone in the organization has the same objective—consumer satisfaction. This is a total and integrated organizational effort.

3. *A profit orientation:* Market those goods and services that will earn the firm a profit and enable it to survive and expand to serve more customer wants and needs.

It took a while for the marketing concept to be implemented by marketers. During the 1980s, businesses began to apply the marketing concept more

◄ **LEARNING GOAL 3**
Describe how relationship marketing differs from traditional marketing.

◄ **CONSIDER USING LECTURE ENHANCER 13-6**
A Brief History of Marketing

◄ **CONSIDER USING OT ACETATE 13-3**
Using the Marketing Concept

marketing concept
A three-part business philosophy: (1) a customer orientation, (2) a service orientation, and (3) a profit orientation.

◄ **CONSIDER USING SUPPLEMENTAL CASE 13-1**
Service Marketing Calls for a Consumer Orientation (SCANS)

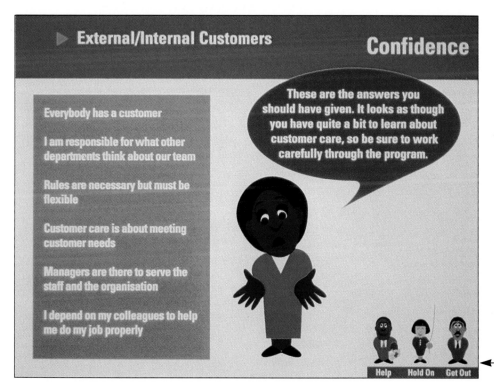

The marketing concept is just another theoretical proposition unless and until employees put it into action. To do that, employees need to be trained to respond to the needs of other employees (internal customers) and external customers (businesses and consumers). Often such training is done on the computer, where employees can learn at their own speed and when it is most convenient for them.

This researcher is interviewing a couple in a shopping mall to get their on-the-spot impression of products. When the goal is to "delight" customers, marketers must constantly gather research data to determine exactly what customers want and then monitor how happy they are with the products and services being offered.

> **CONSIDER USING LECTURE ENHANCER 13-7**
The Power of Marketing

Published Image is just one of many small companies that have formed self-managed teams to get work done quickly and efficiently. Not all companies give employees the freedom to set their own work schedules and do their own budgets, however. What are the advantages and disadvantages you see to giving employees such freedom?

aggressively. In the 1990s, they extended the marketing concept by adopting the concept of total quality management (TQM), which focuses on "delighting" the customer. In the following sections, we'll explore how the marketing concept and total quality management have merged.

••• FROM A CUSTOMER ORIENTATION TO ••• DELIGHTING CUSTOMERS AND OTHER STAKEHOLDERS

Marketing's goal in the past was to provide customer satisfaction. Today the goal of some total quality firms is to please or even delight customers by providing goods and services that exactly meet their requirements or exceed their expectations.[3] One objective of a company's marketing effort, therefore, is to make sure that the response to customer wants and needs is so fast and courteous that customers are truly surprised and pleased by the experience. You can see how TQM is an extension of the marketing concept, especially in the area of customer orientation.

You don't have to look far to see that most organizations haven't yet reached the goal of delighting customers. Retail stores, government agencies, and other organizations may still irritate customers as often as they please them. Nonetheless, global competition is forcing organizations to adopt total quality concepts, which means, above all, adapting organizations to customers.

Businesses have learned that employees won't provide first-class goods and services to customers unless they receive first-class treatment themselves. Marketers must therefore work with others in the firm, such as human resource personnel, to help make sure that employees are pleased. In some firms, such as IBM, employees are called internal customers ≫ P. 209 ≪.

••• FROM TRAINING ALL EMPLOYEES TO ••• UNITING ORGANIZATIONS

Once it became clear that everyone in the firm had to work together to please internal and external customers ≫ P. 209 ≪, many changes started to happen in

organizations, as discussed in Chapter 8. First of all, barriers between departments began to fall. Marketers formed cross-functional teams ➤ P. 242 ◄ with designers, engineers, production personnel, and others in the firm to develop high-quality products.

In Boston, Eric Gershman organized his small newsletter-publishing concern, Published Image, into four self-managed teams. His employees set their own work schedules, prepare their own budgets, and receive group bonuses based on their team's performance. As a consequence, turnover has virtually halted, revenues have doubled, and profit margins increased from 3 percent to 20 percent.

Determining whether organizations are providing first-class service and quality is done through *competitive benchmarking* ➤ P. 247 ◄.[4] That means that companies compare their processes and products with those of the best companies in the industry to learn how to improve them. Xerox Corporation, for example, has benchmarked its functions against corporate leaders such

 This year alone, more than 2,300 companies participating in EPA's Green Lights® and ENERGY STAR® Buildings programs will save nearly $282 million in energy costs, and help prevent over 5 billion pounds of air pollution emissions. This means they'll not only improve their bottom line, but the environment as well. To find out how you can get involved, call EPA's toll-free Hotline at 1-888-STAR-YES.

as American Express (for billing), Ford (for manufacturing floor layout), Westinghouse (for bar coding), Mary Kay Cosmetics (for warehousing and distribution), and Florida Power & Light (for quality processes).

••• MAINTAINING A PROFIT ORIENTATION •••

Marketing managers must make sure that everyone in the organization understands that the purpose behind pleasing customers is to ensure a profit for the firm. Using that profit, the organization can then satisfy other stakeholders of the firm such as stockholders, environmentalists, and the local community.[5] Chris Zane (see the Profile at the beginning of this chapter) provides a good example of community involvement.

It has been estimated that reducing by 5 percent the number of customers who defect—that is, who switch from buying your products to buying another company's—can increase profit by as much as 85 percent (though this figure varies by industry). Some of that profit comes from increased purchases and some from referrals.[6] In the next section, we'll explore the marketing process in more detail so you can see how relationships are established. But first, stop and do the Critical Thinking exercise.

Often, what is best for a company's profits is also best for the environment. For example, using energy-efficient lighting lowers costs and minimizes the pollution caused by power plants. Similarly, recycling lowers costs and keeps the environment cleaner. When a company keeps all stakeholders in mind when making decisions—including employees, suppliers, dealers, and the community—everyone can benefit.

Critical Thinking

The government is now starting to implement total quality concepts, just as business is doing. What barriers will make the process more difficult? For example, why can't the U.S. Postal Service delight customers as UPS and Federal Express do?

Progress Check

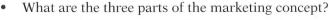

• What are the three parts of the marketing concept?
• Can you define competitive benchmarking?

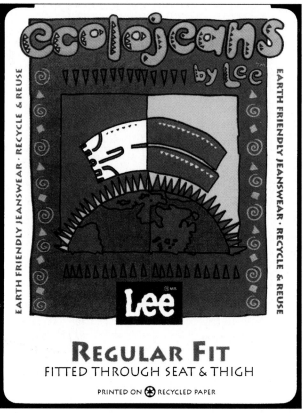

These two images provide a remarkable contrast in terms of the approach of various businesses to stakeholders and social responsibility. On the left you have an example of a timber company in the northwest engaging in clear-cutting of a forest, which is destructive to wildlife habitat, leads to soil erosion, and creates an eyesore. Conversely, Lee's Ecolojeans are made of recycled materials, and the ad itself is even printed on recycled paper. Which company is more environmentally sensitive? Does this make a difference to you as a consumer?

relationship marketing
Establishing and maintaining mutually beneficial exchange relationships with internal and external customers and all the other stakeholders of the organization.

RELATIONSHIP MARKETING

The traditional marketing concept emphasized giving customers what they want. Relationship marketing goes further by recognizing the need to please other stakeholders ⇒ P. 12 ⇐ as well. If you go too far in giving customers what they want, the organization will lose money. That would hurt stockholders. Likewise, you could please customers but harm the environment, thus harming relationships with the community. Balancing the wants and needs of all the firm's stakeholders—employees, suppliers, dealers, and the community—is a much bigger challenge than marketing has attempted in the past.

Relationship marketing, then, is establishing and maintaining mutually beneficial exchange relationships with internal and external customers and all the other stakeholders of the organization. Organizations that adopt relationship marketing take the community's needs into mind when designing and marketing products. For example, many companies have responded to the environmental movement by introducing "green products" into the marketplace. A **green product** is one whose production, use, and disposal doesn't damage the environment. For example, Ventura, California-based Patagonia sells outdoor clothing that uses organically-grown cotton exclusively. That means less fertilizers to pollute the soil. Patagonia also pledges one percent of sales or ten percent of pre-tax profit, whichever is greater, to small, local preservation efforts.[7]

••• THE MOVEMENT AWAY FROM MASS MARKETING •••

In the world of mass production following the Industrial Revolution, marketers responded with mass marketing. **Mass marketing** means developing products and promotions to please large groups of people. The mass marketer tries to sell products to as many people as possible. That means using mass media, such as TV, radio, and newspapers. Although mass marketing led many firms to success, many marketing managers got so caught up with their products and competition that they became less responsive to the market.

Relationship marketing tends to lead away from mass production toward custom-made goods and services. The goal is to keep individual customers over time by offering them products that exactly meet their requirements. The latest in technology enables sellers to work with individual buyers to determine their wants and needs and to develop goods and services specifically designed for them (e.g., hand-tailored shirts and unique vacations). One-way messages in mass media give way to a personal dialogue among participants. The following are two examples of relationship marketing:

- Rental car companies, airlines, and hotels have frequent user programs through which loyal customers can earn special services. For example, a traveler can earn free flights on an airline, special treatment at a car rental agency (e.g., no stopping at the rental desk—just pick up a car and go), and all kinds of special services at a hotel (e.g., faster check-in and check-out procedures, flowers in the room, free breakfasts, free exercise rooms).

- A small express-delivery company established a long-term relationship with a major manufacturer by offering a customized air and ground transportation system. The manufacturer, in turn, offered a guaranteed volume of business.

Relationship marketing is more concerned with retaining old customers than with creating new ones. Special deals, fantastic service, loyalty programs (e.g., frequent flyer programs), and the like are just the beginning. Companies maintain databases that enable them to custom-make products for individuals. For example, some stores sell custom-made Levi's for about $10 more than mass-produced Levi's. Once the company has your measurements, you can be assured of a perfect fit every time (as long as you don't gain or lose weight).

green product
A product whose production, use, and disposal don't damage the environment.

mass marketing
Developing products and promotions to please large groups of people.

◄ **CONSIDER USING OT ACETATE 13-4**
Basics of Relationship Marketing

◄ **CONSIDER USING OT ACETATE 13-5**
Relationship Marketing Builds Customer Loyalty

Relationship marketing is enhanced by developing customized products for individuals on a huge scale. This is called mass customization. A good example is provided by The Custom Foot shoe store in White Plains, New York. Infrared scans are used to customize shoes for each foot. Sizes range from 2AAAAAA to 16EEEEEEEE. The shoes are made in Maine or Italy in three to four weeks.

••• FROM RELATIONSHIP MARKETING TO •••
FORMING COMMUNITIES OF BUYERS

Relationship marketing eventually leads to a dialogue with customers. As we described earlier, a database is established so that every contact with consumers results in more information about them. For example, whenever a customer buys something, the color, the size, and other important data are recorded in the database. If the consumer sends a letter, that letter is also included. Over time, the seller learns more and more about consumers; the next step is to put that knowledge to use in establishing a community of buyers.

Fly & Field, for example, is a small store in Glen Ellyn, Illinois, that sells fly-fishing equipment. Fly fishers are a relatively small market locally, but a nice-sized market nationally. To reach the national audience, Fly & Field has established an interactive Web site (http://www.flyfield.com) where customers and prospects can chat with each other. Naturally, visitors to the site can also access fly-fishing materials and an on-line catalog where they can buy what they want.[8]

Fly & Field is not alone. Many companies are using interactive Web sites as part of the move from relationship marketing to forming communities of buyers. Others are using a wide variety of activities. Harley-Davidson has a 220,000-member club that has its own newsletter, meetings and rallies. The Wally Byam Caravan Club is made up of owners of Airstream trailers and motor homes; they have events where the manufacturer sends merchandise, staff, information, giveaway items, and more. Community bonding leads to a strong commitment to the products and the company. Such loyalty is hard to match.

Companies that use Digital Equipment Corporation's computers have their own user group that shares information, so relationship marketing is also critical in the business-to-business market. Ultimately, companies would like their users to actively recruit other users.[9]

➤ **LEARNING GOAL 4**
List the four Ps of marketing.

➤ **CONSIDER USING OT ACETATE 13-6**
Elements in the Marketing Mix

➤ **CONSIDER USING TM 95**
The Marketing Environment (Figure 13.2 on text page 388)

•••• ▬▬▬ ••••
MARKETING MANAGEMENT AND
THE MARKETING MIX

Marketing managers are responsible for getting everyone in the firm to establish and maintain mutually beneficial relationships with all stakeholders. A *mutually beneficial exchange* is one in which both parties to the exchange

FIGURE **13.2**
••••
THE MARKETING
ENVIRONMENT

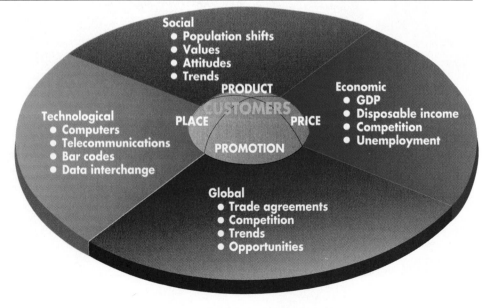

believe they have received good value for their efforts. For example if you buy a hat for a price that you and the dealer find satisfactory, that is a mutually beneficial exchange (money for hat). Traditionally, the main focus of marketing managers has been to please customers. Given that goal, managing the marketing process involves four factors: (1) designing a want-satisfying *product*, (2) setting a *price* for the product, (3) distributing the product to a *place* where people will buy it, and (4) *promoting* the product. These four factors (product, price, place, and promotion) have become known as the four Ps of marketing. Together, they're called the **marketing mix**, because they're the ingredients that go into a marketing program.

Each factor of the marketing mix will be discussed in detail in the following three chapters. Note that the marketing mix is surrounded by the marketing environment (see Figure 13.2). Changes in the social, economic, technological, and global environment force marketers to constantly adapt. The environment of marketing is changing faster today than ever before, so marketers must make changes faster as well. Note also that customers are in the middle of the diagram because they are the focus.

A marketing manager designs a marketing program that effectively combines the ingredients of the marketing mix (see Figure 13.3). **Marketing management**, therefore, is the process of planning and executing the conception, pricing, promotion, and distribution (place) of ideas, goods, and services (products) to create mutually beneficial exchanges. The Legal Briefcase box on page 390 explores one issue that marketing managers face: protecting brand names.

marketing mix
The ingredients that go into a marketing program: product, price, place, and promotion.

◄ **CONSIDER USING TM 96**
The Four Ps and the Marketing Manager's Role (Figure 13.3 on text page 389)

marketing management
The process of planning and executing the conception, pricing, promotion, and distribution of ideas, goods, and services (products) to create mutually beneficial exchanges.

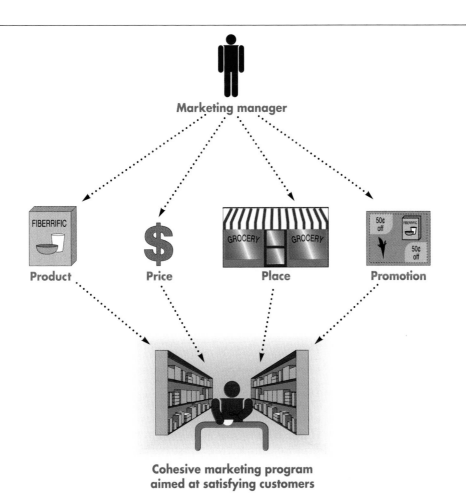

**Cohesive marketing program
aimed at satisfying customers**

FIGURE **13.3**
• • • •
THE FOUR Ps AND THE MARKETING MANAGER'S ROLE

The marketing manager chooses the proper price, promotion, and place to develop a comprehensive marketing program. This figure shows the mix for Fiberrific cereal. Included would be decisions about packaging, couponing, and more.

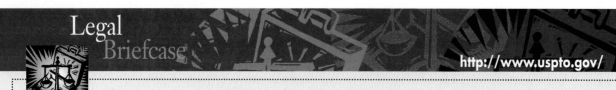

http://www.uspto.gov/

Committing Brand Genericide

Businesses often spend a lot of money developing a brand name, only to find later that the brand name cannot be used or is overused and becomes generic. Furthermore, someone could copy your brand name and take some of its effectiveness away. In short, the legal issues surrounding the branding of a product are quite significant.

To minimize legal problems, it is best to register a brand name with the appropriate state agency and the U.S. Patent and Trademark Office. You first do a records search to ensure that your chosen brand name isn't already in use. The U.S. patent office has libraries throughout the country where you can conduct such a search.

After you have chosen a name, it is important to protect it. One danger a business faces is having its brand name become a generic name; that is, the name of the product category rather than one brand. Aspirin, for example, was once a brand name. So were corn flakes, escalator, cellophane, thermos, yo-yo, and raisin bran. ▲

Allowing your brand name to become a generic name has become known as *genericide*. For example, Pampers became so closely associated with disposable diapers that people simply said "I'm going to buy some Pampers" no matter what brand they actually purchased. When Huggies became a competitor, people would say, "I'm going to buy some Huggies Pampers."

A company's brand name (Pepsi-Cola or Avis) is often an asset worth millions of dollars. One way to protect a brand name is to never use it as a verb, as in "Xerox this for me." Another is to use the generic name with the brand name, as in Kleenex tissues or Pampers disposable diapers. It also pays to protect that name legally so that others cannot destroy your valuable asset.

Sources: Chip Walker, "The Perils of Popularity," *Marketing Tools*, June 1997, pp. 34–37; and Justin Martin, "Is It Mr. Clean or Captain Shine?," *Fortune*, July 7, 1997, p. 206.

••• LEARNING ABOUT THE MARKET •••

market
People with unsatisfied wants and needs who have both the resources and the willingness to buy.

➤ **CONSIDER USING LECTURE ENHANCER 13-8**
Marketing Functions

At the beginning of the word *marketing* is the word *market*. A **market** is defined as people with unsatisfied wants and needs who have both the resources and the willingness to buy. Thus, if there are people who want a high-fiber, low-sugar cereal, like Fiberrific, and if those people have the resources and willingness to buy it, then it is said that there's a market for Fiberrific. We can learn whether there's a market for our cereal by studying consumer wants and needs. We'll look at how marketers determine customer wants and needs after the Progress Check.

Progress Check

• What is relationship marketing? How does it differ from mass marketing?
• What are the four Ps of the marketing mix?

➤ **LEARNING GOAL 5**
Apply the four parts of the marketing research process to a business problem.

DETERMINING WHAT CUSTOMERS WANT

marketing research
The analysis of markets to determine opportunities and challenges.

Marketing research is the analysis of markets to determine opportunities and challenges. One goal of marketing research is to determine exactly what consumers want and need. That isn't easy because consumer wants and needs are constantly changing. Therefore, marketing must maintain close relationships with customers. Marketing research helps determine what customers have purchased in the past, what situational changes have occurred to change what consumers want, and what they're likely to want in the future. In addition, marketers conduct research on business trends, the ecological impact of their decisions, international trends, and more (see Figure 13.4). Businesses need information in order to compete effectively, and marketing research is the activity that gathers that information. Note, too, that in addition to listening to customers, marketing researchers should pay attention to what employees, shareholders, dealers, consumer advocates, and other stakeholders have to say.

◄ **CONSIDER USING LECTURE ENHANCER 13-9**
Using Marketing Research to Identify the Target Market

◄ **CONSIDER USING OT ACETATE 13-7**
Guidelines for Market Research

◄ **CONSIDER USING TM 97**
Marketing Research Topics (Figure 13.4 on text page 391)

••• THE MARKETING RESEARCH PROCESS •••

The marketing research process consists of four key steps:

1. Define the problem and determine the present situation.
2. Collect data.
3. Analyze the research data.
4. Choose the best solutions.

The following sections look at each of these steps.

DEFINE THE PROBLEM AND DETERMINE THE PRESENT SITUATION

It's as important to know what an organization does well as to know what it doesn't do well. Marketing research should report both sides. Marketing researchers should be given the freedom to help discover what the present situation is, what the problems are, what the alternatives are, what information is needed, and how to go about gathering and analyzing data.

┌ FIGURE **13.4** ┐
• • • •
MARKETING RESEARCH TOPICS

Many organizations do research to determine market potential, to evaluate market share, and to learn more about the people in various markets. Most also do short- and long-range sales forecasting and competitor analysis.

Advertising research
1. Motivation research
2. Copy research
3. Media research
4. Studies of ad effectiveness
5. Studies of competitive advertising

Business economics and corporate research
1. Short-range forecasting (up to 1 year)
2. Long-range forecasting (over 1 year)
3. Studies of business trends
4. Pricing studies
5. Plant and warehouse location studies
6. Acquisition studies
7. Export and international studies
8. MIS (management information system)
9. Operations research
10. Internal company employees

Corporate responsibility research
1. Consumers' "right-to-know" studies
2. Ecological impact studies
3. Studies of legal constraints on advertising and promotion
4. Social values and policies studies

Product research
1. New product acceptance and potential
2. Competitive product studies
3. Testing of existing products
4. Packaging research

Sales and market research
1. Measurement of market potentials
2. Market share analysis
3. Determination of market characteristics
4. Sales analysis
5. Establishment of sales quotas and territories
6. Distribution channel studies
7. Test markets and store audits
8. Consumer panel operations
9. Sales compensation studies
10. Promotional studies

Making Ethical Decisions

http://www.findsvp.com/tocs/la468.htm

No Kidding

Marketers have long recognized that children can be an important influence on their parents' buying decisions. In fact, many direct appeals for products are focused on children. At Fiberrific, we've experienced a great response to our new high-fiber, high-protein cereal among health-conscious consumers. The one important group we haven't been able to attract is children. Therefore, the product development team is considering introducing Fiberrific Jr. to expand the product line.

Fiberrific Jr. may have strong market potential if we follow two recommendations of our research department. First, we coat the flakes generously with sugar (significantly changing the cereal's nutritional benefits). Second, we promote the product exclusively on chil-

dren's TV programs. Such a promotional strategy should create a strong demand for the product, especially if we offer a premium (a toy or other "surprise") in each box. The consensus among the research department is that kids will love the new taste, plus parents will agree to buy Fiberrific Jr. because of their positive impression of our best-selling brand. The research director commented, "The chance of a parent actually reading our label and noting the addition of sugar is nil."

Would you introduce Fiberrific Jr. according to the recommendations of your research department? What are the benefits of doing so? What are the risks involved in following the recommendations? What would you do if you were the marketing manager?

➤ SCANS

➤ **CONSIDER USING OT ACETATE 13-8**
Uses of Marketing Research

secondary data
Already-published research reports from journals, trade associations, the government, information services, libraries, and so forth.

primary data
Facts and figures not previously published that you have gathered on your own.

➤ **CONSIDER USING OT ACETATE 13-9**
How to Find Out What's on Customers' Minds

focus group
A small group of people who meet under the direction of a discussion leader to communicate their opinions about an organization, its products, or other given issues.

➤ **CONSIDER USING CRITICAL THINKING EXERCISE 13-2**
Good to the Last Drop (SCANS)

COLLECT DATA Obtaining usable information is vital to the marketing research process. Nevertheless, you must first determine the scope and estimated costs of doing research. Research can become quite expensive, so some trade-off must be made between the need for information and the cost.

To minimize costs, it's best to explore secondary data first. **Secondary data** consist of already-published research reports from journals, trade associations, the government, information services, libraries, and so forth.

Usually, previously published research doesn't provide all the information necessary for important business decisions. When additional, more in-depth information is needed, marketers must do their own studies to gather primary data. **Primary data** are facts and figures not previously published that you gather on your own. One way to gather primary data is the observation method, in which data are collected by observing the actions of potential buyers. Can you think of a way we could use the observation method to gather the information we need to promote Fiberrific?

A more formal way to gather primary data is the survey. Telephone surveys, mail surveys, and personal interviews are the most common methods of gathering survey information.[10] Focus groups have become a popular method of surveying individuals. A **focus group** is a small group of people (8 to 14 individuals) who meet under the direction of a discussion leader to communicate their opinions about an organization, its products, or other given issues.

Figure 13.5 lists the principal sources of both secondary and primary data.

ANALYZE THE RESEARCH DATA Careful, honest interpretation of data you collect can help you find useful alternatives to specific marketing challenges. The same data can mean different things to different people. Sometimes people become so intent on a project that they're tempted to ignore or misinterpret data. For example, if our data indicate the market won't support another brand of cereal, we should accept the information and drop Fiberrific rather than slant the results to show what we'd like to see and go ahead with the project.

CHOOSE THE BEST SOLUTION   After collecting and analyzing data, market researchers determine several alternative strategies and make recommendations as to which strategy may be best and why. In today's customer-driven market, ethics is important in every aspect of marketing. Companies should therefore do what's right as well as what's profitable. This step could add greatly to the social benefits of marketing decisions. (See the box called Making Ethical Decisions.)

The last steps in a research effort involve following up on the actions taken to see if the results were as expected. If not, corrective action can be taken and new research studies done in the ongoing attempt to provide consumer satisfaction at the lowest cost.

◄ CONSIDER USING LECTURE ENHANCER 13-10
Sick Pets, Healthy Market

FIGURE **13.5**
• • • •
SELECTED SOURCES OF SECONDARY AND PRIMARY INFORMATION
You should spend a day or two at the library becoming familiar with these sources. You can read about primary research in any marketing research text from the library.

SECONDARY SOURCES

Government publications
Statistical Abstract of the United States
Survey of Current Business
Census of Retail Trade
Census of Transportation
Annual Survey of Manufacturers

Commercial publications
A. C. Nielsen Company studies on retailing and media
Marketing Research Corporation of America studies on consumer purchases
Selling Areas–Marketing, Inc., reports on food sales

Magazines

Business Week	*Journal of Marketing*	Trade Magazines
Entrepreneur	*Journal of Retailing*	appropriate to your industry
Fortune	*Journal of Consumer Research*	such as *Progressive Grocer*
Inc.	*Journal of Advertising*	Reports from various
Advertising Age	*Journal of Marketing Research*	Chambers of Commerce
Forbes	*Marketing News*	
Harvard Business Review	*Journal of Advertising Research*	

Newspapers
The Wall Street Journal   Internet searches
Barron's   Check your library for various software programs that will research articles in various business and trade publications for you

Internal sources
Company records
Balance sheets
Income statements
Prior research reports

PRINCIPAL SOURCES OF PRIMARY DATA

Observation
Surveys
Experiments
Focus groups
Questionnaires

This Web site, in German, is typical of Web sites available throughout the world, in many different languages. Such sites enable a company to establish a dialogue with customers and to respond quickly to their information and product needs. What would you recommend that companies do to make such sites more attractive and useful to you?

••• USING RESEARCH TO UNDERSTAND CONSUMERS •••

The secret to understanding consumers is to listen to them carefully. There are many techniques for doing that, such as the focus groups mentioned earlier. At this point, it's important to note that effective marketing research calls for getting out of the office and getting close to customers to find out what they want and need. Laboratory research and consumer panels can never replace going into people's homes, watching them use products, and asking them what improvements they seek. Many U.S. producers are now doing this, but others still ignore this important marketing process.

In international markets, the need for marketing research is even greater. One must learn the culture of the people and talk with them directly. Ruine Design International, Inc., is a small business that sells residential and commercial furnishings and accessories. The Ruines say that, in Japan, something as simple as stuffing a potential client's business card into your wallet can turn off that client. Japanese custom requires that business cards, like people, be treated with a high level of formality.[11] Furthermore, Japanese businesspeople often exchange gifts before discussing any transactions. The goal in international business is the same as that of business in the United States: find a need and fill it. To do that, marketers must adapt to all the customs and beliefs of the people they are dealing with.

As mentioned earlier, one way to do marketing research (in both domestic and global markets) is to set up a Web site where customers can interact with the company and each other. The information exchanged in such a manner can be extremely useful in determining what customers want. Keeping that information in a database enables a company to improve its product offerings over time and to design promotions that are geared exactly to meet the needs of specific groups of consumers. Marketing majors often take courses in consumer behavior. The following section briefly reviews what is discussed in those courses.

··· THE CONSUMER DECISION-MAKING PROCESS ···

Figure 13.6 shows the consumer decision-making process and some of the outside factors that influence it. The five steps in the process are often studied in courses on consumer behavior. "Problem recognition" may occur, say, when your washing machine breaks down. This leads to an information search—you look for ads about washing machines and read brochures about them. You may even consult *Consumer Reports* and other information sources. And, most likely, you will seek advice from other people who have purchased washing machines. Then you evaluate alternatives and make a purchase decision. After the purchase, you may ask the people you spoke to previously how their machines perform and do other comparisons. Marketing researchers investigate consumer thought processes and behavior at each stage to determine the best way to facilitate marketing exchanges.

Consumer behavior researchers also study the various influences on consumer behavior. Figure 13.6 shows that such influences include the marketing mix variables; psychological influences, such as perception and attitudes; situational influences, such as the type of purchase and the physical surroundings; and sociocultural influences such as reference groups and culture. Here are some terms whose technical definitions may be unfamiliar to you:

- *Learning* involves changes in an individual's behavior resulting from previous experiences and information. Once you've tried a food you don't like, for example, you may not ever buy it again.

- *Reference group* is the group that an individual uses as a reference point in the formation of his or her beliefs, attitudes, values, or behavior. For example, a college student who carries a briefcase instead of a backpack may see businesspeople as his or her reference group.

◄ **CONSIDER USING OT ACETATE 13-10 AND OT ACETATE 13-11**
Using Market Research

◄ **CONSIDER USING LECTURE ENHANCER 13-11**
Yak Paks

◄ **CONSIDER USING SUPPLEMENTAL CASE 13-2**
Developing the Harley-Davidson Image (SCANS)

◄ **CONSIDER USING TM 98**
The Consumer Decision-Making Process and Outside Influences
(Figure 13.6 on text page 395)

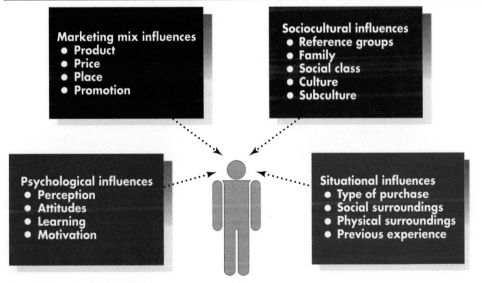

FIGURE 13.6
····
THE CONSUMER DECISION-MAKING PROCESS AND OUTSIDE INFLUENCES

There are many influences on consumers as they decide which goods and services to buy. Marketers have some influence, but it's not usually as strong as sociocultural influences. Helping consumers in their information search and their evaluation of alternatives is a major function of marketing.

Marketing mix influences
- Product
- Price
- Place
- Promotion

Sociocultural influences
- Reference groups
- Family
- Social class
- Culture
- Subculture

Psychological influences
- Perception
- Attitudes
- Learning
- Motivation

Situational influences
- Type of purchase
- Social surroundings
- Physical surroundings
- Previous experience

Decision-making process
- Problem recognition
- Information search
- Alternative evaluation
- Purchase decision
- Postpurchase evaluation (cognitive dissonance)

cognitive dissonance
A type of psychological conflict that can occur after a purchase, when consumers may have doubts about whether they got the best product at the best price.

consumer market
All the individuals or households who want goods and services for personal consumption or use.

business-to-business market
All the individuals and organizations that want goods and services to use in producing other goods and services.

The target market for the Spanish-Language version of *People* magazine is the group of Spanish-speaking people from Mexico, Cuba, Central America, and other parts of the world who have unique cultures and interests. What other languages could *People* magazine use successfully to target people from other countries?

- *Culture* is the set of values, attitudes, and ways of doing things that are transmitted from one generation to another in a given society. The American culture, for example, emphasizes education, freedom, and diversity.

- *Subculture* is the set of values, attitudes, and ways of doing things that result from belonging to a certain ethnic group, religious group, racial group, or other group with which one closely identifies (e.g., teenagers). This group is one small part of the larger culture. Your subculture may prefer rap and hip-hop music, while your parents' subculture may prefer opera.

- **Cognitive dissonance** is a type of psychological conflict that can occur after the purchase. Consumers may have doubts about whether they got the best product at the best price. That means marketers must reassure consumers after the sale if they want to establish a long-term relationship.

···· ▬ ····
RECOGNIZING DIFFERENT MARKETS: CONSUMER AND BUSINESS-TO-BUSINESS

There are two major markets in business: the consumer market and the business-to-business market. The **consumer market** consists of all the individuals or households who want goods and services for personal consumption or use. McDonald's Happy Meals, Toro lawn mowers, and Prudential health insurance policies are examples of items that are commonly considered consumer products but that could be business-to-business products if the buyer were a company rather than an individual. For example, when a landscaping company buys a Toro lawn mower, that is a business-to-business sale.

The **business-to-business market** consists of all the individuals and organizations that want goods and services to use in producing other goods and services or to sell, rent, or supply goods to others. Oil drilling bits, cash registers, display cases, office desks, public accounting audits, and corporate legal advice are examples of such goods and services.

The important thing to remember is that the buyer's reason for buying and the end use of the product determine whether a product is considered a consumer product or a business-to-business product. For example, a box of Fiberrific cereal bought for a family's breakfast is considered a consumer product. However, if the same box of Fiberrific were purchased by Dinnie's Diner to sell to its breakfast customers, it would be considered a business-to-business product.

··· THE CONSUMER MARKET ···

The consumer market consists of the approximately 6 billion people in world markets. Because consumers differ so greatly in age, education

Going Monthly in 1998

Anaheim — **Hot**　　Jalapeño — **Hotter**　　Habanero — **Even Hotter**

PEOPLE EN ESPAÑOL

The Hottest!

Turn up the heat with PEOPLE EN ESPAÑOL

PEOPLE EN ESPAÑOL the hottest Spanish-language magazine in the U.S. - is going monthly in 1998. We'll continue our sizzling coverage of Latino superstars, artists, achievers and news while increasing our rate base to 200,000. This is your chance to reach America's fastest-growing market segment with the country's best-selling Spanish-language magazine. So call your PEOPLE EN ESPAÑOL sales rep now or Publisher Lisa Quiroz at (212) 522-3245 because the next issue of PEOPLE EN ESPAÑOL closes on 11/24/97.

© 1997 Time Inc.

Reaching Beyond
Our Borders

http://www.wnba.com

Men's and Women's Basketball

Compensation of players in the National Basketball Association has changed dramatically since the 1970s. The big stars were paid as much as half a million dollars back then. Today stars such as Shaquille O'Neal may make as much as $120 million through multiyear contracts. Several factors have contributed to this growth, but the two most important ones are television exposure and the promotional efforts of Commissioner David Stern. His marketing expertise has made basketball such a popular sport in the United States that it is now challenging football and baseball for supremacy in viewership. Today's NBA stars come from all over the world. Hakeem Olajuwon is from Nigeria. Toni Kukoc is from Croatia. Rik Smits is from Holland. The Olympics and the participation of the NBA's star players have also contributed to making men's basketball a truly global phenomenon.

In 1997, another product was relaunched: women's professional basketball. There had been several attempts in the past to make women's basketball a professional sport, but they all failed. The Women's National Basketball Association (WNBA) is now televised on NBC, ESPN, and Lifetime. As men's professional basketball once had, women's basketball now has two leagues, the WNBA and the American Basketball League.

Will women's professional basketball become as popular worldwide as men's? Will it develop marquee players like Michael Jordan? It is all a matter of how well the two professional women's leagues are marketed. There are women's teams in many different countries, and many players are being recruited worldwide to play in the two leagues. One aspect of women's basketball is that the players make about $100,000, much less than professional men players now do—although that may change over time. Meanwhile, because the costs are lower, the tickets to women's games are much less expensive, and the women are building their own fans.

Professional women's basketball now has numerous sponsors, the backing of the NBA, TV coverage, and a developing fan base. What research needs to be done next to take the game to a new level and increase its popularity in the United States and around the world? How might you segment the market to ensure women's basketball's long-term success?

Sources: David Halberstam, "David Did It," *World Business,* January–February 1996, pp. 34–39; Edward A. Robinson, "A League or Two of Their Own," *Fortune,* June 23, 1997, p. 32; Joan Hamilton, David Greising, and Richard A. Melcher, "Two Leagues of Their Own?," *Business Week,* May 13, 1996, p. 52; and Tom Knott, "Strange Dynamic Concerns Stern," *The Washington Times,* February 8, 1998, pp. C1 and C2.

---

level, income, and taste, marketers must learn to select different consumer groups to develop products and services specially tailored to their needs. If a consumer group is large enough, a company may design a marketing program to serve only that market.

Take Campbell soups, for example. You know Campbell for its line of traditional soups such as chicken noodle and tomato. If you've been to the grocery lately, you may also know that Campbell has expanded its product line to appeal to a number of different tastes. Recently Campbell noticed the population growth in the South and in the Latino community, so it is experimenting with a Creole soup for the southern market and a red bean soup for the Latino market. In Texas and California, where people like their food with a bit of kick, Campbell makes its nacho cheese soup spicier than in other parts of the country. Campbell is just one company that has had success studying the consumer market, breaking it down into categories, and then developing products for separate groups of consumers.

◄ **LEARNING GOAL 6**
Differentiate between consumer and industrial markets.

◄ **CONSIDER USING OT ACETATE 13-12**
From Boom to Bust to Boom

◄ **CONSIDER USING LECTURE ENHANCER 13-12**
Untapped Markets

◄ **CONSIDER USING LECTURE ENHANCER 13-13**
Bull's Eye Marketing

Spotlight on Small Business

If You Don't Give Great Service, Watch Out, Here Comes the Internet

Few organizations are more annoying to consumers than auto dealers. New no-haggle pricing is helpful, but too many people have had bad experiences buying cars. As a result, consumers are open to a whole new way of buying cars. At least, that's what Pete Ellis thinks. When Ellis opened a small Internet service that sells autos, he expected to receive about 50 inquiries for cars a day. But on the fourth day, he got 1,348 requests! That's when he realized that the Internet is the way mainstream America wants to buy cars.

In 1995, sales at Ellis's company, called Auto-By-Tel Corporation, were $274,000. By 1996, sales were up to over $5 million. The company allows shoppers to research autos on the Internet and then get referrals to a network of reputable dealers that will give them price quotes over the phone. Customers can also get low-cost ▲

auto insurance and financing—plus low prices on used cars and leases. How do people hear about Auto-By-Tel? Word of mouth mostly.

Most customers know exactly what they want in a car, and they are just looking for the best deal. There is no easier or faster way to buy than on the Internet. Promoting a car in a dealership costs a couple of hundred dollars plus over $1,000 in personnel costs. The Internet cuts those costs by as much as 80 percent. People are learning to buy computers, printers, appliances, and other products on the Internet. What are some of the consequences you see for traditional retailers?

Sources: Lynn Beresford, "Full Speed Ahead," *Entrepreneur*, June 1997, pp. 112–13; and "Make Your Small Business an E-Business," an ad in *Nation's Business*, March 1998, pp. 43–50.

---

market segmentation
The process of dividing the total market into several groups whose members have similar characteristics.

target marketing
Marketing directed toward those groups (market segments) an organization decides it can serve profitably.

➤ **CONSIDER USING LECTURE ENHANCER 13-14**
Niche Marketing

➤ **CONSIDER USING LECTURE ENHANCER 13-15**
Another Great Marketing Solution

niche marketing
The process of finding small but profitable market segments and designing custom-made products for them.

one-to-one marketing
Developing a unique mix of goods and services for each individual customer.

The process of dividing the total market into several groups whose members have similar characteristics is called **market segmentation**. The overall market consists of both women and men, children and adults, people in all parts of the world, and people with different wants and needs. Usually a business can't serve all of these groups. Therefore, it must decide which groups to serve. **Target marketing** is marketing directed toward those groups (market segments) an organization decides it can serve profitably. For example, a shoe store may choose to sell only women's shoes, only children's shoes, or only athletic shoes. The box called Reaching Beyond Our Borders explores a new and exciting segmentation problem: promoting women's professional basketball. The issue is finding the right target market for this new venture.

••• REACHING SMALLER MARKET SEGMENTS •••

During the 1990s, marketers became more focused on smaller market segments with large profit potential in spite of their small size. New manufacturing techniques make it possible to develop specialized products for small market groups. **Niche marketing** is the process of finding small but profitable market segments and designing custom-made products for them. For example, a small company called Evergreen makes upgraded central processing units (CPUs) for computers, a market not pursued by giants such as Intel. **One-to-one marketing** means developing a unique mix of goods and services for each individual customer. Travel agencies often develop such packages, including airline reservations, hotel reservations, rental cars, restaurants, and admission to museums and other attractions. This is relatively easy to do in industrial markets where each customer may buy in huge volume. But one-to-one marketing is now becoming possible in consumer markets as well.

••• THE BUSINESS-TO-BUSINESS MARKET •••

The business-to-business market consists of manufacturers, institutions (e.g., hospitals or schools), commercial operations (retail stores), the government, and so on. The basic principle of business-to-business marketing is still "Find a need and fill it," but the strategies differ from consumer marketing because the nature of the buyers is different. Several factors make business-to-business marketing different. Some of the more important include:

1. The *number* of customers in the industrial market is relatively few; that is, there are just a few construction firms or mining operations compared to the 70 million or so households in the U.S. consumer market.

2. The *size* of industrial customers is relatively large; that is, a few large organizations account for most of the employment and production of various goods and services. Nonetheless, there are many small to medium-size firms in the United States that together make an attractive market.

3. Industrial markets tend to be *geographically concentrated.* For example, oil fields tend to be concentrated in the Southwest and in Alaska. Consequently, marketing efforts may be concentrated on a particular geographic area, and distribution problems are often minimized by locating warehouses near industrial centers.

4. Industrial buyers generally are more *rational* than ultimate consumers in their selection of goods and services; they use specifications and often more carefully weigh the "total product offer," including quality, price, and service.

5. Industrial sales tend to be *direct.* Manufacturers sell products, such as tires, directly to auto manufacturers but tend to use intermediaries, such as wholesalers and retailers, to sell to ultimate consumers.

Relationship marketing has always been important in the business-to-business market. For example, Joe Morabito runs a small business that helps companies move from one location to another. Because the company is small, Morabito alone is not able to provide all the services companies need to have an easy, successful move. Therefore, Morabito has established a close relationship with other businesses in the area that provide the complementary services needed to make this complex process easier. The companies work closely together to provide a package of services that exceeds anything even the largest competitors can offer. This is a good example of relationship marketing in the business-to-business area.

By acting as a coordinator of many businesses, Morabito can provide the services of a

◄ **CONSIDER USING CRITICAL THINKING EXERCISE 13-3**
The Marketing Opportunity (SCANS)

◄ **CONSIDER USING OT ACETATE 13-16**
Rare Parts? Call Al

Business-to-business marketers have practiced relationship marketing for years. They know the value of having as much information as possible about potential customers so they can serve them better and faster. Dun & Bradstreet is one company that provides such information. Can you see why businesses need to have close, personal, and long-term relationships with their suppliers and dealers?

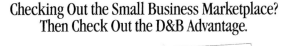

> **CONSIDER USING LECTURE ENHANCER 13-17**
Segmenting the Consumer Market

> **CONSIDER USING LECTURE ENHANCER 13-18**
Federal Express Targets its Customers

> **CONSIDER USING OT ACETATE 13-13**
Guide to Successful Marketing in Small Organizations

> **CONSIDER USING OT ACETATE 13-14**
Marketing Strategies in Nonprofit Organizations

> **CONSIDER USING SUPPLEMENTAL CASE 13-3**
Food Marketing in the Inner City (SCANS)

large company while preserving the closeness and flexibility of a small company. Bob Beck, one of the people who works closely with Mr. Morabito, says, "Business is moving from the transaction era to the relationship era." That is, it is more important to establish and maintain friendly and committed relationships than to simply make the sale.[12]

Critical Thinking

When businesses buy goods and services from other businesses, they usually buy in very large volume. Salespeople in the industrial field usually are paid on a commission basis; that is, they make a certain percentage of every sale. Can you see why industrial sales may be a more rewarding career area (monetarily) than consumer sales? Industrial companies sell goods such as steel, lumber, computers, engines, parts, and supplies. Where would you find the names of such companies?

••• CAREER PROSPECTS IN MARKETING •••

If you were to major in marketing, a wide variety of careers would be available to you. You could work in a retail store or for a wholesaler. You could do marketing research or get involved in product management. You could go into selling, advertising, sales promotion, or public relations. You could get involved in transportation, storage, or international distribution. As you read through the following marketing chapters, consider whether a marketing career would interest you. We'll discuss marketing careers again later, after you have reviewed all the marketing chapters.

Progress Check

- What are the four parts of the marketing research process?
- What's the difference between primary and secondary data?
- What are some of the differences between domestic and international markets?
- Can you define *niche marketing* and *one-to-one marketing*?
- What are four key factors that make industrial markets different from consumer markets?

SUMMARY
• • • • •

1. Define marketing and summarize the steps involved in the marketing process.

1. Marketing is the process of determining customer wants and needs and then providing customers with goods and services that meet or exceed their expectations.
   - ***What is the basic goal of marketing?***
   To find a need and fill it.
   - ***What kinds of organizations are involved in marketing?***
   All kinds of organizations use marketing, both profit and nonprofit organizations (including charities, churches, and nonprofit schools).
   - ***What are the basic steps in the marketing process?***
   After finding a need, the next step in the marketing process is finding a product or the proposed product and testing it in the marketplace. The product development process includes packaging, branding, and pricing. Marketing intermediaries often distribute the product to consumers. The final steps in the marketing process are promoting the product to consumers and building a relationship with customers.

2. The role of marketing changes as the wants and needs of consumers change.

- • **How is the role of marketing changing?**

Marketing is becoming more customer-oriented than ever before. Originally, marketing's goal was simply to satisfy customers. Now marketing tries to please or "delight" customers.

- • **What are the three parts of the marketing concept?**

The three parts of the marketing concept are (1) a customer orientation, (2) a service orientation (this is a total and integrated organizational effort), and (3) a profit orientation (that is, market those goods and services that will earn the firm a profit and enable it to survive and expand to serve more customer wants and needs).

- • **How has the total quality movement affected the marketing concept?**

Total quality has led firms to have a broader orientation than customers. Marketing now is concerned with employees, customers, and other stakeholders of the firm (e.g., suppliers, dealers, and the local communities). Furthermore, marketing is establishing close relationships among firms so that the whole marketing system is customer-oriented. Finally, everyone in the system must keep the profit orientation in mind.

2. Describe marketing's changing role in society and the merging of the marketing concept with total quality management.

3. The marketing process involves research, developing product ideas, branding and pricing products, distributing products to customers, and establishing long-term relationships with customers.

- • **What is relationship marketing?**

Relationship marketing is establishing and maintaining mutually beneficial exchange relationships with internal and external customers and all the other stakeholders of the organization. Organizations that adopt relationship marketing take the community's needs into mind when designing and marketing products.

- • **What's the difference between relationship marketing and mass marketing?**

Mass marketing means developing products and promotions that are designed to please large groups of people. That means using mass media such as TV, radio, and newspapers. Relationship marketing tends to lead away from mass production toward custom-made goods.

3. Describe how relationship marketing differs from traditional marketing.

4. Marketers perform various functions that create value for consumers.

- • **What is the marketing mix?**

The marketing mix consists of the four Ps of marketing: product, price, place, and promotion.

4. List the four Ps of marketing.

5. Marketing research is the first step in the "Find a need and fill it" process.

- • **What are the four steps in the marketing research process?**

The four steps are (1) define the problem and determine the present situation, (2) collect data, (3) analyze the research data, and (4) choose the best solutions.

5. Apply the four parts of the marketing research process to a business problem.

6. There are two major markets: the consumer market and the business-to-business market.

- • **What are the differences between the two markets?**

The consumer market is people who buy products for their own use—people like you and me. The business-to-business market consists of all the individuals and organizations that use goods and services to produce other goods and services or to sell, rent, or supply goods to others.

6. Differentiate between consumer and industrial markets.

> • *How do businesses segment the consumer market?*
> From the total market of men and women, children and adults, and other such groups, businesses choose only those groups (called market segments) that they can serve profitably. This is called target marketing.

KEY TERMS
• • • • • •

brand name 381
business-to-business
 market 396
cognitive dissonance
 396
consumer market 396
focus group 392
green product 387
market 390
market segmentation
 398

marketing 379
marketing concept
 383
marketing
 management 389
marketing mix 389
marketing research
 390
mass marketing 387
niche marketing 398

one-to-one marketing
 398
primary data 392
product 381
promotion 382
relationship
 marketing 386
secondary data 392
target marketing 398
test marketing 381

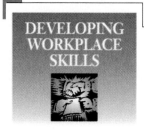

DEVELOPING WORKPLACE SKILLS

1. Imagine that you are the president of a small liberal arts college. Enrollment has declined dramatically. The college is in danger of closing. Show how you might revive the college by applying the marketing concept. Develop an action plan outlining how you would implement the three phases: (1) a customer orientation, (2) a service orientation, and (3) a profit orientation.

2. Think of a product or service that your friends want but cannot get on or near campus. Invent a product or service to fill that need. Evaluate the total market, think of a brand name and a package, develop a promotional scheme, and design a system to distribute it to students.

3. Find a company involved in business-to-business marketing. Interview a member of this firm regarding the ways business-to-business marketing differs from consumer marketing. Report your findings to the class.

4. How would you segment the market for a new, nutritious soft drink that contains no sugar and has all the vitamins required for a day? Describe a target market that you feel would be the most profitable.

5. Divide into groups of four or five students. Conduct a very basic marketing research study that identifies a problem on your campus that your group agrees needs attention. Collect information about that problem, analyze the data, and make written recommendations to the proper authority.

TAKING IT TO THE NET

Purpose

To demonstrate how the Internet can be used to enhance relationship marketing.

Exercise

Procter & Gamble's Clearasil Vertigo Lounge is a Web site that contains simple interactive features on skin care and nutrition. It goes an extra step by offering outside content relationships relevant to teens. Fashion commentary is provided by an editor from the fashion magazine *Black Book*, while sample questions from the Scholastic Aptitude Test (SAT) and tips on test taking are provided by Kaplan Educational Centers. Visit the site at http://www.clearasil.com/home.html.

1. Does Clearasil's Web site help the company strengthen the relationships it has with customers? Give examples to support your answer.

2. How do the elements of the Web site reflect Clearasil's target market?

3. Does Clearasil invite comments from visitors to its Web site? If so, how does this affect its attempt to build positive relationships with its customers?

Practicing Management Decisions

CASE

• • • • • •

APPLYING TOTAL QUALITY MARKETING CONCEPTS AT THERMOS

• • • • • •

Thermos is the company made famous by its Thermos bottles and lunch boxes. Thermos also manufacturers cookout grills. Its competitors include Sunbeam and Weber. To become a world-class competitor, Thermos completely reinvented the way it conducted its marketing operations. By reviewing what Thermos did, you can see how new marketing concepts affect organizations.

First, Thermos modified its corporate culture. It had become a bureaucratic firm organized by function: design, engineering, manufacturing, marketing, and so on. That organizational structure was replaced by flexible, cross-functional, self-managed teams. The idea was to focus on a customer group—for example, buyers of outdoor grills—and build a product development team to create a product for that market.

The product development team for grills consisted of six middle managers from various disciplines, including engineering, manufacturing, finance, and marketing. They called themselves the Lifestyle Team because their job was to study grill users to see how they lived and what they were looking for in an outdoor grill. To get a fresh perspective, the company hired Fitch, Inc., an outside consulting firm, to help with design and marketing research. Team leadership was rotated based on needs of the moment. For example, the marketing person took the lead in doing field research, but the R&D person took over when technical developments became the issue.

The team's first step was to analyze the market. The team spent about a month on the road talking with people, videotaping barbecues, conducting focus groups, and learning what people wanted in an outdoor grill. The company found that people wanted a nice-looking grill that didn't pollute the air and was easy to use. It also had to be safe enough for apartment dwellers, which meant it had to be electric.

As the research results came in, engineering began playing with ways to improve electric grills. Manufacturing kept in touch to make sure that any new ideas could be produced economically. Design people were already building models of the new product. R&D people relied heavily on Thermos's strengths. Thermos's core strength was the vacuum technology it developed to keep hot things hot and cold things cold in Thermos bottles. Drawing on that strength, the engineers developed a domed lid that contained the heat inside the grill.

Once a prototype was developed, the company showed the model to potential customers, who suggested several changes. Employees also took sample grills home and tried to find weaknesses. Using the input from potential customers and employees, the company used continuous improvement to manufacture what became a world-class outdoor grill.

No product can become a success without communicating with the market. The team took the grill on the road, showing it at trade shows and in retail stores. The product was such a success that Thermos is now using self-managed, customer-oriented teams to develop all its product lines.

Decision Questions

1. How could the growth of self-managed cross-functional teams affect marketing departments in other companies? Do you believe that would be a good change or not? Why?

2. Can you see the advantage of having teams of people from auto repair shops researching consumers in the same way Thermos did?
3. Which people in an organization do you anticipate being most resistant to working directly with people in marketing? Why?
4. What do you think the Thermos team would have found if it had asked customers what

they thought about having consumers put the grills together rather than buying them assembled?

Sources: Brian Dumaine, "Payoff from the New Management," *Fortune*, December 13, 1993, pp. 103–10; and Christine Bunish, "Marketers Take Over as Cost-Cutting Ends," *Business Marketing*, April, 1997, pp. 1, 8.

┌ VIDEO CASE ┐

• • • • • •

ALLIGATOR RECORDS HAS THE BLUES (FOR SALE)

In 1971, Bruce Iglauer, a 23-year-old blues fan, used a $2,500 inheritance to follow his heart and start a record company to record and promote his favorite band, Hound Dog Taylor and the HouseRockers. Today that company, Alligator Records, is home to some of the world's premiere blues performers and is regarded as a top label. Its recordings have won more awards than any other contemporary blues label, including a total of 30 Grammy nominations.

When Iglauer was a student at Lawrence University in Appleton, Wisconsin, he hosted the blues show on his college radio station. When the college activities committee was in need of a band, Iglauer convinced them to book blues legend Howlin' Wolf. Iglauer was disappointed with the promotional push given by the university. He knew he could do better, so he offered to guarantee the costs—out of his own pocket—of booking Luther Allison in exchange for full control over the promotion. The two shows were completely sold out. Not long after that, Iglauer started Alligator Records.

Alligator Records is a small business that competes with giants in the music industry. It does that through marketing. Selling the blues is more than a marketing task for Iglauer, however—it is his mission in life.

If marketing is a process of finding a need and filling it, Alligator Records strives to fill blues lovers' need to buy the recordings they like, particularly those made by musicians who are talented but not well known. Iglauer, therefore, became a bridge that linked the two groups (blues musicians and blues lovers). That is what marketing is all about.

Marketing management means managing the four Ps of product, price, place, and promotion. Marketing begins with understanding the wants and needs of customers. Iglauer has been around

blues enthusiasts for so long that he instinctively knows what they will like. Nonetheless, he must still do some research to stay in tune with the market (pun intended).

Once the recordings are produced, Iglauer's job is to distribute the music, not only in the United States but around the world. Like most marketers, he relies on intermediaries like wholesalers and retailers to do that job. He also has to find overseas distributors.

Iglauer deals with both the consumer market and the business-to-business market. He has to convince wholesalers to push his products among retailers. He also has to encourage radio personalities to play the music. Ultimately, however, Iglauer sells his performers and his music to consumers in clubs and on CDs and cassettes. Blues lovers form what is called a niche market, or one small part of the overall music market.

The marketing concept calls for a customer orientation. That means providing value to customers. It also means establishing long-term relationships with a relatively small market segment—those who love the blues. This is known as relationship marketing. One way to maintain such relationships is to establish a Web site where people can hear the latest releases and order them directly from the recording company. Visit Alligator Records' Web site at http://www.alligator.com to sample the sounds or read more about the company and its artists.

Alligator Records is still fueled by the same principles that established the label in 1971. Although the staff has increased to 22 full-time employees, the focus hasn't changed. Iglauer is as driven as he ever was. "I just want to keep bringing the blues to new fans and getting them as excited about it as I am."

Discussion Questions

1. What role will the Internet play in music industry marketing in the future? Will most recordings be sold in stores or over the Internet? What might Iglauer do to prepare for that?

2. Does the marketing of musicians and music differ from the marketing of other products, such as clothes or automobiles? What are the similarities and differences?

3. What role does Iglauer play in creating value for customers? How are the four Ps used to accomplish that goal?

4. What growth prospects do you see in the international promotion of the blues? How would you go about popularizing the blues in other countries?

Developing and Pricing Quality Products and Services

Chapter 14

LEARNING GOALS

*After you have read and studied this chapter,
you should be able to*

1 Explain the difference between a product and a value package.

2 Describe how businesses create product differentiation for their goods and services in both consumer and industrial markets.

3 List and describe the six functions of packaging.

4 Give examples of a brand, a brand name, and a trademark, and explain how to prevent a brand name from becoming generic.

5 Explain the role of product managers and the five steps of the new-product development process.

6 Identify and describe the stages of the product life cycle, and describe marketing strategies at each stage.

7 Give examples of various pricing objectives and show how break-even analysis helps in pricing decisions.

oro Company has long been proud of "producing the best darn lawn mower in the world." Today, however, Kendrick Melrose, the chief executive, knows that Toro must broaden its product base to protect itself from seasonal fluctuations. In addition to lawn mowers, Toro produces snow blowers, but sales of these products are also subject to the weather. For example, Toro expected to sell few snow blowers in 1997 because the winter of 1996 was relatively mild and distributors still had products in stock. The winter of 1998 also turned out to be unusually warm in much of the country.

So what kind of products should Toro add to its product mix? Recently the company added "fertigation" systems to its mix. These systems water and fertilize crops at the same time. They are part of an overall plan to get deeply involved in irrigation systems in general, including watering systems for golf courses and drip irrigation systems for farmers.

Toro has also purchased a company that makes a machine for reducing stumps to sawdust. In fact, about half of Toro's revenues now come from commercial clients, including landscapers, golf-course superintendents, and municipal park operators. This, remember, is called business-to-business marketing ➤ P. 396 ◄.

PROFILE

Kendrick Melrose of Toro

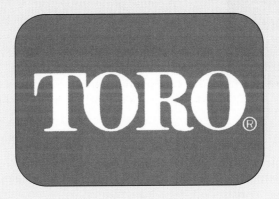

To further diversify its product mix, Toro is providing several different services to customers, including global satellite technology that could tell farmers and golf-course managers when certain areas need watering. The next step for Melrose is to take the company into cyberspace. For example, Toro is developing a system to provide computer monitors on lawns or golf courses that will report nutrient deficiencies or excess water runoff. In short, Toro is adjusting its product mix to assure sales throughout the year.

This chapter will explore issues such as the proper product mix that companies should have. It will also explore how companies can differentiate their products from competitors, make maximum use of brand names, and set an effective pricing strategy. It is important to understand that consumers evaluate many different aspects of a product before buying it. Today, that includes the decision whether to buy the product from a catalog, in a store, or on the Internet.

Sources: Richard Gibson, "Toro Charges into Greener Fields with New Products," *The Wall Street Journal*, July 22, 1997, p. B4, and Stephen Budiansky, "Taking the Measure of El Niño," *U S. News and World Report*, March 9, 1998, p. 7.

····· ▬▬ ·····

PRODUCT DEVELOPMENT AND THE VALUE PACKAGE

International competition today is so strong that American businesses are losing some part of the market to foreign producers. The only way to regain that lost part is to design and promote better products—meaning products that are perceived to have the best *value*—high quality at a fair price.[1] As we'll see in this chapter, whether a consumer perceives a product as the best value depends on many factors. To satisfy consumers, marketers must learn to listen better than they do now and to adapt constantly to changing market demands. Managers must also constantly adapt to price challenges from competitors.

Learning to manage change, especially new-product changes, is critical for tomorrow's managers. An important part of the impression consumers get about products is the price. This chapter, therefore, will explore two key parts of the marketing mix: product and price ➤ P. 388 ◄.

◄ **CONSIDER USING TM 91**
Chapter Outline

◄ **LEARNING GOAL 1**
Explain the difference between a product and a value package.

◄ **CONSIDER USING LECTURE ENHANCER 14-1**
Wolfgang Schmitt of Rubbermaid

Fast-food restaurants such as this one in London are constantly looking for new products to appeal to their customer base. Who would expect a vegetable cheeseburger at KFC? But KFC, like all restaurants, is surveying customers, trying new products, and expanding their product mix to include something for everyone. In this case, a burger for vegetarians and those who are cutting back on meat. We'd like to give it a try. Would you?

value package
Everything that consumers evaluate when deciding whether to buy something.

▶ **CONSIDER USING SUPPLEMENTAL CASE 14-1**
The Value of a Product Offer **(SCANS)**

Toro's Kendrick Melrose and other marketers have learned that adapting products to markets is an ongoing necessity. An organization can't do a one-time survey of consumer wants and needs, design a line of products to meet those needs, put them in the stores, and relax.

Fast-food organizations, for example, must constantly monitor all sources of information for new-product ideas. Wendy's was able to greatly increase its product sales when it added stuffed pitas to its product mix. McDonald's is placing new cooking equipment in its stores to make custom-made sandwiches and expand the menu.[2] CEO Robert Autry of Hardee's Food System claims to bring out more new products than anyone else. Each Hardee's offers 12 to 15 different sandwiches. Offerings differ in various locations, based on the wants of the local community. In Iowa, pork tenderloin is big, but in Oklahoma City, it's tortilla scramblers.

Product development, then, is a key activity in any modern business. There's a lot more to new-product development than merely introducing new products, however. What marketers do to create excitement and demand for those products (product strategy) is as important as the products themselves.[3]

••• DEVELOPING A VALUE PACKAGE •••

From a strategic marketing viewpoint, a value package is more than just the physical good or service. A **value package** (also known as the total product offer) consists of everything that consumers evaluate when deciding whether to buy something. Thus, the basic product or service may be a washing machine, an insurance policy, or a bottle of beer, but the value package also consists of the following:

> Price
>
> Package
>
> Store surroundings (atmospherics)
>
> Image created by advertising
>
> Guarantee
>
> Reputation of the producer
>
> Brand name
>
> Service
>
> Buyer's past experience
>
> Speed of delivery
>
> Accessibility of marketer (e.g., on the Internet)

When people buy a product, they may evaluate and compare value packages on all these dimensions. Therefore, a successful marketer must begin to think like a consumer and evaluate the product offer as a total collection of impressions created by all the factors listed above. It is wise to talk with consumers to see which features and benefits are most important to them.[4]

Let's go back and look at our highly nutritious, high-fiber, low-sugar breakfast cereal, Fiberrific, which we introduced in Chapter 13. The value package as perceived by the consumer is much more than the cereal itself. Anything that affects consumer perceptions about the cereal's benefits and value may determine whether the cereal is purchased. The price certainly is an important part of the perception of product value.

Often a high price indicates exceptional quality. The store surroundings also are important. If the cereal is being sold in an exclusive health food store, it takes on many characteristics of the store (e.g., healthy and upscale). A guarantee of satisfaction can increase the product's value in the mind of consumers, as can a well-known brand name. Advertising can create an attractive image, and word of mouth can enhance the reputation. Thus, the Fiberrific value package is more than a cereal; it's an entire bundle of impressions.

You may think that Gateway sells computer systems, but it sells a lot more than that. It sells "custom-built" computers, for one thing. For another, it offers "hassle-free financing." But customers also demand service, so Gateway offers 24-hour service and support. All of this is available at a competitive price. The value package is one that competitors will find hard to beat. Are you impressed by the value?

◄ CONSIDER USING LECTURE ENHANCER 14-2
Prestige Pricing and Lacoste

Sometimes an organization can use low price to create an attractive value package. For example, Hull Industries, a small company in Twinsburg, Ohio, developed a steering-wheel-locking device (Lockjaw) to compete with The Club, the original and most widely sold such device. Lockjaw's wholesale price is $5 less than The Club's, and Lockjaw comes in one size that fits all cars, whereas The Club comes in multiple sizes. Furthermore, the Lockjaw is said to be stronger and thieves would have to cut the Lockjaw in two places (versus just one for The Club). Despite Lockjaw's lower price and more attractive features, it still needs great promotion to capture the market from the leader.

As you learned earlier, one way to keep customers is to establish a dialogue with them and keep the information they provide in a database. There is no easier way to do this than to establish a Web site where consumers can ask questions, get information, and chat with others. Having a close personal relationship with customers adds to the perceived benefits of products because most people would prefer to buy from someone they know and like. It is difficult for large companies to establish such relationships, which gives an advantage to those smaller companies that can do so more easily. The box called Spotlight on Small Business on page 410 discusses this issue in more depth.

Critical Thinking

What's the product of a library? One branch of the Chicago Public Library actually lends out expensive power tools and such accessories as fiberglass extension ladders. At the Carnegie library in Pittsburgh, volunteer psychologists go to the library, listen to people's troubles, and refer them to appropriate

Spotlight on Small Business

http://www.benchnet.com

Creative Product Design Helps Small Businesses Compete

One major advantage small businesses have over large ones is their ability to get closer to the customer and provide more personal and friendly service. But don't assume that a small business always provides better service. Small-business managers must constantly improve their products and services. To facilitate this objective they should frequently poll their customers and employees to see what they think, using this feedback as the catalyst for change.

Small businesses shouldn't react negatively to the demands that customers place on them. Rather, they must encourage employees to give customers friendly, responsive service. If they fail to do so, competitors that emphasize service will take away business.

Another good idea for small businesses is to benchmark ❖ P. 247 ❖ two major competitors to find weak-

nesses in their products or services. They can then exploit those weak links, using them as a competitive edge. Smaller airlines, for example, are taking advantage of major carriers by offering service to more areas at lower prices. Smaller retailers are taking slices of the market by specializing in one or two products. Thus, you can now find stores selling just sunglasses or just kites.

Small businesses must constantly review their product mix and eliminate those products that no longer appeal to the market niche being served. That means constantly monitoring consumer trends and quickly adapting the product/service mix to meet current demands. Today many of the greatest marketing opportunities are beyond our borders. Adapting products to successfully penetrate such markets will continue to be the challenge of the future.

---

product line
A group of products that are physically similar or are intended for a similar market.

➤ **CONSIDER USING OT ACETATE 14-1**
Mickey Mouse's Product Mix

Kelloggs' product line, shown here in a convenience store in Dublin, Ireland, is purposely broad. Notice All-Bran, Nut Feast, Sultana Bran, Country Store, and more. As many consumers have become more health conscious, cereal companies responded with bran cereals and others whose ingredients are considered healthful. Are you impressed by the sheer quantity of brands you have to choose from?

help. The Broome High School Media Center in Spartanburg, South Carolina, lends out prom, wedding, and mother-of-the-bride dresses donated by members of the community. What do you think prompted libraries to be so creative in their product offers? What's the product of a college or university?

••• PRODUCT LINES AND THE PRODUCT MIX •••

Companies usually don't have just one product that they sell. Rather, they sell several different but complementary products. The Profile about Toro showed that new-product lines can be added continually with the right amount of research. Figure 14.1 shows Procter & Gamble's product lines. A **product line**, as the figure shows, is a group of products that are physically similar or are intended for a similar market. Procter & Gamble's product lines include bar soaps, laundry detergents, and dish-

FIGURE **14.1**
· · · ·
PROCTER & GAMBLE'S
PRODUCT MIX
INCLUDING ALL ITS
PRODUCT LINES

PRODUCT LINES	BRANDS
Bar soaps	Camay, Coast, Ivory, Kirk's, Lava, Monchel, Safeguard, Zest
Laundry detergents	Bold, Cheer, Dash, Dreft, Era, Gain, Ivory Snow, Liquid Bold-3, Liquid Cheer, Liquid Tide, Oxydol, Solo, Tide
Dishwashing detergents	Cascade, Dawn, Ivory Liquid, Joy, Liquid Cascade
Cleaners and cleansers	Comet, Comet Liquid, Mr. Clean, Spic & Span, Spic & Span Pine Liquid, Top Job
Shampoos	Head & Shoulders, Ivory, Lilt, Pert Plus, Prell
Toothpastes	Crest, Denquel, Gleem
Paper tissue products	Banner, Charmin, Puffs, White Cloud
Disposable diapers	Luvs, Pampers
Shortening and cooking oils	Crisco, Crisco Oil, Crisco Corn Oil, Puritan

(Product mix indicated along the left margin of the table.)

Most large companies make more than one product. Here we see the various products and brands Procter & Gamble makes. Note how physically similar the products are.

◄ **CONSIDER USING TM 100**
Procter & Gamble's Product Mix
Including All Its Product Lines
(Figure 14.1 on text page 411)

washing detergents. In one product line, there may be several competing brands. Thus, Procter & Gamble has many brands in its laundry detergent product line, including Bold, Cheer, Tide, and Ivory Snow. All of P&G's product lines make up its product mix.

Product mix is the term used to describe the combination of product lines offered by a manufacturer. As we see in Figure 14.1, P&G's product mix consists of product lines of soap, detergents, toothpastes, shampoos, and so forth.

Service providers have product lines and product mixes as well. For example, a bank may offer a variety of services from savings accounts, automatic teller machines, and computer banking to money market funds. A bank's product mix may include safety deposit boxes, loans (home, car, etc.), traveler's checks, on-line banking, and more.[5] AT&T combines services (telephone) with goods (computers, phones) in its product mix. AT&T is also becoming more consumer oriented than in the past. John Walter, former CEO of AT&T, said in 1997 that, "Every aspect of what we are doing is about the customer. That is a total reversal in our procedures and our strategic intent."[6] Companies must decide what product and service mix is best. The mix includes both goods and services to spread the risk among several industries.

product mix
The combination of product lines offered by a manufacturer.

◄ **LEARNING GOAL 2**
Describe how businesses create product differentiation for their goods and services in both consumer and industrial markets.

· · · · ▬▬▬ · · · ·

PRODUCT DIFFERENTIATION

Product differentiation is the creation of real or perceived product differences. Actual product differences are sometimes quite small, so marketers must use a clever mix of pricing, advertising, and packaging to create a unique, attractive image. Evian, for example, which sells bottled water, successfully attempted product differentiation. The company made its water so attractive through pricing and promotion that often restaurant customers now order it by brand name instead of a Coke or Pepsi.

product differentiation
The creation of real or perceived product differences.

► **CONSIDER USING OT ACETATE 14-2**
Consumer Choices of the Leading Product Innovations of All Time

Candy is a convenience good. That is, you tend to buy what is available where you are at the time. But, given that choice, wouldn't you prefer one that "Melts in your mouth, not on your hands?" This humorous, eye-catching ad is intended to reinforce the brand image in your mind so that you will remember it the next time you're in the market for candy. How effective do you think this ad will be among your age group?

> **CONSIDER USING TM 101**
Various Classes of Consumer and Industrial Goods and Services (Figure 14.2 on text page 412)

convenience goods and services
Products that the consumer wants to purchase frequently and with a minimum of effort.

There's no reason why you couldn't create an attractive image for Fiberrific. With a high price and creative advertising, it could become the Evian of cereals. But different products call for different marketing strategies, as we'll see next.

Small businesses can often win market share with creative product differentiation. For example, yearbook photographer Charlie Clark competes with other yearbook photographers by offering multiple clothing changes, backgrounds, and poses along with special allowances, discounts, and guarantees. He has been so successful that companies use him as a speaker at photography conventions. Small businesses usually have the advantage of being more flexible than big businesses in adapting to customer wants and needs and giving them attractive product differences.

A company can differentiate a product in many ways. Asking the following questions gives you an idea of just how many aspects of the customer's experience with the company's total value package can be improved:[7]

How do consumers become aware of a need for your product? Oral-B added a blue dye to the bristles of its toothbrushes: The dye fades with time to tell people when the brushes are getting old.

How do consumers find your product? Can you reach people better by catalog or on the Internet? A flower shop may buy or rent space in a supermarket to become more accessible to consumers and differentiate itself from the competition. It may also set up an easy-to-remember 800 number such as 1-800-Flowers.

How do consumers order your product? Could your order-processing system be improved? Many fast-food organizations now accept orders by fax. E-mail offers another new way to help customers order easily.

How quickly do you deliver your product? Many firms have won market share by offering overnight delivery.

We could go on and on about the various ways companies interact with customers, but you get the idea. Each time a customer comes in contact with an employee, there is another chance to treat that customer better, faster, or in a more friendly manner than competitors do. That is what differentiation is all about.

••• MARKETING DIFFERENT CLASSES OF •••
CONSUMER GOODS AND SERVICES

Several attempts have been made to classify consumer goods and services. One classification has four general categories—convenience, shopping, specialty, and unsought—based on consumer shopping habits and preferences.

1. **Convenience goods and services** are products that the consumer wants to purchase frequently and with a minimum of effort (e.g., candy, snacks, banking services). Location, brand awareness, and image are important for marketers of convenience goods and services. Banking

and other services are now much more convenient because they are available on the Internet. Companies that don't offer such services are likely to lose market share to those who do unless they offer outstanding service to customers who visit in person.

2. **Shopping goods and services** are those products that the consumer buys only after comparing value, quality, and price from a variety of sellers. Shopping goods and services are sold largely through shopping centers where consumers can "shop around." Because many consumers carefully compare such products, marketers can emphasize price differences, quality differences, or some combination of the two. Examples include clothes, shoes, appliances, and auto repair services. It is so easy to make price comparisons on the Internet today that companies will instead have to compete on service in the future.

Consumers tend to be bombarded with last-minute purchase ideas as they get to the checkout counters of supermarkets and drugstores. How often do you buy such "unsought" items when you go to the store? What is your weakness—gum, candy, magazines? Why do you think supermarkets carry tabloids and position them at the checkout counters?

3. **Specialty goods and services** are products that have a special attraction to consumers who are willing to go out of their way to obtain them. Examples are fur coats, jewelry, chocolates, and cigars as well as services provided by medical specialists or business consultants. These products are often marketed through specialty magazines. For example, specialty skis may be sold through sports magazines and specialty foods through gourmet magazines. By establishing interactive Web sites where customers can place orders, companies that sell specialty goods and services can make buying their goods as easy or easier than shopping at a local mall.

4. **Unsought goods and services** are products that consumers are unaware of, haven't necessarily thought of buying, or find that they need to solve an unexpected problem. Some examples of unsought products are emergency car-towing services and burial services. Others are batteries and magazines, which are often displayed at the checkout counter where they attract consumers who did not intend to buy them when they entered the store. What effects might the Internet have on the sale of unsought goods?

The marketing task varies depending on the kind of product; that is, convenience goods are marketed differently from specialty goods, and so forth. The best way to promote convenience goods is to make them readily available and to create the proper image. Price, quality, and service are the best appeals for shopping goods. Specialty goods rely on reaching special market segments through advertising. Unsought goods are best sold through creative and highly visible in-store displays.

Whether a good or service falls into a particular class depends on the individual consumer. What's a shopping good for one consumer (e.g., coffee) could be a specialty good for another consumer (e.g., flavored gourmet coffee). Some people shop around to compare different dry cleaners, so dry cleaning is a shopping service for them. Others go to the closest store, making it a convenience service. Therefore, marketers must carefully monitor their customer base to determine how consumers perceive their products. Can you see how Fiberrific could be either a convenience good or a shopping good?

shopping goods and services
Those products that the consumer buys only after comparing value, quality, and price from a variety of sellers.

specialty goods and services
Products that have a special attraction to consumers who are willing to go out of their way to obtain them.

unsought goods and services
Products that consumers are unaware of, haven't necessarily thought of buying, or find that they need to solve an unexpected problem.

••• MARKETING INDUSTRIAL GOODS AND SERVICES •••

industrial goods
Products used in the production of other products.

Industrial goods are products used in the production of other products. Some products can be classified as both consumer goods and industrial goods. For example, personal computers could be sold to consumer markets or industrial (business-to-business) markets ⇒ P. 396 ⇐. As a consumer good, the computer might be sold through computer stores like CompUSA or through computer magazines. Most of the promotional task would go to advertising. As an industrial good, personal computers are more likely to be sold by salespeople. Advertising would be less of a factor in the promotion strategy. You can see that classifying goods by user category helps determine the proper marketing mix strategy. Figure 14.2 shows some categories of both consumer and industrial goods and services.

Progress Check

- What's the difference between a product and a value package?
- What's the difference between a product line and a product mix?
- Name the four classes of consumer goods and services, and give examples of each.

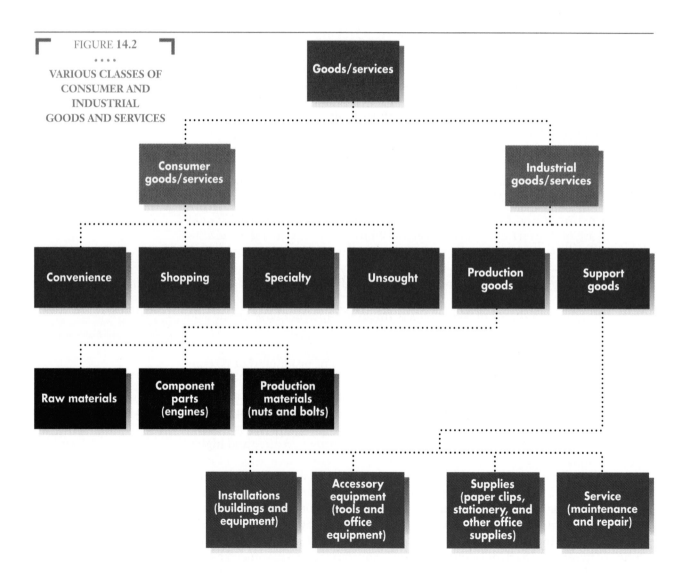

FIGURE **14.2**
••••
VARIOUS CLASSES OF CONSUMER AND INDUSTRIAL GOODS AND SERVICES

···· ━━━ ····

PACKAGING CHANGES THE PRODUCT

◄ **LEARNING GOAL 3**
List and describe the six functions of packaging.

◄ **CONSIDER USING LECTURE ENHANCER 14-3**
New Packaging Trends

We've said that consumers evaluate many aspects of the value package, including the brand. It's surprising how important packaging can be in such evaluations. Many years ago people had problems with table salt because it would stick together and form lumps during humid or damp weather. The Morton Salt Company solved that problem by designing a package that kept salt dry in all kinds of weather, thus the slogan "When it rains, it pours." Packaging made Morton's salt more desirable than competing products, and even though other salt companies developed similar packaging, Morton's is still the best-known salt in the United States.

Other companies have also used packaging to change and improve their basic product. Thus, we've had squeezable catsup bottles, plastic bottles for motor oil that eliminate the need for funnels, stackable potato chips in a can, toothpaste pumps, plastic cans for tennis balls, dinners and other foods (like popcorn) that can be cooked in a microwave

Antilock brakes are largely an industrial good that gets sold in the business-to-business market. However, consumers often have to replace such items if they have their autos long enough. By encouraging consumers to shop at particular dealers, manufacturers can sell more brakes and other goods to those dealers. This is called a pull strategy in marketing. Do you ever shop at auto supply stores to get new brakes and other auto needs?

oven, whipped cream in dispenser cans, and so forth. In each case, the package changed the product in the minds of consumers and opened large markets.[8] Packaging can also help make a product more attractive to retailers. For example, the Universal Product Codes on many packages make it easier to control inventory. In short, packaging changes the product by changing its visibility, usefulness, or attractiveness. A major issue in packaging today is the effect packages have on the environment. The box on Making Ethical Decisions on the next page discusses this topic in depth.

◄ **CONSIDER USING LECTURE ENHANCER 14-4**
Wine Bottle Imitation

··· THE GROWING IMPORTANCE OF PACKAGING ···

Packaging has always been an important aspect of the product offer, but today it's carrying more of the promotional burden than in the past. Many goods that were once sold by salespersons are now being sold in self-service outlets, and the package has been given more sales responsibility. The package must perform the following functions: (1) attract the buyer's attention; (2) describe the contents and give information about the contents; (3) explain the benefits of the good inside; (4) provide information on warranties, warnings, and other

Making Ethical Decisions

http://www.mcdonalds.com/

It's Not Easy Being Green

Manufacturers are increasingly torn between using packages that are good for the environment and those that are good for marketing. Compact discs, for example, were originally packaged in 6-inch by 12-inch cardboard or plastic boxes. This excess packaging created an environmental problem. In Canada and Europe two record producers voluntarily agreed to eliminate the "long box" for CDs. U.S. producers, however, were reluctant to give up the large box, which they saw as an excellent marketing tool. They argued that the large boxes allowed them to use eye-catching graphics and that they discouraged shoplifting. Nonetheless, in a movement spearheaded by the Rykodisc record company, manufacturers responded to environmental concerns and changed the CD package. The cost to retailers was high because they had to put in new display units.

Environmentalists have put great pressure on all U.S. firms to be more environmentally concerned in their packaging. McDonald's, for example, trashed its polystyrene sandwich containers. Both Coke and Pepsi have announced that they plan to use recycled bottles.

Many people are now separating their rubbish into different categories to aid the recycling process. But it turns out that not all such efforts can be justified at this time on a cost basis alone. In fact, until technology improves, in certain instances it can still be more costly to recycle. However, with the goals of cleaning up the environment and saving natural resources recycling is a process businesses must continue to pursue.

When forced to choose between a package that makes a product more marketable and one that's recyclable or less damaging to the environment (e.g., that leads to less litter), which package should a marketer choose? Let's say that you know another form of packaging is better for the environment than coated paper but that you could get a lot of publicity by shifting to paper. Would you shift to paper to get the publicity? What would be the consequences of your actions? Would you have supported new laws to require U.S. producers to make smaller packages for CDs even if the change in packaging resulted in fewer sales? What are the ethical issues?

> SCANS

You may not associate massages and manicures with an airline, but that's exactly what Virgin Atlantic Airlines offers for its first class passengers, in its Clubhouse. And they are complimentary (read free). The total package offered by the airline, therefore, has the image of luxury and personal care. What are some other services an airline could offer to make travel easier and more relaxing?

consumer matters; (5) give some indication of price, value, and uses; and (6) protect the goods inside, stand up under handling and storage, be tamperproof, and yet be easy to open and use. Clearly, packaging has become a critical part of product design. This is true in markets throughout the world. It's a real challenge to design a package that communicates well with people from all countries.[9] Just for fun, you might want to try drawing an attractive package for Fiberrific cereal.

Packaging of *services* has been getting more attention recently. For example, Virgin Airlines includes door-to-door limousine service and in-flight massages in its total package.[10] When combining goods or services into one package, it's important not to include so much that the price

Reaching Beyond Our Borders

Packaging for World Markets

Despite the growth of the electronic supermarket (i.e., the Internet) in global markets, people around the world still enjoy shopping in retail stores. Some 70 to 80 percent of all consumer choices are made in stores, and some 60 percent of these are impulse purchases. Thus, packaging is still "the final salesperson" that attracts customers and tells them about product benefits, price, and more.

Designing a package for world markets is much more difficult than designing one for the United States or some other country alone. When serving global markets, the challenge is to communicate the right message in a way that is understood by widely diverse populations. Imagery often takes the place of words as marketers try ▲

to use a universal language. For example, StarTAC phone communicates the reach of its phone system and the high-tech nature of the product with a symbol that shows the rich terrain of the world on a hand that holds the tiny phone.

Care must be taken in the choice of colors and brand names, because different colors and words have different meanings in various countries. For example, Chevy's Nova *no va* means "no go" in Spanish.

Source: Howard Alport, "Global, Interactive Marketing Call for Innovative Packaging," *Marketing News*, January 6, 1997, p. 30; and Pat Le May Burr and Richard M. Burr, "World Wide Wealth of Information," *International Business*, January–February 1998, pp. 16–17.

gets too high. It's best to work with customers to develop offers that best meet their needs. Packaging goods and services for global markets takes special care, as the box called Reaching Beyond Our Borders shows.

◄ **LEARNING GOAL 4**
Give examples of a brand, a brand name, and a trademark, and explain how to prevent a brand name from becoming generic.

BUILDING BRAND EQUITY

Closely related to packaging is branding. A **brand** is a name, symbol, or design (or combination thereof) that identifies the goods or services of one seller or group of sellers and distinguishes them from the goods and services of competitors. The term *brand* is sufficiently comprehensive to include practically all means of identification of a product. A *brand name*, remember, is that part of the brand consisting of a word, letter, or group of words or letters comprising a name that differentiates a seller's goods or services from those of competitors ➤ P. 381 ◄. Brand names you may be familiar with include QVC, Sony, Del Monte, Campbell, Levi's, Snackwell's, Borden, Michelob, and Macintosh. Such brand names give products a distinction that tends to make them attractive to consumers.

A **trademark** is a brand that has been given exclusive legal protection for both the brand name and the pictorial design. Trademarks such as McDonald's golden arches are widely recognized.

People are often impressed by certain brand names, even though they say they know there's no difference between brands in a given product category. For example, when people say that all aspirin is alike, put two bottles in front of them—one with the Anacin label and one labeled with an unknown brand. See which they choose. Most people choose the brand name even when they say there's no difference.

brand
A name, symbol, or design (or combination thereof) that identifies the goods or services of one seller or group of sellers and distinguishes them from the goods and services of competitors.

trademark
A brand that has been given exclusive legal protection for both the brand name and the pictorial design.

◄ **CONSIDER USING OT ACETATE 14-3**
What Are the Top U.S. Brands?

••• BRAND CATEGORIES •••

Several categories of brands are familiar to you. **Manufacturers' brand names** are the brand names of manufacturers that distribute products nationally—Xerox, Polaroid, Kodak, Sony, and Chevrolet, for example. **Knockoff brands** are illegal copies of national brand-name goods such as Polo shirts or Rolex watches. If you see an expensive brand-name item for sale at a ridiculously low price, you can be pretty sure it's a knockoff.

Dealer (private) brands are products that don't carry the manufacturer's name but carry a distributor or retailer's name instead. Kenmore and Diehard (Sears) are examples. These brands are also known as house brands or distributor brands.

Many manufacturers fear having their brand names become generic names. A **generic name** is the name for a product category. Did you know that aspirin and linoleum, which are now generic names for products, were once brand names? So were nylon, escalator, kerosene, and zipper. All those names became so popular, so identified with the product, that they lost their brand status and became generic. (Such issues are decided in the courts.) Their producers then had to come up with new names. The original Aspirin, for example, became Bayer aspirin. Companies that are working hard to protect their brand names today include Xerox (one ad reads, "Don't say 'Xerox it'; say 'Copy it'"), Styrofoam, and Rollerblade (in-line skates).

Generic goods are nonbranded products that usually sell at a sizable discount compared to national or private brands. They feature basic packaging and are backed with little or no advertising. Some are of poor quality, but many come close to having the same quality as the national brand-name goods they copy. There are generic tissues, generic cigarettes, generic peaches, and so forth. Consumers today are buying more generic products because their overall quality has improved so greatly that it approximates that of more expensive brand names.

••• BUILDING BRAND EQUITY AND LOYALTY •••

A major goal of marketers in the future will be to reestablish the notion of brand equity. **Brand equity** is the combination of factors, such as awareness, loyalty, perceived quality, images, and emotions, people associate with a given brand name. In the past companies tried to boost their short-term performance by offering coupons and price discounts to move goods quickly. This eroded consumers' commitment to brand names. Now companies realize the value of brand equity and are trying to measure the earning power of strong brand names.[11]

The core of brand equity is brand loyalty. **Brand loyalty** is the degree to which customers are satisfied, like the brand, and are committed to further purchases. A loyal group of customers represents substantial value to a firm, and that value can be calculated. Relationship marketing ⇒ P. 386 ⇐ is designed to create brand loyalty.[12]

Brand awareness refers to how quickly or easily a given brand name comes to mind when a product category is mentioned. Advertising helps build strong brand awareness.[13] Older brands, such as Coca-Cola and Pepsi, are usually the highest in brand awareness. Event sponsorship (e.g., the Winston-Salem auto races and Virginia Slims tennis tournament) helps improve brand awareness.[14]

Perceived quality is an important part of brand equity. A product that's perceived as of better quality than its competitors can be priced accordingly. The key to creating a perception of quality is to identify what consumers look for in

---

manufacturers' brand names
The brand names of manufacturers that distribute products nationally.

knockoff brands
Illegal copies of national brand-name goods such as Polo shirts or Rolex watches.

dealer (private) brands
Products that don't carry the manufacturer's name but carry a distributor or retailer's name instead.

generic name
The name for a product category.

➤ **CONSIDER USING LECTURE ENHANCER 14-5**
Quantifying the Value of a Brand Name

generic goods
Nonbranded products that usually sell at a sizable discount compared to national or private brands.

➤ **CONSIDER USING LECTURE ENHANCER 14-6**
Brand Loyalty, Cookies, and Donors

brand equity
The combination of factors such as awareness, loyalty, perceived quality, images, and emotions people associate with a given brand name.

brand loyalty
The degree to which customers are satisfied, like the brand, and are committed to further purchase.

brand awareness
How quickly or easily a given brand name comes to mind when a product category is mentioned.

➤ **CONSIDER USING OT ACETATE 14-4**
What Makes a Good Brand Name?

a high-quality product and then to use that information in every message the company sends out. Quality cues include price, appearance, and reputation. Consumers often develop brand preference (that is, they prefer one brand over another) because of such cues.

It's now so easy to copy a product's benefits that off-brand products are being developed to draw consumers away from brand-name goods. Brand X disposable diapers, for example, has increased its market share from 7 to 20 percent. Paragon Trade Brands gives retailers higher-than-normal margins (the difference between purchasing cost and selling price) and quickly matches the product innovations of the major companies. Brand-name manufacturers, like Intel Corporation, have to develop new products faster and promote their names better than ever before to hold off the challenge of lower-priced competitors.[15]

Quality Like This Takes Three Years Of Oak Barrel Aging!

There's only one TABASCO® brand Pepper Sauce. It's the only one made from specially cultivated, hand-selected peppers mixed in a recipe that has remained the same since 1868. The pepper blend is carefully aged in White Oak barrels for three years according to the time-honored TABASCO® tradition. No other pepper sauce is aged so long, or so carefully. That's why it delivers the distinctive, consistent quality that has made TABASCO® brand Pepper Sauce an American favorite for more than 130 years.

For more information call 1-888-HOT DASH.

More Than A Trend... A Tradition!

http://www.TABASCO.com

Aged tobacco. Aged wine. But aged Tabasco sauce? Yes. Tabasco brand pepper sauce is not like any other. It is aged for three years in oak barrels. It is not easy to communicate a quality image for such a product. How successful do you think this ad is in creating a quality image?

◄ **CONSIDER USING LECTURE ENHANCER 14-7**
World's Most Valuable Brands

••• CREATING BRAND ASSOCIATIONS •••

The name, symbol, and slogan a company uses can assist greatly in brand recognition for that company's products. **Brand association** is the linking of a brand to other favorable images. For example, you can link a brand to other product users, to a popular celebrity, to a particular geographic area, or to competitors. Note, for example, how ads for Mercedes-Benz and Cadillac associate those companies' cars with rich people who may spend their leisure time playing or watching polo. Note too the success of associating basketball shoes with stars such as Shaquille O'Neal and Michael Jordan. What person might we associate with Fiberrific to give the cereal more appeal?

The person responsible for building brands is known as a brand manager or product manager. We'll explore that position right after the Progress Check.

brand association
The linking of a brand to other favorable images.

◄ **CONSIDER USING OT ACETATE 14-5**
Do Brand Names Influence Purchasing by Teenagers?

* What six functions does packaging now perform?
* What's the difference between a brand name and a trademark?
* Can you explain the difference between a manufacturer's brand, a private brand, and a generic brand?
* What are the key components of brand equity?

Progress Check

···· ▬▬ ····

PRODUCT MANAGEMENT

product manager
A manager who has direct responsibility for one brand or one product line.

➤ **LEARNING GOAL 5**
Explain the role of product managers and the five steps of the new-product development process.

➤ **CONSIDER USING OT ACETATE 14-6**
The First Products Produced by Six Major Companies

➤ **CONSIDER USING CRITICAL THINKING EXERCISE 14-1**
Silky Skin Solutions **(SCANS)**

➤ **CONSIDER USING TM 102**
The New-Product Development Process (Figure 14.3 on text page 420)

A **product manager** has direct responsibility for one brand or one product line. This responsibility includes all the elements of the marketing mix: product, price, place, and promotion. Thus, the product manager is like a president of a one-product firm. Imagine being the product manager for Fiberrific. You'd be responsible for everything having to do with that one brand. One reason many large consumer-product companies created the position of product manager is to have greater control over new-product development and product promotion.

Many companies are now challenging the value of product managers. As we mentioned earlier, some manufacturer's brand names have become less important to retailers, and customers' brand loyalty is declining. This gives product managers less power. The product management concept seems to be fading, and cross-functional teams ⇒ P. 242 ⇐ and similar consumer-oriented forms of marketing are taking their place. Remaining product managers are finding that their role is expanding and involves long-range planning skills. Brand managers now must create brand equity and turn all employees into brand ambassadors through indoctrination programs so that the brand name becomes a greater competitive advantage.[16]

••• NEW-PRODUCT SUCCESS •••

Chances that a new product will fail are overwhelmingly high, according to *The Wall Street Journal*, which reported that 86 percent of products introduced in one year failed to reach their business objectives. Not delivering what is promised is a leading cause of new-product failure. Other reasons for failure include poor positioning, not enough differences from competitors, and poor packaging. Smaller firms may experience a lower success rate unless they do proper product planning. We'll discuss such planning next.

┌ FIGURE **14.3** ┐
····
THE NEW-PRODUCT DEVELOPMENT PROCESS

Product development is a five-stage process. Which stage do you believe to be the most important?

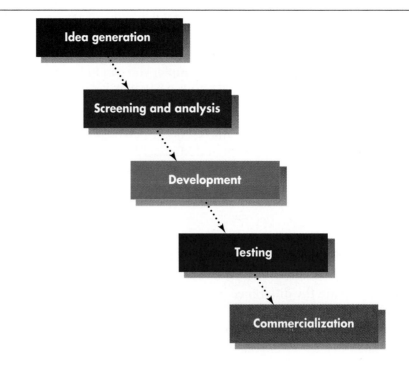

⋯ THE NEW-PRODUCT DEVELOPMENT PROCESS ⋯

As Figure 14.3 shows, product development for producers consists of several stages:

1. Idea generation.
2. Screening and analysis.
3. Development.
4. Testing.
5. Commercialization (bringing the product to the market).

New products continue to pour into the market every year, and the profit potential looks tremendous. Think, for example, of the potential of home video conferencing, interactive TV, large-screen HDTV sets, virtual reality games and products, and other innovations. Where do these ideas come from? How are they tested? What's the life span for an innovation? The following material looks at these issues.

⋯ GENERATING NEW-PRODUCT IDEAS ⋯

Figure 14.4 gives you a good idea of where new-product ideas come from. Note that 38 percent of the new-product ideas for consumer goods come from analyzing competitors (the source of 27 percent of ideas for new industrial products). Such copying of competitors slows the introduction of original ideas.

◄ **CONSIDER USING OT ACETATE 14-7**
Seven Classic Product Failures

◄ **CONSIDER USING LECTURE ENHANCER 14-8**
The Top Ten New Products of All Time

◄ **CONSIDER USING TM 103**
Sources of New-Product Ideas
(Figure 14.4 on text page 421)

CONSUMER PRODUCTS (based on a survey of 79 new products)	
Analysis of the competition	38.0%
Company sources other than research and development	31.6
Consumer research	17.7
Research and development	13.9
Consumer suggestions	12.7
Published information	11.4
Supplier suggestions	3.8
INDUSTRIAL PRODUCTS (based on a survey of 152 new products)	
Company sources other than research and development	36.2
Analysis of the competition	27.0
Research and development	24.3
Product users	15.8
Supplier suggestions	12.5
Product user research	10.5
Published information	7.9

FIGURE 14.4
• • • •
SOURCES OF NEW-PRODUCT IDEAS
This survey shows where ideas for new products originate. As you know, research plays an important role in the development of new products.

FIGURE 14.5

• • • •

CRITERIA FOR
SCREENING NEW-
PRODUCT IDEAS

Ideas for new products
are carefully screened.
This screening helps the
company identify the
areas where new
products are needed and
reduces the chance of a
company working on too
many ideas at a time.

Areas of company strengths and weaknesses	Consumer promotional considerations
Tie-ins with, or potential impact on, other company brands	Nature of competition
	Market segments
Production capabilities	Distribution channels
Consumer attitudes toward category	Trade perceptions of category
Awareness	Turnover rates/optimum inventory allocations
Satisfaction with existing brands	Seasonal characteristics
Regional consumer differences	Price margins
Advertising and merchandising norms, timing, and directions	

➤ CONSIDER USING TM 104
Criteria for Screening New-Product
Ideas (Figure 14.5 on text page 422)

➤ CONSIDER USING OT ACETATE
14-8
Six Clues to New Product Success

A strong point can be made for listening to employee suggestions for new-product ideas. The number one source of ideas for new industrial products has been company sources other than research and development. It was also a major source for new consumer goods. Part of that is due to successful marketing communication systems that monitor suggestions from all sources.

Look through Figure 14.4 carefully and think about the implications. Notice that more than a third of all new-product ideas for industrial products came from users, user research, or supplier suggestions. This finding emphasizes the principle that a firm should listen to its suppliers and customers and give them what they want.

••• PRODUCT SCREENING AND ANALYSIS •••

product screening
A process designed to reduce the number of new-product ideas being worked on at any one time.

Product screening is designed to reduce the number of new-product ideas being worked on at any one time. Criteria needed for screening include whether the product fits in well with present products, profit potential, marketability, and personnel requirements (see Figure 14.5). Each of these factors may be assigned a weight, and total scores are then computed. A new software package called Quick Insight now helps companies analyze the potential of new goods and services. By answering about 60 questions and then reviewing the answers, the user can gain an understanding of the likely problems and potential strengths of the new offering.[17] Nonetheless, it still takes about seven ideas to generate one commercial product.[18] *Product analysis* is done after product screening. It's largely a matter of making cost estimates and sales forecasts to get a feeling for profitability. Products that don't meet the established criteria are withdrawn from consideration.

➤ CONSIDER USING LECTURE
ENHANCER 14-9
Would You Buy a Plastic Car?

➤ CONSIDER USING OT ACETATE
14-9
What Are Consumers' Five Favorite
Technology Products?

➤ CONSIDER USING LECTURE
ENHANCER 14-10
Why Zima Faded

••• PRODUCT DEVELOPMENT AND TESTING •••

If a product passes the screening and analysis phase, the firm begins to develop it further. A product idea can be developed into many different product concepts (alternative product offerings based on the same product idea that have different meanings and values to consumers). For example, a firm that makes packaged meat products may develop the concept of a chicken dog—a hot dog made of chicken that tastes like an all-beef hot dog.

concept testing
Taking a product idea to consumers to test their reactions.

Concept testing involves taking a product idea to consumers to test their reactions (see Figure 14.6). Do they see the benefits of this new product? How frequently would they buy it? At what price? What features do they like and dislike? What changes would they make? Different samples are tested using different packaging, branding, ingredients, and so forth until a product emerges that's

➤ CONSIDER USING TM 105
Steps to Take Before Test Marketing a
Product (Figure 14.6 on text page 423)

PRODUCT DEVELOPMENT	COMMUNICATION DEVELOPMENT	STRATEGY DEVELOPMENT
Identify unfilled need	Select a name	Set marketing goals
Preliminary profit/payout plan for each concept	Design a package and test	Develop marketing mix (after communication developed)
Concept test	Create a copy theme and test	Estimate cost of marketing plan (after product development)
Determine whether the product can be made	Develop complete ads and test	
Test the concept and product (and revise as indicated)		
Develop the product		
Run extended product use tests		

FIGURE 14.6
• • • •
STEPS TO TAKE BEFORE TEST MARKETING A PRODUCT

Product development, communication development, and strategy development all are used as a company develops a new product. Extensive testing is used to guarantee the new product's success.

(left) Concept testing is important for new products. You can imagine the reaction to the concept of a pocket-sized optical scanner that can translate from one language to another instantly. Sounds great, huh? Seiko introduced such a scanner, called Quicktionary, at the Consumer Electronics Show in Las Vegas (1998). What business uses can you imagine for such a product?
(right) Sometimes a concept test shows that a new product idea simply won't work. McDonald's, for example, tested and dropped the concept of a family-style restaurant called Hearth Express.

desirable from both production and marketing perspectives. Can you see the importance of concept testing for Fiberrific?

••• COMMERCIALIZATION •••

Even if a product tests well, it may take quite a while before the product achieves success in the market. Take the zipper, for example, the result of one of the longest development efforts on record for a consumer product. After Whitcomb Judson received his first patents in the early 1890s, it took more than 15 years to perfect the product, but even then consumers weren't interested. Judson's company suffered numerous financial setbacks, name changes, and relocations before settling in Meadville, Pennsylvania. Finally, the U.S. Navy

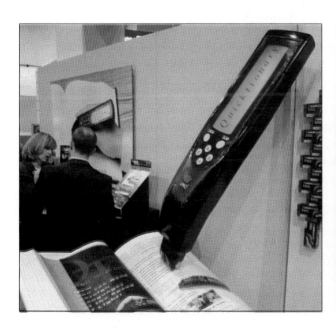

Not long ago, Japan was considered the premier producer of consumer electronics. Now, American brands, such as Xerox, are winning those markets back through high-quality equipment produced quickly. A good example is the WorkCentre 450 from Xerox. It is a five-in-one multifunction system that provides big office productivity for the small or home office. It does color printing, faxing, PC faxing, copying, and scanning. How important do you think its convenience and compact size are to its success? Why?

> **CONSIDER USING LECTURE ENHANCER 14-11**
Taste Testing at R.J. Reynolds

> **CONSIDER USING LECTURE ENHANCER 14-12**
Foreign Brands Sometimes Just Don't Fly

> **LEARNING GOAL 6**
Identify and describe the stages of the product life cycle and describe marketing strategies at each stage.

product life cycle
A theoretical model of what happens to sales and profits for a product class over time.

started using zippers during World War I. Today, Talon Inc. is the leading U.S. maker of zippers, producing some 500 million of them a year.

This example shows that the marketing effort must include commercialization. This includes (1) promoting the product to distributors and retailers to get wide distribution and (2) developing strong advertising and sales campaigns to generate and maintain interest in the product among distributors and consumers. New products are now getting rapid exposure to global markets by being promoted on the Internet. Interactive Web sites enable consumers to view new products, ask questions, and make purchases easily and quickly.[19]

••• **THE INTERNATIONAL CHALLENGE** •••

As described in the profile at the beginning of this chapter, Kendrick Melrose of Toro learned through experience that the secret to success in today's rapidly changing environment is to bring out new products, high in quality, and to bring them out quickly. This is especially true in light of the rapid development process occurring in other countries.

Xerox executives were surprised by Japanese competitors who were developing new copier models twice as fast as Xerox and at half the cost. Xerox had to slash its traditional four-to-five-year product development cycle. After millions of dollars of investment, Xerox can now produce a new model in two years.

The Big Three automakers all recently formed task forces to cut product development cycles that had swollen to nearly five years. The Japanese cycles were taking about three and a half years. To stay competitive in world markets, U.S. businesses must develop an entirely new-product development process. To keep products competitive requires continuous, incremental improvements in function, cost, and quality. Cost-sensitive design and new process technologies are critical.

More attention in the United States must be given the product development process; that is, developing products in cooperation with their users. To implement the new-product development process, managers must go out into the market and interact closely with their dealers and their ultimate customers. Successful new-product development is an interactive process whereby customers present their needs, and new-product designs are prepared to meet those needs. Changes are made over time to make sure that the total product offer exactly meets the customer's needs. The focus shifts from internal product development processes to external customer ➤ P. 209 ◄ responsiveness.

Global marketers today use cross-functional teams to develop new products.[20] Teams from production, marketing, engineering, and other departments go to customers in other countries and learn what they want. The team then works together to quickly meet those customers' needs.

•••• ▬▬▬ ••••

THE PRODUCT LIFE CYCLE

Once a product has been developed, tested, and placed on the market, it often goes through a life cycle consisting of four stages: introduction, growth, maturity, and decline. This is called the product life cycle (see Figure 14.7). The **product life cycle** is a *theoretical* model of what happens to sales and profits for a

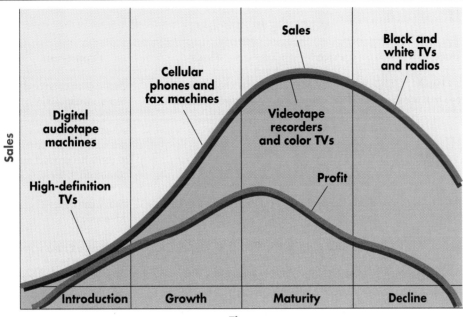

FIGURE 14.7
• • • •
SALES AND PROFITS
DURING THE PRODUCT
LIFE CYCLE

Note that profit levels start to fall *before* sales reach their peak. When profits and sales start to decline, it's time to come out with a new product or to remodel the old one to maintain interest and profits.

product class (e.g., all dishwasher soaps) over time. However, not all products follow the life cycle, and particular brands may act differently. For example, while frozen foods as a generic class may go through the entire cycle, one brand may never get beyond the introduction stage. Nonetheless, the product life cycle may provide some basis for anticipating future market developments and for planning marketing strategies. Some products, such as microwave ovens, stay in the introductory stage for years. Other products, such as fad clothing, may go through the entire cycle in a few months.

◄ CONSIDER USING TM 106
Sales and Profits During the Product Life Cycle (Figure 14.7 on text page 425)

••• EXAMPLE OF THE PRODUCT LIFE CYCLE •••

You can see how the theory works by looking at the product life cycle of instant coffee. When it was introduced, most people didn't like it as well as "regular" coffee, and it took several years for instant coffee to gain general acceptance (introduction stage). At one point, though, instant coffee grew rapidly in popularity, and many brands were introduced (rapid-growth stage). After a while, people became attached to one brand and sales leveled off (maturity stage). Sales then went into a slight decline when freeze-dried coffees were introduced (decline stage). At present, freeze-dried coffee is at the maturity stage. It's extremely important to recognize what stage a product is in because such an analysis may lead to more intelligent and efficient marketing decisions.

◄ CONSIDER USING LECTURE ENHANCER 14-13
The End of the Typewriter

◄ CONSIDER USING LECTURE ENHANCER 14-14
Extending the Life Cycle

••• THE IMPORTANCE OF THE PRODUCT LIFE CYCLE •••

The importance of the product life cycle to marketers is this: Different stages in the product life cycle call for different strategies. Figure 14.8 outlines the marketing mix decisions that might be made. As you go through the table, you'll see that each stage calls for multiple marketing mix changes. Remember, these concepts are largely theoretical and should be used only as guidelines.

Figure 14.9 shows in table form the theory of what happens to sales volume, competition, and profit/loss during the product life cycle. You can compare this table to the graph in Figure 14.7. For instance, both figures show that a product at the mature stage may reach the top in sales growth while profit is

	Marketing Mix Elements			
Life Cycle Stage	Product	Price	Place	Promotion
Introduction	Offer market-tested product; keep mix small	Go after innovators with high introductory price (skimming strategy) or use penetration pricing	Use wholesalers, selective distribution	Dealer promotion and heavy investment in primary demand advertising and sales promotion to get stores to carry the product and consumers to try it.
Growth	Improve product; keep product mix limited	Adjust price to meet competition	Increase distribution	Heavy competitive advertising
Maturity	Differentiate your product to satisfy different market segments	Further reduce price	Take over wholesaling function and intensify distribution	Emphasize brand name as well as product benefits and differences
Decline	Cut product mix; develop new-product ideas	Consider price increase	Consolidate distribution; drop some outlets	Reduce advertising to only loyal customers

FIGURE **14.8**

• • • •

SAMPLE STRATEGIES FOLLOWED DURING THE PRODUCT LIFE CYCLE

▶ **CONSIDER USING TM 107**
Sample Strategies Followed During the Product Life Cycle. (Figure 14.8 on text page 426)

FIGURE **14.9**

• • • •

HOW SALES, PROFITS, AND COMPETITION VARY OVER THE PRODUCT LIFE CYCLE

All products go through these stages at various times in their life cycle. What happens to sales as a product matures?

decreasing. At that stage, a marketing manager may decide to create a new image for the product to start a new growth cycle. You may have noticed, for example, how Arm & Hammer baking soda gets a new image every few years to generate new sales. One year it's positioned as a deodorant for refrigerators and the next as a substitute for harsh chemicals in swimming pools. Knowing what stage in the cycle a product is in helps marketing managers decide when such strategic changes are needed. Figure 14.8 summarizes the decision making that may occur at each level of the product life cycle.

◀ **CONSIDER USING TM 108**
How Sales, Profits, and Competition Vary Over the Product Life Cycle (Figure 14.9 on text page 426)

LIFE CYCLE STAGE	SALES	PROFITS	COMPETITORS
Introduction	Low sales	Losses may occur	Few
Growth	Rapidly rising sales	Very high profits	Growing number
Maturity	Peak sales	Declining profits	Stable number, then declining
Decline	Falling sales	Profits may fall to become losses	Declining number

In what stage of the product life cycle are laptop computers? What does Figure 14.8 indicate firms should do at that stage? What will the next stage be? What might you do at that stage to optimize profits?

Peanut butter is in the maturity or decline stage of the product life cycle. Does that explain why Skippy introduced a reduced-fat version of its peanut butter? What other variations on older products have been introduced in the last few years?

Critical Thinking

Progress Check

• What are the five steps in the new-product development process?
• Can you draw a product life cycle and label its parts?

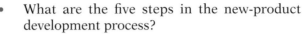
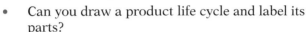

COMPETITIVE PRICING

Pricing is so important to marketing that it has been singled out as one of the four Ps in the marketing mix, along with product, place, and promotion. Price is also a critical ingredient in consumer evaluations of the product. In this section, we'll explore price both as an ingredient of the product and as a strategic marketing tool.

◄ **LEARNING GOAL 7**
Give examples of various pricing objectives and show how break-even analysis helps in pricing decisions.

••• PRICING OBJECTIVES •••

A firm may have several objectives in mind when setting a pricing strategy. When pricing Fiberrific, we may want to promote the product's image. If we price it high and use the right promotion, maybe we can make it the Evian of cereals, as we discussed earlier. We also might price it high to achieve a certain profit objective. We could also price Fiberrific lower than its competitors because we want poor people and older people to be able to afford this nutritional cereal. That is, we could have some social or ethical goal in mind. Low pricing may also discourage competition because the profit potential is less in this case. A low price may also help us capture a larger share of the market. The point is that a firm may have several pricing strategies, and it must formulate these objectives clearly before developing an overall pricing objective. Popular strategies include the following:

◄ **CONSIDER USING OT ACETATE 14-10**
What They Cost When They Were First on the Market

1. *Achieving a target profit.* Ultimately, the goal of marketing is to make a profit by providing goods and services to others. Naturally, one long-run pricing objective of almost all firms is to optimize profit.
2. *Building traffic.* Supermarkets often advertise certain products at or below cost to attract people to the store. These products are called loss leaders. The long-run objective is to make profits by following the short-run objective of building a customer base.
3. *Achieving greater market share.* The auto industry is in a fierce international battle to capture and hold market share. U.S. producers lost market share to foreign producers and have used price incentives (and quality) to win it back.

◄ **CONSIDER USING LECTURE ENHANCER 14-15**
What Would You Pay for a Mars Rock?

4. *Increasing sales.* Sometimes a firm will lower prices to increase sales. Such a move could hurt profit margins in the short run but will enable the company to become more financially secure in the long run. Then prices could again be raised.

5. *Creating an image.* Certain watches, perfumes, and other socially visible products are priced high to give them an image of exclusivity and status.

6. *Furthering social objectives.* A firm may want to price a product low so that people with less money can afford the product. The government often gets involved in pricing farm products so that everyone can get basic needs such as milk and bread at a low price.

Another objective may be to avoid government investigation and control. Large, powerful firms can't price their products so low that they drive out competitors for fear of government involvement. Wal-Mart, for example, gained much of its market share with a simple motto: "Always the low price. Always." But an Arkansas judge ruled that Wal-Mart's prices for pharmaceuticals were too low and that the chain had illegally engaged in predatory pricing tactics (tactics designed to drive competitors out of business). Although the ruling applied only to Arkansas, all Wal-Mart stores may be more careful in setting such low prices in the future.

Note that a firm may have short-run objectives that differ greatly from its long-run objectives. Both should be understood at the beginning and put into the strategic marketing plan. Pricing objectives should be influenced by other marketing decisions regarding product design, packaging, branding, distribution, and promotion. All of these marketing decisions are interrelated. Recent changes in the economic conditions of the world, especially in Asia, have led to deflation ⇒ P. 61 ⇐ in some countries. Such environmental changes force businesses to constantly adjust prices. The box called From the Pages of *Business Week* goes deeper into this issue.

People believe intuitively that the price charged for a product must bear some relation to the cost of producing the product. In fact, we'd generally agree that prices are usually set somewhere above cost. But as we'll see, prices and cost aren't always related.

••• COST-BASED PRICING •••

Producers often use cost as a primary basis for setting price. They develop elaborate cost accounting systems to measure production costs (including materials, labor, and overhead), add in some margin of profit, and come up with a price. The question is whether the price will be satisfactory to the market as well. In the long run, the market—not the producer—determines what the price will be. Pricing should take into account costs, but it should also include the expected costs of product updates, the objectives for each product, and competitor prices.[21]

Cost-driven pricing has been cited as the reason that the United States lost much of the consumer electronics market. The United States had the technology and the products, but because it used cost-based pricing the price ended up being too high. The Japanese, on the other hand, used price-led costing. That is, the Japanese determined what the

► CONSIDER USING LECTURE ENHANCER 14-16
Rival Chip Makers Challenge Intel

► CONSIDER USING OT ACETATE 14.11
Many Names for Price

Who says the government can't compete with private business? Not the United States Postal Service. It takes on private competition head to head with a comparative ad on prices. What's your priority? it asks. If your priority is price, $3 anywhere is a good deal. What non-price factors may lead someone to use UPS or FedEx instead?

Go figure.

$3
ANYWHERE

What's Your Priority?™

Car Prices Finally Dropping

In the past, the price of new cars seemed to rise every year. But car manufacturers actually cut prices in 1998. The Nissan Altima, for example, was down $1,500, and the Ford Taurus was down $740. What led to this price cut? Overcapacity. Auto manufacturers around the world are building more and more cars, while demand is not growing as rapidly. Thus the competitive pricing. The prices look even better when you inspect the cars and find better engines and other improvements.

There is some talk about prices on other products coming down as companies throughout the world produce more goods than people want or need. Too much money chasing too few goods produces inflation. But too many goods and too little money results in deflation. And deflation may well occur. Prices always seem to be going up, but it is quite possible for prices to go down also. But when that happens, businesses lose money, begin laying off workers, and the economy falls into a recession ➽ P. 61 ➹ or, possibly, a depression ➽ P. 61 ➹.

Meanwhile, however, consumers enjoy the benefits of lower prices. Consumers are also enjoying no-haggle shopping for automobiles in both the new and used car markets.

Source: Kathleen Kirwin, "Detroit Finally Gets It," *Business Week*, August 25, 1997, pp. 38–39.

market was willing to pay (price) and then designed products to fit those prices. Eventually, the Japanese won most of the market. Today, many U.S. producers are as good as the best in the world and have recaptured lost market share from international competitors. However, the recent economic collapse in Asia is leading to huge price discounts from Asian firms.[22] U.S. firms will have to respond to these price cuts, which again points out the importance of the economic environment to all aspects of marketing.

••• VALUE PRICING •••

Value pricing is when marketers provide consumers with brand-name goods and services at fair prices. Manufacturers and service organizations, as you might expect, are finding it hard to maintain profits while offering value pricing to consumers. The only way to offer value prices and not go broke is to redesign products from the bottom up and to cut costs wherever possible. Taco Bell, for example, cut its kitchen space to provide more seating and specifically designed its menu to increase the number of items that took little kitchen space to prepare. Now 70 percent of each Taco Bell restaurant is seating, compared with 30 percent in the past. Some companies are refurbishing old equipment and selling it at attractive prices. Again, the idea is to sell brand-name items at low prices.

value pricing
When marketers provide consumers with brand-name goods and services at fair prices.

••• VALUE PRICING IN THE SERVICE SECTOR •••

Value pricing isn't just for fast-food restaurants and grocery stores. It's rapidly expanding to other parts of the service sector as well. Airlines, for example, are struggling to meet the pricing challenge of low-cost carriers such as Southwest Airlines.

Service industries are adopting many of the same pricing tactics as goods-producing firms. They begin by cutting costs as much as possible. Then they

◄ CONSIDER USING CRITICAL
THINKING EXERCISE 14-2
Break-Even Analysis **(SCANS)**

◄ CONSIDER USING OT ACETATE
14-12
How to use Break-Even Analysis

No matter what the cost of a product may be, a seller can't successfully base the final price on that cost if the market won't accept the price. This street vendor in Bangkok, Thailand, is trying to sell goods for half off because the economy there was doing so poorly in 1998. In the long run, the market will determine the price the vendor gets, not the cost of the goods. Have you noticed a drop in prices lately of goods imported from Asian countries due to market conditions in those countries?

break-even analysis
The process used to determine profitability at various levels of sales.

total fixed costs
All the expenses that remain the same no matter how many products are sold.

determine what services are most important to customers; those that aren't important are cut. For example, some airlines have eliminated meals on their flights. Southwest doesn't incur the administrative costs of assigned seats. In return, customers get good value.

Some of the bigger airlines are trying to cut costs but are stuck with high fixed costs. American Airlines often won't even try to match other airlines' prices. It must offer exceptional service to compete. United Airlines is creating an airline within the airline, called U2, that will offer low fares on shorter routes. New airlines, like Midway Airlines out of Raleigh-Durham, North Carolina, also offer low fares for short-haul flights.

With both goods and services, the idea is to give the consumer value. But trying to give the consumer value while maintaining profits is a challenge. Break-even analysis helps an organization relate sales, profit, and price. We'll explore that concept next.

••• BREAK-EVEN ANALYSIS •••

Before we go into the business of producing Fiber-rific cereal, it may be wise to determine how many boxes of cereal we'd have to sell before making a profit. We'd then determine whether we could reach such a sales goal. **Break-even analysis** is the process used to determine profitability at various levels of sales. The break-even point is the point where revenues from sales equal all costs. The formula for calculating the break-even point is as follows:

$$\text{Break-even point (BEP)} = \frac{\text{Total fixed cost (FC)}}{\text{Price of one unit} - \text{Variable cost (VC) of one unit}}$$

Total fixed costs are all the expenses that remain the same no matter how many products are sold. Among the expenses that make up fixed costs are the amount paid to rent a factory or warehouse and the amount paid for business insurance. **Variable costs** change according to the level of production. Included are the expenses for the materials used in making products and the bonuses paid to employees. For example, imagine that you are a manufacturer selling a sweater for $20 and have a fixed cost of $200,000 (for rent, equipment, and so on). Your variable cost per sweater is $10. The break-even point would be 20,000 sweaters. In other words, you wouldn't make any money selling sweaters unless you sold more than 20,000 of them:

$$\text{BEP} = \frac{\$200,000}{\$20 - \$10} = \frac{\$200,000}{\$10} = 20,000 \text{ sweaters}$$

••• PRICING STRATEGIES •••

Let's say a firm has just developed a new line of products, such as high-definition television (HDTV) sets. The firm has to decide how to price these sets at the introductory stage of the product life cycle. One strategy would be to price them high to recover the costs of developing the sets and to take advantage of the fact that there are few competitors. A **skimming price strategy** is one in which a new product is priced high to make optimum profit while there's little competition. Of course, those large profits will attract competitors. That happened when high-priced HDTVs were introduced in the 1990s.

A second strategy would be to price the new HDTVs low. This would attract more buyers and discourage others companies from making sets because the profit is so low. This strategy enables the firm to penetrate or capture a large share of the market quickly. A **penetration strategy**, therefore, is one in which a product is priced low to attract more customers and discourage competitors. The Japanese successfully used a penetration strategy with videocassette recorders. No U.S. firm could compete with the low prices the Japanese offered. Additional pricing strategies are listed in the accompanying chart.

Ultimately, price is determined by supply and demand in the marketplace, as described in Chapter 2. For example, if we charge $3 for our cereal and nobody

One way producers are able to keep prices low is to downsize the product. Usually customers can't tell the difference, and the producer is able to keep prices low and still make a good profit. What are the ethical implications of such practices?

ADDITIONAL PRICING TACTICS

It's impossible to cover all pricing tactics in detail in this book, but you should at least be familiar with the following terms:

1. *Adaptive pricing* allows an organization to vary its prices based on factors such as competition, market conditions, and resource costs. Rather than relying on one set price, the firm adjusts the price to fit different situations.

2. *Cost-oriented pricing* is the "strategy of setting prices primarily on the basis of cost." For example, retailers often use cost plus a certain markup, while producers use a system of cost-plus pricing.

3. *Customary pricing* means that most sellers will adapt the product to some established, universally accepted price such as the price for gum or candy bars. Notice that when the price goes up, almost all producers adjust their price upward.

4. *Product-line pricing* is the procedure used to set prices for a group of products that are similar but aimed at different market segments. For example, a beer producer might have a low-priced beer, a popular-priced beer, and a premium-priced beer.

5. *Target pricing* means that an organization will set some goal such as a certain share of the market or a certain return on investment as a basis for setting a price. Usually, market conditions prevent a firm from establishing prices this way, but such goals do give some direction to pricing policies.

6. *Uniform pricing*, also known as *single-price policy*, means that all customers buying the product (given similar circumstances) pay the same price. Although it's the most common policy in the United States, uniform pricing is unusual in many foreign markets, especially among private sellers.

7. *Odd pricing* or *psychological pricing* means pricing an item a few cents under a round price ($9.98 instead of $10) to make the product appear less expensive.

8. *Price lining* is the practice of offering goods at a few set prices such as $30, $40, and $50. Such a tactic makes both pricing and checkout easier, and it appeals to a market segment interested in that level of pricing.

variable costs
Costs that change according to the level of production.

skimming price strategy
Strategy in which a new product is priced high to make optimum profit while there's little competition.

penetration strategy
Strategy in which a product is priced low to attract many customers and discourage competition.

➤ **CONSIDER USING SUPPLEMEN- TAL CASE 14-2**
Avoid Pricing Mistakes (**SCANS**)

➤ **CONSIDER USING LECTURE ENHANCER 14-17**
What Would You Pay for a Harley?

price leadership
The procedure by which all competitors in an industry follow the pricing practices of one or more dominant firms.

Buy enough Pepsi or Mountain Dew and you can get "stuff" like sports bags and watches. Campaigns of this type are designed to build loyal customers who will demand only those brands so they can pile up points. Consumers can obtain a catalog of such "stuff" from Pepsi. Check out the deal at http://www.pepsi.com

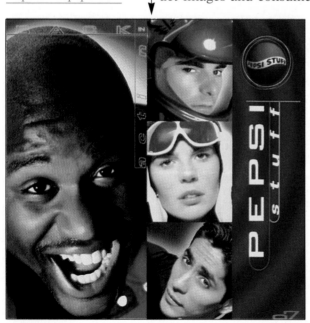

buys it at that price, we'll have to lower the price until we reach a price that's acceptable to customers and to us. The price that results from the interaction of buyers and sellers in the marketplace is called the market price.

Recognizing the fact that different consumers may be willing to pay different prices, marketers sometimes price on the basis of consumer demand rather than cost or some other calculation. That's called *demand-oriented pricing* and is reflected by movie theaters with low rates for children and by drugstores with discounts for senior citizens. The Washington Opera Company in Washington, D.C., for example, raised its prices on prime seating and lowered its pricing on less attractive seating; this strategy raised the company's revenues by 9 percent.[23]

Besides supply and demand forces, another factor in the marketplace is competition. **Price leadership** is the procedure by which all competitors in an industry follow the pricing practices of one or more dominant firms. You may have noticed that practice among oil and cigarette companies. Competition-oriented pricing is a strategy based on what all the other competitors are doing. The price can be at, above, or below competitors' prices. Pricing depends on customer loyalty, perceived differences, and the competitive climate.

Marketers will face a new pricing problem in the next few years. Customers can now compare prices of many goods and services on the Internet. For example, you may want to check out Compare Net at http://www.compare.net for prices on items such as VCRs and minivans. Price competition is likely to heat up as consumers have more access to price information from all around the world. In that case, nonprice competition is likely to increase. We discuss that strategy next.

··· NONPRICE COMPETITION ···

In spite of the emphasis placed on price in microeconomic theory, marketers often compete on product attributes other than price. You may have noted that price differences between products such as gasoline, men's haircuts, candy bars, and even major products such as compact cars and private colleges are often small, if there's any difference at all. Typically, you will not see price used as a major promotional appeal on television. Instead, marketers tend to stress product images and consumer benefits such as comfort, style, convenience, and durability.

Many smaller organizations promote the services that accompany basic products rather than price in order to compete with bigger firms. The idea is to make a relatively homogeneous product "better" by offering more service. Danny O'Neill, for example, is a small wholesaler who sells gourmet coffee to upscale restaurants. He has to watch competitor prices and see what services they offer so that he can charge the premium prices he wants. To charge high prices, he has to offer superior service.

Larger companies often do the same thing. For example, some airlines stress friendliness, promptness, more flights, better meals, and other such services. Higher priced hotels stress "no surprises," cable TV, business services, health clubs, and other extras.

Often marketers emphasize nonprice differences because prices are so easy to match. On the other hand, few competitors can match the image of a friendly, responsive, consumer-oriented company. The following are some other strategies for avoiding price wars:

1. *Add value.* Some drugstores with elderly customers add value by offering home delivery. Training videos add value to any product that's difficult to use. Toro gives lawn parties during which it teaches customers lawn care strategies.

2. *Educate consumers.* Home Depot teaches its customers how to use the equipment it sells and how to build decks and other do-it-yourself projects. The Iowa Beef Processors educate their customers about the value of buying top-grade beef, which has less waste.

3. *Establish relationships.* Customers will pay a little more for products and services when they have a friendly relationship with the seller. Today some auto dealers, like Saturn, may send out cards reminding people when service is needed. They may also have picnics and other special events for customers. Airlines, supermarkets, hotels, and car rental agencies have frequent buyer clubs that offer all kinds of fringe benefits to frequent users. The services aren't less expensive, but they offer more value.

As you can see, this chapter begins and ends with one theme: Give customers value and they'll give you their loyalty.[24]

◄ CONSIDER USING SUPPLEMEN-
TAL CASE 14-3
Pricing and Packaging the Harley Image
(SCANS)

Progress Check

- Can you list two short-term and two long-term pricing objectives? Are the two compatible?
- What's wrong with using a cost-based pricing strategy?
- What's the purpose of break-even analysis?
- Can you calculate a product's break-even point if producing it costs $10,000 and revenue from the sale of one unit is $20?

SUMMARY
· · · · · ·

1. Product development means developing a value package for each product and developing a product mix that will appeal to a variety of consumers.
   - ***What's the difference between a product and a value package?***
   A product is any physical good, service, or idea that satisfies a want or need. A value package is much more than a physical object. A value package consists of everything that consumers evaluate when deciding whether to buy something. A value package includes price, brand name, satisfaction in use, and more.
   - ***What's the difference between a product line and a product mix?***
   A product line is a group of physically similar products. (A product line of gum may include chewing gum, sugarless gum, etc.) A product mix is a company's combination of product lines. (A manufacturer may offer lines of gum, candy bars, chewing tobacco, etc.)

1. Explain the difference between a product and a value package.

2. Product differentiation is what makes one product appear better than the competition in both consumer and industrial markets.
   - ***How do marketers create product differentiation for their goods and services?***
   Marketers use a mix of pricing, advertising, and packaging to make their products seem unique and attractive.

2. Describe how businesses create product differentiation for their goods and services in both consumer and industrial markets.

- ***What are the four classifications of consumer goods and services, and how are they marketed?***
There are convenience goods and services (requiring minimum shopping effort), shopping goods and services (for which people compare price and quality), specialty goods and services (which consumers go out of their way to get), and unsought goods and services (which consumers did not intend to buy when they entered the store). Convenience goods and services are best promoted by location, shopping goods and services by some price/quality appeal, and specialty goods and services by word of mouth. Unsought goods are often displayed at the checkout counter where consumers see them while waiting in line and are attracted to buy them.
- ***What are industrial goods and how are they marketed differently from consumer goods?***
Industrial goods are products used in the production of other products. They're sold largely through salespeople and rely less on advertising.

3. List and describe the six functions of packaging.

3. Packaging changes the product and is becoming increasingly important, taking over much of the sales function for consumer goods.
- ***What are the six functions of packaging?***
The six functions are (1) to attract the buyer's attention; (2) to describe the contents; (3) to explain the benefits of the product inside; (4) to provide information on warranties, warnings, and other consumer matters; (5) to indicate price, value, and uses; and (6) to protect the goods inside, stand up under handling and storage, be tamperproof, and yet be easy to open and use.

4. Give examples of a brand, a brand name, and a trademark, and explain how to prevent a brand name from becoming generic.

4. Branding also changes a product.
- ***Can you give examples of a brand, a brand name, and a trademark?***
There are endless examples. One example of a brand name of crackers is Waverly by Nabisco. The brand consists of the name Waverly as well as the symbol (a red triangle in the corner with Nabisco circled in white). The brand name and the symbol are also trademarks, since Nabisco has been given legal protection for this brand.

5. Explain the role of product managers and the five steps of the new-product development process.

5. Product managers are like presidents of one-product firms.
- ***What are the functions of a product manager?***
Product managers coordinate product, price, place, and promotion decisions for a particular product. In many companies the product manager's role is gradually losing its importance as consumer brand loyalty decreases.
- ***What are the five steps of the product development process?***
The steps are (1) generation of new-product ideas, (2) screening and analysis, (3) development, (4) testing, and (5) commercialization.

6. Identify and describe the stages of the product life cycle and describe marketing strategies at each stage.

6. Once a product is placed on the market, marketing strategy varies as the product goes through various stages of acceptance called the product life cycle.
- ***How do marketing strategies theoretically change at the various stages?***
See Figures 14.7, 14.8, and 14.9.
- ***What are the stages of the product life cycle?***
They are introduction, growth, maturity, and decline.

7. Give examples of various pricing objectives and show how break-even analysis helps in pricing decisions.

7. Pricing is one of the four Ps of marketing.
- ***What are pricing objectives?***
Objectives include achieving a target profit, building traffic, increasing market share, increasing sales, creating an image, and meeting social goals.

- *What's the break-even point?*

At the break-even point, total cost equals total revenue. Sales beyond that point are profitable.

- *What strategies can marketers use to determine a product's price?*

A skimming price strategy is one in which the product is priced high to make optimum profit while there's little competition, whereas a penetration strategy is one in which a product is priced low to attract more customers and discourage competitors. Demand-oriented pricing is based on consumer demand rather than cost. Competition-oriented pricing is based on all competitors' prices. Price leadership occurs when all competitors follow the pricing practice of one or more dominant companies. Please review the box on p. 431 to be sure you understand all the terms used for other pricing tactics.

KEY TERMS

brand 417
brand association 419
brand awareness 418
brand equity 418
brand loyalty 418
break-even analysis 430
concept testing 422
convenience goods and services 412
dealer (private) brands 418
generic goods 418
generic name 418
industrial goods 414

knockoff brands 418
manufacturers' brand names 418
penetration strategy 431
price leadership 432
product differentiation 411
product life cycle 424
product line 410
product manager 420
product mix 411
product screening 422

shopping goods and services 413
skimming price strategy 431
specialty goods and services 413
total fixed costs 430
trademark 417
unsought goods and services 413
value package 408
value pricing 429
variable costs 430

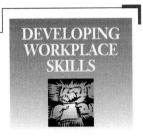

DEVELOPING WORKPLACE SKILLS

1. Look around your classroom and notice the different types of shoes that students are wearing. What product qualities were they looking for when they chose those shoes? What was the importance of price, style, brand name, and color? Describe the product offerings you would feature in a new shoe store designed to appeal to college students.

2. A product offer consists of everything that consumers evaluate when choosing among products, including price, package, service, reputation, and so on. Compose a list of as many factors that consumers might consider when evaluating the following products: a vacation resort, a college, and a new car.

3. Discuss how the faculty at your college could increase student satisfaction by working more closely with students in developing new products (courses) and changing existing products (courses). Would it be a good idea for all marketers to work with their customers that way? Prepare a three-to five-minute presentation explaining your answer.

4. Go to your medicine cabinet and take an inventory of all the branded and nonbranded items. Then discuss with your classmates the brand names they buy for the same goods. Do most students buy brand-name goods or generic goods? Why?

5. Determine where in the product life cycle you would place each of the following products and then prepare a marketing strategy for each product based on the recommendations in this chapter:

   a. Alka Seltzer.

   b. Cellular phones.

   c. Electric automobiles.

   d. Campbell's chicken noodle soup.

TAKING IT TO THE NET

Purpose

To assess how the Internet can be used to differentiate products and build brand equity.

Exercise

Joe Boxer wants to know if you're wearing clean underwear today. The Web seems to be a natural medium for the wacky underwear manufacturer. "It's fun, it's outrageous," observed Nicholas Gramah, chief underpants officer (CUO—aka Joe Boxer). In 1995, the company launched the "world's first interactive electronic outdoor billboard" in Times Square. The 6,000-square-foot billboard has a 100-foot-long electronic message strip, called The Zipper, which allows selected consumers from all around the world to "talk" to New York from their living rooms, laptops, and PCs via e-mail or Joe Boxer's World Wide Web site (http://www.joeboxer.com).

1. How does the Web site reinforce the Joe Boxer brand name and image? Give examples that support your answer.

2. Fruit of the Loom is one of Joe Boxer's competitors. Visit the Fruit of the Loom Web Site (http://www.fruit.com). Compare Fruit of the Loom's brand image with Joe Boxer's. Do you think they are targeting the same market? Defend your answer.

3. Where is Joe Boxer in the product life cycle? Suggest ways that Joe Boxer could extend its product life cycle.

Practicing Management Decisions

CASE
• • • • • •
EVERYDAY LOW PRICING (EDLP)
• • • • • •

Wal-Mart, Kmart, and wholesale clubs such as Price Club have had great success with a concept they call everyday low pricing (EDLP). Rather than have relatively high prices and then barrage consumers with coupons and price discounts, such stores promote the fact that they offer lower prices every day. Similarly, some manufacturers are offering everyday low purchase prices. Instead of having a relatively high price for products sold to retailers, manufacturers such as Procter & Gamble have everyday low purchase prices. It's the same concept as EDLP applied to retailers instead of consumers.

Many retailers have decided to follow the lead of Wal-Mart and others by cutting prices on all their goods. But recent research shows that this isn't always wise. Dominick's Finer Foods, with 28 percent of the Chicago-area food business, tried an EDLP policy and boosted sales by 3 percent. On the other hand, profits declined by 18 percent. It has been calculated, in fact, that supermarket volume would have to increase by 39 percent for supermarkets to avoid losing money after a 7 percent price drop. Consumers say location is usually their most important factor in choosing a supermarket. Thus, supermarkets shouldn't have to have the lowest prices to keep market share.

Usually sales volume falls after the introduction of everyday low prices, but it picks up later. That is true in Europe as well as in the United States.

In spite of the potential drawbacks of every-day low pricing, 7-Eleven implemented it in 250 stores in the Dallas–Fort Worth area. This pricing policy was just one part of an overall revamping of 7-Eleven's image, including updated interiors, fresh produce, and gourmet items. In fact, 7-Eleven no longer wants its former image of a high-priced convenience store, but seeks to appear as a small yet viable alternative to supermarkets.

Decision Questions

1. As a consumer, would you prefer that your local supermarket offer everyday low prices, offer some products at major discounts (half off) periodically, or offer some combination of the two?

2. What could your local supermarket do other than offer low prices or price discounts to win your business (delight you) and still maintain a high profit margin?

3. What advantages and disadvantages do you see for manufacturers to offer everyday low purchase prices to retailers?

4. Are manufacturers and retailers pushing price so much that they're in danger of lowering profits? Why is price competition so common?

Source: "Everyday Low Profits," *Harvard Business Review*, March–April 1994, p. 13; and Dagmar Mussey, "Heat's On Value Pricing," *Advertising Age International*, January 1997, p. 21.

When introducing a new product, a company has two major pricing options. One is to introduce the product at a high price to recapture the cost of researching and developing the product. However, such a strategy invites competition, and is called a skimming strategy. The other strategy is to introduce the product at a low price to discourage competition and draw in addition customers. It is called a penetration strategy because the idea is to capture as large a market share as possible. That is the strategy used by Taco Bell when it priced its products at 59, 79, and 99 cents. It was a successful strategy for them, but not the best strategy for everyone.

Radio Shack asks two key questions when pricing: (1) How much can I charge and still make the sale? (2) Do I want the business at that price? Radio Shack chooses the price range it feels best for its customers. Rather than stock a wide variety of products, Radio Shack chooses a limited number of goods that fit the price range most desired. Customer service and satisfaction are important to its customers. Radio Shack believes that it offers a unique value to customers, making them a little less price sensitive.

Unique value is one of eight factors that determine customers' price sensitivity (the importance that they put on price versus other factors). The other seven are:

1. *Comparison difficulty.* If it is hard to compare the price of one product to others, consumers tend to be less price sensitive.

VIDEO CASE

• • • • • •

HOW MUCH IS THAT DOGGIE ON WINDOWS 98?

For example, consumers often have no idea what the fair charge is for certain medical procedures, so they are less sensitive than they would be if they had more knowledge.

2. *Shared cost.* When business travelers pay a lot of money to fly, other consumers can pay less because the business traveler covers the majority of costs for the airlines.

3. *Awareness of substitutes.* If consumers are not aware of substitutes, they are less price sensitive. For example, if they think that only one airline flies to where they are going, they accept the price because they see few flying alternatives.

4. *Size of total expenditure.* If the price of an item is high (say a Mercedes-Benz car), then consumers tend to be more price sensitive. Mercedes lowers that sensitivity sometimes by offering monthly payments that don't seem so high.

5. *Price-quality factor.* If the perceived quality of a good is very high, consumers may be less concerned about the price. That is the case with Preference by L'Oreal. By stressing the high quality of the product and the fact that "You are worth it," the company lowers price sensitivity.

In business-to-business marketing, the next two pricing factors are key:

6. *Size of total expenditure.* If a company has already spent lots of money on a product (say a computer system), the company is less likely to change systems because the switching cost would be too high. The costs would include the equipment plus training.

7. *The significance of the end event.* This is a fancy way of saying that the cost of an item is important if that item is a major part of what you buy. For example, a company that makes T-shirts would be sensitive to the price of cotton because it is a major cost of production.

The eight factors that affect price sensitivity only touch the surface of the complexities involved in pricing goods and services. Competitive price changes force companies to reevaluate their prices continuously. So do changes in the overall economy and changes in consumer preferences. Because price competition is so difficult, many firms turn to nonprice competition and compete on factors such as service, speed, and friendliness.

Discussion Questions

1. How would you expect Taco Bell to react if the price of a major ingredient, such as beef or tomato paste, were to rise suddenly?

2. How do you minimize the cost of travel to other cities? What pricing or nonpricing strategy might attract you to using some other means of travel?

3. What products do you buy because of superior quality versus price? Would you continue buying that product if the price were even higher?

4. Business travelers often pay as much as $1,200 for a trip that the person sitting next to them paid only $350. The reason they pay more is because they don't stay over the weekend and must pay the higher rate. Is such a pricing system fair? Can you see an airline capturing the business market by using a different pricing strategy? What would that strategy be?

Distributing Products Efficiently and Competitively

Chapter

15

LEARNING GOALS

*After you have read and studied this chapter,
you should be able to*

1 Explain the value of marketing intermediaries.

2 Give examples of how intermediaries perform the six utilities.

3 Discuss how a manufacturer can get wholesalers and retailers in a channel system to cooperate by the formation of systems.

4 Describe in detail what's involved in physical distribution management.

5 Describe the various wholesale organizations in the distribution system.

6 List and explain the ways that retailers compete.

7 Explain the various kinds of nonstore retailing.

The Pacific Coast Feather Company in Seattle, Washington, makes feather beds, feather pillows, and comforters. Sounds like a rather simple company, right? Wrong. President Roy Clothier puts it this way: "We manufacture 2,500 unique products, using 12,000 raw materials, in a make-to-order environment with average turnaround times of three to five days. We have been required to ship pillows to 40,000 different addresses within 24 hours of receiving the order (often to motels, hotels, and other volume purchasers), all the while growing the business at a 20 percent annual rate and building a new plant a year for the past four years." Whew!

There is no way that Pacific Feather could have handled all of those orders without a sophisticated system of supply and distribution that enabled the company to react quickly to customer requests. Such a system began with an enterprise resource planning system ⟫ P. 266 ⟪ that organized the everyday tasks of entering orders, tracking product shipments, scheduling production, and updating sales forecasts and balance sheets.

Once products are made, however, a whole new system kicks in to get those products to customers quickly and efficiently. Tony Friscia, founder of a leading market analysis firm, says, "It is no longer enough to be able to make your products the way that the customer desires. You also have to get it to consumers in the quantities, features, options, sizes,

PROFILE

Roy Clothier of Pacific Coast Feather Company

colors, and mix they want, where and when they want it, while also maintaining an adequate profit margin in the face of ever-increasing competition." Whew, again!

It is clear today that only firms with a superior supply-chain management system will be able to compete in the 21st century.

Companies in different industries must learn to work together to form a seamless flow of materials from the raw material source (e.g., mines) to the ultimate consumers. The firms involved are in mining, manufacturing, wholesaling, retailing, and logistics. To manage such flows requires network resource planning (NRP), which is the networking of multiple systems to allow firms to work together as a single entity to ensure superior customer service.

One can't help but be amazed at the rapid change that has taken place in the field of logistics (moving goods from place to place and storing them when needed). You can now order a product and receive it the next day—or even the same day if you pay more. Such service was unheard of just a few years ago. New technology is revolutionizing the way we buy and sell things and how those things are delivered. This chapter will discuss all of these changes and more.

Sources: Jerry Bowles, "Building a World-Class Supply Chain," a special advertising section in *Fortune*, July 7, 1997, pp. 151ff; and Debra Phillips, "Rush Hour," *Entrepreneur*, February 1998, pp. 114–18.

THE ROLE OF DISTRIBUTION IN BUSINESS

◄ CONSIDER USING TM 109
Chapter Outline

◄ LEARNING GOAL 1
Explain the value of marketing intermediaries.

Thus far, we've looked at two of the four Ps of the marketing mix: product and price. In this chapter, we'll look at the third of the four Ps: place. Products have to be physically moved from where they're produced to a convenient place where consumer and industrial buyers can see and purchase them. **Physical distribution (logistics)** is the movement of goods from producers to industrial and consumer users. It involves functions such as transportation and storage, and activities such as purchasing goods, receiving them, moving them

physical distribution (logistics)
The movement of goods from producers to industrial and consumer users.

This message from Business Express, a British trucking company, recognizes that companies can design the best products and price them attractively and still lose customers if they are unable to deliver the products when the buyer needs them. Usually that means now or sooner. Most manufacturers don't have the facilities to deliver goods overnight or in a couple of days. Instead, they outsource the delivery function to someone else. Business-to-business ads attract them to such experts.

marketing intermediaries
Organizations that assist in moving goods and services from producers to industrial and consumer users.

channel of distribution
Marketing intermediaries, such as wholesalers and retailers, who join together to transport and store goods in their path from producers to consumers.

wholesaler
A marketing intermediary that sells to other organizations.

retailer
An organization that sells to ultimate consumers.

supply-chain management (SCM)
The overall process of minimizing inventory and moving goods through the channel by using computers and other technology.

through the plant, taking inventory of them, storing them, and shipping them to final users (including all the warehousing, reshipping, and physical movements involved).[1]

How efficiently those tasks are performed often makes the difference between success and failure of the whole system.[2] For example, the ultimate success or failure of the emerging capitalist system in the former Soviet Union will depend to a considerable degree on whether Russia and the newly independent states can build effective logistics systems. Such a system is made up of a series of organizations called marketing intermediaries (or middlemen).

Marketing intermediaries are organizations that assist in moving goods and services from producers to industrial and consumer users. They're called intermediaries because they're organizations in the middle of a whole series of organizations that join together to help distribute goods from producers to consumers. You can see, therefore, why a set of these organizations as a group is known as a channel of distribution. A **channel of distribution** consists of marketing intermediaries, such as wholesalers and retailers, who join together to transport and store goods in their path (or channel) from producers to consumers. A **wholesaler** is a marketing intermediary that sells to other organizations, such as retailers and hospitals. A **retailer** is an organization that sells to ultimate consumers. Figure 15.1 pictures channels of distribution for both consumer and industrial goods.

Channels of distribution ensure communication flows and the flow of money and title to goods. They also help ensure that the right quantity and assortment of goods will be available when and where needed.

Few people are aware of how many different wholesale institutions there are, and the careers available in them. Therefore, competition for jobs in physical distribution often isn't as stiff as it is in other areas of business. There are many career opportunities in logistics, and the number of students majoring in that area is lower than the number who will be needed as more and more firms move into international distribution. We'll discuss careers in more detail later. Meanwhile, you should know that the total U.S. logistics bill is $600 to $700 billion per year. Logistics costs are about 10 percent of the total gross domestic product in the United States.[3] Imagine the bill for companies throughout the world. Imagine the opportunities for companies that can lower those costs!

••• FROM LOGISTICS TO SUPPLY-CHAIN MANAGEMENT •••

The management of global distribution flows from the mine, the farm, and other raw materials suppliers to the ultimate consumer has changed so dramatically that a new term has evolved to describe the process: supply-chain management. **Supply-chain management (SCM)** is the overall process of minimizing inventory and moving goods through the channel by using computers and other technology. The goal of SCM is to improve the flow of goods and information among the channel members.[4] The whole system is often called the *value chain* because the value created by its efficiency is so great.

In the past, most firms in the channel of distribution were forced to carry high levels of inventory to ensure that goods were available when needed. Much lower levels of inventory can now be carried because firms now have better communication links with their suppliers, who can thus respond more quickly. **Quick response** is the term used to describe the efforts by producers and suppliers to send goods to retailers and to each other as quickly as possible. One way to minimize response time is to link retailers with suppliers and producers by computer so that suppliers and producers can send replacement stock quickly when something is needed. Computerized checkout machines read the bar codes on goods that are sold and send that information to suppliers instantly so that replacement goods can be sent at just the right time.

quick response
The efforts by producers and suppliers to send goods to retailers and to each other as quickly as possible.

◄ **CONSIDER USING TM 110**
Channels of Distribution for Industrial and Consumer Goods and Services (Figure 15.1 on text page 443)

••• ELECTRONIC DATA INTERCHANGE AND ••• EFFICIENT CONSUMER RESPONSE

Electronic data interchange (EDI) enables producers', wholesalers', and retailers' computers to "talk" with each other. EDI makes it possible for a retailer to be directly linked with a supplier. As a result, the supplier knows when retail sales have been made and can ship new goods accordingly. EDI thus becomes a critical part of an effective supply-chain management system. Target and Ace Hardware were two of the first retailers to use EDI on a global basis. Many retailers are now following suit and are tracking shipments from Asia and other countries minute by minute so that the transportation time is minimized. The next step is to integrate information about where products are at any given moment directly into order-entry, credit, and collections systems. Thus, shippers are assisting their customers by providing helpful information as well as moving goods efficiently.[5]

electronic data interchange (EDI)
Technology that enables producers', wholesalers', and retailers' computers to "talk" with each other.

FIGURE **15.1**
· · · ·
CHANNELS OF DISTRIBUTION FOR INDUSTRIAL AND CONSUMER GOODS AND SERVICES

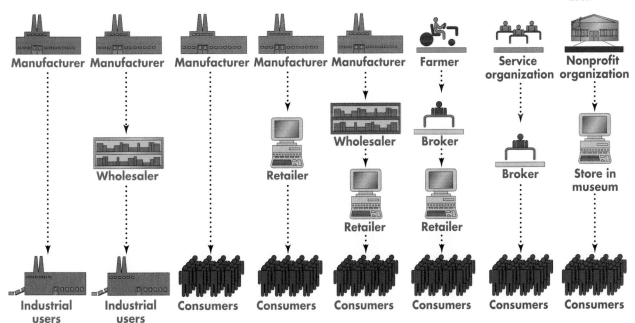

Channels for industrial goods

This is the common channel for industrial products such as glass, tires, and paint for automobiles.

This is the way that lower-cost items such as supplies are distributed. The wholesaler is called an industrial distributor.

This channel is used by craftspeople and small farmers.

This channel is used for cars, furniture, and clothing.

Channels for consumer goods

This channel is the most common channel for consumer goods such as groceries, drugs, and cosmetics.

This is a common channel for food items such as produce.

This is a common channel for consumer services such as real estate, stocks and bonds, insurance, and nonprofit theater groups.

This is a common channel for nonprofit organizations that want to raise funds. Included are museums, government services, and zoos.

Manufacturer	Manufacturer	Manufacturer	Manufacturer	Manufacturer	Farmer	Service organization	Nonprofit organization
	Wholesaler		Retailer	Wholesaler	Broker	Broker	Store in museum
				Retailer	Retailer		
Industrial users	Industrial users	Consumers	Consumers	Consumers	Consumers	Consumers	Consumers

In this computerized warehouse, few people are needed to move goods from place to place. Electronic data interchange equipment makes it possible to read the bar codes on packages and send them quickly on their way. What will the impact of such technology have on warehouse workers and other blue-collar workers?

➤ **CONSIDER USING OT ACETATE 15-1**
How Middlemen Create Efficiency

➤ **CONSIDER USING OT ACETATE 15-2**
Steps Involved in Supply-Chain Management

efficient consumer response (ECR)
The electronic linking of firms to provide more efficient response to consumer needs.

➤ **CONSIDER USING LECTURE ENHANCER 15-1**
Campbell Soup Succeeds with EDI

➤ **CONSIDER USING OT ACETATE 15-3**
Five Steps in Creating Customer Relationships

➤ **CONSIDER USING LECTURE ENHANCER 15-2**
Cutting Costs, Not Quality, to Offer a Better Service

Companies such as Procter & Gamble, Xerox, 3M, Nabisco, and Black & Decker have cut inventory and improved service using supply-chain management. These companies implement the system by working together on forecasting, distribution, and marketing. Data are shared among firms so that the whole system can be operated as a unit and so that globally competitive products can be sent through the system as fast as possible. New EDI computer software makes all this possible. Such high-quality service and management are demanded in the highly competitive global economy.[6] The higher the level of trust becomes among the companies involved, the more efficient the system becomes.[7]

Efficient consumer response (ECR) is the term used in the grocery industry to describe the linking of firms to provide more efficient response to consumer needs. Total cost reductions using supply-chain management have been 30 percent or more. Similar reductions in inventory have also been achieved. Bergin Brunswig, a major distributor of pharmaceuticals and health care products, has cut the time between order placement and product delivery to just 12 hours. With such quick response time, a supermarket can carry much less inventory than ever before and still never run out of a product.[8] The effect of such systems has been to eliminate some intermediaries because the manufacturer is now performing certain distribution functions.

The next section will discuss why marketing needed intermediaries in the first place. Before you go on, however, read the box called Making Ethical Decisions to review a major issue in retailing today.

··· WHY MARKETING NEEDS INTERMEDIARIES ···

Manufacturers don't always need marketing intermediaries to sell their goods to consumer and industrial markets. Recall that Figure 15.1 shows that some manufacturers sell directly to buyers. So why have marketing intermediaries at all? The answer is that intermediaries perform certain marketing tasks such as transporting, storing, selling, and advertising more effectively and efficiently than most manufacturers could. A simple analogy is this: You could deliver packages in person to people anywhere in the world, but usually you don't. Why not? Because it's usually cheaper and faster to have them delivered by the post office or some private agency such as UPS or Emery.

http://www.coams.com/outlook/slot1.htm

Pay Up or What?

Marketers of new grocery products are finding it difficult to get shelf space in supermarkets. Grocery chains are demanding incentive money to place new goods on already-crowded shelves. This money is known as a slotting allowance. Stores claim that slotting allowances are needed to add the product to the computer system, to warehouse the goods, and to promote the new products. The fees are getting higher and higher as new products enter the market. Smaller producers may eventually be forced to drop new-product introductions because of these fees for shelf space.

Imagine that you're a large producer of grocery products and can easily afford such fees. Would you pay them without protest knowing that, in the long run, they'll benefit you by restricting competition? Since this is a common practice, do you feel that such payments are ethical? If you have trouble with the ethics of such payments, whom should you blame: the supermarkets or the businesses that pay supermarkets fees for shelf space?

Similarly, you could sell your home by yourself or buy stock directly from other people, but most people don't. Why? Again, because there are specialists (brokers) who make the process more efficient and easier. **Brokers** are marketing intermediaries who bring buyers and sellers together and assist in negotiating an exchange, but don't take title to (own) the goods. Usually, they don't carry inventory, provide credit, or assume risk. Examples include insurance brokers, real estate brokers, and stock brokers. In California, brokers help in the gathering and sale of produce, and in the airline industry brokers consolidate airline seats and sell them for a discount. You may want to explore brokerage in more detail. If so, you might want to take a course or read a text on logistics.

◄ SCANS

brokers
Marketing intermediaries who bring buyers and sellers together and assist in negotiating an exchange but don't own the goods.

••• HOW INTERMEDIARIES CREATE •••
EXCHANGE EFFICIENCY

The benefits of marketing intermediaries can be illustrated rather easily. Suppose that five manufacturers of various food products each tried to sell directly to five retailers. The number of exchange relationships that would have to be established is 5 times 5, or 25. But picture what happens when a wholesaler enters the system. The five manufacturers would contact one wholesaler to establish five exchange relationships. The wholesaler would have to establish contact with the five retailers. That would mean another five exchange relationships. Note that the number of exchanges is reduced from 25 to only 10 by the addition of a wholesaler. Figure 15.2 on page 446 shows this process.

In the past, intermediaries conducted exchanges not only more efficiently than manufacturers or retailers but more effectively as well. This meant that intermediaries were often better at performing their functions than a manufacturer or retailer could be. Recently, however, technology has made it possible for manufacturers to reach consumers much more efficiently than in the past. For example, some manufacturers reach consumers directly on the Internet. Companies such as Dell Computer are famous for their direct-selling capability. They then outsource their delivery function to a marketing intermediary (a logistics firm). Note, however, that there is no wholesaler in the middle and no need for local storage facilities.

Marketing intermediaries provide invaluable assistance to manufacturers and other marketers. This Spanish version of a UPS ad stresses the importance of time to such companies. If you want your package delivered before 8 AM, UPS will do it. For a little less money, they will guarantee delivery by 10:30 AM What other marketing intermediaries might a manufacturer use?

FIGURE 15.2
••••

HOW MIDDLEMEN CREATE EXCHANGE EFFICIENCY

This figure shows that adding a wholesaler to the channel of distribution cuts the number of contacts from 25 to 10. This makes distribution more efficient.

Similarly, retailers are now so closely linked with manufacturers that they can get delivery as often as once or twice a day. Again, that means that there is often no need for a wholesaler to perform functions such as storage and delivery. Does that mean that wholesalers are obsolete? The answer is *not yet,* but wholesalers need to change their functions to remain viable in today's rapidly changing distribution systems.[9] In the next section, we shall explore the value that intermediaries can provide.

••• THE VALUE CREATED BY ••• INTERMEDIARIES

Marketing intermediaries have always been viewed by the public with some suspicion. Some surveys have shown that about half the cost of the things we buy are marketing costs that go largely to pay for the work of intermediaries. People reason that if we could only get rid of intermediaries, we could greatly reduce the cost of everything we buy. Sounds good, but is the solution really that simple?

Let's take as an example a box of Fiberrific cereal that sells for $4. How could we, as consumers, get the cereal for less? Well, we could all drive to Michigan where some of the cereal is

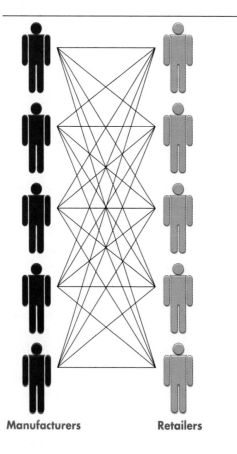

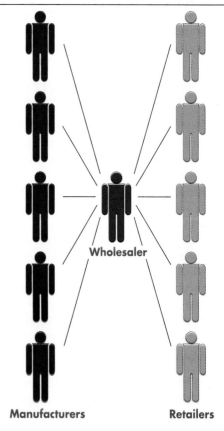

Manufacturers　　**Retailers**　　**Manufacturers**　　**Retailers**

Wholesaler

One of the hottest trends in the restaurant industry today is for top-flight chefs such as Emeril Legasse of New Orleans (and TVFN) and Charlie Trotter of Chicago to establish exclusive relationships with smaller farmers who grow or produce products that meet the precise specifications the chefs and their customers demand, thus bypassing the traditional wholesaler. What could traditional wholesalers do to recapture such customers?

produced and save some shipping costs. But would that be practical? Can you imagine millions of people getting in their cars and driving to Michigan just to buy some cereal? No, it doesn't make sense. It's much cheaper to have intermediaries bring the cereal to major cities. That might involve transportation and warehousing by wholesalers. These steps add cost, don't they? Yes, but they add value as well, the value of not having to drive to Michigan.

The cereal is now in a warehouse somewhere on the outskirts of the city. We could all drive down to the wholesaler and pick it up. But that isn't really the most economical way to buy cereal. If we figure in the cost of gas and time, the cereal would be rather expensive. Instead, we prefer to have someone move the cereal from the warehouse to a truck, drive it to the corner supermarket, unload it, unpack it, stamp it with a price, put it on the shelf, and wait for us to come in to buy it. To make it even more convenient, the supermarket may stay open for 24 hours a day, seven days a week. Think of the costs. But think also of the value! For $4, we can get a box of cereal when we want it, with little effort on our part.

If we were to get rid of the retailer, we could buy a box of cereal for a little less, but we'd have to drive farther and spend time in the warehouse looking through rows of cereals. If we got rid of the wholesaler, we could save a little more money, not counting our drive to Michigan. But a few cents here and a few cents there add up—to the point where marketing may add up to 75 cents for every 25 cents in manufacturing costs. Figure 15.3 shows where your money goes in the distribution process. Notice that the largest percentage goes to people who drive trucks and work in wholesale and retail organizations. Only 3.5 cents goes to profit. Figure 15.4 shows the share of distribution costs that go to various intermediaries. Note that the percentages vary greatly among products. Here are three basic points about intermediaries:

- Marketing intermediaries can be eliminated, but their activities can't; that is, you can eliminate some wholesalers and retailers, but then consumers or someone else would have to perform the retailer's tasks, including transporting and storing goods, finding suppliers, and establishing communication with suppliers. Today, many of those functions are being performed on the World Wide Web (the Internet), and intermediaries *are* being eliminated. The term for eliminating intermediaries is *disintermediation*.[10]

◄ CONSIDER USING TM 111
How Middlemen Create Exchange Efficiency (Figure 15.2 on text page 446)

◄ CONSIDER USING TM 112
Distribution's Effect on Your Food Dollar (Figure 15.3 on text page 448)

FIGURE **15.3**

· · · ·

DISTRIBUTION'S EFFECT ON YOUR FOOD DOLLAR

Note that the farmer gets on 25 cents of your food dollar. The bulk of your money goes to intermediaries to pay distribution costs. Their biggest cost is labor (truck drivers, clerks), followed by warehouses and storage.

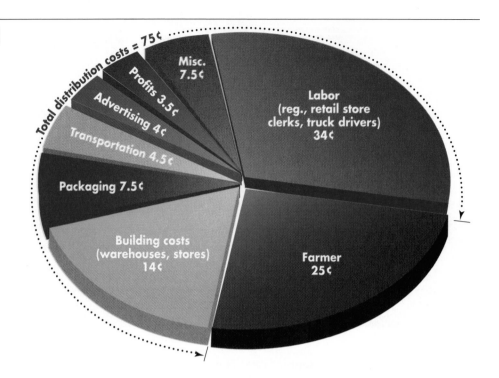

> **CONSIDER USING TM 113**
> How Middlemen Share Your Food
> Dollar (Figure 15.4 on text page 00)

- Intermediary organizations have survived in the past because they have performed marketing functions more effectively and efficiently than others could. To maintain their competitive position in the channel, intermediaries must adopt the latest in technology.[11]

- Intermediaries add costs to products, but these costs are usually more than offset by the values they create.

 Critical Thinking

Imagine that we have eliminated intermediaries and you have to go shopping for groceries and shoes. How would you find out where the shoes and groceries were? How far would you have to travel to get them? How much money do you think you'd save for your time and effort? Which intermediary do you think is most important and why? How might the Internet change your shopping in the future?

FIGURE **15.4**

· · · ·

HOW MIDDLEMEN SHARE YOUR FOOD DOLLAR

ITEM	FARMER	PROCESSOR	WHOLESALER	RETAILER
1 pound choice beef	66.3%	5.4%	7.4%	20.9%
1 dozen grade A large eggs	69.7	11.5	5.1	13.7
1 half-gallon milk	50.8	21.6	19.8	7.8

···· ▬ ····

HOW INTERMEDIARIES ADD UTILITY TO GOODS

◄ **LEARNING GOAL 2**
Give examples of how intermediaries perform the five utilities.

Utility is an economic term that refers to the value or want-satisfying ability that's added to goods or services by organizations when the products are made more useful or accessible to consumers than before. Six utilities are added: form, time, place, possession, information, and service.

··· FORM UTILITY ···

◄ **CONSIDER USING LECTURE ENHANCER 15-3**
The Vet Makes House Calls

◄ **CONSIDER USING LECTURE ENHANCER 15-4**
The Growing Importance of the "Fourth P"

Form utility is performed mostly by producers. It consists of taking raw materials and changing their form so that they become useful products. Thus, a farmer who separates the wheat from the chaff and the processor who turns the wheat into flour are creating form utility. Marketers sometimes perform form utility as well. For example, a retail butcher may cut pork chops from a larger piece of meat and trim off the fat. Normally, however, marketers concentrate on performing the other five utilities: time, place, possession, information, and service. The following are some examples of how they do that.

··· TIME UTILITY ···

Intermediaries, such as retailers, add time utility to products by making them available when they're needed. For example, Devar Tennent lives in Boston. One winter evening while watching TV with his brother, he suddenly got the urge for a hot dog and Coke. The problem was that there were no hot dogs or Cokes in the house. Devar ran down to the corner delicatessen and bought some hot dogs, buns, Cokes, and potato chips. He also bought some frozen strawberries and ice cream. Devar was able to get these groceries at 10 P.M. because the deli was open 24 hours a day. That's time utility.

··· PLACE UTILITY ···

Intermediaries add place utility to products by having them where people want them. For example, while traveling through the badlands of South Dakota, Juanita Ruiz grew hungry and thirsty. There are no stores for miles in this part of the country. Juanita saw one of many signs along the road saying that Wall Drug with fountain service was up ahead. Lured by the signs, she stopped at the store for refreshments. She also bought sunglasses and souvenir items there. The goods and services provided by Wall Drug are in a convenient place for vacationers. 7-Eleven stores remain popular because they are usually located in places where they are easy to reach.

··· POSSESSION UTILITY ···

Intermediaries add possession utility by doing whatever is necessary to transfer ownership from one party to another, including providing credit. Activities associated with possession utility include delivery, installation, guarantees, and follow-up service. For those consumers who don't want to own goods, possession utility makes it possible for them to use goods through renting or leasing.

Does *your* McDonald's deliver? This one in central London does! Of all the marketing utilities, possession utility is the least understood. It is a catch-all utility that means adding value by doing whatever the customer needs to complete the sale, including providing credit, delivery, or whatever. What other products or services might benefit by offering free delivery?

The facts you need before you choose

Consumer Reports is published by Consumers Union, an independent, nonprofit testing and information organization serving only consumers. We are a comprehensive source for unbiased advice about products and services, personal finance, health and nutrition, and other consumer concerns. Since 1936, our mission has been to test products, inform the public, and protect consumers. Our income is derived solely from the sale of CONSUMER REPORTS and our other services, and from nonrestrictive, noncommercial contributions, grants, and fees.

 We buy all the products we test off the shelf, just as you do. We receive no special treatment. We accept no free samples and no gifts; if a manufacturer sends us a free product, we return it.

 We test products in 50 state-of-the-art labs at our National Testing and Research Center in Yonkers, N.Y. Our Ratings are based on lab tests, controlled-use tests, and expert judgments by our technical and research staff. If a product is high in overall quality and relatively low in price, we deem it **A CR Best Buy™**. A Rating refers only to the brand and model listed.

 We survey our millions of readers to bring you information on the reliability of hundreds of auto models and of major products like appliances and electronic gear. Reader-survey data also help us rate insurance and other consumer services.

 We report on current issues of concern to consumers. Our staff of researchers and editors brings you in-depth information on matters that affect your health, your money, and your well-being.

 We accept no ads from companies. We do advertise our own services, which provide impartial information and advice to consumers. We don't let any company use our reports or Ratings for commercial purposes. If that happens, we insist that the company stop, and we take whatever additional steps are open to us.

Marketing intermediaries come in many forms. For example, *Consumer Reports* is a marketing intermediary that provides helpful purchasing information to consumers. What other sources do you turn to for information about products and services you intend to buy?

For example, Larry Rosenberg wanted to buy a nice home in the suburbs. He found just what he wanted, but he didn't have the money he needed. So he went with the real estate broker to a local savings and loan and borrowed the money to buy the home. Both real estate brokers the savings and loan companies are marketing intermediaries.

••• INFORMATION UTILITY •••

Intermediaries add information utility by opening two-way flows of information between marketing participants. For example, Jerome Washington couldn't decide what kind of TV set to buy. He looked at various ads in the newspaper, talked to salespeople at several stores, and read material at the library. He also got some booklets from the government about radiation hazards and consumer buying tips. Newspapers, salespeople, libraries, and government publications are all information sources made available by intermediaries.

••• SERVICE UTILITY •••

Intermediaries add service utility by providing fast, friendly service during and after the sale and by teaching customers how to best use products over time. For example, Sze Leung bought a personal computer (PC) for his office at home. Both the computer manufacturer and the retailer where he bought the computer continue to offer help whenever Sze needs it. He also gets software updates for a small fee to keep his computer up-to-date. What attracted Sze to the retailer in the first place was the helpful, friendly service he received from the salesperson in the store. Service utility is rapidly becoming the most important utility for many retailers, because without it they could lose business to electronic marketing or direct marketing (e.g., marketing by catalog or on the Internet).

For consumers to receive the maximum benefit from marketing intermediaries, the various organizations must work together to ensure a smooth flow of goods and services to the consumer. Historically, there hasn't always been total harmony in the channel of distribution. As a result, channel members have created channel systems that make the flows more efficient. We'll discuss those systems next. The box called Reaching Beyond Our Borders tells what the trends are in international marketing; after reading it, you should better understand the need for sophisticated distribution systems.

> **LEARNING GOAL 3**
> Discuss how a manufacturer can get wholesalers and retailers in a channel system to cooperate by the formation of systems.

•••• ▬▬▬ ••••

BUILDING COOPERATION IN CHANNEL SYSTEMS

How can manufacturers get wholesalers and retailers to cooperate to form an efficient distribution system? One way is to somehow link the firms together in a formal relationship. Four systems have emerged to tie firms together: corporate systems, contractual systems, administered systems, and value chains.

Reaching Beyond Our Borders

http://www.mktplc.com/cfnet/spmenu.html

What Intermediaries to Use

It's one thing to decide to sell a product internationally; it's something else again to try to implement such a program. How are you going to reach the consumer? You could, of course, send sales representatives to contact people directly, but that would be costly and risky. How can you get your product into foreign markets at a minimum cost and still have wide distribution?

- *Use brokers.* A broker is an intermediary who keeps no inventory and takes no risk. A broker can find distributors for you. Brokers sell for you and make a commission on the sale. This is the least expensive way to enter foreign markets, but you still assume the risks of transportation.

- *Use importers and exporters.* Importers and exporters take all the risks of business and sell your products to international markets. Their commission is much higher than that of brokers, but they do much more for you. They may find you distributors or do the selling to ultimate consumers themselves.

- *Call on distributors directly.* You can bypass exporters and brokers and call on distributors yourself. In that case, you actually become your own exporter and deliver directly to distributors, but again you assume the risks of transportation.

- *Sell direct.* The most costly and risky way to sell internationally is to set up your own distribution system of wholesalers and retailers. On the other hand, this maximizes potential profits in the long run. Many firms start out selling through importers and exporters and end up setting up their own distribution system as sales increase.

International distribution will be a major growth area in marketing, with many challenges and opportunities for tomorrow's college graduates. Does a career in this area sound interesting to you?

••• CORPORATE DISTRIBUTION SYSTEMS •••

A **corporate distribution system** is one in which all of the organizations in the channel of distribution are owned by one firm. If the manufacturer owns the retail firm, clearly it can influence much greater control over its operations. Sherwin-Williams, for example, owns its own retail stores and thus coordinates everything: display, pricing, promotion, inventory control, and so on. Other companies that have tried corporate systems include GE, Firestone, and Xerox.

corporate distribution system
A distribution system in which all of the organizations in the channel of distribution are owned by one firm.

••• CONTRACTUAL DISTRIBUTION SYSTEMS •••

If a manufacturer can't buy retail stores, it can try to get retailers to sign a contract to cooperate. A **contractual distribution system** is one in which members are bound to cooperate through contractual agreements. There are three forms of contractual systems:

1. *Franchise systems* such as McDonald's, KFC, Baskin-Robbins, and AAMCO. The franchisee agrees to all of the rules, regulations, and procedures established by the franchisor. This results in the consistent quality and level of service you find in most franchised organizations.

2. *Wholesaler-sponsored chains* such as Ace Hardware and IGA food stores. Each store signs an agreement to use the same name, partici-

contractual distribution system
A distribution system in which members are bound to cooperate through contractual agreements.

◄ **CONSIDER USING LECTURE ENHANCER 15-5**
Tank Parts From Sears

➤ **CONSIDER USING CRITICAL THINKING EXERCISE 15-1**
Distribution Channels (SCANS)

➤ **CONSIDER USING LECTURE ENHANCER 15-6**
Motorola Angers Channel Partners

pate in chain promotions, and cooperate as a unified system of stores even though each store is independently owned and managed.

3. *Retail cooperatives* such as Associated Grocers. This arrangement is much like a wholesaler-sponsored chain except that it's initiated by the retailers. The same cooperation is agreed to, however, and the stores remain independent. The normal way such a system is formed is for retailers to agree to focus their purchases on one wholesaler, but cooperative retailers could also purchase a wholesale organization to ensure better service.

••• ADMINISTERED DISTRIBUTION SYSTEMS •••

administered distribution system
A distribution system in which producers manage all of the marketing functions at the retail level.

If you were a producer, what would you do if you couldn't get retailers to sign an agreement to cooperate? One thing you could do is to manage all the marketing functions yourself, including display, inventory control, pricing, and promotion. A system in which producers manage all of the marketing functions at the retail level is called an **administered distribution system**. Kraft does that for its cheeses; Scott does it for its seed and other lawn care products. Retailers cooperate with producers in such systems because they get so much free help. All the retailer has to do is ring up the sale.

••• VALUE CHAINS •••

value chain
The sequence of linked activities that must be performed by various organizations to move goods from the sources of raw materials to ultimate consumers.

As outlined earlier, the **value chain** is the sequence of linked activities that must be performed by various organizations to move goods from the sources of raw material, such as farms and mines, to ultimate consumers. Because the value chain starts with raw materials and ends with the customer, any one company usually assumes just a few of the activities, relying on suppliers and other members of the channel of distribution to handle the others.[12] What makes this system so efficient is that the various organizations are linked electronically so that information flows from one firm to another are as smooth as information flows once were within a single firm.[13] By sharing information and exchanging fast, efficient service, these united firms are becoming the most competitive entities in the global market.[14]

 Progress Check

• What are the relationships among intermediaries, channels of distribution, and physical distribution?

• Why do we need intermediaries? Can you illustrate how intermediaries create exchange efficiency? How would you defend intermediaries to someone who said that getting rid of them would save millions of dollars?

• Can you give examples of the six utilities and how intermediaries perform them?

• Could you tell a firm how to implement a corporate, a contractual, and an administered system as well as a value chain?

• What are EDI and ECR?

➤ **LEARNING GOAL 4**
Describe in detail what's involved in physical distribution management.

➤ **CONSIDER USING LECTURE ENHANCER 15-7**
A New Fictional Hero: The Logistics Manager

•••• ▬▬▬ ••••

PHYSICAL DISTRIBUTION (LOGISTICS) MANAGEMENT

Historically, intermediaries helped perform the distribution function; that is, they helped move goods from the farm to consumer markets, move raw materials to factories, and so forth. Physical distribution involved moving goods by truck, train, and other modes, and storing goods in warehouses along the way. (A *mode*, in the language of distribution, is any of the various means used to transport goods such as trucks, trains, planes, ships, and pipelines.) Today, logistics systems involve more than simply moving products from place to place. They involve all kinds of activities such as processing orders and taking inventory of products. In other words, logistics systems involve whatever it takes to see that the right products are sent to the right place quickly and efficiently.

Logistics systems, like all marketing activities, are becoming more customer-oriented than ever before. Many firms have introduced customer-oriented logistical strategies such as just-in-time (JIT) inventory controls ➔ P. 267 ◆.[15] Manufacturers that use JIT (1) can cut back substantially on their inventory in warehouses and (2) count on suppliers to deliver needed parts and materials just in time to go onto production lines. None of this would be possible without an efficient, reliable logistics system supported by trucking. Thanks to improved logistics systems, businesses now carry less in inventory and total national logistics costs have decreased dramatically. Some problems have emerged with JIT systems, however. For example, Japan is a heavy user of just-in-time delivery, but the streets of Japan have been jammed with trucks, thus negating some of the benefits. In the United States, distances between firms are often so great that weather and other circumstances may hinder the smooth flow of goods. Therefore, companies often keep a small inventory on hand to ensure that goods will be available when trucks can't get through.

··· METHODS USED TO MOVE RAW MATERIALS ··· AND FINISHED GOODS

A primary concern of distribution managers is selecting a transportation mode that will minimize costs and ensure a certain level of service. The largest percentage of goods in the United States is shipped by rail. Railroad shipment is best for bulky items such as coal, wheat, automobiles, and heavy equipment. Figure 15.5 compares the various modes on several dimensions.

For the past 20 years or so, railroads have handled about 35 to 40 percent of the total volume of goods in the United States. Railroad lines are in a state of transition, but as a result of practices such as piggyback shipments, railroads should continue to hold better than a 38 percent share of the market. (*Piggyback* means that a truck trailer is detached from the cab; loaded onto a railroad flatcar; and taken to a destination where it will be offloaded, attached to a

◀ CONSIDER USING LECTURE ENHANCER 15-8
Doublemint in China

◀ CONSIDER USING LECTURE ENHANCER 15-11
Goodwill Pills or Inventory Dumping?

◀ CONSIDER USING LECTURE ENHANCER 15-10
FedEx Redefines Quick Delivery

◀ CONSIDER USING OT ACETATE 15-4
A Phyiscal Distribution Manager's Job

◀ CONSIDER USING TM 114
Comparing Transportation Modes (Figure 15.5 on text page 453)

FIGURE **15.5**
····
COMPARING TRANSPORTATION MODES
Combining trucks with railroads lowers cost and increases the number of locations reached. The same is true when combining trucks with ships. Combining trucks with airlines speeds goods over long distances and gets them to almost any location.

Mode	Cost	Percentage of domestic volume	Speed	On-time dependability	Flexibility handling products	Frequency of shipments	Reach
Railroad	Medium	38%	Slow	Medium	High	Low	High
Trucks	High	25	Fast	High	Medium	High	Most
Pipeline	Low	21	Medium	Highest	Lowest	Highest	Lowest
Ships (water)	Lowest	15	Slowest	Lowest	Highest	Lowest	Low
Airplane	Highest	1	Fastest	Low	Low	Medium	Medium

More and more companies are learning that the best way to handle logistics is to let someone else, like Penske, handle it for them. As this ad suggests, such companies will provide order fulfillment (shipping out goods), procurement (buying things), inventory management, and transportation. Some will offer credit and information services. Why would so many companies outsource logistics?

truck, and driven to customers' plants.) Railroad shipment is a relatively energy-efficient way to move goods and could therefore experience significant gains if energy prices climb.

The second largest surface transportation mode is motor vehicles (trucks, vans, and so forth). Such vehicles handle a little over 25 percent of the volume. As Figure 15.5 shows, trucks reach more locations than trains. Trucks can deliver almost any commodity door-to-door.

Railroads have joined with trucking firms to further the process of piggybacking. The difference lately is that the new, 20-foot-high railroad cars, called double-stacks, can carry two truck trailers, one on top of the other.

Water transportation moves a greater volume of goods than you might expect. Over the past 20 years, water transportation has carried 15 to 17 percent of the total. If you live near the Mississippi River, you've likely seen towboats hauling as many as 30 barges at a time with a cargo of up to 35,000 tons. On smaller rivers, about eight barges can be hauled, carrying up to 20,000 tons—that's the equivalent of four 100-car railroad trains. Thus, you can see the importance of river traffic. Add to that Great Lakes shipping, shipping from coast to coast and along the coasts, and international shipments, and water transportation takes on a new dimension as a key transportation mode. When truck trailers are placed on ships to travel long distances at lower rates, the process is called *fishyback* (see the explanation of piggyback).

One transportation mode that's not visible to the average consumer is movement by pipeline. About 21 percent of the total volume of goods moves this way. Pipelines are used primarily for transporting petroleum and petroleum products. The Cleveland Electric Illuminating Company has experimented with a coal pipeline, and several more are either planned or in operation now. Here's how it works. The coal is broken down into small pieces, mixed with water to form what's called slurry, and piped to its destination, where it often must be dried before use. Such coal may not burn as cleanly as dry coal, and there's some resistance to coal pipelines from environmentalists. Still, there have been experiments with sending other solids in pipelines, which could be a major mode of distribution in the future.

Today, only a small part of shipping is done by air. Nonetheless, air transportation is a critical factor in many industries. Airlines carry everything from small packages to luxury cars and elephants, and could expand to be a competitive mode for other goods. The primary benefit of air transportation is *speed*. No firm knows this better than Federal Express, whose theme is "When it absolutely, positively has to be there overnight." As just one of several competitors vying for the fast-delivery market, FedEx has used air transport to expand into global markets.

The air freight industry is starting to focus on global distribution. Emery has been an industry pioneer in establishing specialized sales and operations teams aimed at serving the logistics needs of specific industries. KLM Royal Dutch Airlines has cargo/passenger planes that handle high-profit items such as diplomatic pouches and medical supplies. Specializing in such cargo has

Intermodal shipping is done very smoothly today. Here you see containers being moved from a port facility to a flatbed truck that will in turn deliver it to a railroad yard for shipment to its final destination. Containers of this type can be stacked two high on trains. Such innovations make it easier and less expensive to ship goods from coast to coast. Would you be happy to see more trucks off the roads and their cargo on the rails?

enabled KLM to compete with Federal Express, TNT, and DHL, which carry bulk items.

··· INTERMODAL SHIPPING ···

Intermodal shipping uses multiple modes of transportation—highway, air, water, rail—to complete a single long-distance movement of freight. Services that specialize in intermodal shipping are known as intermodal marketing companies. While the United States has developed numerous intermodal shipping systems, Europe is just now catching up.[16] Today railroads are merging with each other and with other transportation companies to offer intermodal distribution. See the box called From the Pages of *Business Week* to see how few railroad companies remain.

intermodal shipping
The use of multiple modes of transportation to complete a single long-distance movement of freight.

··· THE STORAGE FUNCTION ···

About 25 to 30 percent of the total cost of physical distribution is for storage. This includes the cost of the warehouse and its operation plus movement of goods within the warehouse. There are two major kinds of warehouses: storage and distribution. A *storage warehouse* stores products for a relatively long time. Seasonal goods such as lawn mowers would be kept in such a warehouse.

Distribution warehouses are facilities used to gather and redistribute products.[17] You can picture a distribution warehouse for Federal Express or United Parcel Service handling thousands of packages for a very short time. GE's combination storage and distribution facility in San Gabriel Valley, California, gives you a feel for how large such buildings can be. At nearly a half mile long and 465 feet wide, it's big enough to hold three Statues of Liberty, two *Queen Mary*s, and one Empire State Building.

◄ CONSIDER USING LECTURE ENHANCER 15-9
Logistics Management at FedEx

··· MATERIALS HANDLING ···

Materials handling is the movement of goods within a warehouse, factory, or store. The increased use of just-in-time inventory control is cutting back on the significant costs associated with such movement. Many manufacturers have

materials handling
The movement of goods within a warehouse, factory, or store.

From the Pages of **BusinessWeek**

http://deliver-it
.com/train/html

Will There Soon Be Just Two Railroads?

Seventeen years ago there were some 40 sizable railroad carriers crisscrossing the United States. Many were losing money, and the trucking industry was able to grab some of their business. Today, many of the railroad lines have merged (there are only four large ones left, plus a few smaller lines) and the result is more efficiency. The railroads are now handling some 40.6 percent of intercity freight, up from 35 percent in 1970.

Business Week magazine reports that the railroads are contemplating further mergers to the point where

only two companies will remain. But there comes a time when having too few competitors results in less competitiveness. A railroad can get so big that it begins to lose track of railroad cars in the system, and all kinds of problems may emerge. Indeed, that was beginning to happen in 1997. Railroads provide the backbone of the distribution system in the United States. It is important that they remain efficient and competitive.

Source: Joseph Weber, "Highballing Toward Two Big Railroads?," Business Week, March 17, 1997, pp. 32–33.

also installed robots and automated equipment to move goods efficiently within the firm. Nonetheless, materials handling can still be quite costly to some firms.

Progress Check

- What are some activities involved in physical distribution?
- Which transportation mode is fastest, which cheapest, and which most flexible?
- Which transportation modes can be combined?
- What percentage of the distribution cost comes from storage?

► LEARNING GOAL 5
Describe the various wholesale organizations in the distribution system.

► CONSIDER USING OT ACETATE 15-5
Services of Wholesale Middlemen

► CONSIDER USING TM 115
A Full-Function Wholesaler (Figure 15.6 on text page 457)

WHOLESALE INTERMEDIARIES

Now that we've talked about channels of distribution and logistics, we can talk about the organizations that make up the channel. Let's begin with wholesalers. Remember that one goal of this discussion, and similar discussions throughout the text, is to introduce you to the variety of careers in this area. Most college students know little or nothing about wholesaling, yet the rapid growth of warehouse clubs offers many career possibilities.

There's much confusion about the difference between wholesalers and retailers. It's helpful to distinguish wholesaling from retailing and to clearly define the functions performed so that more effective systems of distribution can be designed. Some producers won't sell directly to retailers but will deal only with wholesalers. Some producers give wholesalers a bigger discount than retailers. What confuses the issue is that some organizations sell much of their merchandise to other intermediaries (a wholesale sale) but also sell to ultimate consumers (a retail sale). Warehouse clubs are a good example.

The issue is really rather simple: A *retail sale* is the sale of goods and services to consumers for their own use. A *wholesale sale* is the sale of goods and services to businesses and institutions (e.g., hospitals) for use in the business or to wholesalers or retailers for resale.

••• MERCHANT WHOLESALERS •••

Merchant wholesalers are independently owned firms that take title to (own) goods they handle. About 80 percent of wholesalers fall in this category. There are two types of merchant wholesalers: full-service wholesalers and limited-function wholesalers. **Full-service wholesalers** perform all of the distribution functions: transportation, storage, risk bearing, credit, market information, grading, buying, and selling (see Figure 15.6). **Limited-function wholesalers** perform only selected functions, but try to do them especially well.

Rack jobbers furnish racks or shelves full of merchandise to retailers, display products, and sell on consignment. This means that they keep title to the goods until they're sold, and then they share the profits with the retailer. Merchandise such as toys, hosiery, and health and beauty aids are sold by rack jobbers. (A rack jobber that doesn't supply credit to customers is classified as a limited-function wholesaler.)

Cash-and-carry wholesalers serve mostly smaller retailers with a limited assortment of products. Retailers go to them, pay cash, and carry the goods back to their stores—thus the term *cash-and-carry*. Cash-and-carry wholesalers have begun selling to the general public in what are called warehouse clubs. Warehouse clubs are open to members only and sell merchandise at prices 20 to 40 percent below those of supermarkets and discount stores. One function of such clubs is to provide small businesses (those too small to have wholesalers service them) with merchandise and supplies at low prices.

What makes these new stores different from any in the past is that you and I can become members of them for an annual fee (usually $25) or buy goods at a 5 percent markup if we belong to a credit union, are government employees, or otherwise meet the qualifications. One example is Sam's Clubs, which were started by Sam Walton of Wal-Mart. Another is Price-Costco.

Drop shippers solicit orders from retailers and other wholesalers and have the merchandise shipped directly from a producer to a buyer. They own the

merchant wholesalers
Independently owned firms that take title to (own) the goods they handle.

full-service wholesalers
Merchant wholesalers that perform all of the distribution functions.

limited-function wholesalers
Merchant wholesalers that perform only selected distribution functions but try to do these functions especially well.

rack jobbers
Wholesalers that furnish racks or shelves full of merchandise to retailers, display products, and sell on consignment.

cash-and-carry wholesalers
Wholesalers that serve mostly smaller retailers with a limited assortment of products.

drop shippers
Wholesalers that solicit orders from retailers and other wholesalers and have the merchandise shipped directly from a producer to a buyer.

A FULL-SERVICE WHOLESALER

1. Provide a sales force to sell the goods to retailers and other buyers.
2. Communicate manufacturers' advertising deals and plans.
3. Maintain inventory, thus reducing the level of the inventory suppliers have to carry.
4. Arrange or undertake transportation.
5. Provide capital by paying cash or quick payments for goods.
6. Provide suppliers with market information they can't afford or can't obtain themselves.
7. Undertake credit risk by granting credit to customers and absorbing any bad debts, thus relieving the supplier of this burden.
8. Assume the risk for the product by taking title.

The wholesaler may perform the following services for customers:

1. Buy goods the end market will desire and make them available to customers.
2. Maintain inventory, thus reducing customers' costs.
3. Transport goods to customers quickly.
4. Provide market information and business consulting services.
5. Provide financing through granting credit, which is critical to small retailers especially.
6. Order goods in the types and quantities customers desire.

FIGURE 15.6
••••
A FULL-SERVICE WHOLESALER

Source: Thomas C. Kinnear and Kenneth L. Bernhardt, *Principles of Marketing*, 2d ed. (Glenview, Ill.: Scott, Foresman, 1986), p. 369.

REI is now the nation's largest retail co-op with more than 1.5 million active members. For a $15 membership fee, you get hassle-free camping gear rentals, discounts on other merchandise, and more. Have you joined a members-only club to get such savings on food and other goods and services?

freight forwarder
An organization that puts many small shipments together to create a single large shipment that can be transported cost-effectively to the final destination.

> ▶ **LEARNING GOAL 6**
> List and explain the ways that retailers compete.

> ▶ **CONSIDER USING SUPPLEMEN-TAL CASE 15-1**
> Getting Cooperation From Retailers (SCANS)

> ▶ **CONSIDER USING OT ACETATE 15-6**
> Can You Shop Until You Drop?

merchandise but don't handle, stock, or deliver it. That's done by the producer. Drop shippers tend to handle bulky products such as coal, lumber, and chemicals.

Smaller manufacturers or marketers that don't ship enough products to fill a railcar or truck can get good rates and service by using a freight forwarder. A **freight forwarder** puts many small shipments together to create a single large shipment that can be transported cost-effectively to the final destination. Some freight forwarders also offer warehousing, customs assistance, and other services along with pickup and delivery. You can see the benefits of such a company to a smaller shipper.

Perhaps the most useful marketing intermediaries as far as you're concerned are retailers. They're the ones who bring goods and services to your neighborhood and make them available day and night. Let's look at retailers in more detail.

···· ▬▬▬ ····

RETAIL INTERMEDIARIES

Next time you go to the supermarket to buy groceries, stop for a minute and look at the tremendous variety of products in the store. Think of how many marketing exchanges were involved to bring you the 18,000 or so items that you see. Some products (e.g., spices) may have been imported from halfway around the world. Other products have been processed and frozen so that you can eat them out of season (e.g., corn and green beans).

A supermarket is a retail store. A retailer, remember, is a marketing intermediary that sells to consumers. The United States boasts approximately 2.3 million retail stores selling everything from apples to zoo souvenirs. Retail organizations employ more than 11 million people and are one of the major employers of marketing graduates. There are many careers available in retailing in all kinds of firms.

··· HOW RETAILERS COMPETE: ···
BENCHMARKING AGAINST THE BEST

There are five major ways for retailers to compete for the consumer's dollar: price, service, location, selection, and total quality. Since consumers are constantly comparing retailers on price, service, and variety, it is important for retailers to use benchmarking ⟫ P. 247 ⟪ to compare themselves against the best in the field to make sure that their practices and procedures are the most advanced. The following sections describe the five major ways to compete.

PRICE COMPETITION   Discount stores such as Wal-Mart, Target, Kmart, Marshall's, and Caldor succeed by offering low prices. It's hard to compete with these price discounters over time, especially when they offer good service as well. Warehouse stores are now trying to win the grocery-store market by offering lower prices than neighborhood supermarkets. Price competition from warehouse stores has hurt many retailers. For example, there are few independent retailers left in the office-supply market; the advent of Staples, Office Depot, and other office-supply giants has caused many smaller shops to close. Those stores that have survived have suffered huge sales and profit declines, except for those that offer truly outstanding service and selection.

Service organizations also compete on price. Note, for example, Southwest Airlines' success with its low-price strategy. The same is true of H&R Block in income tax preparation services, Hyatt Legal Plans for legal services, and Motel 6 or Red Roof Inns for motel-room rentals.

SERVICE COMPETITION   A second competitive strategy for retailers is service. Retail service involves putting the customer first. This requires all front-line people to be courteous and accommodating to customers. Retail service also means follow-up service such as on-time delivery, guarantees, and fast installation. Consumers are frequently willing to pay a little more for goods and services if the retailer offers outstanding service.

The benchmark companies in this regard are Dayton's, Lord & Taylor, Dillard's, and Nordstrom. These retailers show that if you hire good people, train them well, and pay them fairly, you will be able to provide world-class service. Service organizations that have successfully competed using service include Scandinavian Airlines, Tokyo's Imperial Hotel, Metropolitan Life Insurance Company, and Florida Power & Light. Small service providers, such as local hair stylists and auto repair shops, also compete by offering superior service.

LOCATION COMPETITION   Many services, especially convenience services like banks and dry cleaners, compete effectively by having good locations. That's why you find automatic teller machines in convenient places such as supermarkets and train stations. Many fast-food stores, such as Burger King and Pizza Hut, now have locations on college campuses where students can reach them quickly. Some dry cleaners pick up and deliver laundry at your home or business, which often makes them more convenient than even the closest dry cleaner.

SELECTION COMPETITION   A fourth competitive strategy for retailers is selection. Selection is the offering of a wide variety of items in the same product category. **Category killer stores** offer wide selection at competitive prices. Toys "R" Us stores carry some 18,000 toys, and the company has over 500 stores around the world. Small, independent toy stores are closing their doors because they simply can't compete with the low prices and selection found at Toys "R" Us. Tower Records carries over 75,000 titles. Borders Books carries some 150,000 different titles. Sportmart carries over 100,000 sporting goods items. Petstuff and other pet food superstores have some 10,000 items each.

Small retailers sometimes compete with category killers by offering wide selection within one or a few categories of items. Thus, you have successful

◄ **CONSIDER USING OT ACETATE 15-7**
Is Service in Retail Stores Better Today Than in 1995?

◄ **CONSIDER USING OT ACETATE 15-8**
Is It Becoming a Wal-Mart World?

◄ **CONSIDER USING CRITICAL THINKING EXERCISE 15-2**
Shop Til You Drop (SCANS)

◄ **CONSIDER USING SUPPLEMENTAL CASE 15-2**
Megamalls Are Here (SCANS)

category killer stores
Large stores that offer wide selection at competitive prices.

◄ **CONSIDER USING LECTURE ENHANCER 15-13**
Color and Retailing

Wal-Mart represents total quality in many dimensions, including its concern for the environment. This store in Lawrence, Kansas, has many environmental features, including mostly wood construction to use a renewable resource. Recycled water is used for watering of plants and lavatories. Recycled asphalt was used in the parking lot. And recycling bins are located at the front door. Would you shop at a store because it was more environmentally concerned than its competitors?

➤ **CONSIDER USING LECTURE ENHANCER 15-12**
Store Design

➤ **CONSIDER USING OT ACETATE 15-9**
Global Retailing Sales

➤ **CONSIDER USING OT ACETATE 15-10**
Can You Identify a Retailer in Your Area?

small stores that sell nothing but coffee or party products. Small retailers also compete with category killers by offering personalized service.

Restoration Hardware, with stores in the Bay Area of California and around the country, is one store that has survived the competition against Home Depot and the other giant lumber and hardware stores. Restoration was able to succeed by offering consumers products that couldn't be found in the other stores.[18]

Service organizations that compete successfully on selection include Blockbuster (wide selection of rental videos), most community colleges (wide selection of courses), and Schwab Mutual Funds (hundreds of funds).

TOTAL QUALITY COMPETITION   A fifth competitive strategy is total quality. A total quality retailer offers low price, good service, wide selection, and total quality management ➤ P. 245 ◀. The benchmark retailer for total quality marketing is Wal-Mart, which treats its salespeople, known as associates, well, gives them ownership incentives, and backs them up with information and the latest in technology to do their job.

Wal-Mart can offer low prices because its marketing process is one of the best in the world. It uses electronic data interchange and supply-chain management to keep its inventories low and its turnover high. Wal-Mart has a societal orientation that recognizes the wants and needs of all its stakeholders, including stockholders, employees, suppliers, and the local community.

Wal-Mart tries to please its customers by offering better service than its competitors do. It believes in continuous improvement and benchmarks on the best in the world for logistics, pricing, and other retail practices. Kmart, Sears, and other competitors are getting stronger by competing with Wal-Mart. Service organizations that compete on total quality include the Ritz-Carlton Hotel Company and Federal Express.

••• RETAILERS AND COMPUTER TECHNOLOGY •••

It has reached the point where few small retailers can thrive without the use of computers. Gene's Books in King of Prussia, Pennsylvania, for example, is a bookstore that tries to compete with the giants. While that's hard to do at any time, it would be nearly impossible today without the creative use of computers. But owner Gene Massey seems up to the challenge. He installed a sophisticated inventory and point-of-sale computer system so he can keep track of the 52,000 book titles in the store along with 4,500 magazines and 110 out-of-town Sunday papers. Such a computer system allows Massey to compete on service. His wide selection wouldn't be possible without the computer. By linking with suppliers' computers, Gene's Books can get a replacement copy soon after a book is sold. That enables the store to carry a very small inventory of each book (sometimes just one) and restock within a day or within hours. Before buying his system, Massey talked to other bookstore owners and hired a reliable computer consultant.

Barry Gainer uses the Internet to boost sales at the Indian River Gift Fruit Company. Gainer discovered that the Internet is an inexpensive way to advertise effectively. His first site was with America Online (*fruit* is the key word) and later on the World Wide Web (giftfruit.com). Now, 25 percent of his revenue is from the Net.[19]

◄ **CONSIDER USING LECTURE ENHANCER 15-14**
Avon's New Salesperson: Barbie

◄ **CONSIDER USING LECTURE ENHANCER 15-15**
The NBA Sets Up Shop in New York

◄ **CONSIDER USING LECTURE ENHANCER 15-16**
Selling Cars in Japan

··· RETAIL DISTRIBUTION STRATEGY ···

A major decision marketers must make is selecting retailers to sell their products. Different products call for different retail distribution strategies. There are three categories of retail distribution: intensive distribution, selective distribution, and exclusive distribution.

Intensive distribution puts products into as many retail outlets as possible, including vending machines. Products that need intensive distribution include candy, cigarettes, gum, and popular magazines (convenience goods).

Selective distribution is the use of only a preferred group of the available retailers in an area. Such selection helps to assure producers of quality sales and service. Manufacturers of appliances, furniture, and clothing (shopping goods) usually use selective distribution.

Exclusive distribution is the use of only one retail outlet in a given geographic area. Because the retailer has exclusive rights to sell the product, he or

intensive distribution
Distribution that puts products into as many retail outlets as possible.

selective distribution
Distribution that sends products to only a preferred group of retailers in an area.

exclusive distribution
Distribution that sends products to only one retail outlet in a given geographic area.

Organizations like The Indian River Gift Fruit Company must completely revamp their advertising plans now that the Internet has become another medium. In fact, 25 percent of their revenue is from Internet sales now. What percentage of their sales would you expect to come from the Internet by the year 2004?

There are literally thousands of vending machines all over Japan selling almost anything you need. In this photo, a woman is using a vending machine that provides photos of men as part of a dating service. Would you like such a machine on campus?

➤ **CONSIDER USING OT ACETATE 15-12**
The Wheel of Retailing

she is more likely to carry more inventory, give better service, and pay more attention to this brand than to others. Auto manufacturers usually use exclusive distribution, as do producers of specialty goods.

➤ **LEARNING GOAL 7**
Explain the various kinds of nonstore retailing.

➤ **CONSIDER USING OT ACETATE 15-11**
Strategies for Covering the Market

NONSTORE RETAILING

For every dollar consumers spend in stores like Safeway and Nordstrom, they spend 37.5 cents at home ordering goods and services by mail and by phone from sources such as Lands' End. The store figures don't include supermarkets, service stations, restaurants, and car dealerships. Still, the out-of-store shopping trend is growing. Categories include telemarketing; vending machines, kiosks, and carts; direct selling; multilevel marketing; and direct marketing.

••• TELEMARKETING •••

telemarketing
The sale of goods and services by telephone.

Telemarketing is the sale of goods and services by telephone. Some 80,000 companies use telemarketing today to supplement or replace in-store selling. Many send a catalog to consumers and let them order by calling a toll-free 800 number. An organization called Occupational Forecasting has predicted that telemarketing will continue to be one of the fastest-growing areas in marketing.

••• VENDING MACHINES, KIOSKS, AND CARTS •••

➤ **CONSIDER USING LECTURE ENHANCER 15-17**
New Trends in Vending Machines

A vending machine dispenses convenience goods when consumers deposit sufficient money in the machine. The benefit of vending machines is their location in airports, office buildings, schools, service stations, and other areas where people want convenience items. Vending machines in Japan sell everything from bandages and face cloths to salads and spiced seafood. Vending by machine will be an interesting area to watch as such innovations are introduced in the United States.

Carts and kiosks have lower overhead costs than stores do; therefore, they can offer lower prices on items such as T-shirts and umbrellas. You often see vending carts outside stores on the sidewalk or along walkways in malls; mall owners often love them because they're colorful and create a marketplace atmosphere. Kiosk workers dispense coupons and provide all kinds of helpful information to consumers, who tend to enjoy the interaction.

··· DIRECT SELLING ···

Direct selling involves selling to consumers in their homes or where they work. Major users of this category include encyclopedia publishers (Britannica), cosmetics producers (Avon), and vacuum cleaner manufacturers (Electrolux). Based on the success of those products, business are now selling lingerie, artwork, plants, and other goods at "house parties" sponsored by sellers.

Because so many women work now and aren't at home during the day, companies based on direct selling are sponsoring parties at workplaces or in the evenings and on weekends.

··· MULTILEVEL MARKETING ···

Over 1,000 companies have had great success using multilevel marketing (MLM.) MLM salespeople work as independent contractors. They earn commissions on their own sales and they also create commissions for the "upliners" who recruited them. In turn, they receive commissions from any "downliners" they recruit to sell. When you have hundreds of downliners—that is, people who have been recruited by the people you recruit—the commissions can be quite sizable. Some people make tens of thousands of dollars a month this way.

Multilevel marketing has been successful around the world in selling a wide variety of products. One fast-growing MLM firm is Rexall Sundown, a company that sells nutritional and health-related products. Salespeople not only earn commissions at Rexall but may also buy stock options.

The main attraction of multilevel marketing for employees, other than the huge potential for making money, is the low cost of entry. For a hundred dollars or less, the average person can start up a business and begin recruiting others. The success of this form of marketing is revealed by the fact that MLM sales overall have reached $18 billion a year.[20] Be careful not to confuse multilevel marketing with "pyramid" schemes, which often aren't involved in the selling of legitimate products and are therefore illegal. They focus on recruiting new people, whose initial "investment" is used to compensate those who have already joined. Pyramid schemes usually involve substantial start-up costs, whereas multilevel marketing programs may cost less than $100 to join.

··· DIRECT MARKETING GOES ON-LINE ···

◄ CONSIDER USING LECTURE ENHANCER 15-18
The Internet: The Fastest Growing Channel

One of the fastest-growing aspects of retailing is direct marketing. Direct marketing includes any activity that directly links manufacturers or intermediaries with the ultimate consumer. Thus, direct retail marketing includes direct mail, catalog sales, telemarketing, and on-line shopping (e.g., Prodigy Information Service shopping). Two popular direct marketing names are L. L. Bean and Lands' End. Direct marketing has created tremendous competition in some high-tech areas as well. For example, direct sales by Dell Computers, Gateway 2000, and other computer manufacturers has led IBM and Compaq to use price-cutting tactics to meet the competition.[21]

Direct marketing has become popular because shopping from home or work is more convenient for consumers than going to stores. Instead of driving to a mall, people can "shop" in catalogs and free-standing advertising supplements in the newspaper and then buy by phone, by mail, or by computer. Interactive on-line selling is expected to provide major competition for retail stores in the near future.

Direct marketing took on a new dimension when consumers became involved with interactive video. Producers now provide all kinds of information on CD-ROMs or on Web sites that consumers access with their computers.[22] The potential of such systems seems almost limitless. Consumers can ask questions, seek the best price, and order goods and services—all by computer. Companies that use interactive video and interactive Web sites have become major competitors for those who market by catalog.[23]

Critical Thinking

How important are intermediaries such as wholesalers, retailers, trucking firms, and warehouse operators to the progress of less-developed countries? Is there a lack of intermediaries in less-developed countries? How do intermediaries contribute to the development of a less-developed country? How will the Internet provide third-world consumers with access to worldwide markets? What intermediaries will be needed most to serve those customers?

Progress Check

*   What are the four major ways retailers compete with each other?
*   What advantages and disadvantages do you see to having an intensive distribution strategy versus an exclusive one?

SUMMARY
......

1. Explain the value of marketing intermediaries.

1. Marketing intermediaries are organizations that assist in moving goods and services from producers to industrial and consumer users.
    *   ***Why do we need marketing intermediaries?***
    We need intermediaries when they perform marketing functions more effectively and efficiently than others can. Marketing intermediaries can be eliminated, but their activities can't. Intermediaries add costs to products, but these costs are usually more than offset by the values they create.

2. Give examples of how intermediaries perform the six utilities.

2. *Utility* is an economic term that refers to the value or want-satisfying ability that's added to goods or services by organizations because the products are made more useful or accessible to consumers.
    *   ***What different types of utilities do intermediaries add?***
    Normally, marketing intermediaries perform the following utilities: form, time, place, possession, information, and service.
    *   ***How do intermediaries perform the six utilities?***
    A retail grocer may cut or trim meat, providing some form utility. But marketers are more often responsible for the five other utilities. Time utility is provided by having goods available when people want them. Place utility is provided by having goods where people want them. Possession utility is provided by making it possible for people to own things by providing them with credit, delivery, installation, guarantees, and anything else that will help complete the sale. Marketers also inform consumers of the availability of goods and services with advertising, publicity, and other means. That provides information utility. Finally, marketers provide fast, friendly, and efficient service during and after the sale (service utility).

3. Discuss how a manufacturer can get wholesalers and retailers in a channel system to cooperate by the formation of systems.

3. One way of getting manufacturers, wholesalers, and retailers to cooperate in distributing products is to form efficient distribution (logistics) systems.
    *   ***What are the four types of distribution systems?***
    The four distribution systems that tie firms together are (1) corporate systems, in which all organizations in the channel are owned by one firm;

(2) contractual systems, in which members are bound to cooperate through contractual agreements; (3) administered systems, in which all marketing functions at the retail level are managed by manufacturers; and (4) value chains, in which the various firms are linked electronically to provide the most efficient movement of information and goods possible.

4. Physical distribution can be a complex process because it involves all the activities needed to get products from producers to consumers as quickly and efficiently as possible.

   • **What's involved in physical distribution management?**

   A primary concern of distribution managers is the selection of a transportation mode that will minimize costs and ensure a certain level of service. Logistics managers must also keep down storage costs. That's why supply-chain management has become so popular. Furthermore, logistics managers are responsible for materials handling, which is moving goods within the warehouse and from the warehouse to the production or selling floor. Less inventory means less materials handling.

4. Describe in detail what's involved in physical distribution management.

5. A wholesaler is a marketing intermediary that sells to organizations and individuals, but not to final consumers.

   • **What are some wholesale organizations that assist in the movement of goods from manufacturers to consumers?**

   Merchant wholesalers are independently owned firms that take title to (own) goods that they handle. Rack jobbers furnish racks or shelves full of merchandise to retailers, display products, and sell on consignment. Cash-and-carry wholesalers serve mostly small retailers with a limited assortment of products. Drop shippers solicit orders from retailers and other wholesalers and have the merchandise shipped directly from a producer to a buyer. Freight forwarders consolidate small shipments into larger ones that can be shipped less expensively.

5. Describe the various wholesale organizations in the distribution system.

6. A retailer is an organization that sells to ultimate consumers.

   • **How do retailers compete in today's market?**

   There are five major ways of competing for the consumer's dollar today: price, service, location, selection, and total quality.

   • **What are three distribution strategies retailers use?**

   Retailers use three basic distribution strategies: Intensive (putting products in as many places as possible, selective (choosing only a few stores in a chosen market), and exclusive (using only one store in each market area).

6. List and explain the ways that retailers compete.

7. For every dollar consumers spend in stores like Safeway and Nordstrom, they spend 37.5 cents at home ordering goods and services by mail and by phone.

   • **What are the various kinds of nonstore retailing?**

   Nonstore retailing includes telemarketing; selling goods in vending machines, kiosks, and carts; multilevel marketing; and other direct marketing.

7. Explain the various kinds of nonstore retailing.

KEY TERMS
. . . . . .

administered distribution system 452	channel of distribution 442	efficient consumer response (ECR) 444
brokers 445	contractual distribution system 451	electronic data interchange (EDI) 443
cash-and-carry wholesaler 457	corporate distribution system 451	exclusive distribution 461
category killer stores 459	drop shippers 457	freight forwarder 458

DEVELOPING WORKPLACE SKILLS

1. The six utilities of marketing are form, time, place, possession, information, and service. Give examples of organizations specifically designed to perform each of these functions.

2. The emergence of the Internet has changed the face of retailing forever. Try shopping for a good or service on the Internet to find the best price. You might begin with Consumer World at http://www.consumerworld.org/. This site lists all kinds of places where you can shop for cars, gifts, computer equipment and more. Be prepared to discuss your findings in class.

3. This text describes five kinds of retail competition: price, service, location, selection, and total quality. Give a five-minute report on your experience as a consumer with each type of competition. Do you prefer one over the others? Why?

4. Visit the newest stores in your community. Compare their prices, products, and services with the older stores. What are the trends in retailing that seem most significant to you?

5. Recall some of the experiences you have had with telemarketers (those people who tend to call at dinnertime trying to sell you things). How could they change their approach so you would be more responsive and positive about their calls? You might practice such approaches on your classmates to see if they really work.

TAKING IT TO THE NET

Purpose

To examine how businesses can use the Internet to distribute their products directly to customers.

Exercise

Many businesses use the Internet to distribute their products to end customers and to strengthen their customer relationships. Relationship marketing moves away from mass production toward custom-made goods. The goal is to keep customers by offering them products that exactly meet their requirements. The latest in technology enables sellers to work with buyers to determine their individual wants and needs and to develop goods and services specifically designed for those individuals. Using the Internet, businesses are able to bypass intermediaries and send their customized products directly to customers. To see this principle in action, go to Gateway 2000's Web site (http://www.gw2k.com/).

1. Do you have a dream machine in mind just in case someone hands you a gift certificate for a new computer? Browse the Gateway Web site and compare computer systems. Do some systems have almost everything you want while others have more than you need? Add and subtract features

until you have just the system you want. From your perspective as a customer, what value does this service add?

2. Explain how Gateway's distribution strategy benefits both the customers and the company.

3. What are the disadvantages of this distribution strategy? What has Gateway done to decrease the effects of these disadvantages?

Practicing Management Decisions

Multilevel marketing often doesn't get the respect it deserves in marketing literature. When multilevel marketing companies succeed, their growth is often unbelievable. At least six multilevel marketing companies have reached the $500 million level in sales.

Multilevel marketing companies work like this: The founders begin by recruiting a few good people to go out and find managers to sell their products and to recruit other supervisors. These supervisors then recruit additional salespeople. That is, 20 people recruit 6 people each. That means 120 salespeople. Those people then recruit 6 people each, and you have 720 salespeople. If in turn those people all recruit 6 people, you then have almost 5,000 salespeople. All supervisors earn commissions on what they sell as well as on what everyone under them sells. When you get thousands of salespeople selling for you, commissions can be quite large. One company promotes the fact that 1 percent from 100 salespeople is as good as 100 percent from one successful salesperson. Companies often add new products or expand to other countries to keep a continuous growth pattern.

CASE
• • • • •
MULTILEVEL MARKETING
• • • • •

Nu Skin will soon have $1 billion in sales. Looking for more growth, the company started a new division, Interior Design Nutrition, to make and sell vitamins and weight-control products. Amway has chosen the international route for growth; in 1996, its sales *increased* by over a billion dollars.

Decision Questions

1. Amway and others have been successful in Japan. To what other countries could you lead such companies so that you could become a top earner?

2. What will happen as multilevel marketing distributors begin selling and recruiting others using the latest in technology such as the Internet and fax on demand?

3. Why do you suppose multilevel marketing hasn't received the same acceptance as other retail innovations such as catalog sales? What could the companies do to improve their image?

4. If multilevel marketing works so well for beauty and health care products, why not use the same concept to sell other products?

The Internet makes it possible to reach consumers all over the world inexpensively and effectively. You can sell almost anything to almost anyone on the Internet. That's the good news. The bad news is that getting products to people all over the world is not nearly as easy. That's where companies like American President's Line come in. They provide the infrastructure necessary to move goods from here to there. Infrastructure is a fancy word that means all the basic organization and structure needed to accomplish a goal. In this case,

VIDEO CASE
• • • • •
AMERICAN PRESIDENT'S LINE EXTENDS OVERSEAS

it means trains, ships, warehouses, trucks, and port facilities to store and move goods quickly and efficiently.

American President's Line (APL) is a key player in the movement of goods to and from the United States. It is conveniently located in the harbor of Los Angeles where containers (actually truck trailers) are loaded onto and unloaded from ships. When a shipment arrives from overseas, the containers are placed on trucks where they are sent to railroad yards and placed on trains (piggyback) for their final destination (Chicago). The movement of the containers is seamless and smooth. A ship can be unloaded and reloaded in three days.

The key to global marketing is keeping shipping costs low. Although ships may be relatively slow, they are the most efficient way to move goods across oceans. But ships are big: two football fields in length (200 yards). The APL shipping yard is 230 acres. It uses huge cranes to lift the containers and place them carefully into the ships. Cranes are also used to double stack the containers on railroad cars. That means the containers are stacked on top of one another.

Physical distribution (logistics) is the movement of goods from producers to industrial and consumer users; it involves functions such as transportation and storage. It adds place utility. The various organizations involved in the movement of goods—wholesalers, retailers, and shippers—are called marketing intermediaries. They help move the goods from producers to consumers. Supply-chain management is the term used to describe the linkages among various firms—usually electronic—that make the process smooth and as inexpensive as possible. In this case, that involves intermodal shipping; that is,

the use of ships, trucks, and trains together. Electronic data interchange is used to trace the movement of goods. Automatic equipment identifiers help trace the movement of containers as they go from one mode, such as trucks, to another, such as trains or ships. APL is just one part of a complex distribution system that moves goods so efficiently that trading in global markets is becoming almost as easy as moving goods from one part of the United States to another.

Discussion Questions

1. How would less developed countries benefit from having port facilities like those provided by APL?
2. How important are business to business relationships to the establishment of a supply chain involving ships, trucks, trains, and warehouses? Can you see the benefit of having one firm do all of these functions?
3. How might a small firm selling a few items at a time compete with huge organizations that use facilities like these?
4. How could airlines capture some of the business that now goes to ships? What would be the benefit to shippers?

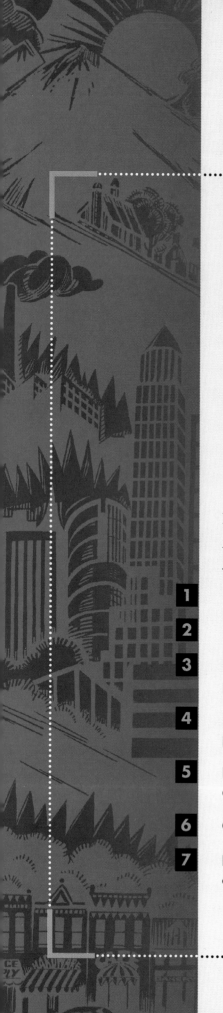

Promoting Products Using Integrated and Interactive Marketing Communication

Chapter 16

LEARNING GOALS

*After you have read and studied this chapter,
you should be able to*

1 List and describe the various elements of the promotion mix.

2 Illustrate the seven steps of the selling process.

3 Describe the functions of the public relations department and the role of publicity.

4 Explain the importance of sales promotion and word of mouth as promotional tools.

5 Describe advantages and disadvantages of various advertising media and explain the latest advertising techniques.

6 Compare and contrast push and pull promotional strategies.

7 Describe integrated marketing communication and the role of interactive communications within it.

Travel and tourism is one of the top industries in the United States. Chris Cavanaugh is the marketing manager of a successful tourist attraction, the Biltmore Estate. Part of his job is to manage the overall promotional effort and to be part of a marketing team that develops advertising, public relations, personal selling, publicity, and sales promotion.

Biltmore is the largest private home in the United States. It was built in 1895 in Asheville, North Carolina, for George Vanderbilt. The estate includes the 250-room Biltmore House, acres of gardens and surrounding grounds, a winery, and restaurants. The whole estate is open to the public, and nearly a million people visit it each year. If you would like to see pictures of many of the estate's magnificent rooms and gardens, go to its Web site at http://www.biltmore.com. The Web site also contains information about the many motels that advertise their proximity to this great tourist attraction.

One goal of the promotional program at the estate is to increase the number of visitors who come annually. To do that, the estate maintains an internal database of customer names and searches external databases for the names of potential visitors. Cavanaugh divides the total visitor market into three categories: passholders (who have one-year admission passes), general visitors (who come to visit for one day), and prospects (people who have never visited but may be interested). He and his marketing team develop separate promotional pieces for each of the market segments: → P. 398 ← passholders, for example, get newsletters, invitations to special events, and other communications.

PROFILE

Chris Cavanaugh of Biltmore Estate

The estate sends direct mail to visitors to encourage them to come back again and to generate word of mouth among their friends. The mailings include colorful brochures and descriptions of special incentives to visit. To encourage first-time visits, the estate uses advertisements in upscale magazines. It uses radio advertisements to promote special events, such as Christmas celebrations. It also uses personal selling techniques when prospects call and when visitors travel the grounds. Cavanaugh's public relations efforts include work with the various media to publish articles and pictures featuring the estate. The publicity includes articles about the estate and special stories about the major events that take place during the year.

Cavanaugh's marketing team integrates all the promotional efforts to form one strong positive image about the estate. Recently, this integrated marketing communication (IMC) approach resulted in a 38 percent increase in daily visits and an average party size increase of 12.5 percent. Everyone at the estate works together to make a visit memorable—so memorable that people want to return over and over to see the gardens and displays at different times of the year.

The Biltmore estate is just one of many organizations seeking new ways of reaching the consumer with database marketing and integrated promotional messages. This chapter will outline the newest promotional strategies. Using such strategies, organizations will become more efficient marketers and get much closer to their customers.

Source: Materials provided by Biltmore Estate, its Web site (http://www.biltmore.com/), and personal contact in 1998.

THE IMPORTANCE OF MARKETING COMMUNICATION AND PROMOTION

Promotion is the last, but not the least, of the four Ps of marketing. Marketers now spend over $175 billion yearly on advertising alone trying to convince industrial and consumer buyers to choose their products.[1] They spend even more on sales promotion efforts such as conventions and trade shows. A **trade show** is an event where many marketers set up displays and potential customers come to see the latest in goods and services.

International trade shows continue to grow and expand as trade barriers fall and global competition increases. As this illustration of the International Dublin Showcase demonstrates, their importance is not limited to large multinational companies. Over 800 Irish manufacturers of all sizes come together once a year with buyers from over 30 countries to transact business.

direct marketing
Marketing that allows customers to buy products by interacting with various advertising media without meeting a salesperson face-to-face.

promotion
An attempt by marketers to inform people about products and to persuade them to participate in an exchange.

Marketers spend the most money sending salespeople into the field to talk personally with customers. Direct marketing is often much cheaper and more effective than personal selling. **Direct marketing** allows customers to buy products by interacting with various advertising media without meeting a salesperson face-to-face. Direct marketing includes direct-mail selling, catalog sales, telemarketing, ➤ P. 462 ◄◄ televised home shopping, and selling on the Internet.

··· THE PROMOTION MIX ···

Promotion is an attempt by marketers to inform people about products and to persuade them to participate in an exchange. Marketers use many different tools to promote their products and services, as you saw in the Biltmore Estate profile. These tools include personal selling, word of mouth, sales promotion, public relations, publicity, and advertising. The combination of promotion tools an organization uses is called its **promotion mix** (see Figure 16.1). The value package ➤ P. 408 ◄◄ is shown in the middle of the figure to illustrate the fact that the product itself can be a promotional tool (e.g., through sampling), and that most promotional efforts are designed to sell products. We'll discuss each of these promotional tools in this chapter. Let's begin by looking at personal selling.

PERSONAL SELLING

Personal selling is the face-to-face presentation and promotion of products and services. It also involves the search for new prospects and follow-up service after the sale. Effective selling isn't simply a matter of persuading others to buy (see Figure 16.2). In fact, it's more accurately described today as helping others to satisfy their wants and needs.

To illustrate personal selling's importance in our economy and the career opportunities it provides, let's look at some numbers. First, U.S. census data show that nearly 10 percent of the total labor force is employed in personal selling. When we add those who sell for nonprofit organizations, we find that over 7 million people are employed in sales.

The average cost of a single sales call to a potential industrial buyer is about $400.[2] Surely no firm would pay that much to send out anyone but a highly skilled, professional marketer and consultant. But how does one get to be that kind of sales representative? What are the steps along the way? Let's take a closer look at the process of selling.

··· STEPS IN THE SELLING PROCESS ···

The best way to get a feel for personal selling is to go through the selling process with a product and see what's involved. One product that you're familiar with is textbooks, like the one you are now reading. A college textbook salesperson has the job of showing faculty the advantages of using a particular book and the

FIGURE **16.1**
. . . .
THE PROMOTION MIX

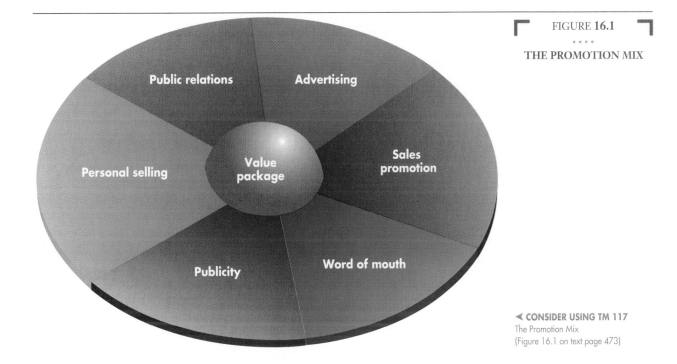

Public relations

Advertising

Personal selling

Value package

Sales promotion

Publicity

Word of mouth

◀ **CONSIDER USING TM 117**
The Promotion Mix
(Figure 16.1 on text page 473)

teaching aids that go with it. Let's go through the selling process with a sales-person to see what can be done to make the sale.

1. *Prospect and qualify.* The first step in the selling process is prospecting. **Prospecting** involves researching potential buyers and choosing those most likely to buy. That selection process is called *qualifying.* To qualify people means to make sure that they have a need for the product, the authority to buy, and the willingness to listen to a sales message.[3] People who meet these criteria are called prospects. You find prospects by asking schools which faculty members are teaching the courses that might assign the book or books you are selling. It is a good idea to develop rapport with the secretaries of the various departments because they can help with faculty office hours and other information. Telemarketing ➤ P. 462 ◀ is often used to find prospects or "leads."[4] Also, faculty members go to professional meetings where publishers set up display booths and where salespeople can discuss various texts and get information for follow-up calls.

2. *Preapproach.* Before making a sales call, the sales representative must do further research. Robert E. Kellar, author of *Negotiating Skills That Sell,* says that 50 percent of a sales negotiation's outcome is determined before you meet the customer face-to-face.[5] As much as possible should be learned about customers and their wants and needs. Before you try to sell a textbook, for example, you would want to know which texts faculty members are now using and some of the subjects they find most important.

3. *Approach.* "You don't have a second chance to make a good first impression." That's why the approach is so important. When you call on a faculty member for the first time, your opening comments are important. The idea is to give an impression of friendly professionalism, to create rapport, and to build credibility. The objective of the initial sales call probably won't be to make a sale that day. Rather, the goal may be to set

promotion mix
The combination of promotion tools an organization uses.

personal selling
The face-to-face presentation and promotion of products and services.

prospecting
Researching potential buyers and choosing those most likely to buy.

◀ **LEARNING GOAL 2.**
Illustrate the seven steps of the selling process.

◀ **CONSIDER USING CRITICAL THINKING EXERCISE 16-1**
Promotional Campaign

◀ **CONSIDER USING LECTURE ENHANCER 16-1**
The Effectiveness of Various Promotional Tools

◀ **CONSIDER USING OT ACETATE 16-1**
Factors that Effect the Promotion Mix

◀ **CONSIDER USING LECTURE ENHANCER 16-2**
"Detail" Selling

► CONSIDER USING TM 118
Steps in the Selling Process (Figure 16.2
on text page 474)

the faculty member at ease. That is, you should listen to the faculty member, learn what his or her textbook and other needs are, and create some interest in the textbook you are selling by pointing out key differences between that book and the competition.

4. *Make presentation.* In the actual presentation of the text and the materials that come with it, the idea is to match the benefits of your value package ⇒ P. 408 ⇐ to the client's needs. The presentation may involve audiovisual aids, such as a Powerpoint presentation on the computer. Since you've done your homework and know the prospect's wants and needs, the presentation will be tailored to his or her needs and will therefore be relatively easy to present. Often different offers may be presented based on the specific needs of that school and its students. For example, the faculty member may be interested in providing students with an inexpensive subscription to *Business Week* as part of the total package.

FIGURE **16.2**

• • • •

**STEPS IN THE
SELLING PROCESS**

Prospect and qualify	This first step involves researching potential buyers and choosing those most likely to buy. These people are called **prospects.** You may learn the names of prospects from present customers, from surveys, from public records, and so forth.
Preapproach	Before making a sales call, the sales representative must do further research. As much as possible should be learned about the customer and his or her wants and needs. What products are they using now? Are they satisfied? Why or why not? Before a call, a salesperson should know the customer well and have a specific objective for the call. This is probably **the most important step in selling.**
Approach	"You don't have a second chance to make a good first impression." That's why the approach is so important. The idea is to give an impression of friendly professionalism, to create rapport, and to build credibility. This is the time to listen carefully to determine customer wants and needs.
Make presentation	This is the actual demonstration or presentation of the product and its benefits to the prospect. This may involve audiovisual aids. Showing advantages versus competition is often included.
Answer objections	Sometimes a prospect may question facts or figures and ask for more information. Often a sales representative must come back several times. The goal is to make sure that the customer is informed and committed to the purchase.
Close sale	You have to "ask for the sale" to finalize the sales process. "Would you like the red one or the green one?" "And when would you want delivery?" are examples of questions used to close the sale.
Follow up	The selling process isn't over until the product is delivered, installed, and working satisfactorily. The selling relationship often continues for years as the salesperson responds to customer requests and introduces new products over time. Selling is a matter of establishing relationships, not just selling goods and services.

Salespeople today are armed with many high-tech tools to help them in satisfying customer needs. In this case, a saleswoman is using a laptop computer to make a presentation in a restaurant. Salespeople may also have fax machines, pagers, and other equipment to help them maintain contact with the company and customers. Can you use PowerPoint and other presentation tools yet?

This ad for an HP Color Palmtop PC shows the power and the benefits of such new high-tech sales tools. Information about the company and the various members of the buying team can be stored in such computers so they are accessible at any time.

5. *Answer objections.* A salesperson should anticipate any objections the prospect may raise and determine proper responses. Questions should be viewed as opportunities for creating better relationships, not as a challenge to what you're saying. Customers have legitimate doubts, and salespeople are there to resolve those doubts. If such a dialogue weren't necessary, salespeople could easily be replaced by advertising. Salespeople are taught several strategies for overcoming objections.

6. *Close sale.* You have to "ask for the sale" to finalize the sales process. A salesperson has limited time and can't spend forever with one faculty member answering questions and objections. Closing techniques include getting a series of small commitments and then asking for the order and showing the client where to sign. Salespeople are taught to remember their "ABCs"—Always Be Closing. For example, the salesperson might say, "Do you want your students to receive the interactive edition of *The Wall Street Journal* with your order? If they order the *Journal,* they will get one free!"

7. *Follow-up.* The selling process isn't over until the order is approved and the customer is happy. The selling relationship often continues for years as the salesperson responds to new requests for information. Selling is a matter of establishing relationships, not just selling goods or services. Thus, follow-up includes handling customer complaints, making sure that the customer's questions are answered, and supplying what the customer wants. Often customer service is as important to the sale as the product itself. Many faculty members today want to maintain a semiconstant

You know Starbucks for its 1,400 stores in 27 states and around the world. But did you know that Starbucks also has many business accounts that contribute 12 percent to the company's revenues? Vincent Eades is the senior vice president of specialty sales. He has formed partnerships with companies like United Airlines, ITT/Sheraton, Barnes & Noble, Nordstrom, and Aramark. What other companies might benefit from partnering with Starbucks?

dialogue with textbook authors and other faculty. Most publishers, therefore, have established Web sites for various texts where information may be obtained and discussions may take place.

The selling process varies somewhat among different goods and services, but the general idea is the same. Your goals as a salesperson are to help the buyer buy and to make sure that the buyer is satisfied after the sale.[6] Companies today are providing many high-tech aids to help salespeople in that process. Salespeople, for example, often have laptop computers that connect to databases. Using those computers, salespeople can track orders, get product information (including prices), and search for all kinds of information. Sales force automation, in fact, includes 400-plus software programs that help salespeople design products, close deals, tap into company intranets, and more. Some salespeople can even conduct virtual reality tours of the manufacturing plant for the customer.[7]

••• BUSINESS-TO-BUSINESS SELLING •••

Business-to-business ➣ P. 396 ≪ salespeople who sell to commercial accounts (wholesalers and retailers), institutional accounts (hospitals and schools), and industrial accounts (manufacturers and service providers) often make more money and have a more challenging experience than those who sell to consumers. Businesses tend to buy in larger quantities, and as a result the salesperson often makes a larger commission.

Business customers are often easier to find than consumers because the government classifies business customers using Standard Industrial Classification (SIC) codes. Books that list such codes are available at most libraries. Once a salesperson has used SIC codes to find one customer in an industry, he or she can easily find other customers with the same SIC code. Business-to-business salespeople are often called marketing consultants because they help their business customers become more effective at marketing. For example, ice cream salespeople can sell more ice cream to dairy stores if they teach the store personnel how to sell more ice cream to ultimate consumers like you and me.

Sales force automation also helps business-to-business salespeople. Using laptop computers, modems, e-mail, fax software, and scanners, salespeople can get specifications by e-mail, get product announcements from the company and then e-mail them to customers, scan documents and fax them to customers, find information in databases and use that data in sales presentations, and more. With such high-tech backing, salespeople have become the eyes and ears of all businesses.[8] When operating overseas, however, salespeople face obstacles they don't face in the United States. The box called Making Ethical Decisions, for example, discusses the issue of bribery in overseas markets.

Critical Thinking

What kind of products do you think you would enjoy selling? Think of the customers for that product. Can you imagine yourself going through the seven-step selling process with them? Which steps would be hardest? Which would be easiest? Which step could you avoid by selling in a retail store? Can you picture yourself going through the sales process on the phone (telemarketing)?

Making Ethical Decisions

http://www.benjerry.com/

What's Ethical Changes in Different Cultures

Ben & Jerry's thought that recent changes in Russia would provide a great opportunity for selling ice cream overseas. It even developed new flavors such as vodka-laced White Russian and Wild Karelian Berry. However, Ben & Jerry's had to pull out of Russia, leaving behind eight scoop shops, a manufacturing facility, and a distribution system. Why? Trying to conduct a business legally and ethically is a challenge, even in the United States. But in overseas markets, where bribery and illegal activities are commonplace, it is difficult if not impossible to compete without acting unethically or illegally. Ben & Jerry's found the system too hard to overcome.

The Foreign Corrupt Practices Act (FCPA) prohibits U.S. citizens from bribing foreign government officials to win business in a foreign country. Disobeying the law can result in felony charges and jail sentences. On the other hand, it is nearly impossible in some countries to conduct business without bribing government officials. So what is a business to do? Either not expand overseas or try its best to follow the law.

Most businesses try their best to follow the law. The relevant concept is called due diligence. A company must do all it can to ensure that its employees follow U.S. laws and maintain high ethical standards when doing business overseas. Without such due diligence a company could lose its global reputation.

Rather than conform to the loose ethical standards of other countries, U.S. businesses are trying hard to get other countries to establish higher standards. Until such standards are established, U.S. businesses must stand out as models for the rest of the world to follow. "Everyone else is doing it" is not a valid defense for behaving unethically or illegally in other countries.

If you were a salesperson in another country and had the opportunity to land a multimillion-dollar sale if you were to bribe the proper officials, what would you do? What would be the potential consequences?

Source: Carol Kurtis, "World Full of Trouble," *International Business*, July–August 1997, pp. 12–18, and Michael Barrier, "Doing the Right Thing," *Nation's Business*, March 1998, pp. 32–38. **SCANS**

- What are the various forms of direct marketing?
- What are the six elements of the promotion mix?
- What are the seven steps in the selling process?

Progress Check

•••• ▬▬▬ ••••

PUBLIC RELATIONS AND PUBLICITY

••• PUBLIC RELATIONS •••

Public relations (PR) is defined by *Public Relations News* as the management function that evaluates public attitudes, identifies the policies and procedures of an individual or an organization with the public interest, and executes a program of action to earn public understanding and acceptance. In other words, a good public relations program has three steps:

1. *Listen to the public.* Public relations starts with good marketing research ("evaluates public attitudes").

2. *Develop policies and procedures in the public interest.* We don't earn understanding by bombarding the public with propaganda; we earn understanding by having programs and practices in the public interest.

3. *Inform people that you're being responsive to their needs.* It's not enough to simply have programs in the public interest. You have to tell the public about those programs so that they know you're being responsive.

◄ **LEARNING GOAL 3.**
Describe the functions of the public relations department and the role of publicity.

public relations (PR)
The management function that evaluates public attitudes, identifies the policies and procedures of an individual or an organization with the public interest, and executes a program of action to earn public understanding and acceptance.

◄ **CONSIDER USING LECTURE ENHANCER 16-3**
How to be Your Own Public Relations Agency

Public relations often takes the lead in generating interest for a company or its products. Note, for example, the success of IBM in publicizing Big Blue's victory over chess champion Kasparov in chess. Such successes show the importance of PR to the overall promotional process.

It is the responsibility of the public relations department to maintain close ties with the media, community leaders, government officials, and other corporate stakeholders. The idea is to establish and maintain a dialogue with those stakeholders so that the company can respond to inquiries, complaints, and suggestions quickly. It is not enough for a company to have programs that support the community, such as donations of computers to schools or "volunteer days"—the company also needs to publicize that involvement. We'll explore the subject of publicity next.

••• PUBLICITY •••

Publicity is one of the major functions of almost all organizations. Here's how it works. Suppose that we want to introduce our new Fiberrific cereal to consumers but that we have very little money to promote it. We need to get some initial sales to generate funds. One effective way to reach the public is through publicity. **Publicity** is any information about an individual, product, or organization that's distributed to the public through the media and that's not paid for, or controlled by, the seller. We might prepare a publicity release describing Fiberrific and the research findings supporting its benefits and send it to the various media. Much skill is involved in writing the story so that the media will want to publish it. Different stories may need to be written for different media. If the stories are published, release of the news about Fiberrific will reach many potential consumers (and investors, distributors, and dealers), and we may be on our way to becoming wealthy marketers.

The best thing about publicity is that the various media will publish stories free of charge if the material seems interesting or newsworthy. The idea, then, is to write publicity that meets those criteria. Besides being free, publicity has several further advantages over other promotional tools, such as advertising. For example, publicity may reach people who wouldn't read an ad. Publicity may be placed on the front page of a newspaper or in some other prominent position, or given air time on a television news show. Perhaps the greatest advantage of publicity is its believability. When a newspaper or magazine publishes a story as news, the reader treats that story as news—and news is more believable than advertising.

There are several disadvantages to publicity as well. For example, you have no control over how, when, or if the media will use the story. The media aren't obligated to use a publicity release, and most are thrown away. Furthermore, the story may be altered so that it's not so positive. There's good publicity (Compaq comes out with a new supercomputer) and bad publicity (GM lays off 10,000 workers). Also, once a story has run, it's not likely to be repeated. Advertising, on the other hand, can be repeated as often as needed. One way to see that publicity is handled well by the media is to establish a friendly relationship with media representatives, cooperating with them when they seek information. Then when you want their support, they're more likely to cooperate.

publicity
Any information about an individual, product, or organization that's distributed to the public through the media and that's not paid for or controlled by the seller.

Publicity is often more powerful than advertising because it can be placed on the front page of newspapers and magazine covers and because it is more believable. That is why companies like Sony Corporation put out publicity releases such as this one that promotes its College JEOPARDY! on-line tournaments for college students.

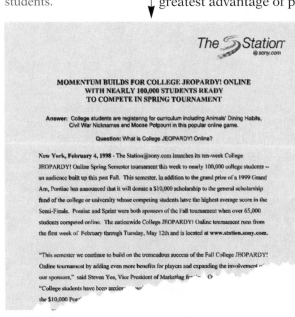

SALES PROMOTION AND WORD OF MOUTH

••• SALES PROMOTION •••

Sales promotion is the promotional tool that stimulates consumer purchasing and dealer interest by means of short-term activities (such things as displays, trade shows and exhibitions, and contests). Figure 16.3 lists some sales promotion techniques.

Those free samples of products that you get in the mail, the cents-off coupons that you clip from newspapers, the contests that various retail stores sponsor, and those premiums you find in Cracker Jack boxes are examples of sales promotion activities. Sales promotion programs are designed to supplement personal selling, advertising, and public relations efforts by creating enthusiasm for the overall promotional program. Coupons were especially popular in the early part of this decade, but manufacturers decided that coupons were costing them too much money and began cutting back on coupon use in the mid-1990s. Leaders in this cutback include such large firms as Procter & Gamble, Philip Morris, and Ralston Purina. However, Del Monte has gained much consumer favor by continuing its couponing strategy.[9]

Sales promotion can take place both internally (within the company) and externally (outside the company). It's just as important to generate employee enthusiasm about a product as it is to attract potential customers. The most important internal sales promotion efforts are directed at salespeople and other customer-contact people, such as complaint handlers and clerks. Internal sales promotion is an attempt to keep salespeople enthusiastic about the company through (1) sales training; (2) the development of sales aids such as flip charts, portable audiovisual displays, and videotapes; and (3) participation in trade shows where salespeople can get leads. Other employees who deal with the public may also be given special training to make them more aware of the company's offerings and a more integral part of the total promotional effort.

After enthusiasm is generated internally, it's important to get distributors and dealers involved so that they too are enthusiastic about helping to promote the product. Trade shows are an important sales promotion tool because marketing intermediaries are able to see products from many different sellers and make comparisons among them. Today, virtual trade shows—trade shows on the Internet—enable buyers to see many products without leaving the office. Furthermore, the information is available 24 hours a day, seven days a week.[10]

After the company's employees and intermediaries have been motivated with sales promotion efforts, the next step is to promote to final consumers using samples, coupons, cents-off deals, displays, store demonstrations, premiums,

◄ **LEARNING GOAL 4.**
Explain the importance of sales promotion and word of mouth as promotional tools.

sales promotion
The promotional tool that stimulates consumer purchasing and dealer interest by means of short-term activities.

◄ **CONSIDER USING SUPPLEMENTAL CASE 16-1**
Developing Effective Sales Promotion Efforts
(SCANS)

◄ **CONSIDER USING TM 119**
Sales Promotion Techniques
(Figure 16.3 on text page 479)

◄ **CONSIDER USING OT ACETATE 16-2**
Tips on Issuing Coupons

◄ **CONSIDER USING LECTURE ENHANCER 16-5**
Sales Promotion in the Auto Industry

Displays (store displays)	Rebates (refunds from producers)
Contests ("You may have won $1 million!")	Lotteries
Samples (toothpaste, soap)	Audiovisual aids
Coupons (25 cents off)	Catalogs
Premiums (free glass when you buy a meal)	Demonstrations
Shows (fashion shows)	Special events
Deals (price reductions)	Exhibits
Trade shows	Portfolios for salespeople
Bonuses (buy one, get one free)	Conventions
Incentives (the gift in a Cracker Jack box)	Sweepstakes

FIGURE 16.3

••••

SALES PROMOTION TECHNIQUES

Spend some time with this list. Most students aren't familiar with all the activities involved in sales promotion. This is the time to learn them.

➤ **CONSIDER USING LECTURE ENHANCER 16-6**
Trade Promotion Wars

➤ **CONSIDER USING LECTURE ENHANCER 16-7**
Avon Streamlines Sales Force

➤ **CONSIDER USING LECTURE ENHANCER 16-8**
Product Placement

contests, trading stamps, rebates, and so on. Sales promotion is an ongoing effort to maintain enthusiasm, so different strategies must be used over time to keep the ideas fresh.

One popular sales promotion tool is sampling—letting consumers have a small sample of the product for no charge. Because many consumers won't buy a new product unless they've had a chance to see it or try it, stores often have people standing in the aisles handing out samples of food and beverage products. Sampling is a quick, effective way of demonstrating a product's superiority at the time when consumers are making a purchase decision.[11] Can you see the importance of sampling textbooks to faculty members? What stores would you target for sampling Fiberrific?

••• WORD OF MOUTH •••

word-of-mouth promotion
A promotional tool that involves people telling other people about products they've purchased.

Word-of-mouth promotion encourages people to tell other people about products they've purchased. Word of mouth is one of the most effective promotional tools, but most marketers don't use it to full effectiveness.[12] Ivan R. Misner's book *The World's Best Known Marketing Secret: Building Your Business with Word-of-Mouth Marketing* is a hands-on, how-to book on managing word-of-mouth promotions. Such books teach marketers the effectiveness of word-of-mouth communication.

➤ **CONSIDER USING OT ACETATE 16-3**
Where Word-of-Mouth Promotion Works Best

Anything that encourages people to talk favorably about an organization is effective word of mouth. Notice, for example, how stores use clowns, banners, music, fairs, and other attention-getting devices to create word of mouth. Clever commercials can generate much word of mouth. Companies can also ask people to tell others about their products or even pay them to do so. Samples are another way to generate word of mouth. But the best way to generate word of mouth is to have a good product, provide good services, and keep customers happy. Word-of-mouth promotion thus includes (1) focusing on customer satisfaction and quality, (2) delivering on promises, and (3) targeting opinion leaders.

One way to encourage word of mouth is to give people information that they can use to tell others about the product. In this case, the product is the movie *Titanic*. By developing a Web site for the movie, producers can both promote the product and at the same time provide information to moviegoers that they can use to sound knowledgeable. Do you often talk with your friends about movies and TV shows? Where do you get your information other than watching the shows themselves?

What's the formula for a successful ad? Apparently Pepsi has it figured out—they've won the *USA Today* Super Bowl ad meter competition an unprecedented five consecutive times. According to the experts (critics), as well as Pepsi and advertising agency executives, it's the use of humor, minimal dialogue, "cool" animals, big stars such as Cindy Crawford, and a good plot that generates an "Ah ha!" reaction from viewers. What other factors cause you to respond to one ad and not another?

Pepsi's Formula

Pepsi-Cola has created a winning formula for Super Bowl ads. Its ads have won USA TODAY's Super Bowl Ad Meter five of 10 years.

PEPSI ADS

Key ingredients in Pepsi ads:

1 Humor

2 Famous people

3 Kicker punchline

3 Animals

CONTAINS: HUMOR, FAMOUS PEOPLE, KICKER PUNCHLINE, ANIMALS, CARBONATED WATER, HIGH FRUCTOSE CORN SYRUP AND/OR SUGAR, CARAMEL COLOR

► A decade of winners in Super Bowl Ad Meter, 3B

Lynn Gordon of French Meadow Bakery in Minneapolis learned about the power of word of mouth when she developed a recipe for old-fashioned bread. Word of mouth from satisfied customers to their friends enlarged her business from selling 40 loaves a week at local co-ops to running her own 13,500-square-foot bakery employing 15 people.

However, negative word of mouth hurts a firm badly. Taking care of consumer complaints quickly and effectively is one of the best ways to reduce the effects of negative word of mouth.

One especially effective strategy for spreading word of mouth is to send testimonials (letters from customers praising your products) to current customers.[13] Most companies use testimonials only in promoting to new customers, but testimonials are also effective in confirming customers' belief that they chose the right company. Positive word of mouth from other users further confirms their choice. Therefore, some companies make it a habit to ask customers for referrals.[14] On the other hand, negative word of mouth can be quite destructive to a firm. Upset customers are now getting on the Internet and publishing their complaints for thousands of people to see.[15] This makes customer relations more critical as we enter the era of the Internet.

Progress Check

- What are the three steps involved in setting up a public relations program?
- What are the advantages and disadvantages of publicity to a marketer?
- Companies spend more money on sales promotion than on advertising. Figure 16.3 lists 20 different sales promotion techniques. How many can you remember?
- How many techniques for generating word of mouth can you describe?

◄ **LEARNING GOAL 5.**
Describe advantages and disadvantages of various advertising media and explain the latest advertising techniques.

◄ **CONSIDER USING LECTURE ENHANCER 16-9**
New Locations for Ads

◄ **CONSIDER USING LECTURE ENHANCER 16-10**
Bang for the Advertising Buck

advertising
Paid, nonpersonal communication through various media by organizations and individuals who are in some way identified in the advertising message.

ADVERTISING

Many people equate promotion with advertising because they are not aware of the differences among promotional tools such as advertising, personal selling, publicity, and word of mouth. Specifically, **advertising** is paid, nonpersonal communication through various media by organizations and individuals who are in some way identified in the advertising message. Word of mouth is not a form of advertising because it doesn't go through a medium (newspaper, TV, etc.), it's not paid for, and it's personal. Publicity is not advertising in that media space for publicity isn't paid for. Personal selling is face-to-face communication and doesn't go through a medium; therefore, it's not advertising.

FIGURE 16.4
••••
ADVERTISING VOLUME
IN THE VARIOUS MEDIA

MEDIUM	SALES ($ MILLIONS)	PERCENTAGE OF TOTAL
Newspapers	$38,402	21.9%
Television	42,484	24.3
Direct Mail	34,509	19.7
Yellow Pages	10,849	6.2
Radio	12,269	7.0
Magazines	9,010	5.1
Business papers	3,808	2.2
Farm publications	297	0.2
Outdoor	1,339	0.7
Miscellaneous	22,263	12.7
Total	175,230	100%

➤ CONSIDER USING TM 120
Advertising Volume in the Various
Media
(Figure 16.4 on text page 482)

➤ CONSIDER USING OT ACETATE
16-4
Where do the Big Spenders Advertise?

➤ CONSIDER USING LECTURE
ENHANCER 16-11
Cramming

••• THE IMPORTANCE OF ADVERTISING •••

The importance of advertising in the United States is easy to document; just look at the numbers in Figure 16.4. The total ad volume exceeds $175 billion yearly. Recently, the number one advertising medium in terms of dollars spent was newspapers, but TV took over the top spot in 1995 and now takes over 24 percent of the total.[16] Newspapers are now number two, with just under 22 percent of the total expenditures. Note that direct mail, one of the fastest-growing advertising media, is now number three.

Advertising costs on TV are very high so that few smaller firms can afford them. What makes the costs so high? Take advertising on sports programs. Superstars now make millions of dollars. To recover those dollars, sports teams need to be on TV, and TV networks pay billions for the rights to show the games.

Medium	Advantages	Disadvantages
Newspapers	Good coverage of local markets; ads can be placed quickly; high consumer acceptance; ads can be clipped and saved.	Ads compete with other features in paper; poor color; ads get thrown away with paper (short life span).
Television	Uses sight, sound, and motion; reaches all audiences; high attention with no competition from other material.	High cost; short exposure time; takes time to prepare ads.
Radio	Low cost; can target specific audiences; very flexible; good for local marketing.	People may not listen to ad; depends on one sense (hearing); short exposure time; audience can't keep ad.
Magazines	Can target specific audiences; good use of color; long life of ad; ads can be clipped and saved.	Inflexible; ads often must be placed weeks before publication; cost is relatively high.
Outdoor	High visibility and repeat exposures; low cost; local market focus.	Limited message; low selectivity of audience.
Direct mail	Best for targeting specific markets; very flexible; ad can be saved.	High cost; consumers may reject ad as "junk mail"; must conform to Post Office regulations.
Yellow Pages advertising	Great coverage of local markets; widely used by consumers; available at point of purchase.	Competition with other ads; cost may be too high for very small businesses.
Internet	Inexpensive global coverage; available at any time; interactive.	Relatively low readership.

FIGURE 16.5

· · · ·

ADVANTAGES AND DISADVANTAGES OF VARIOUS ADVERTISING MEDIA

The most effective media are often very expensive. The inexpensive media may not reach your market. The goal is to use the most efficient medium that can reach your desired market.

◄ **CONSIDER USING LECTURE ENHANCER 16-12**
How Much Time Is Devoted to TV Ads?

◄ **CONSIDER USING OT ACETATE 16-5**
Favorite Budweiser Advertising Slogans

◄ **CONSIDER USING TM 121**
Advantages and Disadvantages of Various Advertising Media
(Figure 16.5 on text page 483)

The public benefits greatly from advertising expenditures. First, ads are informative. The number two medium, newspaper advertising, is full of information about products, prices, features, and more. Are you surprised that businesses spend more on direct mail than on radio or magazine advertising? Direct mail (e.g., catalogs and letters sent by mail to people's homes) is an informative shopping aid for consumers. Each day, consumers receive minicatalogs in their newspapers or in the mail that tell them what's on sale, where, at what price, for how long, and more.

Advertising not only informs us about products; it also provides us with free TV and radio programs because the money advertisers spend for commercial time pays for the production costs. Advertising also covers the major costs of producing newspapers and magazines. When we buy a magazine, we pay mostly for mailing or promotional costs. Figure 16.5 discusses advantages and disadvantages of various advertising media to the advertiser. Newspapers, radio, and the Yellow Pages are especially attractive to local advertisers. Advertising in international markets is a little more difficult. Marketers must learn to adjust to the practices and culture of each country.

TV offers many advantages to national advertisers, but it's expensive. For example, the cost of 30 seconds of advertising during the Super Bowl telecast has risen to $1.3 million. Figure 16.6 discusses the costs of other TV shows. How many bottles of beer or bags of dog food must a company sell to pay for its commercials? The answer may seem to be *a lot,* but few other media besides television allow advertisers to reach so many people with such impact. Marketers must choose which media and which programs can best be used to reach the audience they desire.

FIGURE **16.6**

· · · ·

COST OF 30-SECOND ADVERTISEMENTS ON SELECTED SHOWS (1998)

TV SHOW	30-SECOND AD
Super Bowl	$1,300,000
Home Improvement	105,000
X-Files	92,000
Frasier	62,000
Mad About You	58,000
The Oprah Winfrey Show	52,000
Baywatch	25,000

Source: "Top 50 Syndicated Shows Ranked by Ad Price," *Advertising Age,* January 19, 1998, p. 51; and Steve Hamm, "This Year's Super Bowl Hero?," *Business Week,* January 19, 1998, p. 6.

➤ **CONSIDER USING TM 122**
Cost of 30-Second Advertisements on Selected Shows
(Figure 16.6 on text page 484)

➤ **CONSIDER USING LECTURE ENHANCER 16-13**
Placement of Magazine Ads

➤ **CONSIDER USING OT ACETATE 16-6**
The Surge in Infomercials

It is getting less expensive and more effective to sometimes use the non-network stations and alternative forms of media, such as direct mail. The box titled Major Categories of Advertising lists and defines some of the most widely used forms of advertising.

Some retailers may find it less expensive to run advertisements if they get co-op advertising funds from producers. This means that producers will often pay half of the cost or more of advertisements if a retailer has sold enough of its products.

MAJOR CATEGORIES OF ADVERTISING

Different kinds of advertising are used by various organizations to reach different market targets. Major categories include the following:

- *Retail advertising*—advertising to consumers by various retail stores such as supermarkets and shoe stores.
- *Trade advertising*—advertising to wholesalers and retailers by manufacturers to encourage them to carry their products.
- *Industrial advertising*—advertising from manufacturers to other manufacturers. A firm selling motors to auto companies would use industrial advertising.
- *Institutional advertising*—advertising designed to create an attractive image for an organization rather than for a product. "We Care about You" at Giant Food is an example. "Virginia Is for Lovers" and "I ❤ New York" are two institutional campaigns by government agencies.
- *Product advertising*—advertising for a good or service to create interest among consumer, commercial, and industrial buyers.
- *Advocacy advertising*—advertising that supports a particular view of an issue (e.g., an ad in support of gun control or against nuclear power plants). Such advertising is also known as cause advertising.
- *Comparison advertising*—advertising that compares competitive products. For example, an ad that compares two different cold care products' speed and benefits is a comparative ad.
- *Interactive advertising*—customer-oriented communication that enables customers to choose the information they receive, such as interactive video catalogs that let customers select which items to view.
- *On-line advertising*—advertising messages that are available by computer when customers want to receive them.

••• ADVERTISING USING INFOMERCIALS •••

One fast-growing form of advertising is the infomercial. An **infomercial** is a TV program devoted exclusively to promoting goods and services. Infomercials have been so successful because they show the product in great detail. A great product can sell itself if there's some means to show the public how it works. Infomercials provide that opportunity. People have said that a half-hour infomercial is the equivalent of sending your very best salespeople to a person's home where they can use everything in their power to make the sale: drama, demonstration, testimonials, graphics, and more.

Some products, such as personal development seminars or workout tapes, are hard to sell without showing people a sample of their contents and testimonials. Infomercials have sold such services so well that major companies are now trying to buy time for their own infomercials.

••• USING TECHNOLOGY IN ••• ADVERTISING AND PROMOTION

The technology revolution is having a major impact on advertising. For example, promoters are using interactive TV to carry on a dialogue with customers instead of merely sending them messages, and they're using CD-ROM technology to provide more product information than ever before.[17]

Salespeople are using handheld computers to place orders and to help consumers design custom-made products. Customers can now request information via e-mail or fax and can reach service people from almost any location using cellular phone technology and pagers. In short, the information revolution has greatly affected advertising in a positive way for both seller and buyer. Next, let's look at some specific ways marketers are using technology in advertising.

••• USING ON-LINE COMPUTER SERVICES ••• IN ADVERTISING

On-line services such as Prodigy, America Online, and CompuServe are organizations that provide their subscribers with information on a variety of subjects such as business, entertainment, finance, and sports (see Chapter 17). Recently, marketers have been devising ways to increase the amount of marketing information available to users of on-line services. The first attempts to load on-line services with advertising were rejected by users, but the future is promising. What on-line services can do is provide vast amounts of product information when customers want it.

Once potential customers see what information is available, they can go on-line with sellers (directly contact them by computer) and get additional information immediately. The potential for two-way communication between buyers and sellers is almost endless. Any data that can be put into a computer can be accessed by others. The challenge is to make on-line searches easy for consumers and profitable for companies.

••• CUSTOMIZED ADVERTISING VERSUS ••• GLOBAL ADVERTISING

Harvard professor Theodore Levitt is a big proponent of global marketing and advertising. His idea is to develop a product and promotional strategy that can be implemented worldwide. Certainly that would save companies money in

infomercial
A TV program devoted exclusively to promoting goods and services.

◄ CONSIDER USING OT ACETATE 16-7
Who Watches Infomercials?

◄ CONSIDER USING LECTURE ENHANCER 16-14
The Success of Infomercials

◄ CONSIDER USING OT ACETATE 16-8
Top Celebrity Endorsers

◄ CONSIDER USING OT ACETATE 16-9
Who Are the Top Sport's Endorsers?

◄ CONSIDER USING LECTURE ENHANCER 16-15
America Online Zeroes in on Its Customers

◄ CONSIDER USING LECTURE ENHANCER 16-16
Moonlighting in Japan

◄ CONSIDER USING LECTURE ENHANCER 16-17
Advertising in China

◄ CONSIDER USING LECTURE ENHANCER 16-18
Name That Ice Cream

◄ CONSIDER USING OT ACETATE 16-10
Top U.S. Advertising Categories

◄ CONSIDER USING OT ACETATE 16-11
Number of Movie Theaters Showing Ads

Ads seem to work best when they are designed to meet the special needs of people in various countries. This ad for Maalox, however, could be used almost anywhere in the world, if it were in the local language. But most products are best sold by adapting the ads to the culture and the specific needs of the people in that country. Have you noticed how ads for products from other countries have adapted to the American culture?

mass customization
The design and promotion of products that can be made to order.

push strategy
Promotional strategy in which the producer uses advertising, personal selling, sales promotion, and all other promotional tools to convince wholesalers and retailers to stock and sell merchandise.

research and advertising design. In fact, that is the strategy being used by major companies such as Compaq, IBM, and Intel.[18] However, other experts think that promotion targeted at specific countries may be much more successful than nonspecified global advertising since each country has its own culture, language, and buying habits.[19]

The evidence supports the theory that promotional efforts specifically designed for individual countries often work best. For example, commercials for Camay soap that showed men complimenting women on their appearance were jarring in cultures where men don't express themselves that way. A different campaign is needed in such countries.

People in Brazil rarely eat breakfast and treat Kellogg's Corn Flakes as a dry snack like potato chips. Kellogg is trying a promotional strategy that shows people in Brazil how to eat cereal with cold milk in the morning. The box Reaching Beyond Our Borders gives further examples. Many more situations could be cited to show that international advertising calls for researching the wants and needs of people in each specific country and then designing appropriate ads and testing them.

Even in the United States, selected groups are large enough and different enough to call for specially designed promotions. For example, Maybelline, which makes a wide array of cosmetics, is targeting special promotions to African-American women. In short, much advertising today is moving from the trend toward globalism (one ad for everyone in the world) to regionalism (specific ads for each country and for specific groups within a country). In the future, marketers will prepare more custom-designed promotions to reach smaller audiences—audiences as small as one person. **Mass customization** is the term used to describe the design and promotion of products that can be made to order.[20]

···· ▬ ····

PREPARING THE PROMOTION MIX

Each target group ⇒ P.398 ⇐ calls for a separate promotion mix. For example, large, homogeneous groups of consumers are usually most efficiently reached through advertising. Large organizations are best reached through personal selling. To motivate people to buy now rather than later, sales promotion efforts such as coupons, discounts, special displays, premiums, and so on may be used. Publicity adds support to the other efforts and can create a good impression among all consumers. As mentioned earlier, word of mouth is often the most powerful promotional tool and is generated effectively by listening, being responsive, and creating an impression worth passing on to others. What combination of promotional tools would you use if you were the product manager for Fiberrific? Why?

··· PROMOTIONAL STRATEGIES ···

There are three ways to facilitate the movement of products from producers to consumers. The first is called a push strategy. In a **push strategy,** the producer uses advertising, personal selling, sales promotion, and all other promotional tools

Reaching Beyond Our Borders

Paying Attention to the Culture

Communicating in global advertising is more than a little tricky. For example, using white roses for, say, a wedding scene in a commercial to be shown in China would backfire because white is a symbol of mourning in the Chinese culture. Using a bull's horn as a symbol of a men's product would work against you in Spain. For many Spaniards, the horns symbolize a man whose wife has committed adultery. As you can see, insensitivity to cultural considerations can be embarrassing—and costly.

Lands' End got into trouble in Germany for offering customers an unconditional guarantee on its merchandise it could not, according to German customers, fulfill. It did not state, for example, how many years the guarantee was applicable. Could you return a garment after 20 years? Lands' End had to go to court and is still fighting for its right to use the guarantee.

It makes sense, therefore, when promoting in another country to be careful to adapt to the country's culture. For example, when FedEx wanted to increase its name recognition in Europe, it teamed with Benetton, an established European name in retail clothes. FedEx sponsors one of Benetton's formula racing cars. The racing car had an image FedEx liked: speed and high tech.

Richard Becker, president of the soft-drink company Blue Sky (whose products are found in many health-food stores), addressed the cultural question by contracting with a Japanese distributor to direct his company's marketing campaign in Japan. The American version of a Blue Sky commercial features lots of condensation-covered cans of Blue Sky against a view of the New Mexico desert. The closing line is "Blue Sky: the new taste of the old West." The Japanese ad is more than a little different. It has a blood-red background with just two cans of Blue Sky. The written message is shoved into the lower-left corner: "We are drinking it again in Japan. Direct from Santa Fe's clear blue sky to the Japanese throat. Natural soda, Blue Sky, new introduction. No additives, no artificial color, no caffeine that your mom recommends (against)."

Not every company finds it necessary to make such changes to appeal to global markets. Gillette introduced its Sensor razor to American men in commercials during the Super Bowl. The same spots were also introduced in 19 other countries with little modification. For example, U.S. football scenes were simply replaced with soccer shots in the non-American commercials. Other than that, though the models in Gillette's commercials speak 26 different languages, they all use the same pitch.

Source: Dom Del Prete, "Winning Strategies Lead to Global Marketing Success," *Marketing News*, August 18, 1997, pp. 1 and 2; and "Unconditional Guarantee Puts Lands' End in German Court," *DM News*, July 14, 1997, p. 1.

---

to convince wholesalers and retailers to stock and sell merchandise. If the push strategy works, consumers will then walk into a store, see the product, and buy it. The idea is to push the product through the distribution system to the stores.

A second strategy is called a pull strategy. In a **pull strategy**, heavy advertising and sales promotion efforts are directed toward consumers so that they'll request the products from retailers. If the pull strategy works, consumers will go to the store and order the products. Seeing the demand for the products, the store owner will then order them from the wholesaler. The wholesaler, in turn, will order them from the producer. Products are thus pulled down through the distribution system. Dr. Pepper has used TV advertising in a pull strategy to increase distribution. Tripledge windshield wipers also reached retail stores through a pull strategy. Of course, a company could use both push and pull strategies at the same time in a major promotional effort. The latest in pull and push strategies are being conducted on the Internet, with companies sending

◄ **LEARNING GOAL 6.**
Compare and contrast push and pull promotional strategies.

pull strategy
Promotional strategy in which heavy advertising and sales promotion efforts are directed toward consumers so that they'll request the products from retailers.

◄ **CONSIDER USING CRITICAL THINKING EXERCISE**
16-2
Advertising Appeals
(SCANS)

The Newspaper National Network helps businesses choose from among 1,500 daily papers to target their promotions to select markets. Advertising is just one part of the promotion mix that includes personal selling, publicity, and sales promotion. But newspapers are one of the leading media, and one of the most targeted (reaches specific geographic audiences). How often do you use the newspaper when looking for items to buy versus magazines or other sources ?

messages to both consumers and businesses.[21]

The third way to move goods from producer to consumer is to make promotion part of a total systems approach to marketing. That is, promotion would be part of supply-chain management ➤ P.442 ◀. In such cases, retailers would work with producers and distributors to make the supply chain as efficient as possible. Then a promotional plan would be developed for the whole system. The idea would be to develop a value package ➤ P.408 ◀ that would appeal to everyone: manufacturers, distributors, retailers, and consumers. The trend today is toward everyday low pricing because that results in the greatest profit for sellers and good bargains for consumers. The best deal for consumers is to take advantage of coupons and other money-saving promotions, but those have proven less profitable for sellers and thus may be unsustainable in the long run.

Critical Thinking

What kinds of problems can emerge if a firm doesn't communicate with environmentalists, the news media, and the local community? In your area have you seen examples of firms that aren't responsive to the community? What were the consequences?

➤ CONSIDER USING SUPPLEMENTAL CASE 16-2
NEC Technology
(SCANS)

••• THE AGE OF INTERACTIVE MARKETING •••

New information technologies such as fax on demand, 900 telephone service, the Internet, databases, e-mail, and CD-ROMs have created a whole new way of marketing to consumers and businesses. The new age of marketing could be called the interactive age because marketers are now able to establish and maintain a dialogue with selected customers over time. Control over promotional messages is being shifted from the seller to the buyer.[22] As we have noted throughout this book, buyers can get on the Internet and seek out whatever information they need to make a purchase.

These new developments have had some effect already, and are expected to have a profound effect on promotion and on marketing in general. Marketing practitioners need to learn these new concepts or risk becoming obsolete. Today's students have the advantage of studying information technology in school and applying the concepts immediately without the bias of old-style marketing thinking. We'll explore these new concepts next.

···· ▬▬▬ ····

INTEGRATED MARKETING COMMUNICATION (IMC)

An **integrated marketing communication (IMC)** system is a formal mechanism for uniting all the promotional efforts in an organization to make them more consistent and more responsive to that organization's customers and other stakeholders. In the past, advertising was created by ad agencies, public relations was created by PR firms, and so forth. There was little coordination of promotional efforts. Today, all of that's changing in many companies. To implement an IMC system, you start by gathering data about customers and stakeholders and their information needs. Gathering such data and making them accessible to everyone in the channel of distribution ➤ P.442 ◄ is a key to future marketing success. All messages reaching customers, potential customers, and other stakeholders must be consistent and coordinated.[23]

Effective marketing communication demands a complete restructuring of the communication function. Let's explore the three steps in developing an interactive marketing communication system. An **interactive marketing communication system** is one where consumers can access company information on their own and supply information about themselves in an ongoing dialogue. Here are the basic steps:

1. Gather data constantly about the groups affected by the organization (including customers, potential customers, and other stakeholders) and keep that information in a database. Make the data available to everyone in the organization. An up-to-date information database is critical to any successful program. Today, a company can gather data from sales transactions, letters, e-mail, and faxes. It may also turn to a company that specializes in gathering such data.

2. Respond quickly to customer and other stakeholder information by adjusting company policies and practices and by designing wanted products and services for target markets. A responsive firm adapts to changing wants and needs quickly and captures the market from other, less responsive firms. That's why information is so vital to organizations today and why so much money is spent on computers and information systems. One reason why small firms are capturing markets from large firms is that small firms tend to be better listeners, to have fewer layers of management in which information gets lost, and to be more responsive to changes in the market.

3. Make it possible for customers and potential customers to obtain the information they need to make a purchase. Then make it easy for people to buy your products in stores or from the company directly by placing an order through e-mail, fax, phone, or other means.

··· INTERACTIVE MARKETING ON THE INTERNET ···

The key to marketing success in the future is interactivity: maintaining a dialogue with consumers.[24] Eventually, such open communication will lead marketers from today's emphasis on mass marketing to a greater emphasis on one-to-one marketing or mass customization. The advantages of interactive marketing on the Internet include the following:[25]

1. Customers can access information anytime they want, 24 hours a day. From the company's perspective, product information can reach markets anywhere in the world inexpensively.

◄ LEARNING GOAL 7.
Describe integrated marketing communication and the role of interactive communications within it.

integrated marketing communication (IMC)
A formal mechanism for uniting all the promotional efforts in an organization to make them more consistent and more responsive to that organization's customers and other stakeholders.

interactive marketing communication system
A system in which consumers can access company information on their own and supply information about themselves in an ongoing dialogue.

◄ CONSIDER USING OT ACETATE 16-12
Objectives of Integrated Marketing Communications

◄ CONSIDER USING LECTURE ENHANCER 16-19
"A" Letters

◄ CONSIDER USING SUPPLEMENTAL CASE 16-3
Waking Up the Coffee Industry **(SCANS)**

◄ CONSIDER USING LECTURE ENHANCER 16-20
Looking for Prospects on the Web

◄ CONSIDER USING LECTURE ENHANCER 16-21
Advertising on the World Wide Web

Charles Schwab offers on-line trading for low fees. Thousands of other companies are joining Charles Schwab by offering everything from automobiles to books, cameras, and music videos on-line. Consumers have gone from being passive receivers of information during TV or radio shows to being active searchers of information. In this new era, the Internet has become the medium of the future. The possibilities for interactive dialogue seem endless.

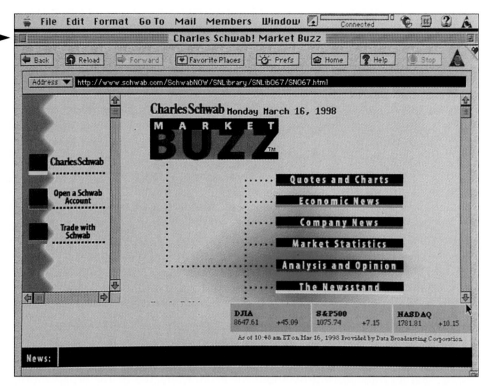

2. Electronic advertisements and catalogs can be updated continually and do not have to be printed, stored, or shipped. Traditional promotional materials, on the other hand, are relatively costly and are difficult to change.

3. Small companies can reach consumers as easily as large firms can, especially if those large firms fail to adjust to the new technologies and market realities.

4. Buyers and sellers can engage in a dialogue over time so that both feel they are getting the best deal. Transactions become interactions.

••• MARKETING SERVICES ON THE INTERNET •••

The promotion of services is often harder than the promotion of goods because the product is intangible and customers can't visualize all the benefits they may receive. A good example of this is brokerage services. What does one financial broker have that others do not? To answer that question, Charles Schwab & Company began to use the Internet to promote its services. Schwab is the leading provider of discount brokerage services and the pioneer of no-transaction-fee mutual funds.

Schwab has a comprehensive line of electronic information services designed to help customers manage their investments through the Internet. "Market Buzz" gives users access to a wealth of stock and market data; One-Source Online provides performance information on the 1,200 or so mutual funds that are part of the on-line supermarket of funds available through Schwab. The latest service is a news and information service that is updated every 15 minutes with information from Dow Online News, PR Newswire, Business Wire, and Newsbytes News Network.

Customers who want to do business with Schwab on-line pay a flat fee of less than $30 per trade for trades up to 1,000 shares and less for larger trades. Schwab is available by phone 24 hours a day, seven days a week. It also has 236 branches where customers can enter and talk to a broker in person.

Legal Briefcase

http://law.house.gov/

Going Global Means Adhering to Global Laws

The Internet makes it inexpensive and relatively easy to reach customers in almost every country of the world. That's the good news. The bad news is that your company will have to learn the many local on-line commerce laws outside of its state and country.

When you conduct transactions on the Internet, you are exposed to the various laws in different states. Although you may be conforming to laws in your own state, you may be sued in another state for some law about which you weren't even aware. The same is true in ▲

other countries. Many countries greatly restrict what you can say and do to promote and sell your products.

Laws in various countries have not kept up with the latest technological changes. Until they do catch up, it would be wise to research the law in various countries before launching a global marketing strategy on the Internet.

Source: "Net Legislation in the Hood," *Home Office Computing,* September 1997, p. 36. William C. Taylor, "Permission Marketing," *Fast Company,* April–May 1998, pp.198–212.

Companies such as Schwab are completely changing how organizations interact with customers. The box called Legal Briefcase outlines some legal issues that may come up for companies that use the Internet to reach global markets. If the legal issues can be managed, global buyers and sellers may enjoy the potential for establishing a dialogue over time where they can discuss goods and services on-line and conduct transactions the same way. But Schwab still uses traditional promotional techniques, such as newspaper advertising, magazine advertising, and direct mail to attract customers to its Web site.

••• THE NEW INTERACTIVE MEDIA •••

One of the newer ways of communicating with customers is through fax on demand. In a **fax-on-demand** arrangement, product information is sent by fax at the request of a customer or potential customer. A company gives a customer or potential customer a phone number to call. When consumers call, they are given a series of numbers to dial in to receive whatever information they desire. That information is then faxed to them immediately.

Integrated marketing communication blends with interactive communications when phone, fax, e-mail, television, and radio are all combined in one promotion. A radio station, for example, may promote a TV show by allowing listeners to participate in a contest in which they answer a series of questions by e-mail, fax, or phone. If participants are required to give their name, address, and phone number, the promoter can build a great database of potential customers. This enables the TV show to get sponsors.

E-mail is an effective way of establishing a dialogue with customers. Customers can leave questions on a company's e-mail system, and the company can answer them quickly. Similarly, 800 and 900 phone numbers enable customers to call and get desired information. Although some companies use automated phone systems, customers don't always like such impersonal service. Therefore, companies may choose to assign telemarketers to answer the phone and provide consumers with personal service.

Sometimes customers need a lot of information about a product and want to see it in action. As we mentioned earlier, infomercials can provide that kind of information, but they are expensive. In the future, customers who need

fax-on-demand
An arrangement in which product information is sent by fax at the request of a customer or potential customer.

Spotlight on Small Business

http://www.sosland.com/MarketFax

Using New Technology to Communicate with Customers

In the past, small businesses have felt that it was their responsibility to advertise to buyers in order to persuade them to buy. However, as a buyer you know that what often prevents you from making a decision to purchase is a lack of information. The question then becomes, How can small businesses make product information available so that buyers can obtain it whenever they want? One answer is to use a system like MarketFax. Here's how it works: You set up a data system at your company that contains all the information you want your potential customers to have. For example, the Boston Computer Exchange took all the documents it normally mailed to clients and put them in a MarketFax system.

Then you give customers and potential customers a special phone number. When they call that number, the ▲

system asks them what information they desire and requests a fax number. Clients key in their fax numbers and then hang up. A few moments later, the system sends the selected information by fax. Thus, all the information needed is sent instantly in printed form. Through this system the Boston Computer Exchange makes available price sheets, news items about popular products, policy statements, order forms, and more. This is just one example of how small companies can use the latest in technology to establish the kinds of communication with their customers that create long-term marketing relationships. Other such technologies include e-mail and inexpensive Web sites tied to other Web sites where consumers can get product information.

---

disk-based advertising
Product information provided on a CD-ROM or computer disk.

detailed information will turn to disk-based advertising. **Disk-based advertising** is product information provided on a CD-ROM or computer disk. That information can be in graphic form and accompanied by sound. Consumers can search the CD or disks for whatever information they want. They then can contact the company by phone, fax, e-mail, or letter to order the product they want, or they can go to the store to complete their purchase.

With the Internet, a whole new world of interactivity develops. Chat rooms can be established where consumers talk with other consumers about products. They can also chat with people from different departments in the company.

The net result of the new technology is that companies will have to totally rethink how marketing and promotion will be done in the future. There is likely to be a big dropoff in TV and other mass advertising, although such advertising will still be needed to establish name recognition and to introduce new products. There is expected to be a huge increase in the use of the Internet as a promotional and marketing tool.[26] The same is true of e-mail, fax, and other communication tools. Students who learn how to communicate interactively with customers—that is, in a dialogue—will rise to the top of marketing firms quickly. Many jobs will be created as well in the management of databases. Salespeople will be intimately linked to the system through laptop computers, modems, fax machines, and e-mail.

Soon there may be as many Internet malls as there are regional malls. Shoppers will be able to request information from multiple firms, compare prices, and make purchases from their homes. What effect will this have on traditional retailers? What will they have to do to encourage customers to keep coming into their stores? Retail location on the Internet will be as important as retail location in cities. How many retailers are prepared for such a shift? Advertising agencies will have to learn to work in the new media or face obsolescence. In short, everyone in marketing will be affected by the interactive age, and that includes you. If you are not familiar with the concepts and terms, now is the time to learn. If you keep up with developments as they occur, you will be in the vanguard and will increase your chances of finding the job you want when you graduate. The box called Spotlight on Small Business explores, for example, how small businesses can use fax machines to compete.

Progress Check

- What are the three steps used in setting up an interactive marketing communication system?
- What are the advantages of interactive marketing on the Internet?
- Could you describe how to implement a push strategy for Fiberrific cereal? A pull strategy?
- What are the new technologies that are making interactivity possible?

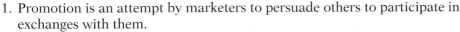

SUMMARY
• • • • • •

1. Promotion is an attempt by marketers to persuade others to participate in exchanges with them.
   - ***What are the six promotional tools that make up the promotion mix?***
   The six promotional tools are advertising, personal selling, word of mouth, sales promotion, public relations, and publicity.

   1. List and describe the various elements of the promotion mix.

2. Personal selling is the face-to-face presentation and promotion of products and services. It also involves the search for new prospects and follow-up service after the sale.
   - ***What are the seven steps of the selling process?***
   The steps of the selling process are (1) prospect and qualify, (2) preapproach, (3) approach, (4) make presentation, (5) answer objections, (6) close sale, and (7) follow-up.

   2. Illustrate the seven steps of the selling process.

3. Public relations is the management function that evaluates public attitudes, identifies the policies and procedures of an organization with the public interest, and executes a program of action to earn public understanding and acceptance.
   - ***What are the three major steps in a good public relations program?***
   (1) Listen to the public—public relations starts with good marketing research; (2) develop policies and procedures in the public interest—one doesn't earn understanding by bombarding the public with propaganda; one earns understanding by having programs and practices in the public interest; and (3) inform people that you're being responsive to their needs.
   - ***What is publicity?***
   Publicity is information distributed by the media that's not paid for, or controlled by, the seller. It's an effective way to reach the public. Publicity's greatest advantage is its believability.

   3. Describe the functions of the public relations department and the role of publicity.

4. Sales promotion motivates people to buy now instead of later, and word of mouth encourages people to talk about an organization and its products.
   - ***How are sales promotion activities used both within and outside the organization?***
   Internal sales promotion efforts are directed at salespeople and other customer-contact people to keep them enthusiastic about the company. Internal sales promotion activities include sales training, sales aids, audiovisual displays, and trade shows. External sales promotion (promotion to consumers) involves using samples, coupons, cents-off deals, displays, store demonstrators, premiums, and other such incentives.

   4. Explain the importance of sales promotion and word of mouth as promotional tools.

- ***What's the best way to generate positive word of mouth?***
The best way to generate positive word of mouth is to have a good product, provide good services, and keep customers happy. Word-of-mouth promotion thus includes (1) focusing on customer satisfaction and quality, (2) delivering on promises, and (3) targeting opinion leaders.

5. Describe advantages and disadvantages of various advertising media and explain the latest advertising techniques.

5. Many people mistake other promotional tools for advertising.
- ***How does advertising differ from the other promotional tools?***
Advertising is limited to paid, nonpersonal (not face-to-face) communication through various media by organizations and individuals who are in some way identified in the advertising message.
- ***What are the advantages of using the various media?***
You can review the advantages and disadvantages of the various advertising media in Figure 16.5.
- ***How is technology used in advertising?***
Rather than passively receive programming (news, entertainment, and commercials), consumers using interactive TV can actively control what they receive and can conduct a dialogue with advertisers. They can eliminate commercials from shows or watch the commercials and respond electronically (responses include product orders). Some on-line services will offer advertising—and nothing but advertising—on demand. There will be databases for "considered purchases," offering consumers in-depth information (via text, pictures, and sound) about cars, travel, consumer electronics, and other high-priced items.

6. Compare and contrast push and pull promotional strategies.

6. Marketers use various promotional strategies to move goods from producers to consumers.
- ***What are the various promotional strategies?***
(1) In a push strategy, the producer uses advertising, personal selling, sales promotion, and all other promotional tools to convince wholesalers and retailers to stock and sell merchandise. (2) In a pull strategy, heavy advertising and sales promotion efforts are directed toward consumers so that they'll request the products from retailers. (3) A final way to move goods from producer to consumer is to make promotion part of a total systems approach to marketing. That is, promotion would be part of supply-chain management, as discussed in Chapter 15. In such cases, retailers would work with producers and distributors to make the supply chain as efficient as possible.

7. Describe integrated marketing communication and the role of interactive communications within it.

7. An integrated marketing communication system is a formal mechanism for uniting all the promotional efforts in an organization to make it more responsive to its customers and other stakeholders.
- ***How do you set up an integrated marketing communication system?***
An integrated marketing communication system consists of three ongoing parts: (1) listen constantly to all groups affected by the organization, keep that information in a database, and make that information available to everyone in the organization; (2) respond quickly to customer and other stakeholder information by adjusting company policies and practices and by designing wanted products and services for target markets; and (3) use integrated marketing communication to let all customers and other stakeholders know that the firm is listening and responding to their needs.
- ***What are some of the new interactive media?***
Interactive media include fax on demand (where consumers can dial a number and get a faxed response to questions), e-mail (where consumers can request information and have an immediate response via computer), and disk-based media (where consumers can access whatever information they want from a CD-ROM or computer disk).

advertising 481	interactive marketing communication system 489	public relations (PR) 477
direct marketing 472		publicity 478
disk-based advertising 492	mass customization 486	pull strategy 487
fax-on-demand 491	personal selling 472	push strategy 486
infomercial 485	promotion 472	sales promotion 479
integrated marketing communication (IMC) system 489	promotion mix 472	trade show 471
	prospecting 473	word-of-mouth promotion 480

DEVELOPING WORKPLACE SKILLS

1. Choose two ads from a newspaper or magazine, one that you consider good and one that you don't consider good. Be prepared to discuss why you feel as you do about each ad.

2. Scan your local newspaper for examples of publicity (stories about new products) and sales promotion (coupons, contests, sweepstakes). Share your examples and discuss the effectiveness of such promotional efforts with the class.

3. Select and bring to class a product that you think others would find interesting. Set up a role-playing situation in which you attempt to sell the product to your classmates in a five-minute sales presentation.

4. Watch for an infomercial or two on TV. Then write a two-page report discussing what made the infomercial good or bad, in your opinion.

5. Make a list of six products (goods and services) that most students own or use and then debate which promotional techniques prompt you to buy these goods and services: advertising, personal selling, publicity, sales promotion, or word-of-mouth.

TAKING IT TO THE NET

Purpose

To recognize the two types of promotional Web sites and to evaluate their effectiveness in meeting a company's marketing goals.

Exercise

There are two types of promotional Web sites: a corporate Web site and a marketing Web site. A corporate Web site might contain information found in a brochure: description of products, phone numbers, addresses, e-mail address, and so on. The URL of the site can appear in a print ad or at the end of a radio or television commercial. Consumers can use the Web to get far more information than they can get from a broadcast or print ad. In addition, they can use the site to request a sales call, to find out the location of the nearest dealer, or to ask a question.

A marketing site is more like a product than an advertisement. Compared to a corporate site, a marketing site is more like a constantly changing magazine than a brochure. It is designed to pull consumers to the site, perhaps with banners or links. It is action oriented, set to move the consumer closer to a sale.

DDB Needham is an advertising agency that applies Web technology to marketing. Visit its site at http://www.ddbniac.com/ and look through the on-line portfolio of Web sites it has developed for products and companies such as Pepsi, Mountain Dew, and GTE.

1. Which of the Web sites developed by DDB are corporate sites? Which are marketing sites? Explain your answers.

2. How does DDB use this medium to present its messages and advance its clients' marketing objectives? Which of these sites do you like and why? Consider these criteria in evaluating the Web sites:

- Achieves marketing objectives (such as consumer awareness, image, trial, accelerating repurchase, attracting job candidates).
- Attracts target market.
- Is useful to target market.
- Is easy to navigate.
- Is graphically pleasing.
- Loads quickly.

3. Choose one of the Web sites designed by DDB and offer suggestions for improving the site. If possible, attempt to redesign the main page of the Web site based on your analysis.

Practicing Management Decisions

CASE
• • • • • •
THE PEPSI CHALLENGE
• • • • • •

Few companies face stronger global competition than the Pepsi-Cola Company, whose main rival is, of course, the Coca-Cola Company. PepsiCo recently decided that the best way to compete with Coke was to get closer to the customer. PepsiCo then concluded that the best means to do that was by gathering more information about customers, its own as well as those of Coke, and then targeting those people with an integrated promotional effort.

As the manager of database marketing at PepsiCo, Jerry Winter had the job of managing information about customers and competitors. But Winter needed help in creating a unified promotional campaign based on that information. He suggested hiring Rapp Collins Worldwide as PepsiCo's first direct marketing agency.

Over the years, Winter's area had gathered extensive information about Pepsi's frequent customers as well as those of Coke. During this period, he also noted that customers for PepsiCo's other products—Frito Lay snack foods—are mostly the same people: teens and families. He determined that it would be possible to develop similar campaigns to reach these targets. Rapp Collins was also commissioned by Pizza Hut to create a program rewarding frequent customers.

Using Rapp Collins's input and PepsiCo's database, the company intends to develop direct mail and other promotional techniques to win Coke customers over to Pepsi. For example, a Diet Pepsi campaign called "Convert a Million" aimed to get Diet Coke users to switch to Diet Pepsi. Sample cases of Diet Pepsi were mailed to 1 million Diet Coke–drinking households. The idea was to send each Diet Coke drinker enough Diet Pepsi to last a while until he or she got used to the taste and, hopefully, became attracted to the product.

Decision Questions

1. What use could Pepsi make of the Internet when trying to establish a relationship with Pepsi users?
2. How could Pepsi target coffee drinkers to win them over to Pepsi as an alternative beverage to perk them up in the afternoon?
3. Who among your fellow students would you target with diet Pepsi versus regular Pepsi?
4. What food companies could Pepsi join with to promote Pepsi with their food?

Airwalk Footwear turned to Lambesis, a full-service promotional firm, to design a promotional strategy for its shoes. The goal was to create a brand image that would appeal to young people, which meant listening to that group more closely than most companies had done before. There was very little research available, so the company had to do its own. They went where teenagers ate, shopped, and hung out. They observed, asked questions, and learned as much as possible about teens' lifestyle, especially among the trendsetters. At first the idea was to target the U.S. market, but Lambesis decided that a global appeal would be more effective. The company's research showed that a 17-year-old in Mexico City or Moscow had the same wants and needs as a 17-year-old in the United States. That may not be true of a different age group, but it was true of this one. Based on that research, Lambesis tried to design a universal message, perhaps one including romance, that would have appeal to teenagers in all countries.

Lambesis took an integrated marketing communication approach. To this company, that meant having all departments working together as a team to develop one unified message in all media and in all communications. Team members from product development, research, broadcast, and Web-site development worked together to develop an overall strategy for Airwalk. The strategy had three themes: (1) entertainment, (2) sports, and (3) style. Every message would try to combine these three elements. even the shoebox was designed in keeping with the themes.

The integrated marketing communication effort included advertising, public relations, sales promotion, word of mouth, direct selling, and the Internet. Advertising vehicles included TV, T-shirts, and posters all over town. A pull strategy was used for advertising. That is, advertising for leading-edge products was directed at teenagers who then went into shoe stores and requested specific Airwalk shoes. The magazines chosen were mostly underground magazines, and the TV shows were ones that appealed to this group but few others.

VIDEO CASE

· · · · · ·

AIRWALK FOOTWEAR

Sales promotion efforts included contests where the winners won trips to various places. Gifts were also sent to people who responded to direct marketing appeals. Much effort also went into public relations and event sponsorship. That included events such as snowboard contests where the participants wore Airwalk snowboarding boots. Rock bands were given free shoes, and special promotions were built around those bands. Every communication tool conveyed the same clear message: these shoes are designed for you and your friends—and they are exciting. Word of mouth spread naturally among the targeted teens.

The Web site was constantly updated to attract people back. It takes all the elements of entertainment, sports, and style to attract people to a Web site and have them spend some time there.

In short, the campaign was targeted precisely to the Airwalk teenage market. As a result of the integrated marketing communication effort, Airwalk sales doubled and then doubled again. Sales globally went from $20 million to $300 million in 14 different countries.

Discussion Questions

1. What are some of the challenges you would face if you were trying to develop a Web site for Airwalk Footwear that would have global appeal (multiple languages) and would allow teens to order by phone, fax, or mail?
2. Could Airwalk expand its market to other market segments? Which segments would offer the greatest opportunities?
3. Would you expand the Airwalk product mix to include clothing for skateboarders and snowboarders? Give reasons why or why not.
4. If you were in charge of developing a promotional strategy for the coming year, what would you do differently to maintain interest among this target audience? Would you emphasize advertising, public relations, sales promotion, word of mouth, direct marketing, or some combination? Justify your strategy.

Part5

Fundamentals of Marketing

Marketing is a challenging and dynamic area in which to choose a career. The field is so varied, it can attract people with a tremendous variety of talents, skills, and interest areas. For example, the "number crunching" person could choose marketing research; artistic individuals might be attracted to advertising or sales promotion; and entrepreneurial types might choose wholesaling or retailing. There are dozens of other combinations.

Marketing is based on the exchange of goods and services. Like every other area of business, it is dynamic and always changing, especially with the current emphasis on international markets. Anyone who wants to be involved in this exciting area must be flexible and able to change with the times as tastes for new products and services change and as new markets open and old ones close. Marketing is an area that remains wide open.

··· SKILLS ···

Although marketing draws on talents from a variety of personality types and skill areas, some realistic generalizations can be made about skills that most marketers have in common. Marketers need to be people oriented, even the number crunchers mentioned above. They also need to be tuned in to the culture of the country or region where they are marketing. They need to sense trends and changing habits of customers. Above all, they must be effective communicators, possessing an ability to be heard and noticed as well as to hear and notice the needs of others. The amount of education required varies widely from position to position, and even firm to firm.

··· CAREER PATHS ···

Many marketing careers start out as sales positions. Sales is a challenging area in which individuals can prove themselves, using that success as a means of moving up to sales manager or other positions of responsibility. Advertising is another avenue of interest, especially for those who are attracted to the tantalizing mixture of psychology, communications, and art that advertisers use. Retailing also offers a variety of opportunities, some more marketing-oriented that others.

Not all positions in marketing require a four-year degree, although one is usually a formally stated requisite. In many companies, your skill level is the important issue. Marketing skills can often be developed in two-year business programs and in real-world experience. On-campus clubs such as FBLA (Future Business Leaders of America) and DECA (Distributive Education Clubs of America) can help you learn to compete in the world of marketing while still in school.

SOME POSSIBLE CAREERS IN MARKETING

Job title	Salary	Job duties	Career path	Prospects
Market researcher	23,000–$34,000 (start) Market research director, as much as $140,000.	Design surveys, opinion polls, and questionnaires; collect data using various methods.	Bachelor's degree with marketing courses. Some positions require only talent and desire to learn.	Good prospects through 2006.
Sales representative	$23,000–$100,000+ (depends both on the company and initiative of the individual).	Call on customers; fulfill needs; provide follow-up; sometimes deal with credit issues; report regularly to home office.	Training programs usually provided by company. Successful representatives are usually promoted to sales manager.	Many new opportunities in the future, especially in high tech and international sales.
Purchasing agent (buyer)	$18,400–$63,000 (median $33,200).	Stay informed about buying opportunities; maintain good relations with company sales force. Maintain positive relations with suppliers.	Usually start out as buyer trainee, or assistant buyer. Can be promoted to purchasing manager or merchandising manager.	Growth through 2006 will be steady.
Advertising agent or manager	$27,000 to start; median $46,000.	Trainee positions are usually in copywriting, layout, or other less responsible positions. Copywriters must have a command of written English. Layout people need a talent for proportion and for predicting reader reaction.	Entry-level positions are usually in specific areas of advertising. A copywriter can be promoted to senior copywriter. The highest promotion will usually be to creative director.	Slow growth through 2006. Growth is in areas of sales promotion.
Public relations specialist	median $46,000; senior $76,900.	Build and maintain a good image for the company. Communicate the goals and purposes of the company to the public and stockholders, if any. Must be good writer and speaker and be comfortable in all areas of the mass media.	College degree with entry-level experience (as an unpaid student trainee, etc.). Many PR people started in some other career, such as journalism, but made this career move later. Can be promoted to management, often outside of public relations, sometimes into market research.	More small companies are now using PR specialists. Future prospects are good to 2006, especially in smaller firms.
Marketing consultant	Varies greatly, because a consultant is in business for himself or herself.	Begin like any service-based entrepreneur. Need especially to make contacts with firms needing your service.	Intensive training needed; essential to be correct in advice. Serve as intern in consulting firm or start on your own with aggressive approach.	Growth good through 2006, especially in areas of international and high tech marketing.

Source: *Occupational Outlook Handbook*, 1998–1999 Edition, Bureau of Labor Statistics.

ISCO Industries, Inc.

Name: Garry Bouvet

Age: 32

Position/title: Regional Sales Manager

Salary range: $30,000 + bonus

Time in this position: Since June 1997 I have been in sales for ISCO Industries. Previously, I was a Manufacturer's Representative and ISCO Industries was one of my accounts. We developed such a great working relationship that they then asked me to come work for them.

Major factors in the decision to take this position: I like the income potential that a sales management position provides. In addition, this position meant a reduction in my travel. With my reduced travel, and the location of my job I can be closer to my family.

Company name: ISCO Industries, Inc.

Company's web address: www.isco-pipe.com

Company description: ISCO Industries, Inc., is a distributor for pipe, fittings, and accessory equipment.

Job description: I sell and promote products for ISCO in numerous markets and various types of industries. My sales position encompasses business to business, or industrial marketing.

Career paths: Previously, I was an independent manufacturer's representative. ISCO was actually one of my accounts. They then asked me to work for them.

Ideal next job: My ideal next job is being a sales manager and managing others.

Best part of your job: I enjoy being my own boss and having the freedom to run my own territory. I also enjoy the satisfaction of solving problems and adding value to projects. Most of all, I enjoy meeting new people.

Worst part of your job: Keeping my paperwork organized can be challenging. I also would rather call on established accounts versus making cold calls.

Educational background: I received an A.A.S. from Lincoln Land Community College in Business Management. I then received my B.A. in Management from the University of Illinois—Springfield, and my M.B.A. from Lindenwood College.

Favorite course: Marketing and management courses.

Best course for your career: The courses that had the most application for what I am doing now were my marketing courses.

Compliments of Professor Robert Redick, Lincoln Land Community College, Springfield, Illinois

Using Technology to Manage Information

Chapter

17

LEARNING GOALS

After you have read and studied this chapter,
you should be able to

1 Outline the changing role of business technology.

2 Compare the scope of the Internet, intranets, and extranets as tools in managing information.

3 List the steps in managing information, and identify the characteristics of useful information.

4 Review the hardware most frequently used in business, and outline the benefits of the move toward computer networks.

5 Classify the computer software most frequently used in business.

6 Evaluate the human resource, security, and privacy issues in management that are affected by information technology.

7 Identify the careers that are gaining or losing workers due to the growth of information technology.

One of the disadvantages of being self-employed is that it is difficult to take time off. With today's technology, however, many entrepreneurs are finding that they don't need to be chained to their desks to keep their businesses running smoothly.

Vance Webster, an insurance services entrepreneur, traded his office for a 44-foot yacht and sailed to the San Juan Islands, taking his business with him. Armed with a cell phone, notebook computer, and pager, Webster kept his business afloat while he enjoyed the sights. He updated his voice mail each morning by referring to the day's date and telling callers that he'd check back for messages later in the day. He sent routine replies (such as those to customers who needed to register cars for insurance) to the database on his notebook computer. He was able to handle long-distance emergencies as well. For example, one client phoned in that his wife had hit a post supporting his carport, which caused the roof to collapse on top of his car. Webster checked the client's policy on his notebook, called him back right away to say everything was covered, and gave him the claims-office phone number.

PROFILE

Vance Webster, Insurance Services Entrepreneur

Technology is changing the way we do business. Technological improvements have made the Internet friendlier and less expensive than it was in the beginning. This technology includes powerful microprocessors and network computers, inexpensive digital storage, improved software development tools, simplified user interfaces, and a low-cost communications bandwidth (the "pipeline" data flows through). For millions of businesspeople, using a computer is now as commonplace as using a telephone.

Businesses small and large will succeed or fail based on their ability to manage information. New technology will enable managers to make informed decisions and to communicate with each other, with customers, and with other companies, including suppliers. The rapid technological developments along the information superhighway make this one of the most exciting times in history. The question is, Will you be able to keep up?

Sources: Dale D. Buss, "Take a Break," *Home Office Computing*, May 1997, pp. 60–64; and Joia Shillingford, "Teleworking," *Financial Times*, September 10, 1997, p. 13.

THE ROLE OF INFORMATION TECHNOLOGY

Throughout this text, we have emphasized the need for managing information flows among businesses and their employees, businesses and their customers, and so on. Those managers who try to rely on the old ways of doing things will simply not be able to compete with those who have the latest in technology and know how to use it.

Business technology has often changed names and changed roles. In the 1970s, business technology was known as **data processing (DP)**. (Although many people use the words *data* and *information* interchangeably, they are different. Data are raw, unanalyzed, and unsummarized facts and figures. Information is the processed and summarized data that can be used for managerial decision making.) DP was used to support an existing business; its primary purpose was to improve the flow of financial information. DP employees tended to be hidden in a back room and rarely came in contact with customers.

In the 1980s, business technology became known as **information systems (IS)**. IS moved out of the back room and into the center of the business.

◄ **LEARNING GOAL 1.**
Outline the changing role of business technology.

◄ **CONSIDER USING TM 123**
Chapter Outline.

data processing (DP)
Technology that supported an existing business; primarily used to improve the flow of financial information.

information systems (IS)
Technology that helps companies *do* business; includes such tools as automated teller machines (ATMs) and voice mail.

Ben Franklin warned us that "time is money." Well, even wise old Ben would be proud of the time that's saved using information technology such as IBM's RS/6000 SP. With the RS/6000 system, companies in the travel, financial, and health care industries can simplify business transactions with just the click of a finger.

information technology (IT)
Technology that helps companies *change* business by allowing them to use new methods.

virtualization
Accessibility through technology that allows business to be conducted independent of location.

➤ **CONSIDER USING OT ACETATE 17-1**
The number of pagers in the U.S.

➤ **CONSIDER USING CRITICAL THINKING EXERCISE 17-1**
Computers Come to College (**SCANS**)

Its role changed from supporting the business to *doing* business. Customers began to interact with a wide array of technological tools, from automated teller machines (ATMs) to voice mail. As business increased its use of information systems, it became more dependent on them.

Until the late 1980s, business technology was just an addition to the existing way of doing business. Keeping up-to-date was a matter of using new technology on *old* methods. But things started to change as the 1990s approached. Businesses shifted to using new technology on *new* methods. Business technology then became known as **information technology (IT)**, and its role became to *change* business.

⋯ HOW INFORMATION TECHNOLOGY ⋯ CHANGES BUSINESS

Time and place have always been at the center of business. Customers had to go to the business during business hours to satisfy their needs. We went *to* the store to buy clothes. We went *to* the bank to arrange for a loan. Businesses decided when and where we did business with them. Today IT allows businesses to deliver products and services whenever and wherever it is convenient for the *customer*. Thus, you can order clothes from the Home Shopping Network and arrange a home mortgage loan by phone, at a time you choose.

Consider how IT has changed the entertainment industry. If you wanted to see a movie 30 years ago, you had to go to a movie theater. Twenty-five years ago you could wait for it to be on television. Fifteen years ago you could wait for it to be on cable television. Ten years ago you could go to a video store and rent it. Now you can order video on demand by satellite or cable.

As IT breaks time and location barriers, it creates organizations and services that are independent of location. For example, NASDAQ and SOFFEX are electronic stock exchanges without trading floors. Buyers and sellers make trades by computer.

Being independent of location brings work to people instead of people to work. With IT, data and information can flow more than 8,000 miles in a second, allowing businesses to conduct work around the globe continuously. We are moving toward what we call **virtualization**; that is, accessibility through technology that allows business to be conducted independent of location. For example, you can carry a virtual office in your pocket or purse. Such tools as cellular phones, pagers, laptop computers, and personal digital assistants allow you to access people and information as if you were in an actual office. Likewise, virtual communities are forming as people who would otherwise not have met communicate with each other through the virtual post office created by computer networks.

Doing business drastically changes when companies increase their technological capabilities. See Figure 17.1 for other examples of how information technology changes business.

⋯ MOVING FROM INFORMATION TECHNOLOGY TOWARD ⋯ KNOWLEDGE TECHNOLOGY

In the mid-1990s, yet another change occurred in the terminology of business technology as we started moving away from information technology and

Organization	Technology is breaking down corporate barriers, allowing functional departments or product groups (even factory workers) to share critical information instantly.
Operations	Technology shrinks cycle times, reduces defects, and cuts waste. Service companies use electronic data interchange to streamline ordering and communication with suppliers and customers.
Staffing	Technology eliminates layers of management and cuts the number of employees. Companies use computers and telecommunication equipment to create "virtual offices" with employees in various locations.
New products	Information technology cuts development cycles by feeding customer and marketing comments to product development teams quickly so that they can revive products and target specific customers.
Customer relations	Customer service representatives can solve customers' problems instantly by using companywide databases to complete tasks from changing addresses to adjusting bills. Information gathered from customer service interactions can further stronger customer relationships.

FIGURE 17.1
• • • •
HOW INFORMATION TECHNOLOGY IS CHANGING BUSINESS

Here are a few ways that information technology is changing businesses, their employees, suppliers, and customers.

◄ **CONSIDER USING TM 124**
How Information Technology is Changing Business (Figure 17.1 on text page 505).

toward **knowledge technology (KT)**. Knowledge is information charged with enough intelligence to make it relevant and useful. KT adds a layer of intelligence to filter appropriate information and deliver it when it is needed. For example, consider the number 70. Alone, it doesn't mean much. Change it to 70 percent and it means a little more but still doesn't tell us a lot. Make it a 70 percent chance of rain and we have more meaning.

Now let's imagine you are the first one on your block with a wristwatch featuring KT. As you walk out the door, the watch signals you that it has a message: "70 percent chance of rain in your city today." KT just gave you relevant and useful information at the moment you needed it. Now you can head for class with an umbrella under your arm, knowing that you made an informed decision.

KT changes the traditional flow of information; instead of an individual going to the database, the data comes to the individual. For example, using KT business training software, AT&T can put a new employee at a workstation and then let the system take over to do everything from laying out a checklist of the tasks required on a shift to answering questions and offering insights that once would have taken up a supervisor's time. Knowledge databases may one day replace the traditional mentors who helped workers up the corporate ladder.[1]

knowledge technology (KT)
Technology that adds a layer of intelligence to filter appropriate information and deliver it when it is needed.

◄ **CONSIDER USING OT ACETATE 17-8**
Why Business Needs Information Technology.

◄ **CONSIDER USING LECTURE ENHANCER 17-1**
Selling Livestock on the Net.

◄ **CONSIDER USING LECTURE ENHANCER 17-2**
Automatic Teller Machines and Humans.

◄ **CONSIDER USING LECTURE ENHANCER 17-3**
Microcomputers Help to Run the Farm. (**SCANS**)

Advancements in technology have made reaching customers a continuous free-for-all among competitors. Home Depot attracts customers in this hotly competitive industry by using a satellite feed to broadcast "Breakfast with Bernie and Arthur" to home improvement wannabes.

KT "thinks" about the facts based on an individual's needs, reducing the time that person must spend on finding and getting information. Businesspeople who use KT can focus on what's important: *deciding* about how to react to problems and opportunities. According to some market analysts, by 2005 more money will be spent on knowledge-based IT than on traditional systems.[2]

Critical Thinking

Knowledge technology allows the database to go to the individual; the individual will no longer need to search through a database. Can you imagine how you could use such a system? If you could design it yourself, what would it look like and what would it do?

Progress Check

- How has the role of information technology changed since the days when it was known as data processing?

- In what way is knowledge technology different from information technology?

As more and more people go on-line, the Internet will continue its informational influence on many facets of our lives. In business, intranets have that same effect on the job. Intranets are companywide networks that use Internet-type technologies, but are closed to public access.

···· ▬▬▬ ····

THE ROAD TO KNOWLEDGE:
THE INTERNET, INTRANETS, AND EXTRANETS

A key issue for business today is how to get the right information to the right people at the right time. Knowledge, more than physical assets, is now the key to successful competition. That is why knowledge has become one of the more important factors of production.[3] The importance of business knowledge is nothing new—what is new is the recognition of the need to manage it like any other asset. To manage knowledge, a company needs to learn how to share information throughout the organization and to implement systems for creating new knowledge. This need is leading to new technologies that support the exchange of information among staff, suppliers, and customers. At the heart of this technology are the Internet, intranets, and extranets.[4]

You already know that the Internet is a network of computer networks. An **intranet** is a companywide network, closed to public access, that uses Internet-type technology. Some companies use intranets only to publish information for employees, such as phone lists and employee policy manuals. These companies do not enjoy as high a return on their investment as other companies that create interactive intranet applications. Such applications include allowing employees to update their addresses or submit company forms such as supply requisitions, timesheets, or payroll forms on-line. These applications save money or generate greater revenue because they eliminate paper handling and enable faster decision making.[5]

Sun designed the first **intranet** back when people thought intranet was a **typo.**

By 2002 between one-half and two-thirds of all businesses will be running intranets.[6] One problem with an intranet occurs when companies don't want others, particularly the competition, to see their site. To solve that problem, companies can construct a "firewall" between themselves and the outside world to protect corporate information from unauthorized users. A firewall can be hardware, software, or both.[7]

Many businesses choose to open their intranets to other, selected companies through the use of extranets.[8] An **extranet** is a semiprivate network that uses Internet technology and allows more than one company to access the same information or allows people on different servers to collaborate. One of the most common uses of extranets is to extend an intranet to outside customers.[9]

The Internet is changing the way we do business. No longer are the advantages of electronic data interchange (EDI) available only to the large companies that can afford such a system ⟫ P. 443 ⟪. Now almost all companies can use the Internet to share data and process orders, specifications, invoices, and payments.[10] "Only about 2 percent of organizations have EDI— but 99 percent have a PC and a telephone. The Internet creates a critical mass of people who can exchange data over the network," explains Matthew Wall, the business unit director at software company EDS.[11]

Another way that the Internet is changing how we do business is by making it easier for small businesses to sell their goods and services globally. Read the Reaching Beyond Our Borders box on page 509 to learn more about how technology can facilitate global business.

If there are no changes in network capacity, the more people use Internet technology, the slower it will become. But Internet computing isn't the only reason for traffic jams on the information superhighway. Remote and mobile workers trying to connect to the corporate networks also add to the congestion.[12] The traffic on the information superhighway has become so intense that early Net settlers—scientists and other scholars—have found that they have been squeezed off the crowded Internet and are unable to access, transmit, and manipulate complex mathematical models, data sets, and other digital

intranet
A companywide network, closed to public access, that uses Internet-type technology.

◄ **CONSIDER USING LECTURE ENHANCER 17-3**
Military Information Logjams.

extranet
A semiprivate network that uses Internet technology and allows more than one company to access the same information or allows people on different servers to collaborate.

◄ **CONSIDER USING OT ACETATE 17-2**
Growth of the On-line Market.

◄ **CONSIDER USING LECTURE ENHANCER 17-4**
How We Got the Internet.

◄ **CONSIDER USING LECTURE ENHANCER 17-5**
A Dictionary for Surfing the Internet.

◄ **CONSIDER USING OT ACETATE 17-3**
Growth Areas for the Internet.

◄ **CONSIDER USING OT ACETATE 17-4**
Most Important Web Site Characteristics.

Ford's intranet system, FOCALpt, is a powerful tool that helps dealers with customer-relationship management. Dealers can record a customer's needs and preferences every time the customer visits their sales or service departments, and then use the information to demonstrate that they remember that customer's needs and wants during later visits. Salespeople can access vehicle data, show a product video, compare vehicles with those of the competition, compare finance versus lease options, and more.

With use of the Internet growing at a frantic pace, traffic is becoming almost as congested as New York City at rush hour. But contain that road rage; a new system—Internet 2—will leave its older sibling in the dust and run 100 to 1,000 times faster than today. Internet 2 should help solve some of the bottlenecks and traffic jams on the information superhighway by 2000.

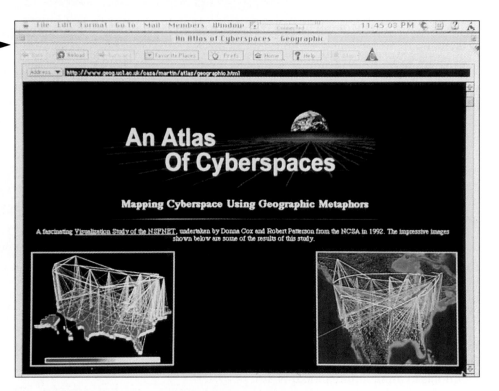

> **CONSIDER USING LECTURE ENHANCER 17-6**
Name That Shangri-la Web Site.

> **CONSIDER USING LECTURE ENHANCER 17-7**
Measure Internet Usage.

Internet 2
The new Internet system that links government supercomputer centers and a select group of universities; it will run 100 to 1,000 times faster than today's public infrastructure and will support heavy-duty applications.

> **CONSIDER USING OT ACETATE 17-4**
Most Important Web Site Characteristics.

> **LEARNING GOAL 3.**
List the steps in managing information and identify the characteristics of useful information.

> **CONSIDER USING OT ACETATE 17-5**
Leading On-line Activities According to Users.

elements of their craft. Their answer? Create another Internet, reserved for research purposes only.

The new system, **Internet 2**, will run 100 to 1,000 times faster than today's infrastructure and will support heavy-duty applications, such as videoconferencing, collaborative research, distance education, digital libraries, and full-body simulation environments known as teleimmersion. A key element of Internet 2 is a network called vBNS, or very high speed Backbone Network Service, which was set up in 1995 as a way to link government supercomputer centers and a select group of universities.[13] Although Internet 2 became available to a few select organizations in late 1997, it is expected to be available to the private sector by 2000. Cynics say that by then Internet 2 itself will be overrun by networked undergrads involved in role-playing games and other resource-hogging pursuits. But the designers of Internet 2 are thinking ahead. Not only do they expect Internet history to repeat itself but they are counting on it. They are planning to filter the Internet 2 technology out to the wider Internet community in such a way that there is plenty of room on the road for all of us—at a price, of course.[14]

···· ▬▬▬ ····

MANAGING INFORMATION

Even before the use of computers, managers had to sift through mountains of information to find what they needed to help them make decisions. Today businesspeople are deluged with information from voice mail, the Internet, fax machines, and e-mail. More than 2.7 *trillion* e-mail messages alone were sent in 1997. One study revealed that the average U.S. office worker sends 57 e-mail messages a day.[15] Businesspeople refer to this information overload as "infoglut."[16] Too much information can confuse issues rather than clarify them. How can managers keep from getting buried in

Reaching Beyond
Our Borders

Using the Internet to Go Global

Many businesses that hadn't had the money, time, or personnel to trade overseas are now using the Internet to reach beyond their borders. The information superhighway allows businesses to keep their doors open to customers in 160 countries 24 hours a day. Export sales account for approximately 18 percent of all business conducted on the Web, according to a research firm that tracks business on the Internet. In 1996, export sales on the Web reached $2.9 billion—six times the 1995 sales. To grow and compete in today's markets, businesses must consider the world their workplace and marketplace. Globalization is no longer merely incidental to growth but is becoming central to growth.

Global businesses have used phones or private data networks to connect with each other. But the Internet and its subset, the World Wide Web, open new opportunities. "Once you're on the Web, going global is a natural," says Irving Wladawsky-Berger, head of IBM's Internet division. "The difference between Peoria and Romania on the Web is not very large."

Here's how you can tap into resource guides and trade sites if you are considering using the Internet to sell your goods or services globally:

1. *Download on-line guides on the basics of exporting.* The Commerce Department's primer, *A Basic Guide to Exporting*, explains the ins and outs of exporting. ▲

You can get it free from the Maingate Corp.'s Web site (http://www.maingate.net/us-exports/bge.html).

2. *Search for possible foreign distributors by surfing buy/sell networks.* These are matchmaking services that specialize in companies looking for foreign agents to market their products. They provide contact information on hundreds of foreign distributors and are listed by country and industry. For example, Trade Compass (http://www.tradecompass.com) lets aspiring exporters lists their products or services free of charge. MultiVend, a New York maker of candy vending machines, increased sales 10 percent in the first year and a half it used Trade Compass.

3. *Visit a virtual trade show.* Save money by going to a trade show at home on the Web. Just like real trade shows with real booths, the computerized trade shows offer virtual booths that display a seller's products with the click of a mouse. Sites such as BemarNet (http://www.bemarnet.es) allow you to participate in a cyberexpo for $750 to $6,000 a booth depending on the number of products you show off. It's the next best thing to being there.

Sources: Peter J. Robinson, Jr., "Net Resources to Help You Export," *Your Company*, February 3–17, 1997; and Kevin Maney, "Technology Is 'Demolishing' Time, Distance," *USA Today*, April 24, 1997, pp. 1–2B.

---

the infoglut? Stepping back to gain perspective is the key to managing the sea of information.

The first step toward gaining perspective is to identify the four or five key goals you wish to reach. Eliminating the information that is not related to those top priorities can reduce the amount of information flowing into your office by half. For example, as we were gathering information to include in this chapter, we collected over 400 journal articles. Feeling the pressure of information overload, we identified the goals we wanted the chapter to accomplish and eliminated all the articles that didn't address those goals. As we further refined our goals, the huge stack of paper gradually dropped to a manageable size.

Obviously, not all of the information that ends up on your desk will be useful. The usefulness of management information depends on four characteristics:

◄ **CONSIDER USING OT ACETATE 17-6**
College and the Internet.

◄ **CONSIDER USING SUPPLEMENTAL CASE 17-1**
Government's Role in Building the Information Highway (**SCANS**)

1. *Quality.* Quality means that the information is accurate and reliable. When the clerk at a fast-food restaurant enters your order into the cash register, it may be automatically fed to a computer, and the day's sales and profits can be calculated as soon as the store closes. The sales and expense data must be accurate, or the rest of the calculations will be wrong. This can be a real problem when, for example, many calculations are based on questionable sales forecasts.

2. *Completeness.* There must be enough information to allow you to make a decision but not so much as to confuse the issue. Today, as we have noted, the problem is often too much information rather than too little.

3. *Timeliness.* Information must reach managers quickly. If a customer has a complaint, that complaint should be handled within a day. In the past, a salesperson would make a report to his or her manager; that report would go to a higher-level manager, and the problem would not be resolved for days, weeks, or months. E-mail and other developments make it possible for marketing, engineering, and production to hear about a problem with a product the same day the salesperson hears about it. Product changes can be made instantly using computer integrated manufacturing, as discussed in Chapter 9.

4. *Relevance.* Different managers have different information needs. Again, the problem today is that information systems often make too much data available. Managers must learn which questions to ask to get the answers they need.

Sorting out the useful information and getting it to the right people are the goals in solving information overload. There are software programs and services available that do just that by filtering information so that users can get the customized information they need. Known as **push technology** because they push the information to users so they don't have to pull it out, these services deliver customized news to individual computers after sorting through thousands of news sources to find information that suits the user's identified needs. The major Web browsers, Netscape Navigator and Microsoft Internet Explorer, include push technology features.[17]

You may be concerned that only getting the information the computer thinks you need will eliminate a lot of other useful information you may find by luck. Software developers envision a program with a fortune dial that will allow you to regulate the amount of random information you receive with your customized news.

The important thing to remember when facing information overload is to relax. You can never read everything that is available. Set goals for yourself and do the best you can. Remember, just because there is a public library doesn't mean you should feel guilty about not reading every book in it. And so it is with the information superhighway: you can't make every stop along the route, so plan your trip wisely and bon voyage!

push technology
Web software that delivers information tailored to a previously defined user profile; it pushes the information to users so that they don't have to pull it out.

···· ▬▬▬ ····

THE ENABLING TECHNOLOGY: HARDWARE

➤ **LEARNING GOAL 4.**
Review the hardware most frequently used in business and outline the benefits of the move toward computer networks.

We hesitate to discuss the advances that have been made in computer hardware because what is powerful as we write this may be obsolete by the time you read it. In the mid-1970s the chairman of Intel Corporation, Gordon E. Moore, predicted that the capacity of computer chips would double every year or so. This has since been called Moore's Law. The million-dollar vacuum-tube computers that awed people in the 1950s couldn't now keep up with a pocket calculator. In fact, a greeting card that plays "Happy Birthday" contains more computing power than existed before 1950.

The speed of evolution in the computer industry has slowed little since Moore's remark, although in 1997, Moore did say that his prediction cannot hold good for much longer because chipmakers will sooner or later run into a fundamental law of nature; that is, the finite size of atomic particles will prevent infinite miniaturization.[18] That won't stop chipmakers from improving chips in other ways than shrinking them. Rapid advances make one product after another obsolete, helping create demand for newer chips. For example, a three-year-old personal computer is considered out-of-date. So rather than add potentially outdated facts to your information overload, we offer you a simple overview of the kind of computer technology available now, at the start of the new millennium.

Hardware includes computers, pagers, cellular phones, printers, scanners, fax machines, personal digital assistants (PDAs), and so on. The mobile worker can find travel-size versions of computers, printers, and fax machines that are almost as powerful and feature-laden as their big brothers. All-in-one devices that address the entire range of your communications needs are now available. For example, there are handheld units that include a wireless portable phone, fax, e-mail, Web browser, and personal information manager (PIM).

Researchers are working on a human computer interface that combines a videocamera and computer. When you approach the PC, it recognizes you, asks you how you feel, and determines what tasks you want to complete that day.[19] Instead of hearing a mechanical beep to remind you of your next class, you'll hear a soothing voice say, "Sam, your Introduction to Business final will begin in 30 minutes." Sorry, it won't take the test for you—some things you still have to do for yourself.

◄ CONSIDER USING LECTURE ENHANCER 17-8
Users' Keyboard Gripes.

◄ CONSIDER USING LECTURE ENHANCER 17-9
IBM's Roots.

◄ CONSIDER USING SUPPLEMEN-TAL CASE 17-2
The Grandfather of Commercial Computers is Now over 40 (SCANS)

◄ CONSIDER USING ACETATE 17-7
Growth of Personal Computers.

◄ CONSIDER USING LECTURE ENHANCER 17-10
John Atanasoff's Computer.

... COMPUTER NETWORKS ...

Perhaps the most dynamic change in business technology in recent years is the move away from mainframe computers that serve as the center of information processing and toward network systems that allow many users to access information at the same time. In an older system, a central computer (mainframe) performed all the tasks and sent the results to a terminal that could not perform those tasks itself. In the new **network computing system** (also called **client/server computing**), the tasks, such as searching sales records, are handled by personal computers ("clients"). The information needed to complete the tasks is stored in huge databases controlled by the "server." Networks connect people to people and people to data.[20]

The major benefits of networks are the following:

Saving time and money. SynOptics Communications found that electronic delivery of mail and files increased the speed of project development by 25 percent.

Providing easy links across functional boundaries. With networks, it's easy to find someone who can offer insightful solutions to a problem. The most common questions on computer bulletin boards begin, "Does anyone know . . . ?" Usually someone does.

Allowing employees to see complete information. In traditional organizations, information is summarized so many times that it often loses its

network computing system (client/server computing)
Computer systems that allow personal computers (clients) to obtain needed information from huge databases in a central computer.

meaning. For example, a sales representative's two-page summary may be cut to a paragraph in the district manager's report and then to a few numbers on a chart in the regional manager's report. Networks, on the other hand, catch raw information.

Here's how networks helped Lotus Development. Instead of waiting for the information gained from 4 million annual phone calls to be summarized by technical support people, Lotus Development now sends information straight into a database, where it's available on demand. Rather than accept someone else's idea of what information is needed, any Lotus development employee can access the data and search according to his or her needs. The result is that many more employees have direct access to market information and can act accordingly.

The move toward networks does not mean that mainframes are dead. Far from it. Using networks requires so many organizational changes that some companies (as many as a third) that try networking go back to mainframes. For the next decade or so, while organizations learn to let go of hierarchical management styles and feel more comfortable entrusting employees with the power of information, the computing world will be a hybrid. PCs will take on more jobs with their speed, flexibility and utility, while mainframes will handle the larger corporations' big jobs of storing, transferring, and processing large amounts of data.

One problem of computer networks is that technical glitches can interrupt the lines of communication. See the box From the Pages of *Business Week* for a remarkable story about how scientists have been able to use what they have learned about ants to improve computer network systems.

Critical Thinking

What are the implications for world peace and world trade given the ability firms and government organizations now have to communicate with one another throughout the world? Could the cooperation needed among telecommunications firms worldwide lead to increased cooperation among other organizations on other issues such as world health care and worldwide exchanges of technical information?

SOFTWARE

➤ CONSIDER USING LECTURE ENHANCER 17-11
Software Piracy.

➤ **LEARNING GOAL 5.**
Classify the computer software most frequently used in business.

Computer software programs provide the instructions that enable you to tell the computer what to do. Although many people looking to buy a computer think first of the equipment, it is important to find the right software before finding the right hardware. Software is like a sound recording. If you want to hear a certain singer or orchestra, you buy that particular recording. The recording may be an old 78 or a new CD. The type of recording you want dictates the kind of equipment you need.

Some software programs are easier to use than others. Some are more sophisticated and can perform more functions than others. A businessperson must decide what functions he or she wants the computer to perform and then choose the appropriate software. That choice will help determine what brand of computer to buy and how much power it should have.

shareware
Software that is copyrighted but distributed to potential customers free of charge.

While most software is distributed commercially through suppliers like retail stores or mail-order houses, there is some software, called **shareware**, that is copyrighted but distributed to potential customers free of charge. The users are asked to send a specified fee to the developer if the program meets their needs and they decide to use it. The shareware concept has become very popular and has dramatically reduced the price of software.[21] **Public domain**

From the Pages of *BusinessWeek*

http://www.bt.com/

It's Only Natural

Researchers at British Telecommunications (BT), one of the world's leading telecommunications companies, studied ant colonies, jellyfish, and slime molds. Why? They hoped that nature could help them solve one of their most critical business problems—overloaded or damaged network lines. It could take BT a decade and over $46 billion to overhaul its phone network the traditional way. So BT asked biologists and entomologists to search the natural world for alternative solutions. "Biological organisms do complex things with very simple software, while man's unbelievably complex systems can only do very simple things," says Peter Cochrane, BT's research head. One of Cochrane's teams modeled a software program on ant colonies. The program sends out "ants," or intelligent agents, to explore alternate routes through overloaded or damaged networks. As each ant returns almost instantaneously with information on how long it takes to travel to different parts of the network, the net-work can reconfigure itself to bypass the problem in less than a second—much faster than the several minutes it now takes to do the same task.

Where is technology headed? Cochrane envisions people and technology converging to create what he calls "homo cyberneticus." For example, we will dress in vests that use heat from our bodies to power all the technology we will wear. Picture a visor that can spray TV-like images or data directly onto the retina, allowing you to read e-mail or study a map while walking down the street. "People will be walking around on-line in the early 21st century," predicts Cochrane. He also believes that desktop boxes will disappear, replaced by more cuddly interfaces. His favorite example is a computerized robot that "looks like a kitten but doesn't bring in dead mice."

Source: Julia Flynn, "British Telecom: Notes from the Ant Colony," *Business Week*, June 23, 1997, p. 108.

---

software is software that is free for the taking. The Making Ethical Decisions box deals with the issue of not paying for software by copying it illegally.

Businesspeople most frequently use software for six major purposes: (1) writing (word processors), (2) manipulating numbers (spreadsheets), (3) filing and retrieving data (databases), (4) presenting information visually (graphics), (5) communicating, and (6) accounting. Today's software can perform many functions in one kind of program known as *integrated software* or *suites*. A new class of software program, called *groupware*, has emerged for use on networks. We shall explore all of these software applications next.

public domain software
Software that is free for the taking.

◄ CONSIDER USING CRITICAL THINKING EXERCISE 17-2
Computer Assistance (**SCANS**)

••• WORD PROCESSING PROGRAMS •••

Many computer users spend most of their time using word processing programs. The most popular of these programs can handle everything from a quick memo to a multichapter book. They can also produce designs that once could be done only by powerful page-layout design programs.

Businesses use word processors to increase office productivity. Standardized letters can be personalized quickly, documents can be updated by changing only the outdated text and leaving the rest intact, and contract forms can be revised to meet the stipulations of specific customers.

Desktop publishing software combines word processing with graphics capabilities. A keystroke or a click of a mouse can change the style of type, the placement of a chart, or the width of the text columns. Businesses can now publish their own professional-looking newsletters and presentations.

Making Ethical Decisions

http://www.xchange.net/computer.html

Superhighway Robbery

Computer software, particularly the applications programs described in this text, can take hundreds of hours to create. Anyone who has taken a basic programming course knows that developing such programs requires tremendous planning, effort, and tenacity. And anyone who has bought a software package knows that programs often cost a lot.

Suppose a friend of yours owns a program that you want to use for writing school term papers. Your friend offers to make a "pirate" (illegal) copy for you. What are your alternatives? What will you do? What are the consequences of your decision?

Of the many word processing software packages on the market, three of the most popular are Corel WordPerfect, Microsoft Word, and WordPro.

••• SPREADSHEET PROGRAMS •••

spreadsheet program
The electronic equivalent of an accountant's worksheet, plus such features as mathematical function libraries, statistical data analysis, and charts.

A **spreadsheet program** is simply the electronic equivalent of an accountant's worksheet plus such features as mathematical function libraries, statistical data analysis, and charts. A spreadsheet is a table made up of rows and columns that enables a manager to organize information. Using the computer's speedy calculations, managers have their questions answered almost as fast as they can ask them. For example, suppose we use a spreadsheet to figure the break-even point ➔ P. 454 ◄ for our Fiberrific cereal. The spreadsheet contains the appropriate formula for calculating the break-even point. Our calculations show that at a price of $2 a box, we must sell 2,000 boxes to break even. We now think we can raise our price, however, since a government study linking eating oat bran with lowering cholesterol levels has caused an increase in demand. We can ask, "What if we raise the price of Fiberiffic to $2.50?" Once we simply insert $2.50 in the price cell (the point where columns and rows intersect), the computer will tell us instantly that we must sell only 1,333 boxes to break even (see Figure 17.2). Of course, this is a simple example. Businesses often develop highly complex spreadsheets, sometimes using hundreds of columns and rows. Some of the most popular spreadsheet programs are Lotus 1-2-3, Quattro Pro, and Excel.

••• DATABASE PROGRAMS •••

database program
Computer program that allows users to work with information that is normally kept in lists: names and addresses, schedules, inventories and so forth.

A **database program** allows users to work with information that is normally kept in lists: names and addresses, schedules, inventories, and so forth. Simple commands allow you to add new information, change incorrect information, and delete out-of-date or unnecessary information. Most programs have features that let you print only certain information, arrange records in the order you want them, and change the way information is displayed. Using database programs, you can create reports that contain exactly the information you want in the form you want it to appear in. Leading database programs include Q&A, Access, Approach, Paradox, PFS: Professional File, PC-File, R base, and FileMaker Pro for Apple computers.

FIGURE 17.2
• • • •

HOW A SPREADSHEET PROGRAM WORKS

In this case, the question is, What would happen to the break-even point if the price of the product were raised to $2.50? You simply type $2.50 in the proper place and the program does the calculations. The answer is 1,333.

	A	B	C	D
	Fixed cost	**Price**	**Unit variable cost**	**Break-even point**
1				
2				
3				
4	**2000**	**2.00**	**1**	**2000**
5	**2000**	**2.50**	**1**	**1333**

Personal information managers (PIMs), or contact managers, are specialized database programs that allow users to track communication with their business contacts. Such programs keep track of everything—every person, every phone call, every e-mail message, every appointment.[22] Some programs have planners that help you identify free blocks of time for yourself and others in your workgroup. The program Goldmine even has a feature that lets you see who's in, who's out, and how long a person has been away from his or her keyboard. Popular PIMs include Goldmine, Lotus Organizer, ACT, and ECCO Pro.

◄ **CONSIDER USING TM 125**
How a Spreadsheet Program Works (Figure 17.2 on text page 515).

◄ **CONSIDER USING LECTURE ENHANCER 17-12**
For Safety Sake: Delete Those Files.

A recent survey asked people about their greatest fear. The majority said speaking in public topped the list. Fear no more. Presentation software makes it possible for the most reluctant presenters to look like seasoned professionals. Computer graphics programs allow presenters to insert sound and video clips as well as animations to make the dullest of topics come alive.

••• GRAPHICS AND PRESENTATION PROGRAMS •••

A picture speaks a thousand words. Why should we study a thousand-word report to identify the leading Fiberrific salesperson when a glance at a computer-generated bar graph can show us in an instant? Computer graphics programs can use data from spreadsheets to visually summarize information by drawing bar graphs, pie charts, line charts, and more. Do you need to change a figure or label? No need to search for the eraser, ruler, and compass. Simply insert the new data and, presto, the computer makes the changes and your new chart is ready for presentation. Would you rather have a pie chart than a bar graph? No problem—for a computer with a good graphics program.

Your software can make your presentation more appealing to the audience's senses. Inserting sound clips, video clips, clip art, and animation could turn a dull presentation into an enlightening presentation. Some popular graphics programs are Illustrator and Freehand for Macintosh computers, PowerPoint, Harvard Graphics, Lotus Freelance Graphics, Active Presenter, and Corel Draw.

••• COMMUNICATIONS PROGRAMS •••

Communications software makes it possible for different brands of computers to transfer data to each other. The software translates the data into a code known as the American Standard Code for Information Interchange (ASCII— pronounced *ask-ee*) which is the common standard all computer manufacturers have agreed to adopt. Communications programs enable a computer to exchange files with other computers, retrieve information from databases, and send and receive electronic mail. Such programs include Microsoft Outlook, ProComm Plus, Eudora, and Telik.

Message center software is more powerful than traditional communications packages. This new generation of programs has teamed up with fax/voice modems to provide an efficient way of making certain that phone calls, e-mail, and faxes are received, sorted, and delivered on time, no matter where you are.[23] Such programs include Communicate, Message Center, and WinFax Pro.

••• ACCOUNTING AND FINANCE PROGRAMS •••

Accounting software helps users record financial transactions and generate financial reports. Some programs include on-line banking features that allow users to pay bills through the computer. Others include "financial advisors" that offer users advice on a variety of financial issues. Popular accounting and finance programs include Peachtree Complete Accounting, Simply Accounting, and QuickBooks Pro.

••• INTEGRATED PROGRAMS •••

It may occur to you that loading your computer with many different software packages might become cumbersome. It may be difficult to cut information generated in one program (such as a spreadsheet) and paste it into, say, a word processing document. One solution is an **integrated software package** (also called a **suite**), which offers two or more applications in one package. With these programs, you can share information across applications easily.

---

communications software
Computer programs that make it possible for different brands of computers to transfer data to each other.

message center software
A new generation of computer programs that use fax/voice modems to receive, sort, and deliver phone calls, e-mail, and faxes.

It's doubtful a person would go to one restaurant for soup, another for salad, another for the main course, and still another for dessert. It's more convenient to go to a single restaurant for all these parts of the meal. Integrated software packages (suites) provide software programs that include word processing, database management, spreadsheet graphics, and communications all in one.

Most such packages include word processing, database management, spreadsheet, graphics, and communications. Suites include Microsoft Office, Lotus SmartSuite, and Corel WordPefect Suite.

··· GROUPWARE ···

As businesses moved toward networking, a new class of software called groupware has emerged. **Groupware** is software that allows people to work collaboratively and share ideas. The programs we discussed above (word processing, databases, etc.) were designed for people working alone at individual computers. Groupware runs on a network and allows people to work on the same project at the same time. Groupware also makes it possible for work teams to communicate together over time. Team members can swap leads, share client information, keep tabs on news events, and make suggestions to one another. The computer becomes a kind of team memory where every memo and idea is stored for quick retrieval at any time. Groupware programs include Lotus Notes, Frontier's Intranet Genie, Metainfo Sendmail, and Radnet Web Share.

- What are the four characteristics of information that make it useful?
- How do computer networks change the way employees gather information?
- Can you list and describe the major types of computer software used in business?

Progress Check

EFFECTS OF INFORMATION TECHNOLOGY ON MANAGEMENT

The increase of information technology has already begun to affect management and will continue to do so. Three major issues arising out of the growing reliance on information technology are human resource changes, security threats, and privacy concerns.

··· HUMAN RESOURCE ISSUES ···

Many bureaucratic functions can be replaced by technology. We talked in Chapter 8 about tall versus flat organization structures. Computers often eliminate middle management functions and thus flatten organization structures.

Perhaps the most revolutionary effect of computers and the increased use of the Internet and intranets is that of telecommuting. In 1997, 11.1 million U.S. employees were classified as telecommuters; by 2000 their ranks are expected to exceed 23 million.[24] Using computers linked to the company's network, employees working at home can transmit their work to the office and back as easily as (and sometimes more easily than) they can walk into the boss's office.

Naturally, such work involves less travel time and fewer costs, and often increases productivity.[25] Telecommuting helps companies save money by allowing them to retain valuable employees during long pregnancy leaves or to tempt experienced employees out of retirement. Companies can also enjoy savings in commercial property costs, since having fewer employees in the office means a company can get by with smaller, and therefore less expensive, offices than before.[26] Telecommuting enables men and women to stay home with small children and is a tremendous boon for disabled workers.[27] Employees who can work after hours on their home computers rather than at the office report less stress and improved morale. Studies show that telecommuting is most successful

integrated software package (suite)
A computer program that offers two or more applications in one package.

groupware
Software that allows people to work collaboratively and share ideas.

◄ LEARNING GOAL 6.
Evaluate the human resource, security, and privacy issues in management that are affected by information technology.

◄ CONSIDER USING LECTURE ENHANCER 17-13
Apocalypse 2000.

◄ CONSIDER USING LECTURE ENHANCER 17-14
The Effects of Keyboard Abuse.

Video conferencing makes it possible to conduct regular business meetings that include all needed company employees without having to fly them from city to city. By using video conferencing, the company can avoid problems (such as scheduling conflicts) and enjoy significant cost savings.

among people who are self-starters, who don't have home distractions, and whose work doesn't require face-to-face interaction with co-workers.

Even as telecommuting has grown in popularity, however, some telecommuters report that a consistent diet of long-distance work gives them a dislocated feeling of being left out of the office loop. Some feel a loss of the increased energy people can get through social interaction. In addition to the isolation issue is the intrusion that work brings into what is normally a personal setting. Often people working from home don't know when to turn the work off.[28] Some companies are pulling away from viewing telecommuting as an either–or proposition: either at home or at the office. Such companies are using telecommuting as a part-time alternative. In fact, industry now defines telecommuting as working at home a minimum of two days a week.

Electronic communication can never replace human communication for creating enthusiasm and esprit de corps. Efficiency and productivity can become so important to a firm that people are treated like robots. In the long run, such treatment results in less efficiency and productivity. Computers are a tool, not a total replacement for managers or workers, and creativity is still a human trait. Computers should aid creativity by giving people more freedom

➤ CONSIDER USING TM 126
When Information Technology Alters the Workplace.
(Figure 17.3 on text page 518)

FIGURE **17.3**
• • • •
WHEN INFORMATION TECHNOLOGY ALTERS THE WORKPLACE

MANAGERS MUST	WORKERS MUST
• Instill commitment in subordinates rather than rule by command and control.	• Become initiators, able to act without management direction.
• Become coaches, training workers in necessary job skills, making sure they have resources to accomplish goals, and explaining links between a job and what happens elsewhere in the company.	• Become financially literate so they can understand the business implications of what they do and changes they suggest.
• Give greater authority to workers over scheduling, priority setting, and even compensation.	• Learn group interaction skills, including how to resolve disputes within their work group and how to work with other functions across the company.
• Use new information technologies to measure workers' performance, possibly based on customer satisfaction or the accomplishment of specific goals.	• Develop new math, technical, and analytical skills to use newly available information on their jobs.

Spotlight on Small Business

http://www.retailadvz.com/

Dear Ernie: On-line Advice for Small Businesses

Many entrepreneurs can't afford to hire consultants to help them set up their new businesses and they don't have time to search for answers to all of their questions. Some of them turn to virtual consultants such as David Wing at the Retail Business Resource Center, an on-line consulting service specializing in small retail and service companies (http://www.retailadvz.com).

Susie Sherman turned to Wing when she decided to start her own office-design business. For $75 a month she communicates with him via e-mail, getting answers within 72 hours—usually sooner. She can either chat with him on-line in real time or attend a group chat for clients. Wing helped Sherman focus her business plan and taught her how to market her service. He also provided moral support during her business's fragile infancy.

Lee Penn, vice president for finance at the SLAM Collaborative, an architectural engineering and design firm, turns to another virtual answer man—Ernie, the folksy name for Ernst & Young's on-line consulting service (http://www.ernie.ey.com). Penn finds that Ernie answers his questions more easily and quickly than the legions of people he once had to search out when he worked at Xerox. Ernie charges a flat $6,000 annual fee for providing a worldwide network of experts to answer business questions related to human resources, real estate, taxes, and information technology. Clients e-mail their questions to Ernie and they are filtered down and passed along through the company's intranet to the appropriate Ernst & Young expert. Answers arrive within 48 hours. When SLAM needed to hire information technicians, Penn needed to know an appropriate pay scale to offer. Instead of buying a salary book for another industry for hundreds of dollars, Penn asked Ernie and quickly received the compensation ranges in his region for that job category.

In addition to providing clients affordable consulting, Ernie also benefits the Ernst & Young experts by keeping them in tune with what their market segment is thinking about. Over time, they will be able to identify trends by industry segment and job function more clearly. Brian Baum, director of Internet Service Delivery at Ernst & Young, considers Ernie the natural extension of a worldwide business. He says, "It's really using the platform, the medium in the most efficient manner. It's applicable to many industries in terms of creating a connected environment."

Source: Robin D. Schatz, "Smaller Businesses Can Turn to Virtual Advisors for Help," *The Wall Street Journal Interactive Edition*, February 20, 1997; and "Small Business Web Sites: Getting Down to Business," *PC Magazine*, January 6, 1998, p. 40.

and more time. Figure 17.3 illustrates how information technology changes the way managers and workers interact.

Information technology also changes the way that small-business owners can access management advice. Read the Spotlight on Small Business box to learn more about how entrepreneurs can benefit from on-line consultants.

◄ CONSIDER USING OT ACETATE 17-9
Company Information Security Threats.

◄ CONSIDER USING OT ACETATE 17-10
High Tech Crimes that Lead to Financial Losses.

◄ CONSIDER USING 17-15
Teen Hackers Toss Electronic Spit Balls.

••• SECURITY ISSUES •••

One current problem with computers that is likely to persist in the future is that they are susceptible to *hackers,* or people who break into computer systems for illegal purposes such as transferring funds from someone's bank account to their own without authorization. In 1994, officials were unable to find the hackers who broke into Pentagon computers through the Internet and stole, altered, and erased numerous records. Ironically, one of the Pentagon systems the hackers gained access to was that of computer security research.

Computer security is more complicated today than ever before. When information was processed in a mainframe environment, the single data center was easier to control since there was limited access to it. Today, however,

Can Regulation and Liberty Coexist On-line?

http://www.equifax.com/

How can you govern the Internet without resorting to the traditionally heavy hand of government? "Attempts at government regulation could act like a vise grip on the Internet when a pair of tweezers might do," says John Ford, vice president of Equifax Inc., an information-services company in Atlanta, Georgia.

Most people in the communications industry consider the current U.S. telecommunications regulations dangerously out-of-date now that we can speed along the information superhighway. Debates rage about how to develop new regulations that protect consumers without prohibiting free trade. The most challenging issues for government policy include the following:

- *Cultivating new technology.* Government and industry must establish common standards in order for information to flow smoothly. However, if the standards are too rigid, the technology will become obsolete rapidly.

- *Deregulation.* The speedy evolution of the information superhighway depends on increased competition among cable, phone, and computer companies. However, one segment may gain unfair advantage if there is too much deregulation.

- *Universal access.* Congress wants to ensure that the telephone-era policy of universal service (everyone has access) survives. Who should pick up the tab of wiring the homes of low-income customers?

- *Balance between privacy and law enforcement.* How can the government keep data safe from criminals while allowing enforcers to tap in when necessary? Who is going to determine when it is necessary for law officers to tap in? Compare the risks of regulation with the risks of unregulated liberty on-line.

Sources: Thomas E. Weber, "Concerned Web Users Ask: Is Public Data Too Public?" *The Wall Street Journal Interactive Edition*, June 19, 1997; "The Encryption Riddle," *The Wall Street Journal Interactive Edition*, October 16, 1997; and Carol Levin, "Let Consumers Govern the Net," *PC Magazine*, November 4, 1997, p. 28.

---

computers are accessible not only in all areas within the company but also in all areas of other companies with which the firm does business.

Another security issue involves the spread of computer viruses over the Internet. A **virus** is a piece of programming code inserted into other programming to cause some unexpected and, for the victim, usually undesirable event. Viruses are spread by downloading infected programming over the Internet or by sharing an infected diskette. Often the source of the file you downloaded is unaware of the virus. The virus lies dormant until circumstances cause its code to be executed by the computer. Some viruses are playful ("Kilroy was here!"), but some can be quite harmful, erasing data or causing your hard disk to crash. There are software programs, such as Norton's AntiVirus, that "inoculate" your computer so that it doesn't catch a known virus. However, new viruses are being developed constantly so that antivirus programs may have only limited success. Therefore, you should keep your antivirus protection program up-to-date and, more importantly, practice "safe computing" by not downloading files from unknown sources and by using your antivirus program to scan diskettes before transferring files from them.

Existing laws do not address the problems of today's direct, real-time communication. As more and more people merge onto the information superhighway, the number of legal issues will likely increase. Already copyright and pornography laws are crashing into the virtual world. Other legal questions—such as those involving intellectual property and contract disputes, on-line sexual and racial harassment, and the use of electronic communication to pro-

virus
A piece of programming code inserted into other programming to cause some unexpected and, for the victim, usually undesirable event.

➤ **CONSIDER USING LECTURE ENHANCER 17-16**
Computer Proves 'Fatal' to Hartford Voters.

➤ **CONSIDER USING LECTURE ENHANCER 17-17**
Computers Meets People.

➤ **CONSIDER USING OT ACETATE 17-11**
Five Top Computer Virus Producing Countries.

mote crooked sales schemes—are being raised as millions of people log on to the Internet.[29]

••• PRIVACY ISSUES •••

Major concerns about privacy are created by the increase of technology, particularly the Internet, as more and more personal information is stored in computers and people are able to access that data, legally or illegally. The Internet allows Web surfers to access all sorts of information about you. For example, some Web sites allow people to search for vehicle ownership from a license number or to find individuals' real estate property records. One key question in the debate over protecting our privacy is, "Isn't this personal information already public anyway?" Civil libertarians have long fought to keep certain kinds of information available to the public. If access to such data is restricted on the Internet, wouldn't we have to reevaluate our policies on public records entirely? The privacy advocates don't think so. After all, the difference is that the Net makes obtaining personal information just too easy.[30] Would your neighbors or friends even consider going to the appropriate local agency and sorting through public records for hours to find out whether you've ever been arrested for drunk driving or to see your divorce settlement. Probably not. But they might if it is as simple as a few clicks of a button.

There's a little geek in all of us.

Average PC users are concerned that Web sites have gotten downright nosy. In fact, some Web servers do secretly track users' movements on-line. Web surfers seem willing to swap personal details for free access to on-line information. This personal information is shared with others without your permission. Web sites often send **cookies** to your computer that stay on your hard drive. These little tidbits often simply contain your name and a password that the Web site recognizes the next time you visit the site so that you don't have to reenter the same information every time you visit. Other cookies track your movements around the Web and then blend that information with a database so that a company can tailor the ads you receive accordingly.[31] Do you mind someone watching over your shoulder while you're on the Web? Tim Berners-Lee, the researcher who invented the World Wide Web, is working on a way to prevent you from receiving cookies without your permission. His Platform for Privacy Preferences, or P3, would allow a Web site to automatically send information on its privacy policies. You would be able to set up your Web browser to communicate only with those Web sites that meet certain criteria.[32] You need to decide how much information about yourself you are willing to give away. Remember, we are living in an information economy, and information is a commodity. The Legal Briefcase box takes a closer look at the potential of government regulation to protect on-line privacy.

▲ Can you expect to advance into a high-paying job of the future without a working knowledge of technology? It's doubtful. Computer proficiency is considered a key to entry into the job market of the new millennium. Unfortunately businesses have already experienced a shortage of trained technology workers.

cookies
Pieces of information, such as registration data or user preferences, sent by a Web site over the Internet to a Web browser that the browser software is expected to save and send back to the server whenever the user returns to that Web site.

◀ **LEARNING GOAL 7.**
Identify the careers that are gaining or losing workers due to the growth of information technology.

TECHNOLOGY AND YOU

If you are beginning to think that being computer illiterate may be occupational suicide, you are getting the point. Workers in every industry come in contact with computers to some degree. Even burger flippers in fast-food chains read orders on computer screens. Nearly 80 percent of the respondents to a 1997 survey said that they believe it is impossible to succeed in the job market without a working knowledge of technology. Respondents who earned $45,000 a year or more were three times more likely to use a computer than those who earned less. More than 80 percent of the women surveyed said that computer proficiency was a key to their entry into traditionally male-dominated fields.[33]

In late 1997, a Commerce Department report warned that the United States is facing an increasing shortage of information technology workers. Such a shortage could have "severe consequences," the department said, for American competitiveness, economic growth, and job creation. The shortage is increasing quickly. According to the report, about 190,000 information technology jobs remain unfilled in 1997. By 2005, U.S. businesses will need more than 1 million new high-tech workers.[34] The increase in demand for skilled information technology workers is driving up pay scales. The average annual salary for a chief information officer rose from $96,000 in 1996 to $123,000 in 1997—a jump of 28 percent.[35] Figure 17.4 illustrates the effects of information technology on careers.

If you are still among those considered computer illiterate, do not feel alone. Researchers who have studied computerphobia (fear of computers), found that 55 percent of Americans have the disorder.[36] Amazingly, half of all white-collar workers say they are afraid of trying new technologies. Gender, age, and income level don't appear to lead to computerphobia. The key variable is exposure. That's why Nintendo era kids take to computers so easily.[37] Computerphobes do not do as well in school as their mouse-clicking classmates. They may get passed up for promotions or lose their jobs. On a psychological level, they often feel inadequate and outdated—sort of like technological outcasts in a digitized world. Here's the good news: computerphobia is curable, and computer training, the best medicine, is readily available. You may want to start out with low-tech learning aids such as videos and computer books and then gradually move up to training classes or CD-ROMs.

As information technology eliminates old jobs while creating new ones, it is up to you to learn the skills you need to be certain you aren't left behind.

FIGURE 17.4

· · · ·

WINNERS AND LOSERS IN THE RACE DOWN THE INFORMATION HIGHWAY

As the information highway accelerates its evolution, many workers are forced from their obsolete jobs while others find higher-paying jobs.

Technological change and office automation will shrink these jobs . . .

PERCENT EMPLOYMENT CHANGE, 1992–2005	
Computer operators	–39%
Billing, posting, and calculating machine operators	–29%
Telephone operators	–28%
Typists and word processors	–16%
Bank tellers	–4%

Data: Bureau of Labor Statistics.

. . . but technology also generates new openings in the info-tech world.

FIVE FASTEST-GROWING OCCUPATIONS REQUIRING A COLLEGE DEGREE, 1992–2005	
Computer engineers and scientists	112%
Systems analysts	110%
Physical therapists	88%
Special education teachers	74%
Operations research analysts	61%

Data: Bureau of Labor Statistics.

- How has information technology changed the way people work?
- What management issues have been affected by the growth of information technology?
- What careers are losing jobs as information technology expands? What careers are gaining jobs?

SUMMARY
. . . . .

1. Business technology is continuously changing names and changing roles.
   - *What are the various names and roles of business technology since 1970?*

   In the 1970s, business technology was called data processing (DP) and its role was to *support* existing business. In the 1980s, its name became information systems (IS) and its role changed to *doing* business. By the 1990s, business technology became information technology (IT) and its role is now to *change* business.
   - *How does information technology change business?*

   Information technology has minimized the importance of time and place to business. Business that is independent of time and location can deliver products and services whenever and wherever it is convenient for the customer. See Figure 17.1 for examples of how information technology changes business.
   - *What is knowledge technology?*

   Knowledge technology adds a layer of intelligence to filter appropriate information and deliver it when it is needed.

1. Outline the changing role of business technology.

2. To become knowledge-based, businesses must know how to share information and design systems for creating new knowledge.
   - *What information technology is available to help business manage information?*

   The heart of information technology involves the Internet, intranets, and extranets. The Internet is a massive network of thousands of smaller networks open to everyone with a computer and a modem. An intranet is a companywide network protected from unauthorized entry by outsiders. An extranet is a semiprivate network that allows more than one company to access the same information.

2. Compare the scope of the Internet, intranets, and extranets as tools in managing information.

3. Information technology multiplies the mountains of information available to businesspeople.
   - *How can one deal with information overload?*

   The most important step in dealing with information overload is to identify your four or five key goals. Eliminate information that will not help you meet your key goals.
   - *What makes information useful?*

   The usefulness of management information depends on four characteristics: quality, completeness, timeliness, and relevance.

3. List the steps in managing information, and identify the characteristics of useful information.

4. Computer hardware changes rapidly.
   - *What was the most dynamic change in computer hardware in the 1990s?*

   Perhaps the most dynamic change was the move away from mainframe computers that serve as the center of information processing toward network systems that allow many users to access information at the same time.

4. Review the hardware most frequently used in business, and outline the benefits of the move toward computer networks.

> • *What are the major benefits of networks?*
> Networks' major benefits are (1) saving time and money, (2) providing easy links across functional boundaries, and (3) allowing employees to see complete information.

5. Classify the computer software most frequently used in business.

5. Computer software provides the instructions that enable you to tell the computer what to do.

> • *What types of software programs are used by managers most frequently?*
> Managers most often use word processing, electronic spreadsheet, database, communication, and accounting programs. A new class of software program, called groupware, allows people to work collaboratively and share ideas.

6. Evaluate the human resource, security, and privacy issues in management that are affected by information technology.

6. Information technology has a tremendous effect on the way we do business.

> • *What effect has information technology had on business management?*
> Computers eliminate some middle management functions and thus flatten organization structures. Computers also allow workers to work from their own homes. On the negative side, computers sometimes allow information to fall into the wrong hands. Managers must find ways to prevent stealing by hackers. Concern for privacy is another issue affected by the vast store of information available on the Internet. Finding the balance between freedom to access private information and individuals' right to privacy will require continued debate.

7. Identify the careers that are gaining or losing workers due to the growth of information technology.

7. Information technology eliminates old jobs while creating new ones.

> • *Which careers are gaining and losing workers because of the growth of information technology?*
> Computer operators and word processors are among the shrinking jobs. As more employees can and do access information themselves, they no longer need others to do it for them. Computer engineers and systems analysts are in demand. See Figure 17.4 for other employment changes caused by the growth of information technology.

KEY TERMS
• • • • •

communications software 516	information technology (IT) 504	network computing system (client/server computing) 511
cookies 521	integrated software package (suite) 517	public domain software 513
data processing (DP) 503	Internet 2 508	push technology 510
database program 514	intranet 507	shareware 512
extranet 507	knowledge technology (KT) 505	spreadsheet program 514
groupware 517	message center software 516	virtualization 504
information systems (IS) 503		virus 520

DEVELOPING WORKPLACE SKILLS

1. Imagine that a rich relative has given you $3,000 to buy a computer system to use for school. Research the latest in hardware and software in computer magazines and then go to a computer store to try out alternatives. Make a list of what you intend to buy and then write a summary explaining the reasons for your choices.

2. Interview someone who bought a computer system to use in his or her business. Ask that person about any problems that occurred in deciding

what to buy or in installing and using the system. What would he or she do differently next time? What software does he or she find especially useful?

3. Imagine that you are a purchasing manager for a large computer store near your campus. Design a two-page research survey to determine what software and hardware features students at the school need. Discuss your research questions and survey implementation strategy with the class.

4. Choose a topic that interests you and then, on the Internet, use two search engines to find information about the topic. If the initial result of your search is a list of thousands of sites, narrow your search using the tips offered by the search engine. Did both search engines find the same Web sites? If not, how were the sites different? Which engine found the most appropriate information?

5. Computers abound on most college campuses. Where are they and what are they used for on your campus? Use a computer graphics program to create a chart that illustrates the types of software used for various activities. For example, the library may record book checkouts and circulation using a database program. In addition to the library, consider computer use in the student records office, food services, athletic department, business school, alumni office, and business office.

TAKING IT TO THE NET

Purpose

To critically evaluate information found on Web sites.

Exercise

Unlike most print resources such as magazines and journals that go through a filtering process (e.g., editing, peer review), information on the Web is mostly unfiltered. The Web has a lot to offer, but not all sources are equally valuable or reliable. Since almost anyone can publish on the Web, accepting information from the Web can be like accepting advice from strangers. It's best to look at all Web sites with critical eyes.

Choose a topic and use a search engine to find a Web site that deals with your topic. Use the following criteria to evaluate the site:

1. *Accuracy.* How reliable and free from error is the information? Are there editors and fact checkers?

2. *Authority.* What is the authority or expertise of the individual or group that created this site? How knowledgeable is the individual or group on the subject matter of the site? Is the site sponsored or co-sponsored by an individual or group that has created other Web sites? Is contact information for the author or producer included in the document?

3. *Objectivity.* Is the information presented with a minimum of bias? To what extent is the information trying to sway the opinion of the audience?

4. *Currency.* Is the content of the work up-to-date? When was the Web item produced? When was the Web site last revised? How up-to-date are the links? How reliable are the links—that is, are there blind links, or references to sites that have moved?

5. *Coverage.* Are the topics included explored in depth? What is the overall value of the content? What does it contribute to the literature in its field? Given the ease of self-publishing on the Web, this is perhaps even more important in reviewing Web resources than in reviewing print resources. Is the arrangement appropriate for the topic, and does it facilitate use? Does the site include a search engine? If so, can the user define search criteria?

Practicing Management Decisions

Couch potatoes may think of the kick-off of the football season as the time to relax and settle in until Super Bowl Sunday, but for the NFL's information technology's networking groups it's the start of frantic work marathon that won't stop until the championship rings are engraved. Imagine keeping 30 teams connected to the NFL's New York headquarters not only during game time but also at off-site summer training camps, at the annual owners' meeting, and during draft announcements. And, of course, during the event of the year, on Super Bowl Sunday, last-minute venue changes and different networking configurations present ample opportunities to fumble.

The networking team must create quick-turn networks that are used for a limited amount of time and then quickly dismantled. In just one month in 1996, the NFL wired more than 3,000 national and international media people, installed 20 miles of telephone cable, set up 800 phone lines and 600 cell phone lines, and created a 140-node network in New Orleans. To make sure that no one drops the ball, the NFL has teamed up with Sprint to create a best-practices playbook for creating quick-turn networks. Having a game plan is definitely worth the effort since the NFL has to do this on a regular basis, according to Craig Johnson, a research analyst at CurrentAnaylsis Inc.

Every year since its creation in 1993, the Carolina Panthers team has built a network at the team's training camp at Wofford College in Spartanburg, South Carolina, connecting it to the team's headquarters in Charlotte. The network designers use encryption to ensure security. Coaches and team managers in the field can use the network to reach key databases at headquarters to access information such as player statistics or salary figures. Even though the networking team has a system for the physical setup and breakdown of the network, it must still go through planning exercises each year because of constant changes in software and networking

CASE
• • • • • •
THE SUPER BOWL OF NETWORKS
• • • • • •

hardware. That means the network's performance must be reevaluated every year.

The most important lesson the NFL/Sprint team learned was to be prepared. Even the best plans can change unexpectedly. For example, just five days before the NFL's highly publicized annual draft announcements, the location was moved from Detroit to Philadelphia. The networking team put a local telecommunications provider in the new locale on alert for establishing a connection in time for the broadcast. You can't plan for everything, so you have to be prepared to move quickly. It's probably safe to say that the venue for the next Super Bowl won't change. But even if it did, the NFL/Sprint networking team will make certain that couch potatoes all over the world aren't denied.

Decision Questions

1. Most businesses don't normally need to create networks quickly, but occasionally it is necessary. Give some examples of situations in which such quick-turn networks might be used.
2. Of course, the NFL doesn't allow general Internet access to its complete network, but you can check out the NFL's Web site (http://www.nfl.com) to get an idea of the kinds of statistics available. What additional kinds of information do you think the NFL manages? As the general manager of an NFL team, how could you use the NFL network in negotiating your players' contracts for the coming year?
3. As the NFL expands its coverage globally, will its quick turn networks be of value in locations such as London, Tokyo, and Moscow?

Sources: Aileen Crowley, "Playbook Calls for On-the-Fly Networks," *PC Week*, September 15, 1997, p. 99; and Bob Wallace, "LAN Blitz Sharpens Panthers' Claws," *Computer World*, September 29, 1997, p. 53.

The World Wide Web is a fast-flowing river of information. Internet surfers have found that navigating the Web takes them to a wide range of sites from homemade personal sites to multimedia corporate sites. Why are businesses willing to invest $200,000 to $1 million to create an impressive Web site? Some want to bolster their corporate image; others want to sell their products on-line.

How companies choose to reach out and hold their audiences' attention depends upon what they intend their sites to accomplish. Some Web sites function as general promotion and brand identity tools. For example, General Mills doesn't use its Web site to sell Betty Crocker cake mix, rather it uses the site to present menu plans and household tips. The goal is to link the brand's image with the information the Web site provides.

Another function of some business Web sites is to conduct on-line business (sometimes called on-line commerce, e-commerce, or transactional sites). For example, you can book airline tickets on Sabre Group's Travelocity site; buy a computer on the Gateway 2000, Dell, and Micron sites; or buy stock from e.Schwab, Datek, and Quick & Reilly.

Unlike e-commerce sites, some broad-based corporate sites don't sell—they give things away. The aim of these sites is to give surfers easy access to huge banks of free information—particularly information about the companies' products. Microsoft is most likely the largest broad-based corporate site on the Web. The information about Microsoft products is so vast that the site changes about eight times a day as new information is added. Web designers have found that the better

VIDEO CASE
• • • • • •
TAKING IN THE SITES

the Web site's organization, the more faith visitors have in the site's information and in the company. Corporate Web sites might contain information found in a brochure: description of products, phone numbers, addresses, e-mail address, and so forth. They can also contain information that might be found in an annual report: shareholder information, corporate mission statements, company history, and press releases.

How companies use the Web, then, depends upon the type of company and on what the company wants their Web site to accomplish. One thing is certain, though, communication remains the main function of this new medium. People want answers to their questions and the Web can be the most efficient way to get them.

Discussion Questions

1. How could your college use a Web site to improve its services to students and the community?

2. The purpose of on-line commerce Web sites is to sell the company's products on-line. Would you feel comfortable buying on-line? What are the advantages and disadvantages of on-line commerce?

3. Suppose you were to design a Web site for our hypothetical product, Fiberiffic. Which of the Web site functions described in this case would you choose (general promotion/ brand identity, on-line business, or broad-based corporate site)? Describe your proposed Web site. What content would you include? Justify using funds to develop this Web site rather than on more traditional promotional/sales tools.

Understanding Financial Information and Accounting

Chapter 18

LEARNING GOALS

After you have read and studied this chapter, you should be able to

1 Understand the importance of financial information and accounting.

2 Define and explain the different areas of the accounting profession.

3 Distinguish between accounting and bookkeeping and list the steps in the accounting cycle.

4 Explain the differences between the major financial statements.

5 Describe the role of depreciation and LIFO and FIFO in reporting financial information.

6 Explain the importance of ratio analysis and the budgeting process in reporting financial information.

7 Describe how computers are used to record and apply accounting information in business.

When Roxanne Coady decided to leave the security of the corporate world and start her own business, her colleagues expected that she would maintain her focus on the new company's bottom line. Coady, a certified public accountant (CPA), worked 20 years for a nationally known accounting firm, where she became the firm's national tax director. She had experience in public and private accounting and was very familiar with financial analysis, healthy balance sheets, and returns on equity and assets. It seemed her bookstore, R. J. Julia Books, was in sound financial hands.

Coady's bookstore enjoyed growth of 30 to 75 percent a year for its first five years, and in 1995 Coady won the honor of Bookseller of the Year by *Publisher's Weekly*. The company published a first-class newsletter and had a large staff, frequent author events, and a customer-friendly ambience. Only one problem plagued the business: the financial numbers were poor. From 1990 to 1992, the company lost $233,000 and was only marginally profitable the next few years. Inventory turnover was too low and business costs were running too high. Coady had invested a significant amount of her own personal funds and still needed approximately $1 million more to keep the company competitive. The irony was that after working 20 years as an accountant, accounting seemed to be Coady's weakest area in the operation of her own business.

Coady realized that she was treating the bookstore as something like a mission outside the rules of business she had worked with for so many years. Financial standards were lax,

 PROFILE

Roxanne Coady of R. J. Julia Books

cash flow was poor, and return on investment was never considered. She eventually faced the uncomfortable fact that the firm had no goal-setting procedures or productivity standards and her staff had never been briefed on meeting financial objectives. The company desperately needed a complete philosophical shift, and so Coady prepared herself to implement it.

The first thing she did was gather employees and announce several major changes. First, Coady refused to put any more of her own money into the business; therefore, everyone had to become more efficient. She began preparing monthly profit-and-loss statements and cash-flow analysis that monitored all business details. The company also focused specifically on costs, since profit margins in the book business are very slim. Most important, Coady recognized that as a small-business owner she was not exempt from the same general financial standards that she had expected from the larger businesses she worked with as a CPA.

Today, R. J. Julia Books is still struggling to survive in an industry where large booksellers dominate. Controlling costs and managing cash flows are two keys to that survival. This chapter will introduce you to the financial information and accounting fundamentals that are so critical to business success. The chapter will also briefly explore the financial ratios that are essential in measuring the performance of a company.

Sources: Roxanne Coady, "The Cobbler's Shoes," *Inc.*, January 1996, pp. 21–22; and Steve Morgenstern, "That Damned Cash Flow," *Home Office Computing,* January 1998, p. 132.

THE IMPORTANCE OF FINANCIAL INFORMATION

Roxanne Coady's story is repeated hundreds of times every day throughout the country. Small and sometimes large businesses falter or even fail because they do not follow good financial procedures. Financial information is the heart that keeps competitive businesses beating. Accounting keeps the heartbeat stable.

Accounting is different from marketing, management, and human resource management in that most of us know almost nothing about accounting from experience. As consumers, we have all had some experience with marketing. As

◄ **LEARNING GOAL 1.**
Understand the importance of financial information and accounting.

◄ **CONSIDER USING TM 127**
Chapter Outline.

◄ **CONSIDER USING OT ACETATE 18-1**
The Influence of Accounting Information.

➤ **CONSIDER USING OT ACETATE 18-3**
Top Business Uses of Accountants.

➤ **CONSIDER USING TM 128**
The Accounting System (Figure 18.1 on text page 530.)

accounting
The recording, classifying, summarizing, and interpreting of financial events and transactions to provide management and other interested parties the information they need to make good decisions.

┌─ FIGURE **18.1** ─┐
 ••••
 THE ACCOUNTING
 SYSTEM

The inputs to an accounting system include sales documents and other documents. The data are recorded, classified, and summarized. They're then put into summary financial statements such as the income statement and balance sheet.

workers or students, we have observed and understand most management concepts. But accounting? What is it? Is it difficult to learn? What do accountants do? Is the work interesting? Is this a career path you may wish to pursue?

The fact is that you have to know something about accounting if you want to understand business. And accounting is not that hard. You will have to learn a few terms; that is mandatory. You also have to understand the relationship of bookkeeping to accounting and how accounts are kept. It's almost impossible to run a business effectively without being able to read, understand, and analyze accounting reports and financial statements.

Accounting reports and financial statements reveal as much about a business's health as pulse rate and blood pressure reports tell us about a person's health. The purpose of this chapter is to introduce you to the importance of obtaining financial information using basic accounting principles. By the end of this chapter, you should have a good idea of what accounting is, how it works, and why it is important. Spend some time learning accounting terms and understanding the purpose of accounting statements. It's important to understand how they are constructed but even more important to know what they mean to the business. A few hours invested in learning this material will pay off repeatedly as you become more involved in business or investing, or simply in understanding what's going on out there in the world of business and finance.

•••• ▬▬▬ ••••
WHAT IS ACCOUNTING?

Financial information is primarily based on information generated from accounting. **Accounting** is the recording, classifying, summarizing, and interpreting of financial events and transactions to provide management and other interested parties the information they need to make good decisions. Financial transactions can include such specifics as buying and selling goods and services, acquiring insurance, paying employees, and using supplies. Once the business's transactions have been recorded, they are usually classified into groups that have common characteristics. For example, all purchases are grouped together, as are all sales transactions. The set of methods used to record and summarize accounting data into reports is called an accounting system (see Figure 18.1).

One purpose of accounting is to help managers evaluate the financial condition and the operating performance of the firm so they may make well-informed decisions. Another major purpose is to report financial information to people outside the firm such as owners, creditors, suppliers, employees, and the government (for tax purposes). In basic terms, accounting is the measurement and reporting of financial information to various users (inside and outside the organization)

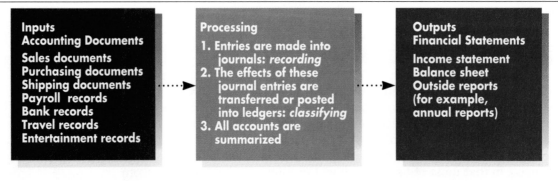

Inputs Accounting Documents	Processing	Outputs Financial Statements
Sales documents **Purchasing documents** **Shipping documents** **Payroll records** **Bank records** **Travel records** **Entertainment records**	1. Entries are made into journals: *recording* 2. The effects of these journal entries are transferred or posted into ledgers: *classifying* 3. All accounts are summarized	**Income statement** **Balance sheet** **Outside reports** **(for example, annual reports)**

FIGURE **18.2**

· · · ·

USERS OF ACCOUNTING
INFORMATION AND THE
REQUIRED REPORTS

Many different types of
organizations use
accounting information
to make business
decisions. The reports
needed vary according to
the information each
user requires. An
accountant must prepare
the appropriate forms.

USERS	TYPE OF REPORT
Government taxing authorities (e.g., the Internal Revenue Service)	Tax returns
Government regulatory agencies	Required reports
People interested in the organization's income and financial position (e.g., owners, creditors, financial analysts, suppliers)	Financial statements found in annual reports (e.g., income statement, balance sheet, statement of cash flows)
Managers of the firm	Financial statements and various internally distributed financial reports

regarding the economic activities of the firm (see Figure 18.2). Accounting work is divided into several major areas. Let's review those areas next.

··· ▬ ··· AREAS OF ACCOUNTING

Accounting has been called the language of business, which may make you think accounting is only for profit-seeking firms. Nothing could be further from the truth. It is also the language used to report financial information about nonprofit organizations such as churches, schools, hospitals, fraternities, and government agencies. The accounting profession is divided into four key working areas: managerial accounting, financial accounting, auditing, and tax accounting. All four areas present career opportunities for students who are willing to put forth the effort.

··· MANAGERIAL ACCOUNTING ···

Managerial accounting is used to provide information and analyses to managers within the organization to assist them in decision making. Managerial accounting is concerned with measuring and reporting costs of production, marketing, and other functions (cost accounting); preparing budgets (planning); checking whether or not units are staying within their budgets (controlling); and designing strategies to minimize taxes (tax accounting).

If you are a business major, it's almost certain you will be required to take a course in managerial accounting. You may even elect to pursue a career as a certified management accountant. A **certified management accountant** is a professional accountant who has met certain educational and experience requirements and been certified by the Institute of Certified Management Accountants. With growing emphasis on global competition, company downsizing, and organizational cost cutting, managerial accounting may be one of the most important courses you study in your college career.

··· FINANCIAL ACCOUNTING ···

Financial accounting differs from managerial accounting because the information and analyses are for people outside of the organization. This information goes to owners and prospective owners, creditors and lenders, employee

◄ **CONSIDER USING TM 129**
Users of Accounting Information and the Required Reports (Figure 18.2 on text page 531.)

◄ **LEARNING GOAL 2.**
Define and explain the different areas of the accounting profession.

◄ **CONSIDER USING OT ACETATE 18-2**
Different Types of Accountants.

◄ **CONSIDER USING LECTURE ENHANCER 18-1**
Other Uses for Managerial Accounting.

managerial accounting
Accounting used to provide information and analyses to managers within the organization to assist them in decision making.

certified management accountant
A professional accountant who has met certain educational and experience requirements and been certified by the Institute of Certified Management Accountants.

◄ **CONSIDER USING OT ACETATE 18-12**
What Investors Think of Annual Reports.

◄ **CONSIDER USING OT ACETATE 18-13**
What to Look For in Reading Financial Reports.

According to Sid Cato, a Michigan consultant on corporate annual reports, U.S. corporations spend over $8.2 billion a year communicating important company information through these yearly updates. Much of the information contained in an annual report is derived from financial accounting statements.

annual report
A yearly statement of the financial condition and progress of an organization covering a one-year period.

private accountants
Accountants who work for a single firm, government agency, or nonprofit organization.

public accountant
An accountant who provides his or her accounting services to individuals or businesses on a fee basis.

certified public accountant (CPA)
An accountant who passes a series of examinations established by the American Institute of Certified Public Accountants.

auditing
The job of reviewing and evaluating the records used to prepare a company's financial statements.

independent audit
An evaluation and unbiased opinion about the accuracy of a company's financial statements.

certified internal auditor
An accountant who has a bachelor's degree and two years of experience in internal auditing, and who has passed an exam administered by the Institute of Internal Auditors.

tax accountant
An accountant who is trained in tax law and is responsible for preparing tax returns or developing tax strategies.

unions, customers, suppliers, government agencies, and the general public. These external users are interested in the organization's profits, its ability to pay its bills, and other financial information. Much of the information derived from financial accounting is contained in the company's **annual report**, a yearly statement of the financial condition and progress of an organization.

It's critical for firms to keep accurate financial information. Because of this, many organizations employ **private accountants**, who work for a single firm, government agency, or nonprofit organization. However, not all firms or nonprofit organizations want or need a full-time accountant. Therefore, thousands of accounting firms in the United States will provide the accounting services an organization needs. An accountant who provides his or her services to individuals or businesses on a fee basis is called a **public accountant**. Public accountants can provide business assistance in many ways. They may design an accounting system for a firm, help select the correct computer and software to run the system, and analyze the financial strength of an organization right from the start. Many big accounting firms earn a sizable percentage of revenues from consulting. Arthur Andersen & Co. (the nation's largest public accounting firm), split off its large client-consulting business into a separate division, Andersen Consulting. The company expects its consulting division to bring in 50 percent of the $4.6 billion in revenues it generates per year.[1]

It's vital for the accounting profession to assure users of financial information that the information is accurate. The independent Financial Accounting Standards Board (FASB) defines the set of generally accepted accounting principles (GAAP) that accountants must follow.[2] If financial reports are prepared "in accordance with GAAP," users know the information is reported according to standards agreed on by accounting professionals. The accounting profession also wants to assure firms the accountants they employ are as professional as doctors or lawyers. An accountant who passes a series of examinations established by the American Institute of Certified Public Accountants (AICPA) and meets the state's requirement for education and experience earns recognition as a **certified public accountant (CPA)**.

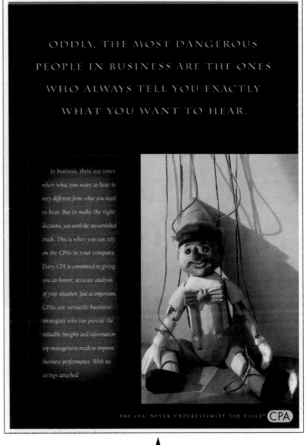

ODDLY, THE MOST DANGEROUS PEOPLE IN BUSINESS ARE THE ONES WHO ALWAYS TELL YOU EXACTLY WHAT YOU WANT TO HEAR.

In business, there are times when what you want to hear is very different from what you need to hear. But to make the right decisions, you need the unvarnished truth. This is when you can rely on the CPAs in your company. Every CPA is committed to giving you an honest, accurate analysis of your situation. Just as important, CPAs are versatile business strategists who can provide the valuable insights and information top management needs to improve business performance. With no strings attached.

THE CPA. NEVER UNDERESTIMATE THE VALUE   CPA

··· AUDITING ···

The job of reviewing and evaluating the records used to prepare a company's financial statements is referred to as **auditing**. Accountants within the organization often perform internal audits to ensure that proper accounting procedures and financial reporting are being carried out within the company. Public accountants also will conduct independent audits of accounting and related records. Financial auditors today not only examine the financial health of an organization but also look into operational efficiencies and effectiveness.[3] An **independent audit** is an evaluation and unbiased opinion about the accuracy of a company's financial statements. A firm's annual report often includes a written opinion from an auditor. An accountant who has a bachelor's degree and two years of experience in internal auditing, and who has passed an exam administered by the Institute of Internal Auditors, can earn standing as a **certified internal auditor**. Internal financial controls are very important for firms of any size, as the From the Pages of *Business Week* box (page 534) highlights.

··· TAX ACCOUNTING ···

Taxes are the price we pay for roads, parks, schools, police protection, and other functions provided by government. Federal, state, and local governments require submission of tax returns that must be filed at specific times and in a precise format. A **tax accountant** is trained in tax law and is responsible for preparing tax returns or developing tax strategies. Since governments often change tax policies according to needs or specific objectives, the job of the tax accountant is certainly challenging. Also, as the burden of taxes grows in the economy, the role of the tax accountant becomes increasingly important to the organization or entrepreneur.

Managerial and financial accounting, auditing, and tax accounting each requires specific training and skill. Yet some people still get confused about the difference between an accountant and a bookkeeper. We'll clarify that difference right after the Progress Check.

If someone experienced extreme chest pains, it's doubtful they would call an auto mechanic. Most likely they would seek the advice of a heart specialist. In financial accounting the specialist to seek for advice is the Certified Public Accountant (CPA). CPAs must pass a series of examinations from the American Institute of Certified Public Accountants and meet state education requirements to qualify for this specialty.

◄ **CONSIDER USING LECTURE ENHANCER 18-2**
How to Choose a CPA Firm.

Progress Check

- Can you explain the difference between managerial and financial accounting?
- Could you define accounting to a friend so that he or she would clearly understand what's involved?
- What's the difference between a private accountant and a public accountant?

Sniffing Out the Missing Loot

As is often the case in life, there's good news and bad news. The bad news is that, each year, companies of all sizes lose money to employee fraud. According to a 1997 study conducted by Arthur Andersen & Company and National Small Business United, companies with fewer than 20 employees fared the best in dealing with fraud. Only 17 percent of these smaller firms faced this problem. However, the number grew to a surprising 35 percent when comparing firms with 20 to 99 employees. This number provided a surprise to the researchers because the 35 percent of companies losing money in this category was very close to the 39 percent recorded among companies of 100 to 500 employees. The average amount of money lost by businesses was $9,800, though many companies lost less than $5,000.

The good news is that companies in all size categories are uncovering lost funds by employing internal financial controls (such as internal audits) that search out business losses such as those caused by employee fraud. Last year, internal financial control systems revealed employee fraud problems in 61 percent of the cases where the fraud was discovered. This percentage far exceeds the 5 percent of the employee fraud problems uncovered from tips provided by honest employees, 12 percent that were found by accident, and 10 percent provided by anonymous tips. It's easy to see how adherence to strict financial controls and auditing can benefit a business of any size.

Source: Edith Hill Updike, "Petty Larceny, Inc." *Business Week*, December 8, 1997.

► **LEARNING GOAL 3.**
Distinguish between accounting and bookkeeping and list the steps in the accounting cycle.

bookkeeping
The recording of business transactions.

► **CONSIDER USING OT ACETATE 18-4**
Business Growth at the Big Accounting Firms.

► **CONSIDER USING OT ACETATE 18-5**
Who are the Big Six?

► **CONSIDER USING LECTURE ENHANCER 18-3**
Is Your CPA a Party Animal?

journal
The book where accounting data are first entered.

► **CONSIDER USING LECTURE ENHANCER 18-4**
Protect Your Business Assets with Internal Controls.

► **CONSIDER USING LECTURE ENHANCER 18-5**
Forensic Accountants Ferret out Fraud.

ACCOUNTING VERSUS BOOKKEEPING

Bookkeeping involves the recording of business transactions. Bookkeeping is an important part of accounting, but accounting goes far beyond the mere recording of data. Accountants classify and summarize the data provided by bookkeepers. They interpret the data and report them to management. They also suggest strategies for improving the financial condition and progress of the firm. Accountants are especially important in financial analysis and for income tax preparation.

If you were a bookkeeper, the first task you would perform is to divide all of the firm's transactions into meaningful categories such as sales documents, purchasing receipts, and shipping documents. The challenge of the bookkeeper is to keep the information organized and manageable. Therefore, the bookkeeper must begin to record the data from the original transaction documents (the sales slips and so forth) into record books. A **journal** is the book where accounting data are first entered. The term journal comes from the French word *jour*, which means day. A journal, therefore, is where the day's transactions are kept.

It is quite possible when recording financial transactions that you could make a mistake. For example, you could easily write or type $10.98 as $10.89. For that reason, bookkeepers record all their transactions in two places. They can then check one list against the other to make sure that they add up to the same amount. If they don't equal the same amount, the bookkeeper knows that he or she made a mistake. The concept of writing every transaction in two

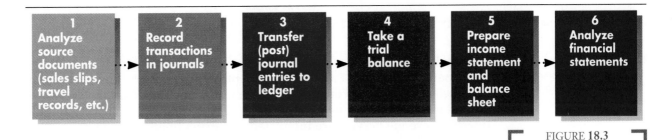

FIGURE **18.3**

····

STEPS IN THE
ACCOUNTING CYCLE

places is called **double-entry bookkeeping**. In double-entry bookkeeping, two entries in the journal are required for each company transaction.

Now, let's suppose a businessperson wanted to determine how much was paid for office supplies in the first quarter of the year. Without a specific bookkeeping tool that would be difficult even with accurate accounting journals. Therefore, bookkeepers make use of a set of books with pages labeled Office Supplies, Cash, and so on. The entries in the journal are transferred (posted) to these pages, and information about various accounts is available quickly and easily. A **ledger**, then, is a specialized accounting book in which information from accounting journals is accumulated into specific categories and posted so that managers can find all the information about a single account in one place. Computerized accounting programs will post information from journals into ledgers daily or instantaneously. This way the financial information is readily available whenever the organization needs it.

double-entry bookkeeping
The concept of writing every transaction in two places.

ledger
A specialized accounting book in which information from accounting journals is accumulated into specific categories and posted so that managers can find all the information about one account in the same place.

··· THE SIX-STEP ACCOUNTING CYCLE ···

The **accounting cycle** is a six-step procedure that results in the preparation and analysis of the two major financial statements: the balance sheet and the income statement (see Figure 18.3). The accounting cycle generally involves the work of both the bookkeeper and the accountant. The first three steps are continual: (1) analyzing and categorizing documents, (2) putting the information into journals, and (3) posting that information into ledgers. The fourth step involves preparing a trial balance. A **trial balance** is a summary of all the data in the account ledgers to show whether the figures are correct and balanced. If the information in the account ledgers is not correct, it must be corrected before the firm's income statement and balance sheet are prepared. The fifth step, then, is to prepare an income statement and balance sheet. The sixth step is for the accountant to analyze the financial statements and evaluate the financial condition of the firm. After the Progress Check, we will look into these two key financial statements and the important information each provides.

accounting cycle
A six-step procedure that results in the preparation and analysis of the two major financial statements: the balance sheet and the income statement.

trial balance
A summary of all the data in the account ledgers to show whether the figures are correct and balanced.

Can you imagine how many different transactions a typical restaurant has in a day? Still, records must be kept of each one to ensure accurate financial information. Can you see why most businesses prefer to hire someone to do this work? Would it be worth the time for an owner to do all the paperwork? Can you also understand why many businesses find it easier to do this work on a computer?

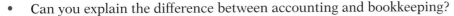

- Can you explain the difference between accounting and bookkeeping?
- What's the difference between an accounting journal and a ledger?
- Why does a bookkeeper prepare a trial balance?

➤ **LEARNING GOAL 4.**
Explain the difference between the major financial statements.

financial statement
A summary of all the transactions that have occurred over a particular period.

➤ **CONSIDER USING TM 130**
Steps in the Accounting Cycle (Figure 18.3 on text page 535.)

➤ **CONSIDER USING LECTURE ENHANCER 18-6**
ABC Accounting

···· ▬ ····
UNDERSTANDING KEY FINANCIAL STATEMENTS

A **financial statement** is a summary of all the transactions that have occurred over a particular period. Financial statements indicate a firm's financial health. That's why stockholders (the owners of the firm), banks and bondholders (people and institutions that lend money to the firm), unions, employees, and the Internal Revenue Service are interested in a firm's financial statements. Two key financial statements are

1. The *balance sheet*, which reports the firm's financial condition on a specific date.
2. The *income statement*, which reports revenues, cost of goods, expenses, and profits (or losses) for a specific period of time, showing the results of operations during that period.

After taking an intensive accounting course, one reporter summarized the difference this way: "The balance sheet is a snapshot, while the income statement is a motion picture. The former tells what the company owns and owes on a certain day; the latter, what it sells its products for and what its selling costs are over a period of time."[4]

To understand important financial information, you must be able to read and understand both the balance sheet and the income statement. Next we'll explore each statement in more detail.

··· THE BALANCE SHEET ···

balance sheet
The financial statement that reports a firm's financial condition at a specific time.

A **balance sheet** is the financial statement that reports a firm's financial condition at a specific time. It's composed of three major accounts: assets, liabilities, and owners' equity. It's called a *balance sheet* because it shows a balance between two figures: the company's assets on the one hand, and its liabilities plus owners' equity on the other. (These terms will be defined in the next sections.)

The following analogy will help explain the idea behind the balance sheet. Let's say that you want to know what your financial condition is at a given point in time. Maybe you want to buy a new house or car and therefore need to calculate the resources you have available. One of the best measuring sticks is your balance sheet.[5] First, you would add up everything you own—cash, property, money owed you, and so forth (assets). Subtract from that the money you owe others—credit card debt, IOUs, car loan, and so forth (liabilities)—and you have a figure that tells you that, as of today, you are worth so much (equity). This is fundamentally what companies are doing in preparing a balance sheet.

··· THE ACCOUNTS OF THE BALANCE SHEET ···

assets
Economic resources owned by a firm.

Assets are economic resources owned by a firm. Assets include productive, tangible items (such as equipment, buildings, land, furniture, fixtures, and motor vehicles) that help generate income, as well as intangibles of value such as patents or copyrights. Think, for example, of the value of brand names such as Coca-Cola, McDonald's, and Intel. Such intangibles as brand names can be among the firm's most valuable assets.[6] Assets are listed on the balance sheet according to their liquidity (see Figure 18.4). **Liquidity** refers to how fast an asset can be converted into cash. For example, land is considered a highly illiquid asset (difficult to turn into cash quickly) because it takes much time and paperwork to sell land. On the other hand, stock is considered highly liquid

liquidity
How fast an asset can be converted into cash.

FIGURE **18.4**

· · · ·

CLASSIFICATIONS OF ASSETS

Assets are classified by how quickly they can be turned into cash (liquidity). The most liquid are called *current assets*. Those that are hard to sell quickly are called *fixed assets* or *property, plant, and equipment*. *Intangible assets* include patents and copyrights.

◄ **CONSIDER USING TM 131**
Classifications of Assets
(Figure 18.4 on text page 537.)

because it can be sold within minutes. Assets are divided into three categories according to how quickly they can be turned into cash:

1. **Current assets** are items that can be converted into cash within one year.
2. **Fixed assets** such as land, buildings, and equipment are assets that are relatively permanent. (These assets are also referred to as property, plant, and equipment.)
3. **Intangible assets** include items of value such as patents and copyrights that have no real physical form.

··· LIABILITIES AND OWNERS' EQUITY ACCOUNTS ···

Another important accounting term is liabilities. **Liabilities** are what the business owes to others. *Current liabilities* are payments due in one year or less; *long-term liabilities* are payments not due for one year or longer. The following are common liability accounts recorded on a balance sheet (see Figure 18.5):

1. *Accounts payable*—money owed to others for merchandise and/or services purchased on credit but not yet paid. If you have a bill you haven't paid, you have an account payable.
2. *Notes payable*—short-term or long-term loans (e.g., from banks) that have a promise for future payment.
3. *Bonds payable*—money lent to the firm that must be paid back. If a firm sells someone a bond, it agrees to pay that person the money he or she lent the company plus interest. (We will discuss bonds in depth in Chapters 19 and 20.)

The value of things you own (assets) minus the amount of money you owe others (liabilities) is called *equity*. The value of what stockholders own in a firm (minus liabilities) is called *stockholders' equity* (or *shareholders' equity*). Because stockholders are the owners of a firm, stockholders' equity can also be called owners' equity or partnership equity.

The formula for **owners' equity,** then, is assets minus liabilities. Differences can exist in the owners' equity account according to the type of organization,

current assets
Items that can be converted into cash within one year.

fixed assets
Assets that are relatively permanent, such as land, buildings, and equipment.

intangible assets
Items of value such as patents and copyrights that have no real physical form.

liabilities
What the business owes to others.

◄ **CONSIDER USING CRITICAL THINKING EXERCISE 18-1**
Income Statements and Balance Sheets (**SCANS**)

◄ **CONSIDER USING TM 132**
Sample Fiberiffic Balance Sheet
(Figure 18.5 on text page 538.)

owners' equity
Assets minus liabilities.

FIGURE **18.5**

· · · ·

**SAMPLE FIBERRIFIC
BALANCE SHEET**

❶ Current assets: Items
that can be converted
to cash within one
year.

❷ Fixed assets: Items
such as land,
buildings, and
equipment that are
relatively permanent.

❸ Intangible assets:
Items of value such as
patents and
copyrights that don't
have a physical form.

❹ Current liabilities:
Payments that are due
in one year or less.

❺ Long-term liabilities:
Payments not due for
one year or longer.

❻ Stockholders' equity:
The value of what
stockholders own in a
firm (also called
owner's equity).

**FIBERRIFIC
Balance Sheet
March 31, 1999**

Assets

❶ Current assets
Cash	$ 15,000	
Accounts receivable	200,000	
Notes receivable	50,000	
Inventory	335,000	
Total current assets		$600,000

❷ Fixed assets
Land		$ 40,000	
Building and improvements	$200,000		
Less: Accumulated depreciation	– 90,000		
		110,000	
Equipment and vehicles	$120,000		
Less: Accumulated depreciation	– 80,000		
		40,000	
Furniture and fixtures	$26,000		
Less: Accumulated depreciation	– 10,000		
		16,000	
Total fixed assets			206,000

❸ Intangible assets
Goodwill	$ 20,000	
Total intangible assets		20,000
Total assets		826,000

Liabilities and Stockholders' Equity
  Liabilities

❹   Current liabilities
Accounts payable	$ 40,000	
Notes payable (due Dec. 1999)	8,000	
Accrued taxes	150,000	
Accrued salaries	90,000	
Total current liabilities		$288,000

❺   Long-term liabilities
Notes payable (due Mar. 2004)	$ 35,000	
Bonds payable (due Dec. 2014)	290,000	
Total long-term liabilities		325,000
Total liabilities		$613,000

❻ Stockholders' equity
Common stock (1,000,000 shares)	$100,000	
Retained earnings	113,000	
Total stockholders' equity		213,000
Total liabilities & stockholders' equity		826,000

however. Businesses not incorporated identify the investment of the sole proprietor or partner(s) through a *capital account.* For such sole proprietors and partners, owners' equity means the value of everything owned by the business minus any liabilities of the owner(s) such as bank loans. For corporations, the owners' equity account records the owners' claims to funds they have invested in the firm (such as capital stock) plus earnings kept in the business and not paid out to stockholders (retained earnings).

The formula given above for owners' equity is the inverse of the fundamental accounting equation. This equation is the basis for the balance sheet, so let's look at it next.

◄ **CONSIDER USING OT ACETATE 18-7**
Fiberiffic's Balance Sheet (Assets).

◄ **CONSIDER USING OT ACETATE 18-8**
Fiberiffic's Balance Sheet (Liabilities and Owner's Equity).

◄ **CONSIDER USING OT ACETATE 18-6**
The Fundamental Accounting Equation.

••• THE FUNDAMENTAL ACCOUNTING EQUATION •••

Imagine that you don't owe anybody money. That is, you don't have any liabilities. Then the assets you have (cash and so forth) are equal to what you own (equity). However, if you borrow some money from a friend, you have incurred a liability. The assets that you hold are now equal to what you owe plus what you own. Translated into business terms,

$$Assets = Liabilities + Owners' \ equity$$

This formula is called the **fundamental accounting equation** and is the basis for the balance sheet. As Figure 18.5 highlights, on the balance sheet, you list assets in a separate column from liabilities and owners' equity. The assets are equal to or are balanced with the liabilities and owners' equity. It's that simple. The only complicated part is determining what is included in the asset account and what is included in the liabilities and owners' equity accounts. It's critical for businesspeople to understand the important financial information the balance sheet provides. Take a few moments and see what facts you can determine about Fiberrific from its balance sheet. Then take a few minutes and try to estimate your net worth, following the directions in the Spotlight on Small Business box on page 540.

fundamental accounting equation
Assets = liabilities + owners' equity; this is the basis for the balance sheet.

Progress
Check

• What does it mean to list various assets by liquidity?
• What goes into the account called liabilities?
• What's the formula for determining owners' equity?
• What's the formula for the balance sheet?

••• THE INCOME STATEMENT •••

The financial statement that shows a firm's "bottom line"—that is, profit after costs, expenses, and taxes—is the income statement (also called the profit and loss statement). The **income statement** summarizes all of the resources (called revenue) that have come into the firm from operating activities, money resources that were used up, expenses incurred in doing business, and what resources were left after all costs and expenses, including taxes, were paid. **Net income or net loss** are the resources left over (see Figure 18.6). The income statement reports the results of operations over a particular period of time (usually a year, a month, or a quarter). It's the financial statement that reveals whether the business is actually turning a profit.[7] The income statement's formula is as follows:

income statement
The financial statement that shows a firm's profit after costs, expenses, and taxes; it summarizes all of the resources that have come into the firm (revenue), all the resources that have left the firm, and the resulting net income or loss.

net income or net loss
Revenue minus expenses.

Spotlight on Small Business

You, Incorporated

How do you think You, Inc., stacks up financially? Let's take a little time and find out. You may be pleasantly surprised, or you may realize that you need to think hard about planning your financial future. Remember, your net worth is nothing more than the difference between what you own (assets) and what you owe (liabilities). Be honest and do your best to give a fair evaluation of your private property's value.

ASSETS		LIABILITIES	
Cash	$_____	Installment loans and interest	$_____
Savings account	_____	Other loans and interest	_____
Checking account	_____	Credit card accounts	_____
Home	_____	Mortgage	_____
Stocks & bonds	_____	Taxes	_____
Automobile	_____	Other debts	_____
IRA or Keogh	_____		
Personal property	_____		
Other assets	_____		
Total assets	_____	Total liabilities	$_____

Determine your net worth:

Total assets	_____
– Total liabilities	– _____
= Net worth	$_____

Revenue – Cost of goods sold = Gross margin (or gross profit)

Gross margin – Operating expenses = Net income before taxes

Net income before taxes – Taxes = Net income (or loss)

The income statement includes valuable financial information for stockholders, lenders, investors (or potential investors), and employees. Because of the importance of this financial report, let's take just a moment to walk through the income statement and learn what each step means. Before we start, take a quick look at how the income statement is arranged according to generally accepted accounting principles:

Revenue
– Cost of goods sold
_____
Gross margin
– Operating expenses
_____
Net income before taxes
– Taxes
_____
Net income or loss

► **CONSIDER USING TM 133**
Sample Fiberiffic Income Statement
(Figure 18.6 on text page 541.)

FIGURE **18.6**
SAMPLE FIBERRIFIC
INCOME STATEMENT

FIBERRIFIC
Income Statement
For the Year Ended December 31, 1999

❶ Revenues

Gross sales		$ 720,000
Less: Sales returns and allowances	$ 12,000	
Sales discounts	8,000	– 20,000
Net sales		$ 700,000

❷ Cost of goods sold

Beginning inventory, Jan. 1		$ 200,000	
Merchandise purchases	$400,000		
Freight	40,000		
Net purchases		440,000	
Cost of goods available for sale	$ 640,000		
Less ending inventory, Dec. 31		– 230,000	
Cost of goods sold			– 410,000

❸ Gross profit $ 290,000

❹ Operating expenses

Selling expenses

Salaries for salespeople	$ 90,000		
Advertising	18,000		
Supplies	2,000		
Total selling expenses		$ 110,000	

General expenses

Office salaries	$ 67,000		
Depreciation	1,500		
Insurance	1,500		
Rent	28,000		
Light, heat, and power	12,000		
Miscellaneous	2,000		
		112,000	
Total operating expenses			222,000
Net income before taxes			$ 68,000
Less: Income tax expense			19,000
❺ Net income after taxes			$ 49,000

❶ Revenue: Value of what's received from goods sold, services rendered, and other financial sources.

❷ Cost of goods sold: Cost of merchandise sold or cost of raw materials or parts of supplies used for producing items for resale.

❸ Gross profit: How much the firm earned by buying or selling merchandise.

❹ Operating expenses: Cost incurred in operating a business.

❺ Net income after taxes: Profit or loss over a specific period after subtracting all costs and expenses including taxes.

··· **REVENUE** ···

Revenue is the value of what is received for goods sold, services rendered, and other financial sources. Note that there is a difference between revenue and sales. Most revenue (money coming into the firm) comes from sales, but there are other sources of revenue, such as rents received, money paid to the firm for use of its patents, and interest earned. Be careful not to confuse the two terms or to use them as if they were synonymous. Also, a quick glance at the income statement shows that revenue is at the top of the statement and income is at

revenue
The value of what is received for goods sold, services rendered.

◄ CONSIDER USING OT ACETATE 18-9
Fiberiffic's Income Statement

the bottom: net income is revenue minus sales returns, costs, expenses, and taxes. Net income can also be referred to as net earnings or net profit.

••• COST OF GOODS SOLD (COST OF GOODS MANUFACTURED) •••

cost of goods sold (or cost of goods manufactured)
A measure of the cost of merchandise sold or cost of raw materials and supplies used for producing items for resale.

The **cost of goods sold (or cost of goods manufactured)** is a measure of the cost of merchandise sold or cost of raw materials and supplies used for producing items for resale. It's simple logic to calculate how much a business earned by selling merchandise over the period evaluated, compared to how much it spent to buy the merchandise from its revenue. The cost of goods sold includes the purchase price plus any freight charges paid to transport goods plus any costs associated with storing the goods. In other words, all the costs of buying and keeping merchandise for sale are included in the cost of goods sold.

When you subtract the cost of goods sold from net sales, you get what is called gross margin or gross profit. **Gross margin (gross profit)** is how much a firm earned by buying (or making) and selling merchandise. In a service firm, there may be no cost of goods sold; therefore, net revenue could equal gross margin. In a manufacturing firm, however, it's necessary to estimate the cost of goods manufactured. In either case (selling goods or services), the gross margin doesn't tell you everything you need to know about the financial performance of the firm. The financial evaluating of an income statement also includes the *net* profit or loss a firm experienced. To get that, you must subtract expenses.

gross margin (gross profit)
How much a firm earned by buying (or making) and selling merchandise.

••• OPERATING EXPENSES •••

expenses
Costs incurred in operating a business, such as rent, utilities, and salaries.

To sell goods or services, a business has certain **expenses**. Obvious expenses include rent, salaries, supplies, utilities, insurance, and even depreciation of equipment. Accountants are trained to help you find these and other expenses you need to deduct.

After all expenses are deducted, the firm's net income before taxes is determined (see again Figure 18.6). After allocating for taxes, we get to what's called the *bottom line*, which is the net income (or perhaps net loss) the firm incurred from operations. It answers the question, How much did the business earn or lose in the reporting period?

Ever think about what goes into the assembly of a jumbo jetliner? Boeing Corporation has to think about that question every day. That's why Boeing has a large contingency of accountants to help coordinate functions such as keeping track of costs and expenses, the purchase and delivery of parts, and the inflows and outflows of cash.

Reaching Beyond
Our Borders

Wanted: Multilingual Financial Statements

If there was ever any doubt, such misfortunes as the Asian financial crisis of the late 1990s reminded us that we live in a global economy. As the news from the Asian markets got more and more distressing, the stock price of many U.S. firms began to tumble. Financial analysts reasoned that the fall was primarily due to concerns about future earnings of U.S. companies given the Asian situation.

Financial analysts from around the globe admit that earnings, determined from accounting statements, reward or punish a firm's stock price accordingly. The problem with using a barometer such as earnings in a global market is that a firm's earnings often differ according to the accounting method from which they were determined. Take Daimler-Benz of Germany, for example. When this company was first listed on the New York Stock Exchange, it reported a $370 million profit under German rules; however, under the U.S. generally accepted accounting principles (U.S. GAAP), the company showed a $1 billion loss. Such incompatibility in financial reporting has led financial specialists around the globe to call on firms to report earnings according to International Accounting Standards (IAS).

The problem with implementing this recommendation, however, is that international regulators, including the U.S. Securities & Exchange Commission (SEC), have flatly refused to accept the international standards—and they show few signs of softening their position in the near future. Arthur Levitt, chairman of the SEC, doesn't expect the United States to compromise on International Accounting Standards, because of many nations' refusal to require companies to provide full financial disclosure on financial statements. Russian companies, for example, often have gaping holes in financial statements due to limited accounting disclosure requirements. Supporters of IAS have countered by blaming the United States for the stalemate, suggesting that the SEC wants to impose its generally accepted accounting principles (which are considered exhaustive and prescriptive) on the world.

Can we expect a quick resolution to this problem? The International Accounting Standards Committee set a goal of resolving key issues by mid-1998. Many hurdles remain, but support is growing among powerful financial institutions such as the New York Stock Exchange. The NYSE has set a goal of attracting more foreign firms than currently trade on it. However, the task of creating a single set of accounting standards to cover companies around the world is not for the fainthearted or impatient. Many observers predict that this job will continue into the next millennium.

Sources: "Global Accounting's Roadblock," *The Economist*, April 27, 1997, pp. 79–82; and Jim Kelly, "A Fair System for Financial Institutions," *Financial Times*, January 8, 1998, pp. 10–13.

You may not be familiar with these terms and may even think they are quite complex, but you use accounting concepts all the time. For example, you know the importance of keeping track of costs and expenses when you prepare your own budget. If your expenses (e.g., rent and utilities) exceed your revenues (how much you earn), you are in deep trouble. If you need more money (revenue), you may need to sell some of the things you own to meet your expenses. The same is true in business. Companies need to keep track of how much money they earn and spend, how much cash they have on hand, and so on. The only difference is that companies tend to have more complex problems and more information to record than you as an individual do. As more firms involve themselves in global markets, accurate financial reporting becomes even more difficult (see the Reaching Beyond Our Borders box). Handling the flow and disbursement of cash is another problem that plagues both businesses and individuals. Keep this in mind as we explore accounting information a bit more in depth in the next section.

◄ CONSIDER USING SUPPLEMEN-
TAL CASE 18-2
When Income Statements Deceive
(SCANS)

Progress Check

➤ **CONSIDER USING OT ACETATE 18-10**
Problems Caused by "Slick Accounting."

➤ **CONSIDER USING LECTURE ENHANCER 18-7**
Connie Connors of CVC Communications.

- What are the three steps in the formula that makes up the income statement?
- What's the difference between revenue and income on the income statement?
- What's the formula for the income statement?

••• THE IMPORTANCE OF CASH FLOW ANALYSIS •••

Understanding cash flow is an important part of financial reporting. If not properly managed it can cause a business much concern. Remember Roxanne Coady's company in the profile? Cash flow analysis is really rather simple to comprehend. Let's say you borrow $100 from a friend to buy a used bike and agree to pay him back at the end of the week. In turn, you sell the used bike for $150 to someone else who also agrees to pay you in a week. Unfortunately, at the end of the week the person who bought the bike from you doesn't have the money and says that she will have to pay you next month. Meanwhile, your friend wants the $100 you agreed to pay him by the end of the week! What seemed like a great opportunity to make a $50 profit is a real cause for concern. Right now you owe $100 and have no cash. What do you do when your friend shows up at the end of the week and demands to be paid? If you were a business, this might cause you to default on the loan and possibly go bankrupt, even though you had the potential for profits.

cash flow
The difference between cash coming in and cash going out of a business.

A business can often increase sales and increase profit, and still suffer deeply from cash flow problems.[8] **Cash flow** is simply the difference between cash coming in and cash going out of a business. Poor cash flow constitutes a major operating problem for many companies and is particularly difficult for small businesses. Cash flow problems can occur even in a growing business like Roxanne Coady's bookstore. In order to meet the demands of customers, more and more goods are bought on credit (no cash is involved). Similarly, more and more goods are sold on credit (no cash is involved). This can go on until the firm uses up all the credit it has with banks that lend it money. When the firm requests more money from the bank to pay a crucial bill, the bank refuses the loan because the credit limit has been reached. All other credit sources refuse a loan as well. The company desperately needs funds to pay its bills or else its creditors could force it into bankruptcy. Unfortunately, all too often, the company does go into bankruptcy simply because there was no cash available when it was most needed.

➤ **CONSIDER USING LECTURE ENHANCER 18-8**
The Value of the Cash Flow Statement.

Cash flow analysis points out that clearly a businessperson's relationship with his or her banker is critical. Maintaining a working relationship with a bank is one possible solution to preventing cash flow problems that often develop. You can also see the value that accounting provides to the firm. Accountants tell the firm if it needs cash and how much. Accounting provides finance managers key insights into how, when, and where to get the money a firm needs. The statement of cash flows is a good barometer of measuring the cash position within a firm.

••• THE STATEMENT OF CASH FLOWS •••

statement of cash flows
Financial statement that reports cash receipts and disbursement related to a firm's major activities: operations, investment, and financing.

In 1988, the Financial Accounting Standards Board required firms to replace the statement of changes in financial position with the statement of cash flows. The **statement of cash flows** reports cash receipts and disbursement related to a firm's major activities:

- *Operations*—cash transactions associated with running the business.
- *Investments*—cash used in or provided by the firm's investment activities.
- *Financing*—cash raised from the issuance of new debt or equity capital or cash used to pay business expenses, past debts, or company dividends.

FIGURE 18.7

· · · ·

FIBERRIFIC STATEMENT
OF CASH FLOWS

FIBERRIFIC
Statement of Cash Flows
For the Year Ended December 31, 1999

Cash flows from operating activities		
Cash received from customers	$150,000	
Cash paid to suppliers and employees	(90,000)	
Interest paid	(5,000)	
Income tax paid	(4,500)	
Interest and dividends received	1,500	
Net cash provided by operating activities		$ 52,000
Cash flows from investing activities		
Proceeds from sale of plant assets	$ 4,000	
Payments for purchase of equipment	(10,000)	
Net cash provided by investing activities		(6,000)
Cash flows from financing activities		
Proceeds from issuance of short-term debt	$ 3,000	
Payment of long-term debt	(7,000)	
Payment of dividends	(15,000)	
Net cash inflow from financing activities		(19,000)
Net change in cash and equivalents		$ 27,000
Cash balance, December 31, 1999		(2,000)
Cash balance, December 31, 1999		$ 25,000

Accountants analyze all of the cash changes that have occurred from operating, investing, and financing and determine the firm's net cash position. The cash flow statement also gives the firm some insight into how to handle cash better so that no cash flow problems occur in the future.

Figure 18.7 shows an example of a statement of cash flows. As you can see from this example, the cash flow statement answers such questions as, How much cash came into the business from current operations? That is, how much cash came into the firm from buying and selling goods and services? Was cash used to buy stocks, bonds, or other investments? Were some investments sold that brought in cash? How much money came in from issuing stock? These and other financial transactions are analyzed to see their effect on the cash position of the firm. Consider these facts and then read the Making Ethical Decisions box (page 546) to see how accountants can sometimes face some tough ethical challenges.

· · · · ▬▬▬ · · · ·

APPLYING ACCOUNTING KNOWLEDGE

If accounting consisted of nothing more than the repetitive function of gathering and recording transactions and preparing financial statements, the major functions could be assigned to computers. In fact, most medium-to large-size firms and growing numbers of small businesses have done just that. But the

◄ **CONSIDER USING TM 134**
Fiberiffic's Statement of Cash Flows
(Figure 18.7 on text page 545.)

◄ **CONSIDER USING SUPPLEMENTAL CASE 18-1**
The Best Laid Plans Often Go Awry
(**SCANS**)

◄ **CONSIDER USING OT ACETATE 18-11**
How to Read a Corporate
Annual Report

◄ **LEARNING GOAL 5.**
Describe the role of depreciation, and
LIFO and FIFO in reporting financial
information.

◄ **CONSIDER USING LECTURE ENHANCER 18-9**
The Oil's Flowing but the Cash Isn't.

To Pad or Not to Pad?

You are the only accountant employed by a small manufacturing firm. You are in charge of keeping the books for the company, which is not in good shape because of an economic downturn that shows no signs of lessening in the near future.

You know that your employer is going to ask the bank for an additional loan so that the company can continue to pay its bills. Unfortunately, the financial statements for the year will not show good results, and you know that the bank will not approve a loan increase based on those figures.

Your boss approaches you in early January before you have closed the books for the year and suggests that perhaps the statements can be "improved" by treating the sales that were made at the beginning of January as

if they were made in December. He also asks you to do a number of other things that will cover up the trail so that the auditors will not discover the "padding" of the year's sales.

You know that it is against the professional rules of your accounting organization, and you argue with your boss. Your boss tells you that if the company does not get the additional bank loan there's a very good chance the business will close. That means you will be out of a job. You believe your boss is probably right and you know that with the current economic downturn it's a bad time to be looking for a job.

What are your alternatives? What are the likely consequences of each alternative? What will you do?

---

depreciation
The systematic write-off of the cost of a tangible asset over its estimated useful life.

➤ **CONSIDER USING LECTURE ENHANCER 18-10**
Pick a Number, Any Number.

➤ **CONSIDER USING LECTURE ENHANCER 18-11**
Favorite Numbers Games.

➤ **CONSIDER USING LECTURE ENHANCER 18-12**
Accounting Tricks in Mergers.

➤ **CONSIDER USING LECTURE ENHANCER 18-13**
Who's Accountable?

➤ **CONSIDER USING LECTURE ENHANCER 18-14**
Accounting Altar Boys?

truth is that *how* you record and report data is also critically important. Take a look at Figure 18.5 again. Note that Fiberrific lists accumulated depreciation on its property, plant, and equipment. What does this mean? Let's take a look.

Depreciation is the systematic write-off of the cost of a tangible asset over its estimated useful life. Have you ever heard the comment that a new car depreciates in market value as soon as you drive it out of the dealership? Well the same thing holds true for equipment and other specific assets of the firm. Companies are permitted to write off the cost of these assets using depreciation as a business operation expense. Subject to certain technical rules, which are beyond the scope of this chapter, a firm may use one of several different techniques for calculating depreciation. Each technique could result in a different net income. Accountants can offer financial advice and recommend ways of handling questions such as depreciation, insurance, investments, and other accounts that affect the firm's financial performance.

Another important issue and interesting example in financial accounting is how to handle inventory. Inventories are a critical part of a company's financial statements and are important in determining a firm's cost of goods sold (or cost of goods manufactured—see Fiberrific's income statement in Figure 18.6). When a firm sells merchandise from its inventory, there could be different ways of calculating the cost of that item. In financial reporting it doesn't matter when a particular item was actually placed in firm's inventory, but it does matter which method an accountant uses to record how much that item cost.

Let's say, for example, that a college bookstore buys textbooks for resale. It buys 100 copies of a particular textbook in July 1998 at a cost of $50 a copy. When classes begin in August, the bookstore sells 50 copies of the text to students for $60 each. In late December the bookstore orders 50 additional copies of the same text to sell for the next term. Unfortunately, the price of the book has increased to $60 due to inflation and other costs. The bookstore now has

	FIFO	LIFO
Revenue	$70	$70
Cost of goods sold	50	60
Income before taxes	20	10
Taxes of 40%	8	4
Net income	12	6

FIGURE **18.8**
• • • •
ACCOUNTING USING LIFO VERSUS FIFO INVENTORY VALUATION

◄ **CONSIDER USING TM 135**
Accounting Using LIFO Versus FIFO
Inventory Valuation (Figure 18.8 on text
page 547.)

copies of the same textbook from both purchase cycles in its inventory. If it sells 50 copies of the book to students for a price of $70 the next term, what was the cost of the book for accounting purposes? Good question. Let's see.

If the accountant used a method called **first in, first out (FIFO)**, the cost of goods sold recorded by the bookstore would be $50, because the textbook that was bought first cost $50. **FIFO** is generally used by businesses such as supermarkets. Supermarket clerks are told to place the old merchandise in front of the new merchandise so that the old merchandise sells first. The accountant, however, could have selected another method, called **last in, first out (LIFO)**. Using this strategy, the bookstore's cost of goods sold for the textbook would be $60. Can you see how the difference in accounting methods could affect the bookstore's bottom line? The books are the same and contain the same information. However, if the book sells for $70, FIFO would report $10 more of net income before taxes than LIFO would (see Figure 18.8).

It's important to understand the methods of valuing inventory and know what method a firm uses in evaluating its financial statements. A switch from LIFO to FIFO could make it appear that the firm made more money when, in fact, nothing changed but the accounting system. That's why the American Institute of Certified Public Accountants (AICPA) insists that readers of financial statements are provided complete information concerning the firm's financial operations. Companies are required to include a notation of any change in inventory valuation in their annual reports.

first in, first out (FIFO)
Accounting method for calculating cost of inventory; it assumes that the first goods to come in are the first to go out.

last in, first out (LIFO)
Accounting method for calculating cost of inventory; it assumes that the last goods to come in are the first to go out.

◄ **CONSIDER USING LECTURE ENHANCER 18-15**
The Smell of Fraud.

◄ **CONSIDER USING CRITICAL THINKING EXERCISE 18-3**
LIFO and FIFO (**SCANS**)

- What is cash flow, and how can a small business protect against cash flow problems before they occur?
- What is the relevance of the statement of cash flows?
- What is the difference between LIFO and FIFO inventory valuation? How could the use of these methods change financial information?

Progress
Check

◄ **LEARNING GOAL 6**
Explain the importance of ratio analysis and the budgeting process in reporting financial information.

• • • • ▬▬▬ • • • •
USING FINANCIAL RATIOS

Every person in an organization should know the importance of accurate financial information. Accurate financial information forms the basis of the analysis performed by accountants and other financial specialists inside and outside the firm. Financial ratios are especially helpful to use in analyzing the actual performance of the company compared to its financial objectives and to other firms in the industry. At first glance ratio analysis may seem somewhat complicated, but most of you already use ratios quite often. For example, in

Looking for that ultimate trip through home improvement land? Well, Home Depot is the spot for you. Home Depot stores stock over 35,000 items that cover over 130,000 square feet. The maintenance of such an enormous inventory is a task the company cannot take lightly. That's why Home Depot depends heavily on financial ratios to make certain they are effectively managing their resources compared to the competition.

> CONSIDER USING CRITICAL
THINKING EXERCISE 18-2
Calculating Financial Ratios (**SCANS**)

basketball, the number of shots made from the foul line is expressed by a ratio: shots made to shots attempted. A player who shoots 85 percent from the foul line is considered an outstanding foul shooter and suggestions are to not foul him or her in a close game. Whether they measure an athlete's performance or the financial health of a business, ratios are easy to compute and provide a good deal of valuable information. Financial ratios particularly provide key insights into how a firm is doing compared to other firms in its industry in the important areas of liquidity (speed of changing assets into cash), debt (leverage), profitability, and activity. Understanding and interpreting business ratios is a key to sound financial analysis. Let's look briefly at four key types of ratios businesspeople use to measure financial performance: liquidity ratios, leverage (debt) ratios, profitability (performance) ratios, and activity ratios.

··· LIQUIDITY RATIOS ···

As explained earlier, liquidity refers to how fast an asset can be converted to cash. Liquidity ratios measure a company's ability to pay its short-term debts. These short-term debts are expected to be repaid within one year and are of particular importance to the firm's creditors who expect to be paid on time. Two key liquidity ratios are the current ratio and the acid-test ratio.

The *current ratio* is the ratio of a firm's current assets to its current liabilities. This information can be found on the firm's balance sheet. Let's say that Miller's Auto Repair has $25,000 of current assets and $10,000 of current liabilities. This firm has a current ratio of 2.5, which means the company has $2.50 of current assets for every $1 of current liabilities.

$$\text{Current ratio} = \frac{\text{Current assets}}{\text{Current liabilities}} = \frac{\$25,000}{\$10,000} = 2.5$$

At first glance, it may appear the firm is well positioned financially for the short term. The current ratio, however, should be compared to that of competing firms within the industry. It's also important for the firm to compare its current ratio with its current ratio from the previous year to note any significant changes.

> CONSIDER USING LECTURE
ENHANCER 18-16
The SEC Pushes Current-value
Accounting.

The second key liquidity ratio, called the *acid-test* or *quick ratio,* measures the cash, marketable securities (such as stocks and bonds), and receivables of a firm, compared to its current liabilities. This ratio is particularly important to firms that have difficulty converting inventory into quick cash. It helps answer such questions as, What if sales drop off and we can't sell our inventory? Can we still pay our short-term debt? Though ratios vary among industries, in general, an acid test ratio of between .50 and 1.0 is satisfactory. An organization that cannot meet its short-term debt often has to go to a high-cost lender for financial assistance.

$$\text{Acid-test ratio} = \frac{\text{Cash + Marketable securities + Receivables}}{\text{Current liabilities}} = \frac{\$15,000}{\$10,000} = 1.5$$

⋯ LEVERAGE (DEBT) RATIOS ⋯

Leverage (debt) ratios measure the degree to which a firm relies on borrowed funds in its operations. A firm that takes on too much debt could experience problems repaying lenders or meeting promises made to stockholders. The *debt to owners' equity ratio* measures the degree to which the company is financed by borrowed funds that must be repaid.

$$\text{Debt to owners' equity ratio} = \frac{\text{Total liabilities}}{\text{Owners' equity}} = \frac{\$150,000}{\$275,000} = 54.5\%$$

A ratio above 1 (i.e., above 100 percent) would show that a firm has more debt than equity. It's a good bet such a firm could be quite risky to both lenders and investors. But remember, it's always important to compare a firm's ratios to those of other firms in the same industry because debt financing is more acceptable in some industries than in others. Comparisons with past ratios can also identify trends that may be occurring within the firm or industry.

⋯ PROFITABILITY (PERFORMANCE) RATIOS ⋯

Profitability (performance) ratios measure how effectively a firm is using its various resources to achieve profits. Management's performance is often accurately reflected in the firm's profitability ratios. Three of the more important ratios used are earnings per share, return on sales, and return on equity.

A new Accounting Standards Board rule that went into effect at the end 1997 requires companies to report their quarterly earnings per share in two ways: basic and diluted.

The *basic earnings per share (basic EPS) ratio* measures the amount of profit earned by a company for each share of outstanding common stock. As you probably guessed, this is a very important ratio for corporations, since earnings help stimulate growth in the company and pay for stockholders' dividends. Continued earnings growth is well received by both investors and lenders. The basic EPS ratio is calculated as follows:

$$\text{Basic earnings per share} = \frac{\text{Net income}}{\substack{\text{Number of} \\ \text{common shares} \\ \text{outstanding}}} = \frac{\$120,000}{100,000} = \$1.20 \text{ per share}$$

The *diluted earnings per share (diluted EPS) ratio* measures the amount of profit earned by a company for each share of outstanding common stock, but also takes into consideration stock options, warrants, preferred stock, and convertible debt securities, which can be converted into common stock.

Diluted EPS shows investors the minimum share of earnings each share of stock is entitled to. This change aligns U.S. accounting standards with evolving international standards, helping investors compare companies globally.[9]

Another reliable indicator of performance is obtained by using a ratio that measures the return on sales. Firms use this ratio to see if they are doing as well as the companies they compete against in generating income from the sales they achieve. *Return on sales* is calculated by comparing a company's net income to its total sales:

$$\text{Return on sales} = \frac{\text{Net income}}{\text{Net sales}} = \frac{\$50,000}{\$500,000} = 10\% \text{ return on sales}$$

Risk is a market variable that concerns investors. The higher the risk involved in an industry, the higher the return investors expect on their investment. Therefore, the level of risk involved in an industry and the return on investment of competing firms is important in comparing the firm's performance. *Return on equity* measures how much was earned for each dollar invested by owners. It is calculated by comparing a company's net income to its total owners' equity.

$$\text{Return on equity} = \frac{\text{Net income}}{\text{Total owners' equity}} = \frac{\$50,000}{\$150,000} = 33\% \text{ return on equity}$$

It's important to remember that profits help companies grow. Therefore, these and other profitability ratios are considered vital measurements of company growth and management performance.

··· ACTIVITY RATIOS ···

Converting the firm's resources to profits is a key function of management. Activity ratios measure the effectiveness of a firm's management in using the assets that are available.

The *inventory turnover ratio* measures the speed of inventory moving through the firm and its conversion into sales. Inventory sitting by idly in a business costs money. The more efficiently a firm manages its inventory, the higher the return. The inventory turnover ratio is measured by:

What's the least popular 10-letter word in business? Bankruptcy! One way to keep this word from becoming part of your company's history is to make sure that inventory management is a key focus of the firm. Using the inventory turnover ratio helps companies stay on track and keyed into acceptable ratios within their industries.

$$\text{Inventory turnover ratio} = \frac{\text{Cost of goods sold}}{\text{Average inventory}} = \frac{\$320,000}{\$116,000} = 2.75 \text{ times}$$

A lower than average inventory turnover ratio often indicates obsolete merchandise on hand or poor buying practices. A higher than average ratio may signal lost sales because of inadequate stock. An acceptable turnover ratio is generally determined industry by industry.

Managers need to be aware of proper inventory control to ensure proper performance. Have you ever worked as a food server in a restaurant? How many times did your employer expect you to "turn over" a table in an evening? The more times a table turns, the higher the return to the owner.

Accountants and other finance professionals use several other specific ratios, in addition to the ones we have discussed, to learn more about a firm's financial condition. The key purpose here is to acquaint you with the idea of what financial ratios are, the relationship they have with the firm's financial statements, and how businesspeople—including investors, creditors, lenders, and managers—use them. If you can't recall what kinds of information are used in ratio analysis, see Figure 18.9 for a quick reference. It's also important for you to note that financial analysis begins where the accounting statements end. The budgeting process also relies on accurate information in financial statements. Let's take a look at budgets next.

◄ CONSIDER USING TM 136
Sample of Specific Account Titles in General Account Classifications (Figure 18.9 on text page 551)

budget
A financial plan that sets forth management's expectations for revenues and, based on those expectations, allocates the use of specific resources throughout the firm.

···· ▬▬▬ ····

ACCOUNTANTS AND THE BUDGETING PROCESS

A budget is a financial plan. To be more specific, a **budget** sets forth management's expectations for revenues and, based on those expectations, allocates the use of specific resources throughout the firm. The balance sheet, income

FIGURE 18.9
····
SAMPLE OF SPECIFIC
ACCOUNT TITLES IN
GENERAL ACCOUNT
CLASSIFICATIONS

FOR THE BALANCE SHEET			FOR THE INCOME STATEMENT			
Assets	Liabilities	Stockholders' or Owners' Equity	Revenues	Cost of Goods Sold	Expenses	
Cash	Accounts payable	Capital stock	Sales revenue	Cost of buying goods	Wages	Interest
Accounts receivable	Notes payable	Retained earnings	Rental revenue	Cost of storing goods	Rent	Donations
Inventory			Commissions revenue		Repairs	Licenses
Investments	Bonds payable	Common stock			Travel	Fees
Equipment	Taxes payable	Treasury stock	Royalty revenue		Insurance	Supplies
Land					Utilities	Advertising
Buildings					Entertainment	Taxes
Motor vehicles					Storage	
Goodwill						

If you ask small businesses for a wish list of items that would make their lives easier, one request that's sure to be close to the top is a simple way to handle the firm's financial information. Well, the fairy godmother has arrived. Peachtree software is one of several companies that offer software packages that address the specific accounting needs of small businesses.

> **LEARNING GOAL 7.**
Describe how computers are used to record and apply accounting information in business.

statement, and statement of cash flows form the basis for the budgeting process because financial information from the past is what's used to project future financial needs. Many companies, both large and small, see the budget process as an opportunity to plan and to improve management of the business. Telecommunications giant Sprint, in fact, has reengineered its budgeting process as part of a larger organizational effort to improve its forecasting and overall business planning.[10] Other innovative companies throughout the business spectrum are intent on determining not only their firms' overall profitability but also the profitability of individual products, individual customers, and individual channels of distribution.[11] Using accurate financial information to make such strategic business decisions is critical. Such reliance on the accounting department and the involvement of accounting professionals reinforces the importance of financial statements being prepared according to legal and accepted accounting principles.

What can be fascinating and challenging is to learn how finance specialists use accounting and financial information to keep the business sound. Accountants are often called on to assist the financial managers in determining what the organization's financial needs specifically include. It's also safe to say that financial planning and budgeting are tasks that tend to be time-consuming, tedious, and labor-intensive. Nonetheless, financial planning and budgeting are vital in both large and small firms and serve as a financial blueprint for the future. We will explore financial planning and the budget process in more depth in Chapter 19. But before we do, let's look at one other trend that has changed the job of reporting financial information in the firm.

···· ▬ ····

THE IMPACT OF COMPUTER TECHNOLOGY ON ACCOUNTING

Financial information and transactions may be recorded by hand or by computer. Of course, today most companies have found that computers greatly simplify the task and enable managers and other employees to get financial reports exactly when they want them. Also, as a business grows, the number of accounts a firm must keep and the reports that need to be generated expand in scope. You no doubt can recognize how computers can help in the accounting process. Even small-business owners have learned that accounting records can be maintained and analyzed best by a computer. Many of the latest small-business accounting packages address the specific needs of small businesses, which are often significantly different from the needs of a *Fortune* 500 company.[12]

Using computers to record and analyze data and to print out financial reports allows managers to obtain up-to-the-minute financial information for the business. It's now even possible, thanks to computers, to have continuous auditing which helps managers prevent cash flow problems and other financial difficulties by allowing them to spot trouble earlier than ever before.

Today there are software programs that allow even novices to do sophisticated financial analyses within days.

◀ CONSIDER USING LECTURE
ENHANCER 18-17
Making Sense of Accounting Software.

It's important to remember, however, that no computer yet has been programmed to make good financial decisions by itself. A computer is a wonderful tool, but business owners should understand exactly what computer system is best suited for their particular needs.[13] That's one reason why we recommend that small-business owners hire or consult with an accountant before they get started in business to identify the particular needs of their firm. Once the exact criteria are determined, it's necessary for a small business to develop its accounting system so that it works within the selected pre-designed package. Today's accounting packages offer enhanced ease of use, better customization, and efficient Internet functionality.

Computers help make accounting work less monotonous. Still, the work of an accountant requires training and very specific competencies. It's interesting that beginning business students sometimes assume that opportunities in accounting are rather limited and narrow in scope. But we hope that you have seen from this chapter that there is more to accounting than meets the eye. Keep in mind that accounting is roughly a $40 billion industry.[14] It can be fascinating and is critical to the firm's operations. As the language of business, accounting is a worthwhile language to learn.

Progress Check

- Look back at the financial statements of Fiberrific in Figures 18.6 and 18.7. Can you calculate the company's current ratio, acid-test ratio, debt to equity ratio, and return on sales ratio?

- What is a budget, and how can accountants assist in the preparation of this important planning tool?

SUMMARY
. . . . . .

1. Understand the importance of financial information and accounting.

1. Financial information is critical to the growth and development of an organization. Accounting provides the information necessary to measure a firm's financial condition.
   - *What is accounting?*
   Accounting is the recording, classifying, summarizing, and interpreting of financial events and transactions that affect an organization. The methods used to record and summarize accounting data into reports are called an accounting system.

2. Define and explain the different areas of the accounting profession.

2. The accounting profession covers four major areas: managerial accounting, financial accounting, auditing, and tax accounting.
   - *How does managerial accounting differ from financial accounting?*
   Managerial accounting provides information and analyses to managers within the firm to assist them in decision making. Financial accounting provides information and analyses to external users of data such as creditors and lenders.
   - *What is the job of an auditor?*
   Auditors review and evaluate the standards used to prepare a company's financial statements. An independent audit is conducted by a public accountant and is an evaluation and unbiased opinion about the accuracy of company financial statements.
   - *What is the difference between a private accountant and a public accountant?*
   A public accountant provides services for a fee to a variety of companies, whereas a private accountant works for a single company. Private and public accountants do essentially the same things with the exception of independent

audits. Private accountants do perform internal audits, but only public accountants supply independent audits.

3. Distinguish between accounting and book-keeping, and list the steps in the accounting cycle.

3. Many people confuse bookkeeping and accounting.
 • *What is the difference between bookkeeping and accounting?*
Bookkeeping is part of accounting, and includes the mechanical part of recording data. Accounting also includes classifying, summarizing, interpreting, and reporting data to management.
 • *What are journals and ledgers?*
Journals are original-entry accounting documents. That means they are the first place transactions are recorded. Summaries of journal entries are recorded (posted) into ledgers. Ledgers are specialized accounting books that arrange the transactions by homogeneous groups (accounts).
 • *What are the six steps of the accounting cycle?*
The six steps of the accounting cycle are (1) analyzing documents, (2) recording information into journals, (3) posting that information into ledgers, (4) developing a trial balance, (5) preparing the income statement and balance sheet and (6) analyzing financial statements.

4. Explain the differences between the major financial statements.

4. Financial statements are a critical part of the firm's financial position.
 • *What is a balance sheet?*
A balance sheet reports the financial position of a firm on a particular day. The fundamental accounting equation used to prepare the balance sheet is Assets = Liabilities + Owners' equity.
 • *What are the major accounts of the balance sheet?*
Assets are economic resources owned by the firm, such as buildings and machinery. Liabilities are amounts owed by the firm to others (e.g., creditors, bondholders). Owners' equity is the value of the things the firm owns (assets) minus any liabilities; thus, owners' equity equals assets minus liabilities.
 • *What is an income statement?*
An income statement reports revenues, costs, and expenses for a specific period of time. (e.g., for year ended December 31, 1998). The formula is Revenue – Cost of goods sold = Gross margin; Gross margin – Operating expenses = Net income before taxes; and Net income before taxes – Taxes = Net income (or net loss). (Note that income and profit mean the same thing.)
 • *What is a statement of cash flows?*
Cash flow is the difference between cash receipts (money coming in) and cash disbursements (money going out). The statement of cash flows reports cash receipts and disbursements related to the firm's major activities: operations, investments, and financing.

5. Describe the role of depreciation and LIFO and FIFO in reporting financial information.

5. Applying accounting knowledge makes the reporting and analysis of data a challenging occupation. Depreciation is a key account that accountants evaluate. Also, two accounting techniques for valuing inventory are known as LIFO and FIFO.
 • *What is depreciation?*
Depreciation is the systematically writing off the value of a tangible asset over its estimated useful life. Depreciation must be noted on both the balance sheet and the income statement.
 • *What are LIFO and FIFO?*
LIFO and FIFO are methods of valuing inventory. LIFO means last in, first out. FIFO means first in, first out. The method you use to value inventory, LIFO or FIFO, affects net income.

6. Financial ratios are a key part of analyzing financial information.
   • *What are the four key categories of ratios?*
   There are four key categories of ratios; liquidity ratios, leverage (debt) ratios, profitability (performance) ratios, and activity ratios.
   • *What is the major value of ratio analysis to the firm?*
   Ratio analysis provides the firm with financial information about its financial position in key areas compared to comparable firms in its industry and its past performance.
   • *What is involved in the budgeting process?*
   A budget is a financial plan that sets forth management's expectations for revenues, and based on the expectations allocates specific resources throughout the firm. Accounting information is a key to setting realistic budgets for the firm.

6. Explain the importance of ratio analysis and the budgeting process in reporting financial information.

7. Computers greatly simplify accounting tasks.
   • *How can computers help accountants?*
   Computers can record and analyze data and provide financial reports. Software is available that can continuously analyze and test accounting systems to be sure they are functioning correctly. Computers can help decision making by providing appropriate information, but they cannot make good financial decisions independently. Accounting creativity is still a human trait.

7. Describe how computers are used to record and apply accounting information in business.

KEY TERMS

accounting 530
accounting cycle 535
annual report 532
assets 536
auditing 532
balance sheet 536
bookkeeping 534
budget 551
cash flow 544
certified internal auditor 532
certified management accountant 531
certified public accountant (CPA) 532
cost of goods sold (or cost of goods manufactured) 542
current assets 537

depreciation 546
double-entry bookkeeping 535
expenses 542
first in, first out (FIFO) 547
financial statement 536
fixed assets 537
fundamental accounting equation 539
gross margin (gross profit) 542
income statement 539
independent audit 532
intangible assets 537
journal 534
ledger 535

liabilities 537
last in, first out (LIFO) 547
liquidity 536
managerial accounting 531
net income or net loss 539
owners' equity 537
private accountants 532
public accountant 532
revenue 541
statement of cash flows 544
tax accountant 532
trial balance 535

DEVELOPING WORKPLACE SKILLS

1. Take a sheet of paper. On every fourth line, write one of the following headings: assets, liabilities, owners' equity, expenses, cost of goods sold (or cost of goods manufactured), and revenues. Then list as many items as you can under each heading. When you are finished, look up the lists in the text and add to your own. Keep the lists for your notes. As you complete the lists, create a mental picture of each account so that you can understand the concepts behind accounts and accounting.

2. Prepare a sample income statement for a real or imaginary company. See how far you can get without looking back to Figure 18.6. Then look in the text to see what you have forgotten, if anything. Actually writing these things down does wonders for remembering the ideas later.

3. Use a computer and spreadsheet software to prepare a balance sheet for a real or imaginary company. Remember the formula: Assets = Liabilities + Owners' equity. Compare your balance sheet to the one in Figure 18.5 in the chapter.

4. Place yourself in the role of a small-business consultant. One of your clients, China Dimensions, is considering opening two new stores. The problem is the business often experiences cash flow problems. Prepare a draft memo to them that proposes an expansion strategy that takes into consideration the potential problems with such rapid growth. Think of several ways the business could avoid such problems.

5. The chapter describes two ways of determining cost of goods sold: FIFO (first in, first out) and LIFO (last in, first out). Compute the net income using FIFO and LIFO with the information listed below. Which strategy is best? What factors should you consider in deciding what inventory valuation method to use?

Beginning inventory:	25,000 units @ $20.00
Purchases (new inventory):	25,000 units @ 25.00
Sales:	25,000 units @ 55.00
Tax rate:	33%

TAKING IT TO THE NET

Purpose

To compute and analyze a sample balance sheet.

Exercise

Find the Interactive Toolbox in the Business Builders section of the Be The Boss Web site (http://www.betheboss.com/). Use the Balance Sheet Tool to create a sample balance sheet for the your shop, Thingamajigs and Things, using the following information:

Cash in savings account	$ 6,300	Equipment	$ 8,000
Cash in checking account	1,400	Fixtures	9,400
Stocks	10,000	Accounts receivable	2,750
Bonds	5,000	Notes payable	2,000
Bank loan	12,000	Employee salaries due	6,000
Money owed to supplier	3,500	Rent	12,000
Inventory	26,000	Depreciation on truck	5,500
Delivery truck	16,500	Taxes payable	12,500

The Balance Sheet Tool uses the information in the balance sheet to compute a current ratio and quick ratio for your business.

1. Is your current ratio greater than or equal to 2? If not, what adjustments might you make? (Hint: the Web site has instructions on how to analyze balance sheets and ratios.)

2. Is your quick ratio (acid-test ratio) satisfactory? Explain. (Hint: again, see the section about how to analyze balance sheets if you need help.)

Practicing Management Decisions

DaVinci Painting and Decorating was started by high school senior Keith Allen. As the business grew, Keith hired several of his friends and is now doing well. At first he did not consider keeping records to be that important. Now he is in a position to begin keeping good records. Keith has written down some of his figures, but he isn't quite sure how to interpret them. He plans to request another loan from a local bank and has been told to prepare a balance sheet to calculate his financial position. These are his figures:

Cash on hand	$5,100
Equipment loan	1,200
Supplies	500
Bank loan	7,500
Truck	13,750
Equipment	4,520
Money owed for materials	900
Office furniture	945
Accounts receivable	2,400
Notes payable	1,900

Keith collected some other figures he felt might be important in determining the performance of his firm. These were put together fast and in no apparent order:

CASE
······
APPLYING FINANCIAL INFORMATION
······

Income from work	$74,000
Salaries to employees	38,000
Advertising expense	1,720
Insurance	2,000
Offices costs (rent, heat, etc.)	8,040
Depreciation on truck	4,000

Keith also recently purchased some wallpapering materials for $1,800 for a job he expects to start in a week.

Decision Questions

1. What additional information, if any, would you need to construct a balance sheet? If DaVinci Painting and Decorating is a sole proprietorship, can you prepare a balance sheet for Keith from the information provided? Is Keith in a strong or poor financial condition? How can you determine this?
2. Prepare an income statement you could use to show Keith how such a financial statement looks. How much did Keith earn before taxes?
3. Is the bank being unreasonable by asking Keith to put together a balance sheet? What other information might interest the bank if Keith wants to get this additional loan?

VIDEO CASE
······
LEARNING THE LANGUAGE OF BUSINESS

Games and sports are more fun to play when you know the rules and regulations. Once you begin playing, it's a challenge to see how well you can do relative to other players. Each game has its own rules and measures of success. In baseball, you can strike out two out of three times at bat yet still be considered a good player. In basketball, on the other hand, if you miss two out of three foul shots you wouldn't seem so good.

Businesses also follow rules and regulations. As in sports, there are various ways of "scoring" and measuring the effectiveness of one business against others in the same field. For example, you can compare supermarkets to other supermarkets in efficiency, return on investment, turnover of goods, and so forth.

The people who keep such records are called accountants. Their function is to act as the score and record keepers of business. Accounting is

thus called the language of business because accounting terms such as assets, liabilities, revenues, expenses, and owners' equity are as important to business as "balls," "strikes," and "outs" are to baseball.

The score sheets in accounting, as you have read in this chapter, include the income statement, the balance sheet, and the statement of cash flows. Such statements tell a business how it is doing internally. But how does the success of the business compare to its competitors. Lots of people would like to know that answer: potential stockholders, union negotiators, potential employees, bankers, and other lenders. Accountants calculate and prepare such comparison measures as return on investment, inventory turnover, debt ratios, price/earnings ratios, and more. In order to be considered a pro in business, you have to know the language and the importance and meaning of key ratios. Just as a professional baseball player can tell you his or her batting average, a professional businessperson can tell you his or her company's return on investment and explain its significance.

Discussion Questions

1. Which accounting terms and concepts do you need to know to prepare a balance sheet? What is the formula?

2. Which terms and concepts do you need to know to prepare an income statement?

3. Why should accountants compare the success of one business against others?

4. Can you prove that you are ready for at least the amateur ranks of business by explaining what return on equity, cash flow, and PE ratio mean?

Part6

Career Portfolio

Managing Information (Information Systems)

Information management is a major growth industry of the future. To understand either the past or the present conditions of a company, we must have information. The process of getting the right information and processing it efficiently is an important part of staying competitive in today's business world. In a world constantly reshaped by new technology, the field of information management plays a key role.

Changing technologies have created a large number of different job titles in this exciting area. Careers are available in: information systems management, computer programming, cost estimating, and troubleshooting, just to name a few. All future forecasts predict that career opportunities in computer-related businesses and industries will continue to grow more rapidly than the average for other occupations.

••• SKILLS •••

Anyone who chooses to work with information technology should be comfortable with change and have a willingness to keep abreast of changes. Such a person also needs to have an interest in and aptitude for data and information and have an ability to see trends and relationships. People in this area are usually involved in some way with problem solving. An aptitude for seeing possible solutions to problems is important.

••• CAREER PATHS •••

In this ever-changing field, up-to-date knowledge is the key. A formal education in computer science, for example, would be almost useless if it was obtained 10 years ago and not updated. Most employers prefer hiring people who have had recent college coursework in software applications, programming, and general business. Business knowledge is important for the employee to place his or her work in context.

Computer skills are taught at public and private vocational schools, community colleges, and universities. Many programmers and systems analysts are college graduates, and a degree is helpful in getting hired. However, vocational schools can often provide the knowledge and skill necessary to excel.

SOME POSSIBLE CAREERS IN INFORMATION SYSTEMS

Job Title	Salary	Job Duties	Career Path	Prospects
Systems analyst	$24,800–$76,200 Median: $46,300	Advise computer programmers on problem solutions. Implement management decision on data processing issues.	Can start as a trainee, then be promoted into management.	One of the fastest-growing occupations through 2006.
Computer programmer	$22,700–$65,200 Median: $40,100	Work for systems analyst to write programs needed by management.	Promotions often mean greater task complexity. Start out as programmer.	Growth will be much faster than average through 2006. Great opportunity.
Cost estimator	$20,000–$30,000 (to start)	Prepare specifications using precedent, math, and computer data to predict cost requirements.	Career path varies greatly from company to company and from industry to industry.	Prospects are average through 2006. Good in construction.
Operations research analyst	$24,300–$65,500 Median: $42,400	Solve problems by the use of computerized data. Nature of problems varies.	Master's degree or Ph.D. very desirable. High level of computer skills is mandatory. Promotion into management quite possible. Bachelor's degree graduates start as research assistants.	Good for those with bachelor's degree. Very good for master's and Ph.D. degree.

Source: *Occupational Outlook Handbook*, 1998–1999 Edition: Bureau of Labor Statistics.

Electronic Data Systems

Name: David Goodman

Age: 29

Position/title: Team Leader for Credited Service, General Motors Pension Administration Center

Salary range: $30,000–$35,000

Time in this position: Two months as a Leader, six months in the position

Major factors in the decision to take this position: Previously, I was working for EDS tracking a Roadside Assistance Program for one of EDS's accounts. I maintained the database that was used to help keep track of customers' needs. After a few years, I was looking for another challenge that would lead me to a supervisor and/or account management position. The Credited Service department was looking for a person to work with the General Motors account, auditing General Motors employees' pension plans and maintaining their pension database.

Company name: Electronic Data Systems (EDS)

Company's Web address: www.eds.com

Company description: EDS excels in shaping how information is created, distributed, shared, enjoyed, and applied for the benefit of enterprises and individuals worldwide.

Job description: I assist in carrying out activities related to credited service audits. I maintain and track the audits through a large database, making sure they are completed and the backlog is kept to a minimum. I also keep the caseloads manageable for personnel.

Career paths: I first discovered my niche was in the data processing area when I was working on computer systems for McDonald's. While still a student, I worked for a hypermarket called Meijer, Inc. I was able to learn various aspects of marketing and data processing. During this time, I also worked for the school newspaper, *The Lookout,* and the *Greater Lansing Business Monthly,* as an advertising manager. I first worked for EDS on a Roadside Assistance Program. When motorists had problems, I would use my data processing resources to solve them. After a few years in working on the Roadside Assistance Program, I was promoted to the Credited Service department where I am today.

Ideal next job: My next ideal position would be as a supervisor, and hopefully that would lead to a manager or account manager position.

Best part of your job: The favorite part of my job is working with people. I enjoy leading and learning from others to effectively achieve our team goals.

Worst part of your job: The worst part of my job is the backlog of audit requests.

Educational background: I have an associate's degree and a bachelor's degree with a double major in marketing and management.

Favorite course: My favorite courses were in marketing, communication, and business.

Best course for your career: Marketing was the best course for my career.

Compliments of Professor Bill Motz, Lansing Community College

Financial Management

Chapter 19

LEARNING GOALS

After you have read and studied this chapter,
you should be able to

1 Explain the role and importance of finance.

2 Describe the responsibilities of financial managers.

3 Outline the steps in financial planning by explaining the process of forecasting financial needs, developing budgets, and establishing financial controls.

4 Recognize the financial needs that must be met with available funds.

5 Distinguish between short-term and long-term financing and between debt capital and equity capital.

6 Identify and describe several sources of short-term financing.

7 Identify and describe several sources of long-term financing.

Judy Lewent has put her education to good use. A graduate of the Massachusetts Institute of Technology's Sloan School of Management, she worked in financial management for 10 years at Pfizer, Inc., before joining another pharmaceutical giant, Merck & Company, Inc., in 1980. After serving three years as company treasurer, Lewent became chief financial officer (CFO) in 1990. She was the first woman in corporate America to hold the title of CFO. Today she sits on the seven-member chairman's staff at Merck and serves on such powerful corporate boards as that of General Mills. Lewent also holds the title of senior vice president at Merck and is considered one of the most powerful women in corporate America.

Lewent's job at Merck is intense and challenging. Think about what she must face in such a competitive industry. The business requires costly, time-consuming research that may not pay off for many years. Merck invests approximately $1 billion a year in research, yet it can take 10 to 12 years and cost over $350 million to develop a new drug. To further compound this problem, only 3 out of 10 drugs brought to the market ever return the cost the company spent on their development. As you might suspect, the question "Do we continue to invest?" is asked often in the course of product development.

Merck also faces the challenge posed by growing consolidation in its industry. In 1994 Merck purchased drug distributor Medco Containment Services for over $6 billion. Such a

huge purchase could have caused serious financial repercussions. But Lewent used $4.2 billion in stock and just $2.4 billion in cash—most of it borrowed—to buy Medco, carefully spreading out the financial impact of the purchase.

In addition to high research costs and growing consolidation, the emerging generic drug market and an unpredictable global market with fluctuating currencies make it easy to see that taking financial risks is an important part of Judy Lewent's job. Lewent believes the challenge facing chief financial officers today is to help change the negative perception many people have that U.S. companies pursue short-term financial gains at the expense of long-term growth. She and her 500-member finance team are charged with developing the financial plan to deal with the high-stakes nature of the changing pharmaceutical industry.

The ideas of risk, complexity, and uncertainty clearly define the global business environment. Add the challenges of fluctuating interest rates and enhanced expectations of investors and lenders, and you see the challenge of sound financial management. Let's explore the role of finance in business and the tools managers use in seeking financial stability and future growth in the firm.

 PROFILE

Judy Lewent, CFO of Merck & Company

Sources: Nancy A. Nichols, "Scientific Management at Merck: An Interview with CFO Judy Lewent," *Harvard Business Review*, January–February 1994, pp. 89–99; "50 World Class Executives," *World Business*, March–April 1996, pp. 21–31; and Joseph Weber, "Merck's Mr. Nice Guy with a Mission," *Business Week*, November 25, 1996.

◄ **LEARNING GOAL 1.**
Explain the role and importance of finance.

◄ **CONSIDER USING TM 137**
Chapter Outline.

THE ROLE OF FINANCE

Before we go any further, let's compare the role of an accountant with that of a financial manager. An accountant is like a skilled laboratory technician who takes blood samples and other measures of a person's health and writes the findings on a health report (in business, the equivalent of a set of financial statements). A financial manager for a business is the doctor who interprets the report and makes recommendations to the patient regarding changes that

➤ CONSIDER USING LECTURE
ENHANCER 19-1
Magic Johnson, All-Star Businessperson.

would improve health. Financial managers use the data prepared by accountants and make recommendations to top management regarding strategies for improving the health (financial strength) of the firm.

It should be clear that a manager cannot make sound financial decisions without understanding accounting information. That's why we examined accounting in Chapter 18. Similarly, a good accountant needs to understand finance. Accounting and finance, finance and accounting—the two go together like peanut butter and jelly. In large and medium-sized organizations, both the accounting and finance functions are generally under the control of a person such as Judy Lewent, who serves as a chief financial officer (CFO). Finance, however, is a critical activity in any size organization.

As you may remember from Chapter 6, financing a *small business* is a difficult but essential function if a firm expects to survive those important first five years. But the need for careful financial management goes beyond the first five years and remains a challenge a business of any size must face throughout its existence. Even a market giant cannot afford to ignore finance; Chrysler Corporation, for example, faced extinction in the late 1970s due to severe financial problems. Had it not been for a government-backed loan of $1 billion, Chrysler might have joined the ranks of other defunct auto companies such as Packard and Hudson. The following are three of the most common ways for any firm to fail financially:

1. Undercapitalization (which means not enough funds to start with).
2. Poor control over cash flow ➤ P. 544 ◄.
3. Inadequate expense control.

••• THE IMPORTANCE OF UNDERSTANDING FINANCE •••

Consider the financial problems encountered by a small organization called Parsley Patch. Two friends, Elizabeth Bertani and Pat Sherwood, started the company on what can best be described as a shoestring budget. It began when Elizabeth Bertani prepared salt-free seasonings for her husband, who was on a no-salt diet. Her friend Pat Sherwood thought the seasonings were good enough to sell. Bertani agreed, and Parsley Patch, Inc., was born.

The business began with an investment of $5,000, which was rapidly eaten up for a logo and a label design. Bertani and Sherwood learned quickly the importance of capital in getting the business going. Eventually, the two women personally invested more than $100,000 to keep the business from experiencing severe undercapitalization.

Everything started well, and hundreds of gourmet shops adopted the product line. But when sales failed to meet expectations, the women decided the health-food market offered more potential than gourmet shops, because salt-free seasonings were a natural for people with restricted diets. The choice was a good one. Sales took off and approached $30,000 a month. Still, the company earned no profits. Bertani and Sherwood were not trained in cash flow procedures or in controlling expenses. In fact, they had been told not to worry about costs, and they hadn't. They eventually hired a certified public accountant and an experienced financial manager who taught them how to compute the costs of the various blends they produced and how to control their expenses. The financial specialists also offered insight into how to control cash coming in and out of the company. Soon Parsley Patch earned a comfortable margin on operations that ran close to $1 million a year. Luckily, they were able to turn things around before they went broke.

If Bertani and Sherwood had understood finance before starting their business, they may have been able to avoid many of the problems they encountered.

➤ CONSIDER USING LECTURE
ENHANCER 19-2
The Pitfalls of Surging Sales.

The key word here is *understand*. One does not have to pursue finance as a career to understand finance. Financial understanding is important to anyone who wants to start a small business, invest in stocks and bonds, or plan a retirement fund. In short, finance and accounting are two areas everyone involved in business needs to study. Let's take a closer look at what finance is all about.

◄ LEARNING GOAL 2.
Describe the responsibilities of financial managers.

WHAT IS FINANCE?

Finance is the function in a business that acquires funds for the firm and manages funds within the firm (e.g., preparing budgets, doing cash flow analysis, and planning for the expenditure of funds on such assets as plant, equipment, and machinery). Without a carefully calculated financial plan, the firm has little chance for survival regardless of its product or marketing effectiveness. **Financial management** is the job of managing a firm's resources so it can meet its goals and objectives. Most organizations will designate a manager in charge of financial operations, generally the chief financial officer (CFO). However, financial management could also be in the hands of a person who serves as the company treasurer or vice president of finance. A comptroller is the chief accounting officer. Figure 19.1 highlights the tasks a financial manager performs. As you can see, the fundamental charge is to obtain money and then control the use of that money effectively. That includes managing cash, accounts receivable, and inventory. Where a company's cash is invested may have a major impact on profits.

finance
The function in a business that acquires funds for the firm and manages funds within the firm.

financial management
The job of managing a firm's resources so it can meet its goals and objectives.

You are probably familiar with such finance functions as buying merchandise on credit and collecting payment from customers. Both of these functions are responsibilities of financial managers. This means that financial managers are responsible for collecting overdue payments and making sure that the company does not lose too much money to bad debts (people or firms that don't pay). While these functions are critical to all types of businesses, they are particularly critical to small and medium-sized businesses, which typically have smaller cash or credit cushions than large corporations.

As Chapter 18 stated, tax payments represent an outflow of cash from the business. Therefore, they too fall under finance. As tax laws and tax liabilities have changed, finance specialists have become increasingly involved in tax management by carefully analyzing the tax implications of various managerial decisions in an attempt to minimize the taxes paid by the business. (Remember Chapter 18's discussion of tax accounting and issues such as LIFO and FIFO?) Businesses of all sizes must concern themselves with managing taxes.

◄ CONSIDER USING LECTURE ENHANCER 19-3
Are Charities Taking Good Care of Other People's Money?

◄ CONSIDER USING LECTURE ENHANCER 19-4
Evaluating Benefits Versus Costs.

◄ CONSIDER USING TM 138
What Financial Managers Do.

It's the internal auditor, usually a member of the firm's finance department, who checks on the journals, ledgers, and financial statements prepared by the accounting department to make sure that all transactions have been treated in accordance with established accounting rules and procedures. If there were no

- Planning
- Budgeting
- Obtaining funds
- Controlling funds (funds management)
- Collecting funds (credit management)

- Auditing
- Managing taxes
- Advising top management on financial matters

FIGURE 19.1

WHAT FINANCIAL MANAGERS DO

All these functions depend greatly on the information provided by the accounting statements discussed in Chapter 18.

such audits, accounting statements would be less reliable. Therefore, it's important that internal auditors be objective and critical of any improprieties or deficiencies they might note in their evaluation. Regular internal audits offer the firm assistance in the important role of financial planning, which we'll look at next.

Critical
Thinking

> CONSIDER USING OT ACETATE 19-1
Financial Planning Process.

Can you see the link between accounting and finance? They're mutually supportive functions in a firm. A firm cannot get along without accounting, but neither can it prosper without finance. The importance of finance is such that many successful finance executives go on to be presidents and chief executive officers. What would be the advantages and disadvantages of having a president with a background in finance versus a marketing background? Do you think Judy Lewent might be in line to become CEO of Merck in the future? Why?

FINANCIAL PLANNING

> LEARNING GOAL 3.
Outline the steps in financial planning by explaining the process of forecasting financial needs, developing budgets, and establishing financial controls.

Planning has been a recurring theme of this book. We've stressed planning's importance as a managerial function and offered insights into planning your career. Financial planning involves analyzing short-term and long-term money flows to and from the firm. The overall objective of financial planning is to optimize the firm's profitability and make the best use of its money. Financial planning is one of the key responsibilities of the financial manager. It's probably safe to assume that we all could use better financial planning in our lives.

Financial planning involves three steps: (1) forecasting both short-term and long-term financial needs, (2) developing budgets to meet those needs, and (3) establishing financial control to see how well the company is doing what it set out to do (see Figure 19.2). Let's look at each step's role in the financial health of an organization.

••• FORECASTING FINANCIAL NEEDS •••

short-term forecast
Forecast that predicts revenues, costs, and expenses for a period of one year or less.

cash flow forecast
Forecast that predicts the expected cash inflows and outflows in future periods, usually months or quarters.

long-term forecast
Forecast that predicts revenues, costs, and expenses for a period longer than 1 year, and sometimes as far as 5 or 10 years into the future.

> CONSIDER USING LECTURE ENHANCER 19-5
Dear Walt & Mickey, Welcome to Realityland.

Forecasting is an important part of any firm's financial plan. A **short-term forecast** predicts revenues, costs, and expenses for a period of one year or less. This forecast is the foundation for most other financial plans, so its accuracy is critical. Part of the short-term forecast may be in the form of a **cash flow forecast**, which predicts the cash inflows and outflows in future periods, usually months or quarters. Naturally, the inflows and outflows of cash recorded in the cash flow forecast are based on expected sales revenues and on various costs and expenses incurred and when they'll come due. The company's sales forecast estimates the company's projected sales for a particular period. A firm often uses its past financial statements as a basis for projecting expected sales and various costs and expenses.

A **long-term forecast** predicts revenues, costs, and expenses for a period longer than 1 year, and sometimes as far as 5 or 10 years into the future. This forecast plays a crucial part in the company's long-term strategic plan. Remember, the strategic plan asks questions such as these: What business are we in, and should we be in it five years from now? How much money should we invest in technology and new plant and equipment over the next decade? Will there be cash available to meet long-term obligations?

The long-term financial forecast gives top management, as well as operations managers, some sense of the income or profit potential possible with different strategic plans. Additionally, long-term projections assist financial managers with the preparation of company budgets.

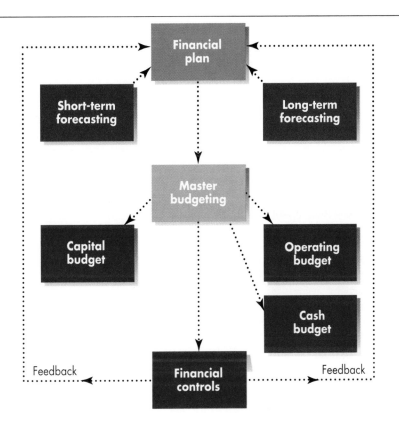

FIGURE **19.2**

. . . .

FINANCIAL PLANNING

Note the close link between financial planning and budgeting.

••• WORKING WITH THE BUDGET PROCESS •••

Chapter 18 identified a budget as a financial plan. You may live under a carefully constructed budget of your own. A business operates in the same way. A budget becomes the primary basis and guide for the firm's financial operations.[1]

Most firms compile yearly budgets from short-term and long-term financial forecasts. Therefore, since budgeting is clearly tied to forecasting, it's important for financial managers to take forecasting responsibilities seriously. There are usually several budgets established in a firm:

- An operating budget.
- A capital budget.
- A cash budget.
- A master budget.

An **operating budget** is the projection of dollar allocations to various costs and expenses needed to run or operate a business, given projected revenues. How much the firm will spend on supplies, travel, rent, advertising, salaries, and so forth is determined in the operating budget.

A **capital budget** highlights a firm's spending plans for major asset purchases that often require large sums of money. The capital budget primarily concerns itself with the purchase of such assets as property, buildings, and equipment.

A **cash budget** estimates a firm's projected cash balance at the end of a given period (e.g., monthly, quarterly). Cash budgets are important guidelines that assist managers in anticipating borrowing, debt repayment, operations expenses, and short-term investments. Cash budgets assist the firm in planning for cash shortages or surpluses. The cash budget is often the last budget that is prepared. A sample cash budget is provided in Figure 19.3.

◄ **CONSIDER USING TM 139**
Financial Planning.

◄ **CONSIDER USING OT ACETATE 19-2**
Business Benefits of the Budgeting Process.

◄ **CONSIDER USING OT ACETATE 19-3**
Forecasted Operating Budget— Fiberiffic.

operating budget
The projection of dollar allocations to various costs and expenses needed to run or operate a business, given projected revenues.

capital budget
A budget that highlights a firm's spending plans for major asset purchases that often require large sums of money.

cash budget
A budget that estimates a firm's projected cash balance at the end of a given period.

FIBERRIFIC
Monthly Cash Budget

	January	February	March
Sales forecast	$50,000	$45,000	$40,000
Collections			
Cash sales (20%)		$ 9,000	$ 8,000
Credit sales (80% of past month)		40,000	36,000
Monthly cash collection		$49,000	$44,000
Payments schedule			
Supplies and material		$11,000	$10,000
Salaries		12,000	12,000
Direct labor		9,000	8,000
Taxes		3,000	3,000
Other expenses		7,000	6,000
Monthly cash payments		$42,000	$39,000
Cash budget			
Cash flow		$ 7,000	$ 5,000
Beginning cash		−1,000	6,000
Total cash		$ 6,000	$11,000
Less minimum cash balance		−6,000	−6,000
Excess cash to market securities		$ 0	$ 5,000
Loans needed for minimum balance		0	0

master budget
The budget that ties together all of a firm's other budgets and summarizes the firm's proposed financial activities.

financial control
A process in which a firm periodically compares its actual revenues, costs, and expenses with its projected ones.

The **master budget** ties together all of a firm's other budgets and summarizes the firm's proposed financial activities.

Clearly, financial planning plays an important role in the operations of the firm. This planning often determines what long-term investments are made, when specific funds will be needed, and how the funds will be generated. Once a company has projected its short-term and long-term financial needs and established budgets to show how funds will be allocated, the final step in financial planning is to establish financial controls.

••• ESTABLISHING FINANCIAL CONTROLS •••

Financial control is a process in which a firm periodically compares its actual revenues, costs, and expenses with its projected ones. Most companies hold at least monthly financial reviews as a way to ensure financial control. This helps managers identify deviations and take corrective action if necessary. Such controls provide feedback to help reveal which accounts, which departments, and which people are varying from the financial plans. Finance managers can judge if such deviations may or may not be justified. In either case, managers can make some financial adjustments to the plan. Read the Making Ethical Decisions box to see a type of situation a manager can face related to financial control. After the Progress Check we shall explore specific reasons why firms need to have funds readily available.

Making Ethical Decisions

On the Road Again

You are the chairperson of the business administration department at a local community college. Like many other colleges, your campus has been affected financially by declining enrollments and increasing expenses. As the end of the college's fiscal year approaches you review your departmental budget and note that your department has some unused travel funds available for faculty and staff development. The faculty and staff have not seemed interested in using the travel money for developmental purposes throughout the year even though it has been readily available. You fear that if the funds are not spent this year there's a good chance the division dean will rec-ommend cutting your travel budget for next year. You consider telling faculty and staff that this money is now available for just about any type of travel they desire on a first-come, first-served basis, with no questions asked concerning the educational or college benefit of the travel request. It's almost certain the division dean will not contest any request you put in for travel funds and you can certainly be a hero in the eyes of your faculty and staff. However you could just return the unused funds to the dean's office for disbursement to the college's general fund. What will you do? What could result from your decision?

Progress Check

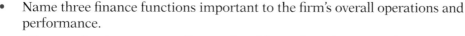

- Name three finance functions important to the firm's overall operations and performance.
- What are the three primary financial problems that often cause firms to fail?
- In what ways do short-term and long-term financial forecasts differ?
- What is the organization's purpose in preparing budgets? Can you identify at least three different types of budgets?

Ever wonder how the average potato dug from the ground becomes tasty munchies such as chips or fries? It all happens with the help of processing equipment such as the type shown here. The firm's capital budget is the financial control that controls the firm's spending plans for major assets such as property, buildings, and equipment.

➤ **LEARNING GOAL 4.**
Recognize the financial needs that must be met with available funds.

➤ **CONSIDER USING LECTURE ENHANCER 19-6**
Advice from the Ice Man.

···· ▬ ····

THE NEED FOR OPERATING FUNDS

In business the need for operating funds never seems to cease. That's why sound financial management is essential to businesses. Like our personal financial needs, the capital needs of a business change over time. For example, as a small business grows, its financial requirements shift considerably. (Remember the example of Parsley Patch.) The same is true with large corporations such as AT&T and PepsiCo. As they venture into new product areas or markets, their capital needs increase. Different firms need funds available for different reasons. However, in virtually all organizations there are certain operational needs for which funds must be available. Let's take a look at these financial needs that affect both the smallest and the largest of businesses.

··· MANAGING DAILY BUSINESS OPERATIONS ···

If workers are to be paid on Friday, they don't want to have to wait until Monday for their paychecks. If tax payments are due on the 15th of the month, the government expects the money on time. If the interest payment on a business loan is due on the 30th, the lender doesn't mean the 1st of the next month. As you can see, funds have to be available to meet the daily operational costs of the business.

The challenge of sound financial management is to see that funds are available to meet these daily cash needs without compromising the firm's investment potential.[2] Money has what is called a time value. In other words, if someone offered to give you $200 today or $200 one year from today, you would benefit by taking the $200 today. Why? A very simple reason. You could start collecting interest or invest the $200 you receive today, and over a year's time, your money would grow. The same thing is true in business; the interest gained on the firm's investments is important in maximizing the profit the company will gain. For this reason, financial managers often try to keep cash expenditures to a minimum, to free funds for investment in interest-bearing accounts.[3] It's not unusual for finance managers to suggest the firm pay bills as late as possible (unless a cash discount is available) and collect what's owed to it as fast as possible. This way they maximize the investment potential of the firm's funds. Efficient cash management is particularly important to small firms in conducting their daily operations.

Think you've got problems? Consider a day in the life of Time Warner. Financial managers at Time Warner are challenged every day to meet the financial needs of the firm's various subsidiaries shown here. What that means is that financial planning is job one if the company expects to meet the obligations of its many daily business operations.

It takes a diverse group of brands to make a great company.
It takes a diverse group of people to make a great brand.

TIME WARNER

AN EQUAL OPPORTUNITY EMPLOYER

··· MANAGING ACCOUNTS RECEIVABLE ···

Financial managers know that making credit available helps keep current customers happy and attracts new customers. In today's highly competitive business environment, many businesses would have trouble surviving without making credit available to customers.

The major problem with selling on credit is that as much as 25 percent or more of the business's assets could be tied up in its accounts receivable. This means that the firm needs to use some of its available funds to pay for the goods or services already given customers who bought on credit. This outflow of funds means financial managers must develop efficient collection procedures. For example, businesses often provide cash or quantity discounts to buyers who pay their accounts by a certain time. Also, finance managers carefully scrutinize old and new credit customers to see if they have a favorable history of meeting their credit obligations on time. In essence, the firm's credit policy reflects its financial position and its desire to expand into new markets.

One way to decrease the time, and therefore expense, involved in collecting accounts receivable is to accept bank credit cards such as MasterCard or Visa. This is convenient for both the customer and the merchant. The banks that issue such credit cards have already established the customer's creditworthiness, which reduces the business's risk. Businesses must pay a fee to accept credit cards, but the fees are not excessive compared to the benefits they provide.

◄ **CONSIDER USING OT ACETATE 19-5**
Financing Daily Operations—Cash Flows.

◄ **CONSIDER USING LECTURE ENHANCER 19-7**
Managing Accounts Receivable.

◄ **CONSIDER USING CRITICAL THINKING EXERCISE 19-1**
Extending Credit. (**SCANS**)

◄ **CONSIDER USING LECTURE ENHANCER 19-8**
Keeping the Money Flowing In.

••• OBTAINING NEEDED INVENTORY •••

As we noted earlier in the text, effective marketing implies a clear customer orientation. ⇒ P. 383 ⇐ This focus on the customer means that high-quality service and availability of goods are vital if a business expects to prosper in today's markets. Therefore, to satisfy customers, businesses must maintain inventories that often involve a sizable expenditure of funds. Although it's true that firms expect to recapture their investment in inventory through sales to customers, a carefully constructed inventory policy assists in managing the use of a firm's available funds and maximizing profitability. For example, an owner of a neighborhood ice cream parlor ties up more funds in inventory (ice cream) in the summer months than in winter. It's obvious why. Demand for ice cream goes up in the summer. As you learned in Chapter 9, innovations such as just-in-time inventory are reducing the amount of funds a firm must tie up in inventory. Also, carefully evaluating its inventory turnover ratio (discussed in Chapter 18) helps a firm control its financial outlays for inventory.

••• MAJOR CAPITAL EXPENDITURES •••

Capital expenditures are major investments in long-term assets such as land, buildings, equipment, or research and development. In many organizations the purchase of major assets—such as land for future expansion, plants to increase production capabilities, research to develop new products, and equipment to maintain or exceed current levels of output—is essential. As you can imagine, these expenditures often require a huge portion of the organization's funds. Remember from the profile at the beginning of this chapter the situation confronting companies such as Merck? They often must spend large sums of money for research to develop products that may not be commercially successful. Therefore, it's critical that companies weigh all the possible options before committing what may be a large portion of their available resources. For this reason, financial managers and analysts evaluate the appropriateness of such purchases or expenditures. Consider the situation in which a firm needs to expand its production capabilities due to increases in demand. One option is to buy land and build a new plant from scratch. Another option would be to purchase an existing plant or consider renting. Can you think of financial and accounting considerations that would come into play in this decision?

The need for available funds raises several questions in any firm: How does the firm obtain funds to finance operations and other business necessities? How long will specific funds be needed by the organization? How much will the needed funds cost? Will these funds come from internal sources or

capital expenditures
Major investments in long-term assets such as land, buildings, equipment, or research and development.

external sources? These questions will be addressed in the next section, after the Progress Check.

Progress Check

• Money is said to have a time value. What does this mean?

• Why are accounts receivable a financial concern to the firm?

• What's the primary reason an organization spends a good deal of its available funds on inventory and major assets?

> **LEARNING GOAL 5.**
Distinguish between short-term and long-term financing and between debt capital and equity capital.

> **CONSIDER USING CRITICAL THINKING EXERCISE 19-2**
Obtaining financing (**SCANS**)

In the life of any business there comes a time when the firm is pressed for additional funds. Short-term financing meets the need for funds to be repaid within one year. Long-term financing refers to capital needs of the firm for a period over one year. One form of long-term financing is equity capital that can be raised through the sale of stock such as the initial public offering (IPO) shown here.

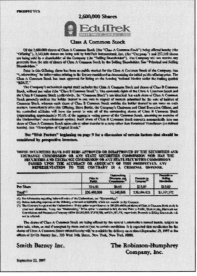

ALTERNATIVE SOURCES OF FUNDS

Earlier in the chapter, you learned that finance is the function in a business that is responsible for acquiring and managing funds for the firm. Determining the amount of money needed for various time periods and finding out the most appropriate sources from which to obtain these funds are fundamental steps in sound financial management. Next we'll look at methods of acquiring funds from a variety of sources. Before we begin this discussion, it's important to highlight some key distinctions involved in funding a firm's operations.

Organizations typically encounter both short-and long-term financing needs. **Short-term financing** refers to borrowed capital that will be repaid within one year. In contrast, **long-term financing** refers to borrowed capital for major purchases that will be repaid over a specific time period longer than one year. We shall explore sources of both short- and long-term financing in the next sections. It's important to know that businesses can use different methods of raising money. A firm can seek to raise money through borrowing money (debt), selling ownership (equity), or earning profits (retained earnings). **Debt capital** refers to funds raised through various forms of borrowing that must be repaid. Funds borrowed could be either short-term, due to be repaid within one year, or long-term, due over a period longer than one year. **Equity capital** is money raised from within the firm or through the sale of ownership in the firm.

short-term financing
Borrowed capital that will be repaid within one year.

long-term financing
Borrowed capital that will be repaid over a specific time period longer than one year.

debt capital
Funds raised through various forms of borrowing that must be repaid.

equity capital
Money raised from within the firm or through the sale of ownership in the firm.

> **LEARNING GOAL 6.**
Identify and describe several sources of short-term financing.

OBTAINING SHORT-TERM FINANCING

The bulk of a finance manager's job does not involve obtaining long-term funds. Instead, the nitty-gritty, day-to-day operation of the firm calls for the careful management of short-term financial needs. Firms need to borrow short-term funds for purchasing additional inventory or for meeting bills that come due unexpectedly. Just as you do, a business sometimes needs to obtain short-term funds when the firm's money is low. This is particularly true of small businesses. It's rare that newly formed small businesses even attempt to find funding for long-term needs. They are concerned more with just staying afloat until they are able to build capital and creditworthiness. Firms can obtain short-term financing in several different ways. Also, suppliers of short-term financing can require that the funds provided be secured or unsecured. Let's look at the major forms of short-term financing.

◄ LECTURE ENHANCER 19-9
Managing Accounts Payable.

••• TRADE CREDIT •••

The most widely used source of short-term funding, trade credit, is the least expensive and most convenient form of short-term financing. **Trade credit** is the practice of buying goods now and paying for them later. When a firm buys merchandise, it receives an invoice (bill) much like the one you receive when you buy something on credit.

It's common for business invoices to contain terms such as *2/10, net 30.* This means that the buyer can take a 2 percent discount for paying within 10 days. The total bill is due (net) in 30 days if the purchaser does not take advantage of the discount. Finance managers need to pay close attention to such discounts because they create opportunities to reduce the cost of financing. Think about it for a moment: if the discount offered to the customer is 2/10, net 30, the customer will pay 2 percent more for waiting an extra 20 days to pay the invoice. Some uninformed businesspeople feel that 2 percent is insignificant and pay their bills after the discount period. In the course of a year, however, 2 percent for 20 days is an annual rate of 36 percent interest (because there are eighteen 20-day periods in the year.) If the firm is capable of paying within 10 days, it is needlessly increasing its cost of financing by not doing so.

trade credit
The practice of buying goods now and paying for them later.

••• PROMISSORY NOTES •••

Some suppliers hesitate to give trade credit to organizations with a poor credit rating, no credit history, or a history of slow payment. In such cases, the supplier may insist that the customer sign a promissory note as a condition for obtaining credit. A **promissory note** is a written contract with a promise to pay. Promissory notes can be sold by the supplier to a bank at a discount (the amount of the note less a fee for the bank's services).

promissory note
A written contract with a promise to pay.

••• FAMILY AND FRIENDS •••

Many small firms obtain short-term funds by borrowing money from family and friends. Because short-term funds are needed for periods of less than a year, friends or relatives are sometimes willing to help. Such loans can be dangerous, however, if the firm does not understand cash flow. As we discussed earlier, the firm may suddenly find several bills coming due at the same time and have no other sources of funds. It is better, therefore, not to borrow from friends or relatives; instead, go to a commercial bank that understands the risk and can help analyze future financial needs. In fact entrepreneurs have come to rely less and less on family and friends, according to the National Federation of Independent Business.[4] However, if you do borrow from family or friends, it's important to be professional about the deal, which means that you must (1) agree on specific loan terms from the beginning, (2) put the agreement in writing, and (3) pay the money back in the same way you would a bank loan.

••• COMMERCIAL BANKS AND OTHER ••• FINANCIAL INSTITUTIONS

Banks are highly sensitive to risk and therefore often reluctant to lend money to small businesses. Nonetheless, a promising and well-organized venture may be able to get a bank loan. If it is able to get such a loan, a small or medium-sized business should have the person in charge of the finance function keep in close touch with the bank. It's wise to see a banker periodically (as often as

◄ CONSIDER USING OT ACETATE
19-6
The Three "T's" of a Good Banking
Relationship.

➤ CONSIDER USING OT ACETATE 19-7
Christmastime and presents, presents, presents in every store you shop. Did you ever wonder where the stores get the money to buy all of these treasures? Department stores and other retailers make extensive use of commercial banks and other financial institutions to borrow the capital needed to stock their shelves with gifts to resell to customers. Ho! Ho! Ho!

➤ CONSIDER USING OT ACETATE
19-7
What Do Bankers Want to Know.

➤ CONSIDER USING LECTURE
ENHANCER 19-10
The Financing Gender Gap.

➤ CONSIDER USING LECTURE
ENHANCER 19-11
The Numbers Speak When Dealing with
Your Banker.

unsecured loan
A loan that's not backed by any specific assets.

secured loan
A loan backed by something valuable, such as property.

pledging
The process of using accounts receivable or other assets as collateral for a loan.

inventory financing
The process of using inventory such as raw materials as collateral for a loan.

line of credit
A given amount of unsecured short-term funds a bank will lend to a business, provided the funds are readily available.

revolving credit agreement
A line of credit that is guaranteed by the bank.

once a month) and send the banker all the firm's financial statements so that the bank continues to supply funds when needed.

If you try to imagine the different types of businesspeople who go to banks for a loan, you'll get a better feel for the role of the financial manager. Picture, for example, a farmer going to the bank to borrow funds for seed, fertilizer, equipment, and other needs. Such supplies may be bought in the spring and paid for when the fall harvest comes in. Now picture a local toy store buying merchandise for Christmas sales. The money for such purchases might be borrowed in June and July and paid back after Christmas. A restaurant may borrow funds at the beginning of the month and pay by the end of the month. Can you see that how much a business borrows and for how long depends on the kind of business it is and how quickly the merchandise purchased with a bank loan can be resold or used to generate funds?

Like you, a business sometimes finds itself in a position where many bills come due at once: utilities, insurance, payroll, new equipment, and more. Most times, such sudden cash demands can be met. But sometimes a business gets so far into debt or so far behind in its payments that the bank refuses to lend it more funds. Suddenly the business is unable to pay its bills. More often than not, the result is that the business fails or files for bankruptcy, a result that can be chalked up to cash flow problems.

We hope you see now how important it is for specialists in the finance and accounting departments to do a cash flow forecast. By anticipating times when many bills will come due, a business can begin early to seek funds or sell other assets to prepare for the crunch. Can you also see why it is important for a businessperson to keep friendly and close relations with his or her banker? The banker may spot cash flow problems early and point out the danger. Or the banker may be more willing to lend money in a crisis if the businessperson has established a strong, friendly relationship built on openness and trust. It's always important to remember that your banker wants you to succeed almost as much as you do. Bankers can be an invaluable support especially to small, growing businesses.

••• DIFFERENT FORMS OF BANK LOANS •••

The most difficult kind of loan to get from a bank or other financial institution is an **unsecured loan** (a loan that's not backed by any specific assets).

Normally, only highly regarded customers of the bank receive unsecured loans.

A **secured loan** is one backed by something valuable, such as property. If the borrower fails to pay the loan, the lender may take possession of the collateral. That takes some of the risk out of lending money. Accounts receivable are assets that can be quickly converted into cash. Therefore, they are often used as security. When accounts receivable or other assets are used as collateral for a loan, the process is called **pledging**. Some percentage of the value of accounts receivable pledged is advanced to the borrowing firm. Then, as customers pay off their accounts, the funds received are forwarded to the firm's lender in repayment of the advance. **Inventory financing** means that inventory such as raw materials (e.g., coal, steel) is used as collateral or security for a loan. Other assets that can be used as collateral include buildings, machinery, and company-owned stocks and bonds.

Another advantage of developing a good relationship with a bank is that often the bank will open a line of credit for you. A **line of credit** is a given amount of unsecured short-term funds a bank will lend to a business, provided the bank has the funds readily available. In other words, a line of credit is not guaranteed to a business. Often entrepreneurs find this out the hard way.[5] The primary purpose of a line of credit is to speed the borrowing process so that a firm does not have to go through the hassle of applying for a new loan every time it needs funds. The funds are generally available as long as the credit ceiling set by the bank is not exceeded. As businesses mature and become more financially secure, the amount of credit often is increased. Some firms will even apply for a **revolving credit agreement**, which is a line of credit that's guaranteed. However, banks usually charge a fee for guaranteeing such an agreement. Both lines of credit and revolving credit agreements are particularly good sources of funds for unexpected cash needs.

A financial manager may also obtain short-term funds from **commercial finance companies**. These organizations make short-term loans to borrowers who offer tangible assets as collateral. Since commercial finance companies are willing to accept higher degrees of risk than commercial banks, the interest rates they charge are usually higher than those of banks. General Electric Capital Corporation is the largest commercial finance company in the United States, with $32.7 billion in annual revenues.[6]

Global Private Banking

WE SPECIALIZE IN
RELATIONSHIP BANKING.
THE LONG-TERM KIND.

In this age of electronic mail and digital everything, private banking by Republic is still a matter of personal relationships.

We believe, and have always believed, that our number one job is to build a close, enduring relationship with each private banking client.

In fact, it's one of the main reasons for Republic's success, worldwide.

As a Republic private banking client you have your own personal Account Officer, someone you can count on to look after your interests. He's there to evaluate investment opportunities, warn you against pitfalls, and make certain your instructions are carried out to the letter.

It is a long-term relationship based on genuine concern and commitment – the rare combination that makes Republic a truly one-of-a-kind bank.

Republic National Bank of New York
Strength. Security. Service.

Relationships with a banker are invaluable to a business. Bankers can assist with financial planning, financial management, and, of course, needed funds. A solid relationship with a banker can also earn the firm a line of credit. A line of credit means a bank will lend a business a set amount of unsecured short-term funds if the bank has the funds readily available.

••• FACTORING •••

One relatively expensive source of short-term funds for a firm is **factoring** (the process of selling accounts receivable for cash). Factoring dates as far back as 4,000 years ago, during the days of ancient Babylon. Here's how it works: Let's say that a firm sells many of its products on credit to consumers and other businesses, creating a number of accounts receivable. Some of the buyers may be slow in paying their bills, causing the firm to have a large amount of money due in accounts receivable. A *factor* is a market intermediary that agrees to buy the accounts receivable from the firm (at a discount) for cash. The factor then collects and keeps the money that was owed the firm. How much this

commercial finance companies
Organizations that make short-term loans to borrowers who offer tangible assets as collateral.

factoring
The process of selling accounts receivable for cash.

◄ **CONSIDER USING LECTURE ENHANCER 19-12**
Managing Debt the Creative Way.

Reaching Beyond Our Borders

http://afia-forfaiting.org/menu.htm

The Global "Factor" in Trade

The trading boom in global markets shows no sign of slowing down. In 1997, the total world export of goods and services grew to over $6 trillion (that's right, *trillion* with a *t*). As more and more businesses look to compete and share in this global largesse, it's important for them to note several financing problems that would-be exporters face.

One concern is that many of the fastest-growing markets are in developing countries where the financial risk of doing business tends to run very high. Problems such as political instability, high loan default rates, and unstable currencies make getting paid for exported products a real challenge. This problem is magnified by the fact that commercial banks are no longer able to finance and underwrite many exporting efforts in such an enormous market by themselves. With many commercial banks tapped out, what's an aspiring businessperson to do?

One option is a form of export financing called forfaiting, a financing technique that is very similar to factoring. Forfaiting allows exporters to sell their future account receivables to an export factor, usually a lending bank. As a financing practice, forfaiting is similar to factoring except that forfaiting agreements are generally of a longer-term nature. The Association of Forfaiters in the Americas Inc. (AFIA) was set up in 1995 to assist in such financing services to exporters.

By using forfaiting agreements, exporters can deal in risky global markets, such as Eastern Europe, Latin America, and Asia, and maintain their financial peace of mind. They may even offer to sell products with terms such as open accounts (a type of trade credit that permits buyers to purchase goods or services and pay for them at a later date without incurring any charges or interest) without having to assume the credit risk. Small exporters can also reap another key benefit from forfaiting: timing. It's not unusual that loans from even established global lenders, such as the Export–Import Bank, can take up to six months to process and close. With forfaiting a deal could be turned around in as fast as 24 hours, if your foreign customer's creditworthiness is judged to be safe by the factor.

While some see export factoring as a relatively new phenomenon, the fact is American colonists used forfaiting as a way to bankroll the cotton trade to England over 200 years ago. While the cost of export factoring can be a bit high and the number of U.S.-based financial institutions offering export financing is still small, the technique offers great opportunity to aspiring firms with poor cash flow or limited creditworthiness the chance to participate in global markets.

Sources: Willy Ostro-Landau, "Pushing Forfaiting Forward," *International Business*, September 1995, p. 12; Kevin Godier and Jon Marks, "Today China, Tomorrow Oman," *Financial Times*, July 10, 1997, p. 10; and Kevin Godier and Jon Marks, "Immunity Comes with a Premium," *Financial Times*, March 11, 1998, p. 13.

costs the firm depends on the discount rate the factor requires. The discount rate, in turn, depends on the age of the accounts receivable, the nature of the business, and the condition of the economy.

Even though factoring can be an expensive way of raising cash, it is popular among small businesses.[7] It's important for you to note that factoring is not a loan; factoring is the sale of an asset. And while it's true that discount rates charged by factors are usually higher than loan rates charged by banks or commercial finance companies, remember that many small businesses cannot qualify for a loan. Also, a company can reduce the cost of factoring if it agrees to reimburse the factor for slow-paying accounts, and it can reduce them even further if it assumes the risk of those people who don't pay at all. Factoring is used, too, in financing global trade ventures. Read the Reaching Beyond Our

Borders box to see why firms are turning to export factoring as a means of financing global trade.

••• COMMERCIAL PAPER •••

Sometimes a large corporation needs funds for a few months and wants to get lower rates than those charged by banks. One strategy is to sell commercial paper. **Commercial paper** consists of unsecured promissory notes, in amounts ranging from $25,000 and up, that mature (come due) in 270 days or less. The promissory note states a fixed amount of money the business agrees to repay to the lender on a specific date. The interest rate being charged is stated in the note. Commercial paper is unsecured (no collateral is offered) and is sold at a public sale, so only financially stable firms (mainly large corporations) are able to sell it. Still, for these companies it's a way to get short-term funds quickly and for less interest than bank rates. Since most commercial paper comes due in 30 to 90 days, it's also an investment opportunity for buyers who can afford to put up cash for short periods to earn some interest.

commercial paper
Unsecured promissory notes of $25,000 and up that mature (come due) in 270 days or less.

Progress
Check

- What do the terms *3/10, net 25* mean?
- What's the difference between trade credit and a line of credit at a bank?
- What is factoring? What are some of the considerations involved in establishing a discount rate in factoring?
- How does commercial paper work, and what's the main advantage of issuing commercial paper?

•••• ▬▬▬ ••••

OBTAINING LONG-TERM FINANCING

◄ **LEARNING GOAL 7.**
Identify and describe several sources of long-term financing.

◄ **CONSIDER USING OT ACETATE 19-8**
Sources of Long-Term Financing.

Financial planning and forecasting help the firm to develop a financial plan. This plan specifies the amount of funding that the firm will need over various time periods and the most appropriate sources of those funds. In setting long-term financing objectives, the firm generally asks three major questions:

1. What are the organization's long-term goals and objectives?
2. What are the financial requirements needed to achieve these long-term goals and objectives?
3. What sources of long-term capital are available, and which will best fit our needs?

In business, long-term capital is used to buy fixed assets such as plant and equipment and to finance expansion of the organization. In major corporations, decisions involving long-term financing normally involve the board of directors and top management, as well as finance and accounting managers. As we mentioned in the chapter profile, Judy Lewent sits on the seven-member chairman's staff at Merck, which makes senior policy decisions involving factors such as long-term financing.[8] In some instances, an expert like an investment banker (we will look at investment bankers in Chapter 20) may also be involved. In smaller businesses, the owners are always actively involved in analyzing financing opportunities.

Initial long-term financing usually comes from one of two major sources: debt capital or equity capital. Let's look at these two sources of long-term funds next.

••• DEBT FINANCING •••

As we described earlier in this chapter, long-term financing of a business can be achieved by securing debt capital. Such capital may be obtained from lending institutions or from the sale of bonds. With debt financing, the company has a *legal obligation* to repay the amount borrowed.

Firms that establish and develop rapport with a bank, insurance company, pension fund, commercial finance company, or other financial institution often secure a long-term loan. Long-term loans are usually repaid within 3 to 7 years but may extend to perhaps 15 or 20 years. For such loans, a business must sign what is called a term-loan agreement. A **term-loan agreement** is a promissory note that requires the borrower to repay the loan in specified installments (e.g., monthly or yearly). A major advantage of this type of financing is that the interest paid on long-term debt is tax deductible.

Because larger amounts of capital are borrowed, long-term loans are often more expensive to the firm than short-term loans are. Also, since the repayment period could be as long as 20 years, the lenders are not assured their capital will be repaid in full. Therefore, most long-term loans require some form of collateral, which may take the form of real estate, machinery, equipment, stock, or other items of value. Lenders will also often require certain restrictions on a firm's operations to force it to act responsibly in its business practices. The interest rate for long-term loans is based on the adequacy of collateral, the firm's credit rating, and the general level of market interest rates. The greater the risk a lender takes in making a loan, the higher the rate of interest it requires. This is known as the **risk/return trade-off**.

If an organization is unable to obtain its long-term financing needs from a lending institution, it may decide to issue bonds. To put it simply, a bond is like a company IOU with a promise to repay on a certain date. It is a binding contract through which the organization issuing the bond agrees to specific terms with investors in return for the money those investors lend to the company. The terms of the agreement in a bond issue are referred to as the **indenture terms**. We will discuss bonds in more depth in Chapter 20. For now, let's see how bonds fit into a firm's long-term financing plans.

••• SECURED AND UNSECURED BONDS •••

A bond is a long-term debt obligation of a corporation or government (see Figure 19.4). You are probably somewhat familiar with bonds. For example, you may own investments like U.S. government savings bonds; or perhaps you volunteered your time to help a local school district pass a bond issue. Maybe your community is building a new stadium or cultural center that requires selling bonds. It's fair to say that businesses compete with government for the sale of bonds. Potential investors in bonds measure the *risk* involved in purchasing a bond with the *return* (interest) the bond promises to pay.

Like other forms of long-term debt, bonds can be secured or unsecured. A **secured bond** is issued with some form of collateral, such as real estate,

---

term-loan agreement
A promissory note that requires the borrower to repay the loan in specified installments.

risk/return trade-off
The principle that the greater a risk a lender takes in making a loan, the higher the interest rate required.

indenture terms
The terms of agreement in a bond issue.

> **CONSIDER USING TM 141**
Who Can Issue Bonds?

secured bond
A bond issued with some form of collateral.

FIGURE 19.4
• • • •
WHO CAN ISSUE BONDS?

1. Federal, state, and local governments
2. Federal government agencies
3. Corporations
4. Foreign governments and corporations

Source: *The Wall Street Journal Guide to Money & Markets.*

FIGURE 19.5

· · · ·

DIFFERENCES BETWEEN
DEBT AND EQUITY
FINANCING

	TYPE OF FINANCING	
CONDITIONS	**DEBT**	**EQUITY**
Management influence	There's usually none unless special conditions have been agreed upon.	Common stockholders have voting rights.
Repayment	Debt has a maturity date. Principal must be repaid.	Stock has no maturity date. The company is never required to repay equity.
Yearly obligations	Payment of interest is a contractual obligation.	The firm isn't legally liable to pay dividends.
Tax benefits	Interest is tax-deductible.	Dividends are paid from aftertax income and aren't deductible.

◄ CONSIDER USING TM 142
Differences Between Debt and Equity Financing.

equipment, or other pledged assets. If the bond's indenture terms are violated, the bondholder can issue a claim on the collateral offered. An **unsecured bond** is a bond backed only by the reputation of the issuer. Bondholders simply have trust in the issuer. These bonds are generally referred to as debenture bonds.

Bonds are a key means of long-term financing for many organizations. If bonds interest you, stay tuned for Chapter 20, where we discuss them in greater detail.

unsecured bond
A bond backed only by the reputation of the issuer.

··· EQUITY FINANCING ···

If a firm cannot obtain a long-term loan from a lending institution, or if it is unable to sell bonds to investors, it may look for long-term financing from equity capital. Equity financing comes from the owners of the firm. Therefore, equity financing involves selling ownership in the firm in the form of stock, or using retained earnings the firm has reinvested in the business. (Figure 19.5 highlights the differences between debt and equity financing.) A business can also seek equity financing from venture capital.

Issuing stock is covered at length in Chapter 20, but a basic understanding of stock as a source of equity financing is important here.

◄ CONSIDER USING OT ACETATE 19-9
Sources of Equity Capital.

··· SELLING STOCK ···

Regardless of whether or not a new firm can obtain debt financing, there usually comes a time when additional funds are needed by a business. One way to obtain such funds is to sell ownership shares (called stock) in the firm to the public. The key word to remember here is *ownership.* The purchasers of stock become owners in the organization. The exact number of shares of stock into which a firm will be divided is generally determined by the organization's board of directors. In seeking equity financing, the board can authorize to sell all the stock of the firm or part of it. Shares of stock the company decides not to offer for sale are referred to as *unissued stock.*

◄ CONSIDER USING LECTURE ENHANCER 19-13
Derivitives are Risky Business.

Spotlight on Small Business

http://plaza.interport.net/witbeer/

Spinning a Web of Capital

Andy Klein was earning a living as a Wall Street lawyer when he was bitten by the entrepreneurial bug and started a small microbrewery called Spring Street Brewing. Spring Street experienced rapid growth in its first three years but, like many emerging businesses, soon faced a capital crunch. The company badly needed funds, but Klein realized the firm was too little to attract the interest of Wall Street underwriters or bankers. He also did not want to risk losing the company to venture capitalists. His entrepreneurial instincts told him it would take innovation to keep the company alive.

Klein was aware of Regulation A, a process whereby small companies can make direct public offerings (DPOs) of a firm's stock to the general public, if approved by the Securities and Exchange Commission (SEC). He decided this was the path to saving Spring Street Brewing. His direct offering, however, was going to be a bit different from any in the past. Spring Street Brewing put a home page on the Internet's World Wide Web to alert the public to the impending sale of stock. The announcement asked potential investors to call or ▲

write for information about the company (in a prepared prospectus) and about how to receive stock order forms. Spring Street attracted 3,500 investors, mostly beer connoisseurs, who bought up 900,000 shares at a price of $1.85 per share. The company raised $1.6 million in new funds through this equity offering without incurring any expensive underwriting fees. The SEC gave Spring Street further approval to operate a permanent trading site on its Web page.

Small businesses with revenues under $25 million can set up DPOs with SEC approval. Still, the task of raising such funds is difficult. Only 30 percent of the firms that filed such offerings met their financing goals. The key to success seems to be uncluttered financial statements and a business plan that investors can understand. With any expected payoff on such investments generally a long way off, a loyal and patient shareholder base is needed.

Sources: Kerry Hannon, "Going Public to the Public," *U.S. News & World Report*, June 17, 1996, pp. 74–75; and Robert Mamis, "Face to Face with Andy Klein," *Inc.*, July 1996, pp. 39–40.

Issuing and selling stock to the public as a means of equity financing is by no means easy or automatic. Companies can issue stock for public purchase only if they meet requirements set by the Securities and Exchange Commission (SEC) as well as various state agencies. As the box Spotlight on Small Business shows, small businesses often make use of creative options. Firms can issue shares of preferred stock, common stock, or both. Preferred and common stock will be discussed in depth in Chapter 20.

••• RETAINED EARNINGS •••

Have you ever heard a businessperson say that he or she puts all the profits right back into the business? You probably remember from Chapter 18 that the profits the company keeps and reinvests in the firm are called retained earnings. Retained earnings often are a major source of long-term funds. This is especially true for small businesses, which have fewer financing alternatives, such as selling bonds or stock, available to them than large businesses do. However, large corporations also depend on retained earnings for needed long-term funding. In fact, retained earnings are usually the most favored source of meeting long-term capital needs since a company that uses them saves interest payments, dividends, and any possible underwriting fees. Also, there is no dilution of ownership, as occurs with selling stock. The major problem with relying on retained earnings as a source of funding is that many organizations do not

From the Pages of BusinessWeek

http://www.nbia.org/

Bless Those Bureaucrats

Business incubators have proven their value to entrepreneurs in many ways. Incubators can provide budding businesspeople with access to low-cost rents, professional services, and interaction with other entrepreneurs. Today, however, changing business trends such as new technology, corporate downsizing, and economic globalization have added another benefit to the incubator-based business: access to early-stage capital.

Dinah Adkins, executive director of the National Business Incubation Association (NBIA), suggests that because of the careful prescreening done by incubators before accepting client companies, investors often see instant value in investing in such firms. Incubators afford investors the chance to pick and choose from a variety of businesses all under one roof rather than search high and low for intriguing new opportunities. It also seems likely that investors feel more assured that their investment will last longer and the business has a chance to grow further in an incubator than in a more conventional business environment. The incubators themselves also provide some security by providing such services as assistance in preparing federal grant proposals and other financial proposals for their clients.

Charles Doty found the Jackson Enterprise Center, a small-business incubator in Jackson, Mississippi, to be very fertile business territory. His firm, Lextron Corporation, started in 1990 at the Jackson Enterprise Center, with financing help coming from a local construction company. He was able to rent 400 square feet of incubator space at below-market rates. Hinds Community College screened job applicants for the company, and experts at the incubator led him to a state-supported project that paid part of his employees' salaries during their training. Today Lextron has 72 employees and does contract work for BellSouth and Lucent Technologies. Most states offer small-business loan subsidies for equipment, working capital, and start-up seed money.

Incubators are growing rapidly to assist small businesses. Just like everyone else, incubators are seeking out companies with real market potential. If such potential is present, investors are not far behind.

Source: Christopher Farrell, "When Bureaucrats Are a Boon," *Business Week*, September 1, 1997.

---

have on hand sufficient retained earnings to finance extensive capital improvements or expansion. If you think about it for a moment, it makes sense. What if you wanted to buy an expensive personal asset such as a new car? The ideal way to purchase the car would be to go to your personal savings account and take out the necessary cash to pay for the car. No hassle! No interest! Unfortunately, few people have such large amounts of cash available. And most businesses are no different. Even though they would like to finance long-term needs from operations, few have the resources on hand to accomplish this.

◄ CONSIDER USING SUPPLEMENTAL CASE 19-1
Becoming a Venture Capitalist.
(SCANS)

••• VENTURE CAPITAL •••

The hardest time for a business to raise money is when it is just starting. The company typically has few assets and no market track record, so the chances of borrowing significant amounts of money from a bank are slim.

Venture capital firms are one of the sources of start-up capital for new companies. **Venture capital**, which is money that is invested in new companies that have great profit potential, helped firms such as Intel, Apple Computer, Compaq, Sun Microsystems, and dozens of other fast-growth companies get started. Take a look at the box called From the Pages of *Business Week* to see an example of venture capital financing at work.

◄ CONSIDER USING OT ACETATE 19-10
Sources of Finding Venture Capital Funding

venture capital
Money that is invested in new companies that have great profit potential.

The venture capital industry began about 50 years ago as an alternative investment vehicle for wealthy families. The Rockefellers financed Sanford McDonnell, for example, when he was operating his company from an airplane hangar. That small venture grew into McDonnell Douglas, the large aerospace and defense contractor that merged with Boeing Corporation in 1997.[9] The venture capital industry grew significantly in the 1980s, when many new high-tech companies were being started. In the 1990s the search for venture capital intensified, especially in high-tech centers such as the Silicon Valley.[10] *Inc.* magazine surveyed 89 fast-growing companies to see how they financed their growth. The number one source of funds was venture capital (44 percent of the firms had used it).

A finance manager has to be careful when choosing a venture capital firm to help finance a new business.[11] For one thing, the venture capital firm generally wants a stake in the ownership of the business. Venture capitalists also expect a very high return on their investment, usually 20 percent or more. More important, the venture capital firm should be able to come up with and be willing to provide more financing if the firm needs it.[12] The search for venture capital actually begins with a good business plan (see Chapter 6). This document must convince investors that the firm will be a success. Part of the business plan should be a clear financing proposal that spells out how much capital the business needs, how it is to be raised, and how it will be paid back.

The dangers of having the wrong venture capital firm are illustrated in the experience of Jon Birck, who started Northwest Instrument Systems with venture capital. Birck worked until 11:00 or 12:00 each night to build the company. One day, after having dedicated three years to the company, he was asked to leave by the venture capital firm, which wanted a more experienced chief executive officer to protect its investment. Birck had left a secure job, put his marriage on the line, taken out a second mortgage on his house, and given himself a below-average salary to get Northwest on its feet; and then, just when the firm was ready for rapid growth, he was asked to resign.

As Jon Birck's story shows, financing a firm's long-term needs clearly involves a high degree of risk. This is particularly true when firms borrow needed funds from venture capitalists. Knowing this, you might be inclined to ask the question, Why do firms borrow funds at all instead of using equity funding? The reason involves the use of leverage. Let's look at this next.

••• MAKING DECISIONS ON USING •••
FINANCIAL LEVERAGE

leverage
Raising needed funds through borrowing to increase a firm's rate of return.

➤ **CONSIDER USING OT ACETATE 19-11**
Making Use of Leverage.

Raising needed funds through borrowing to increase the firm's rate of return is referred to as **leverage**. While it's true that debt increases the risk of the firm, it also enhances the firm's ability to increase profits. Two key jobs of the finance manager or CFO are to forecast the need for borrowed funds and to manage them once they are obtained. (Refer back to Figure 19.5 for a comparison of debt and equity financing alternatives.)

If the firm's earnings are larger than the interest payments on the funds borrowed, business owners can realize a higher rate of return than if equity financing were used. See Figure 19.6 for an example that involves our cereal company, Fiberrific. However, if the firm's earnings are less than the interest paid on borrowed funds, owners could lose money on their investment.

Normally, it's up to each individual firm to determine exactly how to balance debt and equity financing. For example, Viacom, the communications giant, took on $8 billion of new debt in taking control of Paramount and Blockbuster. In contrast, Gillette became a major player in the battery market with its $7 billion purchase of Duracell, all in stock.[13] Some firms, such as Wm. Wrigley Jr. Co. and

Legal Briefcase

Financing a Small Business

If you are starting or running a small business, you know that one of the hardest jobs of a small-business owner is to find money when it is really needed. The text already discusses many sources of funds, such as banks, the SBA, partners, venture capitalists, and other successful entrepreneurs. Here are some other sources you may want to search:

1. *State funds.* The SBA has a booklet available called "Capital Formation in the States," which lists funds operated by some states.
2. *Customers or suppliers.* The *Standard Industrial Classification Manual* or Dun's Marketing Services' *Million Dollar Directory* can help find large companies in your industry.
3. *Small-business investment companies (SBICs).* The best way to find an SBIC is through the National Asso- ▲

ciation of Small Business Investment Companies or the National Association of Investment Companies.

4. *Community development funds.* Ask the National Congress for Community Economic Development or your state's Department of Economic Development about community funds in your area.
5. *Accounting firms.* Some big accounting firms help small businesses by discounting their fees and by introducing you to potential investors. Call the small-business divisions of big accounting firms for the names of people who work with new businesses.
6. *Small-business incubators.* For information, contact the National Business Incubation Association in Carlisle, Pennsylvania. Colleges, universities, and chambers of commerce can also help locate incubators.

Hershey Foods, have little long-term debt. Using leverage ratios (which we discussed in Chapter 18) can offer companies a standard of the comparative leverage of firms in their industries. According to Standard & Poor's and Moody's Investor Services, the average debt of a large industrial corporation ranges between 33 and 40 percent of its total assets. Small-business debt varies considerably. Read the Legal Briefcase box to review some interesting alternatives for small businesses in considering financing. As the requirements of financial

◄ **CONSIDER USING TM 143**
Using Leverage Versus Equity Financing: Fiberrific Inc. Needs to Raise $500,000.

LEVERAGE—SELLING BONDS		EQUITY—SALE OF STOCK	
Common stock	$ 50,000	Common stock	$500,000
Bonds (at 10% interest)	450,000		
	$500,000		$500,000
Earnings	$125,000	Earnings	$125,000
Less bond interest	45,000		
	$ 80,000		$125,000
Return to stockholders $= \dfrac{\$80,000}{\$50,000} = 160\%$		Return to stockholders $= \dfrac{\$125,000}{\$500,000} = 25\%$	

FIGURE **19.6**

· · · ·

USING LEVERAGE VERSUS EQUITY FINANCING: FIBERRIFIC INC. NEEDS TO RAISE $500,000

institutions become more stringent and investors more demanding, it's certain the job of the finance manager will become more difficult and challenging.

Chapter 20 takes a deeper look at stocks and bonds both as financing tools and as investment options. You will learn about the stock exchanges, how to buy and sell stock, how to choose the right investment, how to read the stock and bond quotations in *The Wall Street Journal* and other newspapers, and more. Finance takes on a whole new dimension when you see how you can participate in financial markets yourself.

Progress Check

- What are the two major forms of debt financing available to a firm?
- How does debt financing differ from equity financing?
- What are the two major forms of equity financing available to a firm?
- What is leverage, and why would firms choose to use it?

SUMMARY

2. Describe the responsibilities of financial managers.

1. Sound financial management is critical to the well-being of any business.
   - ***What are the most common ways firms fail financially?***
   The most common financial problems are (1) undercapitalization, (2) poor control over cash flow, and (3) inadequate expense control.

2. *Finance* is that function in a business responsible for acquiring funds for the firm, managing funds within the firm (e.g., preparing budgets and doing cash flow analysis), and planning for the expenditure of funds on various assets.
   - ***What do financial managers do?***
   Financial managers plan, budget, control funds, obtain funds, collect funds, audit, manage taxes, and advise top management on financial matters.

3. Outline the steps in financial planning by explaining the process of forecasting financial needs, developing budgets, and establishing financial controls.

3. Financial planning involves short- and long-term forecasting, budgeting, and financial controls.
   - ***What are the four budgets of finance?***
   The *operating budget* is the projection of dollar allocations to various costs and expenses given various revenues. The *capital budget* is the spending plan for expensive assets such as property, plant, and equipment. The *cash budget* is the projected cash balance at the end of a given period. The *master budget* summarizes the information in the other three budgets.

4. Recognize the financial needs that must be met with available funds.

4. During the course of a business's life, its financial needs shift considerably.
   - ***What are the major needs for funds firms experience?***
   Businesses have financial needs in four major areas: (1) managing daily business operations, (2) managing accounts receivable, (3) obtaining needed inventory, and (4) planning major capital expenditures.

5. Distinguish between short-term and long-term financing and between debt capital and equity capital.

5. Businesses often have needs for short-term and long-term financing and for debt capital and equity capital.
   - ***What's the difference between short-term and long-term financing?***
   Short-term financing refers to funds that will be repaid in less than one year, whereas long-term financing refers to funds that will be repaid over a specific time period of more than one year.
   - ***What's the difference between debt capital and equity capital?***
   Debt capital refers to funds raised by borrowing (going into debt), whereas equity capital is raised from within or by selling ownership (stock) in the company.

6. There are many sources for short-term financing including trade credit, promissory notes, family and friends, commercial banks and other financial institutions, factoring, and commercial paper.

- **Why should businesses use trade credit?**
Trade credit is the least expensive form of short-term financing and the most convenient. Businesses can buy goods today and pay for them sometime in the future.

- **What's a line of credit?**
It is an agreement by a bank to lend a specified amount of money to the business at any time, if the money is available. A revolving credit agreement is a line of credit that guarantees a loan will be available—for a fee.

- **What's the difference between a secured loan and an unsecured loan?**
An unsecured loan has no collateral backing it. Secured loans have collateral backed by assets such as accounts receivable, inventory, or other property of value.

- **Is factoring a form of secured loan?**
No, factoring means *selling* accounts receivable at a discounted rate to a factor.

- **What's commercial paper?**
Commercial paper is a corporation's unsecured promissory note maturing in 270 days or less.

7. One of the important functions of a finance manager is to obtain long-term capital.

- **What are the major sources of long-term financing?**
Debt financing involves the sale of bonds and long-term loans from banks and other financial institutions. Equity financing is obtained through the sale of stock, from venture capital firms, or the firm's retained earnings.

- **What are the two major forms of debt financing?**
Debt capital comes from two sources: selling bonds and borrowing from individuals, banks, and other financial institutions. Bonds can be secured by some form of collateral or can be unsecured. The same is true of loans.

- **What's leverage, and how do firms use it?**
Leverage is raising funds from borrowing. It involves the use of borrowed funds to invest in such undertakings as expansion, research and development. Firms measure the risk of borrowing (leverage) against the potential for higher profits.

KEY TERMS

capital budget 567
capital expenditures 571
cash budget 567
cash flow forecast 566
commercial finance companies 575
commercial paper 577
debt capital 572
equity capital 572
factoring 575
finance 565
financial control 568
financial management 565

indenture terms 578
inventory financing 574
leverage 582
line of credit 574
long-term financing 572
long-term forecast 566
master budget 568
operating budget 567
pledging 574
promissory note 573
revolving credit agreement 574

risk/return trade-off 578
secured bond 578
secured loan 574
short-term financing 572
short-term forecast 566
term-loan agreement 578
trade credit 573
unsecured bond 579
unsecured loan 574
venture capital 581

DEVELOPING WORKPLACE SKILLS

1. Obtain the annual report from at least three different corporations. Compare the balance sheets in each. Which assets are fixed and what is their value? How much has each company borrowed? (Hint: Look under long-term liabilities.) Based on your analysis, which company is in the best financial health? How do you know?

2. Visit a lending officer from a local bank. Ask what the current interest rate is and what rate small businesses would pay for short-term and long-term loans. Ask for blank forms that borrowers use to apply for loans. Share these forms with your class and explain the types of information the bank is looking for.

3. Use information from Standard & Poor's and Moody's Investors Service to investigate three bonds. Ask the librarian what similar references are available. Report what you find to the class.

4. One small-business consultant has commented that the most difficult concept to get across to small-business owners is the need to take all the trade credit (e.g., 2/10, net 30) they can get. He simply could not convince owners that they would save over 36 percent a year by doing that. Explain the concept to the class to show your own understanding.

5. Assume you work as a small-business consultant. Draft a memo to your clients advising them on the best sources for financing available to their businesses.

TAKING IT TO THE NET

Purpose

To summarize discussions with entrepreneurs regarding ways to finance budding businesses.

Exercise

One of the most valuable ways of learning about ways to finance a business is to talk to those who have done it. Find the Starting Your Business discussion group on the EntreWorld Web site (http://www.entreworld.org/). At the time of this writing, there was a discussion thread called Venture Capital: Pot of Gold or Forbidden Fruit? If this thread is no longer available, search the site for a similar discussion about financing a new business.

1. List the major points of advice given by entrepreneurs who have been through the process of obtaining funds for a new business. (Note the addresses for the posts where you found your answers.)

2. List the advantages and disadvantages given in the discussion you found of using venture capital in financing a new business. (Note the addresses for the posts where you found your answers.)

3. It is important for you to keep in mind that you don't know the qualifications of the individuals who post messages in these forums. While information published in textbooks and journals is subjected to critical review, the comments made in these discussions are not. Therefore, it is important that you evaluate information you find in these sources in light of what you read in more reliable sources. Compare and contrast the information you discovered in the thread with the information provided in this chapter.

Practicing Management Decisions

CASE
• • • • • •
FINANCING NONPROFIT ORGANIZATIONS
• • • • • •

Looking for a career that's challenging, with opportunities for advancement, and large numbers of openings? Then welcome to the world of financial management in nonprofit organizations. Nonprofits are crying for the talents of skilled financial managers, who often overlook nonprofits in favor of profit-seeking firms. As the demand for financing soars and the available funds become scarcer, the need for innovative and experienced financial managers grows.

The size and scope of the nonprofit sector often surprises even seasoned business professionals. Also, misconceptions abound about work in nonprofits. For starters, many people assume that the nonprofit sector of the economy is quite small. In reality, it is valued at approximately $500 billion per year. This makes the U.S. nonprofit sector twice as large as the U.S. construction industry. Also, the term nonprofit sometimes brings to mind church-sponsored bingo games or bake sales. But people forget that the nonprofit sector contains such notables as the National Football League, the Smithsonian Institution, and the National Audubon Society, none of which sponsors bingo events.

Work in nonprofits often includes interactions with the profit-seeking sector. For example, the Smithsonian has recently begun a new corporate sponsorship program to help fund its 150th anniversary traveling exhibition. One nonprofit, the Rockland Family Shelter in Rockland County, New York, even enlisted a financial specialist to start a for-profit business to help finance the work of the shelter.

Many nonprofit organizations have experienced problems at the top of their organizations. According to David LaGreca, a manager with the Volunteer Consulting Group (VCG), top management positions at nonprofits are often filled with highly "trained" businesspeople, such as social workers and former dancers. These individuals have creative and specific skills but lack the training and business expertise of executives at profit-seeking firms. LaGreca also notes that it's often difficult to recruit qualified individuals to serve on nonprofit boards. Many feel that the possibility of scandal in the operations of a nonprofit could damage their reputation or tarnish the image of other groups with which they are associated.

Decision Questions

1. How is the job of a financial manager in a nonprofit organization different from that of a financial manager with a profit-seeking firm?
2. Should financial managers in nonprofit organizations be compensated equally to their counterparts in profit-seeking firms? Why or why not?
3. Do you see the job of the nonprofit financial manager as getting easier or more difficult in the future? Where might you get facts to support your conclusions?

Sources: Michael Heyman, "Smithsonian Perspectives," *Smithsonian*, February 1997, pp. 12–14; and "Profiting a Non-Profit," *Nation's Business*, February 1996, p. 5.

VIDEO CASE
• • • • • •
THE ROLE OF THE FINANCIAL MANAGER

The role of the financial manager is one of the most complex roles in business. These managers are responsible for forecasting financial needs, budgeting, obtaining and controlling funds, auditing, managing accounts receivable, and advising management on financial affairs. In addition, financial managers handle tax questions, manage cash, and do internal audits. In short, financial managers are responsible for anything having to do with obtaining, spending, and managing money.

Financial management then can be defined simply as assuming responsibility for acquiring the necessary funds to start a business and then to manage the cash inflow and outflow once it is established. But such a definition doesn't capture the dynamics of financial management. It may be easier to picture part of finance as a four-step process: (1) forecasting financial needs, (2) preparing budgets, (3) establishing controls to ensure the company follows its financial plans, and (4) obtaining short-term and long-term financing.

Short-term financing involves the use of trade credit, issuing promissory notes, borrowing from friends and family, going to commercial banks, and collecting funds from those who owe the company. Financial managers are responsible for minimizing the costs of borrowing and decreasing costs in general.

Long-term financing, on the other hand, is usually provided by retained earnings (profit not distributed in the form of dividends) or from the sale of stock or bonds. When a company sells stock, the ownership is spread among many people. A board of directors represents these owners, and the board selects the company's managers. When a company sells bonds, it obtains funds without losing any of its ownership. A bond is more like a corporate IOU. The rate a company must pay depends on the economy and competition from government bonds.

Clearly, financial managers are in touch with the company's lifeblood—money. In many ways, financial management is a form of risk management. Financial managers must weigh their risks of borrowing money against the potential earnings. They must also weigh the risks of investing the firm's profits, in the stocks or bonds of other companies or in other types of investments. Additionally financial managers play key roles in deciding which of the firm's projects to finance and which to deny or cut off. Given such responsibility, it's easy to see why finance is both a rewarding and challenging career possibility.

Discussion Questions

1. What are the financial conditions of the economy today and how do those conditions affect financial managers?
2. If you were a financial manager today at a major corporation, would you try to raise investment capital through the sale of stock or bonds or some other source? Why?
3. What is the relationship between accounting and finance? Could you be an outstanding financial manager without a good understanding of accounting?
4. Does finance seem like a good career for you? Why or why not?

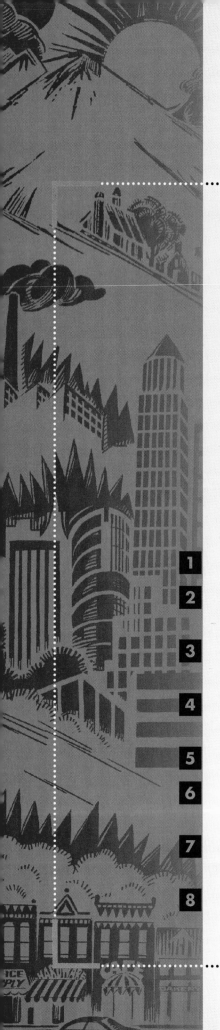

Securities Markets: Financing and Investing

Chapter

20

LEARNING GOALS

*After you have read and studied this chapter,
you should be able to*

1 Examine the functions of securities markets and investment bankers.

2 Compare the advantages and disadvantages of issuing bonds, and identify the classes and features of bonds.

3 Compare the advantages and disadvantages of issuing stock, and outline the differences between common and preferred stock.

4 Identify the various stock exchanges, and describe how to invest in securities markets and choose among different investment strategies.

5 Analyze the opportunities bonds offer as investments.

6 Explain the opportunities stocks and mutual funds offer as investments and the advantages of diversifying investments.

7 Discuss the high risk involved in junk bonds, buying stock on margin, and commodities.

8 Explain securities quotations listed in the financial section of a newspaper, and how the Dow Jones averages affect the market.

I t's a weekday in the nation's capital and Kemp, Lott, and Breaux are deeply involved in a serious meeting. No, they are not discussing another possible minimum wage increase or debating what to do about the nation's budget. You see this beltway meeting involves *Joanne Kemp*, *Tricia* Lott, and *Lois* Breaux, members of the Meager Means Investment Club and wives of Jack Kemp, former Republican vice presidential candidate; Trent Lott, the majority leader of the U.S. Senate; and John Breaux, U.S. Senator from Louisiana.

The "Beltway Ladies" have joined growing numbers of Americans that have pooled their talents and dollars into forming investment clubs that meet once a month and invest regularly in stocks they like. From 1982 to 1997, the number of investment clubs in the United States has grown from approximately 5,000 to almost 33,000. The Meager Means Investment Club is open to both democrats and republicans, and is perhaps the only investment club in the country whose activities have been cleared by the Senate Ethics Committee.

Investment clubs date back to 1900 and tend to vary in popularity according to trends in the stock market. Without question, the tremendous growth and prosperity of the stock market of the late 1990s is certainly a major reason for the continued growth and popularity of investment clubs. The National Association of Investment Clubs (NAIC) claims that in the past two years it has doubled its membership, with growth occurring all across the nation among investors from all economic levels. The NAIC estimates investment clubs are growing at a rate of approximately 900 per month.

PROFILE

The Beltway Ladies Investment Club

Being the wives of influential men who earn well into six figures unfortunately does not guarantee success in the stock market. Mary Clement, wife of Representative Bob Clement of Tennessee laments recommending ICC Technology to the club at $15 per share. The stock quickly fell to $5. So far the Meager Means Club has earned between 15 percent and 20 percent on its investments. While these results are not phenomenal, they are not too shabby either. Like most investment clubs, the Meager Means Investment Club has several common threads in their investment strategy:

- Invest all or nearly all of the club's money in stocks;
- Extensively research new investment ideas and debate the risks before committing any money;
- Invest regularly, regardless of what the market is doing;
- Buy high-quality stocks with good records and growth potential; and
- Keep up with economic news and other market developments.

This chapter discusses securities markets and how they assist both companies and investors in achieving financial goals and objectives. Read this chapter carefully and perhaps you will be the next person calling the National Association of Investment Clubs for membership information.

Sources: Mary Beth Regan, "The Beltway Ladies Investment Guide?" *Business Week*, September 1, 1997, p. 6; and Eileen Kinsella and Nichole M. Christian, "Investment Clubs Catch On With Blacks," *The Wall Street Journal*, October 15, 1997, p. C1.

THE FUNCTION OF SECURITIES MARKETS

Securities markets such as the New York Stock Exchange serve two major functions: They help businesses find long-term funding, and they give investors a place to buy and sell investments such as stocks and bonds. Securities markets can provide businesses the capital they need to finance beginning opera-

➤ **CONSIDER USING OT ACETATE 20-1**
Debt and Equity Financing

tions, expand their businesses, or buy goods and services. Investors benefit from the securities market by buying and selling stocks, bonds, mutual funds, and other investments that will help them build their financial future. In this chapter, we will look at securities from the perspectives of both business owners and investors.

Securities markets are divided into primary and secondary markets. Primary markets handle the sale of new securities. Corporations make money on the sale of their securities only once—when they are first bought on the primary market. After that the secondary market handles the trading of securities between investors, with the proceeds of the sale going to the investor selling the stock, not to the corporation. For example, if we, as the makers of Fiberrific, sell 200,000 shares of stock in our company at $15 a share, we would raise $3 million. However, if Shareholder Jones sells 100 shares of her Fiberrific stock to Investor Smith, we collect nothing. Smith bought the stock from Jones, not from Fiberrific. It's important to note, however, that companies like Fiberrific can offer additional shares of stock in the future to raise additional capital.

The importance of long-term funding to businesses can't be overemphasized. Unfortunately, many new companies start without sufficient capital and many established firms fail to do adequate long-term planning. If given a choice, businesses normally prefer to meet long-term financial needs by using retained earnings or by borrowing from a lending institution. However, if such forms of long-term funding are not available, the company may be able to raise capital by issuing corporate bonds or selling stock (ownership). As Chapter 19 explained, issuing corporate bonds is a form of *debt* financing and selling stock in the corporation is a form of *equity* financing. These forms of debt or equity financing are not available to all companies, but many firms use such financing to meet long-term financial needs.

For example, what if we needed long-term financing to expand our operations at Fiberrific? We know, unfortunately, that the company doesn't have sufficient retained earnings and that it's unlikely we can secure funds from a lender. Our chief financial officer suggests that we might want to offer shares of stock or corporate bonds to the public. She warns, however, that getting such issues approved requires extensive financial disclosures and detailed scrutiny by the U.S. Securities and Exchange Commission (SEC). She thinks the company should turn to an investment banker for assistance. Let's see why.

••• THE ROLE OF INVESTMENT BANKERS •••

investment bankers
Specialists who assist in the issue and sale of new securities.

Investment bankers are specialists who assist in the issue and sale of new securities. Investment banking firms such as Goldman Sachs and Salomon Morgan Stanley help companies like our hypothetical Fiberrific prepare the financial analysis necessary to gain SEC approval for stock or bond issues.

Investment bankers also underwrite new issues of bonds or stocks. In other words, the investment banking firm buys the entire bond or stock issue a company wants to sell at an agreed-on discount (which can be quite sizable), and then sells the issue to private or institutional investors at full price. **Institutional investors** are large investors, such as pension funds, mutual funds, insurance companies, and banks, that invest their own funds or the funds of others. Institutional investors are a powerful force in securities markets because of their buying power.

institutional investors
Large investors such as pension funds, mutual funds, insurance companies, and banks that invest their own funds or the funds of others.

Securities markets, as we have said, help companies raise needed long-term capital through debt financing by issuing bonds or equity financing by selling stock. Let's look first at issuing bonds.

DEBT FINANCING THROUGH SELLING BONDS

Put simply, a **bond** is a corporate certificate indicating that a person has lent money to a firm (see Figure 20.1). A company that issues bonds has a legal obligation to make regular interest payments to investors and to repay the entire bond principal amount at a prescribed time, called the maturity date. Let's explore the language of bonds a bit more carefully so you understand what's involved.

••• LEARNING THE LANGUAGE OF BONDS •••

A more specific definition of a bond than the one given above is that a bond is a contract of indebtedness issued by a corporation or government unit that promises payment of a principal amount at a specified future time. Interest is paid to the holder of the bond until the principal amount is due. Thus, in this context, **interest** is the payment the issuer of the bond makes to the bondholders for use of the borrowed money. The interest rate paid on a bond may also be called the bond's *coupon rate*. This term dates back to when bonds were issued as *bearer bonds* and the holder, or bearer, was considered the owner. The company issuing the bond kept no accounts of transfers in ownership, and the interest on the bond was obtained by clipping "coupons" attached to the bond and sending them to the issuing company. Today bonds are registered, and changes in ownership are recorded. Look again at the bond in Figure 20.1 and see if you can tell whether it is a registered bond or a bearer bond.

bond
A corporate certificate indicating that a person has lent money to a firm.

◄ **LEARNING GOAL 2**
Describe the responsibilities of financial managers.

interest
The payment the issuer of the bond makes to the bondholders for use of the borrowed money.

◄ **CONSIDER USING TM 145**
A Sample Bond Certificate from IBM (Figure 20.1 on text page 593)

FIGURE **20.1**
••••
A SAMPLE BOND CERTIFICATE FROM IBM

➤ **CONSIDER USING OT ACETATE 20-2**
Bonds Are Getting Longer Maturities

The interest rate paid on a bond varies according to factors such as the state of the economy, the reputation of the company, and the going interest rate for bonds of similar companies. The interest rate being paid by U.S. government bonds also clearly affects the interest rate a firm must agree to pay, since government bonds are considered safe investments. (Remember the risk/return trade-off defined in Chapter 19.) Bonds are also rated in terms of their risk by such independent firms as Standard & Poor's and Moody's Investors Service. Figure 20.2 describes the range of ratings these two firms attach to bond issues. Once an interest rate is set for a bond issue, it cannot be changed.

principal
The face value of a bond.

maturity date
The exact date the issuer of a bond must pay the principal to the bondholder.

In reference to bonds, **principal** is the face value of a bond. (Bonds are almost always issued in multiples of $1,000.) The issuing company is legally bound to repay the bond principal to the bondholder in full on the **maturity date**. For example, if Fiberrific issues a $1,000 bond with an interest rate of 9 percent and a maturity date of 2018, we are agreeing to pay bondholders $90 in interest *each year* until a specified date in 2018, when the full $1,000 must be repaid. Since bond issues have no set time limits, different bonds are issued with different maturity dates. In fact, some firms such as Disney and Coca-Cola have issued bonds with 50-year maturity dates.

➤ **CONSIDER USING CRITICAL THINKING EXERCISE 20-1**
Financial Growth (**SCANS**)

➤ **CONSIDER USING TM 146**
Bond Ratings
(Figure 20.2 on text page 594)

••• ADVANTAGES AND DISADVANTAGES OF SELLING BONDS •••

Bonds offer long-term financing advantages to an organization. The decision to issue bonds is generally based on advantages such as the following:

- Bondholders are creditors, not owners, of the firm and have no vote on corporate matters; thus, management maintains control over the firm's operations.
- Interest paid on bonds is tax-deductible. Chapter 18 explained how certain interest expenses can help a firm limit its tax responsibilities to the government.

FIGURE 20.2
••••
BOND RATINGS

RATING		
MOODY'S	**STANDARD & POOR'S**	**DESCRIPTIONS**
Aaa	AAA	Highest quality (lowest default risk)
Aa	AA	High quality
A	A	Upper medium grade
Baa	BBB	Medium grade
Ba	BB	Lower medium grade
B	B	Speculative
Caa	CCC, CC	Poor (high default risk)
Ca	C	Highly speculative
C	D	Lowest grade

- Bonds are a temporary source of funding for a firm. They're eventually repaid and the debt obligation eliminated.

But bonds also have their drawbacks:

- Bonds increase debt (liabilities) and may adversely affect the market's perception of the firm.
- Interest on bonds is a legal obligation. If interest is not paid, bondholders can take legal action to force payment.
- The face value of bonds must be repaid on the maturity date. Without careful planning, this repayment can cause cash flow ⇒ P. 544 ⇐ problems when the bonds come due.

◄ CONSIDER USING LECTURE ENHANCER 20-1
Municipal Bonds: Financing Local Government Public Works

••• DIFFERENT CLASSES OF BONDS •••

As mentioned in Chapter 19, organizations can issue two different classes of corporate bonds. The first class is unsecured bonds, which are not supported by any type of collateral. These bonds are usually referred to as **debenture bonds** and are issued only by well-respected firms with excellent credit ratings, since the only security the bondholder has is the reputation and credit history of the company.

debenture bonds
Bonds that are unsecured (i.e., not backed by any collateral such as equipment).

The second class of bonds is secured bonds, which are backed by some tangible asset that is pledged to the bondholder if interest isn't paid or the principal isn't paid back. There are several kinds of secured bonds:

- *Mortgage bonds* are secured by company assets such as land and buildings. They are the most common form of secured bonds and often the most desirable.
- *Collateral trust bonds* are secured by shares of stock the company owns that are held in trust by a commercial bank (thus the word *trust* in the title).
- *Equipment trust bonds* are backed by equipment the company owns such as trucks, aircraft, and other equipment widely used in industry. Such items make excellent collateral since they can be taken over easily and have good resale value.

Figure 20.3 lists and describes several other types of bonds that compete with U.S. corporate bonds. Different bonds include different features. Let's look at special features bonds sometimes offer.

◄ CONSIDER USING TM 147
Types of Bonds That Compete with Corporate Bonds (Figure 20.3 on text page 595)

Bond	Description
U.S. government bond	Issued by the federal government; considered the safest type of bond investment
Treasury bills (T-bills)	Bonds that mature in less than a year and are issued with a minimum par value of $10,000
Treasury notes and bonds	Bonds that mature in 10 to 25 years and are sold in denominations of $1,000 and $5,000
Municipal bonds	Bonds issued by state or local governments; interest payments are exempt from federal taxes
Yankee bond	Bonds that are issued by a foreign government and are payable in U.S. dollars
Zero-coupon bond	Bonds that pay no interest prior to maturity; the return to the investor comes from the difference between the purchase price and the bond's face value.

FIGURE 20.3

• • • •

TYPES OF BONDS THAT COMPETE WITH CORPORATE BONDS

U.S. government bonds are considered the safest bond investments since they have the full faith and credit of the federal government behind them. There are different kinds of bonds with different risks for every kind of investor.

••• SPECIAL BOND FEATURES •••

sinking fund

Provision of a bond that requires the issuer to retire (put in a trust fund), on a periodic basis, some part of the bond principal prior to maturity.

By now you should know that bonds are issued with an interest rate, are unsecured or secured by collateral, and must be repaid at their maturity date. This repayment requirement often leads companies to establish what is called a sinking fund to ensure that enough money will be available to repay bondholders on the maturity date. **Sinking fund** bond issuers regularly set aside funds in a reserve account (a sinking fund) so that enough capital will be accumulated by the maturity date to pay off the bond. Sinking funds can be attractive to firms for several reasons:

- They provide for an orderly retirement of a bond issue.
- They reduce the risk of the bond not being repaid.
- The market price of the bond is supported because the risk of the firm's not repaying the principal on the maturity date is reduced.

callable bond

A bond that gives the issuer the right to pay off the bond before its maturity.

Another special feature that can be included in a bond issue is a call provision. A **callable bond** permits the bond issuer to pay off the bond's principal prior to its maturity date. Call provisions must be included when a bond is issued and bondholders should be aware that a bond is callable. Callable bonds give companies some discretion in their long-term forecasting. Suppose Fiberrific issued $50 million in 20-year bonds in 1998 with an interest rate of 10 percent. The yearly interest expense would be $5 million ($50 million × .10). If market conditions change in 2003, and bonds of the same quality pay only 7 percent, Fiberrific would be paying 3 percent, or $1.5 million, in excess interest yearly ($50 million × .03). The company could clearly benefit if it could call in (pay off) the old bonds and reissue new bonds at the lower interest rate.

convertible bond

A bond that can be converted into shares of common stock in the issuing company.

A last feature sometimes included in bonds is convertibility. A **convertible bond** is one that can be converted into shares of common stock in the issuing company. Why would bond investors want to convert their investment to stock? If the value of the firm's common stock grows sizably in value over time, bondholders can compare the value of continued bond interest with the possible sizable profit they could gain by converting to a specified number of common shares. Convertibility often adds an incentive for an investor to buy a bond. When we discuss common stock in the next section, this advantage will become more evident to you.

 **Progress Check**

- Why are bonds considered to be a form of debt financing?
- What does it mean when a firm states that it is issuing a 9 percent debenture bond due in 2018?
- Explain the difference between an unsecured and a secured bond.
- Why do companies like to issue callable bonds? Why do investors dislike them?
- Why are convertible bonds attractive to investors?

•••• ▬▬▬ ••••

EQUITY FINANCING THROUGH SELLING STOCK

► LEARNING GOAL 3
Outline the steps in financial planning by explaining the process of forecasting financial needs, developing budgets, and establishing financial controls.

Equity financing is the other form of long-term funding we first introduced in Chapter 19. One form of equity financing is obtaining funds through the sale of ownership (stock) in the corporation. As we did with bonds, let's look at the language of stock.

••• LEARNING THE LANGUAGE OF STOCK •••

Stocks are shares of ownership in a company. A **stock certificate** is evidence of stock ownership that specifies the name of the company, the number of shares it represents, and the type of stock being issued (see Figure 20.4). Today most stock certificates are held electronically for the owners of the stock. Certificates sometimes indicate a stock's **par value**, which is a dollar amount assigned to each share of stock by the corporation's charter. Some states use par value as a basis for calculating the state's incorporation charges and fees but today, since par values do not reflect the market value of the stock, most companies issue "no-par" stock. **Dividends** are part of a firm's profits that may be distributed to stockholders as either cash payments or additional shares of stock. Although companies that issue bonds are required to pay interest, companies that issue stocks are not required to pay dividends.

••• ADVANTAGES AND DISADVANTAGES OF ISSUING STOCK •••

Since securities markets include the names of almost every large company in the United States, companies apparently feel that equity financing is a good way to raise long-term funds. The following are some advantages of issuing stock:

- As owners of the business, stockholders never have to be repaid.
- There's no legal obligation to pay dividends to stockholders; therefore, income (retained earnings) can be reinvested in the firm for future capital needs.
- Selling stock can improve the condition of the firm's balance sheet since the sale creates no debt and makes the company stronger financially.

But, as the saying goes, there is no such thing as a free lunch. Disadvantages of issuing stock include the following:

- As owners, stockholders (usually only common stockholders) have the right to vote for the company's board of directors. Usually one vote is

stocks
Shares of ownership in a company.

stock certificate
Evidence of stock ownership that specifies the name of the company, the number of shares it represents, and the type of stock being issued.

par value
A dollar amount assigned to each share of stock by the corporation's charter.

dividends
Part of a firm's profits that may be distributed to stockholders as either cash payments or additional shares of stock.

◄ **CONSIDER USING LECTURE ENHANCER 20-2**
Initial Public Offerings (IPOs)

◄ **CONSIDER USING TM 148**
Stock Certificate for Pet Inc. (Figure 20.4 on text page 597)

FIGURE **20.4**
••••
STOCK CERTIFICATE FOR PET INC.
Examine this certificate for key information about this stock.

▶ CONSIDER USING LECTURE
ENHANCER 20-3
The Dominican Nuns' Stock Portfolio

▶ CONSIDER USING LECTURE
ENHANCER 20-4
Firms Reassess the Cost of Annual
Meetings

preferred stock
Stock that gives its owners
preference in the payment of
dividends and an earlier claim on
assets than common stockholders if
the company is forced out of
business and its assets sold.

**cumulative preferred
stock**
Preferred stock that accumulates
unpaid dividends.

One option companies
may use to finance
growth is to offer the
firm's stock to the public
in an initial public offering (IPO). However, offering to sell company stock
is no guarantee that
investors will be inter-
ested in buying it. Wired
Ventures, publishers of
Wired magazine, hoped to
raise millions of dollars
from an IPO that unfortu-
nately fell through when
market underwriters
soured on the offering.

granted for each share of stock. Hence, the direction of the firm can be
altered by the sale of stock.

• Dividends are paid out of profit after taxes and thus are not tax-
deductible.

• Management's decisions can be affected by the need to keep stockholders happy.

Companies can issue two classes of stock: preferred and common. Let's
see how these forms of equity financing differ.

··· ISSUING SHARES OF PREFERRED STOCK ···

Preferred stock gives its owners preference in the payment of dividends and
an earlier claim on assets than common stockholders if the company is forced
out of business and its assets sold. Normally, preferred stock does not include
voting rights in the firm. Preferred stock is frequently referred to as a hybrid
investment because it has characteristics of both bonds and stocks. To illustrate this, consider the treatment of preferred stock dividends.

Preferred stock dividends differ from common stock dividends in several
ways. Preferred stock is generally issued with a par value that becomes the
base for the dividend the firm is willing to pay. For example, if a preferred
stock's par value is $100 a share with a dividend rate of 8 percent, the firm is
committing to an $8 dividend for each share of preferred stock the investor
owns (8 percent of $100 = $8). An owner of 100 shares of this preferred stock
is promised a fixed yearly dividend of $800. The owner is also assured that this
dividend must be paid in full before any common stock dividends can be distributed.

Other ways in which preferred stock and bonds are similar are that both
have a face (or par) value and both have a *fixed* rate of return. Preferred stocks
are rated by Standard & Poor's and Moody's Investors Service just like bonds.[1]
So how do they differ? Remember that companies are legally bound to pay
bond interest and to repay the face value of the bond on its maturity date. In
contrast, even though preferred stock dividends are generally fixed, they do
not legally have to be paid, and stock never has
to be repurchased. Though both bonds and
stock can increase in market value, the price of
stock generally increases at a higher percentage
than the price of bonds. Of course, the market
value of both could also go down.

SPECIAL FEATURES OF PREFERRED STOCK
Preferred stock can have special features not
applicable to common stock. For example, like
bonds, preferred stock can be callable. This
means a company could require preferred stockholders to sell back their shares. Preferred stock
can also be convertible to shares of common
stock. An important feature of preferred stock is
that it's often cumulative. That is, if one or more
dividends are not paid when due, the missed
dividends of **cumulative preferred stock** will
be accumulated and paid later. This means that
all dividends, including the back dividends,
must be paid in full before any common stock
dividends can be distributed.

••• ISSUING SHARES OF COMMON STOCK •••

Common stock is the most basic form of ownership in a firm. Holders of common stock have the right (1) to vote for board directors and important issues affecting the company and (2) to share in the firm's profits through dividends, if offered by the firm's board of directors. Having voting rights in a corporation allows stockholders to influence corporate policy since the elected board chooses the firm's top management and makes major policy decisions. Also, common stockholders have what is called a **preemptive right**, which is the first right to purchase any new shares of common stock the firm decides to issue. This right allows common stockholders to maintain a proportional share of ownership in the company.

Now that we have looked at stocks and bonds from a company's perspective, we will look at them from an investor's perspective, after we discuss stock exchanges.

- Name at least two advantages and two disadvantages of issuing stock as a form of equity financing.

- What are the major differences between preferred stock and common stock?

- In what ways are preferred stock and bonds similar? How are they different?

common stock
The most basic form of ownership in a firm; it confers voting rights and the right to share in the firm's profits through dividends, if offered by the firm's board of directors.

preemptive right
Common stockholders' right to purchase any new shares of common stock the firm decides to issue.

Progress Check

◄ **LEARNING GOAL 4**
Recognize the financial needs that must be met with available funds.

STOCK EXCHANGES

As its name implies, a **stock exchange** is an organization whose members can buy and sell (exchange) securities for companies and investors. Brokerage firms purchase memberships, or seats, on the exchanges, but there is a limited number of seats; the New York Stock Exchange (NYSE), for example, has only 1,366 members. This limitation pushed the average price of a seat on the NYSE to $1.3 million in 1997.[2]

Stock exchanges operate all over the world in cities such as Paris, London, Sydney, Buenos Aires, and Tokyo. Even former communist-bloc countries such as Hungary and Poland have opened stock exchanges that

stock exchange
An organization whose members can buy and sell (exchange) securities for companies and investors.

Where's the action in stocks and bonds? The action is global on stock exchanges throughout the world. The largest stock exchange in the United States is the New York Stock Exchange, where as many as one billion shares of stock have been traded in a single day. Though the NYSE often looks like chaos personified, the exchange works efficiently for businesses and investors.

Even though the hectic job of a stock exchange is to bring buyers and sellers together, not all stock exchanges resemble a traffic jam at rush hour. The Hong Kong Exchange is the picture of efficiency and composure compared to the NYSE.

➤ **CONSIDER USING SUPPLEMENTAL CASE 20-1**
Stocks or Bonds? That Is the Question
(SCANS)

enable businesses and individuals to buy securities from companies almost anywhere in the world. If you hear of a foreign company that has great potential for growth, you can usually obtain shares of its stock with little difficulty from U.S. brokers who have access to the foreign stock exchanges. In fact, the number of foreign firms listed on the NYSE has tripled in the past five years.

➤ **CONSIDER USING LECTURE ENHANCER 20-5**
The NYSE and Small Investors

➤ **CONSIDER USING OT ACETATE 20-4**
The Tale of the Tape: NASDAQ v/s the NYSE

••• U.S. EXCHANGES •••

The largest stock exchange in the United States, the New York Stock Exchange (NYSE), lists about 3,100 companies, mostly very large. The second largest U.S. exchange, also located in New York, is the American Stock Exchange (AMEX). The AMEX lists about 800 common and preferred stocks.[3] These two exchanges are national exchanges because they handle stocks of companies from all over the United States. In addition to the national exchanges, there are several regional exchanges in cities such as Chicago, San Francisco, Philadelphia, Cincinnati, Spokane, and Salt Lake City. The regional exchanges deal mostly with firms in their own areas.

••• THE OVER-THE-COUNTER (OTC) MARKET •••

over-the-counter (OTC) market
Exchange that provides a means to trade stocks not listed on the national exchanges.

National Association of Securities Dealers Automated Quotation (NASDAQ)
A nationwide electronic system that communicates over-the-counter trades to brokers.

The **over-the-counter (OTC) market** provides companies and investors with a means to trade stocks not listed on the national securities exchanges. The OTC market is a network of several thousand brokers. These brokers maintain contact with one another and buy and sell securities through a nationwide electronic system known as the **National Association of Securities Dealers Automated Quotation** system (**NASDAQ**—pronounced *nazz-dak*).

Originally, the over-the-counter market dealt mostly with small firms that could not qualify for listing on the national exchanges or did not want to bother with the procedures. Today, however, well-known firms such as Intel and Microsoft have their stock traded on the OTC market because the trades are done electronically. The over-the-counter market also handles corporate and U.S. government bonds as well as many city and state government bonds. The NASDAQ today lists approximately 5,600 stock issues, including many emerging small companies. Figure 20.5 lists the requirements for registering

EXCHANGE	REQUIREMENTS	TYPE OF COMPANY
New York Stock Exchange (NYSE)	Pre-tax income of $2.5 million; 1.1 million shares outstanding at a minimum market value of $18 million	Oldest, largest, and best-known companies
American Stock Exchange (AMEX)	Pre-tax income of $750,000; 500,000 shares publicly held at a minimum market value of $3 million (a second AMEX listing requires only 250,000 shares publicly held at a minimum market value of $2.5 million)	Midsized growth companies
NASDAQ	Pre-tax income of $750,000 or a total market value of all shares outstanding at $1 million; 400 shareholders; net assets of $4 million	Large, midsized, and small growth companies

Source: http://www.nyse.com/public/listed/3b/3bfm.htm.

stocks on the various exchanges. Adding a company to one of the various exchanges is a highly competitive undertaking, and the battle is often outright fierce. This competition is highlighted in the From the Pages of *Business Week* box. You'll read in the box how, in 1998, the boards of NASDAQ and AMEX made strides to improve their competitive position by approving a preliminary merger agreement that would join the two securities markets.[4]

••• SECURITIES REGULATIONS •••

The Securities Act of 1933 protects investors by requiring full disclosure of financial information by firms selling new stocks or bonds. This act was passed to deal with the free-for-all atmosphere that existed in the securities markets during the Roaring Twenties and the early 1930s. The Securities and Exchange Act of 1934 created the **Securities and Exchange Commission (SEC)**, which has responsibility at the federal level for regulating activities in the various exchanges. Companies trading on the national exchanges must register with the SEC and provide annual updates. The act also established specific guidelines that companies must follow when issuing stock.[5] For example, before issuing stock for sale to the public, a company must file with the SEC a registration statement with detailed economic and financial information relevant to the firm. The condensed version of that registration document—called a **prospectus**—must be sent to potential purchasers.

The 1934 act also established guidelines to prevent insiders from taking advantage of their privileged information. **Insider trading** involves the use of knowledge or information that individuals gain through their position that allows them to benefit unfairly from fluctuations in security prices. Originally, the SEC defined the term *insider* rather narrowly as consisting of a company's directors, employees, and relatives. Today the term has been broadened to include just about anyone with securities information that is not available to the general public.[6] For example, say your next-door neighbor, the chief financial officer of Fiberrific, tells you she is finalizing paperwork to sell the company to a major cereal producer. You buy the stock on this information. A court may well consider this insider trading. Penalties for insider trading can include fines or imprisonment. The Making Ethical Decisions box on page 603 describes a manager's dilemma involving insider information.

Most people think of securities markets as sources of investment opportunities for individuals and businesses. Let's look at this side of the market next.

FIGURE 20.5
· · · ·
REQUIREMENTS FOR REGISTERING STOCK ON THE NEW YORK, AMERICAN, AND NASDAQ EXCHANGES

◄ CONSIDER USING TM 149
Requirements for Registering Stock on the New York, American, and NASDAQ Exchanges (Figure 20.5 on text page 601)

Securities and Exchange Commission (SEC)
Federal agency that has responsibility for regulating the various exchanges.

prospectus
A condensed version of economic and financial information that a company must file with the SEC before issuing stock; the prospectus must be sent to potential stock purchasers.

insider trading
The use of knowledge or information that individuals gain through their position that allows them to benefit unfairly from fluctuations in security prices.

From the Pages of **BusinessWeek**

http://www.nyse.com

The Battle of the Boards

The talk on the street is that the battle of the boards is getting fiercer every year. But don't get confused; the talk is not on the streets of Chicago, Los Angeles, or Houston, nor does the battle of the boards refer to basketball fans' analysis of their favorite sport. The street we're talking about is 11 Wall Street, and the boards are the New York Stock Exchange (NYSE) and the National Association of Securities Dealers Automated Quotation system (NASDAQ).

The NYSE controlled the battlefield in the late 1990s. Its roster of foreign companies tripled between 1992 and 1997 and the "big board," as the NYSE is called, feels confident of attracting 500 to 600 non-U.S. companies by 2000. The NYSE even listed its first Russian company, Vimpel Communications, in 1996. But even more important in the battle is that the NYSE is garnering a record number of NASDAQ transfers, including big-name technology companies such as Gateway 2000, America Online, and Iomega. It has even reserved the ticker symbol M in the hopes of attracting Microsoft and is actively seeking initial public offerings of stocks (IPOs), which the NASDAQ has long dominated.

The NASDAQ has not been just sitting by and watching its fortunes decline. In fact, it has also attracted a record number of new companies, though most of them ▲ are small, and it is looking abroad for companies to join its exchange. The major problems that plagued the NASDAQ in the late 1990s were scandals and regulatory problems that called the integrity of the exchange into question.

At the time of this writing, the boards of NASDAQ and AMEX approved a preliminary merger agreement that would join the United States second- and third-largest securities markets. Final approval was scheduled for May 1998. If it passed, the merger created a "market of markets" where companies could choose to list on either the AMEX or the NASDAQ.

The NYSE has invested $1.2 billion in technology during the past 10 years to improve its operations; it now claims that it can process 3 billion shares per day. Not to be left behind, the NASDAQ can now process 2 billion shares per day. Both exchanges also allow price quotes in 16ths rather than 8ths, and both plan to quote prices in decimals in the near future. As the battle goes on, investors can look forward to both lower costs and improved service.

Sources: Suzanne Woolley, "The Big Board Is Booming," *Business Week,* August 4, 1997, pp. 58–64; and Suzanne Woolley, "Market of the Future? Not Likely," *Business Week,* March 30, 1998, p. 36.

···· ▬▬ ····

HOW TO INVEST IN SECURITIES MARKETS

stockbroker
A registered representative who works as a market intermediary to buy and sell securities for clients.

Investing in bonds, stocks, or other securities is not difficult at all. First, you decide what bond or stock you want to buy. Then you need to find someone authorized to trade stocks and bonds to call a member of the stock exchange to execute your order. A **stockbroker** is a registered representative who works as a market intermediary to buy and sell securities for clients. Stockbrokers place an order with a stock exchange member, who goes to the place at the exchange where the bond or stock is traded and negotiates a price. After the transaction is completed, the trade is reported to your broker, who notifies you to confirm your purchase. Large brokerage firms like Merrill Lynch or A. G. Edwards have automated order systems that allow their brokers to enter your order the instant you make it; seconds later, the order can be confirmed.

The same procedure is followed if you wish to *sell* stocks or bonds. Brokers will even hold on to the stock or bond certificate for you to keep it safe or to

▶ **CONSIDER USING LECTURE ENHANCER 20-6**
Wall Street War Stories

Wagging the Dog

After 35 years of hard work you finally made it to the post of chief executive officer of Laddie-Come-Home, a large producer of pet foods. As part of your compensation package, you are offered bonuses based on the company's stock performance. If the stock price of Laddie-Come-Home exceeds $50 during the current fiscal year, you could realize a windfall of close to $3 million in bonuses. It's been brought to your attention by an investment banking firm that a major competitor, Barking-Up-the-Wrong-Tree, has an interest in taking over your company. The investment banker hinted that Barking-Up-the-Wrong-Tree would pay upward of $55 a share for Laddie-Come-Home. You realize that the board of directors would probably follow your recommendation if you suggested selling the company, but you also know that at least half of the current employees would lose their jobs in the takeover.

You plan to retire within the next two years, and $3 million could make life easier. What are the ethical considerations in this situation? What are your alternatives? What are the consequences of each alternative? What will you do?

---

allow you to sell it easily and quickly, with just a telephone call. A broker can also be a valuable source of information about what stocks or bonds would best meet your financial objectives. It's important, however, that you learn about and follow stocks and bonds on your own, because stock analysts' advice may not always meet your specific expectations and needs. In fact, a Stockholm newspaper gave five Swedish stock analysts and a chimpanzee each the equivalent of $1,250 to make as much money as they could in the stock market. The chimp, who made his selections by throwing darts, won the competition.[7] *The Wall Street Journal* also periodically compares the predictions of a panel of "experts" to those of "dart throwers." Make sure to look for these contests in the *Journal.* The results are often interesting.

◄ CONSIDER USING LECTURE ENHANCER 20-7
Investment Strategies to Ponder

◄ CONSIDER USING OT ACETATE 20-5
Differences in Trading Costs

••• INVESTING ON-LINE •••

As we have stressed throughout this book, technology has affected virtually every aspect of business, and trading in investment securities is no exception. Investors can use on-line trading services to buy and sell stocks and bonds. DLJ Direct, Accutrade, and E*Trade are a few of the leading providers of Web-based stock trading services.[8] The commissions charged by these trading services are far less than those of regular stockbrokers. Trades that cost hundreds of dollars with traditional brokerage firms may cost less than $10 on the Web.[9] The on-line trading services are targeted primarily at investors who are willing to do their own research and make their own investment decisions without the assistance of a broker. The leading on-line services, however, do provide important market information such as company financial data, price histories of a stock, and consensus analysts' reports.

◄ CONSIDER USING OT ACETATE 20-6
The Five Lowest-Priced On-line Brokers

◄ CONSIDER USING LECTURE ENHANCER 20-8
Beware of Internet Investment Fraud

◄ CONSIDER USING OT ACETATE 20-3
What Are the Pick of the Investment Clubs?

Whether you use an on-line trading service or a stockbroker, investing means committing capital with the expectation of making a profit. The first step in any investment program is to analyze such factors as desired income, cash requirements, level of risk, and so forth. You are never too young or too old to get involved. Let's look at some alternatives and questions you should consider before investing.

Like other business services, trading in securities has taken it to the net. On-line trading services offer investors the option of buying and selling stocks and bonds at much lower commission charges than the fees charged by traditional brokerage firms such as Merrill Lynch. Web-based services such as Ameritrade offer investors rates as low as $8 per trade.

➤ CONSIDER USING OT ACETATE 20-7
Paying Dividends Through Thick and Thin

••• CHOOSING THE RIGHT INVESTMENT STRATEGY •••

As you might suspect, investment objectives change over the course of a person's life. For example, a young person saving for retirement can afford to invest in more high-risk options (such as stocks) than a person nearing retirement age. The younger person has time to wait for stocks to rise again should they hit a slump. The older person doesn't have that luxury. Inherent in the risk/return trade-off are several questions: Should you consider stocks or bonds? Do you want common or preferred stock? Do you want corporate-issued or government-issued bonds? These tough questions vary investor by investor. That's why you should consider five criteria when selecting investment options:

➤ CONSIDER USING LECTURE ENHANCER 20-9
Stock Dividend Yield

1. *Investment risk*—the chance that an investment and all its accumulated yields will be worth less at some future time than it's worth now.
2. *Yield*—the percentage return on an investment, such as interest or dividends, usually over a period of one year.
3. *Duration*—the length of time assets are committed.
4. *Liquidity*—how quickly you can get back invested funds when you want or need to.
5. *Tax consequences*—how the investment will affect your tax situation.

➤ CONSIDER USING LECTURE ENHANCER 20-10
Not What, but When, Is the Question

Since new investors are not generally well versed in the world of investing or in choosing proper investment strategies, an investment planner or a short course in investments can be very useful. The Spotlight on Small Business box on page 605 offers an interesting example of a growing investment firm.

Next, let's look at the potential of bonds as an investment. Then we'll move on to stocks.

Spotlight on Small Business

http://www.edwardjones.com/

Small Street versus Wall Street

It's hard to imagine a small business with $465 million of capital and a workforce of 3,744 brokers. Yet *small* is how the St. Louis–based brokerage firm Edward D. Jones likes to think of itself. The company has been referred to as the Wal-Mart of Wall Street because of its focus on building business in rural and suburban America. Jones's clients tend to be nontraditional yet conservative as investors. Many clients are farmers or small-town business owners who are not looking to get in the market, make a bundle, and then get out. They know their money could earn a better return, and they look to Edward D. Jones brokers to earn it for them.

The company follows a safety-first perspective in the market and will not generally deal in risky investments such as initial public offerings (IPOs), options, or commodities futures. The firm also takes a negative stand in dealing with penny stocks and will not compensate its brokers for trades on shares priced under $5. The battle cry at Jones is "Buy and hold . . . and hold . . . and hold, then hold a little more." Investors seem to listen. Management guru Peter Drucker believes the firm has created a product Wall Street has never seen before—peace of mind.

The company's brokers are encouraged to think like entrepreneurs. They can get as close to their customers as they choose, and face-to-face customer service is the order of the day. Some brokers even prefer going door-to-door rather than calling cold to introduce themselves to potential customers. Such personal contact allows them to question potential clients very specifically concerning their financial objectives.

Since the company does not earn money in the traditional Wall Street way—that is by shifting clients in and out of investments—the generation of new accounts is essential. Brokers earn a flat commission on trades, with the rest of their earnings coming from a bonus pool tied to the firm's overall profitability. No one seems to complain. Managing partner John Bachmann says that even though the firm has received lucrative buyout offers from larger Wall Street firms, it intends to stay independent. Bachmann's goal is to triple the number of Jones entrepreneurs (brokers) to 10,000 by 2004.

Sources: Richard Teitelbaum, "The Wal-Mart of Wall Street," *Fortune*, October 13, 1997, pp. 128–30; and Juan Carlos Perez, "Brio the Answer for Edward Jones," *PC Week*, October 14, 1996, pp. 37–39.

INVESTING IN BONDS

◄ **LEARNING GOAL 5**
Distinguish between short-term and long-term financing and between debt capital and equity capital.

For investors who desire the least possible risk, U.S. government bonds are a secure investment because they are backed by the full faith and credit of the federal government. Municipal bonds, also secure, are offered by local governments and often have advantages such as tax-free interest.

Two questions often bother first-time bond investors. The first is, if I purchase a corporate bond, do I have to hold it until the maturity date? No! You do not have to hold a bond until maturity. Bonds are bought and sold daily on major exchanges such as the New York Stock Exchange. However, if you sell your bond to another investor before its maturity date, you are not guaranteed to get the face value of the bond (usually $1,000). For example, if your bond does not have features (high interest rate, early maturity, etc.) that make it attractive to other investors, you may be forced to sell your bond at a *discount* (less than the face value). But if your bond is highly valued by other investors, you may be able to sell it at a *premium* (above face value). Bond prices generally fluctuate with current market interest rates; as interest rates go up, bond prices fall, and vice versa. Thus, like all investments, bonds have a degree of risk.

The second question is, How can I assess the investment risk of a particular bond issue? Standard & Poor's and Moody's Investors Service rate the level of risk of many corporate and government bonds (refer back to Figure 20.2). Naturally, the higher the market risk of one bond compared to other bonds, the higher the interest rate the issuer must offer to investors. Remember, investors have many options to consider, one of which is to buy stock. After the Progress Check, let's look at stock as an investment.

Progress Check

- What is the primary purpose of a stock exchange? Can you name the largest stock exchange in the United States?
- What does NASDAQ stand for? How does this exchange work?
- What role do Standard & Poor's and Moody's Investors Service play in bond markets?

► LEARNING GOAL 6
Identify and describe several sources of short-term financing.

► CONSIDER USING CRITICAL THINKING EXERCISE 20-2
Playing the Stock Market (**SCANS**)

► CONSIDER USING LECTURE ENHANCER 20-11
Trying to Predict the Market

► CONSIDER USING LECTURE ENHANCER 20-12
What Is a Bull Market?

growth stocks
Stocks of companies whose earnings are expected to grow faster than other stocks or the overall economy.

income stocks
Stocks that offer investors a high dividend.

blue chip stocks
Stocks of high-quality companies that pay regular dividends and generate consistent growth in the company's stock price.

penny stocks
Stocks that sell for less than $1.

INVESTING IN STOCKS AND MUTUAL FUNDS

Buying stock makes the investor an owner of the firm. Stock investments provide investors an opportunity to share in the success of emerging or expanding companies. In fact, since 1925 the average annual return on stocks has been 10 percent, the highest return of any popular investment. As owners, however, stockholders can also lose money if a company does not do well. It's up to investors to choose the stock investment that best fits their overall investment objectives.

According to investment analysts, the market price (and growth potential) of common stock depends heavily on the overall performance of the corporation in meeting its business objectives. If a company reaches its stated objectives, there are great opportunities for capital gains. For example, a $1,000 investment made in Microsoft stock when it first went public would be worth well over $1 million today. Stocks can be subject to a high degree of risk, however. Drops in the stock market in 1987 and 1997 certainly caught investors' attention. Later in this chapter, we will take a look at both of these market downturns.

Stock investors are often called bulls or bears depending on their perceptions of the market. *Bulls* are investors who believe that stock prices are going to rise, so they buy stock in anticipation of the increase. When overall stock prices are rising, the market is called a bull market. *Bears* are investors who expect stock prices to decline. Bears sell their stocks in anticipation of falling prices. When the prices of stocks decline steadily, the market is called a bear market.

Investors may select several different investment opportunities in stock. **Growth stocks**, for example, are stocks of corporations (often high-tech firms) whose earnings are expected to grow at a rate faster than other stocks in the market. While often considered speculative (very risky) the potential for growth is strong. Another option is **income stocks**, stocks that offer investors a rather high dividend yield on their investment. Public utilities are often considered good income stocks. The stock of high-quality companies such as Coca-Cola, Boeing, and Gillette are referred to as **blue chip stocks**. These stocks pay regular dividends and generate consistent growth in the company's stock price. Investors can also invest in a type of stock called a penny stock. **Penny stocks** are stocks that sell for less than $1. Such stocks frequently represent ownership in firms, such as mining or oil exploration companies, which compete in highly speculative industries. Penny stocks are considered very risky investments. Investors can also choose to invest in the stock of foreign companies. It's important to remember that we live in a global economy and not all investment

Reaching Beyond Our Borders

Going Shopping for Global Investments

Investing in stocks is a risky business. If even blue chip stocks are subject to market fluctuation, should investors consider incorporating international stocks or mutual funds into their portfolios? After all, the U.S. market is less than 40 percent of the total stock market value in the world. Sounds like global investing is a good option! Maybe, but keep in mind that if investing in American stocks is a risky business, investing in international stocks and mutual funds can be even riskier.

The following are tips from the pros on investing in international stocks and mutual funds. The advice is not foolproof, but it may help you in your hunt for that dream stock.

- Consider international stocks and mutual funds as a form of diversification or as downside protection for your account. Even though many economists and market analysts argue that markets are perfectly related, that's not always accurate. Even if the U.S. economy is lagging, another economy may be surging.
- Pick global stocks with solid value and an established track record. Choose companies with steady and uninterrupted sales gains that have a solid niche in the marketplace (e.g., Shell Oil, Nestlé, Siemens). International funds are generally available on a global,

regional, or country basis. Regional and country-based funds tend to be riskier than global funds.

- Be aware of risks such as currency fluctuations and political instability in international investing.
- Look into opportunities such as American depository receipts (ADRs) when investing in global markets. ADRs represent a set number of shares in a foreign company. An ADR certifies ownership held on deposit at a foreign branch of an American bank. This simplifies foreign investing by providing documentation and ensuring payments or dividends that might be hard for individual investors to track. ADRs can be purchased from brokers in the United States.

As more American investors realize the opportunity in international stocks, the demand for them will grow. It's important to remember that conducting research and understanding risk are the keys to long-term success in this volatile investment market.

Sources: Caitlin Mollison, "Playing the Global Game," *Ticker*, April 1997, pp. 61–63; "How to Map Out a Global Investment Strategy," *USA Today*, April 25, 1997, p. 5B; and James Anderson, "The Investor's Passport: ADRs Provide You Access to Companies Abroad," *Black Enterprise*, February 1997, pp. 58–61.

---

opportunities exist in the U.S. Read the box Reaching Beyond Our Borders to look into the challenging investment opportunities globally.

◄ CONSIDER USING LECTURE ENHANCER 20-13
Turning Cash Dividends into Stock

••• BUYING STOCK: MARKET AND LIMIT ORDERS •••

Investors that buy stock have more options for placing an order than investors buying and selling bonds. Stock investors, for example, can place a **market order**, which tells a broker to buy or to sell a stock immediately at the best price available. This type of order can be processed quickly, and the trade price can be given to the investor almost instantaneously. A **limit order** tells the broker to buy or to sell a particular stock at a specific price, if that price becomes available. Let's say, for example, that a stock is selling for $40 a share; you believe that the price will go up eventually but that it might drop a little before it goes higher. You could place a limit order at $36. The broker will buy the stock for you at $36 if the stock drops to that price. If the stock never falls to $36, the broker will not purchase it.

market order
Instructions to a broker to buy or sell a stock immediately at the best price available.

limit order
Instructions to a broker to buy or sell a particular stock at a specific price, if that price becomes available.

••• STOCK SPLITS •••

round lots
Purchases of 100 shares of stock at a time.

Companies and brokers prefer to have stock purchases conducted in **round lots**, that is, purchases of 100 shares at a time. The problem is that many investors cannot afford to buy 100 shares of a stock in companies that may be selling for perhaps $120 per share. Such high prices often induce companies to declare **stock splits**; that is, they issue two or more shares for every share of stock currently outstanding. For example, if Fiberrific stock were selling for $120 a share, Fiberrific could declare a two-for-one split. Investors who owned one share of Fiberrific would now own two shares; each share, however, would now be worth only $60 (one-half as much as before the split). As you can see, there is no change in the firm's ownership structure and no change in the investment's value after the stock split. Investors generally approve of stock splits because often the demand for the stock at $60 per share may be greater than the demand at $120 per share. Thus, the stock price may go up.[10]

stock splits
An action by a company that gives stockholders two or more shares of stock for each one they own.

One of the most popular means of investing is through mutual funds. Let's see why.

➤ **CONSIDER USING OT ACETATE 20-8**
How Stock Splits Work

••• INVESTING IN MUTUAL FUNDS •••

mutual fund
An organization that buys stocks and bonds and then sells shares in those securities to the public.

A **mutual fund** buys stocks and bonds and then sells shares in those securities to the public. Mutual fund managers have the expertise to pick what they consider to be the best stocks and bonds available. Investors can buy shares of the mutual funds and thus take part in the ownership of many different companies they could not afford to invest in individually. Thus, for a normally small fee, mutual funds provide professional investment management and help investors diversify. Today there are more than 9,000 mutual funds, which together control approximately $3 trillion of investors' money.[11]

Buying shares in a mutual fund is probably the best way for a small investor to get started. The funds available range from very conservative ones that invest only in government securities or secure corporate bonds to others that specialize in emerging high-tech firms, foreign companies, precious metals, and other investments with greater risk. Some mutual funds even invest exclusively in socially responsible ➤ P. 101 ◄ companies.[12] A stockbroker, financial planner, or banker can help you find the mutual fund that best fits your investment objectives. The *Morningstar Investor* newsletter is an excellent resource for evaluating mutual funds.

➤ **CONSIDER USING OT ACETATE 20-9**
Number of U.S. Households that Own Mutual Funds

One advantage of mutual funds is that you can buy most funds directly and save any fees. A true *no-load fund* is one that charges no commission to either buy or sell its shares. A *load fund* would charge a commission to investors to buy shares in the fund. It's important to check the costs involved in a mutual fund, such as any fees and charges imposed in the managing of a fund, because these can differ significantly.

Some funds, called *open-end funds,* will accept the investments of any interested investors. *Closed-end funds* offer a specific number of shares for investment; once a closed-end fund reaches its target number, no new investors are admitted.

➤ **CONSIDER USING LECTURE ENHANCER 20-14**
The Beardstown Ladies Investment Club

The key points to remember about mutual funds is that they offer small investors a way to spread the risk of stock ownership and a way to have their investments managed by a trained specialist for a nominal fee. Most financial advisors put mutual funds high on the list of recommended investments for beginning investors.

••• DIVERSIFYING INVESTMENTS •••

diversification
Buying several different investment alternatives to spread the risk of investing.

Diversification involves buying several different investment alternatives to spread the risk of investing. For example, an investor may put 20 percent of his or her money into growth stocks that have relatively high risk. Another 30 percent may be invested in conservative government bonds, 15 percent in income

Legal Briefcase

http://www.schwab.com/

All's Fair in Investment Markets— or Is It?

Some say one good idea is all it takes to make a fortune. Investing in such an idea can also be a path to financial security. Therefore, it's not surprising that the initial public offering (IPO) market is a hotbed of interest for individual investors looking to score big on new ideas and companies. Such enthusiasm has helped investment bankers such as Goldman Sachs raise millions of dollars in equity capital for emerging companies such as Netscape, Boston Chicken, and U.S. Robotics. Did these and other hot IPOs help individual investors realize that dream of scoring big? Not according to many experts who follow this market.

It seems the playing field is not quite level. Large institutional investors (mutual funds, pension funds, etc.) get the first slice—a rather large one—of the IPO pie. Wall Street syndicate managers at many large investment banking firms admit that institutions do get to buy as much as 60 to 80 percent of the shares of certain "hot" deals. Additionally, critics argue that the shares left over for small investors are often distributed according to internal politics and favoritism.

Institutional investors are also given more in-depth information than individual investors are given. Some

firms even provide elaborate "road shows" that promote the stock offering and disclose important information about the company and the deal. Small investors receive only the information in the prospectus, as required by law.

But help may be on the way. Discount broker Charles Schwab & Co. now offers its customers access to the IPOs of three leading investment banking firms. On-line broker E*Trade and Fidelity Brokerage also announced their smaller clients would be able to join the game. However, participation is limited to 10 percent of the new issues.

Small investors can take solace in a study by Prudential Securities that tracked IPOs from 1991 to 1997. Prudential found that while 74 percent of the IPOs beat the market the first week of trading, less than half outperformed the market a year later. Still, many observers feel that the IPO market, even with all its strengths and vast opportunities, is being distorted and is not serving all investors. You be the judge.

Sources: Anne Kates Smith and James M. Pethokoukis, "Looking for the Next Netscape? Dream On," *U.S. News & World Report,* September 22, 1997, pp. 71–73; and Charlie Vestner, "Letting In the Little Guy," *Individual Investor,* October 1997, pp. 28–30.

---

stocks, 20 percent in a mutual fund, and the rest placed in the bank for emergencies and possible other investment opportunities. By diversifying investments, the investor decreases the chance of losing everything. This type of investment strategy is often referred to as a *portfolio strategy.*

Stockbrokers and financial planners are trained to give advice about the portfolio that would best fit each client's financial objectives. However, the more investors read and study the market on their own, the higher the potential for gain. Individual investors, unfortunately, don't always have the same opportunities to buy stocks that institutional investors have. The Legal Briefcase box discusses this. It's also important for potential investors to be aware that some investments carry rather heavy risks. Let's look at several high-risk investments.

◄ CONSIDER USING OT ACETATE 20-10
Risks Associated with Investments

INVESTING IN HIGH-RISK INVESTMENTS

◄ LEARNING GOAL 7
Identify and describe several sources of long-term financing.

At a racetrack some bettors always pick the favorites; others like the long shots. The same thing is true in the investment market. Some investors think that high-rated corporate bonds are clearly the investment of choice; others want to take more market risk. Let's look at three risky investment options: junk bonds, buying on margin, and commodities.

••• INVESTING IN HIGH-RISK (JUNK) BONDS •••

junk bonds
High-risk, high-interest bonds.

> CONSIDER USING OT ACETATE
20-11
Buying Stock on Margin

Although bonds are generally considered relatively safe investments, some investors look for higher returns through riskier bonds called **junk bonds**. Standard & Poor's Investment Advisory Service and Moody's Investor Service consider junk bonds as non-investment-grade bonds because of their high risk and high default rates. Junk bonds rely on the firm's ability to pay investors interest based on the company's asset valuation remaining high and its cash flow staying strong.[13] Although the interest rates are attractive, if the company can't pay off the bond, the investor is left with a bond that isn't worth more than the paper it's written on; in other words junk.

••• BUYING STOCK ON MARGIN •••

buying on margin
Purchasing stocks by borrowing some of the purchase cost from the brokerage firm.

Buying on margin involves purchasing stocks by borrowing some of the purchase cost from the brokerage firm. The *margin* is the amount of money an investor must invest in the stock. The Board of Governors of the Federal Reserve System sets margin rates in the U.S. market. You can read about this in more detail in Chapter 21. Briefly, if the margin rate is 50 percent, an investor may borrow 50 percent of the stock's purchase price from a broker. Although buying on margin sounds like an easy way to buy stocks, the downside is that investors must repay the credit extended by the broker plus interest. Additionally, if the investor's account goes down in market value, the broker will issue a *margin call,* requiring the investor to come up with more money to cover the losses the stock has suffered. If the investor is unable to make the margin call, the broker can legally sell off shares of the investor's stock to reduce the broker's chance of loss. Margin calls can force the investor to repay a significant portion of the loss within days or even hours.

Try to imagine a 60,000-square-foot trading floor packed with traders yelling, pointing, and making undecipherable hand signals to each other. Welcome to the Chicago Board of Trade, where commodities such as corn, wheat, and soybeans are traded for delivery in the future.

••• INVESTING IN COMMODITIES •••

Commodities are high-risk investments for most investors. Investors willing to speculate in commodities hope to profit handsomely from the rise and fall of prices of items such as coffee, wheat, pork bellies, petroleum, and other arti-

cles of commerce (commodities) that are scheduled for delivery at a given (future) date. Trading in commodities demands much expertise. Small shifts in the prices of certain items can result in significant gains and losses. It's estimated, in fact, that 75 to 80 percent of the investors who speculate in commodities lose money in the long term.

Trading in commodities, however, can also be a vehicle for protecting businesspeople, farmers, and others from wide fluctuations in commodity prices and thus can be a very conservative investment strategy. A **commodity exchange** specializes in the buying and selling of precious metals and minerals (e.g., silver, foreign currencies, gasoline) and agricultural goods (e.g., wheat, cattle, sugar). The Chicago Board of Trade (CBOT), with its $182-million, 60,000-square-foot trading floor is the largest commodity exchange.[14] The CBOT is involved with a wide range of commodities, including corn, plywood, silver, gold, and U.S. Treasury bonds. The Chicago Mercantile Exchange is the second largest and deals in commodities such as cattle, pork bellies (bacon), potatoes, and various foreign currencies.

Commodity exchanges operate much like stock exchanges: members of the exchange meet on the exchange's floor to transact deals. Yet the appearance of a commodities exchange is quite different, and interesting to observe. All transactions for a specific commodity take place in a specific trading area, or "pit." Trades result from the meeting of a bid and offer in an open competition among exchange members. The bids and offers are made in a seemingly impossible-to-understand blend of voices, with all participants shouting at once. Surprisingly, the market is quite efficient.

Many companies use commodities markets to their advantage by dealing in the futures market. **Futures markets** involve the purchase and sale of goods for delivery sometime in the future. Take, for example, a farmer who has oats growing in the field. He or she is not sure what price the oats will sell for at harvest time. To be sure of a price, the farmer could sell the oats on the commodity floor for delivery in the future. The price is now fixed, and the farmer can plan his or her budget and expenses accordingly. On the other hand, as producers of Fiberrific, we are worried about the possibility of oat prices rising. If we buy the oats in the futures market, we know what we will have to pay and can plan accordingly. All of this is possible because of commodity exchanges.

commodity exchange
A securities exchange that specializes in the buying and selling of precious metals and minerals (e.g., silver, foreign currencies, gasoline) and agricultural goods (e.g., wheat, cattle, sugar).

futures markets
The purchase and sale of goods for delivery sometime in the future.

◄ CONSIDER USING LECTURE ENHANCER 20-15
The Futures Market Is Tricky Ground

Progress Check

- What is a stock split? Why do companies sometimes split their stock?
- What is a mutual fund? How do mutual funds benefit small investors?
- What is meant by *buying on margin*?
- Why would a restaurant chain be interested in the futures market?

···· ▬▬▬ ····

UNDERSTANDING INFORMATION FROM SECURITIES MARKETS

You can find a wealth of investment information in newspapers, in magazines, and on Web sites. Such information is useless, however, until you understand what it means. Look through *The Wall Street Journal, Barron's, USA Today,* and your local newspaper's business section; listen carefully to business reports on radio and TV for investment analysis and different viewpoints. Investing is an inexact science, and few people are consistently right in predicting future market movements. Every time someone sells a stock believing it will go up no further, someone else is buying it, believing it will go still higher. Read the

◄ LEARNING GOAL 8
Explain securities quotations listed in the financial section of a newspaper, and how the Dow Jones Averages affect the market.

◄ CONSIDER USING TM 150
Understanding Bond Quotations (Figure 20.6 on text page 612)

What's the best way for a new or novice investor to get started in building that envious portfolio? It starts with a commitment to education. Getting acquainted with publications such as *The Wall Street Journal, Barron's, Business Week,* and so forth, helps prepare you for the challenge of becoming the next Warren Buffett (America's most successful investor).

⌐   FIGURE **20.6**   ⌐
· · · ·
UNDERSTANDING BOND QUOTATIONS

following sections carefully and you will begin to understand investment information.

··· UNDERSTANDING BOND QUOTATIONS ···

Bonds, remember, are issued by corporations and governments. Government issues are covered in *The Wall Street Journal* in a table called Treasury Issues. These issues are traded on the over-the-counter market. The price is quoted as a percentage of the face value. The interest rate is often followed by an *s* for easier pronunciation. For example, 9 percent bonds due in 1999 are called 9s of 99.

Figure 20.6 gives a sample of bond quotes for corporations. Look at the quotes and note the variation in interest rates and maturity dates. The more you know about the bond market, the better prepared you will be to talk intelligently with investment counselors and brokers. You want to be sure that their advice is consistent with your best interests.

··· UNDERSTANDING STOCK QUOTATIONS ···

If you look in the Money & Investing section of *The Wall Street Journal,* you will see stock quotations from the New York Stock Exchange, the American Stock Exchange, and the NASDAQ over-the-counter markets. Look at the top of the columns and notice the headings. To understand the headings better, look carefully at Figure 20.7. (This example highlights the information on the New York and American Stock Exchanges.) Stocks are quoted in 16ths of a dollar, illustrated as fractional amounts. For example, a stock listed at $65\%_{16}$ is selling for $65.5625. (Both the NYSE and the NASDAQ plan to switch to decimals in January 2000.)[15] Preferred stocks are identified by the letters *pf* following the abbreviated company name. Corporations can have several different preferred stock issues.

CV means convertible bond.

Bonds	Cur Yld	Vol	High	Low	Close		Net Chg
LaQuin 10s02	cv	4	102	102	102	–	1 $^1/_4$
LearS 10s04	10.0	3	100	100	100	+	1 $^5/_8$
LearS 11$^1/_2$10	11.1	5	103 $^1/_2$	103 $^1/_2$	103$^1/_2$	–	1 $^1/_2$
LearS 11$^1/_4$15	10.8	2	104 $^1/_4$	104 $^1/_4$	104$^1/_4$	–	$^3/_4$
Leget 6$^1/_2$06	cv	36	103	102	102		. . .
LipGp 8$^5/_8$01	9.4	10	92 $^1/_8$	92 $^1/_8$	92$^1/_8$	–	1 $^7/_8$
LincFl 8$^1/_2$09	8.7	5	97 $^1/_2$	97 $^1/_2$	97$^1/_2$	–	1 $^3/_8$
LomN 7s11	cv	4	104	104	104		. . .
LonSI 11$^1/_4$12	11.7	5	100 $^3/_8$	100 $^3/_8$	100$^3/_8$	–	2
Loral 7$^1/_4$10	cv	2	121	121	121	–	$^1/_2$
Lorilld 6$^7/_8$05	7.6	62	90 $^7/_8$	90 $^3/_8$	90$^3/_8$		. . .
LouGs 9$^1/_4$07	9.2	10	101 $^1/_8$	101	101		. . .
Lowen 8$^1/_8$10	9.4	18	90	89	90	+	7
viLykes 7$^1/_2$99	. . .	35	19 $^1/_2$	18	18	–	1
viLykes 7$^1/_2$08	. . .	79	20 $^1/_2$	19 $^7/_8$	20$^1/_2$	+	$^7/_8$
viLykes 11s10	. . .	25	21	20 $^1/_2$	20$^1/_2$	–	$^1/_2$
MACOM 9$^1/_4$06	cv	30	101	99 $^1/_4$	99$^1/_4$	–	1 $^1/_4$

Five bonds were traded that day.

These Lowen bonds are due in 2010 and originally paid 8$^1/_8$%. The current yield is 9.4%.

This bond sold for a high of $900 and the low for the day was $890. It ended the day at $900, up $70 from the previous day.

Let's look at the columns and headings more closely. Moving from left to right, the stock quote tells us the following:

- The highest and lowest price the stock has sold for over the past 52 weeks.
- The abbreviated company name and the company's stock symbol.
- The last dividend paid per share.
- The stock's dividend yield (the return expected).
- The price/earnings (P/E) ratio is the price of the stock divided by the firm's per share earnings.
- The number of shares traded that day in 100s.
- The stock's high, low, and closing price for the day.
- The net change in the stock's price from the previous day.

Look down the columns and find the stock that's had the biggest price change over the past 52 weeks, the stock that pays the highest dividend, and the stock that has the highest price/earnings ratio. The more you look through the figures the more sense they begin to make. You might want to build a hypothetical portfolio of stocks and track how they perform over the next six months. (See the Taking It to the Net exercise at the end of this chapter.)

◄ CONSIDER USING CRITICAL THINKING EXERCISE 20-3
Understanding Stock Quotations
(SCANS)

◄ CONSIDER USING TM 151
Understanding Stock Quotations
(Figure 20.7 on text page 613)

FIGURE 20.7
• • • •
UNDERSTANDING STOCK QUOTATIONS

Hi	Lo	Stock	Sym	Div	Yld %	P/E	Vol 100s	Hi	Lo	Close	Net Chg
$33^5/_8$	$12^5/_8$	Galoob Toys	GAL	...		33	5783	$15^1/_4$	$14^5/_8$	$14^{15}/_{16}$	$+^1/_4$
$106^{11}/_{16}$	69	Gannett	CGI	1.52f	1.4	15	2823	$106^7/_8$	$105^7/_{14}$	$106^7/_8$	$+^{13}/_{16}$
$53^7/_{16}$	26	Gap Inc.	GPS	.30	.6	30	9018	$51^1/_8$	$49^3/_4$	$50^{11}/_{16}$	$+^1/_4$
$38^3/_4$	$14^5/_8$	GardnrDenvr	GDI	...		16	359	$34^1/_8$	$33^{11}/_{16}$	$33^{11}/_{16}$	$-^1/_4$
$46^1/_4$	$22^5/_{16}$	Gateway 2000	GTW	...		19	8946	$33^1/_2$	$32^{11}/_{16}$	$32^7/_8$	$-^3/_8$
$26^1/_2$	$18^3/_4$	GaylrdEntr	GET	.40	1.5	14	2795	26	$25^7/_8$	26	$+^1/_{16}$
31	$13^5/_8$	GenCorp	GY	60	2.1	7	884	$28^7/_8$	$27^5/_8$	28	$-^1/_4$
$59^1/_4$	$52^5/_8$	Genantech	GNE	...		64	449	$58^3/_8$	$57^{11}/_{16}$	$57^{11}/_{16}$	$-^1/_4$
$27^8/_{16}$	$20^3/_8$	GenAmlov	GAM	2.96	0.8		223	$27^1/_2$	$27^1/_8$	$27^1/_2$	...
$36^1/_4$	$20^3/_8$	GenChl	GCN	...			263	36	$35^3/_4$	$35^{11}/_{16}$	$-^1/_4$
$33^5/_8$	$18^3/_8$	GenChemCp	GCG	.20	.6	12	702	31	$30^7/_8$	31	$+^1/_4$
$32^1/_8$	20	GenCigar	MPP	...			499	28	$27^7/_{16}$	$27^3/_8$	$+^1/_4$
$12^3/_8$	$5^3/_8$	GenData	GDC	...		dd	3362	$6^3/_{16}$	$6^1/_{14}$	$6^1/_{16}$	$-^1/_4$
$91^1/_2$	$63^1/_8$	GenDynam	GD	1.64	1.9	1.9	898	$88^3/_{16}$	$88^5/_8$	$86^{11}/_{16}$	$-1^{11}/_{16}$
$74^5/_8$	$45^1/_8$	GenElec	GE	1.04	1.5	30	33297	$69^7/_8$	$67^3/_4$	$69^1/_{16}$	$+^3/_4$
$36^1/_8$	$23^7/_8$	GenGrowProp	GGP	1.80	4.9	10	239	37	$36^1/_4$	37	$+^7/_8$
$4^5/_8$	$2^3/_8$	GenHost	GH	stk	...	dd	143	$3^1/_4$	$3^1/_2$	$3^1/_2$	...
$10^7/_8$	$8^3/_8$	GenHouse	GHW	.32	3.4	29	157	$9^1/_4$	$9^3/_8$	$9^7/_{16}$	$-^7/_{16}$
$71^1/_2$	$56^7/_8$	GenMills	GIS	2.12	3.1	23	5425	$69^1/_4$	$67^3/_4$	$69^1/_4$	$+1^5/_{16}$
$28^1/_2$	$25^{13}/_{16}$	GenMotTOPRS	D	68p	...		18	$26^1/_2$	$25^1/_{16}$	$26^3/_8$	$+^1/_4$
30	$27^1/_2$	GenMotTOPRS	G	78p	...		14	$29^7/_{16}$	$29^3/_8$	$29^7/_{16}$	$+^1/_4$
$69^3/_4$	$46^7/_8$	GenMotor	GM	2.00	3.0	9	25891	$68^{11}/_{16}$	66	$66^{11}/_{16}$	$+^{11}/_{16}$
$67^7/_8$	49	GenMotor H	GMH	1.00	1.5	20	4374	$66^1/_8$	$65^{11}/_{16}$	$65^1/_{16}$	$+^1/_8$
27	$25^3/_4$	GenMotor Pf		1.98	7.4		16	$26^{15}/_{16}$	$26^{11}/_{16}$	$26^{15}/_{16}$	$+^3/_4$
$29^1/_4$	$27^3/_8$	GenMotor PfG		2.28	7.8		5	$29^1/_8$	$29^1/_8$	$29^1/_8$	$-^1/_8$
$27^7/_8$	$26^1/_4$	GenMotor PfQ		2.28	8.4		418	$27^1/_8$	$26^{11}/_{16}$	27	$+^1/_{16}$

High and low price for last 52 weeks.

Abbreviated name of company.

General Dynamics pays a dividend of $1.64 per share.

Pf stands for preferred.

Price of the Gap stock is 30 times its earnings.

70,200 shares of this stock traded today.

General Electric went up $.75 since the previous day's close.

General Mills's highest price was $69^1/_4$. The lowest price was $67^3/_4$. It was up $1^5/_{16}$ from the previous day's close.

This stock yields a 7.8% dividend.

••• UNDERSTANDING MUTUAL FUND QUOTATIONS •••

Remember, one way to get expert investment advice and diversify your investments at a minimum cost is to buy into mutual funds. Look up the listing of mutual funds in *The Wall Street Journal* (see Figure 20.8). You will see that many different companies offer mutual funds. The various funds offer many alternatives to meet investors' objectives. For example, the AIM mutual fund listed in Figure 20.8 highlights many different options. You can learn about the objectives of the various funds by contacting a broker or contacting the fund directly by phone or through its Web page. Business publications can also guide you to free information from various mutual funds.

> **CONSIDER USING TM 152**
> Understanding Mutual Fund Quotations
> (Figure 20.8 on text page 614)

As you look across the columns in the mutual fund quotations, the information is rather simple to understand. The fund's name is in the first column, followed by the fund's net asset value (NAV). The net asset value is the market value of the mutual fund's portfolio divided by the number of shares it has outstanding. (If the fund is a no-load fund, the NAV is the price per share of a mutual fund.) The next column lists the sale price (the net asset value plus charges and fees). The last column displays the net change in the NAV from the previous day's trading. Many mutual funds, remember, are no-load, meaning there is no cost to buy into the fund. It's also simple to change your investment objectives with mutual funds. Switching your money, for example, from a bond fund to a stock fund and back is generally no more difficult than calling an 800 number. Mutual funds are a great way to begin investing to meet your financial objectives.

FIGURE 20.8
••••
UNDERSTANDING
MUTUAL FUND
QUOTATIONS

| | Inv Obj | NAV | Offer Price | NAV Chg | Total Return | | |
					YTD	13 wks	3 yrs
AIM Funds:							
AdlGV p	BST	9.63	9.73		+0.1	+0.2	NS ..
Agrsv p	SML	24.43	25.85	−0.09	−0.1	−1.2	+25.2 A
BalB t	S & B	15.30	15.30	−0.04	−4.2	+0.3	NS ..
Chart p	G & I	8.73	9.24	−0.03	−2.7	0.0	+7.0 D
Const p	CAP	16.57	17.53	−0.16	−5.3	−2.9	+16.8 A
BalA p	S & B	15.29	16.05	−0.05	−3.9	+0.5	+12.3 A
GoScA p	BND	9.38	9.85	+0.01	−2.8k	+0.8k	+6.2k E
GrthA p	GRO	10.29	10.89	−0.09	−9.1	−5.2	+2.1 E
GrthB t	GRO	10.22	10.22	−0.09	−9.6	−5.5	NS ..
HYldA p	BHI	9.34	9.81	. . .	−2.0k	−0.7k	+15.4k B
HYldB t	BHI	9.33	9.33	. . .	−2.4k	−1.0k	NS ..
IncoA p	BND	7.49	7.86	. . .	−7.6k	−0.7k	+8.8k B
IntlE p	ITL	13.02	13.78	−0.07	−0.2	+2.4	NS ..
LimM p	BST	9.96	10.06	+0.01	+0.5	+0.8	+5.5 C
MunlA p	GLM	8.16	8.57	+0.02	−2.2k	+2.2k	+8.4k A
SumIt	GRO	9.14	NA	−0.08	−5.8	−2.2	+7.7 C
TeCt p	SSM	10.72	11.25	+0.03	−2.2k	+1.9k	+7.9k B
TF Int	IDM	10.65	10.76	+0.02	−1.0k	+1.6k	+7.1k B
UtllA p	SEC	12.35	13.07	+0.01	−10.1k	−2.3k	+8.9k C
UtllB t	SEC	12.35	12.35	+0.01	−10.4k	−2.5k	NS ..
ValuA p	GRO	20.83	22.04	−0.11	0.0	−0.5	+17.5 A
ValuB t	GRO	20.74	20.74	−0.12	−0.4	−0.8	NS ..
Weing p	GRO	16.65	17.62	−0.12	−2.9	−1.1	+4.9 E

Price to buy one share.

Investment objective of the fund. GRO means growth fund. (Other mutual fund objective categories can be found in *The Wall Street Journal*.)

Change in NAV (net asset value) from previous day.

Return on investment year-to-date, 13 weeks, and over 3-year periods.

NAV refers to net asset value of the fund.

••• THE DOW JONES AVERAGES •••

When you listen to news reports, you often hear announcers say things like "The Dow Industrials are up 20 points today in active trading." What's going on? The **Dow Jones Industrial Average** is the average cost of 30 selected industrial stocks, used to give an indication of the direction (up or down) of the stock market over time. A man named Charles Dow began the practice of measuring stock averages in 1884 when he added together the prices of 11 important stocks and divided the total by 11 to get an average. The Dow was broadened in 1982 to include 30 stocks.

New stocks are substituted on the Dow when deemed appropriate. For example, the list was changed in 1991 by adding McDonald's to reflect the increase in the service sector.[16] In 1997 the list was again altered with Hewlett-Packard, Johnson & Johnson, Wal-Mart, and insurance giant Travelers Group replacing Texaco, Woolworth, Bethlehem Steel, and Westinghouse.[17] The 30 stocks in the Dow Jones Industrial Average include such notables as Du Pont, General Electric, IBM, Sears, Philip Morris, and Coca-Cola (see Figure 20.9). Critics argue that if the purpose of the Dow is to give an indication of the direction of the broader market over time, the 30-company sample is too small to get a good statistical representation. Many investors and market analysts therefore prefer to follow stock indexes like the Standard & Poor's 500, which tracks the performance of 400 industrial, 40 financial, 40 utility, and 20 transportation stocks.

Dow Jones Industrial Average
The average cost of 30 selected industrial stocks, used to give an indication of the direction (up or down) of the stock market over time.

◄ CONSIDER USING SUPPLEMENTAL CASE 20-2
Investing an Inheritance (SCANS)

◄ CONSIDER USING OT ACETATE 20-12
The Original 12 Dow Stocks

◄ CONSIDER USING OT ACETATE 20-13
The Down Days of the Dow

Critical Thinking

What form of investment seems most appropriate to your needs now? How might your objectives and needs change over time? Would investing other people's money be an interesting career to pursue? What problems might stockbrokers or managers of mutual funds face on their jobs?

••• THE STOCK MARKET SLIDES OF 1987 AND 1997 •••

On October 19, 1987, the stock market suffered the largest one-day drop in its history. The Dow Jones Industrial Average fell 508 points. In just six and one-half hours of trading, a half-trillion dollars vanished before bewildered investors' eyes.[18] How much was a half-trillion dollars worth in 1987? According to economist Paul Erdman, "A half-trillion dollars was more than all the people of Central America plus most of the inhabitants of Eastern Europe earned in an entire year." One brokerage firm (as the joke goes) told its clients to start investing half their money in bonds and the other half in canned goods. The crash

◄ CONSIDER USING LECTURE ENHANCER 20-16
The Crash of 1929

◄ CONSIDER USING TM 153
Dow Jones 30 Industrial Stocks
(Figure 20.9 on text page 615)

Alcoa	Exxon	Merck
Allied Signal	General Electric	3M Corp.
American Express	General Motors	Philip Morris
AT&T	Goodyear	Procter & Gamble
Boeing	Hewlett-Packard	Sears Roebuck
Caterpillar	IBM	Travelers
Chevron	International Paper	Union Carbide
Coca-Cola	Johnson & Johnson	United Technologies
Du Pont	J. P. Morgan	Walt Disney
Eastman Kodak	McDonald's	Wal-Mart

FIGURE **20.9**
••••
THE DOW JONES 30 INDUSTRIAL STOCKS

prompted billionaire H. Ross Perot to caution, "It was God tapping us on the shoulder and warning us to get our act together before we get the big shock."

What caused the market turmoil of 1987? Ask a dozen financial analysts and you might get a dozen different responses. However, many analysts attest that "program trading" was a big cause of stock prices falling to the disastrous levels they reached. In **program trading**, investors give their computers instructions to automatically sell if the price of their stock dips to a certain point to avoid potential losses. On Black Monday (as October 19, 1987, is called), the computers became trigger-happy and sell orders caused many stocks to fall to unbelievable depths.

On October 27, 1997, investors felt the fury of the market once again. The Dow fell 554 points, primarily due to fears of impending economic problems in Asian markets. Analysts believe that the market could have fallen even further had it not been for rules adopted in the wake of the crash of 1987.[19] The 1997 plunge was, in fact, the first real test of the market's new "circuit breakers." Under market rules, if the market fell 350 points, the circuit breakers would kick in and halt trading for half an hour to give investors a chance to assess the situation. Since the 1997 sell-off, U.S. stock exchanges have agreed to halt trading for the day if the Dow Jones Industrial average drops 20 percent.[20]

We can learn a lesson from the market slides of 1987 and 1997. What goes up can also come down. It's also important to remember that we live in a global market today and that all nations' economies and markets are tied together. As the crisis in Asia sent Indonesia, Thailand, and South Korea searching for assistance from the International Monetary Fund, and sent Hong Kong and Japanese stocks plunging, U.S. businesses reevaluated their profit potential.[21] The situation in Asia bears continuous watching and could have a huge effect on global markets as we approach the new millennium.

The lessons you can learn are about the importance of diversifying your investments and understanding the risks of investing with borrowed money that may have to be repaid quickly when stock prices tumble. Taking a long-term perspective is also wise. The market recovered nicely after the 1987 crash and swept back upward shortly after the fall in 1997. However, it's critical for you to know that there's no such thing as easy money or a "sure thing." Investing is a challenging and interesting field that's always changing. If you carefully research companies and industries, keep up with the news, and make use of investment resources such as newspapers, magazines, newsletters, the Internet, and TV programs, the payoff can be highly rewarding. You may want to refer to this chapter again when you read about personal finance in Chapter 22.

program trading
Giving instructions to computers to automatically sell if the price of a stock dips to a certain point to avoid potential losses.

 Progress Check

- What exactly does the Dow Jones Industrial Average measure? Why is it so important?

- Explain program trading and the problems it can create.

SUMMARY
• • • • •

1. Examine the functions of securities markets and investment bankers.

1. Securities markets provide opportunities for businesses and investors.
   - ***What opportunities are provided to businesses and individual investors by securities markets?***
   Businesses are able to raise much-needed capital to help finance major needs of the firm. Individual investors can share in the success and growth of emerging firms by having the opportunity of investing in the firm.
   - ***What role do investment bankers play in securities markets?***
   Investment bankers are specialists who assist in the issue and sale of new securities.

2. Companies can raise capital by debt financing, which involves issuing bonds.

   • ***What are the advantages and disadvantages of issuing bonds?***
   The advantages of issuing bonds include the following: (1) Management retains control since bondholders cannot vote; (2) interest paid on bonds is tax-deductible; and (3) bonds are only a temporary source of finance, and after they are paid off the debt is eliminated. The disadvantages of bonds include the following: (1) Because bonds are an increased debt, they may affect the market's perception of the company adversely, (2) interest on bonds must be paid, and (3) the face value must be repaid on the maturity date.

   • ***Are there different types of bonds?***
   Yes. There are unsecured (debenture) and secured bonds. Unsecured bonds are not supported by collateral, whereas secured bonds are backed by tangible assets such as mortgages, stock, and equipment.

2. Compare the advantages and disadvantages of issuing bonds, and identify the classes and features of bonds.

3. Companies can also raise capital by equity financing, which involves selling stock.

   • ***What are the advantages and disadvantages of selling stock?***
   The advantages of selling stock include the following: (1) The stock price never has to be repaid since stockholders are owners in the company; (2) there is no legal obligation to pay dividends; and (3) no debt is incurred, so the company is financially stronger. The disadvantages are the following: (1) Stockholders become owners of the firm and can affect its management by voting for the board of directors, (2) it is more costly to pay dividends since they are paid after taxes, and (3) managers may be tempted to make stockholders happy in the short term rather than plan for long-term needs.

   • ***What are the differences between common and preferred stock?***
   Common stockholders have voting rights in the company. Preferred stockholders have no voting rights. In exchange for voting privileges, preferred stocks offer a fixed dividend that must be paid in full before common stockholders receive a dividend.

3. Compare the advantages and disadvantages of issuing stock, and outline the differences between common and preferred stock.

4. Stock exchanges afford investors the opportunity of investing in securities markets through the different investment options that are offered.

   • ***What is a stock exchange?***
   An organization whose members can buy and sell securities.

   • ***What are the different exchanges?***
   There are stock exchanges all over the world. The largest U.S. exchange is the New York Stock Exchange (NYSE). It and the American Stock Exchange (ASE) together are known as national exchanges because they handle stock of companies all over the country. In addition, there are several regional exchanges that deal primarily with companies in their own areas.

   • ***What is the over-the-counter (OTC) market?***
   OTC is a system for exchanging stocks not listed on the national exchanges. It also handles bonds issued by city and state governments.

   • ***How do investors normally make purchases in securities markets?***
   Investors generally purchase investments through market intermediaries called stockbrokers, who provide many different services. However, on-line investing is also becoming very popular.

   • ***What are the criteria for selecting investments?***
   Investments should be evaluated with regard to (1) risk, (2) yield, (3) duration, (4) liquidity, and (5) tax consequences.

4. Identify the various stock exchanges and describe how to invest in securities markets and choose among different investment strategies.

- *How are securities exchanges regulated?*

The Securities and Exchange Commission (SEC) is responsible for regulating securities exchanges.

- *What is insider trading?*

Insider trading involves the use of information or knowledge that individuals gain through their position that allows them to benefit unfairly from fluctuations in security prices.

5. Analyze the opportunities bonds offer as investments.

5. Bonds present opportunities for investors.

- *What is the difference between a bond selling at a discount and a bond selling at a premium?*

A bond selling at a premium is a bond that can be sold in securities markets at a price above its face value. A bond selling at a discount is a bond that can be sold in securities markets but at a price below its face value.

6. Explain the opportunities stocks and mutual funds offer as investments, and the advantages of diversifying investments.

6. Stocks and mutual funds present opportunities for investors to enhance their financial position.

- *What is a market order?*

A market order tells a broker to buy or to sell a security immediately at the best price available. A limit order tells the broker to buy or sell at a specific price if the stock reaches that price.

- *What does it mean when a stock splits?*

When a stock splits, stockholders receive two or more shares for each share they own. Each share is then worth half or less of the original share. Therefore, while the number of the shares increases, the total value of the stockholders' holdings stays the same. The lower price per share may increase demand for the stock.

- *How can mutual funds help individuals diversify their investments?*

A mutual fund is an organization that buys stocks and bonds and then sells shares in those securities to the public. Individuals who buy shares in a mutual fund are able to invest in many different companies they could not afford to invest in otherwise.

- *What is diversification?*

Diversification means buying several different types of investments (government bonds, corporate bonds, preferred stock, common stock, etc.) with different degrees of risk. The purpose is to reduce the overall risk an investor would assume by just investing in one type of security.

7. Discuss the high risk involved in junk bonds, buying stock on margin, and commodities.

7. Other types of speculative investments are available for investors seeking large returns on their investments.

- *What is a junk bond?*

Junk bonds are high-risk, high-interest bonds that speculative investors often find attractive.

- *What does buying on margin mean?*

It means that the investor borrows up to 50 percent of the cost of the stock from the broker so he or she can get more shares.

- *What are commodity exchanges?*

Commodity exchanges specialize in the buying and selling of precious metals and minerals (e.g., silver, oil) and agricultural goods (e.g., wheat, cattle, sugar).

8. Explain securities quotations listed in the financial section of a newspaper, and how the Dow Jones averages affect the market.

8. Security quotations and Dow Jones Averages are listed daily in newspapers.

- *What information do stock quotations give you?*

The stock quotations give you all kinds of information: the highest price in the last 52 weeks; the lowest price; the dividend yield; the price/earnings ratio; the total shares traded that day; and the high, low, close, and net change in price from the previous day. The bond quotations give you information regarding trading bonds in securities markets, as do quotations concerning mutual funds.

- *What is the Dow Jones Industrial Average?*

The Dow Jones Industrial Average is the average price of 30 specific stocks traded on the New York Stock Exchange.

KEY TERMS

blue chip stocks 606
bond 593
buying on margin 610
callable bond 596
commodity exchange 611
common stock 599
convertible bond 596
cumulative preferred stock 598
debenture bonds 608
diversification 608
dividends 597
Dow Jones Industrial Average 615
futures markets 611
growth stocks 606
income stocks 606

insider trading 601
institutional investors 592
interest 593
investment bankers 592
junk bonds 610
limit order 607
market order 607
maturity date 594
mutual fund 608
National Association of Securities Dealers Automated Quotation (NASDAQ) 600
over-the-counter (OTC) market 600
par value 597

penny stocks 606
preemptive right 599
preferred stock 598
principal 594
program trading 616
prospectus 601
round lots 608
Securities and Exchange Commission (SEC) 601
sinking fund 596
stockbroker 602
stock certificate 597
stock exchange 599
stock splits 608
stocks 597

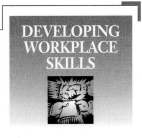

DEVELOPING WORKPLACE SKILLS

1. Write the Education Department of *The Wall Street Journal,* 200 Burnett Road, Chicopee, MA 01020, and request the Student Edition booklet. Look through it at your leisure. It explains all the columns and charts used in investment markets. Discuss this edition with your class.

2. Read *The Wall Street Journal* or *Investor's Business Daily* each day for two weeks and then select a sample stock portfolio. Track the stocks in your portfolio and use a computer to graphically display the trends of each one on a weekly basis. See how market trends and information affect your stocks and write out a brief explanation of why the stock was affected.

3. See if anyone is interested in setting up an investment game in your class. Each student should choose one stock (100 shares) and one mutual fund (100 fund shares). Record each student's selections and the corresponding prices on a chart. In six weeks, look up and chart the prices again. The student with the largest percentage gain would win.

4. Analyze the risk and opportunities of investing in today's market. Prepare a brief written analysis of stocks, bonds, and mutual funds. Then imagine that a distant relative gives you $10,000. Since you don't need additional funds for college at the moment, you can invest the entire $10,000. Plan how to invest your money. Name the investments you chose and explain why you chose them.

5. Many businesses in the late 1990s have tried to raise capital by offering new stock offerings (called IPOs). Go to the library or use the Internet to find two IPOs that have been offered during the past year. Track the performance of each IPO from its introduction to its present price.

TAKING IT TO THE NET

Purpose

To experience investing in the stock market.

Exercise

One of the safest ways to learn about trading stocks is to invest with "virtual" money (the modern name for play money). Go to InvestSmart Stock Game (http://library.advanced.org/10326/market_simulation/index.html). Here you can buy virtual stock on the New York Stock Exchange (NYSE), NASDAQ, or the American Stock Exchange (AMEX). The stock quotes used are actual data from the exchange, delayed 20 minutes because of SEC regulations. You will start out with a virtual $100,000 in your cash account.

1. Research companies and decide which stocks you want to buy or sell. We suggest that you invest in no more than five stocks and that you choose companies in different industries. There will be $15 to $30 commission for every transaction, depending on which brokerage firm you use.

2. You may sign up for this game more than once by entering a different user name each time. That way, you can trade different stocks in each account to test out various investing strategies. A ranking of all the players is generated daily. This ranking will show who can build up stock portfolios with the greatest value.

Practicing Management Decisions

CASE

• • • • • •

SURVIVAL IS THE NAME OF THE GAME

• • • • • •

Carlos Galendez had big dreams but very little money. He had worked more than 10 years as a dishwasher and then as a cook for a major restaurant. Finally, his dream to save enough money to start his own Mexican restaurant came true. Galendez opened his restaurant, Casa de Carlos, with a guaranteed loan from the Small Business Administration. His old family recipes and appealing Hispanic decor helped the business gain immediate success. He repaid his small-business loan within 14 months and immediately opened a second, and then a third, location. Casa de Carlos became one of the largest Mexican restaurant chains in the nation.

Galendez decided the company needed to go public to help finance a nationwide expansion. He believed that continued growth was beneficial to the company, and that offering ownership was the way to bring in loyal investors. Nevertheless, he wanted to make certain his family maintained a controlling interest in the firm's stock. Therefore, in its initial public offering, Casa de Carlos offered to sell only 40 percent of the company's available shares to investors. The Galendez family kept control of the remaining 60 percent.

As the public's craving for Mexican food grew, so did the fortunes of Casa de Carlos, Inc. Heading into the 1990s, the company enjoyed the position of being light on debt and heavy on cash. But the firm's debt position changed when it bought out Captain Al's Seafood Restaurants and, three years later, expanded into full-service wholesale distribution of seafood products with the purchase of Ancient Mariner Wholesalers. The firm's debt increased, but the price of its stock was up and all its business operations were booming.

Then tragedy struck the firm when Carlos Galendez died suddenly from a heart attack. His oldest child, Maria, was selected to take control as chief executive officer. Maria Galendez had learned the business from her father, who had taught her to keep an eye out for opportunities that seemed fiscally responsible. Even so, the fortunes of the firm began to shift. Two major competitors were taking market share from Casa de Carlos, and the seafood venture began to flounder (pun intended). Also, consumer shifts in eating habits and a slight fear of a recession encouraged consumers to spend less, causing some severe cash problems. Maria Galendez had to decide how to get the funds the firm needed for improvements and other expenses. Banks wouldn't expand the firm's credit line, so she considered the possibility of a bond or stock offering to raise capital.

Decision Questions

1. What advantages do bonds offer a company such as Casa de Carlos? What disadvantages do bonds impose?
2. What would be the advantages and disadvantages of the company's offering new stock to investors?
3. Are any other options available to Maria Galendez?
4. What choice would you make and why?

The average small company never gets involved with stocks and bonds. It has to raise money through loans and from other means. Eventually, however, some small companies become bigger, and that's the time when they may want to sell stocks or bonds to raise large amounts of money for growth and expansion.

A bond is like a corporate IOU. The bond certificate is the paper that spells out the terms of the agreement. It states when the bond will be paid, what the interest rate is, and the principal. Most bonds come in $1,000 denominations. One advantage for a company selling bonds rather than stocks is that bondholders do not get a vote in running the company. Furthermore, the interest paid to bondholders is tax deductible. If interest rates are not too high, therefore, bonds are a good way to raise money. However, bonds increase debt, and that doesn't look good on financial statements. Moreover, bonds are a legal obligation; that is, you have to pay the money back. As far as investors are concerned, they would prefer a secured bond, one that is backed by some collateral such as securities, real estate, and equipment. Unsecured bonds are called debentures and are usually issued by financially secure firms such as Xerox.

If you want maximum security in a bond, buy those sold by the U.S. government. Why? The federal government is unlikely to go bankrupt.

In determining when to buy, it's important to recognize that there are favorable and unfavorable times to purchase bonds. The best time to buy bonds is when interest rates are high and falling. Bond prices rise when interest rates fall. It is bad, therefore, to buy bonds when interest rates are low and rising. The bond price will fall in that case. Junk bonds promise high interest rates, but the risk assumed by the buyer is higher also.

Companies may prefer to raise money by selling stock. Stock doesn't pay interest; it pays dividends (some share of profits). The advantage of selling stock is that the money never has to be repaid. After all, the holders of the stock are the owners of the firm. They don't have to pay themselves anything. Furthermore, there is no legal

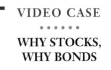

VIDEO CASE

• • • • • •

WHY STOCKS, WHY BONDS

demand that dividends be paid and many companies do not. Profits not paid to stockholders in the form of dividends are called retained earnings.

Common stock is, as it sounds, the most common form sold. Such stock provides its owners with voting rights with respect to certain issues affecting the company. Preferred stock carries no voting right, but the owners have first rights to any dividends the company pays. Generally, owners of common stock make more money in the long run than people who buy bonds—a lot more.

If you are interested in buying stocks, you may want to buy from a mutual fund. A mutual fund buys stock in a variety of companies and then sells shares of those holdings to the public. You get the advantage of a diversified group of stocks and the expertise of those who buy them

The stock market was a great invention because it made it possible for people to invest in companies and it made it easier for companies to raise money. As companies prosper and grow, they hire more people and pay more taxes to the government. They also create wealth for their owners. And since it is relatively easy to become an owner (stockholder), it should be relatively easy to become wealthy. You just have to pick the right stock in the right company. Maybe it's not so easy after all.

Discussion Questions

1. As an investor, what do you see as the advantages of buying stocks versus bonds? What is an easy way to diversify your risk?
2. There are mutual funds that buy both stocks and bonds. What would be the advantages and disadvantages of investing your money in such a fund?
3. Imagine that you are the owner of a small firm and you need to raise money to expand. Which would you prefer to offer first: bonds or stock? Why?
4. People often say that bonds are a safer investment than stock. Do you agree? Why?

Understanding Money and Financial Institutions

Chapter

21

LEARNING GOALS

*After you have read and studied this chapter,
you should be able to*

1 Explain what money is and how its value is determined.

2 Describe how the Federal Reserve controls the money supply.

3 Trace the history of banking and the Federal Reserve System.

4 Classify the various institutions in the U.S. banking system.

5 Explain the importance of the Federal Deposit Insurance Corporation and other organizations that guarantee funds.

6 Weigh the future of the U.S. banking system.

7 Evaluate the role and importance of international banking and the role of the World Bank and the International Monetary Fund.

http://www.bog.frb.fed.us/

PROFILE

Alan Greenspan, Chairman of the Federal Reserve

Alan Greenspan was born in New York, the only son of Herbert (a broker) and Rose Greenspan. He went to George Washington High School, later studied music at Juilliard, and played the clarinet for a year or so in a jazz band.

When music's attraction declined, Greenspan went to New York University, where he majored in economics. He received his degree summa cum laude in 1948. He went on to get his MA in economics at NYU and started doctoral studies under Arthur Burns at Columbia. Arthur Burns later became chairman of the Federal Reserve Board.

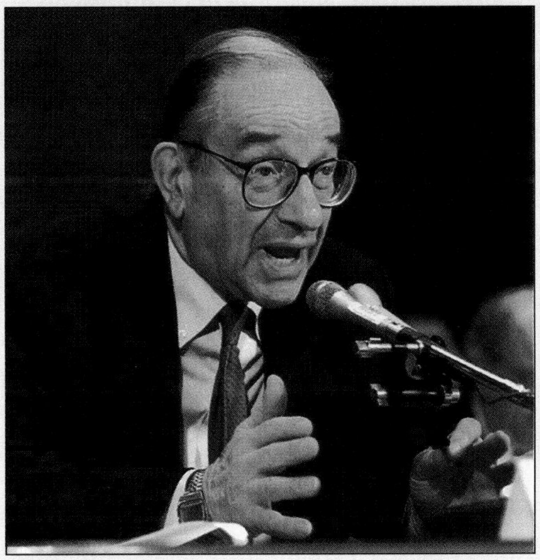

Greenspan began work as an economist for the Conference Board, a nonprofit research group. Later he started his own consulting firm. He went on to teach economics at NYU for a couple of years; the school granted him a doctorate later. His firm, Townsend-Greenspan, provided research, forecasts, and other economic consulting services to major firms. He also devoted his energies to public service and began a distinguished career in government that included service for five presidents.

As one of President Richard Nixon's top economic aides, Greenspan worked on several economic task forces and served as an informal advisor. As chairman of the Council of Economic Advisors under President Gerald Ford, he became an intense inflation fighter. He also argued that government spending must be cut. That's one reason why President Ronald Reagan chose him to be chairman of the Federal Reserve System (the Fed). In 1991, President George Bush reappointed Greenspan to another term, citing his success in fighting inflation and leading the economic recovery from the recession of 1990. President Bill Clinton retained him for much the same reason.

Dr. Greenspan has occupied one of the most powerful positions in the country for the past 10 years. *Fortune* magazine says that "they've been ten of the best years in the history of monetary policy." As chairman of the Federal Reserve, Greenspan has control over the nation's money supply ➢ P. 62 ➣. Price stability is his most important goal. People were watching Greenspan during all of 1997 to see if he would raise interest rates to hold down growth and inflationary ➢ P. 61 ➣ pressures. The stock market reached record highs and the unemployment rate reached record lows, but Greenspan held fast and didn't raise rates. In fact, Greenspan began talking about deflation ➢ P. 61 ➣ late in 1997. Many people will be watching Greenspan in the coming years to see if he can maintain an economy with modest growth and low inflation. If he does, he will go down in history as one of the most brilliant managers of the Federal Reserve. Some people believe he already is.

Sources: Rob Norton, "Greenspan's Decade," *Fortune,* August 4, 1997, pp. 30–32; Therese Eiben with the editors of *Fortune* magazine, *Fortune Adviser 1997* (New York: Fortune Books, 1997), pp. 39–49; Dean Foust, "Alan Greenspan's Brave New World," *Business Week,* July 14, 1997, pp. 45–50; and William Hester, "A Cure for What's Ailing," *Bloomberg Personal,* March 1998, pp. 21–22.

THE IMPORTANCE OF MONEY

◄ LEARNING GOAL 1
Explain what money is and the importance of the money supply to domestic and international exchange.

◄ CONSIDER USING TM 154
Chapter Outline

The U.S. economy depends heavily on money: its availability, its value relative to other currencies, and its cost. Economic growth and the creation of jobs depend on money. Money is so important to the economy that many institutions have evolved to manage money and to make it available to you when you need it. Today you can easily get cash from an automated teller machine (ATM) almost anywhere in the world, but you don't have to have cash anymore to buy things. Most organizations will accept a check, credit card, debit

➤ **CONSIDER USING LECTURE ENHANCER 21-1**
Fixed Assets, or Why a Loan in Yap Is Hard to Roll Over

➤ **CONSIDER USING OT ACETATE 21-1**
Characteristics of a Good Money System

➤ **CONSIDER USING CRITICAL THINKING EXERCISE 21-1**
Bartering: Buying a Box of Fiberrific (SCANS)

card, or smart card to pay for things you buy. Behind the scenes of this free flow of money is a complex system of banking that makes it possible for you to do all these things.[1]

The banking system is becoming more complex all the time because the flow of money from country to country is as free as the flow from state to state. Therefore, what happens to any major country's economy has an effect on the U.S. economy and vice versa. Clearly, there's more to money and its role in the economies of the world than meets the eye. There's no way to understand the U.S. economy without understanding global money exchanges and the various institutions involved in the creation and management of money.[2]

We'll explore such institutions in this chapter. Let's start at the beginning by discussing exactly what people mean when they say "money" and how the supply of money affects the prices you pay for goods and services.

••• WHAT IS MONEY? •••

money
Anything that people generally accept as payment for goods and services.

Money is anything that people generally accept as payment for goods and services. In the past, objects as diverse as salt, feathers, stones, rare shells, tea, and horses have been used as money. *Barter* is the trading of goods and services for other goods and services directly. Many people today still barter goods and services. For example, in Siberia two eggs buy one admission to a movie, and customers of Ukraine's Chernobyl nuclear plant pay in sausages and milk.[3] The problem is that eggs and milk are difficult to carry around. People need some object that's more portable, divisible, durable, and stable so that they can trade goods and services without carrying the actual goods around with them. One answer to that problem over the years was to create coins made of silver or gold. Coins met all the standards of a useful form of money:

➤ **CONSIDER USING LECTURE ENHANCER 21-2**
Dirty Money

➤ **CONSIDER USING LECTURE ENHANCER 21-3**
Funny Money

➤ **CONSIDER USING LECTURE ENHANCER 21-4**
What to Do about the Penny?

➤ **CONSIDER USING LECTURE ENHANCER 21-5**
Is it Legal Tender?

➤ **CONSIDER USING OT ACETATE 21-2**
The Life Span of Currency

➤ **CONSIDER USING LECTURE ENHANCER 21-6**
Community Money Supply Thrives in Ithaca

➤ **CONSIDER USING OT ACETATE 21-3**
Understanding the Money Supply

➤ **CONSIDER USING LECTURE ENHANCER 21-7**
Gold or Silver Standard?

Portability. Coins were a lot easier to take to market than were pigs or other heavy products.

Divisibility. Different-sized coins could be made to represent different values. For example, prior to 1963 a U.S. quarter had half as much silver content as a half dollar and a dollar had four times the silver of a quarter. Because silver is now too expensive, today's coins are made of other metals, but the values remain.

Stability. When everybody agrees on the value of coins, the value of money is relatively stable. In fact, U.S. money has become so stable that much of the world uses the U.S. dollar as the measure of value.

Durability. Coins last for thousands of years, even when they've sunk to the bottom of the ocean, as you've seen when divers find old Roman coins in sunken ships.

Difficult to counterfeit. It's hard to copy elaborately designed and minted coins. But with the latest color copiers, people are able to duplicate the look of paper money relatively easily. Thus, the government has had to go to extra lengths to make sure real dollars are readily identifiable.

When coins and paper money become units of value, they make exchanges easier. Most countries have their own coins and paper money; they're all about equally portable, divisible, and durable. However, they're not always equally stable. For example, the value of money in Russia is so uncertain and so unstable that other countries won't accept Russian money in international trade. For Russia to participate in global markets, it must develop money that's tradable. When Poland made its money more stable in the early 1990s, global trade for that country grew tremendously.

This display of automobiles in the heart of Warsaw, Poland, and the smart clothing store in the background are both signs of the growing capitalism in that country. As a result of the capitalist movement, more products are available, wages are higher, and people are enjoying a higher standard of living and quality of life. One of the secrets to its success was Poland's development of tradeable money.

··· WHAT IS THE MONEY SUPPLY? ···

This chapter's profile says that Alan Greenspan is in control of the money supply. Two questions emerge from that simple statement: (1) What is the money supply? and (2) Why does it need to be controlled? The **money supply** is the amount of money there is to buy available goods and services.

There are several ways of stating the money supply. They're called M-1, M-2, and so on. The *M* stands for money, and the *1* and *2* stand for different definitions of the money supply. **M-1**, for example, includes **currency** (coins and paper bills), money that's available by writing checks, and money that's held in traveler's checks; that is, money that is quickly and easily raised. **M-2** includes everything in M-1 plus money in savings accounts (time deposits) and money in money market accounts, mutual funds, certificates of deposit, and the like; that is, money that may take a little more time to obtain than currency. M-2 is the most commonly used definition of money. You'll learn more about money and the money supply if you study finance and economics. In such courses, you will also learn about M-3 and L, two less-used measures of the money supply.

··· WHY DOES THE MONEY SUPPLY ··· NEED TO BE CONTROLLED?

Imagine what would happen if governments (or in the case of the United States, the Federal Reserve) were to generate twice as much money as exists now. There would be twice as much money available, but there would be the same amount of goods and services. What would happen to prices in that case? Think about the answer for a minute. (Hint: Remember the laws of supply and demand from Chapter 2 » P. 55 «?)

The answer is that prices would go up because more people would try to buy goods and services with their money and would bid up the price to get what they wanted. This is called inflation. Some people define inflation as "too much money chasing too few goods."

Now think about the opposite: What would happen if someone took some of the money out of the economy? What would happen to prices? Prices would go down because there would be an oversupply of goods and services compared to the money available to buy them. Some people say that prices will fall in coming

money supply
How much money there is to buy available goods and services.

M-1
Money that is quickly and easily raised (currency, checks, traveler's checks, etc.).

currency
All coin and paper money issued by the Federal Reserve banks, and all gold coins.

M-2
Money included in M-1 plus money that may take a little more time to raise (savings accounts, money market accounts, mutual funds, certificates of deposit, etc.).

◄ CONSIDER USING SUPPLEMENTAL CASE 21-1
When Money Loses Its Meaning
(SCANS)

years as Asian nations pour goods into the world economy in an effort to strengthen their own weakened economies. We shall explore that issue later in the chapter. For now, recall that if we take too much money out of the economy, a recession ➤ P. 61 ◄ might occur. That is, people would lose jobs and the economy would stop growing.

Now we come to the second question about the money supply: Why does the money supply need to be controlled? The money supply needs to be controlled because doing so allows us to manage the prices of goods and services somewhat. And controlling the money supply affects employment and economic growth or decline. The same is true in international markets.

••• THE GLOBAL EXCHANGE OF MONEY •••

falling dollar
When the amount of goods and services you can buy with a dollar goes down.

rising dollar
When the amount of goods and services you can buy with a dollar goes up.

A **falling dollar** means that the amount of goods and services you can buy with a dollar goes down. A **rising dollar** means that the amount of goods and services you can buy with a dollar goes up. Thus, the price you pay for a Japanese car today is lower than it was a few years ago because the American dollar has been rising relative to the Japanese yen (Japan's unit of currency).

What makes the dollar weak (falling dollar value) or strong (rising dollar value) is the position of the U.S. economy relative to other economies. When the economy is strong, people want to buy dollars and the value of the dollar rises. When the economy is perceived as weakening, however, people no longer desire dollars and the value of the dollar falls. The value of the dollar depends on a strong economy. Clearly, control over the money supply is important. In the following section, we'll discuss who controls the money supply and how it's done. Then we'll explore the U.S. banking system and how it loans money to businesses and individuals, such as you and me.

Critical Thinking

What will happen to the value of the dollar if Japanese businesspeople stop investing in the United States? What will happen to the value of the yen? Can you see that Japanese car prices will rise if the value of the dollar falls?

➤ **LEARNING GOAL 2**
Describe how the Federal Reserve controls the money supply.

CONTROL OF THE MONEY SUPPLY

You already know that money plays a huge role in the American economy and in the economies of the rest of the world. Therefore, it's important to have an organization that controls the money supply to try to keep the U.S. economy from growing too fast or too slow. Theoretically, with the proper monetary policy, you can keep the economy growing without causing inflation. (See Chapter 2 to review monetary policy.) The organization in charge of monetary policy is the Federal Reserve System (the Fed). The head of the Federal Reserve (at the moment, Alan Greenspan) is one of the most influential people not only in the country but also in the world because he or she controls the money that much of the world depends on for trade. Because this is an introductory text, we cannot discuss the Federal Reserve in depth here. Nonetheless, the Fed is so important that you may want to learn more about it on your own. If so, get on the Internet and search for http://www.bog.frb.fed.us/.

••• BASICS ABOUT THE FEDERAL RESERVE •••

The Federal Reserve System consists of five major parts: (1) the board of governors; (2) the Federal Open Market Committee (FOMC); (3) 12 Federal Reserve Banks; (4) three advisory councils; and (5) the member banks of the

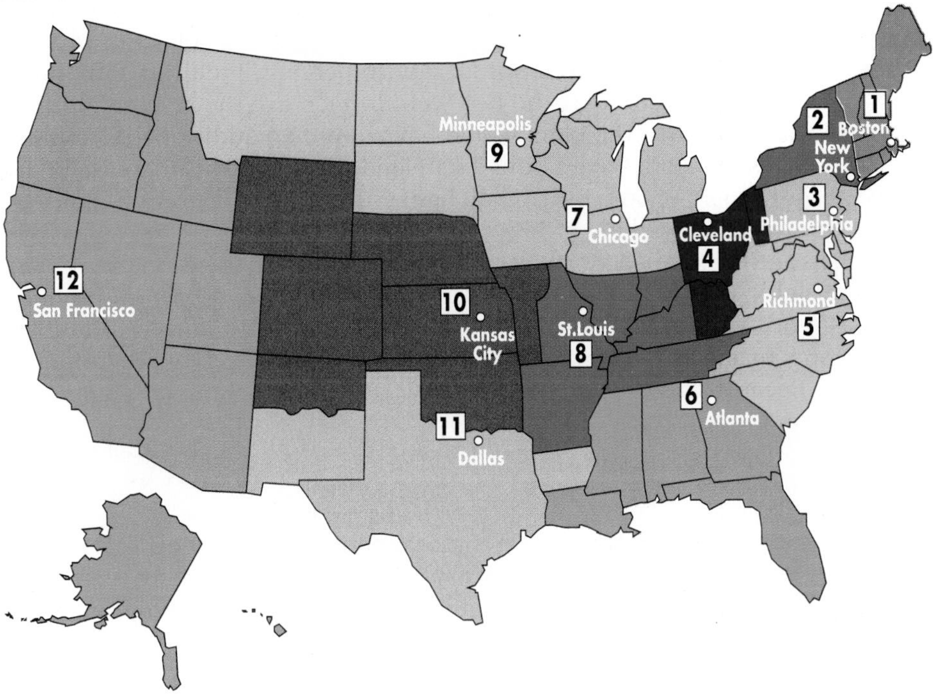

FIGURE 21.1

THE TWELVE FEDERAL RESERVE DISTRICT BANKS

system. Figure 21.1 shows where the 12 Federal Reserve banks are located. Member banks may be chartered by the federal government or by the state in which they're located. See what we mean when we say the system is complex?

◄ **CONSIDER USING TM 156**
The Twelve Federal Reserve District Banks (Figure 21.1 on text page 627)

◄ **CONSIDER USING OT ACETATE 21-4**
The Federal Reserve System

The board of governors administers and supervises the 12 Federal Reserve System banks. The seven members of the board are appointed by the president and confirmed by the Senate. The board's primary function is to set monetary policy » P. 62 «. The Federal Open Market Committee has 12 voting members and is the policymaking body. The committee is made up of the seven-member board of governors plus the president of the New York Reserve Bank. Four others rotate in from the other Reserve Banks. The advisory councils offer suggestions to the board and to the FOMC. The councils represent the various banking districts, consumers, and member institutions, including banks, S&Ls, and credit unions.

The Federal Reserve buys and sells foreign currencies, regulates various types of credit, supervises banks, and collects data on the money supply and other economic activity. As part of monetary policy, the Fed determines the level of reserves that must be kept at the 12 Federal Reserve Banks by all financial institutions. It also lends money to member banks and sets the rate for such loans (called the *discount rate*). Finally, it buys and sells government securities, or open-market operations. It is important to understand *how* the Fed controls the money supply, so we'll explore that in some depth next. The three basic tools the Fed uses to manage the money supply are reserve requirements, open-market operations, and the discount rate. Let's explore how each of these is administered.

••• THE RESERVE REQUIREMENT •••

The **reserve requirement** is a percentage of commercial banks' checking and savings accounts that must be physically kept in the bank (e.g., as cash in the vault) or in a non-interest-bearing deposit at the local Federal Reserve district bank. The reserve requirement is the Fed's most powerful tool. When the Fed increases the reserve requirement, banks have less money for loans and thus

reserve requirement
A percentage of commercial banks' checking and savings accounts that must be physically kept in the bank.

make fewer loans. Money becomes more scarce, which in the long run tends to reduce inflation. For instance, if Omaha Security Bank holds deposits of $100 million and the reserve requirement is, say, 10 percent, then the bank must keep $10 million on reserve. If the Fed were to increase the reserve requirement to 11 percent, then the bank would have to put an additional $1 million on reserve, thus reducing the amount it can lend out. Since this increase in the reserve requirement would affect all banks, the money supply would be reduced and prices would likely fall.

A decrease of the reserve requirement, on the other hand, increases the funds available to banks for loans, so banks make more loans and money becomes more readily available. An increase in the money supply stimulates the economy to achieve higher growth rates, but it can also create inflationary pressures. Because this tool is so potent and can cause such major changes in the U.S. economy, it is rarely used.

➤ CONSIDER USING OT ACETATE 21-5
The Fed Regulates the Money Supply

••• OPEN-MARKET OPERATIONS •••

open-market operations
The buying and selling of U.S. government securities by the Fed with the goal of regulating the money supply.

Open-market operations are the Fed's most commonly used tool. To decrease the money supply, the federal government *sells* U.S. government securities (e.g., bonds) to the public. The money it gets as payment is taken out of circulation, decreasing the money supply. If the Fed wants to increase the money supply, it *buys* government securities from individuals, corporations, or organizations that are willing to sell. The money paid by the Fed in return for these securities enters circulation, resulting in an increase in the money supply.

➤ CONSIDER USING OT ACETATE 21-6
Types of Monetary Policy

••• THE DISCOUNT RATE •••

discount rate
The interest rate that the Fed charges for loans to member banks.

The Fed has often been called the banker's bank. One reason for this is that member banks can borrow money from the Fed and then pass it on to their customers in the form of loans. The **discount rate** is the interest rate that the Fed charges for loans to member banks. An increase in the discount rate by the Fed discourages banks from borrowing and consequently reduces the number of available loans, resulting in a decrease in the money supply. In contrast, lowering the discount rate encourages member banks to borrow money and increases the funds available for loans, which increases the money supply.

As you can see, the whole banking industry is affected by the Federal Reserve System's actions. In the following sections, we'll briefly discuss the history of banking to give you some background information on why the Fed came into existence. Then we'll explore what's happening in banking today.

Progress Check

- What is money?
- What are the characteristics of useful money?
- What is the money supply, and why is it important?
- What are the various ways the Federal Reserve controls the money supply, and how do they work?

➤ LEARNING GOAL 3
Trace the history of banking and the Federal Reserve System.

THE DEVELOPMENT OF THE FEDERAL RESERVE SYSTEM

The system of money and banking was slow to develop in the United States. In the colonies there were no banks at first. Strict laws limited the number of coins that could be brought to the colonies. Thus, colonists were forced to barter for goods; for example, cotton and tobacco may have been traded for shoes and lumber.

The demand for money was so great that Massachusetts issued its own paper money in 1690, and other colonies soon followed suit. But continental currency, the first paper money printed in the United States, became worthless after a few years because people didn't trust its value.[4]

Land banks were established to lend money to farmers. (Note that banks were used as a means to grow the economy.) But Great Britain, still in charge of the colonies at that point, ended land banks by 1741. In fact, in Pennsylvania during the American Revolution, a new bank was formed to finance the war against England.

In 1791, after the United States gained independence, Alexander Hamilton persuaded Congress to form a central bank (a bank where banks could keep their funds and borrow funds if needed), over the objections of Thomas Jefferson and others. This first version of a federal bank closed in 1811, only to be replaced in 1816 because state-chartered banks couldn't support the War of 1812. The battle between the Second (Central) Bank of the United States and state banks got hot in the 1830s. Several banks in President Andrew Jackson's home state were hurt by pressure from the Central Bank. The fight ended when the bank was closed in 1836.

By the time of the Civil War, the banking system was a mess. Many different banks issued different kinds of currencies. During the war, coins were hoarded because they were worth more as gold and silver than as coins. The chaos continued long after the war ended, reaching something of a climax in 1907, when many banks failed. People got nervous about their money and went to banks to withdraw their funds. Shortly thereafter, the cash ran out and some banks had to refuse money to depositors.

The cash shortage problems of 1907 led to the formation of an organization that could lend money to banks—the Federal Reserve System. It was to be a "lender of last resort" in such emergencies. Under the Federal Reserve Act of 1913, all federally chartered banks had to join the Federal Reserve. State banks could also join. The Federal Reserve became the banker's bank. If banks had excess funds, they could deposit them in the Fed; if they needed extra money, they could borrow it from the Fed. The Federal Reserve System has been intimately related to banking ever since.

Not too many years ago, this was a common sign on banks. It says that the FDIC has taken over this San Antonio, Texas, bank and is trying to find a stronger bank to merge it with. Meanwhile, assurance is given that deposits are insured up to $100,000. It is interesting to note that a similar banking collapse is occurring throughout much of Asia at the time of this writing. Is it the responsibility of the United States to help bail out those banks also? What benefits does the United States gain from such support?

••• THE GREAT DEPRESSION •••

The Federal Reserve System was designed to prevent a repeat of the 1907 panic. Nevertheless, the stock market crash of 1929 led to bank failures in the early 1930s. When the stock market began tumbling, people ran to banks to get their money out. In spite of the Federal Reserve System, the banks ran out of money and states were forced to close banks. President Franklin D. Roosevelt extended the period of the bank closings in 1933 to gain time to come up with some solution to the problem.

In 1933 and 1935, Congress passed legislation to strengthen the banking system. The most important move was to establish federal deposit insurance, which you'll learn more about later in this chapter. At this point, it's important for you to know that in the 1930s, during the Great Depression, the government started an insurance program to further protect us from bank failures.

◀ **CONSIDER USING LECTURE ENHANCER 21-8**
Goldsmith Banking

◀ **LEARNING GOAL 4**
Classify the various institutions in the U.S. banking system.

••• THE FEDERAL RESERVE AND THE BANKING INDUSTRY •••

The Federal Reserve is frequently in the news as it tries to keep the economy growing at an even pace. In the early 1990s, the Fed pumped up the money supply and lowered interest rates to get the economy moving. As inflation threatened in 1994, the Fed increased short-term interest rates. That caused bond prices to fall and threatened the stock market. Alan Greenspan became the center of attention as the whole financial community waited for the Fed's next move.

Some people felt that inflation was coming to the United States and applauded the Fed for hiking up interest rates. They knew that such a move would cut inflation and let the economy grow slowly but surely. Others felt that there was no inflation threat and that higher interest rates would slow the economy so much that a new recession would occur. In short, the whole world has been watching and continues to watch the Federal Reserve System to see what direction the U.S. economy will take next. No group of people is more concerned than the nation's bankers.

stagflation
A combination of slow growth and inflation

Businesses are concerned because higher bank rates mean a higher cost of borrowing money. If businesses stop borrowing, then business growth slows, people are fired, and the whole economy stagnates. In fact, it's quite possible to have both slow growth and inflation. (That's called **stagflation**.) Thus, money and banking are critical to business leaders. You now know about money and the money supply. The following sections explore banking and its importance to businesspeople.

•••• ▬▬ ••••

THE AMERICAN BANKING SYSTEM

The American banking system consists of commercial banks, savings and loan associations, credit unions, and mutual savings banks. In addition, various organizations perform several banking functions, although they aren't true banks. These nondeposit institutions (often called **nonbanks**) include pension funds, insurance companies, commercial finance companies, consumer finance companies, and brokerage houses. In the following sections we'll discuss the activities and services provided by each of these institutions, starting with commercial banks.

nonbanks
Financial organizations that accept no deposits but offer many of the services provided by regular banks (pension funds, insurance companies, commercial finance companies, consumer finance companies, and brokerage houses).

••• COMMERCIAL BANKS •••

commercial bank
A profit-making organization that receives deposits from individuals and corporations in the form of checking and savings accounts and then uses some of these funds to make loans.

A **commercial bank** is a profit-making organization that receives deposits from individuals and corporations in the form of checking and savings accounts and then uses some of these funds to make loans. Banks may be chartered by the federal government or the various states. State banks are where entrepreneurs often turn for loans.[5] Commercial banks have two types of customers: depositors and borrowers (those who take out loans). A commercial bank is equally responsible to both types of customers. Commercial banks try to make a profit by efficiently using the funds depositors give them. In essence, a commercial bank uses customer deposits as inputs (on which it pays interest) and invests that money in interest-bearing loans to other customers (mostly businesses). Commercial banks make a profit if the revenue generated by loans exceeds the interest paid to depositors plus all other operating expenses.

••• SERVICES PROVIDED BY COMMERCIAL BANKS •••

Individuals and corporations that deposit money in a checking account have the privilege of writing personal checks to pay for almost any purchase or transaction. The technical name for a checking account is a **demand deposit**, because the money is available on demand from the depositor. Typically, banks impose a service charge for check-writing privileges or demand a minimum deposit. Banks might also charge a small handling fee for each check written. For corporate depositors, the amount of the service charge depends on the average daily balance in the checking account, the number of checks written, and the firm's credit rating and credit history.

In the past, checking accounts paid no interest to depositors, but interest-bearing checking accounts have experienced phenomenal growth in recent years. Most commercial banks offer negotiable order of withdrawal (NOW) and Super NOW accounts to their depositors. A NOW account typically pays an annual interest rate but requires depositors always to maintain a certain minimum balance in the account (e.g., $500) and may restrict the number of checks that depositors can write each month.

A Super NOW account pays higher interest to attract larger deposits. However, Super NOW accounts require a larger minimum balance. They sometimes offer free, unlimited check-writing privileges. Individual banks determine the specific terms for their NOW and Super NOW accounts. The longer you keep your funds in such accounts, the more interest they pay.

In addition to these types of checking accounts, commercial banks offer a variety of savings account options. A savings account is technically called a **time deposit** because the bank can require a prior notice before withdrawal.

A certificate of deposit (CD) is a time-deposit (savings) account that earns interest to be delivered at the end of the certificate's maturity date. The depositor agrees not to withdraw any of the funds in the account until the end of the specified period. CDs are now available for periods of three months up to many years; interest rates vary, depending on the period of the certificate. The interest rates also depend on economic conditions and the prime rate at the time of the deposit. In addition to the checking and savings accounts discussed above, commercial banks offer a variety of other services to their depositors including automated teller machines and credit cards. The box called Making Ethical Decisions (on page 632) discusses the kind of situation that led to more automated banking.

Automated teller machines (ATMs) give customers the convenience of 24-hour banking at a variety of outlets such as supermarkets, department stores, and drugstores in addition to the bank's regular branches. Depositors can now transfer funds, make deposits, and get cash at their own discretion with the use of a computer-coded personalized plastic access card, almost anywhere in the world.

Commercial banks also offer credit cards to creditworthy customers, inexpensive brokerage services, financial counseling, automatic payment of telephone bills, safe-deposit boxes, tax-deferred individual retirement accounts (IRAs) for qualified individuals and couples, traveler's checks, and overdraft checking account privileges. (This means preferred customers can automatically get loans at reasonable rates when they've written checks exceeding their account balance.) Figure 21.2 lists key banking services.

Bank on the environment of Vermont.

VERMONT NATIONAL BANK
Quality People · Quality Service

We'll put your money where your values are.

Vermont National Bank depositors may specify that their accounts be used for loans meeting social criteria. By using deposits for loans for affordable housing, agriculture, education, the environment, and businesses with a dual bottom line (a social and a financial bottom line), the bank allows depositors to influence how their money is put to work for their community.

demand deposit
The technical name for a checking account; the money in a demand deposit can be withdrawn anytime on demand from the owner.

time deposit
The technical name for a savings account; the bank can require prior notice before the owner withdraws money from a time deposit.

automated teller machines (ATMs)
Machines that give customers the convenience of 24-hour banking at a variety of outlets.

Making Ethical Decisions

http://law.house.gov/316.htm

To Tell the Teller or Not

You have been banking at the same bank for some time, but the tellers at the bank keep changing, so it is difficult to establish a relationship with any one teller. You don't like using the automated teller machine because the bank has decided to charge for each transaction. Therefore, you are working with a teller and withdrawing $300 for some expenses you expect to incur. The teller counts out your money and says: "OK, here's your $300." Before you leave the bank, you count the money once more. You notice that the teller has given you $350

by mistake. You return to the teller and say, "I think you have made a mistake in giving me this money." She replies indignantly, "I don't think so. I counted the money in front of you."

You are upset by her quick denial of a mistake and her attitude. You have to decide whether or not to give her back the overpayment of $50. What are your alternatives? What would you do? Is that the ethical thing to do?

➤ **CONSIDER USING OT ACETATE 21-7**
Shrinking Number of Commercial Banks

➤ **CONSIDER USING LECTURE ENHANCER 21-9**
The Convenience of ATM Machines

➤ **CONSIDER USING LECTURE ENHANCER 21-10**
Automated Loan Machines

➤ **CONSIDER USING TM 155**
Services Available at Most Commercial Banks (Figure 21.2 on text page 632)

••• SERVICES TO BORROWERS •••

Commercial banks offer a variety of services to individuals and corporations in need of a loan. Generally, loans are given based on the recipient's creditworthiness. Banks want to manage their funds effectively and are supposed to screen loan applicants carefully to ensure that the loan plus interest will be paid back on time. Small businesses and minority businesses often search out banks that cater to their needs. The box called Spotlight on Small Business discusses such banks in more depth.

••• BUSINESS LOANS •••

Business loans are normally characterized as short-term or long-term, depending on whether they're to be repaid within one year or over a longer period of time. Short-term loans have to be paid within one year. Many businesses borrow on a short-term basis to get urgently needed cash for items such as seasonal inventory. Businesses find it useful to establish a line of credit before they actually need money. This involves getting approval for a specified loan amount beforehand, so the firm can immediately borrow the money whenever it's needed.

FIGURE 21.2
• • • •

SERVICES AVAILABLE AT MOST COMMERCIAL BANKS

The number of services has expanded recently as banks seek to provide more and more assistance to consumers and businesses.

- Demand deposits (checking accounts)
- Time deposits (savings accounts)
- Loans
- Financial counseling
- Safe deposit boxes
- Certified checks
- Overdraft protection
- Insurance

- Traveler's checks
- Credit cards
- Certificates of deposit (CDs)
- NOW accounts
- Super NOW accounts
- On-line banking
- Automated teller machines (ATMs)
- Brokerage services

Spotlight on Small Business

Where Do Small and Minority Businesses Go for Loans?

Louis E. Prezeau, Sr., president and CEO of City National Bank, says that a small-business owner will have a lot more access to somebody who can make decisions in a minority-owned or small bank than in a large bank. That was true for Adetunde Dada when he sought funding for Tunde Dada House of Africa in Orange, New Jersey. He got great service from the African American–owned City National Bank of New Jersey in Newark. Other banks had not turned him down, but they were really slow in responding to his request.

The National Bankers Association (NBA) is a Washington, D.C.–based trade group that represents some 50 minority- and women-owned banks. Its members are committed to providing employment opportunities, entrepreneurial capital, and economic revitalization in neighborhoods that often have little access to financial services. A large bank may hesitate to make a small loan to a small business, but a small bank can get to know that business and that businessperson well. As a result, a small business can get not only money but financial advice and other services as well.

Minority banks usually have more experience dealing with minority borrowers and thus can help them with more than simple banking services. If you are thinking of starting a small business, to impress any banker you should first open a checking and savings account in that bank. The bank will help with the writing of a business plan and make sure you have the kind of financial backing you need to succeed in the long run. The banker is likely to visit your business to see the operation. Such close cooperation and participation makes the link between small businesses and small bankers intimate and beneficial to both.

Sources: Sharon Nelton, "Lending with a Personal Touch," *Nation's Business*, March, 1997, pp. 42–43; and Anne Marriott, "Banking Enters Brave New World," *Business Times*, February 9, 1998, pp. D12–D14.

Long-term loans are those payable in a period that exceeds one year. Typically, long-term loans must be repaid within 2 to 5 years but could also be extended for longer periods (up to 20 years). Banks give long-term loans to individuals, corporations, and domestic and foreign governments. The interest charged for most long-term loans to large corporations and governments is negotiated between the two parties. Often, such loans require a long, exhausting round of bargaining before terms of the loan (interest charged, repayment period, default options, and so forth) are agreed on. Most loans by law require collateral. *Collateral* is some object of value, such as a home or stock, that may be sold if the loan is not paid any other way.

••• SAVINGS AND LOAN ASSOCIATIONS (S&Ls) •••

A **savings and loan association (S&L)** is a financial institution that accepts both savings and checking deposits and provides home mortgage loans. S&Ls are often known as thrift institutions because their original purpose (starting in 1831) was to promote consumer thrift and home ownership. To help them encourage home ownership, thrifts were permitted for many years to offer slightly higher interest rates on savings deposits than banks. Those rates attracted a large pool of funds, which were then used to offer long-term fixed-rate mortgages at whatever the rate was at the time.

Between 1979 and 1983, about 20 percent of the nation's S&Ls failed. Faced with this situation, the federal government permitted S&Ls to offer NOW and

savings and loan association (S&L)
A financial institution that accepts both savings and checking deposits and provides home mortgage loans.

◄ CONSIDER USING OT ACETATE 21-8
Where Businesses Keep Their Money

Shown here is Charles Keating in handcuffs on his way to court. Keating, former head of Lincoln Savings and Loan, became the poster child for the savings and loan industry's failures when he was convicted of defrauding Lincoln's customers. Initially, he received a 10-year prison term, but his conviction was later overturned on appeal.

credit unions
Nonprofit, member-owned financial cooperatives that offer basic banking services such as accepting deposits and making loans to their members.

▶ CONSIDER USING LECTURE ENHANCER 21-11
Ukrainian Washington FCU

Super NOW accounts, to allocate up to 10 percent of their funds to commercial loans, and to offer mortgage loans with adjustable interest rates based on market conditions. In addition, S&Ls were permitted to offer a variety of other banking services, such as financial counseling to small businesses and credit cards. As a result, S&Ls became much more similar to commercial banks than before.

Congress decided to guarantee S&L savings up to $100,000 per account so people would feel secure keeping their money in banks and S&Ls. Those guarantees came back to haunt Congress when banks and S&Ls made risky loans in the 1980s, with the thought that such loans were guaranteed by the government. There was no way the bankers could lose if the loans fell through; after all, deposits were guaranteed. When many of those loans did fail, it cost the government (you and me) about $500 billion. Some S&L directors were sentenced to prison for defrauding investors and mismanaging funds. Today, S&Ls are in better financial shape but, as always, are subject to changing economic conditions. This history is important because Mexico is now going through the same problems, as are several Asian countries. We shall discuss these later in the chapter.

··· CREDIT UNIONS ···

Credit unions are nonprofit, member-owned financial cooperatives that offer basic banking services such as accepting deposits and making loans to their members. Today the 12,000 or so credit unions in the United States hold about 7 percent of all savings and deposits. Typically, credit unions offer their members interest-bearing checking accounts (called share draft accounts) at relatively high rates, short-term loans at relatively low rates, financial counseling, life insurance policies, and a limited number of home mortgage loans.[6] Credit unions may be thought of as financial cooperatives organized by government agencies, corporations, unions, or professional associations. As nonprofit institutions, credit unions enjoy an exemption from federal income taxes. Recently credit unions have been criticized for offering their services to widely diverse groups that many not be eligible for membership. This will be an interesting issue to follow in the next few years.

··· OTHER FINANCIAL INSTITUTIONS ···

As we explained earlier, nonbanks are financial organizations that accept no deposits but offer many of the services provided by regular banks. Nonbanks include life insurance companies, pension funds, brokerage firms, commercial finance companies, and corporate financial services. As competition between these organizations and banks increases, the dividing line between banks and nonbanks is becoming less and less apparent. This is equally true in Europe, where companies from the United States such as Fidelity Investment and GE Capital Corporation compete with European banks.[7] The diversity of financial services and investment alternatives offered by nonbanks has caused banks to expand the services they offer. In fact, banks today are merging with brokerage firms to offer full-service financial assistance.[8]

Life insurance companies provide financial protection for policyholders, who periodically pay premiums. In addition, insurers invest the funds they receive from policyholders in corporate and government bonds. In recent years, more insurance companies have begun to provide long-term financing for real estate development projects.

Pension funds are amounts of money put aside by corporations, nonprofit organizations, or unions to cover part of the financial needs of members when they retire. Contributions to pension funds are made either by employees, by employers, or by both employers and employees. A member may begin to collect a monthly draw on this fund upon reaching a certain retirement age. To generate additional income, pension funds typically invest in low-return but safe corporate stocks or in other conservative investments such as government securities and corporate bonds.

> **pension funds**
> Amounts of money put aside by corporations, nonprofit organizations, or unions to cover part of the financial needs of members when they retire.

Many large pension funds such as the California Public Employees Retirement System (CalPERS) are becoming a major force in U.S. financial markets. Formidable rivals such as the Teachers Insurance & Annuity Association (TIAA) lend money directly to corporations.

Brokerage firms have traditionally offered services related to investments in the various stock exchanges in this country and abroad. However, brokerage houses have made serious inroads into regular banks' domain by offering high-yield combination savings and checking accounts. In addition, brokerage firms offer checking privileges on accounts (money market accounts). Also, investors can get loans from their broker, using their securities as collateral.

Commercial and consumer finance companies offer short-term loans to businesses or individuals who either can't meet the credit requirements of regular banks or have exceeded their credit limit and need more funds. These finance companies' interest rates are higher than regular banks'. The primary customers of these companies are new businesses and individuals with no credit history. In fact, college students often turn to consumer finance companies for loans to pay for their education. One should be careful when borrowing from such institutions, because the interest rates can be quite high.

> **commercial and consumer finance companies**
> Organizations that offer short-term loans to businesses or individuals who either can't meet the credit requirements of regular banks or else have exceeded their credit limit and need more funds.

Corporate financial systems established at major corporations such as General Electric, Sears Roebuck, General Motors, and American Express offer considerable financial services to customers. To compete with such nonbank organizations, banks have had to offer something extra—guaranteed savings.

Critical Thinking

Do you keep your savings in a bank, a S&L, a credit union, or some combination? Have you compared the benefits you could receive from each? Where would you expect to find the best loan values?

Progress Check

- Why did the United States need a Federal Reserve Bank?
- What's the difference between a bank, a savings and loan association, and a credit union?
- What is a nonbank?

HOW THE GOVERNMENT PROTECTS YOUR FUNDS

The American economic system learned a valuable lesson from the depression of the 1930s. To prevent investors from being completely wiped out during an economic downturn, several organizations evolved to protect your money. The

> ◄ **LEARNING GOAL 5**
> Explain the importance of the Federal Deposit Insurance Company and other organizations that guarantee funds.

three major sources of financial protection are the Federal Deposit Insurance Corporation (FDIC); the Savings Association Insurance Fund (SAIF), originally called the Federal Savings and Loan Insurance Corporation or FSLIC; and the National Credit Union Administration (NCUA). All three insure deposits in individual accounts up to $100,000. Let's explore these organizations and the challenges they face.

··· THE FEDERAL DEPOSIT INSURANCE CORPORATION (FDIC) ···

Federal Deposit Insurance Corporation (FDIC)
An independent agency of the U.S. government that insures bank deposits.

The **Federal Deposit Insurance Corporation (FDIC)** is an independent agency of the U.S. government that insures bank deposits. If a bank were to fail, the FDIC would arrange to have its accounts transferred to another bank or pay off depositors up to a certain amount. (As we noted earlier, this amount has increased over the years and is now $100,000 per account.) The FDIC covers about 13,000 institutions, mostly commercial banks. What would happen if one of the top 10 banks in the United States were to fail? The FDIC has a contingency plan to nationalize the bank so that it wouldn't fail.[9] The idea is to maintain confidence in banks so that others don't fail if one happens to falter.

··· THE SAVINGS ASSOCIATION INSURANCE FUND (SAIF) ···

Savings Association Insurance Fund (SAIF)
The part of the FDIC that insures holders of accounts in savings and loan associations.

The **Savings Association Insurance Fund (SAIF)** insures holders of accounts in savings and loan associations. It's now part of the FDIC. As just noted, it was originally called the Federal Savings and Loan Insurance Corporation (FSLIC) and was an independent agency. A brief history will show why the association was created.

Both the FDIC and the FSLIC were started during the Great Depression. The FDIC was begun in 1933, and the FSLIC in 1934. Some 1,700 bank and thrift institutions failed during the previous few years, and people were losing confidence in them. The FDIC and FSLIC were designed to create more confidence in banking institutions.

For some 50 years, the FSLIC and the FDIC were successful in covering losses from thrift and bank institution failures. When the thrift institutions of America began to fail in the 1980s, as we discussed earlier, many banks and S&Ls went out of business and their assets (largely real estate property) were turned over to the government. Remember, the government was responsible for making sure that depositors got their money back. In 1989, the government created the Resolution Trust Corporation (RTC) to sell the real estate. The money from these sales went to pay back the money the government lost from the S&L crisis. Most of the lost money, however, was never regained.

To get more control over the banking system in general, the government placed the FSLIC under the Federal Deposit Insurance Corporation (FDIC) and gave it a new name: the Savings Association Insurance Fund.

··· NATIONAL CREDIT UNION ADMINISTRATION (NCUA) ···

The NCUA provides up to $100,000 coverage per individual depositor per institution. This coverage includes all accounts, including share draft checking, savings or money market accounts, and certificates of deposit. Additional protection can be obtained by holding accounts jointly or in trust. Individual retirement accounts (IRAs) are also separately insured. A family of four can thus have insured accounts totaling over a million dollars. To see how this can be done, check the NCUA Web site at http://www.spefcu.org/chart2.htm.

···· ▬ ····

THE FUTURE OF BANKING

How will banks and savings and loans change in the 21st century? The answer lies in the decisions made by the Federal Reserve (monetary policy) and the U.S. Congress (fiscal policy), and in the overall strength of the U.S. and world economies. As we write, the U.S. financial community and the U.S. economy appear to be in the best shape they've been in for years. However, federal debt and personal debt keep rising, and over a million people are declaring bankruptcy each year. In short, the banking system may not be as strong as it appears on the surface, especially given the collapse of banks in many other countries. Since banks are now connected around the world, those losses will affect U.S. banks, but we don't know yet how major the effects will be. We'll talk more about this issue toward the end of the chapter.

Regardless of the effect of the current international banking crisis, it is certain that banks as we've traditionally known them will change. Banks are readying themselves to sell everything from insurance to mutual funds. Many changes are needed to further strengthen the banking system. It's nearly impossible to accurately predict the future of an economy. By the time you read this text, the economy probably will have changed from how it is as we write. You must find out for yourself what has happened in the meantime. For now, Japan's banks are struggling and banks in Thailand and other parts of Asia are struggling also.[10] Weakness in the world's financial markets has placed a strain on U.S. banks as well. In the next section, we'll discuss recent trends in banking that may strengthen America's financial base.

··· INTERSTATE BANKING ···

From earlier chapters of this text, you've learned that businesses everywhere are reorganizing to become more efficient and effective. Many businesses have done this through a whole series of mergers and acquisitions that created larger, more entrepreneurial organizations. That is, although the businesses are large, they give their individual units more freedom to be responsive to the market.

This trend is also occurring in banking. For example, Citicorp merged with Travelers in the biggest financial merger ever.[11] Such mergers may strengthen banks and allow them to become more efficient. Yet banks are beginning to charge higher fees for everything from ATM use to the use of inside tellers—and the fees are annoying consumers. As a consequence, a countertrend is seen in the opening of community banks that are more user-friendly and convenient than the giants[12]

··· EXPANDING WHAT BANKS DO ···

States have taken the lead in giving banks freedom to go into businesses other than banking through acquisitions. For many years, banks in Minnesota and North Carolina, for example, have been allowed to sell insurance. In states such as Massachusetts and New Jersey, banks can engage in brokerage and underwriting, aspects of the "big three" nonbanking businesses: insurance, securities (stocks and bonds), and real estate. Today, banks may provide services in all three areas. One area of explosive potential growth is bank-sponsored mutual funds.

··· ELECTRONIC BANKING TAKES ON TRADITIONAL BANKING ···

Today, the whole banking system is on the brink of a major revolution in its day-to-day operations. The way things have always been done—depositing

◄ LEARNING GOAL 6
Weigh the future of the U.S. banking system.

◄ CONSIDER USING OT ACETATE 21-10
What Are the Largest U.S. Banks

money, writing checks, protecting against bad checks, and so on—is expensive. Imagine the cost to the bank of approving a check, processing it through the banking system, and mailing it back to you. Bankers have long looked for ways to make the system more efficient.

One step in the past was to issue credit cards. Credit cards cut down on the flow of checks, but they too have their costs: There's still paper to process, and there's a chance for credit card fraud.

The next step was to create the electronic exchange of money. In an **electronic funds transfer system (EFTS)** a bank gives you a card much like a credit card. Retailers put that card into a slot in a cash register (which they call a point-of-sale terminal). When the sale is recorded, an electronic signal is sent to the bank, transferring funds from your account to the store's account automatically. Because of EFTSs some workers today receive no paycheck. Rather, their employer contacts the bank and orders it to transfer funds from the employer's account to the worker's account. You can see why it's called an electronic funds *transfer* system.

"Smart cards" may be the currency of the future.[13] Smart cards are an advanced version of the cards used in EFTSs. American Express, Hilton, American Airlines, and IBM were experimenting with such cards in 1998.[14] You can now buy an airplane ticket by placing your smart card into a special reading device at the gate; you can also use it to rent a car, pay for your hotel, and so on. The card will compile your frequent flyer miles and other information. Such cards are more popular overseas than in the United States now, but they could catch on as consumers see the benefits of cashless buying.

> **electronic funds transfer system (EFTS)**
> A computerized system that electronically performs financial transactions such as making purchases, paying bills, and receiving paychecks.

••• ELECTRONIC BANKING ON THE INTERNET •••

Soon all of the top 200 banks in the United States will have some kind of on-line banking. Banks will add value to such services by merging with credit card companies, brokerage firms, and mutual funds. You will be able to obtain information on every aspect of your personal finances in one central location—on-line. Some banks charge a small monthly service for electronic banking, but others are offering the service free to attract consumers to this new

> ➤ **CONSIDER USING LECTURE ENHANCER 21-12**
> Intuit Sets up Online Financial Bazaar
>
> On-line banking is so new that it does not offer enough conveniences and benefits to appeal to most people. But there is a good chance that the majority of people will do their banking on-line in the future. Just as it took a while to get used to automated teller machines, it will take a while to get used to on-line banking. But when we do, we'll be able to check our account balances, shift funds from one account to another, get mortgages and other loans, buy insurance, and do all kinds of financial transactions, including buying and selling stock, on-line. Does the prospect appeal to you or not? Why?

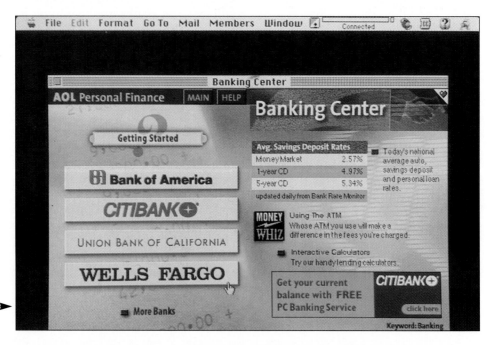

way of banking. In general, on-line bill paying should cost about $6 for 20 payments a month; together, on-line banking and bill paying should total less than $10 a month.[15]

Different on-line sites offer varying degrees of completeness, flexibility, and usability.[16] One of the best is the Banking Center of America Online's Personal Finance Forum, which includes the America Online branches of over 20 banking institutions (keyword: *bank*). Security First Network Bank (SFNB) doesn't have a nationwide network of banks, so it can offer on-line services for less than other banks. Open a $100 checking account and you can get up to 20 free electronic payments a month and free paper checks for emergencies. The first 10 ATM transactions are also free. If you are worried about whether electronic banking is safe, experts say that the latest in technology makes it safer than giving your credit card to a retailer.[17]

Progress Check

- What's the difference between the FDIC and the SAIF?
- What are two major trends in banking today?
- Describe an electronic funds transfer system (EFTS). What are its benefits?
- What are some of the services being offered along with on-line banking?

···· ▬▬▬ ····

INTERNATIONAL BANKING AND BANKING SERVICES

◄ **LEARNING GOAL 7**
Evaluate the role and importance of international banking and the role of the World Bank and the International Monetary Fund.

Banks help companies conduct business in other countries by providing three services: letters of credit, banker's acceptances, and currency exchange. If a U.S. company wants to buy a product from Germany, the company could pay a bank to issue a letter of credit. A **letter of credit** is a promise by the bank to pay the seller a given amount if certain conditions are met. For example, the German company may not be paid until the goods have arrived at the U.S. company's warehouse. A **banker's acceptance** promises that the bank will pay some specified amount at a particular time. No conditions are imposed. Finally, a company can go to a bank and exchange American dollars for German marks; that's called **currency exchange**.

Banks are making it easier than ever before for you and other tourists to buy goods and services overseas as well. Automated teller machines now provide pounds, francs, lira, marks, and other foreign currencies through your personal Visa, MasterCard, Cirrus, Plus, or American Express card. You can usually get a better exchange rate with an ATM than you can from your hotel or corner money exchange facility.

letter of credit
A promise by the bank to pay the seller a given amount if certain conditions are met.

banker's acceptance
A promise that the bank will pay some specified amount at a particular time.

currency exchange
Exchange of currency from one country with currency from another country.

••• LEADERS IN INTERNATIONAL BANKING •••

◄ **CONSIDER USING OT ACETATE 21-9**
The World's Banking Giants

This chapter focused on banking within the United States. In the future, though, it's likely that many crucial financial issues will be international in scope. In today's financial environment, it's foolish to discuss the American economy apart from the world economy. If the Federal Reserve decides to lower interest rates, foreign investors can withdraw their money from the United States in minutes and put it in countries with higher rates. Of course, the Fed's increasing interest rates can draw money to the United States equally quickly.

Today's money markets form a global market system. The United States is just a part, although a major part, of that system. International bankers tend not to be nationalistic in their dealings. That is, they send money to any country

Reaching Beyond Our Borders

http://www.ml.com/

Merrill Lynch Goes Global

The U.S. market for banking services is relatively mature; therefore, the growth markets of the future will be overseas. Few firms understand the potential of international banking better than Merrill Lynch, a leader in brokering and in financing corporations. Nonetheless, the company recognizes the competition from other international banks, insurance companies, mutual fund companies, financial planners, and brokers.

To expand overseas, Merrill Lynch bought the British brokerage Smith New Court; Spain's Iversiones; and stakes in brokerages in India, Thailand, South Africa, Indonesia, and Italy. It is also expanding to Latin America and recently acquired Australia's McIntosh Securities. In all, it is present in over 40 countries. As a consequence, about 30 percent of Merrill Lynch's revenues now come from overseas. Merrill Lynch is using the same concepts it developed in the United States to ▲

develop globally. In fact, it was one of the biggest losers during the Asian banking crisis.

Other leading U.S. bankers are going global as well. Names like Charles Schwab and Travelers Group are becoming familiar all over the world. You can understand the potential when you learn that only 44 percent of the total value of stocks traded worldwide are traded in the United States. That means 56 percent are foreign markets. That is an attractive market for brokers and other financial institutions from all nations. It also means that there will be opportunities for tomorrow's college graduates in finance to work anywhere in the world.

Sources: Matthew Schifrin, "Merrillizing the World," *Forbes*, February 10, 1997, pp. 146–51; and Christine Dugas, "Trading Losses Hurt Merrill Lynch, Morgan the Most," *USA Today*, January 21, 1998, p. 3B.

where they can get a maximum return for their money at a reasonable risk. As a result, some $1.5–$2.0 trillion is traded daily![18] The net result of international banking and finance has been to link the economies of the world into one interrelated system with no regulatory control. American firms must compete for funds with firms all over the world. An efficient firm in London or Tokyo is more likely to get international financing than a less efficient firm in Detroit or Chicago.

What all this means to you is that banking is no longer a domestic issue; it's an international issue. To understand the U.S. financial system, you must learn about the global financial system. To understand America's economic condition, you'll have to learn about the economic condition of countries throughout the world. What has evolved, basically, is a world economy financed by international banks. The United States is just one player in the game. To be a winning player, America must stay financially secure and its businesses must stay competitive in world markets. The box called Reaching Beyond Our Borders discusses how U.S. banks are going global.

••• THE WORLD BANK AND THE ••• INTERNATIONAL MONETARY FUND (IMF)

To understand what is happening in the global banking world, you have to understand what the International Monetary Fund (IMF) is. The World Bank and the IMF are twin intergovernmental pillars that support the structure of the world's banking community. It is beyond the scope of this text to describe in detail the role of each, but a brief rundown follows:

The **World Bank** (also known as the International Bank for Reconstruction and Development) is primarily responsible for financing economic development. For example, it lent money to countries in Western Europe after World War II so they could rebuild. Today, the World Bank lends most of its money to poor nations to improve productivity ❯❯ P. 16 ❮❮ and help raise the standard of living and quality of life ❯❯ P. 2 ❮❮.

In contrast to the World Bank, the **International Monetary Fund (IMF)** was established to assist the smooth flow of money among nations. It requires members (who are voluntary) to allow their currency to be exchanged for foreign currencies freely, to keep the IMF informed about changes in monetary policy, and to modify those policies on the advice of the IMF to accommodate the needs of the entire membership. The IMF is not primarily a lending institution, as is the World Bank. Rather, it is an overseer of member countries' monetary and exchange rate policies. The IMF's goal is to maintain a global monetary system that works best for all nations. Members of the IMF contribute funds (rich countries pay more, poor countries pay less). Those funds are available to countries when they get into financial difficulty. The IMF was in the news almost daily in early 1998 because it was lending money (billions of dollars) to Asian nations whose currencies had fallen dramatically and whose banks were failing. We'll explain that story in detail next.

··· BANKS THROUGHOUT THE WORLD ARE ··· FINANCIALLY WEAK

The brief history of the U.S. banking system you read in this chapter gives you some background for understanding what happened to Asian banks late in the 1990s. In recent years, countries such as Indonesia, Thailand, and Japan were growing rapidly. Real estate prices skyrocketed. Banks were eager to lend money to investors in real estate and other ventures. Money poured into various Asian countries from all over the world, including the United States. Banks became a little careless with their lending practices and took big risks. As we noted such practices were what led to the failure of many S&Ls in the United States. Similar trouble began in Thailand, whose economy began to slow in 1997. People began to sell the baht (the Thai unit of currency), and the Thai central bank spent all of its reserves trying to keep up the value of the baht. It didn't succeed, and Thailand soon owed other countries some $92 billion. By the end of 1997, its currency was worth less than half what it was earlier in the year and its stock market fell by over 35 percent.

The situation in Thailand spread across Asia. The value of Indonesia's currency, for example, dropped almost 70 percent, and the Indonesian stock market dropped by over 35 percent. South Korea's currency dropped by about 45 percent and its stock market fell by about a third. Indonesia owed other countries about $120 billion; South Korea owed about $144 billion.[19]

The Asian countries turned to the IMF to help them out. The IMF responded by lending these countries billions of dollars each.[20] The problem is

World Bank
The bank primarily responsible for financing economic development; also known as the International Bank for Reconstruction and Development.

International Monetary Fund (IMF)
Organization that assists the smooth flow of money among nations.

Workers of the Samsung Group in Korea collected gold items from employees in 1998 to help the financial group pay off part of the $57 billion South Korea owed to the International Monetary Fund. Does the failure of such Asian banks have any effect on U.S. banks?

http://www.hg.org/banking.html

BCCI, The Bank of Crooks and Criminals, International

Many in the banking world felt that the Bank of Credit and Commerce, International (BCCI), was a textbook example of what's wrong in international banking. BCCI was fined for laundering drug money in Florida and was involved in a foreign exchange scandal in Kenya. Its customers included former Panamanian strongman Manuel Noriega and Colombian drug lords. The bank was so bad, in fact, that it earned the name "Bank of Crooks and Criminals, International." Yet for almost 20 years, BCCI stayed one step ahead of the law. This financial reign of terror came to a crashing end in the early 1990s when bank regulators from the United States, Britain, and five other countries shut down BCCI. The estimated losses from BCCI's operations amounted to almost $5 billion, making it one of the world's biggest banking failures. How did all this happen, and what can be done to prevent future BCCIs from developing?

Most experts agree that the absence of any type of global regulatory agency permitted BCCI to remain untouchable. For example, the bank's registered home base was Luxembourg, but its managers worked from London. Its shareholders were wealthy Persian Gulf oil sheiks, and its assets were tangled in a branch network that included 70 different countries. Many operations were channeled through the Cayman Islands. The complexity of the bank prevented any banking authority from performing regulatory audits. Fraud, corruption, and ▲

money laundering became the order of the day. *Time* magazine called the bank "the largest corporate criminal enterprise ever."

BCCI's actions have caused many industrialized nations to consider imposing tighter controls on international banks. The U.S. Senate and the Federal Reserve support global actions to control international banking activity. International banks will undergo more intensive scrutiny in the future in an attempt to prevent another BCCI-type scandal.

Meanwhile, U.S. authorities were able to convince authorities in Abu Dhabi to free BCCI files in return for dropping all criminal charges against Abu Dhabi officials. Furthermore, the Abu Dhabi government allowed the U.S. government to keep some $400 million being held in the United States. Recently, Clark Clifford and his law partner Robert A. Altman—executives in First American Bankshares, one of the banks involved in the scandal—agreed to pay the Federal Reserve $5 million to settle charges related to the case, nine years after the government began to pursue them.

Sources: Jonathan Beaty and S. C. Gwynne, "The Dirtiest Bank of All," *Time*, July 29, 1991, pp. 42–47; Mark Maremont, "BCCI: Justice May Finally Prevail," *Business Week*, January 31, 1994, p. 59; and Sharon Walsh, "Clifford, Altman Settle BCCI Case," *The Washington Post*, February 4, 1998, pp. A1, A9.

that the people who benefited from those dollars were often bankers from around the world who had lent the countries money in the first place. They took high risks and, because of the IMF intervention, were not forced to suffer the full consequences. Many countries are now challenging the policies of the IMF, especially since the IMF aid to international bankers may tempt bankers to take similar risks in the future.

The "Asian crisis" is generating a number of other potential problems. Asian countries are desperate for U.S. dollars and intend to sell their products to the U.S. at greatly reduced prices. This is good for consumers, but not so good for the companies that compete against them. Also, U.S. producers will have trouble selling goods and services in Asia because the people there now have less money to buy than before. The net result is that some U.S. businesses will suffer, some U.S. banks will suffer, and the U.S. economy as a whole may suffer as well. The effects of the Asian crisis have not been fully realized around the world. But this much is certain: The global financial situation is weak and more crises may emerge. Furthermore, the United States is not immune from such problems. For one thing, the United States is expected to put more money into the IMF to provide even more funds for failing banks in other countries.

Since all the world's banks are now so intimately linked, a major failure in any one country has an effect on all countries, especially investors who put their money into international mutual funds. U.S. banks seem to be emerging from the latest crisis and appear to be relatively strong.[21] Nonetheless, the whole U.S. economy could be slowed by the banking crisis that has affected much of the rest of the world. The banking crisis is further damaged by illegal activities that have taken place in international banking. The box called Legal Briefcase looks into one institution plagued by such activities.

••• THE YEAR 2000 PROBLEM •••

You may have heard of the well-publicized Year 2000 problem—which is that most of the world's computer systems will read 1900 instead of 2000 on January 1, 2000. Two digits may seem like a minor thing, but they will likely be a major problem for banks, as well as other businesses.[22] Banks have a special problem because they deal with funds that have dates of deposit. If computers can't read the date *2000*, they simply may not work. That includes the computers at the Federal Reserve. Even worse, computers affected by the Year 2000 problem may miscalculate all kinds of numbers, including mortgage payments and stock prices. Most large banks are trying to fix the problem before it occurs, but many banks are behind schedule. No one knows the extent of this problem now, but it bears watching as the year 2000 approaches.[23]

Progress Check

- What are the major functions of the Federal Reserve? What other functions does it perform?
- How is the Federal Reserve organized?
- How does the Federal Reserve control the money supply?
- What are the roles of the World Bank and the International Monetary Fund?
- What is the Year 2000 problem?

SUMMARY

1. Money is anything that people generally accept as payment for goods and services.

   • ***How is the value of money determined?***
   The value of money depends on the money supply; that is, how much money is available to buy goods and services. Too much money in circulation causes inflation. Too little money causes recession and unemployment.

1. Explain what money is and how its value is determined.

2. Because the value of money is so important to the domestic economy and international trade, an organization was formed to control the money supply.

   • ***What's that organization and how does it work?***
   The Federal Reserve makes financial institutions keep funds in the Federal Reserve System (reserve requirement), buys and sells government securities (open-market operations), and lends money to banks (the discount rate). To increase the money supply, the Fed can cut the reserve requirement, buy government bonds, and lower the discount rate.

2. Describe how the Federal Reserve controls the money supply.

3. Trace the history of banking and the Federal Reserve System.

3. In the American colonies at first there were no banks and coins were limited. The colonists traded goods for goods instead of using money.
   • *How did banking evolve in the United States?*
   Massachusetts issued its own paper money in 1690; other colonies followed suit. British land banks lent money to farmers but ended such loans by 1741. After the revolution, there was much debate about the role of banking, and there were heated battles between the Central Bank of the United States and state banks. The banking system was a mess by the time of the Civil War, with many banks issuing different kinds of currency. Eventually, a federally chartered and state-chartered system was established, but chaos continued until many banks failed in 1907. The system was revived by the Federal Reserve only to fail again during the Great Depression. The Fed, banks, and S&Ls were in the news during the 1990s because many banks and S&Ls failed and the Federal Reserve kept raising interest rates. These events greatly affected the economy.

4. Classify the various institutions in the U.S. banking system.

4. Savings and loans, commercial banks, and credit unions are all part of the banking system.
   • *How do they differ from one another?*
   Before deregulation in 1980, commercial banks were unique in that they handled both deposits and checking accounts. At that time, savings and loans couldn't offer checking services; their main function was to encourage thrift and home ownership by offering high interest rates on savings accounts and providing home mortgages. Deregulation closed the gaps between banks and S&Ls so that they now offer similar services.
   • *What kinds of services do they offer?*
   Banks and thrifts offer such services as savings accounts, NOW accounts, CDs, loans, individual retirement accounts (IRAs), safe-deposit boxes, on-line banking, and traveler's checks.
   • *What is a credit union?*
   A credit union is a member-owned cooperative that operates much like a bank in that it takes deposits, allows you to write checks, and makes loans. It also may sell life insurance and make home loans. Because credit unions are member-owned cooperatives rather than profit-seeking businesses like banks, credit union interest rates are sometimes higher than those from banks, and loan rates are often lower.
   • *What are some of the other financial institutions that make loans and do other banklike things?*
   Nonbanks include life insurance companies that lend out their funds, pension funds that invest in stocks and bonds and make loans, brokerage firms that offer investment services, and commercial finance companies.

5. Explain the importance of the Federal Deposit Insurance Corporation and other organizations that guarantee funds.

5. The government has created organizations to protect depositors from losses such as those experienced during the Great Depression.
   • *What agencies ensure that the money you put into a bank, S&L, or credit union is safe?*
   Money deposited in banks is insured by an independent government agency, the Federal Deposit Insurance Corporation (FDIC). Money in S&Ls is insured by another agency connected to the FDIC, the Savings Association Insurance Fund (SAIF). Money in credit unions is insured by the National Credit Union Administration (NCUA). These organizations protect your savings up to $100,000 per account.

6. Weigh the future of the U.S. banking system.

6. There will be many changes in the banking system in coming years.
   • *What are some major changes?*
   One important change will be the advent of interstate banking. Another change will be more services offered by banks including insurance, securi-

ties (stocks, bonds, and mutual funds), and real estate sales. Electronic funds transfer systems will make it possible to buy goods and services with no money. Automated teller machines enable you to get foreign currency whenever and wherever you want it. On-line banking may change the banking process dramatically as people become more used to paying bills on-line.

7. Today's money markets aren't national; they are global.
  * ***What do we mean by global markets?***
  Global markets mean that banks don't necessarily keep their money in their own countries. They send it where they get the maximum return.
  * ***What are the roles of the World Bank and the IMF?***
  The World Bank (also known as the International Bank for Reconstruction and Development) is primarily responsible for financing economic development. The International Monetary Fund (IMF), in contrast, was established to assist the smooth flow of money among nations. It requires members (who are voluntary) to allow their currency to be exchanged for foreign currencies freely, to keep the IMF informed about changes in monetary policy, and to modify those policies on the advice of the IMF to accommodate the needs of the entire membership.

7. Evaluate the role and importance of international banking and the role of the World Bank and the International Monetary Fund.

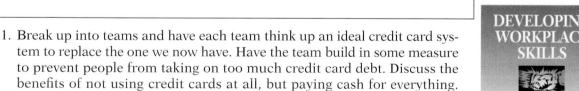

KEY TERMS
• • • • • •

automated teller machines (ATMs) 631
banker's acceptance 639
commercial and consumer finance companies 635
commercial bank 630
credit unions 634
currency 625
currency exchange 639
demand deposit 631
discount rate 628

electronic funds transfer system (EFTS) 638
falling dollar 626
Federal Deposit Insurance Corporation (FDIC) 636
International Monetary Fund (IMF) 641
letter of credit 639
M-1 625
M-2 625
money 624
money supply 625

nonbanks 630
open-market operations 628
pension funds 635
reserve requirement 627
rising dollar 626
savings and loan association (S&L) 633
Savings Association Insurance Fund (SAIF) 636
stagflation 630
time deposit 631
World Bank 641

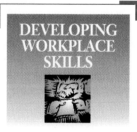

DEVELOPING WORKPLACE SKILLS

1. Break up into teams and have each team think up an ideal credit card system to replace the one we now have. Have the team build in some measure to prevent people from taking on too much credit card debt. Discuss the benefits of not using credit cards at all, but paying cash for everything. Have each team present a brief summary to the class.

2. Examine the business section of your daily newspaper or *The Wall Street Journal* and look at the exchange rates table that lists the equivalent price of foreign currency in U.S. dollars. Note which foreign currencies are priced less than the U.S. dollar and which cost more. Choose one and list the reasons for the difference.

3. Visit a local financial institution and ask about its high-yield interest rates (time deposits). Do you think they provide a satisfactory return on investment (ROI)? What are the pros and cons of such investments?

4. Would you recommend that the government stop guaranteeing deposits in banks and savings and loan associations? What are the advantages and disadvantages of such a proposal? Is there a compromise you can formulate?

5. Research the trends in M-1 and other money measures in *The Wall Street Journal.* What are the trends? See if you can find articles linking the money supply to economic conditions. Report to the class what those articles say and make a prediction about future economic growth given the money supply changes in the last six months.

TAKING IT TO THE NET

Purpose

To review the history of money and to explain the functions of money.

Exercise

It's something you work for and use every day, but how much do you know about money? Visit the Woodrow Federal Reserve Bank of Minneapolis Web site at http://woodrow.mpls.frb.fed.us/econed/curric/money.html. After reading the pages Face of U.S. Currency, Counterfeit Protection, U.S. Currency—New Designs, and History of Money, answer the following questions:

1. Name two ways the United States protects its currency from counterfeiting.
2. True or false: The U.S. government plans to recall all currency and replace it with the newly designed currency.
3. True or false: The Federal Reserve System prints all the money in the United States.
4. What's the difference between representative money and fiat money?
5. What are the three functions of money?
6. Who is credited with making the first paper money?
7. What were some of the commodities people once used as money and why?
8. What system of trade did money replace?

Practicing Management Decisions

Unlike other cases in this text, this case requires you to gather the facts and figures. Consult *The Wall Street Journal* or other business publications to see how the Federal Reserve System is strengthening the economy. This is an important exercise because few people know much about the Federal Reserve.

The Coalition for Monetary Education conducted a random survey of 2,000 people to see what they knew about the Federal Reserve and monetary policy in general. Only about 1 percent (some 20 out of 2,000) understood the monetary basics. Over 75 percent of the respondents knew that the Federal Reserve Board of Governors controlled the money supply. But only 9 percent of those polled were aware that the Federal Reserve's policies influenced the inflation rate, and only 13 percent were aware that the Fed's policies affected interest rates.

Only 31 percent of the people knew that U.S. currency isn't redeemable in gold or silver. Less

CASE
• • • • • •
LEARNING ABOUT THE FEDERAL RESERVE SYSTEM
• • • • • •

than 30 percent knew that bank failures were widespread. Reacting to these findings, the coalition planned a campaign to educate the public about the effect of federal policies on banking.

Decision Questions

1. How do the Federal Reserve's policies affect interest rates and the inflation rate? Why is it important for people to know that?
2. What action, if any, has the Federal Reserve taken in the past year to control the money supply and inflation? What are the results? (The answer to this question can be found in past issues of *The Wall Street Journal.*)
3. Go back to Chapter 2 and read about fiscal and monetary policy. Which seems to be having the greater effect on the U.S. economy today: monetary or fiscal policy? Why?

Get ready to hear the word *virtual* a lot in the next century: virtual shopping, virtual malls, and virtual banking. Virtual, in more common terms, means electronic. So you could call it electronic shopping, electronic malls, and electronic banking. The bottom line is that people will be able to shop, buy stocks and bonds, pay their bills, get price quotes, and conduct all kinds of business using their phone or their computer. Chances are that most will use their computer because it is easier to do transactions when you can see what is happening.

Let's focus for a minute on on-line banking. Imagine the convenience of sitting at your desk and paying your bills, reviewing your accounts at the bank, and even buying and selling stock, insurance, and more—all by computer. It is estimated that about 18 million households will be banking on-line by the year 2002. Some of the advantages are:

1. *Convenience.* With on-line banking, you can bank from anywhere at any time: 24 hours a day, 7 days a week. It takes just a few keystrokes, so you save the time of writing checks, addressing them, stamping the envelopes, and taking them to the mailbox. Money can also be transferred from one account to the other.

2. *Fast information.* You can quickly determine what your balance is in any account.

3. *Financial planning.* You can access all kinds of information dealing with personal financial planning, such as budgeting and forecasting.

4. *Low cost.* Many banks offer free software and charge minimal amounts per month (about $5 for writing 20 checks). Some charge less, as little as nothing.

Potential disadvantages include:

1. *Security.* Some people are worried about sending private information about money matters electronically. But bankers say that the latest encryption technology makes it as safe to bank on-line as to go through a teller.

2. *Computer overuse.* Many people work all day behind a computer. They may not want to come home and spend more time at a com-

┌ **VIDEO CASE** ┐

• • • • • •

ON-LINE BANKING

puter doing their banking. Furthermore, there is the possibility that the system may go down and they'll have to revert to the old banking methods. Some people also prefer having a paper trail to follow their transactions.

3. *Limited services.* You cannot make deposits on-line or get cash. If you're going to the bank anyhow, it may be easier and faster to use the ATM or the teller. Having person to person contact with a banker is comforting to some people. Some organizations won't participate in electronic banking, so you may not be able to pay all your bills that way.

Small businesses may find on-line banking much more advantageous because they have too many bills to pay. The cost savings and convenience are much greater than for consumers, and record keeping may be easier.

Banks are now merging with mutual funds, insurance companies, and other services to offer even more services on-line. Some see the end to traditional banking as banks become more complex financial institutions offering a wider variety of services, including financial counseling, on-line stock reports, and more. Soon you will be able to shop at a virtual mall, check the status of your accounts at the bank, make payments on-line, take out a loan if you need one, and invest money left over—all electronically from your home office.

Discussion Questions

1. Some people enjoy shopping at traditional malls and working with real tellers at the bank. What can banks and retailers do to encourage people to move to on-line banking and shopping?

2. Brainstorm the kinds of services that could be combined with banking services to make your life easier. Don't forget to include government services such as paying for your auto license and paying your taxes.

3. What are some of the dangers you see of conducting your banking, stock transactions, and insurance payments electronically? What happens when the electricity goes out? What happens if files get erased, as so often happens on your home PC? What can be done to minimize such dangers?

Managing Personal Finances: The Road to Entrepreneurship

Chapter

22

LEARNING GOALS

After you have read and studied this chapter, you should be able to

1 Describe the six steps one should take to generate capital.

2 Explain the best way to preserve capital and begin investing.

3 Compare and contrast various types of life, health, and other insurance alternatives.

4 Outline a strategy for retiring with enough money to last a lifetime.

Thomas Stanley has been studying wealthy people for over 20 years. His research is now available in a book called *The Millionaire Next Door: The Surprising Secrets of America's Wealthy*, which he co-authored with William Danko. You may enjoy reading the book yourself, but here are some helpful hints you may use immediately.

First, it is important to note that there are more than 3 million households in the United States with more than $1 million in net worth. Generally speaking, these millionaires are not connected with big companies. Rather, they are entrepreneurs who own the local McDonald's, the local scrap metal company, or some other small business. Self-employed people are four times as likely to be millionaires as people who earn a paycheck working for others.

The average income for the 3 million millionaires is $131,000 a year. So how did they get to be millionaires? They saved their money. To become a millionaire by the time you are 50 or so, you have to save about 15 percent of your income every year—starting when you are in your 20s. If you start later, you have to save an even larger percentage. The secret is to put your money in a place where it will grow without your having to pay taxes on it. You could invest in real estate, but this text emphasizes the benefits of buying and managing your own business. The majority of millionaires in the study took that route.

PROFILE

Thomas Stanley, Expert on Millionaires

To save that 15 percent a year, you have to spend less than you earn. That discipline must begin with your first job and stay with you all your life. To save money, the millionaires in the study tended to own modest homes and to buy used cars (37 percent bought used cars). The rule for house-buying was to spend no more than twice their annual income for a home. The millionaires tried not to spend money on things that had no lasting value: clothing, eating out, dry cleaning, and the like. In short, Stanley and Danko say that becoming a millionaire has more to do with thrift than with how much you earn. Many high-wage earners spend all their money on big homes and fancy cars but have relatively little when they retire.

To start your own business, you need capital (money). Most people use their own money to start their businesses. But how do they get that money in the first place? They save it. The message is clear: If you want to become a millionaire, the best way is through entrepreneurship, and the path to entrepreneurship is to save enough money to buy your own business. But that is easier said than done. It takes discipline and it takes knowledge. In this chapter, you will explore techniques for earning and saving money, regardless of where you choose to work at first.

Sources: Michael Ryan, "You Can Be Rich," *Parade Magazine*, June 22, 1997, pp. 8–10; and "$1 Million Worth of Secrets," *U.S. News and World Report*, June 9, 1997, pp. 90–92.

THE NEED FOR PERSONAL FINANCIAL PLANNING

◄ **LEARNING GOAL 1.**
Describe the six steps one should take to generate capital.

◄ **CONSIDER USING TM 157**
Chapter Outline.

If you talk to successful entrepreneurs, you'll learn that one of the hardest parts of entrepreneurship is raising the money you need to start your business and keep it going. As you ponder your job prospects, you'll see that the chance for finding an excellent job and then moving up through management is much smaller today than it was in the past. Many middle management jobs have been eliminated, which means that many people are competing for a relatively small number of management jobs. Even if you land such a job, you may find, as most millionaires have, that owning your own firm is more interesting and financially rewarding.

Making Ethical Decisions

http://www.abiworld.org/

Bankruptcy

It has been estimated that 10 percent of all U.S. households will declare bankruptcy in the 1990s. In 1996 alone, 1.1 million Americans declared personal bankruptcy. Even more declared bankruptcy in 1997. Such declarations are increasing at a rate of 21 percent a year.

Bankruptcy makes it possible for people to buy a big home, a new car, clothes, and luxury items of all kinds and then declare themselves bankrupt. That means that the courts may relieve them of all or most of the debt. In many states, bankrupts can default on mortgage payments and still keep their homes. In 1996 alone, some $30 billion in household debt was discharged by the bankruptcy courts.

Imagine that you have piled up debts of $15,000 and want to purchase many more items, like an expensive vacation. You could go ahead and take that vacation knowing that you can't possibly pay for it and the government can't take it back. Then you could declare bankruptcy and ask the courts to forgive your debts. Your credit rating would plummet, but you would be able to keep some of what you have and make no further payments. What is the ethical thing to do? What conditions or circumstances would make such a decision more ethical? What would you do? What would be the consequences?

Sources: Damon Darlin, "The Newest American Entitlement," *Forbes,* September 8, 1997, pp. 113–16; and Mary Deibel, "Americans Set Another Record for Going Bust!" *The Washington Times,* February 28, 1998, pp. A11–A14.

But it's not easy to become an entrepreneur. You have to start thinking and acting like an entrepreneur long before you start your own business. You can do that rather easily, however, by learning to manage your own career and finances. The planning, budgeting, controlling, and self-disciplining you need in order to save money will prove invaluable as you start your own firm. Whether or not you intend to become an entrepreneur, it's wise to learn personal financial planning.

When people get into financial trouble, they often make moral and ethical as well as economic mistakes. Read the box Making Ethical Decisions to review such a situation.

••• SIX STEPS IN LEARNING TO ••• CONTROL YOUR ASSETS

It's worth repeating that the only way to accumulate enough money to start your own business, using your own wages as a base, is to make more than you spend! We know you may find it hard to save today, but saving money isn't only possible, it's imperative if you want to accumulate enough to start a business. The following are six steps you can take today to get control of your finances.

➤ **CONSIDER USING CRITICAL THINKING EXERCISE 22-1**
Preparing a Personal Balance Sheet (**SCANS**)

➤ **CONSIDER USING LECTURE ENHANCER 22-1**
In Quicken We Trust.

STEP 1: TAKE AN INVENTORY OF YOUR FINANCIAL ASSETS   To take inventory, you need to develop a balance sheet for yourself. Remember, a balance sheet starts with the fundamental accounting equation: Assets = Liabilities + Owners' equity ➜ P. 537 ⬅. You can develop your own balance sheet by listing assets (e.g., TV, VCR, computer, bicycle, car, jewelry, and clothes) on one side and liabilities (e.g., mortgage, credit card debt, and auto loans) on the other. Assets include anything you own, and should be evaluated based on their current value, not purchase price.

If the value of your liabilities exceeds the value of your assets, you aren't on the path to financial security. In fact, you may be one of those who find the box on bankruptcy particularly interesting. You need some discipline in your life. Since we're talking about accounting, let's talk again about an income statement. ≫ P. 539 ≪. At the top of the statement is revenue. You subtract costs and expenses to get net income or profit. Have you done that for your own enterprise, You, Inc.? The easiest place to begin is to list all your sources of revenue: your job, your investments, and so on. You'll then know how much revenue you have each month and what your net worth is—an excellent start.

This may also be an excellent time to think about how much money you will need to start your own business. The more you visualize your goals, the easier it is to begin saving for them.

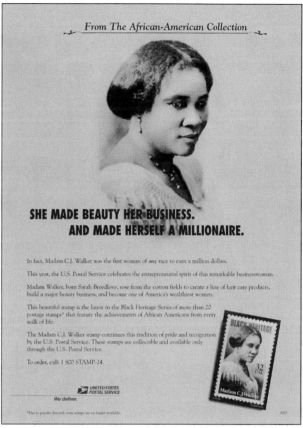

From The African-American Collection

SHE MADE BEAUTY HER BUSINESS. AND MADE HERSELF A MILLIONAIRE.

In fact, Madam C.J. Walker was the first woman of any race to earn a million dollars.

This year, the U.S. Postal Service celebrates the entrepreneurial spirit of this remarkable businesswoman.

Madam Walker, born Sarah Breedlove, rose from the cotton fields to create a line of hair care products, build a major beauty business, and become one of America's wealthiest women.

This beautiful stamp is the latest in the Black Heritage Series of more than 20 postage stamps* that feature the achievements of African Americans from every walk of life.

The Madam C.J. Walker stamp continues this tradition of pride and recognition by the U.S. Postal Service. These stamps are collectible and available only through the U.S. Postal Service.

To order, call: 1 800 STAMP-24.

UNITED STATES POSTAL SERVICE
We deliver.

*Due to popular demand, some stamps are no longer available.

STEP 2: KEEP TRACK OF ALL YOUR EXPENSES
Keeping records of your expenses is a rather tedious but necessary chore if you want to learn discipline. In other words, you have to write down every single penny you spend each day. Most people like to have a category called miscellaneous where they put expenditures for things like *caffe latte*, but you won't believe how much you fritter away on "miscellaneous" items unless you keep a detailed record for at least a couple of months.

You may often find yourself running out of money. In such circumstances, the only way to trace where the money goes is to keep track of every cent you spend. Actually, it can turn out to be an enjoyable task because it gives you such a feeling of control. Here's how to proceed: Carry a notepad with you wherever you go and record what you spend as you go through the day. That notepad is your journal. At the end of the week, record your journal entries into a record book. (Accountants call it a ledger.)

Develop certain categories (accounts) to make the task easier and more informative. For example, you can have a category called Food for all food you bought from the grocery or the convenience store during the week. You might want to have a separate account for meals eaten away from home because you can dramatically cut such costs if you make your lunches at home. Other accounts could include automobile, clothing, utilities, entertainment, donations to charity, and gifts. You can develop your accounts based on what's most important to you or where you spend the most money.

The discipline you develop in keeping track of your personal spending will prove invaluable if you start your own business. Many entrepreneurs spend too much money on furniture, equipment, and other aspects of a business start-up. You are likely to be more cautious with your spending once you have learned to track your expenses and how they affect you and your economic condition.

It has never been easy to become an entrepreneur. But throughout history Americans have saved their money, taken the risks, and realized the benefits of business ownership. Madam C. J. Walker was the first woman to earn a million dollars. She did it by creating a line of hair care products. You too can become a millionaire entrepreneur. Do you have the patience, willingness, and drive that it takes?

STEP 3: PREPARE A BUDGET
Once you know your financial situation and your sources of revenue and expenses, you're prepared to make a personal budget. The budget should be based on your financial goals (e.g., money to start a business). It's important to include large purchases you're likely to make (such as a car or new roof for the house). For such expenditures, it's smart to save so much each month in a separate account. Then when it comes time to make that purchase, you have the cash so you won't have to pay any finance charges. Remember, the idea is to spend less than you take in. When

◄ CONSIDER USING CRITICAL THINKING EXERCISE 22-2
Developing a Budget (**SCANS**)

This couple uses the computer to help manage their finances. Part of that process is to set up a budget so they know where their money will be going and to trace expenditures as they go along.

you do that, you'll see why the government has so much trouble balancing the budget. It's hard to cut back on expenses; nonetheless, it's critical to financial health—for you and the government alike.

Other items that are important in a household budget include life insurance, car insurance, and medical care. You'll learn that running a household's finances is similar to running a small business's. It takes the same careful record keeping, the same budgeting process and forecasting, the same control procedures, and often (sadly) the same need to periodically borrow funds. Suddenly, concepts such as credit and interest rates become only too real. This is where some knowledge of finance, investments, and budgeting pays off. Thus, any time you spend learning budgeting techniques will benefit you throughout your life, especially if you become an entrepreneur.

➤ CONSIDER USING LECTURE ENHANCER 22-2
Turning 25¢ a Week into $44,000.

STEP 4: PAY OFF YOUR DEBTS The first thing to do with any extra money you have is to pay off your debts. Start with the debts that carry the highest interest rates. Credit card debt, for example, may be costing you 16 percent or more a year. Merely paying off such debts will set you on a path toward financial freedom. It's better to pay off such a debt that costs 16 percent than to put the money in a bank account that earns only 5 percent.

➤ CONSIDER USING SUPPLEMENTAL CASE 22-1
Deciding When to Start Your Savings Plan (**SCANS**)

STEP 5: START A SAVINGS PLAN The best way to save money is to pay yourself first. That is, take your paycheck, take out money for savings, and then plan what to do with the rest. You can arrange with your bank or mutual fund to deduct a certain amount every month. You will be pleasantly surprised when the money starts accumulating and earning interest over time. With some discipline, you will soon have enough to start your own business or to invest in someone else's business.

STEP 6: BORROW MONEY ONLY TO BUY ASSETS THAT HAVE THE POTENTIAL TO INCREASE IN VALUE Don't borrow for expenses; you'll only get into more debt that way. If you have budgeted for emergencies, such as car repairs and health care costs, you should be able to stay financially secure. Only the most unexpected of expenses will cause you to borrow. It is hard to wait until you have enough money to buy what you want, but learning to wait is a critical part of self-discipline.

Alex Nevarez has been saving money all of his life. He lives with his parents in Hillside, New Jersey. But saving a quarter here and a few dollars there has added up over time. Now Nevarez has over $40,000 saved and hopes to buy a home in a few years. Do your friends and acquaintances have the same desire to save so that they too can become home-owners and business owners when they are ready? Do you?

If you follow all six of these steps, you'll not only have money for investment but you'll have developed most of the financial techniques needed to run a small business. At first you may find it hard to live within a budget. Nonetheless, the payoff is well worth the pain. One asset you're already accumulating is a college education. As the world moves toward an information economy, education will become a more and more important investment—one you will probably want to keep investing in the rest of your life.

Critical
Thinking

How would your life change if you were to implement the six steps outlined above? Would it be worth the time and effort if you knew you could become a millionaire by following them? What advice would you give college students who are not sure they should follow such a program?

••• EDUCATION: THE FIRST INVESTMENT •••

Throughout history an investment in education has paid off regardless of the state of the economy or political ups and downs. Education became even more important as we entered the information age.[1] When planning for your financial future, it's wise to think of what you'll do when you become financially secure. Life is more than working and making money. An investment in education may expose you to other countries, other languages, new ideas, and different ways of life. If you invest in yourself, you'll be making the best investment of all.

Many people use their education to find successful careers in business and to improve their earning potential, but at retirement they have little to show for their efforts. Making money is one thing; saving, investing, and spending it wisely are something else. *Less than 10 percent of the U.S. population has accumulated enough money by retirement age to live comfortably.*

••• HOW MUCH CAPITAL DOES A •••
BUDDING ENTREPRENEUR NEED?

It's surprising how little capital an entrepreneur needs to get started in business. For example, Richie Stachowski was only 11 when he came up with the idea for Water Talkies, which enable people to talk and hear each other underwater. He took out $275 from his savings account and went to Toys "R" Us to

Reaching Beyond
Our Borders

Outsourcing

Recently, Sara Lee Corporation announced that it would be moving away from making the products it sells. Instead, it outsourced the production of goods to other companies, some of them overseas. Sara Lee is the company that used to make Sara Lee frozen desserts, Kiwi shoe polish, L'eggs hosiery, Wonderbras, and Coach briefcases.

As a result of this restructuring, Sara Lee's stock went up on Wall Street and the company had lots of money available to market its products more fully. The company expected to enhance its competitive position and trim some $125 million in costs annually.

What an entrepreneur can learn from this and other companies that farm out their manufacturing is this: Being successful in business may take a lot less investment than you think, if you learn to work closely with other companies in all parts of the world. You can develop your expertise in brand building and marketing

while leaving manufacturing and distribution to others in other countries. Being one part of an integrated system of companies is a lot less expensive than trying to do everything yourself.

In your personal life, you may have to make similar decisions. Although it is not hard to mow your own lawn and clean your own house, it may be less expensive to hire people to do that while you dedicate yourself to more productive ventures, such as running your business. You could lease cars instead of owning them. All in all, the decisions that a businessperson makes are often very similar to ones that an individual makes in running a household.

Sources: James P. Miller, "Sara Lee to Retreat from Manufacturing," *The Wall Street Journal*, September 16, 1997, p. A3; and "Outsourcing: The New Midas Touch," an ad in *Business Week*, October 15, 1997, pp. 67ff.

---

convince them to try the product in all their stores. The key components of his conception were a soccer cone (that orange device used to mark off the field) and a mouthpiece adapted from a snorkel mask. He then outsourced production to others. The box called Reaching Beyond Our Borders discusses how outsourcing ➤ P. 246 ◀ minimizes the capital outlay for some businesses.

John Schnatter was in his 20s when he started selling pizza from the back of his father's tavern. His start-up cost was $1,600. Now his company, Papa John's, has $840 million in sales. Michael Krause was 14 when he came up with the idea for ExchangeNet. He approached his older brother (then 25) for help. With just $20,000, they started a company that now has some 7,000 corporate and public accounts. Jeff Haugen and Tim Cady were in their 20s when they saw the trend toward cigar smoking. They opened a store in Minnetonka, Minnesota, with an investment of a little over $10,000. Revenues are now about $2.2 million.[2] These stories were taken from an article entitled "Young Millionaires" in *Entrepreneur* magazine. Similar stories can be found in *Inc.*, *Success*, *Nation's Business*, and other magazines that feature small-business entrepreneurs.

Generation Xers, people in their 20s and early 30s, started almost 2 million businesses in 1996. They represent the fastest-growing segment of American entrepreneurs. Anthony Terrell Teat was in his twenties when he started a graphic design and wholesale apparel company called Masai Design in Largo, Maryland. Initial investment: $20,000 borrowed from family, friends, and savings.[3] Alex Nevarez began saving 25 cents a week when he was in second grade. At 12, he delivered newspapers, and in high school he worked in hotels and

Spotlight on
Small Business

http://www.morebusiness.com/

Saving to Become an Entrepreneur

Eillen Dorsey and Walter Hill, Jr., are successful entrepreneurs today because early in life they learned the importance of personal financial planning. The youngest of eight children, Eillen was reared in Harford County, Maryland. Her parents taught her that if she dreamed long and hard enough and was committed to her dream, she could turn it into reality. But that meant saving her money for college and then for investment.

Eillen attended Catonsville and Essex Community Colleges. Both inside and outside of school, Eillen began building a network of people who worked in corporate America and in local government agencies. She developed a particularly strong relationship with Walter Hill, Jr., who had attended Morgan State University and the University of Maryland. Walter also knew the value of savings.

Using the money they saved, Eillen and Walter wanted to start a minority firm in the Baltimore, Maryland, area. They noted that almost every corporation producing machinery had to buy some type of electrical components. They also knew that many of those companies were interested in doing business with a minority firm, so they saw an opportunity to become entrepreneurs.

Each partner contributed $5,000 to get the business started. They secured a $35,000 loan by using their ▲

homes as equity. Their homes thus became an important investment vehicle as well. The partners had already won a contract before they applied for the loan, making it easier for the lender to make the loan. Because the partners had invested their own money and assets, the banks were willing to give them a line of credit totaling $200,000.

Minority entrepreneurs like Eillen and Walter who've saved their money and invested in small firms have had great success all across the United States. In Connecticut, Wiley Mullins is annually selling almost $2 million worth of Wiley's Healthy Southern Classics. In North Carolina, Larry Harris is selling some $3.5 million worth of Harris Electronics' seatbelt chimes and related goods. In Kansas, Cleo and Mitchell Littleton (father and son) are grossing some $1 million a year in the environmental cleanup business. In Dallas, Joyce Foreman owns Foreman Office Products. There are over 23,000 businesses owned by African-Americans in the Los Angeles/Long Beach area alone. There are over 15,000 in Chicago. Many of their stories are much like that of Eillen and Walter. Such success stories usually begin with personal financial planning for accumulating start-up money.

restaurants. He saved enough money to attend Kean College in Union, New Jersey. At 26, Nevarez had an investment portfolio worth over $44,000. Nevarez is proof that a little can build to a lot with the right discipline.[4]

No matter how young you are, it is never too soon to start thinking about saving money to invest. We'll talk about how to do that next.

◀ LEARNING GOAL 2
Explain the best way to preserve capital and begin investing.

···· ▬ ····

BUILDING YOUR CAPITAL ACCOUNT

The path to success in a capitalist system is to have capital (money) to invest, yet the trend today for young graduates is not only to be capital-poor, but to be in debt. As you've read, accumulating capital takes discipline and careful planning.

For a young person, that process may be easier than you might expect. Read through the box called Spotlight on Small Business, which talks about two young people who saved their money and then went into business together.

The first step toward accumulating capital is to find employment. You may want to work for several years before getting married and having children.

You may think it's silly to talk to a college student about retirement, but it is never too soon to do some life planning and never too soon to begin saving money for such times. There is no question that success in life calls for sacrifice. Part of that sacrifice is to delay gratification; that is, to delay buying things now so that you have money to buy things that may be more important to you later. Would it be important to you to have money later to buy a successful business?

During those years, you should try to live as frugally as possible, saving a certain percentage of your income each month. The savings can then be used to generate even more capital. It may be invested in a mutual fund or some other relatively safe investment. Part of it could be invested in more risky investments for rapid capital accumulation. See the Practicing Management Decisions case at the end of this chapter for an example of a couple who followed this program.

Living frugally is extremely difficult for the average young person. Most people are eager to spend their money on a new car, furniture, CDs, clothes, and the like. They tend to look for a fancy apartment with all the amenities. A capital-generating strategy may require forgoing most (though not all) of these purchases to accumulate investment money. The living style required is close to the one adopted by most college students: a relatively inexpensive apartment furnished in hand-me-downs from parents, friends, and resale shops. For five or six years, you can manage with the old stereo, used cars, and a few nice clothes. The living style desired is one of sacrifice, not luxury. It's important not to feel burdened by this plan; instead, feel happy knowing that your financial future will be more secure.

After six years of careful saving, you can accumulate a sizable nest egg. What to do with the money? The first investment might be a low-priced home. This investment should be made as early as possible. The purpose of this investment is to lock in payments for your shelter at a given amount. This is possible by owning but not by renting. Through the years, home ownership has been a wise investment.

••• APPLYING THE STRATEGY •••

Some people have used the seed money from this strategy to buy duplex homes (two attached homes). They live in one and rent out the other. The rent covers a good part of the payments for both homes, so they can be housed very cheaply while their investment in a home appreciates. They learn that it's quite possible to live comfortably, yet inexpensively, for several years. In this way they accumulate capital. As they grow older, they see that such a strategy has put them years ahead of their peers in terms of financial security. They can eventually sell their duplex home and buy a single-family home with the profits. The money saved can also be invested in everything from stocks and bonds to precious metals, insurance, additional real estate, and higher education.

This strategy may seem too restrictive for you, but you still can apply the principles. The idea is to generate capital to invest. After all, this is basically a capitalist society, and in such a society you're lost without capital. People are wise to plan their financial future with the same excitement and dedication as they plan other aspects of their lives. Even a modest saving of $5,000 a year will allow you to buy a small home in a few years and begin an investment program. Remember, money that earns 12 percent annually doubles in just six years! An annual investment of $5,000 for six years can grow with compounding to a total of almost $41,000—a healthy start for anyone.

FIGURE 22.1
• • • •

INCOME	INTEREST RATE			
	7%	8%	9%	10%
$ 25,000	$104,167	$ 94,516	$ 86,180	$ 79,015
50,000	208,333	189,033	172,360	158,030
75,000	312,500	283,549	258,540	237,044
100,000	416,667	378,065	344,720	316,059

Source: National Association of Home Builders.

HOW MUCH HOUSE CAN YOU AFFORD?

Monthly mortgage payments—including interest, principal, real estate taxes, and insurance—generally shouldn't amount to more than 28 percent of monthly income. Assuming that principal and interest equal 25 percent of household income, and taxes and insurance 3 percent, here's how much people in various income categories can afford to pay for a home if they use a 30-year mortgage and make a 10 percent down payment.

◄ **CONSIDER USING TM 158**
How Much House Can You Afford?
(Figure 22.1 on text page 657)

◄ **CONSIDER USING LECTURE ENHANCER 22-3**
The "Rent Versus Buy" Decision.

••• REAL ESTATE: A RELATIVELY SECURE INVESTMENT •••

Historically, one of the better investments a person can make is in his or her own home. Homes may grow in value each year. Home prices in some areas declined during the late 1980s and early 1990s, but in many regions of the country prices are now on the rise again. Homes provide several investment benefits. First, a home is the one investment that you can live in. Second, once you buy a home, the payments are relatively fixed (though taxes and utilities go up). As your income rises, the house payments get easier and easier to make, but renters often find that rents tend to go up at least as fast as income.

Paying for a home is a good way of forcing yourself to save. Every month you must make the payments. Those payments are an investment that will prove very rewarding over time for most people. As mentioned earlier, an investment in a duplex or small apartment building is also an excellent strategy. As capital accumulates and values rise, an investor can sell and buy an even larger apartment complex. Many fortunes have been made in real estate in just such a manner. Furthermore, a home is a good asset to use when applying for a loan. Figure 22.1 will give you some idea of how much house you can afford, given your income.

Once you understand the benefits of owning versus renting, you can decide whether those same principles apply to owning the building where you set up your business—or owning versus renting equipment, trucks, and the like. Furthermore, you may start thinking of real estate as a way to earn a living. You could, for example, buy older homes, fix them up, and sell them.

••• TAX DEDUCTION AND HOME OWNERSHIP •••

Buying a home is likely to be the largest and most important investment you'll make. It's nice to know that the federal government is willing to help you with that investment. Here's how: Interest on your home mortgage payments is tax-deductible. So are your real estate taxes. During the first few years, almost all the mortgage payments go for interest on the loan, so almost all the early payments are tax-deductible—a tremendous benefit for homeowners and investors. If, for example, your payments are $1,000 a month and your income is in the 28 percent tax bracket, then during the early years of your mortgage Uncle Sam will, in effect, give you credit for about $280 of your payment, lowering your real cost to $720. This makes home ownership much more competitive with renting than it may appear on the surface.

Real estate people will tell you that there are three keys to getting the optimum return on a home: location, location, and location. A home in the "best

◄ **CONSIDER USING LECTURE ENHANCER 22-4**
Taxes after the Bomb.

◄ **CONSIDER USING LECTURE ENHANCER 22-5**
What Did You Deduct?

part of town," near schools, shopping, and work, is the best financial investment. Most young people tend to go farther away from town, where homes are less expensive, but such homes may appreciate in value much more slowly. It's important to learn where the best place to buy is. It's better, from a financial viewpoint, to buy a smaller home in a great location. Again, the same concepts often apply to buying a business. Location is a critical factor. Businesses may also deduct mortgage payments and other expenses. So personal finance and business finance are more closely related than you may have thought.

Progress Check

- What are the six steps you can take today to control your finances?
- What's called *the first investment*?
- What steps should a person follow to build capital?
- Why is real estate a good investment?

> **LEARNING GOAL 3.**
Compare and contrast various types of life, health, and other insurance alternatives.

••• WHERE TO PUT YOUR SAVINGS •••

You have learned that one place to invest the money you have saved is in a home. What are some other good places to save your money? For a young person, one of the worst places to keep your long-term investments is in a bank or savings and loan ↝ P. 633 ↜. It is important to have a month or two of savings in the bank for emergencies, but the bank is not the place to invest. A recent survey of high school students found that 85 percent believed that a savings account or a U.S. savings bond would offer the highest growth over the 18 years of saving for a child's education.[5] One of the best places to invest over time has been the stock market. The stock market does tend to go up and down, but over a longer period of time, it has proved to be one of the best investments. Chapter 20 gave you a foundation for starting such an investment program. That chapter also talked about bonds, but bonds have traditionally lagged behind stocks as a long-term investment. It is important to make the maximum return on your investments because that is how you build capital to buy your own business.

••• LEARNING TO MANAGE ••• CREDIT AND INSURANCE

Known as *plastic* to young buyers, credit cards are no doubt familiar to you. Names like Visa, MasterCard, American Express, Discover, Diners Club, and Carte Blanche are well known to most people. In a credit card purchase, finance charges after the first 25 or 30 days usually amount to about 12 to 20 percent annually. This means if you finance a car, home appliances, and other purchases with a credit card, you may end up spending much more than if you pay with cash. A good personal financial manager, like a good businessperson, pays on time and takes advantage of savings made possible by paying early. Those people who've established a capital fund can tap that fund to make large purchases and pay the fund back (with interest if so desired) rather than pay a bank.

Which credit card you get may make a big difference in how much interest you pay. Wachovia, for example, has a Prime for Life card that charges only the prime rate to card owners. However, you have to pay more up front to own the card. Have you sat down and compared the rates charged by the various credit card companies to be sure that you're getting the best deal?

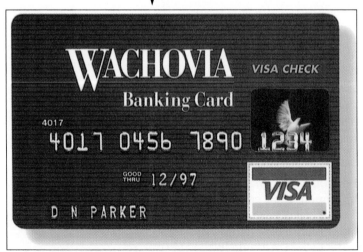

Credit cards are an important element in a personal financial system, even if they're rarely used. First, some merchants request credit cards as a form of identification. It may be difficult to buy certain goods or even rent a car without owning a credit card because businesses use them for identification and assured payment.

Second, credit cards are a way to keep track of purchases. A gasoline credit card, for example, gives you records of purchases over time for income tax and financial planning purposes. It's sometimes easier to write one check at the end of the month for several purchases than to carry cash around. Besides, cash may be stolen or lost.

Finally, a credit card is simply more convenient than cash or checks. If you come upon a special sale and need more money than you usually carry, a credit card is a quick, easy way to pay. You can carry less cash and don't have to worry about keeping your checkbook balanced as often.

If you do use a credit card, you should pay the balance in full during the period when no interest is charged. Not having to pay 16 percent interest is as good as earning 16 percent tax free. Also, choose a card that pays you back in cash, like the Discover card, or in frequent flier miles. The value of these give-backs can be as high as 2 to 5 percent. Rather than *pay* 16 percent, you *earn* a certain percentage—quite a difference.

The danger of a credit card is the flip side of its convenience. Too often, consumers buy goods and services that they wouldn't normally buy if they had to pay cash or write a check on funds in the bank. Using credit cards, consumers often pile up debts to the point where they're unable to pay. If you aren't the type who can stick to a financial plan or household budget, it may be better not to have a credit card at all. Credit cards are a helpful tool to the financially careful buyer. They're a financial disaster to people with little financial restraint and tastes beyond their income. College students take note: Of the debtors seeking help at the National Consumer Counseling Service, more than half were between 18 and 32.[6]

••• BUYING LIFE INSURANCE •••

One of the last things young people think about is the idea that they may get sick or have an accident and die. It's not a pleasant thought. Even more unpleasant, though, is the reality of young people dying every day in accidents and other unexpected ways. You have to know only one of these families to see the emotional and financial havoc such a loss causes.

Today, with so many husbands and wives both working, the loss of a spouse means a sudden drop in income. The same may be true when a top manager in a business dies. To provide protection from such risks, a couple or business should buy life insurance.

Today, the preferred form of life insurance is called term insurance. **Term insurance** is pure insurance protection for a given number of years. Every few years, you must renew the policy, whose fee usually gets higher and higher. Before buying any insurance, it would be wise to consult an insurance expert. See the appendix to this chapter for more details about insurance and its alternatives. Figure 22.2 shows some reasons for choosing term insurance.

term insurance
Pure insurance protection for a given number of years.

••• BUYING HEALTH INSURANCE •••

Both individuals and businesses need to consider protecting themselves from losses due to health problems. At first, you're likely to have health insurance coverage through your employer. If not, you can buy insurance from a health insurance provider (e.g., Blue Cross/Blue Shield), a health maintenance organization

◄ CONSIDER USING OT ACETATE 22-1
Advantages and Disadvantages of Consumer Credit Cards.

◄ CONSIDER USING OT ACETATE 22-2
How College Students Rate Their Credit-Card Behavior.

◄ CONSIDER USING OT ACETATE 22-3
How Often Are Consumers Worried About Credit-Card Debt?

◄ CONSIDER USING OT ACETATE 22-4
The Five "C's" of Credit.

◄ CONSIDER USING LECTURE ENHANCER 22-6
Discredit Report.

◄ CONSIDER USING LECTURE ENHANCER 22-7
Shutting down Credit Repair Fraud.

FIGURE 22.2
••••
WHY BUY TERM
INSURANCE?

INSURANCE NEEDS IN EARLY YEARS ARE HIGH.	INSURANCE NEEDS DECLINE AS YOU GROW OLDER.
1. Children are young and need money for education.	1. Children are grown.
2. Mortgage is high relative to income.	2. Mortgage is low or completely paid off.
3. Often there are auto payments and other bills to pay.	3. Debts are paid off.
4. Loss of income would be disastrous.	4. Insurance needs are few.
	5. Retirement income is needed.

➤ CONSIDER USING TM 159
Why Buy Term Insurance? (Figure 22.2
on text page 660)

(HMO), or a preferred provider organization (PPO). See the appendix to this chapter for details. Small-business owners must also choose among health care providers for themselves and their employees, if they provide such coverage.

It's dangerous financially not to have any health insurance. Hospital costs are simply too high to risk financial ruin by going uninsured. In fact, it's often a good idea to supplement health insurance policies with disability insurance that pays part of the cost of a long-term sickness or an accident. Your chances of becoming disabled at an early age are much higher than your chances of dying from an accident. Therefore, it's important to have the proper amount of disability insurance. (See your agent.) The cost is relatively low to protect yourself from losing your livelihood for an extended period.

••• BUYING OTHER INSURANCE •••

You should buy insurance for your car. Get a large deductible of $500 or so to keep the premiums lower, and cover small damage on your own. You'll also need liability insurance to protect yourself against being sued by someone accidentally injured by you. Often you can get a discount by buying all your insurance with one company. GEICO, for example, gives discounts for safe driving, getting good grades, and more.

➤ LEARNING GOAL 4.
Outline a strategy for retiring with
enough money to last a lifetime.

➤ CONSIDER USING OT ACETATE
22-5
What's the Most Important Goal of
Investors?

PLANNING YOUR RETIREMENT

It may seem too early to begin planning your retirement, but not to do so would be a big mistake. Successful financial planning means long-range planning, and retirement is a critical phase of life. What you do now could make a world of difference in your quality of life after age 65.

••• SOCIAL SECURITY •••

Social Security
The term used to describe the Old-Age, Survivors, and Disability Insurance Program established by the Social Security Act of 1935.

➤ CONSIDER USING LECTURE
ENHANCER 22-8
Social Insecurity and Your Retirement
Strategy.

Social Security is the term used to describe the Old-Age, Survivors, and Disability Insurance Program established by the Social Security Act of 1935. There's no question that by the time you retire, there will have been significant changes in the Social Security system. There is even talk today of making all or part of the system private. The problem is that the number of people retiring and living longer is increasing dramatically, though the number of workers paying into Social Security per retiree is declining. The result is likely to be serious cuts in benefits, a much later average retirement age, reduced cost-of-living adjustments

(COLAs), and/or much higher Social Security taxes. Don't count on Social Security to provide you with ample funds for retirement. Rather, plan now to save funds for your nonworking years (see Figure 22.3). Recognizing Social Security's potential downfall, the government has established incentives for you to save money now for retirement. Here are the specifics.

··· INDIVIDUAL RETIREMENT ACCOUNTS (IRAs) ···

Traditionally an **individual retirement account (IRA)** has been a tax-deferred investment plan that enables you (and your spouse, if you are married) to save part of your income for retirement. A traditional IRA allows people who qualify to deduct from their reported income the money they put into an account. The newest kind of IRA is called a Roth IRA. People who invest in a Roth IRA don't get up-front deductions on their taxes, but withdrawals are tax free. Financial planners highly recommend IRAs, but differ as to which kind is best.[7] Both have advantages and disadvantages, so you should check with a financial advisor to determine which would be best for you.[8] You may decide to have both kinds of accounts. For more details about IRAs, check out http://www.datachimp.com, a site put together by interested amateurs who are not very rich—yet.

If you begin saving now in either type of IRA, the money could compound over and over and become quite a nest egg by the time you retire. Opening an IRA may be one of the wisest investments you make.

A wide range of investment choices is available when you open an IRA. Your local bank, savings and loan, and credit union all have different types of IRAs. Insurance companies offer such plans as well. You may prefer to be a bit aggressive with this money to earn a higher return. In that case, you can put your IRA funds into stocks, bonds, mutual funds, or precious metals. Some mutual funds

individual retirement account (IRA)
Traditionally, a tax-deferred investment plan that enables you (and your spouse, if you are married) to save part of your income for retirement.

◀ CONSIDER USING TM 160
The Fate of Your Social Security Investment (Figure 22.3 on text page 661)

FIGURE 22.3
· · · ·
THE FATE OF YOUR SOCIAL SECURITY INVESTMENT
This chart shows that, at present rates, Social Security funds will run out in the year 2048. That is about 50 years from now. Much sooner than that, the outgo will exceed revenues. It's a good idea to begin your own retirement account to supplement Social Security. You're likely to live a long time after retirement and will need the money.

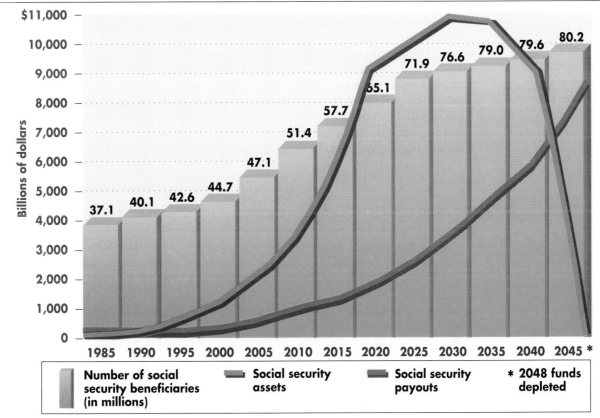

Source: Social Security Administration data.

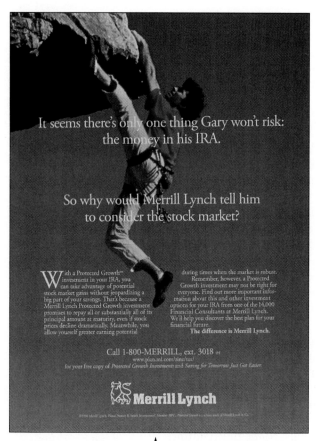

When you put money into a traditional IRA, the government gives you a tax break by deducting that amount from your reported earnings on your income tax form. If you are in the 18–28 percent tax bracket, that means that the government is subsidizing your savings at a rate of 18–28 percent, a rate you're not likely to find elsewhere. Can you see why some folks even borrow money to put into an IRA? Our advice, check it out!

> **CONSIDER USING ACETATE 22-6**
How to Figure Your Net Worth.

> **CONSIDER USING LECTURE ENHANCER 22-9**
Investment Choices for Your IRA.

have multiple options (gold stocks, government securities, high-tech stocks, and more). You can switch from fund to fund or from investment to investment with your IRA funds. You can even open several different IRAs as long as the total amount invested doesn't exceed the government's limit.

Let's see why a traditional IRA is such a good deal for a young investor if you don't have a company-sponsored retirement plan. The tremendous benefit is the fact that the invested money is not taxed. That means fast, and good, returns for you. For example, say you put $2,000 a year into an IRA. Normally, you'd pay taxes on that $2,000. But because you put the money into an IRA, you won't have to pay those taxes. If you're in the 28 percent tax bracket, that means you save $560 in taxes! Put another way, the $2,000 you save only costs you $1,440—a huge bargain.

If you save $2,000 a year for 20 years and earn 12 percent a year, you'll accumulate savings of over $145,000 in just 20 years and nearly $500,000 in 30 years. If you start when you are just out of school, you'll be a millionaire by the time you retire. All you have to do is save $2,000 a year and earn 12 percent. Can you see why investment advisors often say that an IRA is the best way to invest in your retirement?

You can't take the money out until you are 59½ years old without paying a 10 percent penalty and paying taxes on the income. That's really a benefit for you, because it's less tempting to tap the fund when an emergency comes up or you see the car of your dreams. On the other hand, the money is there if a real need or emergency arises. For example, you can take out some funds to invest in an education or a new home. But check the rules; they change over time.

When you make financial plans, be sure to explore IRAs. It's a sure path to being a millionaire someday and to having the funds available to further enjoy your retirement years. You might consider contributing to an IRA through payroll deductions to ensure that the money's invested before you're tempted to spend it. Check the taxes you will have to pay at retirement, however. Your broker may recommend a Roth IRA instead.

••• SIMPLE IRAs •••

Companies with 100 or fewer employees can provide their workers with a simple IRA. Basically, that means that employees can contribute up to $6,000 of their income annually, compared with the $2,000 with regular IRAs. The company matches the contribution. This new plan enables people to save much more money over time and makes for a good employee benefit for smaller companies.[9]

••• 401(k) PLANS •••

More than 220,000 companies now offer 401(k) retirement plans covering some 30 million workers.[10] These plans have three benefits: (1) The money you put in reduces your present taxable income, (2) tax is deferred on the earnings, and (3) employers often match part of your deposit—50 cents or more for every dollar deposited. You should deposit at least as much as your employer matches, often up to 15 percent of your salary. You normally can't withdraw funds from this account until you're 59, but often you can borrow from the account. You can usually select how the money in a 401(k) plan is invested: stocks, bonds, and, in some cases, real estate. If the policy is held until death, no income taxes will ever be due on the investment gains that have built up in the policy.

There is a simple 401(K) plan for those firms that employ 100 or fewer employees. The maximum investment is $6,000, but it is matched by the employer. This is a rather new program, but should prove popular among smaller businesses.

◄ **CONSIDER USING LECTURE ENHANCER 22-10**
The Popularity of Small Business 401(k) Plans.

◄ **CONSIDER USING OT ACETATE 22-7**
Are 401(k) Accounts Being Fully Used?

••• KEOGH PLANS •••

Millions of small-business owners don't have the benefit of a corporate retirement system. Such people can contribute to an IRA, but the amount they can invest is limited. The alternative for all those doctors, lawyers, real estate salespeople, artists, writers, and other self-employed people is to establish their own Keogh plan. It's like an IRA for entrepreneurs. You can also check into simplified employee pension (SEP) plans, which are the best types of IRAs for sole proprietors ➤ P. 134 ◄.

The advantage of Keogh plans is that the maximum that can be invested is more than $30,000 per year. The original amount was much lower, but the government wanted to encourage self-employed people to build retirement funds. Both IRA and Keogh plans could be considered backup plans to protect people against the likely declines in the value of the Social Security system. Even without any cuts, Social Security simply won't provide enough for a comfortable retirement.

Like IRAs, Keogh funds aren't taxed until they are withdrawn, nor are the returns the funds earn. Thus, a person in the 28 percent tax bracket who invests $10,000 yearly in a Keogh saves $2,800 in taxes. That means, in essence, that the government is financing 28 percent of his or her retirement fund. As with an IRA, this is an excellent deal. If a person were to put the full $30,000 a year into a Keogh plan that earns 10 percent a year, he or she would have over $5 million in the account after 30 years.

As with an IRA, there's a 10 percent penalty for early withdrawal. Also like an IRA, funds may be withdrawn in a lump sum or spread out over the years. However, the key decision is the one you make now—to begin early to put funds into an IRA, a Keogh plan, or both, so that the magic of compounding can turn that money into a sizable retirement fund.[11]

◄ **CONSIDER USING OT ACETATE 22-8**
Major Sources of Financial Advice.

••• FINANCIAL PLANNERS •••

If the idea of developing a comprehensive financial plan for yourself or your business seems overwhelming, relax; help is available. The people who assist in developing a comprehensive program that covers investments, taxes, insurance, and other financial matters are called financial planners. Be careful, though; anybody and his brother or sister can claim to be financial planners today. Many so-called planners are simply life insurance salespeople or mutual fund salespeople. Businesspeople often turn to their accountants or finance department for legitimate financial planning help.

In the past few years, there has been an explosion in the number of companies offering financial services. Such companies are sometimes called one-stop financial centers or financial supermarkets because they provide a variety of financial services ranging from banking service to mutual funds, insurance, tax assistance, stocks, bonds, and real estate. It pays to shop around for financial advice. You can go to an independent financial planner or a financial service

◄ **CONSIDER USING OT ACETATE 22-9**
Questions to Ask Your Financial Planner.

◄ **CONSIDER USING OT ACETATE 22-10**
What Do Middle Aged Americans Feel About the Financial Future?

Tim Ulbrich is an investment broker with A. G. Edwards & Sons. In today's complex economic environment, almost everyone could use some investment advice. Be careful to find someone who understands your wants and needs and can meet them effectively. Begin by determining the most reputable firms in your area. Then interview several investment professionals, finding the one that matches your personality and investment objectives. You will be spending much time making important decisions with your investment professional throughout your life. This is why finding the person you can trust and respect, who also has your best interests in mind, will make your professional relationship a lasting one.

company. In either case, ask around among your friends and family. Find someone who understands your situation and is willing to spend some time with you.

Most financial planners begin with life insurance. They feel that most people should have basic term insurance coverage. They also explore your health insurance plans. They look for both medical expense and disability coverage. They may also recommend major medical protection to cover catastrophic illnesses.

Financial planning covers all aspects of investing, all the way to retirement and death. (Planning for estate taxes is important early in life.) Financial planners can steer you into the proper mix of IRAs, stocks, bonds, precious metals, real estate, and so on.[12]

As you can see, accumulating enough funds to start a business is a complex and difficult matter. Investing that money and protecting it from loss makes the process even more involved. It is never too early to start a saving and investment program. As you have learned, there are many, many millionaires in the United States and around the world. They have taken many different paths to their wealth, but the most common paths are entrepreneurship and wise money management. We hope this chapter helps you join their ranks.

Progress Check

- What are three advantages of using a credit card?
- What kind of life insurance is recommended for most people?
- What are the advantages of investing through an IRA? A Keogh account? A 401(k) account?

SUMMARY
......

1. Describe the six steps one should take to generate capital.

1. There are six steps you can take today to get control of your finances.
   - ***What are the six steps to managing personal assets?***
   (1) Take an inventory of your financial assets. That means that you need to develop a balance sheet for yourself: Assets = Liabilities + Owners' equity. (2) Keep track of all your expenses. (3) Prepare a budget. (4) Pay off your debts. (5) Start a savings plan. The best way to save money is to pay yourself first. That is, take your paycheck, take out money for savings, and then

plan what to do with the rest. (6) If you have to borrow money, only borrow it to buy assets that have the potential to increase in value, such as a house or business.

• ***What is called the first investment?***

Education is called the first investment because all through your life you will need to spend time learning not just business but everything about living life.

• ***How much capital does a young entrepreneur need?***

Businesses can be started with a few thousand dollars. Major expenditures for capital equipment are not necessary because those functions can be outsourced to others.

2. To accumulate capital, you must earn more than you spend.

• ***How can a person accumulate enough capital to become financially secure?***

First, find a job. Try to live as frugally as possible. The savings can then be used to generate even more capital. Invest the money wisely: real estate is a great start.

• ***Why is real estate a good investment?***

Over the years real estate has grown in value. Furthermore, the government allows you to deduct interest payments on the mortgage, which allows you to buy more home for the money than you could otherwise.

• ***Where is the best place to keep savings?***

It is not wise to keep long-term savings in a bank or an S&L. It is best, in the long run to invest in stock. Bonds have not traditionally been as good an investment. Although stocks go up and down, in the long run they earn more than most other investments.

3. Term insurance is pure insurance protection for a given number of years.

• ***Why is term insurance preferred?***

You can buy much more term insurance than whole-life insurance for the same amount of money.

• ***Do I need other insurance?***

It's important to have health insurance to protect against large losses. You also need car insurance (get a large deductible—$500 or so) and liability insurance in case you injure someone.

4. It may seem too early to begin planning your retirement, but not to do so would be a big mistake. Successful financial planning means long-range planning, and retirement is a critical phase of life.

• ***What are some basics?***

Supplement Social Security with savings plans of your own. Everyone should have an IRA to begin with. Let the government pay for some of your retirement savings. All tax-free savings are good. That's why a Keogh plan or an IRA-SEP is wise. An IRA-SEP is a savings plan for entrepreneurs. If you work for someone else, check out the 401(k) plan. Find a financial advisor who can recommend the best IRA and help you make other investments.

2. Explain the best way to preserve capital and begin investing.

3. Compare and contrast various types of life, health, and other insurance alternatives.

4. Outline a strategy for retiring with enough money to last a lifetime.

Individual Retirement Account (IRA) 661

Social Security 660

Term insurance 659

KEY TERMS
••••••

DEVELOPING WORKPLACE SKILLS

1. Few things are more surprising to a new college graduate than the cost of living, single or married, in an apartment. To prevent such surprises, research and calculate these costs now and share them with the class. Be sure to include rent, utilities, food, clothes, health care, insurance (life, auto, disability), transportation, vacation, charity, recreation, furniture, and depreciation. Then prepare a two-page paper on the concept of living on one income, given these figures. Older students in class are great for offering realistic facts and figures.

2. Talk with your parents or others you know who have invested in a family home. What appreciation have they gained on the purchase price? What other benefits has the home brought? Compose a list of the benefits and the drawbacks of owning a home and real estate in general as an investment. Be prepared to give a one-minute presentation on what you learned.

3. For one month keep a record of every expenditure you make. Based on the results, share what you learn with your class. Use a computer spreadsheet or personal finance software to establish an annual budget.

4. Debate the following statement: "The best investment one can make is in education, including education in the arts, literature, music, and dance." Take the side you do not now believe to see how others think.

5. Check out the benefits and drawbacks of both traditional and Roth IRAs. The text offers a Web site to use, but such information is also available in the library. Prepare a two-minute presentation on the benefits of each.

TAKING IT TO THE NET

Purpose

To use on-line resources to make smart personal finance decisions.

Exercise

Use the calculators on the FinanCenter Web site (http://www.financenter.com) to answer the following questions:

1. You need $5,000 for a trip to Europe in two years. How much would you have to deposit monthly in a savings account paying 3 percent in order to meet your goal?

2. Investing $1,000 at 6 percent for five years, what is the difference in purchasing power of your savings if inflation increases by 2 percent annually during that time? By 4 percent?

3. Starting today, how much would you need to save each month in order to become a millionaire before you retire?

4. You need a new car. What car can you afford if you have $1,500 for a down payment, can make monthly payments of $300, and get $1,000 for trading in your old clunker?

5. How much house can you afford if you earn $36,000 a year and have $10,000 savings for a down payment, a $6,000 car loan balance, and no credit card debts?

Practicing Management Decisions

CASE
BECOMING FINANCIALLY SECURE

Mike and Priscilla Thomas are a married couple with two incomes and no children. Their cars are both paid for. They've saved enough money to buy a new house without selling their old one. (Real estate is typically a sound investment.) They're renting out their town house for added income. They hope to buy more rental property to use as an income producer so that they can both retire at age 50!

Priscilla runs a company called Cost Reduction Services and Associates. It advises small firms on ways to cut overhead expenses. The couple also owned a window-washing business when they were in college. Priscilla loves being in business for herself because, she says, "when you own your own business, you can work hard and you get paid for your hard work." Mike is a pharmaceutical salesperson.

How did the Thomases get the money to start their own businesses and buy a couple of homes? They committed themselves from the beginning of their marriage to live on Mike's income and to save Priscilla's income. Furthermore, they decided to live frugally. The goal of early retirement was their incentive. They "lived like college kids" for five years, cutting out coupons and saving every cent they could. They don't often go out to eat, and they rent movies for their VCR instead of going to the movie theater. Their first investment was a town house. They used the tax deductions to help offset their income.

Mike puts the maximum amount into his company's 401(k) plan. It's invested in a very aggressive growth fund: half U.S. stocks and half international stocks. Now that the couple is financially secure, they're planning to have children.

Decision Questions

1. What steps would the average young couple have to follow to be like Mike and Priscilla and become financially secure all their lives?
2. What kind of goals could you establish to make it worthwhile to scrimp and save your money rather than spend it on today's pleasures?
3. How much money would one person have to earn to support two people living in an apartment in your area?
4. Can you see now why money management is one of the keys to both entrepreneurship and personal financial security?

Source: Jerry Knight, "Mike and Priscilla's DINK Adventure," *The Washington Post,* July 24, 1994, p. H5.

VIDEO CASE
EMPLOYEE SAVINGS PLANS—WORKING WITH BROKERS

You may feel uncertain when it comes to planning your financial future, but you aren't alone. Even large firms like Mobil Oil need help when it comes to financial planning. At one time, Mobil ran its own savings plan for employees, but it recently outsourced the plan to Merrill Lynch. You too can turn to a brokerage firm to help you manage your investments. Or perhaps helping others plan their investments looks like an interesting career possibility.

By working with a broker like Merrill Lynch, the employees at Mobil found more investment flexibility, more choices, and better investment information than they had found on their own. They can make fund transfers and withdrawals, apply for loans, check savings rate changes, change the direction of their savings plans, and even customize their private investment number—24 hours a day, seven days a week. All of this is done with the utmost of privacy because the broker handling your account deals with numbers and doesn't have to know your name.

Merrill Lynch handles some $510 billion in investments for Mobil and other big corporate accounts as well as smaller accounts for individual investors. After observing what such account people do, you may be interested in being a broker yourself or working for a brokerage firm on corporate accounts.

Merrill Lynch, like most brokerage firms, has several funds where you can invest your money. There are a number of stock funds, including an international fund, that feature investments in different types of companies and industries (e.g., technology). They also manage a group of bond funds. Managing your money in such an account makes it possible to accumulate the funds required to invest in or purchase your own business, buy a home, plan your retirement, and make other financial decisions.

Discussion Questions

1. How appealing does a career in a firm like Merrill Lynch seem to you? What do you find attractive or unattractive about such a career?
2. When you see employees at Mobil and other major firms carefully planning their financial futures, does it motivate you to begin such planning yourself? Why?
3. When you see how easy it is to deal with brokers—by simply picking up a phone and giving them the necessary information—does it encourage you to invest your money in such an account? Why?
4. When you are starting a career, the idea of saving for the future may seem less important. What are the primary benefits of consulting with a financial planning professional early in your career?

Managing Risk

Appendix

THE INCREASING CHALLENGE OF
RISK MANAGEMENT

The management of risk is a major issue for businesses throughout the country. Almost every day you hear about an earthquake, flood, fire, airplane crash, riot, or car accident that destroyed property or injured someone. An accident that involves a major personality, such as Princess Diana, may be front-page news for weeks. Such reports are so much a part of the news that we tend to accept these events as part of everyday life. But events involving loss mean a great deal to the businesspeople involved. They must pay to restore the property and compensate those who are injured. In addition to the newsmaking stories, thousands of other incidents involve businesspeople in lawsuits. Lawsuits in recent years have covered everything from job-related accidents to product liability—for example, a woman who was burned by spilled coffee at McDonald's brought a suit against the company.

◄ CONSIDER USING TM 161
Chapter Outline.

MANAGING RISK

The term **risk** refers to the chance of loss, the degree of probability of loss, and the amount of possible loss. There are two different kinds of risk:

◄ CONSIDER USING OT ACETATE
RM-1
Types of Risk.

risk
The change of loss, the degree of probability of loss, and the amount of possible loss.

- **Speculative risk** involves a chance of either profit or loss. It includes the chance a firm takes to make extra money by buying new machinery, acquiring more inventory, and making other decisions in which

speculative risk
A chance of either profit or loss.

Flood insurance. It's just smart business.

If you own a small business, you know that it's a part of you. That's why you try to be prepared for anything that could jeopardize it. Yet the threat of floods is one thing you may have overlooked. Over 90% of all natural disasters in the United States involve flooding. And a flood can destroy your years of effort in minutes.

Are you covered?

Many small business owners find out too late that most business insurance doesn't cover flood damage. Fortunately, the National Flood Insurance Program

offers flood insurance that covers small businesses like yours.

Give yourself peace of mind.

Everyone runs the risk of being a flood victim. Between 25% to 30% of flood insurance claims come from low to moderate risk areas. So, mail the coupon or call your insurance company, agent or this toll-free number, 1-888-CALL-FLOOD, ext. 152. Act now, since there's a waiting period before your coverage takes effect. Because with floods, you can never say never.

1-888-CALL-FLOOD ext. 152
Please send me information about NFIP.
MAIL TO: FEMA/MSC, PO BOX 1038,
JESSUP, MD 20794-0408

We can't replace your memories, but we can help you build new ones.
NFIP, 500 C Street SW, Washington, D.C. 20472 • TDD #1-800-427-5593 • http://www.fema.gov/fema/nfip96-18.shtm

Often the best way to protect a company against pure risk is to buy insurance. Recently, El Niño has caused much flood damage in many parts of the United States. Is there a better way to protect a business than insurance?

➤ CONSIDER USING LECTURE ENHANCER C-1
Personal Risk Management

pure risk
The threat of loss with no chance for profit.

the probability of loss may be relatively low and the amount of loss is known. An entrepreneur takes speculative risk on the chance of making a profit ⇢ P. 4 ⇠. In business, building a new plant is a speculative risk because it may result in a loss or a profit.

- **Pure risk** is the threat of loss with no chance for profit. Pure risk involves the threat of fire, accident, or loss. If such events occur, a company loses money; but if the events do not occur, the company gains nothing.

The risk that is of most concern to businesspeople is pure risk. Pure risk threatens the very existence of some firms. Once such risks are identified, firms have several options:

1. Reduce the risk.
2. Avoid the risk.
3. Self-insure against the risk.
4. Buy insurance against the risk.

We'll discuss the option of buying insurance in detail later in this appendix. In the next sections, we will discuss each of the alternatives for managing risk. These steps should be taken to lower the need for outside insurance.

••• REDUCING RISK •••

A firm can reduce risk by establishing loss-prevention programs such as fire drills, health education, safety inspections, equipment maintenance, accident prevention programs, and so on. Many retail stores, for example, use mirrors, video cameras, and other devices to prevent shoplifting. Water sprinklers and smoke detectors are used to minimize fire loss. In industry, most machines have safety devices to protect workers' fingers, eyes, and so on.

Employees, as well as managers, can reduce risk. For example, truck drivers can wear seat belts to minimize injuries from accidents, operators of loud machinery can wear earplugs to reduce the chance of hearing loss, and those who lift heavy objects can wear back braces. The beginning of an effective risk management strategy is a good loss-prevention program. However, high insurance rates have forced some people to go beyond merely preventing risks to the point of avoiding risks, and in extreme cases by going out of business.

••• AVOIDING RISK •••

Many risks cannot be avoided. There is always the chance of fire, theft, accident, or injury. But some companies are avoiding risk by not accepting hazardous jobs and by outsourcing ⇢ P. 246 ⇠ shipping and other functions. The threat of lawsuits has driven away some drug companies from manufacturing vaccines, and some consulting engineers refuse to work on hazardous sites. Some companies are losing outside members of their boards of directors for lack of liability coverage protecting them from legal action against the firms they represent.

••• SELF-INSURING •••

Many companies and municipalities have turned to **self-insurance** because they either can't find or can't afford conventional property/casualty policies. Such firms set aside money to cover routine claims and buy only "catastrophe" policies to cover big losses. Self-insurance, then, lowers the cost of insurance by allowing companies to take out insurance only for larger losses.

Self-insurance is most appropriate when a firm has several widely distributed facilities. The risk from fire, theft, or other catastrophe is then more manageable. Firms with huge facilities, in which a major fire or earthquake could destroy the entire operation, usually turn to insurance companies to cover the risk.

One of the more risky strategies for self-insurance is for a company to "go bare," paying claims straight out of its budget. The risk here is that the whole firm could go bankrupt over one claim, if the damages are high enough. A less risky alternative is to form risk retention group-insurance pools that share similar risks. It is estimated that about one-third of the insurance market is using such alternatives.

••• BUYING INSURANCE TO COVER RISK •••

Although well-designed, consistently enforced risk-prevention programs reduce the probability of claims, accidents do happen. Insurance is the armor individuals, businesses, and nonprofit organizations use to protect themselves from various financial risks. For this protection, such organizations spend about 10 percent of GDP on insurance premiums. Some insurance protection is provided by the federal government (See Figure A.1), but most risks must be covered by individuals and businesses on their own. We will continue our discussion of insurance by identifying the types of risks that are uninsurable, followed by those that are insurable.

WHAT RISKS ARE UNINSURABLE?   Not all risks are insurable, even risks that once were covered by insurance. An **uninsurable risk** is one that no insurance company will cover. Examples of things that you cannot insure include market risks (e.g., losses that occur because of price changes, style changes, or new products that make your product obsolete); political risks (e.g., losses from war or government restrictions on trade); some personal risks (such as loss of a job); and some risks of operation (e.g., strikes or inefficient machinery).

WHAT RISKS ARE INSURABLE?   An **insurable risk** is one that the typical insurance company will cover. Generally, insurance companies use the following guidelines when evaluating whether or not a risk is insurable:

    1. The policyholder must have an **insurable interest**, which means that the policyholder is the one at risk to suffer a loss. You cannot, for

Insurance companies will help you do everything you can to eliminate or minimize risk. But that still leaves much risk that is often best covered with insurance. Some insurance coverage is mandatory, but all companies must weigh the risks against the cost. Do you carry any insurance? What factors did you consider when buying it?

self-insurance
The practice of setting aside money to cover routine claims and buying only "catastrophe" policies to cover big losses.

uninsurable risk
A risk that no insurance company will cover.

insurable risk
A risk that the typical insurance company will cover.

insurable interest
The possibility of the policyholder to suffer a loss.

FIGURE A.1

· · · ·

PUBLIC INSURANCE
State or federal government agencies that provide insurance protection.

Type of Insurance	What It Does
Unemployment Compensation	Provides financial benefits, job counseling, and placement services for unemployed workers.
Social Security	Provides retirement benefits, life insurance, health insurance, and disability income insurance.
Federal Housing Administration (FHA)	Provides mortgage insurance to lenders to protect against default by home buyers.
National Flood Insurance Association	Provides compensation for damage caused by flooding and mud slides to properties located in flood-prone areas.
Federal Crime Insurance	Provides insurance to property owners in high-crime areas.
Federal Crop Insurance	Provides compensation for damaged crops.
Pension Benefit Guaranty Corporation	Insures pension plans to prevent loss to employees if the company declares bankruptcy or goes out of business.

➤ **CONSIDER USING TM 162**
Public Insurance (Figure A.1 on text page 672).

➤ **CONSIDER USING LECTURE ENHANCER C-2**
Personal Risk Management.

➤ **CONSIDER USING OT ACETATE RM-2**
Percentage of Employers that Self-Fund Employee Health Insurance.

insurance policy
A written contract between the insured and an insurance company that promises to pay for all or part of a loss.

premium
The fee charged by an insurance company for an insurance policy.

law of large numbers
Principle that if a large number of people are exposed to the same risk, a predictable number of losses will occur during a given period of time.

➤ **CONSIDER USING OT ACETATE-3**
Types of Uninsurable Risks.

rule of indemnity
Rule says that an insured person or organization cannot collect more than the actual loss from an insurable risk.

example, buy fire insurance on your neighbor's house and collect if it burns down.

2. The loss should be measurable.
3. The *chance* of loss should be measurable.
4. The loss should be accidental.
5. The risk should be dispersed; that is, spread among different geographical areas so that a flood or other natural disaster in one area would not bankrupt the company.
6. The insurance company can set standards for accepting risks.

THE LAW OF LARGE NUMBERS   An **insurance policy** is a written contract between the insured (an individual or organization) and an insurance company that promises to pay for all or part of a loss. A **premium** is the fee charged by the insurance company or, in other words, the cost of the insurance policy to the insured.

As in all private businesses, the objective of an insurance company is to make a profit. To ensure that it makes a profit, an insurance company gathers data to determine the extent of the risk. What makes the acceptance of risk possible for insurance companies is the law of large numbers.

The **law of large numbers** states that if a large number of people or organizations are exposed to the same risk, a predictable number of losses will occur during a given period of time. Once the insurance company predicts the number of losses likely to occur, it can determine the appropriate premiums for each policy it issues. The premium is supposed to be high enough to cover expected losses and yet earn a profit for the firm and its stockholders. Today, many insurance companies are charging high premiums, not for past risks but for the anticipated costs associated with the increasing number of court cases and high damage awards.

RULE OF INDEMNITY   The **rule of indemnity** says that an insured person or organization cannot collect more than the actual loss from an insurable risk. One cannot gain from risk management; one can only minimize losses.

One cannot, for example, buy two insurance policies and collect from both for the same loss. If a company or person carried two policies, the two insurance companies would calculate any loss and divide the reimbursement.

SOURCES OF INSURANCE There are two major types of insurance companies. A **stock insurance company** is owned by stockholders, just like any other investor-owned company. A **mutual insurance company** is owned by its policyholders. The largest life insurance company, Prudential, is a mutual insurance company. A mutual insurance company, unlike a stock company, does not earn profits for its owners. It is a nonprofit organization, and any excess funds (over losses, expenses, and growth costs) go to the policyholders/investors in the form of dividends or premium reductions.

stock insurance company
A type of insurance company owned by stockholders.

mutual insurance company
A type of insurance company owned by its policyholders.

.... ▬ ....
TYPES OF INSURANCE

As we have discussed, risk management consists of reducing risk, avoiding risk, self-insuring, and buying insurance. There are many types of insurance that cover various losses: property and liability insurance, health insurance, and life insurance. Property losses result from fires, accidents, theft, or other perils. Liability losses result from property damage or injuries suffered by others for which the policyholder is held responsible. Let's begin our exploration of insurance by looking at health insurance.

◄ **CONSIDER USING OT ACETATE RM-4**
Public and Private Insurance Companies.

··· HEALTH INSURANCE ···

Businesses and nonprofit organizations may offer their employees an array of health care benefits to choose from. Everything from hospitalization to physician fees, eye exams, dental exams, and prescriptions can be covered. Often, employees may choose between options from health care providers (e.g., Blue Cross/Blue Shield); health maintenance organizations (HMOs, e.g., Kaiser Permanente); or preferred provider organizations (PPOs).

◄ **CONSIDER USING OT ACETATE RM-5**
Additional Public Insurance Companies.

HEALTH MAINTENANCE ORGANIZATIONS (HMOs) **Health Maintenance Organizations (HMOs)** offer a full range of health care benefits. Emphasis is on helping members stay healthy instead of on treating illnesses. Two nice features typical of HMOs are that members do not receive bills and do not have to fill out claim forms for routine service. HMOs employ or contract with doctors, hospitals, and other systems of health care, and members must use those providers. In other words, they cannot choose any doctor they wish but can select one doctor from the approved list to be their primary care physician. That doctor will then recommend specialists, if necessary. The HMO system is called managed care.

health maintenance organizations (HMOs)
Health care organizations that require members to choose from a restricted list of doctors.

HMOs are less expensive than comprehensive health insurance providers, but members sometimes complain about not being able to choose doctors or to get the care they want or need. Some physicians also complain because they lose some freedom to do what is needed to make people well and they often receive less compensation than they feel is appropriate for the services they provide.

◄ **CONSIDER USING OT ACETATE RM-6**
Growth of Enrollments in HMOs.

It may seem that HMOs are capturing all the profit for themselves, but that is not true. Kaiser Permanente, for example, the largest of the HMOs, lost $270 million in 1997, even as it expanded membership to 8,970,000 people.[1]

To save money, HMOs usually must approve treatment before it is given. People who prefer to have their doctor make such decisions often choose a PPO, as we shall see next.

PREFERRED PROVIDER ORGANIZATIONS (PPOs)

Preferred provider organizations (PPOs) also contract with hospitals and physicians, but unlike an HMO, a PPO does not require its members to choose only from those physicians. However, members do have to pay more if they don't use a physician on the preferred list. Also, members usually have to pay a deductible (e.g., $250) before the PPO will pay any bills. When the plan does pay, members usually have to pay part of the bill. This payment is called co-insurance. Some people feel that the added expense of PPOs over HMOs is worth the freedom to select their own physicians.

Since both HMOs and PPOs can cost as much as 80 percent less than comprehensive individual health insurance policies, most businesses and individuals choose to join one.

••• DISABILITY INSURANCE •••

Disability insurance replaces part of your income (50 to 70 percent) if you become disabled and unable to work. There usually is a period of time you must be disabled (e.g., 60 days) before you can begin collecting. Many employers provide this type of insurance, but some do not. In either case, insurance experts recommend that you get this type of insurance because the chances of becoming disabled by a disease or accident are much higher than the chance of dying. The premiums for such insurance vary depending on your age, occupation, and income.

••• WORKERS' COMPENSATION •••

Workers' compensation insurance guarantees payment of wages, medical care, and rehabilitation services (e.g., retraining) for employees who are injured on the job. Employers in all 50 states are required to provide this insurance. This insurance also provides benefits to the survivors of workers who die as a result of work-related injuries. The cost of insurance varies by the company's safety record, its payroll, and the types of hazards faced by workers. For example, it costs more to insure a steelworker than an accountant.

••• LIABILITY INSURANCE •••

Professional liability insurance covers people who are found liable for professional negligence. For example, if a lawyer gives advice carelessly and the client loses money, the client may then sue the lawyer for an amount equal to that lost. This type of insurance is also known as malpractice insurance. While you may think of doctors and dentists when you hear that term, the fact is that many professionals, including mortgage brokers and real estate appraisers, are buying this insurance because of large lawsuits their colleagues have faced.

Sometimes it is easier and less expensive to cover as many insurance needs as possible with one carrier. That company will more likely give you better and faster service and will help you minimize your costs. Not all employees will want dental insurance, but most should have disability insurance, whether they now recognize the need or not. Can you see why companies need to work with their employees to develop coverage that is best for everyone involved?

preferred provider organizations (PPOs)
Health care organizations similar to HMOs except that they allow members to choose their own physicians (for a fee).

➤ **CONSIDER USING LECTURE ENHANCER C-3**
Is Your Household Helper Insured?

Product liability insurance provides coverage against liability arising out of products sold. If a person is injured by a ladder or some other household good, he or she may sue the manufacturer for damages. Insurance usually covers such losses.

••• OTHER BUSINESS INSURANCE •••

It is impossible in an introductory course like this to discuss in detail all the insurance coverage that businesses may buy. Naturally, businesses must protect themselves against property damage, and they must buy car and truck insurance and more. Figure A.2 on the next page will give you some idea of the types of insurance available.

The point to be made in this appendix is that risk management is critical in all firms. That includes the risk of investing funds and the risk of opening your own business (speculative risk). Remember from Chapter 1, though, that risk is often matched by opportunity and profits. Taking on risk is one way for an entrepreneur to prosper. Regardless of how careful we are, however, we all face the prospect of death, even entrepreneurs. To ensure that those left behind will be able to continue the business, entrepreneurs often buy life insurance that will pay partners and others what they will need to keep the business going. We'll explore that next.

A small business often suffers tremendous loss when its owner dies. Insurance can provide the funds necessary to find a new owner and cover the costs involved in making the transition. Valued employees may also be insured if their loss would severely impact a company. Risk management is not always the first thought one has when starting a business. What might happen if a businessperson neglects such risks?

••• LIFE INSURANCE FOR BUSINESSES •••

We discussed life insurance in Chapter 22. There, the focus was on life insurance for you and your family. Everything said there applies to life insurance for business executives as well. The best coverage for most individuals is term insurance, but dozens of new policies with interesting features have been emerging recently.

THE RISK OF DAMAGING THE ENVIRONMENT

The risk of environmental harm reaches international proportions in issues such as global warming.[2] One international incident that had dramatic consequences for businesses was the disaster in Bhopal, India, late in the 1980s, in which a chemical gas leak from a Union Carbide plant killed over 2,000 people and seriously injured thousands more. Public concern was later raised over a similar Union Carbide plant in Institute, West Virginia.

The explosion of the Chernobyl nuclear plant in the former Soviet Union caused much concern throughout the world. Due to violations of various safety standards, several U.S. nuclear power plants have been shut down. Yet since coal-fired power plants are said to cause acid rain, and other inexpensive fuel sources haven't been developed, there may be more research into nuclear plants in order to make them safer. Clearly, this will be an issue well into the next century.[3]

Many people feel there is a need for a more careful evaluation of environmental risks than currently is done. How much risk is there in global warming

◄ CONSIDER USING TM 163
Private Insurance (Figure A.2 on text page 676)

┌─   FIGURE A.2   ─┐
└   ┘
            ....
      PRIVATE INSURANCE
Insurance companies not
government-owned
(stock companies or
mutual companies).

Types of Insurance	What It Does
Property and Liability	
Fire	Covers losses to buildings and their contents from fire.
Automobile	Covers property damage, bodily injury, collision, fire, theft, vandalism, and other related vehicle losses.
Homeowners'	Covers the home, other structures on the premises, home contents, expenses if forced from the home because of an insured peril, third-party liability, and medical payments to others.
Computer coverage	Covers loss of equipment from fire, theft, and sometimes spills, power surges, and accidents.
Professional liability	Protects from suits stemming from mistakes made or bad advice given in a professional context.
Business interruption	Provides compensation for loss due to fire, theft, or similar disasters that close a business. Covers lost income, continuing expenses, and utility expenses.
Nonperformance loss protection	Protects from failure of a contractor, supplier, or other person to fulfill an obligation.
Criminal loss protection	Protects from loss due to theft, burglary, or robbery.
Commercial credit insurance	Protects manufacturers and wholesalers from credit losses due to insolvency or default.
Public liability insurance	Provides protection for businesses and individuals against losses resulting from personal injuries or damage to the property of others for which the insured is responsible.
Extended product liability insurance	Covers potentially toxic substances in products; environmental liability; and, for corporations, directors and officer liability.
Fidelity bond	Protects employers from employee dishonesty.
Surety bond	Covers losses resulting from a second party's failure to fulfill a contract.
Title insurance	Protects buyers from losses resulting from a defect in title to property.
Health Insurance	
Basic health insurance	Covers losses due to sickness or accidents.
Major medical insurance	Protects against catastrophic losses by covering expenses beyond the limits of basic policies.
Hospitalization insurance	Pays for most hospital expenses.
Surgical and medical insurance	Pays costs of surgery and doctor's care while recuperating in a hospital.
Dental insurance	Pays a percentage of dental expenses.
Disability income insurance	Pays income while the insured is disabled as a result of accident or illness.
Life Insurance	
Group life insurance	Covers all the employees of a firm or members of a group.
Owner or key executive insurance	Enables businesses of sole proprietors or partnerships to pay bills and continue operating, saving jobs for the employees. Enables corporations to hire and train or relocate another manager with no loss to the firm.
Retirement and pension plans	Provides employees with supplemental retirement and pension plans.
Credit life insurance	Pays the amount due on a loan if the debtor dies.

The environmental damage caused by oil spills, such as this one—the *Exxon Valdez* spill in Alaska—points out the need for all companies to work together to maintain the integrity of the planet. The various governments of the world are working together to explore various environmental risks and the steps that can be taken cooperatively to lessen those risks. All of us must do our part to protect the environment and our communities.

and the depletion of the ozone layer? We don't yet know, but the risks may be substantial.

Clearly, risk management now goes far beyond the protection of individuals, businesses, and nonprofit organizations from known risks. It means the evaluation of worldwide risks such as global warming. It also means prioritizing these risks so that international funds can be spent where they can do the most good.[4] No insurance company can protect humanity from such risks. These risks are the concern of international governments throughout the world, with the assistance of the international scientific community. They should also be your concern as you study risk management in all its dimensions.

KEY TERMS
• • • • •

health maintenance organizations (HMOs) 673
insurable interest 671
insurable risk 671
insurance policy 672
law of large numbers 672

mutual insurance company 673
preferred provider organizations (PPOs) 674
premium 672
pure risk 670

risk 669
rule of indemnity 672
self-insurance 671
speculative risk 669
stock insurance company 673
uninsurable risk 671

Part 7

Career
Portfolio

Financial Management (Finance and Accounting)

Accounting and finance are career areas that have existed for many centuries. Records discovered in the ruins of ancient Babylon dating back to 300 B.C. show that financial records were kept by the ancients. European monarchs, particularly in the 18th and 19th centuries, relied on bankers and other professional financiers to recover from wars and to build the new industrial revolution.

Today, accountants and financial managers are as much in demand as ever. Computerization has enriched both career areas immensely. Because of changing laws and regulations, companies and their personnel in these positions must place a greater emphasis than ever on accurate reporting of financial data. This field, like so many others, is dynamic and changing.

Nearly two million people work in some area of finance or accounting, most as accountants, financial managers, banking personnel, or financial consultants. Nearly every company—whether in manufacturing, transportation, retailing, or a variety of services—employs one or more financial managers. Accountants and bookkeepers are equally in demand.

••• SKILLS •••

Anyone who enters these areas must have a mathematical aptitude, an interest in numbers, and a considerable amount of patience. As with nearly every other area, speaking and writing skills are a must, because the financial information must be communicated to people. Good ethical judgment is also essential, because areas of finance and accounting both contain more "gray areas" than many of us imagine.

••• CAREER PATHS •••

A bachelor's degree in accounting or finance is usually a prerequisite, although accountants with two-year degrees and outstanding abilities have been hired as bookkeepers and accounting assistants. In some states, tax preparers do not need formal degrees, only mastery of current tax law. In all cases, though, continuing education is becoming increasingly important because of the growing complexity of global commerce, changing federal and state laws, and the constant introduction of new, complex financial instruments.

A well-trained, experienced financial manager is a prime candidate for promotion into top management. Junior public accountants usually advance to semi-senior positions within two to five years and to senior positions within six to eight years. Although advancement can be rapid for well-prepared accountants, especially in public accounting, employees without adequate college preparation are often dead-ended in routine jobs. Also, even CPAs must constantly be reeducated in today's changing environment.

SOME POSSIBLE CAREERS IN MARKETING

Job title	Salary	Job duties	Career path	Prospects
Accountant	Entry level: $29,400 (bachelor's degree) Experienced: Median: $87,400	Depends on size and nature of firm as well as specific job title. Public accountants work independently on a fee basis. Private accountants handle financial records in the company where they are salaried employees. The general accountant supervises, installs, and devises systems. The cost accountant determines unit costs of products and services. The auditor examines and vouches for the accuracy of records.	Start with either an accounting degree or many courses in accounting. Certified Public Accountant must take comprehensive exam, then intern as auditor for two years. Able accountants, especially CPAs, can be promoted rapidly. By specializing in certain accounting areas, an accountant can often be promoted.	Openings in all accounting areas are expected to be average through 2006.
Financial Manager	$21,800–$81,000 Median: $40,700.	As with accountants, duties depend on size and nature of firm as well as specific job title. Titles include treasurer, controller, credit manager, cash manager. Controllers direct preparation of financial reports; cash and credit managers monitor and control the flow of receipts and disbursements; risk and insurance managers work to minimize risk and cut risk costs.	Most start with a degree in finance or accounting. A Master of Business Administration degree (MBA) is becoming increasingly required by some companies. Often promoted into top management.	Number of applicants continues to grow and may exceed the number of openings in the next 10 years.
Securities and financial services sales workers	$18,100–$98,400. Once established, changes to commission only. Median: $38,800.	Open accounts for new customers, execute buy and sell orders based on information from the securities exchange. Get information on company's progress from the research dept. Must be able to anticipate buying and selling trends in the markets.	Many brokerage concerns hire trainees, then place them on a probationary track of around six months. Depending on ability and ambition, promotion can be rapid. Bank employees make much less.	For the talented and ambitious person, the opportunities will remain numerous through 2006. But depends on the growth of the economy.

Source: *Occupational Outlook Handbook,* 1998–1999 Edition: Bureau of Labor Statistics.

Parker/Hunter, Incorporated

Name: Donald F. Detts, Jr., CFP

Age: 37

Position/title: Assistant Vice President, Assistant Branch Manager

Salary range: $60,000–$70,000

Time in this position: Overall, I have been in the investment industry as an Investment Executive for 14 years. Two years ago I was promoted as the Assistant Branch Manager, or ABM.

Major factors in the decision to take this position: From the time I was young, I can always remember having an interest in investments. When I was only 12 years old, I purchased my first stocks with the profits from my paper route. I used to go into the local Parker/Hunter office and research my stocks very carefully. I became a familiar face around the office, and got to know the investment executives.

When in college, I always enjoyed my investment, finance, and accounting courses. It was then that I decided to get my B.S. in accounting.

Upon graduation, a Parker/Hunter investment executive whom I had known for 20 years asked me to come work for them.

Company name: Parker/Hunter Incorporated

Company's web address: www.parkerhunter.com

Company description: Parker/Hunter Incorporated is a full-service stock brokerage and investment banking firm. They are headquartered in Pittsburgh, Pennsylvania. They have several branch offices in the surrounding cities and states.

Job description: I help clients set both short-term and long-term financial goals, which includes retirement and estate planning. I then monitor their plans and make adjustments accordingly. In addition, as the Assistant Branch Manager, I have some administrative duties.

Career paths: I started as a registered representative, or broker. I am now the Assistant Branch Manager.

Ideal next job: My ideal next job is Branch Manager.

Best part of your job: I enjoy meeting with people and determining their individual financial needs. I take a great deal of satisfaction when I have helped them meet their needs and achieve their financial goals.

Worst part of your job: Often times the media—television, newspaper, magazines—make blanket recommendations for what stocks people should buy or sell. This often makes my clients react and they insist that I change their portfolios. In every situation, I have to evaluate if the change makes sense to the overall plan. Most often it doesn't. It is very difficult constantly having to battle these blanket recommendations.

Educational background: I received B.S. in accounting, and then received my Certified Financial Planner (CFP) designation.

Favorite course: investments, tax, and accounting.

Best course for your career: investments and finance.

Compliments of Professor William Blosel, California State University, Pennsylvania

CISS®
Campbell™ Interest and Skill Survey

Irwin/McGraw-Hill and the Assessments group of NCS have partnered to offer you the CISS® (Campbell™ Interest and Skill Survey) career planning package. This 12-page personalized report and career planning guide will help you apply the CISS survey information to your personal and professional life. The CISS survey was developed by Dr. David Campbell of the Center for Creative Leadership.

As you begin exploring your career options in the field of business, let the CISS survey provide you with information to assist you with career exploration and career development. With the CISS survey, you will learn how your likes, dislikes, and self-reported skills compare to those of individuals who are happily and successfully employed in occupations that require a post-secondary education.

Complete the survey and return it to NCS with payment according to the instructions at the end of the answer sheet. Please take advantage of this opportunity to use the results of the Campbell Interest and Skill Survey—we believe you will find this a helpful tool in choosing a meaningful career!

Do not record your answers on pages C1–C6. Use the answer sheet that follows the questions. **If there are no answer sheets left in this book, contact NCS at 1-800-627-7271, extension 5151, to request an additional answer sheet.** You will be charged $14.95 plus $3.00 for shipping and handling when you return your completed answer sheet to NCS.

PART I—INTERESTS

The major purpose of this section is to assess your interests to determine the areas of work where you would be most likely to find satisfying activities.

Following are lists of occupations, school subjects, and varied work activities. Indicate how much you like each item by using the following scale:

L = STRONGLY LIKE
L = Like
l = slightly like
d = slightly dislike
D = Dislike
D = STRONGLY DISLIKE

Blacken the circle that corresponds to your answer on the answer sheet that follows. Don't worry about how good you would be at the activity, or whether you would be successful—just whether or not you would enjoy doing it. Don't think about how much money you might make, or how much status or prestige would be involved. Base your answer solely on how much you would like it.

Work quickly. Your first impression is generally most useful. You may wish to look up from your paper every now and then and take a short break. This will help you stay fresh and alert.

1. An actor or actress, performing on the stage, TV, or in movies

2. An architect, designing new homes and buildings

3. An artist, creating works of art

4. An author, writing stories and novels

5. A baker, making breads and pastries

6. A building superintendent, managing a maintenance staff

7. A bulldozer operator, helping to build new roads

8. A bush pilot, flying a small plane in remote regions

9. A cabinetmaker, building fine furniture

10. A career counselor, helping people make important career decisions

11. A carpenter, building new homes

12. A chef, preparing gourmet meals

13. A chemist, working in a research lab

14. A circus clown, making people laugh

15. A city detective, solving crimes

16. A clothing designer, creating new fashions

17. A coach, working with athletic teams

18. A college professor, teaching and doing research

19. A commercial designer, designing new products

20. A computer programmer, creating new computer software

21. A computer salesperson, selling high-technology products

22. A dancer, performing with a professional company

23. A day care worker, caring for children during the day

24. A diplomat, negotiating agreements between countries

25. A drama director, directing plays and TV shows

26. An economist, predicting future economic trends

27. An elected official, developing new public programs

28. An electrician, installing electrical systems

29. An elementary school teacher, helping young children develop

30. An engineer, designing large building projects

31. A factory superintendent, managing a large manufacturing plant

32. A farmer, raising and harvesting crops

33. A fashion buyer, making decisions about purchasing new styles

34. A financial vice president, responsible for a company's finances

35. A foreign language translator, working overseas

36. A forester, managing timber resources

37. A hairstylist, working in an elite salon

38. A health club manager, helping people exercise

39. A high school teacher, working with teenagers

40. An interior designer, planning room layouts

41. An international tour guide, taking people to other countries

42. An inventor, inventing new products

43. A jeweler, selling expensive jewelry

44. A judge, presiding over a courtroom

45. A laboratory researcher, doing scientific experiments

46. A life insurance salesperson, helping people with their estate planning

47. A manager of a fruit grove, growing fruit commercially

48. A manager of a kennel, caring for animals

49. A marketing director, planning marketing strategies

50. A mathematics instructor, teaching math concepts

51. A medical researcher, running experiments in a hospital

52. A military officer, commanding an outstanding military unit

53. A minister, priest, or rabbi, serving a congregation

54. A musician, performing music for audiences

55. A night club entertainer, doing comedy routines

56. A nurse, caring for patients in a hospital

57. A nursery school teacher, working with young children

58. A nutritionist, advising people on their diets

59. An office manager, overseeing a clerical staff

60. An over-the-road truck driver, driving big trucks

61. A paramedic, giving first aid to accident victims

62. A photographer, taking pictures for a news magazine

63. A physical therapist, helping people recover from injuries

64. A physician, helping patients with their health problems

65. A playground director, arranging games and contests

66. A police captain, in charge of a police precinct

67. A probation officer, working with parolees and the courts

68. A professional athlete, competing against others

69. A prospector, looking for minerals in unexplored areas

70. A psychologist, studying human behavior

71. A realtor, selling private homes

72. A religious leader, preaching about spiritual life

73. A reporter, writing articles for a newspaper

74. A restaurant manager, in charge of a well-established restaurant

75. A sales executive, overseeing a chain of retail stores

76. A school principal, managing teachers and students

77. A singer, performing with a band in dinner clubs

78. A speech instructor, helping people improve their speaking techniques

79. A state governor, directing state affairs

80. A stockbroker, advising clients on their investments

81. A symphony conductor, leading a symphony orchestra

82. A technical writer, preparing scientific manuals

83. A top executive, managing a large corporation

84. A trial lawyer, arguing cases in court

85. A university president, overseeing a major university

For questions 86 through 128, indicate how you would feel about studying each of these school subjects by choosing one of the following responses:

Y = **YES, YES, I definitely would like to study this subject.**
Y = YES, I would like to study this subject.
y = yes, I feel slightly more positive than negative about studying this subject.
n = no, I feel slightly more negative than positive about studying this subject.
N = NO, I would not like to study this subject.
N = **NO, NO, I definitely would not like to study this subject.**

Don't worry about your ability, just whether or not you would enjoy studying the subject.

86. Advertising
87. Agriculture
88. Algebra
89. Architecture
90. Art
91. Auto Mechanics
92. Beauty and Hair Care
93. Chemistry
94. Child Development
95. Computer Science
96. Cooking
97. Creative Writing
98. Electronics
99. Engineering
100. First Aid

101. Foreign Languages
102. Forestry
103. Group Dynamics
104. Hotel Management
105. Law Enforcement
106. Leadership
107. Literature
108. Marketing
109. Martial Arts (Judo, Karate, etc.)
110. Mathematics
111. Medicine
112. Military Strategies
113. Music
114. Nursing
115. Office Practices

116. Physics
117. Plants and Gardens
118. Political Science
119. Psychology
120. Public Speaking
121. Real Estate
122. Sales Techniques
123. Social Work
124. Tax Planning
125. Theater Arts
126. Typing
127. Welding
128. Woodworking

Following is a list of activities. Indicate as before how much you would like doing each one.

L = **STRONGLY LIKE**
L = Like
l = slightly like

d = slightly dislike
D = Dislike
D = **STRONGLY DISLIKE**

129. Act in a local theater production
130. Advise others on their wardrobes and grooming
131. Appraise the value of jewelry or antiques
132. Attend religious services
133. Belong to a military drill unit
134. Build an outside deck or balcony on a house
135. Calculate payroll deductions for a working force

136. Care for a herd of cattle or horses
137. Care for sick people
138. Compete in an athletic contest
139. Conduct religious ceremonies
140. Deal with emergencies where people are in danger
141. Design the landscaping for a large garden

142. Develop a marketing strategy for a new consumer product

143. Develop new varieties of plants and flowers

144. Do exercises to improve your body

145. Engage in exciting, dangerous adventures

146. Experiment with new ways of preparing food

147. Explain a complicated scientific concept to others

148. Figure out why a small gasoline engine won't work

149. File a lawsuit to straighten out an injustice

150. Give a speech to a large group

151. Go parachuting or hang gliding

152. Help develop leadership talents in other people

153. Interview people applying for a job

154. Introduce an after-dinner speaker

155. Lay out the advertisements for a magazine

156. Lead the calisthenics in a physical fitness program

157. Maintain an elaborate office filing system

158. Make sales calls on prospective clients or customers

159. Manage a pet shop

160. Manage the work of others

161. Monitor the business expenses for an organization

162. Negotiate conflicts between irate people

163. Operate scientific equipment

164. Organize a political campaign

165. Participate in a search for an escaped criminal

166. Persuade others to adopt new methods

167. Plan an advertising campaign

168. Plan social activities for retired people

169. Plan the long-range budget of an organization

170. Play the stock market

171. Prepare the food for a large banquet

172. Raise and care for show animals

173. Raise exotic plants, such as orchids

174. Repair a broken-down automobile

175. Restore antique furniture

176. Ride in a motorcycle race

177. Run a small specialty shop in a shopping mall

178. Sell expensive merchandise in an exclusive shop

179. Serve as a private secretary to a top executive

180. Set out new trees in a garden

181. Sketch pictures for a local magazine

182. Solve mathematical puzzles

183. Soothe angry or upset people

184. Supervise a large number of clerical workers

185. Take care of small babies

186. Take part in a public debate

187. Tape a sprained ankle

188. Teach new skills to adults

189. Tell jokes to large audiences

190. Tell stories to children

191. Think up new products and services to sell

192. Train an animal to do tricks

193. Train new workers in the operation of office machines

194. Travel independently in foreign countries

195. Type business letters

196. Work as a receptionist for a large company

197. Work overseas in a foreign embassy

198. Work with a young people's religious group

199. Write a newspaper story

200. Write a technical report

PART II—SKILLS

The major purpose of this section is to assess your skills to identify the major themes and then to compare your skills to those reported by others.

Following is a list of activities. Indicate your estimated level of skill in each by filling in the appropriate circle on the answer sheet. If you have never done the activity, estimate how good you think you would be if you did it.

E = **EXPERT:** Widely recognized as excellent in this area
G = Good: Have well-developed skills in this area
sa = slightly above average: Average, or a touch above
sb = slightly below average: Average, or a touch below
P = Poor: Not very skilled in this area
N = **NONE:** Have no skills in this area

Sometimes these responses will seem a bit strange for the activity mentioned, but try to judge your skill level as best you can. Try to be honest and candid.

201. Acquiring the necessary resources to carry out your plans.

202. Acting the lead role in a demanding drama

203. Activating the creative potential in other people

204. Advising others on ways to promote their image as public figures

205. Advising people making career decisions, helping them plan their future

206. Aiding an angry husband and wife to understand each other better

207. Analyzing data, using statistical concepts

208. As a member of a team, inspiring your teammates to superior performance

209. Being patient with children

210. Being responsible for animals in a kennel or stable

211. Being tough with other people when it is necessary for business purposes

212. Building furniture, using power saws and other woodworking equipment

213. Caring for a wild-bird sanctuary, including preparing the proper plantings and feeding stations

214. Carrying out secretarial duties, such as managing someone else's correspondence and schedule

215. Charming and entertaining other people

216. Coaching a highly skilled performance group, motivating them to superior achievements

217. Competing against others in challenging situations

218. Completing income tax returns, taking advantage of all deductions

219. Composing poems or essays, using a lively vocabulary and imaginative ideas

220. Conducting traditional ceremonies for a social or religious group

221. Constructing a psychological analysis of someone, using interviews, tests, and biographical data

222. Constructing outdoor projects such as decks or gazebos

223. Cooking a gourmet meal, including several different courses

224. Counseling an individual who is grappling with a personal moral dilemma, such as an unreported theft

225. Creating a multi-media production, using multiple projectors, lights, and music

226. Cultivating leadership talents in other people

227. Dancing in some structured style, such as folk, ballroom, or modern dancing

228. Debating issues in a public forum

229. Defending someone in physical danger

230. Delegating authority to others

231. Delivering a well-organized and entertaining speech

232. Designing a laboratory experiment, setting up controls, collecting data, and applying the appropriate statistics

233. Designing jewelry, using a combination of metals and gems

234. Developing a long-range, visionary plan for your organization

235. Developing computer programs

236. Devising an arts-and-crafts project for children

237. Diagnosing the physical health of individuals, using various tests and laboratory results

238. Doing major auto repairs such as replacing piston rings or brake pads

239. Drawing people out in conversation so that they talk freely about themselves

240. Deciding how to spend advertising dollars through various media, such as newspaper, radio, TV, or direct mail

241. Dressing in a distinctive style, using imaginative combinations of colors and accessories

242. Editing a weekly food column for a local publication

243. Educating young people, making them feel important, helping them learn new ideas

244. Engaging in high-risk activities, such as hang gliding, driving racing cars, or mountain climbing

245. Establishing budgets and time schedules for your organization

246. Experimenting with new ways of preparing food

247. Explaining scientific terms to lay people

248. Furnishing first-aid assistance to someone badly injured

249. Giving interviews to the media, representing your organization

250. Growing exotic plants, such as orchids or special roses

251. Helping people plan their investment strategies

252. Helping people with their personal appearance; advising about hairstyles, clothing, and grooming

253. Identifying several major symphonies and composers by listening to musical passages

254. In a one-on-one contest, such as tennis, racquetball, or handball, playing well enough to place in tournaments

255. Initiating new creative educational methods

256. Installing built-in lighting, handling all of the carpentry and electrical work yourself

257. Instructing new parents on the care of their infants

258. Investing money for profit

Adapted by the Assessments group of NCS for Irwin/McGraw-Hill with permission of the author.

C5

259. Knowing the names of the major political and historical figures in many different countries

260. Landscaping a garden, including selecting the proper plants and trees

261. Leading exercise sessions for people who want to get their bodies in better shape

262. Leading other people, making important things happen

263. Making the necessary political contacts so that your organization will be well-treated

264. Making up stories for children, keeping the children enthralled

265. Managing a large forest preserve

266. Managing the finances of an organization, emphasizing planning and thrift

267. Monitoring machines and performing the necessary maintenance to prevent future breakdowns

268. Motivating others to perform in dangerous situations requiring teamwork and courage

269. Negotiating compromises between conflicting parties

270. Nursing sick animals back to health

271. Operating scientific instruments such as oscilloscopes or spectrometers

272. Ordering correctly the necessary office supplies for next year's activities for your organization

273. Organizing a political campaign

274. Overcoming sales resistance of potential customers

275. Overseeing a production process involving people, machines, raw materials, and deadlines

276. Participating in endurance sports, such as running, swimming, or bicycling

277. Performing in public, playing the piano or other musical instrument

278. Persuading others to use your ideas or services

279. Planning a marketing campaign for a new consumer product

280. Playing team sports well, with ease, athletic grace, and teamsmanship

281. Preparing detailed financial contracts for complicated business opportunities

282. Presiding as master of ceremonies at a large program

283. Providing medical services to people of varying ages

284. Providing spiritual counseling for individuals and couples

285. Purchasing clothing and accessories for department stores

286. Raising crops, including preparing the land, cultivating the plants, and harvesting the output

287. Redecorating a large living room with the style and flair found in design magazines

288. Remodeling the interior of an old building

289. Researching a historical event, using a wide range of library and other reference materials

290. Running a large-scale agricultural operation, such as a large farm or ranch

291. Scanning an article or book, then using the information to support an idea or decision

292. Scheduling the work flow in an office for maximum efficiency

293. Searching through complex data, identifying trends, and reporting the findings in technical reports

294. Selecting flowers and arranging floral displays

295. Selecting paintings and sculptures for public display

296. Selling a product or concept

297. Serving as a host or hostess at a large dinner, making guests feel socially comfortable

298. Serving as an officer in a national volunteer organization

299. Setting up an efficient office filing system, including correspondence and data processing files

300. Sketching pictures of people or objects

301. Speaking and writing a foreign language

302. Starting conversations with strangers

303. Staying calm and thinking clearly in crisis situations

304. Supervising the work of others

305. Surviving in the wilderness, living off the land

306. Taking people on nature walks, explaining the local plants and animals to them

307. Teaching classes for people interested in converting to a religious faith

308. Teaching mathematics classes

309. Teaching new skills to adults

310. Telling jokes to large audiences

311. Thinking up new advertising slogans

312. Training an animal to do tricks

313. Translating between two people who speak different languages, such as English and French

314. Traveling worldwide, planning your own schedule, handling your own arrangements

315. Using algebra or geometry to solve design or construction problems

316. Utilizing outdoor equipment such as a compass, camping equipment, and climbing gear

317. Visiting sick parishioners to provide comfort and support

318. Working with hand tools and shop machinery

319. Working with rifles, pistols, or other small arms

320. Writing a newspaper story

CISS®
Campbell™ Interest and Skill Survey

Use this answer sheet to record your responses. For each item, completely fill in the circle that corresponds to your answer. Do not make any marks outside of the circles.

PART I—INTERESTS

1. ⓁⓁⓘⓓⒹⒹ
2. ⓁⓁⓘⓓⒹⒹ
3. ⓁⓁⓘⓓⒹⒹ
4. ⓁⓁⓘⓓⒹⒹ
5. ⓁⓁⓘⓓⒹⒹ
6. ⓁⓁⓘⓓⒹⒹ
7. ⓁⓁⓘⓓⒹⒹ
8. ⓁⓁⓘⓓⒹⒹ
9. ⓁⓁⓘⓓⒹⒹ
10. ⓁⓁⓘⓓⒹⒹ
11. ⓁⓁⓘⓓⒹⒹ

12. ⓁⓁⓘⓓⒹⒹ
13. ⓁⓁⓘⓓⒹⒹ
14. ⓁⓁⓘⓓⒹⒹ
15. ⓁⓁⓘⓓⒹⒹ
16. ⓁⓁⓘⓓⒹⒹ
17. ⓁⓁⓘⓓⒹⒹ
18. ⓁⓁⓘⓓⒹⒹ
19. ⓁⓁⓘⓓⒹⒹ
20. ⓁⓁⓘⓓⒹⒹ
21. ⓁⓁⓘⓓⒹⒹ
22. ⓁⓁⓘⓓⒹⒹ

23. ⓁⓁⓘⓓⒹⒹ
24. ⓁⓁⓘⓓⒹⒹ
25. ⓁⓁⓘⓓⒹⒹ
26. ⓁⓁⓘⓓⒹⒹ
27. ⓁⓁⓘⓓⒹⒹ
28. ⓁⓁⓘⓓⒹⒹ
29. ⓁⓁⓘⓓⒹⒹ
30. ⓁⓁⓘⓓⒹⒹ
31. ⓁⓁⓘⓓⒹⒹ
32. ⓁⓁⓘⓓⒹⒹ
33. ⓁⓁⓘⓓⒹⒹ

34. ⓁⓁⓘⓓⒹⒹ
35. ⓁⓁⓘⓓⒹⒹ
36. ⓁⓁⓘⓓⒹⒹ
37. ⓁⓁⓘⓓⒹⒹ
38. ⓁⓁⓘⓓⒹⒹ
39. ⓁⓁⓘⓓⒹⒹ
40. ⓁⓁⓘⓓⒹⒹ
41. ⓁⓁⓘⓓⒹⒹ
42. ⓁⓁⓘⓓⒹⒹ
43. ⓁⓁⓘⓓⒹⒹ
44. ⓁⓁⓘⓓⒹⒹ

45. ⓁⓁⓘⓓⒹⒹ
46. ⓁⓁⓘⓓⒹⒹ
47. ⓁⓁⓘⓓⒹⒹ
48. ⓁⓁⓘⓓⒹⒹ
49. ⓁⓁⓘⓓⒹⒹ
50. ⓁⓁⓘⓓⒹⒹ
51. ⓁⓁⓘⓓⒹⒹ
52. ⓁⓁⓘⓓⒹⒹ
53. ⓁⓁⓘⓓⒹⒹ
54. ⓁⓁⓘⓓⒹⒹ
55. ⓁⓁⓘⓓⒹⒹ

56. ⓁⓁⓘⓓⒹⒹ
57. ⓁⓁⓘⓓⒹⒹ
58. ⓁⓁⓘⓓⒹⒹ
59. ⓁⓁⓘⓓⒹⒹ
60. ⓁⓁⓘⓓⒹⒹ
61. ⓁⓁⓘⓓⒹⒹ
62. ⓁⓁⓘⓓⒹⒹ
63. ⓁⓁⓘⓓⒹⒹ
64. ⓁⓁⓘⓓⒹⒹ
65. ⓁⓁⓘⓓⒹⒹ
66. ⓁⓁⓘⓓⒹⒹ

67. ⓁⓁⓘⓓⒹⒹ
68. ⓁⓁⓘⓓⒹⒹ
69. ⓁⓁⓘⓓⒹⒹ
70. ⓁⓁⓘⓓⒹⒹ
71. ⓁⓁⓘⓓⒹⒹ
72. ⓁⓁⓘⓓⒹⒹ
73. ⓁⓁⓘⓓⒹⒹ
74. ⓁⓁⓘⓓⒹⒹ
75. ⓁⓁⓘⓓⒹⒹ
76. ⓁⓁⓘⓓⒹⒹ
77. ⓁⓁⓘⓓⒹⒹ

78. ⓁⓁⓘⓓⒹⒹ
79. ⓁⓁⓘⓓⒹⒹ
80. ⓁⓁⓘⓓⒹⒹ
81. ⓁⓁⓘⓓⒹⒹ
82. ⓁⓁⓘⓓⒹⒹ
83. ⓁⓁⓘⓓⒹⒹ
84. ⓁⓁⓘⓓⒹⒹ
85. ⓁⓁⓘⓓⒹⒹ

86. ⓎⓎⓨⓝⓃⓃ
87. ⓎⓎⓨⓝⓃⓃ
88. ⓎⓎⓨⓝⓃⓃ
89. ⓎⓎⓨⓝⓃⓃ
90. ⓎⓎⓨⓝⓃⓃ
91. ⓎⓎⓨⓝⓃⓃ
92. ⓎⓎⓨⓝⓃⓃ
93. ⓎⓎⓨⓝⓃⓃ
94. ⓎⓎⓨⓝⓃⓃ
95. ⓎⓎⓨⓝⓃⓃ
96. ⓎⓎⓨⓝⓃⓃ

97. ⓎⓎⓨⓝⓃⓃ
98. ⓎⓎⓨⓝⓃⓃ
99. ⓎⓎⓨⓝⓃⓃ
100. ⓎⓎⓨⓝⓃⓃ
101. ⓎⓎⓨⓝⓃⓃ
102. ⓎⓎⓨⓝⓃⓃ
103. ⓎⓎⓨⓝⓃⓃ
104. ⓎⓎⓨⓝⓃⓃ
105. ⓎⓎⓨⓝⓃⓃ
106. ⓎⓎⓨⓝⓃⓃ
107. ⓎⓎⓨⓝⓃⓃ

108. ⓎⓎⓨⓝⓃⓃ
109. ⓎⓎⓨⓝⓃⓃ
110. ⓎⓎⓨⓝⓃⓃ
111. ⓎⓎⓨⓝⓃⓃ
112. ⓎⓎⓨⓝⓃⓃ
113. ⓎⓎⓨⓝⓃⓃ
114. ⓎⓎⓨⓝⓃⓃ
115. ⓎⓎⓨⓝⓃⓃ
116. ⓎⓎⓨⓝⓃⓃ
117. ⓎⓎⓨⓝⓃⓃ
118. ⓎⓎⓨⓝⓃⓃ

119. ⓎⓎⓨⓝⓃⓃ
120. ⓎⓎⓨⓝⓃⓃ
121. ⓎⓎⓨⓝⓃⓃ
122. ⓎⓎⓨⓝⓃⓃ
123. ⓎⓎⓨⓝⓃⓃ
124. ⓎⓎⓨⓝⓃⓃ
125. ⓎⓎⓨⓝⓃⓃ
126. ⓎⓎⓨⓝⓃⓃ
127. ⓎⓎⓨⓝⓃⓃ
128. ⓎⓎⓨⓝⓃⓃ

129. ⓁⓁⓘⓓⒹⒹ
130. ⓁⓁⓘⓓⒹⒹ
131. ⓁⓁⓘⓓⒹⒹ
132. ⓁⓁⓘⓓⒹⒹ
133. ⓁⓁⓘⓓⒹⒹ
134. ⓁⓁⓘⓓⒹⒹ
135. ⓁⓁⓘⓓⒹⒹ
136. ⓁⓁⓘⓓⒹⒹ
137. ⓁⓁⓘⓓⒹⒹ
138. ⓁⓁⓘⓓⒹⒹ
139. ⓁⓁⓘⓓⒹⒹ

140. ⓁⓁⓘⓓⒹⒹ
141. ⓁⓁⓘⓓⒹⒹ
142. ⓁⓁⓘⓓⒹⒹ
143. ⓁⓁⓘⓓⒹⒹ
144. ⓁⓁⓘⓓⒹⒹ
145. ⓁⓁⓘⓓⒹⒹ
146. ⓁⓁⓘⓓⒹⒹ
147. ⓁⓁⓘⓓⒹⒹ
148. ⓁⓁⓘⓓⒹⒹ
149. ⓁⓁⓘⓓⒹⒹ
150. ⓁⓁⓘⓓⒹⒹ

151. ⓁⓁⓘⓓⒹⒹ
152. ⓁⓁⓘⓓⒹⒹ
153. ⓁⓁⓘⓓⒹⒹ
154. ⓁⓁⓘⓓⒹⒹ
155. ⓁⓁⓘⓓⒹⒹ
156. ⓁⓁⓘⓓⒹⒹ
157. ⓁⓁⓘⓓⒹⒹ
158. ⓁⓁⓘⓓⒹⒹ
159. ⓁⓁⓘⓓⒹⒹ
160. ⓁⓁⓘⓓⒹⒹ
161. ⓁⓁⓘⓓⒹⒹ

162. ⓁⓁⓘⓓⒹⒹ
163. ⓁⓁⓘⓓⒹⒹ
164. ⓁⓁⓘⓓⒹⒹ
165. ⓁⓁⓘⓓⒹⒹ
166. ⓁⓁⓘⓓⒹⒹ
167. ⓁⓁⓘⓓⒹⒹ
168. ⓁⓁⓘⓓⒹⒹ
169. ⓁⓁⓘⓓⒹⒹ
170. ⓁⓁⓘⓓⒹⒹ
171. ⓁⓁⓘⓓⒹⒹ

Adapted by the Assessments group of NCS for Irwin/McGraw-Hill with permission of the author.

C7

172. Ⓛ Ⓛ Ⓘ ⓓ Ⓓ Ⓓ 180. Ⓛ Ⓛ Ⓘ ⓓ Ⓓ Ⓓ 188. Ⓛ Ⓛ Ⓘ ⓓ Ⓓ Ⓓ 196. Ⓛ Ⓛ Ⓘ ⓓ Ⓓ Ⓓ
173. Ⓛ Ⓛ Ⓘ ⓓ Ⓓ Ⓓ 181. Ⓛ Ⓛ Ⓘ ⓓ Ⓓ Ⓓ 189. Ⓛ Ⓛ Ⓘ ⓓ Ⓓ Ⓓ 197. Ⓛ Ⓛ Ⓘ ⓓ Ⓓ Ⓓ
174. Ⓛ Ⓛ Ⓘ ⓓ Ⓓ Ⓓ 182. Ⓛ Ⓛ Ⓘ ⓓ Ⓓ Ⓓ 190. Ⓛ Ⓛ Ⓘ ⓓ Ⓓ Ⓓ 198. Ⓛ Ⓛ Ⓘ ⓓ Ⓓ Ⓓ
175. Ⓛ Ⓛ Ⓘ ⓓ Ⓓ Ⓓ 183. Ⓛ Ⓛ Ⓘ ⓓ Ⓓ Ⓓ 191. Ⓛ Ⓛ Ⓘ ⓓ Ⓓ Ⓓ 199. Ⓛ Ⓛ Ⓘ ⓓ Ⓓ Ⓓ
176. Ⓛ Ⓛ Ⓘ ⓓ Ⓓ Ⓓ 184. Ⓛ Ⓛ Ⓘ ⓓ Ⓓ Ⓓ 192. Ⓛ Ⓛ Ⓘ ⓓ Ⓓ Ⓓ 200. Ⓛ Ⓛ Ⓘ ⓓ Ⓓ Ⓓ
177. Ⓛ Ⓛ Ⓘ ⓓ Ⓓ Ⓓ 185. Ⓛ Ⓛ Ⓘ ⓓ Ⓓ Ⓓ 193. Ⓛ Ⓛ Ⓘ ⓓ Ⓓ Ⓓ
178. Ⓛ Ⓛ Ⓘ ⓓ Ⓓ Ⓓ 186. Ⓛ Ⓛ Ⓘ ⓓ Ⓓ Ⓓ 194. Ⓛ Ⓛ Ⓘ ⓓ Ⓓ Ⓓ
179. Ⓛ Ⓛ Ⓘ ⓓ Ⓓ Ⓓ 187. Ⓛ Ⓛ Ⓘ ⓓ Ⓓ Ⓓ 195. Ⓛ Ⓛ Ⓘ ⓓ Ⓓ Ⓓ

PART II—SKILLS

201. Ⓔ Ⓖ ⓢⓐ ⓢⓑ Ⓟ Ⓝ   231. Ⓔ Ⓖ ⓢⓐ ⓢⓑ Ⓟ Ⓝ   261. Ⓔ Ⓖ ⓢⓐ ⓢⓑ Ⓟ Ⓝ   291. Ⓔ Ⓖ ⓢⓐ ⓢⓑ Ⓟ Ⓝ
202. Ⓔ Ⓖ ⓢⓐ ⓢⓑ Ⓟ Ⓝ   232. Ⓔ Ⓖ ⓢⓐ ⓢⓑ Ⓟ Ⓝ   262. Ⓔ Ⓖ ⓢⓐ ⓢⓑ Ⓟ Ⓝ   292. Ⓔ Ⓖ ⓢⓐ ⓢⓑ Ⓟ Ⓝ
203. Ⓔ Ⓖ ⓢⓐ ⓢⓑ Ⓟ Ⓝ   233. Ⓔ Ⓖ ⓢⓐ ⓢⓑ Ⓟ Ⓝ   263. Ⓔ Ⓖ ⓢⓐ ⓢⓑ Ⓟ Ⓝ   293. Ⓔ Ⓖ ⓢⓐ ⓢⓑ Ⓟ Ⓝ
204. Ⓔ Ⓖ ⓢⓐ ⓢⓑ Ⓟ Ⓝ   234. Ⓔ Ⓖ ⓢⓐ ⓢⓑ Ⓟ Ⓝ   264. Ⓔ Ⓖ ⓢⓐ ⓢⓑ Ⓟ Ⓝ   294. Ⓔ Ⓖ ⓢⓐ ⓢⓑ Ⓟ Ⓝ
205. Ⓔ Ⓖ ⓢⓐ ⓢⓑ Ⓟ Ⓝ   235. Ⓔ Ⓖ ⓢⓐ ⓢⓑ Ⓟ Ⓝ   265. Ⓔ Ⓖ ⓢⓐ ⓢⓑ Ⓟ Ⓝ   295. Ⓔ Ⓖ ⓢⓐ ⓢⓑ Ⓟ Ⓝ
206. Ⓔ Ⓖ ⓢⓐ ⓢⓑ Ⓟ Ⓝ   236. Ⓔ Ⓖ ⓢⓐ ⓢⓑ Ⓟ Ⓝ   266. Ⓔ Ⓖ ⓢⓐ ⓢⓑ Ⓟ Ⓝ   296. Ⓔ Ⓖ ⓢⓐ ⓢⓑ Ⓟ Ⓝ
207. Ⓔ Ⓖ ⓢⓐ ⓢⓑ Ⓟ Ⓝ   237. Ⓔ Ⓖ ⓢⓐ ⓢⓑ Ⓟ Ⓝ   267. Ⓔ Ⓖ ⓢⓐ ⓢⓑ Ⓟ Ⓝ   297. Ⓔ Ⓖ ⓢⓐ ⓢⓑ Ⓟ Ⓝ
208. Ⓔ Ⓖ ⓢⓐ ⓢⓑ Ⓟ Ⓝ   238. Ⓔ Ⓖ ⓢⓐ ⓢⓑ Ⓟ Ⓝ   268. Ⓔ Ⓖ ⓢⓐ ⓢⓑ Ⓟ Ⓝ   298. Ⓔ Ⓖ ⓢⓐ ⓢⓑ Ⓟ Ⓝ
209. Ⓔ Ⓖ ⓢⓐ ⓢⓑ Ⓟ Ⓝ   239. Ⓔ Ⓖ ⓢⓐ ⓢⓑ Ⓟ Ⓝ   269. Ⓔ Ⓖ ⓢⓐ ⓢⓑ Ⓟ Ⓝ   299. Ⓔ Ⓖ ⓢⓐ ⓢⓑ Ⓟ Ⓝ
210. Ⓔ Ⓖ ⓢⓐ ⓢⓑ Ⓟ Ⓝ   240. Ⓔ Ⓖ ⓢⓐ ⓢⓑ Ⓟ Ⓝ   270. Ⓔ Ⓖ ⓢⓐ ⓢⓑ Ⓟ Ⓝ   300. Ⓔ Ⓖ ⓢⓐ ⓢⓑ Ⓟ Ⓝ

211. Ⓔ Ⓖ ⓢⓐ ⓢⓑ Ⓟ Ⓝ   241. Ⓔ Ⓖ ⓢⓐ ⓢⓑ Ⓟ Ⓝ   271. Ⓔ Ⓖ ⓢⓐ ⓢⓑ Ⓟ Ⓝ   301. Ⓔ Ⓖ ⓢⓐ ⓢⓑ Ⓟ Ⓝ
212. Ⓔ Ⓖ ⓢⓐ ⓢⓑ Ⓟ Ⓝ   242. Ⓔ Ⓖ ⓢⓐ ⓢⓑ Ⓟ Ⓝ   272. Ⓔ Ⓖ ⓢⓐ ⓢⓑ Ⓟ Ⓝ   302. Ⓔ Ⓖ ⓢⓐ ⓢⓑ Ⓟ Ⓝ
213. Ⓔ Ⓖ ⓢⓐ ⓢⓑ Ⓟ Ⓝ   243. Ⓔ Ⓖ ⓢⓐ ⓢⓑ Ⓟ Ⓝ   273. Ⓔ Ⓖ ⓢⓐ ⓢⓑ Ⓟ Ⓝ   303. Ⓔ Ⓖ ⓢⓐ ⓢⓑ Ⓟ Ⓝ
214. Ⓔ Ⓖ ⓢⓐ ⓢⓑ Ⓟ Ⓝ   244. Ⓔ Ⓖ ⓢⓐ ⓢⓑ Ⓟ Ⓝ   274. Ⓔ Ⓖ ⓢⓐ ⓢⓑ Ⓟ Ⓝ   304. Ⓔ Ⓖ ⓢⓐ ⓢⓑ Ⓟ Ⓝ
215. Ⓔ Ⓖ ⓢⓐ ⓢⓑ Ⓟ Ⓝ   245. Ⓔ Ⓖ ⓢⓐ ⓢⓑ Ⓟ Ⓝ   275. Ⓔ Ⓖ ⓢⓐ ⓢⓑ Ⓟ Ⓝ   305. Ⓔ Ⓖ ⓢⓐ ⓢⓑ Ⓟ Ⓝ
216. Ⓔ Ⓖ ⓢⓐ ⓢⓑ Ⓟ Ⓝ   246. Ⓔ Ⓖ ⓢⓐ ⓢⓑ Ⓟ Ⓝ   276. Ⓔ Ⓖ ⓢⓐ ⓢⓑ Ⓟ Ⓝ   306. Ⓔ Ⓖ ⓢⓐ ⓢⓑ Ⓟ Ⓝ
217. Ⓔ Ⓖ ⓢⓐ ⓢⓑ Ⓟ Ⓝ   247. Ⓔ Ⓖ ⓢⓐ ⓢⓑ Ⓟ Ⓝ   277. Ⓔ Ⓖ ⓢⓐ ⓢⓑ Ⓟ Ⓝ   307. Ⓔ Ⓖ ⓢⓐ ⓢⓑ Ⓟ Ⓝ
218. Ⓔ Ⓖ ⓢⓐ ⓢⓑ Ⓟ Ⓝ   248. Ⓔ Ⓖ ⓢⓐ ⓢⓑ Ⓟ Ⓝ   278. Ⓔ Ⓖ ⓢⓐ ⓢⓑ Ⓟ Ⓝ   308. Ⓔ Ⓖ ⓢⓐ ⓢⓑ Ⓟ Ⓝ
219. Ⓔ Ⓖ ⓢⓐ ⓢⓑ Ⓟ Ⓝ   249. Ⓔ Ⓖ ⓢⓐ ⓢⓑ Ⓟ Ⓝ   279. Ⓔ Ⓖ ⓢⓐ ⓢⓑ Ⓟ Ⓝ   309. Ⓔ Ⓖ ⓢⓐ ⓢⓑ Ⓟ Ⓝ
220. Ⓔ Ⓖ ⓢⓐ ⓢⓑ Ⓟ Ⓝ   250. Ⓔ Ⓖ ⓢⓐ ⓢⓑ Ⓟ Ⓝ   280. Ⓔ Ⓖ ⓢⓐ ⓢⓑ Ⓟ Ⓝ   310. Ⓔ Ⓖ ⓢⓐ ⓢⓑ Ⓟ Ⓝ

221. Ⓔ Ⓖ ⓢⓐ ⓢⓑ Ⓟ Ⓝ   251. Ⓔ Ⓖ ⓢⓐ ⓢⓑ Ⓟ Ⓝ   281. Ⓔ Ⓖ ⓢⓐ ⓢⓑ Ⓟ Ⓝ   311. Ⓔ Ⓖ ⓢⓐ ⓢⓑ Ⓟ Ⓝ
222. Ⓔ Ⓖ ⓢⓐ ⓢⓑ Ⓟ Ⓝ   252. Ⓔ Ⓖ ⓢⓐ ⓢⓑ Ⓟ Ⓝ   282. Ⓔ Ⓖ ⓢⓐ ⓢⓑ Ⓟ Ⓝ   312. Ⓔ Ⓖ ⓢⓐ ⓢⓑ Ⓟ Ⓝ
223. Ⓔ Ⓖ ⓢⓐ ⓢⓑ Ⓟ Ⓝ   253. Ⓔ Ⓖ ⓢⓐ ⓢⓑ Ⓟ Ⓝ   283. Ⓔ Ⓖ ⓢⓐ ⓢⓑ Ⓟ Ⓝ   313. Ⓔ Ⓖ ⓢⓐ ⓢⓑ Ⓟ Ⓝ
224. Ⓔ Ⓖ ⓢⓐ ⓢⓑ Ⓟ Ⓝ   254. Ⓔ Ⓖ ⓢⓐ ⓢⓑ Ⓟ Ⓝ   284. Ⓔ Ⓖ ⓢⓐ ⓢⓑ Ⓟ Ⓝ   314. Ⓔ Ⓖ ⓢⓐ ⓢⓑ Ⓟ Ⓝ
225. Ⓔ Ⓖ ⓢⓐ ⓢⓑ Ⓟ Ⓝ   255. Ⓔ Ⓖ ⓢⓐ ⓢⓑ Ⓟ Ⓝ   285. Ⓔ Ⓖ ⓢⓐ ⓢⓑ Ⓟ Ⓝ   315. Ⓔ Ⓖ ⓢⓐ ⓢⓑ Ⓟ Ⓝ
226. Ⓔ Ⓖ ⓢⓐ ⓢⓑ Ⓟ Ⓝ   256. Ⓔ Ⓖ ⓢⓐ ⓢⓑ Ⓟ Ⓝ   286. Ⓔ Ⓖ ⓢⓐ ⓢⓑ Ⓟ Ⓝ   316. Ⓔ Ⓖ ⓢⓐ ⓢⓑ Ⓟ Ⓝ
227. Ⓔ Ⓖ ⓢⓐ ⓢⓑ Ⓟ Ⓝ   257. Ⓔ Ⓖ ⓢⓐ ⓢⓑ Ⓟ Ⓝ   287. Ⓔ Ⓖ ⓢⓐ ⓢⓑ Ⓟ Ⓝ   317. Ⓔ Ⓖ ⓢⓐ ⓢⓑ Ⓟ Ⓝ
228. Ⓔ Ⓖ ⓢⓐ ⓢⓑ Ⓟ Ⓝ   258. Ⓔ Ⓖ ⓢⓐ ⓢⓑ Ⓟ Ⓝ   288. Ⓔ Ⓖ ⓢⓐ ⓢⓑ Ⓟ Ⓝ   318. Ⓔ Ⓖ ⓢⓐ ⓢⓑ Ⓟ Ⓝ
229. Ⓔ Ⓖ ⓢⓐ ⓢⓑ Ⓟ Ⓝ   259. Ⓔ Ⓖ ⓢⓐ ⓢⓑ Ⓟ Ⓝ   289. Ⓔ Ⓖ ⓢⓐ ⓢⓑ Ⓟ Ⓝ   319. Ⓔ Ⓖ ⓢⓐ ⓢⓑ Ⓟ Ⓝ
230. Ⓔ Ⓖ ⓢⓐ ⓢⓑ Ⓟ Ⓝ   260. Ⓔ Ⓖ ⓢⓐ ⓢⓑ Ⓟ Ⓝ   290. Ⓔ Ⓖ ⓢⓐ ⓢⓑ Ⓟ Ⓝ   320. Ⓔ Ⓖ ⓢⓐ ⓢⓑ Ⓟ Ⓝ

Order Form

To receive your career planning package with the results of your survey, complete this order form and mail the completed answer sheet with your payment to: **NCS Assessments, Irwin/McGraw-Hill Offer, P.O. Box 1294, Minnetonka, MN 55440.** Allow 2–3 weeks to receive your 12-page personalized report and career planning guide. Offer expires June 30, 2001.

Career planning package $14.95
Shipping and handling ...... $ 3.00
State tax .... _____

(If you are a resident of CT, Washington, DC, FL, HI, IA, NM, PA, TX, or WV, add applicable tax.)

Total .... _____

Name _____

Address _____

City _____ State ____ ZIP _____

Phone (____) _____

Birth Date (MM/DD/YY) _____
(required for proper processing)

❏ My check is enclosed

❏ Credit Card ❏ VISA   ❏ MasterCard   ❏ AMERICAN EXPRESS

Card Number _____

Expiration Date _____

Signature _____

AHN

CISS®
Campbell™ Interest
and Skill
Survey

Use this answer sheet to record your responses. For each item, completely fill in the circle that corresponds to your answer. Do not make any marks outside of the circles.

PART I—INTERESTS

1. Ⓛ Ⓛ Ⓘ Ⓓ Ⓓ Ⓓ
2. Ⓛ Ⓛ Ⓘ Ⓓ Ⓓ Ⓓ
3. Ⓛ Ⓛ Ⓘ Ⓓ Ⓓ Ⓓ
4. Ⓛ Ⓛ Ⓘ Ⓓ Ⓓ Ⓓ
5. Ⓛ Ⓛ Ⓘ Ⓓ Ⓓ Ⓓ
6. Ⓛ Ⓛ Ⓘ Ⓓ Ⓓ Ⓓ
7. Ⓛ Ⓛ Ⓘ Ⓓ Ⓓ Ⓓ
8. Ⓛ Ⓛ Ⓘ Ⓓ Ⓓ Ⓓ
9. Ⓛ Ⓛ Ⓘ Ⓓ Ⓓ Ⓓ
10. Ⓛ Ⓛ Ⓘ Ⓓ Ⓓ Ⓓ
11. Ⓛ Ⓛ Ⓘ Ⓓ Ⓓ Ⓓ

12. Ⓛ Ⓛ Ⓘ Ⓓ Ⓓ Ⓓ
13. Ⓛ Ⓛ Ⓘ Ⓓ Ⓓ Ⓓ
14. Ⓛ Ⓛ Ⓘ Ⓓ Ⓓ Ⓓ
15. Ⓛ Ⓛ Ⓘ Ⓓ Ⓓ Ⓓ
16. Ⓛ Ⓛ Ⓘ Ⓓ Ⓓ Ⓓ
17. Ⓛ Ⓛ Ⓘ Ⓓ Ⓓ Ⓓ
18. Ⓛ Ⓛ Ⓘ Ⓓ Ⓓ Ⓓ
19. Ⓛ Ⓛ Ⓘ Ⓓ Ⓓ Ⓓ
20. Ⓛ Ⓛ Ⓘ Ⓓ Ⓓ Ⓓ
21. Ⓛ Ⓛ Ⓘ Ⓓ Ⓓ Ⓓ
22. Ⓛ Ⓛ Ⓘ Ⓓ Ⓓ Ⓓ

23. Ⓛ Ⓛ Ⓘ Ⓓ Ⓓ Ⓓ
24. Ⓛ Ⓛ Ⓘ Ⓓ Ⓓ Ⓓ
25. Ⓛ Ⓛ Ⓘ Ⓓ Ⓓ Ⓓ
26. Ⓛ Ⓛ Ⓘ Ⓓ Ⓓ Ⓓ
27. Ⓛ Ⓛ Ⓘ Ⓓ Ⓓ Ⓓ
28. Ⓛ Ⓛ Ⓘ Ⓓ Ⓓ Ⓓ
29. Ⓛ Ⓛ Ⓘ Ⓓ Ⓓ Ⓓ
30. Ⓛ Ⓛ Ⓘ Ⓓ Ⓓ Ⓓ
31. Ⓛ Ⓛ Ⓘ Ⓓ Ⓓ Ⓓ
32. Ⓛ Ⓛ Ⓘ Ⓓ Ⓓ Ⓓ
33. Ⓛ Ⓛ Ⓘ Ⓓ Ⓓ Ⓓ

34. Ⓛ Ⓛ Ⓘ Ⓓ Ⓓ Ⓓ
35. Ⓛ Ⓛ Ⓘ Ⓓ Ⓓ Ⓓ
36. Ⓛ Ⓛ Ⓘ Ⓓ Ⓓ Ⓓ
37. Ⓛ Ⓛ Ⓘ Ⓓ Ⓓ Ⓓ
38. Ⓛ Ⓛ Ⓘ Ⓓ Ⓓ Ⓓ
39. Ⓛ Ⓛ Ⓘ Ⓓ Ⓓ Ⓓ
40. Ⓛ Ⓛ Ⓘ Ⓓ Ⓓ Ⓓ
41. Ⓛ Ⓛ Ⓘ Ⓓ Ⓓ Ⓓ
42. Ⓛ Ⓛ Ⓘ Ⓓ Ⓓ Ⓓ
43. Ⓛ Ⓛ Ⓘ Ⓓ Ⓓ Ⓓ
44. Ⓛ Ⓛ Ⓘ Ⓓ Ⓓ Ⓓ

45. Ⓛ Ⓛ Ⓘ Ⓓ Ⓓ Ⓓ
46. Ⓛ Ⓛ Ⓘ Ⓓ Ⓓ Ⓓ
47. Ⓛ Ⓛ Ⓘ Ⓓ Ⓓ Ⓓ
48. Ⓛ Ⓛ Ⓘ Ⓓ Ⓓ Ⓓ
49. Ⓛ Ⓛ Ⓘ Ⓓ Ⓓ Ⓓ
50. Ⓛ Ⓛ Ⓘ Ⓓ Ⓓ Ⓓ
51. Ⓛ Ⓛ Ⓘ Ⓓ Ⓓ Ⓓ
52. Ⓛ Ⓛ Ⓘ Ⓓ Ⓓ Ⓓ
53. Ⓛ Ⓛ Ⓘ Ⓓ Ⓓ Ⓓ
54. Ⓛ Ⓛ Ⓘ Ⓓ Ⓓ Ⓓ
55. Ⓛ Ⓛ Ⓘ Ⓓ Ⓓ Ⓓ

56. Ⓛ Ⓛ Ⓘ Ⓓ Ⓓ Ⓓ
57. Ⓛ Ⓛ Ⓘ Ⓓ Ⓓ Ⓓ
58. Ⓛ Ⓛ Ⓘ Ⓓ Ⓓ Ⓓ
59. Ⓛ Ⓛ Ⓘ Ⓓ Ⓓ Ⓓ
60. Ⓛ Ⓛ Ⓘ Ⓓ Ⓓ Ⓓ
61. Ⓛ Ⓛ Ⓘ Ⓓ Ⓓ Ⓓ
62. Ⓛ Ⓛ Ⓘ Ⓓ Ⓓ Ⓓ
63. Ⓛ Ⓛ Ⓘ Ⓓ Ⓓ Ⓓ
64. Ⓛ Ⓛ Ⓘ Ⓓ Ⓓ Ⓓ
65. Ⓛ Ⓛ Ⓘ Ⓓ Ⓓ Ⓓ
66. Ⓛ Ⓛ Ⓘ Ⓓ Ⓓ Ⓓ

67. Ⓛ Ⓛ Ⓘ Ⓓ Ⓓ Ⓓ
68. Ⓛ Ⓛ Ⓘ Ⓓ Ⓓ Ⓓ
69. Ⓛ Ⓛ Ⓘ Ⓓ Ⓓ Ⓓ
70. Ⓛ Ⓛ Ⓘ Ⓓ Ⓓ Ⓓ
71. Ⓛ Ⓛ Ⓘ Ⓓ Ⓓ Ⓓ
72. Ⓛ Ⓛ Ⓘ Ⓓ Ⓓ Ⓓ
73. Ⓛ Ⓛ Ⓘ Ⓓ Ⓓ Ⓓ
74. Ⓛ Ⓛ Ⓘ Ⓓ Ⓓ Ⓓ
75. Ⓛ Ⓛ Ⓘ Ⓓ Ⓓ Ⓓ
76. Ⓛ Ⓛ Ⓘ Ⓓ Ⓓ Ⓓ
77. Ⓛ Ⓛ Ⓘ Ⓓ Ⓓ Ⓓ

78. Ⓛ Ⓛ Ⓘ Ⓓ Ⓓ Ⓓ
79. Ⓛ Ⓛ Ⓘ Ⓓ Ⓓ Ⓓ
80. Ⓛ Ⓛ Ⓘ Ⓓ Ⓓ Ⓓ
81. Ⓛ Ⓛ Ⓘ Ⓓ Ⓓ Ⓓ
82. Ⓛ Ⓛ Ⓘ Ⓓ Ⓓ Ⓓ
83. Ⓛ Ⓛ Ⓘ Ⓓ Ⓓ Ⓓ
84. Ⓛ Ⓛ Ⓘ Ⓓ Ⓓ Ⓓ
85. Ⓛ Ⓛ Ⓘ Ⓓ Ⓓ Ⓓ

86. Ⓨ Ⓨ Ⓨ Ⓝ Ⓝ Ⓝ
87. Ⓨ Ⓨ Ⓨ Ⓝ Ⓝ Ⓝ
88. Ⓨ Ⓨ Ⓨ Ⓝ Ⓝ Ⓝ
89. Ⓨ Ⓨ Ⓨ Ⓝ Ⓝ Ⓝ
90. Ⓨ Ⓨ Ⓨ Ⓝ Ⓝ Ⓝ
91. Ⓨ Ⓨ Ⓨ Ⓝ Ⓝ Ⓝ
92. Ⓨ Ⓨ Ⓨ Ⓝ Ⓝ Ⓝ
93. Ⓨ Ⓨ Ⓨ Ⓝ Ⓝ Ⓝ
94. Ⓨ Ⓨ Ⓨ Ⓝ Ⓝ Ⓝ
95. Ⓨ Ⓨ Ⓨ Ⓝ Ⓝ Ⓝ
96. Ⓨ Ⓨ Ⓨ Ⓝ Ⓝ Ⓝ

97. Ⓨ Ⓨ Ⓨ Ⓝ Ⓝ Ⓝ
98. Ⓨ Ⓨ Ⓨ Ⓝ Ⓝ Ⓝ
99. Ⓨ Ⓨ Ⓨ Ⓝ Ⓝ Ⓝ
100. Ⓨ Ⓨ Ⓨ Ⓝ Ⓝ Ⓝ
101. Ⓨ Ⓨ Ⓨ Ⓝ Ⓝ Ⓝ
102. Ⓨ Ⓨ Ⓨ Ⓝ Ⓝ Ⓝ
103. Ⓨ Ⓨ Ⓨ Ⓝ Ⓝ Ⓝ
104. Ⓨ Ⓨ Ⓨ Ⓝ Ⓝ Ⓝ
105. Ⓨ Ⓨ Ⓨ Ⓝ Ⓝ Ⓝ
106. Ⓨ Ⓨ Ⓨ Ⓝ Ⓝ Ⓝ
107. Ⓨ Ⓨ Ⓨ Ⓝ Ⓝ Ⓝ

108. Ⓨ Ⓨ Ⓨ Ⓝ Ⓝ Ⓝ
109. Ⓨ Ⓨ Ⓨ Ⓝ Ⓝ Ⓝ
110. Ⓨ Ⓨ Ⓨ Ⓝ Ⓝ Ⓝ
111. Ⓨ Ⓨ Ⓨ Ⓝ Ⓝ Ⓝ
112. Ⓨ Ⓨ Ⓨ Ⓝ Ⓝ Ⓝ
113. Ⓨ Ⓨ Ⓨ Ⓝ Ⓝ Ⓝ
114. Ⓨ Ⓨ Ⓨ Ⓝ Ⓝ Ⓝ
115. Ⓨ Ⓨ Ⓨ Ⓝ Ⓝ Ⓝ
116. Ⓨ Ⓨ Ⓨ Ⓝ Ⓝ Ⓝ
117. Ⓨ Ⓨ Ⓨ Ⓝ Ⓝ Ⓝ
118. Ⓨ Ⓨ Ⓨ Ⓝ Ⓝ Ⓝ

119. Ⓨ Ⓨ Ⓨ Ⓝ Ⓝ Ⓝ
120. Ⓨ Ⓨ Ⓨ Ⓝ Ⓝ Ⓝ
121. Ⓨ Ⓨ Ⓨ Ⓝ Ⓝ Ⓝ
122. Ⓨ Ⓨ Ⓨ Ⓝ Ⓝ Ⓝ
123. Ⓨ Ⓨ Ⓨ Ⓝ Ⓝ Ⓝ
124. Ⓨ Ⓨ Ⓨ Ⓝ Ⓝ Ⓝ
125. Ⓨ Ⓨ Ⓨ Ⓝ Ⓝ Ⓝ
126. Ⓨ Ⓨ Ⓨ Ⓝ Ⓝ Ⓝ
127. Ⓨ Ⓨ Ⓨ Ⓝ Ⓝ Ⓝ
128. Ⓨ Ⓨ Ⓨ Ⓝ Ⓝ Ⓝ

129. Ⓛ Ⓛ Ⓘ Ⓓ Ⓓ Ⓓ
130. Ⓛ Ⓛ Ⓘ Ⓓ Ⓓ Ⓓ
131. Ⓛ Ⓛ Ⓘ Ⓓ Ⓓ Ⓓ
132. Ⓛ Ⓛ Ⓘ Ⓓ Ⓓ Ⓓ
133. Ⓛ Ⓛ Ⓘ Ⓓ Ⓓ Ⓓ
134. Ⓛ Ⓛ Ⓘ Ⓓ Ⓓ Ⓓ
135. Ⓛ Ⓛ Ⓘ Ⓓ Ⓓ Ⓓ
136. Ⓛ Ⓛ Ⓘ Ⓓ Ⓓ Ⓓ
137. Ⓛ Ⓛ Ⓘ Ⓓ Ⓓ Ⓓ
138. Ⓛ Ⓛ Ⓘ Ⓓ Ⓓ Ⓓ
139. Ⓛ Ⓛ Ⓘ Ⓓ Ⓓ Ⓓ

140. Ⓛ Ⓛ Ⓘ Ⓓ Ⓓ Ⓓ
141. Ⓛ Ⓛ Ⓘ Ⓓ Ⓓ Ⓓ
142. Ⓛ Ⓛ Ⓘ Ⓓ Ⓓ Ⓓ
143. Ⓛ Ⓛ Ⓘ Ⓓ Ⓓ Ⓓ
144. Ⓛ Ⓛ Ⓘ Ⓓ Ⓓ Ⓓ
145. Ⓛ Ⓛ Ⓘ Ⓓ Ⓓ Ⓓ
146. Ⓛ Ⓛ Ⓘ Ⓓ Ⓓ Ⓓ
147. Ⓛ Ⓛ Ⓘ Ⓓ Ⓓ Ⓓ
148. Ⓛ Ⓛ Ⓘ Ⓓ Ⓓ Ⓓ
149. Ⓛ Ⓛ Ⓘ Ⓓ Ⓓ Ⓓ
150. Ⓛ Ⓛ Ⓘ Ⓓ Ⓓ Ⓓ

151. Ⓛ Ⓛ Ⓘ Ⓓ Ⓓ Ⓓ
152. Ⓛ Ⓛ Ⓘ Ⓓ Ⓓ Ⓓ
153. Ⓛ Ⓛ Ⓘ Ⓓ Ⓓ Ⓓ
154. Ⓛ Ⓛ Ⓘ Ⓓ Ⓓ Ⓓ
155. Ⓛ Ⓛ Ⓘ Ⓓ Ⓓ Ⓓ
156. Ⓛ Ⓛ Ⓘ Ⓓ Ⓓ Ⓓ
157. Ⓛ Ⓛ Ⓘ Ⓓ Ⓓ Ⓓ
158. Ⓛ Ⓛ Ⓘ Ⓓ Ⓓ Ⓓ
159. Ⓛ Ⓛ Ⓘ Ⓓ Ⓓ Ⓓ
160. Ⓛ Ⓛ Ⓘ Ⓓ Ⓓ Ⓓ
161. Ⓛ Ⓛ Ⓘ Ⓓ Ⓓ Ⓓ

162. Ⓛ Ⓛ Ⓘ Ⓓ Ⓓ Ⓓ
163. Ⓛ Ⓛ Ⓘ Ⓓ Ⓓ Ⓓ
164. Ⓛ Ⓛ Ⓘ Ⓓ Ⓓ Ⓓ
165. Ⓛ Ⓛ Ⓘ Ⓓ Ⓓ Ⓓ
166. Ⓛ Ⓛ Ⓘ Ⓓ Ⓓ Ⓓ
167. Ⓛ Ⓛ Ⓘ Ⓓ Ⓓ Ⓓ
168. Ⓛ Ⓛ Ⓘ Ⓓ Ⓓ Ⓓ
169. Ⓛ Ⓛ Ⓘ Ⓓ Ⓓ Ⓓ
170. Ⓛ Ⓛ Ⓘ Ⓓ Ⓓ Ⓓ
171. Ⓛ Ⓛ Ⓘ Ⓓ Ⓓ Ⓓ

Adapted by the Assessments group of NCS for Irwin/McGraw-Hill with permission of the author.

C9

172. Ⓛ Ⓛ Ⓘ ⓓ Ⓓ Ⓓ   180. Ⓛ Ⓛ Ⓘ ⓓ Ⓓ Ⓓ   188. Ⓛ Ⓛ Ⓘ ⓓ Ⓓ Ⓓ   196. Ⓛ Ⓛ Ⓘ ⓓ Ⓓ Ⓓ
173. Ⓛ Ⓛ Ⓘ ⓓ Ⓓ Ⓓ   181. Ⓛ Ⓛ Ⓘ ⓓ Ⓓ Ⓓ   189. Ⓛ Ⓛ Ⓘ ⓓ Ⓓ Ⓓ   197. Ⓛ Ⓛ Ⓘ ⓓ Ⓓ Ⓓ
174. Ⓛ Ⓛ Ⓘ ⓓ Ⓓ Ⓓ   182. Ⓛ Ⓛ Ⓘ ⓓ Ⓓ Ⓓ   190. Ⓛ Ⓛ Ⓘ ⓓ Ⓓ Ⓓ   198. Ⓛ Ⓛ Ⓘ ⓓ Ⓓ Ⓓ
175. Ⓛ Ⓛ Ⓘ ⓓ Ⓓ Ⓓ   183. Ⓛ Ⓛ Ⓘ ⓓ Ⓓ Ⓓ   191. Ⓛ Ⓛ Ⓘ ⓓ Ⓓ Ⓓ   199. Ⓛ Ⓛ Ⓘ ⓓ Ⓓ Ⓓ
176. Ⓛ Ⓛ Ⓘ ⓓ Ⓓ Ⓓ   184. Ⓛ Ⓛ Ⓘ ⓓ Ⓓ Ⓓ   192. Ⓛ Ⓛ Ⓘ ⓓ Ⓓ Ⓓ   200. Ⓛ Ⓛ Ⓘ ⓓ Ⓓ Ⓓ
177. Ⓛ Ⓛ Ⓘ ⓓ Ⓓ Ⓓ   185. Ⓛ Ⓛ Ⓘ ⓓ Ⓓ Ⓓ   193. Ⓛ Ⓛ Ⓘ ⓓ Ⓓ Ⓓ
178. Ⓛ Ⓛ Ⓘ ⓓ Ⓓ Ⓓ   186. Ⓛ Ⓛ Ⓘ ⓓ Ⓓ Ⓓ   194. Ⓛ Ⓛ Ⓘ ⓓ Ⓓ Ⓓ
179. Ⓛ Ⓛ Ⓘ ⓓ Ⓓ Ⓓ   187. Ⓛ Ⓛ Ⓘ ⓓ Ⓓ Ⓓ   195. Ⓛ Ⓛ Ⓘ ⓓ Ⓓ Ⓓ

PART II—SKILLS

201. Ⓔ Ⓖ ⓢ̲ₐ ⓢ̲ᵦ Ⓟ Ⓝ   231. ...   261. ...   291. ...
202. ...   232. ...   262. ...   292. ...
203. ...   233. ...   263. ...   293. ...
204. ...   234. ...   264. ...   294. ...
205. ...   235. ...   265. ...   295. ...
206. ...   236. ...   266. ...   296. ...
207. ...   237. ...   267. ...   297. ...
208. ...   238. ...   268. ...   298. ...
209. ...   239. ...   269. ...   299. ...
210. ...   240. ...   270. ...   300. ...

211. ...   241. ...   271. ...   301. ...
212. ...   242. ...   272. ...   302. ...
213. ...   243. ...   273. ...   303. ...
214. ...   244. ...   274. ...   304. ...
215. ...   245. ...   275. ...   305. ...
216. ...   246. ...   276. ...   306. ...
217. ...   247. ...   277. ...   307. ...
218. ...   248. ...   278. ...   308. ...
219. ...   249. ...   279. ...   309. ...
220. ...   250. ...   280. ...   310. ...

221. ...   251. ...   281. ...   311. ...
222. ...   252. ...   282. ...   312. ...
223. ...   253. ...   283. ...   313. ...
224. ...   254. ...   284. ...   314. ...
225. ...   255. ...   285. ...   315. ...
226. ...   256. ...   286. ...   316. ...
227. ...   257. ...   287. ...   317. ...
228. ...   258. ...   288. ...   318. ...
229. ...   259. ...   289. ...   319. ...
230. Ⓔ Ⓖ ⓢ̲ₐ ⓢ̲ᵦ Ⓟ Ⓝ   260. ...   290. ...   320. Ⓔ Ⓖ ⓢ̲ₐ ⓢ̲ᵦ Ⓟ Ⓝ

Order Form

To receive your career planning package with the results of your survey, complete this order form and mail the completed answer sheet with your payment to: **NCS Assessments, Irwin/McGraw-Hill Offer, P.O. Box 1294, Minnetonka, MN 55440.** Allow 2–3 weeks to receive your 12-page personalized report and career planning guide. Offer expires June 30, 2001.

Career planning package $14.95
Shipping and handling ...... $ 3.00
State tax .... _____

(If you are a resident of CT, Washington, DC, FL, HI, IA, NM, PA, TX, or WV, add applicable tax.)

Total .... _____

Name _____

Address _____

City _____ State ____ ZIP _____

Phone (____) _____

Birth Date (MM/DD/YY) _____
(required for proper processing)

❏ My check is enclosed

❏ Credit Card   ❏ VISA   ❏ MasterCard   ❏ AMERICAN EXPRESS

Card Number _____

Expiration Date _____

Signature _____

AHN

Chapter Notes

Prologue

1. Gene Koretz, "The Sheepskin Paradox," *Business Week*, October 6, 1997, p. 30.

2. Michael Adams, "Charm Schools: Your Salespeople Are Tough, Taut, Competitive, but a Few Lessons in Etiquette May Help Them Sell Even Better," *Sales & Marketing Management*, April 1996, pp. 72–76.

3. Tracey-Lynn Clough, "Learn How to Mind Your Business Manners," *Dallas Morning News*, January 14, 1997, p. 1B.

4. Carla Joinson, "A Return to Good Manners," *HR Magazine*, February 1997, pp. 84–90.

5. Rhonda Reynolds, "Avoiding the Looks That Kill Careers," *Black Enterprise*, June 1995, pp. 281–85.

Chapter 1

1. Wallace Terry, "I Choose to Change My Life," *Parade*, October 13, 1996, pp. 4–5.

2. "Biggest Employers," *Fortune*, August 4, 1997, p. f-15.

3. Dirk Dusharme and Elizabeth R. Larson, "Customer Service: You Get What You Pay For in Arlington," *Quality Digest*, May 1997, p. 9.

4. Heather R. McLeod, "Cross Over: The State of Small Business 1997," *Inc.*, pp. 100–105.

5. Sharon Nelton, "Minority Businesses," *Nation's Business*, October 1996, p. 8.

6. "Sky's the Limit," *Entrepreneur*, April 1997, p. 16.

7. "Reader's Views on Outsourcing," *Nation's Business*, May 1996, p. 85.

8. Lisa Goff, "Leaper or Creeper?," *Home Office Computing*, May 1997, p. 19.

9. Andy Reinhardt, Joan O'C. Hamilton and Linda Himelstein, "Silicon Valley," *Business Week*, August 25, 1997, pp. 64–72.

10. Gary S. Becker, "Don't Blame High Tech for Europe's Job Woes," *Business Week*, July 7, 1997, p. 26.

11. James Worsham, "Clear Sailing?," *Nation's Business*, January 1997, pp. 16–21.

12. Matthew Shifrin, "The New Enablers—Chief Information Officers," *Forbes*, June 2, 1997, pp. 138–43.

13. Tim McCollum, "High-Tech Marketing Hits the Target," *Nation's Business*, June 1997, pp. 39–42.

14. Marion Harmon, "Quality Leaders Predict the Future," *Quality Digest*, April 1997, pp. 22–28.

15. Rebecca Blumenstein, "GM Is Building Plants in Developing Nations to Woo New Markets," *Wall Street Journal*, August 4, 1997, pp. A1, A4.

16. Norm Brodsky, "We Have Met the Enemy, and His Is Us," *Inc.*, June, 1997, pp. 35–37.

17. John Kay, "Shareholders Aren't Everything," *Fortune*, February 17, 1997, pp. 133–34.

18. Michael Donovan, "Maximizing the Bottom-Line Impact of Self-Directed Work Teams," *Quality Digest*, June, 1996, pp. 34–35.

19. Timothy Aeppel, "Empowerment Style Receives Mixed Reviews From Workers," *Wall Street Journal* (Interactive Edition), September 8, 1997.

20. Sue Shellenbarger, "Work & Family," *Wall Street Journal*, May 14, 1997, p. B1.

21. Kirstin Downey Grimsley, "Telecommuting's Growth Marked by Glaring Glitches," *Washington Post*, July 5, 1997, pp. A1, A10.

22. Malcolm M. McCluskey, "Small Office/Home Office List Market Ready to Explode," *DMNews*, March 3, 1997, p. 21.

23. Mike McNamee, "The Productivity Boom Is Still a Mystery," *Business Week*, August 25, 1997, p. 42.

24. Sidney Weintraub, "In the Debate about NAFTA, Just the Facts Please," *Wall Street Journal*, June 20, 1997, p. A19.

25. Annette Dennis McCully, "Integration and Legal Impacts of EMS Documentation," *Quality Digest*, May, 1997, pp. 49–54.

26. Michael M. Phillips, "Tourism's Role Rises, Creating Some Risks," *Wall Street Journal*, October 7, 1996, p. A1.

Chapter 2

1. Steve Pearlstein, "Understanding the Asian Economic Crisis," *The Washington Post*, January 18, 1998, p. A32.

2. Walter Williams, "Economic Freedom the key to Progress," *The Washington Times*, July 17, 1997, p. A·16.

3. Richard A. Melcher, Keith H. Hammonds, Brad Wolverton, and Paul Judge, "A New Breed of Philanthropist," *Business Week*, October 6, 1997, pp. 40–44.

4. Bill Powell, "The Capitalist Czars," *Newsweek*, March 17, 1997, pp. 30–32.

5. Reuven Brenner, "How Canada Scares Away Investors and Talent," The Wall Street Journal, January 2, 1998, p. 9.

6. Bruce Bartlett, "Jobs in the Balance," *The Washington Times*, January 20, 1997, p. A18.

7. Bill Javetski, Gail Edmonston, and Thane Peterson, "Long Live the Welfare State," *Business Week*, June 16, 1997, pp. 48–50.

8. James Worsham, "Checks, Balances, and the CPI," *Nation's Business*, April, 1997, pp. 34–37.

9. Bruce Bartlett, "Changes in Producer Index," *The Washington Times*, July 28, 1997, p. A13.

10. George Melloan, "Is There a Cloud of Deflation Blowing Up from Asia?," *The Wall Street Journal*, November 25, 1997, p. A23.

11. "Budget Deficit Gone for Now, But National Debt Remains," *The Arizona Daily Star*, January 11, 1998, p. A6.

12. Peter Brimelow, "Bipartisan Blather," *Forbes*, March 10, 1997, pp. 52–54.

Chapter 3

1. Glenn Collins, "Going Global Involves More Than Many U.S. Companies Think," *New York Times*, January 2, 1997.

2. Lori Calabro, "Murky Payback," *CFO*, December 1996, p. 15.

3. Greg Steinmetz and Tara Parker-Pope, "All Over the Map," *The Wall Street Journal*, September 26, 1996, pp. R1–R6.

4. Karl Schoenberger, "Motorola Bets Big On China," *Fortune*, May 27,1996, pp. 116–24.

5. "The Miracle of Trade," *The Economist*, January 27, 1996, p. 61.

6. Amy Borrus, "Small-Business Exporters Get a Boost from Bill," *Business Week*, September 9, 1996, p. 55.

7. Robert Rose and Carl Quintanilla, "More Small U.S. Firms Take Up Exporting with Much Success," *The Wall Street Journal*, December 20, 1996, pp. A1–A8.

8. G. Pascal Zachary, "Major U. S. Companies Expand Efforts to Sell to Consumers Abroad," *The Wall Street Journal*, June 13, 1996, pp. A1–A11.

9. "Gearing Up for Going Global," *Inc.*, January 1997.

10. Leonard K. Cheng and Mordechai E. Kreinin, "Supplier Preferences and Dumping: An Analysis of Japanese Corporate Groups," *Southern Economic Journal*, July 1996, pp. 51–60.

11. Christina Duff, "Trade Deficit Grew 17% in September," *The Wall Street Journal*, September 26, 1996, pp. R4–R6

12. Justin Martin, "Mercedes: Made in Alabama," *Fortune*, July 7, 1997, pp. 150–58.

13. Norbert Gannon, "Export Assistance Centers: The Original One-Stop-Shop for U.S. Exporters," *Business America*, June 1996, p. 14.

14. "A Musical Ride to the Cash Register," *Maclean's*, March 11, 1996, p. 10.

15. Greg Steinmetz and Tara Parker Pope, "All Over the Map," *The Wall Street Journal*, September 26, 1996, pp. R4–R6.

16. Doug Bartholomew, "Chips, Boards, Boxes to Go: Contract Manufacturers Take On Expanded Roles, Designing and Shipping Products for PC Makers," *Industry Week*, April 7, 1997, pp. 121–24.

17. McDonald's Corporation 1996 Annual Report, pp. 20–22.

18. "Think Globally, Bake Locally," *Fortune*, October 14, 1996, p. 205.

19. Carolyn Brown, Partnering for Profit: Strategic Alliances and Joint Ventures Are Advancing Revenue Growth of Small Enterprises," *Black Enterprise*, June 1996, pp. 43–45.

20. Joseph Weber, "What's Not Cooking at Campbell's," *Business Week*, September 23, 1996.

21. David P. Hamilton, "United It Stands," *The Wall Street Journal*, September 26, 1996, p. R19.

22. Rebecca Piirto Heath, "Think Globally," *Marketing Tools*, October 1996, pp. 49–54.

23. Dr. Carol Kinsey Gorman, "The New International Communications Essentials," *Boardroom Reports*, March 15, 1996, p. 11.

24. Rebecca Piirto Heath, "Think Globally," *Marketing Tools*, October 1996, pp. 49–54.

25. Jeffery D. Zbar, "Kid's Networks Mature Into Global Programming Force," *Advertising Age*, March 1997, p. 16.

26. Leonard K. Cheng, "Supplier Preference and Dumping: An Analysis of Japanese Corporate Groups," *Southern Economic Journal*, July 1996, pp. 51–56.

27. Susan Porjes, "Strengthening Diversity," *International Business*, November 1996, pp. 18–24.

28. Michael Elliott, "Hey, Can You Spare a 'Euro'?," *Newsweek*, February 17, 1997, pp. 48–49.

29. "Dollar Dethroned?," *Industry Week*, April 21, 1997, p. 32.

30. Ibid.

31. David Bacon, "Mexico's New Braceros: How NAFTA Promotes Child Labor," *The Nation*, January 27, 1997, pp. 18–22.

32. John Conley, "Enter the Dragon," *International Business*, January, 1997, pp. 40–44.

33. Kathleen Kerwin, Dexter Roberts, and Mark Clifford, "GM's New Promised Land," *Business Week*, June 16, 1997, p. 34.

34. Mark Clifford, Nicloe Harris, Dexter Roberts, and Manjeet Kripalani, "Coke Pours into Asia," *Business Week*, October 28, 1996, pp. 72–77.

35. John Yarbrough, "Asian Horizon," *Sales & Marketing Management*, August, 1996, p. 64.

Chapter 4

1. Cathy Lazere, "Ethically Challenged," *CFO*, April 1997, pp. 40–41.

2. Harriet Webster, "Can Values Be Taught?," *Better Homes and Gardens*, March 1997, pp. 116–20.

3. Kenneth Blanchard and Norman Vincent Peale, *The Power of Ethical Management*, (New York: William Morrow, 1988); and Hal Lancaster, "Managing Your Career," *The Wall Street Journal Interactive Edition*, June 17, 1997.

4. Lynn Sharp Paine, "Managing for Organizational Integrity," *Harvard Business Review*, March–April 1994, pp. 106–17; and "United States Military Academy Faces Ethical Dilemmas in Third Annual Intercollegiate Ethics Bowl," PR Newswire, February 26, 1997.

5. David Carrig, "Money Bookshelf," *USA Today*, May 19, 1997.

6. Colleen Cooper, "Give and Thou Shall Receive," *Sales and Marketing Management*, March 1997, p. 75; and Barbara Sullivan, "Some Bitterness in the Mix at Ben & Jerry's Ice Cream Company," *Chicago Tribune*, May 26, 1997, p. B3.

7. Dan Seligman, "Talking Back to the Ethicists: What Qualifies These Professional Moralists to Tell Us How We Should Behave? Not Much," *Forbes*, May 5, 1997, p. 198.

8. John Dobson, "Are Ethics Programs a Hoax?," *CFO*, January 1997, p. 12.

9. Cooper, "Give and Thou Shall Receive"; and Jonathan Alter, "Down to Business," *Newsweek*, May 12, 1997, p. 57.

10. Alter, "Down to Business"; and Del Jones, "Good Works, Good Business," *USA Today*, April 25, 1997, pp. B1 and B2.

11. Kerry A. Dolan, "Kinder, Gentler MBAs," *Forbes*, June 2, 1997, p. 39.

12. Stuart V. Price, "Community Relations: What Motivates Stakeholders?" *Communication World*, February–March 1997, pp. 36–40; and John Kay, "Shareholders Aren't Everything," *Fortune*, February 17, 1997, pp. 133–34.

13. David Woodruff, "A-Class Damage Control at Daimler Benz," *Business Week*, November 24, 1997.

14. Thomas F. Roeser, "What's Good for the Consumer Is Good for Business," *Chicago Tribune*, May 19, 1997, p. 11.

15. Lazere, "Ethically Challenged."

16. Anna Muoio, "Ways to Give Back," *Fast Company*, December–January 1998, pp. 113–36; and "Affecting the Bottom Line; Coopers & Lybrand/Smith O'Brien Join Forces for Social Responsibility," PR Newswire, January 7, 1998.

17. Keith Hammonds, "A Portfolio With a Heart Still Needs a Brain," *Business Week*, January 26, 1998, p. 100.

18. Greg W. Prince, "Living for the City," *Beverage World*, January 1997, pp. 31–43.

19. Michael Novak, "Profits with Honor," *Policy Review*, May–June, 1996, pp. 50–57.

20. David Fischer, "A New Way to Shine Up Corporate Profits; Firms That Help Workers Polishing Their Skills Prosper," *U.S. News & World Report*, April 15, 1996, pp. 54–55.

21. Martha H. Peak, "Social Action for the Rest of Us," *Management Review*, October 1996, p. 1.

22. William Droel, "The Give and Take of Corporate Stewardship," *U.S. Catholic*, January 1997, pp. 12–18.

23. Steven Greenhouse, "Nike Shoe Plant in Vietnam Is Called Unsafe For Workers," *The New York Times*, November 8, 1997 and Bill Richards, "Nike Hires an Executive from Microsoft for New Post Focusing on Labor Policies," *The Wall Street Journal*, January 15, 1998, p. B14.

24. Jeffrey E, Garten, "Globalism Doesn't Have to be Cruel," *Business Week*, February 9, 1998, p. 26.

Chapter 4 Appendix

1. "Black Women Awarded $4.5 Million in Hair Care Suit," *Jet*, January 20, 1997, p. 12.

2. "Patents," *1996 Information Please™ Almanac*, 1996, p. 597.

3. Rodney Ho, "Inventors Battle Big Firms over Patent Secrets Bill," *The Wall Street Journal*, March 18, 1997, p.A1

4. Frank James, "Releasing Patent Details Sooner Not Inventive Idea to Opponents," *Chicago Tribune*, May 8, 1997.

5. "Despite Protests, U.S. House Passes Amended Patent Bill," *Los Angeles Times*, April 24, 1997, p. D3

6. Andrew F. Pepper, "In Defense of Antitrust Immunity for Collective Ratemeking: Life after the ICC Termination Act of 1995," *Transportation Journal*, Summer 1996, pp. 26–34.

7. Joan C. Szabo, "Bankruptcy: 1990s Style," *Nation's Business*, May 1995, p. 38

8. Daniel McGinn, "Deadbeat Nation," *Newsweek*, April 14, 1997, p. 50.

9. James Carter, "A Fresh Start or a Free Ride?" *St. Louis Post-Dispatch*, January 7, 1997, p. 11B.

10. Ibid.

11. Harvey Wasserman, "Utility Meltdown," *The Nation*, February 10, 1997, p. 6.

12. "Utility Deregulation Heats Up: Is Your Community Ready?," *Nation's Cities Weekly*, January 27, 1997, p. 10.

Chapter 5

1. "Anatomy of a Start-Up: The Hard Part," *Inc.*, April 1991, p. 55.

2. "Lobbyists Battle a Proposed Obstacle to S Corporation Conversions," *The Wall Street Journal Interactive Edition*, March 20, 1997.

3. Gloria Marulla, "Easier Rules Take Effect for S Corporations," *Nation's Business*, February 1997, p. 63.

4. Susan Pace Hamill, "The Limited Liability Company: A Catalyst Exposing the Corporate Integration Question," *Michigan Law Review*, November 1996, pp. 393–446 and "Small Business News: News, Trends, and Help for Growing Companies," *Los Angeles Times*, December 17, 1997, P. D-4.

5. "All About LLCs," *Inc.*, March 1996, p. 100; Roberta Maynard, "Starting a Limited Liability Company," *Nation's Business*, November 1996, p. 12; and Wayne R. Wells and Gary A. Yoshimoto, "Is There a Limited Liability Company in Your Future?" *Review of Business*, Spring 1996, pp. 26–32.

6. Milton Zall, "New Tax Flexibility for Limited-Liability Companies," *Video Business*, August 9, 1996, p. 42.

7. Steven Lipin, "Wave of Corporate Mergers Continues to Gather Force," *The Wall Street Journal Interactive Edition*, February 26, 1997.

8. David Whitford, "Sale of the Century," *Fortune*, February 17, 1997.

9. Shaifali Puri, "Deals of the Year," *Fortune*, February 17, 1997.

10. "Stavro Gets the Gardens," *Maclean's*, August 19, 1996, p. 41.

11. Therese Thilgen, "Corporate Clout Replaces 'Small Is Beautiful,'" *The Wall Street Journal*, March 27, 1997, p. B14.

12. David Segal, "In Hopes of a Chain Reaction: At the Franchise Expo, Images of Rich Rewards Vie with a Harder Reality," *The Washington Post*, April, 30, 1997 p. C11.

13. "McDonald's Celebrates Its Brand at Annual Meeting," company press release, May 22, 1997.

14. Jeffrey A. Tannenbaum, "Franchisors Push Franchisees to Do More Local Marketing," *The Wall Street Journal Interactive Edition*, April 1, 1997.

15. Jeffrey A. Tannenbaum, "Alternative Terms Make Owning a Franchise Easier," *The Wall Street Journal Interactive Edition*, February 4, 1997.

16. David Segal, "Franchisees Unite to Fight for Their Lives; Judgments Against Parent Companies Tip Balance of Power," *The Washington Post*, April 17 1997, p. A1.

17. "Consider Buying a Brand-Name Business," *Home-Office Computing*, http://www.smalloffice.com/maven/archive/bmspot8.htm

18. David Segal, "Franchisees Unite to Fight for Their Lives; Judgments against Parent Companies Tip Balance of Power," *The Washington Post*, April 17, 1997, p. A1; and Nicole Harris and Mike France, "Franchisees Get Feisty," *Business Week*, February 24, 1997.

19. "McDonald's Franchisees Join the McFight Fast Food," *Los Angeles Times,* May 22, 1997, p. D8; Cliff Edwards, "Fast Food Giant's Franchisee group Revolts against Mandates," Associated Press, May 21, 1997; and Richard Gibson, "McDonald's 'Campaign 55' Promotion to Be Clarified and Advertised More," *The Wall Street Journal,* May 20, 1997, p. B14.

20. Greg Burns, "Fast-Food Fight," *Business Week,* June 2, 1997, pp. 34–36.

21. Vicki Torres, "Black Business Expo Assumes a New Tack Trade Show," *Los Angeles Times,* April 24, 1997, p. D1.

22. Ripley Hotch, "Real-Time Info, and No Paperwork," *The Wall Street Journal,* March 27, 1997, p. B16.

Chapter 6

1. Barbara Ettorre, "Is There a Talent Squeeze in Corporate America?" *Management Review,* March 1997, pp. 47–52.

2. Stephanie N. Mehta, "Young Are Business Veterans at Early Age, Study Finds," *The Wall Street Journal Interactive Edition,* March 19, 1997.

3. Martha Groves, "Adventures on the Job," *Los Angeles Times,* June 23, 1997, p. DD-34.

4. Stephanie N. Mehta, "Ideas Sire Many Entrepreneurs But May Follow Business Plan," *The Wall Street Journal Interactive Edition,* February 19, 1997.

5. Richard Ashton, "Upstart Students Start Up," *Inc.,* October 1996, p. 32.

6. Dale Dauten, "Creativity Demands 'Flashlight,' Not Flash of Insight," *St. Louis Post-Dispatch,* January 13, 1997, p. 4BP.

7. Mike Feibus, "Compaq Plays—And Wins—The Numbers Game," *PC Week,* June 23, 1997, p. 91.

8. Charlotte Grimes, "Home-Based Entrepreneurs Have 27 Million Colleagues," *St. Louis Post-Dispatch,* April 28, 1996, p. 8A; and Repps Hudson, "Doing Business Together," *St. Louis Post-Dispatch,* February 9, 1998, pp. BP1 and BP12–13.

9. Scott DeGarmo, "Micropreneurs: What Entrepreneurs Can Learn from Their Work-at-Home Cousins," *Success,* December 1996, p. 6.

10. Teresa McUsic, "'Micropreneurs' Climb Ladder to Success, Step by Step," *St. Louis Post-Dispatch,* January 6, 1997, p. 6BP.

11. Alan Farnham, "Getting the Best from Your Smartest People," *Fortune,* March 17, 1997.

12. Tony Jackson, "Innovation," *The Financial Times,* June 19, 1997, p. 1.

13. Kathy Yakal, "Now You Can Use Your Post-it Notes Electronically," *Computer Shopper,* June 1997, p. 547.

14. "Poll Finds Business Formation in U.S. Slipped 14% Last Year," *The Wall Street Journal interactive edition,* January 6, 1998.

15. Stephanie N. Mehta, "Women Quit Lucrative Jobs to Start Their Own Businesses," *The Wall Street Journal Interactive Edition,* November 11, 1996.

16. Jeffrey A. Tannenbaum, "Minority-Women-Owned Firms Increase by 153% in Nine Years," *The Wall Street Journal Interactive Edition,* June 25, 1997.

17. Gene Koretz, "Startups: Still a Job Engine," *Business Week,* March 24, 1997; and Sherwood Ross, "Entrepreneurs Should Get Credit for the U.S. Employment Miracle,' *St. Louis Post-Dispatch,* January 5, 1998, p. BP4.

18. Jerry Useem, "Surprising Snapshots of Who's Starting Companies—and Where the Money's Coming From," *Inc. Online,* April 4, 1997.

19. Gene Koretz, "Small Business Is Putting Some Snap in the Job Market," *Business Week,* April 25, 1994, p. 26.

20. Richard L. Hudson, "One Field Where Little Guy May Still Have the Edge," *The Wall Street Journal Interactive Edition,* February 4, 1997; and Katy Kelly, "Taking Complaints, for a Very Small Fee," *USA Today,* January 6, 1998, p. 8.

21. Gene Koretz, "A Surprising Finding on New-Business Mortality Rates," *Business Week,* June 14, 1993, p. 22; James Aley, "Debunking the Failure Fallacy," *Fortune,* September 6, 1993, p. 21; and Jerry Useem, "U.S. Business Data Worst in World—and Getting Worse," *Inc.,* October 1996, p. 26.

22. Daniel Grebler, "Try a Business Before You Buy It—You'll Be Gald You Did," *St. Louis Post-Dispatch,* January 5, 1998, p. BP9.

23. Carolyn Brown, "Becoming Your Own Boss: Developing a Solid Business Plan," *Essence,* March 1997, pp. 83–86.

24. Sheryl Nance-Nash, "How to Raise Venture Capital," *Your Company Weekly,* February 10–14, 1997.

25. Joel T. Patz, "Step-by-Step Business Planning," *Home Office Computing,* November 1996, pp. 120–29.

26. Dale Buss, "Bringing New Firms Out of Their Shell," *Nation's Business,* March 1997, pp. 48–51.

27. Stephanie N. Mehta, "Venture Capital Raised by Firms Was a Record $10.1 Billion," *The Wall Street Journal interactive edition,* February 5, 1997; and "Venture Investments Rise," *The Wall Street Journal Interactive Edition,* February 21, 1997.

28. Mitchell Stern, "The Insider's Guide to the SBA," *Working Woman,* October 1996, pp. 44–48.

29. Susan Hodges, "SBA Microloans Fuel Big Ideas," *Nation's Business,* February 1997, pp. 23–35.

30. Earl A. Berner, "City, University Team Up on Business Incubator," *Nation's Cities Weekly,* January 6, 1997, p. 3; and Michele Mohr, "Making Money People Get Good Advice on Organizing and Planning a Small Business," *Chicago Tribune,* May 11, 1997, p. 3.

31. J. Tol Broome Jr., "Changes Make SBA More User-Friendly," *Video Business,* February 3, 1997, pp. 38–39.

32. Patrick Wilson, "Help for Women's Business," *St. Louis Post-Dispatch,* January 8, 1998, p. C7.

33. Anne B. Fisher, "Profiting from Crisis," *Fortune,* February 7, 1994, p. 166.

34. Daniel Grebler, "This Group Helps New Entrepreneurs SCORE," *St. Louis Post-Dispatch,* August 4, 1977, p. 17BP.

35. Laura, M. Litvan, "Small Firms Go International," *Investor's Business Daily,* February 26, 1997, p. A1.

Chapter 7

1. David Greising, "It Is the Best of Times–Or Is It?,'" *Business Week,* January 12, 1998, pp. 36–38.

2. Rebecca A. Fannin, "U.S. Multinationals," *Ad Age International,* January 1998, pp. 17–26.

3. Jack Neff, "Diversity," *Advertising Age,* February 16, 1998, pp. S1 & S14.

4. Richard Pascale, "Change How You Define Leadership, and You Change How You Run a Company," *Fast Company,* April–May 1998, pp. 110–120.

5. Scott Kirsner, "Every Day It's a New Place," *Fast Company,* April–May 1998, pp. 130–134.

6. "A Chat With C. Michael Armstrong," *Business Week,* February 2, 1998, p. 132.

7. Mark Henricks, "Golden Rules," *Entrepreneur,* May 1997, pp. 17–151.

8. Steve Lewis, "All or Nothing: Customers Must Be 'Totally Satisfied,'" *Marketing News,* March 2, 1998, pp. 11–12.

9. Clint Willis, "Super Chiefs," *Worth,* September 1997, pp. 60–84.

10. Thomas A. Stewart, "Why Leadership Matters," *Fortune,* March 2, 1998, pp. 71–82.

11. Francis J. Quinn, "What's the Buzz?," *Logistics Management,* February 1997, pp. 43–46.

12. Stephanie Gruner, "The Secrets of Cross-Promotion," *Inc.,* June 1997, pp. 99–101.

13. Thomas W. Malone, "Is Empowerment Just a Fad? Control, Decision Making, and IT," *Sloan Management Review,* Winter 1997, pp. 23–35.

14. Stephen Covey, "Patterns for Success," *Incentive,* May 1997, p. 23.

15. "Teams Rule," *The Wall Street Journal,* May 28, 1996, p. A1.

16. Joanne Cleaver, "An Inside Job," *Marketing News,* February 16, 1998, pp. 1 & 14.

17. "'Enviropreneurial' Strategy Is a Free-Market Approach," *Marketing News,* February 3, 1997, p. 22.

18. Joel Kurtzman, "Is Your Company Off Course? Now You Can Find Out Why." *Fortune,* February 17, 1997, pp. 128–30.

19. Thomas A. Stewart, "Why Leadership Matters," *Fortune,* March 2, 1998, pp. 71–82.

20. David Garvin, "What Makes for an Authentic Learning Organization?," *Management Update,* June 1997, pp. 7–9.

21. Michael Donovan, "Maximizing the Bottom-Line Impact of Self-Directed Work Teams," *Quality Digest,* June 1996, pp. 34–35.

22. Sharon Nelton, "Leadership for a New Age," *Nation's Business,* May 1997, pp. 18–27.

23. Scott Bistayi, "Delegate—Or Not?," *Forbes,* April 21, 1997, pp. 20–22.

24. Jack Neff, "Diversity," *Advertising Age,* February 16, 1998, pp. S1 and S14.

25. "What Are Your Most Challenging Business Tasks?," *Home Office Computing,* March 1998, p. 80.

26. Gary N. Powell, "Reinforcing and Extending Today's Organizations: The Simultaneous Pursuit of Person–Organization Fit and Diversity," *Organizational Dynamics,* Winter 1998, pp. 50–61.

27. John Helyar and Joann S. Lubin, "The Portable CEO," *The Wall Street Journal,* January 21, 1998, pp. A1 and A10.

Chapter 8

1. Richard K. Lester, Michael J. Piore and Kamal M. Malek, "Interpretive Management: What General Managers Can Learn from Design," *Harvard Business Review,* March–April 1998, pp. 86–96.

2. Gene Koretz, "Will Downsizing Ever Let Up?" *Business Week,* February 16, 1998, p. 26.

3. Gene Koretz, "The Downside of Downsizing," *Business Week,* April 28, 1997, p. 26.

4. Norman R. Augustine, "Reshaping an Industry: Lockheed Martin's Survival Story," May–June, 1997, pp. 83–94.

5. Leonard L. Berry, "Services Marketing at the Turn of the Millennium," *Marketing Management,* Fall 1997, pp. 9–13.

6. A. Blanton Godfrey, "The Quality-Driven Future," *Quality Digest,* January 1998, p. 19.

7. Richard Pascale, "Change How You Define Leadership, and You Change How You Run a Company," *Fast Company,* April–May 1998, pp. 110–120.

8. Gene Koprowski, "Only Connect," *Marketing Tools,* January/February 1998, pp. 30–34.

9. Gene Koprowski, "Intranets: Broader Applications Require New Skills," *The Washington Post,* June 15, 1997, p. M19.

10. Mary J. Cronin, "Intranets Reach the Factory Floor," *Fortune,* August 18, 1997, p. 208.

11. Iris Mohr-Jackson, "Managing a Total Quality Orientation," *Industrial Marketing Management,* March 1998, pp. 109–25.

12. Elizabeth R. Larson, "Profiles in Quality: the 1997 Baldrige Award Winners," *Quality Digest,* January 1998, pp. 26–29.

13. Kenneth Hein, "Reengineering Undergoes Reconstruction," *Incentive,* February 1997, p. 5.

14. James Brian Quinn, Philip Anderson, and Sydney Finkelstein, "Making the Most of the Best," *Harvard Business Review,* March–April 1996, pp. 71–80.

15. Lisa M. Kennedy, "Benchmarking Often Explores Non-Competitors' Bright Ideas," *Business Marketing,* March 1996, p. 7.

16. Melinda Nykamp, "Insourcing vs. Outsourcing: Which Is the Right Choice?," *DM News,* July 21, 1997, p. 30.

17. Paul Mahler, "Strategic Outsourcing Sharpens Big Picture Focus," *DM News,* June 9, 1997, pp. 31 and 52.

18. Thomas A. Stewart, "Another Fad Worth Killing," *Fortune,* February 3, 1997, p. 119.

19. Thomas Petzinger Jr., "Charles Koch Teaches Staff to Run a Firm Like a Free Nation," *The Wall Street Journal,* April 18, 1997, p. B1.

20. Michael Warshaw, "The Good Guy's Guide to Office Politics," *Fast Company,* April–May 1998, pp. 157–178.

Chapter 9

1. Michael van Biema and Bruce Greenwald, "Managing Our Way to Higher Service-Sector Productivity," *Harvard Business Review,* July–August 1997, pp. 87–95.

2. Chris Woodyard, "Mass Production Gives Way to Mass Customization," *USA Today,* February 16, 1998, p. 3B.

3. Russ Banham, "Not-So-Clear Choices," International Business, November–December 1997, pp. 23–25.

4. Kathleen M. Eisenhardt and Shona L. Brown, "Time Pacing: Competing in Markets That Won't Stand Still," *Harvard Business Review,* March–April 1998, pp. 56–69.

5. Brian Steinberg, "Separated At Work," *Entrepreneur,* March 1998, pp. 132–136.

6. Greg Jaffe and Oscar Suris, "Audi May Join Car Makers' Caravan to Southern States," *The Wall Street Journal,* March 13, 1997, pp. B1, B10.

7. Jodie DeJonge, "Allen-Edmonds Tries Milwaukee," *The Washington Times,* April 19, 1997, pp. C11–C14.

8. Don Peppers and Martha Rogers, "Lessons from the Front," *Marketing Tools,* January–February 1998, pp. 39–42.

9. Michael H. Martin, "Smart Managing," *Fortune,* February 2, 1998, pp. 149–151.

10. Robert J. Samuelson, "The Assembly Line," *Newsweek,* special issue, 1997.

11. Sarah Schafer, "Have It Your Way," *Inc. Tech 1997,* No. 4, pp. 56–64.

12. Chris Woodyard, "Virtual Tailors Fashion Apparel," *USA Today,* February 16, 1998, p. 3B.

13. Sarah Schafer, op. cit.

14. Dan Gutman, "Design Your Product in 3D," *Success,* September 1996, p. 66.

15. Roland T. Rust, "The Dawn of Computer Behavior," *Marketing Management,* Fall 1997, pp. 31–33.

16. Shikhar Ghosh, "Making Business Sense of the Internet," *Harvard Business Review,* March–April 1998, pp. 126–135.

Chapter 10

1. Alan Farnham, "The Man Who Changed Work Forever," *Fortune,* July 21, 1997, p. 114.

2. Ibid.

3. Douglas A. Blackmon, "Shippers Pitch Power of Gizmos and Gadgets," *The Wall Street Journal,* June 2, 1997, p. B1.

4. Abraham H. Maslow, *Motivation and Personality* (New York: Harper & Brothers, 1954).

5. David Kirkpatrick, "Intel's Amazing Profit Machine," *Fortune,* February 17, 1997, pp. 60–72.

6. Andrea Gabor, "Hard Work and Common Sense," *Los Angeles Times,* February 8, 1998, p. 5.

7. Jim Collins, "The Human Side of Enterprise," *Inc.,* December 1996, p. 55.

8. "First Discipline Then Empowerment," *The Wall Street Journal,* February 20, 1998, p. A19.

9. Robert Maynard, "How to Motivate Low-Wage Workers," *Nation's Business,* May 1997, pp. 35–39.

10. William G. Ouchi, *Theory Z: How American Business Can Meet the Japanese Challenge* (Menlo Park, CA: Addison-Wesley, 1981).

11. Frederick Herzberg, *Work and the Nature of Man* (World Publishers, 1966).

12. Virginia Baldwin Hick, "What Works at Work: Kind Word from Boss," *St. Louis Post-Dispatch,* January 3, 1994, p. 1C.

13. Meg Carter, "What to Ask the Workers," *Financial Times,* February 18, 1998, p. 23.

14. Bob Nelson, "Dump the Cash, Load On the Praise," *Personnel Journal,* July 1996, p. 65 and Sherwood Ross, "Employees Prize Career Development When Deciding to Change Jobs," *St. Louis Post-Dispatch,* February 2, 1998, p. BP4.

15. Herman Cain, "Leadership Is Common Sense," *Success,* February 1997, pp. 41–48.

16. Theodore H. Poister and Gregory Streib, "MBO in Municipal Government: Variations on a Traditional Management Tool," *Public Administration Review,* January–February 1995, pp. 48–56.

17. Victor H. Vroom, *Work and Motivation* (New York: John Wiley & Sons, 1967).

18. David Nadler and Edward Lawler, "Motivation—a Diagnostic Approach," in *Perspectives on Behavior in Organizations,* ed. Richard Hackman, Edward Lawler, and Lyman Porter (New York: McGraw-Hill, 1977).

19. Ron Frank, "The Inspiration of Experience: Six Bestselling Leadership Principles You Won't Find in a Business Bestseller," *Management Review,* January 1997, pp. 33–38.

20. Joseph B. White and Oscar Suris, "New Pony: How a 'Skunk Works' Kept the Mustang Alive—on a Tight Budget," *The Wall Street Journal,* September 21, 1993 and Anita Lienert, "A Special Delivery From Ford," *Chicago Tribune,* February 12, 1998, p. 11.

21. Diane Summers, "Generation X Comes of Age," *Financial Times,* February 16, 1998, p. 16.

22. Charles L. Parnell, "Teamwork: Not a New Idea, but It's Transforming the Workplace," *Vital Speeches,* November 1, 1996, p. 46.

23. Ronald B. Lieber, "100 Best Companies to Work For in America," *Fortune,* January 12, 1998, pp. 72–85.

24. Stephen Franklin, "Unsettled Past Leads to Remarkable Harmony," *Chicago Tribune,* September 7, 1997, p. 2.

25. Vincent Alonzo, "Recognition? Who Needs It?," *Sales & Marketing Management,* February 1997, p. 26.

26. Linda Grant, "Happy Workers, High Returns," *Fortune,* January 12, 1998.

27. Morey Stettner, "Five Painless Steps to Motivate Colleagues," *Investor's Business Daily,* February 5, 1998, p. A1.

Chapter 11

1. Diane Summers, "When People Really Matter," *Financial Times,* January 8, 1998, p. 18.

2. Philip Manchester, "The Skills Shortage: A Worldwide Problem," *Financial Times,* January 7, 1998.

3. Sherwood Ross, "Employee Recruiting Goes Electronic," *St. Louis Post-Dispatch,* April 1, 1996, p. 19BP; and Regina Kwon, Carol Levin, Sebastian Rupley, and Don Willmott, "Netting a Job," *PC Magazine,* February 4, 1997, p. 10.

4. Sherwood Ross, "Employee Satisfaction Is a Problem for Employers," *St. Louis Post-Dispatch,* April 7, 1997, p. 16BP.

5. Adrienne Fox, "Passing the Educational Buck," *Investor's Business Daily,* January 8, 1998.

6. Sarah Schafer, "Human Resources: Putting IT to the Test," *Inc. Technology,* no. 1 for 1997, p. 74.

7. Eric Rolfe Greenberg, "Drug Testing Now Standard Practice," *HR Focus*, September 1996, p. 24; and Teresa Brady, "Bad Hair Days: Hair Follicle Testing Offers an Alternative to Traditional Drug Tests," *Management Review*, February 1997, pp. 59–61.

8. Stephen Covey, "The Perfect Hire," *Incentive*, June 1997, p. 19.

9. Rivka Tadjer, "Virtual Employees May Be the Way to Strong Expansion," *The Wall Street Journal Interactive Edition*, December 29, 1997.

10. "Outsourcing: Common Alternative Staffing Options," *HR Magazine*, February 1997.

11. Andrew Bolger, "Flexibility in the Workplace Now the Norm," January 29, 1998, p.12.

12. Thomas. C. Greble, "A Leading Role for HR in Alternative Staffing," *HR Magazine*, February 1997.

13. Sherwood Ross, "Are American's Temporary Workers Being Marginalized?," *St. Louis Post-Dispatch*, January 13, 1997, p. 20BP.

14. Linda Stockman Vines, "Make Long-Term Temporary Workers Part of the Team," *HR Magazine*, April 1997, pp. 65–69.

15. Hal Plotkin, "What They Do (and Don't) Teach You in Business School," *The Wall Street Journal Interactive Edition*, January 5, 1998.

16. Hal Lancaster, "How Women Can Find Mentors in a World of Few Role Models," *The Wall Street Journal Interactive Edition*, April 1, 1997.

17. Christopher Caggiano, "How You Gonna Keep 'Em Down on the Firm," *Inc. Online*, January 7, 1998.

18. Margaret A. Jacobs, "'New Girl' Network Is Boon for Women Lawyers," *The Wall Street Journal*, March 4, 1997, pp. B1 and B12; and Linda Himelstein "How Do You Get the Boys to Pass You the Ball?," *Business Week*, February 17, 1997.

19. Jack Stack, "The Curse of the Annual Performance Appraisal," *Inc. Magazine*, March 1997, p. 39.

20. Stephanie Gruner, "Feedback from Everybody," *Inc. Magazine*, February 1997, p. 102.

21. Courtney Price, "What's the Best Kind of Incentive to Give Employees?" *St. Louis Post-Dispatch*, January 6, 1997, p. 20BP.

22. Al Stamborski, "Year-End Bonuses Rarer as Companies Reward Performance," *St. Louis Post-Dispatch*, January 6, 1997, p. 3BP; and Joseph B. White, "The 'In' Thing," *The Wall Street Journal*, April 10, 1997, pp. R10 and R13.

23. John O. Whitney, *The Trust Factor* (New York: McGraw-Hill, 1994).

24. C. James Novak, "Proceed with Caution When Paying Teams," *HR Magazine*, April 1997, pp. 73–77.

25. Perry Pascarella, "Compensating Teams," *Across the Board*, February 1997, pp. 16–23.

26. Richard Donkin, "The Year of the Knowledge Worker," *Financial Times*, January 9, 1998.

27. Donald J. McNerney, "Case Study: Team Compensation," *Management Review*, February 1, 1995, p. 16.

28. Tim Smart, "IBM Has a New Product: Employee Benefits," *Business Week*, May 10, 1993, p. 58.

29. Marie Gendron, "Getting to Yes on Flexible Work Schedules," *Management Update*, May 1997, p. 10.

30. Laura Shapiro, "The Myth of Quality Time," *Newsweek*, May 12, 1997, pp. 62–68.

31. Melanie Warner, "Working at Home—The Right Way to Be a Star in Your Bunny Slippers," *Fortune*, March 3, 1997.

32. Barry Williams, "Trends in Employment Patterns and Policies," Public Management, August 1996, pp. 24–26.

33. David R. Henderson, "Why You Can't Fire Anybody," *Fortune*, June 23, 1997, pp. 38–38.

34. Holman W. Jenkins, Jr. "Jesse Jackson, Rainmaker," *The Wall Street Journal Interactive Edition*, January 7, 1998.

35. Clint Bolick, "A Middle Ground on Affirmative Action," *The Wall Street Journal Interactive Edition*, January 6, 1998.

36. Holman W. Jenkins, Jr. "Think Your Co-Workers Are Crazy? They Are," *The Wall Street Journal*, May 13, 1997, p. A23; "EEOC Says Disabilities Act Applies to the Mentally Ill," *The Wall Street Journal Interactive Edition*, April 30, 1997; Ellen Joan Pollock and Joann S. Lublin, "Employers Remain Wary of Mental-Illness Guidelines," *The Wall Street Journal Interactive Edition*, May 1, 1997; and Robert Pear, "Employers Told to Accommodate the Mentally Ill," *New York Times*, April 30, 1997, p. A1.

Chapter 12

1. Glenn Burkins, "AFL–CIO Plans Campaign for a Rebound," *The Wall Street Journal*, February 18, 1997, p. A24.

2. Kenneth Reich, "State Panel to Examine Standards for Private Judges," *Los Angeles Times*, December 26, 1997, p. A-3.

3. Allison Lucas, "Damage Control: How to Make Sure Sales Don't Suffer When a Work Force Strikes," *Sales & Marketing Management*, June 1996, p. 21.

4. James Worsham, "Labor's New Assault," *Nation's Business*, June 1997, pp. 15–23.

5. Warren Cohen, "A Union Drive to Woo Women," *U.S. News and World Report*, March 3, 1997, p. 43.

6. Sue Shellenberger and Karen Nussbaum, "Plans to Focus Unions on Family Issues," *The Wall Street Journal*, February 19, 1997, p. B1.

7. Michael J. McCarthy, "Thanks a Lot: CEO Gets $102 Million Bonus," *The Wall Street Journal*, March 27, 1997, p. B1.

8. Jennifer Reingold and Amy Borris, "Even Executives Are Wincing at Executive Pay," *Business Week*, May 12, 1997, pp. 40–41.

9. Eric Hardy, "The Prize," *Forbes*, May 19, 1997, pp. 166–69.

10. Rebecca Quick, "Wanna Earn the Bosses Pay? Then Check Out This Site," *The Wall Street Journal*, April 11, 1997, p. B1.

11. Jennifer Reingold, "Executive Pay," *Business Week*, April 21, 1997, pp. 59–66.

12. "Economic Indicators," *The Economist*, November 16, 1996, p. 108; and Ira T. Kay, "High CEO Pay Helps the U.S. Economy Thrive," *The Wall Street Journal*, February 23, 1998, p. A22.

13. Allan Sloan, "How Much Is Too Much?," *Business Week*, March 17, 1997, p. 40 and C. Frederic Wiegold, "The Quest for Shareholder Value: Third Annual Guide to America's Best, Worst Companies," *The Wall Street Journal*, February 26, 1998, p. R1.

14. "Labor's Gender Gap," *Business Week*, January 9, 1997.

15. "Gender Pay Gap a Bit Less at Top," *St. Louis Post Dispatch*, December 18, 1996, p. 8C.

16. Deborah Anderson, "Sex Discrimination in the Labor Market: The Case for Comparable Worth," *Industrial and Labor Relations Review*, October 1996, pp. 170–72.

17. Richard J. Newman, "Did We Say Zero Tolerance? A Legal Dilemma over Sexual Harassment," *U.S. World & News Report*, March 10, 1997, p. 33.

18. Leslie Kaufman, "A Report from the Front," *Newsweek*, January 13, 1997, p. 32.

19. Steven C. Bahls and Jane Easter Bahls, "Hands-Off Policy," *Entrepreneur*, July 1997, pp. 74–77; and Anne Fisher, "After All This Time, Why Don't People Know What Sexual Harassment Means?" *Fortune*, January 12, 1998, p. 156.

20. Larry Reynolds, "Sex Harassment Claims Surge," *HR Focus*, March 1997, p. 8.

21. Warren Cohen, "The Long Road to a Model Workplace," *U.S. News & World Report*, February 24, 1997, p. 57; and Rochelle Sharp, "Mitsubishi Deceived Press, Ex–Official Says," *The Wall Street Journal*, January 12, 1998, p. A22.

22. Reynolds, "Sexual Harassment Claims Surge."

23. Rana Dogar, "Corporate Relief for Desperate Parents," *Working Woman*, March 1995, p. 15; and Judith Graham and Carol Kleinman, "Clinton Asks $21 Billion for Child-Care Package from Perk to Trend to Real Progress," *Chicago Tribune*, January 8, 1998, p. 1.

24. Maureen Minehan, "The Aging Baby Boomers," *HR Magazine*, April 1997, p. 208.

25. "Fleet Financial Vice President Briefs Congress on Effect of Aging Parents and Elder Care on Work-Life Balance," *PR Newswire*, June 12, 1997.

26. Sue Shellengarger, "We Take Better Care of Parents Than Most Americans Realize," *The Wall Street Journal*, March 12, 1997, p. B1.

27. "AIDS in the Workplace Survey: 'Wake Up Call for American Business," *AIDS Weekly Plus*, July 29, 1997, p. 18.

28. "ABC's of AIDS Are Slow to Be Taught in the American Workplace," *AIDS Weekly Plus*, February 24, 1997, p. 14.

29. Peggy Kochner, "Drug-Testing Is Becoming Standard Practice," *St. Louis Small Business Monthly*, June 1997, p. 31.

30. John K. Slage, "Attack on Violence: Debate Rages about the Extent of Workplace Violence and What, If Anything, Can Be Done about It," *Industry Week*, February 17, 1997, p. 15.

31. Ibid.

32. Steve Kaufman, "ESOPs' Appeal on the Increase," *Nation's Business*, June 1997, p. 43.

33. Dominic Bencivenga, "Employee-Owners Help Bolster the Bottom Line," *HR Magazine*, February 1997 and Tamara Chuang, "Stock Ownership Plans Don't Only Benefit Worker," *The Dallas Morning News*, November 25, 1997, p. 1C.

34. Aaron Bernstein, "Why ESOP Deals Have Slowed to a Crawl," *Business Week*, March 18, 1996, p. 101–102.

35. Susan Chandler, "United We Own," *Business Week*, March 18, 1996, pp. 96–100.

36. Bernstein, "Why ESOP Deals Have Slowed to a Crawl."

Chapter 13

1. Jim Mateja, "Customer Wants to Fuel the Market," *The Washington Times*, February 27, 1998, pp. E1 and E9.

2. Paul Mahler, "Strategic Outsourcing Sharpens Big Picture Focus," *DM News*, June 9, 1997, pp. 31, 52.

3. Steve Lewis, "All or Nothing: Customers Must Be Totally Satisfied," *Marketing News*, March 2, 1998, pp. 11–12.

4. "Dime Yankee," *Inc.*, May 1997, p. 16.

5. John Kay, "Shareholders Aren't Everything," *Fortune*, February 17, 1997, p. 133.

6. Jesus Mena, "Looking for Mr. Goodbuy," *Marketing Tools*, June 1997, pp. 24–27.

7. Jacquelyn Ottman, "Proven Environmental Commitment Helps Create Committed Customers," *Marketing News*, February 2, 1998, pp. 5–6.

8. "Fly & Field—A Website Worth Studying," *MaxiMarketing Insights*, March 1996, p.11.

9. Mark McLaughlin, "Drive Customer Loyalty to Increase Profit," *DM News*, February 9, 1998, p. 6.

10. David Kay, "Go Where the Consumers Are and Talk to Them," *Marketing News*, January 6, 1997, p. 14.

11. Paul Ruine and Cheryl Stuart Ruine, "Being a Global Winner," *Nation's Business*, December 1997, p. 6.

13. Thomas Petzinger, Jr., "Joe Morabito Beats the Competition with Cooperation," *The Wall Street Journal*, February 7, 1997, p. B1; and Frequent Shopper Review, *Supermarket Strategic Alert*, December 1996, p. 4.

Chapter 14

1. William C. Symonds, "Dunkin' Donuts Is on Coffee Rush," *Business Week*, March 16, 1998, pp. 107–108.

2. David Leonhardt, "McDonald's," *Business Week*, March 9, 1998, pp. 70–77.

3. "Polaroid Retouches Faded Image," *Chicago Tribune*, January 5, 1998, Sec. 4, p. 5.

4. Ruth O'Brien, "Developing a World Class Solutions Philosophy," *TeleServices News*, March 9, 1998, p. 19.

5. Steven D. Kage, "Megamerger," *U.S. News & World Report*, April 20, 1998, pp. 60–62.

6. Steve Rosenbush, "Putting the Buzz Back into AT&T," *USA Today Money*, April 2, 1997, p. 1.

7. Ian C. MacMillan and Rita Gunther McGrath, "Discovering New Points of Differentiation," *Harvard Business Review*, July–August 1997, pp. 133–45.

8. Ian P. Murphy, "Study: Packaging Important in Trial Purchases," *Marketing News*, February 3, 1997, p. 14.

9. Howard Alport, "Global, Interactive Marketing Call for Innovative Packaging," *Marketing News*, January 6, 1997, p. 30.

10. John T. Landry, "Make a Bundle Bundling," *Harvard Business Review*, November–December 1997, pp. 18–19.

11. Rebecca Piirto Heath, "The Once and Future King," *Marketing Tools*, March 1998, pp. 38–43.

12. Kurt Johnson, "Loyalty Marketing: Choosing the Right Program," *Relationship Marketing Report*, March 1998, pp. 1 and 5–7.

13. Margaret Webb Pressler, "The Power of Branding," *The Washington Post*, July 27, 1997, pp. H1, H5.

14. Harry Hurt III, "Parks Brought to You By . . . ," *U.S. News and World Report*, August 11, 1997, pp. 42–45.

15. Dean Takahashi, "How the Competition got Ahead of Intel in Making Cheap Chips," *The Wall Street Journal*, February 12, 1998, pp. A1, A11.

16. Alan J. Bergstrom, "Brand Management Poised for Change," *Marketing News*, May 7, 1997, p. 5.

17. "Instant Market Analysis," *Success*, February 1996, p. 10.

18. "Got a Good Idea for a New Product?," *The Wall Street Journal*, May 1, 1997, p. 1.

19. Shikhar Ghosh, "Making Business Sense of the Internet," *Harvard Business Review*, March–April 1998, pp. 126–35.

20. Richard Pascale, "Change How You Define Leadership and You Change How You Run a Company," *Fast Company*, April–May 1998, pp. 110–120.

21. Roberta Maynard, "Taking the Guesswork Out of Pricing," *Nation's Business*, December 1997, pp. 27–29.

22. William Claiborne, "Asian Monetary Crisis Sends Ripples to the U.S. West Coast," *The Washington Post*, February 10, 1998, p. A3.

23. Susan Greco, "Are Your Prices Right?," *Inc.*, January 1997, pp. 88–89.

24. Mark McLaughlin, "Drive Customer Loyalty to Increase Profit," *DM News*, February 9, 1998, p. 6.

Chapter 15

1. Laurie Joan Aron, "The Changing Course of Logistics Education," *Inbound Logistics*, April 1997, pp. 24–30.

2. Michael Warshaw, "Guts and Glory," *Success*, March 1997, pp. 28–33.

3. Francis J. Quinn, "Logistics' New Customer Focus," *Business Week*, March 10, 1997, pp. 53.

4. Leigh Buchanan, "From Steer to Eternity," *Inc. Tech 1998, No. 1*, pp. 66–77.

5. Lisa H. Harrington, "Logistics for Profit," *Fortune*, April 1, 1997, pp. 137–44.

6. John Conley, "The Shakeout in Global Logistics," *International Business*, December 1995–January 1996, pp. 50–57.

7. John T. Landry, "The Value of Trust," *Harvard Business Review*, January–February 1998, pp. 18–19.

8. Judann Pollack, "The Food Chain," *Advertising Age*, May 6, 1996, pp. 28–30.

9. William Davidow, "The Buck No Longer Stops Here," *Forbes ASAP*, February 24 1997, p. 24.

10. Gary Hamel, "Strategy as Revolution," *Harvard Business Review*, July–August 1996, pp. 69–82.

11. "Super Smart Transportation and Logistics," *Fortune*, March 31, 1997, pp. 47–53.

12. William G. Nickels and Marian Burk Wood, *Marketing: Relationships, Quality, Value* (New York: Worth Publishers, 1997).

13. Debra Phillips, "Rush Hour," *Entrepreneur*, February 1998, pp. 114–18.

14. Joan Magretta, "The Power of Virtual Integration: An Interview with Dell Computer's Michael Dell," *Harvard Business Review*, March–April 1998, pp. 73–84.

15. David L. Levy, "Lean Production in the Supply Chain," *Sloan Management Review*, Winter 1997, pp. 94–102.

16. Russ Banham, "Getting on Track," *International Business*, March 1997, pp. 14–15.

17. Margaret Webb Pressler, "Coming to a Store Near You," *Washington Business*, February 24, 1997, pp. 12–14.

18. Ann March, "Not Your Dad's Hardware Store," *Forbes*, January 26, 1998, p. 45.

19. Heather Page, "Fruitful Idea," *Entrepreneur*, January 1997, p. 20.

20. Dale D. Buss, "A Direct Route to Customers," *Nation's Business*, September 1997, pp. 46–51.

21. David Kirkpatrick, "Why Compaq Envies Dell," *Fortune*, February 17, 1997, p. 26.

22. Joseph Alba, John Lynch, Barton Weitz, Chris Janiszewski, Richard Lutz, Alan Sawyer and Stacy Wood, "Interactive Home Shopping: Consumer, Retailer, and Manufacturer Incentives to Participate in Electronic Marketplaces," *Journal of Marketing*, July 1997, pp. 38–53.

23. Ron Copfer, "Tomorrow Is Yesterday," *Strategies & News*, February 1998, p. 34.

Chapter 16

1. Robert J. Coen, "Coen: Ad Spending Tops $175 Billion During Robust '96," *Advertising Age*, May 12, 1997, p. 20.

2. Anne Fisher, "Willy Loman Couldn't Cut It," *Fortune*, November 11, 1996, p. 210.

3. Kristin Dunlap Godsey, "Back on Track," *Success*, May 1997, p. 52.

4. Marianne Seiler and Jody Marinez, "Leads on the Line," *Marketing Tools*, July 1997, pp. 20–25.

5. Kristin Dunlap Godsey, "Critical Steps in the Sales Process," *Success*, May 1997, pp. 24–25.

6. Ron Gajewski, "The Winning Team," *Strategies & News*, February 1998, pp. 14–17.

7. Sarah Schafer, "Supercharged Sell," *Inc. Tech*, 1997, no. 2, pp. 42–51.

8. Karen E. Starr, "Relationship Management," *Selling Power*, January–February 1998, pp. 88–94.

9. "One for the Clippers," *Marketing Tools*, August 1997, p. 11.

10. Mollie Neal, "Virtual Trade Shows Offer Real Results," *Business Marketing*, June 1997, pp. 1, 43.

11. Jeanne Whalen, "A Feast of Free Food," *Advertising Age*, June 9, 1997, pp. 22, 46.

12. Mark Henricks, "Spread the Word," *Entrepreneur*, February 1998, pp. 120–25.

13. Mark Henricks, "Spread the Word," *Entrepreneur*, February 1998, pp. 120–25.

14. Stephanie Gruner, "We Want More Referrals. What Can We Do?," *Inc.*, June 1997, p. 96.

15. Bob Donath, "Shed Some Light: Handling On-Line Threats to Firm's Image," *Marketing News*, February 16, 1998, p. 12.

16. Robert J. Coen, "U.S. Advertising Volume," *Advertising Age,* May 12, 1997, p. 20.

17. Edward W. Desmond, "Interactive TV Has Arrived," *Fortune,* February 2, 1998, pp. 135–36.

18. Bradley Johnson and Mercedes M. Cardona, "Compaq Paves the Way for Global Ads," *Advertising Age,* June 9, 1997, p. 10.

19. Kerry Pechter, "Intel Wants to Be 'Nike' of Computer Business' in China," *Advertising Age International,* June 1997, pp. I-2, I-6.

20. James H. Gilmore and B. Joseph Pine II, "The Four Faces of Mass Customization," *Harvard Business Review,* January–February 1997, pp. 91–101.

21. J.D. Mosley-Matchett, "Webcasting: It's Important to Learn Pros and Cons of Push and Pull," *Marketing News,* April 14, 1997, p. 31.

22. Jeffrey Spencer, "Route Info with E-Mail Robots," *Home Office Computing,* January 1998, pp. 46–47.

23. Minna Levine, "Consistency Counts in Sealing Interactive Brand Identity," *Marketing News,* January 19, 1998, p. 8.

24. Thomas R. Schori and Michael L. Garee, "Capitalize on the Interactive Nature of the Internet," *Marketing News,* January 19, 1998, p. 12.

25. Regina Brady, Edward Forrest and Richard Mizerski, *Cybermarketing* (Lincolnwood, IL: NTC Business Books, 1997).

26. Tom Hyland, "Web Advertising: A Year of Growth," *IAB Online Advertising Guide* (a supplement to *Advertising Age*), Spring 1998, 20A–24A, 66A.

Chapter 17

1. James Coates, "Classroom in a Box," *Chicago Tribune,* January 5, 1998, section 4, p. 1.

2. Nuala Moran, "Knowledge Management," *Financial Times,* October 1, 1997, p. 8; and Jeff Angus, "Knowledge Management: Great Concept . . . But What Is It?," *Information Week,* March 16, 1998, p. 38.

3. Dave Ulrich, "Intellectual Capital = Competence × Commitment," *Sloan Management Review,* Winter 1998, pp. 15–21.

4. Vanessa Houlder, "The High Price of Know How," *Financial Times,* July 14, 1997, p. 10; and Carol Levin, "Business Class Net," *PC Magazine,* February 24, 1998, p. 28.

5. "Intranets Yield Returns for Most User Firms, According to Survey," *The Wall Street Journal,* June 19, 1997; and Joe Mullich, "Enjoying the Intranet Ride," *PC Week,* March 9, 1998, p. 31.

6. George Black, "Growth of the Intranet," *Financial Times,* September 10, 1997, p. 9.

7. John Gilroy, "Ask the Computer Guy," *The Washington Post,* September 1, 1997, p. F19.

8. George Melloan, "Where Is the Information Technology Payoff?," *The Wall Street Journal,* August 11, 1997, p. A15.

9. Tamara E. Holmes, "Choosing a Database or Contact Manager; Getting to Know Bots," *USA Today,* August 28, 1997, p. 5D; and Bob Wallace, "Extranet Service Helps Users Tailor Info Access," *Computer World,* March 9, 1998, p. 4.

10. Jeff Moad, "Forging Flexible Links," *PC Week,* September 15, 1997, p. 74; and Daniel Grebler, "Survey Points Out Growing Internet Use by Small Businesses," *St. Louis Post-Dispatch,* February 6, 1998, p. BP14.

11. Philip Manchester, "Impact of the Internet," *Financial Times,* October 1, 1997, p. 4.

12. Joia Shillingford, "Enterprise Networks," *Financial Times,* June 4, 1997, p. 6.

13. Matt Kelley, "Scientists and Supercompanies Turn to vBNS for High Speed," *The Wall Street Journal Interactive Edition,* February 3, 1997.

14. Reva Basch, "The Next Net," *Computer Life,* September 1997, pp. 48–49; Cary Lu, "Make Room for Data," *Inc. Technology,* March 18, 1997, p. 33; and Jeff Caruso, "Cisco Weaves Faster Fabric—Frames, Not Cells, Will Dominate Gigabit Enterprise Networking," *Internet Week,* February 9. 1998, p. 1.

15. Geoffrey Nairn, "Office Communications," *Financial Times,* October 1, 1997, p. 9.

16. Geoffrey Wheelwright, "Information Overload," Financial Times, October 1, 1997, p. 9.

17. Walter S. Mossberg, "Average Home Users May Find Push Services Slow, Irritating," *The Wall Street Journal Interactive Edition,* October 16, 1997.

18. Louise Kehoe, "A Block on the Old Chip," *Financial Times,* October 3, 1997, p. 19.

19. Philip Albinus, "The Shape of Things to Come," *Home Office Computing,* November 1997, pp. 70–76.

20. N. MacDonald and C. Goodhue, "What Is a Networked Computing Device?," *The Wall Street Journal Interactive Edition,* July 21, 1997; and "Boise Cascade Office Products: Intelligent Technology," *Selling Power,* January/February 1998, p. 78.

21. Virginia Baldwin Hick, "Shareware is Now More Than a Hobby," *St. Louis Post-Dispatch,"* January 12, 1998, pp. BP1, 14.

22. Carol Venezia, "PIM Improvements," *PC Magazine,* March 24, 1998, p. 80; and Dan Gillmor, "Old Technology Keeps Coming Back in Smaller, Practical Uses," *St. Louis Post-Dispatch,* March 16, 1998, p. BP16.

23. Charles H. Gajeway, "Message Centers," *Home Office Computing,* November 1997, p. 103.

24. Carla Lazzareschi, "Telecommuters Still Feel Pull of Office," *Los Angeles Times,* September 13, 1997, p. D1.

25. Jerri Stroud, "Home Suite. . . Office" *St. Louis Post-Dispatch,* October 19, 1997, p. 1E; and Carol Kleiman, "Many Would Take a Home Office Over a Corner Office,". *St. Louis Post-Dispatch,* March 12, 1998, p. C8.

26. Joia Shillingford, "Teleworking," *Financial Times,* September 10, 1997, p. 13.

27. "Advances Let Disabled into Computer World," *St. Louis Post-Dispatch,* January 14, 1998, p. C7.

28. Michelle V. Rafter, "Too Much Time on the 'Net Can Leave You Stressed Out," *St. Louis Post-Dispatch,* January 17, 1998, p. C7.

29. Richard Behar, "Who's Reading Your E-Mail?" *Fortune,* February 3, 1997, pp. 57–70.

30. "The Privacy Debate," *The Wall Street Journal Interactive Edition,* October 16, 1997.

31. "Internet-based Commerce Needs Better Security," *USA Today,* October 1, 1997, p. 12A; and Heather Newman, "Cookies are Good For You," *Home Office Computing,* March 1998, p. 16.

32. Thomas E. Weber, "Concerned Web Users Ask: Is Public Data Too Public?" *The Wall Street Journal Interactive Edition*, June 19, 1997; and "Cookie Managers," *PC Magazine*, March 24, 1998, p. 182.

33. Michele Weldon, "High-Tech Skills Ease the Gender Gap," *Chicago Tribune*, June 8, 1997, p. 3.

34. Noah Isackson, "U.S. Issues Warning on Lack of Information Technology Workers," *Chicago Tribune*, September 30, 1997, p. 1; and Diana Kunde, "Companies Go to Great Lengths to Fill High-Tech Jobs," *St. Louis Post-Dispatch*, January 21, 1998, p. E1.

35. James Coates, Jon Bigness, and Jon Van, "Magazine's Survey Finds Chicago Leads in Geek Gold Rush," *Chicago Tribune*, September 8, 1997, p. 2; and Carol Levin, "High-Tech Salary Surge," *PC Magazine*, March 24, 1998, p. 10.

36. Reid Goldsborough, "Computers Scare You Bitless?," *MSNBC*, March 17, 1997.

37. Sherwood Ross, "The Internet Generation Will Shake Corporations, Author Says," *St. Louis Post-Dispatch*, February 23, 1998, p. BP4.

Chapter 18

1. David Whitford, "Arthur, Arthur . . ." *Fortune*, November 10, 1997.

2. "Financial Misstatements," *The Economist*, January 17, 1998, p. 59.

3. Greg Hutchins, "Certified Quality Auditor Exam: More Than Just Number Crunching," *Quality Digest*, April 1997, pp. 34–38.

4. Lee Berton, "Last In, First Out, and Keep the Flies off the Lemonade," *The Wall Street Journal*, May 13, 1989, pp. 1, 9.

5. Jeannie Mandelker, "Track Your Assets," *Small Business Computing*, September 1997, pp. 77–80.

6. Tom Peters, "The Brand Called You," *Fast Company*, August–September 1997, pp. 83–94.

7. Jeannie Mandelker, "Books in Order," *Small Business Computing*, August 1997, pp. 65–68.

8. Steve Morgenstern, "That Damned Cash Flow," *Home Office Computing*, January 1998, p. 132.

9. "New and Improved Earnings Per Share," *St. Louis Post-Dispatch*, February 16, 1998, BP6.

10. Susan Arterian, "Sprint Retools the Budget Process," *CFO*, September 1997, pp. 88–91.

11. Srikumar S. Rao, "Overhead Can Kill You," *Forbes*, February 10, 1997, pp. 97–98.

12. Yvonne Koulouthros, "Accounting 101," *PC Magazine*, February 4, 1997, p. 36.

13. Ibid.

14. Jill Andresdy Fraser, "How Many Accountants Does It Take to Change an Industry?" *Inc.*, April 1997, p. 67.

Chapter 19

1. Albert B. Crenshaw, "Why the Budgeted Life Can Be Worth Examining," *The Washington Post*, January 11, 1998, p. H1.

2. Cyndia Zwahlen, "Small Business Black Belt Must Get Out of the Red or Bow Out," *Los Angeles Times*, January 21, 1998, p. D-1.

3. Juan Hovy, "Trends and Help for Growing Companies," *Los Angeles Times*, January 14, 1998, p. D-4.

4. Michael Selz, "Businesses Are Less Dependent on Funds from Family, Friends," *The Wall Street Journal*, April 8, 1997.

5. Sharon Nelton, "Capital Ideas for Financing," *Nation's Business*, September 1997, pp. 18–27.

6. John Curran, "GE Capital: Jack Welch's Secret Weapon," *Fortune*, November 10, 1997, pp. 116–34.

7. "Passing the Buck," Home Office Computing, May 1997, p.19.

8. Stefan Wagstyl, "When Even a Rival Can Be a Best Friend," *Financial Times*, October 22, 1997, p. 17.

9. David Whitford and Carolyn Bollinger, "Sales of the Century," *Fortune*, February 17, 1997.

10. Linda Himelstein, Peter Burrows, and Andy Reinhardt, "The Great Hunt for Hot Ideas," *Business Week*, August 25, 1997, pp. 106–10.

11. David R. Evanson and Art Beroff, "Perfect Pitch," *Entrepreneur*, March 1998, pp. 60–63.

12. Norm Brodsky and Bo Burlington, "My Life as an Angel," *Inc.*, July 1997, pp. 43–48.

13. Steven Lipin, "Wave of Corporate Mergers Continues to Gather Force," *The Wall Street Journal*, February 26, 1997.

Chapter 20

1. Lorayne Fiorillo, "Uncommon Valor," *Entrepreneur*, April 1997, pp. 67–69.

2. Suzanne Woolley, "The Booming Big Board," *Business Week*, August 4, 1997, pp. 58–64.

3. AMEX and NASDAQ Discuss Merger," *St. Louis Post-Dispatch*, March 13, 1998, p. B1.

4. Deborah Lohse, "NASD, AMEX Boards Approve Agreement to Merge Markets," *The Wall Street Journal Interactive Edition*, March 19, 1998.

5. Paula Dwyer, "Hardball at the SEC," *Business Week*, September 29, 1997, pp. 50–52.

6. Anne Kates Smith, "Betrayers of Trust: Who's an Inside Trader? After Last Week, Almost Anybody," *U.S. News & World Report*, July 7, 1997, pp. 72–76.

7. "Chimpanzee Beats 5 Swedish Analysts at Picking Stocks," *St. Louis Post-Dispatch*, September 8, 1993, p. C1.

8. Mike Hogan, "Do-it Yourself Cybertrading," *PC/Computing*, October 1997, pp. 98–100; Kim Komando, "Online Stock Trading Is Just a Mouse Click Away," *Los Angeles Times*, December 22, 1997, p. D–4; and Dan Gillmor, "Riding the Bulls, Bears Online Can Provide Quite a Scare," *St. Louis Post-Dispatch*, January 12, 1998, p. BP14.

9. Jack Egan, "Online Trading: How Low Can It Go?," *U.S. News & World Report*, October 20, 1997, p. 59; and Bill Howard, "Things Can Only Get Better," *PC Magazine*, March 10, 1998, p. 97.

10. Lorayne Fiorillo, "Tricks of the Trade," *Entrepreneur*, March 1998, pp. 71–73.

11. David Brindly, "Ten Pros Pick 30 Funds," *U.S. News & World Report*, June 9, 1997, pp. 95–100.

12. Amy Dunkin, "Want To Put Your Money Where Your Conscience Is?," *Business Week*, September 8, 1997, pp. 134–35.

13. Lorayne Fiorillo, "Garbage Collectors," *Entrepreneur*, August 1997, pp. 62–65.

14. "CBOT Traders Embrace New Floor," *Futures*, April 1997, p. 12.

15. Anne Kates Smith, "NYSE and NASDAQ: Dollars and Common Cents," *U.S. News and World Report*, June 16, 1997, p. 54.

16. Ken Sheets, "Texaco Shareholders Ask: Is There Life after the Dow?," *Kiplinger's Personal Finance*, July 1997, pp. 20–22.

17. Out with the Old, In with the New," *U.S. News & World Report*, March 24, 1997, p. 60.

18. James M. Pethokoukis, "You Call that a Crash?," *U.S. News & World Report*, October 20, 1997, p. 8

19. Floyd Norris, "Stocks Fall 554 Points, Off 7%, Forcing Suspension in Trading," *New York Times*, October 28, 1997.

20. Dow Jones Newswires, "U.S. Stock Exchanges Agree to Halt Trading if Dow Drops 20%," *The Wall Street Journal Interactive Edition*, January 26, 1998.

21. William Murray, Dow Jones Newswires, "Greenspan Tempers Inflation Worries with Dose of Asia," *The Wall Street Interactive Edition*, January 29, 1998.

Chapter 21

1. Anne Marriott, "Banking Enters Brave New World," *Business Times*, February 9, 1998, pp. 12–14.

2. Jerry Knight, "Banks Now Shift to Global Markets," *The Washington Post*, April 14, 1998, p. A6.

3. Matthew Brzezinski, "Where Cash Isn't King: Barter Lines the Pockets in Ex-Soviet States," *The Wall Street Journal*, May 1, 1997, p. A14.

4. Peter M. Rexford, "A Second Chance at First-Rate Design," *Metropolitan Times*, January 12, 1996, p. C23.

5. Jill Andresky Fraser, "How to Finance Anything," *Inc.*, February 1998, pp. 34–42.

6. Kristin Davis, "Banks Vs. Credit Unions: You Haven't Heard the End of It," *Kiplinger's Personal Finance Magazine*, May 1998, pp. 17–18.

7. Charles Fleming, "With Spread of 'Nonbanks' from U.S. to Europe, Financial Turf War Begins," *The Wall Street Journal*, August 27, 1997, p. A8.

8. Vanessa O'Connell, "It's a Broker! It's a Banker! It's a Mutual Fund.," *The Wall Street Journal*, February 19, 1998, pp. C1, C27.

9. Jack Anderson and Michael Binstein, "On Deposit, the Belly-Up Scenario," *The Washington Post*, January 4, 1996, p. D.19.

10. Steven Butler, "Good Life, Bad Loans: A Japanese Scandal," *U.S. News and World Report*, February 9, 1998, p. 47.

11. Michael Meyer, "Sure, It's Big," *Newsweek*, April 20, 1998, pp. 36–37.

12. Roy S. Johnson, "Banking on Urban America," *Fortune*, March 2, 1998, pp. 128–32.

13. Gina Imperato, "Wow, What a Smart Card," *Fast Company*, February–March 1998, p. 64.

14. Peter Pae and Devon Spurgeon, "Smart Cards Get Off to a Slow Start," *The Washington Post*, March 21, 1998, pp. D1 & D2.

15. "Banking with a Net," *Home Office Computing*, March 1997, p. 73.

16. Renee Wijnen, "First Tennessee Goes Online with Full-Service Banking," *DM News*, February 9, 1998, p. 10.

17. Damon Darlin, "Try E-Banking," *Forbes*, January 13, 1997, pp. 68–69.

18. George P. Shultz, William E. Simon, and Walter B. Wriston, "Who Needs the IMF?," *The Wall Street Journal*, February 3, 1998, p. A22.

19. "Understanding the Asian Economic Crisis," *The Washington Post*, January 18, 1998, p. A32.

20. Robert J. Samuelson, "Primer on Panic," *The Washington Post*, January 14, 1998, p. A19.

21. Shawn Tulley, "Despite Asia's Woes, U.S. Banks Are Standing Tall," *Fortune*, February 16, 1998, pp. 26–27.

22. "Year 2000 Bug Has Already Bit Some Businesses," *St. Louis Post-Dispatch*, February 4, 1998, p. C7.

23. Debra Sparks, "Will Your Bank Live to See the Millennium?," *Business Week*, January 26, 1998, pp. 74–75.

Chapter 22

1. "Sheepskins Are Golden Fleeces," *Business Week*, July 28, 1997, p. 24.

2. "Young Millionaires," *Entrepreneur*, November 1997, pp. 108–18.

3. Heather Salerno, "The Young Entrepreneurs," *Washington Business*, December 22, 1997, pp. 9–12.

4. Sandra Block, "25¢-a-Week Savings Habit Grew," *USA Today*, February 2, 1998, p. B3.

5. "Students Flunk on Personal Finance," *The Washington Post*, May 23, 1997, p. A8.

6. Joshua Wolf Shenk, "In Debt All the Way Up to Their Nose Rings," *U.S. News and World Report*, June 9, 1997, pp. 38–39.

7. Jane Bryant Quinn, "IRAs: Should You Roth It?," *Newsweek*, January 19, 1998, pp. 54–55.

8. Charles A. Jaffe, "New IRA, New Era," *The Washington Times*, January 11, 1998, pp. A1, A14.

9. Jill Andresky Fraser, "The ABCs of Retirement Planning," *Inc.*, April 1997, p. 103.

10. "401(k)s and Beyond," an ad in *Inc.*, February 1998.

11. Joan Szabo, "In the Market," *Entrepreneur*, March 1998, pp. 65–68.

12. Lorayne Fiorillo, "Rope One In," *Entrepreneur*, December 1997, pp. 70–71.

Chapter 22 Appendix

1. George Anders, "Kaiser's Red Ink Signals Trouble for HMOs," *The Wall Street Journal*, February 17, 1998, p. B1.

2. David Stipp, "Trouble in the Air," *Fortune*, December 8, 1997, pp. 113–20.

3. Rob Gordon, "Deadly Critter Control Concept," *The Washington Times*, February 8, 1998, p. B4.

4. Charles Oliver, "Is Cleanup of Greenhouse Gases Really Worth the Big Price Tag?," *Investor's Business Daily*, November 11, 1997, p. A8.

Glossary*

absolute advantage (p. 75) When a country has a monopoly on producing a product or is able to produce it at a cost below that of all other countries.

accounting (p. 530) The recording, classifying, summarizing, and interpreting of financial events and transactions to provide management and other interested parties the information they need to make good decisions.

accounting cycle (p. 535) A six-step procedure that results in the preparation and analysis of the two major financial statements: the balance sheet and the income statement.

acquisition (p. 147) A company's purchase of the property and obligations of another company.

Active Corps of Executives (ACE) (p. 182) SBA volunteers from industry, trade associations, and education who counsel small businesses.

administered distribution system (p. 452) A distribution system in which producers manage all of the marketing functions at the retail level.

administrative agencies (p. 119) Institutions created by Congress with delegated power to pass rules and regulations within their mandated area of authority.

advertising (p. 481) Paid, nonpersonal communication through various media by organizations and individuals who are in some way identified in the advertising message.

affirmative action (p. 338) Employment activities designed to "right past wrongs" by increasing opportunities for minorities and women.

agency shop agreement (p. 353) Clause in a labor–management agreement that says employers may hire nonunion workers who are not required to join the union but must pay a union fee.

American Federation of Labor (AFL) (p. 349) An organization of craft unions that championed bread-and-butter labor issues.

analytic system (p. 265) Manufacturing system that breaks down raw materials into components to extract other products.

annual report (p. 532) A yearly statement of the financial condition and progress of an organization covering a one year period.

apprentice programs (p. 326) Training programs involving a period during which a learner works alongside an experienced employee to master the skills and procedures of a craft.

arbitration (p. 356) The agreement to bring in an impartial third party (an arbitrator) to render a binding decision in a labor dispute.

assembly process (p. 265) Production process that puts together components.

assets (p. 536) Economic resources owned by a firm.

auditing (p. 532) The job of reviewing and evaluating the records used to prepare a company's financial statements.

autocratic leadership (p. 213) Leadership style that involves making managerial decisions without consulting others.

automated teller machines (ATMs) (p. 631) Machines that give customers the convenience of 24-hour banking at a variety of outlets.

balance of payments (p. 77) The difference between money coming into a country (from exports) and money leaving the country (for imports) plus money flows from other factors such as tourism, foreign aid, military expenditures, and foreign investment.

balance of trade (p. 77) The relationship of exports to imports.

balance sheet (p. 536) The financial statement that reports a firm's financial condition at a specific time.

banker's acceptance (p. 639) A promise that the bank will pay some specified amount at a particular time.

bankruptcy (p. 128) The legal process by which a person, business, or government entity unable to meet financial obligations is relieved of those obligations by having the court divide any assets among creditors, freeing the debtor to begin anew.

bargaining zone (p. 356) Range of options between the initial and final offer that each party will consider before negotiations dissolve or reach an impasse.

*Terms and definitions printed in italic are considered business slang, or jargon.

bartering (p. 82) The exchange of goods or services for goods or services.

bitten by the entrepreneurial bug *We are driven to become an entrepreneur as if we were infected by a bug bite.*

blue chip stocks (p. 606) Stocks of high-quality companies that pay regular dividends and generate consistent growth in the company's stock price.

bond (p. 593) A corporate certificate indicating that a person has lent money to a firm.

bookkeeping (p. 534) The recording of business transactions.

bottom line *The last line of the income statement, or net profit after taxes; thus the bottom line is the final result.*

brand (p. 417) A name, symbol, or design (or combination thereof) that identifies the goods or services of one seller or group of sellers and distinguishes them from the goods and services of competitors.

brand association (p. 419) The linking of a brand to other favorable images.

brand awareness (p. 418) How quickly or easily a given brand name comes to mind when a product category is mentioned.

brand equity (p. 418) The combination of factors such as awareness, loyalty, perceived quality, images, and emotions people associate with a given brand name.

brand loyalty (p. 418) The degree to which customers are satisfied, like the brand, and are committed to further purchase.

brand name (p. 381) A word, letter, or group of words or letters that differentiates one seller's goods and services from those of competitors.

breach of contract (p. 124) When one party fails to follow the terms of a contract.

break-even analysis (p. 430) The process used to determine profitability at various levels of sales.

brokers (p. 445) Marketing intermediaries who bring buyers and sellers together and assist in negotiating an exchange but don't own the goods.

budget (p. 551) A financial plan that sets forth management's expectations for revenues and, based on those expectations, allocates the use of specific resources throughout the firm.

bureaucracy (p. 230) An organization with many layers of managers who set rules and regulations and oversee all decisions.

business (p. 1) Any activity that seeks profit by providing needed goods and services to others.

business law (p. 119) Rules, statutes, codes, and regulations that are established to provide a legal framework within which business may be conducted and that are enforceable by court action.

business may be shot down *A war metaphor meaning that a business may be destroyed by someone else just as a plane may be shot down in a war.*

business plan (p. 175) A detailed written statement that describes the nature of the business, the target market, the advantages the business will have in relation to competition, and the resources and qualifications of the owner(s).

business-to-business market (p. 396) All the individuals and organizations that want goods and services to use in producing other goods and services.

buying on margin (p. 610) The purchase of stocks by borrowing some of the purchase cost from the brokerage firm.

cafeteria-style fringe benefits (p. 333) Fringe benefits plan that allows employees to choose the benefits they want up to a certain dollar amount.

callable bond (p. 596) A bond that gives the issuer the right to pay off the bond before its maturity.

capital budget (p. 567) A budget that highlights a firm's spending plans for major asset purchases that often require large sums of money.

capital expenditures (p. 571) Major investments in long-term assets such as land, buildings, equipment, or research and development.

capitalism (p. 45) An economic system in which all or most of the means of production and distribution are privately owned and operated for profit.

cash budget (p. 567) A budget that estimates a firm's projected cash balance at the end of a given period.

cash flow (p. 544) The difference between cash coming in and cash going out of a business.

cash flow forecast (p. 566) Forecast that predicts the expected cash inflows and outflows in future periods, usually months or quarters.

cash-and-carry wholesalers (p. 457) Wholesalers that serve mostly smaller retailers with a limited assortment of products.

category killer stores (p. 459) Large stores that offer wide selection at competitive prices.

centralized authority (p. 239) When decision-making authority is maintained at the top level of management at the company's headquarters.

certification (p. 351) Process of a union's becoming recognized by the NLRB as the bargaining agent for a group of employees.

certified internal auditor (p. 532) An accountant who has a bachelor's degree and two years of experience in internal auditing, and who has passed an exam administered by the Institute of Internal Auditors.

certified management accountant (p. 531) A professional accountant who has met certain educational and experience requirements and been certified by the Institute of Certified Management Accountants.

certified public accountant (CPA) (p. 532) An accountant who passes a series of examinations established by the American Institute of Certified Public Accountants.

channel of distribution (p. 442) Marketing intermediaries, such as wholesalers and retailers, who join together to transport and store goods in their path from producers to consumers.

closed-shop agreement (p. 353) Clause in a labor–management agreement that specified that workers had to be members of a union before being hired (outlawed in 1947).

cognitive dissonance (p. 396) A type of psychological conflict that can occur after a purchase, when consumers may have doubts about whether they got the best product at the best price.

collective bargaining (p. 350) The process whereby union and management representatives put together a contract for workers.

command economies (p. 48) Economic systems in which the government largely decides what goods and services will be produced, who will get them, and how the economy will grow.

commercial and consumer finance companies (p. 635) Organizations that offer short-term loans to businesses or individuals who either can't meet the credit requirements of regular banks or else have exceeded their credit limit and need more funds.

commercial bank (p. 630) A profit-making organization that receives deposits from individuals and corporations in the form of checking and saving accounts and uses some of these funds to make loans.

commercial finance companies (p. 575) Organizations that make short-term loans to borrowers who offer tangible assets as collateral.

commercial paper (p. 577) Unsecured promissory notes of $25,000 and up that mature (come due) in 270 days or less.

commodity exchange (p. 611) A securities exchange that specializes in the buying and selling of precious metals and minerals (e.g., silver, foreign currencies, gasoline) and agricultural goods (e.g., wheat, cattle, sugar).

common law (p. 119) The body of law that comes from judges' decisions; also referred to as *unwritten law.*

common market (p. 90) A regional group of countries that have no internal tariffs, a common external tariff, and a coordination of laws to facilitate exchange; an example is the European Union.

common stock (p. 599) The most basic form of ownership in a firm; it confers voting rights and the right to share in the firm's profits through dividends, if offered by the firm's board of directors.

communications software (p. 516) Computer programs that make it possible for different brands of computers to transfer data to each other.

communism (p. 47) A system in which the state makes all economic decisions and owns all the major forms of production.

comparable worth (p. 363) The concept that people in jobs that require similar levels of education, training, or skills should receive equal pay.

comparative advantage theory (p. 74) Theory which asserts that a country should produce and sell to other countries those products that it produces most efficiently.

competitive benchmarking (p. 246) Rating an organization's practices, processes, and products against the world's best.

compliance-based ethics codes (p. 106) Ethical standards that emphasize preventing unlawful behavior by increasing control and by penalizing wrongdoers.

compressed workweek (p. 334) Work schedule that allows an employee to work a full number of hours per week but in fewer days.

computer-aided design (CAD) (p. 271) The use of computers in the design of products.

computer-aided manufacturing (CAM) (p. 272) The use of computers in the manufacturing of products.

concept testing (p. 422) Taking a product idea to consumers to test their reactions.

conceptual skills (p. 217) Skills that involve the ability to picture the organization as a whole and the relationship among its various parts.

conglomerate merger (p. 147) The joining of firms in completely unrelated industries.

Congress of Industrial Organizations (CIO) (p. 350) Union organization of unskilled workers; broke away from the AFL in 1935 and rejoined it in 1955.

consideration (p. 123) Something of value; consideration is one of the requirements of a legal contract.

consumer market (p. 396) All the individuals or households who want goods and services for personal consumption or use.

consumer price index (CPI) (p. 59) Monthly statistics that measure changes in the prices of about 400 goods and services that consumers buy.

consumerism (p. 126) A social movement that seeks to increase and strengthen the rights and powers of buyers in relation to sellers.

contingency planning (p. 203) The process of preparing alternative courses of action that may be used if the primary plans do not achieve the objectives of the organization.

contingent workers (p. 325) Workers who do not have the expectation of regular, full-time employment.

continuous improvement (p. 245) Constantly improving the way the organization does things so that customer needs can be better satisfied.

contract (p. 123) A legally enforceable agreement between two or more parties.

contract law (p. 123) Laws that specify what constitutes a legally enforceable agreement.

contract manufacturing (p. 81) Production of private-label goods by a company to which another company then attaches its brand name or trademark.

contractual distribution system (p. 451) A distribution system in which members are bound to cooperate through contractual agreements.

controlling (p. 200) A management function that involves determining whether or not an organization is progressing toward its goals and objectives, and taking corrective action if it is not.

convenience goods and services (p. 412) Products that the consumer wants to purchase frequently and with a minimum of effort.

conventional (C) corporation (p. 139) A state-chartered legal entity with authority to act and have liability separate from its owners.

convertible bond (p. 596) A bond that can be converted into shares of common stock in the issuing company.

cookies (p. 521) Pieces of information, such as registration data or user preferences, sent by a Web site over the Internet to a Web browser that the browser software is expected to save and to send back to the server whenever the user returns to that Web site.

cooling-off period (p. 357) When workers in a critical industry return to their jobs while the union and management continue negotiations.

cooperative (p. 155) A business owned and controlled by the people who use it—producers, consumers, or workers with similar needs who pool their resources for mutual gain.

copyright (p. 122) Exclusive rights to materials such as books, articles, photos, and cartoons.

core competencies (p. 246) Those functions that the organization can do as well or better than any other organization in the world.

core time (p. 334) In a flextime plan, the period when all employees are expected to be at their job stations.

corporate distribution system (p. 451) A distribution system in which all of the organizations in the channel of distribution are owned by one firm.

corporate philanthropy (p. 107) Dimension of social responsibility that includes charitable donations.

corporate policy (p. 107) Dimension of social responsibility that refers to the position a firm takes on social and political issues.

corporate responsibility (p. 107) Dimension of social responsibility that includes everything from minority hiring practices to the making of safe products.

corporation (p. 134) A legal entity with authority to act and have liability separate from its owners.

cost of goods sold (or cost of goods manufactured) (p. 542) A measure of the cost of merchandise sold or cost of raw materials and supplies used for producing items for resale.

countertrading (p. 82) Bartering among several countries.

craft union (p. 349) An organization of skilled specialists in a particular craft or trade.

credit unions (p. 634) Nonprofit, member-owned financial cooperatives that offer basic banking services such as accepting deposits and making loans to their members.

critical path (p. 273) The sequence of tasks that takes the longest time to complete.

cross-functional teams (p. 242) Groups of employees from different departments who work together on a semipermanent basis.

cumulative preferred stock (p. 598) Preferred stock that accumulates unpaid dividends.

currency (p. 625) All coin and paper money issued by the Federal Reserve banks, and all gold coins.

currency exchange (p. 639) Exchange of currency from one country with currency from another country.

current assets (p. 537) Items that can be converted into cash within one year.

damages (p. 124) The monetary settlement awarded to a person who is injured by a breach of contract.

data processing (DP) (p. 502) Technology that supported an existing business; primarily used to improve the flow of financial information.

databank (p. 10) Electronic storage file for information.

database program (p. 514) Computer program that allows users to work with information that is normally kept in lists: names and addresses, schedules, inventories and so forth.

dealer (private) brands (p. 418) Products that don't carry the manufacturer's name but carry a distributor or retailer's name instead.

debenture bonds (p. 595) Bond that are unsecured (i.e., not backed by any collateral such as equipment).

debt capital (p. 572) Funds raised through various forms of borrowing that must be repaid.

debtor nation (p. 79) Country that owes more money to other nations than they owe it.

decentralized authority (p. 239) When decision-making authority is delegated to lower-level managers more familiar with local conditions than headquarters management could be.

decertification (p. 351) The process by which workers take away a union's right to represent them.

decision making (p. 218) Choosing among two or more alternatives.

deflation (p. 61) A situation where prices are actually declining.

delegating (p. 218) Assigning authority and accountability to others while retaining responsibility for results.

demand (p. 53) The quantity of products that people are willing to buy at different prices at a specific time.

demand deposit (p. 631) The technical name for a checking account; the money can be withdrawn anytime on demand from the owner.

demography (p. 14) The statistical study of human population to learn its size, density, and other characteristics.

departmentalization (p. 236) The dividing of organizational functions into separate units.

depreciation (p. 546) The systematic write-off of the cost of a tangible asset over its estimated useful life.

depression (p. 62) A severe recession.

deregulation (p. 130) Government withdrawal of certain laws and regulations that seem to hinder competition.

devaluation (p. 87) Lowering the value of a nation's currency relative to other currencies.

direct marketing (p. 472) Marketing that allows consumers to buy products by interacting with various advertising media without meeting a salesperson face-to-face.

discount rate (p. 628) The interest rate that the Fed charges for loans to member banks.

disinflation (p. 61) A condition where price increases are slowing (the inflation rate is declining).

disk-based advertising (p. 492) Product information provided on a CD-ROM or computer disk.

diversification (p. 608) Buying several different investment alternatives to spread the risk of investing.

dividends (p. 597) Part of a firm's profits that may be distributed to stockholders as either cash payments or additional shares of stock.

double-entry bookkeeping (p. 535) The concept of writing every transaction in two places.

Dow Jones Industrial Average (p. 615) The average cost of 30 selected industrial stocks; used to give an indication of the direction (up or down) of the stock market over time.

down and dirty *Getting so deeply involved in something so that getting dirty doing it doesn't matter.*

downsizing (p. 4) Making organizations more efficient by laying off workers.

drop shippers (p. 457) Wholesalers that solicit orders from retailers and other wholesalers and have the merchandise shipped directly from a producer to a buyer.

dumping (p. 78) Selling products for less in a foreign country than is charged in the producing country.

economics (p. 44) The study of how society chooses to employ resources to produce goods and services and distribute them for consumption among various competing groups and individuals.

efficient consumer response (ECR) (p. 444) The electronic linking of firms to provide more efficient response to consumer needs.

electronic data interchange (EDI) (p. 443) Technology that enables producers', wholesalers', and retailers' computers to "talk" with each other.

electronic funds transfer system (EFTS) (p. 638)   A computerized system that electronically performs financial transactions such as making purchases, paying bills, and receiving paychecks.

embargo (p. 89)   A complete ban on the import or export of certain products.

employee orientation (p. 326)   The activity that introduces new employees to the organization; to fellow employees; to their immediate supervisors; and to the policies, practices, and objectives of the firm.

employee stock ownership plans (ESOPs) (p. 368)   Programs that enable employees to buy part or total ownership of the firm.

empowerment (p. 207)   Giving employees the authority and responsibility to respond quickly to customer requests.

enabling (p. 207)   Giving workers the education and tools needed to assume their new decision-making powers.

enterprise resource planning (ERP) (p. 266)   Computer-based production and operations system that links multiple firms into one integrated production unit.

entrepreneur (p. 4)   A person who takes the risk of starting and managing a business.

entrepreneurial team (p. 166)   A group of experienced people from different areas of business who join together to form a managerial team with the skills needed to develop, make, and market a new product.

entrepreneurship (p. 163)   Accepting the risk of starting and running a business.

equity capital (p. 572)   Money raised from within the firm or through the sale of ownership in the firm.

equity theory (p. 302)   Theory that employees try to maintain equity between inputs and outputs compared to others in similar positions.

ethics (p. 102)   Standards of moral behavior; that is, behavior that is accepted by society as right versus wrong.

ethnocentricity (p. 83)   The feeling that one's culture is superior to all others.

exchange rate (p. 86)   The value of one currency relative to the currencies of other countries.

exclusive distribution (p. 461)   Distribution that sends products to only one retail outlet in a given geographic area.

expectancy theory (p. 301)   Victor Vroom's theory that the amount of effort employees exert on a specific task depends on their expectations of the outcome.

expenses (p. 542)   Costs incurred in operating a business, such as rent, utilities, and salaries.

Export Assistance Centers (EACs) (p. 80)   Created to provide hands-on exporting assistance and trade-finance support for small and medium-sized businesses.

export trading companies (p. 80)   Companies that attempt to match buyers and sellers from different countries.

exporting (p. 74)   Sellling products to another country.

express warranties (p. 123)   Specific representations by the seller regarding the goods.

external customers (p. 209)   Dealers, who buy products to sell to others, and ultimate customers (or end users), who buy products for their own personal use.

extranet (pp. 243, 507)   An extended Internet that connects suppliers, customers, and other organizations via secure Web sites.

extrinsic reward (p. 288)   Something given to you by someone else as recognition for good work; extrinsic rewards include pay increases, praise, and promotions.

factoring (p. 575)   The process of selling accounts receivable for cash.

factors of production (p. 6)   The resources used to create wealth: land, labor, capital, entrepreneurship, and knowledge.

fairy godmother   *A fictional character who provides you with things unexpectedly; thus it means relying on something not real.*

falling dollar (p. 626)   When the amount of goods and services you can buy with a dollar goes down.

fax-on-demand (p. 491)   An arrangement in which product information is sent by fax at the request of a customer or potential customer.

Federal Deposit Insurance Corporation (FDIC) (p. 636)   An independent U.S. government agency that insures bank deposits.

federal deficit (p. 63)   The difference between federal revenue and federal spending in any given year.

finance (p. 565)   The function in a business that acquires funds for the firm and manages funds within the firm.

financial control (p. 568)   A process in which a firm periodically compares its actual revenues, costs, and expenses with its projected ones.

financial management (p. 565)   The job of managing a firm's resources so it can meet its goals and objectives.

financial statement (p. 536)   A summary of all the transactions that have occurred over a particular period.

first in, first out (FIFO) (p. 547)   Accounting method for calculating cost of inventory; it assumes that the first goods to come in are the first to go out.

fiscal policy (p. 62)   Government efforts to keep the economy stable by increasing or decreasing taxes or government spending.

fixed assets (p. 537)   Assets that are relatively permanent, such as land, buildings, and equipment.

flexible manufacturing systems (p. 269)   The design of machines to do multiple tasks so that they can produce a variety of products.

flextime plan (p. 334)   Work schedule that gives employees some freedom to choose when to work, as long as they work the required number of hours.

floating exchange rates (p. 87)   Value of currencies fluctuate according to the supply and demand in the market for the currency.

focus group (p. 392)   A small group of people who meet under the direction of a discussion leader to communicate their feelings concerning an organization, its products, or other given issues.

Foreign Corrupt Practices Act of 1978 (p. 85)   Law that prohibits "questionable" or "dubious" payments to foreign officials to secure business contracts.

foreign direct investment (p. 79)   Buying of permanent property and businesses in foreign nations.

foreign subsidiary (p. 81)   A company owned by another company (parent company) in a foreign country.

form utility (p. 261)   The value added by the creation of finished goods and services using raw materials, components, and other inputs.

formal organization (p. 250)   The structure that details lines of responsibility, authority, and position; the structure shown on organization charts.

franchise (p. 149)   The right to use a specific business's name and sell its products or services in a given territory.

franchise agreement (p. 149)   An arrangement whereby someone with a good idea for a business sells the rights to use the business name and sell its products or services to others in a given territory.

franchisee (p. 149)   A person who buys a franchise.

franchisor (p. 149)   A company that develops a product concept and sells others the rights to make and sell the products.

free trade (p. 74)   The movement of goods and services among nations without political or economic obstruction.

free-market economies (p. 48)   Economic systems in which decisions about what to produce and in what quantities are decided by the market, that is, by buyers and sellers negotiating prices for goods and services.

free-trade area (p. 92)   Market in which nations can trade freely without tariffs or other trade barriers.

freight forwarder (p. 458)   An organization that puts many small shipments together to create a single large shipment that can be transported cost-efficiently to the final destination.

fringe benefits (p. 333)   Benefits such as sick-leave pay, vacation pay, pension plans, and health plans that represent additional compensation to employees.

full-service wholesalers (p. 457)   Merchant wholesalers that perform all of the distribution functions.

fundamental accounting equation (p. 539)   Assets = liabilities + owners' equity; this is the basis for the balance sheet.

futures market (p. 611)   The purchase and sale of goods for delivery sometime in the future.

game plan   *A sports metaphor that refers to the strategy to be used during a game; thus any plan for accomplishing something.*

Gantt chart (p. 274)   Bar graph showing production managers what projects are being worked on and what stage they are in on a daily basis.

General Agreement on Tariffs and Trade (GATT) (p. 90)   Agreement among 124 countries which provided a forum for negotiating mutual reductions in trade restrictions.

general partner (p. 136)   An owner (partner) who has unlimited liability and is active in managing the firm.

general partnership (p. 136)   A partnership in which all owners share in operating the business and in assuming liability for the business's debts.

generic goods (p. 418)   Nonbranded products that usually sell at a sizable discount compared to national or private brands.

generic name (p. 418)   The name for a product category.

getting into the swing of things   *Getting involved in something rather than just watching.*

givebacks (p. 359)   Concessions made by union members to management; gains from labor negotiations are given back to management to help employers remain competitive and thereby save jobs.

global marketing (p. 84) Selling the same product in essentially the same way everywhere in the world.

glowing example *An example that makes a good impression, like a glowing lamp.*

goal-setting theory (p. 300) Theory that setting specific, attainable goals can motivate workers and improve performance if the goals are accepted, are accompanied by feedback, and are facilitated by organizational conditions.

goals (p. 201) The broad, long-term accomplishments an organization wishes to attain.

goods (p. 20) Tangible products such as houses, food, and clothing.

green product (p. 387) A product whose production, use, and disposal don't damage the environment.

grievance (p. 355) A charge by employees that management is not abiding by the terms of the negotiated labor agreement.

gross domestic product (GDP) (p. 58) The total value of goods and services produced in a country in a given year.

gross margin (gross profit) (p. 542) How much a firm earned by buying (or making) and selling merchandise.

groupware (p. 517) Software that allows people to work collaboratively and share ideas.

growth stocks (p. 606) Stocks of companies whose earnings are expected to grow faster than other stocks or the overall economy.

hard nosed *A sports metaphor from boxing meaning that a person can be hit on the nose and not hurt; thus a hard-nosed person is one that doesn't easily give in or is "stubborn."*

hatchet man *From the person in earlier times who cut off people's heads with an ax and refers to anyone who is responsible for punishing others for misdeeds or who keeps others in line through intimidation.*

Hawthorne effect (p. 292) The tendency for people to behave differently when they know they are being studied.

health maintenance organizations (HMOs) (p. 673) Health care organizations that require members to choose from a restricted list of doctors.

hierarchy (p. 230) A system in which one person is at the top of the organization and many levels of managers are responsible to that person.

hit the hurdles and tumbled *A sports metaphor from running the hurdles in track; sometimes the runners hit the hurdles and lose their balance—thus this phrase refers to setbacks that occur when trying to do something.*

high fives *A way of celebrating where people slap their upraised hand against someone else's upraised hand; thus it is a way of recognizing accomplishments.*

horizontal merger (p. 147) The joining of two firms in the same industry.

human relations skills (p. 217) Skills that involve communication and motivation; they enable managers to work through and with people.

human resource management (p. 316) The process of evaluating human resource needs, finding people to fill those needs, and getting the best work from each employee by providing the right incentives and job environment, all with the goal of meeting the objectives of the organization.

hygiene factors (p. 297) Factors that can cause dissatisfaction if missing but do not necessarily motivate employees if increased.

implied warranties (p. 123) Guarantees legally imposed on the seller.

import quota (p. 89) Limiting the number of products in certain categories that can be imported.

importing (p. 74) Buying products from another country.

income statement (p. 539) The financial statement that shows a firm's profit after costs, expenses, and taxes; it summarizes all of the resources that have come into the firm (revenue), all the resources that have left the firm, and the resulting net income or loss.

income stocks (p. 606) Stocks that offer investors a high dividend.

incubators (p. 176) Centers that offer new businesses low-cost offices with basic business services.

indenture terms (p. 578) The terms of agreement in a bond issue.

independent audit (p. 532) An evaluation and unbiased opinion about the accuracy of a company's financial statements.

Individual Retirement Account (IRA) (p. 661) Traditionally, a tax-deferred investment plan that enables you (and your spouse, if you are married) to save part of your income for retirement.

industrial goods (p. 414) Products used in the production of other products.

industrial unions (p. 349) Labor organizations of unskilled workers in mass-production-related industries such as automobiles and mining.

inflation (p. 61) A general rise in the prices of goods and services over time.

infomercial (p. 485) A TV program devoted exclusively to promoting goods and services.

informal organization (p. 250) The system of relationships and lines of authority that develops spontaneously as employees meet and form power centers; the human side of the organization that does not appear on any organization chart.

information systems (IS) (p. 503) Technology that helps companies *do* business; includes such tools as automated teller machines (ATMs) and voice mail.

information technology (IT) (p. 504) Technology that helps companies *change* business by allowing them to use new methods.

injunction (p. 359) A court order directing someone to do something or refrain from doing something.

insider trading (p. 601) The use of knowledge or information that individuals gain through their position that allows them to benefit unfairly from fluctuations in security prices.

institutional investors (p. 592) Large investors such as pension funds, mutual funds, insurance companies, and banks that invest their own funds or the funds of others.

insurable interest (p. 671) The possibility of the policyholder to suffer a loss.

insurable risk (p. 671) A risk that the typical insurance company will cover.

insurance policy (p. 672) A written contract between the insured and an insurance company that promises to pay for all or part of a loss.

intangible assets (p. 537) Items of value such as patents and copyrights that have no real physical form.

integrated marketing communication (IMC) (p. 489) A formal mechanism for uniting all the promotional efforts in an organization to make them more consistent and more responsive to that organization's customers and other stakeholders.

integrated software package (suite) (p. 517) A computer program that offers two or more applications in one package.

integrity-based ethics codes (p. 106) Ethical standards that define the organization's guiding values, create an environment that supports ethically sound behavior, and stress a shared accountability among employees.

intensive distribution (p. 461) Distribution that puts products into as many retail outlets as possible.

interactive marketing communication system (p. 489) A system in which consumers can access company information on their own and supply information about themselves in an ongoing dialogue.

interest (p. 593) The payment the issuer of the bond makes to the bondholders for the use of borrowed money.

intermodal shipping (p. 455) The use of multiple modes of transportation to complete a single long-distance movement of freight.

internal customers (p. 209) Individuals and units within the firm that receive services from other individuals or units.

International Monetary Fund (IMF) (p. 641) Organization that assists the smooth flow of money among nations.

Internet (p. 9) A connection of tens of thousands of interconnected computer networks that includes 1.7 million host computers.

Internet 2 (p. 508) The new Internet system that links government supercomputer centers and a select group of universities; it will run 100 to 1,000 times faster than today's public infrastructure and will support heavy-duty applications.

in the trenches A war metaphor from World War I where soldiers fought from trenches; thus, in business, it means getting ready for battle or being actively engaged in competition.

in-the-black To be profitable.

in-the-red To be unprofitable (or in red ink).

intranet (pp. 243, 507) A companywide network, closed to public access, that uses Internet-type technology.

intrapreneurs (p. 169) Creative people who work as entrepreneurs within corporations.

intrinsic reward (p. 288) The good feeling you have when you have a job well.

inventory financing (p. 574) The process of using inventory such as raw materials as collateral for a loan.

inverted organization (p. 245) An organization that has contact people at the top and the chief executive officer at the bottom of the organization chart.

investment bankers (p. 592) Specialists who assist in the issue and sale of new securities.

invisible hand (p. 45) The term coined by Adam Smith to describe the social benefits that come from businesspeople trying to improve their own lives.

involuntary bankruptcy (p. 128) Bankruptcy procedures filed by a debtor's creditors.

ISO 9000 (p. 19) Quality management and assurance standards published by the International Organization for Standardization (ISO).

ISO 14000 (p. 20) A collection of the best practices for managing an organization's environmental impacts.

job analysis (p. 320) A study of what is by employees who hold various job titles.

job description (p. 320) A summary of the objectives of a job, the type of work to be , the responsibilities and duties, the working conditions, and the relationship of the job to other functions.

job enlargement (p. 300) Job enrichment strategy involving combining a series of tasks into one assignment that is more challenging and interesting.

job enrichment (p. 299) A motivational strategy that emphasizes motivating the worker through the job itself.

job rotation (p. 300) Job enrichment strategy involving moving employees from one job to another.

job sharing (p. 335) An arrangement whereby two part-time employees share one full-time job.

job simplification (p. 300) Process of producing task efficiency by breaking down the job into simple steps and assigning people to each of those steps.

job simulation (p. 327) The use of equipment that duplicates job conditions and tasks so that trainees can learn skills before attempting them on the job.

job specifications (p. 320) A written summary of the minimum qualifications required of workers to do a particular job.

joint venture (p. 82) A partnership in which companies (often from two or more different countries) join to undertake a major project.

journal (p. 534) The book where accounting data are first entered.

judiciary (p. 119) The branch of government chosen to oversee the legal system.

junk bonds (p. 610) High-risk, high-interest bonds.

keep the throttle at full speed A car-racing metaphor that means going as fast as you can.

Knights of Labor (p. 349) The first national labor union; formed in 1869.

knockoff brands (p. 418) Illegal copies of national brand-name goods such as Polo shirts or Rolex watches.

knowledge technology (KT) (p. 505) Technology that adds a layer of intelligence to filter appropriate information and deliver it when it is needed.

laissez-faire (free-reign) leadership (p. 213) Leadership style that involves managers setting objectives and employees being relatively free to do whatever it takes to accomplish those objectives.

last in, first out (LIFO) (p. 547) Accounting method for calculating cost of inventory; it assumes that the last goods to come in are the first to go out.

law of large numbers (p. 672) Principle that if a large number of people are exposed to the same risk, a predictable number of losses will occur during a given period of time.

leadership (p. 210) Creating a vision for others to follow, establishing corporate values and ethics, and transforming the way the organization does business in order to improve its effectiveness and efficiency.

leading (p. 200) A management function that involves creating a vision for the organization and guiding, training, coaching, and motivating others to work effectively to achieve the organization's goals and objectives.

lean manufacturing (p. 269) The production of goods using less of everything compared to mass production.

leaner and meaner A sports metaphor meaning that a person has lost weight to be a more agile and tougher player or fighter, and doing so makes one mean and determined to win.

learning organization (p. 212) An organization skilled at creating, acquiring, interpreting, retaining, and transferring knowledge; it also purposefully modifies its behavior based on new knowledge, including that which it gains from making mistakes.

ledger (p. 535) A specialized accounting book in which information from accounting journals is accumulated into specific categories and posted so that managers can find all the information about one account in the same place.

letter of credit (p. 639) A promise by the bank to pay the seller a given amount if certain conditions are met.

leverage (p. 582) Raising needed funds through borrowing to increase a firm's rate of return.

leveraged buyout (LBO) (p. 147) An attempt by employees, management, or a group of investors to purchase an organization primarily through borrowing.

liabilities (p. 537) What the business owes to others.

licensing (p. 80) Agreement in which a producer allows a foreign company to produce its product in exchange for royalties.

limit order (p. 607)   Instructions to a broker to buy or sell a particular stock at a specific price, if that price becomes available.

limited liability (p. 136)   The responsibility of a business's owners for losses only up to the amount they invest; limited partners and shareholders have limited liability.

limited partner (p. 136)   An owner who invests money in the business but does not have any management responsibility or liability for losses beyond the investment.

limited partnership (p. 136)   A partnership with one or more general partners and one or more limited partners.

limited-function wholesaler (p. 457)   Merchant wholesalers that perform only selected distribution functions but try to do these functions especially well.

limited-liability company (LLC) (p. 145)   A company similar to an S corporation but without the special eligibility requirements.

line of credit (p. 574)   A given amount of unsecured short-term funds a bank will lend to a business, provided the funds are readily available.

line personnel (p. 240)   Employees who perform functions that contribute directly to the primary goals of the organization.

liquidity (p. 536)   How fast an asset can be converted into cash.

lockout (p. 358)   When management temporarily closes the business to put pressure on unions.

long shot   *The chances of accomplishing something are not good, such as trying to hit a target from a long distance, a long shot.*

long-term financing (p. 580)   Borrowed capital that will be repaid over a specific time period longer than one year.

long-term forecast (p. 566)   Forecast that predicts revenues, costs, and expenses for a period longer than 1 year, and sometimes for as long as 5 or 10 years into the future.

looking to score big   *A sports metaphor that means trying to get as many points as possible; thus any effort to win decisively and/or make a large profit.*

loss (p. 5)   When a business's costs and expenses are more than its revenues.

M-1 (p. 625)   Money that is quickly and easily raised (currency, checks, travelers' checks, etc.).

M-2 (p. 625)   Money included in M-1 plus money that may take a little more time to raise (savings accounts, money market accounts, mutual funds, certificates of deposit, etc.).

management (pp. 199, 210)   The process used to accomplish organizational goals through planning, organizing, leading, and controlling people and other organizational resources.

management by objectives (MBO) (p. 301)   A system of goal setting and implementation that involves a cycle of discussion, review, and evaluation of objectives among top and middle-level managers, supervisors, and employees.

management development (p. 327)   The process of training and educating employees to become good managers and then monitoring the progress of their managerial skills over time.

managerial accounting (p. 531)   Accounting used to provide information and analyses to managers within the organization to assist them in decision making.

managing diversity (p. 221)   Building systems and a climate that unite different people in a common pursuit without undermining their diversity.

manufacturers' brand names (p. 418)   The brand names of manufacturers that distribute products nationally.

market (pp. 390, 180)   People with unsatisfied wants and needs who have both the resources and the willingness to buy.

market order (p. 607)   Instructions to a broker to buy stock immediately at the best price available.

market segmentation (p. 398)   The process of dividing the total market into several groups whose members have similar characteristics.

marketing (p. 379)   The process of determining customer wants and needs and then providing customers with goods and services that meet or exceed their expectations.

marketing concept (p. 383)   A three-part business philosophy: (1) a consumer orientation, (2) a service orientation, and (3) a profit orientation.

marketing intermediaries (p. 442)   Organizations that assist in the movement of goods and services from producers to industrial and consumer users.

marketing management (p. 389)   The process of planning and executing the conception, pricing, promotion, and distribution of ideas, goods, and services (products) to create mutually beneficial exchanges.

marketing mix (p. 389)   The ingredients that go into a marketing program: product, price, place, and promotion.

marketing research (p. 390) The analysis of markets to determine opportunities and challenges.

Maslow's hierarchy of needs (p. 292) Theory of motivation that places different types of human needs in order of importance, from basic physiological needs to safety, social, and esteem needs, to self-actualization needs.

mass customization (p. 270) Tailoring products to meet the needs of individual customers.

mass customization (p. 486) The design and promotion of products that can be made to order.

mass marketing (p. 387) Developing products and promotions to please large groups of people.

master budget (p. 568) The budget that ties together all of a firm's other budgets and summarizes the firm's proposed financial activities.

master limited partnership (p. 136) A partnership that looks much like a corporation in that it acts like a corporation and is traded on the stock exchanges like a corporation, but is taxed like a partnership and thus avoids the corporate income tax.

materials handling (p. 455) The movement of goods within a warehouse, factory, or store.

matrix organization (p. 241) Organization in which specialists from different parts of the organization are brought together to work on specific projects but still remain part of a traditional line-and-staff structure.

maturity date (p. 594) The exact date the issuer of a bond must pay the principal to the bondholder.

mediation (p. 356) The use of a third party, called a mediator, who encourages both sides to continue negotiating and often makes suggestions for resolving the dispute.

mentor (p. 328) An experienced employee who supervises, coaches, and guides lower level employees by introducing them to the right people and generally being their organizational sponsor.

mercantilism (p. 89) The economic principle advocating the selling of more goods to other nations than a country buys.

merchant wholesalers (p. 457) Independently owned firms that take title to (own) the goods they handle.

merger (p. 147) The result of two firms forming one company.

message center software (p. 516) A new generation of computer programs that use fax/voice modems to receive, sort, and deliver phone calls, e-mail, and faxes.

micropreneurs (p. 167) Those who are willing to accept the risk of starting and managing the type of business that remains small, lets them do the kind of work they want to do, and offers them a balanced lifestyle.

middle management (p. 203) The level of management that includes general managers, division managers, and branch and plant managers who are responsible for tactical planning and controlling.

missing the boat *Losing out because you did something wrong, like turn up late–often means someone who doesn't understand.*

mission statement (p. 200) An outline of the fundamental purposes of the organization.

mixed economies (p. 49) Economic systems in which some allocation of resources is made by the market and some is made by the government.

monetary policy (p. 62) The management of the money supply and interest rates.

money (p. 624) Anything that people generally accept as payment for goods and services.

money supply (p. 625) How much money there is to buy available goods and services.

monopolistic competition (p. 55) The market situation where there are a large number of sellers that produce similar products, but the products are perceived by buyers as different.

monopoly (p. 56) A market in which there is only one seller.

more than meets the eye *There is much happening that you can't see just by looking at things.*

motivators (p. 297) Factors that can cause employees to be productive and that give them satisfaction.

multiculturalism (p. 14) Process of optimizing the contribution of people from different cultures.

multinational corporation (MNC) (p. 92) An organization that does manufacturing and marketing in many different countries; it has multinational stock ownership and multinational management.

mutual fund (p. 608) An organization that buys stocks and bonds and then sells shares in those securities to the public.

mutual insurance company (p. 673) A type of insurance company owned by its policyholders.

name of the game *That's the way things are.*

National Association of Securities Dealers Automated Quotation (NASDAQ) (p. 600) A nationwide electronic system which communicates over-the-counter trades to brokers.

national debt (p. 63) The sum of all the federal deficits over time.

negotiable instruments (p. 123) Forms of commercial paper (such as checks) that are transferable among businesses and individuals and represent a promise to pay a specified amount.

negotiated labor–management agreement (p. 352) Settlement that sets the tone and clarifies the terms under which management and labor agree to function over a period of time.

net income or net loss (p. 539) Revenue minus expenses.

network computing system (client/server computing) (p. 511) Computer systems that allow personal computers (clients) to obtain needed information from huge databases in a central computer.

networking (p. 328) Using communications technology and other means to link organizations and allow them to work together on common objectives. **(p. 330)** The process of establishing and maintaining contacts with key managers in one's own organization and other organizations and using those contacts to weave strong relationships that serve as informal development systems.

niche marketing (p. 398) The process of finding small but profitable market segments and designing custom-made products for them.

nonbanks (p. 630) Financial organizations that accept no deposits but offer many of the services provided by regular banks (pension funds, insurance companies, commercial finance companies, consumer finance companies, and brokerage houses).

nonprofit organization (p. 3) An organization whose goals do not include making a profit for its owners.

objectives (p. 201) Specific, short-term statements detailing how to achieve the goals.

off-the-job training (p. 327) Training that occurs away from the workplace and consists of internal or external programs to develop any of a variety of skills or to foster personal development.

oligopoly (p. 55) A form of competition where the market is dominated by just a few sellers.

on cloud nine *Feeling great, like the feeling of winning the game or being in love.*

on-the-job training (p. 326) Training program in which the employee immediately begins his or her tasks and learns by doing, or watches others for a while and then imitates them, all right at the workplace.

on the wrong foot *Having a poor start.*

one-to-one marketing (p. 398) Developing a unique mix of goods and services for each individual customer.

open shop agreement (p. 353) Agreement in right-to-work states that gives workers the option to join or not join a union, if one exists in their workplace.

open-market operations (p. 628) The buying and selling of U.S. government securities by the Fed with the goal of regulating the money supply.

operating budget (p. 567) The projection of dollar allocations to various costs and expenses needed to run or operate a business, given projected revenues.

operational planning (p. 203) The process of setting work standards and schedules necessary to implement the tactical objectives.

organizational culture (p. 249) Widely shared values within an organization that provide coherence and cooperation to achieve common goals.

organizational design (p. 230) The structuring of workers so that they can best accomplish the firm's goals.

organizing (p. 200) A management function that involves designing the organizational structure, attracting people to the organization (staffing), and creating conditions and systems that ensure that everyone and everything work together to achieve the objectives of the organization.

outsourcing (p. 246) Assigning various functions, such as accounting and legal work, to outside organizations.

over-the-counter (OTC) market (p. 600) Exchange that provides a means to trade stocks not listed on the national exchanges.

owners' equity (p. 537) Assets minus liabilities.

par value (p. 597) A dollar amount assigned to each share of stock by the corporation's charter.

participative (democratic) leadership (p. 213) Leadership style that consists of managers and employees working together to make decisions.

partnership (p. 134) A legal form of business with two or more owners.

patent (p. 121) A document that gives inventors exclusive rights to their inventions for 20 years.

penetration strategy (p. 431) Strategy in which a product is priced low to attract many customers and discourage competition.

penny stocks (p. 606)   Stocks that sell for less than $1.

pension funds (p. 635)   Amounts of money put aside by corporations, nonprofit organizations, or unions to cover part of the financial needs of members when they retire.

perfect competition (p. 55)   The market situation where there are many sellers of nearly identical products and no seller is large enough to dictate the price of the product.

performance appraisal (p. 329)   An evaluation in which the performance level of employees is measured against established standards to make decisions about promotions, compensation, additional training, or firing.

personal selling (p. 473)   The face-to-face presentation and promotion of products and services.

physical distribution (logistics) (p. 441)   The movement of goods from producers to industrial and consumer users.

pitch in to help   *To accept your fair share of the work.*

planning (p. 199)   A management function that involves anticipating trends and determining the best strategies and tactics to achieve organizational objectives.

pledging (p. 574)   The process of using accounts receivable or other assets as collateral for a loan.

preemptive right (p. 599)   Common stockholders' right to purchase any new shares of common stock the firm decides to issue.

preferred provider organizations (PPOs) (p. 674)   Health care organizations similar to HMOs except that they allow members to choose their own physicians (for a fee).

preferred stock (p. 598)   Stock that gives its owners preference in the payment of dividends and an earlier claim on assets than common stockholders, if the company is forced out of business and its assets sold.

premium (p. 672)   The fee charged by an insurance company for an insurance policy.

prepare for the crunch   *To be ready for times when things get busy by getting organized and having adequate inventory or personnel, etc., to compete and satisfy customers.*

price leadership (p. 432)   The procedure by which all competitors in an industry follow the pricing practices of one or more dominant firms.

primary boycott (p. 358)   When a union encourages both its members and the general public not to buy the products of a firm involved in a labor dispute.

primary data (p. 392)   Facts and figures not previously published that you have gathered on your own.

principal (p. 594)   The face value of a bond.

principle of motion economy (p. 289)   Theory that every job can be broken down into a series of elementary motions.

private accountants (p. 532)   Accountants who work for a single firm, government agency, or nonprofit organization.

process manufacturing (p. 265)   Production process that physically or chemically changes materials.

product (p. 381)   Any physical good, service, or idea that satisfies a want or need.

product differentiation (p. 411)   The creation of real or perceived product differences.

product liability (p. 120)   Part of tort law that holds businesses liable for negligence in the production, design, sale, or use of products they market.

product life cycle (p. 424)   A theoretical model of what happens to sales and profits for a product class over time.

product line (p. 410)   A group of products that are physically similar or are intended for a similar market.

product manager (p. 420)   A manager who has direct responsibility for one brand or one product line.

product mix (p. 411)   The combination of product lines offered by a manufacturer.

product screening (p. 422)   A process designed to reduce the number of new-product ideas being worked on at any one time.

production (p. 261)   The creation of finished goods and services using the factors of production: land, labor, capital, entrepreneurship, and knowledge.

production and operations management (p. 261)   The set of activities managers do to create goods and services.

productivity (p. 16)   The total output of goods and services in a given period of time divided by work hours (output per work hour).

profit (p. 4)   Earnings above and beyond what a business spends for salaries, expenses, and other costs.

program evaluation and review technique (PERT) (p. 273)   A method for analyzing the tasks involved in completing a given project, estimating the time needed to complete each task, and identifying the minimum time needed to complete the total project.

program trading (p. 616) Giving instructions to computers to automatically sell if the price of stock dips to a certain point to avoid potential losses.

promissory note (p. 573) A written contract with a promise to pay.

promotion (p. 382) All the techniques sellers use to motivate people to buy products or services.

promotion (p. 472) An attempt by marketers to inform people about products and to persuade them to participate in an exchange.

promotion mix (p. 473) The combination of tools an organization uses.

prospecting (p. 473) Researching potential buyers and choosing those most likely to buy.

prospectus (p. 610) A condensed version of economic and financial information that a company must file with the SEC before issuing stock; the prospectus must be sent to potential stock purchasers.

protective tariff (p. 89) Import tax designed to raise the price of imported products so that domestic products are more competitive.

public accountant (p. 532) An accountant who provides his or her accounting services to individuals or businesses on a fee basis.

public domain software (p. 513) Software that is free for the taking.

public relations (PR) (p. 477) The management function that evaluates public attitudes, identifies the policies and procedures of an individual or an organization with the public interest, and executes a program of action to earn public understanding and acceptance.

publicity (p. 478) Any information about an individual, product, or organization that's distributed to the public through the media and that's not paid for or controlled by the seller.

pull strategy (p. 487) Promotional strategy in which heavy advertising and sales promotion efforts are directed toward consumers so that they'll request the products from retailers.

pure risk (p. 670) The threat of loss with no chance for profit.

push strategy (p. 486) Promotional strategy in which the producer uses advertising, personal selling, sales promotion, and all other promotional tools to convince wholesalers and retailers to stock and sell merchandise.

push technology (p. 510) Web software that delivers information tailored to a previously defined user profile; it pushes the information to users so that they don't have to pull it out.

put to pasture *To retire someone, just as you would put an old horse to pasture rather than breed it.*

quality (p. 19) Providing customers with high quality goods and services that go beyond the expected.

quality control (p. 274) The measurement of products and services against set standards.

quality of life (p. 2) The general well-being of a society.

quick response (p. 443) The efforts by producers and suppliers to send goods to retailers and to each other as quickly as possible.

rack jobbers (p. 457) Wholesalers that furnish racks or shelves full of merchandise to retailers, display products, and sell on consignment.

recession (p. 62) Two consecutive quarters of decline in the GDP.

recruitment (p. 321) The set of activities used to obtain a sufficient number of the right people at the right time; its purpose is to select those who best meet the needs of the organization.

reengineering (p. 245) The fundamental rethinking and radical redesign of organizational processes to achieve dramatic improvements in critical measures of performance.

relationship marketing (p. 386) Establishing and maintaining mutually beneficial exchange relationships with internal and external customers and all the other stakeholders of the organization.

reserve requirement (p. 627) A percentage of commercial banks' checking and savings accounts that must be physically kept in the bank.

restructuring (p. 231) Redesigning an organization so that it can more effectively and efficiently serve its customers.

retailer (p. 442) An organization that sells to ultimate consumers.

revenue (pp. 5, 541) The value of what is received for goods sold, services rendered, and other sources.

revenue tariff (p. 89) Import tax designed to raise money for the government.

reverse discrimination (p. 339) Discrimination against whites or males in hiring or promoting.

revolving credit agreement (p. 574) A line of credit that is guaranteed by the bank.

right-to-work laws (p. 353) Legislation which gives workers the right, under an open shop, to join or not join a union if it is present.

rising dollar (p. 626) When the amount of goods and services you can buy with a dollar goes up.

risk (p. 5) The chance you take of losing time and money on a business that may not prove profitable. **(p. 669)** The chance of loss, the degree of probability of loss, and the amount of possible loss.

risk/return trade-off (p. 578) The principle that the greater a risk a lender takes in making a loan, the higher the interest rate required.

robot (p. 270) A computer-controlled machine capable of performing many tasks requiring the use of materials and tools.

round lots (p. 608) Purchases of 100 shares of stock at a time.

rule of indemnity (p. 672) Rule says that an insured person or organization cannot collect more than the actual loss from an insurable risk.

S corporation (p. 143) A unique government creation that looks like a corporation but is taxed like sole proprietorships and partnerships.

sales promotion (p. 479) The promotional tool that stimulates consumer purchasing and dealer interest by means of short-term activities.

Savings Association Insurance Fund (SAIF) (p. 636) The part of the FDIC that insures holders of accounts in savings and loan associations.

savings and loan association (S&L) (p. 633) A financial institution that accepts both savings and checking deposits and provides home mortgage loans.

scientific management (p. 289) Studying workers to find the most efficient way of doing things and then teaching people those techniques.

secondary boycott (p. 358) An attempt by labor to convince others to stop doing business with a firm that is the subject of a primary boycott.

secondary data (p. 392) Already-published research reports from journals, trade associations, the government, information services, libraries, and so forth.

secured bond (p. 578) A bond issued with some form of collateral.

secured loan (p. 574) A loan backed by something valuable, such as property.

Securities and Exchange Commission (SEC) (p. 601) Federal agency that has responsibility for regulating the various exchanges.

selection (p. 322) The process of gathering information and deciding who should be hired, under legal guidelines, for the best interests of the individual and the organization.

selective distribution (p. 461) Distribution that sends products to only a preferred group of retailers in an area.

self-insurance (p. 671) The practice of setting aside money to cover routine claims and buying only "catastrophe" policies to cover big losses.

Service Corps of Retired Executives (SCORE) (p. 182) An SBA office with 13,000 volunteers who provide consulting services for small businesses free (except for expenses).

services (p. 21) Intangible products such as education, health care, and insurance.

sexual harassment (p. 363) Unwelcome sexual advances, requests for sexual favors, and other conduct of a sexual nature (verbal or physical).

share of economic pie *Getting your fair share of resources just as one would want his or her piece of apple pie to be the same as others get.*

shareware (p. 512) Software that is copyrighted but distributed to potential customers free of charge.

shop steward (p. 355) A labor official who works permanently in an organization and represents employee interests on a daily basis.

shopping goods and services (p. 413) Those products that the consumer buys only after comparing value, quality, and price from a variety of sellers.

short-term financing (p. 572) Borrowed capital that will be repaid within one year.

short-term forecast (p. 566) Forecast that predicts revenues, costs, and expenses for a period of one year or less.

sinking fund (p. 596) A bond whose issuers regularly set aside funds in a reserve account (a sinking fund) so that enough capital will be accumulated by the maturity date to pay off the bond.

skimming price strategy (p. 431) Strategy in which a new product is priced high to make optimum profit while there's little competition.

Small Business Investment Companies (SBICs) (p. 179) Private investment companies licensed by the Small Business Administration to lend money to small businesses.

small business (p. 170) A business that is independently owned and operated, is not dominant in its field of operation, and meets certain standards of size in terms of employees or annual receipts.

Social Security (p. 660) The term used to describe the Old-Age, Survivors, and Disability Insurance Program established by the Social Security Act of 1935.

social audit (p. 111) A systematic evaluation of an organization's progress toward implementing programs that are socially responsible and responsive.

social responsibility (p. 101) A business's concern for the welfare of society as a whole.

socialism (p. 47) An economic system based on the premise that some businesses should be owned by the government.

sole proprietorship (p. 134) A business that is owned, and usually managed, by one person.

span of control (p. 235) The optimum number of subordinates a manager supervises or should supervise.

specialty goods and services (p. 413) Products that have a special attraction to consumers who are willing to go out of their way to obtain them.

speculative risk (p. 669) A chance of either profit or loss.

spreadsheet program (p. 514) The electronic equivalent of an accountant's worksheet, plus such features as mathematical function libraries, statistical data analysis, and charts.

staff personnel (p. 240) Employees who perform functions that assist line personnel in achieving their goals.

stagflation (p. 630) A combination of slow growth and inflation.

stakeholders (p. 12) Those people who stand to gain or lose by the policies and activities of an organization.

standard of living (p. 2) The level of ability to buy goods and services.

statement of cash flows (p. 544) Financial statement that reports cash receipts and disbursement related to a firm's major activities: operations, investment, and financing.

statutory law (p. 119) State and federal constitutions, legislative enactments, treaties, and ordinances (written laws).

stay tuned *A radio metaphor meaning to keep listening; thus to stay tuned means to keep paying attention to what is happening.*

stock certificate (p. 597) Evidence of ownership that specifies the name of the company, the number of shares it represents, and the type of stock being issued.

stock exchange (p. 599) An organization whose members can buy and sell (exchange) securities for companies and investors.

stock insurance company (p. 673) A type of insurance company owned by stockholders.

stock splits (p. 608) An action by a company that gives stockholders two or more shares of stock for each one they own.

stockbroker (p. 602) A registered representative who works as a market intermediary to buy and sell securities for clients.

stocks (p. 597) Shares of ownership in a company.

strategic (long-range) planning (p. 202) The process of determining the major goals of the organization and the policies and strategies for obtaining and using resources to achieve those goals.

strike (p. 357) A union strategy in which workers refuse to go to work; the purpose is to further workers' objectives after an impasse in collective bargaining.

strikebreakers (p. 359) Workers hired to do the jobs of striking workers until the labor dispute is resolved.

supervisory (first-line) management (p. 204) Managers who are directly responsible for supervising workers and evaluating their daily performance.

supply (p. 53) The quantity of products that manufacturers or owners are willing to sell at different prices at a specific time.

supply-chain management (SCM) (p. 442) The overall process of minimizing inventory and moving goods through the channel by using computers and other technology.

SWOT analysis (p. 201) An analysis of an organization's strengths, weaknesses, opportunities, and threats.

synthetic systems (p. 265) Systems that either change raw materials into other products (process manufacturing) or combine raw materials or parts into a finished product (assembly process).

tactical (short-range) planning (p. 202) The process of developing detailed, short-term decisions about what is to be done, who is to do it, and how it is to be done.

tapped out *Exhausted (as in financial resources), just as a keg of beer may be empty from being drained.*

target marketing (p. 398) Marketing directed toward those groups (market segments) an organization decided it can serve profitably.

tax accountant (p. 532) An accountant who is trained in tax law and is responsible for preparing tax returns or developing tax strategies.

taxes (p. 126) How the government (federal, state, and local) raises money.

technical skills (p. 217) Skills that involve the ability to perform tasks in a specific discipline or department.

telecommuting (pp. 15, 263) Working at home via computer and modem.

telemarketing (p. 462) The sale of goods and services by telephone.

term insurance (p. 659) Pure insurance protection for a given number of years.

term-loan agreement (p. 578) A promissory note that requires the borrower to repay the loan in specified installments.

test marketing (p. 381) The process of testing products among potential users.

the hard way *Doing things in a way that is inefficient, thus there is a better way of doing it.*

the rest is history *You know the rest of the story because it has been reported in so many places.*

time deposit (p. 631) The technical name for a savings account; the bank can require prior notice before the owner withdraws money from a time deposit.

time-motion studies (p. 289) Studies of the tasks performed to complete a job and the time needed to do each task.

top management (p. 203) Highest level of management, consisting of the president and other key company executives who develop strategic plans.

tort (p. 119) A wrongful act that causes injury to another person's body, property, or reputation.

total fixed costs (p. 430) All the expenses that remain the same no matter how many products are sold.

total quality management (TQM) (p. 245) The practice of striving for customer satisfaction by ensuring quality from all departments in an organization.

trade credit (p. 573) The practice of buying goods now and paying for them later.

trade deficit (p. 77) Buying more goods from other nations than are sold to them.

trade protectionism (p. 88) The use of government regulations to limit the import of goods and services; based on the theory that domestic producers can survive and grow, producing more jobs.

trade show (p. 471) An event where many marketers set up displays and potential customers come to see the latest in goods and services.

trademark (p. 122) A legally protected name, symbol, or design (or combination of these) that identifies the goods or services of one seller and distinguishes them from those of competitors.

trademark (p. 417) A brand that has been given exclusive legal protection for both the brand name and the pictorial design.

training and development (p. 326) All attempts to improve productivity by increasing an employee's ability to perform.

trial balance (p. 535) A summary of all the data in the account ledgers to show whether the figures are correct and balanced.

trigger happy *Someone who shoots a gun indiscriminately without thinking, thus anyone in business who does things quickly without thinking.*

turned a deaf ear *A person isn't listening to what you have to say.*

unemployment rate (p. 58) The number of civilians who are unemployed and tried to find a job within the prior four weeks.

Uniform Commercial Code (UCC) (p. 123) A comprehensive commercial law adopted by every state in the United States; it covers sales laws and other commercial laws.

uninsurable risk (p. 671) A risk that no insurance company will cover.

union security clause (p. 353) Provision in a negotiated labor–management agreement that stipulates that employees who benefit from a union must either join or pay dues to the union.

union shop agreement (p. 353) Clause in labor–management agreement that says workers do not have to be members of a union to be hired, but must agree to join the union within a prescribed period.

unions (p. 348) Employee organizations that have the main goal of representing members in employee–management bargaining over job-related issues.

unlimited liability (p. 135) The responsibility of business owners for all of the debts of the business.

unsecured bonds (p. 579) A bond backed only by the reputation of the issuer.

unsecured loan (p. 574) A loan that's not backed by any specific assets.

unsought goods and services (p. 413) Products that consumers are unaware of, haven't necessarily thought of buying, or find that they need to solve an unexpected problem.

value chain (p. 452) The sequence of linked activities that must be performed by various organizations to move goods from the sources of raw materials to ultimate consumers.

value package (p. 408) Everything that consumers evaluate when deciding whether to buy something.

value pricing (p. 429)   When marketers provide consumers with brand name goods and services at fair prices.

variable costs (p. 430)   Costs that change according to the level of production.

venture capital (p. 581)   Money that is invested in new companies that have great profit potential.

venture capitalists (p. 178)   Individuals or companies that invest in new businesses in exchange for partial ownership of those businesses.

vertical merger (p. 147)   The joining of two companies involved in different stages of related businesses.

vestibule training (p. 327)   Training in schools where employees are taught on equipment similar to that used on the job.

virtualization (p. 504)   Accessibility through technology that allows business to be conducted independent of location.

virus (p. 520)   A piece of programming code inserted into other programming to cause some unexpected and, for the victim, usually undesirable event.

vision (p. 200)   An explanation of why the organization exists and where it's trying to head.

voluntary bankruptcy (p. 128)   Legal procedures initiated by a debtor.

walking the walk   *Actually doing something as opposed to talking the talk which means talking about doing something, but not really doing it or being able to do it.*

wholesaler (p. 442)   A marketing intermediary that sells to other organizations.

win-win   *Everyone comes out ahead from doing something as opposed to win-lose where one person gains by beating someone else or taking something from someone else.*

word-of-mouth promotion (p. 480)   A promotional tool that involves people telling other people about products they've purchased.

World Bank (p. 641)   The bank primarily responsible for financing economic development; also known as the International Bank for Reconstruction and Development.

World Trade Organization (WTO) (p. 90)   An independent institution governing cross-border trade issues and business practices.

yellow-dog contracts (p. 358)   A contract that required employees to agree, as a condition of employment, not to join a union.

Credits

Chapter 12

p. 349, John Thoeming. p. 350, AP/Wide World Photos. p. 352, PhotoDisc. p. 356, AP/Wide World Photos. p. 361, Jeff Greenberg/PhotoEdit. p. 361, PhotoDisc. p. 364, John Thoeming. p. 366, AP/Wide World Photos. p. 369, John Thoeming. p. 370, Courtesy of United Airlines.

Chapter 13

p. 381, Earl Coulter Studio. p. 384, GTE Sprint. p. 386, Courtesy of GTE Sprint. p. 387, Robert E. Daemmrich/Tony Stone Images. p. 388, Video Arts. p. 388, Published Image. p. 389, EPA. p. 390 (left), Paul Conklin/PhotoEdit. p. 390 (right), Lee VF Jeanswear. p. 391, © Norman Y. Lono, 1998. p. 398, John Thoeming. p. 403, Courtesy of Dun & Bradstreet.

Chapter 14

p. 411, Courtesy of Toro. p. 412, Burrston House. p. 413, Courtesy of Gateway 2000. p. 414, Burrston House. p. 416, Courtesy of M&M Mars. p. 417, John Thoeming. p. 418, Courtesy of Ford Motor Corporation. p. 420, Courtesy of Virgin Atlantic Airlines. p. 423, Courtesy of McIlhenny Co. p. 427 (left), AP/Wide World Photos. p. 427 (right), John Thoeming. p. 428, Courtesy of Xerox Corporation. p. 430, John Thoeming. p. 432 Courtesy of the U.S. Postal Service. p. 433, AP/Wide World Photos. p. 435, John Thoeming. p. 436, Courtesy of Pepsico.

Chapter 15

p. 445, John Thoeming. p. 446, John Thoeming. p. 448, Cindy Charles/PhotoEdit. p. 450, Courtesy of UPS. p. 451, PhotoDisc. p. 453, Burrston House. p. 454, © 1998 by Consumers Union of U.S., Inc., Yonkers, NY 10703-1057. Reprinted by permission from CONSUMER REPORTS, March 1998. p. 458, © Penske Truck Leasing. p. 459, PhotoDisc. p. 462, John Thoeming. p. 464, Courtesy of Wal-Mart. p. 465, John Thoeming. p. 466, Kaku Kirita/Gamma Liaison.

Chapter 16

p. 475, Courtesy of the Biltmore Estate. p. 476, Burrston House. p. 479, Christopher Bissell/Tony Stone Images. p. 479, Courtesy of Hewlett Packard. p. 480, Gary Benson. p. 481, (Pepsi's formula) 1998, USA TODAY. Reprinted with permission. p. 482, Courtesy of Sony. p. 484, John Thoeming. p. 488, AP/Wide World Photos. p. 490, Courtesy of Rhone-Poulenc Rorer Inc. p. 492, Courtesy of NNN/Culver Associates, Ltd. p. 494, John Thoeming.

Chapter 17

p. 507, PhotoDisk. p. 508, Courtesy of IBM. p. 509, Courtesy of Home Depot. p. 511, Courtesy of Sun. p. 511, Courtesy of Ford Motor Company. p. 512, John Thoeming. p. 515, Courtesy of Intel. p. 520, Courtesy of In Focus Systems, Inc. p. 521, Courtesy of Claris. p. 522, The Stock Market. p. 525, Courtesy of ZDTV.

Chapter 18

p. 535, Courtesy of R. J. Julia Book Seller. p. 538, Anthony James Dugal Photography. p. 539, Courtesy of the American Institute of Certified Public Accountants. p. 548, Courtesy of Boeing Corporation. p. 554, Courtesy Home Depot. p. 556, Burrston House. p. 558, Courtesy of Peachtree Software, Inc.

Chapter 19

p. 571, Courtesy of Merck & Company. p. 576, Jeff Greenberg/PhotoEdit. p. 578, Courtesy of Time Warner. p. 580, Courtesy of EduTrek International, Inc. p. 582, R. Crandall/The Image Works. p. 583, Courtesy of the Republic National Bank of New York.

Chapter 20

p. 599, John Thoeming. p. 600, © 1998 Matthew Gilson/All rights reserved. p. 607, Richard Laird/FPG International/Aaron Goodman Illus. p. 608 (left), Tony Savino/The Image Works. p. 609 (right), James Marshall/The Image Works. p. 613, John Thoeming. p. 619 (left), Courtesy of the Chicago Board of Trade. p. 619 (right), PhotoDisc. p. 621, PhotoDisc.

Chapter 21

p. 633, AP/Wide World Photos. p. 635, John Eastcott/YVA Momatiuk/The Image Works. p. 640, B. Daemmrich/The Image Works. p. 641, Courtesy of Vermont National Bank. p. 644, John Barr/The Gamma Liaison Network. p. 648, John Thoeming. p. 651, AP/Wide World Photos.

Chapter 22

p. 659, John Thoeming. p. 661, Courtesy of the U.S. Postal Service. p. 662, J. Carini/The Image Works. p. 663, © Norman Y. Lono, 1998. p. 666, Courtesy of Founders Funds. p. 668, Courtesy of Wachovia Bank of Georgia. p. 672, Courtesy of Merrill Lynch. p. 674, Courtesy of A.G. Edwards & Sons, Inc. p. 680, Courtesy of the National Flood Insurance Program. p. 681, Courtesy of Liberty Mutual. p. 684, Courtesy of the Principal Financial Group. p. 685, Courtesy of Northwestern Mutual Life. p. 687, Anchorage Daily News/Gamma Liaison.

Name Index

Organization Index

Subject Index